GAAP 2001

UK financial reporting and accounting

GAAP 2001

UK financial reporting and accounting

by

Ken Wild
Brian Creighton

and the

Deloitte & Touche technical department

Deloitte & Touche

www.deloitte.co.uk

abg
professional
information

40 Bernard Street
London WC1N 1LD
Tel: 020 7920 8991
Fax: 020 7920 8992
E-mail: info@abgpublications.co.uk
Website: www.abgweb.com

British Library Cataloguing-in-Publication Data
A catalogue record for this book is available from the British Library

ISBN 1 84140 086 6

Typeset by YHT Ltd, London
Printed by The Bath Press.

Foreword by Sir David Tweedie

When I penned the Foreword to the launch edition of this book a year ago, I mentioned that I was quite shaken to see on reading it how accounting for so much had been changed by the institution of the Accounting Standards Board. This year, as people start to implement FRS 15, and to wrestle with the cost, valuation and depreciation of tangible fixed assets, covered by this new edition, it could be said that the ASB has now made its mark on every significant part of the balance sheet, with the exception only of the valuation of liabilities – and that work is well in hand. I do believe that the balance sheet has acquired so much more meaning as a result that it is beginning to play its proper part in the work of analysts and in the eyes of users generally. And about time too!

When we at the ASB set standards, we do not try to deal with every single situation. We try to set what we call 80 per cent standards, that is we will deal with 80 per cent of the problem and can perhaps accomplish that objective in 50 or 60 pages. If we were required to deal with 95 per cent of the problem, we could double or treble the size of the standard. That is the reason we aim for the shorter statements consisting mainly of principle, leaving the remaining 20 per cent to the judgement of the finance director and auditor. If poor judgement based on the 'where does it say that I can't do that' philosophy emerges, then the Board will intervene, either by amending the standard or by using the offices of the Urgent Issues Task Force – neither of these routes has been used with any frequency.

GAAP 2001: UK financial reporting and accounting not only outlines the essential thrust of the Board's standards and its direction but also goes that step further and moves into the 20 per cent area which the ASB has left alone – clearly using the experience of the authors in dealing with the accounting problems of the firm's clients. The book is based on sound practical experience and will save many a rash enthusiast from getting into unnecessary difficulty.

I said last year that I could see that this manual would become a lifesaver for the hard-pressed company accountant and the equally hard-pressed auditor. I can well imagine it becoming a standard fixture on the office shelves of accountants at every level, from the finance director down. Certainly one cannot fail to notice it on the shelf, by virtue both of its size and of its extraordinarily bold cover that shouts across the room! Nothing that is happening today suggests that financial reporting is going to get any simpler as the years go by. Indeed, as the globalisation of accounting approaches, and financial deals and, consequently, financial reporting become ever more complex, the needs for manuals such as this will increase. I suspect that *GAAP 2015* will be just as vital to accountants as *GAAP 2000* appeared to be last year and *GAAP 2001* will be this year. May the solutions to your problems be found herein.

Sir David Tweedie
June 2000

Acknowledgements

The associate authors who contributed to this book were Elizabeth Buckley, Margaret Cassidy, Elizabeth Chrispin, Sasha Dorofeyev, Haydn Everitt, Veronica Poole, Gary Romain, Andy Simmonds, Robert Stenhouse and Gillian Sutherland. Our thanks are also extended to John Belsey and Chris Jones for their assistance.

Contents

Contents

3   The Accounting Standards Board's Statement of Principles

4   Preparation, filing and publishing of financial statements

5 General requirements as to financial statements

Contents

Contents

11 Statement of total recognised gains and losses

12 Balance sheet: general

Contents

Contents

17 Liabilities, provisions and contingencies

Contents

18   Share capital and reserves

Contents

20 Segmental information

21 Other disclosure requirements, including derivatives

Contents

24 Consolidation techniques

Contents

25 Associates and joint ventures

Contents

Contents

29 Leasing

30 Pension costs

31 Government grants

32 Related-party transactions, including directors' loans

Contents

33 Requirements concerning share capital and distributions

Contents

39 Reports on audited financial statements

Contents

40 Reports on listed companies

41 Reports on the appropriateness of the going concern basis

42 Other audit reports

Contents

46 Model report and financial statements

Appendices

Table of Financial Reporting Standards

Table of Statements of Standard Accounting Practice

Table of Urgent Issue Task Force Abstracts

Table of Statutes

Table of Statutory Instruments

1 Introduction

1   Introduction

Purpose of the manual

1.1   The purpose of this manual is to suggest best practice in respect of:

     (a)   the form and content of financial statements;

     (b)   best practice and acceptable alternatives in respect of accounting policies and disclosures adopted for the presentation of financial information; and

     (c)   the form and content of auditors' and accountants' reports.

How to use the manual

1.2   Each chapter is ordered as follows:

     (a)   key changes since the previous issue of the book. This will only appear in those chapters where key changes have occurred;

     (b)   discussion and analysis of those standards in force at 31 March 2000 (i.e., year ends on or after that date) or of standards issued at 31 March 2000 where no previous standard existed;

     (c)   discussion and analysis of standards issued at 31 March 2000 but not mandatory where an earlier standard is in issue and in force at 31 March 2000;

     (d)   discussion of any likely developments, including Exposure Drafts and discussion documents, with an indication, where available, of when they are likely to become requirements.

1.3   The format of the manual has been devised to give guidance on reporting and accounting matters as clearly as possible. Each chapter sets out the requirements of the law, accounting standards and other requirements appropriate to the subject matter. In many areas of reporting and accounting, there are generally areas of choice between alternative interpretations, whether of accounting method or of presentation. The manual gives not only compliance guidance, but also highlights those areas where the formal guidance is ambiguous or deficient. The paragraphs of the manual that give interpretations are highlighted as shown below.

32.28   A loan made to an employee before he is appointed to the board is not of itself illegal, since it is the making of a loan to a director, rather than the existence of the loan, which is addressed by the Act. However, once the employee becomes a director, any increase in the loan due to further advances or the accruing of interest would be subject to the restrictions.

1.4   Changes to a chapter brought about by a new standard, or key proposals for change, are highlighted at the start of the relevant chapter as follows.

Para.	*Topic*	*Summary*
30.67	FRED 20 *Retirement benefits*	Proposes radical changes for defined benefit schemes leading to increased volatility in the balance sheet as actuarial gains and losses are recognised immediately in the STRGL and scheme assets are valued at fair values.

Contents of this edition

1.5   This edition of the manual includes the reporting and accounting requirements contained in:

(a)   the Companies Act 1985, as amended by the Companies Act 1989;

(b)   relevant statutory instruments issued up to 31 March 2000;

(c)   FRSs 1 to 16;

(d)   SSAPs 2, 4, 5, 9, 13, 15, 17, 19 to 21, 24 and 25;

(e)   UITF Abstracts 4 to 7, 9 to 15 and 17 to 23;

(f)   Statements of Auditing Standards, Statements of Standards for Reporting Accountants, Practice Notes and Bulletins issued by the Auditing Practices Board (APB) up to 31 March 2000;

(g)   auditing standards and guidelines issued by the Auditing Practices Committee (APC) and adopted by the APB; and

(h)   the Listing Rules issued by the UK Listing Authority.

Small companies

1.6   Certain small companies are permitted by the Companies Act to pre-
       pare their reports and accounts in accordance with special rules
       which are contained in sections 246, 248 and 248A of and Schedule 8
       to the Act. Such companies are also permitted to follow the FRS for
       Smaller Entities (FRSSE) rather than normal accounting standards.
       Chapters 34 and 35 deal in general with small and medium-sized
       companies, but this manual does not deal in detail with the rules for
       small companies.

Specialised industry practice

1.7   Banking and insurance companies and groups should prepare their
       accounts in accordance with special rules which are contained in sec-
       tions 255, 255A and 255B of the Companies Act. This manual does
       not deal in detail with these rules nor with specialised accounting
       practices followed by various industries. It does, however, give guid-
       ance on audit reports for specialised industries.

References and abbreviations used

1.8   Unless otherwise stated all references to 'the Act' in this manual are
       to the Companies Act 1985 as amended by the Companies Act 1989
       and statutory instruments issued up to 31 March 2000. For example:

       s227(2)   Section 227 subsection (2) of the Act

       Sch 4: 58(3)   Paragraph 58, subparagraph (3) of Schedule 4 to
                        the Act

1.9   References to accounting standards, UITF Abstracts, auditing stan-
       dards and other technical material are indicated as follows:

       FRS 2(19)   Paragraph 19 of FRS 2

       SSAP 19(13)   Paragraph 13 of SSAP 19

       UITF Abstract 4(3)   Paragraph 3 of UITF Abstract 4

       SAS 600(3)   Paragraph 3 of Statement of Auditing
                            Standards 600

1.10   A glossary of abbreviations used in the text of this manual is con-
       tained in Appendix I.

Disclosure checklist

1.11 A checklist of disclosures which are required by the Act, FRSs, SSAPs, UITF Abstracts, Listing Rules and the London Stock Exchange to be included in the directors' report and financial statements is included in Appendix II. The checklist indicates the authority for each requirement. Disclosures in respect of corporate governance required by the Listing Rules are given separately in Appendix V.

2 Accounting requirements and their enforcement

2 Accounting requirements and their enforcement

Summary of changes since the previous issue of this publication

Para.	*Topic*	*Summary*
2.21	Company law review	The DTI are currently undertaking a large scale review of company law in the UK. The review commenced in 1998 and five consultation documents have so far been issued.

Sources of accounting requirements

Introduction

2.1 The sources and status of accounting principles and disclosures required of UK companies may be described under two headings: mandatory and advisory.

Mandatory sources

2.2 Those sources which are mandatory include:

    (a) legal requirements contained in the Act or, particularly for concerns which are not incorporated under the Companies Acts, any rules laid down by other Acts or regulatory bodies. EU Directives are only mandatory when enacted into legislation by Parliament; other EU Directives are to be regarded as advisory;

    (b) Financial Reporting Standards (FRSs) and Statements of Standard Accounting Practice (SSAPs) issued or adopted by the Accounting Standards Board (ASB) (referred to as accounting standards). A number of accounting standards contain exemptions for companies of particular sizes from certain disclosure requirements; these are indicated in the text of this manual where applicable;

    (c) UITF Abstracts issued by the ASB's Urgent Issues Task Force;

    (d) the requirements contained in the 'Listing Rules' and in chapter 16 of the rules of the London Stock Exchange (not to be confused with the Listing Rules). These requirements relate respectively to listed companies and to companies whose shares are dealt in on the alternative investment market (AIM). References in this manual to 'Listed companies' are those companies admitted to the official list by the UK Listing Authority. The UK Listing Authority was transferred from the London Stock Exchange to the Financial Services Authority in May 2000 (see **5.52** below).

2.3 The status of accounting standards and UITF Abstracts under UK legislation is addressed in a written opinion by Miss Mary Arden QC obtained by the ASB. This opinion is included as an appendix to the ASB's *Foreword to Accounting Standards.*

Advisory sources

2.4 Those sources which are advisory in nature include:

(a) Statements of Recommended Practice (SORPs), which give guidance on current best practice on topics which are not of major or fundamental importance;

(b) Financial Reporting Exposure Drafts (FREDs) issued by the ASB in advance of the issue of the final FRS. Although substantial alterations may be made in the light of comments received, these FREDs are a useful indicator of the eventual requirements. The ASB also issues discussion documents prior to the issuance of FRSs and FREDs and these give the likely direction to be taken by the ASB on a particular practice;

(c) other statements issued by the ASB;

(d) Technical Releases issued by the UK accountancy bodies to publicise views on various matters. Although these releases and recommendations are not mandatory, they are, nevertheless, strongly persuasive;

(e) the report of the Committee on the Financial Aspects of Corporate Governance (Cadbury Committee), issued 1 December 1992;

(f) the report of the Study Group on Directors' Remuneration (Greenbury Committee), issued in July 1995;

(g) the report of the Committee on Corporate Governance (Hampel Committee), issued in January 1998;

(h) the Combined Code, issued in June 1998 (derived by the Hampel Committee from their report and from the Cadbury and Greenbury reports);

(i) pronouncements of international committees and professional bodies in other countries (e.g., statements and exposure drafts issued by the IAS, Statements of Financial Accounting Standards (SFASs) issued by the US FASB, and Accounting Principles Board Opinions of the American Institute of Certified Public Accountants).

Legal requirements

The Companies Act

2.5   The Companies Act 1985 consolidated all previous Companies Acts. The Companies Act 1989 made a number of amendments to the 1985 Act, the principal changes which affect accounts being as a consequence of the introduction into law of accounting principles underlying the preparation of consolidated accounts as specified by the EU Seventh Directive on company law. Part VII of and Schedules 4 to 11 to the Act (as amended) set out the legislation relating to the preparation, form and content, audit and publication of company and group accounts.

Accounting standards

Introduction

2.6   The Companies Act 1989 gave accounting standards legal definition for the first time; it defined them as 'statements of standard accounting practice issued by such body or bodies as may be prescribed by regulations'. To date, the only body prescribed for this purpose is The Accounting Standards Board Limited.

2.7   On its formation, the ASB adopted the extant SSAPs and these (other than those subsequently withdrawn by the ASB), together with FRSs issued since, are 'accounting standards' for the purpose of the Act.

Scope and authority

2.8   In its *Foreword to Accounting Standards*, which explains the authority, scope and application of accounting standards, the ASB states that accounting standards are applicable to financial statements of a reporting entity (not just companies) that are intended to give a true and fair view of its state of affairs at the balance sheet date and of its profit or loss (or income and expenditure) for the financial period ending on that date. The *Foreword to Accounting Standards* also states that, as accounting standards are authoritative statements of how particular types of transaction and other events should be reflected in financial statements, compliance with them will normally be necessary for financial statements to give a true and fair view.

2.9   The appendix to the *Foreword to Accounting Standards* contains a written opinion from counsel on the meaning of 'true and fair', with particular reference to the role of accounting standards. In summary, the opinion notes that accounting standards are an authoritative source of accounting practice and, in consequence, it is now the norm for financial statements to comply with them. Courts may, therefore, take accounting standards into account when forming an opinion on whether the financial statements being considered by them give a true and fair view.

Disclosure of compliance

2.10   Companies, other than small and medium-sized companies (see **34.4** to **34.17** below for definitions), are required by the Act to state whether their financial statements have been prepared in accordance with applicable accounting standards and particulars of any material departure and the reasons for it shall be given. [Sch 4: 36A] Small and medium-sized companies are not required to state that their financial statements have been prepared in accordance with applicable accounting standards, but the *Foreword to Accounting Standards* requires all companies to disclose in their financial statements particulars of any material departure from an accounting standard, the reasons for it and its financial effects. [*Foreword* (19)]

Urgent Issues Task Force

Introduction

2.11   The ASB has established the Urgent Issues Task Force (UITF) to assist it in areas where an accounting standard or Companies Act provision exists, but where unsatisfactory or conflicting interpretations have developed or seem likely to develop. The results of the UITF's deliberations on a subject are promulgated by means of published Abstracts.

UITF Abstracts

2.12   In its *Foreword to UITF Abstracts*, which explains the authority, scope and application of UITF Abstracts, the ASB states that UITF Abstracts are applicable to financial statements of a reporting entity (not just companies) that are intended to give a true and fair view of its state of affairs at the balance sheet date and of its profit or loss (or income and expenditure) for the financial period ending on that date. UITF Abstracts should be considered to be part of the corpus of practices forming the basis for determining what constitutes a true and fair view.

2.13   The opinion from counsel on the meaning of 'true and fair' referred to in **2.9** above notes that Courts are likely to treat UITF Abstracts as of considerable standing when forming an opinion on whether the financial statements being considered by them give a true and fair view.

Enforcement of accounting requirements

Introduction

2.14 Companies incorporated under the Companies Acts are required by the Act to prepare annual accounts that give a true and fair view and comply with the accounting requirements of the Act. Prior to the Companies Act 1989, responsibility for 'policing' these requirements rested with the Department of Trade and Industry (DTI). The 1989 Act introduced new procedures for the revision of defective accounts. These procedures included allowing a person, authorised by the Secretary of State, the power to apply to the court for an order requiring the directors of a company to prepare revised accounts. The Secretary of State has authorised the Financial Reporting Review Panel (Review Panel) for this purpose.

2.15 The Councils of the Consultative Committee of Accountancy Bodies (CCAB) expect their members who assume responsibility for the preparation or audit of financial statements to observe accounting standards and UITF Abstracts. The CCAB bodies, through appropriate committees, may enquire into apparent failures by their members to observe accounting standards and UITF Abstracts or to ensure adequate disclosure of material departures.

Enforcement by the Secretary of State

2.16 Where the Secretary of State believes that the accounts may not comply with the requirements of the Act, he may give notice to the directors indicating the matters in question. If, after a specified period (not less than one month), the directors have not given the Secretary of State a satisfactory explanation or have not revised the accounts so as to comply with the Act, the Secretary of State may apply to the court to order the directors to do so. [s245A] The court may give directions with respect to the auditing of the revised accounts, the revision of any directors' report or summary financial statement, and the steps required by the directors to bring the making of the court order to the notice of persons likely to rely on the previous accounts. If the court finds that the accounts did not comply with the Act, it may order all costs or any part of the costs in connection with the application and the revision of the accounts to be borne by those directors who had approved the defective accounts. [s245B]

Enforcement by the Financial Reporting Review Panel

2.17 The role of the Review Panel is to examine departures from the accounting requirements of the Act and, if necessary, to seek an order from the court to remedy them. By agreement with the DTI, the normal ambit of the Review Panel is public and large private companies; the DTI deals with all other cases.

2.18 The cases investigated by the Review Panel arise from:

(a) referral by the UK Listing Authority of companies whose auditors have qualified their reports on the financial statements;

(b) unfavourable press comments on companies' financial statements; or

(c) complaints from members of the public.

2.19 The Review Panel's investigations include consideration of any material departure from an accounting standard or UITF Abstract where, as a result, the financial statements do not give a true and fair view.

2.20 The Review Panel normally aims to discharge its task by seeking voluntary agreement with the directors of the company concerned; to date, no applications to the Court have been made. In most of the cases reported so far, the Review Panel has accepted undertakings from the company's directors to make additional disclosures or changes to the comparative figures in the following year's financial statements.

Future developments

Company law review

2.21 The DTI are currently undertaking a large scale review of company law in the UK.

2.22 An initial consultation paper *Modern Company Law for a Competitive Economy* was published in March 1998. It set out the background to the present position as regards company law and sketched out the way in which the review would be handled, outlining the scope and arrangements for the review including the terms of reference. The review is based on the following structure:

(a) A Steering Group will oversee the management of the project and ensure that its outcome is clear in concept, internally coherent, well articulated and expressed, and workable.

(b) A widely-based Consultative Committee including members of the Steering Group, but also including wider legal representation and key groups such as the CBI, TUC and the accountancy bodies, as well as other Government Departments.

(c)   Various Working Groups addressing the detailed work in specified areas.

2.23   The Steering Group's first consultation document *The Strategic
Framework* was published in February 1999. It described the work to
date, issues identified and analysed, and proposals for taking the
work forward. The main issues identified were:

(a)   the scope of company law;

(b)   the needs of small and closely-held companies;

(c)   company formation;

(d)   capital maintenance;

(e)   regulation and boundaries of law;

(f)   international issues;

(g)   information and communications technology; and

(h)   high-level reporting and accounting issues.

2.24   In October 1999 the Steering Group issued three further consultation documents building on the results of the earlier consultation
process and taking forward the review's work in key areas of company law. The topics covered by those documents were:

(a)   company general meetings and shareholder communication;

(b)   company formation and capital maintenance; and

(c)   reforming the law concerning overseas companies.

2.25   The Steering Group's fifth consultation document *Developing the
Framework* was published in March 2000. It summarises the process
to date and the way forward. The two main technical issues identified are corporate governance; and small and private companies and
alternative vehicles. The consideration of corporate governance
includes duties and roles of directors, shares and shareholders and
reporting and accounting (see chapter 6 below as regards this latter
topic). The discussion on small and private companies includes proposals relating to their reports and accounts (see chapters 34 and 35
below).

2.26   Up-to-date reports on the review project together with downloadable texts of the consultation documents can be obtained from the
DTI website www.dti.gov.uk/cld/review.htm.

3 The Accounting Standards Board's Statement of Principles

3   The Accounting Standards Board's Statement of Principles

Summary of changes since the previous issue of this publication

Para.	Topic	Summary
3.1 to 3.27	Statement of Principles for Financial Reporting	In December 1999 the ASB issued its *Statement of Principles for Financial Reporting*. This is not an accounting standard and conse-quently does not have an imple mentation date.

Introduction

Background

3.1   One of the recommendations of the Dearing report on the setting of accounting standards (the report that gave rise to the new financial reporting regime at the end of the 1980s) was that the successor body to the Accounting Standards Committee (ASC) should develop a statement on the principles that underlie accounting and financial reporting.

3.2   In December 1999 the ASB issued its *Statement of Principles* for Financial Reporting (Statement of Principles). These were developed from a series of discussion papers issued in the early 1990s and two Exposure Drafts issued in 1995 and March 1999. In addition to the Statement of Principles, which, with appendices, is over 140 pages long, the ASB have produced an 11 page introduction which may be downloaded from the ASB's website (www.asb.org.uk).

Purpose

3.3   The primary purpose of the Statement of Principles is to assist the ASB both in the development of future accounting standards and in its review of existing accounting standards by providing a 'coherent frame of reference'. This will also benefit those who interact with the ASB during the standard setting-process. Knowledge of the Statement of Principles should also assist others (such as preparers, auditors and users) in:

(a) understanding the Board's approach to the formulation of accounting standards;

(b) understanding the nature and function of information reported in general purpose financial statements; and

(c) analysing issues relating to new or emerging issues in the absence of applicable accounting standards.

Status, implementation and scope

3.4 The Statement of Principles is not an accounting standard and does not have the status of an accounting standard. Therefore it does not contain requirements as to how financial statements should be prepared or presented, nor does it have an implementation date. Paragraph 17 of the introduction to the Statement of Principles notes, 'It will be made clear in each accounting standard how the standard relates to the Statement of Principles'.

3.5 The Statement of Principles is primarily concerned with financial statements that are intended to give a true and fair view. While the statement gives some consideration to the meaning of true and fair it does not define it.

3.6 The Statement remains an evolving document and may be revised from time to time in the light of the Board's experience of working with it and in response to developments in accounting thought.

Chapters of the Statement of Principles

Introduction

3.7 It is beyond the scope of this manual to give full details of each chapter of the Statement of Principles, therefore the following sections outline the provisions very briefly.

The objective of financial statements (chapter 1)

3.8 This chapter identifies that the objective of financial statements is to provide information about the financial position and performance of an entity that is useful to a wide range of users for assessing the stewardship of management and for making economic decisions. This objective can usually be met by focusing on the information needs of present and potential investors who require information useful in assessing the entity's ability to generate cash and in assessing its financial adaptability. The chapter also notes that there are limitations on financial statements as they will not meet all of the information needs of users and have various inherent limitations.

Thus, users will usually need additional sources of information to supplement the financial statements.

The reporting entity (chapter 2)

3.9 This chapter identifies that an entity ought to prepare and publish financial statements if there is a legitimate demand for the information and the entity is a cohesive economic unit. It also considers what determines the boundary when circumscribing the relevant activities and resources on which the entity reports. Two boundaries are identified and used as the model in the remainder of the statement:

(a) direct control – single entity accounts; and

(b) direct plus indirect control – consolidated accounts.

Chapter 8 of the statement addresses accounting for entities influenced by, but not controlled by, the reporting entity (see **3.24** below).

The qualitative characteristics of financial information (chapter 3)

3.10 Qualitative characteristics of financial information are the characteristics that make the information useful and determine whether, when and how it is to be presented in financial statements so that they yield information useful to the users for assessing the financial position, performance and financial adaptability of an entity. This chapter identifies the qualities of financial information that make it useful as relevance, reliability, comparability, understandability and materiality. A trade-off will be needed in instances where the characteristics are mutually exclusive. An example raised in the Statement of Principles is that of relevance vs. reliability, i.e., that which is most relevant may not be the most reliable and vice versa. The approach suggested is one that maximises the relevance of the information provided by using the most relevant of the reliable information.

The elements of financial statements (chapter 4)

3.11 In this chapter, the definitions of the elements of financial statements are set out and discussed. The elements and their definitions are:

(a) *assets*: 'Assets are rights or other access to future economic benefits controlled by an entity as a result of past transactions or events';

(b) *liabilities*: 'Liabilities are obligations of an entity to transfer economic benefits as a result of past transactions or events':

(c) *ownership interest*: 'Ownership interest is the residual amount found by deducting all of the entity's liabilities from all of the entity's assets';

(d) *gains*: 'Gains are increases in ownership interest not resulting from contributions from owners';

(e) *losses*: 'Losses are decreases in ownership interest not resulting from distributions to owners';

(f) *contributions from owners*: 'Contributions from owners are increases in ownership interest resulting from transfers from owners in their capacity as owners';

(g) *distributions to owners*: 'Distributions to owners are decreases in ownership interest resulting from transfers made to owners in their capacity as owners'.

3.12 This chapter also considers offsetting of assets and liabilities and gains and losses. The presentation issue is addressed in chapter 7 (see **3.21** below). Considerations applying to the offset of assets and liabilities are:

(a) as a matter of recognition, rights that represent an asset and obligations that represent a liability are not combined and recognised as a single item;

(b) a right and obligation represent a single asset or liability, if the reporting entity has an assured ability to insist on net settlement; and

(c) rights and obligations relating to an unperformed executory contract, or to the equally proportionally unperformed parts of a partially completed contract, together represent a single asset or liability.

[Statement of Principles (4.33 to 4.36)]

Recognition in financial statements (chapter 5)

3.13 Recognition involves depiction of elements of financial statements both in words and by a monetary amount. This chapter identifies three stages of recognition (i.e., initial recognition, subsequent remeasurement (see **3.17**), and derecognition) and sets three principles (see **3.14** to **3.16** below). In some cases derecognition of an asset or liability may require recognition of a new asset or liability.

Initial recognition

3.14 If a transaction or other event has created a new asset or liability or added to an existing asset or liability, that effect will be recognised if:

(a) sufficient evidence exists that the new asset or liability has been created or that there has been an addition to an existing asset or liability; and

(b) the new asset or liability or the addition to the existing asset or liability can be measured at a monetary amount with sufficient reliability.

3.15 In a transaction involving the provision of services or goods for a net gain, the recognition criteria described above will be met on the occurrence of the critical event in the operating cycle involved.

Derecognition

3.16 An asset or liability will be wholly or partly derecognised if:

(a) sufficient evidence exists that a transaction or other past event has eliminated a previously recognised asset or liability; or

(b) although the item continues to be an asset or a liability, the criteria for recognition are no longer met.

Measurement in financial statements (chapter 6)

3.17 This chapter deals with the principles underlying the measurement of the elements of the balance sheet and of the statements of financial performance. It also discusses measurement issues such as going concern, discounting, uncertainty and capital maintenance adjustments and changing prices.

3.18 Two measurement bases are identified:

(a) *Historical cost*: lower of cost and recoverable amount;

(b) *Current value*: value to the business which is the lower of replacement cost and recoverable amount, where the latter is the higher of value in use and net realisable value (see pictorial representation below).

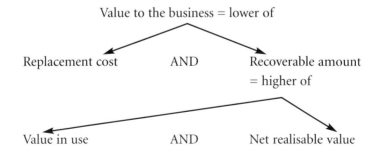

3.19 In practice some categories of assets and liabilities will be measured on a historical cost basis and some on a current value basis. The statement envisages that such a 'mixed measurement system' will be used.

3.20   Assets and liabilities arising from transactions at fair value will be initially recognised at the same amount – their transaction cost. Where a current value basis is used, assets and liabilities will need to be remeasured each time financial statements are drawn up to ensure they are included at an up-to-date value. There must be sufficient evidence and reliability of the change in value. A limited amount of remeasurement is required under the historical cost basis to ensure that assets are not carried at a value in excess of recoverable amount and that monetary amounts denominated in a foreign currency are carried at an amount based on up-to-date exchange rates.

Presentation of financial information (chapter 7)

3.21   This chapter analyses the way in which information should be presented in financial statements. The objective is to communicate clearly, effectively and in a simple and straightforward manner, without losing the relevance and reliability of the information, or unnecessarily lengthening the financial statements.

3.22   Financial information is presented in the form of a structured set of financial statements comprising primary financial statements and supporting notes and, in some cases, in accompanying information. The primary statements identified are:

•   the statement of financial performance (e.g., the profit and loss account and the statement of total recognised gains and losses);

•   the statement of financial position or balance sheet; and

•   the cash flow statement.

3.23   The role of the supporting notes is to amplify and explain the primary statements; disclosure of information in the notes does not correct or justify a misrepresentation or omission in the primary financial statements.

Accounting for interests in other entities (chapter 8)

3.24   This chapter deals with the measurement and presentation issues of the effect on a reporting entity's financial performance and position of its interest in other entities. It considers both single entity and consolidated financial statements. In the latter case the way that the interests are dealt with will vary with the degree of influence concerned.

3.25   In single entity financial statements (where the boundary is set by direct control – see **3.9** above) only the income and (depending on the measurement basis adopted) capital growth arising from the interest are reflected.

3.26   In consolidated financial statements (where the boundary is set by both direct and indirect control – see **3.9** above) the interests are addressed in one of three ways depending on the degree of influence as follows:

    (a)   *control*: incorporate the controlled entity as part of the reporting entity (i.e., consolidation of a subsidiary);

    (b)   *joint control or significant influence*: recognise a share of the other entity's result and resources but not as if they were controlled by the reporting entity (i.e., equity of gross equity basis);

    (c)   *not control, joint control or significant influence*: recognise as any other asset (i.e., as for a single entity – see **3.25** above).

3.27   The chapter also considers the amalgamation of two or more businesses and concludes that such business combinations may be categorised as a purchase (acquisition) or a uniting of interests (merger).

4 Preparation, filing and publishing of financial statements

4 Preparation, filing and publishing of financial statements

Summary of changes since the previous issue of this publication

Para.	Topic	Summary
4.150	Dormant companies	In March 1999 the DTI issued proposals for reform of dormant companies.
4.152	Consultation document *Oversea companies*	Issued in October 1999 as part of the company law review. The document sets out proposals for reforming the law concerning overseas companies.
4.154	Consultation document *Developing the framework*	Issued by Company Law Review in March 2000. The proposals include making preliminary announcements a statutory requirement and publishing them on a website, and requiring the full report to be filed within 90 days of the year end and published on the web.
4.156	*Limited Liability Partnerships*	Proposed legislation to create a new form of corporate business entity, the limited liability partnership (LLP), issued in the form of the Limited Liability Partnerships Bill and draft regulations which apply and modify the requirements of the Companies Act in various areas.
4.158	*Electronic transmission of documents*	In February 2000 the DTI issued a consultative document of an order under the Electronic Communications Bill entitled *Electronic Communications for Companies.*

| 4.162 | Discussion paper *Year-end financial reports: Improving communication* | Issued by the ASB in February 2000, the paper proposes that, for listed companies, both summary financial statements and full audited financial statements should be distributed within 80 days of the year end and within 30 days of the preliminary announcement. It also considers financial reporting on the Internet. |

Rules for preparing and filing financial statements

Preparation of accounts

4.1 Every UK company registered under the Companies Acts is required to prepare a balance sheet and profit and loss account for each financial year (individual accounts) which give a true and fair view (see **23.131** below as regards a parent company's individual profit and loss account) and which comply with Schedule 4 to the Act as regards format and additional information provided by way of note (certain types of company may use a Schedule other than Schedule 4 – see **1.5** and **1.6** above). [s226] If the company is a parent company, consolidated accounts (group accounts) must also be prepared. [s227] An exemption from the requirement to prepare group accounts is given to groups which qualify as small or medium-sized groups (see **34.23** below). For consistency, the remainder of this chapter refers to financial statements rather than accounts and notes (see **5.6** and **5.7** below).

Presentation of company name

4.2 Although there are no statutory or other requirements in this respect, it is good practice to state clearly the name of the company at the head of each page of the financial statements.

4.3 A change in the company's name during the period or since the end of the period should be disclosed by mentioning the former name in the heading on each page of the financial statements.

Example 4.3

Delto Plastics Limited
(formerly Delto Plastics (Birmingham) Limited)

Approval and signing of financial statements

4.4   The annual financial statements must be approved by the board of directors and signed on their behalf by a director on the face of the balance sheet. The name of the signatory must also be stated. The copy of the balance sheet which is delivered to the Registrar of Companies must be signed. Any copies of the balance sheet which are laid before the company in general meeting or otherwise issued must state the name of the signatory. [s233]

4.5   When group financial statements are prepared, it is normal practice for the consolidated balance sheet to be signed as well.

4.6   Financial statements of unincorporated concerns, prepared with or without audit, should be approved by the board of management (or its equivalent) before the auditors' or accountants' report is signed. Normally, the board of management's approval of the financial statements is evidenced by a declaration along the lines of 'We approve these financial statements' or 'Approved by the Board of Management', together with a signature or signatures. There may be circumstances where a fuller declaration, such as 'We approve these financial statements and confirm that we have made available all relevant records and information for their preparation', would be appropriate.

4.7   In the case of partnerships, the declaration should be signed either by all the partners or by the partner(s) duly authorised to sign on behalf of all the partners.

4.8   The date on which the financial statements are approved by the board of directors (or the board of management, or equivalent, of an organisation which does not have directors) should be disclosed in the financial statements. [SSAP 17(26)] This date is defined as the date when the board approves formally a set of documents as the financial statements (these need not be the final printed or typewritten documents to be submitted to members, but they should be complete in all material respects). [SSAP 17(5)] This date is important in establishing the date to which the directors are responsible for disclosing material post balance sheet events (see chapter 22).

4.9   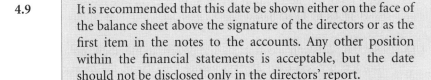It is recommended that this date be shown either on the face of the balance sheet above the signature of the directors or as the first item in the notes to the accounts. Any other position within the financial statements is acceptable, but the date should not be disclosed only in the directors' report.

> **Example 4.9**
>
> Approved by the Board of Directors on 24 July 2000.

Persons entitled to receive copies of accounts and reports

4.10   A copy of the financial statements, together with the auditors' report and directors' report, must be sent to every member and debenture holder. The timing is considered in **4.20** to **4.24** below. Dormant companies and certain categories of small company are not required to appoint auditors or to obtain an auditors' report, but, in some instances (i.e., charitable companies), a report prepared by a reporting accountant under s249A(2) may be required (see **4.57** and **34.48** to **34.62** below).

4.11   Normally the financial statements and reports sent to members and debenture holders will be the same as those filed at Companies House. However, differences may arise:

   (a)   Small and medium-sized companies are entitled to different levels of exemption in the financial statements and directors' reports sent to members, etc., and those filed at Companies House (see **4.25** to **4.27** below);

   (b)   Listed companies (which does not include AIM companies) need not, in certain circumstances, send copies of annual financial statements to those members who do not wish to receive them, but may instead send them a summary financial statement. [s251] The form and content of such statements are dealt with in chapter 36. Listed companies are those admitted to the official list of the UK Listing Authority.

Laying of accounts and reports at the annual general meeting

4.12   The directors must lay copies of the annual accounts, together with the auditors' report and directors' report, before the company in general meeting (normally the AGM – see **4.20** below for time limits). [s241] Dormant companies and certain categories of small company are not required to appoint auditors or to obtain an auditors' report, but, in some instances (i.e., charitable companies), a report prepared by a reporting accountant under s249A(2) may be required (see **4.57** and **34.48** to **34.62** below).

4.13   Such reports and accounts should be sent to members and debenture holders not less than 21 days before the date of the meeting. [s238] Members of a private company may, however, elect not to lay accounts and reports at that meeting. [s252] Where this election is made, every member must be sent a copy of the accounts and reports not less than 28 days before the end of the period allowed for laying and delivering financial statements (normally 10 months after the last day of the relevant accounting reference period – see **4.20** below), together with a notice informing the member of his right to require the laying of financial statements and reports before a general meeting. Any member or auditor of the company may, by giving written notice within 28 days beginning with the date on which the financial statements are sent out, require that a general meeting be held for the purpose of laying the financial statements and reports. [s253]

4.14   At least 21 days' notice of the AGM must be given in writing. [s369] In addition the Combined Code (which applies to certain listed companies – see chapter 7) requires the notice of the AGM and related papers to be sent to shareholders at least 20 working days prior to the AGM. Timetables for the publication of financial statements should take into consideration this statutory requirement, particularly where the notice of meeting is contained in the annual report and financial statements.

Delivery of financial statements and reports to the Registrar

4.15   The directors of every company (including overseas companies having a place of business in the UK, but excluding an unlimited company which is not a qualifying company or a subsidiary undertaking or parent company of a limited company – see **4.51** to **4.56** below) must deliver a copy of the annual financial statements, auditors' report and directors' report to the Registrar of Companies (see **4.20** below for time limits). [s242] These documents may take the form of abbreviated accounts in the case of small and medium-sized companies which qualify for this exemption (see **4.26** below). Dormant companies and certain categories of small company are not required to appoint auditors or to obtain an auditors' report; in which case, an auditors' report is not required, but (for charitable companies) a report by a reporting accountant prepared under s249A(2) may be required (see **4.57** and **34.48** to **34.62** below).

4.16   A copy of the annual financial statements (together with a copy of the auditors' report where this is required by law) of certain subsidiary undertakings must be appended to the copy of the parent company's annual financial statements delivered to the Registrar. Undertakings affected are those which are unincorporated or are incorporated outside Great Britain and have no place of business in Great Britain and which are excluded from consolidation on the grounds of differing activities. (See **23.79** to **23.83** below, which cover the circumstances when a subsidiary undertaking should be excluded from consolidation on the grounds of differing activities.) The principal exceptions to this requirement are provided where the financial statements of such undertakings would not otherwise be required to be published or made available for public inspection any-where in the world; in such a case, the reason for not appending the financial statements must be stated in a note to the parent company's financial statements. [s243]

4.17   A company that is a member of a qualifying partnership at the end of that partnership's financial year should, unless an exemption applies, append a copy of the partnership's financial statements to the copy of its own annual financial statements which is next deliv-ered to the Registrar of Companies in accordance with s242 (see **4.117** to **4.132** below).

4.18   All statutory documents submitted to the Registrar, including finan-cial statements and reports, are required to show, in a prominent position, the registered number of the company to which they relate. [s706(2)(a)] This is normally shown on the front page with the com-pany's name and the accounting period.

4.19   The Registrar is empowered to set requirements to ensure successful copying of documents delivered to him. The Registrar is likely to reject statutory financial statements that cannot be copied easily. Problems typically arise with 'glossy' financial statements which make use of shading to highlight figures.

Time limits for laying and delivering financial statements and reports

4.20   The time periods from the end of the accounting reference period in which the annual financial statements and reports must be laid before the company at general meeting and delivered to the Registrar of Companies are:
[s244(1)]

- public company: 7 months;
- private company: 10 months.

Special provisions apply to:

(a)   a company's first accounting period;
[s244(2)]

(b)   an accounting period shortened by virtue of a notice given under s225.
[s244(4)]

4.21   Companies which have businesses or interests outside the UK, Channel Islands and the Isle of Man can apply for a three-month extension. [s244(3)]

4.22 Companies are liable to a civil penalty if they fail to deliver to the Registrar of Companies a copy of the annual financial statements and reports within the prescribed period from the financial year end. The amount of the penalty is determined by reference to whether the company is public or private and the length of the period between the end of the period allowed for delivering financial statements (or 1 July 1992 if later) and the day on which the financial statements are actually delivered to the Registrar. [s242A] The table of penalties is as follows:

Length of period	Public company	Private company
Not more than 3 months	£500	£100
More than 3 months but not more than 6 months	£1,000	£250
More than 6 months but not more than 12 months	£2,000	£500
More than 12 months	£5,000	£1,000

4.23 The penalties in **4.22** above are in addition to, not in place of, the penalties payable by directors under ss241 and 242.

Listing Rules and Stock Exchange requirements

4.24 Listed companies and AIM companies are required to issue their annual reports and financial statements within six months following the date of the end of the financial period. Companies with significant overseas interests may apply for an extension.

Disclosure exemptions given to small and medium-sized companies

Financial statements sent to members

4.25 The Act contains certain exemptions that are available to small and medium-sized companies and groups in respect of the annual financial statements that are sent to members. In addition, certain small companies have the option of complying with the FRSSE rather than normal accounting standards; and some accounting standards include exemptions for certain smaller entities. These exemptions are dealt with in chapter 34.

Financial statements filed with the Registrar of Companies

4.26 In most cases, the financial statements to be delivered to the Registrar of Companies will be the same as those required under s241 to be laid before the company in a general meeting. However, companies which qualify as small or medium-sized may take advantage of some or all of the exemptions given under ss246 and 246A and file 'abbreviated accounts' with the Registrar. The form and content of abbreviated accounts is dealt with in chapter 35.

4.27

> Taking advantage of this exemption will require the preparation of another set of financial statements solely for this purpose and companies may, therefore, not consider it worthwhile to take advantage of the exemption.

Revision of defective financial statements

4.28   The Companies Act 1989 introduced new procedures for the revision of defective financial statements. These procedures include:

(a)   voluntary revision by the directors (see **4.30** to **4.32** below) [s245]; and

(b)   allowing the Secretary of State, or a person authorised by him, the power to apply to the court for an order requiring the directors of a company to prepare revised financial statements. [ss245A and 245B]

4.29   The Secretary of State has authorised the Financial Reporting Review Panel (Review Panel) for the purposes of s245B. The role of the Financial Reporting Review Panel is explained in **2.17** to **2.20** above.

Voluntary revision

4.30   If it appears to the directors of a company that the annual financial statements of the company, or any directors' report, did not comply with the requirements of the Act, they may prepare revised financial statements or a revised report. Where copies of the previous financial statements or report have been laid before the company in general meeting or delivered to the Registrar of Companies, the revisions shall be confined to:
[s245]

(a)   the correction of those respects in which the previous financial statements or report did not comply with the requirements of the Act; and

(b)   the making of any necessary consequential alterations.

4.31   The regulations provide two methods of revision: full revision, entailing the preparation of a new set of financial statements and/or report, and partial revision, requiring a supplementary note to the original financial statements and/or report. The method used should be that which the directors consider most appropriate. Auditors' (or reporting accountants') responsibilities and reports on revised financial statements and directors' reports are covered in **43.54** to **43.59** below.

4.32   The regulations do not preclude the issue of an erratum slip if a small typographical error occurs during the printing process. Where discovery of the matter that might give rise to revision occurs close to the publication of the subsequent year's financial statements, the directors should consider whether the correction would best be dealt with in those financial statements, as a prior year adjustment if it represents a fundamental error (see chapter 9), or whether the interests of the users justifies the additional costs of voluntary revision.

Requirements of subsidiary companies

Introduction

4.33   Subsidiary companies (incorporated in the UK) are subject to the same general requirements to prepare, publish and file annual financial statements and reports as are companies generally. However, there are special rules applying to the disclosures required of subsidiaries. These both add disclosures and provide relief from certain disclosure requirements.

Additional disclosures required by the Act

Guarantees and financial commitments undertaken for group undertakings

4.34   Subsidiary (or parent) companies are required to disclose the amounts of guarantees and financial commitments undertaken for: [Sch 4: 50 and 59A]

(a)   any parent undertaking or fellow subsidiary undertaking; or

(b)   any subsidiary undertaking;

The analysis must be given for each of the following items:

(a)   any charge on the assets of the company;

(b)   contingent liability;

(c)   capital expenditure not provided for;

(d)   pension commitments, both provided and unprovided; and

(e)   any other unprovided commitments relevant to assessing the company's affairs.

> The requirement to produce a similar analysis of amounts included in the balance sheet (due to or from any parent undertaking or fellow subsidiary undertaking; or any

> subsidiary undertaking) was repealed in 1996. [Sch 4: 59 – now repealed]

Information about parent undertakings

4.35 The Act requires a subsidiary company to disclose details concerning:
[Sch 5: 11, 12, 30 and 31]

(a) the company (if any) regarded by the directors as the company's ultimate parent company; and

(b) the parent undertaking of the largest group of undertakings for which group financial statements are drawn up and of which the reporting company is a member, and also the parent undertaking of the smallest such group.

In (a) above references to company include any body corporate, e.g., a foreign company.

4.36 The details to be disclosed for each parent company or undertaking identified above are:

• its name; and

• its country of incorporation, if not Great Britain.

4.37 In addition, in respect of the parent undertakings of the largest and smallest group for which group financial statements are drawn up and of which the reporting company is a member (see **4.35** above), the following should be disclosed:

(a) the address from which copies of the groups financial statements can be obtained (if publicly available); and

(b) the principal place of business (if the parent undertaking is unincorporated).

Example 4.37

*An illustrative disclosure in respect of the requirements outlined in **4.35** to **4.37** above is given below*

In the opinion of the directors, the company's ultimate parent company is Saffron Sarl, a company incorporated in Luxembourg. The parent undertaking of the largest group which includes the company and for which group financial statements are prepared is Sapphire Limited, a company incorporated in Great Britain. The parent undertaking of the smallest such group is Ruby Limited, a company

---

incorporated in New Zealand. Copies of the group financial statements of Sapphire Limited are available from Companies House, Crown Way, Maindy, Cardiff CF4 3UZ. Copies of the group financial statements of Ruby Limited are available from The Registrar of Companies, Companies House, Wellington, New Zealand.

4.38   The Act does not specify the date in respect of which the disclosures on parent undertakings are to be given. It is suggested that the appropriate date is the balance sheet date. However, FRS 8's provisions on the disclosure of control could be interpreted more widely as requiring disclosure of information on all controlling parties from the beginning of the period up until the date of approval of the financial statements. See **32.78** to **32.91** below for more information on FRS 8's requirements.

4.39   The Secretary of State may give an exemption from these requirements to disclose information about a parent where the parent is established under the law of a country outside the UK or it carries on business outside the UK and, in the opinion of the directors, disclosure would be seriously prejudicial to the business of the parent or of the reporting company. [s231(3)] Where advantage is taken of this exemption, that fact shall be stated in a note to the financial statements.

Additional disclosures required by accounting standards

4.40   Additional disclosures are required of a subsidiary company in respect of deferred taxation and pension costs.

(a)   A subsidiary company should state the assumptions made as regards the availability of group relief and disclose any payment for that purpose. The full disclosure details are given in **27.99** and **27.137** to **27.141** below.

(b)   A subsidiary which is a member of a group pension scheme should disclose that fact and the nature of the group scheme, indicating, if appropriate, that the contributions are based upon pension costs across the whole group. If the holding company is registered in the UK or the Republic of Ireland, the subsidiary may omit disclosing actuarial details concerning the group scheme, but should state the name of the holding company in whose financial statements such details are disclosed. See **30.42** and **30.64** below for further details on this subject.

Exemption from producing consolidated financial statements

4.41 A subsidiary company, which is itself a parent company is, in certain cases, exempt from the requirement to prepare and deliver consolidated financial statements. [s228] This exemption does not apply if the subsidiary company is listed on an EU Stock Exchange.

4.42 The conditions that must be met if the exemption is to apply are that the subsidiary:

(a) is wholly owned by an EU parent undertaking, or more than 50 per cent of the shares are held by an EU parent undertaking and the subsidiary has no minority interests who request group financial statements in the prescribed manner;

(b) is included in the consolidated financial statements of a larger group drawn up by an EU parent to the same date or an earlier date in the same financial year and those financial statements are drawn up and audited and that parent's annual report is drawn up in compliance with the EU Seventh Directive on company law;

(c) discloses in its financial statements the fact that it has taken advantage of the exemption;

(d) discloses in its financial statements:

(i) the name of the EU parent undertaking drawing up group accounts as referred to in (b) above; and

(ii) the country of incorporation of that parent undertaking, if not Great Britain, or, if unincorporated, the address of that parent undertaking's principal place of business; and

(e) copies of those group financial statements, the parent undertaking's annual report and the auditors' report on them, all in English, are delivered to the Registrar within the period allowed for the subsidiary to deliver its individual financial statements (see **4.20** above).

Exemptions from accounting standards

4.43 There are exemptions in respect of some elements of pension cost disclosure, segmental reporting, cash flow statements and related party transaction disclosures, as follows:

(a) in certain cases, subsidiary companies are exempt from disclosing the actuarial details of the group pension scheme in which they participate (see **30.64** below);

(b) a 'large' subsidiary (see **20.11**(c) below) that is not a public company, banking or insurance company need not comply with the additional segmental disclosure required by SSAP 25, as long as its parent provides segmental disclosures in compliance with SSAP 25 (see **20.14** and **20.15** below). The disclosures required by SSAP 25 are considered in chapter 20;

(c)   a subsidiary undertaking, 90 per cent or more of whose voting rights are controlled within the group, need not prepare a cash flow statement in certain circumstances. These are considered in **19.9** below;

(d)   a subsidiary undertaking, 90 per cent or more of whose voting rights are controlled within the group, need not disclose certain intra-group related party transactions. This exemption is considered in **32.64** below.

Requirements of companies limited by guarantee

Definition

4.44   A company limited by guarantee is defined by the Act [s1(2)(b)] as a company having the liability of its members limited by its Memorandum to such amount as the members have undertaken to contribute to the assets of the company in the event of its being wound up.

Requirements to prepare and file financial statements

4.45   The requirements of the Act relating to the financial statements and audit of a guarantee company are the same as for a limited company.

4.46   Although there is no statutory requirement, it is good practice to indicate in the financial statements when a company is limited by guarantee. This could be done either as a note to the financial statements or in the title of the financial statements.

Example 4.46

DELTO CHARITABLE TRUST LIMITED
(A company limited by guarantee)

4.47   In addition, it is useful to disclose, as a note to the financial statements, the liability of the members in the event of a winding-up.

> **Example 4.47**
>
> **Guarantee**
>
> The four members of the company have agreed to contribute £1 each to the assets of the company in the event of it being wound up.

Requirements of unlimited companies

Definition

4.48   An unlimited company is defined by the Act [s1(2)(c)] as a company not having any limit on the liability of its members. An unlimited company will always be a private company. This follows from the definitions of public and private companies in the Act which state that 'a public company is a company limited by shares or limited by guarantee and having a share capital ....' and '.... a private company is a company that is not a public company'. [s1(3)]

4.49   An unlimited company which is formed and registered under the Act is a separate legal entity and should not be confused with an unincorporated business using the term 'company' in its name. Unlike an unincorporated entity, an unlimited company is bound by the requirements imposed on companies by the Act. An unlimited company enjoys the benefits of separate legal identity, e.g., perpetual succession, no limit on the number of members, and the ability to hold property and investments in its own name.

4.50   Members of unlimited companies can be made liable without limit for the debts and obligations of the company. If creditors cannot be repaid out of the assets of the company on a winding up, the members are liable to contribute an amount sufficient to cover the company's liabilities and the expenses of winding up. This means that such companies appear to offer greater security to those who deal with them and consequently they are given the benefit of greater privacy of affairs through an exemption from filing accounts with the Registrar (see **4.51** below). Unlimited companies are therefore usually formed where the privacy of the entity's financial affairs is important and the loss of limited liability is of less significance e.g., where companies are formed merely to hold property or investments.

Requirements to prepare and file financial statements

4.51   An unlimited company is exempt, subject to the conditions in **4.52** to **4.55** below, from the requirement to file financial statements with the Registrar of Companies. [s254(1)] Nevertheless, it must still prepare financial statements, have them audited (unless one of the exemptions applies – see **4.57** and **34.48** below) and deliver them to its members in the same way as a limited company.

4.52 The exemption from the requirement to file financial statements mentioned in **4.51** above does not apply where, at any time during the accounting period, the unlimited company was:

(a)   a parent company of an undertaking which was then limited; or

(b)   to its knowledge, a subsidiary undertaking of an undertaking which was then limited; or

(c)   where, to its knowledge, there were outstanding rights exercisable by or on behalf of two or more limited companies which, if exercised by one of them, would have made the company a subsidiary of it.

The references above to an undertaking being limited at a particular time are to an undertaking (under whatever law established), the liability of whose members is at that time limited, and so extends to foreign entities such as foreign limited companies. [s254(2)]

4.53   The 'rights' referred to in **4.52**(c) above are understood as being those set out in s258(2), dealing with when an undertaking is the parent undertaking of another undertaking (a subsidiary undertaking) (see **23.11** below). It therefore means that if, in aggregate, limited companies (or limited undertakings) which are members of the unlimited company possess such rights over it, the exemption from delivering accounts does not apply.

4.54 The filing exemption in **4.51** does not apply to an unlimited company that:
[s254(3)]

(a)   is a banking or insurance company or the parent company of a banking or insurance group; or

(b)   a 'qualifying company' (see **4.55** below), or

(c)   if at any time in the relevant accounting period the company carried on business as the promoter of trading stamp scheme within the Trading Stamps Act 1964.

4.55 In **4.54**(b) above, an unlimited company is a qualifying company if each of its members is:
[SI 1993 No 1820 reg 9]

(a)   a limited company; or

(b)   another unlimited company, or a Scottish firm, each of whose members is a limited company.

In this definition, any reference to a limited company, another unlimited company or a Scottish firm includes a reference to any comparable undertaking incorporated in or formed under the law of any country or territory outside Great Britain. See **15.22** below as regards disclosure requirements in respect of interests in 'qualifying undertakings' (i.e., 'qualifying companies' and 'qualifying partnerships').

4.56   Unlimited companies are not required to refer to the existence of branches outside of the UK in their directors' report (see **6.67** below). In addition the requirements of the Act relating to the return of capital to members, e.g., by capital reduction or purchase of shares (see chapter 33) apply to limited companies so that unlimited companies are less constrained in this area. It should be noted that Table E of The Companies (Tables A to F) Regulations 1985 [SI 1985/805], which gives a Memorandum and Articles of Association for an unlimited company having a share capital, requires the company to pass a special resolution to cancel share capital.

Dormant companies

4.57   Providing it satisfies certain conditions a dormant company may exempt itself from the provisions of Part VII of the Act relating to the audit of financial statements [s250(1)] and from the obligation to appoint auditors [s388A] (see **4.59** to **4.64** below). This is achieved by passing a special resolution under section 250. The significance of the s250 exemption has diminished since the issue of 'The Companies Act 1985 (Audit Exemption) Regulations 1994' which widened the scope of audit exemption to include certain small companies (see **34.48** below). Nevertheless, it remains appropriate for certain companies which wish to exempt themselves from the audit requirements of the Act but which are unable to meet the relevant small company qualification criteria. For example:

(a)   public companies;

(b)   members of an ineligible group (see **34.20** below);

(c)   a company which was at any time in the financial year:
   (i)   enrolled in the list maintained by the Insurance Brokers Registration Council under section 4 of the Insurance Brokers (Registration) Act 1977;
   (ii)   an appointed representative under the Financial Services Act 1986; or
   (iii)   a special register body as defined in section 117(1) of the Trade Union and Labour Relations (Consolidation) Act 1992 or an employers' association as defined in section 122 of that Act;
(d)   companies with net assets in excess of £1,400,000.

4.58   A company cannot pass a special resolution making itself exempt from the obligation to appoint auditors if its Articles contain a specific requirement to appoint auditors. This is likely to be the position of most companies incorporated before 1 July 1985 (the date the Companies (Tables A to F) Regulations 1985 replaced the version of Table A previously set out in Sch 1 to the 1948 Act). In these circumstances, the company's Articles must be suitably amended before the special resolution can validly be passed. Some companies may have taken advantage of audit exemption but overlooked the need to amend their articles of association. Having taken appropriate legal advice such companies may find that a practical solution would be to pass a special resolution ratifying the previous decision not to appoint auditors, and then to pass a special resolution amending the articles of association.

Conditions for passing the special resolution

4.59 A company may pass the special resolution referred to in **4.57** above if it:
[s250(1)]

(a) has been dormant (see **4.63** below) from the time of its formation; or

(b) has been dormant (see **4.63** below) since the end of the previous financial year and meets all of the following three criteria:

 (i) it was entitled in respect of its individual financial statements for that year to the exemptions available under s246 to small companies, or would have been entitled save for being a public company or a member of an ineligible group (see **4.62** below for explanation and example);

 (ii) it was not required to prepare group financial statements for that year; and

 (iii) it passes the special resolution after copies of the annual financial statements and reports for that year have been sent out in accordance with s238(1).

A company may not pass such a resolution if it is a banking or insurance company or an authorised person under the Financial Services Act 1986. [s250(2)]

4.60 The special resolution no longer has to be passed at a general meeting at which financial statements are laid, so it could be passed using the written resolution procedures available to private companies.

4.61 An ambiguity arises because the Act does not define what is meant by the 'previous financial year'. Two readings seem possible:

(a) the Act may be referring to the last financial year prior to that for which the company proposes to claim exemption from audit. Under this reading, the company would be able to pass the resolution retrospectively, i.e., after the end of the year for which dormant status is being claimed.

(b) an alternative reading is that the Act is literally referring to the last financial year prior to the date on which the resolution is to be passed. Under this reading, the window in which the resolution may be passed will be restricted; for example, if a private company delays sending out its accounts until the end of the permitted ten months after the year end, it will only have a two month window in which to pass the resolution. It will not be possible to pass the resolution retrospectively.

It is not immediately clear why the restriction implicit in the latter reading would have been intended. Nevertheless, a company which adopts the former interpretation should recognise that its approach could be challenged.

If a company subsequently ceases to be dormant, or ceases to satisfy the conditions noted above, it will cease to be exempt under s250. It may, however, remain exempt from audit by satisfying instead the audit exemption conditions for small companies.

4.62 Where a dormant company has not been dormant since its formation, note that the test (in **4.59** above) is that it was entitled to prepare small company financial statements for the previous financial year in accordance with s246(2). This involves, inter alia, consideration of whether it would qualify as a small company in respect of the previous financial year.

> ### *Example 4.62*
>
> If Company A was a small company with a December year end, which became dormant during 2000, it could pass the required special resolution in 2001.
>
> If the company met the criteria to be classed as small in 2000 (the year in which it became dormant) but had not done so previously, it would first become entitled to prepare small company financial statements in respect of the year 2001 (it would need to meet the criteria for two years in succession – see chapter 34) and could pass the resolution to dispense with the requirement to appoint auditors in 2002.
>
> If it was not a small company in 2000, the earliest date at which it would be able to pass the resolution would be 2003, since 2002 would be the first possible year in which it would be entitled to prepare small company financial statements.

Definition of dormant

4.63   For a company to be dormant during any period, it must have no transactions during that period which are required by s221 to be entered in the company's accounting records, other than the taking up of shares by the subscribers to the Memorandum in pursuance of an undertaking in the Memorandum ('significant accounting transactions'). [s250(3)] The transactions required to be entered under s221 include all sums of money received and expended by the company, the matters in respect of which the receipt and expenditure takes place, and a record of the assets and liabilities of the company.

4.64   For practical purposes, a significant accounting transaction is any transaction, however 'immaterial', except for the issue of subscriber shares. Thus, many non-trading companies will not qualify as dormant (see **4.74** and **4.75** below) e.g., because of immaterial accounting transactions, such as bank charges, movement on intercompany accounts, ongoing expenses and asset write-downs.

Requirements to prepare and file financial statements

4.65   A dormant company may exempt itself from the obligation to appoint auditors and the provisions relating to the audit of financial statements but not from preparing financial statements, filing those financial statements or from issuing them. However a dormant company will be eligible for certain exemptions (see **4.67** below). Dormant companies would appear to fall within the scope of the guidance in 'Audit 1/95' (see **45.3** to **45.13** below).

4.66   If a dormant company's financial statements are not audited, then the balance sheet delivered to the Registrar of Companies must include a statement by the directors, placed above the signature on the balance sheet, to the effect that the company was dormant throughout the financial year. [s250(4)(c)] As is the case for small companies claiming exemption from audit, no statement of directors' responsibility is needed.

> ### *Example 4.66*
>
> The company was dormant throughout the financial year within the meaning of section 250 of the Companies Act 1985.

4.67   If a dormant company traded in the previous period, a profit and loss account will be required in the annual financial statements in order to set out comparative figures. Headings and subheadings may only be omitted if there are no figures for the current and comparative year. If the company has not traded in either the current or preceding period, so that there are no figures to be included in the profit and loss account for either period, the requirement to prepare a profit and loss account could be met by having a heading 'Profit and loss account', followed by a statement to that effect as illustrated in example **4.66** below. Such a statement addresses both the requirement of the Act to produce a profit and loss account and the requirement of FRS 3 for a statement of total recognised gains and losses.

Example 4.67

The company did not trade during the current or preceding period and has made neither profit nor loss, nor any other recognised gain or loss.

Accounting exemptions

4.68   A company which satisfies the dormant criteria will automatically satisfy the small company criteria except that it may be a public company or a member of an ineligible group (see **4.59**(b)(i) above). Section 250(4)(d) states that a company which has passed a valid section 250 resolution 'shall be treated as a company entitled to prepare accounts in accordance with section 246(2) notwithstanding that it is a member of an ineligible group'.

4.69   It appears possible to interpret s250(4)(d) in more than one way. Only a company which meets the small company qualification criteria is entitled to prepare accounts in accordance with s246(2). Note also that section 250(4)(d) does not merely say that the company 'shall be entitled to prepare accounts in accordance with s246(2)' – it says it 'shall be *treated as a company* entitled to prepare accounts in accordance with section 246(2)'. Does this mean:

(a)   that a dormant company is to be treated as meeting the small company qualification criteria *for all purposes* (this is to take the Act's wording at face value); or

(b)   merely that it may produce accounts in accordance with s246(2)?

Whichever interpretation in (a) or (b) above is correct, such a company is certainly, under s246(2), eligible to produce accounts for members which contain reduced disclosures compared to those required of other companies, i.e., in accordance with Schedule 8 to the Companies Act 1985. If the former interpretation is correct, presumably such a company may also file abbreviated accounts; claim an exemption from FRS 1 (although being dormant there should not be any cash flows); and claim an exemption from certain other accounting standards if they comply with the FRSSE (see chapters 34 and 35).

4.70 Since a dormant company will generally have very little in its balance sheet anyway, the impact of claiming such further exemptions, as discussed in **4.69** above, would usually be very slight. If, nevertheless, a company wishes to do so, it should bear in mind the uncertainty described and consider whether legal advice should be sought. A dormant company which is neither a public company nor a member of an ineligible group will of course be entitled to all the exemptions described above.

4.71 Where a dormant company chooses to file abbreviated accounts with the Registrar of Companies, it is exempt from the requirement that the abbreviated accounts be accompanied by a copy of a special auditors' report (see **43.5** below).

Ceasing to be dormant

4.72 If a dormant company, which has passed the special resolution referred to above, subsequently ceases to be dormant (as a result of entering into a transaction which must be recorded in the accounting records), or ceases to qualify for the exemptions for any other reason, auditors must be appointed to audit the annual financial statements for the financial year in which the company ceased to qualify for the exemptions.

4.73 The general rule is that auditors are appointed at the general meeting at which financial statements are laid or, for a private company that does not lay financial statements, at the general meeting held within 28 days of the financial statements being sent to members. [ss384, 385 and 385A] However, there may be a prolonged period between the date at which dormant status is lost and the next general meeting. Indeed, the next financial statements to be laid or sent to members may be the ones that relate to the period in which the dormant status is lost and therefore will need to be audited. The Act recognises this situation and provides that the directors of a company that has lost its dormant status (or ceased to be exempt from appointing auditors under s249A) may appoint auditors at an earlier opportunity. Namely:

(a) before the next general meeting at which financial statements are to be laid before the company; [s388A(3)]

(b) if the company, being a private company, has elected not to lay financial statements under s385A, before the end of the 28-day period beginning with the day on which copies of the company's annual financial statements are next sent to members or if notice has been given requiring the laying of financial statements before a general meeting, before that meeting. [s388A(4)]

4.74

It is important to plan properly when intentionally making a company dormant. As noted above, a single immaterial transaction may cause the company to lose its dormant status. For example, a bank account may be left open in the name of the company, inter-company balances left outstanding or ongoing expenses incurred. Significant accounting transactions may arise if charges were incurred or interest earned on the bank account or if the inter-company balances were written off or written back.

Non-trading companies

4.75

Dormant and non-trading are not synonymous terms. The fact that a company is non-trading is not, of itself, a reason for not appointing auditors. Significant accounting transactions, such as bank charges and asset write-downs can arise in a non-trading company.

Agency companies

4.76

It is often found that a 'dormant' company acts as an agent and allows its name to be used by another company which is trading. The company trading as principal is frequently another company in the same group as the agency company. Whether or not the agency company can be considered to be dormant (for the purposes of section 250) will depend upon the nature of the agency arrangement. In particular it will depend on whether the agency arrangement is disclosed or undisclosed – in other words, whether or not a third party entering into a transaction is aware of the agency arrangement. Travel agencies, for example, usually make it clear on the customer booking forms that the contractual relationship is between the customer and the travel company, not the travel agent. On the other hand, agency arrangements may be undisclosed.

For example:

(a) A company wishing to lease equipment to customers may enter into an arrangement with a financier whereby the financier assumes the legal rights and obligations of the company's agreement with the customer. The paperwork (invoices, correspondence, etc.) indicates, however, that the customer has entered into a contract with the company itself.

(b) A subsidiary transfers its business to the parent company, but the subsidiary's name is still used for trading purposes (in effect, creating an agency).

4.77 The key issue in determining whether or not the agent may qualify as dormant under s250 is whether or not it is required to record the transactions in its books. In particular, in example (b) in **4.76** above, the subsidiary may seek to file financial statements as a dormant company.

4.78 From a legal perspective, only a disclosed agency is effective in allowing the complete removal of the transactions from the agent's books. Thus, the agent should state clearly on all paperwork that it is acting as agent and state the name of the principal. Otherwise, the company is holding itself out as principal and therefore incurs legal obligations, resulting in transactions which should be reflected in the financial statements.

4.79 From an accounting perspective, however, it is necessary to look at the substance of transactions and the economic benefit accruing to the company acting as agent. Under FRS 5, where a transaction results in an item that meets the definition of an asset or liability, that item should be recognised in the balance sheet if there is sufficient evidence of its existence and it can be measured with sufficient reliability.

4.80 There is therefore a potential conflict between FRS 5 and the strict legal position. As a result, it is necessary to consider carefully the accounting treatment of agency arrangements in each case. As a general rule, the accounting treatment which should be adopted is as follows:

(a) where the agency arrangements are fully disclosed to the customer and the agent has no economic interest in the transactions, they should not be recorded and, provided there are no other transactions, it will be appropriate for the agent to prepare dormant company financial statements. There may, however, be a contractual duty to maintain memorandum accounts on behalf of the principal.

If those memorandum accounts are regarded as part of the company's accounting records, the entries in those memorandum accounts will be significant accounting transactions, with the result that it would not be appropriate for the agency company to prepare dormant company financial statements;

(b) where the agency arrangements are undisclosed, the agent should record the original transaction, followed by a disposal to the principal, provided that the conditions for derecognition under FRS 5 are met (see chapter 28). Derecognition requires that all significant rights or other access to benefits relating to an asset and all significant exposure to the risks inherent in those benefits have been transferred to a third party. Consequently, an undisclosed agent will not be entitled to the s250 exemption as it will have recorded significant accounting transactions,

Nominee companies

4.81   A company is not dormant simply because it does not have a beneficial interest in the transactions which it records. For example, a nominee company may not receive any income or incur any expenditure which needs to be shown in its profit and loss account or hold any assets or liabilities in its own right. Nevertheless, it would:

(a) acquire, dispose of and transfer investments on behalf of the beneficial owners; and

(b) receive and disburse cash on behalf of others.

Such transactions could be classified as significant accounting transactions and the company would be unable to claim dormant status.

Requirements of overseas companies

Introduction

4.82   A company incorporated in a foreign country may operate part of its business in Great Britain in one of three ways: by extending its own activities through a branch (see **4.89** below), by extending its own activities through a place of business or by setting up or purchasing a subsidiary company. In the first two cases, the foreign company is referred to as an 'oversea company'. The formal definition included in the Act [s744] is a company incorporated elsewhere than in Great Britain which establishes a place of business in Great Britain. For this purpose, England, Scotland and Wales are regarded as forming Great Britain (i.e., the Channel Islands, Isle of Man and Northern Ireland are not included) and the United Kingdom comprises Great Britain together with Northern Ireland.

4.83 The Act lays down separate rules, both in respect of registration and in respect of the delivery of reports and financial statements, to be applied to:

(a) limited companies which were incorporated outside the United Kingdom and Gibraltar but have a branch in Great Britain; and

(b) other oversea companies (for example, those with a place of business, but not a branch, in Great Britain).

This publication only addresses the requirements in respect of the delivery of reports and financial statements

4.84 Slightly different rules in respect of the delivery of reports and accounts apply to credit and financial institutions, with a branch in Great Britain, which were incorporated or formed and have a head office outside the United Kingdom and Gibraltar (see **4.95** below). In addition, certain types of oversea company are required neither to register nor to deliver reports and accounts (see **4.106** below).

4.85 It is worth emphasising that, where an oversea company is required to file financial statements, those financial statements will be for the *company*, not for the branch or place of business.

4.86 The Act does not give a comprehensive definition of what constitutes a 'place of business', but the following paragraphs provide guidance based on legal rulings.

4.87 A place of business includes:

(a) A specified or identifiable place at which the company carries on business [*Banque des Marchands de Moscou (Koupetschesky) v Kindesley* (1951)];

(b) A 'local habitation' of its own, such as an office [*Lord Advocate v Huron and Erie Loan and Savings Co* (1911)];

(c) A place with some 'visible sign or physical indication' of connection with the company [*Deverall v Grant Advertising Inc.* (1954)];

(d) A share transfer or share registration office. [s744]

4.88   A place of business is not established as a result of:

(a)   The carrying on of business through an agent [*Re Lloyd Generale – Italiano* (1885)];

(b)   Owning a resident subsidiary company [*Deverall v Grant Advertising Inc.* (1954)];

(c)   The carrying on of business from an occasional place of business, such as an hotel at which an officer of a foreign company regularly resides when he visits Great Britain [*Re Tovarishestro Manufactur Lindrig Rabenek* (1944)];

(d)   Operating as a property holding company with investments, but no further activity in Great Britain [Companies House Guidance Notes].

4.89   The Act defines a branch (other than of a credit or financial institution) as a branch within the meaning of the Council Directive concerning disclosure requirements in respect of branches opened in a Member State by certain types of company governed by the law of another State (the Eleventh Company Law Directive 89/666/EEC). [s698(2)] The Eleventh Company Law Directive does not define a branch. Its meaning is ultimately to be determined by the European Court of Justice. Guidance Notes issued by Companies House take the meaning of a branch from the judgements given in the European Court of Justice in Etablissements *Somafer SA v Saar-Ferngas AG* and in *Blanckaert and Willems v Trost*. At a meeting in 1994 of the EC Accounts Contact Committee, all delegations confirmed that the definition given by the European Court of Justice in *Somafer SA v Saar-Ferngas AG* was essentially the same as that in Article 1 of the Directive.

4.90   Using this definition, a branch will be a part of a company which is organised so as to conduct business on behalf of the company. This means that a person will be able to deal directly with the branch in Great Britain, instead of with the company in its home state. It should be noted that the term 'branch' is not used in the commonly understood sense of a local bank branch or an office branch at a single locality. Rather, it is used in a sense closer to the concept of a subsidiary, although it will not be a separate corporate body. It may, however, operate from a number of locations within a common management structure. Any activity which is an integral part of the company's business as a whole (and not just its principal activity) is included. For example, an airline selling tickets through its own outlet in Great Britain is likely to have established a branch and will thus need to register under the branch regime. The Companies House Guidance Notes explain that if such a

> company set up its main advertising and promotional opera-
> tions in Great Britain, this similarly is likely to constitute a
> branch. A place of business will not amount to a branch if the
> business carried on at that place is only ancillary or incidental
> to the company's business as a whole. The Companies House
> Guidance Notes explain that such incidental operations
> include warehouse facilities or administrative offices for the
> company and internal data processing facilities.

4.91   The Act defines a branch (of a credit or financial institution) as a
place of business which forms a legally dependent part of the institution and which conducts directly all or some of the operations
inherent in its business. [s699A(3)]

4.92   Since the branch or place of business is not a legal person in its own
right, and is not regulated as an incorporated UK company, the Act
contains specific provisions relating to business names, registration
and financial statements. The following paragraphs set out the provisions on financial statements only.

Requirement to prepare financial statements

4.93   As discussed above, there are three categories of oversea company for
the purposes of financial statements and reports:

(a)   credit or financial institutions incorporated or otherwise
formed outside, and having a head office outside, the UK and
Gibraltar, but having a branch in Great Britain (*credit or financial institutions*); [s699A(2)]

(b)   limited companies incorporated outside the UK and Gibraltar
(other than credit or financial institutions in (a) above) with a
branch in Great Britain (*branches*); [s699AA(2)] and

(c)   oversea companies other than those in (a) and (b) above and
other than limited companies incorporated outside the UK and
Gibraltar and having a branch in Northern Ireland (*place of
business*). [s699B]

4.94   Northern Ireland is referred to in **4.93**(c) above as the Act dis-
applies the 'place of business' regime for the financial statements and reports of a limited company which is incorporated
outside of the United Kingdom (Great Britain together with
Northern Ireland) and Gibraltar and having a branch in the
United Kingdom.

Credit or financial institutions

4.95   Credit or financial institutions incorporated or otherwise formed outside, and having a head office outside, the UK and Gibraltar, but having a branch within Great Britain are required to comply with Sch 21C [s699A], to which reference should be made for further details. Further discussion is outside the scope of this publication.

Branches

4.96   Limited companies incorporated outside the UK and Gibraltar having a branch in Great Britain, but not being a credit or financial institution, are required to comply with Sch 21D. [s699AA] The requirements are summarised in the following paragraphs and distinguish between those oversea companies:

(a)   that are required by their parent law to prepare, have audited and publicly disclose accounts (see **4.97** below); and

(b)   those which are not (see **4.99** below).

Branches required by their parent law to prepare, have audited and publicly disclose accounts

4.97   If the company is required by the law of the country in which it is incorporated (its 'home country') to prepare, have audited and disclose financial statements, then the Act requires those financial statements to be filed with the relevant Registrar in Great Britain. If the financial statements filed in the home country are in a modified form, the modified financial statements can be filed here. The financial statements have to be filed with the Registrar within three months of the date on which the financial statements are first disclosed in the home country. If the financial statements are not in English, a translation into English should be provided. [Sch 21D, Part I]

4.98

> The legislation relating to oversea companies does not require that the accounts which are filed have been audited. Nevertheless, one of the conditions for an oversea company to fall within Part I of Schedule 21D is that it is required by its parent law to have its accounts audited (see **4.97** above). If this is not the case, even if the company elects voluntarily to have its accounts audited, it will not fall within the scope of this section; instead it will fall within the scope of Part II of Schedule 21D (see **4.99** below) and will prepare accounts under the 'place of business' regime.
>
> This will not automatically prevent the company from filing the accounts prepared in its country of incorporation – this will depend in part upon whether or not they comply with the detailed reporting requirements (see **4.104** to **4.114** below).

Branches not required by their parent law to prepare, have audited and publicly disclose accounts

4.99   If the company is not required by the law of its 'home country' to prepare, have audited and publicly disclose financial statements then the Act requires the company to prepare financial statements (for the company as a whole, rather than just for the branch) as if it were under the 'place of business' regime (see **4.104** to **4.114** below). If the financial statements are not in English, a translation into English should be provided. [Sch 21D, Part II]

4.100 Under Part I of Schedule 21D, the company's accounting period is the same as that in its country of incorporation; under the 'place of business' regime, it will instead usually begin on the date that a place of business is established in Great Britain (see **4.101** and **4.113** below). Accordingly, even if the company elects to change its British accounting reference date so as to bring it into line with that in its country of incorporation, it will (almost always) need to produce separate accounts for its first British accounting period, since the start of that period is unlikely to coincide with the start of an accounting period in its country of incorporation (see **4.101** below).

4.101 The rules relating to the company's accounting reference periods are similar to those set out in sections 223 to 225 of the Act. The two points of difference are:
[Sch 21D: 9]

(a)   references in those sections to the date of incorporation should be read as references to the date on which the company fell within the scope of Part II of Schedule 21D (usually the date on which it first established a branch in Great Britain); and

(b)   the restriction that the accounting reference date may not be extended twice within five years does not apply to oversea companies.

4.102 The financial statements normally have to be filed with the registrar within 13 months of the end of the relevant accounting reference period. Special rules apply in certain circumstances:

(a)   if the company's first accounting period exceeds 12 months, the filing deadline is 25 months after the start of that period;

(b)   if the company's accounting reference period is shortened by a notice under section 225 of the Act, the filing deadline will be the date based on the revised period (normally 13 months after its end) or 3 months after the date of the notice, whichever is later.

The Secretary of State has the power to extend a company's filing deadline if application is made to him in writing before the filing deadline has expired. [Sch 21D: 12]

Oversea companies with more than one branch

4.103 If an oversea company has more than one branch in Great Britain, the financial statements referred to in each of the two cases above (**4.97** and **4.99**) have to be filed by each branch. Alternatively, the financial statements can be filed by just one branch, provided that the particulars filed on registration of the branches which are not filing financial statements specify which branch is to file financial statements, where it is registered and what its registered number is. [Sch 21A: 1 and Sch 21D: 3 and 11]

Place of business regime

4.104 This regime applies to all oversea companies (see **4.82** above) apart from:

(a) credit and financial institutions (see **4.95**);

(b) other branches (see **4.96** to **4.103**);

(b) limited companies incorporated outside the United Kingdom and Gibraltar which have a branch in Northern Ireland and a place of business (other than a branch) in Great Britain (England, Scotland and Wales). [s699B]

4.105 Accordingly, the requirements discussed below will apply to:

(a) oversea companies with a place of business, other than a branch, in Great Britain (unless they have a branch in Northern Ireland);

(b) companies incorporated in Gibraltar and in Northern Ireland having a branch in Great Britain; and

(c) unlimited oversea companies having a branch in Great Britain.

4.106 Limited companies incorporated outside the United Kingdom and Gibraltar which have a branch in Northern Ireland and a place of business (other than a branch) in Great Britain are required, by the Act, neither to register [s690B] nor to deliver accounts and reports. [s699B] Such companies will, however, be caught by broadly equivalent legislation in Northern Ireland and will normally be required to deliver reports and accounts to the registrar in Northern Ireland.

4.107 The Act [s700(1)] includes a general requirement for an oversea company to prepare financial statements and directors' reports and have the financial statements audited as if it were a UK company; the Act also gives power to the Secretary of State to make modifications to and exemptions from the requirements. [s700(2)] The Secretary of State has exercised his powers under s700(2) by issuing a statutory instrument – the Oversea Companies (Accounts) (Modifications and Exemptions) Order 1990 (SI 1990 No 440).

4.108   The Order exempts an unlimited oversea company from the requirement to prepare and file accounts, provided it satisfies the criteria set out in section 241(4) to the unamended 1985 Act, namely that: [SI 1990 No 440 art 2(3)]

(a)   at no time during the year was it a subsidiary of a limited company (or body corporate);

(b)   at no time during the year have there been, to its knowledge, rights exercisable by or on behalf of two or more limited companies (or bodies corporate) which, if exercisable by one of them, would have made the company a subsidiary of it;

(c)   at no time during the year was it the parent of a limited company (or body corporate); and

(d)   at no time during the year was it the promoter of a trading stamp scheme within the Trading Stamps Act 1964.

4.109   The general requirements for financial statements are:

(a)   Part VII of the Act shall apply as if it had not been amended by the 1989 Act and as if any provision of the 1985 Act necessary for the interpretation of that Part had not been amended or repealed by the 1989 Act (the 'unamended 1985 Act'); [SI 1990 No 440 art 2(1)(a)]

(b)   financial statements are to be prepared in accordance with the reduced requirements applicable to banking and insurance companies in the UK under the unamended 1985 Act; [SI 1990 No 440 art 2(1)(b)]

(c)   exemptions available to small and medium-sized companies and dormant companies are not available to oversea companies; [SI 1990 No 440 art 2(1)(c)]

(d)   Where the financial statements are not in English, a translation into English must be provided; [s702(1)]

(e)   additional information, such as that normally required by Sch 4, may be given.

4.110   The reporting exemptions [SI 1990 No 440 Schedule] applicable to oversea companies mean that the following need not be given:

(a) an auditors' report (exempt from s236 of the unamended 1985 Act';

(b) a directors' report (exempt from s235 of the unamended 1985 Act);

(c) regarding form and content of financial statements (Sch 9 to the unamended 1985 Act):

- the basis of computation of UK corporation and income tax liability and charges;

- amount of UK and non-UK tax charged;

- amount of and method of computing turnover;

(d) regarding miscellaneous notes disclosures (Sch 5 to the unamended 1985 Act):

- details of subsidiaries (names, countries of incorporation/registration and percentage held etc.);

- details of investment holdings of 10 per cent or more;

- identity of ultimate holding company;

- chairman's and highest paid director's emoluments, banding of all directors' emoluments into £5,000 brackets, and directors' emoluments waived;

(e) regarding transactions (Sch 6 to the unamended 1985 Act):

- disclosure of transactions with directors and officers of the company.

4.111 The financial statements have to give a true and fair view. Accordingly, they should be consolidated financial statements if the oversea company has subsidiary undertakings. They should contain a cash flow statement, a statement of total recognised gains and losses and a reconciliation of shareholders' funds. In addition some disclosures which are exempted in **4.109** and **4.110** above may still be required by accounting standards (for example, transactions with directors will be required by Financial Reporting Standard 8 'Related Party Disclosures').

4.112 Accounts prepared, as required above, in accordance with the rules for special category companies set out in the unamended 1985 Act will differ in a number of respects from accounts prepared in accordance with section 226 of the 1985 Act as amended by the Companies Act 1989. One of the main differences, however, is that the exemption for small and medium-sized groups from the requirement to produce group accounts will not be available. This is because this exemption was introduced by the Companies Act 1989. Accordingly, unless oversea

> parent companies of such groups can claim one of the exemptions set out in section 229 of the unamended 1985 Act, they will need to produce and file group accounts.

4.113 Except as noted, the rules relating to the company's accounting reference periods are those set out in sections 223 to 225 of the Act – the same rules which apply to a company incorporated in Great Britain. The two differences are that:

(a) references in those sections to the date of incorporation should be read as references to the date on which the company established a place of business in Great Britain; and

(b) the restriction that the accounting reference date may not be extended twice within five years does not apply to oversea companies. [s701]

4.114 The accounts normally have to be filed with the registrar within 13 months of the end of the relevant accounting reference period. Special rules apply in certain circumstances:

(a) if the company's first accounting period exceeds 12 months, the filing deadline is 25 months after the start of that period;

(b) if the company's accounting reference period is shortened by a notice under section 225 of the Act, the filing deadline will be the date based on the revised period (normally 13 months after its end) or 3 months after the date of the notice, whichever is later.

The Secretary of State has the power to extend a company's filing deadline if application is made to him before the filing deadline has expired. [s702]

Listed overseas companies

4.115 An overseas company with securities listed in the UK will be bound by chapter 17 of the Listing Rules (while the Act refers to an "oversea company" the Listing Rules refers to an "overseas company"). Compliance with these obligations will result in an overseas company being unable to take advantage of many of the exemptions normally available to overseas companies (see **7.14** to **7.16** below). Nevertheless, the Listing Rules specify certain exemptions for overseas companies. Such companies need not comply with the following paragraphs of the Listing Rules:

(a) **para. 12.43(v)** – an overseas company need not include a statement by the directors that the business is a going concern;

(b) **para. 12.43A** – an overseas company need not make the disclosures required in relation to the principles and provision of the Combined Code nor give a directors' remuneration report (save that it must include in its annual report and accounts a statement as required by para. 12.43A(c)(vii) – unexpired term of directors service contract).

4.116 Where specific Listing Rules refer to a company incorporated in the United Kingdom, an overseas company need not comply if to do so would be contrary to the law in its country of incorporation. [Listing Rules, paragraph 17.12]

Requirements of qualifying partnerships

Introduction

4.117 The Partnerships and Unlimited Companies (Accounts) Regulations 1993 (SI 1993 No 1820) require certain 'qualifying partnerships' to prepare and have audited annual financial statements and reports. These financial statements and reports, which should be prepared and audited in accordance with Part VII of the Act (the normal rules applying to companies generally), subject to modifications set out in the Regulations, should then be appended to the annual financial statements filed by limited company members of the partnership.

4.118 These requirements result from an EU Directive and are likely to have little impact in the UK because they do not apply if the partnership is dealt with by the method of full or proportional consolidation or by the equity method in the group financial statements of one of the limited company members that is established under the law of a Member State of the EU (see **4.124** to **4.126** below).

Definitions

Qualifying partnership

4.119 A 'qualifying partnership' for the purposes of the Regulations is a partnership governed by the laws of any part of Great Britain, each of whose members is:
[SI 1993 No 1820 reg 3]

(a) a limited company; or

(b) an unlimited company, or a Scottish firm, each of whose members is a limited company.

References to limited companies, unlimited companies or a Scottish firm include comparable undertakings incorporated or formed outside Great Britain.

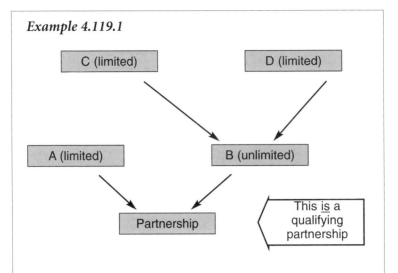

Example 4.119.1

A partnership has two members: A, a limited company, and B, an unlimited company. B itself has two members, C and D, both limited companies.

Accordingly the partnership is a qualifying partnership.

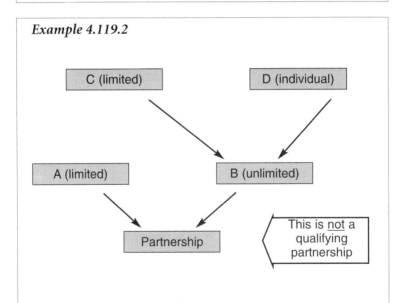

Example 4.119.2

A partnership has two members: A, a limited company, and B, an unlimited company. B itself has two members: C, a limited company, and D an individual.

Accordingly the partnership is not a qualifying partnership because D is not a limited company.

4.120

Examples 4.119.1 and 4.119.2 help to illustrate that a partnership will only be a qualifying partnership if all its "members" are limited companies, either directly or via an "intermediate" unlimited company or Scottish firm. It should not be concluded, however, that any partnership for which this is true will automatically be a qualifying partnership, since the definition is more narrow than this as illustrated in example 4.120 below. If the intention of the EU directive giving rise to the Regulations was to prevent limited companies from using partnerships to get round legislation drafted only for companies, it is not clear why the Regulations should not have been drafted so as to encompass this last example

Example 4.120

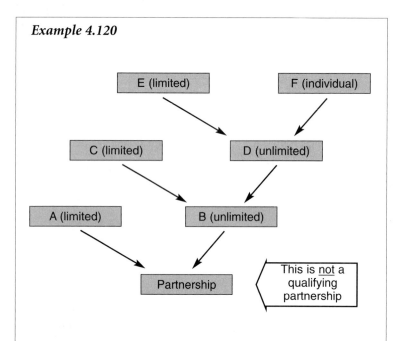

A partnership has two members: A, a limited company, and B, an unlimited company. B itself has two members: C, a limited company, and D an unlimited company. Finally, D itself has two members, E and F, both limited companies.

Accordingly the partnership does not appear to be a qualifying partnership, even though the "ultimate members" A, C, E and F are all limited companies, because it does not meet the definition: specifically, not all of B's members are unlimited companies.

Members of a qualifying partnership

4.121 Where the members of a qualifying partnership include:

(a) an unlimited company, or a Scottish firm, each of whose members is a limited company; or

(b) a member of another partnership each of whose members is:

    (i) a limited company; or

    (ii) an unlimited company, or a Scottish firm, each of whose members is a limited company,

any reference to the members of the qualifying partnership in Regulations 4 to 8 (which deal with the requirements to prepare, file and make available financial statements for the qualifying partnership, the exemptions available and penalties for non-compliance) includes a reference to the members of that company, firm or other partnership. [SI 1993 No 1820 reg 3]

Example 4.121

A partnership has two members: A, a limited company, and B, an unlimited company. B itself has two members, C and D, both limited companies.

Accordingly the partnership is a qualifying partnership. For the purposes of regulations 4 to 8, the members of the partnership will be A, B, C and D.

4.122   Part (b) of **4.121** above is less straightforward. It apparently states that, where a member of a qualifying partnership is also a member of another qualifying partnership (the latter extended to include partnerships which are not governed by the laws of any part of Great Britain), then all members of the latter partnership shall be treated as members of the former partnership for the purposes of Regulations 4 to 8. This may be illustrated by way of example.

Example 4.122

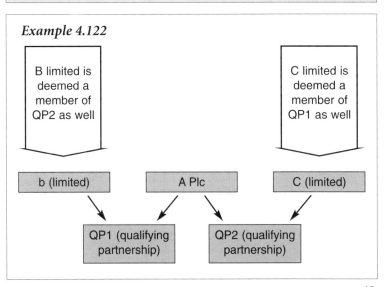

QP1, a qualifying partnership, has two limited company members, A Plc and B Limited.

QP2, a qualifying partnership, has two limited company members, A Plc and C Limited.

A Plc is a large listed company which enters into many qualifying partnerships with different companies. B Limited and C Limited are smaller private companies, which are completely unrelated to each other.

Under the Regulations it appears that B Limited is to be treated as a member of QP2 and C Limited as a member of QP1. Accordingly, unless an exemption is available, they may both be required to file with their accounts the financial statements of a qualifying partnership with which they are not involved.

4.123 Following on from example 4.122 above, if QP1 went into liquidation, under joint and several liability it appears that a liquidator might have recourse not only to the assets of A and B but also, through A, to the assets of QP2. This may be the explanation underlying this requirement, which is otherwise not entirely clear. Nevertheless, from a practical standpoint, if C tries to comply with this Regulation, it may find it difficult to obtain the financial statements of QP1 since it is not a partner.

Exemption

4.124 The requirements set out in **4.127** to **4.132** below do not apply if the partnership is dealt with on a consolidated basis (full or proportional consolidation or equity accounted) in group financial statements prepared by:

(a) a member of the partnership which is established under the law of a Member State of the EU; or

(b) a parent undertaking of such a member which is so established,

and (in either case):

(c) the group financial statements are prepared and audited under the law of the Member State concerned in accordance with the provisions of the EU Seventh Directive on company law; and

(d) the notes to those financial statements disclose that advantage has been taken of the exemption conferred by the Regulations.

Example 4.124

These financial statements include on a consolidated basis the results and financial position of the group's 45 per cent interest in the 'Vector/Delto Joint Venture' partnership. Accordingly, advantage has been taken of the exemptions provided by Regulation 7 of the Partnerships and Unlimited Companies (Accounts) Regulations 1993.

4.125 Where advantage is taken of this exemption, any member of the qualifying partnership which is a limited company must disclose on request the name of at least one member or parent undertaking in whose group financial statements the partnership has been or is to be dealt with on a consolidated basis.

4.126 In practice, these exemptions should often be available. Where a partnership has a small number of partners, it will often be the case that at least one partner will have sufficient influence that either consolidation or equity accounting will be appropriate. Nevertheless, some partnerships will be set up so that no partner has significant influence. In addition, some partnerships may be between small or medium-sized companies which may therefore be exempt from the requirement to produce group accounts. In such cases the exemptions provided by Regulation 7 will not be available.

Requirements

4.127 Unless the exemption set out in **4.124** above applies, the Regulations require qualifying partnerships to prepare annual financial statements and an annual report (directors' report) and to have the financial statements audited as would be required by Part VII of the Act, subject to the modifications and adaptations set out in the Schedule to the Regulations. [SI 1993 No 1820 reg 4 and Schedule] Such financial statements will normally need to include the equivalent of a directors' report, a profit and loss account, balance sheet, cash flow statement, statement of total recognised gains and losses and reconciliation of movements in partners' funds, and all the disclosures required of a company by the Companies Act 1985 and applicable accounting standards, other than those which are specifically excluded. A limited partnership which qualifies as small or medium-sized may, however, be entitled to some or all of the following:

(a) exemption from producing consolidated financial statements;

(b) entitlement to prepare financial statements in accordance with Schedule 8 (the special provisions for small companies);

(c) entitlement to prepare financial statements in accordance with the Financial Reporting Standard for Smaller Entities;

(d) entitlement to file abbreviated accounts;

(e)   exemption from audit.

4.128   Such financial statements should be prepared within 10 months of the qualifying partnership's financial year end and should state that they are prepared under Regulation 4. [SI 1993 No 1820 reg 4]

Example 4.128

These financial statements have been prepared under Regulation 4 of the Partnerships and Unlimited Companies (Accounts) Regulations 1993.

4.129   A limited company that is a member of a qualifying partnership at the end of that partnership's financial year should, unless the exemption set out in **4.124** above applies, append a copy of the partnership's financial statements to the copy of its own annual financial statements which is next delivered to the Registrar of Companies in accordance with s242. [SI 1993 No 1820 reg 5]

4.130   Unless the exemption set out in **4.124** above applies, a limited company which is a member of a qualifying partnership shall supply to any person upon request:
[SI 1993 No 1820 reg 5]

(a)   the name of each member which is to deliver, or has delivered, a copy of the latest financial statements of the partnership to the Registrar of Companies (see **4.129** above); and

(b)   the name of each member incorporated in a Member State of the EU other than the UK which is to publish, or has published, the latest financial statements of the partnership in accordance with the provisions of the EU Fourth or Seventh Directives on company law.

4.131   The Regulations also make provision for the members of a qualifying partnership with a head office in Great Britain to make the partnership's financial statements available at its head office or to supply them on request in certain cases. Broadly this provision applies to qualifying partnerships other than those:

(a)   where exemption is available under **4.124** above;

(b)   whose members include a UK limited company (which will therefore have a UK filing requirement); or

(c)   whose members include a limited company incorporated in a European Community member state, which has published the partnership accounts.

If the financial statements include information in a language other than English, a translation into English should be annexed to the financial statements available for inspection. [SI 1993 No 1820 reg 6]

4.132   The requirements of the Regulations apply without regard to any change in the members of a qualifying partnership which does not result in it ceasing to be such a partnership.

Publication of financial statements

Statutory and non-statutory accounts

4.133   The Act [s240] requires that where a company or group:

(a)   publishes any of its statutory accounts (i.e., its individual or group financial statements for a financial year as required to be delivered to the Registrar of Companies under s242), they must be accompanied by the relevant auditors' report required by s235 or, as the case may be, the relevant report made for the purposes of s249A(2) (report by a reporting accountant on the financial statements of certain small companies); if the company is a parent company, it may not publish its own statutory accounts without also publishing its group statutory accounts;

(b)   publishes non-statutory accounts (i.e., any balance sheet or profit and loss account relating to any financial year of the company otherwise than as part of the company's statutory accounts, such as a preliminary announcement of annual results or employee reports which contain information which can be regarded as a balance sheet or profit and loss account), it shall publish with them a statement indicating:

(i)   that the accounts are not the company's statutory financial statements;

(ii)   whether statutory financial statements dealing with any financial year with which the non-statutory accounts purport to deal have been delivered to the Registrar of Companies;

(iii)   whether the auditors or reporting accountant have made a report in respect of the statutory financial statements and, if so, whether the report was qualified or contained a statement under s237(2) or (3) (i.e., accounting records or returns inadequate, accounts not agreeing with records and returns or failure to obtain necessary information and explanations) or whether any report made for the purposes of s249A(2) (report by a reporting accountant on the financial statements of certain small companies) was qualified.

The company must not publish the auditors' report under s235 or any report made for the purposes of s249A(2) (report by a reporting accountant on the financial statements of certain small companies) with the non-statutory accounts.

4.134 The term 'publishes' in this context means that the company publishes, issues or circulates the document or otherwise makes it available for public inspection in a manner calculated to invite any member of the public to read it. [s240(4)]

Interim accounts and other statements

4.135

> The publication of a statement covering an interim period, such as an interim profit announcement, is not of itself covered by the requirements set out in **4.133** above as it does not relate to a financial year (rather it relates to part of a financial year). However, some interim profit announcements contain comparable information covering the preceding financial year and these figures should be regarded as constituting non-statutory accounts. In these circumstances, a statement along the lines of the following example should be made.

> ### *Example 4.135*
>
> The results for the year ended (date) are not statutory accounts. A copy of the statutory accounts for that year has been delivered to the Registrar of Companies. The auditors' report on those accounts was not qualified.

Rules regarding company year ends and accounting periods

Introduction

4.136 The Act requires the directors to prepare for each financial year a balance sheet as at the last day of the year and a profit and loss account. [s226] The following sections summarise the rules regarding accounting periods and give guidance on the procedures for varying the statutorily determined length of accounting reference periods.

Definitions

4.137 Accounting reference date (ARD): the date on which the accounting reference period ends in each calendar year (see **4.140** below). [s224]

4.138 Accounting reference period (ARP): the period by reference to which financial statements have to be prepared and presented to members (see **4.141**, **4.142** and **4.144** to **4.149** below). [s224]

4.139   Financial year: the period covered by the statutory profit and loss account, whether this is a year or not (see **4.143** below). [s223]

Accounting reference date

4.140   The ARD of a company incorporated on or after 1 April 1996 is the last day of the month in which the anniversary of its incorporation falls. [s224(3A)] Thus, a company incorporated on 15 April 1998 would have an ARD of 30 April. If the directors wish to change this ARD, they may do so – see **4.144** to **4.148** below.

Accounting reference periods

4.141   The first ARP begins on the date of incorporation and ends on the ARD and is a period of more than six months and not more than 18 months. [s224(4)]

4.142   Succeeding ARPs will be for 12 months, unless valid notice is given of an alteration in ARD. They start on the day after that on which the preceding ARP ends. [s224(5)]

Financial year

4.143   The financial year of a company will normally be the same as its ARP (see **4.141** and **4.142** above). However, to accommodate 52-week accounting, the financial year may begin or end on dates which are not more than seven days before or after the ARD. [s223(3)]

Changes in accounting reference periods

4.144   To change an ARP [s225], notice must be given in the prescribed form to the Registrar of Companies specifying a new ARD having effect in relation to:

(a)   the company's current ARP and subsequent periods; or

(b)   the company's previous ARP and subsequent periods.

A notice may only be given in respect of a previous accounting period if the period allowed for laying and delivering financial statements and reports in relation to that period has not already expired. [s225(5)] The notice should state whether the current or previous ARP is to be treated as being shortened or lengthened. [s225(3)]

4.145   If a listed company changes its accounting reference date, it must notify the Company Announcements Office without delay. Where the change in accounting reference date results in the extension of the accounting period to more than 14 months, the company must prepare and publish a second interim report (see **38.3** below).

4.146   Accounting periods may be lengthened only if:

(a) at least five years have passed from the end of any earlier ARP which itself had been extended; or

(b) the new ARD is that of its parent company or its subsidiary undertaking and that parent or subsidiary undertaking is established under the law of any part of the UK or the law of any other European Economic Area (EEA) State. [s225(4)]

The ARP must not exceed 18 months. [s225(6)]

4.147 There are no restrictions on making changes that shorten the ARP.

4.148

The prohibition in **4.141** above is something of a hangover of a past regime and in practice a newly incorporated company could produce its first set of financial statements for a period less than six months as follows:

(a) on incorporation a company is assigned an ARD of the last day of the month of the anniversary of incorporation – therefore, every company other than one incorporated on the last day of any given month will initially have a first accounting period of more than 12 but less than 13 months.

(b) the first ARP can be altered (either shortened or extended) by notice under s225 (see **4.144** to **4.147** above). This is not precluded by s224 which notes that: 'This section has effect subject to the provisions of section 225 relating to the alteration of accounting reference dates and the consequences of such alteration.' [s224(6)]

Example 4.148

A company is incorporated on 16 March 1999. Its automatic ARD is therefore 31 March.

First financial statements are required for the period 16 March 1999 to 31 March 2000.

Period ending/ended 31 March 2000 can be altered (either shortened or extended) by notice under s225 CA 1985 filed and accepted any time up to the deadline for filing financial statements for the period ended 31 March 2000.

4.149

It will be noticed that certain changes can only be made if the new ARD is that of the parent company or subsidiary undertaking. There appears to be nothing to prevent the formation

> of a subsidiary company for this purpose, even if the new company is formed after the end of the ARP which is to be changed.

Future developments

Dormant companies

4.150   As part of its programme for company law reform, the Department of Trade and Industry in March 1999 issued proposals for reform of dormant companies. The issues exposed for comment were:

(a)   whether there is a continuing need for a separate dormant company regime in order to secure exemption from audit for those companies not entitled by other means;

(b)   whether there is a need for dormant companies to pass and file special resolutions;

(c)   the advantages and disadvantages of seeking to remove dormant companies from the scope of the Fourth Directive in order to avoid having to file accounts;

(d)   whether the scope of transactions that a dormant company may undertake without breaching its status should be extended to include payment of annual return fee, late filing penalties, change of name fee and re-registration fee; and

(e)   the status and disclosures required of companies who act as agents.

Company law review

4.151   The DTI are currently undertaking a large scale review of company law in the UK (see **2.21** to **2.26** above). As part of this process they issued a consultation document in October 1999 on *Reforming the law concerning overseas companies* (see **4.152** below). In March 2000 another consultation document *Developing the framework* was issued (see **4.162** below). Up-to-date reports on the review project together with downloadable texts of the consultation documents can be obtained from the DTI website www.dti.gov.uk/cld/review.htm.

4.152   The consultation paper on overseas companies notes that the existence of two separate regimes at present (i.e., the branch or the place of business regime) gives rise to a number of problems:

(a)   it creates some confusion and uncertainty for oversea companies wishing to register as it is not always clear which regime is applicable;

(b) there are complex transitional provisions which apply when a company needs to transfer from the branch to place of business regime, or vice versa, and by the fact that companies may need to register separately in England and Wales and in Scotland; and

(c) there is no obvious reason why less information should be available in respect of some oversea companies than others.

4.153 The main proposals are to move to a single regime based upon the stricter branch requirements, which in turn derive from the requirements of the Eleventh Directive. It is also proposed to simplify the requirements for those overseas companies that do not have a local requirement to prepare financial statements by specifying the contents of the financial statements required to be filed with Companies House in a separate schedule to the Act rather than, as at present, by referring back to the unamended 1985 Act.

4.154 The consultation paper *Developing the framework* addresses a number of topics including reporting and accounting. It proposes that for listed companies the preliminary statement should become a statutory document distributed to all shareholders and published on a company website. It also proposes that the full report should be filed within 90 days of the year end and published on the website.

4.155 The proposed timetable thereafter is for a further consultation document in November 2000 and then a final report in spring 2001.

Limited Liability Partnerships

4.156 The Limited Liability Partnerships Bill was published in late 1999. It is intended to allow firms to incorporate as limited liability partnerships (LLPs) which will have the organisational flexibility and tax status of a partnership. The partners, however, will have limited liability, subject to safeguards for those with whom they deal. These will include public disclosure and filing of information about the partnership, and in particular its finances (broadly equivalent to that required of companies), and also safeguards in the event of insolvency. In addition draft regulations have been published which apply and modify the requirements of the Companies Act in various areas, including the provisions of Part VII of the Act on Accounts and Audit. The progress of the Bill can be followed on the DTI website at www.dti.gov.uk/cld/llpbill/index.htm.

4.157 LLPs, as discussed in **4.156** above, should be differentiated from existing limited partnerships established under the Limited Partnerships Act 1907. Such limited partnerships must always have at least one partner with unlimited liability. Except where the Limited Partnerships Act 1907 specifies otherwise, limited partnerships are subject to the provisions of the Partnership Act 1890. [s7 of the

Limited Partnerships Act 1907] Accordingly, there is no general requirement either for a limited partnership to file its financial statements, or for its financial statements to be audited, and in fact there is no general requirement for a limited partnership to prepare financial statements. In practice, however, the partnership agreement will usually specify that financial statements must be prepared, since they will be needed both by the partners and by the Inland Revenue. Partnership agreements often also require the financial statements to be audited. In addition, a limited partnership may be required to file audited financial statements if it is also a qualifying partnership (see **4.117** to **4.132** above). Accounting for an interest in a limited partnership is considered in **23.36** above.

Electronic communications for companies

4.158 In February 2000 the DTI issued a consultative document of an order under the Electronic Communications Bill entitled Electronic Communications for Companies. The proposals are to facilitate the use of electronic communication in the following circumstances:

(a) between the company and Companies House to incorporate or to register as a different type of company;

(b) between a company and its members relating to the sending of annual reports, annual financial statements, summary financial statements and notices of meetings;

(c) between members or the auditors and the company as regards requiring the laying of the annual reports and financial statements where an elective resolution not to do so is in force; and

(c) between members and the company as regards the appointment of proxies.

4.159 The proposals are not compulsory and are designed to permit, rather than require, electronic communication to be used. So, for example, both sides to the communication would have to be in agreement that the method could be used. The proposals do not address the holding of meetings electronically. A separate paper on this subject was issued in late 1999 as part of the wider company law review (see **2.21** to **2.26** above).

4.160 Electronic transmission of the annual financial statements and reports, or of summary financial statements, would encompass publication on the internet. The Institute of Chartered Secretaries and Administrators has drawn up a proposed Best Practice Guide to accompany the consultative document (www.icsa.org.uk/icsa/). The consultative document notes that the IASC have issued a Discussion Paper *Business reporting on the internet* (www.iasc.org.uk/frame/cen3_26.htm).

4.161   The subject of electronic filing with the Listing Authority of documentation produced by listed companies is also discussed in consultation Paper 37 *The transfer of UK Listing Authority to the FSA* issued
by the FSA (see chapter 5).

Year end financial reports

4.162   In February 2000 the ASB issued a discussion paper *Year-End
Financial Reports: Improving communication* addressing certain
issues surrounding listed companies communications with private
shareholders (see **6.141** to **6.143** below). One of the proposals is that
both summary financial statements and full audited financial statements should be distributed within 80 days of the year end and
within 30 days of the preliminary announcement.

4.163   The paper also considers financial reporting on the Internet (see
4.158 to **4.161** above) noting that there is a case for developing business standards for such reporting.

5   General requirements as to financial statements

5 General requirements as to financial statements

Summary of changes since the previous issue of this publication

Para.	*Topic*	*Summary*
5.52	Listing Rules	Republished by the Financial Services Authority (FSA) following the transfer on 1 May 2000 of the UK Listing Authority function from the London Stock Exchange.
5.53	FRED 21 *Accounting policies*	Issued by the ASB in December 1999, it proposes an update on the guidance on accounting policies contained in SSAP 2, to be consistent with the Statement of Principles and other recent pronouncements, including FRS 12 (*Provisions*) and FRS 5 (*Substance of transactions*).
5.59	Consultation Document *Developing the framework*	Issued by company law review in March 2000. The paper addresses a number of topics including reporting and accounting.

Financial statements required

Introduction

5.1 The directors of every company registered under the Companies Acts (see **4.1** above) are required to prepare financial statements in respect of each accounting reference period and these financial statements should include a balance sheet, profit and loss account and additional information provided by way of notes. [ss226, 227 and 735] These statements should comply with the requirements of the Act as to their form and content. (See chapter 4 for further requirements in respect of the preparation, filing and publishing of financial statements.)

5.2   In addition to the statutory requirements, the financial statements should contain other financial information and additional disclosures as required by accounting standards. Listed companies also need to comply with the reporting requirements set out in the Listing Rules (see **5.52** below). AIM companies also need to comply with the reporting requirements set out in chapter 16 of the rules of the London Stock Exchange.

5.3   Small and medium-sized companies (as defined by the Act) may take advantage of exemptions from certain of the disclosure requirements of the Act. These exemptions are dealt with in chapter 34.

5.4   In addition, small and medium-sized companies may opt to prepare condensed versions of their financial statements solely for the purpose of filing with the Registrar of Companies. These 'abbreviated accounts' are discussed in chapter 35.

5.5   Listed companies are allowed to issue to their members summary financial statements. The rules in this respect are outlined in chapter 36.

Definitions of 'financial statements' and 'accounts'

5.6   The term 'financial statements' has been adopted by the ASB. The Statement of Principles (see Chapter 3) indicates that a complete set of financial statements contains a balance sheet, profit and loss account, statement of total recognised gains and losses and cash flow statement, together with those notes and other statements and explanatory material that are specified as an integral part of the financial statements.

5.7   The general term 'accounts' has not been formally defined in the past, but is usually taken to refer to the formal accounting statements, i.e., balance sheets and profit and loss accounts (both group and company), and possibly other 'primary' statements, such as the cash flow statement, required by accounting standards. The notes which amplify these statements are not normally taken to be part of the accounts. This is the meaning assigned to the term in this manual. Thus it is correct to refer to 'notes to the accounts' but not to 'notes to the financial statements'. This may be contrasted with specific terms in the Act and the reference in Part VII to 'a company's annual accounts, or to a balance sheet or profit and loss account, include notes to the accounts giving information which is required by any provision of this Act, and required or allowed by any such provision to be given in a note to company accounts'. [s261(2)]

True and fair view

Companies Act requirements

5.8 Financial statements are required to give a true and fair view of the profit or loss for the financial year and the state of affairs at the end of it. [ss226(1) and (2) and 227(2) and (3)] This requirement over-rides all other accounting requirements of the Act and accounting standards.

5.9 If the financial statements drawn up in compliance with the Act do not provide sufficient information to give a true and fair view, then the necessary additional information should be given in the accounts or in the notes thereto. [ss226(4) and 227(5)]

5.10 In rare circumstances, it is possible that compliance with any of the provisions of the Act, even when supplemented by additional infor-mation, would be inconsistent with the requirement to give a true and fair view. In these cases, the directors should depart from the specific provisions to the extent necessary to give a true and fair view (i.e., use the 'true and fair override'), but disclosure should be made in a note of the particulars of the departure, the reasons for it and its effect. (see **21.17** to **21.19** below). [ss226(5) and 227(6)]

5.11 The statutory disclosures required when the true and fair override is used should be interpreted as follows:
[UITF Abstract 7(4)]

(a) 'particulars of any such departure': a statement of the treat-ment which the Act would normally require in the circum-stances and a description of the treatment actually adopted;

(b) 'the reasons for it': a statement why the treatment prescribed would not give a true and fair view;

(c) 'its effect': a description of how the position shown in the accounts is different as a result of the departure, normally with quantification (see **5.12** below), except:

(i) where quantification is already evident in the financial statements; or

(ii) whenever the effect cannot reasonably be quantified,

in which case, the directors should explain the circumstances.

The UITF 7 disclosures should be included in, or cross-referenced to, the disclosures required by Sch 4: 36A (see **5.42** and **21.19** below). [UITF Abstract 7(7)]

5.12 Thus, 'normally with quantification' (see **5.11** above) appears to mean always with quantification unless it is not possible.

Accounting Standards

5.13   While the Act requires disclosure of whether applicable accounting standards have been followed (see **5.42** and **21.10** below) it does not mandate their application. This follows from the requirement on directors' to produce true and fair financial statements. The ASB has obtained a written opinion from counsel on the meaning of 'true and fair', with particular reference to the role of accounting standards. In summary, the opinion notes that accounting standards are an authoritative source of accounting practice and, in consequence, it is now the norm for financial statements to comply with them. The courts may, therefore, take accounting standards into account when forming an opinion on whether the financial statements being considered by them give a true and fair view. The opinion also notes that the courts are likely to treat UITF Abstracts as of considerable standing. The forewords to accounting standards and to UITFs require similar disclosures to those noted in **5.10** above where financial statements include significant departures from accounting standards or UITF Abstracts (see **21.11** and **21.20**).

Fundamental accounting principles

Introduction

5.14   The Act prescribes the fundamental accounting principles that are to be applied in determining the amounts to be included in respect of all items shown in financial statements. [Sch 4: 9 to 14] A departure from these accounting principles is only permitted if there are special reasons for it; in which case, the financial statements should include a note giving particulars of the departure, the reasons for it and its effect. [Sch 4: 15]

5.15   Four of the fundamental accounting principles set out in the Act follow closely the 'fundamental accounting concepts' recognised by SSAP 2 *Disclosure of accounting policies* (i.e., going concern, consistency, prudence and accruals). If financial statements are prepared on the basis of assumptions which differ in material respects from any of these four fundamental concepts the facts should be explained. In the absence of a clear statement to the contrary, there is a presumption that the fundamental concepts have been observed. [SSAP 2(17)] FRED 21 *Accounting polices* (see **5.53** below) proposes an update to the guidance on accounting policies contained in SSAP 2, to be consistent with the Statement of Principles and other recent pronouncements, including FRS 12 (*Provisions*) and FRS 5 (*Substance of transactions*).

5.16   The prescribed accounting principles (set out in the Act) and the fundamental accounting concepts (set out in SSAP 2) are dealt with in **5.17** to **5.31** below.

Going concern

5.17   An entity is presumed to be carrying on business as a going concern. [Sch 4: 10] This assumes that it will continue in operational existence for the foreseeable future and that there is no intention or necessity to liquidate or curtail significantly the scale of operation (see chapter 41). [SSAP 2(14a)]

Consistency

5.18   The concept of consistency requires that there is consistency of accounting treatment of like items within each accounting period and from one period to the next. [SSAP 2(14c)] The Act specifies that accounting policies should be applied consistently within the same accounts and from one financial year to the next. [Sch 4: 11] (See also **23.118** to **23.122** below, which deal with uniformity of accounting policies within a group of companies.)

5.19   The only 'special reason' which would justify a departure from the principle of consistency of accounting policies is that the new policy is preferable to the one it replaces because it will give a fairer presentation of the result and of the financial position of the entity. [FRS 3(62)] Normally, this will arise from new legislation or the publication of a new FRS, UITF Abstract or SORP.

5.20   Changes in accounting policies are sometimes confused with changes in estimates which arise from new information or developments. A change in accounting policy results from a choice between two or more accounting bases and not from the occurrence of transactions or events that are clearly different in substance from those previously occurring or which in the past were insignificant in their impact on the financial statements. [FRS 3(62)]

5.21   Where a corresponding amount in the financial statements is not comparable, the Act requires that amount to be adjusted and the particulars of the adjustment and the reasons for it to be disclosed. [Sch 4: 4(2) and 58(2)] Comparative figures should only be restated in two circumstances, i.e., as a result of a prior period adjustment and to reclassify the results of discontinued activities. [FRS 3(60)]

5.22   Prior period adjustments are limited to items arising from changes in accounting policies or from the correction of fundamental errors (see **9.251** below). [FRS 3(60)] Corresponding amounts should not be adjusted for changes in circumstances or estimates, which should normally be dealt with in the current year's results.

5.23   Comparative figures in respect of the profit and loss account should include in the continuing operations category only the results of those operations included in the current period's continuing operations. [FRS 3(30)] Thus, an entity that reports discontinued operations in the current financial year should adjust the analysis between continuing and discontinued operations in the comparative figures accordingly (see **9.161** to **9.163** below).

Prudence

5.24   The amount of any item should be determined on a prudent basis and in particular:
[Sch 4: 12]

   (a)   only profits realised at the balance sheet date may be included in the profit and loss account; and

   (b)   all liabilities and losses which have arisen or are liable to arise in respect of any period prior to the balance sheet date should be taken into account (including all those which become apparent before the balance sheet is signed on behalf of the board of directors).

5.25   Realised profits are defined as those which fall to be treated as realised in accordance with generally accepted accounting principles at the time when the accounts are prepared. [s262(3)]

5.26   Revenue and profits are not anticipated, but are recognised by inclusion in the profit and loss account only when realised in the form either of cash or other assets the ultimate cash realisation of which can be assessed with reasonable certainty; provision is made for all known liabilities whether the amount of these is known with certainty or is a best estimate in the light of the information available. [SSAP 2(14d)]

5.27   Provisioning is addressed in chapter 17. The subject of realised profits is discussed in detail in chapter 33.

5.28   The Act gives no indication of how to determine what principles are 'generally accepted', but the point was considered by the Court of Appeal in the case of *Associated Portland Cement Manufacturers Ltd v Prices Commission* [1975] ICR 27. The Court concluded that generally accepted accounting principles are those principles which are generally regarded as permissible or legitimate by the accountancy profession, irrespective of the degree of use.

Accruals

5.29   Income and charges relating to the financial year should be taken into account without regard to the date of receipt or payment. [Sch 4: 13] For this purpose, the accruals concept in SSAP 2 is more explicit, i.e., the recognition of revenue and costs as they are earned or incurred not as money is received or paid. Revenue and profits dealt with in the profit and loss account are 'matched' by including in the same period the costs incurred in earning them. [SSAP 2(14b)]

5.30 Not infrequently, there is a conflict between the prudence concept on the one hand and the accruals concept on the other. This conflict is not recognised in Sch 4, but is in SSAP 2 which indicates that where the accruals concept is inconsistent with the prudence concept, it is prudence which prevails. [SSAP 2(14b)]

Separate determination of items

5.31 In determining the aggregate amount of any item, the amount of each individual asset or liability that falls to be taken into account shall be determined separately. [Sch 4: 14] Thus, a 'portfolio' approach to the determination of asset values (i.e., the aggregation of two or more items for the purpose of determining whether a diminution in value of one of them has to be recognised) is not compatible with this principle.

General rules as to form and content of financial statements

Introduction

5.32 With the exception of small companies and banking and insurance companies and groups, statutory financial statements are required to comply with the general requirements as to their form and content set out in **5.38** to **5.43** below.

5.33 Small companies may prepare their accounts in accordance with s246 and Sch 8. Accounts so prepared should contain a statement that they are prepared in accordance with the special provisions relating to small companies. [s246(8)] This is considered in chapter 34.

5.34 Banking and insurance companies and groups should prepare accounts in accordance with Sch 9 and Sch 9A. Accounts so prepared should contain a statement that they are prepared in accordance with the special provisions relating to banking or insurance companies and groups, as the case may be. [ss255 and 255A]

5.35 A banking company means a company which is authorised under the Banking Act 1987. [s744] A banking group is a group where either the parent company is a banking company, or where the parent company's principal subsidiary undertakings are wholly or mainly credit institutions, and the parent company does not itself carry on any material business apart from the acquisition, management and disposal of interests in subsidiary undertakings. [s255A(4)]

5.36   Insurance company means the same as in the Insurance Companies Act 1982. [s744] An insurance group is a group where either the parent company is an insurance company, or where the parent company's principal subsidiary undertakings are wholly or mainly insurance companies, and the parent company does not itself carry on any material business apart from the acquisition, management and disposal of interests in subsidiary undertakings. [s255A(5)]

5.37   This manual does not deal in detail with the rules for the preparation of accounts for banking and insurance companies and groups.

General requirements of Schedule 4 to the Act

5.38   A company is required to follow one of the two formats for the balance sheet and four formats for the profit and loss account prescribed in Sch 4. [Sch 4: 1] The formats chosen cannot be changed to an alternative format unless, in the opinion of the directors, there are special reasons for a change. A note to the accounts will then be required, giving particulars of the change in the format and explaining the reasons for it. [Sch 4: 2]

5.39   The Sch 4 formats are reproduced in Appendix III of this manual. Balance sheet format 1 and profit and loss account formats 1 and 2 follow the 'vertical' arrangement of items which is customarily followed in the UK.

5.40
The alternative formats place the same items in a 'double-sided', or 'horizontal', arrangement. The double-sided formats, particularly the double-sided profit and loss account, are usually unsatisfactory, as they tend to confuse rather than clarify (e.g., it is usually impossible to extend important subtotals such as gross profit or net current assets).

5.41   The general rules contained in Sch 4 with respect to the form and content of a company's statutory financial statements are as follows. [Sch 4: 1 to 5 and 86]

(a)   Items listed in the formats (except those designated by Arabic numbers) should be shown on the face of the balance sheet and profit and loss account and in the order and under the headings and subheadings given in the format adopted (the letters and numbers are for identification purposes only and need not be shown in the statements). The precise headings and subheadings specified in the formats should be used.

(b)   Items designated in the formats by Arabic numbers should be adapted in terms of arrangement and headings where the special nature of the company's business requires. They may be combined if an amount is immaterial or the combination facilitates the assessment of the company's state of affairs or profit or loss, but, in the latter case, the items so combined should be disclosed in a note to the accounts.

(c)   If no amount falls to be shown under a heading for both the current and the preceding financial year, the heading should be omitted.

(d)   Any amount which, in the context of any provision of Sch 4, is not material may be disregarded.

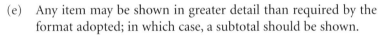

> Whether an amount is or is not material should be judged by reference to the needs of the users of the financial statements and, in cases of doubt, it should be treated as material. What must be decided is whether the item or matter is of significance to the user of the financial statements in relation to the specific provision of Sch 4 under consideration. No arbitrary percentage yardstick can be applied in judging whether an amount or other disclosure is not material. Qualitative factors must also be considered. In this respect, disclosure of an item, e.g., auditors' remuneration, cannot be considered immaterial, regardless of its size in relation to other costs shown in the profit and loss account.

(e)   Any item may be shown in greater detail than required by the format adopted; in which case, a subtotal should be shown.

(f)   Corresponding amounts for the preceding year should be shown. [Sch 4: 4(1) and 58(2)] This applies both to the accounts and to information stated in the notes to the accounts with the exception of:

   (i)   details of accounting treatment of acquisitions required by Sch 4A: 13;

   (ii)   shareholdings in other undertakings required by Sch 5: 2, 8(3), 16, 21(1)(d), 22(4) and (5), 24(3) and (4) and 27(3) and (4);

   (iii) particulars of certain loans, etc. to directors and others as required by Sch 6: Parts II and III; and

   (iv)   the details of movements on fixed assets, reserves and provisions required by Sch 4: 42 and 46.

(g)   The financial statements may include an item not otherwise covered by the items listed in the format adopted, but preliminary expenses, expenses of and commissions on issue of shares or debentures, and cost of research cannot be shown as assets in the balance sheet. [Sch 4: 3]

(h)   Offsets of assets against liabilities or of income against expenditure are not allowed.

> This requirement is interpreted as prohibiting the offset of any material amounts which fall into one of the items in the formats against another item. For example, amounts owed to a customer (credit balance) should not be offset within debtors against amounts owed by other customers. Similarly, a bank overdraft owing to one bank cannot be offset by cash held at another bank, but it will be appropriate to offset overdrafts against bank balances held with the same bank where a legal right of offset exists.

FRS 5's rules on offset are explained in **28.52** to **28.60** below.

(i) Any information required by Sch 4 which is not shown on the face of the accounts should be given by way of note.

5.42 The notes to the accounts should state whether the accounts have been prepared in accordance with applicable accounting standards and particulars of any material departure from those standards and the reason for it should be given. [Sch 4: 36A] A company that qualifies as a small or medium-sized company in relation to a financial year is exempt from this requirement (see chapter 34).

5.43 The Financial Reporting Review Panel announced (Press Notice FRRP PN 3, dated 28 January 1992) that it has taken legal advice which confirms that a statement that satisfies Sch 4: 36A does not satisfy the requirement of Sch 4 :36 to state the accounting policies (see **21.3** to **21.9** below), whether those accounting policies are required by accounting standards or otherwise.

Reporting currency

Statutory accounts

5.44

> While it is customary for a UK company to produce its statutory financial statements in pounds sterling, there are no restrictions in UK company law which would prevent a company from using a foreign currency for this purpose (e.g., the currency of the economic environment in which the company operates and in which most of its transactions are carried out (i.e., the functional currency)), if there are good reasons for doing so. A number of companies have recently switched their reporting currency from sterling to US dollars (e.g., HSBC Holdings plc, The Royal Dutch/Shell Group of Companies and BP Amoco plc).

> **Extract 5.44**
>
> HSBC Holdings plc
>
> 31 December 1998
>
> Notes on the accounts
>
> 1   Basis of preparation
>
> Since the US dollar and currencies closely linked to it form the main currency bloc in which the Group's business is transacted, the Group changed its reporting currency from sterling to US dollars with effect from 1 January 1998.
>
> For comparative purposes, the 1997 sterling reported profit and loss account has been translated into US dollars at the quarterly average exchange rates. The 1997 sterling-reported balance sheets have been translated into US dollars at the closing rate.

5.45   The reporting currency, if it is other than sterling, should be disclosed in a prominent manner on every page in which financial figures are shown.

5.46   Where the reporting currency is changed to another currency, the new currency being the functional currency, the new currency amounts for the current and preceding financial years should be determined using the temporal method of translation (see **26.29** to **26.31** below). This method is preferred, as it achieves the same currency balances as would have been obtained had the company accounted in the new currency from its inception. In some cases, the company may have changed the economic environment in which it operates, and hence its functional currency, after inception. In that case, it would be appropriate to apply the temporal method from the date of change, rather than inception, reflecting the period in which the company has been exposed to fluctuations between the new reporting currency and other currencies. Balances at the date of change would be converted at the exchange rate at that date.

5.47   A company may additionally choose to report in a currency other than its functional currency. To apply the principles above could be potentially misleading, as the accounts would reflect exchange movements to which the company had not been exposed, while hiding those to which it had been exposed, resulting in a potentially misleading profit trend being reported. Simply restating the current and prior period figures at a single exchange rate (such as the year end rate) would preserve the underlying trend reported in the company's functional currency. In such a case, it would be helpful if the notes to the financial statements explained the basis of translation, the exchange rate used and that the trends over the years are exactly the same as if the financial statements for all periods have been expressed in the functional currency. See **42.107** to **42.109** below regarding the audit report on a second set of accounts in a foreign currency.

5.48   A company may choose to draw up its main financial statements (i.e., its annual accounts) in a reporting currency which is not its functional currency. Three approaches may be taken:

(a)   report as in **5.47** above – this approach would not seem appropriate as it would lead to the statutory accounts having unexplained movements in the comparative figures in the current period when compared with the figures reported in the previous year's financial statements;

(b)   report on a temporal basis (see **26.29** to **26.31** below) – for the same reasons as noted in **5.47** above, a temporal method would not seem appropriate as the profit and loss account would reflect exchange movements to which the company had not been exposed;

(c)   report using the closing rate method (see **26.19** to **26.24**) below – this would reflect the fluctuations between the reporting currency and the functional currency in reserves rather than on the face of the profit and loss account. Given that the reporting entity is not exposed to these fluctuations, such an approach is to be preferred. It treats the functional currency operation as an autonomous branch of the 'reporting currency' reporting entity (see **26.14** to **26.18** below).

If the reporting entity were to change reporting currencies, but not to the functional currency (see **5.46** above), it may be necessary to recalculate accumulated currency movements – being the difference between the exchange rate at which the asset or liability was acquired and that at the reporting date – in the new reporting currency.

The Euro

5.49   The euro (the European single currency) came into being on 1 January 1999. As noted in **5.44** above, there are no restrictions in UK company law which would prevent a company from using the euro to produce its statutory financial statements from this date, as it is just another currency. This is a key difference from the old ecu which was not a currency and, accordingly, it was not possible to file principal statutory accounts if they were drawn up in ecus. SI 1992 No 2452 introduced an optional facility for companies to prepare and file, at Companies House, an additional set of statutory accounts, translated into ecus.

5.50   It should be noted that EU regulations (European Council Regulation 1103/97 of 17 June 1997) provide that 'every reference to the ecu in a legal instrument shall be replaced by a reference to the euro at a rate of one euro to one ecu'.

5.51   Those companies producing accounts in euros should have regard to the appendix to UITF Abstract 21 (issued 5 March 1998) on further accounting issues arising from the introduction of the euro. The appendix deals mainly with issues that arise for those companies with a functional (or, in SSAP 20's terms, 'local') currency that is participating in monetary union. The disclosures required by UITF 21, where the potential impact of preparing to change over to the euro is significant, are considered in chapter 6.

The UK Listing Authority

5.52   The UK Listing Authority function was transferred from the London Stock Exchange to the Financial Services Authority (FSA) on 1 May 2000. The Listing Rules were reissued at that date. The FSAs approach is to maintain 'business as usual' and the Listing Rules preserve the previous arrangements as far as possible. The principal changes relate to the transfer of the UK Listing Authority and the separation of the responsibility for admission of securities to listing (admission to the Official List) from admission of securities to trading on a recognised investment exchange (such as the London Stock Exchange).

Future developments

Accounting policies – FRED 21

5.53   ASB has deemed it to be an appropriate time to take another look at the guidance contained in SSAP 2 (see **5.15** above) which was issued in 1971. Since then numerous accounting standards have been issued and certain of these would suggest that a revision of these concepts is necessary. The emergence of the new Statement of Principles to act as a basis for such a revision makes such a review particularly timely.

5.54   FRED 21 *Accounting policies* distinguishes between accounting policies and estimation techniques giving specific definitions of both. It notes that 'different accounting policies present the same set of facts in different ways or different aspects of the same set of facts. By contrast, estimation techniques are used to arrive at the facts that are to be presented'. Measurement bases (i.e., historical cost vs current replacement cost) are a matter of accounting policy whereas the methods used to arrive at the appropriate values corresponding to the measurement bases selected are not.

5.55 Two of the SSAP 2 principles are noted as playing a pervasive role in financial statements and the selection of accounting policies; namely the going concern assumption and the accruals concept. The FRED notes that if either of these notions is not appropriate to a reporting entity there will be fundamental implications for its financial reporting and its selection of accounting policies.

5.56 The FRED sets out four objectives to measure the appropriateness of accounting policies to an entity's particular circumstances: relevance; reliability; comparability and understandability (see **3.10** above). The remaining principles of SSAP 2 (prudence and consistency) are considered in the discussion on these objectives.

(a) Prudence – recognising changes in the nature and complexity of markets have moved the recognition criteria for gains from 'is it reasonably certain that the gain will be realised as cash?' to 'is there sufficient evidence that it exists and that it can be measured reliably?'. The concept of prudence is, however, maintained by the FRED's acknowledgement that, in conditions of uncertainty, greater evidence of existence and reliability of measurement will be required to recognise a gain or asset, than a loss or liability. This change in emphasis is consistent with the recent standard concerning provisions, FRS 12, which prohibits a provision being made if there is no obligation to transfer economic benefits.

(b) The FRED sets an objective of comparability rather than of consistency but notes that comparability will usually be achieved through a combination of consistency and disclosure.

5.57 The FRED includes a number of disclosures which broadly are:

(a) a description of each accounting policy and estimation technique relating to material items;

(b) details of changes in accounting policy or estimation technique;

(c) details where the financial statements are prepared on the basis of assumptions that differ from either the going concern assumption or accruals concept; and

(d) details of a departure from an accounting standard or companies legislation.

5.58 The ASB issued a supplement to FRED 21 in March 2000 *Accounting*

Policies: Compliance with Statements of Recommended Practice (SORP). This requires disclosure, where a reporting entity's activities fall within the scope of a SORP, of:

(a)   the name of the SORP;

(b)   whether the financial statements have been prepared in accordance with it; and

(c)   details of departures (i.e., how and why).

Company law review

5.59   The DTI are currently undertaking a large scale review of company law in the UK (see **2.21** to **2.26** above). As part of this process they issued a consultation document in March 2000 *Developing the framework*. The paper addresses a number of topics including reporting and accounting. It proposes changes for listed companies (see **4.154** above and **36.20** below) and small and private companies (see **34.84** below). The paper also proposes that rules on the format and content of accounts and reports be delegated to an appropriate rule making body, so that legislation would provide only an overall framework, and that public and large private companies should produce a statutory operating and financial review (see **6.144** below).

5.60   The proposed timetable is for a further consultation document in November 2000 and then a final report in spring 2001. Up-to-date reports on the review project together with downloadable texts of the consultation documents can be obtained from the DTI website www.dti.gov.uk/cld/review.htm.

6 Documents accompanying the financial statements

6 Documents accompanying the financial statements

Summary of changes since the previous issue of this publication

Para.	*Topic*	*Summary*
6.131	*No Surprises: The case for better risk reporting*	ICAEW paper that encourages the reporting of risks facing a company. It refines the proposals contained in and responds to comments on, an earlier paper and also includes the results of a study on risk disclosures.
6.137	*Inside Out: Reporting on shareholder value*	ICAEW paper which encourages the reporting of information about a company's potential for creating shareholder value.
6.141	*Year end financial reports:: Improving communication*	ASB discussion paper which seeks to address concerns that financial statements are becoming less accessible to private shareholders.
6.144	Consultation document *Developing the framework*	Issued as part of the company law review in March 2000. The proposals include replacing the directors' report and requiring a statutory OFR from public and very large private companies.

Introduction

6.1 All financial statements are required by the Act to be accompanied by a directors' report. The information to be included within the directors' report is specified in the Act. In addition, for listed companies, there are a number of mandatory 'miscellaneous' disclosures which are normally included in the directors' report. The Listing Rules also require listed companies to provide disclosures relating to directors' emoluments and corporate governance. This information is usually included in a separate statement (see chapters 7 and 8 below). Also

UITFs 20 and 21 include discursive disclosures which may be located in the directors' report, or the operating and financial review, or any other statement included in the annual report.

6.2 UITF Abstract 20 requires disclosures to be made of the potential impact and extent of the year 2000 problem. In January 2000 the UITF issued Information Sheet 34 in response to questions raised regarding the disclosure requirements of Abstract 20 following the date change on 1 January 2000. They indicated that the Abstract would be withdrawn in due course, but that it would be premature to do this immediately, as problems were likely to emerge, not just on 1 January, but over the succeeding months (see **6.78** below). UITF Abstract 21 (see **6.83**) requires similar disclosure in respect of the potential impact of the changeover to the euro. Companies in the UK, as a non-participating Member State, may find the euro impacting in a number of ways, from introducing another foreign currency, through suppliers or customers requiring transactions to be based in euros, to preparing a financial statement in euros if part of an EU group (see **5.44** to **5.51** above).

6.3 Many large companies also like to accompany the financial statements with a general review of performance in the year. Recommendations to provide this type of information come from two sources:

(a) *chairman's statement*: the London Stock Exchange issued a letter in 1964 which recommended that a chairman's statement, providing details of operating and trading activities, be included in annual reports;

(b) *operating and financial review*: due to the wide variation from one company to another in the extent of reviews accompanying the financial statements, the ASB issued a Statement *Operating and financial review,* which makes recommendations on the content of such reviews (see **6.89** below). It suggests the information can be in a stand-alone section or incorporated into other sections, such as the chairman's review.

6.4 A further disclosure recommended by the Stock Exchange's letter of 1964 to be included in annual report and accounts was 'tables of relevant comparative figures for the last ten years'. In practice, most companies do provide comparative tables, with a preference for five rather than ten years' information, and, although non-mandatory, it is likely that non-disclosure will be questioned (see **6.86** below).

6.5 This chapter covers these recommendations and requirements, with the exception of the Listing Rules disclosures on corporate governance matters and directors' remuneration (including the recommendations of UITF Abstract 10), these are covered in chapter 7 and chapter 8 respectively, and the following Listing Rules disclosures which more naturally fall within other chapters:

(a)   interest capitalised (see **14.18** below);

(b)   waiver of directors' emoluments (see **8.106** below);

(c)   allotments for cash (see **18.18** below);

(d)   parent participation in a placing (see **21.33** below);

(e)   contracts of significance, transactions with controlling share-holders and small related party transactions (see **32.37** et seq. below);

(f)   long-term incentive schemes (see **8.104** below);

(g)   going concern statement (see **7.87** below).

Also covered are examples of the type of information companies are providing in their wish to address the wider interests of all their 'stakeholders'.

6.6   The future developments section (see **6.129** below) deals with two reports issued by the Institute of Chartered Accountants in England and Wales (ICAEW) and a discussion paper issued by the ASB, all three of which address communication issues and are aimed at listed companies. The ICAEW reports are:

–   *No Surprises – The case for better risk reporting* which considers the means of improving the way businesses communicate information about risk; and

–   *Inside Out – Reporting on shareholder value* which considers the reporting of information concerning a company's potential for creating shareholder value.

The ASB discussion paper *Year-end financial reports: improving communication* is primarily concerned with improving accessibility of financial statements for private shareholders.

Directors' report

General requirements

6.7   The requirement to produce a directors' report is contained in s234 of the Act. The information required to be disclosed is detailed in this section and in Sch 7.

6.8   The directors' report should be approved by the board of directors and signed on behalf of the board by a director or the secretary of the company. The copy of the report which is to be sent to the Registrar of Companies should also be signed, but copies which are laid before the company at the annual general meeting or which are otherwise issued may just state the name of the signatory. [s234A]

6.9   Difficulties of interpretation and application of the relevant disclosure provisions of the Act arise particularly where disclosure is required only if an item is 'material', 'significant' or 'substantial', as no definitions of these terms are given. It should be emphasised that, except where the Act gives an exemption on the grounds of materiality or significance, the information should be given even if it is considered unimportant or immaterial by the directors.

6.10

In general, comparative figures are not required in the directors' report other than for directors' interests (see **6.42** below). In practice many companies do include comparative figures so that the reader can better appreciate changes in performance. For this reason it is recommended that comparative information be given in the review of developments section of the report (see **6.16** to **6.20** below).

Principal activities of the company

6.11   The directors' report should state the principal activities of the company and its subsidiaries during the financial year and details of any significant change in these activities during the year. [s234(2)] A definition of 'principal activities' or 'significant change' is not given in the Act, but the following guidelines are suggested.

6.12

Principal activities disclosed are usually taken to mean categories of important horizontal diversification representing distinct classes of industry and commerce (e.g., textiles, oil, publishing, electrical equipment). Vertical analysis (e.g., wholesale, retail, manufacturing, factored, domestic, export) may be made for internal management and other reporting purposes, but is usually not meaningful for the reader of the financial statements.

6.13   It is not always an easy matter to decide whether differing types of business are sufficiently significant to require separate disclosure. Although no precise rule can be laid down, it is suggested that those activities which constitute less than 10 per cent of the total of turnover or profits before taxation should not be separately disclosed.

Example 6.13

The company and its subsidiaries are engaged principally in the manufacture, distribution and sale of food products, in hotel and catering operations and in property development.

6.14 A change in activities which is disclosed usually involves the commencement or cessation of a complete activity rather than a change in degree of activity. Frequently, a change in activities involves the acquisition or disposal of a subsidiary company. It is not sufficient to disclose details of such acquisitions or disposals without also disclosing any resultant change in the group's activities. Unless informed otherwise, the reader will assume that the acquisition or disposal does not involve any such change.

Example 6.14

The principal activities of the group continue to be consumer electronics, music, films, video, software and leisure, and domestic appliances. During the year, the group withdrew from the medical electronics business and from the hotel and restaurant activities.

6.15 Where no change in activities has taken place during the year, it is recommended that this fact be disclosed.

Example 6.15.1

There has been no change in these activities during the year.

Example 6.15.2

The principal activities of the company continue to be those of a holding company with subsidiaries engaged in ...

Review of developments

6.16 The directors' report should contain a fair review of the developments of the business of the company and its subsidiaries during the financial year and of their position at the end of it. [s234(1)(a)]

Review of developments during the year

6.17 What constitutes 'a fair review' for this purpose is a matter to be determined by the directors. Current reporting practices by public companies indicate a wide variation in the extent of disclosure, ranging from brief generalised statements to comprehensive reviews covering separately each major activity.

6.18 No clear guidelines have emerged as to the form and content of the review of developments necessary to comply with this requirement of the Act. The ASB Statement *Operating and* *financial review* provides larger companies with the recommended contents of a comprehensive review (see **6.89** to **6.121** below). It is envisaged that the matters which the Act intended to be shown under this heading are similar to those the ASB Statement states as example matters to be discussed in relation to operating results for the period (see **6.95** to **6.98** below). Larger companies are encouraged to provide a full operating and financial review; for smaller companies, it is suggested that it is good practice to deal with the matters discussed below.

(a)   The review should highlight the significant measures of performance (i.e., turnover, profits from ordinary activities, exceptional and extraordinary items), indicating comparisons with the preceding year and, where relevant, with other prior years. The directors' report on the model financial statements of Delto PLC (see chapter 46) illustrates the use of percentage changes to emphasise the extent of growth in activities and performance.

(b)   The main factors which have contributed to any significant change in results should be disclosed. This can best be done by discussing the results and developments by significantly different activities. This should contribute to a better understanding of the financial breakdowns of turnover and profits which are required to be given in the notes to the accounts.

(c)   The review should include a discussion of any significant acquisitions and disposals of businesses and fixed assets, and exceptional trading conditions. Separate headings could be given to any of these topics.

6.19   There appears to be no uniformity as to where the review is shown in the report. The ASB Statement does not encourage the information to be given in any one place. Many companies include their reviews in the chairman's statement or in a review report separate from the directors' report. Most of these reviews are referred to in the directors' report and this seems necessary to comply with the requirements of the Act.

Review of position at the end of year

6.20   To deal adequately with the position of the company and its subsidiaries at the end of the year, the following matters should be considered:

(a)   changes in and adequacy of working capital, levels of

> stocks, debtors, creditors and borrowings as compared with the preceding year;
>
> (b) proposals for financing any major commitments; and
>
> (c) ratios such as gearing, current assets: current liabilities and net assets per share.

Published forecasts

6.21 Listed companies should give an explanation if the results for the period under review differ by 10 per cent or more from any published forecast or estimate by the company. [Listing Rules 12.43(b)]

6.22
> This latter requirement could refer not only to the obvious example of a forecast given in an offer or rebuttal document, but also any forecast given in an earlier chairman's statement or directors' report.

Future developments in the business

6.23 The report should contain an indication of the likely future developments in the business of the company and its subsidiaries. [Sch 7: 6(b)]

6.24
> This seems to require:
>
> (a) a statement, in general terms, of the expectation of the directors regarding the trend of earnings in the forthcoming year;
>
> (b) details of decisions made which will have a significant impact on earnings or on the course of the business (e.g., new products, plans for expansion/rationalisation, proposed disposals/acquisitions); and
>
> (c) the effect of significant events beyond the control of the company which have occurred or are expected to occur (e.g., restrictive legislation, technological changes, loss of markets or shortage of supplies, political or economic disturbances in the company's markets, interest rate changes).

6.25 This is another area of overlap with the recommendations of the ASB Statement *Operating and financial review.* Larger companies are encouraged to provide the wider disclosures recommended by the ASB Statement; the example matters included under the headings 'dynamics of the business' and 'investment for the future' seem particularly relevant in this respect (see **6.99** to **6.103** below).

Dividends

6.26   The directors' report should state the amount, if any, recommended to be paid as dividend. [s234(1)(b)] Where the directors do not propose a dividend, it is customary to state this. Listed companies should give details of any agreement whereby a shareholder has waived or has agreed to waive dividends, for both future dividends and dividends for the period under review. [Listing Rules 12.43(e)]

Post balance sheet events

6.27   The directors' report should contain particulars of any important events affecting the company or any of its subsidiaries which have occurred since the end of the financial year. [Sch 7: 6(a)] There is a similar requirement in SSAP 17 for disclosure in the notes to the accounts of 'non-adjusting post balance sheet events' which are of such materiality that their non-disclosure would affect the ability of users of financial statements to reach a proper understanding of the financial position. While an event might be thought sufficiently important to require disclosure in the directors' report, it may not be necessary for a proper understanding of the financial position and therefore would not need to be disclosed under SSAP 17; however, clearly any event which needs to be disclosed in the notes to the accounts under SSAP 17 is also an important event to be disclosed in the directors' report to comply with the Act. It is suggested that, in these circumstances, it is appropriate to make only a brief mention of the matter in the directors' report, with a reference to the relevant note in the financial statements. This is the approach adopted in the directors' report included in the model report and accounts of Delto PLC (see chapter 46).

Fixed assets

6.28   The directors' report should contain particulars of any substantial difference between the market value and balance sheet value of interests in land held by the company or any of its subsidiary undertakings if the directors decide that this is significant to shareholders or debenture holders. [Sch 7: 1(2)]

6.29   'Land' is usually taken to include buildings and other capitalised building improvements such as car parks, drainage, etc.

6.30   No guidance is provided by the Act as to what is 'substantial' and as to the circumstances in which the information should be regarded as 'significant'. A substantial difference between book and market value is usually significant to shareholders or debenture holders where land and buildings are suitable for alternative uses or redevelopment so that their current value

> greatly exceeds book value. Since the realisation of such a difference could often only be achieved by the company selling the property in question, a fair presentation would also disclose any tax liabilities which would arise as a result of such a sale.

Research and development

6.31 The directors' report should contain an indication of the activities (if any) of the company and its subsidiaries in the field of research and development. [Sch 7: 6(c)] This appears to require a description of the progress of projects which are expected to result in new or improved products, services, or production techniques. Additional disclosure regarding the level of expenditure on research and development is required to be given in the financial statements (see **9.223** to **9.225** below).

Acquisition of own shares

6.32 Where a company purchases its own shares during the year, the following information should be given in the directors' report:
[Sch 7: Part II]

(a) the number and nominal value of shares purchased and the percentage of the called-up share capital which those shares represent;

(b) the consideration paid; and

(c) the reasons for the purchases.

6.33 Other dealings in own shares, which should also be disclosed under Sch 7: 7, include own shares which are:

(a) acquired by the company through forfeiture or gift; or

(b) acquired by the company's nominee or by others with company financial assistance, where the company has a beneficial interest; or

(c) made subject to a lien or charge by the company.

The disclosures required in these circumstances, which are expected to be rare, are contained in Sch 7: 8.

6.34 The Listing Rules require listed companies to disclose the following additional information regarding arrangements for the acquisition of their own shares:
[Listing Rules 12.43(n)]

(a) any authority given by the shareholders for the company to purchase its own shares which exists at the end of the year (i.e., authority which has not yet been exercised and is still valid);

(b) where acquisitions have been made (or are proposed) other than by a tender or partial offer to all shareholders, or by purchases through the market, the names of the sellers of the shares being purchased or proposed to be purchased in the year; and

(c) where purchases, or options or contracts for purchase have been entered into since the end of the financial year covered by the report, the same particulars as are required by the Act in respect of purchases during the year (see **6.32** above).

6.35   The circumstances under which a company may legally purchase or redeem its own shares and the requirements to ensure maintenance of capital are discussed in chapter 33.

Directors

Directors' names and details of non-executive directors

6.36   Disclosure is required of the names of the persons who were directors of the company at any time during the financial year. [s234(2)] This can be achieved either by listing the names of the directors or referring the reader to the page where this information may be found.

6.37   The following information, which is not required by the Act, or any other regulation, is also often given either in the directors' report or in the board's remuneration report to shareholders (see chapter 8 below):

(a)   the dates of appointments or resignations occurring during the period;

(b)   changes in the directors since the end of the financial year; and

(c)   the directors who retire at the annual general meeting and whether they offer themselves for re-election.

6.38   The requirement for listed companies to disclose the identity of independent non-executive directors, together with a short biographical note on each, was removed by amendment 13 to the Listing Rules with effect from January 1999. [Listing Rules 12.43(i)] However, Code Provision A.3.2 requires non-excutive directors considered to be independent to be identified in the annual report (see **7.31** below).

6.39   Provision A.6.2 of the Combined Code requires disclosure of the names of directors submitted for election or re-election, together with sufficient biographical detail to enable shareholders to take an informed decision on their election. Such disclosure might appear in the notice of the AGM or the notes to it.

Membership of committees

6.40 The Combined Code recommends disclosure of the membership of three committees:

(a) the members of the remuneration committee in the board's remuneration report to members (Code provision B.2.3 – see **8.111** below);

(b) the identification of the chairman and members of the nominations committee (Code provision A.5.1 – see **7.85** below); and

(c) the members of the audit committee (Code provision D.3.1 – see **7.85** below).

Although there is no guidance as to where in the annual report the last two disclosures are made, it is suggested that the information be given with the other information concerning directors in the narrative statement (see **7.32** below).

Directors' interests in shares or debentures

6.41 The interests in shares or debentures of the company and other group companies, which for these purposes includes a body corporate (i.e., including a foreign company) in the same group, of each person who was a director at the end of the financial year should be stated in the directors' report or, alternatively, in the notes to the accounts. [Sch 7: 2A] If a director has no such interest, this should be stated. The interests to be reported are those shown in the register of directors' interests kept under s325. A body corporate is in the same group as the reporting company if it is a subsidiary or holding company of the reporting company, or it is another subsidiary of the holding company of the reporting company (i.e., a fellow subsidiary. [Sch 7: 2(2)(b)] Thus interests in associates or joint ventures of the group are not caught by this requirement.

6.42 If a director has an interest at the year end, both the interests at the beginning of the year (or at the date of appointment) and the interests at the end of the year should be disclosed. The details to be disclosed are the number of shares in and amount of debentures of each company (specifying it) in which each director was interested as recorded in the register of directors' interests. The interests of a director's spouse and infant children (other than any who are also directors of the company) are to be treated as interests of the director. [s328] There are reliefs from these disclosures in certain cases given by SI 1985 No 802 (see **6.44** below).

6.43   Part 1 of Sch 13 contains rules for interpretation of the requirements. It states that:

(a)   an interest in shares or debentures includes any interest of any kind whatsoever; [Sch 13: 1(1)]

(b)   any restraints or restrictions on the exercise of any rights attached to the interest is disregarded; [Sch 13: 1(2)]

(c)   it is immaterial that the shares or debentures in which a person has an interest are unidentifiable; [Sch 13: 8] and

(d)   particulars of any duplication in holdings (i.e., joint holdings) should be given as interests of each of the holders. [Sch 13: 7]

6.44   The following table summarises the specific rules for determining the interests which are included in and excluded from the register and hence from the disclosure requirements (see **6.41** above).

Included:

(a)   an interest as a beneficiary under a trust; [Sch 13: 2]

(b)   joint interests (each notifiable); [Sch 13: 7]

(c)   an interest arising from a contract for the purchase of shares or debentures; [Sch 13: 3]

(d)   an entitlement to exercise any right conferred by the holding of shares or debentures (except as holder of a proxy for a specified meeting); [Sch 13: 3]

(e)   a right to call for delivery of shares or debentures, a right to acquire an interest, or an obligation to take an interest in shares or debentures (but excluding a right to subscribe for shares or debentures – see **6.49** below); [Sch 13: 6]

(f)   an interest acquired through another body corporate, if that body corporate is interested and:

    (i)   that body corporate or its directors are accustomed to act in accordance with the instructions of the notifying director; or

    (ii)   the notifying director controls one-third of the voting power in that body corporate. [Sch 13: 4]

Excluded:

(a)   interests of a director of a reporting company, which is a wholly owned subsidiary, and the director is also a director of the parent body corporate which will report the interest (the exemption is from notifying the reporting company); [SI 1985 No 802: 3(1)(b)]

(b)   where a reporting company is a wholly owned subsidiary of a body corporate incorporated outside Great Britain, interests in any body corporate in the group incorporated outside Great Britain (the exemption is from notifying the reporting company); [SI 1985 No 802: 3(1)(a)]

(c) a person holding shares or debentures as a bare trustee or custodian trustee (see **6.45** below); [Sch 13: 10]

(d) interests arising as a trustee or personal representative where the public trustee is also a trustee or personal representative (the exemption is from notifying the reporting company); [SI 1985 No 802: 2(a)]

(e) a remainder interest in trust property, so long as the life interest subsists; [Sch 13: 9]

(f) interests in shares arising solely on account of a limitation in the Memorandum or Articles on a person's rights of disposal of shares (the exemption is from notifying the reporting company); [SI 1985 No 802: 2(g)]

(g) interests in shares or debentures of a society registered under the Industrial and Provident Societies Act 1965 (the exemption is from notifying the reporting company); [SI 1985 No 802: 2(b)]

(h) interests as a trustee or beneficiary of an approved superannuation fund or retirement benefit scheme (the exemption is from notifying the reporting company). [SI 1985 No 802: 2(c)]

6.45 The definitions of trustees for purpose of the exclusion stated at **6.44**(c) above are:

(a) *bare trustee*: a trustee with no duties, except to convey the assets to or by the direction of the beneficiaries. He should have no beneficial interest in the context of these rules (e.g., a nominee);

(b) *custodian trustee*: a trustee in whose name assets have been vested, but who has no powers of administration. He is bound to act in accordance with the directions of the managing trustees as long as there is no breach of trust (e.g., a bank which holds the assets of a unit trust).

6.46 Each director is obliged, within five days of his appointment [s324 and Sch 13: Part II], to notify the company in writing of his interests in shares or debentures of the company and group companies. Any subsequent change in the interests should be notified to the company within five days of the 'event' which causes the change. An event is normally a sale, purchase or inheritance. Part III of Sch 13 to the Act covers most circumstances which constitute an event and specifies the information to be included in the notice.

6.47 A director for this purpose includes a shadow director (i.e., any person in accordance with whose directions or instructions the directors are accustomed to act, unless they do so only on advice given by this person in a professional capacity). [s324(6)]

6.48 It also includes an alternate director from the moment he is appointed to the time he is relieved of his post and not just when he is performing the duties of a director.

6.49 The Act requires disclosure of registered rights to subscribe for shares or debentures of group companies (again includes a body corporate) granted to, or exercised by, directors and immediate families during the year. [Sch 7: 2B] (Such rights are not deemed to be interests in shares or debentures under Sch 13, but s325 requires them to be notified and recorded in the register of directors' interests.)

Additional requirement for listed companies

6.50 Listed companies incorporated in the UK should also disclose the beneficial and non-beneficial interest of each director of the company disclosed to the company under the Companies Act 1985 at the end of the financial period, together with any changes in those interests which have occurred between the end of the financial year and a date not more than one month prior to the date of the notice of the general meeting at which the accounts are to be laid before the company. If there has been no change, this fact should be disclosed. [Listing Rules 12.43(k)] An interest should be shown as non-beneficial only if the director, his spouse and infant children have no beneficial interests.

UITF Abstract 10 Disclosure of directors' share options

6.51 The disclosures on directors' share options that are recommended by UITF Abstract 10 are dealt with in chapter 8 below.

Employees

Employee involvement in affairs, policy and performance

6.52 Sch 7: 11 requires the directors' report to contain a statement describing the action that has been taken during the financial year to introduce, maintain or develop arrangements aimed at:

(a) providing employees systematically with information on matters of concern to them as employees;

(b) consulting employees or their representatives on a regular basis, so that the views of employees can be taken into account in making decisions which are likely to affect their interests;

(c)　encouraging the involvement of employees in the company's performance through an employees' share scheme or by some other means; and

(d)　achieving a common awareness on the part of all employees of the financial and economic factors affecting the performance of the company.

6.53　This requirement applies only where the average number of persons employed during the financial year exceeds 250. The number of employees for this purpose is determined by dividing the sum of the number of employees employed under contracts of service in each week (whether throughout the week or not, but excluding those persons who worked wholly or mainly outside the UK) by the number of weeks in the financial year.

6.54　The DTI has stated that the disclosure is intended to refer to individual companies where such information would be relevant and not to groups of companies. Thus, a holding company which employed less than 251 people need not make the above disclosure in the group directors' report even though the total of group employees exceeded 250.

6.55　An example of appropriate wording is contained in the directors' report of Delto PLC in chapter 46.

Disabled persons

6.56　Sch 7: 9 requires the directors' report to contain a statement describing the company's policy in respect of employment of disabled persons as it has been applied during the financial year:

(a)　for giving full and fair consideration to applications for employment by the company made by disabled persons, having regard to their particular aptitudes and abilities;

(b)　for continuing the employment of, and for arranging appropriate training for, employees of the company who have become disabled persons during the period when they were employed by the company; and

(c)　otherwise for the training, career development and promotion of disabled persons employed by the company.

6.57　This requirement applies to a company which employs more than 250 persons for each week of the financial year. The calculation of the number of employees for this purpose is the same as for the disclosures applicable to employee involvement in affairs, policy and performance (see **6.53** and **6.54** above).

6.58 As with the requirement to report the policy regarding employee involvement in affairs, policy and performance, this requirement applies only to individual companies which employ more than 250 people and not to groups (see **6.54** above).

Interests in contracts

6.59 The Listing Rules require listed companies to disclose any contracts of significance:
[Listing Rules 12.43(q), (r) and (s)]

(a) where a director of the company is or was materially interested in such a contract to which a group company is party; and

(b) between any group company and a controlling shareholder, including a contract for the provision of services to a group company by a controlling shareholder.

6.60 These requirements are discussed in detail in **32.37** to **32.48** below.

Major holdings

6.61 Listed companies are required to include in their annual report and accounts a statement of the major interests of any persons in the share capital of the company. [Listing Rules 12.43(l)] The statement should be made of the position at a date not more than one month prior to the date of the notice calling the annual meeting and should state the names of the persons interested and the amounts of their interests. If no such major interests have been notified to the company, this should be stated. It is customary to give this information in the directors' report.

6.62 The interests which are to be stated are those which are disclosed to the company in accordance with ss198 to 208. The register should include 'material interests' of three per cent or more and all interests (whether including 'material interests' or not) of 10 per cent or more notified to the company.

6.63 The rules for notification of substantial interests are complex and are contained in ss198 to 210A. Notification is required as soon as a person has a material interest in three per cent or more of the voting shares of a public company or an interest of 10 per cent or more [s199(4) or they cease to have such an interest [s199(5)(a)], and changes should be notified when they result in the interest to be reported changing by one per cent or more [s199(5)(b)]. In calculating a change of interest for the purposes of s199(5)(b) the percentage change should, if it is not a whole number, be rounded down to the next whole number. [s200(1)] The term 'interest' is very widely construed; a person's interest is not restricted to a beneficial interest and it includes the interests of his close family and of bodies corporate which are accustomed to act on his instructions or of which he controls one-third or more of the voting power. A 'material interest' is defined in s199; it excludes such interests as those managed on behalf of others or operated under a unit trust scheme. In addition, ss204 to 206 catch the situation where two or more people agree together to acquire voting shares in a 'target company' (i.e., concert parties).

Auditors' trustee appointments

6.64 When a partner or member of staff (or a person connected with either) of an audit firm is the trustee of a trust holding shares in an audit client, then there is a potential threat to objectivity and independence. The ICAEW *Guide to Professional Ethics* provides guidance relating to such trustee appointments. This guide requires disclosure of the trust investment in the accounts, in the directors' report or in the auditors' report, save in the case of trustee shareholdings where the aggregate of all relevant shareholdings is less than one per cent of the issued capital of the company. [Members handbook statement 1.201: 4.46(c)]

Example 6.64

XYZ Trustees Limited, a company wholly owned by the company's auditors, acts as a trustee for trusts which own five per cent of the issued ordinary share capital of the company.

Political and charitable gifts

6.65 If a company and its subsidiaries have given money for political or charitable purposes, or both, which aggregate more than £200 in the financial year, then the following should be disclosed in the report: [Sch 7: 3 and 4]

(a) the amount given for charitable purposes;

(b) the amount given for political purposes;

(c) the name of each person or political party to which an amount in excess of £200 was given for political purposes and the amount given.

Money given for charitable purposes to persons not ordinarily resident in the UK are excluded for the purposes of this requirement.

6.66 Wholly owned subsidiaries of companies incorporated in Great Britain are exempt from this requirement.

Branches outside the UK

6.67 Where a limited company has branches outside the UK, the directors' report is required to give an indication of the existence of these branches. [Sch 7: 6(d)]

6.68 The definition of a branch contained in s698(2) is not helpful. Companies House has provided guidance by stating that:

(a) 'A "branch" is part of an oversea limited company organised to conduct business through local representatives in Great Britain rather than referring it abroad.'; and

(b) 'A "place of business" is for companies who cannot register as a branch because:

- they are from within the UK (Northern Ireland or Gibraltar); or
- they are not limited companies; or
- their activities in Great Britain are not sufficient to define it as a branch. Such activities might include internal computer processing, warehousing, or simply a representative office.

6.69 The Channel Islands and Isle of Man are outside the UK and therefore branches located there should be disclosed.

Policy on the payment of creditors

6.70 The directors' report of a company which at any time during the year was:

(a) a public company; or

(b) a member of a group of which the parent was a public company, and the company did not qualify as small or medium-sized under s247,

should include a statement setting out the company's policy for the next financial year in respect of the payment of trade creditors and should disclose 'creditor days' in respect of amounts due at the year end. [Sch 7: Part VI]

Extract 6.70.1

Imperial Chemical Industries PLC

Year ended 31 December 1999

Extract from directors' report

Payment to suppliers

The Company agrees terms and conditions for its business transactions with suppliers. Payment is then made to these terms, subject to

---

the terms and conditions being met by the supplier. Payment terms can differ in the many markets in which ICI trades.

Trade creditors of the Company at 31 December 1999 were equivalent to 56 days purchases, based on the average daily amount invoiced by suppliers to the Company during this year.

Extract 6.70.2

Hanson plc

Year ended 31 December 1999

Extract from directors' report

Creditor payment policy

Hanson companies aim to pay all of their suppliers within a reasonable period of the invoice being received and in any case within the supplier's own standard payment period and in accordance with the Confederation of British Industry prompt payment code (copies available from the C.B.I. Centre Point, 103 New Oxford Street, London WC1A 1DU). At December 31, 1999 the group trade creditors represented 49 days of trade purchases. The holding company, Hanson PLC, does not have any trade creditors.

6.71   The statement of policy should disclose:

(a)   whether, in respect of some or all of its suppliers, it is the company's policy to follow a code or standard payment practice and, if so, the name of the code or standard and where information about, and copies of, it can be obtained;

(b)   whether, in respect of some or all of its suppliers, it is the company's policy to:

(i)   agree the terms of payment when agreeing the terms of the transaction;

(ii)   ensure that the supplier is aware of the terms of payment; and

(iii)   abide by those terms; and

(c)   the policy in respect of those suppliers that do not fall within (a) or (b) above.

The statement should identify the suppliers or classes of suppliers to which the various policies apply.

> ### Example 6.71
>
> The policies that the company follows for the payment of creditors in the current financial year is:
>
> (a) for those suppliers that specify terms of payment in advance of the goods or services being ordered, payment is made in accordance with those terms;
>
> (b) for other suppliers, payment is made the later of 45 days after the receipt of the invoice or 45 days after receipt of the goods or services concerned.

6.72 In calculating 'creditor days'.

(a) Creditor days is defined by the regulations as:

[X/Y multiplied by the number of days in the financial year]; where

X = the aggregate of the amounts which were owed to trade creditors at the end of the year; and

Y = the aggregate of the amounts which the company was invoiced by suppliers during the year.

(b) The amounts which were owed to trade creditors are taken to be the amounts shown under the heading 'Trade creditors' (amounts falling due within one year) within the various balance sheet formats set out in the Act.

> ### Example 6.72
>
> Trade creditor days of the company at 31 March 2000, calculated in accordance with the requirements of the Companies Act 1985, were 29.5 days. This represents the ratio, expressed in days, between the amounts invoiced to the company in the year by its suppliers and the amounts due, at the year end, to trade creditors falling due for payment within one year.

6.73 A person is a supplier of a company at any time if:

(a) at that time, he is owed an amount in respect of goods and services supplied; and

(b) that amount would be included under the heading corresponding to trade creditors falling due within one year if accounts were prepared in accordance with the Act at that time.

6.74

The requirements to disclose payment policy and creditor days are in respect of an individual company. In consolidated accounts, it is therefore the policy and creditor days of the parent company that are required to be disclosed. In some groups, the parent company is solely a holding company and in these cases such information appears to have little value. Some groups therefore choose to include as additional information the payment policy and creditor days for the group (see extract 6.70.2 above).

6.75   The fixed formula for calculating creditor days can produce a strange result in certain circumstances, e.g., in a seasonal business with particularly high activity before the year end. In such circumstances, although the figure given by applying the formula should not be adjusted, it is acceptable to include a sentence stating why the figure does not appear to reflect the payment policy.

Reappointment of auditors

6.76   Although there is no statutory requirement for the directors' report to refer to the reappointment of the auditor, it is normal for it to do this. The first example below deals with the situation where the auditors are to be reappointed at a general meeting under s385 or s385A. The second example addresses the situation where a private company has dispensed with the annual appointment of auditors under s386.

Example 6.76.1

A resolution to reappoint Verry and Fire as auditors will be proposed at the forthcoming Annual General Meeting.

Example 6.76.2

Pursuant to s386 Companies Act 1985, an elective resolution was passed on 7 April 1998 dispensing with the requirement to appoint auditors annually. Therefore, Verry and Fire are deemed to continue as auditors.

UITF Abstract 20 and UITF Abstract 21 discursive disclosures

6.77   In March 1998, the UITF issued UITF Abstract 20 *Year 2000 issues* and UITF Abstract 21 *Accounting issues arising from the proposed introduction of the euro*. In August 1998, the UITF issued an appendix to UITF Abstract 21, which addressed how certain requirements, principally matters covered by SSAP 20 *Foreign currency translation*, should be applied in the context of the introduction of the euro. The appendix is mainly concerned with issues that arise for those companies with a functional (or, in SSAP 20's terms, 'local') currency that is participating in monetary union.

6.78 UITF Abstract 20 states that having considered the potential impact and extent of the year 2000 problem on the business and operations, disclosure should be made of:

(a) the risks and uncertainties associated with the year 2000 problem. If the entity has not made an assessment of this problem or has not determined its materiality, that fact;

(b) the entity's general plans to address the year 2000 issues relating to its business and operations and, if material, its relationship with customers, suppliers and other relevant parties; and

(c) whether the total estimated costs of these plans, including amounts to be spent in future periods, have been quantified and, where applicable, an indication of the total costs likely to be incurred, with an explanation of the basis on which the figures are calculated (e.g., the treatment of internal costs and replacement expenditure).

6.79 In complying with these disclosure requirements, companies should take care to ensure that all the disclosures are factually correct, supported by underlying papers, and that they do not give guarantees that cannot be met.

6.80 In January 2000 the UITF issued Information Sheet 34 following questions regarding the disclosure requirements of UITF 20: 11 following the date change on 1 January 2000. While the Abstract will be withdrawn in due course, it was decided that it would be premature to do this immediately, as it had been indicated that problems were likely to arise from the date change over the succeeding months. Thus 'the UITF believe that entities should consider what disclosure would be appropriate over the coming months, for example regarding any residual risks and uncertainties, or any exceptional costs or likely costs arising from inadequate preparation or in fixing problems that have or may emerge'.

6.81 Where, to the date of signing the financial statements, no significant impact from year 2000 problems has been experienced, or is expected, these disclosure requirements are best satisfied by updating the disclosure from the previous year for costs and events to the date of the report. For example, costs still to be incurred as part of a year 2000 plan should continue to be disclosed. Confirmation should also be given as to whether the directors continue to be alert to issues that may arise from the year 2000 problems.

6.82 In March 1999, the London Stock Exchange (which was then the UK Listing Authority – see **5.52**) issued a letter and Listing Rules Guidance Note 01/99 The year 2000 issue. This made it clear that all listed companies should disclose the potential impact of year 2000 on the company prominently in all listing particulars and class 1 circulars, in order to fully comply with paragraph 6.G.1(b) (and 6.N.1(b)) of the Listing Rules. The Guidance Note also reminds listed companies that the disclosures required by the ASB's UITF Abstract 20 should continue to be made in all annual reports published before 1 January 2000. The guidance note also requested listed companies to provide equivalent information in interim reports published during 1999, so that investors will be informed of progress towards resolution of this important issue. To date the UK Listing Authority have not issued any further guidance nor have they revoked Guidance Note 01/99.

Extract 6.82

Imperial Chemical Industries PLC

Year ended 31 December 1999

Extract from operating and financial review

YEAR 2000

The Group's Year 2000 Project, which started in 1995, is now effectively complete. It was a comprehensive programme designed to ensure that ICI's operations and relationships with its business partners were not adversely affected by problems resulting from computer programs and equipment being unable to distinguish between the year 1900 and the year 2000. Indications to date are that the work was successful.

Responsibilities

Project teams addressed all aspects of Year 2000 issues including potential Year 2000 failures relating to:

- business critical information systems;
- the information technology infrastructure;
- manufacturing areas including control systems and building systems, and
- the external supply chain

Contingency plans relating to any other residual risks including, in particular, those that could have SHE (Safety, Health and Environment) or significant financial consequences were also considered.

The Project covered more than 400 sites in over 35 countries. There was a small central team which acted as a centre of expertise to support the efforts of the business-based teams, to ensure consistency of approach, to share information, and report progress to the Executive Management Team and the Audit Committee of the Board. Where appropriate, external consultants and suppliers were also engaged to

---

review progress, manage risk and provide external benchmarking. Progress was reviewed quarterly by the Audit Committee of the Board as well as by the Executive Management Team. In addition, the Group's internal auditors periodically reviewed the Project status and progress.

Operations within ICI have been unaffected by the century date change. The situation continues to be monitored in case any related event should arise but actions taken ahead of the date change seem to have ensured that Businesses have continued to operate without interruption.

Costs

Year 2000 expenditure was funded from cash flow from the Group's operations and costs to meet Year 2000 readiness did not have a material adverse effect on the Group's financial position, results or liquidity.

The costs of the Year 2000 Project have been expensed as incurred, with the exception of capitalisable expenditure. Management estimates that the total costs for Year 2000 projects in respect of continuing operations is in the order of £120m which includes any expenditure associated with Year 2000 contingency measures. Less than 3% of the expenditure is outstanding. Internal staff costs have not been included, for example, where Year 2000 issues form only a part of the staff's activity. The costs of accelerating investment decisions, such as the introduction of packaged software for commercial reasons have not been included in the costs, although the millennium-driven upgrade costs of these systems, where not covered by maintenance contracts, have been included.

Risk management and contingency planning

ICI is unable to determine at this time whether future consequences of any Year 2000 failure may have a material impact on ICI's results of operations, liquidity or financial position. However, to date ICI is not aware of any such failures and believes that the completion of the Year 2000 Project has reduced the possibility that significant interruptions to normal operations will arise. However, due to the general uncertainty inherent in the Year 2000 problem, including the readiness of the external supply chain, there may yet be an interruption in, or a failure of, certain normal business activities or operations due to a Year 2000 problem, which may not yet have been detected. There may also be legal risks associated with discontinued products, divested businesses, or the very few products that have ever contained date dependent devices.

Readers are cautioned that forward-looking statements contained in this Year 2000 disclosure should be read in conjunction with ICI's disclosures under the heading "Cautionary Statement for the Purposes of the 'Safe Harbor' Provisions of the Private Securities Litigation Reform Act of 1995" on page 2. (*Note: not reproduced in this publication.*)

UITF 21

6.83   UITF Abstract 21 requires that where the potential impact of preparing to change over to the euro is significant, information and discussion should be given, together with an indication of the total costs likely to be incurred.

6.84

> The UITF Abstract has not been withdrawn following the introduction of the euro for participating Member States from 1 January 1999. Companies in the UK, as a non-participating Member State, may find the euro impacting in a number of ways:
>
> (a)   introducing another foreign currency into their accounting systems;
>
> (b)   suppliers or customers requiring transactions to be based in euros;
>
> (c)   a requirement to preparing a financial statement in euros if part of an EU group.
>
> In addition there will be a future impact as and when it is decided that the UK will participate in the euro.
>
> Where disclosure has previously been made as to the euro's potential impact and that impact has ceased, it would be helpful to the reader for the subsequent report to clarify the matter.

6.85   FRS 3 and the Act respectively require disclosures of any exceptional items and significant commitments, which would include those in respect of year 2000 or euro costs, to be given in the financial statements. The discursive nature of the additional disclosures required by UITF Abstract 20 and UITF Abstract 21 make the directors' report or operating and financial review a more appropriate location for these.

> ### Extract 6.85
>
> The BOC Group plc
>
> 30 September 1999
>
> Extract from finance and treasury review
>
> **Economic and monetary union (EMU)**
>
> Europe's single currency, the euro, was launched for business-to-business use on 1 January 1999 in the 11 countries that are currently participating. There is now a three year transition period, after which the euro will be adopted for all purposes in those countries participating. Sterling will continue unaffected for use in the UK.

BOC businesses in continental Europe were able to operate in euros from January 1999. The degree of interest by customers and suppliers in using the new currency has varied but the take up to date has been small. This has given us an opportunity to refine our systems and processes for euro conversion and no material problems have been encountered. We believe interest in using the euro will grow strongly in the period up to January 2002.

The UK government has no timetable for the use of the euro in the UK. Some changes to BOC's existing systems will be needed before all UK businesses have full euro functionality. This will be achieved as part of the periodic upgrading of systems. A systems upgrade will be required before our Irish business can achieve full euro functionality but there are no obstacles to full implementation of euro compatible systems and processes in Ireland well before the end of 2001.

Costs to date have been fully expensed and any future costs will also be expensed as incurred and identified separately in the accounts if they are significant. We do not believe that the introduction of the euro will be material to the Group's financial condition, operations or liquidity.

Five-year record

6.86   Although the Stock Exchange letter (see **6.4** above) referred to comparative figures for the last ten years, in practice, many companies prefer to provide a five-year record (i.e., figures for the current year and the four previous years). The Stock Exchange seems to have accepted this practice. Although there is no formal requirement, the practice of providing some form of table of comparative figures is now so well established that it is likely that the Stock Exchange or UK Listing Authority would raise objections if one was not given.

6.87   The figures disclosed have in the past tended to be key profit and loss account numbers such as:

- turnover;
- operating profit;
- pre-tax profit;
- post-tax profit;
- dividends; and
- retained profit.

6.88   More recently, many companies have also provided balance sheet and, in some cases, cash flow information. See chapter 10 below as regards earnings per share.

Operating and financial review

Recommendation to provide an operating and financial review

6.89   The ASB Statement *Operating and financial review* (OFR), issued in July 1993, sets out the recommended contents of an OFR which would supplement the accounts of large companies. The ASB Statement is not an accounting standard and therefore its use is not mandatory. However, the Financial Reporting Council, the 100 Group of Finance Directors and the London Stock Exchange have given their strong support to the issue of the Statement and many listed companies, particularly the larger ones, have adopted it.

Presentation of an operating and financial review in annual reports

6.90   The matters to be reported in an OFR, as proposed in the ASB Statement, need not be reported together in a separate, stand-alone section, as the proposals are not intended to result in the duplication of information already provided in the annual report. Therefore, some of the matters can be incorporated in other sections, e.g., the chairman's statement, the chief executive's report or the finance director's report.

Features of an operating and financial review

6.91   The OFR aims to provide a framework for directors to discuss and analyse the business's performance and the factors underlying its results and financial position, in order to assist users to assess for themselves the future potential of the business.

6.92   To achieve this objective, the ASB has indicated that an OFR should:

(a)   be written in a clear and succinct style;

(b)   be balanced and objective;

(c)   refer to comments made in previous statements where these have not been borne out by events;

(d)   contain analytical discussion rather than just numerical analysis;

(e)   discuss individual aspects of the business in the context of a discussion of the business as a whole;

(f)   explain the reason for, and effect of, any changes in accounting policies;

(g)   clearly relate any ratios and numerical information given in the OFR to the financial statements;

(h)   include discussion of trends and factors underlying the results but not expected to continue and known events likely to have an impact on the business in the future.

6.93   The two main sections in an OFR are the operating review and the financial review. The guidance given below is based on the ASB Statement, which is designed as a guideline rather than a rigid format. Directors should develop the presentation of their OFR in a way that best complements the format of their annual report as a whole.

Operating review

6.94   The operating review identifies and explains the main factors that underlie the business and, in particular, those which either have varied in the past or are expected to change in the future. The ASB Statement suggests that the matters to be discussed are as set out below.

Operating results for the period

6.95   This section of the OFR should discuss the significant features of operating performance for the financial period, including all aspects of the profit and loss account to the level of profit on ordinary activities before taxation. The focus should be on the overall business and on those segments/divisions that are relevant to an understanding of the performance as a whole. Examples include:

(a)   changes in market conditions;

(b)   new products and services introduced or announced;

(c)   changes in market share or position;

(d)   changes in turnover and margins;

(e)   changes in exchange rates and inflation rates; and

(f)   new activities, discontinued activities and other acquisitions and disposals.

6.96   Where there have been material acquisitions, the extent to which the expectations at the time of acquisition have been realised should be discussed.

6.97   If seasonal businesses have been acquired during the period under review and the results included in the consolidated accounts are not indicative of those for a full year, an indication of this fact should be given.

6.98   Any other special factors that have affected the results for the period should be discussed.

Dynamics of the business

6.99 This section should discuss the main factors and influences that may have a major effect on future results, whether or not they were significant in the period under review. This would include a discussion identifying the principal risks and uncertainties in the main lines of business, together with a commentary on the approach to managing these risks and, in qualitative terms, the nature of the potential impact on results. Examples of matters that may be relevant are :

- scarcity of raw materials;
- skill shortages and expertise of uncertain supply;
- patents, licences or franchises;
- dependence on major suppliers or customers;
- product liability;
- health and safety;
- environmental protection costs and potential environmental liabilities;
- self insurance;
- exchange rate fluctuations;
- rates of inflation differing between costs and revenues, or between different markets.

Investment for the future

6.100 This section should discuss the business's main activities in the area of maintaining and enhancing future income or profits. This includes discussion of activities and expenditure of the period under review which are intended wholly or partly to enhance future profitability and which can be varied, at the discretion of management, over a relatively wide range without significantly affecting current trading. Such expenditure falls into two broad categories: capital expenditure and 'revenue investment'.

6.101 The following features of capital expenditure should be covered:

(a) the current level of capital expenditure, together with planned future expenditure (both committed, and authorised but not committed), indicating the overall level of expenditure, the major business segments and geographical areas accounting for material elements of the total, and the major projects involved;

(b) the likely benefits expected from capital expenditure.

6.102 'Revenue investment' (a term used in FRED 1, the precursor of

FRS 3, but not in the ASB Statement on OFR) is expenditure charged in the profit and loss account that nevertheless can be regarded as a form of investing in the future.

6.103 Revenue investment should be discussed, with particular emphasis on changes in the level of activity and management policy. The benefits expected from such activities should also be discussed. Examples of such activities will vary greatly from company to company and from industry to industry, but examples include:

- marketing and advertising campaigns;
- training programmes;
- refurbishment and maintenance programmes;
- pure and applied research;
- development of new products and services;
- technical support to customers.

Profit for the financial year, total recognised gains and losses and shareholders' perspective

6.104 The OFR should discuss the overall return attributable to shareholders, in terms of dividends and increases in shareholders' funds, commenting on the contributions from the operating performance of the various business units and on the other items reported as part of total recognised gains and losses. The discussion should include any significant gains and losses that were previously simply accounted for as reserve movements and which are now given prominence in the statement of total recognised gains and losses.

Profit for the financial year, dividends and earnings per share

6.105 The OFR should comment on the comparison between profit for the financial year and dividends, both in total and in per share terms, indicating the directors' overall dividend policy. If the accounts include additional measures of earnings per share, as permitted by FRS 3, these should also be discussed.

Accounting policies

6.106 An indication and explanation of any subjective judgements to which the financial statements are particularly sensitive should be given.

Financial review

6.107 The financial review explains the capital structure of the business, its treasury policy and the dynamics of its financial position. The ASB

Statement suggests that the matters to be addressed/discussed are as follows.

Capital structure and treasury policy

6.108 The OFR should include discussion of the capital structure of the business, in terms of maturity profile of debt, type of capital instrument used, currency, and interest rate structure, including comments on relevant ratios such as interest cover and gearing ratios. The capital funding and treasury policies and objectives, covering management of interest rate risk, maturity profile of borrowings and management of exchange rate risk, should be stated. The OFR should also discuss the implementation of capital funding and treasury policies in the period under review, in terms of:

(a) manner in which treasury activities are controlled;

(b) currencies in which borrowings are made and in which cash and cash equivalents are held;

(c) extent to which borrowings are at fixed interest rates;

(d) use of financial instruments for hedging purposes; and

(e) extent to which foreign currency net investments are hedged by currency borrowings and other hedging instruments.

6.109 The purpose and effect of major financing transactions undertaken up to the date of approval of the financial statements should be explained.

6.110 The effect of interest costs on profits and the potential impact of interest rate changes should be discussed.

Taxation

6.111 Where the overall tax charge is significantly different from a 'standard' charge (i.e., the normal UK tax rate applied to the profit before taxation), the main components of the reconciliation between the actual and 'standard' tax charges should be discussed.

Funds from operating activities and other sources of cash

6.112 The cash generated from operations and other cash inflows during the period and any special factors that influenced these cash flows should be discussed. Where segmental cash flows are significantly out of line with segmental profits, an indication and explanation of this fact should be given.

Current liquidity

6.113   The business's liquidity at the year end should be discussed, including comments on:

(a)   the level of borrowings at year end;

(b)   the seasonality of borrowing requirements, as indicated by the peak level of borrowings during the period; and

(c)   the maturity profile of both borrowings and committed borrowing facilities.

Reference should also be made to the funding requirements for capital expenditure commitments and authorisations.

6.114   Any restrictions on the ability to transfer funds from one part of the group to meet the obligations of another part of the group (e.g., exchange controls or adverse taxation consequences of transfers) should be discussed.

6.115   Where the business has entered into covenants with lenders, which could have the effect of restricting the use of credit facilities, and negotiations with lenders on the operation of these covenants are taking place or are expected to take place, an indication of this fact should be given. Where a breach of a covenant has occurred or is expected to occur, details of the measures taken or proposed to remedy the situation should be given.

Going concern

6.116   The Combined Code (see chapter 7 below) states that directors of listed companies incorporated in the UK should report that the business is a going concern, with supporting assumptions or qualifications as necessary (see **7.87** below). This is also specifically required by the Listing Rules [12.43(v)]. The detailed guidance for directors states that such statements should be included in the OFR. Directors' statements on going concern are dealt with further in **7.87** to **7.112** below.

Balance sheet value

6.117   A commentary on strengths and resources of the business whose value is not reflected in the balance sheet (or only partially shown in the balance sheet) should be given. Such a commentary might include brands and other intangible assets, tangible fixed assets, e.g., properties, which have not been revalued, and investments which have not been revalued.

Disclosure in the operating and financial review of information on derivatives

6.118   The ASB published, in September 1998, FRS 13 *Derivatives and other financial instruments: Disclosures*, an accounting standard, on the disclosure of information about derivatives and other financial instruments.

6.119   Two types of disclosure are required: numerical information, to be included in the notes to the accounts, and discursive disclosures, which may be included in the OFR (or directors' report, in the absence of an OFR). The requirements of FRS 13 are considered in chapter 21.

Compliance with the ASB Statement

6.120   Directors are not expected to give any formal confirmation that they have complied with the principles set out in the ASB Statement, as it is intended to be a statement of best practice. However, as it would be helpful to users of annual reports, it is recommended that directors include some comment on the extent to which the Statement has been followed.

6.121   The ASB Statement states that where it is implied, through the use of the words 'operating and financial review' or otherwise, that the directors have endeavoured to follow the principles set out in the ASB Statement, any significant departure from them should be reported.

Addressing stakeholders

Developments in practice

6.122   There appears to be a growing regard shown in the annual reports of some leading companies to the interests of all their 'stakeholders'. There are no statutory or other requirements currently underlying this development. Instead, the driving force seems to be one of strategic self-interest, as discussed below. Unlike the earlier parts of this chapter, therefore, the purpose of the following paragraphs is to raise awareness of existing practice in this area rather than to inter-pret any standards or guidelines.

6.123   However, as noted in **6.129** et seq. below, there are a number of proj-ects currently reviewing the scope of a reporting entity's 'audience'.

Underlying concepts

6.124   Businesses deal with, and draw on, the resources of a wide spectrum of groups of individuals and entities: their customers, suppliers, employees, shareholders, bankers and financiers, and the communities in which they operate. These groups have a corresponding interest in the business – hence the term 'stakeholder'. The concept of stakeholder recognises that the continued success of the business depends upon its performance across a range of goals that are relevant to the needs and expectations of these various interest groups.

6.125 There would seem to be broadly three reasons for companies seeking to reflect these aspects of performance in their annual reports. The first is a desire to give a fuller picture of the capacity of the company to generate wealth on a sustainable basis. The results of the company's efforts, e.g., its initiatives to improve quality of customer service or its educational programmes, may not immediately be measurable in financial terms. The second is to demonstrate to stakeholders the importance the company attaches to actively managing relationships with them, a genuine commitment that is underwritten by significant levels of investment. The third reason is one of internal motivation: it is suggested that the prospect of external reporting of particular aspects of performance may act as a spur to the company's own management.

Examples of issues addressed

6.126 Set out below are examples of matters affecting particular groups of stakeholders that are included in company annual reports.

Customers:

- data on customer satisfaction;
- degree of customer loyalty/product loyalty;
- product awareness;
- new products/enhancements;
- length of innovation cycle;
- service delivery/after-sales care;
- marketing initiatives.

Lenders and financiers:

- treasury policy;
- capital structure;
- gearing/interest cover;
- liquidity/cash flows.

Shareholders:

- share price performance;
- shareholder services;
- investment in intangibles and infrastructure.

Suppliers:

- degree of supplier loyalty;
- quality initiatives;
- involvement in product design;
- cooperative ventures.

Employees:

- training and development efforts;
- profit sharing;
- employee ownership;
- pensions;
- retention statistics;
- health and safety;
- equal opportunity;
- team building.

The community:

- involvement in community projects;
- educational programmes – schools and universities;
- influencing regulators, governments and policy makers;
- environmental policies and issues.

6.127   In some cases, companies segregate and label disclosures relating to a group of stakeholders, e.g., disclosures relating to employees or to the community, particularly on environmental issues, often appear under separate headings within the annual report. In other cases, these disclosures are subsumed within the reviews of operations and finance.

6.128   Some general observations can be made about certain characteristics of these disclosures. Quantified results tend to have a greater impact on the reader than qualitative statements, particularly where accompanied by comparatives from previous years. Some disclosures, e.g., on environmental issues, can be highly technical and require special effort to make them understandable to stakeholder groups. Cosmetic disclosures that are intended to disguise a lack of genuine commitment are generally counter-productive – they leave readers inclined to downgrade other information in the annual report.

Future developments

Creating quality dialogue – responding to change in the capital market

6.129 A DTI report, *Creating quality dialogue'*, was published in February 1999 calling for improved dialogue between smaller quoted companies (SQCs) and fund managers. Its recommendations for SQCs include:

(a) an investor communication statement to underpin their investor relations policy and programme;

(b) inclusion in the annual report of a statement of prospects; and

(c) quarterly trading statements to improve timeliness and quality of communication.

6.130 The contents of the statement of prospects would include:

(a) investment criteria applied in capital investment decisions;

(b) comments on funding structure and weighted average cost of capital;

(c) assessment of current and future rates of return in comparison with cost of capital;

(d) key internal performance indicators and competitor benchmarking;

(e) major operational risks and sensitivities; and

(f) future trading prospects.

The case for better risk reporting

6.131 In July 1999 the ICAEW published a paper entitled *No surprises: The case for better risk reporting*. This refines the proposals contained in and responds to comments on, an earlier 1997 discussion paper, *Financial reporting of risk: Proposals for a statement of business risk*. The new paper also includes the results of a study on risk disclosures.

6.132 One change from the 1997 paper is that it is no longer proposed that a separate statement of business risk be published. This reflects concern that it would be difficult to summarise risks and the related actions and measures in a single report and some opposition to including another separate report.

6.133   The report expresses the view that improving the reporting of an entity's risks in the broadest sense and the actions taken to manage them would act towards the ultimate aim of reducing its cost of capital. It would also be beneficial to replace the current emphasis on downside risk with a broader view, in terms of uncertainty and volatility.

6.134   The analysis of current disclosures established that, typically, extensive risk disclosures are made in the prospectus, with rather less information appearing in subsequent annual reports. Unsurprisingly, it is the view of the Steering Group that maintaining, at least, the risk reporting practices evolving in recent prospectuses would be a beneficial and realistic aim.

6.135   The suggested goal that companies should set for themselves is to avoid surprising the capital market (i.e., no surprises). This requires:

(a)   improving risk management;

(b)   helping investors to expect and understand volatility; and

(c)   'telling it as it is'.

6.136   The report contains guidance only – the suggestions contained therein are not mandatory. It is important that any risk disclosures do not create legal exposure. The 1997 paper recommended that any statement of business risk be prefaced with a general statement that 'Any list of risks cannot be comprehensive and the nature of the group's business means that risks will change as a result of controllable and uncontrollable events occurring after the date of this statement.'

Reporting on shareholder value

6.137   In 1999 the ICAEW published a paper entitled *Inside out: Reporting on shareholder value* which encourages the reporting of information about a company's potential for creating shareholder value. It is the latest in a series of papers on reporting financial performance and risk (see also **6.131** above) that considers the need for enhanced information about business performance which reflects a more forward looking focus.

6.138   To this end, the ICAEW are reviewing the external communication of information about a company in *The Corporate Report – New Horizons* project which will also consider the need for information on intangibles, future prospects and stakeholder issues; as well as the impact of globalisation and information technology on reporting.

6.139   The *Inside out* paper believes that there are key issues that need to be communicated widely and not just in briefing meetings for analysts.

They include:

- What is the company's strategic vision and strategy for achieving it?

- Why is that the appropriate direction?

- Does the organisation have the capability to implement the chosen strategy?

- What then does management need to manage in order to achieve its objectives?

6.140 Thus the paper proposes external reporting of key elements of information used internally to manage the business. For listed companies it is proposed that there should be disclosed in either the OFR (see **6.89** to **6.121** above) or a similar statement:

(a) For the company as a whole:

    (i) Its ambitions;

    (ii) Its strategic direction, together with targets or milestones towards achieving its objectives;

    (iii) A description of the strategic decision making process;

    (iv) A description of the performance management process;

    (v) The preferred measures used internally to monitor economic performance.

(b) For each significant business activity for management purposes:

    (i) A description of the key drivers of value in the business derived from inter alia:

        - A description of the market in which the business operates, using both qualitative terms and quantitative data;

        - Why management believes it is the right market to be in;

        - The business's competitive position within the market;

        - Future trends anticipated in the market;

        - How management intends to maintain or alter the business's position within the market.

    (ii) Measure of performance appropriate to the business, including non-financial measures, and/or lead indicators, derived from the key drivers of value, that are used internally to monitor potential in that business.

Year end financial reports

6.141 In February 2000 the ASB issued a discussion paper *Year-end financial reports: improving communication,* which seeks to address concerns that financial statements are becoming less accessible to private shareholders. In general, the changes suggested would require existing legal requirements to be amended.

6.142 The key proposals relate to the 'paper' communications sent to shareholders and include:

(a) Summary financial statements – should become the main report for shareholders so that all listed companies would be required to prepare them. The contents should comprise at least the information recommended in the ASB guidance on preliminary announcements (see chapters 36 and 37);

(b) Full audited financial statements – should still be produced for those who want them and for filing purposes. They may evolve into 'plain paper' statements similar to the 10-K document prepared for companies listed in the USA;

(c) Timing – both summary financial statements and full audited financial statements should be distributed within 80 days of the year-end and within 30 days of the preliminary announcement; and

(d) Simplified financial review – a plain language document reporting and commenting on a standardised set of financial highlights (without tabular profit and loss account, balance sheet etc.) that could be sent to shareholders instead of the summary financial statements and full audited financial statements.

6.143 The paper also considers financial reporting on the internet (see **4.158** to **4.161** above) noting that there is a case for developing business standards for such reporting.

Company law review

6.144 The DTI is currently undertaking a large scale review of company law in the UK (see **2.21** to **2.26** above). As part of this process it issued a consultation document in March 2000 *Developing the framework*. The paper addresses a number of topics including governance and reporting. It proposes changes for listed companies (see **4.154** above and **36.20** below) and small and private companies (see **34.84** below). The paper also proposes that public and large private companies should produce a statutory operating and financial review. The content of the review would be partly prescribed by statute, with the detailed requirements laid down in standards. The paper envisages the rules on the form and content of accounts and reports being delegated to an appropriate rule making body. The statutory OFR, together with a supplementary statement dealing with prescribed public interest disclosures, would replace the directors' report for large companies. For small companies the directors' report would be replaced by a cover sheet dealing with prescribed public interest disclosures.

6.145   The paper notes that the two key components as regards governance are an inclusive duty and broader accountability. These components are intended to highlight the need for directors to have due regard to the company's business, and wider external, relationships. In the case of the inclusive duty, the proposed statement of directors' duties requires directors to act in the collective best interests of shareholders, but recognises that this can only be achieved by taking due account of wider interests. The transparency element is provided by a wider reporting requirement which, for public and larger private companies, will encompass a statutory Operating and Financial Review.

6.146   The proposed timetable is for a further consultation document in November 2000 and then a final report in spring 2001. Up-to-date reports on the review project together with downloadable texts of the consultation documents can be obtained from the DTI website www.dti.gov.uk/cld/review.htm.

7 Corporate governance disclosures

7 Corporate governance disclosures

Summary of changes since the previous issue of this publication

Para.	*Topic*	*Summary*
7.40 and 7.66 to 7.82	*Internal Control – Guidance for Directors on the Combined Code*	The Head of Listings wrote to all listed companies in September 1999 formally endorsing the guidance issued by the Turnbull Working Party and also setting out implementation arrangements. This guidance is the final piece in the corporate governance jigsaw. Under the implementation arrangements, companies are now able to fully comply with the requirements of the Combined Code although there is a transitional approach available for the first year which most listed companies are following.
7.121 to 7.123	*APB Bulletin 1999/5*	Consolidates previous guidance for external auditors on how to perform their review of the seven provisions specified for review by the Listing Rules.

Introduction

7.1   Save for certain exemptions (see **7.11** below), listed companies are subject to Listing Rule 12.43A and the Principles and provisions contained within the Combined Code which reflect the recommendations of the Committee on Corporate Governance ('the Hampel Committee').

7.2   The challenge for the directors of these companies is now considerable. While it was hoped that the Combined Code would reduce the 'box ticking' approach which some people apply to governance, in reality the extent of corporate governance disclosures has increased considerably. Also, various governance organisations have been busy analysing disclosures with the hope of finding matters which could embarrass directors.

7.3   This chapter explains the considerations relating to disclosures under the post-Hampel regime, covering both the compliance and narrative statements. It also puts particular emphasis on the recently issued Turnbull guidance on the wider aspects of internal control as well as describing developments relating to statements on going concern and directors' responsibilities. It also describes the position of AIM companies and of those listed companies which can avail themselves of exemptions.

7.4   Although no more changes in the area of governance disclosures are in the pipeline, corporate governance disclosures have been subject to considerable changes. Therefore, there should be a check before an annual report is finalised that further changes have not occurred.

7.5   This chapter does not deal with disclosures relating to directors' remuneration, which are dealt with in chapter 8.

Brief history

7.6   The corporate governance path has been a busy one. As a result of major companies failing in the late 1980's, the Cadbury Committee published 'The Financial Aspects of Corporate Governance' in 1992 which gave directors guidance on what was expected of them. This was followed in 1994 by the Rutteman guidance on internal financial control and guidance on going concern. In 1995, following media interest about the amount of remuneration directors of large companies were earning, the Greenbury Committee published a report requiring various additional disclosures to be made in listed company accounts. These 'remuneration' requirements have been incorporated into the Listing Rules and are discussed in chapter 8. The Hampel Committee hoped to reduce the box-ticking approach to governance which had surfaced, and so produced a report in 1998 which, following discussions with the London Stock Exchange, was tailored to form the Combined Code. From December 1998, the Combined Code has formed part of the appendix to the Listing Rules and is the focus of current corporate governance discussions.

The Relevant Listing Rule

7.7   The main disclosure requirements of the Listing Rule on corporate governance are as follows:

'In the case of a company incorporated in the United Kingdom, the following additional items must be included in its annual report and accounts:

(a)   a narrative statement of how it has applied the Principles set out in Section 1 of the Combined Code, providing explanations which enable its shareholders to evaluate how the Principles have been applied; (see **7.32** to **7.37** below)

(b)   a statement as to whether or not it has complied throughout the accounting period with the Code provisions set out in Section 1 of the Combined Code. A company that has not complied with the Code provisions or (in the case of provisions whose requirements are of a continuing nature) complied for only part of an accounting period, must specify the Code provisions with which it has not complied, and (where relevant) for what part of the period such non-compliance continued, and give reasons for any non-compliance.' (See **7.26** to **7.31** below.)

[Listing Rules 12.43 (A)]

Timing considerations

7.8   Listing Rule 12.43A, which requires both a narrative and compliance statement to be made on corporate governance matters, applies to all listed companies with year ends on or after 31 December 1998 (save limited exceptions – see **7.11** below).

7.9   When the Listing Rule was originally published in June 1998, the London Stock Exchange created a problem by expecting disclosures by companies on how they have applied the Principles and complied with the detailed provisions of the Combined Code, in respect of the whole of the first accounting period ending on or after 31 December 1998. The London Stock Exchange acknowledged that a limited number of Code provisions were new and that, where these provisions were of a continuing nature, companies may not have complied with them throughout the accounting period and the disclosure statement made would need to reflect this. In these circumstances, the London Stock Exchange recommended that shareholders and others monitoring compliance with the Combined Code should do so with flexibility, using common sense and with regard to the individual companies' circumstances, particularly in the first year of reporting compliance.

7.10   As companies are now into their second (or later) year of disclosures relating to the Combined Code, it is now not realistic to use the timing of the publication of the Combined Code as a reason for non-compliance with a Code provision (see **7.9** above). Institutional shareholders and various governance organisations may have accepted non-compliance in the first year following the Combined Code's publication on the grounds that insufficient time was given for the company to comply with every provision. This is unlikely to be the case in subsequent years.

Exemptions for certain listed companies

7.11   Following amendment 14 of the Listing Rules issued in January 2000, exemptions from disclosures relating to corporate governance and directors' remuneration are available for various categories of companies. The exemptions available vary for each of the categories of companies and are described in **7.13** to **7.19** below. The extent of the exemption should be considered carefully as in certain cases some governance or remuneration disclosures are still required. It is worth the company secretary checking the position with the UK Listing Authority if a company wishes to avail itself of an exemption to ensure a further amendment has not been made.

7.12   If a company avails itself of one of the exemptions, the directors should ideally disclose which exemption the company has availed itself of and the grounds for doing so. Such a disclosure would assist readers of annual reports and accounts who otherwise may mistakenly believe that the directors have omitted information on aspects of the company's corporate governance. Suggested wording, which could be included in the directors' report, is given in example **7.12.1** below. Such an indication would normally be given in the directors' report and not within the audited financial statements. Companies that can avail themselves of an exemption from corporate governance disclosures but are choosing to provide all disclosures may wish to include a sentence explaining that they are eligible for an exemption, but have decided not to take it. Suggested wording is given in example **7.12.2** below.

Example 7.12.1

As the company is not incorporated/trust is not constituted* within the UK, it has availed itself of an exemption from the Listing Rules to make corporate governance disclosures and for auditor review thereof.

*Delete as appropriate

Example 7.12.2

The company is eligible to exemption from the Listing Rules requirements relating to corporate governance disclosures but the directors have decided to provide such disclosures which are set out on page x/below.'

Specialist debt securities

7.13   The annual reports and accounts of companies that have only specialist debt securities listed need not comply with the continuing obligations on corporate governance, directors' remuneration or going concern disclosures. [Listing Rule 23.22] Specialist debt securities are defined by paragraph 23.1 of the Listing Rules as 'securities which, because of their nature, are normally bought and traded by a limited number of investors who are particularly knowledgeable in investment matters'. Directors who believe that their company has only specialist debt securities listed should agree this position with the UK Listing Authority, via the company's broker, before taking advantage of the exemption.

Other debt securities and fixed income shares

7.14   The annual reports and accounts of companies with only debt securities or with only fixed income shares listed need not comply with the Listing Rule paragraphs on corporate governance and directors' remuneration. [Listing Rules 9.46 and 9.47] They must, however, comply with the Listing Rule 12.43(v) on going concern statements.

Overseas companies with a primary listing by the UK Listing Authority

7.15   Except as indicated in **7.16** below, the annual report and accounts of overseas companies with a primary listing by the UK Listing Authority need not comply with the Listing Rule 12.43A on corporate governance and directors' remuneration. [Listing Rule 17.12] They also do not need to comply with the Listing Rule 12.43(v) on going concern.

7.16   Overseas companies with a primary listing by the UK Listing Authority are, however, required to comply with Listing Rule 12.43A(c)(vii) and disclose the unexpired term of any service contract of a director proposed for election or re-election at the forthcoming AGM. If any director proposed for election or re-election does not have a service contract, a statement to that effect must be made.

Overseas companies with a secondary listing by the UK Listing Authority

7.17   Overseas companies with a secondary listing by the UK Listing Authority need not comply with Listing Rules on corporate governance, directors' remuneration or going concern disclosures. [Listing Rule 17.14]

Investment companies (including investment trusts)

7.18   The annual report and accounts of investment companies (including investment trusts) that have no executive directors should note that under Listing Rule 21.20(i):

(a)   the narrative statement required under 12.43A(a) does not apply in respect of Combined Code Principles B1 to B3 on directors' remuneration;

(b)   the statement of compliance under 12.43A(b) does not apply in respect of Combined Code provisions B.1.1 to B.1.10, B.2.1 to B.2.6 and B.3.1 to B.3.5 on directors' remuneration; and

(c)   paragraph 12.43A(c) on directors' remuneration disclosures does not apply.

They must, however, comply with the other aspects of the Listing Rules on corporate governance and directors' remuneration disclosures and the Listing Rule on going concern statements.

Venture capital trusts

7.19   The exemptions available to venture capital trusts with no executive directors are the same as those available to investment companies [Listing Rule 26.9(c)].

Alternative investment market companies

7.20   Companies that have securities traded on the AIM are required to prepare annual reports and accounts in accordance with chapter 16 of the rules of the London Stock Exchange (which should not be confused with the Listing Rules). These rules do not require AIM companies to comply with the post-Hampel disclosures and nor did they previously require AIM companies to comply with the Cadbury or Greenbury recommendations.

7.21   However, guidance for AIM companies, issued in February 1995, states that a 'way of generating investor confidence is by adopting some or all of the guidelines on the Code of Best Practice on the Financial Aspects of Corporate Governance, known as "the Cadbury Code", although neither compliance, nor a statement on the degree of compliance, is a requirement of AIM'. The guidance goes on to say that 'Companies should take into account [the Cadbury Code] with a view to adopting adequate corporate governance'. This statement applies equally to the new 'Combined Code', and is therefore a matter worthy of consideration by directors of AIM companies and their nominated advisers. AIM companies may, therefore, wish to make a statement on the degree of compliance with the Code provisions within section 1 of the Combined Code and may wish to state how they have applied the Principles within section 1 of the Combined Code. Similarly, although there is no requirement for the annual report and accounts of AIM companies to include additional disclosures on directors' remuneration, AIM companies might wish to give the disclosures required by the Listing Rules. The 'Guidance for Smaller Quoted Companies' issued by the City Group for Smaller Companies (CISCO) in March 1999 backs up this view and it encourages AIM companies, in relation to corporate governance, to 'aspire to the standards set for listed companies, insofar as they relate to their particular circumstances'. It is recommended that the directors disclose that they are volunteering the information. Suggested wording is:

> **_Example 7.21_**
>
> Although not required to, the directors have decided to provide corporate governance and directors' remuneration* disclosures.
>
> * delete as appropriate

The Combined Code

7.22   The Combined Code (reproduced in Appendix IV) is appended to, but does not form part of, the Listing Rules. It was derived from the Hampel Committee's final report and from the predecessor Cadbury and Greenbury reports. It is seen by the Hampel Committee as a consolidation of the work of the three committees, not as a new departure.

7.23   Section 1 of the Combined Code contains 14 corporate governance Principles and 45 provisions which are covered by the disclosure requirements referred to in **7.7** above. This chapter focuses mainly on these disclosure requirements. The Principles and provisions apply to individual companies unless stated otherwise.

7.24   Section 2 of the Combined Code contains three Principles and three provisions applicable to institutional shareholders with regard to their voting, dialogue with companies and evaluation of a company's governance arrangements. The Hampel Committee did not believe that the latter were matters which are appropriate to include with the mandatory disclosure requirements. However, it expressed the hope that at least the major institutions would voluntarily disclose to their clients and the public the extent to which they are able to give effect to these provisions:

(a)   the elimination of unnecessary variations in the criteria which

apply to the corporate governance arrangements and performance of the companies in which they invest;

(b) the making available on request to their clients information on
the proportion of resolutions on which votes were cast and
non-discretionary proxies lodged;

(c) the steps taken to ensure that their voting intentions are being
translated into practice. [Code provisions E.1.1 to E.1.3]

7.25 The Principles and provisions within section 1 of the Combined
Code fall under the following headings:

A   Directors

  –   The board
  –   Chairman and chief executive officer
  –   Board balance
  –   Supply of information
  –   Appointments to the board
  –   Re-election

B   Directors' remuneration

  –   The level and make-up of remuneration (an underlying
      provision B.1.6 is supported by Schedule A to the Code,
      which sets out further provisions on the design of per-
      formance related remuneration).
  –   Procedure
  –   Disclosure (an underlying provision B.3.3 is supported by
      Schedule B to the Code, which sets out related provisions
      on what should be included in a remuneration report).

C   Relations with shareholders

  –   Dialogue with institutional shareholders
  –   Constructive use of the AGM

D   Accountability and audit

  –   Financial reporting
  –   Internal control
  –   Audit committee and auditors

The full text is reproduced in Appendix IV.

Statements of compliance

7.26 Where there is compliance with all/some of the Combined Code
provisions, the statement of compliance required by Listing Rule
12.43A(b) (see **7.7** above) might be worded along the following lines:

> ### *Example 7.26.1*
>
> Throughout the year ended 31 March 2000, the company has been in compliance with the Code provisions set out in section 1 of the Combined Code on Corporate Governance which is appended to the Listing Rules.

> ### *Example 7.26.2*
>
> [Save for the exceptions outlined below within this report*], the company has been in compliance with the Code provisions set out in section 1 of the Combined Code on Corporate Governance which is appended to the Listing Rules for the year ended 31 March 2000.
>
> * Note: [to be modified as appropriate]
>
> The companies must then disclose clearly the exceptions, their respective periods of non-compliance and their reasons for non-compliance.

> The Listing Rules do not prescribe where such a statement should be given, but it seems sensible to include it within a 'corporate governance statement' or, if no separate corporate governance statement is included, in the directors' report, following the narrative statement (see **7.32** to **7.37** below).

7.27 Where there are non-compliances, the annual report will need to specify the Code provisions with which the company has not complied and (where relevant) for what part of the period such non-compliance continued in addition to giving reasons for the non-compliance.

7.28 In the first year following the publication of the Code, many companies explained that the reason for certain non-compliances was because the Code was issued during their reporting period and hence the company was unable to comply with the Code for the full accounting period. As companies are now into their second (or later) accounting period following the Code's publication it is unlikely that analysts will accept the timing of the Code's publication as a satisfactory reason for non-compliance.

7.29 Key areas where companies are reporting non-compliance include:

(a) identification of a senior independent non-executive director (A.2.1);

(b) service contract periods for executive directors exceed the recommended one year (B.1.7);

(c)   directors are appointed for more than 3 years (A.6.2);

(d)   board composition (at least one-third should be non-executive) (A.3.1);

(e)   the membership of the audit committee (D.3.1 states that no executive directors should be on the audit committee);

(f)   directors' remuneration (where a significant element needs to be linked to performance) (B.1.4); and

(g)   the existence or not of a nominations committee (the only exception is where the board is small) (A.5.1).

(a) to (c) above are the most common non-compliance disclosed in the December 1999 annual reports published to date. The others, although common previously, appear to have been addressed by the majority of companies.

7.30   No definition is given in the Combined Code of words such as 'small, significant or independent' which are key adjectives used in Code provisions and, therefore, directors may be asked to justify how they interpreted such terms. Consequently, it will be useful to minute the bases for any judgements relating to such words when they are critical to determining whether there has been compliance.

Independent non-executive directors

7.31   The decision as to whether a non-executive is independent has been the subject of many debates at both the company and institutional investor levels. The Combined Code does not define what is meant by 'independent' other than stating that 'the majority of non-executive directors should be independent of management and free from any business or other relationship which could materially interfere with the exercise of their independent judgement' (Code Provision A.3.2). Therefore, it is ultimately down to the Board to decide whether its non-executives meet these requirements. However, various institutions have formed their own view on how 'independence' should be interpreted and have published their rules which they expect their investments to comply with. These rules are non-mandatory and companies with institutions with large shareholdings which have such rules should consider discussing any potential breaches of these rules with the institution prior to making a decision on independence.

Narrative statements

7.32   No official guidance has been issued on the form of the narrative statement, required by Listing Rule 12.43A(a) (see **7.7** above), on how the Principles of good governance have been applied. The London Stock Exchange indicated, on publication of the Code, that companies should have a free hand to explain their governance policies in the light of the Principles, including any special circumstances which have led to a particular approach. However, a representative of the London Stock Exchange indicated that brief, bland statements of appliance will be treated as a rule breach.

7.33   Similarly, no official guidance has been issued on the location of the narrative statement. Companies are including it either in a separate 'corporate governance statement' or within the directors' report. It is useful if it could precede the statement of compliance in order to enable the directors to explain their approach to governance before they deal with how it reconciles with the Code provisions.

7.34   To date, numerous types of disclosures have been published, stemming from brief statements to detailed information on every Principle and provision. Given that directors have to use their judgement as to whether certain provisions have been complied with or not, the more information given about the reason behind a decision the more helpful this is to investors and the fewer questions are likely to be raised at the AGM.

7.35   It is advisable for directors to arrange for a check to be carried out to satisfy themselves that all 14 Principles are covered in the narrative. Even though the London Stock Exchange, to date, has not been very active in monitoring disclosures, this may very well change as the authority for the Listing Rules has transferred to the Financial Services Authority and this body is expected to be more forceful in its monitoring (see **5.52** above). The current pressure for disclosures is coming from various shareholder bodies who perform detailed analyses of corporate governance disclosures with a view to embarrassing companies which do not address all the Principles.

7.36   When drafting a narrative statement, it is useful to consider whether:

(a)   it should either be in one continuous statement or be in different places but cross-referenced;

(b)   to include the control statement in (or cross-refer it to) the narrative statement, as one of Principles, D.2, is on internal control;

(c)   the board wishes to describe the steps which it has carried out in the year to improve its governance arrangements;

(d) to organise the statement under the headings for the Principles set out in the Combined Code (see **7.25** above). (However, directors may find such an approach difficult or too mechanistic);

(e) there are key issues relating to the size of the business, the nature of the risks faced, the type of management information which the board uses, the identity of the providers of external advice and the organisation of the board and its subcommittees which require explanation.

Extract from published annual reports

7.37   There are numerous ways the narrative statement can be presented. In addition to the extract below, see the model corporate governance statement in Delto plc in chapter 46 for sample disclosures.

Extract 7.37

Alliance & Leicester 31 December 1999

Principles of Corporate Governance

The Company's Board appreciates the value of good corporate governance not only in the areas of accountability and risk management but also as a positive contribution to business prosperity. It believes that corporate governance involves more than a simple box ticking approach to establish whether a company has met the requirements of a number of specific rules and regulations. Rather the issue is one of applying corporate governance principles (including those set out in Section 1 of the Principles of Good Governance and Code of Best Practice (the Combined Code) published by the Stock Exchange in June 1998) in a sensible and pragmatic fashion having regard to the individual circumstances of a particular company's business. The key objective is to enhance and protect shareholder value.

Board Structure

The Company's Board comprises the Executive Chairman, five non-executive directors and four executive directors who have the collective responsibility for ensuring that the affairs of the Company and its subsidiaries are managed competently and with integrity. The Executive Chairman is Mr John Windeler who has assumed, as an interim arrangement, the executive role of Group Chief Executive pending appointment of a permanent successor. This combination of the roles of the Chairman and Chief Executive is balanced by non-executive directors who bring independent judgement and wide business experience to the Board. The senior independent non-executive director is the Deputy Chairman, Sir Michael Thompson.

The Board meets regularly and approves and closely monitors the Alliance & Leicester Group's business strategy. There is a formal

---

schedule of matters specifically reserved to the Board for decision including major capital expenditure, annual budgets and corporate objectives. Procedures are in place which allow directors to take independent professional advice in the course of their duties and all directors have access to the advice and services of the Company Secretary. Day-to-day conduct of the Group's business is entrusted to the Executive Chairman and his senior management colleagues.

The Board receives regular management performance and internal control reports and operates a system of Board reviews of individual business units and their performance against key business targets and objectives.

The non-executive directors are not employees of the Company and the Board considers that all the non-executive directors are independent of management and free from business or other relationships which could materially interfere with the exercise of their independent judgement. It should be noted in this context that the pension entitlements of two non-executive directors are fully accrued in accordance with the details disclosed in the Report on Directors' Remuneration. The non-executive directors do, however, play a full part as members of the Board 'team' and share responsibility for Board decisions. They bring a diversity of business perspective and objectivity which complements the 'hands on' expertise of their executive director colleagues. In his present executive role, Mr Windeler is an employee of the Company.

The composition of the Board is kept under review with the aim of ensuring that the Board collectively possesses the necessary skills and experience for the proper direction of the Group's business activities.

Newly appointed directors submit themselves for election by shareholders at the first opportunity after their appointment and at three yearly intervals thereafter. They receive induction training upon appointment.

The Board has established several committees with specified terms of reference which assist the full Board in the exercise of its responsibilities:

Nomination Committee

Under the chairmanship of Mr Windeler, this Committee has the task of recommending new appointments to the Board and reviewing re-appointments when they become due. It has formal Terms of Reference and its current membership comprises the Executive Chairman, the Deputy Chairman (non-executive) and Miss F A Cairncross (non-executive).

Remuneration Committee

Under the chairmanship of Sir Michael Thompson, non-executive Deputy Chairman, this Committee determines the remuneration and contractual arrangements of individual executive directors having regard to a general policy framework for executive remuneration established by the Board. The Board's Report on Directors' Remuneration appears on pages 28 to 32.

The Committees Terms of Reference require membership of the Committee to be confined to non-executive directors. The present members of the Committee are:

Sir Michael Thompson (Chairman)
Mr G N Corah
Miss F A Cairncross

Mr J R Windeler stepped down from the membership of the Committee upon his appointment as Executive Chairman.

Audit Committee

Under the chairmanship of Mr Corah (non-executive director) the duties of the Committee fall into two main areas: internal control and financial reporting.

Internal Control: the Committee reviews the effectiveness of the Groups systems of internal control and risk management and monitors compliance with regulatory requirements. To do this, the Committee approves the annual Internal Audit and Compliance plans, which are based on thorough risk assessments of the full scope of the Groups business activities, and monitors progress against the plans. Each meeting of the Audit Committee receives a report regarding the state of internal control within the Group and the salient points of this report are presented to the next Board meeting.

Financial Reporting: the Committee's role is to review, on behalf of the Board, the annual report and accounts, the interim report and internal audit reports. The Committee focuses on reviewing any changes in accounting policy, major areas of judgement and estimates, and compliance with accounting principles and regulatory requirements.

Membership of the Committee comprises Mr Corah, Sir Michael Thompson and Mr M P S Barton (all of whom are non-executive directors). Meetings of the Committee are normally attended by the Group Finance Director, the Head of Internal Audit, the Head of Group Compliance and the external auditors. The Chairman of the Committee has independent access to both internal and external auditors (and to the Groups key external regulator, the Financial Services Authority).

The Committee recognises the importance of maintaining a sound system of internal control to safeguard shareholders investments and the Companys assets. Further information on the systems of business control appears later in this Statement. The Committee has formal Terms of Reference. The Companys auditors are present at meetings of the Committee and the Committee keeps under review the overall financial relationship between the Company and its auditors in order to ensure a proper balance between the maintenance of objectivity and obtaining value for money.

Other Committees

The Board has also established two other committees. The Group Credit Policy Committee reviews all aspects of lending credit risk and the Group Assets and Liabilities Committee establishes strategies for, and monitors and controls, the levels of balance sheet risk including liquidity, funding and currency exposures across the Group.

Pension Funds

The Groups pension funds are held and controlled by Trustees separately from the Group; in particular no scheme assets are directly invested in or loaned to the Company or its subsidiaries. Independence is reinforced by strong employee trustee representation.

Relations with Shareholders

The Company values dialogue with its institutional shareholders through meetings and results briefings. The Annual General Meeting and the documents sent to shareholders before that meeting provide an opportunity for the Board to account to shareholders for its stewardship of the Group's business.

Compliance Statement

All directors in post at the time of flotation of the Company in April 1997 will have stood for re-election by May 2000 which will ensure an orderly transition to a system of retirements at three yearly intervals thereafter. Subject to this exception, in the directors opinion the Company complied with the provisions of Section 1 of the Combined Code throughout the year ended 31 December 1999.

Internal Control

The Board has adopted the transitional approach for implementing the Combined Code set out in the letter from the London Stock Exchange to listed companies at the end of September 1999.

The Board reviewed the Group's system of non-financial internal controls in comparison to Internal Control: Guidance for Directors on the Combined Code. The review identified that financial and non-financial controls (see Systems of Business Control below) had been implemented and embedded but that more formal reporting to the Board would be required to achieve full compliance. The Board can confirm that, by the year end, it had changed internal reporting procedures in order to implement the guidance fully.

In accordance with the Combined Code, the Board has reviewed the effectiveness of the Group's system of internal control for the year to

31 December 1999 and has taken account of any material developments that may have taken place since the year end.

Systems of Business Control

The Board is responsible for the Group's system of internal controls and for monitoring its effectiveness. The systems of internal control are designed to provide reasonable assurance as to the effectiveness of the safeguards protecting the business against the risk of material error, loss or fraud, but it must be recognised that they cannot provide absolute assurance.

The directors are additionally required by law to establish systems for the control of the conduct of the business in accordance with Schedule 3 of the Banking Act 1987 (the Act). The directors are required to conduct the business with prudence and integrity, ensuring that there are adequate reserves and other capital resources and assets in liquid form for the protection of depositors.

The key features of the system of business control established by the Board are:

¥ a Group Internal Control Policy requiring senior management to identify major risks and monitor the effectiveness of internal controls through key performance indicators and certify to the Board on a twice yearly basis that they are effective. The results of this self-certification are subject to internal audit scrutiny and are reported via the Audit Committee;

¥ a well defined management structure with clear accountabilities;

¥ management information systems, including a budgetary and financial control system;

¥ Risk Management and Compliance functions to identify and monitor all major risks to which the Group is exposed;

¥ an Internal Audit function to report to the Board on the effectiveness of key internal controls in relation to these major risks; and

¥ documented procedures and authority levels to ensure that risks involved in major projects are properly assessed and controlled.

The activities of the Group, including the systems of business control, are subject to supervision by the Financial Services Authority. The Group is required on a regular basis to submit detailed prudential and statistical returns covering all areas of its business and meets regularly with its supervisors, conducting the relationship in an open and constructive manner.

Going Concern

The directors confirm that they are satisfied that the Group has adequate resources to continue in business for the foreseeable future. For this reason, they continue to adopt the going concern basis in preparing the accounts.

Internal control statements

Introduction

7.38 Principle of good governance D.2 states that 'The board should maintain a sound system of internal control to safeguard shareholders' investment and the company's assets'. In addition, Code provision D.2.1 of the Combined Code states that 'the directors should, at least annually, conduct a review of the effectiveness of the group's system of internal control and should report to the shareholders that they have done so. The review should cover all controls including financial, operational and compliance controls and risk management'.

7.39 When the Combined Code was issued, the only guidance the directors had on internal control was the Rutteman guidance (see **7.52** below) which focused only on internal *financial* control, not on the wider aspects of control as intended by D.2.1 (see **7.38** above). The London Stock Exchange wrote to listed companies on 10 December 1998 explaining this situation and gave transitional arrangements on how companies should interpret D.2.1 pending the publication of the guidance for directors on the wider aspects of internal control which was being prepared by the ICAEW. This transitional guidance was as follows:

> 'Until the guidance has been published, a company's statement will, in our opinion, meet the requirements of paragraph 12.43(A) in respect of Code provision D.2.1 if a company complies with the existing arrangements on internal controls, by reporting on their internal financial controls pursuant to the guidance for directors on internal controls and financial reporting that was issued by the Rutteman Working Group in December 1994. A company which has adopted this approach should indicate in its statement of compliance that it has done so. Companies may wish to reflect this approach as part of their narrative statement under paragraph 12.43A(a) in relation to internal controls (Code Principle D.2).'

7.40 The ICAEW's working party (commonly known as the Turnbull working party) issued its guidance *Internal Control – Guidance for Directors on the Combined Code* on 27 September 1999 (see **7.66** below). The London Stock Exchange wrote to all listed companies on that date explaining its timescale for the implementation for the guidance. This letter supersedes the previous transitional arrangements set out in the 10 December 1998 letter (see **7.39** above) for accounting periods ending on or after 23 December 1999, and is as follows:

> 'When we wrote to you on 10 December 1998 on the Combined Code and Internal Control, we undertook to provide a further update on the implementation of the internal control aspects of the Combined

Code, once new guidance had been prepared. With the publication of this guidance, we consider that compliance with all aspects of the Combined Code and, in particular, with those aspects of it relating to internal control, will now be possible. Consequently, full compliance by listed companies with paragraph 12.43A(a) and (b) of the Listing Rules will now be possible and will be required for accounting periods ending on or after 23 December 2000.

In the intervening period, the transitional arrangements set out in our letter of 10 December 1998 will cease to have effect for accounting periods ending on or after 23 December 1999. They will be replaced by the implementation arrangements set out below.

Accounting periods ending on or after 23 December 1999

To allow all companies to take the steps necessary to adopt the new guidance, a company will have satisfied its disclosure requirements in respect of internal controls, if it either:

(a) complies in full with those requirements (see paragraph 12.43A(a) and (b) of the Listing Rules); or

(b) adopts the following approach to disclosure for accounting periods ending on or after 23 December 1999 and up to 22 December 2000:

Paragraph 12.43A(a) of the Listing Rules

(i) as a minimum, in respect of the application of Code Principle D.2, state in their annual report and accounts that they have established the procedures necessary to implement the guidance (*Internal Control: Guidance for Directors on the Combined Code*) or provide an explanation of when they expect to have those procedures in place; and

Paragraph 12.43A(b) of the Listing Rules

(ii) in respect of Code provision D.2.1, report on their internal financial controls pursuant to "Internal Control and Financial Reporting – Guidance for directors of listed companies registered in the UK" (the Rutteman Guidance).

A company which adopts this transitional approach should indicate within its corporate governance disclosures that it has done so.

Accounting periods ending on or after 23 December 2000

For accounting periods ending on or after 23 December 2000, full compliance by all companies with paragraph 12.43A(a) and (b) of the Listing Rules will be required.'

Turnbull implementation arrangements

7.41 The disclosures which are required to be included in the annual report relating to Code principal D.2 and provision D.2.1 depend on when a company's accounting period ends. A summary of the arrangements for various different year ends is as follows:

(a) **Accounting periods ending before 23 December 1999:**

The London Stock Exchange letter of 10 December 1998 can apply (see **7.39** above). No mention of the Turnbull guidance is necessary and the company should refer to its right to report only on internal financial control in its compliance statement (see disclosure in **7.43** below) and follow the Rutteman guidance on internal financial control as detailed in **7.52** to **7.61** below.

(b) **Accounting periods ending between 23 December 1999 and 22 December 2000:**

The London Stock Exchange letter of 27 September 1999 applies (see **7.40** above). Companies can either:

(i) comply with the Turnbull guidance in full; or

(ii) adopt the transitional approach which requires:

- a statement that they are adopting the transitional approach;

- as a minimum, a statement that the procedures to implement the Turnbull guidance are in place or an explanation of when the procedures are expected to be in place; and

- a review of internal financial controls as described in the Rutteman guidance (see **7.52** to **7.61** below).

(c) **Accounting periods ending on or after 23 December 2000:**

The London Stock Exchange letter of 27 September 1999 applies (see **7.40** above). Full compliance with the Turnbull guidance is required (see **7.62** to **7.82** below).

Accounting periods ending pre 23 December 1999

7.42 Companies which are reporting on accounting periods ending before 23 December 1999 can still follow the London Stock Exchange letter dated 10 December 1998 and report on internal financial control in accordance with the 1994 Rutteman guidance (see **7.52** to **7.61** below). No mention of the Turnbull guidance is needed and companies should avoid making statements in its annual report which could be misleading. Depending on the circumstances of the company such a statement could be that, even though not required at the current time, the company is already in a position to comply with the Turnbull guidance in full.

7.43

Companies which are following the London Stock Exchange's letter dated 10 December 1998 (see **7.39** above) and are restricting their internal control review confirmation to 'internal financial control' until the first accounting period ending on or after 23 December 1999, are required to indicate that they have done so. It is normal that a sentence is included in the statement of compliance along the lines set out in Example **7.43** below. This statement is only needed for accounting periods ending before 23 December 1999 and will not be required for accounting periods ending on or after this date.

Example 7.43

As permitted by the Listing Rules, the company has complied with Code provision D.2.1 by reporting on internal financial control in accordance with the guidance for directors on internal control and financial reporting that was issued in December 1994.

Accounting periods ending between 23 December 1999 and 22 December 2000

7.44   In its letter dated 27 September 1999 (see **7.40** above), the London Stock Exchange allowed companies to adopt one of two approaches in their first accounting period ending on or after 23 December 1999. These options were to either:

(a)   comply in full with the Turnbull guidance; or

(b)   adopt the transitional approach which involves, as a minimum, a statement that the procedures to implement the Turnbull guidance are in place or an explanation of when the company expects to have those procedures in place, a statement that the transitional approach has been adopted and a review of internal financial controls in accordance with the 1994 Rutteman guidance.

7.45   Disclosures to be made when complying with the guidance in full are discussed in **7.62** to **7.82** below. Full compliance will be difficult for most companies as the guidance was not published in its final form until late September 1999. One disclosure which is required by the Turnbull guidance (see **7.67**(a) below) is a statement saying that there is an ongoing process of review which has been in place for the full accounting period and which accords with the Turnbull guidance. This statement will be difficult for most companies to meet given the timing of the publication of the final guidance. It will be difficult for companies, with say a December 1999 year end, to have had a system in place for the whole accounting period given the fact that the guidance was only issued in draft form in April 1999. Neither the Exchange nor the Turnbull working party encourages early full compliance.

7.46   Given the reasons in **7.45** above, the transitional approach is the more likely approach to be adopted by the vast majority of companies in accounting periods ending between 23 December 1999 and 22 December 2000. The disclosures required under this approach are threefold (see **7.44** above). Firstly, a statement needs to be made that the transitional approach is being adopted. Wording of this statement could be as follows:

Example 7.46

Internal Control

The group has adopted the transactional approach to the internal control aspects of the Combined Code as set out in the letter from the London Stock Exchange to listed companies dated 27 September 1999.

7.47   Secondly, as a minimum, a statement needs to be made that the procedures to prepare the company for the Turnbull guidance are either in place or an explanation provided of when the company expects to have those procedures in place. Wording of this statement could be as follows:

Example 7.47

Wider aspects of internal control

The board confirms that it has established [as from (insert date)]* the procedures necessary to implement the guidance 'Internal Control: Guidance for Directors on the Combined Code'.

Or:

The board expects to have the procedures in place in May 2000 necessary to implement the guidance 'Internal Control: Guidance for Directors on the Combined Code'. This takes account of the time that needs to be taken to put in place the procedures which the board has agreed should be established.

*Companies can state when the procedures were established. This may aid users understanding of the next year's internal control disclosure (see **7.63** below).

This is the minimum amount of information which needs to be disclosed. Companies are not precluded from giving more information, and indeed, this is to be encouraged in order to help users understand the impact the Turnbull guidance has had on the company. It is up to individual companies to decide whether additional information is given and, if it is, its nature and quantity. Wording to follow the statement made above could be as follows:

> The procedures which have been/are to be* established include holding a risk management workshop, attended by all board members, together with prioritising change issues, the group's objectives and risks and determining a control strategy for each of the significant risks. A risk management policy document has been/is also being* sent to all employees setting out the board's attitude to risk to the achievement of the business objectives. The monthly management information has/is* also being improved with the addition of some key risk indicators.
>
> The board has changed/is to change* its meeting calendar and agenda so that risk management and internal control will be considered on a regular basis during the year and there will be a full risk and control assessment before reporting on the year ending 31 December 2000.
>
> *The tense depends on whether the procedures have already been established or are still to be established.

7.48 As discussed in **7.63** below, if procedures to implement the guidance have been established at any point after the balance sheet date for the first accounting period ending on or after 23 December 1999, there will be an impact on the full compliance disclosures given in the next accounting period (i.e., the first accounting period ending on or after 23 December 2000).

7.49 Thirdly, under the transitional approach, the board must make a statement in accordance with the Rutteman guidance and report on a review of effectiveness of internal financial control. The Rutteman guidance is discussed in **7.52** to **7.60** below.

Extracts from published annual reports

7.50 Some examples of recently published transitional disclosures follow:

> ***Extract 7.50.1***
>
> ***Hanson plc 31 December 1999***
>
> **Internal control**
>
> The board recognises that it is responsible for the company's system of internal control and for reviewing its effectiveness. Such a system

can only provide reasonable and not absolute assurance against material misstatement or loss, as it is designed to manage rather than eliminate the risk of failure to achieve business objectives.

The Combined Code introduced a requirement that the effectiveness of the system of internal control, including financial, operational, compliance and risk management, is reviewed by the board at least annually. In addition, *Internal Control: Guidance for Directors on the Combined Code* ('The Turnbull Report') was published in September 1999 to provide guidance to directors in respect of this requirement. In this respect, the board has adopted the transitional approach for the Combined Code set out in the letter from the London Stock Exchange to listed companies at the end of September 1999.

The board expects that it will fully comply with the guidance with effect from 1 April 2000. In respect of the accounting period to 31 December 1999 the board acknowledges responsibility for Hanson's system of internal financial control, the effectiveness of which has been reviewed and reported upon to the board by the audit committee (as permitted by the London Stock Exchange in accordance with the guidance for directors on internal control and financial reporting issued in December 1994).

Hanson operates a clearly defined decentralised structure which delegates authority, responsibility and accountability to management of the operating companies thus ensuring that internal control becomes embedded in the operations. The key ongoing processes and features of the internal risk-based control system that will be operative effective from 1 April 2000 will include:

- a process to identify and evaluate business risks;
- a control environment and control activities;
- information and communication processes;
- a monitoring system and board review for effectiveness.

Internal audit

The board has considered the need to introduce a group internal audit function but has decided that the current control mechanisms, which include internal audit functions within certain operating units, are appropriate for the group. The board continues to review this decision.

Extract 7.50.2

George Wimpy plc 31 December 1999

The Board is responsible for the Group's system of internal financial control and for reviewing its effectiveness. The system can only provide reasonable and not absolute assurance against material misstatement or loss.

During 1999 the Group operated under an established internal financial control framework which can be described under four headings:

Financial and Operating Reporting – there is a comprehensive budgeting system with an annual budget approved by the Board. Forecasts are prepared three times a year. Monthly actual performance of each business unit is reviewed by Divisional management and subsequently reported to the Board against both budget and forecast. Particular emphasis is placed on cash flow as well as profit and loss and balance sheet reporting, and on key operating issues.

Business Unit Controls – controls and procedures, including information systems controls, are detailed in procedures manuals and confirmed by internal control questionnaires completed by each business unit. Compliance with these procedures is reviewed by the Company's internal auditors and management at Divisional level.

Functional Reporting – the Group has identified a number of key areas which are subject to regular review such as Treasury Operations, Tax, Health and Safety, Legal Environment, and Risk Management.

Land Purchase and Investment Appraisal – the Group has clearly defined guidelines for purchase of land and for capital expenditure. These include annual budgets, detailed appraisal and review procedures, levels of authority and due diligence requirements.

The Audit Committee has reviewed the operation and effectiveness of this framework and will continue to do so on a regular basis.

At the year end the Group adopted the transitional approach for the Combined Code set out in the letter from the London Stock Exchange to listed companies at the end of September 1999.

The Board is able to confirm that it has established the procedures necessary to implement the guidance 'Internal Control: Guidance for Directors on the Combined Code' for its financial year beginning 1 January 2000. As part of the process the Board identified and agreed key 'high level' risks, which affect the Group, the acceptable level of such risks, and the controls and reporting procedures. The risk assessment document has been communicated in an appropriate form to each of the Group's business units.

Extract 7.50.3

Woolwich plc 31 December 1999

Internal control

The Board of directors has overall responsibility for the Group's system of internal control and for reviewing its effectiveness. Although no system of internal control can provide absolute assurance to the directors, the Group's systems are designed to manage the risk of failure to achieve business objectives and to provide the directors with reasonable assurance against material misstatement or loss.

The Combined Code introduced a requirement that the directors' review of internal controls extend to all controls, including financial and operational controls, compliance and risk management. Until clarification was provided on this, the London Stock Exchange introduced transitional rules enabling companies to continue to review and report on internal financial controls in accordance with the ICAEW's 1994 guidance: *Internal Controls and Financial Reporting* (the Rutteman guidance). Further guidance for directors on the Combined Code requirement was published in September 1999 (the Turnbull guidance). The Board confirms that the procedures necessary to implement the Turnbull guidance have been established so that they will be fully complied with for the accounting period ending on 31 December 2000. For 1999, the directors have continued to use the transitional rules and accordingly have reviewed and report on internal financial controls in the light of the Rutteman guidance.

Key elements of the internal financial control system include:

- A planning framework which includes the Board approving a three-year business plan and annual budget covering all the Group's activities.

- A comprehensive system of financial reporting to the Board, based on the annual budget with monthly reports against actual results, review of variances and key indicators, plus regular forecasting.

- A Group Risk Committee which is responsible for the establishment and monitoring of effective financial risk management practices across the Group and ensuring that control limits for financial risk, including credit, market, liquidity and funding, are strictly adhered to.

- The existence of controls and procedures to limit the Group's exposure to loss of assets and to fraud and other irregularities.

- The use of control manuals for documenting key controls against identified risks within the business units.

- The regular review by the internal audit function of all business activities to verify the existence and effective operation of appropriate controls.

Monitoring of the effectiveness of internal financial control is undertaken by the Audit Committee, which receives regular reports from the internal audit function and, where appropriate, from external auditors. The Audit Committee has reviewed the effectiveness of the system of internal financial control which operated during 1999.

External auditors

7.51   Failure to provide any disclosure under either set of options is likely to result in the external auditors being forced to refer to the matter in their report to the members (see **7.121** to **7.123** below and chapter 40). As the disclosures are subject to auditor review, there is a need to keep them factual and avoid misleading statements.

Internal financial control

7.52   The Rutteman guidance focuses only on internal financial control and has been the source of guidance on internal control since 1994. Under this guidance, most listed companies have had to review the effectiveness of internal financial control and to make a statement in the annual report to this affect. In order to comply with the December 1994 Rutteman guidance, directors should include a statement on the system of internal financial control covering the period of the financial statements and taking account of material developments between the balance sheet date and the date on which the financial statements are signed, including:

(a)   an acknowledgement by the directors that they are responsible for the company's/group's system of internal financial control;

(b)   an explanation that such a system of internal financial control can provide only reasonable and not absolute assurance against material misstatement or loss;

(c)   a description of the key procedures that the directors have established and which are designed to provide effective internal financial control, having regard to paragraph 11 of the Rutteman guidance and the section of the guidance entitled 'Criteria for assessing effectiveness';

(d)   a confirmation that the directors (or a board committee) have reviewed the effectiveness of the system of internal financial control;

(e)   where weaknesses in internal financial control have resulted in material losses, contingencies or uncertainties which require disclosure in the financial statements or auditor's report, the statement should:

  (i)   describe what corrective action has been taken or is intended to be taken; or
  (ii)   explain why no changes are considered necessary.

7.53   Where the company is a parent company preparing group financial statements, the directors' statement regarding internal financial control should be in respect of the group as a whole.

7.54   The Rutteman guidance states that directors may wish, and are encouraged, to extend their statement to cover their responsibility for wider aspects of internal control rather than just internal financial control. However, caution should be taken in this area especially if the company has not yet established all the procedures necessary to implement the Turnbull guidance.

7.55 | It is advisable for directors to avoid expressing any form of opinion on the control system, on the grounds that there is no requirement to express an opinion. The previous Cadbury Code provision 4.5, which recommended a report on the effectiveness of the system of internal control, has been superseded by Combined Code provision D.2.1, which recommends instead a report on whether the directors have reviewed the effectiveness of the system of internal control. If, despite this change in the Code provisions, directors still wish to give an opinion, it should be confined to internal financial control, confined to a point in time, expressed in reasonableness rather than effectiveness terms and not attempt to convey the impression of perfection.

7.56 | The control statement should preferably be included in (or cross-referred to) the narrative statement describing how the Principles are applied (see **7.32** above).

Criteria for assessing effectiveness

7.57 Under the Rutteman guidance, directors should have regard to the criteria for assessing the effectiveness of internal financial control as set out in the 1994 guidance, recognising that criteria can be addressed in different ways. Control procedures should be appropriate to the organisation and its activities and the need for formal systems is likely to increase with the size and public interest in the entity concerned. The criteria set out in the guidance are included under the headings set out below:

- Control environment;
- Identification and evaluation of risks and control objectives;
- Information and communication;
- Control procedures; and
- Monitoring and corrective action.

Reporting on internal financial control

7.58 The Rutteman guidance does not include examples of statements by directors. However, paragraph 11 of the guidance states that the description of the key procedures that the directors have established should include:

(a) the steps taken to ensure an appropriate control environment (e.g., clear management responsibilities in relation to internal financial control, unambiguous responses to control failures);

(b) the process used to identify major business risks (including optionally a brief explanation of the major financial risks identified) and to evaluate their financial implications (e.g., board or committee review of the risk implications of new treasury products);

(c) the major information systems that are in place (e.g., annual budgeting, monthly forecasting and comparison with budgets and forecasting);

(d) the major control procedures which address the financial implications of the major business risks (e.g., authorisation limits, segregation of duties); and

(e) the monitoring system the board uses to check that the system is operating effectively (e.g., the role of the audit committee, management reviews, internal audit function and/or reports from independent accountants).

The description should avoid excessive detail, recognising that the way in which major business risks are identified and evaluated, the Principles that are applied and the high-level monitoring procedures are more relevant in the context of public reporting than descriptions of the accounting system and its related low-level controls.

Example 7.58

A statement of internal financial control

The directors are responsible for the company's system of internal financial control. Such a system can provide only reasonable and not absolute assurance against material misstatement or loss. Key procedures that have been established and are designed to provide effective internal financial control can be described under five headings.

(a) *Financial reporting* – the group has a comprehensive system for reporting financial results to the board; each operating unit prepares monthly results with a comparison against budget. Towards the end of each financial year, the operating units prepare detailed budgets for the following year and update their rolling five-year outline plans. Budgets and plans are reviewed by the board before being adopted formally.

(b) *Quality and integrity of personnel* – one of the group's five core values is integrity; this is regarded as vital to the maintenance of the group's system of internal financial control. The group's policies are detailed in the Corporate Policy Manual, to which all operating units are required to adhere.

(c) *Operating unit controls* – the executive management has defined the financial controls and procedures with which each operating unit is required to comply. Key controls over major business risks include reviews against performance indicators and exception reporting. The operating units make regular assessments of the extent of their compliance with these controls and procedures. These management assessments are checked by visits by internal auditors. The reports arising from such visits are given to both the executive and unit management and the audit committee.

(d) *Computer systems* – much of the group's financial and management information is processed by and stored on computer systems. Accordingly, the group has established controls and procedures over the security of data held on computer systems. Also, the group has put in place arrangements for computer processing to continue and data to be retained in the event of the complete failure of the group's own data processing facility. These arrangements are tested regularly and reviewed by the group's internal audit department.

(e) *Controls over central functions* – a number of the group's key functions, including treasury, taxation, environmental monitoring and insurance, are dealt with centrally. Each of these functions has detailed procedures manuals and is required to report to the board on a monthly basis. The treasury department also reports daily to the finance director or, in his absence, to the managing director. These central functions are also subject to self-assessment and visits by the group's internal auditors. The external auditors have also performed a special review engagement during the year and reported to the audit committee on controls over treasury activities, including the use of derivative instruments.

The board has reviewed the effectiveness of the system of internal financial control in accordance with criteria set out in the Rutteman guidance for directors *Internal Control and Financial Reporting*. It has considered the major financial risks, the control environment, information on and arising from control procedures and the results of the internal audit department's work.

7.59   The next example showing how a weakness in the system of internal financial control that gives rise to a material loss (in this case, as a result of entering into unauthorised derivative contracts) should be disclosed.

Example 7.59

Loss on derivative contracts

As referred to in the chairman's statement and note 17 to the accounts, a year of progress at the trading level was masked by the impact of £183 million currency trading losses related to derivative contracts.

> The losses arose as a result of the unauthorised speculative 'writing' of currency options by a member of the group's central treasury operation. The transactions assumed that the sterling/dollar exchange rate would rise above 1.80 before 30 June 1999. A regular visit by the group's internal audit department discovered the irregularities and immediately informed the audit committee. A special board meeting was convened and the decision was taken to immediately 'close out' the unauthorised contracts; the £/$ rate at the time was 1.55, which resulted in a loss of £183 million.
>
> Since the discovery of the irregularities by the internal audit department, the board, with the assistance of the audit committee, has put in place measures to prevent the group from again being exposed to such 'one-off' losses from unauthorised transactions. These measures include:
>
> (a) the appointment of a new head of the treasury department who is required to report daily positions to the finance director; she is also required to report each month's treasury activities to the board at its regular monthly meetings;
>
> (b) revision of the treasury department's exposure limits;
>
> (c) retraining of all treasury department employees; and
>
> (d) more regular monitoring of treasury functions by the internal audit department.
>
> The new procedures, the board believes, should ensure that there is no possibility of such losses recurring.

7.60   The Rutteman guidance also states that the statement of directors' responsibilities should refer to the directors' responsibilities for the company's system of internal financial control. The example in **7.115** below includes appropriate wording.

Adopting the transitional approach and reporting on the wider aspects

7.61

> An issue which is arising with some listed companies is that they are adopting the transitional approach but also providing a Rutteman statement which refers to internal control rather than internal financial control. This is permissible as the Rutteman guidance does include encouragement for companies to report on the wider aspects of internal control. However, it is suggested that, if a company does go down this route (which may not be uncommon as some large companies were already reporting on the wider aspects in previous years), there be a clear explanation given. For instance, wording could be added such as:
>
> 'The review covers the wider aspects of internal control in response to the encouragement given in the 1994 guidance.'

This would also accord with Rutteman's requirement that, if the wider aspects of internal control are discussed, a statement should be made which allows the shareholders to understand its scope.

Extract 7.61

Internal control

The Board of Directors has overall responsibility for the system of internal control and for reviewing its effectiveness throughout the Abbey National Group. However, it is important to note that the size and complexity of the Group's operations mean that such a system can only provide reasonable and not absolute assurance against material misstatement or loss. The effectiveness of the internal control system is reviewed by the Audit Committee on behalf of the Board.

The rationale of the system of internal control is to enable the Group to achieve its corporate objectives within an acceptable risk profile, not to eliminate the risk, and the effectiveness of internal control has to be viewed in this context. The Board and executive management structures summarised above describe the processes for determining strategies, policies and the control environment.

The Audit Committee has, on behalf of the Board, reviewed the effectiveness of the system of internal control during the period covered by the Annual Report and Accounts. The basis of the review predated the Turnbull Working Party's guidance ('the guidance') for directors but did cover financial, operational, and compliance control and risk management. Following the publication of the guidance, the Board confirms that procedures have been established to implement it fully for the year ending 31 December 2000. The directors are also of the view that as from 1 January 2000 there is an on-going process for identifying, evaluating and managing the Group's significant risks that is regularly reviewed by the Board and accords with the guidance.

For the purposes of this statement, the Board has adopted the transitional approach as permitted by the London Stock Exchange letter dated 27 September 1999 and therefore sets out below a description of the control procedures. However, it also sets out additional information to assist the understanding of the Company's risk management processes and the system of internal control including financial control. The key elements are as follows:

–   Risk management and control embedded within the operations of the Group.

–   A framework of high-level authorities (see 'The Board' section above).

–   A high-level risk management framework which outlines the risk management philosophy and resultant control environment.

- A planning framework which incorporates a Board approved rolling three-year plan, with detailed annual operating objectives and milestones to business unit levels together with the related key risks and sensitivities.

- A Group high-level risk map which identifies the policy mechanisms and independent risk monitoring functions for all risks within broad risk categories; credit, market position, liquidity, insurance, business event, strategic and operational. Ian Treacy, Director and Secretary, heads the Group Risk Division responsible for independent risk monitoring functions which regularly report on financial, compliance and operational risk exposures.

- A comprehensive system of reporting to the Board, based on an annual budget with monthly reports against actual results, analysis of variances, scrutiny of key performance indicators, plus regular reforecasting.

- Well-defined regulations governing appraisal and approval of capital expenditure. These include an annual budget, detailed project approval procedures, incorporating appropriate levels of authority, and a post-investment review process.

- The use of control manuals to document key controls against identified risks, supplemented by procedure manuals at the operating level.

The Board has established a process for reviewing the effectiveness of the system of internal control through reports it receives from these Committees and various independent monitoring functions. The procedures to enable this to operate throughout 2000 have been put in hand. As part of this process, management including executive directors submit Self Certification Statements on the effectiveness of risk management and internal controls against material risks. The Board will undertake a formal annual assessment in 2000 and annually thereafter to form its own view on the effectiveness of the system of internal control.

There is a long established internal audit function with requisite expertise. Its role is to provide independent and objective assurance to the Board that the processes by which significant risks are identified, assessed and managed are appropriate and effectively applied, and achieve residual risk exposures consistent with management's risk policy, reporting any material exceptions and following up management responses to ensure effective resolution of issues. The Audit Committee approves the annual plans for internal audit which cover the scope, authority and resources of the function.

Accounting periods ending on or after 23 December 2000

7.62 For accounting periods ending on or after 23 December 2000, full compliance with the Turnbull guidance is expected as per the

London Stock Exchange letter dated 27 September 1999 (see **7.40** above). The disclosures recommended by the Turnbull guidance for full compliance are discussed in **7.67** below.

7.63   An issue may arise in relation to one of the required full compliance disclosures (see **7.67**(a) below) when, for the accounting period ending between 23 December 1999 and 22 December 2000, the transitional approach to implementing Turnbull has been adopted (see **7.41** above). When procedures to implement the guidance were still being established during the accounting period ending on or after 23 December 2000, then the company will be unable to state that there has been an ongoing process for identifying, evaluating and managing the group's significant risks that has been in place for the *full* year ended on or after 23 December 2000. As required by the Turnbull guidance (see **7.68** below), when this statement cannot be made, this should be stated and an explanation given. This could be done as follows.

Example 7.63

A company has a 31 December year end. In the annual report for the year ended 31 December 1999 published in March 2000, it adopted the transitional approach as permitted by the Listing Rules and stated that the procedures to implement the Turnbull guidance would be in place by the end of May 2000. In the annual report for the year ended 31 December 2000, the board cannot state that it has complied with the guidance in full as the company took five months to establish procedures. Wording which could be included in the 31 December 2000 annual report is as follows:

'The board is of the view that there is an ongoing process for identifying, evaluating and managing the group's significant risks that has been in place for the period from the beginning of June 2000 up to the date of approval of the annual report and accounts. This process is regularly reviewed by the board and accords with the internal control guidance for directors on the Combined Code. The board is unable to state that the process has been in place for the first five months of the year as this period was needed to put in place the procedures which the board agreed should be established.'

7.64   The Listing Rules require companies to state whether or not they have complied with the Code's provisions during the year. Therefore, this rule would require the board to disclose if it has failed to conduct a review of the effectiveness of the company's system of internal control (as required by Code provision D.2.1). This non-compliance disclosure would fall within the compliance statement (see **7.26** to **7.31** above).

External auditors

7.65   Failure to provide any disclosure is likely to result in the external auditors being forced to refer to the matter in their report to the members (see **7.123** below and chapter 40). As the disclosures are subject to auditor review, there is a need to keep them factual and avoid misleading statements.

Turnbull guidance

7.66   The ICAEW working party, chaired by Nigel Turnbull, published their report on the wider aspects of internal control in September 1999 titled *Internal Control – Guidance for Directors on the Combined Code* (the Turnbull guidance). Its objectives, inter alia, are to help boards of directors in:

(a)   assessing how the company has applied Code Principle D.2;

(b)   implementing the requirements of Code provisions D.2.1 and D.2.2; and

(c)   reporting on these matters to shareholders in the annual report and accounts.

The guidance contains few surprises, but some challenges. It extends the board's review of effectiveness of internal control to the wider aspects of risk. A key feature is that a company's system of internal control should have, as its principal aim, the management of risks that are significant to the fulfilment of its business objectives, with a view to safeguarding the company's assets and enhancing over time the value of the shareholders' investment.

7.67   The disclosures recommended by the Turnbull guidance for full compliance are as follows:

(a)   As a minimum, in its narrative statement of how it has applied Code Principle D.2, disclosure that there is an ongoing process for identifying, evaluating and managing the significant risks faced by the company that:

(i)   has been in place for the year under review and up to the date of the approval of the annual report and accounts;

(ii)   is regularly reviewed by the board; and

(iii) accords with the Turnbull guidance.

(b)   In relation to the application of Principle D.2, an acknowledgement by the board that it is responsible for the company's system of internal control and for reviewing its effectiveness.

(c)   An explanation that the system of internal control is designed to manage rather than eliminate the risk of failure to achieve business objectives, and can only provide reasonable and not absolute assurance against material misstatement or loss.

(d) In relation to Code provision D.2.1, a summary of the processes the board (where applicable, through its committees) has applied in reviewing the effectiveness of the system of internal control.

(e) The processes applied by the board to deal with material internal control aspects of any significant issues disclosed in the annual report and accounts.

(f) Where material joint ventures and associates have not been dealt with as part of the group for the purposes of applying this guidance, this should be stated.

The board may wish to provide additional information to assist understanding of the company's risk management processes and system of internal control. Directors should also ensure that disclosures are concise, provide meaningful, high-level information and do not give a misleading impression.

7.68 Where a company has not made one or more of the disclosures in (a), (d) or (e) in **7.67** above, the Turnbull guidance requires that this fact should be stated and an explanation provided.

7.69 Neither the Exchange nor the Turnbull Working Party encourage any opinions on the effectiveness of the system of internal control.

7.70 Some companies will wish to adopt a minimalist approach to disclosure. Others will wish to go further. Indeed this is specifically catered for in the reference that the board may wish to provide additional information (see **7.67** above).

7.71 Disclosure is expected in relation to the processes the board has applied to deal with material internal control aspects of any significant issues disclosed in the annual report and accounts. The board should preferably minute the rationale for their decisions where there is any possibility that a reported issue deemed to be insignificant could be construed as significant by other parties. It may need to be able to justify such decisions later.

7.72 The full annual report and accounts, the interims and other statements made during the year should be read to ensure that there are no references to significant problems (which arise from material internal control issues) which are not responded to in the new statement of internal control under the full compliance regime. Otherwise, criticisms could be made of the directors.

7.73   An impression of perfection should be avoided. It is useful to refer to reports received by the board on risk and control which include recommendations for improvement.

7.74   The guidance stresses that there should be appropriate documentation to support the statement on internal control. The guidance for auditors, APB Bulletin 1999/5, was finalised in November 1999 and requires that auditors understand the review process and review the documentation prepared by or for the directors which supports the internal control statement.

7.75   Where the company is the parent of a group, the statement on internal control should be from the perspective of the group as a whole.

7.76   The *Internal Control Guidance for Directors on the Combined Code* (the Turnbull guidance) is more onerous than the Rutteman guidance on internal financial control (see **7.52** to **7.61** above). The recommendations which are tougher include the following:

(a)   There is a need for directors to be publicly accountable not only for internal control which helps ensure the quality of internal and external reporting, but also internal control which facilitates the effectiveness and efficiency of operations and helps ensure compliance with laws and regulations.

(b)   The directors are not only required to perform an annual assessment of internal control, but also to consider reports relating to internal control regularly during the year.

(c)   There is specific reference that the system of internal control should:

(i)   be embedded in the operations of the company and form part of its culture;

(ii)   be capable of responding quickly to evolving risks to the business arising from factors within the company and changes in the business environment; and

(iii)   include procedures for reporting immediately to appropriate levels of management any significant control failings or weaknesses that are identified along with details of corrective action being undertaken.

(d)   There is much greater clarity about the respective roles of the board and management. The guidance states that reviewing the effectiveness of internal control is an essential part of the board's responsibilities and that the board will need to form its own view on effectiveness after due and careful enquiry based on the information and assurances provided to it. It also states that management is accountable to the board for monitoring the system of internal control and for providing assurance that it has done so.

(e)   There is more guidance on what is expected from reports to the board and on the matters to be considered regularly during the year.

(f)   There is more clarity about the matters which the annual assessment needs to include.

(g)   There are a number of questions set out in the appendix which the guidance says the board may wish to consider and discuss with management when regularly reviewing reports. Guidance is given to assist boards of companies which do not have an internal audit function, to meet the recommendation of Combined Code provision D.2.2 that they should from time to time review the need for one.

7.77   Companies will fall in various categories of compliance, from leading edge to laggards. However, all will find some challenges in complying with these guidelines. For example, even leading edge companies may find the following matters referred to in the guidance as challenging:

(a)   installing key risk indicators which allow management to monitor risks and identify developments which require interventions;

(b)   ensuring that their system is actually 'ongoing';

(c)   ensuring that all employees collectively possess the necessary skills, technical knowledge, objectivity and understanding of the organisation and the industries and markets in which the company operates;

(d)   creating an environment that promotes learning within the company on risk and control issues, including the provision of relevant training;

(e)   improving their internal reporting on risk and control, especially where currently there is only reporting by exception;

(f)   making risk management and control more explicit across the organisation; and

(g)   strengthening and repositioning internal audit.

7.78   Key questions for a board to consider include the following:

(a)   Is the process for identifying, evaluating and managing the key risks ongoing?

(b)   Does this process accord with the guidance?

(c)   What work needs to be done to ensure that the directors have established the necessary procedures to implement the guidance?

> (d) Is sufficient resource being applied to create the level of control environment specified by the guidance?
>
> (e) Does the group have key risk indicators which enable immediate reporting of major control weaknesses?
>
> (f) Is there an environment that promotes learning within the company on risk and control issues, including the provision of relevant training as now expected by the guidance?

7.79 Pitfalls for directors to avoid include:

(a) treating Turnbull only as a disclosure issue;

(b) continuing with too narrow a definition of risk;

(c) concentrating only on comfort areas (e.g., internal financial controls);

(d) identifying too many risks;

(e) not creating a top down process. Such a process would usefully involve members of the board participating at the outset and taking into account the views of the executive committee on the key business risks;

(f) not putting in place procedures to find out from all levels of the organisation other significant risks or risk which they perceive as poorly controlled;

(g) not addressing cultural issues;

(h) not creating a process which is embedded and ongoing;

(i) creating a situation where one person/department (i.e., the Financial Director, the Head of Risk Assessment, the Head of Internal Audit or the Audit Committee) is accountable for management of all risks; accountability for managing risk should be allocated across the organisation to relevant people and there should be a collective sense of concern to ensure that key risks are kept under control;

(j) a lack of linkage between the strategy review and risk management processes;

(k) 'throwing the baby out with the bathwater', i.e., not keeping the key elements of the system of control that are already successful.

7.80 Specimen and recently published internal control statements which comply with the Turnbull guidance in full are as follows:

Example 7.80.1

SPECIMEN INTERNAL CONTROL STATEMENT

(for the first accounting period ending on or after 23 December 2000)

The Board is responsible for the group's system of internal control and for reviewing its effectiveness. Such a system is designed to manage rather than eliminate the risk of failure to achieve business objectives and can only provide reasonable and not absolute assurance against material misstatement or loss.

The board is of the view that there is an on-going process for identifying, evaluating and managing the group's significant risks that has been in place for the year ended 31 December 2000 and up to the date of approval of the annual report and accounts, is regularly reviewed by the Board and accords with the internal control guidance for directors of the Combined Code.[1]

Or

The board is of the view that there is an ongoing process for identifying, evaluating and managing the group's significant risks that has been in place for the period from the beginning of June 2000 up to the date of approval of the annual report and accounts. This process is regularly reviewed by the board and accords with the internal control guidance for directors on the Combined Code. The board is unable to state that the process has been in place for the first five months of the year as this period was needed to put in place the procedures which the board agreed should be established.[2]

The Executive Committee receives reports setting out key performance and risk indicators and considers possible control issues brought to their attention by early warning mechanisms which are embedded within the operational units and reinforced by risk awareness training. The Executive Committee and the Audit Committee also receive regular reports from the internal audit and 'health, safety and environmental monitoring' functions which include recommendations for improvement. The Audit Committee's role in this area is confined to a high level review of the arrangements for internal financial control.

The board's agenda includes a regular item for consideration of risk and control and receives reports thereon from the Executive Committee and the Audit Committee. The emphasis is on obtaining the relevant degree of assurance and not merely reporting by exception. At its February 2001 meeting, the board carried out the annual assessment for the year 2000, also taking account of events since 31 December 2000.

Following the precautionary recall of the drinks lines in May 2000, which is discussed in the Operating and Financial Review on page y, a full investigation was performed by the group's health, safety and environmental monitoring team. The resulting report was considered by the Board. This has resulted in further training of relevant workers and the introduction of enhanced monitoring equipment. The risk of such an eventuality occurring again has been reduced.

1   This assumes that full compliance has been achieved for the whole accounting period and the period up to approval of the annual report and accounts.

2   This assumes that the group could only achieve full compliance for part of the accounting period. This would be likely to occur if, for the first accounting period ended on or after 23 December 1999 (i.e., 31 December 1999 in this example), the directors provided an explanation of when (during the year to 31 December 2000) they expected to have the procedures necessary to implement the guidance in place.

Example 7.80.2

SmithKline Beecham plc 31 December 1999

Internal control

The Board of Directors has overall responsibility for the system of internal control and for reviewing its effectiveness throughout the Abbey National Group. However, it is important to note that the size and complexity of the Group's operations mean that such a system can only provide reasonable and not absolute assurance against material misstatement or loss. The effectiveness of the internal control system is reviewed by the Audit Committee on behalf of the Board.

The rationale of the system of internal control is to enable the Group to achieve its corporate objectives within an acceptable risk profile, not to eliminate the risk, and the effectiveness of internal control has to be viewed in this context. The Board and executive management structures summarised above describe the processes for determining strategies, policies and the control environment.

The Audit Committee has, on behalf of the Board, reviewed the effectiveness of the system of internal control during the period covered by the Annual Report and Accounts. The basis of the review predated the Turnbull Working Party's guidance ('the guidance') for directors but did cover financial, operational, and compliance control and risk management. Following the publication of the guidance, the Board confirms that procedures have been established to implement it fully for the year ending 31 December 2000. The directors are also of the view that as from 1 January 2000 there is an on-going process for identifying, evaluating and managing the Group's significant risks that is regularly reviewed by the Board and accords with the guidance.

For the purposes of this statement, the Board has adopted the transitional approach as permitted by the London Stock Exchange letter dated 27 September 1999 and therefore sets out below a description of the control procedures. However, it also sets out additional information to assist the understanding of the Company's risk management processes and the system of internal control including financial control. The key elements are as follows:

- Risk management and control embedded within the operations of the Group.

- A framework of high-level authorities (see 'The Board' section above).

- A high-level risk management framework which outlines the risk management philosophy and resultant control environment.

- A planning framework which incorporates a Board approved rolling three year plan, with detailed annual operating objectives and milestones to business unit levels together with the related key risks and sensitivities.

- A Group high-level risk map which identifies the policy mechanisms and independent risk monitoring functions for all risks within broad risk categories; credit, market position, liquidity, insurance, business event, strategic and operational. Ian Treacy, Director and Secretary, heads the Group Risk Division responsible for independent risk monitoring functions which regularly report on financial, compliance and operational risk exposures.

- A comprehensive system of reporting to the Board, based on an annual budget with monthly reports against actual results, analysis of variances, scrutiny of key performance indicators, plus regular reforecasting.

- Well-defined regulations governing appraisal and approval of capital expenditure. These include an annual budget, detailed project approval procedures, incorporating appropriate levels of authority, and a post-investment review process

- The use of control manuals to document key controls against identified risks, supplemented by procedure manuals at the operating level.

The Board has established a process for reviewing the effectiveness of the system of internal control through reports it receives from these Committees and various independent monitoring functions. The procedures to enable this to operate throughout 2000 have been put in hand. As part of this process, management including executive directors submit Self Certification Statements on the effectiveness of risk management and internal controls against material risks. The Board will undertake a formal annual assessment in 2000 and annually thereafter to form its own view on the effectiveness of the system of internal control.

There is a long established internal audit function with requisite expertise. Its role is to provide independent and objective assurance to the Board that the processes by which significant risks are identified, assessed and managed are appropriate and effectively applied, and achieve residual risk exposures consistent with management's risk policy, reporting any material exceptions and following up management responses to ensure effective resolution of issues. The Audit Committee approves the annual plans for internal audit which cover the scope, authority and resources of the function.

Location of statement on internal control

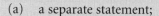

7.81 The positioning of the directors' internal control statements is not prescribed, but it is possible that it will appear in:

(a) a separate statement;

(b) the narrative statement;

(c) the OFR; or

(d) the directors' report

7.82 It is preferable that the statement on internal control should be included in or cross-referred to the narrative statement (see **7.7** above). The reason for this is that the maintenance of the system of internal control is expected under Principle D.2 and there is a need to describe how the Principles are applied in the narrative statement.

Assessment of the company's position and prospects

7.83 Code Principle D.1 recommends that the board should present a balanced and understandable assessment of the company's position and prospects. Most larger companies provide such an assessment in their directors' report or chairman's statement. These reviews may be adapted to satisfy this requirement. Alternatively, an OFR (see **6.89** above) is likely to provide the relevant information.

7.84 Code provision D.1.2 also states that the board's responsibility to present a balanced and understandable assessment extends to interim and other price-sensitive public reports and reports to regulators, as well as information required to be presented by the statutory requirements.

Other governance disclosures

7.85 Excluding directors' remuneration disclosures, the Code provisions of the Combined Code recommend other governance disclosures in the annual report. These include the identification of:

(a) the chairman, chief executive and senior independent director; [Code provision A.2.1]

(b) the non-executive directors considered by the board to be independent of management and free from any business or other relationship which could materially interfere with the exercise of their independent judgement; [Code provision A.3.2]

(c) the chairman and members of the nominations committee; [Code provision A.5.1] and

(d) the members of the audit committee. [Code provision D.3.1]

7.86   Code provision A.2.1 recommends that a decision to combine the posts of chairman and chief executive in one person be publicly justified. Such justification is not required to be in the annual report, but it is best practice to disclose the justification in the annual report.

Extract 7.86

Anglo American plc 31 December 1999

In compliance statement:

Since Anglo American was listed on 24 May 1999 the principles and detailed provisions of the Combined Code have been complied with except that the chairman of the board is also the chief executive. This is commented on below.

In the narrative statement:

The Board considers that J Ogilvie Thompsons combined role as chairman and chief executive is in Anglo American's best interests. This combined role will continue for a limited period until such time as conditions are appropriate, but no later than the annual general meeting to be held in 2002, whereafter it is intended that the functions of chairman and chief executive will be split.

Going concern statements

7.87   Combined Code provision D.1.3 states that directors should report that the business is a going concern, with supporting assumptions or qualifications as necessary. This was originally provision 4.6 of the Cadbury Code. Neither the Cadbury nor Hampel Committees produced guidance on how this should be carried out or on the form or content of the report; it was decided that this was better carried out by a Joint Working Group comprising members of the accountancy profession and representatives of preparers of accounts.

7.88   The Joint Working Group published its final guidance, entitled *Going Concern and Financial Reporting*, on 7 November 1994. The purpose of the guidance is to:

(a)   explain the significance of going concern in relation to the financial statements;

(b)   describe the procedures that an explicit statement on going concern may entail; and

(c)   recommend appropriate disclosure.

7.89   The Listing Rules require listed companies incorporated in the UK to include in their annual report and accounts a statement by the directors that the business is a going concern, with supporting assumptions or qualifications as necessary, as interpreted by the guidance *Going Concern and Financial Reporting*. [Listing Rules 12.43(v)] This requirement does not apply to various categories of company (see **7.11** to **7.19** above).

7.90   Although the November 1994 guidance is intended principally for directors of listed companies incorporated in the UK, the Joint Working Group notes that it may also be of assistance to directors of other companies and, in particular, large private companies and 'public interest' companies.

7.91   The November 1994 guidance specifies that directors should carry out an assessment of their company's financial position, to determine whether the company will continue in operational existence for the foreseeable future and hence is a going concern, and make disclosures in the financial statements based on that assessment.

7.92   The November 1994 guidance does not define 'foreseeable future' as a specific period. It states that the foreseeable future depends on the specific circumstances at a point in time, including the nature of the company's business, associated risks and external influences.

7.93   However, where the foreseeable future considered by the directors has been limited to a period of less than one year from the date of approval of the financial statements, the November 1994 guidance states that the directors should determine whether the financial statements require any additional disclosures to explain adequately the assumptions that underlie the use of the going concern basis.

7.94   In these circumstances, even though the directors are not required to state that they have considered a period of less than one year from the date of approval of the financial statements, it is likely that they will do so because, in the absence of such disclosure, the auditors are required to make such disclosure in their report (see **41.73** below). [SAS 130(45)]

7.95 The directors' statement on going concern should be made based on what is known at the date on which they approve the financial statements; in practice, most of their work will be performed before the date of approval and updated as appropriate.

7.96 The following areas are identified in the November 1994 guidance as ones which directors will need to consider to determine whether they are or could become significant:

- forecasts and budgets;
- borrowing requirements;
- liability management;
- contingent liabilities;
- products and markets;
- financial risk management; and
- financial adaptability.

The appendix to the November 1994 guidance includes detailed procedures that may need to be performed under each of the above headings. The list of procedures is not intended to be used as a checklist, since there may be other procedures which are relevant and not all the procedures listed will be appropriate for every company.

7.97 However, directors are best placed to know which factors are likely to be of greater significance in relation to their company. The relative importance of the factors will vary by industry and from company to company within a particular industry. The relative significance of the factors can also vary over time.

7.98 The November 1994 guidance identifies three conclusions which the directors can reach when considering the results of their procedures:

(a) they have a reasonable expectation that the company will continue in operational existence for the foreseeable future and have therefore used the going concern basis in preparing the financial statements;

(b) they have identified factors that cast doubt on the ability of the company to continue in operational existence for the foreseeable future, but that they consider that it is appropriate to use the going concern basis in preparing the financial statements;

(c) they consider that the company is unlikely to continue in operational existence for the foreseeable future and therefore the going concern basis is not an appropriate one on which to draw up the financial statements.

The November 1994 guidance includes example wording of the directors' statement for the first two situations, but suggests that legal advice be sought if directors find themselves in the third situation, i.e., they consider that the company is unlikely to continue in operational existence.

7.99 The statement should be included in the OFR (see **6.89** and **6.116** above); the November 1994 guidance does not seem to envisage the situation in which an OFR is not prepared as a separate statement. In addition, there needs to be a specific cross-reference between the going concern statement in the OFR and the accounting policy note.

7.100 If the annual report and accounts do not include an OFR as a separate section, it is suggested that the going concern disclosures by the directors be included either in a separate statement on corporate governance or, in the absence of such a statement, in the directors' report.

7.101 Where the directors are satisfied that the company will continue in operational existence, they should make a statement to that effect.

7.102 The example wording included in the November 1994 guidance does not indicate that the judgement is formed at a point in time. However, it is important that readers of a statement on going concern understand that this is the case and thus the example set out below differs from the example wording set out in the guidance, by making specific reference to this.

> ### Example 7.102
>
> After making enquiries, the directors have formed a judgement, at the time of approving the financial statements, that there is a reasonable expectation that the company has adequate resources to continue in operational existence for the foreseeable future. For this reason, the directors continue to adopt the going concern basis in preparing the financial statements.

7.103 Where the directors have identified factors which cast doubt on the appropriateness of the going concern assumption, the directors should explain the circumstances so as to identify the factors which give rise to the problem (including any external factors outside their control which may affect the outcome) and an explanation of how they intend to deal with the problem so as to resolve it.

7.104 Paragraph 44 of SAS 130 gives guidance for auditors when assessing whether the disclosures on going concern in financial statements are adequate for the purposes of giving a true and fair view. Disclosures are not normally regarded as adequate unless they include:

(a)   a statement that the financial statements have been prepared on the going concern basis;

(b)   a statement of the pertinent facts;

(c)   the nature of the concern;

(d)   a statement of the assumptions adopted by the directors, which should be clearly distinguishable from the pertinent facts;

(e)   (where appropriate and practical) a statement regarding the directors' plans for resolving the matters giving rise to the concern; and

(f)   details of any relevant actions by the directors.

7.105   The November 1994 guidance includes an example of disclosure which may be appropriate where there is doubt about the appropriateness of the going concern assumption. The example below is based on that example.

> ### Example 7.105
>
> The company is in breach of certain loan covenants at its balance sheet date and so the company's bankers could recall their loans at any time. The directors continue to be involved in negotiations with the company's bankers and as yet no demands for repayments have been received. The negotiations are at an early stage and, although the directors are optimistic about the outcome, it is as yet too early to make predictions with any certainty.
>
> In the light of the actions described elsewhere in the operating and financial review, the directors have formed a judgement, at the time of approving the financial statements, that it is appropriate to adopt the going concern basis in preparing the financial statements.

7.106   While doubts about the ability of a company to remain as a going concern do not necessarily mean that the company is or is likely to become insolvent, directors are rightly concerned that disclosure of such doubts may have an adverse effect on the public's perception of the company's position which, in turn, might exacerbate the company's future operations. They nevertheless have a responsibility to make a reasonable judgement based on all available information at the time the financial statements are approved by them and report accordingly.

7.107   Where the directors consider that the company is not a going concern, they should no longer prepare the financial statements using the going concern assumption and an alternative basis will have to be used. The November 1994 guidance suggests that legal advice be sought on the wording of any directors' statement. The fact that the company is not a going concern does not necessarily mean that the company is insolvent. However, the directors will need to consider whether the company may be or become insolvent. Lawyers should be consulted when the directors know or ought to have concluded that there is no reasonable prospect that the company would avoid going into insolvent liquidation (i.e., possibility of action for wrongful trading).

7.108 A problem which has been identified by the APB in Bulletin 1999/5 is that the statement by the directors should not be inconsistent with the disclosures regarding going concern either in the financial statements or the auditors' report thereon. The Bulletin therefore states that where going concern matters are discussed in the financial statements, one method of achieving consistency is for the directors' statement to include a cross-reference to the relevant note in the financial statements.

7.109 Even in straightforward situations, directors should take care not to extend their responsibilities unnecessarily by making gratuitous statements that go beyond those set out in the guidance. To limit any additional responsibility, directors are likely to wish to consult with their auditors and, in some circumstances, their legal advisers, regarding the form of disclosure that they should make.

Groups

7.110 In respect of groups, the November 1994 guidance states that the directors of the parent company should make their statement regarding going concern in respect of both the parent company and the group as a whole. A statement regarding the going concern status of the group does not mean that each of the companies within the group is a going concern. It is possible that the directors may have doubts about the going concern status of a member of the group (other than the parent) and still conclude that the group is a going concern for the foreseeable future.

Interim reporting

7.111 Although the primary purpose of the November 1994 guidance is to outline procedures and disclosures for year end reporting, it also includes a paragraph on interim reporting. At the half-year stage, the guidance suggests that directors review the work performed at the previous year end to determine whether any of the significant factors which they had identified at that time have changed to such an extent as to affect the appropriateness of the going concern presumption. However, no guidance is given on reporting at the interim stage.

7.112 Where there are doubts about the appropriateness of the going concern presumption at the interim stage, directors are likely to increase the extent of their procedures in the going concern area. They should also consider including wording on the appropriateness of the going concern basis in the explanatory statement required by Listing Rule 12.56 to be contained in the half-yearly report.

Statements of directors' responsibilities

7.113 The Combined Code requires the directors to explain their responsibility for preparing the accounts (Combined Code provision D.1.1). Unlike the Cadbury Code, the Combined Code does not specify where in the annual report and accounts this responsibility statement should be located. However, paragraph 4 of SAS 600 states that: 'It will aid communication with the reader if ... and, where, the directors set out their responsibilities themselves, if this description is immediately before the auditors' report'.

7.114 The Combined Code contains no prescribed contents for the directors' responsibilities statement. However, paragraph 21 of SAS 600 states that the statement should cover:

(a) the legal requirement for directors to prepare financial statements for each financial year which give a true and fair view of the state of affairs of the company (or group) as at the end of the financial year and of the profit or loss for the year then ended;

(b) the requirement for directors, in preparing financial statements, to select suitable accounting policies and then apply them on a consistent basis, making judgements and estimates that are prudent and reasonable;

(c) (large companies only – all listed companies will meet the definition of large) the requirement for directors in preparing financial statements to state whether applicable accounting standards have been followed, subject to any material departures disclosed and explained in the notes to the accounts. (This does not obviate the need for a formal statement in the notes disclosing whether the financial statements have been prepared in accordance with applicable accounting standards);

(d) (where no separate statement on going concern is made by the directors – this should therefore not apply to listed companies) the requirement for directors in preparing financial statements to prepare the financial statements on the going concern basis unless it is not appropriate to presume that the company/group will continue in business;

(e) the responsibility of the directors for keeping proper accounting records, for safeguarding the assets of the company (or
group) and for taking reasonable steps for the prevention and
detection of fraud and other irregularities.

7.115 Points (a) to (e) in **7.114** above are from SAS 600. In addition, Note
12 to the Cadbury Code (which was not mandatory) contained guidance on the points to be included in the directors' responsibility
statement – the points are the same as the ones above, but excluding
point (d). Note 12 to the Cadbury Code, however, called for confirmation by the directors that they had complied with points (b) and
(c) above (rather than simply stating the responsibility).

7.116 In the absence of guidance in the Combined Code on the required
contents, it is suggested that a directors' responsibility statement that
complies with SAS 600, whether or not it also complies with Note 12
to the Cadbury Code, would satisfy the recommendation in Code
provision D.1.1 of the Combined Code.

7.117 The following example is based on the wording given in appendix 3
to SAS 600.

Example 7.117

Statements of directors' responsibilities

Company law requires the directors to prepare financial statements
for each financial year which give a true and fair view of the state of
affairs of the company as at the end of the financial year and of the
profit or loss of the company for that period. In preparing those
financial statements, the directors are required to:

(a) select suitable accounting policies and then apply them consistently;

(b) make judgements and estimates that are reasonable and prudent;

(c) (large companies only*) state whether applicable accounting
standards have been followed, *subject to any material departures
disclosed and explained in the financial statements;***

(d) prepare the financial statements on the going concern basis,
unless it is inappropriate to presume that the company will
continue in business.****

The directors are responsible for keeping proper accounting records
which disclose with reasonable accuracy at any time the financial
position of the company and to enable them to ensure that the financial statements comply with the Companies Act 1985. They are also
responsible for the company's system of internal [financial] con-
trol*** and for safeguarding the assets of the company and hence for

---

taking reasonable steps for the prevention and detection of fraud and other irregularities.

   *   Large companies are those that do not fall within the Act's definitions of small or medium sized – see chapter 34 – all listed companies will meet the definition of large.

   **   See **7.118** below.

   ***   This requirement comes from internal control guidance (both Rutteman and Turnbull), and is necessary when acknowledgement for responsibility is not made in the internal control or narrative statements. When using Rutteman (see **7.52** to **7.61** above) confirmation should be for internal financial control, when using Turnbull (see **7.66** to **7.81** above), confirmation should be for internal control. If this statement is given within the internal control statement, it does not need to be repeated here.

   ****   Per **7.87** to **7.112** above, listed companies need to give a separate statement on going concern. Therefore, this point does not need to be included in the directors' responsibilities statement for listed companies.

7.118   It is suggested that the words in *italics* in the example in **7.117** above be included only if there is a material departure from applicable accounting standards. Otherwise, they may give the misleading impression that there has been a material departure in circumstances in which there is no such departure.

7.119   If the report and accounts do not include a description of the directors' responsibilities, then the auditors' report will need to include such a description. If the statement of compliance with the Code (see **7.26** to **7.31** above) does not refer to this departure from the Code, the auditors will also need to draw attention to the departure in their report on the financial statements or alternatively in a separate report on the statement of compliance if such a report is given. The requirements of SAS 600 in respect of auditors' reports are dealt with in more detail in chapter 39.

7.120   Wording is now included in the auditors' report regarding the nationality of the accounting standards and of the applicable law following an agreement between the International Forum on Accounting Developments and legal global regulators who were concerned that it is not always apparent to international investors which standards are being followed (see chapter 39).

APB Bulletin 1999/5

7.121 The APB issued Bulletin 1999/5 in November 1999 which is effective for periods ending on or after 23 December 1999. The Bulletin provides guidance for external auditors when reviewing the directors' report to shareholders concerning the directors' review of the effectiveness of internal control. It also consolidates, into one Bulletin, all of the APB's extant guidance on corporate governance as it supersedes Bulletins 1995/1, 1996/3, 1997/2 and 1998/10.

7.122 The Bulletin makes clear what the external auditors' responsibilities are over various aspects of corporate governance, namely:

(a) Narrative statement;

(b) Compliance statement, focusing on the seven provisions specified for external auditor review;

(c) Internal control;

(d) Directors' remuneration; and

(e) Going concern statement.

7.123 The Bulletin reiterates the guidance previously given to explain the auditors' different responsibilities for auditing the accounts, reviewing the corporate governance disclosures, in so far as they relate to the seven Code provisions specified for our review by the Lisiting Rules, and for reading other parts of the annual report. However, it also goes further in one key respect – it now suggests that where the auditor finds corporate governance disclosures, other than those which they are formally required to review, to be misleading or inconsistent they should draw attention to the fact in an additional paragraph in their audit report (see chapter 40).

8   Directors' remuneration

8 Directors' remuneration

Summary of changes since the previous issue of this publication

Para.	Topic	Summary
8.117	*Directors' remuneration*	The principal focus of this DTI consultative document is the remuneration of executive directors of quoted companies. Some of the issues raised are, however, relevant also to the remuneration of non-executive directors.

Introduction

8.1 The requirements to give disclosures on directors' remuneration in the annual Report and Accounts are contained in the Act and the Listing Rules. The requirements contained in the Listing Rules, which are based on the recommendations of the Greenbury Committee and the Combined Code (see chapter 7), go further than the requirements of the Act. The requirements of the Act are dealt with in **8.2** to **8.62** below. The requirements contained in the Listing Rules are covered in **8.63** to **8.109** below. In addition **8.110** to **8.114** below describe some further disclosures which are recommended by the Combined Code. Where the disclosures described in **8.111** and **8.112** below are not given it will be necessary to list them as departures from compliance with the Code provisions of the Combined Code (see **7.27** above). For listed companies, the disclosures will be subject to scrutiny by various regulatory bodies, including the Financial Reporting Review Panel, and by the various governance bodies.

Requirements of the Act

Disclosure requirements

8.2 The Act requires disclosure of various amounts which fall under four general headings: remuneration; pensions and other retirement benefits; compensation payments; and payments to third parties. The disclosures, which are required to be in the notes to the accounts, are as follows:

(a) *Remuneration*: disclosure is required of the aggregate for each of the following:

  (i) emoluments (including salary, fees and bonuses), sums paid by way of expenses allowance so far as chargeable to UK income tax and the estimated money value of non-cash benefits but excluding:

   – options granted to a director;
   – gains made on the exercise of options;
   – contributions paid or treated as paid to a pension scheme by a person other than the director in respect of whom the contributions are made;
   – any benefits to which a director is entitled under a pension scheme;
   – any money or other assets paid to or received or receivable by the director under a long-term incentive scheme);

   paid to or receivable by directors in respect of qualifying services; [Sch 6: 1]

  (ii) (for companies with securities admitted to the Official List and companies whose securities are traded on AIM) gains made by directors on the exercise of share options (being the difference between the market price of the shares on the date of exercise less the price paid for the shares); [Sch 6: 1]

  (iii) (for companies with securities neither admitted to the Official List nor traded on AIM) the number of directors who exercised share options; [Sch 6: 1]

  (iv) (for companies with securities admitted to the Official List and companies whose securities are traded on AIM) money paid to or receivable by directors, together with the net value of other assets (other than share options) received or receivable by directors under long-term incentive schemes in respect of qualifying services; [Sch 6: 1]

  (v) (for companies with securities neither admitted to the Official List nor traded on AIM) money paid to or receivable by directors, together with the net value of other assets (other than shares and share options) received or receivable by directors under long-term incentive schemes in respect of qualifying services; [Sch 6: 1]

  (vi) (for companies with securities neither admitted to the Official List nor traded on AIM) the number of directors in respect of whose qualifying services shares were received or receivable under long-term incentive schemes; [Sch 6: 1]

(vii) the value of contributions paid, or treated as paid, to a pension scheme by a person other than the director to whom retirement benefits are accruing in respect of directors' qualifying services to the extent that the contributions might lead to money purchase benefits being payable [Sch 6: 1] (see **8.9** and **8.38** to **8.44** below);

(viii) the number of directors, if any, to whom retirement benefits are accruing in respect of qualifying services in respect of each of:

- money purchase schemes; and
- defined benefit schemes; [Sch 6: 1]

(b) *Pensions and other retirement benefits*: the aggregate of directors' and past directors' pensions and other retirement benefits payable under pension schemes in excess of the pensions and other benefits to which they were entitled on the later of the date the pensions and other benefits first became payable and 31 March 1997. The nature of any non-cash benefit must also be disclosed [Sch 6: 7] (see **8.45** to **8.51** below). In addition, particulars have to be given of any commitments to pay pensions to past directors [Sch 4: 50(4)] (see **8.51** below);

(c) *Compensation for loss of office*: aggregate compensation to directors or past directors in respect of loss of office. The nature of any non-cash benefit must also be disclosed [Sch 6: 8] (see **8.52** to **8.56** below);

(d) *Consideration paid to third parties*: aggregate consideration paid to or receivable by third parties for making available the services of any person as a director of the company or, while director of the company, as director of any of its subsidiaries or otherwise in connection with the management of the affairs of the company or any of its subsidiaries. The nature of any non-cash consideration must also be disclosed [Sch 6: 9] (see **8.57** to **8.58** below).

In addition, in certain instances specified details have to be disclosed in respect of the highest paid director (see **8.59** to **8.62** below).

8.3 The amounts to be disclosed under each heading must include all relevant sums paid by or receivable from:
[Sch 6: 10(2)]

- the company,

- the company's subsidiary undertakings, and

- any other person.

8.4 The amounts to be shown for any financial year are the sums receivable by a director in respect of that year, even if not actually paid during it or, in the case of sums not receivable in respect of a period, the sums paid during that year. [Sch 6: 11(1)]

8.5

> For example, directors' fees paid in respect of the financial year should be included at their proposed amount, even if they do not become due until approved by the shareholders in general meeting.

8.6

> Where the financial statements cover a financial year which is shorter or longer than 12 months, the remuneration will be that for the financial year and thus will not be for a 12-month period. To avoid misinterpretation of comparative information, the periods covered by the information should be described clearly. The amounts should not be annualised.

8.7 Amounts paid to or receivable by a director include amounts paid to or receivable by a person connected with him or a body corporate controlled by him (but not so as to require an amount to be counted twice). [Sch 6: 10(4)]

8.8 It should be noted that the information to be given concerns directors of the reporting company. Thus, in the notes to the accounts of a group, it is only payments to the directors of the parent company that should be disclosed. Payments made to a person who is a director of a subsidiary company, but not of the parent, should be excluded from the disclosures even if he receives some or all of his remuneration from the parent company.

8.9

> The definition of 'pension scheme' within the Act is generally interpreted as extending to unfunded arrangements.

8.10 Further details of the requirements are given in the following sections.

Qualifying services

8.11 Qualifying services means a person's services as a director of the company and, while a director of the company, his services:
[Sch 6: 1(5)]

(a) as a director of any of its subsidiary undertakings; or

(b) otherwise in connection with the management of the affairs of the company or any of its subsidiary undertakings.

8.12

> Whether the director is receiving remuneration for services as a director of a company or otherwise in connection with the management of its affairs is a question of fact. The presumption must be that any payments he receives from the company (which are not reimbursements of expenses) must come within this category unless it can be demonstrated clearly that they do

not. One exception could be payments made to a director in a professional capacity (e.g., as a solicitor) as payment for professional services performed for the company. Here, it is usually a question of degree. For example, if a solicitor is a director and occasionally performs (or his firm performs) intermittent conveyancing work for which the normal scale fees are paid, it could be accepted that these payments were not caught by Sch 6 para 1, particularly if the director was non-executive. However, if his main work for the company was conveyancing (e.g., as director of a property company), it would be difficult to accept this view.

8.13 The position is less obvious if a non-executive director is a management consultant. It can be argued that intermittent advice given by the director to the chief executive for which the director's firm charges professional fees on its normal basis does not involve services in connection with the management of the company and therefore such fees should not be included as directors' emoluments. Obviously, the facts must be considered closely.

8.14 Sometimes, the details of a service agreement between the company and the director confirm that certain payments are part of his remuneration and the minutes also may give confirmation. Absence of such confirmation is, of course, not conclusive nor would a negative agreement (e.g., confirming that the payments made to a director were not in respect of his services as a director) provide irrefutable evidence.

8.15 Where a person is appointed as a director of the company part way through an accounting period, it is only his remuneration since he became a director of the company that is disclosed.

> ### Example 8.15
>
> A Limited's accounting period ends on 31 December each year. On 1 September 1999, Mr X was appointed as a director of A Limited. Mr X received emoluments of £35,000 from 1 January to 31 August 1999 and £25,000 for the remainder of 1999. In A Limited's financial statements for 1999, the amount in respect of Mr X included in the aggregate emoluments will be the £25,000 payable to him since his appointment as a director.

8.16 Where a parent company is not preparing group accounts, say, because it heads up a medium-sized group or is an intermediate holding company, the remuneration disclosed will still be the remuneration its directors receive for their services to its subsidiaries as well as to the company.

Example 8.16

A Limited has three subsidiaries, B Limited, C Limited and D Limited. Mr X is a director of all four companies and receives emoluments of £25,000 for his services to each of the four companies. In A Limited's financial statements, the amount in respect of Mr X included in the aggregate emoluments will be £100,000, irrespective of whether group or individual company financial statements are prepared.

8.17 Where a company is a member of a group other than as the parent, care is necessary to identify the appropriate directors' remuneration disclosures. The following should be noted:

(a) only remuneration of directors of the company should be included;

(b) all of the remuneration disclosures other than the gains made on the exercise of options (or, for unlisted companies, i.e., companies with securities neither admitted to the Official List nor traded on AIM, the number of directors who exercised options) are for remuneration in respect of qualifying services, i.e., are in respect of services to the company and its subsidiaries (if any);

(c) remuneration in respect of services to its parent company or any fellow subsidiaries should be excluded, whether or not the director concerned is also a director of these companies.

Exanple 8.17.1

Mr X is a director of ABC Ltd and receives emoluments of £8,000 in respect of his services to ABC Ltd plus £10,000 in respect of his services to its subsidiary A Ltd. The emoluments to be included in the financial statements of ABC Ltd are £18,000. The emoluments to be included in the financial statements of A Ltd are £10,000 if Mr X is a director of A Ltd and nil if he is not. Pension benefits are accruing, under the group defined benefit pension scheme, in respect of his services to both ABC Ltd and A Ltd. In the financial statements of ABC Ltd, Mr X will be included in the number of directors disclosed as accruing benefits under the defined benefit scheme. If Mr X is also a director of A Ltd, he will also be included in the number of directors disclosed as accruing benefits under the defined benefit scheme in its financial statements.

Example 8.17.2

Mr Y is employed as a manager of ABC Ltd at a salary of £9,000 per year. He also acts as a director of its subsidiary B Ltd at a fee of £5,000. No disclosure is required in the financial statements of ABC Ltd, since

---

Mr Y is not a director of that company. The emoluments to be disclosed in the financial statements of B Ltd are £5,000. The group operates a pension scheme under which Mr Y is accruing benefits in respect of his services to ABC Ltd and is not accruing benefits in respect of his role as a director of B Ltd. Since Mr Y is not a director of ABC Ltd, there is nothing to disclose in respect of his pension entitlements in its financial statements. Similarly, there is nothing to disclose in respect of his pension entitlements in the financial statements of B Ltd, since pension benefits do not accrue to him in respect of his role as director of B Ltd.

Example 8.17.3

Mr Z is a director of ABC plc, a listed company. He also acts as a director of its subsidiary C Ltd. During the year ended 31 December 1999, Mr Z exercised options over 3,000 shares at £2.50 per share. At the date of exercise, the market price of the shares was £3.50 per share. In the financial statements of ABC plc, £3,000 (being 3,000 x (£3.50 − £2.50)) is included in respect of this transaction within the aggregate of gains made on the exercise of options. In addition, in the financial statements of C Ltd, Mr Z will be included in the disclosure of the number of directors who exercised options (see **8.33** below).

8.18   A situation which sometimes arises and which can cause difficulty is where directors of subsidiary companies are paid a single salary in respect of their services to the whole group and no allocation is made between the separate companies.

8.19   Schedule 6 para 12 states that the directors may apportion any payments in such manner as they think appropriate. However, directors do not always feel able to make an appropriate apportionment. In such cases, it is necessary to give adequate disclosure.

Example 8.19

ABC Ltd has three subsidiaries: A Ltd, B Ltd and C Ltd.

X, Y and Z are directors of each of the subsidiary undertakings and executives of ABC Ltd, the holding company. ABC Ltd pays X, Y and Z £20,000 per annum each, but no allocation between their services, as executives of ABC Ltd and directors of each of the subsidiary undertakings, is made nor is ABC Ltd prepared to attempt such allocation. The directors accrue benefits under the group pension scheme, which pays a pension based on final salary and the total £20,000 is pensionable.

> The best disclosure in the financial statements of each of the subsidiary undertakings would be a recital of the facts, for example:
>
> The directors are executives of the holding company, ABC Ltd, and are also directors of A Ltd, B Ltd and C Ltd. The directors received total emoluments of £60,000 from ABC Ltd during the year, but it is not practicable to allocate this between their services as executives of ABC Ltd and their services as directors of A Ltd, B Ltd and C Ltd. In addition, the three directors are each accruing benefits under the ABC Ltd group pension scheme, which is a defined benefit scheme, in respect of their services to the four group companies.

Readily ascertained test

8.20   The Act specifically states that (other than in respect of the aggregate of gains made on the exercise of options, in respect of pensions to directors and former directors and in respect of sums paid to third parties) information shall be treated as shown if it is capable of being readily ascertained from other information which is shown. Thus, for example, if a listed company complying with the Listing Rules discloses sufficient information about each individual director to enable the aggregate emoluments paid to or receivable by the directors to be derived, it need not also disclose the aggregate figure. [Sch 6: 1(6)]

Golden hellos

8.21   Emoluments paid or receivable or share options granted in respect of a person's accepting office as a director are to be treated as emoluments paid or receivable or share options granted in respect of his services as a director. [Sch 6: 1(6)(b)]

8.22

> The inclusion in the above of share options granted is puzzling. Share options *granted* during a year are not disclosed as directors' remuneration under the disclosure requirements. The Act only requires options to be disclosed as part of directors' remuneration when they are exercised. Accordingly, share options *granted* as part of a 'golden hello' will not be disclosed under the Act's directors' remuneration requirements (although they will be disclosed under the Listing Rules' directors' remuneration disclosure requirements).

Emoluments

8.23   Emoluments include any sums paid by way of expenses allowance which are chargeable to UK income tax. This might arise if a director was granted a round sum allowance for expenses which he could not justify to the Inland Revenue. If any payments of this nature are not disclosed in the appropriate year (on the grounds that they are not expected to be charged to tax), but they are charged to tax subsequently, then they should be shown separately in the first accounts in which it is practicable to do so. [Sch 6: 11(2)]

8.24 Emoluments include the estimated value of benefits received otherwise than in cash (other than share options and benefits under a pension scheme and under long-term incentive schemes). [Sch 6: 1(3)] A common example is the private use by a director of a company car. Because benefits in kind enjoyed by a director are assessable to income tax, this requirement is often interpreted as requiring disclosure of any of those amounts which are assessed to income tax. While, in many cases, the amount will be similar, it is emphasised that the disclosure requirement is not directly related to assessment to income tax and that the estimated value of all benefits in kind, even if they are not so assessed, should be included.

8.25 When the London Stock Exchange first issued its Listing Rule requiring disclosure of pension entitlements, it also issued a summary of the comments received on its earlier consultation. In this, the London Stock Exchange explained that a number of commentators asked whether death in service benefits should be included in pension entitlements. The London Stock Exchange's view was that these benefits should be included in 'benefits in kind' in the detailed analysis of individual director's remuneration (see **8.72** below). However, as explained above, benefits under pension schemes should be excluded from the 'emoluments' disclosure under the Act. Accordingly, where a company is combining the disclosures under both the Act and the Listing Rules, it should disclose separately the value of the death in service benefit, so that the Act's information can be derived.

8.26 Awards under annual bonus schemes are included in emoluments whether payable to directors in cash, shares or some other assets. The inclusion of shares is irrespective of whether the company's securities have been admitted to the Official List, traded on AIM or neither. This contrasts with awards in the form of shares under long-term incentive schemes where there is one treatment for companies whose securities have been admitted to the Official List or traded on AIM and another treatment for all other companies.

Options

8.27 Set out below are the Act's rules on disclosure of options. The disclosures required by the Listing Rules are set out in **8.78** to **8.82** below.

8.28 Usually, the director has to remain with the company for a set period of time (e.g., three years) before he is able to exercise the options. Executive options are often exercisable at a price equal to the market price of the shares on the date the option was granted. The Act specifically states that the grant of an option is excluded from the definition of emoluments; instead, listed companies (i.e., companies with securities admitted to the Official List and companies whose securities are traded on AIM) are required to disclose the gains made on the exercise of options and other companies have the less demanding requirement to disclose the number of directors who exercised options; neither the number of shares nor the exercise price has to be disclosed.

8.29 The gain on the exercise of an option is the difference between the market price on the date of exercise and the price actually paid for the shares.

8.30 In many cases, directors do not pay anything to acquire the option; the options being granted to them for nil consideration as part of their remuneration package. Where, however, a director has paid to acquire the option (maybe because it was not granted as part of a remuneration package, but instead he purchased it on the open market), the question arises as to whether the Act's phrase 'price actually paid for the shares' includes the cost of the option itself. It might at first be thought that the phrase refers only to the exercise price of the option. However, in substance, the total 'price' paid by the director for the shares will include the cost of acquiring the option. Accordingly, it is suggested that the cost of acquiring the option is included in the calculation of the gain on exercise and the fact that it has been included is clearly explained.

8.31 The disclosure requirements for both listed and unlisted companies are not linked in any way to 'qualifying services'. Therefore, disclosure is not limited to options granted for qualifying services and exercised now, i.e., granted and exercised since the person had been appointed as a director of the company.

Example 8.31

The accounting period of ABC plc, a listed company, ends on 31 December each year. Mr X was appointed as a director of ABC plc on 1 January 1999. On 1 October 1999, he exercised 2,000 options granted to him (at nil cost) in 1995 at an exercise price of £4 per share. The market price on the date of exercise was £5 per share. In ABC plc's financial statements for 1999, the amount in respect of Mr X included in the aggregate gains on the exercise of options will be £2,000, irrespective of whether Mr X retains or sells the shares.

8.32   The requirement, for listed companies (i.e., companies with securities admitted to the Official List and companies whose securities are traded on AIM) is to disclose the aggregate of the amount of gains made by *directors* on the exercise of share options and, for unlisted companies, is to disclose the number of *directors* who exercised share options. Although there is no reference to 'qualifying services', the reference to 'directors' does mean that it is only options exercised *after* becoming a director that are disclosed.

Example 8.32

The accounting period of ABC plc, a listed company, ends on 31 December each year. Mr X was appointed as a director of ABC plc on 1 July 1999. On 1 March 1999, he exercised 2,000 options granted to him in 1995 at an exercise price of £4 per share. The market price on the date of exercise was £5 per share. He exercised no other options at any time during the year. In ABC plc's financial statements for 1999, no amount will be included in the aggregate gains on the exercise of options in respect of Mr X.

8.33   The disclosure on options applies to options over shares and share warrants in the company, or any undertaking which is a group undertaking in relation to the company.

Bonuses

8.34   Bonuses other than those payable under long-term incentive schemes will be classified as emoluments.

8.35   Long-term incentive schemes, particularly those under which directors are rewarded in shares, have become increasingly popular since the Greenbury Report was issued. Long-term incentive schemes are defined by the Act [Sch 6: 1(4)] as 'any agreement or arrangement under which money or other assets may become receivable by a director and which includes one or more qualifying conditions with respect to service or performance which cannot be fulfilled within a single financial year; and for this purpose the following shall be disregarded, namely:

(a)   bonuses the amount of which falls to be determined by reference to service or performance within a single financial year;

(b)   compensation for loss of office, payments for breach of contract and other termination payments; and

(c)   retirement benefits'.

8.36   The requirements of the Act are to disclose the amount of emoluments and of awards under long-term incentive schemes paid to or receivable by directors. In addition, the Act provides that the amounts to be shown for any financial year are the sums receivable by a director in respect of that year, even if not actually paid during it or, in the case of sums not receivable in respect of a period, the sums paid during that year. [Sch 6: 11(1)] Problems arise in determining which is the appropriate year in which to disclose bonuses where the performance criteria relating to a bonus end in one financial year but the bonus is only given to the directors if they are still in employment at a specified date in a later financial year.

Example 8.36

The accounting period of ABC plc, a listed company, ends on 31 December each year. In respect of its year ended 31 December 1999, it had both an annual bonus scheme and a long-term incentive scheme. Relevant details are as follows.

Annual bonus scheme – the earnings per share for 1998 exceeded a predetermined target, so each director still in employment on 1 July 1999 received a bonus of £10,000 on that date. The earnings per share for 1999 exceeded a predetermined target, so each director still in employment on 1 July 2000 will receive a bonus of £12,000 on that date.

Long-term incentive scheme – the company's total shareholder return (TSR) for the three years ended 31 December 1998 was in the top quartile for a predetermined group of comparator companies. Accordingly, the directors still in employment on 1 July 1999 received shares with an aggregate market value on that date of £100,000. The company's TSR for the three years ended 31 December 1999 was also in the top quartile for a predetermined group of comparator companies. Accordingly, each director still in employment on 1 July 2000 will receive the shares provisionally awarded to them on 1 January 1997, the start of the three-year period. This will total 25,000 shares for the directors in aggregate. The market price of the shares at

31 December 1999 was £5.17 and immediately before signing the 1999 financial statements was £5.20.

In disclosing directors' remuneration in its 1999 financial statements, the company should:

Either:

include the £12,000 per director annual bonus in aggregate emoluments and disclose under long-term incentive schemes the 25,000 shares receivable by directors in respect of the scheme with performance criteria ending on 31 December 1999;

Or:

include the £10,000 per director annual bonus in aggregate emoluments and disclose under long-term incentive schemes the shares worth £100,000 received by directors in respect of the scheme with performance criteria ending on 31 December 1998.

Before the Act's requirements were changed, it was generally accepted that an annual bonus would be disclosed as directors' remuneration in the financial statements of the year to which the performance criteria related. In the above example, the bonus of £12,000 per director would have been disclosed in the 1999 financial statements, since its payment was dependent upon the earnings per share for that year. The Act's requirements have not changed in this respect. Consequently, although companies can choose which of the above two options to follow in disclosing directors' remuneration, the first suggestion is the preferable one.

If ABC plc chose to disclose using the first option, it would have to estimate the value of the shares receivable by the directors under the long-term incentive scheme ending 31 December 1999, if its financial statements are approved before 1 July 2000. The Act requires shares received or receivable under long-term incentive schemes to be valued at the market price of the shares on the day they are received or receivable by the director, less any money paid or other value given by the director (which is nil in this case). Since the financial statements are being prepared before the day the shares are to be given to the directors, ABC plc has to estimate the value. It would be appropriate for the company to value the shares using the market price on the day as close to approving the financial statements as is possible and to state in the financial statements that this has been done. Thus, ABC plc would value the shares at £5.20 per share and state this in its financial statements. If the market price on 1 July 2000 were different, the difference would be disclosed in the subsequent year's financial statements.

8.37   The disclosures required by the Listing Rules on long-term incentive schemes are set out in **8.83** to **8.88** below.

Pension schemes

8.38   The following sets out the Act's rules on disclosure of pension scheme information. The disclosures required by the Listing Rules are set out in **8.96** to **8.103** below. The Listing Rules use the definitions set out in the Act.

8.39   As stated in **8.2** above, the Act requires disclosure of:

(a)   the value of contributions paid, or treated as paid, to a pension scheme by a person other than the director to whom retirement benefits are accruing in respect of directors' qualifying services to the extent that the contributions might lead to money purchase benefits being payable; and

(b)   the number of directors, if any, to whom retirement benefits are accruing in respect of qualifying services in respect of each of:

(i)   money purchase schemes; and
(ii)   defined benefit schemes;

(c)   in respect of the highest-paid director:

(i)   the amount of contributions to pension schemes attributable to qualifying services in respect of which money purchase benefits may be payable; and
(ii)   (where the pension accruing in respect of qualifying services is either defined benefit or is under a hybrid scheme that might make defined benefit payments) the amount at the end of the year of the accrued pension, and the amount, if any, of the accrued lump sum.

8.40   The definition of pension scheme within the Act is generally interpreted as extending to unfunded arrangements.

8.41   The Act defines a money purchase scheme, in relation to a director, as a pension scheme under which all of the benefits that may become payable to or in respect of the director are money purchase benefits.

> 'Money purchase benefits, in relation to a director, means retirement benefits payable under a pension scheme the rate or amount of which is calculated by reference to payments made, or treated as made, by the director or by any other person in respect of the director and which are not average salary benefits.'

A defined benefit scheme, in relation to a director, is a pension scheme other than a money purchase scheme.

8.42
> Hybrid schemes which pay either money purchase benefits or defined benefits, whichever is the higher, will therefore meet the definition of a 'defined benefit scheme'.

8.43   For the purposes of the disclosures on remuneration, including the disclosure of the highest paid director's remuneration, the Act permits companies operating such a hybrid scheme in respect of a director to classify the scheme by reference to the type of benefits which appear more likely in respect of the director at the end of the company's financial year.

Example 8.43

ABC plc has four directors, all of whom are members of the company's pension scheme. The scheme is funded as if it were a defined benefit scheme paying out a maximum pension of two-thirds of basic salary after 20 years' service. However, the actual pension payable will be the higher of the defined benefits calculated in this way and the pension that would have accrued had the company instead paid contributions, equal to six per cent of basic salary, into a money purchase scheme that invested these contributions in FTSE 100 tracker funds.

In preparing the company's financial statements for its year ended 31 December 1999, the company considers the scheme to determine which benefits appear to be the higher. If it concludes that the money purchase benefits would be the higher, it will disclose:

(a)   the amount of contributions for the directors in aggregate upon which the money purchase benefits are calculated, i.e., six per cent of basic salary;

(b)   all four directors as being members of a money purchase scheme;

(c)   the amount of contributions in respect of the highest paid director upon which the money purchase benefits are calculated, i.e., six per cent of basic salary (see **8.61** below).

If, instead, it had concluded that the defined benefits would be the higher, it would disclose:

(a)   all four directors as being members of a defined benefit scheme;

(b)   the amount of the accrued benefit for the highest paid director (see **8.61** below).

8.44   In the above example, the company could choose not to estimate which of the benefits it thinks will be the higher. If so, it would disclose:

(a)   the amount of contributions for the directors in aggregate upon which the money purchase benefits are calculated, i.e., six per cent of basic salary (even if it is defined benefits that might be payable);

(b)   all four directors as being members of a defined benefit scheme;

(c) the amount of contributions in respect of the highest paid director upon which the money purchase benefits are calculated, i.e., six per cent of basic salary (see **8.61** below); and

(d) the amount of the accrued benefit for the highest paid director (see **8.61** below).

Pensions and other retirement benefits receivable by directors and past directors under pension schemes

8.45   The DTI has decided that the disclosures about pensions to be made while a person is a director will be sufficient to put the user of the financial statements on notice about the pension arrangements and it has, sensibly, made this comprehensive by requiring the information for all schemes, not just funded schemes. The disclosure of retirement benefits to directors and former directors is a sort of 'anti-avoidance' disclosure, calling for the disclosure of any discretionary increases to the retirement benefits being paid to directors and former directors.

8.46   The amount to be disclosed is the amount of retirement benefits paid to or receivable by directors and past directors under pension schemes in excess of the amount they were entitled to on the later of the date the benefit first became payable and 31 March 1997. [Sch 6: 7(1)] The definition of 'retirement benefits' is:

> 'any pension, lump sum, gratuity or other like benefit given or to be given on retirement or on death, or by virtue of a pension sharing order or provision, or in anticipation of retirement, or in connection with past service, after retirement or death, or to be given on or in anticipation of or in connection with any change in the nature of the service of the employee in question, except that it does not include any benefit which is to be afforded solely by reason of the disablement by accident of a person occurring during his service or of his death by accident so occurring and for no other reason.'

8.47   Thus the disclosure is of any pension, lump sum, gratuity or other benefit, whether payable in cash or otherwise. The nature of any benefits in kind included in pensions and other retirement benefits must be disclosed in the notes to the accounts. [Sch 6: 7(3)]

8.48   Once a director or former director who is receiving retirement benefits is awarded an increase in those benefits, disclosure will be required in each subsequent set of accounts until the increased payments cease.

8.49   The definition of 'pension scheme' is 'a scheme for the provision of benefits consisting of or including relevant benefits, but not including any national scheme providing such benefits'. The definition of pension scheme encompasses unfunded, as well as funded, schemes. Accordingly, the disclosure applies irrespective of whether the scheme is funded or unfunded.

8.50   An increase in the retirement benefits payable need not be disclosed where the funding of the scheme was such that the amounts were, or could have been, paid without recourse to additional contributions *and* amounts were paid to or receivable by *all* pensioner members of the scheme on the same basis. [Sch 6: 7(2)]

8.51   In addition to the above disclosures required by Sch 6 to the Act, Sch 4, para 50, in requiring disclosures of guarantees and other financial commitments, specifically requires disclosure of particulars of any commitments, provided and unprovided, to pay pensions to past directors [Sch 4: 50(4)] – see **21.28** below.

Compensation to directors or past directors in respect of loss of office

8.52   Disclosure is required of the aggregate amount of any compensation to directors or past directors in respect of loss of office.

8.53   The amount disclosed must include any sums (including the money value of any benefits in kind) received or receivable by a director or past director by way of compensation for the loss of office as director of the company or for the loss, while director of the company or on or in connection with his ceasing to be a director of the company, of any other office in connection with the management of the company's affairs or of any office as director or otherwise in connection with the management of the affairs of any subsidiary undertaking of the company. The nature of any benefits in kind included in such compensation should be disclosed in the notes to the accounts. [Sch 6: 8(2) and (3)]

8.54   Compensation for which the director concerned is liable to account to the company, its subsidiary undertakings, or past or present members under the Act [ss314 and 315] is to be excluded (i.e., compensation paid to a director for loss of office in connection with an offer for the company's shares, unless it is disclosed to and approved by the shareholders before the transfer of the shares). [Sch 6: 10(2)] However, if the director's liability is subsequently released or is not enforced within two years, then the amount involved must be disclosed separately in the first accounts in which it is practicable to disclose it. [Sch 6: 11(2)]

8.55   The Act clarifies that where retirement from the office of director is because of a breach of contract, any damages or settlements in respect of the breach shall be disclosed as compensation for loss of office. [Sch 6: 8(4)]

8.56 When a director's pension entitlements are increased as part of his ceasing to be a director, the question arises as to whether this should be disclosed as part of compensation for loss of office or pensions to directors and former directors. Where the increase is made as part of his ceasing to be a director, the capital cost of the increase should be disclosed as part of compensation for loss of office, irrespective of whether the employer directly pays additional contributions (to cover the increase) into the pension scheme or whether the increase is funded by an existing surplus in the scheme. Any increase in pension entitlements after a person has ceased to be a director would be disclosed under pensions to directors and former directors (see **8.45** to **8.51** above).

Consideration paid to third parties

8.57 Disclosure is required of the aggregate consideration (including the money value of any non-cash consideration) paid to or receivable by third parties for making available the services of any person as a director of the company or, while a director of the company, as a director of any of its subsidiary undertakings or otherwise in connection with the management of the affairs of the company or any of its subsidiary undertakings. The nature of any non-cash consideration should be disclosed. [Sch 6: 9(1) and (3)]

8.58 Third parties are persons other than:

(a) the director;

(b) persons connected with the director;

(c) a body corporate controlled by the director;

(d) the company; and

(e) any of the company's subsidiary undertakings. [Sch 6: 9(3)]

Highest paid director

8.59 Certain details about the highest paid director have to be disclosed for any company where the total of the following three elements of aggregate directors' remuneration is £200,000 or more in any accounting period (regardless of its length):

(a) total emoluments paid to or receivable by directors;

(b) gains made by directors on the exercise of options*; and

(c) money and other assets paid to or receivable by directors under long-term incentive schemes*.

*   For companies with securities neither admitted to the Official List nor traded on AIM omit (b) and exclude shares from (c).

8.60   The highest paid director is the one to whom is attributable the greatest part of the total of the three items listed in **8.59** above. This is regardless of whether any director performed his duties as director wholly or mainly outside the UK.

8.61   The details that have to be disclosed about the highest paid director are:

(a)   the total of the three items in **8.59** above that is attributable to the highest paid director;

(b)   the amount of contributions to pension schemes attributable to the highest paid director's qualifying services in respect of which money purchase benefits may be payable;

(c)   (for companies with securities neither admitted to the Official List nor traded on AIM) whether the highest paid director exercised any share options and whether any shares were received or receivable by that director in respect of qualifying services under a long-term incentive scheme. Where the highest paid director has not been involved in any of these transactions, that fact need not be stated;

(d)   where the pension accruing to the highest paid director as a result of his qualifying services is either of the defined benefit type or is under a hybrid scheme that might make defined benefit payments, the following has to be disclosed:

(i)   the amount at the end of the year of the accrued pension; and

(ii)   the amount, if any, of the accrued lump sum.

In disclosing the accrued pension and the accrued lump sum, no account shall be taken of the possible effect of commutation of the pension or inverse commutation of the lump sum. Two examples of the calculation of the amount of accrued pension are included in **8.101** below.

The following extract illustrates the disclosure of the highest paid director's remuneration included in Glaxo Wellcome plc's 1998 report and accounts.

Extract 8.61

Glaxo Wellcome plc

Year ended 31 December 1998

Remuneration report (extract)

Highest paid Director	The highest paid Director in 1998 and 1997 was Sir Richard Sykes.		
		1998	**1997**
		£000	**£000**
	Total emoluments	1,863	1,723
	Amounts receivable under Long-Term Incentive Plan	1,777	–
	Gains made on exercise of share options	–	1,775
		£000	£000
		p.a.	p.a.
	Defined benefit pension: Accrued pension at end of year	494	426

8.62

In determining which director is the highest paid director, companies with securities admitted to the Official List and companies whose securities are traded on AIM have to include gains made on the exercise of options. This could result in the person meeting the definition of highest paid director changing from one year to the next. Comparatives are required to all the directors' remuneration disclosures. Accordingly, where one director is the highest paid in the current year and a different director was the highest paid in the previous year, the comparative to the current disclosure will be in respect of the person who was the highest paid director in that previous year (rather than giving last year's remuneration for the director who is the highest paid in the current year). An example of disclosure where one person is the highest paid director in the current year and someone else was the highest paid director in the previous year can be seen in Example **8.75.1** (Marks and Spencer plc) – see footnote 4.

Requirements of the Listing Rules

Introduction

8.63   This section deals with the disclosure requirements that are included in the Listing Rules; these mainly result from recommendations in the Greenbury Report and the Combined Code.

Scope

8.64   The disclosures on directors' remuneration dealt with in this section are those required by the Listing Rules paragraphs 12.43A(c), 12.43(d) and 12.43(u). Various exemptions are, however, available from these disclosure requirements. The exemptions are as follows:

(a)   companies that have only specialist debt securities listed – exempt from all the above disclosures [Listing Rules 23.22];

(b)   companies with only debt securities or with only fixed income shares listed – exempt from all the above disclosures except 12.43(u) [Listing Rules 9.46 and 9.47];

(c)   overseas companies with a primary listing by the UK Listing Authority – exempt from all the above disclosures except 12.43A(c)(vii), 12.43(d) and 12.43(u) [Listing Rules 17.12(b)];

(d)   overseas companies with a secondary listing by the UK Listing Authority – exempt from all the above disclosures [Listing Rules 17.14];

(e)   investment companies (including investment trusts) and venture capital trusts with no executive directors – exempt from all the disclosures except 12.43(d) and 12.43(u). [Listing Rules 21.20(i) and 26.9(d)]

Requirements

Remuneration report by the board

8.65   Listed companies (other than those exempted from the requirement – see **8.64** above) should include in their annual report and accounts a remuneration report by the board to shareholders. [Listing Rules 12.43A(c)] This report should be the main vehicle through which the company reports to shareholders on directors' remuneration. The form and content of this report as required by the Listing Rules is dealt with in the following sections. Paragraphs **8.110** to **8.114** below set out further recommended contents. Where the disclosures in **8.111** and **8.112** are not given it will be necessary to list them as departures from compliance with the Combined Code (see **7.27**). An example of a remuneration report by the board is included in the model financial statements of Delto PLC (see chapter 46).

8.66

The board's remuneration report is generally presented as a separate report, although it could be presented as a section within the directors' report as was done by Whitbread plc in its report and accounts for the year ended 27 February 1999.

8.67

> Some of the disclosures required to be disclosed in the report, i.e., the elements of each director's pay, the information on share options, the details of long-term incentive schemes and details of pension entitlements, are required to be included in the scope of the auditors' report on the financial statements. This is most easily achieved by including this information within the notes to the financial statements and making a cross-reference from the board's remuneration report.

Example 8.67

Extract from the remuneration report of the board

This report should be read in conjunction with notes x and y to the accounts which also constitute part of this report. Full details of all elements in the remuneration package of each director, full details of each director's interest in the long-term incentive scheme together with details of each director's pension entitlements are given in note x to the accounts. Details of each director's share options are given in note y to the accounts.

8.68

> As an alternative to including in the notes to the financial statements the disclosures described above, some companies may wish to include them within the board's remuneration report. If so, it is preferable for them to be incorporated into the audited financial statements by means of an appropriate cross-reference which indicates unambiguously which disclosures fall within the scope of audit. The Act's disclosures on directors' remuneration are required to be included in the financial statements. Thus, where a company includes the Act's disclosures in the board's remuneration report, the company will also be required to include in the financial statements an unambiguous cross-reference to those disclosures. The example wording below assumes that all disclosures on directors' remuneration are included in the board's remuneration report and that the cross-reference in the financial statements is to the disclosures required by both the Act and the Listing Rules.

Example 8.68

Disclosures on directors' remuneration*, share options*, long-term incentive schemes*, pension contributions* and pension entitlements* required by the Companies Act 1985 and those specified for audit by the UK Listing Authority are on pages 20† and 21† within the board's remuneration report and form part of these audited financial statements.

* Delete any not relevant to the company.

† The page references must be unambiguous. It is assumed in this example that all of the information required to be audited is on pages 20 and 21 and that these pages contain no other information. Where these pages contain information that has not been audited, the reference would need to be more specific, e.g., 'paragraphs 6 to 10 of the board's remuneration report on pages 19 to 21'.

Policy on executive directors' remuneration

8.69 The board's remuneration report should contain a statement setting out the company's policy with respect to executive directors' remuneration. [Listing Rules 12.43A(c)(i)]

8.70

As well as being a requirement of the Listing Rules, this is also a recommendation in the Combined Code. Although principle B.3 of the Combined Code says no more than there should be a statement of remuneration policy, Code provision B.3.2 states that the statement on policy 'should draw attention to factors specific to the company'.

In addition, the Hampel Committee in its final report, paragraph 4.15, commented that: 'We have reviewed the value of a general statement of remuneration policy. A number of companies have met the letter of this requirement with anodyne references to the need to "recruit, retain and motivate" or to pay "market rates". We consider that a policy statement is potentially helpful, to set the context for the more detailed information; we hope that companies will provide more informative statements, drawing attention to factors specific to the company'. To this end, the disclosure on general policy could usefully cover those matters set out in paragraph 5.5 of the Greenbury report that are relevant to the company, that is:

(a) the total level of remuneration;

(b) the main components of remuneration and the arrangements for determining them;

(c) the comparator groups of companies considered;

(d) the main parameters and rationale for annual bonus schemes, including caps;

(e) the main parameters for any share option or other long-term incentive schemes;

> (f) how performance is measured and how these measures link to the company objectives;
>
> (g) the policy on allowing executives to accept outside appointments;
>
> (h) the policy on contracts of service and early termination; and
>
> (i) the main elements of remuneration that are pensionable, the type of scheme, including whether it is part of the main scheme or not, and how the Inland Revenue pensions cap has been accommodated.

8.71   The statement should relate only to executive directors, including directors based wholly or mainly overseas. The Greenbury Report, in its elaboration of its recommendations, suggested that the remuneration policy with respect to non-executive directors' pay should also be stated. However, neither the Combined Code nor the Listing Rules have picked up this recommendation and it therefore remains non-mandatory. All of the other information required in the report is in respect of all directors and therefore includes both executive and non-executive directors.

The amount of each element of remuneration for the period

8.72   For each director by name, the amount of each element of the remuneration package should be shown for the period under review including:

- basic salary and fees;

- the estimated money value of benefits in kind;

- annual bonuses;

- deferred bonuses;

- compensation for loss of office and payments for breach of contract or other termination payments.

The total for each director should also be shown. For the corresponding period, it is sufficient to show only the total figure per director. [Listing Rules 12.43A(c)(ii)]

8.73   Significant payments made to former directors during the period under review should also be disclosed. (see **8.76** to **8.77** below).

8.74   The Listing Rules require the information in **8.72** and **8.73** to be presented in tabular form, unless inappropriate, together with explanatory notes as necessary.

8.75   The following extracts illustrate the disclosure given by Marks and Spencer plc and by Reuters Group plc.

Extract 8.75.1

Marks and Spencer plc

Year ended 31 March 1999

Remuneration report (extract)

1 DIRECTORS' EMOLUMENTS

	Salary £000	Profit Share £000 (5)	Benefits £000 (6)	Bonus £000 (7)	Total 1999 £000	Total 1998 £000
Chairman						
Sir Richard Greenbury [(1)(4)]	772	n/a	38	n/a	**810**	969
Executive directors						
P L Salsbury (Chief Executive) [(2)]	420	12	7	–	**439**	435
P G McCracken	380	11	18	–	**409**	435
Lord Stone of Blackheath	393	11	12	–	**416**	427
R Aldridge	278	8	26	–	**312**	300
J R Benfield	248	8	19	–	**275**	286
R W C Colvill	320	10	12	–	**342**	344
Mrs C E M Freeman	210	6	14	–	**230**	229
B S Morris	210	6	14	–	**230**	226
J T Rowe	275	8	19	–	**302**	292
Non-executive directors						
B F Baldock	50	n/a	n/a	n/a	**50**	50
Sir Martin Jacomb	34	n/a	n/a	n/a	**34**	34
Sir Michael Perry	34	n/a	n/a	n/a	**34**	34
Dame Stella Rimington	34	n/a	n/a	n/a	**34**	34
Sir Ralph Robins	34	n/a	n/a	n/a	**34**	34
The Hon David Sieff	34	n/a	11	n/a	**45**	43
Retired directors						
(with effect from)						
D K Hayes (31 May 1999)	230	7	38	–	**275**	275
C Littmoden (31 May 1999) [(8)]	251	n/a	336	–	**587**	595
S J Sacher (31 May 1999)	262	8	23	–	**293**	310
P P D Smith (31 March 1999) [(8)(9)]	318	n/a	361	–	**679**	624
J K Oates (31 January 1999) [(3)(4)(9)]	510	n/a	35	–	**545**	646
D G Trangmar (31 March 1998)	n/a	n/a	n/a	n/a	**n/a**	341
D G Lanigan (31 July 1997)	n/a	n/a	n/a	n/a	**n/a**	37
The Rt Hon The Baroness						
Young (31 July 1997)	n/a	n/a	n/a	n/a	**n/a**	13
Total	5,297	95	983	–	**6,375**	7,013

(1)   The roles of Chairman and Chief Executive were split from 1 February 1999. Sir Richard Greenbury, the Chairman and Chief Executive, relinquished the role of Chief Executive on 31 January 1999. As Chairman he receives a salary of £450,000 pa. As a non-executive director he no longer participates in the profit share or bonus schemes, but retains share options

---

previously granted under the Senior Staff Share Option Scheme and SAYE Option Scheme.

(2)   P L Salsbury, formerly Managing Director, was appointed Chief Executive from 1 February 1999, on a salary of £560,000 pa.

(3)   J K Oates resigned from the Board and took early retirement on 31 January 1999. Terms concerning the termination of employment have been implemented in accordance with his contract of employment amounting to £587,000. This relates to salary and benefits for the 11 months outstanding on his employment contract. Additionally, should a senior management bonus be payable for the 31 March 2000 financial year, he will receive a further amount equal to 9/12ths of that bonus (maximum £85,000), which will be shown in next year's Annual Report. He has been awarded an Early Retirement Pension (see section 3(ii) of this report) of £166,000 pa payable for three and a half years, until the normal senior management retirement age of 60.

(4)   The highest paid director was Sir Richard Greenbury, whose emoluments were £810,000. No gains were made on his share options this year. His accrued pension entitlement at the end of the year was £465,000. Last year, the highest paid director was J K Oates, whose emoluments, including gains on share options, were £1,393,000 with an accrued pension entitlement at the end of last year of £268,000.

(5)   In line with all other members of staff, executive directors performing their duties mainly in the UK are allocated a profit share based on a percentage of their salary. Further information on profit sharing is given in note 9C to the financial statements.

(6)   Benefits for UK directors relate mainly to the provision of cars, fuel and travel. For expatriate directors see footnote (8).

(7)   A bonus is not payable for the year under review as the Group performance targets were not achieved. (Last year a bonus of 14.5% amounting to £2.3m was paid.)

(8)   Expatriate directors carrying out their duties overseas have their remuneration adjusted to take account of local living costs. This adjustment is to put them in a position, after taking into account taxation differentials, where they are no better or worse off as a result of carrying out their duties overseas. Payments made to them, or on their behalf, such as allowances for working overseas and the provision of accommodation are treated as benefits for the purpose of the above table and are non-pensionable.

(9)   Included in the salary figure for J K Oates and P P D Smith is a non-pensionable payment in lieu of holidays.

Extract 8.75.2

Reuters Group plc

Year ended 31 December 1999

Report on remuneration and related matters

DIRECTORS' REMUNERATION

	1999					1998
	Salary/ Fees	Salary/ Fees increase	Bonus	Benefits	Total	Remuner- ation total
	£000	%	£000	£000	£000	£000
Chairman:						
Sir Christopher Hogg	203	5.2	–	10	**213**	203
Non-executive directors:						
R P Bauman	43	–	–	–	**43**	42
Sir John Craven	33	–	–	–	**33**	33
M P Green (resigned 20 April 1999)	11	–	–	–	**11**	33
R Mendoza (appointed 18 February 1998)	33	–	–	–	**33**	29
R L Olver	33	–	–	–	**33**	33
C J F Sinclair	43	–	–	–	**43**	43
Sir David Walker	33	–	–	–	**33**	33
Total for non-executive directors (excluding Chairman)	229	–	–	–	**229**	246
Executive directors:						
P Job, Chief Executive	550	5.3	328	27	**905**	791
J-C Marchand	362	7.4	196	33	**591**	530
J M C Parcell	300	22.0	179	16	**495**	377
R O Rowley	338	4.3	201	17	**556**	492
D G Ure	355	4.4	141	20	**516**	518
A-F H Villeneuve	355	4.4	141	55	**551**	524
Total for executive directors	2,260	–	1,186	168	**3,614**	3,232
TOTAL EMOLUMENTS	2,692	–	1,186	178	**4,056**	3,681

8.76   As with most of the Listing Rules' requirements on directors' remuneration, the requirement to disclose significant payments made to former directors during the period under review (see **8.73** above) was originally introduced in response to the Greenbury report. The wording in the Greenbury report is, 'Also disclosed should be any payments and benefits not previously disclosed, including any additional pension provisions, receivable by Directors who have retired during the accounting period or the previous accounting period'.

8.77   Clearly, what is included in the Listing Rules is much wider. It would require disclosure, for example, of payments made to a former director for consultancy services in the current year. An example of disclosure under this requirement is set out below.

Extract 8.77

Hanson plc

Year ended 31 December 1999

Remuneration report (extract)

Directors' remuneration (extract)

Amounts paid to directors retiring during the year to December 31, 1999;

	Salary/ fees £'000	Annual bonus £'000	Benefits £'000	Total 1999 £'000	Total 1998 £'000
The Hon. Charles H Price II	31	–	–	31	30

Remuneration paid to former directors during the year to December 31, 1999;

	£'000
Lord Hanson	25
B A Hellings	15

Information on share options

8.78   Information on share options, including SAYE options, should be given for each director by name in accordance with the recommendations of UITF Abstract 10 *Disclosure of directors' share options*. The information should be given in tabular form, together with explanatory notes as necessary. [Listing Rules 12.43A(c)(iii)]

8.79   UITF Abstract 10 recommends disclosure of information, including exercise prices, in respect of individual directors' options, together with market price information at the year end and at the date of exercise if this occurred during the period. The appendix to UITF Abstract 10 suggests that the following information should be given for each director, by name, for each combination of exercise prices and dates:

(a)   the number of shares under option at the start of the year (or date of appointment if later) and at the end of the year;

(b)   the number of options:

(i)   granted;
(ii)   exercised; and
(iii)   lapsed during the year;

(c)   the exercise prices;

(d)   the dates from which the options may be exercised and the expiry dates;

(e)   the cost of the options (if any);

(f)   the market price of the shares at the date of exercise of any options; and

(g)   a concise summary of any performance criteria conditional upon which the options are exercisable.

In addition, it suggests that the market price of the shares at the end of the year and the range (high and low) during the year should be disclosed. UITF Abstract 10 includes a suggested table of disclosures which could be used. This is reproduced below. If the table is included within the notes to the accounts, no further disclosure in respect of directors' options would be required in the directors' report.

Example 8.79

Example illustration from the appendix to UITF Abstract 10

Directors [names]	Number of options during the year				Exercise price	Market price at date of exercise	Date from which exercisable	Expiry date
	At 01.01.93	Granted	Exercised	At 31.12.93				
A	100	–	(100)	–	50p	130p	–	–
B	100	–	–	100	50p	–	31.12.92	31.12.99
	–	50	–	50	120p	–	31.12.95	31.12.02
C	200	–	(100)	100	50p	120p	31.12.92	31.12.99
D	100	–	–	100	150p	–	31.12.94	31.12.01
	–	50	–	50	120p	–	31.12.95	31.12.02

No options lapsed during the year. The market price of the shares at 31.12.93 was 140p and the range during 1993 was 106p to 142p.

8.80   Where information might be excessive in length because of the number of different options granted at different dates, the appendix to UITF Abstract 10 accepts that a more concise disclosure, using weighted average exercise prices for each director, would be a satisfactory alternative, although some additional disclosure may be necessary. For example, it would be relevant to distinguish options which are 'in the money' from those 'out of the money'. Also, unusually large individual items may need to be noted to prevent misleading conclusions being drawn from an average (taking account of when such options are exercisable). Paragraph A3 of the appendix states that this more concise approach would involve disclosure of the following:

(a) total shares under option at the beginning and end of the year for each director, with appropriate weighted average exercise prices applicable to shares under option at the end of the year;

(b) full details of any movements during the year (covering options granted and lapsed during the year with disclosure of the exercise price and options exercised in the year disclosing the exercise price and the share price at date of exercise); and

(c) the fact that the company's Register of Directors' Interests (which is open to inspection) contains full details of directors' shareholdings and options to subscribe.

8.81 The extract below illustrates the disclosure using the more concise approach.

Example 8.81

Bass plc

Year ended 30 September 1999

Remuneration report (extract)

| 6 DIRECTORS' OPTIONS | Ordinary shares under option | | | | Price | |
| | | | | | Weighted average option | Option |
	30.9.99	Granted	Lapsed	1.10.98	price	price
Tim Clarke		23,300 *				798p
		1,319 **				734p
A	24,600				554p	
B	65,100				812p	
C	61,919				877p	
Total	151,619	24,619	–	127,000	796p	
Iain Napier		23,300 *				798p
		1,319 **				734p
			1,100			
A	43,100				591p	
B	16,600				812p	
C	89,019				919p	
Total	148,719	24,619	1,100	125,200	812p	
Richard North		21,900 *				798p
A	146,400				642p	
B	12,300				812p	
C	37,700				868p	
Total	196,400	21,900	–	174,500	696p	
Tom Oliver		59,000 *				798p
C	200,300				833p	
Total	200,300	59,000	–	141,300	833p	
Sir Ian Prosser		38,200 *				798p
A	30,000				545p	
B	10,200				812p	
C	277,135				855p	
Total	317,335	38,200	–	279,135	824p	

No option was exercised during the year 1998/99. The 1997/98 gain on exercise by Sir Ian Prosser, the highest paid director, was £8,216 and by the Board in aggregate was £461,582.

Options are held under the Bass Executive Share Option and Bass Employee Savings Share Schemes. Option grants marked* above were made under the Executive Share Option Scheme and are exercisable between 2002 and 2009. Grants marked ** were made under the Employee Savings Share Scheme and are exercisable between 1 September 2002 and 28 February 2003.

Shares under option at 30 September 1999 are designated as:

A   where the options are exercisable and the market price per share at 30 September 1999 was above the option price;

B   where the options are exercisable but the market price at 30 September 1999 was below the option price; and

C   where the options are not yet exercisable.

The market price on 30 September 1999 was 732.5p per share and the range during the year was 642p to 1,000.5p per share.

The Company's Register of Directors' Interests, which is open to inspection at the Registered Office, contains full details of directors' shareholdings and share options.

8.82   Neither the Listing Rules nor UITF Abstract 10 specifies in respect of which directors the information should be given. When UITF Abstract 10 was first published, it was often seen as expanding on the information given under the Act. The Act, however, only requires information on options to be disclosed in respect of a person who was a director *at the end of the company's financial year.* The UITF Abstract 10 disclosures have now been incorporated into the Listing Rules as part of remuneration disclosures. The spirit of the Listing Rules requirements would therefore suggest giving the disclosures in respect of a person who was a director *at any time during the year.* Where a person ceased to be a director during the year, his options lapsed upon his ceasing to be a director and he exercised no options during the year prior to ceasing to be a director, this information could be by way of footnote rather than incorporated in a table if wished.

Long-term incentive schemes

8.83   The Listing Rules state that details should be given of any long-term incentive schemes, other than share option information included under the requirements of the previous section (see **8.78** to **8.82** above). [Listing Rules 12.43A(c)(iv)]

8.84 Long-term incentive schemes are those involving any arrangement (other than a retirement benefit plan or other arrangement specified in Listing Rules 12.43A(c)(ii) (e.g., a deferred bonus)) requiring, *inter alia*, one or more conditions in relation to service and/or performance to be satisfied over more than one financial year.

8.85 For each director by name, who was in the scheme(s) at any time during the accounting period, the following information should be disclosed:

(a) the interests in the schemes at the beginning of the period;

(b) entitlements and awards granted and commitments made under the schemes during the period, showing which crystallise in the period or subsequent periods;

(c) the money value and number of shares, cash payments or other benefits received during the period;

(d) the interests in the schemes at the end of the period.

8.86 The following extract illustrates the disclosure requirement.

Extract 8.86

Whitbread plc

Year ended 27 February 1999

Remuneration report (extract)

Long Term Incentive Plan

Potential awards held by the executive directors under the Plan at the beginning and end of the year, and details of the actual awards during the year and their value, are as follows:

	POTENTIAL AWARDS HELD AT 1/3/98	POTENTIAL AWARD FOR THE THREE-YEAR PERFORMANCE PERIOD ENDING ON 28/2/01[(i)]	ACTUAL AWARDS FOR THE PERFORMANCE PERIOD ENDED ON 28/2/98 Shares	Value £[(ii)]	POTENTIAL AWARDS HELD AT 27/2/99
A S Perelman	52,862	13,982	11,843	92,494	46,424
D H Richardson	29,821	8,907	6,276	48,200	27,906
W M F C Shannon	41,489	12,351	8,613	68,042	38,989
M H Templeman	48,181	13,143	10,497	104,445	43,225
D M Thomas[(ii)]	50,557	19,419	10,228	91,029*	52,341

Notes

(i)

The share price used to calculate the potential share entitlement maximum for the three-year performance period ending on 28 February 2001 was 965.5p.

(ii)

The value shown is that of the shares given to each director on the day he called for his award. *Mr D M Thomas has not yet called for his shares and a notional value is therefore shown, calculated using the price at 27 February 1999.

(iii)

For the performance period ending on 27 February 1999, the company's TSR performance was ranked fifty-eighth (1997/8 – forty-sixth) relative to other companies in the FT-SE 100 index; accordingly, the participants in the Plan are entitled to 34% (1997/8 – 58%) of their maximum possible award. The actual awards to the executive directors for the performance period ended on 27 February 1999 were as follows:

	SHARES
A S Perelman	5,604
D H Richardson	2,987
W M F C Shannon	4,173
M H Templeman	5,127
D M Thomas	5,008

(iv)

The company funds an employee share ownership plan trust ('ESOP') to enable it to acquire and hold the necessary shares. The ESOP currently holds 345,262 shares; the executive directors each have a technical interest in all these shares. All dividends on shares in the ESOP are waived by the Trustee.

(v)

During the period from 27 February 1999 to 4 May 1999 no director has exercised his option to call for the transfer of his shares out of the Plan. The balance of the potential awards to the executive directors for this performance period, totalling 44,458, has lapsed.

8.87 In the extract from Whitbread's remuneration report in **8.86** above the figures do not 'add across'. This is because, although the Listing Rules do not use the words 'maximum potential', the interpretation of (a) and (b) in **8.85** above is that the maximum potential awards have to be disclosed. The disclosure under (c) is of the actual award, which in the Whitbread extract is 58 per cent of the maximum potential award.

8.88 Listing Rule 12.43(u) requires that for long-term incentive schemes in which the only participant is a director of the company (or an individual whose appointment as a director is in contemplation) and the arrangement is established specially to facilitate, in unusual circumstances, the recruitment or retention of the relevant individual, the following information should be disclosed in the first annual report published following the date on which the individual becomes eligible to participate in the arrangement:

(a)   the name of the sole participant;

(b)   the date on which the individual first became eligible to participate in the arrangement;

(c)   explanation of why the circumstances in which the arrangement was established were unusual;

(d)   the conditions to be satisfied under the terms of the arrangement;

(e)   the maximum award(s) under the terms of the arrangement or, if there is no maximum, the basis on which awards will be determined;

(f)   the information set out in paragraph 13.14(a) to (d) of the Listing Rules.

Explanation of pensionable remuneration

8.89   It is normally the case that only basic salary is pensionable. The Listing Rules therefore require that if any element of remuneration, other than basic salary, is pensionable then the board's remuneration report should give an explanation and justification of why this is the case. [Listing Rules 12.43A(c)(v)]

8.90   The following extract illustrates the disclosure.

Extract 8.90

Glaxo Wellcome plc

Year ended 31 December 1998

Remuneration report (extract)

Post-retirement benefits

Executive Directors participate in pension schemes established by Group companies to provide pensions to staff in retirement. The schemes are mostly non-contributory. Pensions are normally equivalent to two-thirds of final salary, excluding bonus and other forms of remuneration, assuming approximately 20 years of service at senior executive level. In the case of Mr Ingram, in accordance with normal US practice, pension entitlement is based on salary plus annual bonus. Executive Directors are also entitled to the post-retirement benefit of medical insurance.

Directors' service contracts

8.91   Large compensation payments to directors on loss of office, particularly those on three-year rolling contracts have given rise to much high-profile criticism. It is recommended, therefore, that directors' service contracts should normally have notice periods of no more than one year.

8.92   Although the Listing Rules do not require notice periods to be set at or reduced to one year, they do require disclosure in the board's remuneration report of any service contracts with a notice period in excess of one year, or which have provisions for predetermined termination payments which would exceed one year's salary and benefits in kind. The reasons for such notice periods should also be disclosed. [Listing Rules 12.43A(c)(vi)]

8.93   The following extract illustrates the disclosure.

Extract 8.93

The BOC Group plc

Year ended 30 September 1999

Report on remuneration (extract)

Service contracts

All executive directors have terms of service which can be terminated by the company on not more than two years' notice, and by the individual director on six months' notice. This is in line with current market practice. It provides directors with a reasonable degree of security, thus enabling them to concentrate on the challenges involved in securing the long-term future of the Group. However, the committee has agreed that for new appointees to the board a one-year service contract will generally apply.

The MRC considers carefully any arrangements for early termination to ensure that failure is not 'rewarded'.

Unexpired service periods

8.94   The unexpired period of any service contract of any director proposed for election or re-election at the AGM should be given in the board's remuneration report. Where any such director does not have a service contract, a statement to that effect in the remuneration report is required. [Listing Rules 12.43A(c)(vii)]

8.95   The Listing Rules define directors' service contract as 'a service contract with a director of the issuer with a notice or contract period of one year or more or with provisions for predetermining compensation on termination of an amount which equals or exceeds one year's salary and benefits in kind'.

Pension entitlements

8.96 The remuneration report of the board should include information on directors' pension entitlements. [Listing Rules 12.43A(c)(ix) and (x)]

8.97 For money purchase pension schemes (as defined in the Act), details of the contribution or allowance payable or made by the company in respect of each director during the period should be disclosed.

8.98 For defined benefit pension schemes (as defined in the Act), the following information should be given for each individual director who served during the accounting period:

(a) details of the amount of the increase during the period (excluding inflation) and of the accumulated total amount at the end of the period in respect of the accrued benefit to which the director would be entitled on leaving service or is entitled having left service during the period; and

(b) either the transfer value (less director's contributions) of the relevant increase in accrued benefit (to be calculated in accordance with Actuarial Guidance Note GN11, but making no deduction for underfunding) as at the end of the period (see extract **8.99** below) or, alternatively (see extract **8.100** below), so much of the following information as is necessary to make a reasonable assessment of the transfer value:

    (i)   current age;
    (ii)   normal retirement age;
    (iii) the amount of any contributions paid or payable by the director under the terms of the scheme during the period;
    (iv) details of spouse's and dependants' benefits;
    (v)   early retirement rights and options;
    (vi) expectations of pension increases after retirement (whether guaranteed or discretionary);
    (vii) discretionary benefits for which allowance is made in transfer values on leaving; and
    (viii) any other relevant information which will significantly affect the value of the benefits.

The Listing Rules state that contributions made by the directors voluntarily and the benefits accrued in respect of such voluntary contributions should not be disclosed.

An example of the disclosures required can be found in the model report and financial statements for Delto PLC (see chapter 46).

8.99   The following extract illustrates the disclosure under the former option.

Extract 8.99

The BOC Group plc

Year ended 30 September 1999

Report on remuneration (extract)

iii)   Pensions
A E Isaac, age 58: Pension to contractual retirement age 60 is being funded in the UK through a combination of tax-approved personal pension plan and a funded unapproved retirement benefit scheme, which is underpinned by a guarantee for which provision is being made in the accounts.

Sir David John, age 61: Pension to contractual retirement age 65 is a defined benefit unfunded arrangement for which provision is being made in the accounts.

Executive directors retiring in the year
Dr D Chatterji, age 55: Pension was covered under the US cash balance retirement plan which entitled Dr Chatterji to a lump sum benefit on termination of employment of US$261,000.

F D Rosenkranz, age 54: Pension benefits are funded under the UK senior executive pension scheme. Following his ceasing to be an employee, his pension was augmented under the rules of the scheme to meet the terms of his contract of employment and address the loss of pension expectation. As a consequence, he became entitled to an annual pension of £323,825 payable from age 55. A cash contribution of £1.3 million will be made in 2000 to meet the cost of augmentation.

	Defined benefit plans				Defined contribution plans	
	Deferred benefit at 30 September		Increase in year net of inflation	Increase in transfer value less members' contributions	Company contributions in year	
	Pension £000	Lump sum £000	£000	£000	£000	
UK-based directors						
A E Isaac	**1999**	–	**1,010**	**180**	**156**	–
	1998	–	805	184	151	–
Sir David John	**1999**	**30**	–	**3**	**53**	–
	1998	26	–	8	129	–
Executive directors retiring in the year						
Dr D Chatterji	**1999**	–	–	–	–	–
	1998	–	411	117	117	10

| F D Rosenkranz | 1999 | 288 | – | 31 | 425 | – |
| | 1998 | 249 | – | 19 | 214 | – |

The transfer value equivalent excludes directors' contributions and has been calculated in accordance with Actuarial Guidance Note GN11.

8.100   The following extract illustrates the disclosure under the latter option.

Extract 8.100

Bass plc

Year ended 30 September 1999

Remuneration report (extract)

4   DIRECTORS' PENSIONS

The following information relates to the pension arrangements provided for the United Kingdom based executive directors except for Tom Oliver, under the Bass Executive Pension Plan (the Plan) and, in the cases of Tim Clarke, Iain Napier and Richard North, under the unfunded Bass Executive Top-Up Scheme (BETUS).

The Plan is a funded, Inland Revenue approved, final salary, occupational pension scheme. Its main features applicable to the executive directors are:

i   a normal pension age of 60;

ii   pension accrual of 1/30th of final pensionable salary for each year of pensionable service;

iii life assurance cover of four times pensionable salary;

iv   pensions payable in the event of ill health; and

v   spouse's and dependants' pensions on death.

All Plan benefits are subject to Inland Revenue limits. Where such limitation is due to the earnings 'cap', BETUS is used to increase pension and death benefits to the level that would otherwise have applied.

Tom Oliver, the executive director formerly based in the US, has retirement benefits provided via the Bass Hotels & Resorts plans: Savings & Retirement Plan (S&RP), Non-Qualified Savings Plan (NQSP) and Supplemental Executive Retirement Plan (SERP).

i   The S&RP is a tax qualified 401(k) plan. The benefits are provided on a money purchase basis with the member and Company both contributing.

ii   The NQSP is a non-tax qualified plan. The benefits are provided on a money purchase basis with the member and Company both contributing.

---

iii The SERP is also a non-tax qualified plan. The pension accrual rate is 2.5% of salary per year of service, and the pension is payable without reduction from age 62. The death in service benefit is a return of the member's contributions plus interest, there is no death in retirement dependant's benefit, except by a surrender of the member's pension, and there are no guaranteed pension increases.

Directors' pension benefits	Age at 30 Sept 1999	Directors' contributions (note 1) £	Increase in accrued pension (note 2) £ pa	Accrued pension at 30 Sept 1999 (note 3) £ pa
Tim Clarke	42	12,000	19,200	76,200
Iain Napier	50	12,000	24,100	107,700
Richard North	49	13,100	18,100	61,500
Tom Oliver (note 4)	58	17,200	5,200	9,700
Sir Ian Prosser (note 5)	56	33,600	73,800	422,400

note 1 Contributions paid in the year by the directors under the terms of the Plan.

note 2 The increase in accrued pension during the year excludes any increase for inflation.

note 3 Accrued pension is that which would be paid annually on retirement at 60 (62 for Tom Oliver), based on service to 30 September 1999.

note 4 The figures for Tom Oliver apply only to the SERP. Over the same period he contributed £6,500 to the S&RP and £8,600 to the NQSP. The Company contributed £5,500 to the SERP and £5,400 to the NQSP on his behalf.

note 5 The accrued pension at 30 September 1998 for Sir Ian Prosser, the highest paid director, was £344,200.

note 6 Members of the Plan joining before 1998 have the option to pay Additional Voluntary Contributions subject to Inland Revenue limits; neither the contributions, nor the resulting benefits are included in the above table.

The following is additional information relating to directors' pensions under the Plan and BETUS:

a   Normal pension age
The normal pension age is 60. Sir Ian Prosser's pension arrangements have already been funded and charged in the Company's accounts in previous years so that the accrued pension can be drawn as of right without reduction on his 58th birthday, or earlier if the Company consents. If such consent were given, which is at the Company's absolute discretion, the accrued pension would be £466,700 per annum.

b   Dependants' pensions

On the death of a director before his normal retirement age, a widow's pension equal to one-third of his own pension is payable; a child's pension of one-sixth of his pension is payable for each of a maximum of two eligible children.

On the death of a director after payment of his pension commences, a widow's pension of two-thirds of the director's full pension entitlement is payable; in addition, a child's pension of one-sixth of his full pension entitlement is payable for each of a maximum of two eligible children.

c   Early retirement rights

After leaving the service of the Company, the member has the right to draw his accrued pension at any time after his 50th birthday, subject to a discount for early payment.

d   Pension increases

All pensions (in excess of Guaranteed Minimum Pensions) are subject to contractual annual increases in line with the annual rise in the RPI subject to a maximum of 5% per annum. In addition, it is the Company's present aim to pay additional increases based on two-thirds of any rise in the RPI above 5% per annum.

e   Other discretionary benefits

Other than the discretionary pension increases mentioned in (d), there are no discretionary practices which are taken into account in calculating transfer values on leaving service.

8.101

The calculation of the accrued benefit at the end of the year is the same under the Listing Rules as under the Act. The following examples illustrate how the amount should be calculated. The exact calculation will be determined by the particular scheme rules.

Example 8.101.1

Director A had 15 years of pensionable service at 31 December 1999, 12 of which were as an employee of the company prior to his appointment as a director and his basic salary for the year then ended was £140,000 (1998 – £125,000). His pension accrues at the rate of one-thirtieth per annum, with the maximum pension payable being equal to two-thirds of basic salary in the final year before retirement.

The calculation of the amount of the accrued pension at 31 December 1999 for A is as follows.

What annual pension (excluding any attributable to voluntary contributions paid by the director) would A be entitled to if he left the group's service at the end of the year and there was no increase in the general level of prices between the year end and A reaching normal pension age?

i.e., Number of years' service (whether as a director or not)

divided by

Rate of accrual of pension

multiplied by

Remuneration on which pension would be calculated if A left the group's service on the balance sheet date.

i.e., 15/30 × £140,000 per annum

i.e., £70,000 per annum

Similarly, the calculation of the amount of the accrued pension at 31 December 1998 is as follows:

14/30 × £125,000 per annum or £58,333 per annum

The difference between the two figures is £11,667 per annum.

The relevant rate of inflation for 1999 is 3.2 per cent therefore the increase in accrued pension attributable to inflation is:

Rate of inflation multiplied by Annual pension entitlement for the previous year

i.e., 0.032× £58,333 = £1,867

Accordingly, the increase for the year excluding inflation is £9,800.

The inflation rate to be used should be that rate published by the Secretary of State for Social Security each year in accordance with Sch 3 Pension Schemes Act 1993; the published rate is updated annually by Statutory Instrument, titled 'The Occupational Pensions (Revaluation) Order [1999]'.

Example 8.101.2

Assume that in the above example Mr A's basic salary was made up of £90,000 relating to his services to the listed parent company and £50,000 relating to his services to one of its subsidiaries, X Ltd. Assume also that during the year Mr A was the highest paid director of X Ltd.

Under the Act's requirements, X Ltd would have to disclose the amount of Mr A's accrued pension at the end of the year. There is no requirement to apportion the amount disclosed depending on the

> allocation of salary between the two group companies. Therefore, the amount disclosed will be exactly the same as that in the above example:
>
> 15/30 × £140,000 per annum
>
> i.e., £70,000 per annum

8.102 The Listing Rule requirement is silent on the issue of comparatives. The requirement for the detailed analysis of remuneration (see **8.72** to **8.77** above) does explicitly require a comparative. Accordingly, this would suggest that the Exchange does not require comparatives to the pension entitlements disclosure. With limited exceptions, the Act requires comparatives 'in respect of every item stated in a note to the accounts'. Where the board's remuneration report is located outside the financial statements, comparatives would not be required to the pension disclosure. However, where the information is located within the financial statements, comparatives should be given.

8.103 The Listing Rules state that the scope of the auditors' report on the financial statements should cover, inter alia, the pension disclosures; failure to provide the required disclosures would result in the auditors providing the required particulars in their report.

Policy on granting of options or awards under employee share and other long-term incentive schemes

8.104 The Board's remuneration report should include a statement of the company's policy on the granting of options or awards under employee share schemes and other long-term incentive schemes. The statement should include explanation and justification of any departure from that policy in the period under review and any change in policy from the preceding year. [Listing Rules 12.43A(c)(viii)] As with most of the disclosure requirements on directors' remuneration, this requirement was introduced in response to the Greenbury report. The recommendations in the Greenbury report that led to the requirement were:

(a) a recommendation that grants under executive share option and other long-term incentive schemes should normally be phased rather than awarded in one large block; and

(b) the recommendation that if such awards were in one large block rather than phased, the remuneration report should contain an explanation and justification.

The London Stock Exchange consulted extensively and no consensus emerged on the definition of 'one large block'. Consequently the Listing Rules instead called for disclosure of the company's policy on the granting of options or awards. However (see **8.112** below), the original disclosure has now also been introduced via the Combined Code.

8.105 Long-term incentive schemes are those involving any arrangement (other than a retirement benefit plan or other arrangement specified in Listing Rules 12.43A(c)(ii) (e.g., a deferred bonus)) requiring, inter alia, one or more conditions in relation to service and/or performance to be satisfied over more than one financial year.

Waiver of emoluments

8.106 Companies are required to disclose 'details of any arrangement under which a director of the company has waived or agreed to waive any emoluments from the company or any subsidiary undertaking'. This requirement extends to particulars of any agreement to waive future emoluments as well as waivers of emoluments in respect of the financial year. Where a director has agreed to waive future emoluments, details of that waiver have to be given separately from details of the emoluments waived during the period. [Listing Rules 12.43(d)]

8.107 This disclosure requirement uses the term 'emoluments' and not 'remuneration'. The term 'emoluments' is not defined in the Listing Rules. At one point the term 'emoluments' was used to refer to the total remuneration package. More recently, however, emoluments has been used to refer to just a part of the total remuneration package. This disclosure requirement was introduced before the change in the meaning of emoluments. It is therefore suggested that its requirements are followed in respect of the waiver of any element in the remuneration package.

Period covered by remuneration disclosures

8.108 The Listing Rules do not specify the period to be covered by the directors' remuneration disclosures, although there are several references to the 'period under review'. This is generally interpreted as the company's statutory reporting period. This interpretation is supported by the Companies Act disclosures which have to be given for the statutory reporting period.

8.109 It can arise that a new company is formed, say, on a merger or demerger, that has its first statutory accounting period shorter or longer than 12 months and for which the underlying business has existed for many years. In these instances companies often present pro forma financial results for 12 months (together with comparatives for 12 months) in addition to giving the financial results for the statutory period, say, seven months. The question therefore arises for which period should the directors' remuneration disclosures be given in the Board's remuneration report. Where such a company believes that giving the disclosure required by the Listing Rules for the statutory reporting period would not be as meaningful as giving the information for the 12 month period, and would prefer not to give the disclosure for both periods, it should approach the UK Listing Authority to enquire whether it could give the disclosures for 12 months and not for the statutory reporting period. The Companies Act disclosures will, nevertheless, have to be given for the statutory reporting period.

Additional disclosures recommended by the Combined Code

8.110   The following disclosures are recommended by the Combined Code.

8.111   Membership of the remuneration committee. The Combined Code provision B.2.3 states that the members of the remuneration committee should be disclosed in the board's remuneration report. Non-compliance with this recommendation would have to be disclosed in the statement of compliance.

8.112   Schedule B, para 3 of the Combined Code states that the remuneration report should explain and justify if grants under executive share option or other long-term incentive schemes are awarded in one large block rather than phased. Non-compliance with this recommendation would have to be disclosed in the statement of compliance. What is meant by 'one large block' is not explained – see **8.104** above.

8.113   Paragraph 4 of Schedule B to the Combined Code states, inter alia, that 'Companies may wish to make clear that the transfer value represents a liability of the company, not a sum paid or due to the individual'.

8.114   The disclosure in **8.113** above applies where companies disclose the transfer value of the increase in directors' accrued pension benefits (see **8.98**(b) above). In some cases the wording set out in paragraph 4 of Schedule B to the Combined Code may not be correct. The following wording may be preferable:

'The transfer values disclosed above do not represent a sum paid or payable to the individual director. Instead they represent a potential liability of the company/pension scheme.'

> 'Company' will be appropriate if the scheme is unfunded and 'pension scheme' will be appropriate if the scheme is funded.
>
> Companies not giving this disclosure will not have to disclose it in the statement of compliance providing they considered whether they wished to make the disclosures.

Other disclosures

8.115 The Greenbury Report included a number of recommendations for disclosures that the London Stock Exchange decided not to include in the Listing Rules. One such disclosure that companies might wish to make is disclosure of the extent to which performance criteria have been met, together with any particular performance criteria on which individual directors' entitlements depend.

Future developments

8.116 In March 1998, the then President of the Board of Trade, Margaret Beckett, made a speech launching the green paper from the DTI on company law reform. In that speech, she made it clear that she would prefer to see effective self-regulation of corporate governance rather than legislation. However, if the City was not prepared to improve in this area, then she threatened that legislation within the new Companies Act might be the only way forward. Part of that threat related to the introduction of a statutory vote on the remuneration report of the board and/or the re-election of directors every year. These suggestions drew criticism from companies at the time. Greenbury, endorsed by Hampel, recommended that the remuneration report be put to shareholders at the AGM, although there seemed to be no sanctions proposed for companies which lose such a vote. The salaries, long-term incentives and bonuses would not be reversed; however, the credibility of the board may be damaged.

8.117 In July 1999 the DTI issued a consultative document 'Directors' remuneration', stating in it, inter alia, that:

> 'The Government believes that there is a sufficient level of concern about the ability of the current best practice framework to deliver the key Greenbury objectives – accountability, transparency, and linkage of rewards to performance – to justify consultation on further measures to strengthen the independence of the remuneration committee, full disclosure of directors' remuneration, and the board's accountability to shareholders.'

8.118 The topics discussed in the document are under the following headings:

237

(a)   the role of the remuneration committee;

(b)   linkage between rewards and performance;

(c)   disclosure of directors' remuneration;

(d)   contracts and compensation; and

(e)   directors' accountability to shareholders.

It is under (e) above that the DTI invites comments on whether quoted companies should be required to ask shareholders to vote on the board's remuneration report every year or whether any of the four other options is more favoured.

8.119   On the topic of disclosure of directors' remuneration, the DTI has said that:

(a)   there should be scope for simplifying the disclosure require-ments on individual directors' remuneration – one of the examples given is to require disclosure of the amount of gains made by directors on the exercise of share options rather than to require disclosure in accordance with UITF 10 (see **8.78** to **8.82** above); and

(b)   new disclosure requirements should be introduced to improve the disclosure of the linkage between pay and performance, specifically:

'companies might, for example, be required to state or other-wise show:

- the longer-term objectives that the company is seeking to achieve in relation to the performance of the board;

- the criteria which the company will use to measure the performance of the directors against those objectives;

- whether the company will be measuring its perform-ance against a comparator group of companies (and, if so, the names of the comparator companies or, where applicable, the relevant index);

- how the company has performed in relation to the comparator group of companies in respect of its objec-tives during the preceding financial years; (companies could, for example, be required to provide a perform-ance graph which allows investors to evaluate how both the company and its main competitors have performed against the relevant performance criteria over a three or five year period)

- the proposed balance between elements in the package which are and are not related to performance;

- the relationship between awards made under incentive schemes and the company's performance in the year in which the awards were earned.'

9 Profit and loss account

9 Profit and loss account

Summary of changes since the previous issue of this publication

Para.	Topic	Summary
9.264	Discussion paper *Reporting financial performance: proposals for change*	Issued by the ASB in June 1999, the discussion paper proposes that financial performance would be presented in a single statement – effectively combining the profit and loss account and statement of total recognised gains and losses.

General requirements

Introduction

9.1 The Act provides that every profit and loss account shall give a true and fair view of the profit or loss for the financial year and shall comply with Sch 4 as to its form and content. [s226] The Act allows certain exemptions from its requirements for companies that qualify as small or medium-sized. These exemptions are dealt with in chapter 34.

9.2 FRS 3 *Reporting financial performance* aims to require reporting entities to highlight a range of important components of financial performance to aid users in understanding the performance achieved by a reporting entity in a period and to assist them in forming a basis for their assessment of future results and cash flows. [FRS 3(1)] To this end, FRS 3 sets out additional requirements as to the form and content of the profit and loss account.

9.3 FRS 3 requires all gains and losses recognised in the financial statements for the period to be included in the profit and loss account, except for those items specifically permitted or required by accounting standards to be taken directly to reserves or, in the absence of a relevant accounting standard, specifically permitted or required by law to be taken directly to reserves. [FRS 3(13), (37) and (65)] Such items are discussed in **18.33** below.

9.4 Some companies' constitutions include clauses that either require certain items of revenue or expense to be taken to reserves or preclude certain gains from being distributed. For example, the articles of property or investment holding companies frequently require that profits on sale of properties or investments should be taken to a capital reserve or other non-distributable reserve.

9.5 Investment companies, as defined in companies legislation, (which are required to include such a clause in their constitutions) should include in the profit and loss account only those profits available for distribution. [FRS 3(31)]

9.6 For other entities with such a clause in their constitution, it is generally accepted that, for the purposes of FRS 3, the clause does not mean that such gains are 'specifically permitted or required by law to be taken directly to reserves', although each situation will need to be considered on its own merit. Thus, in most cases, the gains and losses concerned should be dealt with in accordance with the normal rules and, if appropriate, a transfer between the profit for the year and the appropriate reserve should be made of any amount recognised in the profit and loss account.

9.7 Having stated the principle set out in **9.3** above, the main provisions of FRS 3 address the way in which results are disclosed in the profit and loss account rather than what is included.

9.8 Guidance is given in the remainder of this chapter on the accounting treatment and disclosures required in respect of the items to be shown on the face of the profit and loss account or in the notes to the profit and loss account as follows:

9.9 to 9.10	Discusses the four format headings
9.11 to 9.101	Reviews each of the format 1 statutory headings in turn.
9.102 to 9.112	Reviews additional format 2 and 4 headings
9.113 to 9.124	Exceptional items
9.125 to 9.163	Continuing and discontinued activities
9.164 to 9.180	Consequences of a decision to sell or terminate an operation
9.181 to 9.189	Directors and employee information
9.190 to 9.199	Employee share schemes
9.200 to 9.215	Depreciation and diminution in value of fixed assets
9.216 to 9.222	Amortisation and impairment of goodwill and other intangible assets
9.223 to 9.225	Research and Development
9.226 to 9.227	Operating leases

Formats

Companies Act formats

9.9 Schedule 4 permits four alternative formats for profit and loss accounts. These formats are reproduced in Appendix III. Format 1 classifies operating expenses by function in a 'vertical' arrangement and relegates details of certain expenditure to the notes. Format 2, also 'vertical' in arrangement, summarises expenditure by type rather than by function. Formats 3 and 4 are 'two-sided' arrangements of the items in formats 1 and 2 respectively.

9.10 All four headings include 'turnover' and 'other operating income'. The headings for operating expenditure used under the different formats are as follows:

Format 1	*Format 2*
Cost of sales	Changes in stocks of finished goods and work in progress
Distribution costs	Own work capitalised
Administrative expenses	Raw materials and consumables
	Other external charges
	Staff costs
	Depreciation and other amounts written off tangible and intangible fixed assets
	Exceptional amounts written off current assets
	Other operating charges

9.11 Companies are free to select whichever format is most suitable to them, but the selected format may not be changed in subsequent years, unless there are special reasons (see **5.38** above).

9.12 Format 1 may be more suitable for a manufacturing company, since format 2 does not permit the calculation of cost of sales and gross profit which is a significant measure of performance for such a company. It is also suggested that 'vertical' formats 1 and 2 give a more logical presentation than the 'two-sided' formats 3 and 4 in most cases.

9.13 There are three headings not included in the formats which the Act states should be shown separately in each profit and loss account, namely:
[Sch 4: 3(6) and (7)]

(a) profit or loss on ordinary activities before taxation;

(b) the aggregate amount of dividends paid and proposed; and

(c) any amount set aside or proposed to be set aside to, or withdrawn or proposed to be withdrawn from, reserves.

The profit and loss account should also disclose the aggregate amount of any dividends proposed, unless the disclosure is made in the notes to the accounts. [Sch 4: 3(7)(c)]

FRS 3 formats

9.14 FRS 3 requires each statutory profit and loss account heading between turnover and operating profit inclusive to be analysed between continuing and discontinued operations; results of acquisitions are to be disclosed separately as a component of continuing operations. Such analyses are dealt with in **9.125** to **9.163** below. The FRS also sets a minimum for the level of disclosure on the face of the profit and loss account (see **9.19** below).

9.15 In consolidated accounts, the information required by FRS 3 will be given on a consolidated basis.

9.16 In addition to the headings required by the Act, FRS 3 requires a subtotal entitled 'Operating profit'. Operating profit for non-financial reporting entities is normally profit before income from shares in group undertakings (i.e., profit after all operating costs and income, but before investment income and interest). [FRS 3(14)]

9.17 The FRS also specifies additional format headings for three special categories of item:

(a) profits or losses on the sale or termination of an operation;

(b) costs of a fundamental reorganisation or restructuring having a material effect on the nature and focus of the reporting entity's operations; and

(c) profits or losses on the disposal of fixed assets.

These are described in **9.41** to **9.59** below.

Format headings – format 1

Introduction

9.18 The items discussed below are dealt with in the order of items shown in format 1 in **9.23** to **9.101** below, taking into account the additional disclosures required by the Act and FRS 3. The additional items required under formats 2 and 4 are discussed in **9.102** to **9.112** below.

9.19 The 'standard' headings required by the Act and FRS 3 are set out below. Headings with Arabic numbers are those headings set out in the format in Sch 4.

1. **Turnover**(2)
2. Cost of sales(2)
3. Gross profit or loss(2)
4. Distribution costs(2)
5. Administrative expenses(2)
6. Other operating income(2)
   Operating profit or loss(2), (4)
   Profits or losses on the sale or termination of an operation(1)
   Costs of a fundamental reorganisation or restructuring(1)
   Profits or losses on the disposal of fixed assets(1)
7. Income from shares in group undertakings
8. Income from participating interests(3), (4)
9. Income from other fixed asset investments
10. Other interest receivable and similar income
11. Amounts written off investments
12. Interest payable and similar charges
    Profit or loss on ordinary activities before taxation
13. Tax on profit or loss on ordinary activities
14. Profit or loss on ordinary activities after taxation
15. Minority interests
16. Extraordinary income
17. Extraordinary charges
18. Extraordinary profit or loss
19. Tax on extraordinary profit or loss
20. Minority interests
21. Other taxes not shown under the above items
22. Profit or loss for the financial year
    Dividends
    Any amount set aside or proposed to be set aside to, or withdrawn or proposed to be withdrawn from, reserves

Headings in **bold** type should be shown on the face of the profit and loss account.

(1)   These headings should be analysed between continuing and discontinued operations on the face of the profit and loss account. Where practicable, this analysis should identify, either on the face of the profit and loss account or in the notes, the amounts arising in respect of acquisitions.

(2)   These headings should be analysed between continuing (with acquisitions specified separately) and discontinued operations. Of these headings, the analysis of turnover and operating profit must be on the face of the profit and loss account; the other headings may be analysed in the notes.

(3)   Where group financial statements are being prepared and the group has associated undertakings, the Act updates the format by requiring item 8 to be replaced by two items: 'Income from interests in associated undertakings' and 'Income from other participating interests'. Prior to FRS 9, a number of companies nevertheless recognised the results of associates in the profit and loss account immediately before the operating profit/loss line. FRS 9 contains provisions on where a reporting entity's share of its joint ventures' and associates' results should be included in the consolidated profit and loss account (see note (4) immediately following).

(4)   In consolidated financial statements, FRS 9 requires that the group's share of its joint ventures' and associates' operating profit be shown immediately after the group operating profit and before the FRS 3 paragraph 20 items. The group's share of its joint ventures' and associates' FRS 3 paragraph 20 items would be with, but shown separately from, the group's FRS 3 paragraph 20 items. This is discussed more fully in chapter 25.

9.20   The effect must be stated of any transactions that are exceptional by virtue of size or incidence though they fall within the ordinary activities of the company. [Sch 4: 57(3)] Such exceptional items are dealt with in **9.113** to **9.124** below.

9.21   All of the headings required by the Act in the profit and loss account formats have Arabic numerals and accordingly they may be combined on the face of the profit and loss account, with the subdivisions shown in the notes, if this combination facilitates the assessment of the profit or loss of the company. In practice, full advantage is taken of this flexibility and there is little uniformity of presentation, but the most common combinations of items under format 1 seem to be:

4, 5 and 6   Distribution costs, administrative expenses, and other operating income;

| 7, 8, 9 and 10 | Investment income; |
| 10 and 12 | Net interest receivable/(payable). |

Further, the directors are required to adapt the arrangement and headings 'in any case where the special nature of the company's business requires such adaptation'.

9.22 Many companies continue the practice followed prior to the enactment of the Companies Act 1981 whereby only key headings are shown on the face of the profit and loss account; the remaining items being given in the notes to the accounts. While this presentation complies with the wording of the Act, the spirit of the requirement seems to be that all main headings of income and expenditure should be included on the face of the profit and loss account, even if on an aggregated basis, so that the reader can readily appreciate the major factors which have contributed to the operating results for the period.

Turnover

9.23 All formats given in Sch 4 require the disclosure of turnover and FRS 3 requires that this item be shown on the face of the profit and loss account.

9.24 Turnover is defined by the Act [s262] as the amounts derived from the provision of goods and services falling within the company's ordinary activities after deduction of trade discounts, value added tax (VAT) and any other taxes based on amounts so derived.

9.25 Under this definition, the turnover of agents, such as insurance brokers, stockbrokers, and estate agents, consists of gross commissions receivable and not the total amounts billed to customers; the turnover of a market maker, on the other hand, consists of sales of investments; the turnover of a construction company would exclude the value of work done on speculative developments not sold at the year end. The treatment of turnover in respect of long-term contracts is discussed in **16.44** to **16.57** below.

9.26 In consolidated financial statements, turnover is total sales made by group undertakings to external customers. It should not include turnover of associates and joint ventures, nor should intra-group turnover be included. However, it should include turnover from the group to associates and to joint ventures. Eliminations of transactions with joint ventures and associates is considered in **25.101** and **25.102** below. FRS 9 requires the group's share of its joint ventures' turnover to be shown on the face of the profit and loss account but separately from the group turnover. There is no such requirement in respect of the group's share of its associates' turnover, although FRS 9 states that: 'Where it is helpful to give an indication of the size of the business as a whole, a total combining the investor's share of its associates' turnover with group turnover may be shown as a memorandum item in the profit and loss account but the investor's share of its associates' turnover should be clearly distinguished from group turnover'. See chapter 25 for a fuller discussion. The example below is an extract from one of the examples appended to FRS 9 under which the option to highlight the group's share of associates' turnover has not been taken up.

Example 9.26

Consolidated profit and loss account (extract)

	£ million	£ million
Turnover: group and share of joint ventures	320	
Less: share of joint ventures' turnover	(120)	
Group turnover		200
Cost of sales		(120)

9.27 Where turnover arises from sales to a related party, FRS 8 requires, *inter alia*, it to be disclosed if material and not covered by an exemption. See chapter 32 for a discussion of FRS 8's requirements.

9.28 The Act and SSAP 25 require disclosure of turnover and profits analysed by business and geographical segment. Full details of the disclosures required are discussed in chapter 20.

Cost of sales

9.29 The cost of sales will normally include the following elements of cost of ordinary activities:

(a) opening stocks and work in progress;

(b) direct materials and other external charges;

(c) direct labour (see **9.190** below in respect of ESOPs);

(d) fixed and variable production overheads, including depreciation or diminution in value of productive assets (see **9.200** to **9.215** below);

(e) amortisation (or impairment losses) of goodwill arising on the acquisition of a manufacturing business (see **9.216** to **9.222** below);

(f) research and development costs (to the extent to which they relate to production – see **9.225** below);

(g) variances from standard where a standard costing system is in use (see **16.35** below).

Less:

(a) own work capitalised;

(b) closing stocks and work in progress.

9.30 The practice of excluding production overheads from cost of sales is not permitted by the Act.

9.31 The elements of cost of sales identified above are appropriate for companies which manufacture or purchase for resale tangible products. It is also appropriate for companies which provide a service to include under this heading the costs of providing that service; the costs should normally be identified as those which are carried forward in work in progress if the related service has not been completed. Where costs cannot be identified reasonably easily with units of service provided, it may well be that format 2 is more appropriate to the needs of a service company.

Gross profit or loss

9.32 Under format 1, the gross profit or loss, being the difference between turnover and the cost of sales, should be shown as a separate item. The gross profit or loss can also be determined from format 3, but it need not be shown in the profit and loss account.

9.33 The manner in which expenditure is analysed in formats 2 and 4 generally prevents the determination of gross profit or loss, unless additional information beyond that required by the Act is given.

Distribution costs

9.34 Distribution costs should include all expenses related to the holding of goods for sale, selling costs and the transfer of goods to the customer, such as:

(a) sales salaries and commissions and related National Insurance (NI) and pension costs (see **9.190** below in respect of ESOPs);

(b) advertising, trade shows;

(c) warehousing costs of finished products;

(d) travelling and entertainment;

(e) outward transportation costs, including depreciation of vehicles;

(f)   rent, rates, insurance, utilities, depreciation (see **9.200** to **9.215** below) and maintenance of sales outlets;

(g)   cash discounts on sales;

(h)   amortisation (or impairment losses) of goodwill arising on the acquisition of a distribution business (see **9.216** to **9.222** below).

Administrative expenses

9.35   This category includes all other operating costs except those associated with the production and distribution of products and services and interest costs which are shown under separate headings. The following expenditure is normally included in administrative expenses:

(a)   salary costs of administrative personnel (e.g., accounting department, directors' salaries attributable to the general management of the company) and related NI and pension costs (see **9.190** below in respect of ESOPs);

(b)   rent, rates, insurance, utilities, depreciation (see **9.200** to **9.215** below) and maintenance of administration buildings;

(c)   professional fees;

(d)   research and development (to the extent that it is not appropriately classified as cost of sales – see **9.225** below);

(e)   bad debts;

(f)   amortisation (or impairment losses) of goodwill (see **9.216** to **9.222** below).

Amortisation of negative goodwill

9.36   Where the amortisation of negative goodwill is included in cost of sales, distribution costs or administrative expenses and the amounts of negative goodwill offsetting the expenses is material, it is necessary to analyse it separately on the face of the profit and loss account to avoid breaching the Act's requirement not to offset positive and negative items. See **9.216** to **9.222** below for a fuller discussion on goodwill amortisation.

Other operating income

9.37   'Other operating income' includes all other income derived from sources associated with the ordinary activities of the business, with the exception of income from investments and other interest receivable which should be shown under separate headings unless they are immaterial. Examples of other operating income include:

• royalties;

• commissions;

- canteen sales;

- rental income from surplus facilities;

- amortisation of negative goodwill (see **9.221** below).

9.38
> For many companies, the amount of other operating income will not be material and will be included as part of turnover or administrative expenses.

Operating profit or loss

9.39   In addition to the headings required by the Act, FRS 3 requires a sub-total entitled 'Operating profit'. In FRS 3, the ASB states that operating profit for non-financial entities is normally profit before income from shares in group undertakings (i.e., profit after all operating costs and income but before investment income and interest). [FRS 3(14)]

9.40   In some cases (e.g., investment holding companies), income from associated companies or other participating interests may be considered part of the operating profit. [FRS 3(39)] See also **9.61** and **25.77** below. In consolidated accounts FRS 9 requires the share of operating profit of joint ventures and associates to be shown immediately after group operating profit (see chapter 25). [FRS 9(21) and (29)]

Profits or losses on the sale or termination of an operation

9.41   FRS 3 does not identify which items should be included within 'profits or losses on the sale or termination of an operation'. However, the standard requires the operating results of a discontinued operation to be shown under each of the statutory format headings. Therefore, results from sold or terminated activities (whether or not meeting the definition of discontinued operations) up to the date of sale or termination do not form part of the profit or loss on sale or termination and should be included as part of the ordinary operating activities of the business. An example of a problem likely to be encountered is illustrated in the following example.

Example 9.41

A manufacturing and retail operation has been terminated. Certain stocks were sold at reduced prices, other stocks scrapped and fixed assets were sold off giving rise to a loss on disposal. Which, if any, of these losses should be included within 'profits or losses on the sale or termination of an operation'?

If losses on the scrapping or selling of stocks at reduced prices were part of the normal business of the entity (e.g., where stocks are perishable) then the losses could be included under the normal statutory headings (e.g., cost of sales) with additional disclosure being given if the losses are larger than normal. If the losses have arisen purely as a result of the termination, it does not seem inappropriate to include them within profits or losses on termination. Similar considerations apply to the disposal of fixed assets.

9.42 The wording of the FRS is vague in this area and thus it is important that reporting entities follow a sensible and consistent approach and give an appropriate level of disclosure.

9.43 This heading should also include provisions in respect of the sale or termination of an operation. Such provisions, which are covered in **9.164** to **9.180** below, should be disclosed on the face of the profit and loss account. In contrast to an actual profit or loss which excludes operating results, a provision for a loss on sale or termination of an operation *includes* expected operating losses from the balance sheet date to the date of sale or termination (see **9.168** below).

9.44 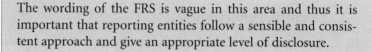 FRS 3 does not contain a definition of 'operation'. This adds to the difficulties in interpreting what should be included in this heading. Where a company operates, say, six retail stores, one in each of six major cities, the closure of one of the stores might constitute the termination of an operation. However, if the store were closed and the customers in that area were serviced by mail order from one of the other stores this might not constitute the termination of an operation; the answer might depend, in part, on the extent that the customer base is depleted. If another company operates six retail stores which sell goods manufactured by the company's four manufacturing plants, then the closure of one of the manufacturing plants would not constitute the termination of an operation if the other three plants continue to manufacture whatever the, now closed, fourth plant used to manufacture.

9.45 FRS 10 and FRS 2 require that the profit or loss on disposal of a previously acquired business should be determined by including the attributable amount of purchased goodwill where it has not previously been charged in the profit and loss account. FRS 10 paragraph 71(c)(ii) requires that where goodwill was eliminated against reserves as a matter of accounting policy in the past and the business with which the goodwill was acquired is now disposed of or closed, the amount of purchased goodwill included in the profit or loss calculation should be disclosed as a component of the profit or loss.

9.46 In requiring that the profit or loss on disposal of a previously acquired business should be determined by including the attributable amount of purchased goodwill where it has not previously been charged in the profit and loss account, FRS 10 has simply picked up the requirement that had been in UITF Abstract 3. However, the UITF believed that UITF Abstract 3 was being abused and so issued a document clarifying the application of UITF Abstracts. In this statement, the UITF emphasised that it is important to follow the spirit of UITF Abstracts. In particular, the UITF pointed out that UITF Abstract 3 requires the goodwill component to be included as part of the profit or loss on disposal and that where the item is presented as two components there should be, in addition, a single subtotal showing the profit or loss on disposal. The caption 'loss on sale of subsidiary' should not be used to describe an item that does not take account of related goodwill. Since the ASB's *Foreword to Accounting Standards* similarly calls for the spirit of standards to be followed, the guidance above applies equally to the rule in FRS 10.

9.47 FRS 10 paragraph 54 requires the profit or loss on each material disposal of a previously acquired business or business segment to be disclosed in financial statements. FRS 3 paragraph 15 requires that where a sale or termination has a material impact on a major business segment this should be disclosed and explained.

Profit/Loss on disposal of a stake in a subsidiary undertaking

9.48 When a company disposes of part of its stake in a subsidiary undertaking, but such that the stake that it retains still falls to be classified as a subsidiary undertaking, a profit or loss on disposal will arise. The calculation of profit or loss for the company's own accounts will be the difference between the proceeds received and the carrying value of the shares now sold. The calculation for the group accounts is set out in **24.134** et seq. below. In the company's own accounts, this will be a profit or loss on disposal of a fixed asset and should be recognised on the face of the profit and loss account as set out in **9.51** to **9.59** below. In the group accounts, the presentation is not so clear; since the group still has a subsidiary undertaking, it has not disposed of an operation; instead, it has bought in a minority interest. The reported operating profit is unaffected by the transaction since 100 per cent of the subsidiary's operating profit is included in the group operating profit regardless of whether the subsidiary is owned 100 per cent or less.

> Accordingly, it seems inappropriate to include the profit or loss on disposal before operating profit. The transaction is a disposal of a fixed asset in the company's own accounts and so it is a logical extension in this instance to recognise the profit or loss arising in the group accounts as an 'FRS 3 paragraph 20' item. If, as a result of the disposal, the undertaking ceases to be a subsidiary (e.g., it becomes an associate or a simple investment); or if a full disposal takes place, then the profit or loss arising in the group accounts will also fall as an 'FRS 3 paragraph 20' item (see extract **9.117** below).

Costs of a fundamental reorganisation or restructuring

9.49 Costs included under this heading should be restricted to those relating to a fundamental reorganisation or restructuring having a material effect on the nature and focus of operations. FRS 6[19] specifies that 'Merger expenses ... should be charged to the profit and loss account of the combined entity at the effective date of the merger, as reorganisation or restructuring expenses, in accordance with paragraph 20 of FRS 3 *Reporting financial performance*'. Given this specific reference in FRS 6, costs of a successful merger will generally be treated as FRS 3(20) items. However, costs of a failed merger or acquisition, or defence costs would normally be charged in arriving at operating profit (see extract **9.117** below).

9.50

> FRS 3 does not define what 'having a material effect on the nature and focus of operations' means in this context (it defines it in the context of a discontinued operation – see **9.155** and **9.156** below). However, it appears that the heading should cover only strategic restructurings where there is a consequent change in the customer base or end product/service provided to customers; normal ongoing reorganisation costs should be charged in arriving at operating profit.

Profits or losses on the disposal of fixed assets

9.51 This heading comprises profits or losses on the disposal of fixed assets, and certain provisions in respect of such items (see **9.208** to **9.212** below). However, such profits and losses are to be included under this heading only to the extent that they do not represent marginal adjustments to depreciation previously charged. [FRS 3(46)]

9.52

> The FRS does not specify the treatment of profits and losses that are such adjustments, but it is most appropriate to recognise them under the same statutory format heading as the normal depreciation charge.

9.53   A common situation encountered in practice is illustrated by the following example.

Example 9.53

Car hire companies regularly dispose of surplus vehicles and, prior to FRS 3, often included the gain or loss in operating profit. The depreciation of the vehicles is calculated to write them down to their estimated residual value over their estimated useful life. If the company regularly disposes of vehicles, then the disposal will not be exceptional by virtue of incidence. Any gain or loss will be an adjustment to depreciation previously charged, although if the gain or loss is material it might be considered exceptional by virtue of its size and thus will require separate disclosure, but within operating profit.

On the other hand, if the company disposed of its head office building that it had held for many years and the disposal gave rise to a material profit, principally due to inflation, then such a profit should be separately disclosed after operating profit.

Profit/Loss on disposal of revalued assets

9.54   FRS 3 has narrowed the options available for accounting for the disposal of assets by requiring the profit or loss on disposal of an asset to be accounted for in the profit and loss account by reference to the net carrying amount of the asset, whether carried at historical cost or at a valuation. [FRS 3(21) and (27)] Any past revaluation surpluses or deficits (representing temporary diminutions in value passed through the revaluation reserve) in the revaluation reserve relating to such an asset must be dealt with as a reserve transfer and cannot be taken through the face of the profit and loss account.

Example 9.54

Disposal of a building:

Original cost in 1988	£10 million
Revalued amount at the 30 June 1999 balance sheet date	£13 million
Net sales proceeds of sale on 30 April 2000	£14 million

Profit on disposal calculated in accordance with FRS 3:

	£ million
Net sales proceeds	14
Less: balance sheet carrying value	13
Profit on sale	1

Profit on disposal calculated based on original cost:

	£ million
Net sales proceeds	14
Less: original cost	10
Profit on sale	4

9.55 It has been suggested that an adverse impact on the profit and loss account can be avoided by changing valuation policy prior to disposal and restating the asset to be sold at its depreciated historical cost. This is obviously a device to avoid the provision of FRS 3. Changing policies (and thus using a prior period adjustment) to change back to the historical cost basis cannot be justified unless all revalued assets are restated at depreciated historical cost. If the asset being sold is the only asset carried at valuation, the company could not argue a change in policy, as the move would be seen only to be circumventing FRS 3's rules and not actually achieving a change in policy. Also, it is not acceptable to carry out a 'revaluation' back to depreciated historical cost, as this would not be a legitimate revaluation and thus such a transfer from the revaluation reserve is prohibited by Sch 4 para 34.

9.56 It has also been suggested that the asset to be sold could be revalued (at sale proceeds in most cases) immediately prior to the sale. The FRS does not appear to prevent such a revaluation and the revaluation surplus or deficit being taken to the revaluation reserve, but in the case of a deficit only to the extent that the revaluation reserve contains earlier revaluation surpluses in respect of that asset. This would result in the profit and loss account showing neither profit nor loss in those circumstances where the asset is sold for more than its depreciated historical cost.

9.57 This treatment is not inconsistent with the principle set out in FRS 3 that individual gains or losses should be recognised only once, either in the profit and loss account or in the statement of total recognised gains and losses.

9.58 Although the ASB proposed such 'deathbed' revaluations in FRED 17, this proposal was heavily criticised and has been omitted from FRS 15. The ASB has deferred consideration of this proposal to its review of FRS 3. Until such a proposal is incorporated in a standard, it would normally be unwise to adopt the above treatment, unless it can be demonstrated that a policy of continuous revaluation has been in place for some time and followed consistently. It may be possible to demonstrate this in the case of, for example, investment properties which have been revalued at every accounting date and where gains/losses on disposal have consistently been taken to the statement of total recognised gains and losses. However, a listed company not normally revaluing its investment properties for its interim statement could be challenged if, during the year of sale, it revalued a property and thus avoided taking a loss to its profit and loss account.

Tax on the profit of revalued assets

9.59   A company that has revalued an asset without providing for deferred tax may find that on disposal the tax arising is out of all proportion to the gain recognised in the profit and loss account because a proportion of the tax relates to the gains previously recorded in the revaluation reserve. In extreme cases there may even be an accounting loss but a taxable gain. FRS 16(6) (effective for periods ending on or after 23 March 2000 – see chapter 27) requires that where a gain or loss is or has been recognised in the statement of total recognised gains and losses the attributable tax should also be recognised directly in the statement of total recognised gains and losses (see **27.44** to **27.48** below).

Example 9.59

	£'000
Profit on disposal calculated in accordance with FRS 3	100
Profit on disposal calculated based on depreciated original cost	1,000
Revaluation reserve in respect of asset	900
Tax on profit on disposal	200

In these circumstances, the tax of £200,000 could reasonably be apportioned: £20,000 to profit and loss account and £180,000 to the statement of total recognised gains and losses, i.e., in the same proportion as the gains themselves.

Income from shares in group undertakings

9.60   'Income from shares in group undertakings' should, in individual company accounts, include dividends received and receivable from subsidiary undertakings and fellow subsidiaries where a company holds shares in a group undertaking. In a consolidated profit and loss account, the heading should include dividends received and receivable in respect of unconsolidated subsidiaries, other than those dealt with under the equity method.

Income from participating interests

9.61   Participating interests are defined in **23.37** to **23.40** below and further discussed in chapter 25. If a company prepares its own profit and loss account, the amount to be shown under this heading is the amount of dividends received and receivable from participating interests, such as associated companies.

9.62   In any consolidated profit and loss account, joint ventures and associates would be accounted for by the equity method and chapter 25 explains how FRS 9 requires the group's share of its joint ventures' and associates' results to be recognised in the consolidated profit and loss account. See also **9.19**(3) and (4) above.

9.63

> It will usually be the case that participating interests are associated companies or joint ventures as defined by FRS 9 and it is likely that the requirements of FRS 9 will continue to be used instead of the one line 'Income from participating interests'.

Income from other fixed asset investments

9.64   Any amounts of income and interest from group undertakings included under this heading must be shown separately. [Sch 4: Formats (note 15)]

Other interest receivable and similar income

9.65   Any amounts of income and interest from group undertakings included under this heading must be shown separately. [Sch 4: Formats (note 15)]

Amounts written off investments

9.66

> In general, the amount to be included under this heading should normally be that portion of an impairment loss which reduces the carrying value of an investment below its cost; any write-off of amounts previously credited to the revaluation reserve in respect of the same investment, and which have not been otherwise eliminated from that reserve (e.g., by capitalisation of the reserve), should be deducted from that reserve and disclosed in the statement of total recognised gains and losses. Accounting for such impairment losses is dealt with more fully in **14.237** et seq, **15.29** et seq and **16.80** et seq below.

9.67   Where a provision to write down an investment below cost is subsequently written back, the relevant credit should be shown under this heading and identified separately.

9.68   A distinction should be noted between the presentation of impairment losses incurred on operating fixed assets and investments. As described in **9.66** above, impairment losses on investments are recognised below operating profit. However, impairment losses incurred on operating fixed assets are presented in the same profit and loss heading as the related depreciation and are thus included in arriving at operating profit. See **9.207** below.

Interest payable and similar charges

9.69   'Interest payable and similar charges' should include:

(a) finance cost of borrowings (which includes interest, the amortisation of discount or premium on the borrowings and the amortisation of issue costs);

(b) imputed interest element of finance leases and similar obligations;

(c) commitment fees in connection with obtaining credit facilities; and

(d) the unwinding of a discount related to a long-term provision,

less: finance cost of borrowings capitalised.

The amounts payable to group undertakings should be shown separately [Sch 4: Formats (note 15)] and other amounts analysed between interest and similar charges on:
[Sch 4: 53]

• bank loans and overdrafts; and

• loans of any other kind made to the company.

Example 9.69

Interest payable and similar charges

	1998	1997
	£'000	£'000
Group company loans	390	125
Bank loans and overdrafts	1,445	974
Other loans	202	200
	2,037	1,299

The investor's share of its joint ventures' and associates' interest should be shown separately from the amounts for the group. The share of joint ventures' interest should be shown separately from the share of associates' interest unless individually they are not material.

When calculating the finance costs of convertible debt, it should be assumed that the debt will never be converted. [FRS 4(25)] Finance costs are dealt with further in chapter 17 (see specifically **17.33** to **17.45** below).

9.70 Gains and losses arising on the repurchase or early settlement of debt should be disclosed in the profit and loss account as separate items within or adjacent to 'interest payable and similar charges'. [FRS 4(64)]

9.71 Where provisions have been discounted to present value, the passage of time will result in the unwinding of the discount. Each year, this amount should be included within or shown adjacent to 'interest payable and other similar charges' on the face of the profit and loss account or in a note. [FRS 12(48)] See chapter 17 (see specifically **17.243** to **17.245** below) for a discussion of calculation of the annual unwinding.

9.72   Under certain circumstances, the finance cost of borrowings to finance the production of an asset may be added to the cost of production rather than be written off as an expense and this subject is discussed in detail in **14.15** to **14.18** below. FRS 4 requires the amount of finance cost capitalised in the year to be charged in the profit and loss account with a simultaneous transfer out of the profit and loss account which is separately disclosed. [FRS 4(76)] The Act requires disclosure of the fact that interest has been capitalised into the cost of an asset and of the amount of interest so included. [Sch 4: 26(2)] Note that the Act refers to interest while FRS 4 refers to finance costs which may include amortised issue costs or redemption premium. Listed companies are required to disclose the amount of interest capitalised during the year and the amount and treatment of any related tax relief. Although there is no legal requirement to do so, it is recommended that entities not subject to the Listing Rules should provide similar information, rather than limiting their disclosure to that required by FRS 4. One convenient method of meeting the requirement is to include it in the note regarding interest payable, as in the following example.

Example 9.72

Interest payable and similar charges

	2000 £'000	1999 £'000
Interest on bank loans and overdrafts	7,200	6,400
Other interest	2,500	2,200
	9,700	8,600
Less: amount of interest added to cost of properties under development	1,430	544
	8,270	8,056

The tax relief obtained in the year in respect of interest costs capitalised has reduced the tax charge by £500,500 (1999 – £190,400). No provision has been made for the potential tax liability which might arise in respect of the capitalised interest element of properties if these properties are sold, since it is anticipated that any tax liability will be rolled over into a replacement property.

Profit or loss on ordinary activities before taxation

9.73   The Act requires the profit and loss account to show the company's profit or loss on ordinary activities before taxation. [Sch 4: 3(6)] Unlike the items listed in the profit and loss account formats, this figure may not be relegated to the notes. It will represent the balance of all items mentioned in the previous sections which relate to the ordinary activities of the company. It should include exceptional items, but exclude taxation and extraordinary items.

Tax on profit or loss on ordinary activities

9.74   The presentation and disclosure of taxation in the profit and loss account are discussed in chapter 27 (see specifically **27.4** to **27.10** below).

9.75   Any special circumstances that affect the overall tax charge or credit for the period, or that may affect those of future periods, should be disclosed in a note to the profit and loss account and the individual effects quantified. [FRS 3(23)] This would include any special circumstances relating to tax attributable to the three exceptional items discussed in **9.41** to **9.59** above. This is largely a restatement of the requirements of the Act. [Sch 4: 54(2)] The effects of a fundamental change in the basis of taxation should be shown in the tax charge or credit for the period and disclosed separately on the face of the profit and loss account. [FRS 3(23)]

9.76   For companies adopting FRS 16 (mandatory for periods ending on or after 23 March 2000) it is a requirement that both incoming and outgoing dividends, interest and other amounts receivable/payable should be recognised at an amount that includes withholding tax but excludes any other taxes (e.g., attributable tax credits, not payable wholly on behalf of the recipient (see **27.54** to **27.72** below). These requirements differ from those of SSAP 8 which required dividends from UK companies to be 'grossed up'.

Profit or loss on ordinary activities after taxation

9.77   All the formats require separate disclosure of 'Profit or loss on ordinary activities after taxation'.

9.78   If there are no extraordinary items or minority interests in both the current and preceding financial years, this amount will be the same as 'Profit or loss for the financial year' (see **9.89** below). In such cases, it is suggested that it is unnecessary to show both headings; the amount might be disclosed as 'Profit or loss for the financial year'.

Minority interests

9.79   The Act requires the minority's share of the profit or loss on ordinary activities to be included in consolidated accounts under formats 1 and 2 as a separate item after 'Profit or loss on ordinary activities after taxation'. [Sch 4A: 17(2)] The amount should be analysed between equity and non-equity minority interests. [FRS 4(60)] The finance costs relating to non-equity minority interests should be calculated in the same manner as those for non-equity shares (see **18.64** to **18.73** below). [FRS 4(51)]

Extraordinary items

9.80   All the formats set out in the Act require separate disclosure on the face of the profit and loss account or in the notes to the accounts of:

- extraordinary income;
- extraordinary charges;
- tax on extraordinary profit or loss;
- minority interests.

Formats 1 and 2 require a further subtotal for 'Extraordinary profit or loss' (stated after extraordinary income and extraordinary charges, but before tax and minority interests).

9.81   Extraordinary items are not defined in the Act, but are defined in the EU Fourth Directive on company law as 'income and charges that arise otherwise than in the course of the company's ordinary activities'. The definition contained in FRS 3 is:
[FRS 3(6)]

> 'Material items possessing a high degree of abnormality which arise from events or transactions that fall outside the ordinary activities of the reporting entity and which are not expected to recur. They do not include exceptional items nor do they include prior period items merely because they relate to a prior period.'

9.82   The definition in FRS 3 is thus apparently more restrictive than that in the Directive, since it introduces the additional test concerning the expectation of recurrence. One of the implicit intentions of FRS 3 is that there should be a severe decrease in the number of items reported as extraordinary.

9.83   The critical distinction between an extraordinary item and one that is included within ordinary activities is whether the item derives from transactions or other events that fall outside the ordinary activities of the reporting entity or from transactions or events that fall within those activities. One of the ways in which FRS 3 reduced the incidence of extraordinary items was by giving a wide definition to the term 'ordinary activities'. It defines ordinary activities as: [FRS 3(2)]

> 'Any activities which are undertaken by a reporting entity as part of its business and such related activities in which the reporting entity engages in furtherance of, incidental to, or arising from, these activities. Ordinary activities include the effects on the reporting entity of any event in the various environments in which it operates, including the political, regulatory, economic and geographical environments, irrespective of the frequency or unusual nature of the events.'

9.84   The ASB was unable to envisage any extraordinary items and accordingly FRS 3 does not give any examples; the extraordinary item has effectively been abolished. In practice, most items previously shown as extraordinary are now disclosed as exceptional.

Disclosure of extraordinary items

9.85   In the unlikely event that a reporting entity has an extraordinary item to report, any extraordinary profit or loss should be shown separately on the face of the profit and loss account. The amount of each extraordinary item should be shown individually either on the face of the profit and loss account or in a note and an adequate description of each extraordinary item should be given to enable its nature to be understood. The tax on the extraordinary profit and loss and any minority interest should be shown separately either in a note or on the face of the profit and loss account. [FRS 3(22)]

9.86   The group's share of any extraordinary items of its associated undertakings or joint ventures should be included with the group's extraordinary items to the extent that the group's share of the items involved would be classified as extraordinary in the context of the financial statements of the group. Where that share is material in the context of the group's results, it should be disclosed separately from other extraordinary items. [FRS 9(27)]

9.87   The tax on extraordinary items should be determined by comparing the notional tax charge, calculated as if the extraordinary items and any items of the type listed in FRS 3 paragraph 20 (see **9.119** below) did not exist, and the actual charge. The difference is apportioned between extraordinary items and the items of the type listed in FRS 3 paragraph 20 in relation to their respective amounts, unless a more appropriate basis of apportionment is available. If a more appropriate basis is adopted, the method of apportionment should be disclosed. [FRS 3(24)]

9.88   Adjustments in subsequent periods to the tax on extraordinary items should be shown as an extraordinary item. [FRS 3(22)]

Profit or loss for the financial year

9.89   All the formats require separate disclosure of 'Profit or loss for the financial year'.

9.90   If there are no extraordinary items or minority interests in both the current and preceding financial years, this amount will be the same as 'Profit on ordinary activities after taxation' (see **9.77** above). In such cases, it is suggested that it is unnecessary to show both headings; the amount might be disclosed as 'Profit or loss for the financial year'.

Dividends

9.91   The aggregate amount of dividends paid and proposed must be shown separately in the profit and loss account. [Sch 4: 3(7)(b)] Dividends should be deducted from 'Profit or loss for the financial year'. Dividends should be expressed in the profit and loss account at the actual cash amount paid (or proposed to be paid) to the shareholders. It is best practice also to disclose the dividend rate per share, so that individual shareholders will be able to calculate their dividend entitlement. Following the amendment of UITF 13 by FRS 14, dividend income on shares held by an ESOP trust is now excluded in arriving at profit before tax. Instead, it is deducted from the aggregate of dividends paid and proposed. If material, the deduction should be disclosed on the face of the profit and loss account (see example **9.94** below); otherwise, it should be disclosed in a note. [FRS 14 (81)] (See **28.103** below for further discussion on accounting for ESOPs.)

9.92   It is not uncommon for the amount of a company's proposed final dividend to be determined after the year end. It is unclear whether the length of the period extending from the balance sheet date to the date the amount of the dividend is determined is limited in law. See **33.79** to **33.81** below for a discussion on when a parent company can recognise in its profit and loss account a dividend receivable from a subsidiary undertaking.

9.93   Where the finance costs for non-equity shares are not equal to the dividends, the difference should be accounted for in the profit and loss account as an appropriation of profits. [FRS 4 (44)]

9.94   Because the Act requires the aggregate amount of dividends paid and proposed to be shown separately in the profit and loss account, any difference between the finance costs and the amount of dividends paid and proposed should also be shown separately on the face of the profit and loss account.

Example 9.94

Extract from the profit and loss account

	Note	2000 £'000	1999 £'000
Profit for the financial year		1,256	910
Dividends paid and proposed (including dividends on non-equity shares)	10	(300)	(250)
Equity dividends paid and payable to ESOP trust	12	20	15
Difference between non-equity finance costs and the related dividends	14	80	(50)
Profit retained for the financial year		1,056	625

9.95   The aggregate amount of dividends proposed should also be shown on the face of the profit and loss account unless it is shown in a note to the accounts. [Sch 4: 3(7)(c)]

9.96   In addition, FRS 4 paragraph 59 requires disclosure of:

(a)   aggregate dividends for each class of share, including the total amount in respect of each of:

   (i)   dividends on equity shares;
   (ii)   participating dividends; and
   (iii)   other dividends on non-equity shares;

(b)   any other appropriation of profit in respect of non-equity shares.

Where this information is not given on the face of the profit and loss account, FRS 4 paragraph 59 requires the relevant caption on the face of the profit and loss account to make it clear where amounts relating to non-equity shares are included.

9.97   If a company gives its shareholders the option of receiving shares in lieu of a cash dividend (i.e., a scrip dividend), the dividend should be expressed in the profit and loss account at the amount of the cash alternative (i.e., the amount of cash that the company would pay to its shareholders if none of them opted to take the scrip dividend). [FRS 4(48)] Accounting for scrip dividends is dealt with in **18.123** to **18.133** below.

9.98

> This treatment should be adopted even if the scrip dividend is enhanced (i.e., the scrip dividend is worth more than the cash alternative) to make it more attractive to shareholders.

9.99 Listed companies are required to disclose particulars of any arrangement under which a shareholder has waived or agreed to waive any dividends. This requirement applies to waivers of future dividends, as well as to waivers of dividends payable during the past financial year. Waivers of minor amounts (less than one per cent of the total value of any dividend) may be disregarded, provided some payment has been made on each share of the relevant class during the relevant calendar year. [Listing Rules 12.43(e)]

Amount set aside to or withdrawn from reserves

9.100 Any amount set aside or proposed to be set aside to, or withdrawn or proposed to be withdrawn from, reserves should be disclosed separately on the face of the profit and loss account. [Sch 4: 3(7)(a)] It is widespread practice to conclude the profit and loss account with a figure derived by deducting the amount of dividends paid and proposed and any other appropriation under FRS 4 from the profit or loss for the financial year. This figure is commonly described by a title such as 'Retained profit' or 'Transferred to/from reserves'.

9.101

> Other transfers, such as transfers from revaluation reserve to distributable profits, often are not disclosed on the face of the profit and loss account but are dealt with in the statement of movements on reserves. This treatment may not comply with a strict interpretation of the requirement that every profit and loss account must show separately as an additional item any amount set aside to, or withdrawn from, reserves. However, it could be argued that a transfer between two reserves is not an amount set aside to, or withdrawn from, reserves.

Additional disclosures under other formats

Introduction

9.102 Formats 2 and 4 require more detailed disclosure of certain profit and loss items. The headings required under these formats which have not been dealt with in the preceding sections are:

(a) changes in stocks of finished goods and work in progress;

(b) own work capitalised;

(c) raw materials and consumables;

(d) other external charges;

(e) staff costs;

(f) depreciation and other amounts written off tangible and intangible fixed assets;

(g) exceptional amounts written off current assets;

(h) other operating charges.

Changes in stocks of finished goods and work in progress

9.103 The difference between opening and closing stocks of finished goods and work in progress is to be shown under this heading. Finished goods would include bought-in components, as well as items manufactured by the company. Progress payments, which would be deducted from the valuation of stocks for balance sheet purposes, are not to be taken into account. Since this heading requires a clear distinction between stocks of finished goods and work in progress on the one hand and stocks of purchased items (such as raw materials and consumables) on the other, it seems that it will only be used by manufacturing companies.

Own work capitalised

9.104 This caption will include the value of direct materials and labour and appropriate overhead costs capitalised in connection with the company's own construction of tangible fixed assets. The cost elements shown under the other profit and loss headings will be shown at their gross amount.

Raw materials and consumables

9.105 The difference between the opening and closing stocks of raw materials and consumables will be deducted from or added to the total cost of purchases of these items in arriving at the amount to be shown under this heading. Purchases of components should be included as forming part of raw materials. Companies in the retail trade which adopt this format should use more appropriate wording for this heading, e.g., 'Goods for resale'.

Other external charges and other operating charges

9.106 No guidance is provided as to what items should be included in 'Other external charges' as opposed to 'Other operating charges'. Since it is linked in the formats with raw materials and consumables, it is suggested that as a minimum 'Other external charges' should include those production costs from external sources which are not included as raw materials and consumables, e.g., subcontractors' costs, equipment rentals and appropriate production overheads. 'Other operating charges' would then include selling and administrative costs which were not shown under the other headings. However, it is impossible to refute the argument that any charge which is neither a staff cost nor depreciation must be an external charge; on this basis, everything that was not specifically included elsewhere would be included in 'Other external charges' and 'Other operating charges' would become redundant.

9.107 It is unlikely that any authoritative interpretation of the division between these two headings will ever be attempted and companies should adopt whatever reasonable division is most convenient to them. The important point is that whatever division is adopted must be adhered to consistently from year to year.

Staff costs

9.108 The information required to be shown under this heading is explained in **9.186** to **9.189** below. The formats indicate that staff costs be divided between wages and salaries paid or payable, social security costs and other pension costs. It is probably clearer to show staff costs as one amount in the profit and loss account and the required details in the notes.

Depreciation and other amounts written off fixed assets

9.109 The information required to be shown under this heading is explained in **9.200** to **9.202** below.

Exceptional amounts written off current assets

9.110 This heading seems to be intended to record necessary reductions from the cost of current assets to arrive at net realisable value, e.g., amounts written off debtors. However, it seems equally possible to deal with these items in some other way: amounts written off debtors could be included in 'Other operating charges' and reductions in net realisable value of stocks under either 'Changes in stocks of finished goods and work in progress' or 'Raw materials and consumables' as appropriate.

Operating profit under formats 3 and 4

9.111 FRS 3 does not give any guidance as to the degree of analysis required in profit and loss accounts which do not enable the inclusion of the heading 'operating profit'.

9.112

> In such a situation, it is suggested that disclosure should still be made equivalent to that which would have been given in a profit and loss account which included the heading 'operating profit'. For formats 3 and 4, this would normally require an analysis of all charges above 'amounts written off investments' and of all income above 'income from shares in group undertakings'.

Exceptional items

Definition

9.113 FRS 3(5) defines exceptional items as:

> 'Material items which derive from events or transactions that fall within the ordinary activities of the reporting entity and which individually or, if of a similar type, in aggregate, need to be disclosed by virtue of their size or incidence if the financial statements are to give a true and fair view.'

Disclosure

9.114 Exceptional items fall within the ordinary activities of a reporting entity and, therefore, it follows that they should be charged or credited in arriving at the 'profit or loss on ordinary activities'. They should be included under the natural statutory format heading to which they relate, unless they fall within one of the three categories of 'non-operating exceptional items' listed in FRS 3(20) (profits or losses on the sale or termination of an operation, costs of a fundamental reorganisation or restructuring and exceptional profits or losses on the disposal of fixed assets) (see **9.119** below). FRS 3(46) states that exceptional items 'should not be aggregated on the face of the profit and loss account under one heading of exceptional items ....'

9.115 Unlike some of the forms of presentation often adopted under the superseded SSAP 6, the FRS 3 approach does not conflict with the requirement of the Act to give the full amount of income and expenditure in respect of each of the statutory headings.

9.116 The amount of each exceptional item, either individually or as an aggregate of items of a similar type, should be disclosed separately by way of note, or on the face of the profit and loss account if that degree of prominence is necessary to give a true and fair view. The items should also be attributed to continuing or discontinued operations as appropriate and an adequate description of each item should be given to enable its nature to be understood. [FRS 3(19)] In showing the amount of each exceptional item, individual items or groups of items should not be combined if separately they relate to continuing and to discontinued operations. [FRS 3(47)]

9.117 Where an exceptional item is shown separately on the face of the profit and loss account, it could be shown in one of the following ways:

Example 9.117.1

	Note	2000 £'000	1999 £'000
Cost of sales (including in 2000 an exceptional loss on a major contract of £8,600,000)	x	114,740	86,900

Example 9.117.2

	Note	2000 £'000	2000 £'000	1999 £'000	1999 £'000
Cost of sales					
Exceptional loss on a major contract	x	8,600		–	
Other cost of sales		106,140		86,900	
Total cost of sales			114,740		86,900

A growing practice, certainly among listed companies, has been to present a columnar profit and loss account with columns disclosing, for each format and FRS 3 heading, the results before exceptional items, exceptional items and total results.

Extract 9.117

Cannons Group Plc

Year ended 31 December 1999

Extract from Consolidated Profit and Loss Account

	Note	Before Exceptional Items £'000	1999 Exceptional Items (note 4) £'000	Total £'000	1998 Total £'000
Turnover					
Existing operations		55,747		55,747	40,698
Acquisitions		13,397		13,397	
Continuing operations		69,144		69,144	40,698
Discontinued operations		–		–	26,449
Total Turnover	1	69,144		69,144	67,147
Cost of sales		(5,253)		(5,253)	(5,444)
Gross Profit		63,891		63,891	(61,703)
Net operating expenses		(47,855)	(2,669)	(50,524)	(47,633)

Operating Profit				
Existing operations		12,570	(1,949)	10,621	9,492
Acquisitions		3,466	(720)	2,746	–
Continuing operations		16,036	(2,669)	13,367	9,492
Discontinued operations		–	–	–	4,578
Total Operating Profit	1	16,036	(2,669)	13,367	14,070
Income from interest in associated undertaking		–	–	–	36
Profit/(loss) on disposal of discontinued operations	4	–	505	505	(12,337)
Profit on Ordinary Activities Before Taxation		16,036	(2,164)	13,872	1,769
Net interest payable and other similar charges	5	(2,448)	–	(2,448)	(1,262)
Profit on Ordinary Activities Before Taxation	2	13,588	(2,164)	11,424	507

Extract from notes to the Accounts

Exceptional Items
(a)   Operating profit is arrived at after charging the following exceptional items:

	1999 £'000	1998 £'000
Board restructuring	(519)	–
Bonus payments on successful Group restructuring	(561)	–
Pinnacle Group restructuring	(720)	–
Aborted merger costs	(869)	–
	(2,669)	–

Board restructuring costs of £519,000 were incurred in the period. On 24 February 1999 it was announced that Mr Chamberlain had resigned from the Board and that Mr Iren's role as Chairman would become non-executive from 13 April 1999.

The Group paid Directors' bonuses totalling £561,000 following the successful disposal of its non Health & Fitness activities.

On 16 June 1999 the Company acquired Pinnacle. Exceptional costs of £720,000 have been incurred in rebranding Pinnacle to Cannons, aligning employment benefit terms and restructuring Pinnacle.

In April 1999 the Company announced that talks concerning the proposed merger of the Company with the health & fitness division of the First Leisure Corporation PLC ("FLC") had been terminated by joint agreement of all parties. Aborted merger costs incurred by the Company amounted to £374,000. The Company also received a claim from FLC for an alleged breach of the terms of an exclusivity agreement between FLC and the Company. Including legal expenses, this claim was settled for £495,000.

> (b) Profit before tax is arrived at after crediting/(charging) the following exceptional items:
>
> | | 1999 £'000 | 1998 £'000 |
> |---|---|---|
> | Disposal of other discontinued activities | 261 | (5,514) |
> | Disposal of Vardon Attractions Ltd | | |
> | Related goodwill previously written off to reserves | – | (6005) |
> | Provision for loss or disposal | 818 | (818) |
> | Actual loss on disposal | (574) | – |
> | Exceptional gain/(loss) on discontinued operations | 505 | (12,337) |
>
> The Company completed the disposal of Vardon Bingo Ltd in 1997. During the year it received £140,000 of deferred consideration. In addition the Group received £121,000 of deferred consideration relating to the earlier disposal of an Attractions business.
>
> The Group completed the disposal of Vardon Attractions Ltd on 18 January 1999. The transaction realised a loss of £574,000.

9.118   Any reference to profit or loss, including or excluding exceptional items, should include an explanation of the relevance of their inclusion or exclusion in the context of considering the results of a period or assessing maintainable earnings. [FRS 3(46)]

Non-operating exceptional items

9.119   As stated above, most exceptional items must now be recognised within the appropriate statutory heading. The three exceptions, all of which are required to be shown separately on the face of the profit and loss account after operating profit and before interest, and included under the appropriate heading of continuing or discontinued operations, are:
[FRS 3(20)]

(a)   profits or losses on the sale or termination of an operation;

(b)   costs of a fundamental reorganisation or restructuring having a material effect on the nature and focus of the reporting entity's operations; and

(c)   profits or losses on the disposal of fixed assets.

These are dealt with more fully in **9.41** to **9.59** above.

9.120   Any tax or minority interest related to these three items should be shown in a note to the profit and loss account. As a minimum, aggregate figures should be given for the related tax and for the related minority interest. If the impact differs for the various categories, further information should be given.

9.121 The tax on the above three non-operating exceptional items should be determined by comparing the notional tax charge, calculated as if the non-operating exceptional items and any extraordinary items did not exist, and the actual charge. The difference is apportioned between the three non-operating exceptional items and any extraordinary items in relation to their respective amounts, unless a more appropriate basis of apportionment is available. If a more appropriate basis is adopted, the method of apportionment should be disclosed. [FRS 3(24)]

9.122 Sufficient information should be disclosed to enable the informed reader of the financial statements to be in a position to make his own evaluation of how each item should be treated and to make any necessary adjustment to earnings per share for his own purposes if the treatment of any item is different from the one which he prefers.

9.123 In addition to the three items listed in **9.119** above, there could be other 'non-operating exceptional items'. These other items would be exceptional items where the natural statutory format heading is below operating profit, such as 'Tax on profit or loss on ordinary activities'. Such exceptional items should be dealt with in accordance with FRS 3(19) (see **9.116** above).

Examples of exceptional items

9.124 SSAP 6 included a list of items which may have been exceptional and a list of those which may have been extraordinary. Under FRS 3, these are all likely to be exceptional items. The lists included:

(a) abnormal charges for bad debts, stock obsolescence or losses on long-term contracts;

(b) redundancy and reorganisation costs unrelated to the discontinuance of a business segment;

(c) previously capitalised intangible assets written off other than as part of a process of amortisation;

(d) the expropriation of assets;

(e) surpluses arising on settlement of insurance claims;

(f) amounts received in respect of insurance claims for consequential loss of profits;

(g) change in basis of taxation, or significant change in government fiscal policy.

In addition, UITF Abstract 20 and UITF Abstract 21 point out that year 2000 software costs and expenditure incurred in preparing for the changeover to the euro might require disclosure as exceptional items.

Analysis of continuing and discontinued operations

Introduction

9.125 The headings in the profit and loss account set out below should be analysed between continuing and discontinued activities:

    (a) each of the statutory format headings between turnover and operating profit, inclusive;

    (b) profits or losses on the sale or termination of an operation;

    (c) costs of a fundamental reorganisation or restructuring;

    (d) profits or losses on the disposal of fixed assets.

In addition, for each of the statutory format headings between turnover and operating profit, inclusive, acquisitions as a component of continuing activities should be disclosed separately. [FRS 3(14)] Where practicable, the analysis of the three FRS 3 paragraph 20 items should identify, either on the face of the profit and loss account or in the notes, the amounts arising in respect of acquisitions.

9.126 As a minimum, turnover and operating profit for the current period should be analysed between continuing operations, acquisitions (as a component of continuing operations) and discontinued operations on the face of the profit and loss account, with the analysis for the remaining headings between turnover and operating profit being given in a note. [FRS 3(14)]

9.127 An analysis between continuing and discontinued operations is required on the face of the profit and loss account for those items required to be disclosed by FRS 3 paragraph 20 (see **9.119** above). Where practicable, the analysis of these items should identify amounts arising in respect of acquisitions either on the face of the profit and loss account or in the notes. [FRS 3(39)]

9.128 In circumstances where there are no discontinued operations or acquisitions to disclose (most years in the case of smaller companies), all that is necessary is to indicate on the face of the profit and loss account that turnover and operating profit all derive from continuing operations. This can be done as shown in the example or by way of a statement at the foot of the profit and loss account.

Example 9.128

	2000	1999
	£	£
Turnover – continuing operations	125,645	122,323
Operating profit – continuing operations	25,687	16,194

Alternatively, giving no analysis implies that there are only continuing operations and this could be confirmed in a note to the financial statements.

9.129 The regular sale and replacement of material assets, undertaken as part of a reporting entity's routine maintenance of its portfolio of assets, should not be classified as discontinuances or acquisitions. [FRS 3(42)]

Finance costs

9.130 Non-financial entities normally strike operating profit before interest payable or receivable. If this is the case, FRS 3 does not require an analysis of interest between continuing and discontinued activities. Should such entities voluntarily disclose such an analysis, they should also state the method and assumptions used in making the allocations. [FRS 3(14)] These details are required, as funding policy may be made on an entity-wide basis and is likely to require a considerable degree of subjectivity in allocating interest between operations. [FRS 3(40)]

Tax

9.131 If entities voluntarily disclose an analysis of tax between continuing and discontinued activities, they should state the method and assumptions used in making the allocations. [FRS 3(14)]

Continuing operations

9.132 Continuing operations are operations that are not discontinued (see **9.141** to **9.148** below). [FRS 3(4)]

Acquisitions

9.133 Acquisitions are operations that are acquired in the period other than those which are also discontinued in the same period. [FRS 3(3) and (14)]

9.134 The aggregate results of acquisitions should be disclosed separately as a component of continuing operations. [FRS 3(14)] If an acquisition has a material impact on a major business segment, this should be disclosed and explained. [FRS 3(15)]

9.135 Where it is not practicable to determine the post-acquisition results of an acquired operation, an indication should be given of the contribution of the acquisition to the turnover and operating profit. If an indication of the contribution of the acquisition to the results of the period cannot be given, this fact and the reason should be explained. [FRS 3(16)]

9.136   In most cases, acquisitions will be made part way through the acquiring entity's financial year and, accordingly, the results will only be reflected for part of the period. In such cases, FRS 3 suggests that it may be helpful to users for the results of acquisitions for the first full financial year for which they are a part of the reporting entity to be disclosed in the notes to the financial statements. [FRS 3(38)]

9.137   The disclosure of post-acquisition results required by FRS 3 is in addition to the disclosure of pre-acquisition results required by the Act and FRS 6. FRS 6's disclosure requirements in respect of pre-acquisition results are covered in **23.142** to **23.159** below.

9.138   Where, in financial statements for the previous year, a reporting entity discloses the post-acquisition results of its acquisitions in accordance with FRS 3, it will not include the analysis in the comparative column in its current year's financial statements. This is because, in order to be an acquisition under FRS 3, the operations must be *acquired in the period*. The exception to not including acquisitions in the comparative column is explained in **9.139** below.

9.139   FRS 3 assumes that acquisitions are accounted for using the acquisition method. It does not discuss the disclosure required in the profit and loss account when merger accounting is used. Obviously, it will be meaningless to restrict the analysis to post-acquisition results, as the profit and loss account would include the full results of the acquired entity for both the current and prior period. In such cases, best practice would be to disclose the results of the acquired operations under the 'acquisitions' heading for both the current period and the prior period. Such disclosures would complement those required by FRS 6 *Acquisitions and mergers*.

9.140   FRS 6 paragraph 28 extends the FRS 3 disclosures on acquisitions and requires them to be given for each material acquisition, where there is more than one in an accounting period. This added analysis can be in the notes to the financial statements rather than on the face of the profit and loss account (see **23.150** below).

Discontinued operations

9.141   Various criteria must be met if an operation is to be treated as discontinued. Operations may only be treated as discontinued if they are sold or terminated and meet all of the following conditions: [FRS 3(4)]

(a)   the sale or termination is completed either in the period or before the earlier of three months after the commencement of the subsequent period and the date on which the financial statements are approved;

(b)   if a termination, the former activities have ceased permanently;

(c)   the sale or termination has a material effect on the nature and focus of the reporting entity's operations and represents a material reduction in its operating facilities resulting either from its withdrawal from a particular market (whether class of business or geographical) or from a material reduction in turnover in the reporting entity's continuing markets;

(d)   the assets, liabilities, results of operations and activities are clearly distinguishable, physically, operationally and for financial reporting purposes.

In addition, the sale or termination must have resulted from a strategic decision by the reporting entity to withdraw from a market or to curtail materially its presence in a continuing market. [FRS 3(43)]

9.142   Operations that fail to meet all these criteria must be treated as continuing even if they have ceased by the time the financial statements are finalised or if it is public knowledge that they are in the process of being sold or terminated. Thus, it may not be possible to treat operations with long decommissioning periods as discontinued until the decommissioning is completed. In recognition of this, the standard suggests the results of discontinuing operations (i.e., operations in the process of being sold or terminated, but which do not meet FRS 3's definition of discontinued) are disclosed by way of note. [FRS 3(41)]

9.143   In addition, there will be some operations that, even though they are sold or terminated during the accounting period, fail to meet the definition of 'discontinued operations'. This might be, for example, because the sale or termination does not have a material effect on the nature and focus of the operations; the profit or loss arising might have a material impact on the reported profit figure for the year, but the loss of the operations will not have a material effect on the nature and focus of the operations. In such instances, these operations will always be reported as 'continuing operations'. Entities may nevertheless wish to highlight such results in the notes to the financial statements.

9.144   If a sale or termination has a material impact on a major business segment, this should be disclosed and explained. [FRS 3(15)]

9.145   The question of whether an operation falls to be treated as discontinued is rather subjective. See **9.149** to **9.160** below, which cover a number of the more subjective tests.

9.146 Only income and costs directly related to discontinued operations should be included under the heading of discontinued operations. [FRS 3(17)] The costs of reorganising or restructuring continuing operations as a result of a discontinuance form part of continuing operations, but may be disclosed separately as exceptional.

9.147

FRS 3 does not make clear what course should be followed if the results of a discontinued operation are identifiable separately but include certain income or cost allocations from other group companies (e.g., central overheads allocated across autonomous divisions). Two possibilities are to:

(a) include only those results of the operation that are identifiable separately under discontinued operations, with the allocated costs being classified as continuing;

(b) include the results of the operation, including all or part of the allocated costs, under discontinued operations.

9.148 One of the aims of the analysis between continuing and discontinued operations is to help users in deciding on the extent to which past results are useful in helping to assess potential future results. Thus, the latter approach noted above would appear to be acceptable only if the sale or termination was expected to lead to a real reduction in the costs to be allocated in future periods and the portion of allocated costs analysed as discontinued was a reasonable estimate of that saving. If the aggregate of the allocated costs was expected to remain unchanged despite the sale or termination of the operation, the latter approach would give a misleading basis from which to assess potential future results and would breach the requirement that only costs directly related to discontinued operations should be included under the heading of discontinued operations. Accordingly, that approach should not be followed.

Interpretation of the definition of discontinued operations

Date of sale or termination

9.149

Although the date of sale or termination forms part of the definition of discontinued activities, the standard does not define that date.

9.150 There are five important dates connected with the sale or termination of an operation:

(a) the date that management make the decision;

(b)   the date when they are 'committed' to the decision;

(c)   the date of completing the sale or termination and relinquishing control;

(d)   the period end to which the financial statements are being prepared; and

(e)   the date of approving those financial statements.

Whether or not an operation can be classified as discontinued depends upon the relationship of the last three dates. The date on which the reporting entity decided to sell or terminate or on which it became demonstrably committed are not relevant to this classification problem but are relevant to whether or not provisions may be made (see **9.164** to **9.177** below).

9.151   Defining the date of disposal as the date on which the entity relinquishes its control over the discontinued operation is consistent with the guidance on the date of disposal of a subsidiary in FRS 2. This is not inconsistent with FRS 3 paragraph 18 (the requirements relating to the making of provisions), which implies that the date of disposal and the date on which a legally binding agreement are made may be different.

9.152   Since a terminated operation cannot be classified as discontinued unless all the former activities have ceased permanently, it is reasonable to assume that the date of termination is the date at which those activities ceased and all the associated assets and liabilities have been disposed of. This is discussed further in **9.154** below.

9.153   The example below illustrates this test applied to the sale of an operation post-year end that was not anticipated at the year end.

Example 9.153

A group with a 31 December 1999 year end receives an offer for a subsidiary in January 2000 that is too good to refuse. The sale was completed in March 2000. The group had no intention of selling the subsidiary at the year end. How should this be treated in the 1999 financial statements which are approved in April 2000?

If the sale has a material effect on the nature and focus of operations and represents a material reduction in operating facilities or turnover, then the results of the operation should be analysed as discontinued, as the sale took place within three months of the year end.

'Ceased permanently' in the context of a termination

9.154 A common problem likely to be encountered is where a company has wound down an operation but still retains the building or factory in which the operation was carried out. Whether such an operation has ceased permanently will depend on the fungibility of the building or factory. If it can be used for a variety of purposes, particularly if the company had used it for differing purposes in the past, then, if the ownership of the factory can be separated from the operation in question, the operation can be treated as discontinued. If the property was designed for a specific purpose and could only be used for that purpose and the operation has effectively been 'mothballed', then the operation is not discontinued. Similarly, if the building is going to be sold off as a direct consequence of ceasing the activity, the activity cannot be treated as discontinued until the property is sold. However, this might result in not being able to treat the activity as discontinued until such time that there are no results, other than the profit or loss on disposal of the property, to be classified as discontinued. Accordingly, it is necessary to consider very carefully whether the building can be used only for one purpose.

'Material effect on the nature and focus' of a company's operations

9.155 FRS 3 does not require that an operation must be a separate business segment, for the purposes of SSAP 25, if it is to be classified as discontinued. The FRS illustrates the requirement for a change in nature and focus by using the example of a hotel company which switches from the lower end of the market to a chain of luxury hotels. By the same justification, a company which ran hotels in both ends of the market, but which decided to sell the 'budget' chain, would be able to treat it as a discontinued operation even though both chains were 'bundled' under one category in the segmental analysis required by SSAP 25.

9.156 The example below illustrates a situation which is not a material change in nature and focus even though there has been a substantial change in the way in which the company concerned carries out its businesses.

Example 9.156

A company in the business of manufacturing and selling widgets carried out an assessment of its manufacturing process and came to the conclusion that it would be more cost-effective in the long term to subcontract manufacturing. The company ceased manufacturing widgets prior to the year end, but continued to sell to the same customer base using supplies from subcontractors. Does this constitute a material effect on the nature and focus of operations?

The fact that a company ceases manufacturing goods does not necessarily mean that there has been a change in the nature and focus of operations. The ultimate purpose of producing the widgets was the generation of profits by selling them to customers. In this example, these activities are still continuing, but the company has found it more cost-effective to have a third party manufacture the goods in future. In this case, the cessation of the manufacturing activities does not constitute a discontinued activity. Also, as there has not been a material effect on the nature and focus of operations, the costs would not fall to be classified as cost of a fundamental reorganisation or restructuring and would thus be charged in arriving at operating profit (see **9.49** above).

Material reduction in operating facilities

9.157 A material reduction in operating facilities results either from a company withdrawing from a particular market (whether class of business or geographical) or from a material reduction in turnover in its continuing markets.

9.158 The example below illustrates this test applied to the merger of operations supplying the same market.

Example 9.158

In the year, a company closed one of its two plant hire depots. The staff were all made redundant but the assets were transferred to the other depot and it is anticipated that there will be no overall reduction in the customer base. Is there a material reduction in operating facilities?

The closure is not expected to lead to a material reduction in turnover in the continuing market and thus does not meet the conditions of paragraph 4c of FRS 3. The operations of the closed depot are not, therefore, discontinued. If the costs are material, they may need to be separately disclosed. They do not appear to fall into one of the categories listed in paragraph 20 of FRS 3 (see **9.119** above), as there is no material effect on the nature and focus of the reporting entity's operations. Therefore, the costs would be charged in arriving at operating profit.

Severe downsizing

9.159 A sale or termination resulting from a decision to curtail materially (downsize) a presence in a continuing market may meet the definition of a discontinued activity. However, the downsizing must have a material effect on the aggregate turnover of the reporting entity and, of course, all the conditions noted in **9.141** above would need to be met. Among other things, this would require that the assets, financial results and activities of the curtailed part of the operation were clearly distinguishable from those of the ongoing 'rump' and from other operations. Classification as discontinued would be precluded if it was necessary to make allocations of income or expenses to a material extent. [FRS 3(44)]

Example 9.159

Dilution of participating interest

A parent company sells 30 per cent of its holding in a previously wholly owned electronics subsidiary. The subsidiary has a material effect on the nature and focus of the group's operations and is the only part of the group involved in the electronics industry. Does this constitute a material reduction in turnover in continuing markets?

There has been no material effect on the nature and focus of the group's operations, no withdrawal from a particular market and no material reduction in turnover in continuing markets. What has decreased is the group's share of the subsidiary's post-tax profits. Even if the transaction had not failed the nature and focus test, it would be difficult to argue that the assets, results and activities of the 30 per cent owned by the minority interest would be distinguishable physically, operationally and for financial reporting purposes from the 70 per cent held by group.

If the dilution had been such that the group's interest was now simply an investment, say, by selling 90 per cent and withdrawing from the management of the company, then the transaction may meet the definition of a discontinued activity. The group would no longer have an electronics division, therefore the nature and focus of operations would have changed and there would have been a withdrawal from a particular market. There would also be a distinguishability of assets, liabilities and results, as instead of bringing in a share of the net assets or results by consolidation or equity accounting, the group would simply show the investment in shares and dividends received.

If the dilution had been such that the group's electronics subsidiary became an associate, the situation is more complicated. If, for example, the group had effectively merged its electronics interests with similar electronics interests of another party such that the group now has a 50 per cent interest in a business twice the size of its original business, then the dilution probably does not constitute a discontinued activity because the overall contribution to the group's results has

---

> not changed significantly. However, if the dilution resulted from a third party taking new shares in the electronics business, then there may have been a severe downsizing in the group's interest, say, down to 30 per cent, with a reduced board representation. In such a case, the results of the former subsidiary should be treated as discontinued.

Strategic decision

9.160 Although not mentioned in the definition in FRS 3 paragraph 4, FRS 3 paragraph 43 states that 'to be classified as discontinued a sale or termination should have resulted from a strategic decision by the reporting entity either to withdraw from a particular market ... or to curtail materially its presence in a continuing market'. This implies that if an entity ceases an activity for external reasons then it should not be classified as discontinued. For example, downsizing in a market because demand for the product has reduced because of the expansion of a competitor would not enable the activity to be classified as discontinued.

Comparative figures

9.161 The same level of analysis between continuing and discontinued activities is required for the comparative figures as is required for the current period. However, the analysis of the comparative figures is not required on the face of the profit and loss account. [FRS 3(30) and (64)]

9.162 Analysis of the comparative figures should be based upon the status of an operation in the financial statements of the period under review. If an operation has been classified as discontinued in the current period, its comparative results must also be classified as discontinued even if they were shown as continuing in the financial statements of the previous period. Thus, the comparative figures for discontinued operations will include, in addition to operations discontinued in the previous period, those operations discontinued in the current period which had previously been analysed as continuing. [FRS 3(30) and (64)]

9.163 The requirement to restate comparatives based upon the status of an operation in the period under review will, of course, result in there never being any amount for 'acquisitions' in the comparative figures (unless merger accounting is used – see **9.139** above). Thus, the comparative figures appearing under continuing may include the figures that were shown under 'acquisitions', as a subdivision of continuing, in the previous period.

Consequences of a decision to sell or terminate an operation

Circumstances in which provisions may be made

9.164 Under FRS 3, provision should be made for the losses arising as a consequence of a decision to sell or terminate an operation only where the entity is 'demonstrably committed' to the sale or termination. This requirement applies irrespective of whether the operation falls to be treated as discontinued in the current, or any, period. [FRS 3(18)]

9.165 FRS 12 deals with provisions generally. However, where another FRS or SSAP deals with a more specific type of provision, an entity applies that standard instead of FRS 12 [FRS 12(8)]. In this case, the rules in FRS 3 related to provisions arising as a consequence of a decision to sell or terminate an operation should be applied rather than those set out in FRS 12. The distinction between FRS 3 and FRS 12 is discussed further in **17.194** to **17.196** below.

9.166 The term 'demonstrably committed' is not defined by the FRS, but it does indicate that, for a termination, evidence is given by:

(a)   a detailed formal termination plan from which withdrawal is not realistic (see **17.204** to **17.210** below as regards guidance on a similar requirement in FRS 12);

(b)   public announcement of plans;

(c)   commencement of implementation; or

(d)   other circumstances obliging the entity to complete the termination.

Similarly, for a sale, evidence is given by a binding sale agreement entered into before the year end or other circumstances obliging the entity to complete the sale. [FRS 3(18)]

9.167 FRS 3 paragraph 45 refers to a post balance sheet contract providing additional evidence of asset values *and commitments* at the balance sheet date. The reference to commitments may be construed as providing evidence that the entity is demonstrably committed at the balance sheet date. However, the remainder of FRS 3 paragraph 45, together with FRS 12 paragraph 83, require a binding sale agreement to be entered into by the year end.

The nature of the provisions

9.168 In the event that an entity is 'demonstrably committed', provision should be made for:

(a) the direct costs of the sale or termination; and

(b) any operating losses of the operation up to the date of termination or sale;

(c) *less* the aggregate profit, if any, to be recognised in the profit and loss account from the future profits of the operation. [FRS 3(18)]

9.169 In accordance with normal practice, irrespective of whether an entity is 'demonstrably committed' to the sale or termination, any impairments in asset values should be recorded. [FRS 3(45)]

9.170

It should be noted that FRS 12 forbids provisions for future operating losses. However, as noted in **9.165** above, the rules in FRS 3 related to provisions arising as a consequence of a decision to sell or terminate an operation override the FRS 12 rules which apply to most other provisions.

9.171 The nature of the provisions required are illustrated in the following table.

Nature of provision	Demonstrably committed to sale or termination	Not demonstrably committed to sale or termination
Direct costs of the sale or termination	Provision required	Do not provide
Operating loss of the operation up to the date of termination or sale	Provision required	Do not provide
Impairment in asset values	Provision required	Provision required

9.172 The examples below illustrate the provisions required where a company is not demonstrably committed.

Example 9.172.1

Company A's board has taken a decision (on 25 March 2000) to close an operation that is loss making. At the company's year end (31 March 2000), it is estimated that it will take one year to close the operation and that it will lose a further £2.5 million over that time. Fixed assets with a book value of £1.8 million are expected to have a recoverable amount not exceeding £1.2 million as a result of the closure

---

decision. No impairment in fixed assets has previously been recognised. Implementation of the decision had not commenced at the balance sheet date and no public announcements had been made. What costs should be provided for at 31 March 2000?

The company is clearly not demonstrably committed to the termination at 31 March 2000 and therefore the only provision that should be made is the £600,000 to reduce fixed assets to their recoverable amount. The operation is not discontinued and thus the provisions should be classified as continuing operations.

Example 9.172.2

A group with a 31 March 2000 year end receives an offer for a subsidiary in April 2000 that is too good to refuse. The sale was completed in June 2000. The group had no intention of selling the subsidiary at the year end. How should this be treated in the 31 March 2000 accounts?

As the group was not demonstrably committed to the sale at the year end, it should not provide for operating losses up to the date of sale or for any direct costs of the sale; any provision would be restricted to a write-down of assets for a permanent diminution in value. However, the operation may be treated as discontinued if the requirements of **9.141** above are met.

9.173

It is not clear whether goodwill previously eliminated against reserves should be taken into account when determining the provision to be made on the sale or termination of an operation. Best practice appears to be to take account of such goodwill as soon as the entity becomes 'demonstrably committed' to the sale or termination (see also **9.45** above).

Example 9.173

ABC Ltd has taken a decision to sell one of its subsidiary undertakings, B Ltd. At the year end (31 March 2000), ABC Ltd was demonstrably committed to the sale; completion is expected to take place on 30 April 2000 and B Ltd is expected to break even in April 2000. The loss on sale is expected to be £1 million before taking into account goodwill of £5 million that was eliminated against reserves when B Ltd was originally acquired.

Taking into account the goodwill, a provision of £6 million is required in the 31 March 2000 financial statements.

9.174 In the above example, if the goodwill is not taken into account in the 2000 financial statements then a provision of £1 million would be made in the 2000 financial statements, with a further loss of £5 million reflected in the 2001 financial statements. This approach is not recommended, as the 2000 financial statements could reasonably be expected to take account of all losses expected to be incurred in respect of the disposal.

9.175 Similar considerations apply to negative goodwill.

Example 9.175

ABC Ltd has taken a decision to sell one of its subsidiary undertakings, B Ltd. At the year end (31 March 2000), ABC Ltd was demonstrably committed to the sale; completion is expected to take place on 30 April 2000 and B Ltd is expected to break even in April 2000. The loss on sale is expected to be £1 million before taking into account negative goodwill of £0.6 million that was credited to a capital reserve when B Ltd was originally acquired.

Taking into account this negative goodwill, a provision of £0.4 million is required in the 2000 financial statements.

9.176 In the above example, if the negative goodwill is not taken into account in the 2000 financial statements then the 2000 financial statements will show a provision for a loss of £1 million and the 2001 financial statements will show a net profit of £0.4 million. Thus, the 2000 financial statements will contain a provision for a loss that will not be incurred.

9.177 If provisions which are created for the costs of a discontinuance subsequently prove to be inaccurate or incomplete, any necessary material adjustment in a subsequent period should also be reflected as a 'non-operating exceptional item' in the profit and loss account.

Disclosure of provisions

9.178 The creation or release of the provisions and the actual profits and losses as they occur should each be analysed as continuing or discontinued, depending upon the classification of the operation in the period for which financial statements are being prepared. [FRS 3(18)] For example, if an entity with a December year end was demonstrably committed to terminating an operation in 1999 but did not cease all activities until June 2000, the operation would be classified as continuing in the financial statements for 1999 and as discontinued in 2000, where the comparatives would be reclassified accordingly.

9.179 The utilisation of any provisions made in respect of the sale or termination of an operation should be analysed as necessary between the operating loss and the loss on sale or termination arising in respect of the discontinuing operation. The utilisation should be disclosed on the face of the profit and loss account immediately below the relevant items. [FRS 3(18)]

9.180   The making and release of provisions is illustrated in the example below.

Example 9.180

Provision of £30 million was made in 1999 for operating losses up to the date of disposal (£10 million) and for the loss on disposal (£20 million). This provision is shown separately on the face of the profit and loss account in the 1999 comparative figures as an exceptional item. In 2000, the trading losses are recognised under the statutory headings and the £10 million provision reversed on the face of the profit and loss account. Similarly, the actual loss on disposal of £17 million is recognised as an exceptional item and the related provision of £20 million released on the face of the profit and loss account.

The relevant extract from the 2000 profit and loss account is as follows:

	2000 £ million	2000 £ million	1999 £ million	1999 £ million
Operating profit				
Continuing operations	56		62	
Discontinued operations	(15)		(10)	
Less release of provision made in 1999	10		–	
Total operating profit		51		52
Exceptional items				
Provision for operations to be discontinued	–		(30)	
Loss on sale of discontinued operations	(17)		–	
Less release of provision made in 1999	20		–	
Total exceptional items		3		(30)

Directors' remuneration, pensions, compensation payments and payments to third parties

9.181   The Act and the Listing Rules include requirements to make disclosures on directors' remuneration in the notes to the accounts. These rules are dealt with in chapter 8.

Other supplementary profit and loss information

Employee information

Number of employees

9.182   The total average number of employees in the financial year and a division of this total by categories determined by the directors having regard to the manner in which the company's activities are organised should be disclosed. [Sch 4: 56(1)]

9.183   The average number of employees is derived by dividing the sum of the number of employees employed under contracts of service in each month by the number of months in the financial year. [Sch 4: 56(2) and (3)]

9.184   The term 'under contracts of service' is not defined, but does not appear to be restricted to those employees who have a written service contract. It seems appropriate that all employees, other than occasional casual workers, should be presumed as being employed under contracts of service. However, a director who acts purely in a non-executive capacity is not employed under a contract of service for this purpose. It should be noted that employees to be included are not restricted to those who are employed in the UK.

9.185   The directors have considerable flexibility as to how they divide employees into categories, e.g., by function (production, selling and distribution, administration), by activity (drilling and exploration, chemicals, textiles), by job description (managers and supervisors, factory workers, clerical staff, salesmen, researchers).

Staff costs

9.186   Disclosure is required of the following costs in respect of all employees who are taken into account in determining the number of employees in **9.183** above:
[Sch 4: 56(4)]

(a)   wages and salaries paid and payable;

(b)   social security costs incurred by the company;

(c)   other pension costs.

Under formats 2 and 4, this information is to be shown separately in the profit and loss account (see **9.102** and **9.108** above).

9.187 Wages and salaries should include bonuses and other incentive payments, whether payable under contract or not, and the emoluments of directors (other than non-executive directors). Redundancy payments should be excluded, as they do not constitute wages or salaries, but they should be disclosed separately if the amount is material.

9.188 The costs of post-retirement benefits other than pensions, if material, could be included as a separate category.

9.189 The charge to the profit and loss account under UITF Abstract 17 *Employee share schemes* should be included in 'wages and salaries' (see **9.190** to **9.199** below).

Employee share schemes

9.190 UITF Abstract 17 requires the amount recognised in the profit and loss account in respect of employee share schemes (whether bonus or option schemes) to be based on the fair value of the shares at the date of award, being the date of conditional grant of shares or rights to shares. The minimum amount will be the difference between: [UITF 17(13(c))]

(a) EITHER the fair value of the shares at the date of award OR the book value of shares purchased at fair value and held by an employee share ownership plan (ESOP) trust which are available for the award; AND

(b) the amount of any consideration participants are required to pay for the shares.

The fair value will not be revised to reflect subsequent movements in the value of shares, nor will it be adjusted in respect of any conditions requiring the participants to retain the shares after the performance criteria have been satisfied. The manner in which the costs of ESOP trusts are dealt with in the profit and loss account should be disclosed. [UITF 13(9(b))]

The UITF concluded that SAYE and similar types of schemes should be outside the scope of the Abstract (see **9.199** below).

9.191 In UITF Information Sheet 26, the UITF explained that it had discussed the application of UITF Abstract 17 where employees of a company are given the opportunity on the occasion of the initial listing of the company to subscribe for shares at a discount to the float price payable by public investors. The UITF Information Sheet explains that the UITF agreed that

> UITF Abstract 17 applied in this situation; consequently, the discount should be treated as a charge in the profit and loss account.

9.192 UITF Abstract 13 (see **28.103** below) deals with the profit and loss charge to be recognised in the sponsoring company in respect of the cost of shares held by an ESOP trust. UITF Abstract 17 extends these rules to require measurement of all share awards to be based on fair value. For companies where the award is via an ESOP trust which subscribes for shares at nominal value, it will result in an increased profit and loss charge based on the fair value of shares at the date of conditional grant rather than just cost to the ESOP trust. Where the ESOP trust acquires shares from the market the UITF 17 charge continues to be based on the cost to the ESOP.

9.193 The timing of the charge is:

(a) in the case of an annual bonus – the year to which the bonus relates; [UITF 17(13(a))]

(b) in the case of long-term incentive schemes – spread over the period to which the performance criteria relate; [UITF 17(13(a))]

(c) where no performance criteria exist and the award is clearly unrelated to past performance – spread over the period from the date of award to the date of unconditional entitlement to shares. [UITF 17(14)]

Where share awards are conditional upon continued employment, the cost is not normally spread over this further period, unless there is a clear intention to reward services provided in this period (e.g., see **9.193**(c) above). [UITF 17(13(d))]

9.194 In the case of long-term incentive schemes, the charge expensed over initial periods of performance will be based on a reasonable estimate of the extent to which the performance criteria are expected to be met. That amount would be charged to the profit and loss account on a straight-line basis unless another basis more fairly reflects the services rendered. Adjustments for changes to the estimate, whether debits or credits, will be made to the subsequent profit and loss charge. [UITF 17(13(d))]

9.195 There are three possibilities as regards the other side of the double entry:

(a) where new shares are to be issued, the other half of the entry is reported in the reconciliation of movements in shareholders' funds, not in the statement of total recognised gains and losses.

[UITF 17(16)] It is appropriate to present this as 'shares to be issued' within the other reserves statutory heading in the balance sheet (see example 1 in **9.196** below);

(b) to the extent that the accrual is covered by shares held in an ESOP trust (see chapter 28), the other side of the entry will be against those shares shown in the balance sheet as 'own shares' (see examples 2 and 4 in **9.196** below);

(c) where it is intended to buy shares in the market, or it is undecided whether new shares are to be issued or new shares bought in the market, (a) above should be followed until the shares are acquired then the charge should be adjusted in line with approach (b) (see examples 3 and 5 in **9.196** below).

9.196 The following examples are reproduced from the appendix to UITF Abstract 17.

Example 9.196

Background for examples 1 to 5

Scheme participants receive a conditional long-term investment plan (L-TIP) award of up to 1,000 shares (with a nominal value of 10p each) on 1 January 1997, when the market price of the shares is £5. The maximum number of shares will be transferred to participants after three years, provided various performance targets are fully met. A lesser number of shares will be transferred if the targets are only partially met. Participants make no contribution for any shares transferred to them.

When the accounts for the year ended 31 December 1997 are being finalised, it is considered that 50 per cent of the maximum number of shares is likely to be awarded.

This estimate was reassessed at 80 per cent of the 1998 accounts. At the end of the three-year period, 75 per cent of the maximum number of shares was awarded and these were transferred on 1 January 2000. The market price of the shares at that date, whether higher or lower than £5, has no relevance for the purpose of accounting required by the Abstract.

Example 1

750 new shares issued on 1 January 2000, when the share price was £8.

By 31 December 1997, the company would accrue one-third of 1,000 x £5 x 50%, i.e., £833.

By 31 December 1998, the company would accrue two-thirds of 1,000 x £5 x 80%, i.e., £2,667.

By 31 December 1999, the company would accrue 750 x £5, i.e., £3,750.

In the balance sheet, the amount accrued would be included within shareholders' funds. On issue of the shares on 1 January 2000, the total amount accrued of £3,750 would be allocated between share capital (£75) and reserves other than share premium account (£3,675). As shares cannot be issued at a discount, it is assumed that an ESOP has paid cash equal to the par value of the shares.

Example 2

1,000 shares acquired on 1 January 1997 are held in an ESOP at a cost of £5,000 until 750 shares transferred to participants on 1 January 2000. The remaining 250 shares continue to be held in the ESOP.

The accounting is as for Example 1 above, except that in the balance sheet the shares will be shown as 'own shares' within fixed assets in accordance with UITF Abstract 13, with the accrual reflecting a diminution in value of those shares.

Example 3

1,000 shares acquired on 30 June 1998 at a cost of £6,000 and held in an ESOP until 750 shares transferred to participants on 1 January 2000.

By 31 December 1997, the company would accrue £833 (as Example 1).

By 31 December 1998, the company would accrue two-thirds of £6,000 x 80%, i.e., £3,200.

By 31 December 1999, the company would accrue 750 x £6, i.e., £4,500.

N.B. The profit and loss account charge is higher than in Example 1 because the shares were acquired at a cost higher than their value at the time of the initial award.

Example 4

Shares already held in an ESOP at 1 January 1997 at a cost of £4,000.

The accounting would be as Example 2, but based on a cost of £4 each rather than £5.

Example 5

750 shares acquired on 31 December 1999 at a cost of £5,250.

The accounting for 1997 and 1998 would be as Example 1.

By 31 December 1999, the company would accrue £5,250.

9.197   The UITF has received legal advice suggesting that the services of employees do not normally form part of the legal consideration received for the issue of shares. On this basis, at the date the shares are issued, any difference between the cash received for the shares (subscribed by the ESOP of the employee) and the fair value at the date of award will not be taken to the share premium account but to some other reserve – which could be the profit and loss reserve.

Example 9.197

Extension of example 1 in 9.196

Scheme participants receive 750 shares the fair value of which at the date of grant was £5 per share. As noted above, the charge to P&L over the 3 years is £3,750 which is first credited to 'shares to be issued'. On issue of the shares on 1 January 2000, the following journal is required assuming that the ESOP has paid cash equal to the par value of the shares:

Shares to be issued	3,750	
Share capital		75
Another reserve – which could be P&L reserve		3,675

If the ESOP subscribed an amount in excess of the 10p nominal value, say £1 a share, the following journal is required:

Shares to be issued	3,750	
Share capital		75
Share premium		675
Another reserve – which could be P&L reserve		3,000

9.198   There are a number of areas not addressed by the abstract:

(a)   What happens if the shares held by an ESOP have been written down to recoverable amount, being the contribution payable by the employee on exercise, but the option lapses unexercised? The shares should be restated to original cost – unwinding the cumulative UITF 17 charge back through the face of the profit and loss account – with disclosure of the effect. However, the shares should not be stated at more than market value. If the option lapsed because it was out of the money there will be a charge to profit and loss as the shares are written down from the exercise price to market value.

(b)   How should shares that have been acquired from the market at different times and prices be allocated to outstanding options in order to compute the cost? The lower the carrying value of the shares applied, the lower the UITF 17 charge to profit and loss. Thus different allocation methods will give rise to differing profit and loss charges and different carrying values in respect of unallocated shares. For accounting purposes, a policy should be adopted and applied consistently. Similar considerations to those applying to valuation of stock apply (see **16.34** below) so that FIFO or an average basis, where shares are being 'turned over' on a regular basis, is most appropriate.

9.199 The UITF concluded that SAYE and similar types of schemes should be outside the scope of the Abstract. It defines such schemes as those under which 'participation is offered on similar terms to all or substantially all employees of the issuer and any of its subsidiary undertakings whose employees are eligible to participate in the scheme (providing that all or substantially all employees are not directors of the issuer)'. Much attention has been focused on the wording of this exemption; in particular, on how widely it could be interpreted. In response, Sir David Tweedie, Chairman of the ASB and the UITF, issued a statement warning against creative interpretations of UITF Abstract 17 and urging preparers and auditors to act in the spirit of the Abstract; the spirit of the exemption being to exempt SAYE, and their overseas equivalents, schemes. The exemption was not intended to apply to profit-sharing and similar employee remuneration arrangements. The full text of Sir David's statement is set out below:

'It has become apparent that some creative advisers are, or may be, seeking to interpret Abstract 17 more broadly than the UITF intended when the Abstract was drafted. The point at issue concerns paragraph 17 which states that "This Abstract need not be applied in accounting for an employees' share scheme under which participation is offered on similar terms to all or substantially all employees of the issuer and any of its subsidiary undertakings whose employees are eligible to participate in the scheme (providing that all or substantially all employees are not directors of the issuer)". (This is very similar wording to that used in The Stock Exchange Yellow Book[1] in connection with the exemption of schemes from the requirement for prior approval by shareholders.)

As indicated in earlier explanatory paragraphs of the Abstract (particularly paragraphs 2 and 12), this exemption was principally intended to apply to SAYE-type schemes (including equivalent overseas schemes), about which there was much debate during the development of the Abstract. The UITF did not intend the exemption to apply to schemes that clearly involved employee remuneration, such as approved profit-sharing schemes under the Income and Corporation Taxes Act 1988 (where the established practice is for a charge to be made to the profit and loss account).

The ASB is very mindful of the frequently expressed wish that the number of accounting rules should be kept to a minimum. I hope therefore that it will not be necessary for the UITF to issue supplementary rules to elaborate on Abstract 17, which, read as a whole, is clear as to the intended limits of the exemption. The UK accounting community has a choice; does it want the UITF and the ASB to produce a detailed cookbook of rules for every possible situation or, as I hope, can we rely on preparers and auditors to act in the spirit of the pronouncements? I would remind all concerned of the ASB's Foreword to UITF Abstracts which states that "it is important when applying UITF Abstracts to be guided by the spirit and reasoning behind them ... set out in the individual UITF Abstracts .... Abstracts are intended to be as concise as the nature of a particular topic allows rather than detailed rules dealing with every conceivable circumstance". I very much hope that we can continue to rely on the support of the financial community and the accounting profession to ensure that the ASB and UITF are not driven to the issue of a proliferation of Abstracts. The choice lies in their hands.'

Note 1 Now issued as the Listing Rules of the UK Listing Authority.

Depreciation

9.200 Under formats 1 and 3, depreciation does not appear as a separate item in the profit and loss account, but the amount of any provisions for depreciation should be disclosed in a note to the accounts. [Sch 4: 18 and 19] Under formats 2 and 4, this amount is shown as a separate item on the face of the profit and loss account.

9.201 FRS 15 requires that the depreciation charge in the profit and loss account be based on the carrying amount of the asset in the balance sheet, whether at historical cost or revalued amount. Where depreciation is based on revalued amounts, the Act [Sch 4: 32(3)] permits the amount of depreciation shown on the face of the profit and loss account under formats 2 and 4 or in the notes to the accounts under formats 1 and 3 to be based on historical cost, but when this is done the additional depreciation on the revaluation surplus must also be shown either on the face of the profit and loss account or in the notes to the accounts. **This provision merely affects the way in which the depreciation charge is disclosed, not the amount charged in the profit and loss account**. No part of the depreciation charge is permitted to be set directly against reserves.

9.202 Depreciation is dealt with further in chapter 14.

Provisions for diminution in value of fixed assets

9.203 The following must be disclosed separately in the profit and loss account or in the notes to the accounts:
[Sch 4: 19]

(a) any provision made for diminution in value of a fixed asset investment;

(b) any provision made for the permanent diminution in value of any other fixed asset (separate from and in addition to the systematic provision for depreciation); and

(c)   any such provisions previously made which are written back on the grounds that they are no longer required.

9.204   Although the Act does not make clear whether all such provisions should be charged to the profit and loss account, FRS 11 provides guidance in this area. This subject is discussed in **14.237** to **14.250** below.

9.205   Prior to the issue of FRS 11, there was considerable debate over what constituted a permanent diminution in asset values. FRS 11 refers to impairment rather than permanent diminutions in value. Nevertheless, the distinction between permanent and temporary diminutions in value is effectively resolved by the FRS. A principle is established that impairment is measured by comparing carrying value with 'recoverable amount', which is the higher of net realisable value and value in use, i.e., respectively, what you could sell the asset for and what you could make it earn for you over its useful economic life. As those two values cover between them all possible outcomes, based on the best estimates currently available, any impairment so measured must logically be regarded as a permanent diminution.

9.206   In order to comply with Sch 4 para 19, where a permanent diminution is deemed to have arisen and the asset has been carried at cost, this diminution is required to be recognised and should be taken to the profit and loss account for the period.

9.207   FRS 11 requires that impairment losses which are appropriately recognised in the profit and loss account should be included within operating profit under the appropriate statutory heading and disclosed as an exceptional item if appropriate. [FRS 11(67)] Such treatment may at times conflict with FRS 3 (see **9.208** to **9.212** below). See **14.282** to **14.283** and **14.265** to **14.272** below for a discussion of when it is appropriate to recognise impairment losses in the profit and loss account as opposed to the statement of total recognised gains and losses.

9.208   In certain cases, it may be appropriate to disclose impairment losses as exceptional items as required by FRS 3 and, in very rare cases, as described below, it may be appropriate for the loss to be shown as one of the exceptional items after operating profit. [FRS 3(20)] FRS 3 requires the profit or loss on disposal of a fixed asset, where it is material and does not represent marginal adjustments to depreciation previously charged, to be shown as one of the exceptional items after operating profit.

9.209   Although the FRS refers specifically to profits and losses on disposal and provisions for loss on disposal, it is also appropriate to show the provision for impairment as an exceptional item after operating profit where the provision:

(a)   is caused by the anticipation of a disposal; or

(b)   represents a disposal of part of the operating capability of an asset as a result of some disastrous event.

This assumes that the impairment has not occurred independently and the events above have merely brought this fact to light.

9.210   Not recognising provisions made in anticipation of a disposal as an exceptional item after operating profit would lead to an inconsistency in the treatment of situations which were identical except for a difference in timing. Therefore, where the fall in value becomes apparent before the year end but the actual disposal takes place after the year end, the treatment should be the same as if disposal had taken place before the year end.

9.211   Whether the individual circumstances of a 'disastrous event' can be regarded as resulting in a disposal of part of the operating capability will depend upon the particular circumstances of each case.

Example 9.211

Consider the situation where an entity acquired land some years ago on which it built two factories. It has now discovered that one of the factories was built on a part of the land which was a landfill site and dangerous gases are collecting under the building, rendering it unsafe to use. The affected factory is now worthless and unsaleable; however, the entity can continue to use the second factory. Because of the discovery of the dangerous gases, the entity has lost half of its manufacturing capacity. Although the contaminated land and factory cannot actually be sold, there has been an effective disposal of part of the operating capacity and it would be appropriate to reflect the loss of value of the factory and land as a disposal.

9.212   One situation which entities often cite as appropriate to treat as non-operating is the destruction of an uninsured asset. Such an act would constitute a disposal of a fixed asset and, as such, falls to be disclosed as a 'paragraph 20' item below operating profit.

Reversal of an impairment loss

9.213 If at any time the reason for making a provision for a permanent diminution in value ceases to apply, Sch 4 para 19 requires that the provision, to the extent that it was charged to the profit and loss account, be written back through the profit and loss account for the period to the extent that it is no longer applicable.

9.214 FRS 11 is more prescriptive and states that if, after an impairment loss has been recognised, the recoverable amount of a tangible fixed asset or investment increases because of a change in either:

- economic conditions; or

- the expected use of the asset,

the resulting reversal of the impairment loss should be recognised in the current period to the extent that it increases the carrying amount of the fixed asset up to the amount that it would have been had the original impairment not occurred. [FRS 11(56)]

The reversal of an impairment loss should be recognised in the profit and loss account to the extent that the original impairment loss (adjusted for depreciation that would have been charged on the unimpaired asset) was recognised in the profit and loss account. Any remaining balance of the reversal of an impairment should be recognised in the statement of total recognised gains and losses. [FRS 11(66)] See chapter 14 (specifically **14.284** below) for a discussion of when the above two criteria are met.

9.215 Although not addressed specifically in FRS 11, it would be logical for the placement in the profit and loss account of an impairment reversal to follow that of the original impairment loss.

Amortisation and impairment of goodwill and other intangible assets

9.216 FRS 10 requires goodwill and certain other intangible assets to be capitalised and subject to systematic amortisation and/or impairment reviews. See chapter 13 for a fuller discussion. The FRS is silent on which profit and loss account heading(s) should include the goodwill amortisation and any impairment charge. The profit and loss account formats in Sch 4 prescribe the headings in which depreciation of tangible and intangible fixed assets should be included:

Formats 1 and 3:	'cost of sales', 'distribution costs' or 'administrative expenses';
Formats 2 and 4:	'depreciation and other amounts written off tangible and intangible fixed assets'.

9.217

> The most appropriate heading to use under formats 1 and 3 might be obvious from the nature of the business. For example, amortisation of goodwill arising on the acquisition of a distribution business might be best included within distribution costs. Where the goodwill has arisen from the purchase of a customer list, 'cost of sales' might be the appropriate category. However, in other circumstances, it might be that none of the permitted headings seems very appropriate. In such circumstances, the 'administrative expenses' heading could usefully be used.

9.218 When an impairment loss or a reversal of such a loss related to goodwill or other intangible assets should be presented in the profit and loss account, the presentation follows the same rules as for other impairment losses, as described in **9.203** to **9.215** above.

9.219 If the goodwill charge is particularly material, it should be disclosed on the face of the profit and loss account, within the relevant statutory format heading, if this degree of prominence is necessary to give a true and fair view.

9.220

> Including goodwill amortisation in a separate heading below operating profit would probably constitute a breach of the Act. The Review Panel, in a press release about the 1997 accounts of Reuters Holdings PLC, stated that 'in the Panel's view a charge for the amortisation of goodwill should be classified as an operating charge and thus deducted before operating profit is arrived at'. It would, however, be acceptable for the heading in which the goodwill amortisation had been included to be analysed on the face of the profit and loss account, providing that the total for that heading was also shown, with its prescribed title.

9.221 Neither FRS 10 nor the Act specifies a profit and loss account heading for the release of negative goodwill. Negative goodwill should be treated consistently with positive goodwill, i.e., in one of the headings above operating profit. An appropriate heading might be 'other operating income' (see **9.37** below). Another appropriate heading might be that used for positive goodwill amortisation (e.g., administrative expenses), which would be consistent with the balance sheet treatment. However, if the amounts of negative goodwill offsetting the expenses were material, it would be necessary to analyse it separately on the face of the profit and loss account to avoid breaching the Act's requirement not to offset positive and negative items.

9.222   The amortisation charge for revalued intangible assets should be based on the revalued amounts and the remaining useful economic lives of the assets. Amortisation charged before the revaluation should not be written back in the profit and loss account. [FRS 10(47)]

Research and development

9.223   The total amount of research and development expenditure charged in the year is required by SSAP 13 to be disclosed, analysed between current year's expenditure and amounts amortised from deferred expenditure. See **13.14** et seq below for a discussion of SSAP 13.

9.224   This disclosure need not be made by an entity that:

(a)   is not a public company, banking company or insurance company or a holding company that has a public company, banking company or insurance company as a subsidiary; and

(b)   satisfies the criteria, multiplied in each case by 10, for defining a medium-sized company (see chapter 34).

9.225   To the extent that research and development relates to goods produced or services provided by the company, it will normally be appropriate for these costs to be included in 'Cost of sales'. Other research and development, including 'pure research' will normally be included in 'Administrative expenses'.

Operaing lease costs

9.226   SSAP 21 requires the disclosure:

(a)   by the lessee, of:

(i)   the operating lease rentals charged to profit and loss during the period, analysed between hire of plant and machinery, and other operating leases;

(ii)   aggregate finance charges for the period in respect of finance leases;

(iii)   total depreciation for the period in respect of assets under finance lease, disclosed by each major class of asset or the total charged where the analysis by class is integrated with that for own assets;

(b)   by the lessor, of the aggregate rentals receivable in the periods in respect of:

(i)   finance leases; and
(ii)   operating leases.

9.227 Leasing is dealt with further in chapter 29.

Auditors' remuneration

Audit fees

9.228 The amount required to be disclosed in the notes is the sum of the audit fee and the related expenses charged in the profit and loss account. This amount will be after adding or deducting, respectively, any under or over provisions for the previous accounting period. The amount of remuneration should include the estimated money value of any benefits in kind. The nature of any such benefits should also be disclosed. The disclosure is required in respect of the audit fee for both the company and the group. [s390A and Sch 4(1)(1)]

Non-audit fees

9.229 Disclosure is required of amounts paid to the company's auditors and to associates of the company's auditors in respect of other services such as accountancy, taxation advice and management consultancy. [SI 1991 No 2128] Companies that qualify as small or medium-sized are exempt from this requirement (see chapter 34).

9.230 The amount to be disclosed is the aggregate amount of the remuneration, if any, in respect of work carried out in that year for services supplied to:

(a)   the company; and

(b)   any UK subsidiary undertaking of the company which is audited by the company's auditors or any associates of the company's auditors.

9.231 Associates of a company's auditors (where the auditors are a partnership) include:

(a)   any partner in the auditors;

(b)   any other partnership which had, at any time in the financial year, a partner in common with the auditors;

(c)   any body corporate (and members of the same group) which was, at any time in the financial year, a partner in the auditors;

(d)   any body corporate (and members of the same group) in which, whether alone or with any associates of the auditors, the auditors or any partner in the auditors was, at any time in the financial year, entitled to exercise, or control the exercise of, 20 per cent or more of the voting rights at any general meeting (excluding a body corporate in which the auditors or the relevant partner in the auditors were or was entitled to exercise, or control the exercise of, 20 per cent or more of the voting rights at any general meeting of such body corporate solely by virtue of acting as an insolvency practitioner in relation to any person, or in his capacity as a receiver, or a receiver or manager, of the property of a company, or a judicial factor on the estate of any person); and

(e) any person who was, at any time in that financial year, entitled to receive 20 per cent or more of the auditors' profits and any person of whose profits the auditors were, in that financial year, entitled to receive 20 per cent or more.

Auditors have a duty to assist directors in identifying associates of the auditors.

9.232 Associates of a company's auditor where the auditor is a body corporate or an individual are defined by SI 1991 No 2128 reg 3(2), (4), (5) and (7) respectively.

Exchange gains and losses

9.233 Neither the Act nor the 'Standard Accounting Practice' section of the relevant accounting standard (SSAP 20) give any guidance as to which heading should be credited or charged with exchange gains and losses which are required to be recognised in the profit and loss account. However, the consideration of the legal requirements in the SSAP notes:

> 'For this reason it is necessary to consider the nature of each foreign exchange gain or loss and to allocate each accordingly. Gains or losses arising from trading transactions should normally be included under "Other operating income or expense" while those arising from arrangements which may be considered as financing should be disclosed separately as part of "Other interest receivable/payable and similar income/expense".'

(See **26.9** to **26.12** below for further discussion of the subject.)

Note of historical cost profits and losses

Introduction

9.234 The note of historical cost profits and losses is a memorandum statement that is an abbreviated restatement of the profit and loss account, adjusting the reported profit or loss, if necessary, so as to show it as if no asset revaluations had been made. [FRS 3(54)]

9.235 The note is a response to concerns that:

(a) there should be a comparable measure of performance, and that historical cost profit or loss gives this, while discretion exists as to whether assets should be revalued or not; and

(b)   certain users may wish to measure the profit or loss on disposal of assets by reference to historical cost rather than, as required by FRS 3, by reference to revalued carrying amount.

Requirement to provide a note of historical cost profits and losses

9.236   A 'Note of historical cost profits and losses' is required where there is a material difference between the result as disclosed in the profit and loss account and the result on an unmodified historical cost basis. [FRS 3(26)]

9.237   FRS 3 does not define 'result' for this purpose. However, as the note of historical cost profits and losses itself covers 'profit or loss on ordinary activities before taxation' and 'retained profit (or transfer from reserves) for the financial year', such a note should be presented if there is a material difference in the results measured at either of these two levels.

9.238   A reasonable inference from the above is that a note of historical cost profits and losses is not required unless an entity has revalued some of its assets and those revaluations have a material impact on the profit and loss account.

9.239   FRS 3 does not state whether the note of historical cost profits and losses need only be prepared for the group or whether it should also be prepared for a parent company where the parent prepares consolidated financial statements. FRS 3 is addressed to reporting entities; when group financial statements are prepared, the group is the reporting entity. Accordingly, parents need not disclose a historical cost profit or loss for the financial year if they do not wish to do so. In addition parent companies producing consolidated financial statements normally take advantage of s230 and do not present their own profit and loss account; they are, however, required to disclose their profit or loss for the financial year. In such circumstances, there seems little point in including the full note of historical cost profits and losses for the parent; parents may, however, wish to disclose a historical cost profit or loss for the financial year

9.240   Where a note of historical cost profits and losses is not presented because there is not a material difference between the reported results and the results on an unmodified historical cost basis, there is no need to give an explanatory note setting out the reason for not presenting the note.

Content

9.241 The note of historical cost profits and losses should reconcile the reported profit on ordinary activities before taxation to the equivalent historical cost amount and should also show the retained profit for the financial year reported on a historical cost basis. [FRS 3(26)] The reconciling items will include adjustments for: [FRS 3(54)]

(a) gains and losses recognised in prior periods in the statement of total recognised gains and losses and realised in the current period, e.g., the difference between the profit on the disposal of an asset calculated on depreciated historical cost and that calculated on a revalued amount; and

(b) the difference between a historical cost depreciation charge and the depreciation charge calculated on the revalued amount included in the profit and loss account for the period.

9.242 The following two categories are not deemed to be departures from the historical cost convention and should not appear in the note as reconciling items: [FRS 3(55)]

(a) adjustments necessarily made to cope with the impact of hyperinflation on foreign operations; and

(b) the practice of market makers and other dealers in investments of marking to market where this is an established industry practice.

9.243 Where full historical cost information is unavailable or cannot be obtained without unreasonable expense or delay, the earliest available values should be used. [FRS 3(26)] In practice, companies should already have most of the historical cost information in order to give the additional information required by Sch 4 para 33 in the event of a departure from the Act's historical cost accounting rules.

9.244 In consolidated financial statements, the profit and loss account figure for minority interests should be amended in calculating retained profit for the year, to reflect the adjustments made where they affect subsidiary companies with a minority interest. [FRS 3(55)]

9.245 Where deferred tax is provided on revaluations, an adjustment will be required to the tax line when computing the retained profit for the year on a historical cost basis in the year of sale of the revalued asset.

9.246 The note of historical cost profits and losses should be adjusted for any prior period adjustments by restating the comparative figures. [FRS 3(29)]

Format and positioning

9.247   The note of historical cost profits and losses should be presented immediately following the profit and loss account or the statement of total recognised gains and losses. [FRS 3(26)] Comparative figures are required. [FRS 3(30)]

9.248   FRS 3 does not stipulate a format for the note. The format below is based upon the illustrative examples which accompany FRS 3. The most appropriate form of disclosure will depend upon the circumstances.

Example 9.248

Note of historical cost profits and losses

	2000 *£ million*	*1999* *£ million*
Reported profit on ordinary activities before taxation	12	43
Realisation of property revaluation gains of earlier years	3	10
Difference between an historical cost depreciation charge and the actual depreciation charge for the year calculated on the revalued amount	3	4
Historical cost profit on ordinary activities before taxation	18	57
Historical cost profit for the year retained, after taxation, minority interests, extraordinary items and dividends	7	34

Prior period items

Introduction

9.249   The Act requires that where any amount relating to any preceding financial year is included in the profit and loss account, the effect shall be stated. [Sch 4: 57(1)]

9.250   The majority of prior period items arise mainly from the corrections and adjustments which are the natural result of estimates inherent in the accounting process and particularly in the periodic preparation of financial statements. Such items should be dealt with in the profit and loss account of the period in which they are identified and shown separately if material. It is specifically stated in FRS 3 that prior period items are not exceptional or extraordinary merely because they relate to a prior period. [FRS 3(60)]

Prior period adjustments

9.251   Prior period adjustments, which are not reflected in the profits of the current financial year, are required and permitted by FRS 3 only in two rare sets of circumstances:
[FRS 3(7)]

(a)   where there has been a change in accounting policy; or

(b)   where it is discovered that a prior period's financial statements included a fundamental error.

9.252   As stated in **5.18** to **5.23** above, accounting policies should be applied consistently from one financial year to the next and policies should be changed only when this can be justified if there are 'special reasons' [Sch 4: 15], i.e., on the grounds of better financial reporting.

9.253   A fundamental error is one which is of such significance as to destroy the true and fair view and hence the validity of the financial statements. [FRS 3(63)]

9.254   It is suggested that a fundamental error should be recognised only in the very rare circumstances when it is acknowledged that the financial statements should not have been issued in the form in which they were. An error in an accounting estimate, however large, which is apparent with the benefit of hindsight is not a fundamental error if the estimate was reasonably made on the basis of the information available at the time.

9.255   Such changes in accounting policy or correction of fundamental errors should be accounted for by restating the comparative figures for the preceding period in the primary financial statements and notes and adjusting the opening balance of reserves for the cumulative effect. In addition, the cumulative effect of the adjustments should be noted at the foot of the statement of total recognised gains and losses of the current period. [FRS 3(29)]

9.256   Where a company changes an accounting policy in 1999 and records the cumulative effect of the adjustments at the foot of its statement of total recognised gains and losses for that year, it need not also include the cumulative effect of the adjustments at the foot of the 1999 column of the statement of total recognised gains and losses presented in the 2000 financial statements.

9.257 The effect of prior period adjustments on the results for the preceding period should be disclosed where practicable (see **9.262** below). [FRS 3(29)]

9.258 The cumulative adjustments arising from prior period adjustments should also be included in the reconciliation of movements in shareholders' funds. [FRS 3(62) and (63)]

9.259

> Where prior period figures have been restated, it is good practice to indicate this in the heading to the comparative figures on each page of the financial statements, together with a reference to the note explaining the prior period adjustment.

Example 9.259

	2000	1999 as restated (see note 2)
	£'000	£'000
Turnover	2,543	2,487

9.260 Schedule 4 para 15 states that 'if it appears to the directors of a company that there are special reasons for departing from any of the principles stated above in preparing the company's accounts in respect of any financial year they may do so, but particulars of the departure, the reasons for it and its effect shall be given in a note to the accounts'. One of the 'principles stated above' is that accounting policies shall be applied consistently from year to year. Accordingly, these disclosures are required to be given when a company changes any of its accounting policies. These disclosures are in addition to the requirements of FRS 3.

9.261

> Where an accounting policy is changed, the reasons for that change should therefore be disclosed. The directors should take particular care in drafting the note to the accounts indicating why they believe the new policy is preferable to the old policy where the change in accounting policy is other than as a result of the adoption of a new or amended accounting standard or UITF Abstract. The Review Panel has already stated that it did not believe that the reasons for a change of policy by a listed company had been adequately disclosed in the financial statements; the company gave a fuller explanation in its subsequent financial statements.

9.262 In the past, it had generally been accepted that the Act's requirement to disclose the effect of a change in accounting policy would be fulfilled by giving the disclosure, required by FRS 3, of the effect of the prior period adjustment on the results of the preceding period (see

9.257 above). However, in November 1995, UITF Abstract 14 was issued, in which the UITF explained that it had received legal advice that the Act required the effect on the current year to be disclosed. In those cases where the effect on the current year is either immaterial or similar to the quantified effect on the prior year, a simple statement saying this will suffice. Where it is not practicable to give the effect on the current year, that fact, together with the reasons, should be stated. [UITF Abstract 14(3)]

9.263 The extract below illustrates the accounting presentation and disclosure of a prior period adjustment arising from a change in accounting policy as a result of adopting FRS 12.

Extract 9.263

Hanson PLC

Year ended 31 December 1999

Extract from consolidated profit and loss account

	Notes	Before Exceptional Items £m	Exceptional Items £m	Total £m
Turnover	1			
continuing operations		1,778.6	–	1,778.6
acquisition	20	141.9	–	141.9
		1,920.5	–	19,20.5
discontinued operations		–	–	–
Costs and overheads less other income	3	(1,607.5)	–	(1,607.5)
Group operating profit		313.0	–	313.0
Share of operating profit of associates		10.6	–	10.3
Operating profit including associates		323.4	–	323.6
continuing operations		300.9	–	300.9
acquisitions	20	22.7	–	22.7
		323.6	–	323.6
discontinued operations		–	–	–
Operating profit including associates	1	323.6	–	323.6
Exceptional items	5			
(Loss) on disposal of operations discontinued operations		–	(3.7)	(3.7)
Release and settlement of environmental and related provisions discontinued operation		–	–	–
Profit (Loss) on disposal and writedown of fixed assets discontinued operations		–	5.8	5.8
		–	2.1	2.1
Net Interest (payable) and similar charges 6				
Net interest (payable) receivable		(1.5)	–	(1.5)
Unwinding of discount (net)		(7.8)	–	(7.8)

				(9.3)	–	(9.3)
Profit (Loss) on ordinary activities before taxation				314.3	2.1	316.4

	Notes	Before Exceptional Items £m	1998 Exceptional Items £m	Total £m
Turnover	1			
continuing operations		1,590.3	–	1,590.3
acquisitions	20	–	–	–
		1,590.3	–	1,590.3
discontinued operations		234.9	–	234.9
		1,825.2	–	1,825.2
Costs and overheads less other income	3	(1,575.8)	–	(1,575.8)
Group operating profit		249.4	–	249.4
Share of operating profit of associates		11.7	–	11.7
Operating profit including associates		261.1	–	261.1
continuing operations		257.5	–	257.5
acquisitions	20	–	–	–
		257.5	–	257.5
discontinued operations		3.6	–	3.6
Operating profit including associates	1	261.1	–	261.1
Exceptional items	5			
(Loss) on disposal of operations discontinued operations		–	(56.1)	(56.1)
Release and settlement of environmental and related provisions discontinued operation		–	132.2	132.2
Profit (Loss) on disposal and writedown of fixed assets discounted operations		–	(155.8)	(155.8)
		–	(79.7)	(79.7)
Net Interest (payable) and similar charges 6				
Net interest (payable) receivable		5.4	–	5.4
Unwinding of discount (net)		(6.7)	–	(6.7)
		(1.3)	–	(1.3)
Profit (Loss) on ordinary activities before taxation		259.8	(79.7)	180.1

The consolidated profit and loss account for the year ended December 31, 1998 has been restated for the adoption of FRS 12 (see note 29).

Extract from statement of total recognised gains and losses

	1999 £m	1998 £m
Profit on ordinary activities	**334.3**	338.5
Currency translation differences on foreign net equity	**6.9**	(1.4)
Total recognised gains and losses in the period	**341.2**	337.1
Prior year adjustment (note 29)	**52.9**	–

Total recognised gains and losses recognised since last annual report	394.1	337.1

The statement of total recognised gains and losses for the year ended December 31, 1998 has been restated for the adoption of FRS 12.

Extract from the notes to the accounts

29 Reinstatement of comparatives

The adoption of Financial Reporting Standard 12 'Provisions, Contingent Liabilities and Contingent Assets' (FRS 12) has required changes in the method of accounting for reclamation costs, health care obligations in respect of US employees, environmental obligations, decommissioning costs and other liabilities.

As a result of these changes in accounting policy the comparatives have been restated as follows:

a) Consolidated balance sheet

	Tangible Fixed assets £m	Prepayments £m	Koppers Liabilities transferred to insurers £m	Provision For liabilities and charges £m	Shareholders' Funds £m
1998 as previously reported	2,000.3	–	–	(684.6)	(1,539.4)
Adoption of FRS 12 at January 1, 1998	(1.0)	164.3	(164.3)	70.3	(69.3)
During 1998 (see below)	–	–	–	(16.4)	16.4
Adoption of FRS 12 at December 31, 1998	(1.0)	164.3	(164.3)	53.9	(52.9)
1998 restated	999.3	164.3	(164.3)	(630.7)	(1,592.3)

The principal changes arise from the elimination, increase and reclassification of provisions for liabilities and charges. In the case of Koppers environmental liabilities the obligation is recognised in provisions with a corresponding asset representing the amounts receivable under the insurance arrangements entered into in 1998. Under these arrangements the funding and risk of the environmental liabilities relating to the former Koppers company operations of Beazer PLC have been transferred to and underwritten by subsidiaries of two of the world's largest reinsurance companies, Centre Solutions (a member of the Zurich Group) and Swiss Re.

b) Consolidated profit and loss account

	Exceptional Items £m	Operating Costs £m	Net interest (payable) Income £m
Year to December 1998 reported	(68.7)	(1,577.1)	5.4
Adoption of FRS 12	(11.0)	1.3	(6.7)
1998 restated	(79.7)	(1,575.8)	(1.3)

The changes arise from the unwinding of the discount on provisions shown as interest together with adjustments arising from FRS 12 shown under operating costs and exceptional items. The impact of adopting FRS 12 on the 1999 results amounted to a charge of £8.4m which represents the unwinding of the discount on provisions in the year and an adjustment to operating costs.

Future developments

9.264 The ASB issued a discussion paper *Reporting financial performance: proposals for change* in June 1999. It presents a position paper developed by the G4+1 group of accounting standard setters. In the UK, the proposals contained therein will be developed with the intention of revising FRS 3 *Reporting financial performance*. The most significant proposal is that financial performance should be reported in a single statement – effectively combining the profit and loss account with the statement of total recognised gains and losses (STRGL).

9.265 The proposed single statement reporting financial performance would present all changes in equity, other than those arising from transactions with shareholders, and divide items into three main components of financial performance:

(a) the results of operating (or trading) activities;

(b) the results of financing and other treasury activities; and

(c) other gains and losses.

In general, the first two components correspond to the profit and loss account, while the third largely comprises items currently reported in the statement of total recognised gains and losses (see **11.20** below).

9.266 See **11.22** and **11.23** below as regards Items which would typically be reported within 'Other gains and losses' and the option to include certain of these within operating/trading activities if appropriate.

9.267 If the contents of the paper were implemented in the UK without amendment, the main effects on FRS 3 (in addition to the introduction of a 'single statement', as described above) would be:

(a) Separately disclosed exceptional items (as per FRS 3(20)) would be reported as part of operating activities (in the case of the costs of a fundamental reorganisation or restructuring) or within the 'other' section (for a profit/loss on the sale/termination of a business, or disposal of a fixed asset), rather than below 'operating profit'. However, such items would still be separately disclosed, if material.

(b) Where there is (voluntary) separate disclosure of 'pre-exceptional results', comparable disclosures relating to each of the past five, or so, years would need to be given.

(c) The total tax expense would be allocated to two amounts – one relating to the total of operating activities and financing, etc, and the other to the 'other gains and losses' component.

(d) All material errors discovered after the financial statements have been issued would be corrected by way of a prior period adjustment, rather than only 'fundamental errors' as is the case under FRS 3.

9.268 Additionally, amendments would be required to:

(a) FRS 15 – regarding the presentation of gains or losses on disposal, as discussed above; and

(b) FRS 11 (and FRS 15) – all impairment losses would be reported as operating activities. The treatment consistent with current standards would be to split such losses between operating activities and other gains and losses (depending upon whether or not a consumption of economic benefits has occurred).

9.269 As a 'transaction with shareholders', dividends would be excluded from the face of the performance statement. In the UK, this creates a legal problem since the Companies Act 1985 (Schedule 4) requires dividends to be disclosed. This could be addressed by including dividends as a memorandum item on the face of the statement.

9.270 Companies operating in certain sectors are likely to be particularly affected by the proposals. For example:

(a) The performance of property investment companies is largely measured in terms of items such as realised and unrealised revaluation gains and losses, disposal gains and losses, interest costs and depreciation. These items might be spread throughout the three main components of the proposed performance statement, disguising the 'true' performance of the business. This is currently the case, with items being split between the profit and loss account and STRGL. However, this paper would appear an ideal opportunity to address the issue.

(b) Investment trust companies currently present the STRGL, under the title of 'Statement of Total Return', as their primary statement of performance. This statement includes those items which would normally be included in the profit and loss account (a separate P&L is usually not presented at all).

(c) The primary performance measures of companies operating in the banking and finance industries would appear in the 'results of financing ...' section of the statement, rather than as the results of operating activities. The discussion paper raises the possibility of merging these two components into one in certain circumstances.

(d) Insurance companies are currently required to include both realised and unrealised gains and losses on investments in the profit and loss account.

9.271 A particular problem with the potential implementation of the proposals, both in the UK and elsewhere, is that revised standards will still have to be consistent with the relevant company law framework. In domestic terms, any revised FRS 3 could not contradict the requirements of the Companies Act 1985 – in particular, Schedule 4, which specifies the form and content of company accounts. Schedule 4 specifies both the statutory headings which must appear in a set of company accounts and the order in which they should appear. The Schedule does not appear consistent with the likely format of the proposed performance statement (the exclusion of dividends, for example, is mentioned above). It should, therefore, be borne in mind that the paper has been written from a, largely, international perspective and the domestic issues arising will be addressed by the ASB in any future revision to FRS 3.

10 Earnings per share

10 Earnings per share

General requirements

Introduction

10.1 FRS 14 *Earnings per share* was issued on 1 October 1998, replacing SSAP 3, which was also entitled *Earnings per share*, and amending UITF Abstract 13 *Accounting for ESOP trusts*. The FRS, which is effective for accounting periods ending on or after 23 December 1998, was developed not through any dissatisfaction with SSAP 3, but exploiting an opportunity to align the UK with international developments.

10.2 Although the bulk of the FRS comprises guidance on how to calculate basic and diluted earnings per share (eps), the disclosure requirements (albeit greater than in SSAP 3) are relatively modest compared to recent standards.

10.3 For entities within the scope of FRS 14, the standard requires both a basic and a diluted eps to be presented on the face of the profit and loss account in respect of each class of ordinary share that has a different right to share in the profit or loss of the period. Diluted eps always has to be disclosed – even if basic eps is a loss per share or dilution is not material (see **10.22** to **10.24** below).

10.4 The numerators used in calculating basic and diluted eps should be disclosed together with a reconciliation of those amounts to the net profit or loss for the period. In addition, the denominators should be disclosed and reconciled to each other. Four further disclosures are stipulated but each of these only has to be given in certain circumstances (see **10.22** and **10.25** to **10.42** below).

10.5 Much of the FRS comprises guidance on how to calculate basic and diluted eps. For example, the FRS stipulates rules: to be applied in determining whether potential ordinary shares are dilutive and thus whether they are to be used to calculate diluted eps; on how to bring share options into the calculation of diluted eps; and on how to deal with contingently issuable shares.

10.6 In a controversial move, the FRS requires certain post-year end share transactions to be reflected in the eps calculation. Where an entity has a bonus issue, share split, share consolidation, bonus element in a rights issue or some other change in capital that alters the number of shares in issue with no corresponding change in the entity's resources (other than on the conversion of potential ordinary shares), the basic and diluted eps calculations should reflect the new number of shares whether the change took place during the year or between the balance sheet date and the date of approval of the financial statements (see **10.89** and **10.90** below).

10.7 Although the FRS is drafted principally in the context of earnings (or other components of profit) per share, the FRS recommends that its requirements also be applied to the calculation of other amounts per share, e.g., net assets per share.

Scope of FRS 14

Scope

10.8 FRS 14 applies to entities:

(a) whose ordinary or potential ordinary shares are publicly traded;

(b) in the process of issuing ordinary or potential ordinary shares in public securities markets; and

(c) voluntarily choosing to present an eps.

For the meaning of 'ordinary share' and 'potential ordinary share' see paragraphs **10.11** to **10.15** below.

10.9 Where an entity presents financial statements for both itself and, on a consolidated basis, for the group that it heads, the disclosures required by the FRS only have to be given in respect of the consolidated information.

10.10 The title of the FRS is *Earnings per share* and thus, with the exception of the section on historical summaries, the FRS deals with the calculation of components of net profit per share. Nevertheless, the requirements of the FRS, to the extent they deal with the 'per share' aspect of the calculation (rather than the earnings component of the calculation), can also be applied to other amounts per share, e.g., net assets per share.

Meaning of ordinary share

10.11 The FRS defines 'ordinary share' as 'an instrument falling within the definition of equity shares as defined in FRS 4 *Capital instruments*'. [FRS 14(2)] FRS 4 defines equity shares as 'shares other than non-equity shares'. Non-equity shares are shares possessing any of the following characteristics:

(a) any of the rights of the shares to receive payments (whether in respect of dividends, in respect of redemption or otherwise) are for a limited amount that is not calculated by reference to the company's assets or profits or the dividends on any class of equity share;

(b) any of their rights to participate in a surplus in a winding-up are limited to a specific amount that is not calculated by reference to the company's assets or profits and such limitation had a commercial effect in practice at the time the shares were issued or, if later, at the time the limitation was introduced; or

(c) the shares are redeemable either according to their terms, or because the holder, or any party other than the issuer, can require their redemption. [FRS 4(12)]

10.12   FRS 14 explains that 'ordinary shares participate in the net profit for the period only after any other types of shares such as preference shares'. In FRS 4's application note on participating preference shares, the implication is also that priority in respect of paying dividends over other classes of shares contributes to the classification as non-equity shares. However, as can be seen from the above definition of non-equity share, although priority of paying dividends might have been behind the thinking when the definition was drafted, prioritisation does not itself feature as part of the definition. Accordingly, although a company may have more than one class of share, the class of shares receiving its dividends last after all the other classes is not automatically defined as equity. Indeed, it may be that a company only has non-equity shares as defined by FRS 4. The legal definition of equity shares differs from that in FRS 4. Accordingly, a company might have equity shares in accordance with the Companies Act 1985 but only have non-equity shares in accordance with FRS 4.

10.13   For FRS 4 analysis purposes, some investment trusts have only non-equity shares. Such an investment trust would therefore not be required to comply with FRS 14 in its annual financial statements (assuming it does not have any potential ordinary shares publicly traded or about to be publicly traded). Nevertheless, if the company wished to disclose an eps figure in its annual financial statements, the requirements of FRS 14 would have to be applied, since the FRS applies to entities voluntarily choosing to present an eps. Ironically, the Listing Rules require a listed company to present an eps as part of its interim financial information and as part of its preliminary announcement. Consequently, a listed investment trust or any other listed company with only non-equity shares choosing not to present voluntarily an eps in its annual financial statements is recommended to consult the UK Listing Authority over the preparation of its interim financial information and preliminary announcements.

Potential ordinary shares

10.14 Potential ordinary shares are defined as 'a financial instrument or a right that may entitle its holder to ordinary shares'. [FRS 14(2)]

10.15

> Examples of potential ordinary shares include:
>
> (a) debentures convertible into ordinary shares;
>
> (b) preference shares convertible into ordinary shares;
>
> (c) warrants and options to purchase or subscribe for ordinary shares;
>
> (d) an award granted under a long-term incentive plan entitling an employee to a specified number of ordinary shares if targets are met over a number of years; and
>
> (e) an acquisition agreement under which the purchaser will issue additional shares to the vendor if the profits of the acquired business over a number of years exceeds a target.

Publicly traded and public securities markets

10.16 Despite being fundamental to the scope of the standard, the terms 'publicly traded' and 'public securities markets' are not defined. FRS 13, issued only one week before FRS 14, refers in the scope of part A to 'a reporting entity that has any of its capital instruments listed or publicly traded on a stock exchange or market'. [FRS 13(3)] The subsequent paragraph explains that 'the term "stock exchange or market" includes domestic and foreign exchanges and markets and it also includes markets other than the main market. It therefore includes markets such as the London and Irish Stock Exchanges, EASDAQ, NASDAQ and the Alternative Investment Market'.

> The above quotation from FRS 13 appears to be equally applicable in interpreting the terms 'publicly traded' and 'public securities markets' for FRS 14 purposes.

Financial statements intended to give a true and fair view

10.17 As stated in **10.8** above, FRS 14 applies to entities:

(a) whose ordinary or potential ordinary shares are publicly traded;

(b) in the process of issuing ordinary or potential ordinary shares in public securities markets; and

(c) voluntarily choosing to present an eps. [FRS 14(3)]

There is no mention in FRS 14 that it applies only to the 'true and fair' financial statements of the above entities. Although the scope paragraph of SSAP 3 similarly omitted any mention of true and fair financial statements, the paragraphs preceding the SSAP explained that the SSAP was 'intended to apply to the audited accounts of listed companies'. FRS 13, issued only one week before FRS 14, is more explicit. The scope paragraph for part A states that, part A applies 'to all financial statements that are intended to give a true and fair view of the reporting entity's financial position and profit or loss (or income and expenditure) for a period and are prepared by a reporting entity that has any of its capital instruments listed or publicly traded …'.

10.18   The question arises as to whether the explicit reference to true and fair in FRS 13, coupled with the omission of any reference to true and fair in FRS 14, means that the scope of FRS 14 is wider than true and fair financial statements. Subject to three exceptions, it is considered that FRS 14 applies only to true and fair financial statements for the following reasons:

    (a)   the text of FRS 14 follows as closely as possible the text of IAS 33. Thus, the omission of a reference to true and fair financial statements probably arises because there is no such reference in IAS 33, rather than as a result of a conscious decision to depart from the usual scope wording of accounting standards;

    (b)   any decision to make the scope wider than true and fair financial statements would probably have been documented in appendix II to FRS 14 on the development of the FRS and there is no such reference in appendix II; and

    (c)   the ASB's *Foreword to Accounting Standards* states (paragraph 13) that 'accounting standards are applicable to financial statements of a reporting entity that are intended to give a true and fair view of its state of affairs at the balance sheet date and of its profit or loss (or income and expenditure) for the financial period ending on that date'.

10.19   The three exceptions referred to in **10.18** above are:

    (a)   interim financial information;

    (b)   historical summaries; and

    (c)   summary financial statements.

> As mentioned in **10.13** above, the Listing Rules require listed companies to present an eps as part of their interim financial information. Although there is no explicit reference in the Listing Rules that the eps should be calculated in accordance with the relevant accounting standard, it is inconceivable that a calculation on any other basis would be acceptable. Presenting eps in historical summaries is dealt with in **10.199** to **10.202** below.

Relationship with international accounting standards

10.20   Earnings per share was added to the ASB's agenda in the light of international developments, rather than because of dissatisfaction with SSAP 3. The International Accounting Standards Committee (IASC) and the US Financial Accounting Standards Board (FASB) worked together on developing guidance on eps. By the exposure draft stage, not only had the two bodies reached agreement on many of the points of principle, but the resulting drafts were closer to SSAP 3 than to the original US standard. Accordingly, the ASB reproduced the full text of the IASC's exposure draft, together with a covering note as a UK discussion paper. Following the support of commentators, and in the interests of international harmonisation, the ASB added the topic to its agenda with a view to aligning the UK guidance to that being developed by the IASC and the FASB.

10.21   FRS 14 therefore follows quite closely not only the requirements of, but also the text of, IAS 33 *Earnings per share*. The ASB has kept departures from IAS 33 to a minimum and in some areas has added guidance, based on the US standard, on the application of IAS 33's principles.

Requirement to disclose earnings per share

Disclosures required in all financial statements

Disclosures

10.22   FRS 14 requires the following to be disclosed in an entity's financial statements:

(a)   basic and diluted eps: to be disclosed on the face of the profit and loss account for each class of ordinary share that has a different right to share in the net profit for the period; basic and diluted eps have to be presented with equal prominence for all periods presented [FRS 14(69)];

(b)   the amounts used as the numerators in calculating basic and diluted eps and a reconciliation of those amounts to the net profit or loss for the period [FRS 14(71)]; and

(c)   the weighted average number of ordinary shares used as the denominators in calculating basic and diluted eps and, excepting figures given in respect of different classes of ordinary share, a reconciliation of these denominators to each other [FRS 14(71)].

Commentary and example disclosures

10.23   Under FRS 14 both basic and diluted eps always have to be disclosed, irrespective of whether basic eps is a loss per share or whether there is an immaterial difference between basic and diluted eps. Where basic and diluted eps are identical to one another (because there are no dilutive potential ordinary shares) the following disclosure is suggested:

Example 10.23

Profit and loss account

For the year ended 31 December 1999 (extract)

	Note	1999 £ million	1998 £ million
Turnover	2	28,759	25,814
⋮		⋮	⋮
Retained Profit		271	239
Earnings per share - basic and diluted		23.9p	22.0p

10.24   Basic and diluted eps have to be disclosed for each class of ordinary share. FRS 14 explains that, for this purpose, ordinary shares having the same rights to receive dividends constitute one class of share.

Example 10.24

Classes of shares

A company has two classes of shares: 'A' ordinary shares and 'B' ordinary shares. Although the voting rights differ between the two classes of shares, the rights to dividends are identical: the 'B' shares are entitled to the same dividend per share as declared by the directors on the 'A' shares. For FRS 14 purposes, there is only one class of share.

10.25 The requirement in **10.22**(b) above is to reconcile the numerators used to calculate basic and diluted eps to the net profit or loss for the period. The net profit or loss for the period is the profit or loss before deduction of any dividends or other appropriations.

10.26 The disclosures called for under **10.22**(b) and (c) above were new to UK financial reporting on the introduction of FRS 14. There is no example disclosure illustrated in FRS 14. However, the US SFAS 128, which was developed concurrently with IAS 33 (on which FRS 14 is based), does have some example disclosures. The following, based on example disclosure appended to SFAS 128, illustrates how this information might be presented.

Example 10.26

Year ended 31 December 1999

	Profit (numerator) £'000	Shares (denominator) Number (000)	Per-share amount Pence
Profit for the financial year	57,500		
Less: preference dividends and other appropriations	(7,500)		
Basic eps			
Profit attributable to ordinary shareholders	50,000	100,000	50
Effect of dilutive potential ordinary shares			
Options	–	10,000	
5% convertible debentures	5,000	15,000	
Convertible preference shares	7,500	20,000	
Diluted eps			
Profit attributable to ordinary shareholders + assumed conversions	62,500	145,000	43p

---

10.27 The following two extracts illustrate disclosure given by companies in their accounts.

Extract 10.27.1

Imperial Chemical Industries plc
Year ended 31 December 1999

11   Earnings (loss) per £1 Ordinary Share (extract)

	Continuing operations £m	Discontinued operations £m	Total £m
1999			
Net profit for the financial year before			
exceptional items	168	64	232
Exceptional items after tax and minorities	(52)	72	20
Net profit for the financial year	116	136	252
	million	million	million
Weighted average Ordinary Shares in issue			
during year	728	728	728
Weighted average shares held by Group's			
employee share ownership plan	(7)	(7)	(7)
Basic weighted average Ordinary Shares in			
issue during year	721	721	721
Dilutive effect of share options	2	2	2
Diluted weighted average Ordinary Shares	723	723	723
	pence	pence	pence
Basic earnings per £1 Ordinary Share			
before exceptional items	23.3	8.9	32.2
after exceptional items	16.1	18.9	35.0
Diluted earnings per £1 Ordinary Share			
before exceptional items	23.2	8.9	32.1
after exceptional items	16.0	18.9	34.9
1998 (as restated – note 1)	£m	£m	£m
Net profit for the financial year before			
exceptional items	94	127	221
Exceptional items after tax and minorities	(191)	53	(138)
Net profit (loss) for the financial year	(97)	180	83
	million	million	million
Weighted average Ordinary Shares in issue			
during year	728	728	728
Weighted average shares held by Group's			
employee share ownership plan	(4)	(4)	(4)
Basic weighted average Ordinary Shares			
in issue during year	724	724	724
Dilutive effect of share options	2	2	2
Diluted weighted average Ordinary Shares	726	726	726
	pence	pence	pence
Basic earnings (loss) per £1 Ordinary Share			
before exceptional items	13.0	17.5	30.5
after exceptional items	(13.4)	24.9	11.5
Diluted earnings (loss) per £1 Ordinary Share			
before exceptional items	12.9	17.5	30.4
after exceptional items	(13.4)	24.8	11.4

There are no options, warrants or rights outstanding in respect of unissued shares except for the share option scheme for employees (note 24).

Earnings per £1 Ordinary Share before exceptional items has been calculated to show the impact of exceptional items as these can have a distorting effect on earnings and therefore warrant separate consideration.

Extract 10.27.2

Reckitt & Colman plc
52 weeks ended 2 January 1999

8   Earnings per ordinary share (extract)

The reconciliations between profit for the financial year and the weighted average number of shares used in the calculations of the diluted earnings per share are set out below:

	1998			1997		
	Profit for the year £m	Average number of shares	Earnings per share pence	Profit for the year £m	Average number of shares	Earnings per share restated pence
Profit attributable to ordinary shareholders	165.3	407,572,659	40.6	215.8	406,061,743	53.1
Dilution for Executive options outstanding	–	767,211		–	603,986	
Dilution for Employee Sharesave Scheme options outstanding	–	721,484		–	377,760	
Dilution for convertible capital bonds outstanding*	12.8	39,233,910		12.6	39,758,610	
On a diluted basis	178.1	448,295,264	39.7	228.4	446,802,099	51.1

* After the appropriate tax adjustment, the profit for the year impact represents the coupon on the convertible capital bonds. The earnings per share impact reflects the effect of that profit and the assumption of the issue of shares on conversion of bonds.

Additional disclosures required in special circumstances

Disclosures

10.28   Where relevant, the following should be disclosed.

10.29   *Additional earnings per share.* Where an additional eps is disclosed, a reconciliation between the additional basic or diluted eps (calculated using a different profit figure) and the equivalent eps is required by FRS 14, together with the reason for calculating the additional version. [FRS 14(74)] The reconciliation should list the items for which an adjustment is being made and disclose their individual effect on the calculation. Either the reconciliation and explanation should appear adjacent to the eps disclosure or the eps disclosure should contain a reference to where the reconciliation and explanation are located. Where both additional basic and diluted amounts per share are presented, they should be disclosed with equal prominence and any additional version of eps presented should not be more prominent than the eps required by the FRS. This essentially repeats the requirement introduced by FRS 3 and adds an explicit reference to diluted eps.

10.30 *Restatement for bonus and similar issues.* The fact that the eps calculations have been adjusted for a bonus issue, share consolidation or other change in capital without a corresponding change in resources, occurring either during the period, or after the balance sheet date but before the date of approval of the financial statements. [FRS 14(63)]

10.31 *Share consolidation combined with special dividend.* The fact that prior periods' eps have not been adjusted for a share consolidation because it was combined with a special dividend and the overall commercial effect is of a share repurchase at fair value. [FRS 14(64)]

10.32 *Post balance sheet changes in share capital.* A description of any other post balance sheet changes in ordinary shares or potential ordinary shares if they are of such importance that non-disclosure would affect the ability of the users of the financial statements to make proper evaluations and decisions. [FRS 14(66)]

Commentary and example disclosures

10.33 The disclosure called for under **10.29** above essentially repeats the requirement in FRS 3 paragraph 25 and adds an explicit reference to diluted eps. In the light of the other changes introduced by FRS 3, presenting an additional eps has become quite common. See **10.38** below for the results of a survey carried out by *Company Reporting* on the incidence of additional eps. When an entity calculates an additional eps, basic or diluted, the amount should be calculated using the weighted average number of ordinary shares determined in accordance with FRS 14 [FRS 14 (73)]. FRS 14 requires an entity presenting an additional eps to present it on a consistent basis over time. [FRS 14 (74)]

10.34 Before disclosing additional earnings per share figures, companies' directors should think carefully about the message that they are attempting to convey and whether this message is best conveyed in the statutory accounts or by some other method. Any additional measure chosen to present a particular aspect of a company's performance that has improved may show the company in a different light in future years as the additional measure will need to be presented on the same basis in those years.

10.35 In the Financial Reporting Review Panel case involving H and C Furnishings plc (now renamed Harveys Furnishing plc), the company agreed to revise its 1997 financial statements for a number of issues; one being computational (calculation of purchase consideration) and the others all being disclosure and presentation. One of the disclosure issues that the company had to correct was that, although it had presented an additional eps, it had not disclosed the required reconciliation and explanation. Clearly, the Review Panel regards the disclosure as important. In disclosing the reason for calculating the additional eps, directors should take care not to imply that the additional eps is in any way more preferable to or meaningful than the FRS 14 eps.

10.36 The following extract illustrates the disclosure of a reconciliation and explanation.

Extract 10.36

Marks and Spencer plc

Year ended 31 March 1999

8.   Earnings per share (extract)

An adjusted earnings per share figure has been calculated in addition to the earnings per share required by FRS 14, 'Earnings per Share' and is based on earnings excluding the effect of the exceptional operating charges/income. It has been calculated to allow the shareholders to gain a clearer understanding of the trading performance of the Group. Details of the adjusted earnings per share are set out below:

| | 1999 | | 1998 As restated | |
	Basic	Diluted	Basic	Diluted
	p	p	p	p
Basic earnings per share	13.0	12.9	28.6	28.4
Exceptional restructuring costs	0.6	0.6	–	–
Exceptional fixed asset provision	2.2	2.2	–	–
Exceptional operating income	–	–	(1.3)	(1.3)
Adjusted earnings per share	15.8	15.7	27.3	27.1

10.37 Another example, illustrating a different additional eps, is set out below.

Extract 10.37

HSBC Holdings plc
Year ended 31 December 1998

9   Earnings per ordinary share (extract)

Headline earnings per share continues to have widespread acceptance and has been calculated in accordance with the definition in the Institute of Investment Management Research ('IIMR') Statement of Investment Practice No. 1, 'The Definition of IIMR Headline Earnings', as follows:

	1998 US$	1997 US$
Basic earnings per ordinary share	**1.61**	2.06
Adjustments:		
Gains on disposal of tangible fixed assets	**(0.01)**	(0.01)
Gains on disposal of subsidiary undertaking	**–**	(0.01)
Headline earnings per ordinary share	**1.60**	2.04

The additional eps disclosed in the example is headline earnings per share. This is discussed in **10.193** to **10.198** below.

10.38 *Company Reporting* included in its July 1997 edition the results of its survey on the incidence of additional eps. The results were:

Example 10.40

Calculation adopted for earnings per share ratio	1997 Total	(1995) Total
Number of companies	505	(475)
	%	%
FRS 3 earnings per share	100	(100)
Additional measure of earnings per share:		
FRS 3 before exceptional items	25	(17)
FRS 3 continuing operations	2	(3)
IIMR	5	(11)
Other measure	9	(10)
Two or more additional measures published	3	(3)
No disclosure of earnings per share	–	(–)

The IIMR eps is discussed in **10.193** to **10.198** below.

10.39

In giving the disclosure under **10.31** above, it would be helpful to add the positive statement that the special dividend and share consolidation have been dealt with in the eps calculation as if they were a share repurchase at fair value.

10.40 The transactions required to be disclosed under **10.32** above will not, by definition, be taken into account in calculating the eps for the period; instead, they will be reflected in the eps calculation for the period in which the transaction takes place. FRS 14 lists the following as examples of such transactions that might need to be disclosed:

(a) issue of shares for cash;

(b) the issue of shares when the proceeds are used to repay debt or preference shares outstanding at the balance sheet date;

(c) the redemption of ordinary shares;

(d) the issue of potential ordinary shares;

(e) the buy-back of ordinary shares outstanding;

(f) the conversion of potential ordinary shares, outstanding at the balance sheet date, into ordinary shares; and

(g) the achievement of conditions that would result in the issue of contingently issuable shares. [FRS 14(67)]

10.41

Under the disclosure requirement, such transactions are only disclosed if 'they are of such importance that non-disclosure would affect the ability of the users of the financial statements to make proper evaluations and decisions'. No explanation is given as to how FRS 14 intends this phrase to be interpreted.

10.42 Paragraph 41 of SFAS 128 contains a slightly different disclosure requirement. It calls for the disclosure of post balance sheet transactions 'that would have changed materially the number of [ordinary] shares or potential [ordinary] shares outstanding at the end of the period if the transaction had occurred before the end of the period'. This seems a reasonable interpretation of the FRS 14 phrase.

Further recommended disclosure

Disclosure

10.43 Where the terms and conditions of an instrument that generates potential ordinary shares affect the measurement of basic and diluted eps, disclosure of the terms and conditions is encouraged, but not required, whether or not disclosure is already required by FRS 4. [FRS 14(72)] FRS 14 notes that the terms and conditions may determine whether any potential ordinary shares are dilutive and, if so, determine the effect on the weighted average number of shares outstanding, together with any consequent adjustments to the net profit attributable to ordinary shareholders.

Commentary

10.44
> FRS 14 encourages the disclosure whether or not it is required by FRS 4. In practice, therefore, the paragraph only has effect to encourage disclosure where it is not already required by FRS 4. The only potential ordinary shares that might affect *basic* eps are contingently issuable shares.

Computation of basic earnings per share

Calculation of basic earnings per shares

10.45   Basic eps is calculated as: [FRS 14(9)]

$$\frac{\text{Net profit/loss for the period less non-equity dividends and other appropriations}}{\text{Weighted average number of ordinary shares outstanding during the period}}$$

The numerator is the net profit/loss attributable to the ordinary shareholders. [FRS 14(10)] This is divided by the weighted average number of ordinary shares outstanding to give the earnings per ordinary share.

Unit of presentation

10.46   Unlike SSAP 3, which stipulated that the eps had to be presented in pence, FRS 14 does not mandate the unit in which the eps has to be presented.

Ordinary shares

10.47   The meaning of ordinary shares is explained in **10.11** to **10.13** above.

Earnings – basic earnings per share

10.48   The principle is for the numerator to be the net profit/loss for the period attributable to ordinary shareholders. [FRS 14(10)] Since ordinary shares are defined as FRS 4 equity shares, it follows that the numerator is the profit or loss for the period less any appropriations, including dividends, to non-equity shareholders. The starting point for the profit figure is the profit after tax, after minority interests and after all exceptional and extraordinary items. [FRS 14(11)]

10.49

> The most common type of non-equity share likely to be of relevance is the preference share, whether or not redeemable. Examples of appropriations to non-equity shareholders are therefore likely to include:
>
> (a) Preference dividends;
>
> (b) Amortisation of issue costs over the term of redeemable preference shares; and
>
> (c) Accrued redemption premium on redeemable preference shares.

10.50 FRS 14 contains guidance on the amount of preference dividends to be deducted from net profit in calculating eps. [FRS 14(12)] The amount of dividends to be deducted is:

(a) for non-cumulative preference shares, the amount of preference dividends declared in respect of the period; and

(b) for cumulative preference shares, the full amount of the dividend accrued under FRS 4 for the period irrespective of whether the dividend has been declared. Dividends on the cumulative shares in respect of an earlier period but declared and/or paid during the current period are excluded.

10.51

> In practice, the amount of dividend or other appropriation on non-equity shares to be deducted in calculating eps should be the amount, calculated in accordance with FRS 4, deducted at the foot of the profit and loss account for the year in respect of non-equity appropriations.

10.52 As stated in **10.22** above, eps has to be calculated and disclosed for each separate class of ordinary share [FRS 14(13)], different classes having different rights to receive dividends. FRS 14 explains that 'where an entity has more than one class of ordinary shares the earnings for the period are apportioned over the different classes of shares in accordance with their dividend rights or other rights to participate in profits'.

10.53

> It is suggested that profits are divided between two (or more) classes on the following basis:
>
> (a) Allocate the dividend(s) declared for the period to each class of share in accordance with the amount payable to each class; and

(b) Allocate the retained profit between the classes as if it were distributed in full to the shareholders on the balance sheet date.

10.54 This principle is illustrated in the following example.

Example 10.54

Classes of shares

Assume a company has two classes of ordinary shares, 'A' and 'B', and that the 'B' shares are entitled to half the dividend per share declared by the directors on the 'A' shares. Assuming that there were an equal number of 'A' and 'B' shares in issue throughout the period, the total amount of profit less non-equity appropriations would be divided into three with two-thirds used to calculate the eps for the 'A' shares and the remaining third used to calculate the eps for the 'B' shares.

What if there were 200,000 'A' shares and 100,000 'B' shares in issue throughout the period and the net profit after non-equity appropriations totalled £300,000? FRS 14 does not explicitly state that the number of shares should be taken into account; it simply refers to apportioning the profits 'in accordance with their dividend rights or other rights to participate in profits'. However, if the total profit for the period were to be paid out to shareholders, £240,000 would be paid to the 'A' shareholders and £60,000 to the 'B' shareholders. Accordingly, it appears appropriate to reflect the number of shares in the division of profits. Thus, in this example, the profit of £300,000 would be split in the ratio of 4:1.

What if there were 200,000 'A' and 100,000 'B' shares in issue on the last day of the accounting period, but, because of share transactions during the period, the weighted average number of shares during the period was 120,000 'A' shares and 30,000 'B' shares? It is appropriate to split the retained profit in the ratio of 4:1 and add to this the dividends actually declared in respect of the period for each class.

If the dividends declared for the period were £77,143 to the 'A' shareholders and £15,000 to the 'B' shareholders, the net profit of £300,000 would be divided as:

'A' shareholders	£243,429	$(77,143 + \frac{4}{5}(300,000 - 92,143))$
'B' shareholders	£ 56,571	$(15,000 + \frac{1}{5}(300,000 - 92,143))$
	£300,000	

Now consider a variation. Assume the 'B' shares are entitled to half of the dividend per share declared by the directors on the 'A' shares, while the dividend on the 'A' shares is up to £1 per share or less, and one-quarter of the dividend per share declared on the 'A' shares for any 'A' share dividend in excess of £1.

Throughout the period, there were 100,000 'A' and 100,000 'B' shares in issue. The interim and proposed final dividends for the period for the 'A' shares were 30 pence and 50 pence respectively. Consequently, the total dividends declared on the shares for the period are:

'A' shares	£ 80,000
'B' shares	£ 40,000
	£120,000

The profit for the period (before deducting any equity dividends) attributable to the 'A' and 'B' shareholders totals £400,000.

If the company has never in the past declared a dividend on the 'A' shares in excess of £1, should the retained profit of £280,000 be divided in the ratio 2:1? Alternatively, if the profit were all distributed at the balance sheet date, it would be distributed in a ratio other than 2:1; does this mean 2:1 is not the correct ratio to use? If the eps calculations are to assume that the retained profit is all distributed on the balance sheet date, the retained profit of £280,000 could be allocated in two ways as follows:

Method one:	'A' shares	£204,000
	'B' shares	£ 76,000
		£280,000

Method two:	'A' shares	£214,000
	'B' shares	£ 66,000
		£280,000

Under method one, the first £150,000 of retained profit (i.e., a dividend of £1 per share for the 'A' shares) is divided in the ratio 2:1 and the remaining retained profit of £130,000 is divided in the ratio of 4:1. With method two, however, only £75,000 of the retained profit is divided in the ratio of 2:1 and the remaining £205,000 is divided in the ratio of 4:1.

> The reason for dividing only £75,000 in the ratio of 2:1 in method two is acknowledging the proposed final dividend on the 'A' shares of 50 pence per share and thus including the proposed final dividend in with the hypothetical dividend in determining the £1 cut-off.
>
> FRS 14 offers no guidance on which method is correct. Indeed, there is no guidance on whether or not to assume the profits are distributed on the balance sheet date or on some other date. An appropriate approach is not to divide all the retained profits in the ratio of 2:1, even if the dividend per 'A' share has never in the past been beyond £1 per share. Rather, assume that the retained profit is distributed in full on the balance sheet date. The more logical preference is method two if there is either an interim dividend declared on the balance sheet date or a proposed final dividend.

Number of shares – basic earnings per share

Weighted average

10.55   The number of shares used in the denominator should be the *weighted average* number of ordinary shares outstanding during the period. [FRS 14(14)] The weighted average number of ordinary shares outstanding during the period is the number of shares outstanding at the beginning of the period, adjusted by the number of ordinary shares bought back or issued during the period multiplied by a time-weighting factor. [FRS 14(15)] The time-weighting factor is:

$$\frac{\text{Number of days the shares are outstanding}}{\text{Number of days in the year}}$$

10.56   FRS 14 explains that, in many circumstances, a reasonable approximation of the weighted average is adequate. Indeed, in example 1 in FRS 14, an illustration of the calculation of the weighted average number of shares, new shares are issued on the last day of a month and shares are bought back on the first day of a month, and the time-weighting factor has been calculated using months, not days. The following example illustrates the calculation.

> **Example 10.56**
>
> **Computation of weighted average cost of shares**
>
> On 1 January 1999, X plc had 100,000 ordinary shares outstanding. The company purchased for cash, and cancelled, 8,000 shares on 15 June 1999, leaving 92,000 shares in issue. An additional 15,000 shares were issued in a share-for-share exchange to acquire a new

subsidiary; the acquisition date was 30 November 1999. There were no other share transactions during the year, giving 107,000 shares in issue at 31 December 1999, X's year end.

The computation of the weighted average number of shares outstanding can be done in two ways:

$$Either: \left(100,000 \times \frac{12}{12}\right) - \left(8,000 \times \frac{6\frac{1}{2}}{12}\right) + \left(15,000 \times \frac{1}{12}\right) = 96,917$$

$$Or: \left(100,000 \times \frac{5\frac{1}{2}}{12}\right) + \left(92,000 \times \frac{5\frac{1}{2}}{12}\right) + \left(107,000 \times \frac{1}{12}\right) = 96,917$$

Date of including new shares

10.57 FRS 14 contains some specific guidance on calculating the weighted average number of shares.

10.58 The general principle in the FRS is that 'in most cases, shares are included in the weighted average number of shares from the date consideration is receivable (which is generally the date of their issue)'. [FRS 14(17)] Thus, while SSAP 3 included shares on an 'output basis', i.e., the date from which they shared in the distribution of profits, FRS 14 adopts an 'input basis', i.e., the date that funds from shares contribute to earning profits. The FRS provides the following examples:

Example 10.58

Ordinary shares issued	Date from which included in weighted average computation
For cash	Date cash is receivable (see **10.63** below)
Under scrip dividend (see **10.60–10.62** below)	Dividend payment date
On conversion of debt instrument to ordinary shares	Date interest ceases accruing
In place of interest or principal	Date interest ceases accruing
In exchange for the settlement of a liability	Settlement date
As consideration for the acquisition of a non-cash asset	Date the acquisition is recognised (see **10.64** below)

10.59 The timing of the inclusion of the ordinary shares is determined by the specific terms and conditions attaching to their issue. In addition, FRS 14 calls for the substance of any contract associated with the share issue to be considered.

Scrip dividends

10.60 Legally, a scrip dividend can take one of two forms: a bonus issue or a reinvestment of a cash dividend. Under FRS 4 *Capital instruments*, the treatment on the face of the profit and loss account is identical (include in the dividend line at the amount of the cash dividend foregone) whichever of the two forms of scrip dividend is used. However, the reserves section of the balance sheet has to reflect the legal form of the scrip dividend.

10.61 FRS 14 does not actually use the term 'scrip dividend'. Instead, the wording used is 'ordinary shares issued on the voluntary reinvestment of dividends on ordinary or preference shares are included at the dividend payment date'. This could be read to imply that the treatment specified applies only to scrip dividends taking the legal form of the reinvestment of a cash dividend. If this is the case, how are scrip dividends that legally take the form of a bonus issue to be dealt with in the eps calculation: as a bonus issue or as a dividend reinvested on the dividend payment date?

10.62 The examples in FRS 14 paragraph 17 are not intended to be an exhaustive list. Accordingly, the omission of a scrip dividend with the legal form of a bonus issue does not automatically mean that FRS 14 intends them to be dealt with in the eps calculation as a bonus issue. In addition, the FRS stresses that 'due consideration is given to the substance of any contract associated with the issue'. For profit and loss account purposes, FRS 4 treats the substance of both kinds of scrip dividend in the same way: as a dividend. This approach would be similarly appropriate for eps purposes. Therefore, irrespective of the legal form of the scrip dividend, for eps purposes, it should be treated as shares issued on the dividend payment date.

Shares issued for cash

10.63 Even with the above guidance, it is not always clear from which date the shares should be included when they are issued for cash. Consider the following example.

Example 10.63

Shares issued for cash

X plc is making a rights issue. Provisional allotment letters in respect of the new shares are posted, by first class post, on 19 October 1999. Shareholders wishing to take up their entitlement must return the provisional allotment letter together with a remittance for the full amount payable so as to be received not later than 3.00pm on 17 November 1999.

Consequently, X will receive cash on a number of days, up to and including 17 November. X's earnings will benefit from the date the cash is received; the cash being available for investment when received. However, FRS 14 requires the shares to be included in the weighted average calculation from the date the cash is receivable.

In this example, 17 November 1998 is the date the cash is receivable (since this is the date by which X has asked to receive the cash and if X received no cash until this date it would still validly issue the shares). Accordingly, X should include the shares in its weighted average calculation from 17 November 1999.

Business combinations

10.64 For a business combination accounted for as an acquisition, the shares issued are included from the date the acquirer starts to recognise the results of the acquired entity's operations in its group profit and loss account. [FRS 14(18)] For a business combination accounted for as a merger, the shares issued are included for all periods presented because the financial statements of the group are presented as if the merged entities had always been merged.

Example 10.64

Shares issued in a merger

From 1 January 1999 to 31 May 1999, inclusive, A plc had 100,000 shares in issue. On 1 June 1999, A plc issued a further 100,000 shares to acquire the whole of the issued share capital of B plc. A plc changed its name to AB plc. No further share transactions took place during the remainder of 1999.

In AB plc's group financial statements for 1999, the combination with B plc was accounted for, in accordance with FRS 6, as a merger.

The shares in issue for AB plc and B plc during 1998 and 1999 were as follows:

	A plc/AB plc	B plc
1 January 1998	90,000	40,000
1 July 1998: shares issued for cash at market price	10,000	–
1 October 1998: shares issued for cash at market price	–	10,000
1 January 1999	100,000	50,000
1 June 1999: shares issued to shareholders of B plc	100,000	–
31 December 1999	200,000	50,000

Paragraph 18 of FRS 14 states that the number of shares to use in calculating eps for the merged results is the aggregate of the weighted average number of shares of the combined entities, adjusted to equivalent shares of the entity whose shares are outstanding after the combination.

Consequently, the weighted average number of shares to be used by AB plc in its group accounts is:

1999

$$\left(\left(100,000+\left(50,000\times\frac{2}{1}\right)\right)\times\frac{5}{12}\right)+\left(200,000\times\frac{7}{12}\right)=200,000$$

1998 (comparative)

$$90,000+\left(100,000\times\frac{6}{12}\right)+\left[\left\{40,000+\left(10,000\times\frac{3}{12}\right)\right\}\times\frac{2}{1}\right]=180,000$$

The above number for 1998 (180,000) is the number to be used in presenting a comparative in the 1999 group financial statements.

In A plc's financial statements for 1998 (i.e., before the merger), the weighted average number of shares that would have been used would have been 95,000, i.e.,

$$\left\{90,000+\left(10,000\times\frac{6}{12}\right)\right\}.$$

Shares held by a group company or ESOP trust

10.65 Shares that are held by an ESOP trust and, in accordance with UITF Abstract 13, are included as assets in the employer's balance sheet (because they have not yet vested unconditionally with the employees) are to be treated for eps purposes as if they had been cancelled [FRS 14(16)].

> *Example 10.65*
>
> **Shares in an ESOP**
>
> X plc has 250,000 £1 ordinary shares in issue on 1 January 1999 and throughout 1999.
>
> On 1 May 1999, the ESOP trust set up by X acquired 35,000 shares in X at the then market price of £4.80 per share. The ESOP trust previously held no shares in X.
>
> The shares held by the ESOP trust had not vested in the employees by 31 December 1999, X's balance sheet date, and accordingly the shares were included as assets in X's balance sheet.
>
> The weighted average number of shares in issue during 1999 to be used by X in calculating its eps is:
>
> $$\left(250,000 \times \frac{12}{12}\right) - \left(35,000 \times \frac{8}{12}\right) = 226,667$$

10.66   Where shares in a company are held by a group member and are not cancelled, FRS 14 requires the shares to be treated for eps purposes as if they had been cancelled. This is consistent with the treatment required by the FRS for shares held by an ESOP trust.

10.67

FRS 14 does not specify whether, for the rule in paragraph **10.66** above to apply, the group company holding the shares has to be one whose financial statements are included in the consolidated financial statements of the company presenting the eps. To illustrate this point, consider two listed companies, A plc and B plc.

(a)   Five per cent of A plc's shares are owned by one of A's subsidiaries. The shares in A have not been cancelled. The subsidiary is included on a consolidated basis in A's group accounts. In calculating its eps under FRS 14, A should treat these shares as if they had been cancelled.

(b)   Sixty per cent of B plc's shares are owned by C Inc, its parent undertaking. Although the shares in B are owned by an entity which is a group entity, the FRS does not appear to intend such shares to be treated for eps purposes as if they had been cancelled.

The rule in FRS 14 paragraph 16 should apply only to group entities included in the consolidated financial statements of the group headed by the company presenting an eps in accordance with FRS 14.

10.68   The following extract illustrates adjustments in respect of shares held by an ESOP trust and by group undertakings.

Extract 10.68

Reuters Group plc
Year ended 31 December 1998

7.   Earnings per ordinary share (extract)

The weighted average number of shares in issue may be reconciled to the number used in the basic and fully diluted earnings per ordinary share calculations as follows:

Weighted average number in millions	1998	1997	1996
Ordinary shares in issue	1,449	1,692	1,684
Ordinary shares held by group undertakings	–	(59)	(59)
Non vested shares held by employee share ownership trusts	(11)	(10)	(9)
Basic earnings per share denominator	1,438	1,623	1,616
Issuable on conversion of options	5	13	22
Fully diluted earnings per share denominator	1,443	1,636	1,638

Partly paid shares

10.69   As can be seen from **10.58** above, the thrust of FRS 14 appears to be to include shares in the calculation of eps from the date the share proceeds start to generate earnings. The FRS's treatment of partly paid shares is thus surprising. Rather than treat partly paid shares as a fraction of a share based on the proportion of the proceeds received, the FRS calls for them to be treated as a fraction of a share to the extent that they are entitled to participate in dividends relative to a fully paid up ordinary share during the period. Shares that are fully paid up are included in the eps calculation from the date the consideration is receivable, irrespective of whether they rank for dividends. [FRS 14(19)]

10.70   Thus, two £1 shares each not ranking for dividend, one 100p paid and the other 99p paid, will be treated differently in the eps computation. Both have contributed to earnings, but, while the first is included in basic eps, the second is excluded.

Contingently issuable shares

10.71   Contingently issuable shares are shares that will be issued at a future date only upon the satisfaction of certain conditions. An example would be shares to be issued under an earn-out agreement. See also **10.146** and **10.148** to **10.150** below for details of when awards under employee remuneration schemes are treated as contingently issuable shares. Under FRS 14, contingently issuable shares are included in basic eps from the date that all necessary conditions have been satisfied and thus, although issuing the shares is still a future transaction, it is no longer contingent; the reason is that there are no circumstances under which the shares will not be issued. [FRS 14(20)]

Example 10.71.1

Contingency based on an event

Company A acquires company B on 1 January 1999. Company A agrees to issue 100,000 shares to the vendor on 1 January 2001 if at any point prior to that date a new product developed, prior to the acquisition, by B is granted a licence.

Company A's year end is 31 December. The 1999 financial statements are approved on 22 March 2000. The product is granted a licence on 4 March 2000.

The 100,000 shares would be excluded from the basic eps for 1999 and would be included in the basic eps for 2000 as if the shares had been issued on 4 March 2000 (the date the licence was granted).

(See **10.154** and **10.155** and example **10.159.2** below for how such shares are dealt with in the diluted eps computation.)

Example 10.71.2

Contingency based on average profits

Company A acquires company B on 1 January 1999. Company A agrees to issue 100,000 shares to the vendor on 1 January 2002 if B's profits for the three years to 31 December 2001 average £1 million or more.

Company B's profits in each of 1999 and 2000 are £1.7 million.

The shares are excluded from both the 1999 and 2000 basic eps. Even if profits for the year 2001 are expected to be above £1, such that the earnings condition will be met, the shares are excluded from basic eps until the contingency period has ended; until then, it is not known for certain whether all the necessary conditions will be satisfied since, however unlikely, a loss could be made in the year 2001 and thus the earnings condition not be met.

(See **10.154**, **10.155**, **10.160** and **10.161** and the example in **10.161** below for how such shares are dealt with in the diluted eps computation.)

Deferred shares

10.72   FRS 14 contains no guidance at all on how to deal with
deferred shares. In this context, a distinction can be drawn
between deferred shares and contingently issuable shares.
Whereas contingently issuable shares are shares that will be
issued at a future date only upon the satisfaction of certain
conditions, deferred shares are shares that will be issued at a
future date and are not subject to any conditions. Deferred
shares typically arise under acquisition agreements. For example, X plc might purchase Y Limited, paying 500,000 shares at
the date of acquisition and a further 100,000 shares one year
after the date of acquisition. Although the FRS does not
address deferred shares, it follows from the guidance on contingently issuable shares that deferred shares are included in
the calculation of basic eps as if they had been issued on the
date that the consideration for the shares is receivable. In the
above example, therefore, all 600,000 shares should be included
in the calculation of basic eps from the date that Y Limited is
brought into X plc's group financial statements.

10.73   An acquisition agreement may provide for further shares to be issued
but the exact number of shares has not been specified. For example,
an agreement may provide that shares valued at £500,000 on a specified future date will be issued, the number of shares to be determined by dividing £500,000 by the share price on the specified future
date. Such shares would be contingently issuable shares rather than
deferred shares.

*Changes in share capital with no corresponding change in the
entity's resources*

10.74   When there is, for example, a bonus issue, the number of shares outstanding increases but the resources available to the entity do not
change. Consider, for example, a company with the following balance sheet as at 31 December 1998:

Net assets	£900,000
Share capital	100,000
Reserves	800,000
	£900,000

On 31 December 1998 and throughout the year then ended, the
share capital comprised 100,000 £1 ordinary shares. On 1 January
1999, the company made a 1:1 bonus issue. The balance sheet immediately after the bonus issue would be as follows:

Net assets	£900,000
Share capital	£200,000
Reserves (800,000 – 100,000)	700,000
	£900,000

The company's net assets do not alter and so the revenue generating ability of the company is unchanged. Consequently, there is no expectation that earnings will alter as a result of the change in share capital. Assuming that profit attributable to ordinary shareholders for each of 1998 and 1999 was £20,000, then treating the bonus issue as an issue of shares for consideration would give eps results as follows:

Example 10.74

	1999	1998
Earnings per share	10 pence	20 pence

Clearly, these results are not comparable; the profits are identical in each of the years and, if no shareholders had sold their shares, the number of shareholders would be identical. Yet the above eps results gives the appearance that the company was less profitable in 1999 than in 1998.

10.75 Consequently, FRS 14 requires that if the number of ordinary shares outstanding is changed by events, other than the conversion of potential ordinary shares and other than when certain share consolidations are combined with a special dividend (see **10.94** below) with no corresponding change in resources, the weighted average number of shares used in calculating basic eps is adjusted as if the change in the number of ordinary shares had taken place at the start of the earliest period for which an eps will be presented. [FRS 14(21)] See **10.80** to **10.93** below for further details. The effect is similar to taking an identical amount of earnings and cutting it into a larger number of smaller slices. Thus, in the example in **10.74** above, the eps calculated in accordance with FRS 14 would be:

Example 10.75

	1999	1998
Earnings per share	10 pence	10 pence

10.76 Bonus issues are not the only example of a change to the number of shares in issue with no corresponding change in resources. The FRS lists the following examples: [FRS 14(22)]

(a) a bonus issue;

(b) a bonus element in any other issue or buy-back, e.g., a bonus element in a rights issue to existing shareholders, or a put warrant, involving the repurchase of shares at significantly more than their fair value (see **10.79** below);

(c) a share split; and

(d) a share consolidation.

The list is not exhaustive.

10.77 Bonus issues, share splits and share consolidations are all adjusted for in the same way, i.e., by adjusting the number of shares outstanding as if the bonus issue, share split or share consolidation had occurred at the start of the earliest period for which an eps is presented (see **10.80** below for further details).

10.78 For rights issues, and bonus elements in any other issue or buy-back, the FRS specifies a formula to be used to calculate the adjustment to the shares in issue before the rights issue (see **10.81** below).

10.79

> The inclusion of the second example in **10.76**(b) above is curious. The principle is to adjust all eps calculations when there is a change in the number of shares *with no corresponding change in resources*. However, the specific example given is where there is a put warrant involving the repurchase of shares at significantly more than fair value. This does involve a change in resources and could equally be seen as equivalent to buying shares back at fair value and paying a special dividend of the excess above fair value. Viewed in this way, there would not be any adjustment to eps, since FRS 14 does not make adjustment for special dividends. However, given such an explicit example in the FRS, any entity issuing warrants to repurchase shares at significantly more than fair value should follow the treatment outlined in the FRS. This is illustrated in the following example.

Example 10.79

Bonus element in put warrant

X plc has 50,000 ordinary shares in issue before issuing put warrants.

X issues put warrants to shareholders, issuing one warrant for every 50 shares held. Each put warrant entitles the shareholders to sell one share to the company for £14. The last date the put warrants can be exercised is 1 July 1999. The fair value of one ordinary share immediately before exercise of the warrants on 1 July 1999 was £10.

The theoretical ex-warrant price per share is:

$$\frac{(50{,}000 \times £10) - (1{,}000 \times £14)}{(50{,}000 - 1{,}000)} = \frac{£486{,}000}{49{,}000} = £9.92$$

The adjustment factor as explained in **10.88** is therefore:

$$\frac{£10}{£9.92}$$

X's profit for the year ended 31 December 1999 was £45,000.

Basic eps for 1998 is:

$$\frac{£45{,}000}{\left(500 \times \dfrac{10}{9.92} \times \dfrac{6}{12}\right) + \left(49{,}000 \times \dfrac{6}{12}\right)} = £0.90$$

Bonus issue, share split or share consolidation

10.80 Here, the number of ordinary shares outstanding is adjusted as if the bonus issue, share split or share consolidation had taken place at the start of the earliest period for which an eps is presented. [FRS 14(23) and (25)]

Example 10.80

Bonus issue

	1999	1998
Profit attributable to ordinary shareholders	£22,631	19,000

Number of shares:

	1999	1998
1 January	120,000	100,000
1 April: issue for cash at fair value		20,000
1 July: issue for cash at fair value	10,000	
1 October: 1:2 bonus issue	65,000	
31 December	195,000	120,000

The weighted average number of shares is calculated as follows:

$$1999 \quad \left(120{,}000 \times \frac{3}{2} \times \frac{12}{12}\right) + \left(10{,}000 \times \frac{3}{2} \times \frac{6}{12}\right) = 187{,}500$$

$$1998 \quad \left(100{,}000 \times \frac{3}{2} \times \frac{12}{12}\right) + \left(20{,}000 \times \frac{3}{2} \times \frac{9}{12}\right) = 172{,}500$$

Therefore, the eps is as follows:

$$1999 \qquad \frac{£22,631}{187,500} = 12.1 \text{ pence}$$

$$1998 \qquad \frac{£19,000}{172,500} = 11.0 \text{ pence}$$

Rights issue

10.81 When shares are offered to shareholders in a rights issue, the price at which they are offered is often less than the fair value of the shares. Consider, for example, a company whose shares are priced at £10. The company offers its shareholders one new share for every four held, giving 100,000 new shares, at £8 per share. Share proceeds of £800,000 will be received and 100,000 shares issued. This is equivalent to issuing 80,000 shares at fair value (of £10 per share) and making a bonus issue of 20,000 shares. This is the bonus element in the rights issue.

10.82 Where there is a bonus element in the rights issue, the eps is calculated as if the bonus element (but not the total rights) arose at the start of the earliest period for which an eps is presented. If there is no bonus element in the rights issue, the new shares issued are treated as an issue for cash at fair value (since that is what they are).

10.83 In order to calculate basic eps where there is a bonus element, however, the above transaction would not be treated as an issue of 80,000 shares at fair value and a bonus issue of 20,000 shares. Instead, as did SSAP 3, the FRS specifies a formula to be used. [FRS 14(24)] If the fair value used to calculate the number of shares issued for no consideration ("the bonus issue") is the same as the fair value of the shares immediately before the exercise of rights, the two methods give identical answers. The formula specified in the FRS is discussed and illustrated in the paragraphs below.

10.84 In calculating basic eps when there has been a rights issue, the number of ordinary shares outstanding prior to the rights issue is multiplied by:

$$\frac{\text{Fair value per share immediately before exercise of rights}}{\text{Theoretical ex-rights fair value per share}}$$

10.85 The FRS specifies that where, before the exercise date, the rights are to be publicly traded separately from the shares, the numerator is the fair value of the shares at the close of the last day on which the shares are traded together with the rights.

10.86 The appendix to SSAP 3 specified that the numerator was the 'cum-rights' share price. It is clear from the above that FRS 14's numerator should also be the 'cum-rights' price. A company is likely to have this information available in its company secretarial department. If not, its brokers are likely to be able to supply the information.

10.87 The theoretical ex-rights fair value per share is:

$$\frac{\text{Fair value of shares outstanding immediately before exercise of rights plus proceeds from exercise of rights}}{\text{Number of shares oustanding after exercise of rights}}$$

Example 10.87

Rights issue

	1999	1998
Profit attributable to ordinary shareholders	£610,000	£455,000

Number of shares:		
1 January	350,000	350,000
1 April: issue for cash at fair value	50,000	
1 July: 1:4 rights issue	100,000	
31 December	500,000	350,000

1 July 1999 was the last day on which the rights could be exercised. The fair value of the ordinary shares on 1 July 1999 immediately before exercise was £10. The exercise price of the rights was £8.

Theoretical ex-rights value per share:

$$\frac{(400,000 \times £10) + (100,000 \times £8)}{(400,000 + 100,000)} = £9.60$$

Adjustment factor:

$$\frac{£10}{£9.60} = £1.04$$

The weighted average number of shares is:

$$1999 \left(350,000 \times 1.04 \times \frac{6}{12}\right) + \left(50,000 \times 1.04 \times \frac{3}{12}\right) + \left(500,000 \times \frac{6}{12}\right) = 445,000$$

$$1998 \left(350,000 \times 1.04 \times \frac{12}{12}\right) = 364,000$$

Therefore, the eps is as follows:

$$1999 \quad \frac{£610,000}{445,000} = £1.37$$

$$1998 \quad \frac{£445,000}{364,000} = £1.25$$

In this example, it is important that the factor of 1.04 is multiplied by the number of shares outstanding prior to the rights issue only for the period up to the rights issue.

Thus, the weighted average number of shares for 1999 can be calculated as:

Either: $\left(350,000 \times 1.04 \times \frac{6}{12}\right) + \left(50,000 \times 1.04 \times \frac{3}{12}\right) + \left(500,00 \times \frac{6}{12}\right)$, as above,

Or: $\left(350,000 \times 1.04 \times \frac{3}{12}\right) + \left(400,000 \times 1.04 \times \frac{3}{12}\right) + \left(500,000 \times \frac{6}{12}\right)$

But *not* as $\left(350,000 \times 1.04 \times \frac{12}{12}\right) + \left(50,000 \times 1.04 \times \frac{9}{12}\right) + \left(100,000 \times \frac{6}{12}\right)$

The latter calculation has adjusted the 350,000 and 50,000 shares for the whole year, and not just the pre-rights issue period.

10.88 Consider an entity that makes a rights issue containing a bonus element and also has some contingently issuable shares for which all the necessary conditions have been met.

Example 10.88

Impact of bonus issue on contingently issuable shares

A company has 1,000,000 ordinary shares in issue from 1 January 1999 to 30 September 1999. On 1 October 1999, the company made a rights issue and issued 200,000 additional shares. The adjustment factor for the bonus element in the rights issue is 1.1. There were no further share transactions during the year.

However, during 1998, the company had acquired a subsidiary and, under the acquisition agreement, had agreed to issue 100,000 shares on 11 May 2000 if certain conditions were met at any point prior to 11 May 2000. All the conditions were satisfied on 1 July 1999. Thus, in calculating basic eps for 1999, the shares are treated as though they had been issued on 1 July 1999.

Exactly how the weighted average number of shares is calculated for 1999 will depend upon the precise terms of the contingently issuable shares.

If the number of shares to be issued on 11 May 2000 is to be increased by the bonus factor of 1.1, the calculation will be as follows:

$$1999 \left(1,000,000 \times 1.1 \times \frac{9}{12}\right) + \left(100,000 \times 1.1 \times \frac{6}{12}\right) + \left(1,200,000 \times \frac{3}{12}\right) = 1,180,000$$

If the number of shares to be issued on 11 May 2000 is not adjusted in any way to take account of the rights issue, but will remain at 100,000, the calculation will be as follows:

$$1999 \left(1,000,000 \times 1.1 \times \frac{9}{12}\right) + \left(100,000 \times \frac{6}{12}\right) + \left(1,200,000 \times \frac{3}{12}\right) = 1,175,000$$

Post-year end changes

10.89 The paragraphs above describe adjustments to eps for bonus, issues, and other changes in the number of shares without a corresponding change in resources. FRS 14 does not limit the adjustment to bonus, and similar, issues taking place before the balance sheet dates but extends the adjustments to issues taking place after the balance sheet date but before the date that the accounts are approved [FRS 14(63)].

Example 10.89

Post balance sheet date issue of shares

A company has 1,000,000 ordinary shares in issue throughout 1998 and 1999. Earnings attributable to ordinary shareholders for 1999 total £330,000 (1998 – £220,000). On 1 February 2000, the company issues 100,000 ordinary shares in a 1:10 bonus issue. The financial statements for 1999 are not approved until 22 March 2000.

In producing the 2000 financial statements, FRS 14 requires the company to take account of the bonus issue as though it had taken place at the start of the earliest period for which an eps is presented. Thus, the 1999 eps that is presented as a comparative to the 2000 eps will be adjusted as if the bonus issue had been at the start of 1999, making the 1999 eps 30p (£330,000 divided by 1,100,000 shares).

FRS 14 extends this principle and requires that if the bonus issue (or any other change in the number of shares in issue with no correspon-ding change in resources) takes place before the 1999 financial state-ments are approved, the eps disclosed in those 1999 financial statements, together with any comparatives to the 1999 eps, are adjusted for the bonus issue (or other change in the number of shares with no corresponding change in resources) as if this took place at the start of the earliest period for which an eps is presented. Consequently, in the 1999 financial statements, the eps will be presented as:

1999   30p   (£330,000 divided by 1,100,000 shares)

1998   20p   (£220,000 divided by 1,100,000 shares)

This treatment means that, in order to interpret a company's eps for a year, it is necessary to know both the date that the financial statements were approved and what, if any, changes to share capital took place by this date.

10.90 FRS 14 requires a post-year end, but pre-approval of the financial statements, change in capital to be reflected in the financial statements only when the change in shares does not result in a corresponding change in resources. FRS 14 paragraph 22 lists examples of such share issue. In the above example, had the 100,000 shares issued on 1 February 2000 been an issue for cash at fair value, no restatement would have been necessary and the 1999 financial statements would have presented eps information as:

1999   33p   (£330,000 divided by 1,000,000 shares)

1998   22p   (£220,000 divided by 1,000,000 shares)

A note would give details of the post-year end share issue for cash.

Conversion of potential ordinary shares

10.91 In discussing the treatment where an entity issues shares but receives no corresponding increase in resources, both FRS 14 paragraph 21 and FRS 14 paragraph 63 (both of which are **bold** typeface paragraphs and are therefore mandatory) exclude from their scope 'the conversion of potential ordinary shares'. However FRS 14 paragraph 24, which deals with rights issues, opens with the sentence: 'The issue of ordinary shares at the time of exercise or conversion of potential ordinary shares *will not usually* give rise to a bonus element, since the potential ordinary shares will usually have been issued for full value, resulting in a proportionate change in the resources available to the entity' (our emphasis).

10.92 This raises a number of questions:

(a)   does this mean that FRS 14 paragraphs 21 and 63 cannot be relied upon and that an entity must consider each conversion of potential ordinary shares to see whether or not it contained a bonus element?

(b) executive options are usually issued with an exercise price equal to the market price on the date of grant. This can be considerably below the market price on the date of exercise. Should these be treated as containing a bonus element?

(c) options issued under SAYE schemes usually have an exercise price below the market price at the date of grant. Should such options be treated as containing a bonus element?

10.93

FRS 14 paragraph 24 talks about the entity issuing the shares for 'full value'; it does not specify that this all has to be cash. Accordingly, if the full value (whether for a rights issue, share option, converting a debenture, etc.) is made up of cash plus employees' services, no bonus element would be present. It is considered that, generally, the conversion of potential ordinary shares should not be treated as containing a bonus element. Where an entity wishes to make a bonus issue, rights issue containing a bonus element, etc., but does so not by conventional means, but through the use of potential ordinary shares, then FRS 14 paragraphs 21 and 63 cannot be relied upon. Instead, the substance of the transaction(s) has to be considered.

In-substance share buy-backs

10.94 A number of companies have in recent years gone into the market and bought back, and cancelled, some of their issued share capital. Other companies have achieved the same effect, although the legal form of the transaction has been different. An example of the latter would be Southern Electric plc. During its year ended 31 March 1996, Southern Electric paid a special dividend and at the same time carried out a share consolidation. The two transactions were designed to achieve the same overall effect as a buy-back of shares at market value.

10.95 Ordinarily, under FRS 14, dividends on ordinary shares do not affect the eps calculation, whereas, as seen above, a share consolidation is dealt with by adjusting the shares in issue as if the share consolidation had happened at the start of the earliest period for which an eps is presented. The position was the same under SSAP 3.

Example 10.95

Share repurchase effected by a special dividend and consolidation

A company has 500,000 ordinary shares in issue on 1 January 1999. The company wishes to effect a share buy-back. Accordingly, on 1 July

1999, when its share price is £6, it pays a special dividend of £300,000 and undertakes a 10:9 share consolidation, issuing nine new shares for every 10 old shares held. As a result, only 450,000 shares are in issue for the remainder of 1999.

Earnings for 1999 total £360,000.

If eps is calculated by treating the special dividend as a dividend and the share consolidation as a share consolidation, the result is:

$$\text{1999 eps} \quad \frac{£360,000}{450,000} = 80\text{p}$$

However, had the company gone into the market and purchased 50,000 shares at the market price of £6 per share, it would also have paid out £300,000 and reduced the number of shares in issue to 450,000. Had it done this, the eps would be:

$$\text{1999 eps} \quad \frac{£360,000}{\left(500,000 \times \frac{12}{12}\right) - \left(50,000 \times \frac{6}{12}\right)} = 75.79\text{p}$$

10.96 In the above example, the substance of the first transaction is the same as a purchase of shares at fair value, the difference being that some capital is returned to each shareholder rather than only to those wishing to sell in the market.

10.97 SSAP 3 did not address this combination of events. The following extract from Southern Electric's 1996 financial statements shows that it calculated and presented the eps as if there had been a share buy-back (rather than in accordance with the actual legal form of the transactions).

Example 10.97

Southern Electric plc

Year ended 31 March 1996 (extract)

11. Dividends

	1996	1995
	£ m	*£ m*
Interim paid: 10.5 per 50p share (1995: 8.3p)	28.8	22.7
Final proposed: 27.0p per 53^{71}/$_{93}$p share		
(1995: 20.2p per 50p share)	69.9	55.2
	98.7	77.9
Special paid: 50p per 50p share (1995: Nil)	137.1	–

Distribution of National Grid Group plc shares at a value of 127.1p per 50p share (1995: Nil)	348.2	–
	584.0	77.9

At the Extraordinary General Meeting held on 23 January 1996, the shareholders approved the payment of a special dividend of 50p per ordinary share, amounting to £137.1 million and a consolidation of the share capital by the issue of 93 new ordinary shares of $53^{71}/_{93}$p each for every 100 existing 50p ordinary shares.

The shareholders also approved the distribution of shares in The National Grid Group plc in the proportion of 0.66 NGG shares for each 50p ordinary share held.

12. Earnings per share

The earnings per ordinary share of 196.3p have been calculated by dividing the profit for the financial year of £530.1 million (1995: £155.5 million) by 270,106,219 ordinary shares, being the weighted average number of shares in issue during the year (1995: 272,328,210).

As described in note 11, during the year the Company paid a special dividend of £137.1 million and at the same time carried out a consolidation of its share capital. These transactions were designed and intended to achieve the same overall effect on the Company's capital structure as a buy-back of shares, but in a way in which all shareholders could participate. Accordingly, the directors consider it appropriate to present the earnings per share on the basis that in substance a share buy-back has occurred.

The earnings per share would have been 208.3p if it had been calculated on the basis that the share consolidation had occurred at the commencement of the financial year.

An earnings per share before exceptional items of 86.9p based on profits of £234.7 million and weighted shares in issue of 270,106,219 has been given in order to provide a fairer indication of the trend in earnings.

10.98 FRS 14 explicitly provides that where a share consolidation is combined with a special dividend and the overall commercial effect in terms of net assets, earnings and number of shares is of a repurchase at fair value, the eps is calculated as if there had been a repurchase of shares at fair value on the date that the special dividend is paid (i.e., when the resources leave the entity). [FRS 14(26)] Consequently, the dividend and share consolidation are not treated for eps purposes as a dividend and a share consolidation respectively. Instead, the eps is calculated in accordance with the substance of the transactions.

10.99 Combining a special dividend with a share consolidation is not the only way of achieving an in-substance share buy-back. However, FRS 14 deals only with the one specific example of a special dividend being combined with a share consolidation; disappointingly, it does not lay down a general principle that an in-substance buy-back can be treated as if it were an actual buy-back.

10.100 In FRS 14 appendix II 'The development of the FRS', the ASB explains that, although it was asked by respondents to the FRED 16 supplement to extend the treatment to other forms of in-substance share buy-back, it restricted its *discussions* to special dividends combined with a share repurchase 'given the additional time and research that would be required in order to satisfy itself that other types of combinations achieved a similar effect through different routes'.

10.101 In the light of this explanation, it would be possible for the UITF to issue pronouncements as to whether other specific combinations of transactions could be dealt with as if they were a share repurchase at fair value. Additionally, in the absence of more specific guidance, directors could cite the spirit of FRS 14 paragraph 26 and FRS 14 paragraph 64 to apply the in-substance treatment to some other combination of transactions. Before doing so, directors should ensure that their arguments are robust enough to withstand a challenge from the Financial Reporting Review Panel.

Impact of bonus issues on terms of potential ordinary shares

10.102 Bonus issues (and other similar issues listed in FRS 14 paragraph 22) have the effect of diluting shareholders funds into a larger number of smaller units. It follows that the terms under which potential ordinary shares, such as options and convertible stocks, are issued will need to be revised to reflect the dilution.

Example 10.102

Effect of bonus issue on option terms

A company has granted options to 100,000 shares at £1.20. The company makes a one for five bonus issue to its ordinary shareholders, such that a shareholder with five shares receives a sixth share as a bonus.

The terms of the option issue will be restated to reflect the bonus issue as follows:

Number of options increased by bonus ratio.

Price paid to exercise decreased by bonus ratio.

Thus:

$$\text{Revised number of options} = 100{,}000 \times \frac{6}{5} = 120{,}000$$

$$\text{Exercise price} = \pounds 1.20 \times \frac{5}{6} = \pounds 1$$

The effect is that the proceeds of all options being exercised is unchanged.

Demergers

10.103 Most commonly, a reduction in the number of an entity's shares will result from a repurchase at fair value. A further example arises where part of a group is demerged through the distribution of shares to shareholders *in specie*. FRS 14 does not deal with this situation. The following treatment is suggested as appropriate:

(a) consolidated financial statements for each part of the demerged group are prepared as if the separate parts had always been independent; the effect is similar to merger accounting under FRS 6, except that balance sheets and profit and loss accounts are disaggregated rather than aggregated;

(b) earnings, before and after the demerger, will be based on the separate disaggregated information; and

(c) number of shares will be based on the share structure after the demerger as if that share structure had been in place throughout all periods covered by the eps (subject to other changes in share capital).

Computation of diluted earnings per share

Structure of FRS requirement

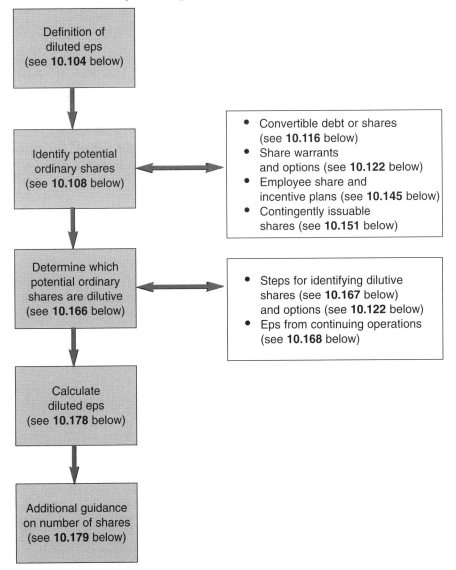

Diluted earnings per share

Definition and general principles

10.104 Diluted eps is calculated as:

$$\frac{\text{Earnings per basic eps} + \text{adjustment for dilutive potential ordinary shares}}{\text{No. of shares per basic eps} + \text{adjustment for dilutive potential ordinary shares}}$$

10.105 Diluted eps should be calculated by an entity if it had dilutive potential ordinary shares outstanding at any point during the year (see **10.188** to **10.190** below).

(a) Potential ordinary shares are considered in **10.108** below, including the definition, examples, and adjustments which are reflected in the dilutive eps calculation for each type of potential ordinary share.

(b) Potential ordinary shares are dilutive if their conversion to ordinary shares would decrease net profit, or increase net loss, per share from continuing operations (see **10.166** below). [FRS 14(56)]

(c) Dilutive potential ordinary shares are taken into the calculation of diluted eps as if the potential ordinary shares had been converted to ordinary shares at the start of the period (or date of issue of potential ordinary shares if later). [FRS 14(29)]

(d) Anti-dilutive potential ordinary shares are disregarded in the calculation of diluted eps.

10.106 Diluted eps as required by FRS 14 is not the same as SSAP 3's fully diluted eps:

(a) FRS 14 'is drafted on the basis that diluted earnings per share is an additional past performance measure, consistent with that of basic earnings per share while giving effect to all dilutive potential ordinary shares';

(b) SSAP 3's fully diluted eps was a forward-looking measure based on the worst case future dilution.

10.107 One difference is that while SSAP 3 started with the total number of shares in issue at the balance sheet date, FRS 14 starts with the weighted average number of shares used in the basic eps calculation. A second difference is contingently issuable shares; as will be explained in **10.154** below, if the conditions for issuing the shares have not been met at the balance sheet date, the shares are excluded from the calculation of diluted eps even if, by the date the financial statements are approved, the conditions have been met and cannot be reversed and thus the directors know that the shares will ultimately be issued.

Potential ordinary shares

Objective

10.108 Before diluted eps can be calculated, it is necessary to identify:

(a) what potential ordinary shares exist;

(b) what adjustment would be made, to earnings and to the number of shares, for these potential ordinary shares in the event that they are dilutive.

N.B. This information is needed before proceeding to determine whether each potential ordinary share is dilutive. How to determine whether potential ordinary shares are dilutive is considered in **10.166** below.

Definition and examples

10.109 Potential ordinary shares are defined as 'a financial instrument or a right that may entitle its holder to ordinary shares'. [FRS 14(2)]

10.110

> Examples of potential ordinary shares include:
>
> (a)   debentures convertible into ordinary shares;
>
> (b)   preference shares convertible into ordinary shares;
>
> (c)   warrants and options to purchase or subscribe for ordinary shares;
>
> (d)   an award granted under a long-term incentive plan entitling an employee to a specified number of ordinary shares if targets are met over a number of years; and
>
> (e)   Shares to be issued by a purchaser to the vendor, in accordance with an acquisition agreement, if the profits of the acquired business over a number of years exceeds a target.

Summary of impact on earnings and on number of shares

10.111 The general principle is that to calculate diluted eps both the numerator (earnings) and denominator (number of shares) used to calculate basic eps are adjusted as though the dilutive potential ordinary shares had been converted to ordinary shares at the start of the period or, if later, the date the potential ordinary shares were issued.

10.112 Summary of adjustments in the diluted eps calculation for potential ordinary shares:

Potential ordinary share	Adjustment to earnings	Adjustment to number of shares
Convertible debentures and preference shares	Add interest, dividends, and other finance costs charged in the period, net of tax (see **10.117** below)	Add number of new shares assuming full conversion (see **10.121** below)
Warrants and options	Generally none (see **10.124** below)	Add number of shares deemed to be issued free of charge (see **10.125** below)

Employee share plans with performance conditions	As for contingently issuable shares	As for contingently issuable shares
Employee share plans without performance conditions	As for warrants and options (no adjustment to earnings to remove UITF Abstract 17 charge) (see **10.146**(b) and **10.152** below)	As for warrants and options (adding future UITF Abstract 17 charges to the deemed proceeds of exercise) (see **10.146**(b) and **10.151** below)
Contingently issuable shares	None (see **10.156** below)	Add number of shares issued based on whether conditions were met at the balance sheet date (see **10.158** below)

Further points on diluted earnings adjustment

10.113 The diluted earnings adjustment is generally the actual charge to the profit and loss account in the year which would have been avoided had the potential ordinary shares been converted to actual ordinary shares. However, in addition to interest and dividends, adjustment is required for 'any other changes in income or expense that would result from the conversion of the dilutive potential ordinary shares'. [FRS 14(53)]

10.114 This further adjustment is intended to cover any consequential changes in income or expense arising from the dilutive potential ordinary shares being ordinary shares rather than potential ordinary shares. [FRS 14(55)] For example, for convertible redeemable bonds, it is likely that the amount of tax charged through the profit and loss account would have been different had the bonds been converted into ordinary shares on the first day of the period. If so, the adjustment must include the consequential adjustment to the tax charge.

10.115 Similarly, the company might operate a profit-related pay or other bonus scheme. Where the charge to the profit and loss account in respect of the scheme would be different had the bonds been converted to ordinary shares on the first day of the period then, again, the adjustment to earnings would include the adjustment to the charge in respect of the scheme.

Convertible debt or shares

Approach

10.116 Convertible debt and convertible shares follow the general principle and have no peculiarities.

Adjustment to earnings

10.117 The adjustment is the post-tax amount recognised in the profit and loss account in respect of finance costs. [FRS 14(54)]

10.118 For a debt instrument, this will be:

- interest charged;

- amortisation of issue costs; and

- amortisation of redemption premium or discount.

In each case, an adjustment is made for tax at a marginal rate.

10.119 For equity and non-equity shares, the adjustment will be:

- dividends charged;

- amortisation of issue costs; and

- amortisation of redemption premium.

10.120

A question arises whether issue costs should be adjusted, since they have already been incurred in full. Nevertheless, it is considered that all three, interest, amortisation of redemption premium and amortisation of issue costs, should be adjusted. This is because all three would have been absent from the profit and loss account for the year had the instrument been converted into shares on the first day of the year. In addition, when the instrument is actually converted, any unamortised issue costs at that point will not be charged in that or any subsequent annual profit and loss account.

Example 10.120

Effect of potential ordinary shares on earnings

A company has a profit attributable to ordinary shareholders for the year ended 31 December 1999 of £740,000. The company has three different potential ordinary shares, all of which are dilutive, which are as follows:

- £100,000 6% convertible redeemable bonds (issued in 1996);

- £100,000 8% convertible bonds (issued 1 July 1999); and

- 100,000 × £1 17% convertible preference shares (issued in 1997).

The finance charge and associated tax effect recognised in the profit and loss (P&L) account for the year ended 31 December 1999 in respect of the above:

	Finance charge recognised in P&L account for year	Associated tax credit	Net of tax cost
	£	£	£
Dilutive potential ordinary shares:			
6% bonds*	7,000	2,800	4,200
8% bonds**	4,000	1,600	2,400
Preference shares	17,000	–	17,000

The right-hand column above, headed 'net of tax cost', is used to adjust earnings in diluted eps calculations. In respect of the 8% bonds issued during 1999, only £2,400 (£4,000 less £1,600) has been charged against earnings. Consequently, only £2,400 can be added back to the earnings number in calculating diluted eps.

*   Including accrued redemption premium.

**   The bonds were only issued on 1 July 1999 and so the finance cost is charged from that date.

Adjustment to number of shares

10.121 The adjustment assumes that all convertible instrument holders exercise all rights to convert to ordinary shares. Where different conversion ratios are allowed at different dates, the ratio used should assume the maximum number of new ordinary shares being issued (see **10.179** below).

Share warrants and share options

Approach

10.122 SSAP 3 assumed that any cash proceeds received on exercising options and warrants would be, for the purposes of calculating fully diluted eps, invested in $2^1/_2$ per cent consolidated stock and thus earnings were increased by the notional interest (less tax) that such investment would have earned and the shares were adjusted by the number of shares that would be issued assuming that all options are exercised. FRS 14 assumes that the proceeds of issuing options (or other potential ordinary shares that lead to cash proceeds) could have been raised by issuing shares at fair value, i.e., based on market value during the period. To the extent that the number of shares actually issuable exceeds the equivalent number at fair value, the excess is deemed to be shares issued for no consideration, and is added in full to the diluted eps adjustment. A similar approach, using different underlying logic but achieving the same answer, is used in other countries, particularly the USA, and is referred to as the 'treasury stock' method.

10.123 For simplicity, the remainder of this section refers just to options, rather than to warrants and options.

Adjustment to earnings

10.124 Generally, there will be no adjustment to earnings. However, there may be occasions when FRS 14 (53)(c) would require an adjustment to earnings. An example where adjustment would be required is where: an ESOP trust holds shares that are used when options are exercised; the ESOP trust had purchased the shares in the market using a loan it had received directly from a third-party bank; and the proceeds received by the ESOP trust on the exercise of options are used immediately to repay an equivalent amount of the bank borrowings. In such circumstances the interest payable on the bank borrowings, together with the tax effect, if any, would be adjusted out of the earnings.

Adjustment to number of shares

10.125 The number of shares is adjusted by the number of shares deemed to be issued free of charge.

Summary of method

10.126 (a) Calculate the cash proceeds which would be received if all options were exercised at the contracted exercise price.

(b) Calculate the number of shares which if issued at the average fair value share price for the period would generate the same proceeds:

   (i) compute the average fair value of ordinary shares for the accounting period;
   (ii) divide the cash proceeds from step (a) by this average fair value.

(c) Compute the number of shares deemed to be issued for no consideration:

   (i) compute the total number of shares which would be created if all options are exercised;
   (ii) deduct from this total the number of shares deemed to be issued at fair value from step (b).
   (iii) treat the resulting number of shares as shares issued for no consideration.

> ### *Example 10.126*
>
> **Impact of exercising options**
>
> In 1997 a company granted 10,000 options exercisable at £8 per share. The average fair value of its shares during the year ended 31 December 1999 was £10.
>
> In order to calculate diluted eps for 1999, the options are assumed to be exercised on 1 January 1999, thus it is assumed that 10,000 shares are issued and £80,000 cash is received. The £80,000 cash received is now treated as though it were received from issuing shares at the average fair value during the period. Thus, 8,000 shares are assumed to have been issued at £10 each. In calculating diluted eps, the difference between the number of shares that would have been issued had all the options been exercised (10,000) and the number of shares assumed to be issued at fair value (8,000), 2,000, is added to the number of shares used in the denominator. Consider whether there should be an adjustment to the earnings figure used in the numerator (see **10.124** above).

All options or just some options?

10.127 Only dilutive potential ordinary shares are included in the calculation of diluted eps. Thus, the above exercise applies only to dilutive options. See **10.166** below, which covers the guidance in FRS 14 on determining which potential ordinary shares are dilutive and thus should be included in the calculation on diluted eps. There are two additional factors to consider with respect to options; these are discussed in **10.128** to **10.135** below.

10.128 When an option holder exercises options, the company will fulfil its side of the contract either by:

(a)   issuing new shares; or

(b)   by buying existing shares in the market at the exercise date; or

(c)   by using shares held for that purpose by an ESOP trust.

10.129 Clearly, in the case of (b), the total number of shares in issue is unaffected by the exercise of options. Where, under the terms of the grant of options, the shares (to satisfy the exercise of the options) have to be purchased in the market at the exercise date, the options would not be dilutive and thus would be excluded from the calculation of diluted eps.

10.130 In the case of (a), the total number of shares in issue is affected by the exercise of options and thus the options might be dilutive and the company has to consider whether the options are in or out-of-the-money (see **10.133** to **10.135** below).

10.131 Where a company can choose whether to issue new shares or buy existing shares in the market at the exercise date then, following the principle in FRS 14(32) (see **10.180** below), if the company has either a stated policy or past experience of always buying the shares in the market, the options would not be treated as dilutive; otherwise the options might be dilutive and the company has to consider whether the options are in or out-of-the-money (see **10.133** to **10.135** below).

10.132 In the case of (c), shares are purchased in the market by an ESOP trust which holds them for use when option holders exercise options. When calculating basic eps the shares are treated as though they had been cancelled (see **10.65** above). Consequently, such shares should be brought into the calculation of diluted eps and treated like case (a) above.

10.133 The FRS contains specific guidance for determining whether share options and share warrants are dilutive for a profitable company. FRS 14 paragraph 37 states that 'options and other share purchase arrangements are dilutive when they would result in the issue of ordinary shares for less than fair value. The amount of the dilution is fair value less the issue price'. In other words, it is saying that in-the-money options are dilutive and out-of-money options are anti-dilutive and can therefore be disregarded. The following examples demonstrate that while this is true for a profitable company, it is false for a loss-making company.

Example 10.133.1

In-the-money options are dilutive for a profitable company

During the year ended 31 December 1999, the profit attributable to the ordinary shareholders of X plc was £2,000,000. All the operations during the year were continuing operations.

The weighted average number of ordinary shares in issue during the year was 5,000,000.

The basic eps for the year was therefore 40p.

During the year, X plc had 1,000,000 shares under option at an exercise price of £3.50.

X had no other potential ordinary shares in issue during the year.

In-the-money

Assume that the average fair value of X's shares during the year was £4.

The proceeds received on exercise of the options = £3,500,000.

This is equivalent to issuing 875,000 shares at fair value.

Thus, 125,000 shares are deemed to be issued for no proceeds.

Diluted eps is therefore 39p (£2,000,000 divided by 5,125,000 shares).

Out-of-the-money

Assume now that the average fair value of X's shares during the year was £3.

The proceeds received on exercise of the options would be £3,500,000.

This is equivalent to issuing 1,166,667 shares at fair value.

This is 166,667 shares more than would actually be issued. Hence, it is equivalent to issuing 1,166,667 shares at fair value together with a share consolidation, or buying shares back for no consideration.

This would give an eps of 41p (£2,000,000 divided by 4,833,333 shares).

Example 10.133.2

In-the-money options are anti-dilutive for a loss-making company

The details are the same as the previous example except that, instead of making a profit in 1999, X plc made a loss attributable to ordinary shareholders of £3,000,000. The basic loss per share is therefore 60p.

In-the-money

This was equivalent to issuing 875,000 shares at fair value and 125,000 shares for no consideration.

Thus, 'dilutive' loss per share would be 59p.

Out-of-the-money

This was equivalent to issuing 1,166,667 shares at fair value and then buying 166,667 shares back for no consideration, giving a 'diluted' loss per share of 62p.

10.134

FRS 14 paragraph 56, which has a **bold** typeface and therefore is a mandatory paragraph, states that 'potential ordinary shares should be treated as dilutive when, and only when, their conversion to ordinary shares would decrease net profit *or increase net loss per share from continuing operations*' (our emphasis). The in-the-money options in the above example reduce the loss per share and thus are not dilutive as defined in the FRS. The out-of-the money options increased the loss per share and so met the FRS's criteria for being dilutive. However, option holders would not usually exercise out-of-the-money options. Does this mean a company should follow the guidance in FRS

14 paragraph 37 and disregard all out-of-the-money options? This is unlikely to be possible: FRS 14 paragraph 37 is not a bold typeface paragraph, whereas FRS 14 paragraph 56 is **bold** typeface. Accordingly, it appears that where an entity has losses attributable to ordinary shareholders from continuing operations, out-of-the-money (and not in-the-money) options are dilutive.

10.135 In summary:

	In-the-money options	Out-of-the-money options
Loss from continuing operations:	Anti-dilutive	Dilutive
Profit from continuing operations:	Dilutive	Anti-dilutive

Calculating average fair value during the period

10.136 In order to bring options into the adjustment for diluted eps, it is necessary for the entity to know the average fair value of its ordinary shares during the period. However, the FRS contains no guidance at all on how this should be calculated.

10.137 The US standard, SFAS 128, does contain guidance. It starts by pointing out that the average shall represent a 'meaningful average' and that, theoretically, the average could be determined by using every market transaction in the entity's shares during the year. From a practical standpoint, however, it acknowledges that a simple average of weekly or monthly closing prices will usually be adequate. Where prices fluctuate widely over the period, week or month, being used the US guidance suggests that an average of the high and low prices for the period would produce a more representative price than simply using the closing price for the period. The US guidance concludes with: 'The method used to compute the average market price shall be used consistently unless it is no longer representative because of changed conditions. For example, an entity that uses closing market prices to compute the average market price for several years of relatively stable market prices might need to change to an average of high and low prices if prices start fluctuating greatly and the closing market prices no longer produce a representative average market price'.

10.138 It seems preferable, where an average is not based on actual transactions, to calculate the average by using the price at the close of each day in the year. Where there has been very little change throughout the year, then the closing price at the end of each week or month could instead be used. However, since the principles underlying the US standard are so similar to those underlying FRS 14, it would be acceptable for an entity to apply the US guidance, rather than calculate the average using daily information.

10.139   A company is likely to have the share price information available in its company secretarial department. If not, its brokers are likely to be able to supply the information.

Options granted during the year

10.140

Options, as with any potential ordinary shares, are included in the calculation of diluted eps as if conversion into ordinary shares had occurred on the first day of the accounting period or, if later, the date on which the option or other potential ordinary shares were granted. Where options are granted part way through a year, the question arises whether the average fair value should be the average from the date the option is granted to the end of the year or the average for the entire accounting period.

Example 10.140

Average share price

X plc's share price is £3 for the four months 1 January to 30 April, £4 for the four months 1 May to 31 August and £5 for the four months 1 September to 31 December. The average price for the year is therefore £4.

On 1 July, X plc grants 10,000 options exercisable at £4 per share, the then market price.

The average price from 1 July to 31 December is £4.67.

Thus, the shares are neither dilutive nor anti-dilutive if compared with the average for the year, but are dilutive if compared to the average price since the date the options were granted.

10.141

The only references in FRS 14 are to the average price 'during the reporting period', implying that the average for the year should be used in all cases. The reference in paragraph 17 of SFAS 128 clearly implies using the average for the year, even though earlier in the paragraph it refers to granting options during the year in question.

10.142   In the above example, using the average for the year results in no dilution, whereas using the average since the date of grant of the options results in dilution. It can be argued that following the requirements of FRS 14 to use the average for the whole period gives an answer in this case which does not reflect the substance. In view of the wording in FRS 14, the average for the whole year should generally be used, but in cases where this gives a distorted answer, as in the above example, the average for the period that the options are in issue may be used.

Options exercised during the year

10.143 Considerations similar to those applying when options are granted in the year apply when options are exercised during the year. Consequently the guidance in **10.142** above should also be applied in respect of options exercised during the year.

Does each option issue have to be looked at separately?

10.144 A company might have granted options in each of the last, say, ten years and at its balance sheet date have some options outstanding from each of the ten issues. The question arises whether the company would have to consider each option issue separately or on an aggregated basis. The company should first decide, using the average price for the period, which options are dilutive; for a profitable company, this will be those options with an exercise price below the average price for the period. Once the dilutive options have been identified, these can then be dealt with on an aggregated basis.

Example 10.144

Identifying dilutive options

At 1 January and 31 December 1999, X plc, which had made a profit from continuing operations during the year, had the following options outstanding:

Number of shares under option	Exercise price	Average share price during year	Dilutive or anti-dilutive	Number of shares deemed issued for no consideration
10,000	£7	£10	D	3,000
5,000	£8	£10	D	1,000
15,000	£9	£10	D	1,500
10,000	£12	£10	A	–
20,000	£11	£10	A	–
				5,500

Alternatively, the company could have calculated the 5,500 shares to be added to the numerator of the diluted eps calculation as:

$$(10,000 + 5,000 + 15,000) - \frac{\{(10,000 \times £7) + (5,000 \times £8) + (15,000 \times £9)\}}{10}$$

Employee share and incentive plans

Approach

10.145 Incentive plans forming part of employee remuneration have changed quite considerably in recent years. A few years ago, incentive plans might have comprised a bonus payable in cash and/or share options with no performance conditions attaching. Now, while some bonuses are still based on one year's performance, it is increasingly common to have bonuses with a performance period of three or four years. Also, while some bonuses are still payable in cash, it is increasingly common for long-term bonuses to be payable in the company's shares or for options to be exercisable only if certain performance conditions have been met.

10.146 The FRS draws a distinction only between incentive schemes in which awards are based on performance criteria, and any other scheme generating potential ordinary shares.

(a) Performance-based awards are to be treated as contingently issuable shares, since their issue or exercise is contingent upon factors other than the passing of time, such as the level of future earnings (see **10.154** below). [FRS 14(40)] Examples are given in **10.149** below.

(b) All other awards made under an employee share or other incentive scheme are regarded as options for the purpose of calculating diluted earnings per share. [FRS 14(41)] They are to be regarded as outstanding as of the grant date, even though their exercise may be contingent upon vesting. They are to be included in the computation, even if the employee may not receive (or be able to sell) the shares until some future date. Accordingly, all shares to be issued are included in calculating diluted eps if the effect is dilutive. Where the awards are granted during the period, the shares to be issued are weighted to reflect that fact (see **10.122** above). Further detailed guidance, in particular, in respect of the impact of UITF 17 charges, and an example are given in **10.151** to **10.153** below.

(c) Any bonuses to be settled in cash have no impact on eps beyond the impact of payments on earnings.

10.147 Share arrangements which may be satisfied by the purchase of shares in the market or cash are considered in **10.180** below. [FRS 14(44)]

Awards based on performance criteria – examples

10.148 FRS 14 paragraph 40 calls for awards based on performance criteria to be treated as contingently issuable shares. Whether or not shares are issued depends upon whether or not the conditions are satisfied.

10.149 The following example illustrates how a performance-based award might impact on the calculation of diluted eps.

Example 10.149

Performance award of shares

X plc operates a long-term incentive scheme as follows. At the start of each three-year period, a conditional award of shares is made to each participating employee, the initial award being 30 per cent of basic salary divided by the share price on the date the conditional award is made. Whether or not the shares vest in the participating employee depends upon the company's TSR relative to the TSR for the FTSE 100 over the three-year period immediately following the date the conditional award is granted. If, at the end of the three-year period, the company's TSR is in the first (upper) quartile, all the shares vest in the employees; if the TSR is in the second quartile, 50 per cent of the shares vest in the employees and no shares vest if the TSR is below the second quartile.

This scheme has been running for a number of years and, during the year ended 31 December 1999, the following conditional awards were outstanding:

Scheme	Note	Maximum potential Share awards
1996–1998	1	70,000
1997–1999	2	68,000
1998–2000	3	72,000
1999–2001	4	70,000

Notes

1   The maximum potential share award for the scheme running from 1 January 1996 to 31 December 1998 was paid out in full on 1 May 1999.

2   The TSR for the three years to 31 December 1999 was in the second quartile. Therefore, 50 per cent of the shares will be paid on 30 April 2000.

---

3   The company's TSR for the two years ended 31 December 1999 is in the second quartile relative to the FTSE 100.

4   The company's TSR for the year ended 31 December 1999 is in the third quartile relative to the FTSE 100.

1996-1998 scheme

The conditions attaching to the 1996–1998 scheme were all met at 31 December 1998. Thus, the 70,000 shares would be included in the calculation of basic eps for the whole of 1999.

1997-1999 scheme

The performance period for the 1997–1999 scheme ended on 31 December 1999, giving rise to an award of 50 per cent of the maximum potential award. Therefore, 34,000 shares would be included in the calculation of diluted eps for 1999. The shares would be excluded from the basic eps calculation of 1999.

1998–2000 and 1999–2001 schemes

The performance periods for the 1998–2000 and 1999–2001 schemes have not ended by 31 December 1999. FRS 14 paragraph 46 specifies that contingently issuable shares are included in diluted eps 'on the assumption that the current amount of earnings or status of the condition, as appropriate, were to remain unchanged until the end of the agreement, if the effect is dilutive'. This suggests, therefore, that the company's TSR relative to the FTSE 100 is considered at 31 December 1999 and the relative position is assumed to remain unaltered until the end of the relevant scheme period. On this basis, no shares are included in the 1999 diluted (or basic) eps calculation in respect of the 1999–2001 scheme and there are two possible ways of calculating the number of shares to be included in the 1999 diluted eps calculation in respect of the 1998–2000 scheme. There will be no impact on the 1999 basic eps in respect of the 1998–2000 scheme. The two methods of calculating the shares to be included in the 1999 diluted eps in respect of the 1998–2000 scheme are:

Method one

36,000 shares (being 50 per cent of 72,000 shares).

Method two

(Assume for this that the UITF Abstract 17 charge in respect of the 1998–2000 scheme is £108,000 in each of the three years 1998 to 2000 inclusive and that the fair value of a share during the year is £10.) Thus, 36,000 shares (being 50 per cent of 72,000 shares) are deemed to be issued for consideration of £108,000 (being the UITF Abstract 17 charge that has not yet been debited to the profit and loss account).

Using the 'options' method of calculation, this would suggest including 25,200 shares (being 36,000 less (108,000 divided by £10)) in the diluted eps calculation.

> *Which of the two methods should be used?*
>
> Although method two is consistent with the treatment set out in the FRS for option schemes not related to performance, FRS 14 paragraph 42 rules it out. Accordingly, method one should be followed.

10.150 FRS 14 paragraph 40, in justifying why performance-based awards are to be treated as contingently issuable shares, explains that 'their issue *or exercise* is contingent upon factors other than the passing of time, such as the level of future earnings' (emphasis added). The reference to 'or exercise' implies that options whose exercise is conditional upon the satisfaction of performance criteria can also be classified as performance-based awards. The difference between treating such options as contingently issuable shares and all other contingently issuable shares is that the options are the only kind of 'contingently issuable share' where cash proceeds are received on conversion. The FRS does not explicitly state how such options are to be dealt with in the diluted eps computation. The following example provides a suitable treatment.

Example 10.150

Options exercisable based on performance

On 1 May 1998, X plc granted 50,000 share options exercisable from 1 May 2002 to 30 April 2008 at a price of £10 per share, providing the rise in basic eps from the 1998 figure over the three calendar years to 31 December 2001 exceeds the movement in retail price index (RPI) by at least five per cent.

The average fair value of the company's share during the year ended 31 December 1999 was £11.50.

In calculating the diluted eps for the year ended 31 December 1999, the options should be treated as follows:

First, ascertain whether the 1999 basic eps exceeds the 1998 eps by the movement in RPI plus five per cent or more: if so, the options will be included in the diluted eps.

Second, calculate the number of shares to include in the diluted eps computation (using the usual method for options). This is done by subtracting from the number of shares that will be issued the number that could have been issued for fair value to generate the same proceeds, namely:

$$\left(50,000 - \frac{(50,000 \times £10)}{£11.50}\right) = 6,522$$

Non-performance related awards – further guidance and example

10.151   The dilutive effect of options is explained and examples are given in **10.122** to **10.126** above. In applying that method, FRS 14 states that 'the assumed proceeds of the potential ordinary shares may need to be adjusted to reflect the fact that they have been earned by past services. This will be the case for those schemes to which UITF Abstract 17 *Employee share schemes* is applied and which are not considered as contingently issuable shares. Here, the assumed proceeds consist of the consideration, if any, the employee must pay upon exercise of the award and the cost of the shares calculated in accordance with UITF Abstract 17 but not yet recognised in the profit and loss account. Initially, dilution is less because part of the consideration consists of future services not yet received. It becomes greater, over time, as the entity's earnings reflect the benefits of having received those services'. [FRS 14(42)] This is illustrated in example **10.153** below.

10.152   However, when adjusting net profit for the purpose of diluted earnings per share, no adjustment is permitted in respect of the UITF Abstract 17 charge to the profit and loss account, as the charge represents a cost of issuing the potential ordinary shares that would not be saved on conversion. [FRS 14(43)]

10.153   FRS 14's argument is that the charge represents a cost of issuing the potential ordinary shares that would not be saved on conversion. However, after conversion the charge will no longer be in the profit and loss account, so the argument appears strange. Nevertheless, the guidance in the FRS should be followed and no adjustment made.

Example 10.153

Non-performance related awards

X plc granted, on 1 May 1998, 100,000 share options to employees. The options are exercisable at £3 per share from 1 May 2001 to 30 April 2008, providing the employee is still employed by X plc at the date of exercise. There are no performance conditions attaching to the options.

The UITF Abstract 17 charge is £3 per share option, to be charged over the period from 1 May 1998 to 30 April 2001. Thus the UITF Abstract 17 charge in each of 1999 and 2000 is £100,000. The charge in 1998 was £66,667 and in 2001 will be £33,333.

The average fair value of a share during 1999 was £6.50 and during 2000 was £7.

The number of shares to be included in the diluted eps calculation for each of 1999 and 2000 is as follows:

1999 $100,000 - \dfrac{(100,000 \times £3) + £133,333}{£6.50} = 33,333 \text{ shares}$

2000 $100,000 - \dfrac{(100,000 \times £3) + £33,333}{£7} = 47,619 \text{ shares}$

Contingently issuable shares

Approach

10.154 Contingently issuable shares are shares that will be issued at a future date, subject to the satisfaction of conditions. The conditions can be linked to earnings, the market price of the shares or something else. Although contingently issuable shares are another example of potential ordinary shares, they are nevertheless sometimes included in the calculation of basic eps. This is dealt with in **10.71** above while **10.155** et seq. discusses how they impact on diluted eps.

10.155 The approach of FRS 14 is to assume that the balance sheet date of the reporting period was the end of the contingency period. [FRS 14(46)] The diluted eps computation includes those shares, if the effect is dilutive, that would be issued under the terms of the contingency on the assumption that the current amount of earnings or status of the condition, as appropriate, were to remain unchanged until the end of the agreement.

Adjustment to earnings

10.156 Contingently issuable shares have no impact on the earnings figure used to calculate diluted eps. This applies even if the condition is itself earnings. The reason for this is that the number of contingently issuable shares included in the diluted eps calculation is always based on the status of the condition at the balance sheet date. Thus, when the condition is earnings, shares are not included in the calculation unless they require an earnings level that has already been achieved.

10.157 Under SSAP 3, shares would sometimes be included in the calculation of fully diluted eps that required an earnings level that had not yet been achieved. In such circumstances, as well as increasing the number of shares used in the calculation, the earnings figure would also have been adjusted to reflect the additional earnings required in order to trigger the share issue. This can never arise under FRS 14, because the number of shares assumed issued is always based on an earnings level already achieved.

Adjustment to number of shares

10.158 The number of contingently issuable shares to be included in the calculation is based on the number of shares that would be issuable if the end of the reporting period was the end of the contingency period.

  (a) Where a condition is expressed as an average over a period, it has the same effect as if it were expressed as a cumulative amount over the period – the performance achieved to date is deemed to be that achieved over the whole of the contingency period. [FRS 14(46)] For example, if the number of shares to be issued depends on whether profits average £100,000 over a three-year period, the condition is expressed in terms of a cumulative target of £300,000 over the three-year period. If, at the end of the first year, profits are £150,000, no additional shares are brought into the calculation.

  (b) Where the number of shares that may be issued in the future depends upon the market price of the shares of the issuing company, the number of shares to be included in the calculation of diluted eps, if dilutive, is based on the number that would be issued, based on the current market price at the end of the current reporting period or the average over a specified period, depending on the terms of the underlying contract. [FRS 14(47)]

  (c) For deferred consideration agreements, in which the consideration is fixed but the number of shares issuable is not known, the number of shares to be included in the calculation is based on the market price at the balance sheet date as if it were the end of the contingency period. [FRS 14(48)]

  (d) If the contingency is based on a condition other than earnings or market price, the contingently issuable shares are included on the assumption that the status of the condition at the end of the reporting period will remain unchanged until the end of the contingency period. [FRS 14(49)] For example, if a further issue of shares is generated on the opening of the tenth new retail outlet and at the year end only five have been opened, no contingently issuable shares are included in the diluted eps computation.

10.159 Although the number of additional shares is based on the year end position, the shares are included (as with all potential ordinary shares) as if they had been issued on the first day of the year or, if later, the date the potential ordinary shares came into existence. [FRS 14(45)]

Example 10.159.1

Condition based on share price movements

X plc is to issue the following number of shares to a third party on 1 October 2000, dependent upon X's share price on 30 September 2000:

Number of shares	Share price on 30 September 2000
Nil	£10 or less
10,000	>£10 and <£11
15,000	£11 or above

If, on 31 December 1999, the last day of X's reporting period, the share price was £9.92, no shares would be included in the diluted eps calculation, whereas an additional 10,000 shares would be included if the share price on 31 December 1999 were £10.21.

What if the share price had been above £10 every day between 21 November 1999 and the date the financial statements were signed other than on 31 December 1999 when the price dipped to £9.98? Under the guidance in the FRS, none of these shares would be included in the diluted eps calculation.

What if the condition had been conditional upon the average share price for the last five business days up to and including 30 September 2000? The diluted eps would be computed by looking at the share price on the last five business days up to and including 31 December 1999 and comparing this with the target average price.

Example 10.159.2

Condition based upon successful event

Company A acquires company B on 1 January 1999. Company A agrees to issue 100,000 shares to the vendor on 1 January 2001 if at any point prior to that date a new product developed, prior to the acquisition, by B is granted a licence.

Company A's year end is 31 December. The 1999 financial statements are approved on 22 March 2000. The product is granted a licence on 4 March 2000.

Even though the directors of company A know, at the date they approve the 1999 financial statements, that the additional 100,000 shares will be issued to the vendor on 1 January 2001, the shares are excluded from the calculation of diluted eps for 1999, because, as at the balance sheet date, the licence had not been granted.

The 100,000 shares would be included in the calculation of diluted eps for 2000; they would be included as if they had been in issue throughout the entire year.

See example **10.71.1** above for how the shares would be included in basic eps.

10.160 Particular problems arise evaluating conditions that contain an average. FRS 14 states that 'where a condition is expressed as an average over a period it has the same effect as if it were expressed as a cumulative amount over the period – the performance achieved to date is deemed to be that achieved over the whole of the contingency period'.

10.161 Hence, if shares are to be issued based on attaining a target of opening an average of three new retail stores each year for three years, the FRS would say this is equivalent to requiring nine new retail stores to be opened over the three years. If, at the end of year one, four new stores had been opened then, in accordance with the FRS, the additional shares will be excluded from the calculation of diluted eps, since four stores falls short of the requirement of nine and activity post-year end has to be assumed to be nil. Similarly, a condition requiring average profit of £0.7 million per annum over two years, under the FRS, is treated as if it were a requirement for profits in total of £1.4 million over the two years.

Example 10.161

Condition based on average profits

Company A acquires company B on 1 January 1999. Company A agrees to issue 100,000 shares to the vendor on 1 January 2002 if B's profits for the three years to 31 December 2001 average £1 million or more.

Company B's profits in each of 1999 and 2000 are £1.7 million.

Under FRS 14, a requirement for average profits of £1 million over three years is to be treated as a requirement for total profits of £3 million over the three years.

Actual profits in 1999 of £1.7 million are below the target of £3 million and, accordingly, the 100,000 shares are excluded from the diluted eps calculation for 1999.

Actual profits for 1999 and 2000 together total £3.4 million. This exceeds the target and thus the 100,000 shares would be included in the diluted eps for 2000. The shares would be included even if B were expected to make a loss of £0.4 million or more in 2001.

See example **10.75.2** in **10.75** above for how the shares would be included in basic eps.

10.162 When the share issue is dependent on a number of conditions being met, e.g., a product licence being granted before a certain date *and* a profit target over the same period, then the diluted eps calculation only includes those shares when all (both in the case of the example) the conditions have been met at the balance sheet date. [FRS 14(50)]

Contingently issuable potential ordinary shares

10.163 The guidance set out in **10.158** above in respect of contingently issuable shares also applies to contingently issuable share options, warrants, convertibles and any other potential ordinary shares.

10.164 FRS 14 states that 'where an entity has contingently issuable potential ordinary shares (e.g., contingently issuable warrants) in respect of the same class of ordinary shares and on the same terms as warrants, etc. currently in issue then, for consistency, the former may be included in the diluted earnings per share calculation only if conversion or exercise of the warrants, etc. already in issue is also assumed'. [FRS 14(51)]

10.165

> This appears to imply that if a company has, say, contingently issuable options and, in addition, has options with identical terms (exercise price, date, etc.) in issue, the contingently issuable options are only included in the calculation of diluted eps if the options in issue are themselves dilutive.

Example 10.165

Contingently issuable options

On 1 July 1998, X plc granted 10,000 share options exercisable at £5 per share from 1 July 2001 to 30 June 2008. On the same date, X plc agreed to issue on 1 July 2000 a further 10,000 share options with identical exercise price and dates, providing X's profit over the two years to 30 June 2000 exceeds a specified target.

X's financial year runs to 31 December.

The average fair value of X's ordinary shares during the year ended 31 December 1999 was £5.50 and during this year X had a profit attributable to ordinary shareholders.

For 1999, the share options are dilutive and the 10,000 that were granted on 1 July 1998 will be included in the calculation of diluted eps for 1999 as if 9,091 shares were issued for fair value (and thus are not dilutive) and 909 shares were issued for no consideration (and thus are dilutive).

The 10,000 options that might be issued on 1 July 2000 will similarly be included in the 1999 diluted eps calculation as if they were the issue of 9,091 shares that are not dilutive and 909 shares that are

> dilutive, but only if the profit target has been reached at the balance sheet date (31 December 1999). If the profit target has not been reached by the balance sheet date, nothing is included in the 1999 diluted eps in respect of the options that might be issued on 1 July 2000.

Dilutive potential ordinary shares

10.166   Potential ordinary shares are treated as dilutive if their conversion to ordinary shares would decrease net profit or increase net loss per share from *continuing* operations. [FRS 14(56)]

Steps for identifying dilutive potential ordinary shares

10.167   FRS 14 stipulates the steps to be followed in determining which potential ordinary shares are dilutive. Each different category of potential ordinary shares is tested; the order in which they are tested is not left to each entity to choose, but is set out in the FRS. [FRS 14(61)] The steps are as follows:

(a)   An entity lists each different category of potential ordinary shares that it has, e.g., a five per cent convertible bond would be considered separately from a seven per cent convertible bond.

(b)   For each category of potential ordinary shares, the entity determines how the earnings would have been affected had the potential ordinary shares been converted to shares on the first day of the year (or date of issue of potential ordinary shares if later). The adjustment to earnings for this purpose will be the same as the adjustment detailed in **10.112** above. The earnings will either be increased (increased profit or reduced loss) as a result of a convertible security or will not be affected at all if converting the potential ordinary shares injects cash into the entity.

(c)   For each category of potential ordinary shares, the entity then determines (in accordance with the rules in the FRS) the number of shares that would be issued if the potential ordinary shares were converted to shares. Thus, if an entity has bonds convertible into 100,000 ordinary shares, the number of shares will be 100,000. However, if the same entity has granted 100,000 share options, the number of shares to be used in the calculation is not 100,000, but is the number that are deemed to be issued for nil proceeds (see **10.122** and **10.126** above). In addition, not all options are considered at this stage (see **10.127** to **10.135** above for a discussion on which options to include in this exercise).

(d)   The adjustment to earnings is then divided by the number of shares that would be issued on conversion to give, for each category of potential ordinary shares, the additional earnings per additional share that would have been generated had the additional shares been issued.

(e) These additional earnings per additional share are ranked, the lowest being ranked first and the largest increase in earnings per new share being ranked last.

(f) The continuing earnings per share (see **10.168** below) is calculated.

(g) The continuing earnings per share is then adjusted, for the category of potential ordinary shares ranked first, by increasing the continuing earnings and increasing the number of shares.

(h) The 'before' and 'after' eps are compared: if the new eps is less the potential ordinary shares are dilutive.

(i) Steps (g) and (h) are repeated for each category of potential ordinary shares in turn in accordance with its ranking.

Some examples and further explanation are included in **10.178** below.

Profit/Loss per share from continuing operations

10.168 In order to determine which potential ordinary shares are dilutive, FRS 14 requires an analysis of the effect of conversion to ordinary shares on net profit or loss from continuing operations. A potential ordinary share is dilutive when conversion decreases net profit or increases net loss per share from continuing operations.

10.169 Profit/Loss per share from continuing operations is calculated as: [FRS 14(58)]

$$\frac{\text{Profit attributable to ordinary shareholders from continuing operations excluding extraordinary items}}{\text{Weighted average number of shares used to calculate basic eps}}$$

10.170 The FRS does not contain a definition of continuing operations. However, it is evident from FRS 14 paragraph 59 that the definition in FRS 3 is intended to apply.

10.171 Under FRS 3 *Reporting financial performance*, the analysis of the profit and loss account items into continuing operations, acquisitions (as a component of continuing operations) and discontinued operations is not required below profit before interest. However, for FRS 14 purposes, it will be necessary to divide the results down to profit/loss attributable to ordinary shareholders into those from continuing operations and those from discontinued operations. [FRS 14(59)]

10.172 The FRS requires that where interest and tax can be allocated between continuing and discontinued operations in a meaningful manner, this should be done. [FRS 14(60)] Where this cannot be done or can only be done in respect of some, but not all, of the interest and tax, the FRS permits the remaining allocation between continuing and discontinued operations to be estimated in the proportion of profit from continuing operations to total profit at the operating profit level.

10.173 The FRS adds that 'in practice a profit-based allocation method may be more suitable for taxation, which is levied on profits, than for interest, which finances capital'. This statement appears to undermine the principle of estimating the allocation of interest between continuing and discontinued operations in the proportion of operating profit. However, the FRS does not put forward a more favoured basis of estimation of interest.

10.174 The overriding principle in FRS 14 is that interest and tax are allocated between continuing and discontinued operations in a meaningful manner. It follows from this that it is only the interest expense that will be extinguished when the discontinued operations are sold or terminated that should be allocated to discontinued operations. All other interest expense should be allocated to continuing operations.

Example 10.174

Calculation of profit from continuing operations

A company's profit and loss account, from the operating profit line onwards, is as follows:

	Continuing Operations £ million	Discontinued operations £ million	Total £ million
Group operating profit	500	100	600
Share of associate's operating profit	20	–	20
	520	100	620
Profit on disposal of fixed assets	40	10	50
Profit on sale of operations	–	300	300
	560	410	970
Net interest payable			(43)

Profit from ordinary activities before tax		927
Taxation		(214)
		713
Dividends: non-equity	(50)	
equity	(220)	
	(270)	
Retained profit		443

The discontinued operations comprise a discrete business segment, made up of four subsidiary undertakings, which was sold during the year.

The group had a central treasury department. Accordingly, the four subsidiaries sold had no external borrowings, only inter-company borrowings from the treasury company. The inter-company borrowings were repaid on disposal of the subsidiaries and the treasury company accordingly repaid external borrowings of an equivalent amount. Interest on the repaid external borrowings during the year had totalled £8 million.

The company was able to attribute tax of £10 million to the continuing non-operating exceptional items and of £51 million to the discontinued non-operating exceptional items. It was unable to allocate the remaining tax between continuing and discontinued operations.

In accordance with the FRS, the remaining tax of £153 million is allocated in the proportion of operating profit. The tax is therefore allocated as:

Continuing operations: $10 + \left(153 \times \dfrac{500}{600} \right) = 138$

Discontinued operations: $51 + \left(153 \times \dfrac{100}{600} \right) = 76$

The profit attributable to ordinary shareholders from continuing operations is therefore:

	£ million
Profit before interest	560
Net interest payable (43 – 8)	(35)
Taxation	(138)
	387
Non-equity dividends	50
	337

10.175 A group may incur a penalty when repaying debt no longer required upon the sale or termination of a discontinued operation. If so, the penalty should also be allocated to discontinued operations.

Can diluted eps ever be greater than basic eps?

10.176 Rather surprisingly, the answer to this question is yes: diluted eps could be greater than basic eps. The reason for this is that, under the FRS, potential ordinary shares are treated as dilutive if their conversion decreases net profit or increases net loss per share *from continuing operations*. Both basic and diluted eps, on the other hand, are calculated using total earnings. It is therefore possible for the particular combination of continuing earnings, total earnings and potential ordinary shares to result in the potential ordinary shares being dilutive as defined by the FRS, but in the potential ordinary shares being anti-dilutive when calculated using total earnings. Consider the following example.

Example 10.176

Diluted eps greater than basic eps

Net profit attributable to ordinary shareholders	£6 million
Net loss attributable to discontinued operations	£4 million
Ordinary shares outstanding – weighted average	2 million

The only potential ordinary shares outstanding during the year are 12 million convertible preference shares. Every 19 preference shares are convertible into one ordinary share. The finance charge recognised in the profit and loss account in respect of the preference shares was £2.4 million.

Are the potential ordinary shares dilutive?

	Net profit attributable to continuing operations £	*Number of ordinary shares* Number	*Per share* £
Continuing eps	10,000,000	2,000,000	5.00
Convertible preference shares	2,400,000	631,579	
	12,400,000	2,631,579	4.71 D

Calculating basic eps:

$$\frac{£6,000,000}{2,000,000} = £3.00$$

Calculating diluted eps:

$$\frac{£(6,000,000 + 2,400,000)}{2,631,579} = £3.19$$

10.177 In the above example, diluted eps is higher than basic eps. If this happened in practice, the diluted eps would nevertheless have to be disclosed in order to comply with the FRS. However, it would seem helpful if the entity adds an explanation. A suggestion is as follows:

Suggested explanation based on above example:

Basic and diluted eps have both been calculated in accordance with the rules in FRS 14. By following these rules, diluted eps has, unusually, come out at a higher profit number per share than basic eps, giving the appearance that the potential ordinary shares are in fact anti-dilutive. This has happened because the rules in the FRS require us to determine whether or not potential ordinary shares are dilutive by looking only at earnings from continuing operations, whereas, to calculate basic and diluted eps, the FRS requires us to use earnings from both continuing and discontinued operations.

Had basic and diluted eps been calculated using results from continuing operations only, the basic eps would have been £5.00 per share and diluted eps would have been £4.71 per share.

Comprehensive examples

Summary of calculation method

10.178 (a) Calculate the additional profit per potential new ordinary share. For each category of potential ordinary shares: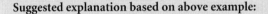

     (i) calculate the additional (post-tax) profit (or reduced loss), if any, that would have been recognised in the profit and loss account for the current year had the potential ordinary shares been converted into ordinary shares;*

     (ii) similarly calculate the additional number of ordinary shares that would have been issued had the potential ordinary shares been converted;

(iii) divide the additional profit by the additional number of shares.

* Where shares are issued for consideration, e.g., options, warrants, earn-outs, there will be no additional profit. Where shares are issued on conversion of an instrument, e.g., convertible debentures and preference shares, the additional profit will arise because the interest or dividends payable would not arise post-conversion.

(b) Rank these: first = lowest additional profit per new share;

last = highest additional profit per new share.

(c) Calculate the basic eps for **continuing** operations: divide profit attributable to ordinary shareholders from continuing operations by the number of shares used to calculate basic eps.

(d) Determine which potential ordinary shares are dilutive, and which are anti-dilutive. For each category of potential ordinary shares, in order of their ranking from step (b):

(i) add the additional profit to the continuing earnings and the additional shares to the number of shares (used at step (c));
(ii) calculate the new continuing eps;
(iii) if the new continuing eps is lower, the category of potential ordinary shares is dilutive.

(e) Calculate diluted eps based on adjustments for dilutive potential ordinary shares.

Example 10.178.1

Convertible bonds and options

Information

Net profit attributable to ordinary shareholders	£20 million
Net profit attributable to discontinued operations	£5 million
Ordinary shares outstanding – weighted average	25 million
Average fair value of ordinary share during year	£5
Tax rate	40%
Year end	31 December 1999

Potential ordinary shares outstanding during year:

6% convertible bond:	Issued on 1 July 1999. Nominal amount £100 million. Each £100 bond is converted to eight ordinary shares. The amortisation of issue costs charged in the profit and loss account during the year was £0.5 million.
8% convertible bond:	Nominal amount £100 million. Each £200 bond is converted into 17 ordinary shares. The amortisation of issue costs charged in the profit and loss account during the year was £1 million.
Options (no performance conditions):	1 million with exercise price of £2 2 million with exercise price of £4 2 million with exercise price of £5.50 In respect of the options with an exercise price of £2, the UITF Abstract 17 charges that have not yet been recognised in the profit and loss account total £0.5 million. There are no UITF Abstract 17 charges in respect of the other options.

Determining the additional earnings per additional share had the potential ordinary shares been converted into ordinary shares:

	Increase in Earnings	Increase in number of ordinary shares	Additional earnings per additional share
	£million	millions	£
6% convertible bond			
$= [(0.06 \times 100 \times 0.5) + 0.5] \times 0.6$	2.1		
$= \dfrac{£100m}{£100} \times 8 \times 0.5$ *		4	
$= 2.1 \div 4$			0.53
8% convertible bond			
$= [(0.08 \times 100) + 1] \times 0.6$	5.4		
$= \dfrac{£100m}{£200} \times 17$		8.5	
$= 5.4 \div 8.5$			0.64
Options †			
= earnings impact	nil		
$= 3m - \dfrac{(1m \times £2) + £0.5m + (2m \times £4)}{£5}$		0.9	
$= nil \div 0.9$			nil

Ranking these gives:

Position	Types of potential ordinary shares	Additional earnings per additional share
1st	Options	nil
2nd	6% convertible bond	£0.53
3rd	8% convertible bond	£0.64

* The 6% bonds were issued during the year. Accordingly, the number of shares assumed issued is weighted.

† The options exercisable at £5.50 per share are out-of-the-money and so are anti-dilutive. Accordingly, they are excluded from the calculations at this stage.

Determining continuing eps:

$$\frac{£20m - £5m}{25m} = 60 \text{ pence}$$

Determining which potential ordinary shares to include in diluted eps:

	Net profit attributable to continuing operations	Number of ordinary shares	Per share
	£	Number	£
Continuing eps	15,000,000	25,000,000	0.60
Options	–	900,000	
	15,000,000	25,900,000	0.58 D
6% convertible bond	2,100,000	4,000,000	
	17,100,000	29,900,000	0.57 D
8% convertible bond	5,400,000	8,500,000	
	22,500,000	38,400,000	0.59 A

D = Dilutive
A = Anti-dilutive

Calculating basic eps:

$$\frac{£20,000,000}{25,000,000} = 80p$$

Calculating diluted eps:

$$\frac{£20,000,000 + £2,100,000}{29,900,000} = 74p$$

Example 10.178.2

Contingently issuable shares and convertible preference shares

Information

Net profit attributable to ordinary shareholders	£15 million
Net profit attributable to discontinued operations	£4 million
Ordinary shares outstanding – weighted average	18 million
Average fair value of ordinary share during year	£6.50
Tax rate	40%
Year end	31 December 1999

Potential ordinary shares outstanding during year:

Convertible preference shares:	2,000,000 entitled to a cumulative dividend of £0.15 per share. Every two shares is convertible into one ordinary share. There is no amortisation of issue costs or redemption premium.
Options (no performance conditions):	One million with exercise price of £4.50. There is no UITF Abstract 17 charge.
Ordinary shares to be issued under acquisition agreement:	500,000 shares to be issued if profits of recently acquired subsidiary average £2 million or more over three years to 31 December 2000. Profits of the subsidiary for 1998 were £2.9 million and for 1999 were £3.3 million.
7% convertible bond:	Nominal amount £10 million. Each £100 bond is converted into 10 ordinary shares.

Determining the additional earnings per additional share had the potential ordinary shares been converted into ordinary shares:

	Increase in earnings	Increase in number of ordinary shares	Additional earnings per additional share
	£	Number	£
Convertible preference shares			
$= 2,000,000 \times £0.15$	300,000		
$= \dfrac{2,000,000}{2}$		1,000,000	
$= 300,000 \div 1,000,000$			0.3
Options			
= earnings impact	nil		
$= 1,000,000 - \dfrac{(1,000,000 \times £4.50)}{£6.50}$		307,692	
$= nil \div 307,692$			nil
Acquisition agreement†			
= earnings impact	nil		
= no. of shares to be issued		500,000	
$= nil \div 500,000$			nil
Convertible bond			
$= (0.07 \times £10,000,000) \times 0.6$	420,000		

$$= \frac{£10,000,000}{£100} \times 10 \qquad\qquad 1,000,000$$

$$= £420,000 \div 1,000,000 \qquad\qquad\qquad 0.42$$

†*The shares to be issued under the acquisition agreement are included in this step because using the balance sheet date (31 December 1999) position the conditions had been met. Average profits of £2 million over three years is equivalent to cumulative profits of £6 million over the three years. At 31 December 1999, cumulative profits were £6.2 million.*

Ranking these gives:

Position	Type of potential ordinary shares	Additional earnings per additional share
1st =	Options	Nil
1st =	Acquisition agreement	Nil
3rd	Convertible preference shares	£0.30
4th	Convertible bond	£0.42

Determining continuing eps:

$$\frac{£15,000,000 - £4,000,000}{18,000,000} = 61p$$

Determining which potential ordinary shares to include in diluted eps:

	Net profit attributable to continuing operations	Number of ordinary shares	Per share
	£	Number	£
Continuing eps	11,000,000	18,000,000	0.61
Options*	–	307,692	
	11,000,000	18,307,692	0.60 D
Acquisition agreement*	–	500,000	
	11,000,000	18,807,692	0.58 D
Convertible preference shares	300,000	1,000,000	
	11,300,000	19,807,692	0.57 D
Convertible bond	420,000	1,000,000	
	11,720,000	20,807,692	0.56 D

i.e., all potential ordinary shares are dilutive.

* The answer is unaffected by whether the options or the acquisition agreement is listed first. If the acquisition agreement were included directly before the options, the post-convertible preference shares per share figure would still be compared to a per share figure of £0.58.

Calculating basic eps:

$$\frac{£15,000,000}{18,000,000} = 83p$$

Calculating diluted eps:

$$\frac{£15,000,000 + £300,000 + £420,000}{20,807,692} = 76p$$

Example 10.178.3

Long-term employee share incentive plan and share options with performance conditions attaching

Information

Net profit attributable to ordinary shareholders	£20 million
Net profit attributable to discontinued operations	£5 million
Ordinary shares outstanding – weighted average	25 million
Ordinary shares owned throughout the year by ESOP trust	3 million
Average fair value of ordinary share during year	£7
Tax rate	40%
Year end	31 December 1999

Potential ordinary shares outstanding during year:

Options (no performance conditions):	500,000 with an exercise price of £5.50. No UITF Abstract 17 charge.
5% convertible bond:	Nominal amount £10 million. Each £100 is convertible into 10 ordinary shares.
Options:	One million with exercise price of £5 granted on 1 January 1998 and one million with exercise price of £6 granted on 1 January 1999. The options are exercisable only if the company's TSR exceeds the average TSR for the FTSE 100 over the three years following the date of grant.
	There is no UITF Abstract 17 charge. For each of 1998 and 1999, the company's TSR exceeded the average for the FTSE 100.
Long-term incentive plan:	The plan commenced on 1 January 1998. The maximum potential award for the 1998–2000 scheme and the 1999–2001 scheme is 400,000 shares and 600,000 shares respectively.
	100% of the shares will be awarded if the company's TSR is in the top (first) quartile for the FTSE 100, 50% will be awarded if the TSR is in the second quartile and no shares will be awarded if the TSR is below that level.
	At 31 December 1999, the company's TSR was in the top quartile for the FTSE 100 when looking at 1998 and 1999 in aggregate and for both 1998 and 1999 in isolation.

The charge arising under UITF Abstracts 13 and 17 is:

1998–2000 plan: £666,666 per annum

1999–2001 plan: £1,200,000 per annum

The shares in the ESOP trust are to be used for the LTIP and the share options with performance conditions attaching. The ESOP trust's purchase of shares was not funded with finance outside the group.

Determining the additional earnings per additional share had the potential ordinary shares been converted into ordinary shares:

	Increase in earnings	*Increase in number of ordinary shares*	*Additional earnings per additional share*
	£m	*Number*	*£*
Options (no performance conditions)			
= earnings impact	nil		
$= 500,000 - \dfrac{(500,000 \times £5.50)}{£7}$		107,142	
$= nil \div 107,142$			nil
5% convertible bonds			
$= (0.05 \times 10,000,000) \times 0.6$	300,000		
$= \dfrac{£10,000,000}{£100} \times 10$		1,000,000	
$= 300,000 \div 1,000,000$			0.3
Options (performance conditions)†			
= earnings impact	nil		
$= 2,000,000 - \dfrac{(1m \times £5) + (1m \times £6)}{£7}$		428,571	
$= nil \div 428,571$			nil
LTIP†			
= earnings impact	nil		
$= (400,000 + 600,000)$		1,000,000	
$= nil \div 1,000,000$			nil

†The shares to be issued under the option scheme with performance conditions and under the LTIP are included in this step because using the balance sheet date (31 December 1999) position the conditions had been met.

Ranking these gives:

Position	*Types of potential ordinary shares*	*Additional earnings per additional share*
1st =	Options (no performance conditions)	nil
1st =	Options (performance conditions)	nil
1st =	LTIP	nil
4th	5% convertible bonds	£0.30

Determining continuing eps:

$$\frac{£20m - £5m}{25m - 3m} = 68p$$

Determining which potential ordinary shares to include in diluted eps:

	Net profit attributable to continuing operations	Number of ordinary shares	Per share
	£	Number	£
Continuing eps	15,000,000	22,000,000	0.68
Options (no performance conditions)	–	107,142	
	15,000,000	22,107,142	0.678 D
Options (performance conditions)	–	428,571	
	15,000,000	22,535,713	0.67 D
LTIP	–	1,000,000	
	15,000,000	23,535,713	0.64 D
5% bond	300,000	1,000,000	
	15,300,000	24,535,713	0.62 D

Thus, all the potential ordinary shares are dilutive. The two types of options have not been added together because, under the FRS, the options with no performance conditions are treated as options, while the options with performance conditions attached are treated as contingently issuable shares.

Calculating basic eps:

$$\frac{£20,000,000}{25,000,000 - 3,000,000} = 91p$$

Calculating diluted eps:

$$\frac{£20,000,000 + £300,000}{24,535,713} = 83p$$

Additional guidance on the number of shares

Assume the most advantageous conversion

10.179 The terms of the financial instrument or rights generating the potential ordinary shares, e.g, acquisition agreement in the case of an earn-out or share option agreement, are what determines the number of ordinary shares that will be issued when potential ordinary shares are converted to ordinary shares. Where there is a choice, the most advantageous conversion rate or exercise price, from the standpoint of the holder of the potential ordinary shares, is used to calculate diluted eps. [FRS 14(31)]

Contracts to be settled in cash or shares

10.180 An entity may have issued a contract that may be settled in cash or shares. FRS 14 states that, irrespective of whether the choice of cash or shares rests with the recipient or issuer, how this is reflected in diluted eps depends upon the facts available in the particular accounting period. Past experience or a stated policy should be followed where that provides a reasonable basis for concluding how the contract will be satisfied. The contract is presumed to be settled by the more dilutive method where there is no stated policy or the entity has no past experience of settling such contracts. [FRS 14(32)]

10.181 If, under an acquisition agreement, a vendor can determine whether to take contingent consideration in the form of cash or shares and the vendor states that it will take shares, those shares (calculated in accordance with the FRS's guidance on contingently issuable shares) would be included in the calculation of diluted eps. FRS 7 *Fair values in acquisition accounting*, on the other hand, would require the estimated contingent consideration to be shown as a liability in the group balance sheet until such time as the shares are issued (or the cash is paid) (see **24.18** below). [FRS 7(83)]

10.182 If an entity has issued convertible redeemable bonds that are dilutive, it should assume conversion when calculating diluted eps, unless the bondholder has stated an intention to redeem the bonds.

Potential ordinary shares issued by subsidiary, joint venture or associate

10.183 Where a subsidiary, joint venture or associate issues potential ordinary shares that are exchangeable for either ordinary shares of itself or of the reporting entity, they should be included in calculating the reporting entity's diluted eps if, on conversion, they would have a 'dilutive effect on the consolidated basic earnings per share'. [FRS 14(33)]

10.184 Interestingly, the FRS refers to a dilutive effect on basic eps rather than, as with potential ordinary shares issued by the reporting entity, a dilutive effect on continuing eps.

10.185 Where a subsidiary has issued potential ordinary shares exchangeable for its own ordinary shares, there will be no impact on the denominator of the group's diluted eps. However, the group's future earnings will be affected if the group and minority shareholders do not take up entitlement in proportion to their holding and conversion takes place. Firstly,

> the reporting entity will have a gain or loss arising on a deemed disposal. Such a gain or loss is most appropriately recognised in the statement of total recognised gains and losses rather than in the profit and loss account (see **24.148** below). The expected gain or loss should be excluded from the numerator of the diluted eps calculation irrespective of whether it will be reported in the profit and loss account or the STRGL. Secondly, the minority interest in the subsidiary's post-conversion results will be higher than pre-conversion. This change in expected ongoing group results should be reflected in the numerator of the diluted eps if dilutive; it will be dilutive if the subsidiary is profit-making and anti-dilutive if the subsidiary is loss-making.

Partly paid shares

10.186 The FRS states that *to the extent* that partly paid shares are not entitled to participate in dividends during the financial period, they are to be regarded as the equivalent of share warrants or options. [FRS 14(34)]

10.187 The words 'to the extent', together with the guidance on how to include such shares in basic eps (see **10.69** above), imply that if a company has, say, 9,000 ordinary shares, two-thirds paid up and entitled to two-thirds of the dividend declared on fully paid shares, then, in calculating diluted eps, the company includes the partly paid shares as if they were options over 3,000 shares (one-third of 9,000) where the exercise price of the options is equal to the amount remaining to be paid on the shares.

Potential ordinary shares outstanding for part of an accounting period

10.188 Where potential ordinary shares are issued during a period, say, convertible bonds are issued four months before the end of the accounting period, diluted eps is calculated as if the potential ordinary shares had been converted to ordinary shares on the date the potential ordinary shares were issued. [FRS 14(62)] Thus, in the example, the convertible bonds would be included in diluted eps as if they had been converted into ordinary shares four months before the end of the accounting period.

10.189 Similarly, where potential ordinary shares are converted into ordinary shares, are cancelled, or lapsed, they are included in the calculation of diluted eps for the period the potential ordinary shares were in existence as potential ordinary shares.

| 10.190 | Having no potential ordinary shares outstanding at the balance sheet date does not automatically mean that the company does not have to calculate diluted eps. Where a company has no potential ordinary shares in existence at its year end but had potential ordinary shares outstanding at some point during the year, the company should still calculate diluted eps. |

Example 10.190

Potential ordinary shares in issue for part of a period

A company has 1,000,000 ordinary shares in issue at the start of its accounting period, 1 January 1999.

In addition, on 1 January, it has £100,000 convertible bonds in issue. The bonds were converted into 100,000 ordinary shares on 1 April 1999. The finance charge recognised in the profit and loss account in respect of the bonds from 1 January to 31 March was £2,500 and the associated tax relief was £1,000.

The net profit attributable to ordinary shareholders (all from continuing operations) for 1999 was £100,000.

The weighted average number of shares outstanding during 1999 and used to calculate basic eps is:

$$\left(1,000,000 \times \frac{12}{12}\right) + \left(100,000 \times \frac{9}{12}\right) = 1,075,000$$

Thus, basic eps is $\dfrac{\text{£}100,000}{1,075,000} = 9.3\text{p}$

Diluted eps is calculated as:

$$\frac{\text{£}100,000 + \text{£}2,500 - \text{£}1,000}{1,075,000 + (100,000 \times 0.25)} = \frac{\text{£}101,500}{1,100,000} = 9.2\text{p}$$

Other matters

Restatement of earnings per share

10.191 Earnings per share is restated in three circumstances.

(a) *Bonus and equivalent issues:* **10.74** above explained that if the number of ordinary shares outstanding is changed by events with no corresponding change in resources, other than the conversion of potential ordinary shares and other than when certain share consolidations are combined with a special dividend, the weighted average number of shares used in calculating basic eps is adjusted as if the change in the number of ordinary shares had taken place at the start of the earliest period for which an eps will be presented. In addition, if the number of potential ordinary shares outstanding changes, with no corresponding change in resources, the calculation of basic and diluted eps should be adjusted as if the change had taken place at the start of the earliest period for which an eps is presented. [FRS 14(63)] The only potential ordinary shares to affect the calculation of basic eps is contingently issuable shares. If any of these changes to ordinary shares or to potential ordinary shares occur after the balance sheet date but before the financial statements are approved, the basic and diluted eps calculations should still be restated.

(b) *Merger accounting:* when a business combination is accounted for on a merger basis, the group results are presented as if the combining entities had always been merged. Accordingly, it is necessary to present eps, basic and diluted, as if the combining entities had always been merged. Example **10.64** above illustrates the calculation of the number of shares to be used for basic eps.

(c) *Prior year adjustment:* whenever a new standard is adopted or a fundamental error is discovered that requires the preceding year's earnings as recognised in the profit and loss account to be altered, the earnings figure used to calculate that year's eps will correspondingly alter.

10.192 Diluted eps of an earlier period, presented in financial statements as a comparative, should not be restated for:

(a) changes in the assumptions used;

(b) conditions (on which contingently issuable shares are subject) not being met; or

(c) the conversion of potential ordinary shares into ordinary shares.

Example 10.192

Circumstances where comparative diluted eps is not restated

X plc calculated diluted eps for the year ended 31 December 1998 on the assumption that, *inter alia*:

(a) £100,000 convertible redeemable bonds would be converted into 100,000 ordinary shares; and

(b) based on the share price at 31 December 1998, 150,000 ordinary shares would be issued under an acquisition agreement.

During 1999:

(a)   the bonds were redeemed in full; and

(b)   using the share price on 1 August 1999, the date stipulated in the acquisition agreement, only 130,000 ordinary shares were issued.

In presenting its diluted eps for 1999, X plc gives as the comparative the diluted eps for 1998 that was presented in the 1998 financial statements; the 1998 figure is not recalculated in the light of the transactions in 1999.

IIMR, or 'headline', eps

10.193   An additional eps that directors may wish to consider presenting (see **10.29** above) is the IIMR, or 'headline', earnings per share.

10.194   When FRS 3 was issued, it effectively abolished extraordinary items. Accordingly, items previously categorised as extraordinary were re-classified as exceptional and thus were brought within the definition of earnings used to calculate earnings per share under the now superceded SSAP 3 (FRS 14 explicity states earnings is after all extrodinary items – see **10.48** above).

10.195   Analysts did not necessarily view a number of the items now included in earnings, for example, profits and losses on the sale of many capital items, as 'earnings'. The Institute of Investment Management and Research (IIMR) therefore set up a subcommittee to define a different 'earnings' number (one that analysts regarded as 'earnings') which could be used to calculate an additional earnings per share figure. The subcommittee considered two concepts: maintainable earnings; and headline earnings. It was concluded that 'in view of the judgements required the calculation of maintainable earnings figures cannot be put on a standardised basis'. Accordingly the subcommittee defined headline earnings (see the IIMR's Statement of Investment Practice No. 1 (SoIP 1), 'The definition of headline earnings'). The headline earnings figure is a factual figure for historic earnings which can be a benchmark figure for the trading outcome for the year; it is intended to provide accounts' users, the press and statistical companies with an unambiguous reference point for the reporting of trading profit. *The Financial Times* publishes price earnings ratios based on IIMR headline earnings. The results of a survey by *Company Reporting*, set out in **10.38** above, show that in 1997 five per cent of companies disclosed the IIMR eps as an additional earnings per share.

10.196   SoIP 1 includes both a detailed definition and explanation. In summary, IIMR headline earnings will be calculated to remove the following items from FRS 3 based profit after tax and extraordinary items:

(a)   profit (loss) on the sale or termination of an operation [FRS 3(20a)] (but no adjustment for the operating results of discontinued operations);

(b)   profit (loss) on the sale of fixed assets [FRS 3(20c)] or businesses, or their permanent diminution in value (includes trade investments, but excludes assets acquired for resale, such as marketable securities);

(c)   profit (loss) arising from reorganisation of long-term debt (such as under FRS 4(32));

(d)   profit (loss) from prior period adjustments (although under FRS 3 these should be excluded from the annual profit and loss account);

(e)   provision for exceptional items listed in FRS 3(20) (which should be allocated to the period in which the expense occurs, rather than the period when provision is made);

(f)   bid defence costs;

(g)   goodwill amortisation and impairment and any goodwill included in the calculation of profit/loss on disposal;

(h)   extraordinary profits (losses) as defined by FRS 3;

(i)   tax and minority interest effects related to the above adjustments.

10.197   It follows that no adjustment should be made for the following items:

(a)   notional interest on any of the above items;

(b)   exceptional items (for example, reorganisation or restructuring) other than those listed above;

(c)   acquisitions or discontinued operations to the extent included in operating profit;

(d)   pension (and other post-retirement benefit) charges and credits including one-off items;

(e)   foreign currency items (unless attaching to an excluded item);

(f)   abortive bid costs;

(g)   one-off costs of complying with major new legislation;

(h)   litigation costs (whether normal or abnormal);

(i)   diminution in value of current assets.

10.198   Extract **10.37** above illustrates the disclosure given by HSBC Holdings plc in its 1998 financial statements when it presented the headline earnings per share as an additional earnings per share number.

Financial statistics in a historical summary

10.199 The FRS contains recommendations on three aspects of reporting financial statistics in a historical summary. The recommendations, which are consistent with those in appendix 2 to SSAP 3, and are not contained in IAS 33, are detailed below.

10.200 First, the FRS recommends that basic and diluted eps disclosed in a historical summary are restated for the effects of a change in the number of ordinary shares or potential ordinary shares with no corresponding change in resources (other than on conversion of potential ordinary shares or when certain share consolidations are combined with a special dividend) as if the change had taken place at the start of the earliest period for which eps information is disclosed. This guidance is consistent with **10.74** and **10.75** above. [FRS 14(76)] The restated eps figures are to be described as restated and clearly distinguished from other non-adjusted data.

10.201 Second, the FRS recommends that where equity dividends per share are disclosed in a historical summary, they are similarly adjusted by the factors used to adjust eps set out in **10.200** above. Again, the FRS calls for the restated dividend per share to be described as restated and, together with the restated eps, to be clearly distinguished from other non-adjusted data. [FRS 14(77)]

10.202 Third, the FRS points out that although dividend cover is normally found by dividing earnings by dividends, this will not give the correct answer if the payment of additional dividends results in the company paying further tax. [FRS 14(78)] Consequently, the FRS recommends that dividend cover is calculated as the theoretical maximum dividend that can be paid out of the current period's earnings (after taking into account any additional tax that would be payable) divided by the actual dividend.

11 Statement of total recognised gains and losses

11   Statement of total recognised gains and losses

Summary of changes since the previous issue of this publication

Para.	Topic	Summary
11.20	Reporting financial performance – proposals for change	Proposes that financial perform-ance would be presented in a single statement – effectively com bining the profit and loss account and statement of total recognised gains and losses.

General requirements
Requirement to provide a statement of total recognised gains and losses

11.1   Not all components of an entity's financial performance will flow through the profit and loss account. Therefore, FRS 3 requires finan-cial statements to include, as a primary statement, a 'statement of total recognised gains and losses' (STRGL) to highlight the gains and losses that are recognised in a period. [FRS 3(27)] The statement deals with gains or losses recognised, not necessarily realised, in a period. Therefore, certain gains, such as revaluation surpluses, may be recognised in one period and realised in a subsequent period.

11.2   The ASB regards both the STRGL and the profit and loss account as performance statements. The STRGL includes all recognised gains and losses, being all increases or decreases in shareholders' funds other than contributions from or distributions to shareholders and goodwill written off directly to reserves (permitted prior to imple-mentation of FRS 10 – see chapter 13) or reinstated on subsequent sale or closure of the business. The profit or loss for the period is included in the statement as a one line entry. The other items repre-sent transactions that were taken directly to reserves (other than goodwill and capital transactions with owners) rather than being included in the profit and loss account. Because the ASB regards the STRGL as a performance statement, it regards transactions as being taken to reserves via either the profit and loss account or the STRGL.

11.3   The STRGL should only be omitted if there are both:
[FRS 3(57)]

(a)   no recognised gains or losses other than the profit or loss for the period in both the current and prior period; and

(b)   a statement to that effect is given at the base of the profit and loss account.

Example 11.3

There are no recognised gains and losses for the current financial year and preceding financial year other than the profit of £123,862 (1999 – profit of £119,665) shown above.

Presentation

11.4   The STRGL is a 'primary statement' and should be presented with the same prominence as the other primary statements (i.e., the profit and loss account, balance sheet and cash flow statement). [FRS 3(27)] It should not be included as a note to the accounts.

Format and content of the statement

Gains and losses

11.5   FRS 3 does not discuss what is meant by 'gains' or 'losses'. However, chapter 4 of the ASB's *Statement of Principles for Financial Reporting* includes the following definitions:

'Gains are increases in ownership interest not resulting from contributions from owners.

Losses are decreases in ownership interest not resulting from distributions to owners.

Ownership interest is the residual amount found by deducting all of the entity's liabilities from all of the entity's assets.'

These definitions are substantially the same as those in the draft version that was in issue when FRS 3 was first published.

11.6   Based upon these definitions and the illustrative examples given in FRS 3 and FRS 4, it is clear that contributions from or distributions to shareholders (e.g., capital contributions from or dividends to shareholders) should be excluded from the statement.

11.7   The total of all recognised gains and losses attributable to shareholders of a reporting entity includes the following components:
[FRS 3(36)]

(a) profit or loss before the deduction of dividends;

(b) adjustments to the valuation of assets; and

(c) differences in the net investment in foreign enterprises arising from changes in foreign currency exchange rates.
The statement should not include:

- the proceeds of a share issue;

- share issue costs (see **18.56** below);

- redemption or purchase of own shares;

- dividends or distributions.

Goodwill

11.8 The footnote to FRS 3 paragraph 27 notes that: 'As explained in UITF Abstract 3 and paragraphs 6 and 7 of SSAP 22 "Accounting for goodwill", the immediate write-off to reserves of purchased goodwill is not a recognised loss'. Accordingly, the immediate write-off of goodwill should not appear in the STRGL but in the reconciliation of movements in shareholders' funds. FRS 10 *Goodwill and intangible assets* no longer permits immediate write-off of goodwill to reserves (see chapter 13).

Investment companies

11.9 Investment companies, as defined in s266, should include in the profit and loss account only profits available for distribution. [FRS 3(31)] Therefore, all non-distributable profits recognised in the period should be shown in the STRGL. These may include both realised and unrealised gains and losses.

11.10 Investment companies may include:

(a) the finance costs in respect of capital instruments; and

(b) any gains or losses arising on the repurchase or early settlement of debt,

in the STRGL to the extent that these items relate to capital. Any amounts so treated should be disclosed separately within the statement. The accounting policy for determining the allocation of such costs between revenue and capital should be stated. [FRS 4(52)] The SORP *Financial statements of investment trust companies* contains recommendations for investment trust companies.

Format

11.11 FRS 3 discusses the contents rather than setting strict formats for the STRGL. Therefore, entities will need to consider which format and level of disclosure is most appropriate to their business. The most appropriate form of disclosure will depend upon the circumstances. The format of the example below is based upon the illustrative examples that accompany FRS 3.

Example 11.11

Statement of total recognised gains and losses

	2000 £ million	1999 £ million
Profit attributable to members of the company	15	10
Unrealised (deficit)/surplus on revaluation of investment properties	(3)	6
Unrealised (loss)/gain on trade investment	(4)	6
	8	22
Foreign exchange translation differences on foreign currency net investment in subsidiaries	(2)	5
Total recognised gains and losses for the year	6	27

The subtotal in the example above has been included because the ASB included one in its example. However, there is no requirement in FRS 3 to include such a subtotal and, in practice, it is rarely seen.

Comparative figures

11.12 Comparative figures are required for the STRGL. [FRS 3(30)]

Consolidated financial statements

11.13 In consolidated financial statements, the information required by FRS 3 will be given on a consolidated basis. A suitable title would be 'Consolidated Statement of Total Recognised Gains and Losses'.

11.14

FRS 3 does not state whether the STRGL need be prepared only for the group or whether it must also be prepared for a parent company where the parent prepares consolidated financial statements. Given that the other primary statement of financial performance of the parent, the profit and loss account, will not be present in the financial statements if, as normal, the parent takes advantage of s230 (see **23.131** below), there seems little point in including a STRGL for the parent. In addition, FRS 3 is addressed to reporting entities; when group financial statements are prepared the group is the reporting entity. Accordingly, it is not necessary to present a STRGL for the parent.

Prior period adjustments

11.15 As discussed in **9.248** to **9.262** above, prior period adjustments should be accounted for by restating the comparative figures in the primary statements, including the STRGL, and notes. In addition, the cumulative effect of the adjustment should be noted at the bottom of the STRGL of the current period. [FRS 3(29)]

Example 11.15

Background information

A prior period adjustment gives rise to a cumulative debit adjustment to reserves of £7,000,000 in the 2000 accounts, of which £2,000,000 relates to 1999 and the balance of £5,000,000 relates to 1998 and prior periods.

Statement of total recognised gains and losses

	2000	1999 as restated (see note x)
	£ million	£ million
Profit attributable to shareholders of the company	25	19
Unrealised (loss)/surplus on revaluation of properties	(4)	7
Total recognised gains and losses related to the year	21	26
Note on prior period adjustment		
Total recognised gains and losses related to the year as above	21	
Prior period adjustment (as explained in note x)	(7)	
Total gains and losses recognised since the last annual report	14	

In the above example, the full £7,000,000 is included at the foot of the 2000 column of the STRGL, even though the profit attributable to shareholders of the company of £19,000,000 shown for 1999 has been adjusted by £2,000,000 of the total adjustment of £7,000,000.

11.16 Continuing the above example, in presenting their 2001 accounts, the directors are not required to include the prior period adjustment of £7,000,000 at the foot of the 2000 column of the STRGL.

Current tax

11.17 FRS 16 *Current Tax* was issued in December 1999 and applies to accounting periods ending on or after 23 March 2000. Where gains or losses are included in the STRGL, this standard makes it clear that any attributable tax should be treated in the same way. This effectively extends the consensus under UITF 19 *Tax on gains and losses on foreign currency borrowings that hedge an investment in a foreign enterprise* to all gains and losses in the STRGL.

11.18   In exceptional circumstances it may be difficult to determine the amount of current tax that is attributable to gains or losses that have been recognised directly in the statement of total recognised gains and losses. In such circumstances, the attributable tax is based on a reasonable pro rata allocation, or another allocation that is more appropriate in the circumstances. [FRS 16(7)]

11.19   The FRS 16 treatment of current tax would also be extended to deferred tax under the proposals of FRED 19 *Deferred Tax*. It would be appropriate to treat deferred tax attributable to gains and losses included in the STRGL in this manner, in advance of the issue of a final standard.

Future developments

11.20   During 1999, the ASB issued a Discussion Paper *Reporting Financial Performance – Proposals For Change* which presents a Position Paper developed by the G4+1 group (comprising the national standard-setters of Australia, Canada, New Zealand, the UK and the USA, together with the IASC). In the UK, the proposals contained therein will be developed with the intention of revising FRS 3. The major proposal of the paper was that financial performance would be presented in a single statement – effectively combining the profit and loss account and STRGL.

11.21   This statement would present all changes in equity, other than those arising from transactions with shareholders, and divide items into three main components of financial performance:

(a)   the results of operating (or trading) activities;

(b)   the results of financing and other treasury activities; and

(c)   other gains and losses.

11.22   In general, it would be the third of these that would essentially correspond to the STRGL. Under the proposals of the paper, the following would typically be included in this section:

(a)   foreign currency translation gains and losses;

(b) revaluation and disposal gains and losses on fixed assets (excluding impairments and their reversals and adjustments to depreciation); and

(c) actuarial gains and losses relating to pensions.

11.23 It is indicated, however, that domestic standard-setters (e.g., the ASB) may decide to grant an option to include certain of these items within operating/trading activities if appropriate (in the case of property investment companies).

11.24 While this 'other' section would, in essence, be the equivalent of the STRGL, certain of the items in **11.22** would currently be included in the profit and loss account under FRS 3. Proposed changes here have occurred as the result of attempts to increase international harmonisation, as well as due to the deliberate reclassification of certain items.

11.25 The paper also includes a matrix summarising criteria that might be useful in distinguishing between 'operating' and 'other' items.

12   Balance sheet: general

12 Balance sheet: general

General requirements

Introduction

12.1   The Act provides that every balance sheet shall give a true and fair view of the state of the company's affairs at the end of its financial year and shall comply with Sch 4 as to its form and content. [s226]

12.2   Guidance is given in this and the following six chapters on the accounting treatment and disclosures required in respect of items to be included under each balance sheet heading.

Formats

12.3   Two alternative formats are permitted and these are reproduced in Appendix III. Format 1 arranges the balance sheet headings vertically, assets above liabilities, which is the practice customarily followed in the UK and is the preferred arrangement. Format 2 presents a two-sided arrangement, with assets on one side and liabilities, capital and reserves on the other. [Sch 4: 1 and section B]

12.4   In practice, most companies that have adopted format 1 strike a total for total assets less liabilities, which equates to the total for capital and reserves below, and this treatment is considered best practice. However, some companies draw a total line at the heading 'Total assets less current liabilities', and then combine long-term liabilities with capital and reserves to give a total which is sometimes described as 'capital employed'. This presentation cannot be said to be precluded by the Act, because the format does not require a heading equivalent to 'Total assets less total liabilities'. It is not recommended, but is acceptable if presented with clarity.

12.5   A practice has grown up involving separating out two elements of long-term liabilities to show what has been described as the 'finance element' with share capital and reserves. The elements of long-term liabilities are shown in the order prescribed by the formats, but a total, sometimes described as 'Total net assets employed', is struck part way through the long-term liabilities.

The next section of the balance sheet is then headed 'Financed by' and commences with the remaining ('finance') element of long-term liabilities, followed by share capital and reserves. While this retains the prescribed order of the balance sheet elements, it omits one prescribed total, that for 'Creditors: amounts falling due after more than one year', which must be shown on the face of the balance sheet. This can be overcome by listing the components of both parts of the split 'long-term' category in a common unique column, enabling them to be both added in to the balance sheet totals and summed to their own total, as demonstrated in the following example. While not easy to present without making the balance sheet appear cluttered, this does avoid a failure to comply with the letter of the Act.

Example 12.5

Assets employed

	£'000	£'000
Fixed assets		1,345
Current assets		4,312
Creditors: amounts falling due within one year		(3,589)
Net current assets		723
Total assets less current liabilities		2,068
Creditors: amounts falling due after more than one year		
Bank loans and overdrafts	1,000	
Trade creditors	168	
	1,168	(1,168)
Total net assets employed		900
Financed by		
Debenture loans	1,100	1,100
	2,268	
Capital and reserves		(200)
Total financing		900

12.6 A further practice that may be found is to extend the distancing of the 'finance' element of the long-term liabilities from the balance by showing the 'finance' element after share capital and reserves rather than before. Because this practice ignores the prescribed order in which items should appear, it does not

> appear to be in compliance with the requirements of the Act. The only argument that could justify this practice, therefore, is a need to change the order in order to give a true and fair view. Again, it is difficult to see how this claim may be sustained, as the method described in the previous paragraph is available and would appear to meet any presentational needs without offending against the requirements of the Act. Consequently, it appears most unlikely that this presentation would be acceptable.

Headings

12.7   Balance sheet headings which have been assigned letters or Roman numerals must be shown in the order and under the headings and subheadings given in the format adopted. [Sch 4: 1] No flexibility is permitted in the description of the headings or in their position in the balance sheet. The only exceptions are the headings for 'Prepayments and accrued income' and 'Accruals and deferred income', which may be shown either as main headings in their own right or as subheadings within debtors and creditors respectively. [Sch 4 Part I, section B, Notes on the balance sheet formats (10)]

12.8   Subheadings preceded by Arabic numerals are permitted greater flexibility. [Sch 4: 3(4)] The arrangement and description of these items shall be adapted in any case where the special nature of the company's business requires it. In addition, they may be combined as one amount where such combination facilitates the assessment of the state of affairs, provided that the details of each item so combined are shown by way of note to the accounts. Items which are not material for such assessment may be combined with other items without such disclosure.

Classification of assets and liabilities

Current assets and fixed assets

12.9   The balance sheet formats require classification of all assets under the heading of 'Current assets' or 'Fixed assets'. There are only two exceptions to this requirement, 'Prepayments and accrued income' and 'Called up share capital not paid'. These categories may be shown as separate main headings or as subheadings under 'Debtors'.

12.10   > The use of separate main headings for these categories would only be encouraged in the unusual situation where the amounts involved were very significant.

12.11   The definition of fixed and current assets given in s262 is based on the intended use of the asset in the business. A fixed asset is one which is intended for use on a continuing basis in the company's activities and a current asset is one which is not intended for such use. This formulation ensures that there is no third category of assets which are neither fixed nor current.

12.12   The term 'current assets' often gives rise to an assumption that such assets are necessarily short-term, particularly as there is no statutory requirement to split current assets between those realisable within one year and those which will be held for longer, to parallel the required split of liabilities. Consequently, any longer-term non-fixed assets must be included within current assets – examples include pension fund surpluses and long-term lease debtors. In recognition of the fact that this could mislead, the UITF has given guidance on where it is necessary to give further disclosure of longer-term current assets, and this is discussed in **12.17** below.

12.13   There is no definition of an asset in the Act. However, in FRS 5 and in the ASB's Statement of Principles, assets are defined as 'rights or other access to future economic benefits controlled by an entity as a result of past transactions or events'. (The Statement of Principles is explained in chapter 3.)

Current liabilities

12.14   The classification of liabilities in the balance sheet formats is made by reference to whether the liability falls due within one year or after more than one year. An exception to this rule is that 'Accruals and deferred income' may be shown separately as a main heading or as a subheading under either of the two 'Creditors' headings.

12.15   The definition of a liability for accounting purposes is given in FRS 5 (with a similar definition in ASB's Statement of Principles) as 'obligations of an entity to transfer economic benefits as a result of past transactions or events'. (The Statement of Principles is explained in chapter 3.)

Net current assets/(liabilities)

12.16   The balance sheet format 1 requires a subtotal for current assets less current liabilities, designated 'Net current assets/(liabilities)'. This subtotal must include 'Prepayments and accrued income' even when this item is shown under a heading separate from that of current assets.

12.17   Since the subheading 'Net current assets/(liabilities)' may include certain assets not realisable within one year while it will recognise only those liabilities which are payable within one year, it may well not give a meaningful indication of liquidity. The UITF has recognised this problem, and UITF Abstract 4 requires that, where the amount of debtors due after more than one year is so material in the context of total net current assets that readers may misinterpret the accounts unless that amount is disclosed separately on the face of the balance sheet rather than just in the notes to the accounts, then that amount should be so disclosed. However, that disclosure must still leave such debtors within the totals for current assets and for net current assets, in order to maintain compliance with the balance sheet formats, so debtors due after more than one year will be shown, if necessary, as a subheading within current assets.

Asset valuation rules

Introduction

12.18   Schedule 4 lays down rules for the amounts at which balance sheet items may be carried. These, for the most part, are consistent with the valuation bases required by accounting standards. The rules distinguish between the historical cost rules and alternative rules. The alternative rules permit companies to adopt the current cost accounting convention in the preparation of their statutory financial statements or to adopt a mixture of historical costs and alternative valuations. However, FRS 15 has introduced certain constraints upon the ability to mix cost and valuation in this way, by requiring consistency by class of asset. This is dealt with in **14.92** below. The current cost convention is not defined in the Act. However, FRS 15 gives chapter and verse on acceptable valuation bases.

12.19   The general valuation rules are stated below. The rules applicable to specific assets are given in the sections of the manual dealing with those assets.

Gross value of assets

12.20   Under the historical cost accounting rules, the gross amount recorded for assets shall be their purchase price or production cost. [Sch 4: 17 and 22]

12.21   The alternative accounting rules permit assets to be valued on the following bases:

(a)   *Tangible fixed assets*: at market value determined as at their last valuation date or at current cost [Sch 4: 31(2)]; but FRS 15 goes into significantly more detail on both how and when to determine market value or current cost.

(b) *Intangible fixed assets, excluding goodwill*: at current cost. [Sch 4: 31(1)].

(c) *Investments included in fixed assets*: at market value determined as at their last valuation date or at a value determined on any basis considered by the directors to be appropriate in the circumstances. [Sch 4: 31(3)]

(d) *Investments included in current assets*: at current cost [Sch 4: 31(4)].

(e) *Stocks*: at current cost [Sch 4: 31(5)].

The term 'current cost' is not defined in the Act but is addressed in FRS 15 in respect of tangible fixed assets (see **14.143** below).

Depreciation

12.22   Whether a fixed asset is carried at cost or alternatively at a valuation, if that asset has a limited useful economic life, the carrying amount must be reduced systematically by a provision for depreciation to write off the difference between the cost or value and any residual amount, over the asset's useful economic life. [Sch 4: 18 and 32] Depreciation is dealt with further in chapter 14.

Provisions for reduction in value

12.23   The Companies Act rules regarding provisions for reduction in value of assets are as follows:

(a) *All fixed assets carried at cost or market value*: a provision **must** be made where the reduction is expected to be permanent. [Sch 4: 19(2) and 32(2)]

This has been interpreted by FRS 11 *Impairment of fixed assets and goodwill* to mean that a permanent reduction has occurred wherever an asset's recoverable amount has fallen below carrying value (see **14.239** and **13.242** below).

(b) *All fixed assets carried at current cost*: by revaluing to current cost each year, a provision for diminution in value will be made where current cost has fallen.

(c) *Fixed asset investments*: a provision for diminution in value **may** be made (even if not expected to be permanent). [Sch 4: 19(1)]

(d) *Current assets*: a write-down to net realisable value **shall** be made if lower than cost or alternative valuation. [Sch 4: 23(1)]

12.24   Where the reasons for making all or part of any of these provisions no longer apply, the provisions shall be written back to the extent that they are no longer necessary. [Sch 4: 19(3)]

Price or cost unknown

12.25   Where the purchase price or production cost of an asset cannot be determined from the records without unreasonable expense or delay, the value ascribed to it in the earliest available record of its value made on or after its acquisition or production shall be used in place of the purchase price or production cost. [Sch 4: 51(1)]

12.26   This concession is likely to have practical significance now only in the context of group accounts when accounting for newly acquired overseas subsidiaries, and then only when merger accounted, i.e., not fair valued.

Valuers' guidance

12.27   The principal source of guidance on valuations for professional valuers is the *Appraisal and Valuation manual* of the Royal Institution of Chartered Surveyors (RICS). This looseleaf handbook (also available on CD-ROM) is updated periodically, and the contents have been developed over a number of years, taking account of parallel developments in the accounting world. Certain definitions therein are significant as a guide to how valuers will probably have arrived at valuation figures presented in individual companies' financial statements. Several of these definitions have now been adopted by the ASB for financial reporting purposes, in FRS 15. Where appropriate, these definitions are referred to later in this text.

Statement of Principles

12.28   The ASB has issued its Statement of Principles for financial reporting (October 1999) which includes chapter 6 'Measurement in financial statements', outlining the principles for measuring elements in the balance sheet and the different concepts of capital maintenance.

12.29   The principal feature of chapter 6 of the Statement of Principles is its endorsement of the 'value to the business' logic for selecting the appropriate basis for valuing any asset or liability under the prevailing circumstances, once a decision has been taken (or the need has arisen because of the possibility of impairment) to revalue the asset. The choice of bases is between entry value, exit value and value in use (briefly, replacement cost, market value and present value of cash flows to termination/disposal). The choice of appropriate basis is made by determining what the entity owning an asset would lose if it were peremptorily deprived of it. Normally, the loss of an asset would be measured as the cost of replacing it (at its current age and condition) but, where it would not economically be worth replacing, the loss would be its recoverable amount, which would be the higher of its sale value or its residual earning power.

12.30 This logic is not new. It was attributed originally to Professor JC Bonbright in 1937 and it formed the basis of the methodology developed for accommodating current cost accounting valuations in the 1970s. It was never one of the contentious aspects of current cost accounting and has already become a part of generally accepted accounting practice. This principle has now been incorporated into FRS 11 as the basis for determining whether and when asset value has been impaired (see **14.240** to **14.250** below) and also into FRS 15.

13   Intangible fixed assets

13 Intangible fixed assets

Introduction

13.1 The accounting treatment of intangible assets changed as a result of the introduction of FRS 10 *Goodwill and intangible assets*, which became mandatory for accounting periods ending on or after 23 December 1998, superseding SSAP 22. FRS 10 does **not** affect the treatment of research and development costs (which are covered by SSAP 13) or oil and gas exploration and development costs (covered by the relevant SORP). FRS 10 also does not affect entities applying the FRSSE, unless they are preparing consolidated financial statements. However, the latest version of the FRSSE includes requirements for dealing with goodwill in entity accounts which are modifications of FRS 10's requirements – see **34.63** below.

Disclosure requirements

Statutory headings

13.2 'Intangible assets' is a main heading which should appear on the face of the balance sheet. The following subheadings are required but may be shown either on the face of the balance sheet or in the notes:

- Development costs;

- Concessions, patents, licences, trademarks, and similar rights and assets;

- Goodwill (note that, as a result of the introduction of FRS 10, this includes negative goodwill – see **13.64** below);

- Payments on account.

Movements

13.3 For each subheading there should be shown:
[Sch 4: 42]

    (a)   in respect of the gross amount:

        (i)   the balances at the beginning and end of the year;
        (ii) acquisitions and disposals during the year; and
        (iii) transfers of assets to and from that item during the year;

(b)   in respect of provisions for depreciation or diminution in value:

    (i)   the balances at the beginning and end of the year;
    (ii)   provision made during the year;
    (iii) adjustments of provisions arising from disposals; and
    (iv) any other adjustments made.

Comparative figures for the preceding year are not required.

Accounting policies

13.4   The Act requires disclosure of the accounting policies with respect to the depreciation and diminution in value of assets, including intangibles. [Sch 4: 36] Generally, this will include the disclosure of the method of amortisation and period of write-off as required by FRS 10 (see **13.5**(c) below).

Additional disclosures mandated by FRS 10

13.5   For (separately) positive goodwill and each class of intangible asset other than those covered by SSAP 13:

(a)   a description of the method used to value intangible assets; [FRS 10(52)]

> As this requirement is listed in the standard under the heading, 'Disclosures – recognition and measurement' and not under 'Disclosures – revaluations', it seems probable that this is intended to refer to those situations where the intangible is carried at a cost which has been established by fair valuing on acquisition at any point in the past. This therefore requires a description of the method originally used to arrive at that value;

(b)   for each class of intangible asset capitalised on the balance sheet:

    (i)   the cost or revalued amount at the beginning and end of the period; [FRS 10(53)(a)]

    (ii)   the cumulative amount of provisions for amortisation or impairment at the beginning and end of the period; [FRS 10(53)(b)]

    (iii) a reconciliation of the movements, separately disclosing additions, disposals, revaluations, transfers, amortisation, impairment losses and reversals of past impairment losses in the financial period; [FRS 10(53)(c)] and

        (iv)   the net carrying amount at the balance sheet date; [FRS 10(53)(d)]

(c)   the methods and periods of amortisation of goodwill and intangible assets and the reasons for choosing those periods; [FRS 10(55)]

(d)   where an amortisation period is shortened or extended, following a review of the remaining useful economic lives, the reason and the effect, if material, should be disclosed in the year of change; [FRS 10(56)]

(e)   where there has been a change in the amortisation method used, the reason and the effect, if material, should be disclosed in the year of change; [FRS 10(57)]

(f)   where goodwill or an intangible asset is either not amortised or is amortised over longer than 20 years since acquisition, the grounds for rebutting the 20-year presumption (a reasoned explanation based on specific factors contributing to the durability of the acquired business or intangible asset) should be given; [FRS 10(58)]

(g)   where a class of intangible assets has been revalued, the year of revaluation, the values, the bases of valuation, the original cost or fair value and the amount of amortisation that would have been recognised if the asset(s) had not been revalued; [FRS 10(61)]

(h)   where any asset has been revalued during the year, the name and qualifications of the valuer; [FRS 10(62)]

(i)   the profit or loss on each material disposal of a previously acquired business or business segment. [FRS 10(54)]

Other disclosures

13.6   Disclosures applicable to specific intangible fixed assets and to negative goodwill are given in the relevant sections below.

Basis of carrying value

Statutory requirements

13.7   Schedule 4 requires that intangible fixed assets should be recognised initially at purchase price or production cost and, except in the case of goodwill, allows the subsequent alternative of revaluing to the current cost basis.

13.8 Intangible assets, other than goodwill, should be depreciated to their residual value over their useful economic life. [Sch 4: 18] Where goodwill is carried as an asset, its cost should be written off over a period not exceeding its useful economic life (see **13.52** to **13.59** below), which precludes the possibility of attributing any residual value to goodwill.

13.9

> Although it is not provided for in the Act, it is considered good practice in respect of any intangible fixed asset which has been fully written down to remove both the cost and the corresponding depreciation from the aggregate amounts disclosed.

Additional requirements imposed by FRS 10

13.10 FRS 10 does not change the requirements relating to initial recognition of goodwill (see **13.45** to **13.50** below). An intangible asset purchased separately from a business should be capitalised at its cost. [FRS 10(9)] Where an intangible asset is purchased as part of the acquisition of a business, there is a potential limitation on the amount at which it may be recognised separately – where such an intangible asset's value can be measured reliably, it should be recorded at its fair value (per FRS 7), but that is subject to the constraint that, unless it has a readily ascertainable market value (see **13.12** below), that fair value should be limited to an amount that does not create or increase any negative goodwill arising on the acquisition. [FRS 10(10)]

13.11 There is a further limitation, which affects only internally generated intangible assets. Such assets may only be capitalised if they have a readily ascertainable market value. [FRS 10(14)]

13.12 A readily ascertainable market value is defined as a value that is established by reference to a market where:
[FRS 10(2)]

    (a)   the asset belongs to a homogeneous population of assets that are equivalent in all material respects; and

    (b)   an active market, evidenced by frequent transactions, exists for that population of assets.

The standard goes on to give examples of intangible assets which might meet these conditions ('certain operating licences, franchises and quotas') and of ones which would not do so ('brands, publishing titles, patented drugs and engineering design patents').

13.13 Some examples may help in interpretation here.

Example 13.13.1

Taxi licences

The taxi licences granted within a certain city give identical rights to each licence holder. The licences are traded actively and, at any point in time, there will be a clearly defined market price. Such licences therefore have a readily ascertainable market value.

Example 13.13.2

Cable television operating licences

Cable television operating licences cover different regions with different populations and geographies and hence may not be homogeneous. Although such licences change hands, it is unlikely that the value of one licence would equal the prices at which others have been traded. Such licences do not have a readily ascertainable market value.

Example 13.13.3

Databases of names and addresses

A market research company builds up databases of names and addresses of individuals with certain socio-economic characteristics. It sells the names and addresses on the list to consumer goods companies wishing to market their products. The fact that the company sells the rights to use the names and addresses does not mean that the database itself is traded. Only if there is a market in which the databases are sold outright to other market research companies and there is an established market price for such databases (say, £x per 1,000 names) could the database have a readily ascertainable market value.

Development costs and expenditure on research

Disclosure requirements

13.14   If any amount is included under 'Development costs' there should be stated in a note to the accounts:
[Sch 4: 20]

(a)   the period over which costs originally capitalised are being or are to be written off; and

(b)   the reasons for capitalising the development costs.

13.15   Development costs are not defined in the Act, but the definition of development (see **13.26** below) given in SSAP 13 may be assumed to be effective for this purpose.

13.16 A development expenditure note which meets these requirements would be as follows:

> ### *Example 13.16*
>
> Development costs on product X which came into production in 1999 are being amortised in equal amounts over the three years 1999–2001, since most of the benefit of the development is expected to fall in these years.
>
> Development costs on product Y are capitalised and carried forward, since product Y is not yet in commercial production. The costs will be amortised over two years, commencing with commercial production, which is expected to be in 2001.

13.17 SSAP 13 requires that the accounting policy followed in relation to expenditure on research and development should be clearly explained.

13.18 Disclosure is required of:

(a) the accounting policy followed in respect of research and development, together with an explanation of that policy; [SSAP 13(30)]

(b) the total amount of research and development expenditure charged in the profit and loss account, analysed between current year's expenditure and amounts amortised from deferred expenditure; [SSAP 13(31)] and

(c) the opening and closing balances of, and movements on, deferred development expenditure. [SSAP 13(32)]

13.19 The information in (b) above need not be given by any company or other entity (provided it is not a public company, bank or insurance company or a parent company which has as a subsidiary any of these types of companies) which satisfies the Act's current criteria, multiplied in each case by 10, for defining a medium-sized company (see chapter 34).

Accounting methods

13.20 The Act provides that the costs of research may not be treated as assets in any company's balance sheet and that an amount may only be included in a balance sheet in respect of development costs in special circumstances. [Sch 4: 3(2) and 20(1)]

13.21 The normal interpretation of 'special circumstances' in this context is that they are those that are defined in and by SSAP 13.

13.22   SSAP 13 subdivides research and development expenditure under three headings.

(a)   *Pure (or basic) research*: experimental or theoretical investigation undertaken to acquire new scientific or technical knowledge for its own sake, rather than directed towards any specific aim or application.

(b)   *Applied research*: original or critical investigation undertaken to gain new scientific or technical knowledge and directed towards a specific practical aim or objective.

(c)   *Development*: the use of scientific or technical knowledge to produce new or substantially improved materials, devices, products, processes, systems or services prior to the commencement of commercial production. The standard specifically excludes from this definition expenditure incurred in locating and exploiting oil, gas and mineral deposits in the extractive industry.

13.23   The SORP *Accounting for oil and gas exploration and development activities* deals only with the accounting treatment of expenditure in exploring, developing and extracting oil and gas. As the SORP does not deal with development expenditure as defined in SSAP 13, development or improvement of processes and techniques in this industry, including those employed in drilling and extraction, fall within SSAP 13's definition.

13.24   Expenditure which is reimbursable by third parties either directly or under a firm contract should be treated in the same way as stocks and work in progress.

13.25   Expenditure on the first two categories, pure and applied research, should be written off as incurred, except that the cost of tangible fixed assets acquired in order to provide facilities for research and development should be treated in the same way as other tangible fixed assets.

13.26   Development expenditure should also be written off as incurred except where all the following circumstances apply:
[SSAP 13(25)]

(a)   there is a clearly defined project;

(b)   the related expenditure is separately identifiable;

(c)   the outcome of the project has been assessed with reasonable certainty as to its technical feasibility and its ultimate commercial viability considered in the light of factors such as likely market conditions (including competing products), public opinion, consumer and environmental legislation;

(d)   if further development costs are to be incurred on the same project, the aggregate of such costs together with related production, selling and administration costs are reasonably expected to be exceeded by related future sales and other revenues; and

(e)   adequate resources exist, or are reasonably expected to be available, to enable the project to be completed and to provide any consequential increases in working capital.

13.27   Where these circumstances apply, development expenditure may be deferred (capitalised) to the extent that its recovery can reasonably be regarded as assured.

13.28   If development costs are deferred to future periods, their amortisation should commence with the commercial production of the product or process. It should then be allocated on a systematic basis to each accounting period, by reference to either the sale or use of the product or process (e.g., by volume) or to the time period over which the product or process is expected to be sold or used.

13.29   It is expected that the period of amortisation will be short, as otherwise it will normally be difficult to have a reasonable certainty of recovery. At the end of each year, the balance of deferred development expenditure for each project should be reviewed in the light of latest available information (e.g., actual sales compared with estimates) and, where the circumstances which justified the deferral in the first instance (the criteria stated above) no longer apply or are considered doubtful, the amount of the balance which is considered to be irrecoverable should be written off immediately.

13.30   SSAP 13 was revised in 1989, so that it no longer prohibited the reinstatement of previously expensed development expenditure where the uncertainties which led to its being written off no longer applied. Consequently, expenditure on a project which could not be deferred in one year because it did not meet the onerous criteria for deferral, and was therefore expensed in that year, may be reinstated in a subsequent year if the criteria are then met. Such a reinstatement represents a change in accounting estimate and should therefore be reflected in the profit and loss account of the year in which the reinstatement is made; in addition it should be separately disclosed in the movements on the deferred balance of development expenditure. However, while the level of uncertainty which led to the initial expensing may reduce, on the grounds of prudence such reinstatement is not recommended.

13.31 This voluntary reinstatement needs to be distinguished from the reversal of provisions made for capitalised development expenditure that were made when it appeared that the project might not be capable of generating sufficient income to cover all that expenditure. As with other provisions for the diminution in value of fixed assets, writing them back by crediting the profit and loss account is required by the Act when and to the extent that such provisions are no longer necessary. [Sch 4: 19(3)]

Concessions, patents, licences, trade marks and similar rights

Introduction

13.32 The Act states that amounts may only be included in a balance sheet under this item if either the assets were acquired for valuable consideration and are not required to be shown under goodwill or the assets were created by the company itself. [Sch 4: Note 2 on the balance sheet formats]

13.33 FRS 10 lays down the ground rules for what may and may not be capitalised as an intangible asset, and this heading is necessarily the one under which such intangible assets would be included. The following table summarises the situation.

Capitalise as goodwill	Capitalise as intangible assets	Do not capitalise
1. Purchased goodwill.	1. Intangible assets purchased separately from a business.	1. Internally generated goodwill.
2. Intangible assets purchased with a business if they are not identifiable from the goodwill or their values cannot be measured reliably.	2. Intangible assets purchased with a business providing they are identifiable from the goodwill and their values can be measured reliably.	
	3. Internally developed intangible assets with a readily ascertainable market value.	2. Internally developed intangible assets with no readily ascertainable market value.

The UITF considered the issue (UITF Information Sheet 34, 26/1/2000) of whether licences and similar rights may fail to qualify as separable intangibles under FRS 10, but confirmed that they do so qualify.

13.34 The wording of the Act raises a doubt over whether such assets may be revalued after acquisition if no cost (i.e., fair value) had

> been ascribed to them on acquisition. This would imply that they were acquired for no valuable consideration. If it can be claimed that the consideration was valuable but, in the context of the net assets as a whole, immaterial, subsequent revaluation is probably acceptable within the meaning of the Act. However, FRS 10 establishes that no intangible assets falling within this Companies Act format heading may be revalued unless they have a readily ascertainable market value. Such assets are more likely to have been recognised at a fair value on acquisition, so the need to interpret this section of the Act is now less likely to arise.

13.35 Amortisation of such intangible assets is governed by the same rules as govern the amortisation of goodwill (see **13.52** to **13.59** below). Additionally, where they are regarded as having limited useful economic lives (i.e., legal rights have been granted for a finite period), the period over which they are to be amortised should be the shorter of the anticipated period of profitable exploitation and the period to the expiry of the right. Renewal periods should only be included if the holder has the option to renew and renewal is assured. The amount of the asset that is treated as having the longer useful economic life should exclude those costs that will recur each time the legal right is renewed (i.e., such costs need to be amortised over the period to renewal). [FRS 10(24)]

13.36 Renewal may be regarded as assured if:
[FRS 10(26)]

(a) the value does not reduce as the initial expiry date approaches (except to reflect the cost of renewal);

(b) there is evidence (possibly experience-based) that the right will be renewed; and

(c) where breach of certain conditions may prevent renewal, there is no evidence of existing or likely future breaches.

Consequently, adoption of an indefinite life is possible only where legal rights can remain in force indefinitely or are renewable indefinitely with each renewal process being assured. [FRS 10(27)]

Brand names and publishing titles

13.37 Brand names are one form of asset falling within the intangible category. A number of prominent companies have taken advantage of the Companies Act option to revalue intangibles by putting a value on the names of their own brands in their balance sheets. In the absence of an accounting standard, there has been no formal prohibition on the capitalisation of brand names. However, as discussed in

13.38 to **13.42** below, FRS 10 extends a serious challenge to the previous practice of either capitalising the costs of developing own brands or revaluing any brands already owned. The only amount at which brands may continue to be carried on the balance sheet is at the cost for which they were purchased (either individually or as part of a business acquisition). In the standard, publishing titles are classed with brands, to be treated in the same way. [FRS 10(2) and (12)]

Capitalisation of own costs

13.38

> Although the Act permits the production cost of intangibles to be included in the balance sheet, FRS 10 seeks to prohibit this treatment in respect of brands and publishing titles. The standard makes it clear that internally generated intangible assets may only be capitalised if they have a readily ascertainable market value. [FRS 10(14)] The definition of a readily ascertainable market value (see **13.12** above) specifically refers to brands and publishing titles as examples of assets which, being by their nature unique, do not have readily ascertainable market values. The ASB seeks to preclude costs of the development of own brands or publishing titles from being capitalised.

Capitalisation of purchased brands or publishing titles

13.39   One factor which in the past attracted companies to recognising the fair value of acquired brands or publishing titles was the opportunity that such an approach offered to side-step certain of the regulations relating to the treatment of goodwill. However, FRS 10 eliminated the potential differences in accounting treatment which created that attraction. A brand or publishing title may be either acquired as part of the purchase of an ongoing business or purchased in isolation. The Act permits the purchase price of intangibles to be included in the balance sheet. FRS 7 requires fair values to be placed on identifiable assets and liabilities as part of the fair value exercise in allocating the purchase consideration for the business to its separable net assets, with any balance being attributed to goodwill or negative goodwill. 'Identifiable' is defined as meaning 'capable of being disposed of separately, without disposing of a business of the entity'. [FRS 7(2)] Any material intangible asset meeting this definition must therefore be included in the acquiring group or company's balance sheet at a fair value. If an intangible asset fails this test, it may not be so included.

13.40   If any brand or publishing title acquired as part of a business meets this test, then it should be valued at the fair value of acquiring it, excluding any value attaching to other aspects of the business which contribute to the earnings potential of the product with which the brand is associated. FRS 7 indicates that 'where an intangible asset is recognised, its fair value should be based on its replacement cost, which is normally its estimated market value'. [FRS 7(10)] FRS 10 strengthens this requirement by adding that its value must be capable of being measured reliably, indicating that techniques have been developed for measuring such assets indirectly, without reference to market values. [FRS 10(10)]

13.41

> The difficulty of establishing objectively a separable market value for a brand is the principal barrier to giving brands a fair value on acquisition and consequently the main reason for them not appearing frequently as a post-acquisition group asset. It is rarely practicable to find objective evidence of a marketplace or market price at which the asset could be exchanged in an arm's-length transaction between informed and willing parties; furthermore, other methods of valuing brands, e.g., independent valuers, do not always address convincingly the question of separability from the business of the entity, posing a potential problem of compliance with FRS 7. Also, FRS 10 has now removed any advantage from separating such assets from goodwill. For these reasons, it is now even less likely that many post-acquisition examples will appear.

Revaluation of brands

13.42 The Act permits intangibles other than goodwill to be valued at current cost. However, FRS 10 puts a constraint on this by limiting it to those intangible assets that have a readily ascertainable market value and, as examples of intangibles that could have such a value, mentions 'certain operating licences, franchises and quotas' (see examples in **13.13** above). [FRS 10(43) and (45)] As the standard also makes clear that it is not possible to establish a readily ascertainable market value for brands or titles, the revaluation of brands or titles is not allowed under the standard. [FRS 10(12)]

Amortisation of intangibles

13.43 FRS 10 has common requirements in respect of amortisation for both goodwill and other intangible assets. This is dealt with in **13.52** to **13.59** below.

Goodwill

Introduction

13.44   Goodwill is a contentious area, internationally and in the UK. Its nature is not well understood and accounting for it varies considerably both by and within different jurisdictions. The UK's approach has been distinctive, inconsistent and hard to justify, but FRS 10 now addresses many of the problem areas, eliminates the previous choice between two very different accounting methods and brings the UK more nearly into line with the treatments adopted in other countries.

13.45   Purchased goodwill is defined as the difference between the cost of an acquired entity and the aggregate of the fair values of that entity's identifiable assets and liabilities. [FRS 10(2)] Successful businesses are worth more than the sum of the net assets they control and so generate their own goodwill (through commercial connections, regular customers, good reputation, efficient management, etc.), but such self-generated goodwill does not appear in the financial statements, and companies are precluded from including it in their balance sheets. The Act provides that goodwill may only be included in a balance sheet to the extent that it was acquired for valuable consideration. [Sch 4: Note 3 on the balance sheet formats and Sch 4: 31(1)]

13.46   The purchase of any business or undertaking may give rise to goodwill, whether the purchase is made directly or through the purchase of shares in a company that owns the business. The provisions of FRS 10 cover both types of goodwill: that arising in an individual entity when it acquires a business and that arising on consolidation when the group has acquired a new company or a sufficient stake in a part-owned company.

13.47   It is necessary at the outset to be able to distinguish between transactions for the purchase of a business, in which goodwill may or may not arise, and the purchase of specific assets. In order to treat a transaction as the purchase of a business, it is considered that two criteria should be met: the benefit of customers' accounts should have passed to the purchaser, and employees should continue in the same employment, albeit with the acquiring company. In other words, the business carries on substantially as before under the responsibility of the new owners.

13.48   Where specific assets are purchased, the total consideration represents the cost of those assets to the purchaser, irrespective of the values attributed to them in the books of the vendor, and therefore no goodwill arises. Where more than one asset or

> group of assets is acquired, it will be necessary to allocate the purchase price to the respective assets on the basis of fair values, in order to record their cost to the purchaser as required by the Act. Where there is a vending agreement which attributes values to the various assets, this may give some guidance but it is unlikely to be authoritative. There is the possibility that the process of attribution may be driven by tax or other considerations, rather than by the need to attribute fair values. Such values should always be considered carefully, in the light of all the circumstances, to check that they represent fair and arm's-length prices, before they may safely be adopted as costs to the purchaser.

13.49 Where a business is purchased, the consideration will reflect not only the net assets being acquired but also any goodwill that the purchaser recognises in the business. It will be necessary to determine the fair value to the purchaser of the net assets acquired in order to identify the amount of goodwill involved. The determination of fair values of assets and liabilities is considered in **24.27** to **24.51** below. It is the fair values, not the net book values carried in the financial statements of the acquired business or of its previous owner, that should be reflected in the balance sheet as their cost to the acquiring company or group. Any excess of the purchase consideration over the fair value of the net assets acquired represents purchased goodwill. Where the business purchased is incorporated, and it becomes a subsidiary or related company, the goodwill element arises in the consolidation process, appearing only in the group balance sheet, and is commonly referred to as 'goodwill on consolidation'.

13.50 Sometimes the total fair value of the net assets acquired (after making provision for all costs which were taken into account in determining the purchase price) exceeds the consideration paid. This excess is referred to as 'negative goodwill' (see **13.64** below).

Accounting for purchased goodwill: introduction

13.51 SSAP 22 provided for two alternative standard practices to be followed in relation to purchased goodwill: immediate elimination and amortisation. The choice between them could be made afresh for each succeeding acquisition, as consistency of practice within each entity was not required. This choice has now been removed by FRS 10; elimination (SSAP 22's preferred method) is no longer an option. Goodwill is required to be capitalised and shown among fixed assets (with negative goodwill shown in the same place – see **13.64** below). However, depending upon circumstances, there may still be an option in respect of amortisation. Also, certain consequences of SSAP 22's preferred method will linger on for some years, as FRS 10's transitional provisions (see **13.66** below) permit rather than require the reinstatement of goodwill previously written off to reserves.

Amortisation

13.52 FRS 10 lays down a common set of requirements regarding the treatment of both goodwill and other intangible assets. Where they are regarded as having limited useful economic lives, they should be amortised on a systematic basis over those lives. [FRS 10(15)] Where they are regarded as having indefinite useful economic lives, they should not be amortised. [FRS 10(17)] Because the Companies Act requires goodwill that is treated as an asset to be amortised systematically and does not allow recognition of any residual value for goodwill at the end of useful economic life, not amortising is a departure from the Companies Act requirement and involves invoking the overriding purpose of providing a true and fair view, with the disclosures that that involves (see **5.11** above). (Because other intangible assets may have a residual value, non-amortisation of those assets does not require the use of a true and fair view override.)

13.53 The ASB explains the need to invoke the true and fair override in the following way:

'The Board has been advised that non-amortisation of goodwill constitutes a departure from the specific requirement of companies legislation to depreciate the value attributed to goodwill over a limited period that does not exceed its useful economic life. However departure from specific requirements such as this one is permitted by companies legislation in exceptional circumstances where it is necessary for the overriding purpose of providing a true and fair view. Accordingly, the Board has limited the circumstances in which it proposes that goodwill is not amortised to those circumstances where systematic amortisation would not provide a true and fair view. It has also incorporated within the disclosure requirements the disclosures that are required by companies legislation where advantage has been taken of the true and fair override provisions.' [FRS 10, appendix III, paragraph 36]

13.54 The ASB is treading a very careful path in order to keep within the terms of the Companies Act, and the term 'exceptional circumstances' in FRS 10, appendix III, paragraph 36 (above) must be regarded as formal rather than real. This is analogous to the requirement that those holding investment properties comply with SSAP 19 and justify non-depreciation by using the true and fair override. Evidence so far suggests that the choice of non-amortisation will prove to be exceptional rather than routine.

13.55   The useful economic life of goodwill or any intangible asset is presumed to be 20 years or less. That presumption may be rebutted and either a longer life or an indefinite life may be substituted, provided both of two conditions are met:
[FRS 10(19)]

(a)   the durability of the acquired business or intangible asset can be demonstrated and justifies estimating the useful economic life to exceed 20 years; and

(b)   the goodwill or intangible asset is capable of continued measurement (so that annual impairment reviews will be feasible).

Durability depends upon such factors as nature of business, stability of the industry, typical lifespan of products, the extent to which the acquisition overcomes market entry barriers which will continue to exist, and the expected future impact of competition. [FRS 10(20)] Continued measurement will be impracticable if its cost is unjustifiably high. [FRS 10(23)] The uncertainty inherent in estimating useful economic life is neither a justification for treating that life as indefinite or for adopting a 20-year life by default, nor an excuse for adopting an unrealistically short life. [FRS 10(21) and (22)] If both conditions (a) and (b) are met, the goodwill or intangible asset will either be carried indefinitely or amortised over the longer period than 20 years that has been identified as appropriate. In either case, they become subject to the impairment testing provisions described in **13.60** to **13.63** below.

13.56   Early indications are that the additional obligations imposed on entities that are successful in rebutting the '20 years or less' assumption are discouraging a high proportion of managements from attempting the rebuttal. Non-amortisation will, it appears, be very much the exception to the rule. One notable exception is entities with purchased brands on the balance sheet, which may well feel that it is worth continuing to claim an indefinite life and carrying out an annual impairment review. SmithKline Beecham and Diageo were amongst early adopters of this policy.

Extract 13.56

SmithKline Beecham plc – 1998

Accounting policies – intangible fixed assets and amortisation

Brands are valued independently as part of the fair value of assets acquired from third parties where the brand has a value which is substantial and long term and where the brands can be sold separately from the rest of the businesses acquired. Brands are amortised over

---

the estimated useful lives but no longer than 20 years except where the end of the useful economic life of the brand cannot be foreseen. The carrying value of brands with an indefinite life is subject to annual review by the Directors and any amortisation or provision for permanent impairment is charged against profit in the year concerned.

13.57 When determining a life and method for amortising an intangible asset, it is also necessary to consider any residual value. A residual value should only be assigned to it if it can be measured reliably. No residual value may be assigned to goodwill. [FRS 10(28)] The standard suggests that the residual value of an intangible asset will only be significant and capable of reliable measurement when that value is either a readily ascertainable market value or a legal or contractual right to receive a certain sum. [FRS 10(29)]

13.58 A straight-line method of amortisation should be selected, unless another method can be demonstrated to be more appropriate, i.e., to reflect better the expected pattern of depletion. [FRS 10(30)] The standard makes it clear that it is not likely that a less conservative method than straight-line can be justified for amortising goodwill and that a method such as 'reverse sum of digits' which aims to produce a constant rate of return on carrying value is not appropriate for amortising goodwill. [FRS 10(31) and (32)]

13.59 Useful economic lives should be reviewed at the end of every reporting period and revised if necessary and the effect of any revision should be spread over the revised life. However, if the effect is to increase life to more than 20 years since acquisition, the additional requirements relating to goodwill and intangible assets amortised over more than 20 years (see **13.60** to **13.63** below) become applicable. [FRS 10(33)]

Impairment testing

13.60 FRS 10 requires that goodwill and intangible assets that are amortised over 20 years or less shall be subject to impairment reviews which take two forms:
[FRS 10(34)]

(a) the 'first year review' – a review at the end of the first full financial year following acquisition; and

(b) a review at the end of any period when events or changes of circumstances indicate that the carrying value may not be recoverable.

However, goodwill and intangible assets which are to be regarded as having lives that are either indefinite or in excess of 20 years since acquisition, i.e., those where the presumption of a maximum life of 20 years has been rebutted (see **13.55** above), shall be subject to an impairment review at the end of **every** reporting period.

13.61 FRS 10 lays down that a first-year impairment review (see **13.60**(a) above) may be performed in two stages:
[FRS 10(40)]

(a) by comparing the first year's performance after acquisition with pre-acquisition forecasts used to support the purchase price; and

(b) by carrying out a full impairment review **only** if either the results of (a) indicate a shortfall from expectations or if any other previously unforeseen events or changes in circumstances indicate that the carrying values may not be recoverable.

13.62 The intention is that a first full year review should be a relatively simple matter, provided that a credible, competently prepared investment appraisal supporting the purchase price was carried out prior to purchase. If net cash flows for the elapsed period since the appraisal are in line with or better than those forecast for that period in the appraisal report, and if there are no indicators suggesting future cash flows will struggle to meet forecast, then no further work will be necessary.

13.63 Where a full impairment review is required, it will be carried out in accordance with FRS 11 *Impairment of fixed assets and goodwill* (see **14.240** et seq. below and appendix X 'Testing for impairment' and appendix XI 'Weighted average cost of capital').

The treatment of negative goodwill

13.64 FRS 10 has changed the treatment of negative goodwill. Firstly, there is a formal requirement, wherever negative goodwill appears to arise on an acquisition, to test the fair values of all the acquired assets for impairment and to check the fair values of acquired liabilities to ensure that none has been omitted or understated. [FRS 10(48)] (The ASB appears to believe that it is improbable that negative goodwill would arise under normal circumstances and that its frequent appearance in the past suggests a lack of rigour in the fair valuing process.) Secondly, negative goodwill may no longer be disclosed as a direct credit to reserves. Instead, it should be separately disclosed with the assets on the face of the balance sheet, immediately below the goodwill heading, followed by a subtotal showing the net amount of positive and negative goodwill. [FRS 10(48)] (It now becomes possible, in theory, to show negative total fixed assets, in the very unlikely event that the negative goodwill exceeds all recorded fixed assets – a figure which, if it ever occurs, will give rise to some surprise.) Purchased goodwill (positive or negative) arising on a single transaction should not be divided into positive and negative components. [FRS 10(51)] (Note also restriction on amount of negative goodwill recognisable in respect of the fair value of an intangible asset with no readily ascertainable market value (see **13.10** above).)

13.65 The standard expects the figure for negative goodwill to be recognised as realised in the profit and loss accounts for subsequent periods (see **9.221** above). Negative goodwill up to the amount of the fair value of the non-monetary assets acquired should be recognised in the profit and loss account in the periods in which the non-monetary assets are recovered, whether through depreciation or by disposal. [FRS 10(49)] Any negative goodwill in excess of the fair value of the non-monetary assets acquired should be recognised in the profit and loss account in the periods expected to benefit. [FRS 10(48)]

Transitional arrangements on the implementation of FRS 10

13.66 Companies (apart from those complying with the FRSSE) were obliged to apply FRS 10 in their first accounting reference period ending on or after 23 December 1998. The standard had to be adopted in respect of all existing goodwill and intangibles carried as assets, with consequent changes in accounting policy treated as prior period adjustments. [FRS 10(66)] (See **13.69** below for impairment losses.) However, each company had to make a choice as to how to deal with any balance of goodwill that had previously been eliminated against reserves and that related to the acquisition of businesses or companies that had not been terminated or disposed of. Each company could choose to reinstate all of that goodwill or it could choose to leave some or all of it eliminated against reserves. However, if it chose the latter, it had to adopt consistently one of three policies:

(a) leave eliminated all previously eliminated goodwill; or

(b) leave eliminated that part of it which was eliminated before the implementation of FRS 7 (FRS 7 was implemented mandatorily for business combinations first accounted for in financial statements relating to accounting periods commencing on or after 23 December 1994); or

(c) leave eliminated that part of it relating to acquisitions made before 23 December 1989, but only in respect of acquisitions where the necessary information was unavailable or could not be obtained without unreasonable expense or delay.

It was not acceptable to choose different policies for different elements in the balance of eliminated goodwill. [FRS 10(69)]

13.67 Where a choice of policy on transition was adopted which resulted in the reinstatement of an element of goodwill, any impairment that was attributed to prior periods had to be determined on the basis of impairment reviews performed in accordance with FRS 11 *Impairment of fixed assets and goodwill.*

13.68 On the subsequent disposal or closure of the business with which that goodwill (i.e., any element that remains eliminated against reserves) was acquired, the calculation of profit or loss on disposal or closure, to be included in the profit and loss account for that period, should take account of attributable goodwill (except to the extent that it has previously been charged to the profit and loss account) and that amount of attributable goodwill should be disclosed (see **13.70** below). [FRS 10(71)(c)]

Measurement of profit on disposal

13.69 Any impairment loss relating to previously capitalised goodwill or intangible assets that is recognised on first implementing the standard should be charged as an expense in that period. [FRS 10(74)]

13.70 FRS 10 picked up the requirements of UITF Abstract 3 (which was therefore withdrawn) by requiring that, on disposal of the business to which any goodwill relates, any element of that attributable goodwill which has previously been eliminated against reserves as a matter of accounting policy (in compliance with SSAP 22) and has not been expensed through the annual profit and loss should be taken into account in determining profit or loss on disposal. [FRS 10(71)(c)(i)] This is to ensure that the total amount of any purchased goodwill is reflected in the profit and loss account at some point by the time of either exhaustion or disposal. This principle is incorporated in FRS 2 which indicates that it applies to both direct and deemed disposals (see **24.134** below). [FRS 2(47)] (Note that, when FRS 10 was implemented, where an entity chose to reinstate goodwill previously written off to reserves, any amortisation of that goodwill figure reckoned to have occurred prior to reinstatement was expensed at that point by prior period adjustment and consequently does not fall to be taken into account in determining profit or loss on subsequent disposal.)

13.71 Logically partial disposals should be dealt with in the same way. This applies whether they are achieved by the actual disposal of shares or by the dilution of the group's holding by means of the issue of further shares in the subsidiary or associate to third parties (a deemed disposal). It also applies whether the partial disposal results in the subsidiary or associate retaining that status or changing to an associate (from subsidiary) or a trade investment. In each case, an appropriate proportion of any goodwill on acquisition which has not yet been expensed through the profit and loss account should be taken into account in determining the gain or loss on disposal.

Disclosure requirements

13.72   In addition to the statutory requirement to disclose movements both in gross amounts and depreciation of intangibles (see **13.3** above), the following information is required to be given, by FRS 6, FRS 10 and the Act:

(a)   the composition and fair value of the consideration given by the acquiring company and its subsidiary undertakings, including the nature of any deferred or contingent purchase consideration and, for contingent consideration, the range of possible outcomes and the principal factors that affect the outcome; [FRS 6(24)]*

(b)   where goodwill is amortised, the period and method selected for amortising the goodwill relating to each major acquisition. Schedule 4 para 21(4) also requires disclosure of 'the reasons for choosing that period', i.e., a statement that the period chosen represents the estimated useful economic life; [FRS 10(55)]

(c)   a table showing for each class of assets and liabilities of each material entity acquired during the period: [FRS 6(25)]

(i)   the book values, as recorded in the acquired entity's books immediately before the acquisition and before any fair value adjustments;

(ii)   the fair value adjustments, analysed into: revaluations; adjustments to achieve consistency of accounting policies; and other significant adjustments, giving the reasons for the adjustments; and

(iii)   the fair values at the date of acquisition,

and including a statement of the amount of purchased goodwill or negative goodwill arising on each material acquisition. [FRS 6(25)] (An example of the disclosures required to be given in the table is given in **13.74** below.) This table also meets the disclosure requirements of Schedule 4A para 13(5);*

(d)   (in the table referred to above) provisions for reorganisation and restructuring costs that are included in the liabilities of the acquired entity, and related asset write-downs, made in the 12 months up to the date of acquisition; [FRS 6(26)]*

(e)   movements on provisions or accruals for costs related to an acquisition, analysed between the amounts used for the specific purpose for which they were created and the amounts released unused; [FRS 6(32)]*

(f)   where the fair values of the assets and liabilities, or the consideration, can only be determined on a provisional basis at the end of the accounting period in which the acquisition took place, this should be stated and the reasons given; subsequent material adjustments to such provisional fair values, with corresponding adjustments to goodwill, should be disclosed and explained. [FRS 6(27)]* The Financial Reporting Review Panel's decision in respect of Reckitt & Colman PLC's accounts (15 April 1997) suggests that it is important that disclosures of adjustments to provisional fair values need 'a similar level of disclosure and explanation' to that required when the acquisition is first accounted for;

(g)   in respect of any goodwill that remains eliminated against reserves: the accounting policy followed in respect of that goodwill; the cumulative amounts of positive goodwill eliminated against reserves and negative goodwill added to reserves, net of any goodwill attributable to businesses disposed of before the balance sheet date, and the fact that this goodwill has been eliminated as a matter of accounting policy and would be charged or credited in the profit and loss account on subsequent disposal of the business to which it relates. [FRS 10(71)(a)] This eliminated goodwill should not be shown as a debit balance on a separate goodwill write-off reserve, but should be offset against the profit and loss account or another appropriate reserve. The amount by which the reserve has been reduced by the elimination of goodwill (or increased by the addition of negative goodwill) **should not be shown separately** on the face of the balance sheet; [FRS 10(71)(b)]

(h)   in respect of each material disposal of a previously acquired business or business segment, the following is to be given:

   (i)   the profit or loss on disposal [FRS 10(54)];
   (ii)   in the case of any goodwill from acquisitions prior to the

implementation of FRS 10 which remains eliminated against reserves, the amount of such goodwill attributable to the business or business segment disposed of and how it has been treated in determining the profit or loss on disposal. [FRS 10(71)(c)(ii)]

Where, on disposal of a business that was acquired before 1 January 1989, it is impossible or impractical to ascertain the goodwill attributable to that business, this should be stated and the reasons given; [FRS 10(71)(c)]

(i) the cumulative amount of goodwill resulting from acquisitions in earlier financial years which has been written off to reserves, i.e., not through the profit and loss account in any year; [Sch 4A: 14]

(j) where capitalised goodwill is not amortised, a statement that the financial statements depart from the specific requirement of companies legislation to amortise goodwill over a finite period for the overriding purpose of giving a true and fair view. This statement therefore needs to include particulars of the departure, the reasons for it and its effect, in sufficient detail to convey to the reader of the financial statements the circumstances justifying the use of the true and fair override. Reasons for the departure should incorporate the explanation of the specific factors contributing to the durability of the acquired business. [FRS 10(59)] When dealing with the effect of the departure, in view of the impossibility of quantifying any effect, it will be necessary to follow the guidance in UITF Abstract 7, i.e., 'whenever the effect cannot reasonably be quantified, the directors should explain the circumstances' (see **5.11** above); [UITF Abstract 7(4)(c)(ii)]

(k) in respect of negative goodwill, the period(s) in which negative goodwill is being written back in the profit and loss account and, where negative goodwill exceeds the fair values of non-monetary assets, the amount and source of the 'excess' negative goodwill and the period(s) in which such excess is being written back should be explained. [FRS 10(63) and (64)]

Disclosures required by paragraphs indicated by '*' above should be made separately for each material acquisition and in aggregate for other acquisitions. [FRS 6(23)]

13.73   On implementation of FRS 10, where any goodwill that was previously eliminated against reserves is reinstated, the notes to the financial statements should disclose the original cost of the goodwill and the amounts attributed to prior period amortisation and, separately, prior period impairment. [FRS 10(70)(b)] It is not necessary to identify separately intangible assets that are subsumed within the goodwill. [FRS 10(70)(c)]

13.74 The following example indicates a format for the fair value table and adjustments.

Example 13.74

XYZ Ltd was acquired on 19 February 2000 and 100,000 £1 ordinary shares were issued as consideration for the acquisition. The assets acquired are set out below. The fair value of the consideration, using the mid-market price on 10 February 2000 of £3.06, was £306,000, giving rise to goodwill of £100,000.

	Book amount	Revaluation	Accounting alignment	Other major items	Fair value to the group
	£'000	£'000	£'000	£'000	£'000
FIXED ASSETS					
Intangible	–	–	–	[d] 80	80
Tangible	160	[a]20	–	–	180
Investments	20	[b] 5	–	–	25
CURRENT ASSETS					
Stocks	31	–	[c] (2)	–	29
Debtors	35	–	–	–	35
Investments	10	–	–	–	10
Cash at bank	12	–	–	–	12
TOTAL ASSETS	268	25	(2)	80	371
PROVISIONS					
Pensions	30	–	–	–	30
Deferred taxation	45	–	–	[e] 10	55
Other	18	–	–	–	18
CREDITORS					
Debenture	2	–	–	–	2
Bank loans	15	–	–	–	15
Trade creditors	30	–	–	–	30
Other creditors	10	–	–	–	10
Accruals	5	–	–	–	5
TOTAL LIABILITIES	155	–	–	10	165
NET ASSETS	113	25	(2)	70	206

---

[a]   Increases in value of freehold properties since last revaluation in 1993.

[b]   Increase in value of investment since purchase in 1995.

[c]   Change of stock valuation from weighted average cost to FIFO which is used by the group.

[d]   Recognition of intangibles – relating to publishing titles and brands acquired.

[e]   Adjustment to deferred tax arising from the incorporation of fair values.

It is worth noting that the Financial Reporting Review Panel appears to attach particular importance to compliance with the detailed requirements of this table – there have been several examples of companies criticised by the Panel for failures in this respect, and each company has been obliged to make subsequent disclosure of the missing information.

14 Tangible fixed assets

14   Tangible fixed assets

Summary of changes since the previous issue of this publication

Para.	*Topic*	*Summary*
Whole chapter	FRS 15 *Tangible fixed assets*	FRS 15 was issued in February 1999 and it replaces SSAP 12 when implemented. It is applicable for years ending on or after 23 March 2000 although early adoption is encouraged.
14.302 to 14.310	*Application of the transitional rules in FRS 15*	UITF 23 was issued in May 2000 to interpret the transitional rules in FRS 15(106) and FRS 15(108). The accounting treatment required by this consensus should be adopted as soon as practicable, but in any event in financial statements relating to accounting periods ending on or after 23 March 2000 (the effective date of FRS 15).

Introduction

14.1   Accounting for tangible fixed assets is now regulated not only by the Companies Act and by SSAP 19, *Accounting for investment properties*, but also by FRS 15, published in February 1999 and taking effect for accounting periods ending on or after 23 March 2000.

Financial statements to which FRS 15 applies

14.2   FRS 15 applies to all financial statements that are intended to give a true and fair view of a reporting entity's financial position and profit or loss (or income and expenditure) for a period, other than individual entity statements prepared in accordance with the Financial Reporting Standard for Smaller Entities.

Tangible fixed assets to which FRS 15 applies

14.3   The requirements of FRS 15 apply to all tangible fixed assets, with the exception of investment properties as defined in SSAP 19, *Accounting for investment properties.* However, as assets under construction do not qualify as investment properties until completed, they fall within the scope of FRS 15 and the Standard's rules on initial capitalisation therefore apply to investment properties (see **14.55** to **14.70** below). Tangible fixed assets are defined as assets that have physical substance and are held for use in the production or supply of goods or services, for rental to others, or for administrative purposes on a continuing basis in the reporting entity's activities.

14.4   FRS 15 supersedes SSAP 12 *Accounting for depreciation,* when implemented. It also withdraws SSAP 19(9), which gave charities exemption from accounting for investment properties under the standard. The charities' SORP already requires charities to carry their investment properties at market value, so the withdrawal of SSAP 19(9) brings the standard into line with existing practice.

Implementation date

14.5   The accounting practices set out in FRS 15 should be regarded as standard in respect of financial statements relating to accounting periods ending on or after 23 March 2000. Earlier adoption is encouraged.

Disclosure requirements

Statutory headings

14.6   'Tangible assets' is a main heading which should appear on the face of the balance sheet. The following subheadings are required but may be shown either on the face of the balance sheet or in the notes:

- Land and buildings;

- Plant and machinery;

- Fixtures, fittings, tools and equipment;

- Payments on account and assets in course of construction.

Movements

14.7   For each subheading there should be shown:
[Sch 4: 42]

(a)   in respect of the gross amounts (i.e., cost or other valuation basis):

    (i)   the balances at the beginning and end of the year;

    (ii) any revision of the amount made during the year arising from a revaluation;

    (iii) acquisitions and disposals during the year; and

    (iv) transfers of assets to or from that asset category during the year;

(b) in respect of provisions for depreciation or diminution in value:

    (i)   the balances at the beginning and end of the year;

    (ii) provisions made during the year;

    (iii) adjustments of provisions arising from disposals; and

    (iv) any other adjustment made in respect of such provisions during the year.

Comparative figures for movements in the preceding year are not required.

Information on valuation bases

14.8   Where tangible fixed assets are valued in accordance with the alternative valuation rules permitted in Sch 4 (i.e., market value or current cost), the Companies Act requires the following information to be given:

(a)   the items (i.e., account headings) affected and the bases of valuation [Sch 4: 33(2)];

(b)   the year of revaluation (particularly in the case of market values, as 'current cost' implies a value arrived at for the current year) and the values; also in the year of valuation, the name of the valuers (or particulars of their qualifications) and basis of valuation [Sch 4: 43]; and

(c)   the comparable historical cost amounts, or the difference between these amounts and the valuation, including the comparable amount or difference in the cumulative provision for depreciation [Sch 4: 33(3)] (but FRS 15 accepts only the former – see **14.9**(a)(iv) below). If the historical cost of any asset is not readily ascertainable, then the value ascribed to it in the earliest available record of its value may be used instead.

14.9   FRS 15 has expanded the disclosure requirements where a policy of revaluing any class of tangible fixed asset has been adopted. 'Class' is defined in FRS 15(2) as: 'A category of tangible fixed assets having a similar nature, function or use in the business of the entity' (see **14.92** to **14.98** below). Every class defined for revaluation purposes needs to be shown separately on the tangible fixed asset note, and all the appropriate disclosures given. The following information should be disclosed in **each** reporting period.

FRS 15 requirements	Comments
(a) For each class of revalued assets:	
(i) the name and qualifications of the valuer(s) or the valuer's organisation and a description of its nature [Companies Act only asks for names or particulars of their qualifications];	There will be cases where the latest interim valuation and the last full valuation have not been performed by the same person/firm. FRS 15 is imprecise on what needs to be disclosed (i.e., details of the interim valuer, the full valuer or both). It is best, therefore, to give details of both valuers. The information given can be either the name of the valuer and his/her qualifications, or the firm's name and authorisation to perform valuations.
(ii) the basis or bases of valuation (including whether notional directly attributable acquisition costs have been included or expected selling costs deducted);	Companies Act asks for the base used. N.B. The requirement to disclose the amount of the notional costs for revalued properties is included in (b)(ii) below.
(iii) the date and amounts of the valuations;	Same requirement as under CA 1985.
(iv) where historical cost records are available, the carrying amount that would have been included in the financial statements had the tangible fixed assets been carried at historical cost less depreciation;	CA 85 accepts either the comparable amounts determined according to the historical cost accounting rules or the differences between those amounts and the revalued amounts. FRS 15 only accepts the former.
(v) whether the person(s) carrying out the valuation is (are) internal or external to the entity;	Under SSAP 19 this is required for investment properties, but it is new for other tangible fixed assets.
(vi) where the directors are not aware of any material change in value and therefore the valuation(s) have not been updated, a statement to that effect;	New requirement. N.B. This is when a 'review' carried out in years 1, 2 and 4 (following the general five-year revaluation cycle – see **14.105** below) indicates no need for an interim valuation, as the carrying value of the assets is still 'current'.
(vii) where the valuation has not been updated, or is not a full valuation, the date of the last full valuation.	New requirement.

(b) Additionally, for properties that are revalued:	
(i) where properties have been valued as fully-equipped operational entities having regard to their trading potential, a statement to that effect and the carrying amount of those properties;	New requirement – types of properties commonly revalued on this basis include hotels, pubs, and petrol filling stations.
(ii) the total amount of notional directly attributable acquisition costs added to (or the total amount of expected selling costs deducted from) the carrying amount, where material.	New requirement.
(c) Where an asset has been excluded from a class for valuation purposes as a reliable valuation cannot be determined, this fact must be stated and the carrying amount of the asset given.	New requirement. The exemption in FRS 15 is limited to assets held outside the UK and the Republic of Ireland. [FRS 15 (61)]

14.10 FRS 15 recognises that other additional disclosures may be required by other professional bodies. For example, the RICS requires confirmation, in any published document containing a reference to a valuation report, that the valuation has been made in accordance with the RICS Appraisal and Valuation Manual or a (named) alternative pursuant to Practice Statement 1.2.2, or the extent of and reason(s) for departure therefrom. [FRS 15(75)]

14.11 'In addition, companies legislation requires disclosure, in the directors' report, of the difference, with such precision as is practicable, between the carrying amount and market value of interests in land, where, in the opinion of the directors, it is of such significance that it needs to be drawn to the attention of the members of the entity.' [FRS 15(76)]

14.12 SSAP 19 requires that, if the valuer of investment properties is an employee of the company or group, this fact should be disclosed. FRS 15 now applies the same requirement to other tangible fixed assets (see **14.9**(a)(v) above).

14.13 An example of disclosure in respect of a property revaluation during the year is as follows:

> ### *Example 14.13*
>
> The company's freehold property was valued by Messrs King & Co,
> Chartered Surveyors, on 31 July 1999. In their opinion, the open mar-
> ket value for the existing use at that time was £750,000, as compared
> with the net book amount of £218,000. A potential tax liability of
> £105,000 will become due if the property is sold at the above value.
> The valuation has been incorporated in the balance sheet and the sur-
> plus over net book amount of £532,000 has been added to the reval-
> uation reserve. Depreciation for the year has been based on the
> amount of the valuation, resulting in an increased depreciation
> charge of £5,100.

Analysis of land and buildings

14.14   The item of 'Land and buildings' should be analysed between free-
holds, long leaseholds (not less than 50 years unexpired) and short
leaseholds. [Sch 4: 44 and 83]

Interest capitalised

14.15   Where interest has been included in the cost of an asset, the amount
of interest so included should be disclosed in a note to the accounts.
[Sch 4: 26(3)] FRS 15(31) expands that disclosure by requiring that,
where a policy of capitalisation of finance costs is adopted, the financial statements should disclose the following:

Disclosure required	Acceptable position	Frequency of disclosure
The accounting policy adopted	In policy note	Every year
The aggregate amount of finance costs included in the cost of tangible fixed assets (see **14.17** below when assets are revalued)	At foot of tangible fixed asset note	Every year
The amount of finance costs capitalised during the period	At foot of tangible fixed asset note or as separate line in the fixed asset table	In year interest capitalised
The amount of finance costs recognised in the profit and loss account during the period	Within 'Interest payable and similar charges' note in accordance with FRS 4(28) and (76)	In year interest capitalised
The capitalisation rate used to determine the amount of finance costs capitalised during the period	In policy note or at foot of tangible fixed asset note	In year interest capitalised

14.16 FRS 15 does not state where this disclosure should appear, or whether it all needs to be in the same note. It seems logical to include the profit and loss charge in the appropriate note where the finance charges have been made and the amounts included in the production cost to be in the fixed asset note. The interest cost required to be disclosed would not include any non-interest element of finance charges, e.g., issue costs, premium on redemption, required by FRS 4 to be spread over the life of an instrument, even if that element has been capitalised in the asset cost alongside the relevant interest.

14.17 The above disclosure requirements apply even if the asset has been revalued. There are two requirements: to disclose the entity's policy regarding interest capitalisation; and to disclose the aggregate amount of finance costs included in 'cost'. In the case of revalued assets, no additional finance charges can be added to the valuation. As there is a requirement to disclose the depreciated historical cost carrying amount, then it appears that the finance costs originally capitalised should also be disclosed, normally as part of the historic cost disclosures (see **14.9** above).

14.18 Listed companies are required to state the amount of interest capitalised during the year, together with the amount and treatment of any related tax relief. [Listing Rule 12.43 (c)]

Treatment of depreciation

14.19 The accounting policies with respect to the depreciation and diminution in value of assets should be disclosed. [Sch 4: 36] FRS 15's requirements are more extensive. The following information regarding depreciation should be disclosed annually in the financial statements for each class of tangible fixed assets:

Disclosure	Acceptable position
The depreciation methods used	Policy note
The useful economic lives or the depreciation rates used	Policy note
Total depreciation charged for the period	Operating profit/loss note and/or Fixed asset table
Where material, the financial effect of **a change** during the period in either the estimate of useful economic lives (made in accordance with FRS 15 para 93) or the estimate of residual values (made in accordance with FRS 15 para 95)	Fixed asset table
The cost or revalued amount at the beginning of the financial period and at the balance sheet date	Fixed asset table

	Fixed asset table
The cumulative amount of provisions for depreciation or impairment at the beginning of the financial period and at the balance sheet date	Fixed asset table
A reconciliation of the movements, separately disclosing additions, disposals, revaluations, transfers, depreciation, impairment losses, and reversals of past impairment losses written back in the financial period	Fixed asset table
The net carrying amount at the beginning of the financial period and at the balance sheet date	Fixed asset table
Where there has been a change in the depreciation method used, the effect, if material, should be disclosed in the period of change. The reason for the change should also be disclosed	Fixed asset table

Example 14.19: Tangible fixed asset note

	Freehold office buildings £'000	Freehold warehouse buildings £'000	Fixtures and fittings £'000	Total £'000
Cost at 1/4/1999	1,000	100	56	1,156
Additions		580	35	615
Interest capitalised		100		100
Revaluations	440			440
Disposals			(13)	(13)
Cost/valuation at 31/3/2000	1,440	780		2,298
Depreciation at 1/4/1999	80	0	28	108
Charge in year	31	10	8	49
Revaluations	(111)			(111)
Disposals			(10)	(10)
Depreciation at 31/3/2000	0	10	26	36
Net book value at 31/3/2000	1,440	770	52	2,262
Net book value at 31/3/2000	920	100	28	1,048

An interim valuation was performed in the year by Messrs Smith and Jones, qualified chartered surveyors who are independent to the company. The valuation was based on existing use value as at 31 March 2000 and includes £40,000 of directly attributable acquisition costs. The last full valuation was performed in 1998 by Simon Gregg, a qualified surveyor who was working for the company at that time, and reviewed by Knight and Co, quantity surveyors. The historical cost

> carrying amount would be £900,000. Included within freehold ware-house buildings cost carried forward are finance costs worth £116,000 which have been capitalised. £100,000 out of a total finance charge of £326,000, has been capitalised in the period which is based on a specific loan rate of 6.75% which has been used to finance the construction.

Provision for diminution in value

14.20 Any provisions for diminution in value of fixed assets which are required in addition to normal charges for depreciation, and any such provisions which have been written back because they are no longer required, should be disclosed separately either in the profit and loss account or in a note to the accounts. [Sch 4: 19(2) and (3)]

Gross amount of depreciable assets

14.21 FRS 15 requires disclosure of the gross amount and the related accumulated depreciation for each 'class' of tangible fixed asset (which would coincide with the entity's choice of classes of asset for revaluation purposes where a revaluation policy is adopted). The principal fixed asset which is not depreciated is land (unless it is a 'wasting asset', e.g. is being exploited for its mineral deposits) and this asset is often combined in the item of 'Land and buildings'. SSAP 12 used to require disclosure of a gross figure for 'depreciable assets', which could not be derived from the customary tabulation of fixed asset information unless the land element not subject to depreciation were separately disclosed. As FRS 15 has not repeated this requirement, it appears that it is no longer necessary to disclose the carrying amount for land separately. However, as readers of accounts are accustomed to having this information, it might be thought good practice to continue to disclose it.

Leased assets

14.22 There are special rules for accounting for leases which define the circumstances under which leased assets should be treated as fixed assets in the accounts. The appropriate treatment is determined by the nature of the lease rather than by the nature of the asset. The subject is dealt with in detail in chapter 29.

Determination of cost

Statutory requirements

14.23 Under the historical cost accounting rules of the Companies Act the amount to be included in respect of any fixed asset is its purchase price or production cost. [Sch 4: 17]

14.24 Purchase price is the actual price paid plus any expenses incidental to the acquisition. [Sch 4: 26(1)]

14.25 Production cost consists of the purchase price of the raw materials and consumables used plus the amount of the costs incurred which are directly attributable to the production of the asset. In addition, production cost may include a reasonable proportion of indirect costs of the production of the asset, but only to the extent that they relate to the period of production, and interest on capital borrowed to finance the production of the asset to the extent that it accrues in respect of the period of production. [Sch 4: 26]

14.26 FRS 15 has added detailed rules to interpret and expand on the Companies Act requirements. In essence, it interprets 'directly attributable to production' as limited to 'those costs to the entity that would have been avoided only if the tangible fixed asset had not been constructed or acquired'. The 'period of production' is interpreted as ceasing when 'substantially all the activities necessary to get the tangible fixed asset ready for use are complete', and ready for use means 'physical construction completed'. In respect of capitalising finance costs, a time of commencement is also specified; and certain costs, including finance costs, should be expensed and not capitalised during periods when construction activity is suspended.

Costs other than finance costs

14.27 A tangible fixed asset should initially be measured at its costs, but only those costs, that are directly attributable to bringing the asset into working condition for its intended use should be included in its measurement. [FRS 15(6)and (7)]

14.28 The wording of FRS 15(7) makes it clear that this is not just a question of establishing which types of cost **may** be capitalised. If a cost is directly attributable within the meaning of the Companies Act and FRS 15, then it **must** be capitalised and **must not** be expensed (unless there is evidence of immediate impairment of the asset, with a consequential instant write-off of part of cost to profit and loss account). FRS 15(8)–(11) then clarify and offer examples to explain what is intended by these statements in respect of costs other than finance costs.

Maximum amount which may be capitalised

14.29 FRS 15(32)–(33) establishes that the maximum that may be capitalised in respect of an asset is the recoverable amount of the asset as defined by FRS 11 *Impairment of fixed assets and goodwill*. A review for impairment on initial recognition should be undertaken where there is evidence that impairment has occurred. Guidance on possible circumstances is given in FRS 11(8)–(13) (see **14.246** below).

Non-finance costs included

14.30 Costs mentioned by FRS 15(8)–(10) as suitable for capitalisation are:

(a) purchase price less trade discounts and rebates;

(b) labour costs of own employees arising directly from construction or acquisition, e.g., site workers, in-house architects, surveyors;

(c) stamp duty, import duties, non-refundable purchase tax; site preparation and clearance costs; initial delivery and handling costs; installations costs; professional fees; and

(d) where under FRS 12 a provision needs to be recognised to dismantle the asset and/or restore the site at the end of its useful economic life, the estimated cost of so doing (discounted to present value in accordance with FRS 12).

The overriding consideration laid down by FRS 15 is that directly attributable (i.e., capitalisable) costs are those that are incremental and would have been avoided only if the asset in question had not been constructed or acquired.

14.31 **Consistency.** The illustrations in **14.30** above both impose restrictions on what may be capitalised and identify types of cost which **must** be capitalised. A 'prudent' approach to capitalisation, i.e., selectivity as to what to capitalise and when, is now precluded in principle. The temptation, in good years, to expense rather than capitalise, and so reduce future depreciation charges, has been removed. The implementation of FRS 15 imposes a need to review capitalisation policies and procedures in order to achieve consistency. If a cost is both directly related to the construction or installation of the asset and incremental (i.e., avoidable if the asset were not acquired), it must be capitalised as part of the cost of the asset.

14.32 **Site preparation costs.** Demolition costs are an illustration of applying the principle that capitalisable costs are limited to those that are incremental. Where existing structures must be demolished in order to build on a site, the cost of demolition may be incremental to the construction cost or it may be associated with the gain or loss on disposal of the existing asset – it depends on whether the existing structures have previously been in use in the entity's business or were acquired as a part of the site with the specific intention of demolishing them. In the latter case, the demolition costs are clearly incremental and should be capitalised; but, in the former case, they form a part of the gain or loss on disposal.

Non-finance costs excluded

14.33 Costs mentioned in FRS 15(9) and (11) as unsuitable for capitalisation and therefore to be expensed as incurred include:

(a) administration and general costs;

(b) site selection activities;

(c) abnormal costs – such as those relating to design errors; industrial disputes; idle capacity; wasted materials, labour or other resources; production delays; and

(d) operating losses as a result of the suspension of a revenue activity while the asset is constructed.

FRS 15 makes no specific mention of marketing or training costs. However, marketing costs are not necessary for bringing an asset into working condition for its intended use, so may **not** therefore be capitalised. Costs of training staff to use the asset, on the other hand, could be regarded exceptionally as necessary for that purpose where the asset is so specialised that staff cannot be hired ready-trained (although see **14.34** below following UITF's publication of Information Sheet 36). Even then, it is not permissible to capitalise training costs if they are incurred after the asset's construction is physically complete.

14.34

Training and similar costs. Where such costs may not be included in the carrying value of a tangible fixed asset, the possibility of recognising them as an asset, normally a prepayment, in their own right might be considered. However, in order to qualify, costs should meet the definition of an asset in FRS 5 *Substance of transactions.* This will require justification that the cost gives rise to future benefits which are **sufficiently certain to occur,** and **sufficiently large to cover the present costs.** Uncertainty of future benefits normally precludes training costs from qualifying as an asset, leading to treatment as an expense. Nevertheless, essential staff training prior to opening a new asset such as a hotel may sometimes qualify; in such cases, the useful life for amortisation will be comparatively short, one or at most two years. (The UITF, in Information Sheet 36, has issued a draft abstract, as this manual goes to press, which seeks to prevent carrying forward such costs – 'expenditure on training, advertising or promotion' – as prepayments, so this practice may have to cease – see Future Developments, **14.320** below.)

14.35 **Directors' remuneration.** The practice of capitalising some part of a director's remuneration where he has responsibility for overseeing construction is now unsafe. A director necessar-

> ily has responsibilities broader than a single management task, so a director's remuneration cannot arise incrementally in consequence of the construction of an asset.

14.36 **Internal relocations.** The cost of relocating machinery within a factory or to another location should not be capitalised, as it cannot add value in itself.

Start-up or commissioning period

14.37 The costs associated with a start-up or commissioning period should be included in the cost of the tangible fixed asset only where the asset is available for use but incapable of operating at normal levels without such a start-up or commissioning period. [FRS 15(14)–(16)] FRS 15 distinguishes between acceptable and non-acceptable circumstances:

(a) **Acceptable** – a commissioning period in which it is impossible to operate at normal levels because of the need to run machinery, test equipment or ensure the proper function of the equipment. This circumstance generally relates to the physical preparation for use. An example would be a printing press where it is necessary to run for a period in order to achieve optimum performance.

(b) **Not acceptable** – an initial operating period when the asset is capable of use, but demand has not yet built up. Examples could be a hotel or retail outlet in the post-opening period. Past practices of capitalised operating losses for the first few months following opening are no longer acceptable. (Consideration may be given to whether some costs may qualify for recognition as assets in their own right – see 'Training and similar costs', **14.34** above.)

Timing – when does capitalisation cease?

14.38 Capitalisation of directly attributable costs should cease when substantially all the activities that are necessary to get the tangible fixed asset ready for use are complete, even if the asset has not yet been brought into use. A tangible fixed asset is ready for use when its physical construction is complete. [FRS 15(12)–(13)]

14.39 **Cut-off date for capitalisation.** FRS 15 introduces a firm cut-off point to settle the issue of when capitalisation must cease. This will challenge existing practice, so all entities that self-construct or instal major tangible fixed assets will need to review their own practices. A decision should be documented as to what event or activity characterises the moment when an

> asset's physical construction is complete (i.e., when substan-
> tially all the activities to achieve completion are themselves
> complete), so that all costs incurred after that point are identi-
> fied and expensed. Where a commissioning period is involved,
> it will similarly be essential to determine in principle the point
> which characterises reaching the capability of operating at nor-
> mal levels, and then to ensure that costs incurred after reaching
> that point are captured and expensed.

14.40   The starting point for determining when 'substantially all' activities
are complete will normally be materiality – when there are no further activities to be completed which could make a material difference to cost, then that would normally be the right moment to cease
capitalising. Deliberate delay in achieving final physical completion
would cause costs occurring during the period of delay to fall into
the category of abnormal cost; or, if the time-related element was a
finance cost, it would be excluded by the requirement that capitalisation should cease when active development is suspended (see **14.49**
and **14.50** below).

14.41   **Regulatory consents.** Regulatory consents, e.g., health and
> safety clearance, are sometimes essential before an asset may be
> used legally. However, cost capitalisation may not necessarily
> continue until such consents are in place. Management will
> normally seek to ensure that such consents are in place very
> close to the time-frame for physical completion and testing,
> and that they do not slow down the start of operations.
> Avoidable delays in obtaining consents which prevent the start
> of operations should be seen as abnormal and similar in effect
> to an industrial dispute, creating an hiatus during which capi-
> talisation should cease. There should be no room for manipu-
> lation of the process of obtaining consents in order to extend
> the capitalisation period.

Finance costs

Companies Act and interest capitalisation

14.42   There may be included in the production cost of an asset interest on
capital borrowed to finance the production of that asset, to the extent
that it accrues in respect of the period of production. [Sch 4: 26(3)]

The nature of finance costs

14.43   FRS 15(2) has interpreted interest to include all finance costs as
defined in FRS 4: 'The difference between the net proceeds of an
instrument and the total amount of the payments (or other transfers
of economic benefits) that the issuer may be required to make in

respect of the instrument'. In other words, capitalisation is not limited to interest payments alone, but encompasses all the costs associated with the relevant borrowings such as the amortisation of a redemption premium.

Policy and consistency

14.44 Where an entity adopts a policy of capitalising finance costs, finance costs that are directly attributable to the construction of tangible fixed assets should be capitalised as part of the cost of those assets [FRS 15(19)–(20)]. This is one of the standard's more significant constraints upon previous practice. Prior to FRS 15, companies could vary their interest capitalisation policy according to circumstance, the nature of the asset under construction and their concern in a given year for the level of reported profit. FRS 15 now requires each entity to choose its policy, either to capitalise finance costs whenever they represent a material element of the cost of any tangible fixed asset, or to eschew such capitalisation altogether. FRS 15 does not proclaim a bias either way, but does require that the choice be made and applied consistently.

Directly attributable

14.45 'Directly attributable to the construction' means only those costs that would have been avoided if there had been no expenditure on the asset. [FRS 15(21)] If funds spent on the asset either arose by borrowing more money or used existing cash which could otherwise have been used to repay existing borrowing, then those funds are 'directly attributable'. Such funds may have been borrowed specifically for the purpose of funding the construction of the asset in question, but FRS 15 does not limit capitalisation to specific funding. Funding may equally come from the general pool of borrowing. If it does, the rate of finance cost to be applied to the construction of a specific asset will be the weighted average rate applicable to the general borrowings outstanding over the period applied to the weighted average carrying amount of the asset over the period. General borrowings will exclude costs associated with borrowings specific to other purposes, i.e., lease costs or loans used to hedge foreign investments. [FRS 15(23)] FRS 15 recognises that judgement will be necessary in making a selection of which borrowings to include in determining the weighted average, but offers guidance that the objective is to arrive at 'a reasonable measure of the finance costs that are directly attributable to the construction of the asset'. The total amount of finance costs capitalised during a period should not exceed the total amount of finance costs incurred during that period. For an example of a calculation, see example **14.54** below.

Intra-group borrowing

14.46 The limitation to total finance costs actually incurred will be significant in the context of consolidated accounts. Where subsidiaries draw their funding for asset construction from within the group, the amount of finance costs correctly capitalised at subsidiary level may exceed in total the finance costs incurred by the group as a whole. This will lead to consolidation adjustments to reduce the carrying amount of such assets at group level. Also, where intra-group interest rates and other finance charges vary significantly from the group's weighted average, consolidation adjustments will again be called for to bring non-specific borrowings into line with the group's rate.

When does capitalisation of finance costs commence?

14.47 Where finance costs are capitalised, capitalisation should begin when:
[FRS 15(25)]

(a) finance costs are being incurred; and

(b) expenditures for the asset are being incurred; and

(c) activities that are necessary to get the asset ready for use are in progress.

All three of these conditions have to be met before capitalisation may commence, so it will be necessary to establish a system to keep track of timing. When specific funding costs are to be capitalised, it will be necessary to establish for each project when (a) and (b) above commenced so that the later of the two is the date when both are operative; and then it must be apparent that, at that date, (c) applied, i.e., that date did not coincide with some temporary hiatus or hold-up such as an industrial dispute. When the rate to be capitalised is to be drawn from the weighted average of general funding, capitalisation should commence as soon as expenditures are being incurred, provided again that does not coincide with some hold-up in activity.

14.48 For this reason, it is not possible to capitalise finance costs to fund holding development land until such time as development activity commences (and is sustained – see **14.49** to **14.50** below). [FRS 15 (26)]

When is capitalisation of finance costs suspended?

14.49 Capitalisation of finance costs should be suspended during extended periods in which active development is interrupted. [FRS 15(27)]

14.50
> No guidance is offered on the meaning of 'extended periods'. Presumably the intention is to avoid the inclusion in cost of any material element of what FRS 15 refers to as 'costs of holding partially completed assets'. [FRS 15(28)] Materiality is therefore the principal determinant of whether it is necessary to class any hiatus (or the aggregation of the effects of more than one hiatus) as lasting for an extended period and therefore suspending capitalisation.

When does capitalisation of finance costs cease?

14.51 Capitalisation of finance costs should cease when substantially all the activities that are necessary to get the tangible fixed asset ready for use are complete. [FRS 15(29)] FRS 15 uses the same wording in para 29 as in para 12 in respect of the end of capitalising costs generally, but in para 13 it makes clear that an asset is ready for use when it is physically complete. Capitalisation of finance costs ends, therefore, when the asset is effectively physically complete.

14.52 When construction of a tangible fixed asset is completed in parts and each part is capable of being used while construction continues on other parts, capitalisation of finance costs relating to a part should cease when substantially all the activities that are necessary to get that part ready for use are completed. [FRS 15(29)]

14.53 If all of a group of assets are necessary in order to enable them to be used together to earn their keep, e.g., a process industry where materials pass through several stages before emerging in saleable form, construction is not complete until all elements are in place. However, parts of a set of assets may be capable of independent use. FRS 15 (30) instances a business park, where each building may be let out or put to use separately. In that event, each independent part is to be judged as if it were a separate asset, and capitalisation of finance costs relating to that part ceases when it is physically complete on its own.

Weighted average finance costs

14.54 Where an entity finances an asset from general borrowings, the amount of capitalised finance cost is found by applying a weighted average finance cost to the weighted average carrying amount of the asset. [FRS 15(23)–(24)] Example **14.54** illustrates such a calculation.

> ### Example 14.54: Weighted average capitalisation rate
>
> A company with a 31 December 2001 year end has been constructing a new office building since August 1999. It is using existing borrowings to finance the construction which is expected to be ready to use

in April 2002 and has a policy of capitalising finance costs by calculating a capitalisation rate in accordance with FRS 15.

Costs incurred to date are as follows:

Costs brought forward at 1/1/2001	£1,000,000
Additions:	
March 2001	£150,000
June 2001	£100,000
September 2001	£250,000
December 2001	£150,000
Cost c/f at 31 December 2001 (excluding finance costs for 2001)	£1,650,000

The weighted average carrying amount of the asset is calculated as follows:

Cost b/f	£1,000,000
Additions:	
March £150k × 9/12 months	£112,500
June £100k × 6/12 months	£50,000
Sept. £250k × 3/12 months	£62,500
Dec. £150k × 0/12 months	–
∴ Weighted average carrying value of the asset	£1,225,000

Existing borrowings which are not used for any specific purpose are as follows:

£800,000	@	6.5%
£600,000	@	7.5%
£725,000	@	6.75%
£150,000	@	8%
Total amount of loans £2,275,000		

Calculation of the capitalisation rate:

{800/2275 × 6.5%} + {600/2275 × 7.5%} + {725/2275 × 6.75%} + {150/2275 × 8%}

= 6.94%

The amount of finance costs which can be capitalised in the year ended 31 December 2000 is:

£1,225,000 × 6.94% = £85,015

Investment properties: capitalisation or expense of development costs

The scope of FRS 15

14.55 The requirements of FRS 15 apply to all tangible fixed assets, with the exception of investment properties as defined in SSAP 19 *Accounting* *for investment properties.* [FRS 15(4)] SSAP 19 defines investment properties as 'an interest in land and/or buildings in respect of which construction work and development **have been completed'**. [SSAP 19: 7]. Therefore, when a property company or group builds its own investment properties, the capitalisation rules of FRS 15 apply to those buildings because, at that point, **they have not yet become investment properties as defined by SSAP 19.**

The constraints on initial measurement

14.56   Practices that have been prevalent up to now and that are now challenged by FRS 15 include capitalising:

(a)   the costs of inducements offered to those 'big-name' prospective tenants whose presence in development schemes will attract other tenants to take their place in the development (discussed in **14.60** to **14.64** below);

(b)   marketing costs directed specifically at attracting tenants (discussed in **14.67** below);

(c)   marketing costs directed at publicising the development in order to attract customers for prospective tenants, thereby creating a more attractive commercial environment for those tenants (discussed in **14.66** below); and

(d)   finance costs incurred during the period between physical completion and letting most of the property (discussed in **14.58** and **14.68** to **14.70** below).

Categories (a), (b) and (c) are not costs that have to be incurred in order to bring the asset into working condition, and they may well be incurred, wholly or partly, after physical completion has been achieved. They also represent three different degrees of closeness of association with the value of the asset: (a) will enhance the asset directly, as the cost is only incurred if the objective is achieved; (b) is less certain of achieving that effect; and (c) is more remote still and unpredictable in its impact.

14.57   Where costs are incurred after physical completion, it could be argued that they are not affected by FRS 15 because, after completion, the properties qualify as investment properties under SSAP 19. Such an argument would be unsafe, as it could result in costs incurred before completion point being rejected as unsuitable for capitalisation whilst costs that are identical in nature would be capitalisable because incurred later, after completion. The Review Panel could regard such a conclusion as absurd.

14.58   Category (d) in **14.56** above is different in kind. FRS 15 specifically precludes capitalising finance costs for periods after physical completion. It even uses the separate buildings in a business park as an illustration of assets 'of which parts are usable while construction continues on other parts', and on which, therefore, capitalisation of finance costs on the usable parts should cease. [FRS 15(30)] The use of this illustration suggests that the ASB fully intends that initial capitalisation of investment properties should be accounted for within FRS 15's rules.

Suggested solutions for investment properties – the accounting choices

14.59 These are the possible approaches in principle. They are discussed below to identify which may be appropriate to particular costs:

(a) capitalise these costs as a part of the asset, but as 'subsequent expenditure' rather than 'initial cost';

(b) carry forward these costs as a prepayment/deferred expenditure and expense them over the period thought to benefit from them; or

(c) class them initially as a prepayment but, at the year end, assimilate them into the valuation of the investment property so that the costs are effectively transferred to Revaluation Reserve.

Inducements to tenants – the accounting choice

14.60 It is useful to start with inducements to prospective tenants because there is a stronger case for regarding these costs as enhancing the investment than any of the others. SSAP 19 ensures that the accounting for investment properties differs from that for all other tangible fixed assets in two crucial respects – they are not depreciated, and they must be revalued in the balance sheet annually, at open market value (OMV). Under FRS 15, when other properties held in continuing use are revalued, that must be at existing use value (EUV). This conforms with the guidance issued to valuers by the Royal Institution of Chartered Surveyors (RICS), and the ASB has incorporated into FRS 15 the RICS definitions of OMV and EUV. The difference between these two bases is enlightening.

14.61 The two definitions are identical except that an EUV has two additional conditions, of which only one is relevant in this context. This condition is that the property is valued on the basis that 'vacant possession is provided on completion of the sale of all parts of the property occupied by the business'. It follows, therefore, that an EUV value cannot take account of any risks or benefits associated with the existence of a sitting tenant. An OMV on the other hand must take account of the existence of a sitting tenant. If the existing tenancy confers additional value, the OMV basis will assess and include that additional value.

14.62 | **Recommended treatment.** Against this background, the effect of each of the options in **14.59** above can be compared.

(a) The words of FRS 15 could be used to justify capitalising the inducement not as part of initial cost but as subsequent expenditure on the asset. FRS 15 requires capitalisation of expenditure that 'provides an enhancement of the economic benefits … in excess of the previously assessed standard of performance'. It is likely that third party evidence could be obtained to demonstrate that the inducement has enhanced the asset, by obtaining a valuer's confirmation that the asset's OMV exceeds its EUV (see above) by more than the amount of the inducement. Although this argument is persuasive, it remains possible that the Review Panel could view this as a stratagem to bypass the FRS 15 rules relating to initial cost.

(b) The inducement could be carried as a prepayment. It will probably qualify as an asset within the meaning of the term, as laid down in FRS 5, and (another good test, though only by analogy) it would probably meet the tests of a capitalisable development cost in SSAP 13. The essential components of both tests are that there are future benefits resulting from the expenditure which are both sufficiently large to cover the present costs, and sufficiently certain to arise. Clearly the value of the inducement payment will last at least for the period to the next tenancy review, and arguably for the full life of the tenancy. However, it challenges conventional practice to carry a prepayment for several years and/or to amortise it over that period. It also risks double-counting because the year end revaluation will necessarily reflect the benefit of the inducement payment and would need to be deliberately reduced by that amount if the prepayment were retained. And finally, as this manual goes to press, the UITF has issued a draft abstract which seeks to preclude carrying forward certain types of cost as a prepayment – see Future Developments, see **14.320** below. For these reasons, it may be preferable to seek a solution with a lower profile.

(c) The preferred solution is to set up the inducement as a prepayment in principle but to then absorb it in the revaluation process so that it will not appear in the balance sheet or need to be expensed over a more or less arbitrary period. The investment property is revalued as required at the year end, and the gain credited to the Revaluation Reserve via the STRGL. However, recognising that a part of that uplift relates to the pre-payment as well as to the carrying cost of the asset, debit the prepayment to the STRGL, so that only the net uplift (OMV less both cost of asset and cost of inducement) is credited to Revaluation Reserve.

14.63 This third option in **14.62** above does not risk offending against FRS 15 because it has no bearing on the carrying cost of the asset. It does not introduce the concept of amortisation, alien in the context of current assets, into the treatment of a prepayment. It is transparent, passing matching items together through the STRGL with full explanation.

14.64 **Expensing inducements**. The one alternative not recom-mended is expensing the inducement cost to the profit and loss account, as that appears not to be a valid option. When, in a single reporting period, a cost is automatically directed to the profit and loss account whilst its benefit is equally automati-cally accounted for and reflected, via the STRGL, in a revalua-tion reserve, proper matching has been compromised. It consequently appears not to be the right answer. (It is not yet clear whether the UITF's proposed abstract on start-up costs – see **14.320** below – seeks to capture and expense this type of cost too. It is hoped that, for the reasons explained above, the final abstract will not require a mismatch between the treat-ments of related gains and losses.)

Marketing costs – the accounting choice

14.65 In categories (b) and (c) in **14.56** above, we looked at two different kinds of marketing costs, those directly associated with attracting tenants for properties and those only indirectly so associated because they are targeted at raising the awareness of the tenants' own prospective customers.

14.66 **Recommended treatment**. It is hard to see any case at all for carrying forward in any way costs of indirect marketing, cate-gory (c) in **14.56** above. While it is likely that, taken in the round, such costs will be well spent and will produce the desired beneficial effect, they will not in themselves carry a guarantee of the 'reasonable certainty' of value required to jus-tify carrying forward any costs as an asset in the balance sheet.

14.67 The case is less clear cut when one comes to look at marketing directly to prospective tenants in order to let the properties. Inducement payments (see **14.60** above) are merely the most direct and precisely targeted of such marketing costs. The one important distinction is that inducement costs are only incurred when they are certain in their effect, because they are only paid when they result in a contract. Most marketing costs are spent in hope, not in certainty, and fall into the same category as the indirect costs discussed above. They are 'soft' costs, the benefits of which are not susceptible to any certainty of measurement. These are the kind of costs that FRS 15 actively seeks to exclude from the balance sheet, and FRS 15's advent increases the risks associated with seeking to continue to carry them. Conclusion: they should be expensed. The UITF's just issued draft abstract (Information Sheet 36, 23 March 2000 – see **14.320** below) has the clear intention of seeking to enforce this conclusion.

Finance costs post completion – the accounting choice

14.68   Because physical completion marks the point at which a development becomes an investment property under SSAP 19, finance costs incurred after physical completion fall outside FRS 15. This is of potential practical importance because it has been the practice of some companies to continue to capitalise finance costs until a property development was about 75% let. However, there is a danger inherent in ignoring FRS 15 because:

(a)   there is no standard specifically addressing capitalisation of interest in respect of investment properties; and

(b)   the only authoritative guidance extant on interest capitalisation generally is that in FRS 15.

It is well established that, when searching for generally accepted accounting practice in the absence of specific guidance, it is wise to look for extant guidance by analogy, i.e., in the closest broadly comparable situation. For that reason, it would be wise to recognise that the Review Panel may well choose to challenge practices relating to investment properties which appear contradictory to what it may take as general principles of GAAP laid down in FRS 15.

14.69   **Recommended treatment.** The difficulties here are twofold. The first is that it is impracticable to regard finance costs as in any sense enhancing an asset. The second is that, because FRS 15 chooses to continue to allow a choice of whether to have a policy of capitalising finance costs, and because the OMV of an asset at the end of the year will be the same whether or not finance costs have been capitalised, the argument that expensing finance costs results in failing to match them with the amount inherent in the valuation holds no water. The same would be true in all those situations where companies have chosen **not** to capitalise any finance costs, before or after completion – and they are entitled to make that choice.

14.70   For these reasons, FRS 15 would appear effectively to oblige owners of investment properties, whatever their policy on capitalising finance costs relating to the period of construction, to expense finance costs relating to the post-completion period.

Special considerations affecting certain categories of tangible fixed assets

Tools

14.71   Tools may be divided into two classes: machine tools and hand tools. Machine tools are relatively expensive and will normally need to be capitalised. They are generally a component part of a larger machine but, because they usually wear out more rapidly than the machine itself and have to be replaced more frequently, they need to be recorded and depreciated separately from the machine. [FRS 15(83)] Hand tools are normally recorded in a separate account and depreciated over quite a short life, unless they are immaterial or short-lived, in which case they should be written off in the year of purchase. The two principal methods of accounting for hand tools (without keeping a register) are to hold them at cost less depreciation and to value them at a fixed amount (see **14.178** below). Both methods will need to be supplemented by periodic stocktakes.

Furniture and fixtures and equipment

14.72   This group of assets should include the cost of moderately long-lifed property, such as showcases and counters, shelving, display fixtures, safes, office equipment and furniture. Although some entities have not separated these from the property asset that houses them and may therefore have been depreciating them over that asset's longer life, FRS 15 now requires components of a larger asset that have materially different useful economic lives from that asset to be depreciated separately over those different lives (see **14.205** below).

14.73   The cost of computer equipment may include software costs. Indeed, FRS 10 paragraph 2, in its definition of intangible assets, actively encourages this treatment where software development costs are directly attributable to bringing a computer system or computer-operated machinery into working condition for its intended use. However, because of the likelihood of rapid operating and technological changes, these costs are often expensed as incurred. If capitalised, they are normally

> written off over a relatively short period of time, because the likelihood of most software still being in effective operation after four or five years is low because of the pace of technological change; FRS 15's 'component accounting' approach encourages this treatment (see **14.210** below).

Payments on account and assets in course of construction

14.74   This heading should include deposits against delivery of fixed assets and payments made to contractors for work completed to date. Although all formats include a separate heading of 'Payments on account and assets in course of construction', the amounts involved are often insufficiently material to justify separate disclosure. Where they are not material, they should be included in the heading appropriate to the asset being acquired.

Subsequent expenditure

Expensing subsequent expenditure

14.75   Subsequent expenditure to ensure that the tangible fixed asset maintains its previously assessed standard of performance should be recognised in the profit and loss account as it is incurred. [FRS 15(34)]

14.76   When an asset is first acquired, it is assessed to determine its probable useful economic life and its residual value at the end of that life, in order to establish an appropriate process of charging depreciation (see **14.179** et seq. below). In order to make that assessment of life and residual value, it is necessary to take into account the standard of maintenance appropriate to keep the asset operating effectively. All expenditure made with that end in view, i.e., to keep the asset running without enhancing its performance beyond its original capacities, should be expensed as occurred.

Materiality of replaced components

14.77   In principle, any complex asset could be disaggregated into all of its components – sections, girders, nuts, bolts, coats of paint – that last for more than one year, and then each component could be depreciated over its life to replacement (and each replacement then capitalised). FRS 15 requires this approach with **major** components (see **14.205** below). However, applying such an approach to minor components would not add value, because the simpler method of setting a life for the entire asset that anticipates regular maintenance, and expenses the maintenance when it is incurred, will give materially the same annual charge to the profit and loss account in total.

Capitalising subsequent expenditure

14.78   Subsequent expenditure should be capitalised in three circumstances.

Circumstance	Examples
(a) Where the subsequent expenditure provides an enhancement of the economic benefits of the tangible fixed asset in excess of the previously assessed standard of performance, for example, by modifying an asset to increase its life or capacity, or upgrading to achieve improved quality or reduced costs [FRS 15(36a), (37)];	(i) adding a conference suite to a hotel; (ii) adding a floor or a wing to an office building;
(b) Where a component of the tangible fixed asset, that has been treated separately for depreciation purposes and depreciated over its individual useful economic life, is replaced or restored [FRS 15 (36b), (38)];	(i) replacing the engines of an aircraft in an existing airframe; (ii) relining a brick furnace; (iii) re-equipping the kitchen of a restaurant; (iv) replacing a lift;
(c) Where the subsequent expenditure relates to a major inspection or overhaul of a tangible fixed asset that restores the economic benefits of the asset that have been consumed by the entity and have already been reflected in depreciation [FRS 15(36c), (39)].	(i) putting a ship into its periodic dry-dock overhaul to enable it to retain its certificate of seaworthiness; (ii) putting an aircraft through its periodic testing for airworthiness. Only inspections or overhauls with a material cost will feature in this category.

14.79   Essentially, expenditure should be capitalised if it enhances an asset by giving it some capacity that it did not have in the first place (**14.78**(a) above) or if it replaces or restores capacity which has been consumed and already charged in the profit and loss account (**14.78** (b) and (c)). Both (a) and (b) may be present where an entity is replacing one life-expired element of machinery in a production line with a faster, more efficient or less wasteful element such that the line becomes more productive.

14.80   FRS 15(40) provides further guidance on whether to identify elements for depreciation over a shorter useful life than that of the 'parent' fixed asset (see also **14.205** below). Examples given are:

(a) components with substantially different lives to the remainder of the asset;

(b) the degree of irregularity in the level of expenditure; and

(c) materiality in the context of the financial statements.

Where separate components are not capitalised, then their replacement is dealt with as a profit and loss account item.

Gifts, donated assets and exchanged assets

Replacement using insurance proceeds

14.81   Where an asset (or a component) is **replaced**, its carrying amount is removed from the balance sheet (by eliminating its cost or revalued amount and related accumulated depreciation) and the resulting gain or loss on disposal is recorded. If material, as required by FRS 3 paragraph 20, it should be disclosed as a 'below the line' exceptional item. This includes replacement of a fixed asset out of insurance proceeds when a tangible fixed asset has been lost or destroyed. In such cases, the loss is treated as a disposal, and the lost/destroyed asset is removed from the balance sheet. The resulting gain or loss on disposal (being the difference between the carrying amount and the insurance proceeds) is recognised. The replacement asset is recorded at its cost.

Exchange of similar and dissimilar assets

14.82   FRS 15 does not explain what is expected when an asset is **exchanged** for another asset. Various practices exist, from maintaining the old asset's carrying amount (with a debit going through the profit and loss account if the new asset's recoverable amount is lower, or a credit to revaluation reserve if higher), to recognising gains or losses based on fair values on exchange.

14.83
The following general guidelines are suggested:

(a) An exchanged asset should continue to be recorded at the predecessor's cost only where the new asset is substantially the same asset. For example, an entity holds all the shares in a company that owns a single property. If the company were liquidated so that the entity held the property directly, this would represent substantially the same asset. Consequently, the property should be recorded at the same carrying value previously attributed to the shares in the company.

(b) Where an exchanged asset is not substantially the same as its predecessor, the exchange should be treated as a disposal followed by an acquisition at fair value. Where the

> profit arising does not amount to a realised profit available for distribution, it may be transferred to a non-distributable reserve. Such a reserve is similar in nature to a revaluation since it arises from an increase in the carrying value of an asset. It becomes realised through depreciation or disposal of the new asset.

Gifts and donated assets

14.84 FRS 15 requires charities to record tangible fixed assets received as gifts and donations at their current value. This is consistent with the requirement of the Charities' SORP.

14.85

> FRS 15 does not address the initial recognition of donated assets by entities other than charities, for example, the vesting of former public assets in a privatised entity. It is reasonable that the same principle of recognising current value would apply (rather than a literal reading of the Companies Act, concluding that the purchase cost was zero, because this will not usually portray the substance of the transaction). It is not yet clear whether any gain arising would be realised or unrealised. (The ASB withdrew its proposal, included in FRED 17, the predecessor exposure draft to FRS 15, requiring fair valuation of all donated assets, apparently as a result of this uncertainty.) If necessary, legal advice should be sought.

Alternative bases of valuation

Overview

14.86 Prior to FRS 15, authoritative guidance on the accounting treatment of revalued fixed assets (other than investment properties) came only from the Companies Act 1985, in the form of 'the alternative accounting rules'. [Sch 4, paras 19–34 CA 1985] Under these rules, a company could revalue tangible fixed assets selectively. There were no rules as to how often or by whom the revaluations might be made, and the only guidance on bases was that assets should be revalued either at market value or at current cost.

14.87 Where assets are revalued, the Companies Act, FRS 3 and FRS 15 require additional disclosure of some equivalent historical cost figures, as if no revaluation had taken place.

14.88 FRS 15 seeks to achieve a greater level of consistency than previously. It addresses the following issues:

(a)   which assets should be revalued (see **14.92** to **14.103** below);

(b) when and how frequently revaluations should be performed (see **14.104** to **14.134** below);

(c) who should perform the revaluations (see **14.135** to **14.141** below); and

(d) on what basis the revaluations should be performed (see **14.142** to **14.178** below).

14.89 In the interests of greater consistency, the ASB has adopted the Royal Institution of Chartered Surveyors' (RICS) definitions of different types of bases of valuations. Some of these definitions have been included in this chapter.

14.90 FRS 15 allows companies the choice of adopting a revaluation policy. When such a policy is adopted, the company should carry all revalued assets at their **current** value at the balance sheet date. It should apply its revaluation policy to individual classes of asset by revaluing **every asset** in that class. This valuation should be performed by a qualified valuer, on an approved basis. Additional disclosure is needed for every class of revalued assets.

14.91 In summary, if an entity chooses to revalue, then it must:

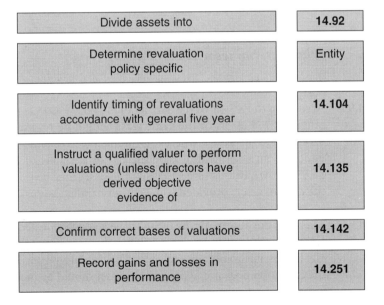

Which assets should be revalued?

14.92 FRS 15(42) allows tangible fixed assets to be revalued only where an entity adopts a policy of revaluation. Where such a policy has been adopted, it should be applied to **all assets in the same class**. This is intended to prevent the distortions caused by selective use of revaluation, known colloquially as 'cherry picking', so as to take credit for gains without acknowledging falls in the value of similar assets.

> ### Example 14.92: Classes of fixed assets
>
> A company has the following fixed assets:
>
> > Land and buildings:
> > Freehold
> > Offices
> > Factories
> > Leasehold
> > Plant and machinery
> > Motor vehicles
>
> Under FRS 15, it can choose to adopt a revaluation policy on any identifiable 'class' of fixed asset but does not need to revalue every asset it owns. Therefore, as long as, say, the 'Freehold factories' are deemed to be one 'class', the company can choose to adopt a revaluation policy over those assets only, and keep the remainder at historical cost. Alternatively, 'Freehold factories' could be split into two or more classes, providing that each class meets the requirements of the standard, by for example separating the factories manufacturing cement from those manufacturing electronic components (see **14.99** below). The company could then validly choose to revalue only one of the classes within 'Freehold factories'.

What determines a 'class' of asset?

General rule and exception

14.93 According to FRS 15(61), where a tangible fixed asset is revalued, **all** tangible fixed assets **of the same class** should be revalued. The one exception to this rule is where it is impossible to obtain a reliable valuation of an asset held outside the UK or Republic of Ireland (see **14.95** below). In this rare situation, this asset may be excluded from the class of assets provided some additional disclosures are made.

14.94 This does not automatically mean that every asset located outside the UK or Republic of Ireland will fall into this exemption. It will generally be possible to obtain a reliable valuation of overseas assets. If so, the exception does not apply and the asset should be included in the class and revalued as normal. It is only in situations where any valuation that would be obtained is not a reliable estimate of value that the asset can be excluded.

14.95 **Interpretation of 'a reliable valuation'.** FRS 15 does not explain what is meant by 'a reliable valuation' (see **14.93** above). A reasonable interpretation is that a valuation of assets which are located outside the UK or Republic of Ireland is not reliable if:

> (a) the valuation cannot be performed by a qualified valuer; or
>
> (b) regular valuations cannot be performed; or
>
> (c) other factors exist that seriously limit the reliability of any valuation obtained.

Definition of class

14.96 The only guidance in FRS 15 as to what constitutes a 'class' is given in the definition section at the beginning of the standard. [FRS 15 (2)] A class of tangible fixed assets is defined as: 'A category of tangible fixed assets having a similar nature, function or use in the business of the entity.'

Interpretation of 'definition of class'

14.97 The classes mentioned by FRS 15(62) are those shown in the formats in Sch 4 CA 1985. These are:

(a) land and buildings;

(b) plant and machinery; and

(c) fixtures, fittings, tools and equipment.

These are very broad, and it is unlikely that companies will limit themselves to these classifications. Regard should be had to the specific assets that companies have and distinctions should be made between them.

14.98 Entities may wish to adopt narrower classes, as permitted by FRS 15, as long as the classes adopted are 'within reason'. It gives an example of splitting 'land and buildings' into specialised properties, non-specialised properties and short leaseholds. It would then be possible to adopt a policy to revalue any individual class or a combination of classes.

Similar nature, function or use

14.99 **Interpretation of 'similar nature, function or use'.** The definition of 'class', given in **14.96** above includes the phrase 'similar nature, function or use'. There are two ways to interpret this phrase:

(a) it could mean that **any** asset that has **any** similarities at all, in its nature, function or use, to any other asset held by the company should be classified with that asset;

(b) it could also be interpreted to mean that assets should be classified according to their '**main**' nature, function or use.

Example 14.99.1

Illustration of interpretation (a) – assets with similarities

A company has four buildings which are used and located as follows:

Head office	Glasgow
Additional office building	Edinburgh
Warehouse	Stirling
Warehouse and administration	Ayr

It seems clear that the offices in Glasgow and Edinburgh have similar nature, function and use, and that the warehouses in Stirling and Ayr are in a similar position. However, the building in Ayr has an administrative function in it, which is similar to the administrative function in both the Glasgow and Edinburgh offices. Therefore, there could be a case for including the building in Ayr with the head offices on the grounds that it comes within the FRS 15 definition of 'tangible fixed assets having a similar **function** in the business of the entity'.

If Ayr were to be included, then because Stirling has a similar function to Ayr (albeit a completely different function to Glasgow and Edinburgh), it could be argued that it too should be included in the class.

This suggests that on this criteria all four buildings would be classed together.

Example 14.99.2

Illustration of interpretation (b) – main function

A company has two buildings as follows.

Office in Aberdeen which focuses on selling the company's products. Salesmen and marketeers are based here. The office contains primarily furniture and equipment needed to carry out telephone sales.

Office in Inverness which deals with the accounting function. Paperwork is passed from Aberdeen to Inverness to record the sales, account for the stock, etc. All the accounts staff and administrators are based here. The office is nearly identical to the Aberdeen office in terms of furnishings.

Under FRS 15, these buildings have a different **use**, and so could be regarded as having distinct asset classifications. The Aberdeen office's function is to sell, whereas the Inverness office's function is to account for all transactions.

Neither of the above appears to be a sufficiently robust interpretation of FRS 15. From a sensible perspective, it is clear that:

(a) from the first example, the warehouse at Stirling has no similarities with the head office in Glasgow and therefore does not necessarily belong in the same class;

(b) from the second example, the buildings are both general offices used to carry on the business of the company and therefore should be included in the same class.

So where should the line be drawn? The starting point will always be the recognition that the safest and most robust approach is normally the simplest, which is to treat all land and buildings as a single class. However, if it is seen as necessary to make more precise distinctions in order to narrow the scope of the revaluation policy, then those distinctions should be easily understood and not obviously open to challenge. One key feature is that the classification should be capable of consistent application from year to year.

Dual-purpose assets

14.100 Particular problems arise with dual-purpose assets. For example, taking illustration **14.99.1** above, the building in Ayr which has a dual purpose should be looked at closely and the following established:

(a) whether the building can be easily split between the two functions (i.e., the majority of the building is for storage with a separate extension for administration);

(b) what the principal purpose for the building is (i.e., is the administration just a 'tag-on' after using the building for storage?);

(c) how is the building viewed by the management (i.e., as a place for storage or as an administrative site?);

(d) what type of administration is performed there? Is it merely recording when the stock stored in the warehouse was received/despatched (i.e., the administration is directly tied in to the use of the building as a warehouse), or is the function similar to the administrative functions performed by the other offices in Glasgow and Edinburgh?

14.101 In the majority of cases, the decision as to which class the dual-purpose asset belongs to should be made by following the above approach. There may be some cases where it is not possible to decide which class is the more appropriate and it is not possible to split the valuation between both purposes. In these situations, the options are:

> (a)   to make a decision as to which class is more appropriate and apply the classification consistently year on year; or
>
> (b)   to include, in a single revaluation class, both the dual-purpose asset and other assets serving each of the two purposes.

14.102 The ASB has made it clear that FRS 15 is designed to eliminate the 'cherry picking' of selective revaluations as a way of manipulating the balance sheet. Consequently, the Review Panel will be expected to look at companies' revaluation policies quite carefully, and may well be prepared to challenge any which seem unusually selective or where the distinctions drawn in describing a revalued class of asset seem tenuous. Companies will be wise to bear this in mind when formulating their revaluation strategies.

Disclosure of classes

14.103 As detailed in paragraph **14.9** above, each class which has been revalued must be disclosed separately in the notes to the accounts. This should be borne in mind when distinguishing classes, as multiple different classes could lead to voluminous disclosures.

Frequency of valuations

Overview

14.104 FRS 15(43) requires that, once a revaluation policy has been adopted, the assets should be carried at their 'current value as at the balance sheet date'. An entity can perform a full valuation every year if it wishes, but FRS 15 does give guidance on how the 'current value as at the balance sheet date' can be achieved without performing such a rigorous (and costly) exercise. This guidance is described in **14.105** below as the 'general five-year cycle'. It is recommended that entities, as a minimum, follow these guidelines.

General five-year cycle

14.105 FRS 15(45) states that the requirement to 'carry at current value' will be met, subject to the exceptions detailed in **14.114** to **14.119** below, by:

(a)   having a qualified valuer perform a full, detailed valuation at least once every five years;

(b)   having a qualified valuer carry out an interim valuation in year 3; and

(c)   performing a review in years 1, 2 and 4. If this review indicates that it is likely that there has been a material change in value, an interim valuation must then be performed by a qualified valuer.

Details of who can become a qualified valuer within the meaning of FRS 15 are given in **14.136** below.

Example 14.105: General five-year cycle

A company has a 31 March 2000 year end and is choosing to revalue its office buildings. It has not revalued in the past. The company's revaluation diary will depend on whether the review in years 1, 2 and 4 indicate any 'material changes in value'.

For simplicity, assume that the reviews in years 1, 2 and 4 indicate no 'material changes in value'. The work to be done is as follows:

Year ending	Work to be done
31/3/2000	Full valuation – adjust carrying value as necessary
31/3/2001 (year 1)	Perform a review. No 'material change in value' detected (after allowing for depreciation where charged)
31/3/2002 (year 2)	Perform a review. No 'material change in value' detected
31/3/2003 (year 3)	Interim valuation – adjust carrying value as necessary
31/3/2004 (year 4)	Perform a review. No 'material change in value' detected
31/3/2005 (year 5)	Full valuation – adjust carrying value as necessary

From 31 March 2006, the cycle repeats itself.

This means that **some form of review/valuation** will be performed every year in order to 'refresh' the value and ensure that it remains 'current'. It does not necessarily mean a full valuation every year.

Revaluing all assets in a class at the same time

14.106

Valuation at different dates. FRS 15 does not give guidance as to whether every asset in the class needs to be revalued at the same time. Given the absence of anything to the contrary, it does seem possible that different assets in the same class could be at different stages of the five-year cycle. However, the requirements in **14.9** above to disclose the details of valuers and the dates of the last full valuations of every class of asset need to be considered, as the disclosure notes may become excessively long.

14.107   For example, a company has five classes of asset. Within one class, there are, say, four subclasses of assets all with different full valuation dates and (for arguments sake) different valuers. If the other four classes of assets are in similar positions, then there will be a very detailed disclosure note in the financial statements which will have around 20 different dates and valuers.

14.108   It is recommended that, for simplicity of disclosure, every asset in the same class follows the same five-year cycle.

Need for annual revaluations

14.109   FRS 15 does not insist on annual revaluations (although these are optional), but has tried to give guidance on how the requirement to carry at current value can be met in practice, when practicalities such as the benefits to the user of annual revaluations and the cost of, and time spent on, valuations are taken into account.

14.110   These are just guidelines given by FRS 15 and therefore are not mandatory. However, as the requirement is to 'carry at current value', entities will have to perform **some** work each year. Management must be able to provide evidence that the figures they are claiming to be 'current values at the balance sheet date' are actually current. Having a 'general five-year cycle' will, in most cases, reduce the cost, burden and hassle of having to decide, each year, just exactly how the evidence of the 'current value as at the balance sheet date' is to be obtained. All entities are strongly advised to follow the general guidelines in **14.105** above. In addition, long periods between full valuations may be questioned by the Review Panel (given the requirement to disclose in the accounts the date of the last full valuation – see section **14.9** above).

14.111   **Interim valuation in year 2 or 3**. FRS 15 specifies an interim valuation in year 3 (see **14.105** above). This is presumably intended to be half way through the five-year cycle, but rounded up to the nearest integer. If this logic is sound, it could be permissible to perform the interim valuation in year 2.

14.112   Paragraphs **14.105** to **14.111** above explain FRS 15's guidelines on how to interpret what is meant by the requirement to carry assets at the 'current value at the balance sheet date'. If the company wishes to perform more frequent full valuations, or to perform an interim valuation for the years required to have a 'review', that is clearly acceptable.

Review in year 1, 2 or 4 indicates a 'material change in value'

14.113 The following questions can be posed when a material change in value has been detected.

Question	Response
Is an interim valuation necessary in a year when a review indicates a 'material change in value'?	Yes, per FRS 15 (45).
Does it have to be an interim valuation or can a full valuation be performed instead?	There is nothing in FRS 15 that prevents entities performing full valuations every year.
If full, what would be the effect on the general five-year cycle (see **14.105** above)?	If a full valuation has been made, then the general five-year cycle has been 'restarted' from this year.
If an interim valuation (following identification of a 'material change in value' at the review) is performed in year 1, does another interim valuation have to be performed before the next full valuation in year 5?	No formal guidance has been given. It is unlikely that the entity will be able to meet the requirement to 'carry at current value' for the next four years by only doing 'reviews' and not carrying out either an interim or a full valuation. It seems logical to follow the general five-year cycle and perform an interim in year 3. If, however, an interim valuation is performed at the end of year 2, then for the reasons stated in **14.111** to **14.112** above, it is possible that no further interim valuation would be necessary until the full valuation in year 5.

Exceptions to the general five-year cycle

Charities, not-for-profit and public sector organisations

14.114 For cost/benefit reasons, these entities may find the general five-year cycle in **14.105** above to be inappropriate. They are allowed, by FRS 15(44), to adopt 'an acceptable alternative approach'. Generally, such approaches will be addressed in relevant sector-specific guidance and SORPs. For example, for charities, the SORP issued in October 1995 would be relevant. (The draft revised Charities SORP, issued December 1999, specifically addresses compliance with FRS 15, and may be taken to constitute best available guidance on acceptable practice in advance of the issue of the final revised SORP.)

Portfolios of non-specialised properties

14.115 FRS 15 suggests that, as an alternative to the general five-year cycle in **14.105** above companies which have portfolios of non-specialised properties (see **14.153** below for definition) can adopt a 'rolling basis' full valuation policy (subject to the conditions below). This entails splitting the properties into five groups and, in rotation, performing a full valuation on one group every year. An interim valuation must be performed on the remaining four-fifths of the portfolio if it is likely that there has been a material change in value (see **14.124** below on how to determine a material change of value).

14.116 The intention appears to be to value the whole portfolio by sample. If property values do not move much, then one-fifth of total assets gets uplifted every year. If values move materially, then the full portfolio will be revalued (one-fifth by a full valuation and the remaining by an interim valuation). This approach means that, unlike the general five-year cycle, there is no required interim valuation in year 3. The disadvantage is that five small full valuations need to be carried out, one in each year.

14.117 FRS 15 states that this approach is appropriate only where the properties held by the entity have certain characteristics. The rules in FRS 15 and examples are given in the table below.

FRS 15 paragraph 46 rules	Examples
(a) Consist of a number of broadly similar properties whose characteristics are such that their values are likely to be affected by the same market forces; or	A portfolio of 50 pubs, all of which are similar. These would be divided into five groups of 10 pubs.
(b) Can be divided on a continuing basis into five groups of a broadly similar spread.	A portfolio of 50 pubs, 15 restaurants and five hotels. A broadly similar spread would be achieved by allocating 10 pubs, three restaurants and one hotel to each group. Other examples of how the portfolio could be spread are based on: (a) a mixture of different assets from different regions; (b) sizes; (c) urban versus rural situations.

The main questions would seem to be:

(a) Is there a portfolio of assets (even within a larger class of assets)?

(b) Can the portfolio be broken down into five groups, each of which is reasonably representative of the whole?

If these conditions are met, then the entity can choose to adopt a rolling-basis full valuation policy over its non-specialised portfolio of properties.

Assets other than properties

14.118 This section covers tangible fixed assets which would fall into Companies Act 1985 categories:

(a) plant and machinery; and

(b) fixtures, fittings, tools and equipment.

For certain types of fixed assets falling within the above categories, it is possible for directors themselves (without using the services of a qualified valuer – see **14.136** below for definition) to obtain a reasonably reliable valuation at the balance sheet date. This could involve using:

(a) an active second-hand market (i.e., for company cars); or

(b) appropriate indices.

If this is done, then the valuation should be updated **annually**, normally by the entity's directors (see **14.141** below).

14.119 If directors are not able to obtain a reasonable valuation annually because there is neither an active second-hand market nor reliable indices of price-change available, then they must use a qualified valuer and perform regular full/interim valuations (i.e., apply the general five-year cycle in **14.105** above).

Types of annual review

14.120 As stated in **14.105** above, the general five-year cycle to meet FRS 15's requirement to 'carry at current value' is:

(a) having a qualified valuer perform a full, detailed valuation at least once every five years; and

(b) having a qualified valuer carry out an interim valuation in year 3; and

(c) performing a review in years 1, 2 and 4. If this review indicates that it is likely that there has been a material change in value, an interim valuation must then be performed by a qualified valuer.

A full valuation, an interim valuation and what constitutes a 'review' are discussed in **14.121** to **14.126** below.

Full valuation

14.121 A full valuation of a property will be carried out by a qualified valuer. Every full valuation performed by a qualified internal valuer must be reviewed by a qualified external valuer (see **14.139** below). A full valuation normally involves, inter alia, the following:

(a) detailed inspection of the interior and exterior of the property (on an initial valuation this will involve detailed measurement of floor space etc., but this would need to be re-performed in future full valuations only if there was evidence of a physical change to the buildings);

(b) inspection of the locality;

(c) enquiries of the local planning and similar authorities;

(d) enquiries of the entity or its solicitors; and

(e) research into market transactions in similar properties, identification of market trends, and the application of these to determine the value of the property under consideration. [FRS 15(47)]

14.122 It would be advisable, when qualified valuers are commissioned to carry out the valuation, to draw their attention to these requirements in order to ensure that the valuation is carried out in accordance with FRS 15.

Interim valuation

14.123 An interim valuation of a property is conducted by a qualified (external or internal) valuer and consists of:

(a) research into market transactions in similar properties, identification of market trends, and the application of these to determine the value of the property under consideration [as in FRS 15(47e)];

(b) confirmation that there have been no changes of significance to the physical buildings, the legal rights, or local planning considerations; and

(c) an inspection of the property or the locality by the valuer to the extent that this is regarded as professionally necessary, having regard to all the circumstances of the case, including recent changes to the property or the locality and the date on which the valuer previously inspected the property.

Again, entities should inform the qualified valuer of these requirements to ensure that the valuation is carried out in accordance with
FRS 15.

Review to assess whether a 'material change in value' has occurred

14.124 As explained in **14.113** above, valuations are to be updated where it
is likely that there has been a material change in value. It is defined
in FRS 15(52) in this way:

> 'A material change in value is a change in value that would reasonably
> influence the decisions of a user of the accounts. In assessing whether
> a material change in value is likely, the combined impact of all rele-
> vant factors (e.g. physical deterioration in the property, general move-
> ments in market prices in the area etc) should be considered.'

14.125 As it is the directors' responsibility to ensure that carrying values
may properly be described as 'current' each year end, FRS 15 lays on
them an implicit duty to review those values in each year when neither a full nor an interim valuation is performed.

14.126 ***Factors which determine the need for an updated valuation.*** Factors
that directors will need to keep in mind when performing their
review include:

(a)   the fact that they are not just looking out for evidence that values may have fallen. Evidence of potential increases in value
will cast just as much doubt on the current status of carrying
value as evidence of a possible fall;

(b)   indicators of possible falls in value will include all those indicators of possible impairments listed in FRS 11(10); and

(c)   systematic collection of objective evidence that changes in
value have been minimal will be best suited to reassuring auditors that no unscheduled interim valuation is required.

Applying the general five-year cycle in the transitional period

14.127 The requirement to carry assets at their current value at the balance
sheet date is met by applying the 'general five-year cycle' (set out in
14.105 above).

Revaluing for the first time

14.128 If an entity has not previously adopted a revaluation policy for a
given class of tangible fixed asset, and chooses to adopt such a policy
for the first time either on implementing FRS 15 or at a later date,
then a full valuation on all assets in the class must be performed in
the year it adopts a revaluation policy (see the general five-year cycle
in **14.105** above).

14.129 For assets other than properties which have a readily accessible market value and do not need a qualified valuer to produce the valuation, first year valuations can be carried out using the appropriate second-hand market value or index (see section **14.118** above).

Further guidance is given in **14.258** and **14.291** below.

Continuing to revalue – all assets in the class previously revalued

14.130 If a company has revalued some assets in the past and is continuing to do so under FRS 15, then for the first period ending on or after 23 March 2000, the company has to decide at which stage of the 'five-year cycle' (as explained in the general five-year cycle, **14.105** above) they have reached. Further guidance is given in **14.299** below.

Example 14.130: Introduction of five-year cycle where all assets revalued

A company, with a 31 March 2000 year end, has had a revaluation policy on all office buildings for the past 10 years. It is continuing this policy under FRS 15. The timing of the last full valuation (as defined in FRS 15) decides what type of valuation/review needs to be carried out this year.

Date and type of valuation carried out previously	Situation at 31/3/2000, and work to be performed this year
Full valuation performed in year to 31/3/99. (Assuming full valuation meets the FRS 15 definition.)	This is year 1 in the five-year cycle and a review is needed to ensure no material change in value has occurred.
Full valuation performed in year to 31/3/98. (Assuming full valuation meets the FRS 15 definition.)	This is year 2 in the five-year cycle and a review is needed to ensure no material change in value has occurred.
Full valuation performed in year to 31/3/97. (Assuming full valuation meets the FRS 15 definition.)	This is year 3 in the five-year cycle and an interim valuation is needed to ensure that the valuation is current.
Full valuation performed in year to 31/3/96. (Assuming full valuation meets the FRS 15 definition.)	This is year 4 in the five-year cycle. As no review/valuation has been performed in 4 years, a more up-to-date valuation is needed. As a minimum, this will involve an interim valuation, but entities may decide that a full valuation is more appropriate.

Full valuation performed in year to 31/3/95 or earlier.	The valuation will be outside the normal 'five-year cycle' and so is unlikely to give a reliable estimate of the current value at the balance sheet date. Therefore, perform a full valuation.
Valuation performed in year to 31/3/99. (Assuming valuation does *not* meet the FRS 15 definition, but falls short in some significant way.)	Where the entity is in the general five-year cycle depends on the reason why the previous valuation did not meet FRS 15's requirements. The amount of work needed comes down to whether the entity has sufficient evidence to prove the year end value is 'current'. E.g., if last year's valuation was performed internally, then this could mean that the entity is in year 4 of the general five-year cycle and a review will be carried out this year.

Summary	In order to not automatically need a full FRS 15 defined valuation in the first year of adopting the standard, the last previous valuation should have met the requirements of FRS 15 and occurred less than five years earlier.

Continuing to revalue – some assets in the class previously revalued

14.131   An entity may have decided to revalue a class of asset, and the newly formed 'class' (see **14.93** above) includes both assets which have been revalued in the past and assets which have not. As FRS 15 requires that all valuations should be 'current' at the year end, it is unlikely that any previous valuation that is now more than one year old could be considered current without, at the very least, performing an interim valuation on it at this stage. In order to put the entire class of revalued assets onto a sound footing for operating an effective five-year cycle of valuation thereafter, a full valuation in the first year on all assets in the class may be advisable.

14.132   Judgement will have to be exercised in respect of any assets carried on the basis of a full valuation only a year ago. In the absence of evidence of significant change in value, it **may** be acceptable (subject to materiality) to incorporate that figure with the current valuations of the other assets in the same class

> as an appropriate starting point for the five-year cycle for the class. FRS 15 does not state that all assets in the same class have to be revalued at the same time. However, for simplicity (and as the date of each most recent full valuation needs to be given in the financial statements), it is recommended that a class should not be split into different subclasses with different valuation timings. In most situations where there is a mixture of assets, some previously revalued and some carried at historic cost, carrying out a full valuation on **all** assets in the class in the year FRS 15 is adopted is likely to give the soundest and most effective basis for not just that year but also future years.

Timing of valuations

14.133 FRS 15 lays some emphasis on the need for valuations to be 'current' at the year end and on the need for a defined frequency of both full and interim valuations. The less current the valuations/reviews are, the less likely they are to meet ASB's intentions.

14.134

> **Meaning of 'current'.** For example, a full valuation carried out in the first three months of a financial year could not be assured to be current at the end of the year. Equally, it would be unrealistic to expect any valuations to take place at the last day of the year. Some judgement must be exercised, and FRS 15 is silent on this. It is suggested that, to be acceptable as a current figure at the year end, any valuation, full or interim, would normally need to be carried out within a 'window' running from a few months prior to the year end to two months after. It would also be advisable, in case of valuations dated close to either end of this spectrum, to have the valuers review their work and indicate (if appropriate) that they have no reason to believe that their valuation would have been materially different had it been dated at the year end.

Valuers

14.135 FRS 15 gives guidance on who should perform most valuations to ensure that the carrying value at the balance sheet reflects current value. Qualified valuers should be used for all property valuations, and also for other assets where there is neither an active second-hand market nor the availability of relevant indices. (Where such evidence exists reliably for non-property assets, directors may use it to arrive at their own valuations and make annual updates themselves.)

Definition of a qualified valuer

14.136 A qualified valuer is a person who:

   (a)   holds a recognised and relevant professional qualification; and

   (b)   has recent post-qualification experience; and

   (c)   has sufficient knowledge of the state of the market, in the location and category of the tangible fixed asset being valued.

A qualified valuer can be either an internal or an external person. As described in **14.138** below, there are restrictions as to which valuations internal valuers can perform without a check being made on their work.

A qualified internal valuer

14.137 An internal valuer must have appropriate qualifications which will need to be verified by auditors (see **14.136** above). It is common for large companies to employ staff with such qualifications. They could be directors, officers or employees of the entity. Additionally, any external valuer who has a significant financial interest in the entity is not independent and will therefore not qualify as an external valuer (see **14.139** to **14.140** below), but could qualify as an internal valuer.

14.138 A qualified internal valuer can perform both interim and full valuations. However, every full valuation performed by a qualified internal valuer must be reviewed by a qualified external valuer. FRS 15 expects this review to involve the external valuer in:

   (a)   valuing a cross-section sample of the entity's revalued properties;

   (b)   comparing the valuations with those of the internal valuer; and

   (c)   expressing an opinion on the accuracy of the internal valuer's estimated valuation figure.

Therefore, if a full valuation is to be included in the financial statements based on an internal valuer's views, this must be checked as being a reasonably accurate figure by a qualified valuer who is external to the business. Relevant documentation needs to be obtained to prove this has been done as details of both the internal and external valuers need to be disclosed in the financial statements.

A qualified external valuer

14.139 A qualified external valuer is someone who:

   (a)   has the appropriate qualifications (see **14.136** above); and

   (b)   is not an internal valuer; and

   (c)   does not have a significant financial interest in the entity.

An external valuer can perform either interim or full valuations, and must also review a full valuation performed by an internal valuer.

14.140 **Surveyors' independence.** FRS 15 does not explain what is meant by a 'significant financial interest'. Judgement should be applied when deciding whether or not an external valuer meets FRS 15's requirements. The main question is whether the interest of the valuer is enough to challenge his/her independence.

Directors establishing annual valuations on other assets

14.141 As noted in **14.118** above, directors may be able to update valuations annually by referring to an active second-hand market or appropriate indices which can be used to give reliable estimations of values at the balance sheet date. Such valuations should be demonstrably objective, i.e., the value that the directors obtain is the same value as any other person would have obtained if they had 'performed' the valuation.

Valuation bases

14.142 FRS 15 has detailed the appropriate bases to be used when valuing assets. The requirements are supported by definitions taken from the Royal Institution of Chartered Surveyors (RICS) *Appraisal and Valuation Manual* (the 'Red Book') which are set out in FRS 15 Appendix 1. Entities that revalue are required to follow FRS 15 and value certain classes of asset on the stated relevant basis.

14.143 The main principle is that, where an asset is revalued, it should be carried at its current value at the balance sheet date. [FRS 15 (43)] This amount is the value of an asset to the business, i.e., the loss that the entity would suffer if it were deprived of the asset. 'Deprival value' will normally be equal to replacement cost because, to put an entity back into the same economic position it occupied before deprival, it would be necessary to replace the asset with another one of the same age, condition and economic potential. As FRS 11 explains, only when the asset has suffered an impairment would it be valued at recoverable amount rather than replacement cost. An unimpaired asset will be valued under FRS 15, at its replacement cost.

14.144 In summary, the bases to be used are as follows.

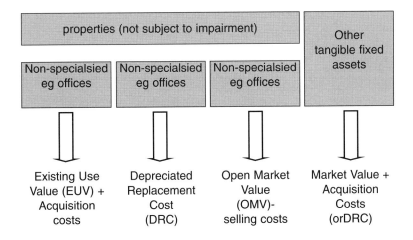

N.B. Per FRS 15(54) assets for which there is an indication of impairment would follow the requirements of FRS 11 *Impairment of fixed assets and goodwill*, and value properties at the lower of replacement cost and recoverable amount (see **14.240** to **14.250** below).

Assets other than properties

14.145 The general rule for tangible fixed assets other than properties, is that they should be valued using market value, where possible. Market value is the best evidence available of what it would cost the entity to replace the asset. The value of plant and machinery to the business is defined in FRS 15 Appendix 1 as:

> 'An opinion of the price at which an interest in the plant and machinery utilised in a business would have been transferred at the date of valuation assuming:
>
> (a) that the plant and machinery will continue in its present uses in the business;
>
> (b) adequate potential profitability of the business, or continuing viability of the undertaking, both having due regard to the value of the total assets employed and the nature of the operation; and
>
> (c) that the transfer is part of an arm's length sale of the business wherein both parties acted knowledgeably, prudently and without compulsion.'

Where market value is not obtainable, the assets should be valued on the basis of depreciated replacement cost, most commonly by using an appropriate index. [FRS 15(59)] These assets can be split into two categories as detailed in **14.146** and **14.149** below.

Assets other than properties with active second-hand markets or appropriate indices

14.146 Assets (other than properties) which can be revalued every year by directors without the assistance of professional valuers are those where an accurate estimate can be made of their value using published, reliable information (see **14.118** and **14.141** above). There is no guidance in FRS 15 as to what constitutes an 'active second-hand market'. FRS 10(2) within the definition of a 'readily ascertainable market value', defines an active market as one 'evidenced by frequent transactions'. Therefore, any asset that has a market which meets this definition or has published second-hand price lists (e.g., cars) will probably be acceptable. In addition, certain notional costs should be added if material (see **14.151** below).

14.147 FRS 15(51) explains that, for an index to be appropriate for use by directors, the index table will:

(a) be appropriate to the class of asset to which it is to be applied, as well as to the asset's location and condition, and take into account technological change; and

(b) have a proven record of regular publication and use and be expected to be available in the foreseeable future.

14.148 One of the main sources of indices which could be used is *Price Index Numbers for Current Cost Accounting* published monthly by the Office for National Statistics.

> ### Example 14.148: Valuation using an index
>
> A company constructed a specialised building in 1994 for £35m. In the year ended 30/9/96, it decided to revalue the building to £55m. Two years later, the valuation was updated using figures in *Price Index Numbers for Current Cost Accounting* (Construction output price index private sector – industrial), published by the Office for National Statistics.
>
> | | | |
> |---|---|---|
> | 1996 Quarter 3 | index figure | 98.8 |
> | 1998 Quarter 3 | index figure | 107.0 |
>
> The new valuation can be calculated as follows:
>
> $$107.0/98.8 \times £55m = £59.56m$$

Assets other than properties which do not have active second-hand markets or appropriate indices

14.149 An appropriate market value should be obtained from a qualified valuer in accordance with the general five-year cycle. In 'The development of the FRS' included in FRS 15 Appendix 4, it explains that valuation bases used should be similar to those used on properties.

Assets other than properties which are surplus to requirements

14.150 Any asset which is expected to be sold should be valued at its net realisable value, i.e., expected selling prices less notional selling costs (see **14.151** below).

Notional costs

14.151 In addition to market value, certain estimated costs should be added or deducted depending on whether the asset is needed in the business or surplus to requirements. This is demonstrated in the table below.

Asset needed in the business	Asset surplus to requirements
Add estimated acquisition costs	*Deduct* estimated selling costs
Why? This gives the best estimate of how much in total the entity would have to pay in order to replace the asset to continue using it in business, i.e., this is *replacement cost*.	*Why?* If the asset is not needed by an entity, this gives the amount that would be received if the asset was sold, i.e., this is *net realisable value (NRV)*.
Only costs which would fall to be capitalised under FRS 15 on initial acquisition will be allowable.	Only those expenses which are unavoidable when selling the asset can be included. (FRS 15 gives no further guidance so the principles for NRV under SSAP 9 *Stock* (see chapter 16) will be relevant.)

Properties

14.152 Properties are split into three main categories as discussed below.

Non-specialised properties – general

14.153 Non-specialised properties are defined in FRS 15 Appendix 1 'RICS Definitions' as:

> 'all properties except those coming within the definition of specialised properties. Hence they are those for which there is a general demand, with or without adaptation, and which are commonly bought, sold or leased on the open market for their existing or similar uses, either with vacant possession for single occupation, or (whether tenanted or

vacant) as investments or for development. Residential properties, shops, offices, standard industrial and warehouse buildings, public houses, petrol filling stations, and many others, are usually non-specialised properties.'

These properties should be valued on the 'existing use' basis (see below). This differs from open market value in two important respects, in that it assumes that:

(a) the property will only be used for the same purpose for the foreseeable future (i.e., no account is taken of the alternative uses that the property may have); and

(b) the property will be sold with vacant possession (i.e., it will not take into account any risks or benefits associated with the existence of a sitting tenant).

14.154 Appendix I of FRS 15 gives the full definition of 'existing use value' as:

'An opinion of the best price at which the sale of an interest in property would have been completed unconditionally for cash consideration on the date of valuation, assuming:

(a) a willing seller;

(b) that, prior to the date of valuation, there had been a reasonable period (having regard to the nature of the property and the state of the market) for the proper marketing of the interest, for the agreement of the price and terms and for the completion of the sale;

(c) that the state of the market, level of values and other circumstances were, on any earlier assumed date of exchange of contracts, the same as on the date of valuation;

(d) that no account is taken of any additional bid by a prospective purchaser with a special interest;

(e) that both parties to the transaction had acted knowledgeably, prudently and without compulsion;

(f) that the property can be used for the foreseeable future only for the existing use; and

(g) that vacant possession is provided on completion of the sale of all parts of the property occupied by the business.'

Thus, existing use takes into account:

(a) the specific job the property is fulfilling (e.g., office building, warehouse, factory etc.) and not the potential it has to be used in a more beneficial way; and

(b) the fact that, should the company need to replace the property with property of similar capability in order to continue to trade as normal, the property must be free from tenants so that the entity could move in without encumbrance.

14.155 'Open market value' is defined by the RICS (FRS 15 Appendix I) in identical terms to those used for 'existing use value' except that they omit conditions **14.154** (f) and (g) above as explained in **14.153** above.

14.156 **Notional direct costs**. Additionally, FRS 15 (53) states that notional directly attributable acquisition costs should be included in the valued amount, e.g., dealing costs such as professional fees, non-recoverable taxes (VAT in certain circumstances) and duties. This is because the value being placed on the property is 'replacement cost'. Any costs that would fall to be capitalised under FRS 15 on initial purchase of the property (should the company have to go out and buy the property now) should be included. This does not include expenditure to enhance the site value such as site improvement costs, planning consents, and site preparation and clearance.

14.157 **Adaptation works**. Structural changes or special fittings which are required to meet the particular needs of the business, for example specialised shop fronts on a retail unit, which have low or 'nil' market value may be dealt with separately from the shell of the property. The shell would be valued at EUV, and the 'adaptation works' at depreciated replacement cost (or even depreciated historical cost if they are regarded as a separate class of asset). [FRS 15(57)]

14.158 **Assets with no commercial use.** FRS 11(20) provides that it may be inappropriate to measure such an asset on the basis of future cash flows, and consequently inappropriate to conclude that an impairment has happened. An alternative measure of service potential, based on a reasonable estimate of useful life, will be more appropriate.

14.159 **Assets with trading potential**. FRS 15(56) and (85) goes along with the RICS valuation rules in allowing properties to be valued as fully operational entities having regard to their trading potential. If this is the basis for valuation, it needs to be disclosed in the financial statements (see **14.9** above). Where the trading potential would not qualify for recognition as a separate intangible asset in accordance with FRS 10 *Goodwill and intangible assets* (see chapter 13), FRS 15 requires the inherent goodwill to be included in the property value.

14.160 Examples given by the RICS Manual of assets which are valued including trading potential are hotels, public houses, cinemas, theatres, bingo clubs, gaming clubs, petrol filling stations, betting shops, specialised sporting and leisure facilities. As a result of the valuation method, an element of value will represent goodwill and other intangible assets. Where such an intangible meets the recognition criteria of FRS 10, that standard would

> appear to encourage separate recognition of the intangible element with 'intangible fixed assets'. For example, a betting shop consists of a retail site (often with little value) together with a licence (which carries significant value). As noted above, FRS 15 requires inseparable assets to be recognised wholly within 'tangible fixed assets'. In cases such as betting shops, companies would appear to have a choice of classification methods. The depreciation of such properties is considered in **14.205** below.

Non-specialised properties where interest is capitalised

14.161 As the valuation basis used in valuing non-specialised properties is EUV, this value shows what it would cost the entity to replace the asset with a fully constructed identical asset. Therefore, even if the entity's policy is to capitalise interest costs in the course of construction, **no** amounts relating to finance charges should be included in the current valuation as the valuation basis uses fully constructed assets (i.e., including compensation to the seller for his costs of finance), and not assets in the process of construction.

14.162 The amount of finance charge which was originally capitalised would be disclosed as part of the historic cost disclosures (see **14.17** above).

Specialised properties – general

14.163 Specialised properties are defined in FRS 15 Appendix 1 'RICS Definitions' as properties which:

> 'due to their specialised nature, are rarely, if ever, sold on the open market for single occupation for a continuation of their existing use, except as part of a sale of the business in occupation. Their specialised nature may arise from the construction, arrangement, size or location of the property, or a combination of these factors, or may be due to the nature of the plant and machinery and items of equipment which the buildings are designed to house, or the function, or the purpose for which the buildings are provided.

> Examples of specialised properties are:

> - oil refineries and chemical works where, usually, the buildings are no more than housings or cladding for highly specialised plant;

> - power stations and dock installations where the buildings and site engineering works are related directly to the business of the owner, it being highly unlikely that they would have a value to anyone other than a company acquiring the undertaking;

- properties of such construction, arrangement, size or specification that there would be no market (for a sale to a single owner occupier for the continuation of existing use) for those buildings;

- standard properties in particular geographical areas and remote from main business centres, located there for operational or business reasons, which are of such an abnormal size for that district, that there would be no market for such buildings there;

- schools, colleges, universities and research establishments where there is no competing market demand from other organisations using these types of property in the locality;

- hospitals, other specialised health care premises and leisure centres where there is no competing market demand from other organisations wishing to use these types of property in the locality; and

- museums, libraries, and other similar premises provided by the public sector.'

14.164 Due to their specialised nature, no EUV or OMV can be determined for these type of assets. Such specialised properties are therefore valued on the basis of depreciated replacement cost (DRC). This is defined in FRS 15 Appendix 1 as:

> 'The aggregate amount of the value of the land for the existing use or a notional replacement site in the same locality, and the gross replacement cost of the buildings and other site works, from which appropriate deductions may then be made to allow for the age, condition, economic or functional obsolescence, environmental and other relevant factors; all of these might result in the existing property being worth less to the undertaking in occupation than would a new replacement.'

14.165 FRS 15 does allow specialised properties to be valued as fully operational entities having regard to their trading potential. This applies particularly where properties fall into categories which are normally valued on this basis (see **14.159** above). If this is the basis for valuation, it needs to be disclosed in the financial statements.

Specialised properties when interest is capitalised

14.166 As explained in **14.164** above, non-specialised properties are valued using depreciated replacement cost (DRC). This identifies what the net value of a replacement asset would be. It may be possible to take the view that, as this is a valuation, then no additional finance charges can be added to the 'gross cost' even if the entity has a policy of capitalising finance costs as this would increase the carrying value of the asset above a notional 'market value'. However, there is an alternative view which we regard as more persuasive. The intention of the DRC method is to determine what it would cost to replace an asset by constructing it from scratch (Gross Replacement Cost) and then deducting from that an appropriate proportion to allow for the existing asset's age and condition to arrive at DRC. If an entity has a policy of capitalising interest, its GRC would logically include interest incurred in funding construction. A simplistic assumption would be that the same proportion of the asset would be funded on replacement as occurred on original construction and at similar rates, so the amount of interest capitalised would change only in direct proportion to the increase in construction prices. Calculation (whether by directors or by valuers) would normally be achieved by applying an index of construction costs to original cost **including** interest capitalised.

14.167 As FRS 15 is silent on this point, it is not yet possible to forecast which view will prevail. In our view, the inclusion of interest is both justifiable and preferable as more closely in line with the underlying concept of value to the business based on replacement cost. The overriding requirement however is for consistency of treatment. An entity needs to decide which view to take and apply it consistently.

14.168 If the entity has a policy of capitalising interest on the original construction of assets, then the amount of finance charges originally capitalised on the revalued asset should be disclosed as part of the historic cost disclosures.

Properties surplus to requirements

14.169 Properties surplus to an entity's requirements (but retained in fixed assets) should be valued on the basis of 'Open Market Value' (see **14.155** above), with expected directly attributable selling costs deducted where material. [FRS 15(53c)] This is a 'net realisable value' (NRV). (For reclassification of fixed assets as current assets, see **14.175** to **14.177** below.)

Valuation of investment properties

14.170 Investment properties, as defined in **14.171** below, are excluded from the scope of FRS 15 because they are covered by SSAP 19. They are required by SSAP 19 to be included in the balance sheet at their open market value (to be determined annually) and, except for leased property having an unexpired term of 20 years or less, are not subject to depreciation. The failure to depreciate investment properties is a departure from the requirement of Schedule 4 para 18 to depreciate fixed assets having limited useful economic lives. Disclosure of such departure and its effect is required by the Act to be given in the notes; UITF Abstract 7 has indicated the level of detail needed to meet this requirement (see **21.17** to **21.19** below). It is not necessary to show the effects of depreciation, even on an arbitrary basis.

14.171 An investment property is defined by SSAP 19 as an interest in land and/or buildings:

(a)   in respect of which construction work and development have been completed; and

(b)   which is held for its investment potential, any rental income being negotiated at arm's length.

Note that, because the exclusion of investment properties from the scope of FRS 15 refers specifically to this definition of an investment property in SSAP 19, properties under construction fall within FRS 15's scope and outside that of SSAP 19, regardless of the fact that they are being constructed with every intention of using them as investment properties.

14.172 Property owned and occupied by a company for its own use and property let to and occupied by group companies are specifically excluded from this definition.

14.173   FRS 15 does not address the classification of part-occupied premises. There will be instances where the proportion of a property which is self-occupied is so small that it would be unreasonable to disregard the claim that it is an investment property on those grounds alone. It is suggested that the most appropriate criterion for making this judgement will be the proportion of the total value of the property represented by the self-occupied part, and that a proportion that exceeds 10 per cent of that value is most unlikely to be small enough to disregard in this respect.

14.174 While the standard does not require the valuer of investment properties to hold professional qualifications or to be independent, the explanatory notes to SSAP 19 suggest that, where investment properties represent a substantial proportion of the total assets of a major enterprise (e.g., a listed company), their valuation would normally be carried out annually by persons who do hold a recognised professional qualification with experience in the location and category of the properties concerned and at least every five years by an external valuer.

Fixed assets surplus to requirements

14.175 Fixed assets are defined as those which are intended for use on a continuing basis in the company's activities. [s262] Thus, when there is no possibility of any doubt that a particular asset is no longer intended for use on a continuing basis, it ceases to be a fixed asset and should be reclassified as current.

14.176

> The definition has been interpreted in various ways. It is suggested that an item which has been defined as a fixed asset should normally continue to be so defined as long as it, in fact, continues to be available for use, even if there is an intention to dispose of it on suitable terms when a buyer can be found. Thus, it is not uncommon for a company to conclude that it would like to sell a particular piece of plant, but to continue to have it on site, available for use. Unless it has been put permanently out of commission (damaged, dismantled or crucial elements disposed of), such an item should continue to be classified as a fixed asset. Similarly, an investment property should be treated as a fixed asset until sold. It is a feature of investment properties that they are always available for sale (at the right price), but, until a sale takes place, they continue to be held for the purposes of the company's business, i.e., to obtain rental income and capital appreciation.

14.177 In the very rare situations when it is wholly appropriate to reclassify a fixed asset as current (for example, where it ceases to be used), it should be revalued at the lower of cost and net realisable value. [Sch 4: 23(1)] If the asset is an item of plant which has been carried at historical cost less depreciation, it is appropriate to treat the net book amount as equivalent to cost for this purpose; it represents the balance of cost which has not yet been charged against profits. If net realisable value is lower than the net book amount, the difference should be charged in the profit and loss account as a provision for diminution in value. However, if the asset has previously been revalued and as a result the asset is included in the balance sheet at an amount which is greater than original cost, it is necessary to reduce it to cost by a transfer from revaluation reserve.

Assets included at a fixed amount

14.178 A further alternative basis of valuation is permitted for tangible fixed assets, provided that they:

(a)   are not material to assessing the company's state of affairs;

(b)   are constantly being replaced; and

(c)   are not subject to material variation as to quantity, value or composition.

Fixed assets which meet all of these conditions may be stated at a fixed quantity and value. [Sch 4: 25] This basis is best suited to low value, short-life assets, such as tools and moulds. The only reason why such assets can escape the requirements of FRS 15 is because the amount involved is immaterial ((a) above).

Depreciation of tangible fixed assets

Overview

14.179 FRS 15 has replaced SSAP 12 as the source of rules relating to depreciation. It has not made radical changes in approach. As most entities have few and/or quite simple fixed asset structures, they will not find much difference. However, for those companies with many or complex depreciating fixed assets, there are a number of significant changes, especially if the measurement of the depreciation of those assets has proved at all complex or contentious in the past. FRS 15 repeats SSAP 12 in insisting that, where material depreciation has taken place, it must be measured and charged systematically. Where FRS 15 goes beyond SSAP 12 is in describing both the circumstances under which depreciation may properly be regarded as immaterial and also the subsets of those circumstances where, as a price to be paid for that concession of a nil or very small depreciation charge, the assets concerned must be the subject of an FRS 11 impairment test **every year** (see **14.240** to **14.250** below).

Companies Act 1985 requirements

14.180 The basis for charging depreciation on depreciating fixed assets is laid down initially by the Companies Act. The requirements are that, in the case of fixed assets carried under the historical cost accounting rules:

'In the case of any fixed asset which has a limited useful economic life, the amount of:

(a) its purchase price or production cost; or

(b) where it is estimated that any such asset will have a residual value at the end of the period of its useful economic life, its purchase price or production cost less that estimated residual value;

shall be reduced by provisions for depreciation calculated to write off that amount systematically over the period of the asset's useful economic life'

and Sch 4 para 32 extends that requirement to fixed assets carried at a revaluation, i.e., under the 'alternative accounting rules', substituting value for cost.

Elements of SSAP 12 retained

14.181 SSAP 12 was first issued in 1977 and is familiar to most UK accountants, so it may be helpful to establish first which of the elements of SSAP 12 are unchanged in FRS 15, and do not have to be relearned.

The principal **unchanged** elements are these:

(a) What must be depreciated is 'the depreciable amount', which is still the difference between cost or revalued amount and residual value.

(b) Residual value is measured at prices prevailing at the date of acquisition or revaluation, i.e., it must **not** take account of subsequent/future price change.

(c) The depreciable amount must be allocated on a systematic basis over its useful economic life.

(d) The pattern of consumption must be reflected as fairly as possible.

(e) Depreciation is charged to the profit and loss account unless it can be capitalised as part of the cost of another asset.

(f) Asset lives must be reviewed at the end of each reporting period and revised if necessary.

(g) The method of depreciation may be changed only when a new method gives a fairer presentation of results and of financial position.

It is therefore apparent that FRS 15 has not changed the framework for measuring and charging depreciation.

Definition of depreciation

14.182 FRS 15 defines depreciation in this way:

> 'The measure of the cost or revalued amount of the economic benefits of the tangible fixed asset that have been consumed during the period.
>
> Consumption includes the wearing out, using up or other reduction in the useful economic life of a tangible fixed asset whether arising from use, effluxion of time or obsolescence through either changes in technology or demand for the goods and services produced by the asset.'

14.183 This clarifies what was intended by the SSAP 12 definition without making any change of substance. The useful clarifications are:

(a) the insertion of the reference to 'cost or revalued amount of the economic benefits'; and

(b)   the substitution of 'through either changes in technology or demand for the goods and services produced by the asset' for the SSAP 12 phrase, 'through technological or market changes'.

Although these wording changes reduce any doubt about what is intended, it is doubtful whether they will make any significant changes to interpretations in practice.

The depreciable amount

14.184   The depreciable amount is defined in FRS 15(77) as the difference between cost or revalued amount and residual value. This must be allocated to the profit and loss account on a systematic basis over useful economic life, by a method that reflects as fairly as possible the pattern of consumption of benefits. The only exception to charging to the profit and loss account is where the cost forms a part of the cost of constructing a capitalisable asset.

14.185   Some guidance is given on these points. It is stressed that (subject to materiality) there must be a cost charged to the profit and loss account even if the asset has risen in value because it cannot be denied that some part of the economic benefits inherent in the asset has been consumed during the period. [FRS 15(78)] In essence, unless that part is measured and charged, the cost of activities will not be properly matched with the revenue from activities and the profit and loss account may thereby fail to give a true and fair view.

14.186   Where the depreciation charge relates to an asset which falls into a class which is being revalued (and that valuation is therefore being reviewed and, if necessary, adjusted each period to keep it current), ideally the depreciation charge should be calculated based on the average value of the asset for the period. [FRS 15(79)] However, the guidance concedes that, in practice, the charge may be based on either the opening or the closing balance. This raises several issues, both of principle and of practice, including those relating to the timing of both acquisitions and revaluations (see **14.187** to **14.191** below).

Depreciation of revalued assets – the ideal approach

14.187   **Use of monthly figures.** The closest approximation to accurate measurement of the benefits consumed period by period is achieved by measuring value consumed on a monthly basis and aggregating those monthly charges to arrive at an annual charge. Many entities use their monthly management accounts in this way. Acquisitions may be depreciated from the month in which they are first capitalised. Where assets are being carried at current value, any that are revalued during the year may be depreciated on the basis of that revaluation from the month in which the revaluation is recorded. Alternatively, the annual depreciation figure may be calculated on the average of opening and closing cost or of opening and closing value giving, in all probability, a close approximation to using the total of monthly charges.

14.188   As FRS 15 indicates, this approach is ideal. However, it has practical disadvantages so simpler solutions have often been the norm. Simplicity often encourages the calculation, for both monthly and annual accounts, of a depreciation charge based on the opening asset figure, coinciding with budgeted depreciation and obviating one variable between budget and actual. When dealing with revalued figures, there is a further complication when the basis of valuation is depreciated replacement cost (DRC), because the year end DRC balance – the valuation – necessarily assumes that it is preceded by a depreciation charge for the year based on the year end gross replacement cost, involving an extra adjustment to revaluation reserve. For these reasons and because the effect of the differences between these routes is so rarely material, simpler methods are generally acceptable.

14.189   *Exception when changing from historical cost.* However, there is one exception, because it can often result in a materially incorrect answer. Although FRS 15(79) concedes that depreciation may be based on the opening balance for the period rather than the closing balance, it should be noted that the paragraph commences with the phrase 'where an asset has been revalued'. It would be unwise and unjustifiable to regard this concession as extending to an accounting period in which the decision is first made to commence revaluing the asset. It does not justify charging depreciation based on either opening cost or the average of opening cost and closing value whilst carrying the asset in the balance sheet at a revalued figure (unless there is no material difference between cost and value). It is important to remember the overriding requirement that 'the depreciation method chosen should reflect **as fairly as possible** the pattern in which the asset's economic benefits are consumed by the entity'. [FRS 15: 77] Once an asset's value has been incorporated into the balance sheet, it is inappropriate to base the depreciation charge on cost in the accompanying profit and loss account, as the two bases cannot be combined. A charge based on an average of cost and value is inappropriate because it is not an average of value covering the reporting period but an average of two 'values' generally many years apart, i.e., an average spanning all those years. For the same reason, on first adopting FRS 15 for a class of assets, it would not be appropriate to use an average of closing value and an opening value brought forward from several years earlier. Therefore, depreciation should be calculated on the basis of closing value as illustrated in Example **14.230** below.

Depreciation of revalued assets – the practical approach

14.190 **Use of opening values.** In many situations, it will be more straightforward to adopt an approach that is more broad-brush than the averaging approach. The choice will be between basing the annual depreciation charge on either the opening balance or the closing balance, of cost or current value respectively (but not mixing the two – see **14.189** above). In the case of additions during the period, some entities modify the 'opening amount' basis by depreciating the additions separately on a broad-brush assumption that they were all bought at mid year, so half of the annual rate is charged.

14.191 Because the difference between using opening or closing cost is not likely to be material in effect, practicability will dictate each entity's choice (and the same is true of the difference between using opening or closing current value). The use of the closing balance is often more prudent in its impact because the effect of price change means that, even in stable situations, both additions and revaluations tend to produce larger closing balances than opening balances. In the case of revaluations, the use of the closing balance has the theoretical correctness of articulating the balance sheet and the profit and loss account; each takes into account assets on the same basis. None the less, the use of opening balances as a basis for depreciation can have the virtue of relative simplicity without normally detracting materially from the truth and fairness of the accounts. For that reason, the examples shown in **14.230** to **14.235** below, illustrating the calculation of the charges to the profit and loss account and their impact in particular on the entries needed to record revaluations, are all based on the opening value method.

Useful economic life and residual value

Factors in determining useful economic life and residual value

14.192 FRS 15(80) lists the following factors as potentially significant when considering what useful economic life and residual value to assign to an asset:

(a)   expected rate of use of the asset, by reference to expected capacity and physical output;

(b)   expected rate of physical deterioration through use or time passing, taking into account intended maintenance plans;

(c)   expected rate of economic or technological obsolescence;

(d)   legal or similar limits on use (e.g., lease terms).

The question of projected maintenance expenditure is also dealt with in FRS 15 under 'subsequent expenditure' (see **14.75** to **14.80** above).

14.193   FRS 15 makes clear that the existence of subsequent expenditure which qualifies for capitalisation (see **14.78** to **14.80** above) does not negate the need for depreciation.

14.194   **Reflecting maintenance expenditure.** There is a trade-off between the assessment of economic life and hence the rate of providing depreciation on the one hand and the question of whether maintenance expenditure should be expensed or capitalised as enhancing the asset. The basic rule is that, if you spend money replacing an economic benefit for the consumption of which you have previously provided via the depreciation charge, then you capitalise the expenditure. For practical reasons, this decision depends systematically on your assumptions about future maintenance and about its regularity when you first set an economic life for depreciation purposes. At one extreme are the utilities like the water industry where the use of renewals accounting (see **14.220** to **14.226** below) allows nil to be charged as depreciation but a systematic sum to be provided against which to expense all maintenance and replacement costs as they occur. At the other extreme lies the adoption of very short lives, maximum depreciation provision and capitalisation of relatively minor replacement expenditure. The important point is that, taken together, the two elements must result in a charge to the profit and loss account that reflects consumption of economic benefit reasonably accurately and consistently. The choice at the outset of where to place any asset along the spectrum between no depreciation and very speedy depreciation depends on expectations and on an assessment of how to reflect those expectations most effectively. Once adopted, in the absence of any evidence that the expectations were seriously mistaken, the most important thing is that the policy should be followed consistently.

Need to review useful economic life and residual value

14.195 Both useful economic life and residual value (if material) should be reviewed at the end of each reporting period and revised if expectations have changed significantly. [FRS 15(93)–(96)] The only change here compared with SSAP 12 is that the need to review residual value in the same way as economic life is made explicit. The review of residual value at the end of each reporting period should take account of reasonably expected technological changes. Where assets are carried at a valuation, in every year when a full or an interim valuation produces a material change in the carrying value, the residual value must be updated also for any expected impact of the change in price levels since the previous carrying value was established.

14.196 The definition of residual value in FRS 15(2) makes it explicit that changes in price levels, whether since the date of acquisition or since the latest revaluation or those expected up to the end of economic life, must **not** be taken into account when determining residual value. The reference to revising residual value 'if expectations are significantly different from previous estimates' [FRS 15(93)] does not therefore include changed expectations of inflation. There is one exception to this rule given in FRS 15(96). Where restatement at such prices is 'not practicable' (no examples are given, but presumably this may relate to inadequacy of records) **and** where restatement of residual value using prices current at the date of restatement gives a figure below the existing estimate, then current prices may be used. If restatement at current prices would increase residual value (and consequently reduce the depreciation charge) **and** restatement at original price levels is impracticable, then residual value should be left unchanged.

Effects of any change in useful economic life or residual value

14.197 The effects of any change in the assessment of remaining useful economic life and/or residual value must be expensed over the revised remaining life. [FRS 15(93) and (95)] The only exception to this is where it coincides with an impairment of the asset, in which case the impairment must be recognised immediately in accordance with FRS 11. (However, as explained in **14.200** below, this requirement has no effect in respect of assets revalued in accordance with FRS 15.)

14.198 This represents a noteworthy change from SSAP 12. Although SSAP 12 had the same basic requirement, it also offered an exception to this general rule, and FRS 15 has ruled out that exception. SSAP 12 (18) stated that:

'Usually, when asset lives are reviewed regularly, there will be no material distortion of future results or financial position if the net book amount is written off over the revised remaining useful economic life. Where, however, future results would be materially distorted, the adjustment to accumulated depreciation should be recognised in the accounts in accordance with FRS 3 as an exceptional item included under the same statutory format heading as the ongoing depreciation charge.'

This was itself an amendment to SSAP 12, made in 1981, principally to avoid a clash with the proposed standard, SSAP 16, on current cost accounting when dealing with depreciated replacement cost. The effect of FRS 15's change is to rule out the possibility of passing a material adjustment through the current year's profit and loss account as an exceptional item. (Where lengthening life or increasing residual value reduced the annual depreciation charge and produced a large credit to current year's P&L, companies could be tempted to take advantage of this concession, now removed.)

Example 14.198: Revision of useful economic life

An asset has a cost of 1,200, and an assessed useful economic life of four years. After two years, accumulated depreciation stands at 600, and net book value is also 600. The remaining estimated useful economic life is reassessed as six years, making a revised total life of eight years.

Under FRS 15, the net book value at the end of year 2 is allocated over the remaining life of six years. The charge for years 1 and 2 is 300 per annum. The charge for years 3 to 8 is 100 per annum. The asset's net book value will appear to decline thus:

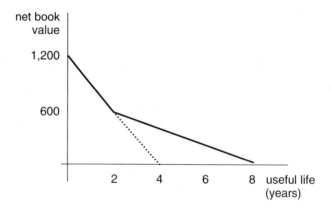

Under SSAP 12, it was possible to adjust the net book value at the end of year 2 to the figure it would have been had the revised life been used throughout, that is, 900. However, this results in a credit to the profit and loss account at the time of revision. The depreciation charge for years 1 and 2 is 300 per annum. In year 3 there is a credit to profit and loss account of 300. For years 3 to 8 annual depreciation is 150. On this basis, the asset's net book value will appear to decline thus:

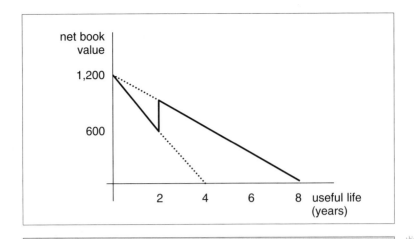

14.199 **True and fair view override**. This change from SSAP 12 is significant and moreover may be thought to take immediate effect. The apparent intention of the SSAP 12 concession was to avoid an extreme situation where the financial statements might fail to give a true and fair view. The Companies Act still requires an override of other requirements if that is the only way to give a true and fair view. The unusual element in SSAP 12(18) was that it conceded an adjustment to **this year's** accounts apparently in order to avoid the risk of distorting the true and fair view in a **future year's** accounts. Since it is for the auditor to report whether or not the accounts give a true and fair view, and since the auditor is necessarily limited to reporting on a year at a time, it would be a bold auditor indeed who accepted a true and fair override on these grounds alone. Moreover, any attempt to make one final use of the SSAP 12 concession in the last year before implementing FRS 15 may also be untenable. A charge in a future year cannot logically be said to materially distort the results of that year when the method of arriving at that charge in that year is in conformity with the financial reporting standard (FRS 15) that necessarily applies for that future year.

Change in useful economic life or residual value of revalued assets

14.200 The ASB has not specifically addressed the issue of change of asset life where assets are being carried on the basis of current value. This may be because the issue is a simple one because there is only one solution; alternatively, the ASB may have failed to notice the point. As FRS 15 requires that any asset carried at a valuation must be revisited every year end to check that that value is 'current', it follows that the value must, in principle, consist of the value remaining after charging for depreciation for the current period. The figure which the valuer either provides or confirms is still 'current' constitutes the value left to be consumed over remaining periods and therefore takes account of any value that has been consumed already. This is true whether the basis of valuation is existing use value (based on market prices) or depreciated replacement cost (based on a new cost less notional past provisions for depreciation at current prices). The balance carried forward is therefore fixed by the valuation process. If a change has been made in the set of assumptions relating to remaining useful economic life, that will necessarily have been factored in to the valuation. The balance carried cannot therefore be 'fudged' by spreading a previously brought forward balance over a new remaining life. For this reason, it is simply impossible to comply both with the standard's requirements to maintain revalued assets at current value and to spread the effect of a change in asset life over future years. What happens in effect is that the necessary retrospective adjustment to past depreciation passes to Revaluation Reserve as a part of the gain or loss on revaluation. (The only exception to this will be where the change in asset life is caused by or coincides with an impairment to the asset.) Consequently, FRS 15(93)–(96)cannot be applied to revalued assets, and should be ignored in that context.

Method of depreciation

14.201 FRS 15's guidance on methods of depreciation is straightforward. The standard concedes that a variety of methods can be used to meet the requirement that the depreciable amount should be allocated on a systematic basis over useful economic life. It endorses the straight-line method and the reducing balance method as acceptable. It goes on to say that 'the method chosen should result in a depreciation charge throughout the asset's useful economic life and not just towards the end of its useful economic life or when the asset is falling in value'; and adds that, where the pattern of consumption of an asset's benefits is uncertain, the straight-line method is 'usually adopted'. [FRS 15(81)]

14.202 However, another useful basis is the unit of production method which apportions the cost of the fixed asset over its productive life measured in terms of the units produced or machine hours utilised in relation to the total of such units or hours estimated to comprise the productive life of the asset. This method is theoretically superior to the straight-line or reducing balance methods, in that it more accurately matches costs with revenue where the life of the asset can be measured with some precision in terms of its ultimate total output. One regular application of this method is in oil, gas and other extractive industries, where the production assets have no further value once mineral reserves have been extracted. However, in these industries precision depends on the accuracy of the prediction of total extractable reserves.

Annuity and other back-end loaded methods

14.203 FRS 15 endorses methods that result in an even depreciation charge in every year or in a charge which is higher in earlier years and reduces over time. It does not comment on any of the methods in use which result in a lower charge in earlier years, rising over time. Consequently, it does not rule such a method out, provided it can be justified. It merely seeks to rule out any method whereby nil or derisory levels of depreciation are charged in earlier years and material depreciation is charged only in the latter years of life. Equally, it makes no comment on the 'unit of production' method common particularly in the extractive industries, whereby an assessment is made of the volume of extractable minerals available and the annual depreciation charge is based on what proportion of the total available has actually been extracted during the period, so that the asset is written down proportionally over the period of extraction. While silence on these points should not be taken as indicating that FRS 15 rules out such methods, the ASB is currently reviewing this issue and it is possible that a proposal may be made shortly, seeking to regulate their use. (See **29.90** below for use of annuity depreciation in relation to lease accounting.)

Changing the method of depreciation

14.204 A change in method is only permissible 'on the grounds that the new method will give a fairer presentation of the results and of the financial position'. [FRS 15(82)] This is identical wording to that used in SSAP 12. Again as in SSAP 12, FRS 15 states that such a change does not constitute a change in accounting policy and therefore the effect of the change is spread forward. In the period of adopting a new method, that method must be applied to the existing carrying balance (or revalued figure if it coincides with a revaluation) to depreciate it over the remaining useful economic life. [FRS 15(83)]

Assets with components with materially different lives

14.205 FRS 15 lays stress on one aspect of determining the depreciation charge that SSAP 12 had ignored, but this does not involve any change in principle: 'Where the tangible fixed asset comprises two or more major components with substantially different useful economic lives, each component should be accounted for separately for depreciation purposes and depreciated over its individual useful economic life.' [FRS 15(83)]

14.206 This effects a change in practice but not a change in principle. FRS 15 reinforces FRS 12, in encouraging entities that have previously made provision in advance for expenditure on replacing material components or on periodic major overhauls now to make provision instead by means of the depreciation charge, because FRS 12 has precluded the use of a provision as such. Examples 11A and 11B in FRS 12, based on furnace linings and aircraft overhauls, are useful illustrations.

FRS 12 Appendix III Example 11

Repairs and maintenance – some assets require, in addition to routine maintenance, substantial expenditure every few years for major refits or refurbishment and the replacement of major components.

Example 11A: *Refurbishment costs – no legislative requirement*

A furnace has a lining that needs to be replaced every five years for technical reasons. At the balance sheet date, the lining has been in use for three years. Present obligation as a result of a past obligating event – There is no present obligation.

Conclusion – No provision is recognised. The cost of replacing the lining is not recognised because, at the balance sheet date, no obligation to replace the lining exists independently of the entity's future actions – even the intention to incur the expenditure depends on the entity deciding to continue operating the furnace or to replace the lining. Instead of a provision being recognised, the depreciation of the lining takes account of its consumption, i.e., it is depreciated over five years. The re-lining costs then incurred are capitalised with the consumption of each new lining shown by depreciation over the subsequent five years.

Example 11B: *Refurbishment costs – legislative requirement*

An airline is required by law to overhaul its aircraft once every three years.

Present obligation as a result of a past obligating event – There is no present obligation.

Conclusion – No provision is recognised. The costs of overhauling aircraft are not recognised as a provision for the same reasons as the cost of replacing the lining is not recognised as a provision in example 11A. Even a legal requirement to overhaul does not make the costs of overhaul a liability because no obligation exists to overhaul the

---

> aircraft independently of the entity's future actions – the entity could avoid the future expenditure by its future actions, for example by selling the aircraft. Instead of a provision being recognised, the depreciation of the aircraft takes account of the future incidence of maintenance costs, i.e., an amount equivalent to the expected maintenance costs is depreciated over three years.'

14.207 Common sense has previously encouraged entities to apply different rates of depreciation to materially different elements. FRS 15 provides two examples: land separate from buildings; and the structure of a building separate from the items within the structure. Common examples have been a building and the lifts and fittings within it. Another example is an aircraft airframe and engines. FRS 15 now makes it explicit that one should account for elements separately where to do so would have a material effect. (See Extract **14.310** below, Marks & Spencer plc.)

Assets valued with trading potential

14.208 FRS 15 does draw attention to one situation where this would not be appropriate, and this is specific to properties valued as operational entities such as pubs and hotels. It says it would not be appropriate to separate out the trading potential element in the valuation from the building itself where the value and life is inseparable from that of the building.[FRS 15(85)]

14.209
> The alternative name for that trading potential is of course 'goodwill'. This highlights the anomalous nature of the valuation of such premises. The ASB has so far taken valuers' practice of valuing them as businesses rather than just bricks and mortar as a reason for not bringing the goodwill element in such valuations within the scope of the goodwill standard, FRS 10. In the long run, it may prove difficult to sustain the logic of this, as the range of premises valued in this way appears to be on the increase. Valuation of such properties is discussed further in **14.159** and **14.160** above.

Computer hardware and software

14.210
> One example of the application of the 'components' approach to depreciating an asset could be the treatment of computer hardware and software. For many years, computer software was often capitalised under the heading of intangible assets. FRS 10 made that more difficult to justify, and encourages capitalising the software as a component of the hardware under tangible fixed assets. It is very possible that the assessed useful economic

> life may differ materially between the software and the hardware. FRS 15 endorses the approach of depreciating each over different asset lives, but as components of a single tangible fixed asset.

Freehold land

14.211 Freehold land which is not subject to depletion (e.g., by the extraction of minerals) does not have a limited useful life and therefore should not be depreciated. [FRS 15(84)] In consequence, it is necessary where freehold property is purchased to allocate the purchase consideration between the respective components, the value of the land and that of the buildings. Similarly, any revaluations of freehold property should distinguish between land and buildings (valuers should provide a figure for the depreciable element in the value). Where the value of freehold land is adversely affected by long-term environmental factors, it should be written down to reflect any permanent diminution in value.

Non-depreciation

Non-depreciation – the justification and the price

14.212 One of the principal problems about depreciation practices over the past 20 years has been inconsistency in the perceived need to charge any depreciation at all. Many companies advanced arguments to justify charging no depreciation. Most of those arguments revolved around immateriality, on the grounds that the life of an asset was very long and/or the residual value was maintained at a very high level, close to the carrying value, by a high level of maintenance expenditure. There was some feeling that this view could and should be challenged and many companies chose to adopt policies that were seen as more conservative and perhaps more apparently compliant with the Companies Act and SSAP 12. In fact, the two views are not in principle contradictory and can be complementary. However, in consequence, companies have been perceived as having freedom to adopt any policy that suited them, and the results were felt to be inconsistent and lacking in comparability.

14.213 The ASB initially, in both a discussion paper and in FRED 17, threatened to adopt a hard line, requiring a depreciation charge almost regardless of circumstance. In the light of the submissions made to it, a careful review has produced a more thoughtful solution in FRS 15. The ASB has accepted the evidence that depreciation may genuinely be immaterial, either because of the estimated length of remaining useful economic life or because residual value at the end of that life is not materially different from carrying amount. However, companies may no longer opt for the alternative of immaterial depreciation simply as an act of faith and policy. Instead, they must go through due process to justify the carrying value each year. Justification must take the form of an FRS 11 impairment review each year. This is seen as a sufficient price to pay to force companies to adopt this approach only when they are sure that the evidence will support it for the foreseeable future.

> 'Tangible fixed assets, other than non-depreciable land, should be reviewed for impairment, in accordance with FRS 11, at the end of each reporting period when either:
>
> (a) no depreciation charge is made on the grounds that it would be immaterial (either because of the length of the estimated remaining useful economic life or because the estimated residual value of the tangible fixed asset is not materially different from the carrying amount of the asset); or
>
> (b) the estimated remaining useful economic life of the tangible fixed asset exceeds 50 years.' (See **14.218** to **14.219** below.)

[FRS 15(89)]

14.214 FRS 15(92) makes it clear that, following a full initial review in the first period of justifying non-depreciation (or depreciating over a life in excess of 50 years), it may only be necessary to update that review in succeeding years. The standard adds that 'if there have been no adverse changes in the key assumptions and variables, or if the estimated recoverable amount was previously substantially in excess of the carrying amount, it may even be possible to ascertain immediately that the asset or income-generating unit is not impaired'.

14.215 **_Year of change._** Not providing depreciation on grounds of immateriality is strictly not an accounting policy, but an accounting estimate. Consequently, in a period when depreciation becomes material (unless it is covered by the transitional provisions explained in **14.301** below) any depreciation should start to be charged to the profit and loss account, spread over the remaining useful economic life. Similarly, in a period when depreciation becomes immaterial, there should be no adjustment to past depreciation charged to the profit and loss account.

Non-depreciation – the meaning of immaterial

14.216 The ASB also clarifies what in this context is meant by immaterial. First, the annual charge and the amount of accumulated depreciation must both be immaterial. [FRS 15(90)] Second, they are only immaterial if they would not reasonably influence the decisions of a user of accounts. Three sets of circumstances are used to illustrate conditions giving rise to immateriality. They are:

[per FRS 15(91)]

(a) a policy and practice of maintenance such that the asset is kept to its previously assessed standard of performance;

(b) no likelihood of suffering from economic or technological obsolescence;

(c) where estimated residual values are material, the entity has a policy and practice of disposal of similar assets well before the end of their economic life and disposal proceeds (excluding the effects of price change) have not been less than carrying amounts.

However, FRS 15 does not appear to suggest that these are the only circumstances under which it is possible to claim immateriality.

14.217 **Materiality judged on annual charge and accumulated balance.** FRS 15 stresses that immateriality must apply both to the annual charge and to the accumulated balance of depreciation. The accumulated balance is clearly a factor when the asset is being carried at cost, because it must be shown on the balance sheet. The same does not necessarily apply in the case of assets carried at a valuation. In the year of a full or interim revaluation, any asset carried at market value will be restated at that new valuation with any accumulated depreciation disappearing from the balance sheet with the previous gross carrying amount. In years between full or interim valuations, a balance of accumulated depreciation will mount up in principle until the next valuation and it is the materiality of that balance that apparently needs to be assessed. Assets revalued at depreciated replacement cost may be shown at gross replacement cost with cumulative depreciation calculated on a replacement cost basis shown separately, and the difference is depreciated replacement cost. However, there is no requirement to show anything but the net figure, i.e., the valuation itself. In that case, exactly the same considerations would apply to a DRC valuation as to a full or interim market value, with no disclosure of an accumulated balance of depreciation, so no question of its materiality could arise.

Assets with remaining lives in excess of 50 years

14.218 It has not been unusual in the past for buildings of various kinds to be assessed as having a useful economic life in excess of 50 years. Possibly this is because, in the UK, there are many examples of buildings already well past 50 and which may well continue for at least another 50 years. However, the ASB has decided that such buildings should be subject to the FRS 11 annual impairment test, whether depreciated or not. Whether it is decided to invoke the immateriality clause described in **14.213** above or to opt for annual depreciation, if a remaining useful economic life of more than 50 years is ascribed to any asset, it (or the income generating unit of which it is a part, if necessary) must be fully tested for impairment every year.

14.219 | **Limiting life to 50 years when it may be longer.** What is not perfectly clear is whether there is a right to choose to select a useful economic life of 50 years or less, and so avoid the annual impairment test, in spite of convincing evidence that the asset's life will in fact exceed that. It seems unlikely that such a decision would be challenged and indeed may well be in line with the ASB's intentions. It is unlikely that the difference between one-fiftieth and (say) one-sixtieth (or even one-hundredth) of the carrying amount of the relevant asset(s) will be material in context. There may, therefore, be a strong case for avoiding the over-50 year category where it is intended to charge depreciation anyway.

Renewals ('infrastructure') accounting

14.220 One of the less commonly claimed justifications for making a nil charge for depreciation has been very specific to a limited number of industries, the water industry in particular. The water industry uses an approach known as 'renewals accounting', applied to its infrastructure of (mainly) underground assets. That industry can probably claim to be unique in certain crucial respects which led to the adoption of this approach in the first place, but companies in other industries, mainly other privatised utilities such as railways, have also adopted it.

14.221 Renewals accounting involves charging to the profit and loss account, in respect of a system or network of infrastructure assets, a figure representing the assessed level of annual expenditure necessary to maintain the operating capacity of the infrastructure network. The actual expenditure incurred each year to maintain the asset is capitalised. The network or system is thus treated as a single infrastructure asset, and not as a collection of separate parts. [FRS 15 (98)–(99)]

14.222 FRS 15(97) makes it clear that renewals accounting does not apply to definable major assets or components of an infrastructure system or network which have determinable finite lives. These must be separated out and depreciated conventionally in accordance with the other provisions of FRS 15.

14.223 It goes on to indicate that the renewals method does not constitute (as it has commonly been represented) a justification for not charging depreciation. Instead, it is an alternative method for estimating the amount of depreciation that should be charged.

14.224 The standard offers the following circumstances as those in which renewals accounting may be used in this:

(a) the infrastructure asset is a system or network that as a whole is intended to be maintained at a specified level of service potential by the continuing replacement and refurbishment of its components; and

(b) the level of annual expenditure required to maintain the operating capacity (or service capability) of the infrastructure asset is calculated from an asset management plan that is certified by a person who is appropriately qualified and independent; and

(c) the system or network is in a mature or steady state (see **14.225** below).

[FRS 15(97)]

14.225 **Mature or steady state.** The standard does not discuss what constitutes 'a mature or steady state'. Evidence for that state should logically take the form of both recent past and forecast future levels of annual expenditure being 'steady', i.e., not varying substantially from year to year, except as accounted for by inflation, or varying only in proportion to changes in the scale of the infrastructure system being maintained.

14.226 **Water industry.** The water industry has two claims to justify adopting renewals accounting. One is the unique nature of water – no other industry can be so certain that its product will remain in demand indefinitely. The other is the age, underground location and historically poor recording of its pipeline etc. assets, such that any approach to determining elapsed age and likely remaining useful life on an asset by asset basis was impracticable – they cannot be seen most of the time and are only dug up when they go wrong. Therefore, any practicable approach to measuring depreciation has to be a relatively broad-brush and theoretical construct. This is important to note because it follows that almost every other industry can probably derive better estimates of depreciation from a less broad-brush, more asset-specific analysis.

Depreciation of revalued assets

14.227 Three scenarios are explored in this section. These focus on how to calculate depreciation when, on revaluation:

(a) the asset has not previously been revalued (i.e., going from historical net book value to a valuation) (see **14.228** to **14.232** below);

(b) the asset has been carried at an existing valuation and this has not been altered in the year (e.g., when a review has occurred in the year and no material change in value has been identified) (see **14.233** below); and

(c) the asset has been carried at an existing valuation and this has been updated in the year (e.g., following an interim or full valuation) (see **14.234** to **14.235** below).

Restatement of comparative figures is discussed in **14.258** below. Adjustments to accumulated depreciation on revaluation are discussed in **14.256** below.

First time revaluation (historical cost to valuation)

14.228 All entities with depreciating assets adopt specific depreciation policies, using either opening, average or closing balances as the base for calculation. FRS 15(79) states that 'where an asset has been revalued the current period's depreciation charge is based on the revalued amount and the remaining useful economic life'.

14.229 FRS 15 does **not** explain how the depreciation should be calculated when an entity decides to revalue for the first time, i.e., where the opening balance is historic cost, but the closing balance is a valuation.

14.230

In the year a revaluation policy is adopted for the first time, the depreciation should be based on the revalued amount, not on the opening historical cost amount. As no valuation will be available for the beginning of the year, the closing value is used to determine an appropriate future annual charge, based on the remaining useful life, and that figure is interpolated as the current year charge.

> ### *Example 14.230: Depreciation charge where asset is revalued for the first time*
>
> A company with a year ended 31 March 2000 has tangible fixed assets with a brought forward net book value of £80,000. The asset cost £100,000 on 1 April 1997 and had a useful economic life (UEL) of 10 years. The annual depreciation charge for years ending 31 March 1998 and 31 March 1999 was £10,000.
>
> The company decides to revalue all of its assets and the qualified valuer provides a figure, as at 31 March 2000, of £120,000. UEL remains as originally estimated.

Depreciation calculations

Value at year end   £120,000 with 7 years' life left

Extrapolated value, start of year   £120,000 x 8/7 = £137,143

Depreciation charge for year to 31/3/2000   £137,143 ÷ 8 = £17,143

From 1 April 2000, the £120,000 will be written off over the remaining seven years at the rate of £17,143 a year, subject to any adjustments to the valuation in the future.

The entries to record the revaluation are explained in **14.255** to **14.257** below.

14.231 The calculation in Example **14.230** above of depreciation is irrespective of the entity's general accounting policy. If the entity charges depreciation on either the opening (historic cost) or average (of cost and value) balance, then this will not meet FRS 15's requirement that 'where an asset has been revalued the current period's depreciation charge is based on the revalued amount'.

14.232 **Management accounts.** In practice, most entities calculate depreciation for management accounts on a weekly, monthly or quarterly basis. If this has been done, and the management accounts are used as a basis for the financial statements, the depreciation charge will need to be adjusted to ensure the depreciation charge is based on the revalued year end balance (i.e., using the simple example in **14.230** above, the depreciation charge in the management accounts would be £10,000 (using historic cost) and must be adjusted up to £17,143 for the financial statements).

Revaluation policy but no movement in the period

14.233 The following example focuses on the effect on depreciation when the value of an asset, which has been carried at an existing valuation, is not altered in the year (e.g., when a valuation review has occurred in the year and no material change in value has been identified). The depreciation charge for the year should be calculated using the company's existing depreciation policy. FRS 15 recommends that this policy uses 'average values' but recognises that, in practice, as long it is consistently applied, either the opening or closing valuation balance may be used. Where there has been no change to the carrying valuation, there will be no difference between the depreciation charge under these alternative methods.

> ### Example 14.233: Depreciation of static revalued asset using different accounting policies
>
> An entity with a year end of 31 March 2000, on adoption of FRS 15, continues revaluing all of its office buildings. A valuation was performed at 31 March 1999 which meets the requirements of a full valuation per FRS 15. A review was carried out at 31 March 2000 which did not identify any material changes in value.
>
> The value brought forward was £2 million with an estimated remaining UEL, at that time, of 40 years.
>
> | | |
> |---|---|
> | Opening value | £2m |
> | Closing value | £2m |
> | Average value | £2m |
> | Depreciation on all bases | £2m ÷ 40 = £50,000 per annum. |
>
> The entries to record the revaluation are explained in **14.255** to **14.257** below.

Revaluation policy with movement in the period

14.234 The example in **14.235** below focuses on the effect on depreciation of different policies when the value of an asset, which has been carried at an existing valuation, is updated in the year (e.g., following an interim or full valuation). Ideally, the depreciation policy should be based on 'average values' but FRS 15 recognises that, in practice, as long it is consistently applied, either the opening or closing valuation balance may be used.

14.235

> **Opening balance.** In practice, it is likely that the opening balance will be used. This figure would have been used in management accounts and, provided there is no material difference, update to average value is unlikely to be made.

> ### Example 14.235: Depreciation of moving revalued asset using different accounting policies
>
> A company with a year end of 31 March 2000, on adoption of FRS 15, continues revaluing all of its office buildings. A full valuation was performed in the year as the previous valuation at 31 March 1999 did not qualify as a full valuation under FRS 15 and therefore a full valuation has been performed at 31 March 2000.
>
> Opening valuation balance was £2 million (no accumulated depreciation) with a useful economic life (UEL), at that time, of 40 years. The year end revaluation showed a value at 31 March 2000 of £2.6 million with 39 years remaining UEL.

Opening value	£2m
Closing value	£2.6m
Average value	£2.3m.

Depreciation on alternative basis (based on 1/40th):

Opening value	£50,000
Closing value	£65,000
Average value	£57,500

The entries to record the revaluation are explained in **14.255** to **14.257** below.

Summary of effect that different depreciation policies have on revaluations

14.236 The following summarises the effect different depreciation policies have on revaluations.

(a) Entities are required to adopt depreciation policies which reflect, as fairly as possible, the pattern in which the asset's economic benefits are consumed.

(b) When an entity revalues a depreciating asset for the first time, charging depreciation on opening or average balance will not meet FRS 15's requirement to charge depreciation based on the revalued amount. Therefore, in these situations, although the entity's policy is to charge depreciation based on opening or average balances, an exception must be made in the year the revaluation first takes place.

(c) When an entity revalues a previously revalued asset, the amount of charge to the profit and loss account can vary depending on the policy adopted by the entity. In this specific situation it seems practical, given that entities normally only perform a revaluation exercise for the period end financial statements, to include a depreciation charge on the opening balance method.

Given the above, the **most practical** depreciation policy for entities with revalued assets is as follows.

First year of revaluation	Depreciation is based on the period end revalued amount 'backdated' to the opening date. Depreciation based on historical cost opening balance will not meet the requirements of FRS 15.
Future years	Ideally, depreciation is based on the average value. In practice, depreciation based on an opening value is acceptable provided it is applied consistently.

Provision for permanent diminution in value

Determining the amount of a provision

14.237 The Companies Act requires that a provision for diminution in value shall be made in respect of any fixed asset if the reduction in its value is expected to be permanent. [Sch 4: 19(2) and (3)] The interpretation of the meaning of 'permanent' in this context has been a long-standing contentious issue, but this has now been resolved by FRS 11 *Impairment of fixed assets and goodwill.* Most fixed assets fall within the scope of that standard, so the determination and treatment of all kinds of impairment diminutions fall within the scope of that standard (see **14.240** below).

14.238 A limited number of types of fixed asset falls outside the scope of FRS 11, so there is therefore still a formal need to interpret the meaning of the words of Schedule 4 para 19(2) and (3) in respect of those types of asset, that is:

(a)   fixed assets within the scope of FRS 13 *Derivatives and other financial instruments*;

(b)   investment properties;

(c)   an entity's own shares held by an ESOP and required by UITF Abstract 13 to be included on the entity's balance sheet; and

(d)   costs capitalised pending determination, under the SORP *Accounting for oil and gas exploration and development activities.*

14.239   The process laid down by FRS 11 for determining the existence and extent of an impairment is a logical one and not limited in principle to those assets captured within the scope of FRS 15. In assessing whether or not any diminution is permanent within the meaning of the Act, it is appropriate that the FRS 11 process (involving determining whether carrying value is higher or lower than recoverable amount) should be used (see **14.240** below). The same principle applies in respect of decisions as to whether impairment losses should pass to the profit and loss account or the statement of total recognised gains and losses, and when and to what extent reversals of impairments are to be recognised; FRS 11's requirements should be regarded as the best available guidance (see **14.240** et seq. below).

Impairment of fixed assets and goodwill

14.240 FRS 11 *Impairment of fixed assets and goodwill,* applies to all true and fair financial statements for accounting periods ending on or after 23 December 1998.

14.241 FRS 11 applies to purchased goodwill recognised in the balance sheet and to all fixed assets except for:

(a) fixed assets within the scope of FRS 13 *Derivatives and other financial instruments*;

(b) investment properties;

(c) an entity's own shares held by an ESOP and required by UITF Abstract 13 to be included on the entity's balance sheet; and

(d) costs capitalised pending determination, under the SORP *Accounting for oil and gas exploration and development activities.*

It does not apply to entities applying the original FRSSE, except to the extent that they are preparing consolidated accounts. The revised (effective March 1999 and subsequent versions) FRSSE (see **34.65**) incorporates only the key principle that assets held at above recoverable amount should be written down to recoverable amount, and also the conditions for recognising the reversal of a write-down (see **14.284** below).

14.242 Accounting for impairment of tangible fixed assets has been based since 1981 on the Companies Act's sections relating to provision for impairment. [Sch 4: 19(2) and 32(2) and (3)] These make it mandatory to provide for permanent diminution in value, so debate has until now focused on the meaning of 'permanent'. However, FRS 11 has introduced a more rigorous process for measuring and recognising impairment to the carrying value of fixed assets and purchased goodwill. It removes any uncertainty inherent in the Act's emphasis on the distinction between permanent and temporary diminutions in value, by introducing a process for determining whether or not a diminution is permanent. It requires the determination of a 'recoverable amount' and then requires that the carrying value shall never exceed that amount.

14.243 Impairment is measured by comparing the carrying amount of a fixed asset or of an income-generating unit with the higher of its net realisable value and its value in use. Value in use is to be calculated by discounting the expected future cash flows, using a discount rate based on an estimate of the rate that the market would expect on an equally risky investment. (See Appendix X 'Testing for impairment' for the standard's guidance on how to determine the income generating units whose future cash flows are the basis for arriving at value in use.)

14.244 The objective of FRS 11 is to ensure that:

(a) fixed assets and goodwill are recorded in the financial statements at no more than their recoverable amount;

(b)   any resulting impairment loss is measured and recognised on a consistent basis; and

(c)   sufficient information is disclosed to enable users to understand the impact of the impairment.

The basis of the impairment standard

14.245   FRS 11 requires that a review for impairment be carried out if events or changes in circumstances indicate that the carrying amount of a fixed asset or goodwill may not be recoverable. [FRS 11(8)] However, in the case of goodwill or intangible assets amortised over longer than 20 years from date of acquisition, or not amortised at all, such an impairment review must be carried out every year. [FRS 10(37)] In each case, that review will compare carrying amount with the higher of net realisable value (if known) and value in use, and write down any shortfall.

Indicators of impairment

14.246   FRS 11 gives examples of what it means by 'events and changes in circumstance that indicate an impairment may have occurred', evidence of which would trigger the need to carry out a full impairment review if they are relevant to the measurement of goodwill or assets. They include:

(a)   a current period operating loss in the business in which the fixed asset or goodwill is involved or net cash outflow from the operating activities of that business, combined with either past operating losses or net cash outflows from such operating activities or an expectation of continuing operating losses or net cash outflows from such operating activities;

(b)   a significant decline in a fixed asset's market value during the period;

(c)   evidence of obsolescence or physical damage to the fixed asset;

(d)   a significant adverse change in:

 –   either the business or the market in which the fixed asset or goodwill is involved, such as the entrance of a major competitor;
 –   the statutory or other regulatory environment in which the business operates;
 –   any 'indicator of value' (e.g., turnover) used to measure the fair value of a fixed asset on acquisition;

(e)   a commitment by management to undertake a significant reorganisation;

(f)   a major loss of key employees;

(g)   a significant increase in market interest rates or other market rates of return that are likely to affect materially the fixed asset's recoverable amount.

Net realisable value

14.247 The process of carrying out an impairment review that involves the determination of value in use is dealt with separately in Appendix X 'Testing for impairment' and Appendix XI 'Weighted average cost of capital'. However, a prior step in checking for impairment would be to determine whether or not the asset has a net realisable value because, where such a value exists, it is simpler to arrive at than value in use. Net realisable value is defined in FRS 11 as the amount at which an asset could be disposed of, less any direct selling costs (a market value, if it is traded on an active market). FRS 11 explains that direct selling costs will include legal costs and stamp duty, and also costs relating to the removal of a sitting tenant. However, it adds that costs associated with reorganising the business rather than selling the fixed asset (such as redundancy costs on sale of a factory) are not to be classed as direct selling costs. [FRS 11(23)]

Subsequent review of recoverable amount based on value in use

14.248 There is an ongoing annual requirement for companies that have carried out an impairment review which has resulted in retaining the existing carrying value, if the justification for retention was dependent upon a recoverable amount based on value in use. In each of the five succeeding years after that impairment review, the cash flows achieved should be compared with those used in the forecasts on which the value in use has been based. If the actual cash flows are so much less than those forecast that they would have resulted in an impairment at the time of the original review, that review should be reperformed (but changing none of the other assumptions on which the original forecast was based) and any impairment now so determined should be charged to the current period. [FRS 11(54)]

14.249 The standard recognises that this review in one of the following five years may reveal both that an impairment should have been recognised originally, based on better forecasts, and that it no longer needs to be recognised because a current calculation of value in use, based on changed circumstances, shows that that impairment has reversed. In this situation, no impairment should be recognised, but both the impairment and its reversal should be disclosed. [FRS 11(54)]

14.250   Paragraph 54 of FRS 11 is an ASB anti-avoidance device. Entities may seek to avoid recognising an impairment by, to put it brutally, fiddling their cash flow forecasts. The ASB wants to deter entities from taking this course by requiring a process of self-audit, whereby the entity checks forecast against actual and recognises any adverse consequences. The wording of FRS 15 does not make it absolutely clear that the same five-year checking process is required when an impairment based on value in use has actually been recognised, but clearly the ASB would be similarly concerned if an entity were to massage its cash flow forecasts so as to minimise the size of the impairment recognised. For this reason, together with the requirements in both FRS 15 and the Companies Act to recognise immediately any reversal of a provision for impairment, it is advisable to carry out this review comparison for the five years following any impairment review the result of which depended upon a value in use calculation.

Reporting gains and losses

Introduction

14.251 Impairment losses, measured in accordance with FRS 11, are discussed in **14.240** to **14.250** above. FRS 15 deals with the other two kinds of gains and losses an entity can make in relation to tangible fixed assets:

(a) gains/losses on the revaluation of assets using the alternative accounting rules as permitted by the Companies Act; and/or

(b) profits/losses made on the ultimate disposal of the asset.

In summary, gains and losses on changes in carrying value are allocated between the Statement of Recognised Gains and Losses (STRGL) and the Profit and Loss account (P&L) as follows:

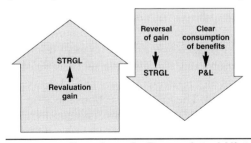

Benchmark: Depreciated Historical Cost

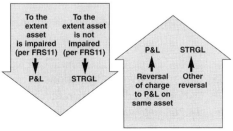

Companies Act 1985 requirements

14.252 Before implementation of FRS 15, an entity could choose to revalue any tangible fixed asset under the alternative accounting rules included in the Companies Act 1985. Requirements for treatment of gains and losses was provided in two ways:

(a) instructions on the creation and use of a revaluation reserve; and

(b) replacement of cost with revalued amount as the starting point for applying the depreciation rules.

14.253 The revaluation reserve holds accumulated gains (or losses) when a valuation based on the alternative valuation rules are included in the financial statements. A gain is recognised when the revalued amount exceeded the existing net book value (and a loss vice versa). The reserve is required to be disclosed on the balance sheet just below 'Share premium account' per Companies Act formats and is included in the reserves note (as required by legislation and FRS 3). The revaluation reserve is not required to be called by that name.

14.254 Application of the depreciation rules could result in two types of write down:

(a) a permanent diminution in value, which is charged to the profit and loss account; and

(b) a temporary diminution in value, which is charged to the revaluation reserve (even if it resulted in a debit balance on the reserve).

In practice the distinction between permanent and temporary gave rise to inconsistent judgements. However, this has now been resolved through the issue of FRS 11 *Impairment of fixed assets and goodwill*. For the purpose of compliance with the Companies Act, an impairment under FRS 11 is taken to mean a permanent diminution, and a reduction in carrying value (for example, as a matter of accounting policy) which is not an impairment under FRS 11 is taken to mean a temporary diminution. The following sections focus on how FRS 15 accounts for gains and losses arising on revaluations, and also discusses how the revaluation reserve should be treated and when it becomes distributable.

Revaluation gains

Basics

14.255 The majority of revaluations performed produce gains, i.e., the valuation exceeds the current carrying value. With the exception of **14.262** below, all revaluation gains are reported in the Statement of

Total Recognised Gains and Losses (STRGL). Since this treatment is specifically required by Companies Act 1985 Schedule 4: 34(1), it meets the requirement of FRS 3 to be included in the STRGL.

The amount of the revaluation gain will be:

Revalued amount of asset	x
Less: Net book value of revalued asset	(x)

The balance sheet note analysing fixed assets will describe the class of revalued assets as being at valuation.

Example 14.255: Revaluation of a non-depreciable asset

A company has a property which cost £50m in August 1997. No depreciation has been charged as it is immaterial given the extended life of the property. In the year ended 31 March 2000, the company decides to revalue the asset. A full valuation is performed resulting in a value of £75m. The gain of £25m is recorded in reserves and shown as a gain in the STRGL for the year ended 31 March 2000.

Double entry is as follows:

Dr	Cost of asset (renamed 'Valuation')	£25m
Cr	Revaluation reserve (reported in STRGL)	£25m

Revaluation of depreciable assets

Assets at a market value

14.256 **Removal of accumulated depreciation**. A valuation establishes a single carrying value for an asset at the date of valuation (but note **14.257** below). It follows that any accumulated depreciation carried prior to the revaluation will be removed from the balance sheet. Where depreciation continues to be charged, it will again be removed at the date of the next valuation. Since FRS 15 requires revalued assets to be carried at current value, accumulated depreciation will always be zero in subsequent balance sheets. Note, however, that an interim review carried out in years 1, 2 and 4 does not necessarily amount to a valuation, and therefore accumulated depreciation will not normally be removed.

Example 14.256: Revaluation of a depreciable asset

A company has a single property which cost £50m on 1 January 1997, and is assessed to have a 50 year life. At 31 December 1999, the balance sheet disclosed the asset at cost with accumulated depreciation of £3m. During 2000 the company applied FRS 15, deciding to revalue this asset. Valuations were as follows:

31 December 2000 (external valuation)	£55m
31 December 2001	Review – no incidence of change
31 December 2002 (interim valuation)	£58m

There is no change to estimated useful economic life.

Depreciation for 2000

Calculation (based on the revalued amount at 31/12/2000)

	£55m x 1/46	£1.2m

Double entry:

Dr	P&L account	£1.2m
Cr	Accumulated depreciation	£1.2m

Revaluation at 31 December 2000

Calculation:

Revalued amount	£55.0m
Net book value (£50m – £4.2m)	£45.8m
Revaluation surplus	£9.2m

Double entry:

Dr	Asset cost (renamed 'Valuation')	£5.0m
Dr	Accumulated depreciation (£3m + £1.2m)	£4.2m
Cr	Revaluation reserve	£9.2m

Depreciation for 2001

Dr	P&L (£55m x 1/46)	£1.2m
Cr	Accumulated depreciation	£1.2m

Depreciation for 2002

Dr	P&L (£55m x 1/46)	£1.2m
Cr	Accumulated depreciation	£1.2m

Revaluation at 31 December 2002

Dr	Asset valuation	£3.0m
Dr	Accumulated depreciation	£2.4m
Cr	Revaluation reserve	£5.4m

Assets at depreciated replacement cost (DRC)

14.257 **Separate figures for cost and depreciation.** To be consistent with other valuation bases, a DRC basis will normally be recorded as a single net amount. Nevertheless, since a DRC basis of valuation produces a gross replacement cost which is equivalent to the cost at which an asset would be purchased new, and a notional amount of accumulated depreciation which reflects the consumption of the actual asset being valued compared to a new asset, it would be acceptable (but not essential) to maintain and adjust both cost and accumulated depreciation within the balance sheet analysis of fixed assets.

Restatement of comparatives following a revaluation

14.258   **Cost to valuation basis.** FRS 15 appears to perpetuate the view
that use of cost or valuation is an accounting policy (and this
will be confirmed if FRED 21 (see chapter 5 above) is ratified
in due course). If this is the case, then restatement of comparatives following a change from cost basis to valuation basis
would be appropriate. Such a restatement would have the following implications:

(a)   assets in comparative balance sheets would be restated to
values current at those balance sheet dates;

(b)   depreciation would be recalculated using estimates of
residual value and useful economic life which would have
been used at those balance sheet dates.

14.259   There are practical constraints in producing appropriate comparable data, particularly the absence of a valuation at the
comparative balance sheet date. Even were it thought to be
cost-effective to have a backdated valuation carried out, it is in
fact virtually impossible to make the same valuation judgements that would have been made at that time, untainted by
hindsight. For this reason, valuers are reluctant to provide such
figures.

14.260   In practice, both restatement (if information is available) and
non-restatement options would seem acceptable.

14.261   **Valuation to cost basis.** In the alternative situation of an entity
changing from a valuation policy back to historical cost, there
are few practical problems of producing comparable information based on cost. Consequently, restatement of comparative
figures is recommended.

Gain which reverses a previously recognised loss

14.262   The exception to the rule that all revaluation gains are taken to the
revaluation reserve and disclosed in the STRGL occurs where a gain
represents the reversal of a loss which has, in a previous period, been
charged as an expense in the profit and loss account. The amount of
gain that can be recognised in the current year is adjusted for any
extra depreciation that **would have been charged** to the profit and
loss account if the loss had not been recognised in the first place. (For
a discussion of the circumstances in which FRS 11 allows such a gain
to be recognised, see **14.284** below.)

Reversal of a previously recognised loss – new valuation exceeds cost

14.263 There may be occasions where an increase in an asset value exceeds the equivalent depreciated historical cost (DHC) amount.

New valuation   >   DHC   >   Carrying value

The depreciation that would have been charged to the profit and loss account in the event that the original loss had not been accounted for will be higher than the amount that has actually been charged. Therefore, an adjustment will be needed to the gain recognised in the profit and loss account this year.

> **Example 14.263: Reversal of a loss with an adjustment to depreciation**
>
> N.B. The general rule in **14.266** below should be understood prior to reading this example.
>
> A company has previously recorded revaluation gains on its assets. In the profit and loss account to 30 June 1997, it recognised a revaluation loss of £35,000, being the fall below depreciated historical cost to current valuation.
>
> Relevant information is:
>
> (a) depreciation would have been £10,000 per annum based on the historic cost;
>
> (b) actual depreciation charged in years to 30 June 1998 and 30 June 1999 was £7,000;
>
> (c) in the year to 30 June 2000, the value of the asset increased (above depreciated historical cost) and the full amount of the loss recorded in 1997 can be reversed.
>
> The amount of the loss charged to the profit and loss account in 1997 that can be credited in 2000 is as follows:
>
> | Depreciation charge if loss had not been recognised in 1997 | | Depreciation charge that has actually been charged | | Difference in depreciation | |
> |---|---|---|---|---|---|
> | 1998 | £10,000 | 1998 | £7,000 | 1998 | £3,000 |
> | 1999 | £10,000 | 1999 | £7,000 | 1999 | £3,000 |
> | 2000 | £10,000 | 2000 | £10,000 | | |
> | **Total** | **£30,000** | **Total** | **£24,000** | **Total** | **£6,000** |
>
> The profit and loss account (in 1998 and 1999) has been undercharged by a total of £6,000 due to the loss being recorded in the profit and loss account in 1997. Therefore, the gain arising on the reversal of the loss in 1997 of £35,000 must be reduced by £6,000 in order to achieve the same overall effect in the profit and loss account

that would have been reached had the original downward revaluation reflected in the profit and loss account not occurred.

The result is that £29,000 is credited to the profit and loss account in the year to 30 June 2000. This can be reconciled as follows.

Amount *that should have been* charged in the profit and loss account:		Amount *actually* charged in the profit and loss account:	
Depreciation to 2000	£30,000	Loss in 1997	£35,000
		Depreciation to 2000	£24,000
		Gain in 2000	(£29,000)
Total	**£30,000**	**Total**	**£30,000**

Reversal of a previously recognised loss – new valuation less than cost

14.264 There may be occasions where an increase in an asset value does not exceed the equivalent depreciated historical cost (DHC) amount:

DHC   >   New valuation   >   Carrying value

In these situations, the gain that will be taken to the profit and loss account this year will be the difference between the current carrying amount and the new valuation. No adjustment needs to be made for any depreciation as this has effectively been done by comparing the two balances.

Revaluation losses

14.265 Where an entity has a policy for revaluing all assets in a class, there may be a time when one (or more) assets will fall in value below the current carrying amount. These losses must be recognised in the performance statements in the year of the loss. Losses cannot be netted off any gains arising on other assets in the same, or another, class as FRS 15 specifically states that 'material gains and losses on individual assets in a class of asset should not be aggregated'. [FRS 15(67)]

General rule

14.266 Where an entity suffers a fall in value in an asset, an attempt should be made to establish the reason for the fall. It will be due to:

(a)   an impairment in the asset (through consumption of economic benefits or other reduction in recoverable amount); and/or

(b)   a general fall in market prices.

14.267 FRS 15(68) and (69) recognises that, in some cases, it will be hard to distinguish a loss between that relating to an impairment and that relating to a fall in general prices. If it is 'obvious' that there has been a consumption of benefits, then the asset has been impaired, and the loss should be recognised in the profit and loss account. If this is not the case, then it is assumed that:

(a) the fall in value from the asset's previous carrying amount to depreciated historical cost is due to a general fall in prices (which is recognised in the statement of total recognised gains and losses, as a valuation adjustment); and

(b) the fall in value from depreciated historical cost to the revalued amount is due to a consumption of economic benefits (and therefore recognised in the profit and loss account).

This general rule can be expressed diagrammatically as follows.

Carrying value

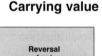
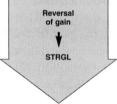

Depreciated Historical Cost

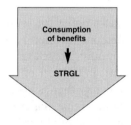

Exceptions to general rule

Clear consumption of benefits

14.268 'All revaluation losses that are caused by a clear consumption of economic benefits should be recognised in the profit and loss account.' [FRS 15(65)]

If there has been a clear indication that there has been a consumption of economic benefits in the year, then the fall in value should be recognised in the profit and loss account. This is done in order to ensure the cost is charged (to the period in which the irreversible loss occurred) as an operating cost similar to depreciation. Some examples of when to recognise a consumption of economic benefits are given in FRS 15(68). These are when there has been:

(a)   any physical damage to the asset; or

(b)   any deterioration in the quality of the service that it can provide.

14.269   FRS 11 also requires that, in the case of impairment of revalued assets, a judgement shall be made as to the nature of the cause of the impairment. It uses the same criteria as FRS 15, asking the entity to decide whether the impairment is, in reality, accelerated depreciation (e.g., physical damage to the asset or some other deterioration in the quality of service that it can provide) in which case it should be charged to the profit and loss account, or whether it arises from more general causes such as a general fall in prices. Both standards use the phrase 'caused by a clear consumption of economic benefit', which appears to indicate that the loss should pass to the STRGL unless it is clear that a consumption of economic benefits can be identified, i.e., if in doubt, charge to the STRGL. Both standards also indicate that a loss may be caused partly by consumption of benefits and partly by general price change; in which case, an appropriate apportionment between profit and loss account and STRGL will be required. [FRS 11(63) to (65) and FRS 15(65) to (69)]

Recoverable amount exceeds valuation

14.270   FRS 15(65) states:

'... Other revaluation losses should be recognised:

(a)   in the statement of total recognised gains and losses until the carrying amount reaches its depreciated historical cost; and

(b)   thereafter, in the profit and loss account unless it can be demonstrated that the recoverable amount of the asset is greater than its revalued amount, in which case the loss should be recognised in the statement of total recognised gains and losses to the extent that the recoverable amount of the asset is greater than its revalued amount.'

Recoverable amount is as defined in FRS 11 *Impairment of fixed assets and goodwill* para 2, 'The higher of net realisable value and value in use'.

14.271 Focusing on FRS 15 (65b), if the asset is worth more to an entity by keeping it and using it in its business (i.e., value in use), than if it sold the asset on the open market, then the difference between the value in use and the new (lower) valuation should **not** be charged to the profit and loss account as it is clearly not an impairment. Instead, it should be charged to the revaluation reserve and recognised in the STRGL as a valuation adjustment.

14.272 This situation only arises because FRS 15 lays down an inflexible rule about the basis on which an entity is allowed to revalue each asset. In the case, for example, of a non-specialised property, existing use market value must be used. Most such properties have a higher inherent value to the business to which they are used than their market value – or it would be more economical and more logical to sell them than to use them. (In technical terms, their recoverable amount will be based on value in use, which will be higher than their market value.) So, if an entity is carrying an asset at a valuation and its market value falls, this fact must be reflected in the balance sheet even if it has no economic significance to the entity, i.e., even if the entity has suffered no real loss because its value in use has not been impaired. It is for this reason that no charge should be made to the profit and loss account for such a fall. Where market value has fallen below value in use, the difference is charged, not to the profit and loss account, but to the STRGL.

This exception can be expressed diagrammatically as follows:

Carrying value

Reversal
of gain

↓

STRGL

benchmark: Depreciated Historical Cost

Impairment
(per FRS11)

↓

P&L

Recoverable amount

No impairment
- valuation reduced for
accounting policy

↓

STRGL

Valuation

Example 14.272: Loss where recoverable amount exceeds valuation

A company has a policy of revaluing factory buildings. The brought forward carrying value was £1 million with a historical cost of £925,000. Depreciation is immaterial as the life of the buildings exceeds 50 years.

For the year ended 31 March 2000, due to the current market conditions, the valuation figure based on 'existing use value' (for non-specialised properties) was £750,000. This is the amount that is recorded in the balance sheet.

However, an exercise was carried out to split the factory into 'income generating units', as detailed in FRS 11 in order to calculate 'value-in-use'. This meant estimating the future cash flows and discounting them using an appropriate discount rate. The 'value-in-use' was estimated to be £800,000, i.e., the factory is worth more to the company if it keeps carrying out the existing trade than if it were sold for its existing use.

If the 'general rule' in **14.266** above were applied, the fall in value would be recognised as follows:

(a) from the carrying value of £1 million down to historical cost of £925,000, in the revaluation reserve, via the STRGL;

(b) from the historical cost of £925,000 to the valuation of £750,000, in the profit and loss account.

This would mean a charge of £50,000 (the difference between the value-in-use £800,000 and the valuation amount of £750,000) in the profit and loss account, which is expected to be recovered in the future. For the reasons explained above, it would be unfair and over prudent to charge this to the profit and loss account.

Therefore, the loss should be recognised as follows:

Carrying value £1,000,000

 Fall in value of £75,000 should be charged to the STRGL.

Historical cost £925,000

 Fall in value of £125,000 should be charged to the profit and loss account.

Value in use £800,000

 Fall in value of £50,000 should be charged to the STRGL.

Valuation £750,000

Debit balance on revaluation reserve

14.273 It follows from the previous section that it **is** possible to have a debit balance on the revaluation reserve. This will result where although there has been no impairment, a company's valuation policy results in an asset being carried at an amount below its recoverable amount. This situation occurred with a number of banks in the early 1990s when market values of high street banking premises fell, but the business carried on within the properties (and hence recoverable amount) was maintained.

Example 14.273: Debit balance on revaluation reserve

A company runs a caravan park and owns land which cost £100,000 10 years ago. It was revalued to £250,000 in the year ended 31 December 1998 with the gain of £150,000 being credited to the revaluation reserve. In the year ended 31 December 1998, the council granted permission for a nuclear power station to be built on the neighbouring land. The market value of the land plummeted to £70,000 although, given that the site was not going to be developed for six years, the value in use was estimated at £80,000.

Balances are as follows:

Carrying value	£250,000
Historic cost	£100,000
Value in use	£80,000
Current valuation	£70,000

The fall in value of £180,000 will be allocated as follows:

(a) £150,000 (£250,000 – £100,000) will be debited to the revaluation reserve, which removes the current balance;

(b) £20,000 (£100,000 – £80,000) will be charged to the profit and loss account showing the 'impairment in value', given that the value in use exceeds the valuation; and

(c) the remaining £10,000 (£80,000 – £70,000) will be debited to the revaluation reserve.

This then leaves a £10,000 debit balance on the reserve which will be transferred to the profit and loss reserve over the remaining life of the asset and disclosed each year in the historical cost profit and loss note.

Miscellaneous points on revaluation gains and losses

Transfers between revaluation reserve and profit and loss reserve

14.274 The Companies Act provides that an amount 'may be transferred from the revaluation reserve ... to the profit and loss account, if the amount was previously charged to that account or represents realised profit'. The Companies Act refers to the profit and loss 'account' and this has been interpreted to mean the 'reserve' not the detailed annual profit and loss account.

14.275 Two types of transfers normally take place:

(a) Annually, the transfer of the excess depreciation that has been charged in the profit and loss annual account which relates to the revalued portion of the asset.

> **Example 14.275.1: Annual transfer of realised revaluation surplus**
>
> Pre-revaluation, annual depreciation charge was £10,000. Post-revaluation, annual depreciation charge is £15,000. The difference of £5,000 should be transferred from the revaluation reserve to the profit and loss reserve annually to realise the part of the revaluation reserve which becomes realised by depreciation being charged to the profit and loss account. This means that only the historical cost depreciation charge impacts on the balance of realised reserves available for distribution.

(b) On disposal of the asset, the balance remaining on the reserve relating to that asset.

> **Example 14.275.2: Realised revaluation surplus on sale**
>
> The balance on the revaluation reserve is £160,000. £50,000 relates to an asset which has been disposed of in the year. A transfer of £50,000 should be made from the revaluation reserve to the profit and loss reserve.

14.276 Any reserve transfer will be disclosed in the reserves note in the year. The above two transfers are bringing the profit and loss reserve to the balance it would have been if no revaluation had happened. Therefore, both transfers will be disclosed in the 'Historical cost profit and loss note' as required by FRS 3.

Netting off revaluation gains and losses

14.277 In determining in which performance statement gains and losses on revaluation should be recognised, material gains and losses on individual assets in a class of asset should not be aggregated.

> **Example 14.277: Netting off gains and losses**
>
> A company has three assets in one class. During the year, all three assets were revalued. Two assets increased in value, and one fell in value. The gains on the two which increased in value can be aggregated and taken to the revaluation reserve as one amount. (Obviously, the amounts of each must be separately noted in order to be able to

545

> make future transfers from the revaluation reserve.) The loss on the asset which has fallen in value will be dealt with according to whether the loss was due to an impairment or through a general fall in market prices.

It is **not** possible to net the loss off with the gains in order to avoid a charge in the profit and loss account.

Insurance companies

14.278 The requirements for reporting gains and losses in FRS 15 do not apply to assets held by insurance companies and insurance groups (including assets of the long-term business), as part of their insurance operations. In these entities, revaluation changes are included in the profit and loss account.

Reporting gains and losses on disposal of tangible fixed assets

14.279 The profit or loss on the disposal of a tangible fixed asset should be accounted for in the profit and loss account of the period in which the disposal occurs as the difference between the net sale proceeds and the carrying amount, whether carried at historical cost (less any provisions made) or at a valuation. Profits or losses on the disposal of fixed assets should be shown in accordance with FRS 3 *Reporting financial performance*.

14.280 Where an asset (or a component of an asset) is **replaced**, its carrying amount is removed from the balance sheet (by eliminating its cost (or revalued amount) and related accumulated depreciation) and the resulting gain or loss on disposal is recorded as normal. If material, as required by FRS 3(20), it should be disclosed as a 'below the line' exceptional item.

14.281 It is expected that the ASB, as part of its review of FRS 3, will re-examine the inclusion of gains and losses on disposal in the profit and loss account. One possible outcome is that a disposal gain could be included with other unrealised revaluation gains as a single grouping of holding gains.

Recognition of impairment losses

14.282 Any impairment loss on an asset carried at (depreciated) historical cost should be recognised in the period's profit and loss account. [FRS 11(14)] (For an impairment loss affecting a revalued asset, see **14.265** et seq. above.)

14.283 An immediate consequence of recognising an impairment loss is that both the remaining useful life and the residual value of the affected asset(s) should be reviewed and, if necessary, revised. The revised carrying amount is then written off over the revised estimate of remaining useful economic life. [FRS 11(21)]

Reversal of past impairments

14.284 In the years that follow recognition of an impairment loss, the relevant goodwill, asset or income-generating unit (see Appendix X 'Testing for impairment') may increase in value. Only in limited circumstances does FRS 11 allow a consequent recognition of a reversal of the impairment loss:

(a) *tangible fixed assets and investments in subsidiaries, associates and joint ventures* – the impairment should be reversed if the increase in value occurs because of a change in economic conditions or a change in the expected use of the asset. If the increase arises merely from mechanical factors affecting the discounted present value, such as the simple passage of time either bringing future inflows closer or overtaking future outflows, such increases are not a reversal of the events or circumstances which led to the impairment in the first place. If they are recognised at all, it will be as, and under the rules affecting, revaluations. [FRS 11(56)] The recognition of a reversal should follow the form of the recognition of the preceding impairment, i.e., to the extent that the original recognition was in the profit and loss account, its reversal should be recognised there too (but note that this does not extend to reversing depreciation charged subsequent to the impairment, as that would constitute a revaluation). Otherwise, recognition will be in the statement of total recognised gains and losses [FRS 11(56) and (66)];

(b) *goodwill and intangible assets* – the impairment should be reversed only if:

(i) an external event caused the previous recognition of the impairment and subsequent external events clearly and demonstrably reverse the effects of that event in a way that was not foreseen in the original impairment calculations; or

(ii) the impairment arose on an intangible fixed asset with a readily ascertainable market value and that market value has increased to above its post-impairment carrying amount [FRS 11(60)].

The reversal of an impairment loss relating to goodwill or an intangible asset should be recognised only to the extent that it restores the carrying amount to the amount at which it would have stood had the original impairment not occurred. [FRS 11(61)]

Disclosure of impairment losses and reversals

14.285 FRS 11 requires that:

(a) impairment losses recognised in the profit and loss account shall be included within operating profit under the appropriate statutory heading, as an exceptional item if appropriate [FRS 11(67)];

(b) impairment losses recognised in the statement of total recognised gains and losses shall be shown as a separate disclosure on the face of that statement [FRS 11(67)];

(c) disclosure of the effect of impairment losses in the notes to the financial statements shall be:

(i) for assets carried at historical cost, inclusion within cumulative depreciation with no reduction of gross cost;

(ii) for revalued assets held at market value, absorption within the revalued carrying amount; and

(iii) for revalued assets held at depreciated replacement cost, treatment will depend upon whether the loss was charged to the profit and loss account or to the statement of total recognised gains and losses; if the former, follow (i) above; if the latter, (ii) [FRS 11(68)];

(d) the discount rate(s) used in any value in use calculation used to determine an impairment loss shall be shown plus, if a risk-free rate is used, some indication of the risk adjustments made to the cash flows [FRS 11(69)];

(e) the reasons shall be given for the reversal of any impairments recognised in previous periods, including any changes in the assumptions upon which calculation of recoverable amount has been based [FRS 11(70)];

(f) both impairment and reversal shall be disclosed where, in the same period, it is recognised that, with more accurate forecasting, an impairment would have been recognised in an earlier period, but that impairment has now reversed (see **14.284** above) [FRS 11(71)]; and

(g) where (exceptionally) cash flow projections incorporate a growth rate which is projected to continue for more than five years before settling down to a steady or declining rate, the notes shall disclose both the length of that longer period and the circumstances justifying it [FRS 11(72)]; and

(h) where (exceptionally) cash flow projections incorporate growth rates in excess of the long-term average for the country concerned and cover more than five years, the notes shall disclose how long, what growth rate is assumed and why [FRS 11(73)].

Transitional rules

14.286 The transitional rules for adopting FRS 11 are relatively straightforward and simple to state. Those for FRS 15, on the other hand, have been bedevilled by unclear drafting and, in consequence, the ASB has issued an interpretation in the form of UITF Abstract 23.

Implementation of FRS 11

14.287 FRS 11 lays down that impairment losses recognised when the standard is implemented for the first time (periods ending on or after 23 December 1998) are not the result of a change in accounting policy and should be recognised in accordance with the requirements of the standard and not as prior period adjustments. [FRS 11(75)]

14.288 This statement is made in a **bold** (mandatory) paragraph, and not merely as guidance. It would appear therefore that the standard simply does not allow the recognition of a past impairment loss as a prior period adjustment. However, it is reasonable to assume that it is not the ASB's intention to override FRS 3, which is the more specific standard in respect of prior period adjustments. Consequently, it remains possible in principle to demonstrate that a genuine fundamental error occurred in an earlier period which led to a failure to provide for an impairment at that time. Given the precise wording of paragraph 75 of FRS 11, the evidence for a fundamental error will need to be overwhelming before that paragraph can safely be ignored.

Implementation of FRS 15

14.289 There are few transitional rules as FRS 15 really only codifies what has been best practice for years. They should be simple – but in one respect they are not. The main transitional rules apply to entities which:

(a) have previously revalued assets but are **not** adopting a policy of revaluation on implementation of FRS 15 (see **14.292** below); and/or

(b) are separating assets into component parts which have significantly different depreciation rates (see **14.301** below).

Valuation policy

14.290 The options entities face relating to the carrying amount of tangible fixed assets on adoption of FRS 15 can be summarised as follows.

Valuation basis used prior to FRS 15	Valuation basis used post FRS 15	Guidance section
Historical cost	(a) Historical cost	Assuming all costs capitalised are valid costs under FRS 15, no special issues arise.
	(b) Revalued amount	**14.291**
Revalued amount	(a) Historical cost	**14.297**
	(b) 'Freeze' existing revalued amount	**14.293**
	(c) New revalued amount (i.e., continuing to revalue)	**14.298**

Entities changing from historical cost to revalued amount

14.291 FRS 15 does not explain what kind of valuation is expected in the first year of adopting a revaluation policy. In order to ensure that the carrying value is the market value at the balance sheet date, there seems no other option than to perform a full valuation in the first year. This will then signal the start of the five-year 'general rule' as explained in **14.105** above. Calculation of depreciation is discussed in **14.228** above. Adjustments to accumulated depreciation on revaluation are discussed in **14.256** above. Restatement of comparative figures is discussed in **14.258** above.

Entities not continuing a revaluation policy

14.292 This is one of the main transitional rules. An entity which decides to cease a previously valuation policy has two choices:

(a) retain the carrying book amounts (see **14.293** below); or

(b) restate the revalued carrying amounts back to historical cost (see **14.297** below).

Retain previously revalued carrying amounts

14.293 An entity may retain the carrying value relating to the previous (pre-FRS 15) valuation and carry this forward as the 'value' to write off in future (FRS 15(104a)). This means that entities which have 'cherry picked' assets for revaluation purposes in the past can carry forward the valuation existing at the date that FRS 15 is first implemented. This provision is **only** allowed on **first** implementation of FRS 15 (i.e., for the first accounting period ending on or after 23 March 2000, or for any earlier accounting period if FRS 15 has been adopted early). Entities cannot then revert at a later date to the previously revalued carrying amounts.

14.294 The entity must disclose, in the year FRS 15 is first implemented, that the transitional provisions are being adopted, the fact that the valuation is not being updated and also the date of the last valuation (see **14.316** below).

14.295 As the carrying value is not original historic cost, CA 1985 still requires various disclosures to be made in the accounts. These are as follows:

(a)   a statement that it is the entity's policy to maintain specified assets at a valuation;

(b)   the comparable historical amounts of those assets (i.e., disclosing either original historic cost and accumulated historical depreciation, or the difference between the revalued amounts and its depreciated historical cost); and

(c)   the year and the amount of the valuation.

14.296   Companies Act disclosure requirements relating to original historical cost still apply. The policy statement in years subsequent to the transitional year should make reference to the transitional provisions in FRS 15 which permit the entity to maintain a valuation in the accounts which is not subject to the provisions of FRS 15. Also, an annual 'depreciation difference' transfer from the revaluation reserve to the profit and loss reserve will still be needed (as detailed in the uses of revaluation reserve in **14.273** above) and that difference in depreciation between the carrying value and historic cost bases will be disclosed in the 'Historical cost profit and loss' note. See Example **14.297** below for sample disclosures.

Restate to historical cost

14.297 On first adoption of FRS 15, entities which have previously revalued can, if they do want to discontinue their policy of carrying certain assets at a revaluation, remove the carrying (revalued) amounts and restate back to depreciated historic cost. This would be done as a prior year adjustment following a change in accounting policy (see discussion in **14.261** above). The adjustment would be to bring the asset to the historical cost-based carrying value which would have appeared in the accounts now if the valuation had never taken place.

Example 14.297.1: Restatement from revalued amount to depreciated historical cost

An asset cost £1m and has a UEL of 50 years. Depreciation was £20,000 p.a.

Five years after acquisition, when NBV equalled £900,000, it was revalued to £1,350,000 with a remaining UEL of 45 years. Depreciation was adjusted to £30,000 p.a.

A further five years later, the carrying amount and equivalent historic cost balances were:

	Carrying value (valuation)	Equivalent historic cost
Valuation/Cost	£1,350,000	£1,000,000
Accumulated depreciation	£150,000	£200,000*
Net book value	£1,200,000	£800,000

*Historic cost accumulated depreciation 10 years @ £20,000.

On implementation of FRS 15, the company wishes to restate the current carrying value of £1,200,000 back to its historic cost. This is done by the following entries which adjust the opening balances of the accounts:

Cr Valuation b/f (removing the valuation)	£350,000
Cr Accumulated depreciation b/f (correcting the balance)	£50,000
Dr Revaluation reserve b/f (removing the balance)	£400,000

N.B. The balance on the revaluation reserve is the amount which is unrealised on the initial revaluation. An unrealised gain of £450,000 was made, but a transfer of £10,000 (being the difference between the actual depreciation charged of £30,000, and the historic depreciation that would have been charged £20,000), has been made annually for five years.

A note explaining the prior year adjustment is needed, detailing:

(a) the reason for the change in accounting policy;

(b) the cumulative effect on reserves;

(c) the effect on current year's profits;

(d) the effect on the results for the preceding period (where practicable).

Where prior period figures have been restated it is good practice to indicate this in the heading to the comparative figures on each page of the financial statements together with a reference to the note explaining the prior period adjustment. Additionally, the adjustment to the revaluation reserve will be disclosed at the foot of the STRGL and in the shareholders' funds note (in the year the prior period adjustment is made).

Summary of non-revaluation options

Example 14.297.2: Options when revaluation policy ceases

A company has a year end of 31 March. Prior to 31 March 2000, the company revalued one of its three office buildings from a historic cost of £100,000 to a valuation of £250,000 (depreciation is ignored in this simple example).

Year ended 31 March 2000

The company has the following options:

Option 1

It could keep the value of £250,000 as the carrying value of the building (assuming there has been no impairment in value). The disclosure in the tangible fixed asset note could look like:

'The transitional arrangements of FRS 15 are being adopted in the case of one office building included within "Land and buildings" where the valuation of £250,000 has not been updated since 20 December 1998. The company is not continuing the revaluation policy relating to this asset. The effects of this change in policy are detailed in note x.'

From 31 March 2000 onwards, the company will treat the £250,000 as the equivalent 'value' of the asset.

Option 2

It could restate the carrying amount back to the historic cost amount of £100,000 by adjusting the cost and revaluation reserve brought forward (i.e. a prior year adjustment). Additionally, all the relevant prior period adjustment disclosures will be made.

Year ended 31 March 2001

The treatment in the accounts depends on which option was adopted for the year to 31 March 2000.

If the company has followed **option 1** above and kept the carrying value at £250,000 (subject to depreciation last year), then the disclosure needed is the appropriate Companies Act disclosures. Some of this could be done in the policy note as follows:

'The company's policy is to carry all assets at historical cost, except one office building which has been included in the balance sheet at a valuation existing on 31 March 2000 when the company implemented FRS 15 for the first time.'

Within the tangible fixed asset note, the following could be disclosed:

'As stated in the policy note x, the company carries one office building at a net valuation of £250,000. The asset was revalued in 1997 and has not been updated since. The historic cost of this asset is £100,000.'

If the company has followed **option 2** above and restated back to cost, then there are no additional disclosures to make.

N.B. If option 2 has been followed, then the company can **never** revert to the value of £250,000 which was in the books at the date FRS 15 was first implemented. Option 2 is **only** available when FRS 15 is applied for the **first** time.

Continuation of revaluation policy

14.298 Entities which are continuing a revaluation policy must decide whether current methods meet the conditions of FRS 15. Possible causes of changes could be:

(a) The need to have more regular valuations performed. Entities have to decide where in the five-year cycle they fall (explained in **14.105** above), and carry out the appropriate amount of work in the transitional year.

(b) They may need to have a different valuer, someone who meets the definition of a qualified valuer in FRS 15 (see **14.136** above), to perform the valuations. Again, this may mean that additional work is needed in the transitional year to meet the requirements of FRS 15.

(c) The need to allocate assets into appropriate distinct 'classes' and to revalue all assets in that class. Paragraph **14.94** above looks at issues which may arise from this.

Issues which may arise when allocating 'classes' for the first time

14.299 Some entities may have had a previous revaluation policy which 'cherry picked' assets. On implementation of FRS 15, this is no longer allowed and entities must separate out assets into different classes. This may lead to the following situations.

Assets within a class	What needs to be done	Paragraph references
All assets in class **have not** previously been revalued (i.e., all on cost basis).	All assets need a full valuation to be performed in the year.	**14.291**
All assets in class **have** previously been revalued.	Need to decide which stage of the general five-year revaluation cycle the entity is at.	**14.130**

Some of the assets in the class **have** been revalued and some **have not**.	Perform a full valuation on the assets **not** previously revalued, and then decide, for the previously revalued assets, the entity's position within the general five-year revaluation cycle. N.B. It is recommended that the same revaluation cycle is chosen for all assets in the class.	14.131

Revision of useful economic lives and residual values

General rule

14.300 The standard states that, with specified exceptions, revisions to the useful economic lives and residual values of tangible fixed assets recognised on adoption of FRS 15 are **not** the result of a change in accounting policy and should be treated in accordance with the normal (prospective) rules. Therefore, they are not prior period adjustments.

> 'Revisions to the useful economic lives or residual values of tangible fixed assets may result in the depreciation of tangible fixed assets that were previously not depreciated by the entity on the grounds of immateriality. In such cases, the carrying amounts of the tangible fixed assets should be depreciated prospectively over the remaining useful economic lives of the assets.'

[FRS 15(107)]

Exception to general rule – separate component parts

14.301 However, on adopting FRS 15, entities may separate their tangible fixed assets into different **component parts** which have different UEL's and residual values. There may be adjustments to correct the accumulated depreciation brought forward to account for the changes made. Under certain circumstances, the adjustments can be made to the opening figures and disclosed as a prior year adjustment following a change in accounting policy. [FRS 15(108)]

> ### Example 14.301: Components approach
>
> A plane had been carried in the accounts at a book value of £700,000 (being its historic cost of £1 million less 15 years depreciation at £20,000 per annum – total UEL = 50 years). On adoption of FRS 15, the company decides to separate the plane into the following parts, and allocates UELs accordingly:
>
> | | |
> |---|---|
> | Body of plane | 50 years |
> | Engine | 10 years |

> An engine normally costs £100,000 to replace (this is the amount esti-mated at the time the plane was acquired). The first replacement engine was purchased after ten years, and the cost of £100,000 was expensed to P&L.
>
> The asset's accumulated depreciation should be as follows:
>
> | | | |
> |---|---|---:|
> | Body of plane | £900,000 / 50 years $\times$ 15 years = | £270,000 |
> | Engine (first replacement) | £100,000 / 10 years $\times$ 5 years = | £50,000 |
> | Total accumulated depreciation to date should be: | | £320,000 |
> | Actual depreciation to date: | | £300,000 |
>
> Therefore, the adjustment of £20,000 which needs to be made to bring the accumulated depreciation to the correct amount is treated as a prior year adjustment.

Potential conflict between FRS 15(106) and (108)

14.302 FRS 15(108) introduces a single exception to the prohibition in para 106 of making the transitional adjustments as a prior period adjust-ment. FRS 15(108) states:

> 'Where, on adoption of the FRS, entities separate tangible fixed assets into different components with significantly different useful eco-nomic lives for depreciation purposes, in accordance with paragraphs 36–41 and 83–85, the changes should be dealt with as prior period adjustments, as a change in accounting policy.'

14.303 The ASB's intention, as has become clearer from its recent publica-tion of the UITF's Abstract 23 (see **14.306** below), appears to be to limit the application of para 108 to those circumstances to which both paras 36–41 and 83–85 apply. This limits it to those situations where a tangible fixed asset comprises two or more major compo-nents with substantially different useful economic lives (83–85) **and** where there has been subsequent expenditure either to replace a major component (36(b)) or to restore economic benefits by means of a major inspection or overhaul (36(c)).

14.304   Taken at simple face value, para 108 could appear to address every situation where a decision is taken on implementation of FRS 15 to disaggregate a single asset into a set of components, and to allocate asset lives to each component that are signifi-cantly different from that used previously for the single asset. There have been some indications from early applications of the standard that some companies have made this simplistic interpretation.

14.305 However, this would provide a potential route whereby almost every asset could be disaggregated in this way, allowing such a

> wide range of exemptions to the basic rule in para 106 as to render it largely void. This cannot have been the ASB's intention and therefore it would always have been unsafe to assume that the Review Panel would be indifferent to widespread avoidance of para 106. In fact, over a year after the publication of FRS 15, UITF has recognised that there is a problem and has issued Abstract 23 which seeks to interpret these paragraphs.

14.306   UITF Abstract 23, issued 18 May 2000, reads as follows:

'The UITF reached a consensus that the prior period adjustment required by paragraph 108 of FRS 15, where components of an asset are identified, should be restricted to the effects of treating separately only those components in respect of which:

(a)   any provision for repairs and maintenance (including replacement expenditure) was itself eliminated by prior period adjustment on adoption of FRS 12 or

(b)   there has been a change from a previous policy of writing off as incurred relevant repairs and maintenance expenditure (including replacement expenditure) to a policy whereby such expenditure is capitalised because it replaces a separately depreciated component.

In particular, any prior period adjustment should not embrace any changes to the useful economic lives or residual values of the remainder of the asset.'

14.307   The UITF explains this as follows:

'Prior to the adoption of FRS 15 an entity may have based its depreciation policy on the whole of an asset, such as property, while recognising that certain components, such as lifts, had a substantially shorter life than the property as a whole: the cost of replacement of such components would have been provided for by means of a provision (prior to FRS 12) or written off as incurred. On adoption of FRS 15 an entity may at the same time (a) identify one or more separate components with significantly different useful economic lives from the remainder of the asset and (b) amend the residual value and/or economic useful life of the remainder of the asset. A typical example would be where the lifts within a building are to be treated as a separate component and depreciated separately and at the same time the building itself is to be depreciated for the first time. The question is whether the effect of both aspects can be combined into a single prior period adjustment under paragraph 108.

Since paragraph 106 is expressed as being subject to paragraph 108, it could be read as placing no limits on the extent to which prior period adjustments could be set up in respect of changes to depreciation rates on the introduction of component accounting. The UITF took the view that paragraph 108 should not be taken as disapplying paragraph 106 with regard to all elements of an asset in which one or more components had been identified on the adoption of FRS 15, but rather as introducing a limited exemption to deal with the situation discussed in paragraph 3 above. The UITF noted that paragraph 106 itself reflects the ongoing requirements for revisions of residual values and/or economic lives (set out in paragraphs 93–96) which is that they should be reflected prospectively over the remaining useful life of the asset. Allocating a shorter life to components of an asset does not itself involve changing the life/residual value placed previously on the asset as a whole. However, reviewing the asset as a whole may also give rise to changes in the estimates of its life/residual value: such changes should be dealt with prospectively.'

14.308   'FRS 15 notes that land and buildings are separable components and are dealt with separately for accounting purposes, even when they are acquired together (paragraph 84). Where they had not previously been treated separately and there had been no charge for depreciation, any depreciation of the buildings component arising from the introduction of FRS 15 should be dealt with prospectively.

Before the adoption of FRS 12 "Provisions, Contingent Liabilities and Contingent Assets" and FRS 15, the fact that some components deteriorated faster than the asset as a whole might have been recognised by a provision for repairs and maintenance (including major refits or refurbishment and the replacement of major components) rather than by different depreciation rates on the components. On adoption of FRS 12 any such provision would have been eliminated by a prior period adjustment. It follows that it was necessary in FRS 15 to allow prior period treatment in respect of the corresponding adjustment resulting from recomputing cumulative depreciation by reference to components of an asset rather than the asset as a whole.'

14.309 Reporting entities applying the Financial Reporting Standard for Smaller Entities currently applicable are exempt from Abstract 23.

14.310 The accounting treatment required by this consensus should be adopted as soon as practicable, but in any event in financial statements relating to accounting periods ending on or after 23 March 2000 (the effective date of FRS 15).

> ### Extract 14.310: Marks & Spencer plc
>
> **Extract from Tangible Fixed Assets Note, from financial statements for year ending 31 March 1999**
>
> Change of Accounting Policy
>
> The Group has adopted FRS 15, and has followed the transitional provisions to retain the book value of land and buildings, certain of which were revalued in 1988.
>
> Adoption has resulted in two key changes:
>
> (i) The FRS encourages the separation of assets into components where they have very different useful economic lives and states that these changes should be dealt with as prior year adjustments. The cost of fitting out properties, which has up to now been included within the cost of buildings, has been separately identified and disclosed together with fixtures, fittings and equipment. Fit out has previously been accounted for on a replacement basis but under this policy will be depreciated evenly over periods ranging from 10–25 years depending on its nature. As a result, £53.2m of fit out which had been expensed in previous years has now been capitalised as at 31 March 1998. In addition, £264.1m of accumulated depreciation has also been recognised as at that date, being the depreciation on fit out which would have been recognised had the new policy been in place in previous years. As a consequence of the prior year adjustment, the net book value of Group tangible fixed assets as at 31 March 1998 has been reduced by £210.9m with a corresponding reduction in the profit and loss account reserve. The effect of this on reported profits has been an additional Group depreciation charge in the current year of £28.6m (last year £23.5m) and a reduction in the charge for repairs and renewals of £18.3m (last year £10.5m).

Revalued assets with component parts

14.311 The conflict between FRS 15(106) and (108) does not extend to an asset which, in the transitional period, is being revalued, as the value that is placed on an asset should be the current market value at a specific date, which will then be depreciated prospectively over its remaining life.

Recognition of costs

14.312 Cost figures should reflect FRS 15 rules relating to what can and cannot be included in purchase price/production cost. This means that entities should review their asset cost on implementation of FRS 15 to ensure that all costs carried forward are valid deferred expenditure. In most cases, the figures carried as 'cost' will not need to be changed because either:

(a)   the carried costs are not materially different from the costs that would fall to be recognised under FRS 15; or

(b) the information to determine the 'correct cost' under FRS 15 is not available because of the length of time since acquisition.

14.313

> **Past policies 'grand-fathered'.** One further factor which suggests that past practice will not be challenged is the general approach of the transitional rules. The fact that the ASB is content to allow old valuations to be 'frozen' in financial statements suggests that the ASB does not feel that it is necessary to carry out expensive analyses and amendments of past transactions, provided that all future transactions are accounted for in compliance with FRS 15.

Summary of impact of implementing FRS 15

14.314

Area where FRS 15 will have an impact	Effect on implementation of FRS 15
Recognition of costs in the future	Entities will have to ensure that cost capitalisation procedures meet all the requirements of FRS 15. Certain types of cost capitalised in the past may in future have to be expensed (see **14.313** above).
Previously capitalised costs which do not fall within the scope of FRS 15	It is not expected that many entities' carrying values will need to be amended because material amounts of inappropriate costs are being carried forward. If an entity decides to review carrying costs, all such costs should be reviewed (see **14.313** above).
Separating assets into component parts	If, on implementation of FRS 15, an entity separates assets which have significantly different UELs into different component parts, then the adjustment to correct the accumulated depreciation for those components will be a prior year adjustment (see **14.301** above).
Changing UELs or residual values as a result of the provisions in FRS 15	This has to be accounted for prospectively over the remaining life of the asset (see **14.300** above).
Deciding to adopt a revaluation policy for the first time	A full valuation must be carried out in the first year in order to obtain a current market value at the balance sheet date (see **14.291** above).

Not continuing with a revaluation policy	Entities have the choice whether to restate back to depreciated historical cost or to continue with the 'old' valuation, as long as the choice is clearly disclosed (see **14.292** above).
Continuing an existing revaluation policy	Entities must ensure that they have allocated all assets into classes; their revaluation policy has been adjusted to take account of the increased/decreased number of assets being revalued; they have a qualified valuer performing the valuations on the correct basis, and they have met the requirements of FRS 15 by performing appropriate work (either a review or a full or interim valuation) (see **14.298** above).

Disclosure on transition

14.315 Where an entity has adopted the transitional arrangements in FRS 15 (104) as detailed in **14.292** above, FRS 15 additional disclosures are required.

When an entity 'freezes' previously revalued assets at carrying value

14.316 An entity which opts to carry forward the existing (pre-FRS 15) 'frozen' values (see **14.293** above) is required to disclose the following:

(a) the fact that the transitional rules have been followed;

(b) the fact that the values have not been updated; and

(c) the date of the last valuation.

14.317 These will be in addition to the disclosure requirements of the Companies Act. As the carrying value is not original historical cost, CA 1985 still requires various disclosures to be made in the accounts. These are:

(a) a statement that it is the entity's policy to maintain specified assets at a valuation;

(b) the comparable historical amounts of those assets (i.e. disclosing either original historic cost and accumulated historical depreciation, or the difference between the revalued amounts and its depreciated historical cost); and

(c) the year and the amount of the valuation.

These disclosures will need to be made for all years where the carrying amount of the 'frozen' assets are material.

When an entity restates a previously revalued asset back to historical cost

14.318 A change from a revaluation policy to historical cost (see **14.297** above) will be treated as a change in accounting policy resulting in a prior year adjustment. A note explaining the prior year adjustment is needed, detailing:

(a) the reason for the change in accounting policy;

(b) the cumulative effect on reserves;

(c) the effect on current year's profits;

(d) the effect on the results for the preceding period (where practicable).

> ### *Extract 14.318: George Wimpey PLC*
>
> ***Extract from Tangible Assets Note, from financial statements for year ending 31 December 1999***
>
> FRS 15 has been adopted this year and on implementation the carrying value of group occupied properties, shown as Other Property, has been restated to historical cost (less restated accumulated depreciation) as a change in accounting policy. Prior year figures for other property have been restated accordingly, reducing the carrying value of Other Property by £4.3 million with a corresponding reduction in the Revaluation Reserve (note 27). This change in accounting policy has had no effect on the profit and loss accounts for the years ending 31 December 1999 and 1998. The Directors are confident that valuations of these properties are in excess of historical cost.

14.319 **Disclosure that comparatives have been restated.** Where prior period figures have been restated it is good practice to indicate this in the heading to the comparative figures on each page of the financial statements together with a reference to the note explaining the prior period adjustment. Additionally, the adjustment to the revaluation reserve will be disclosed at the foot of the STRGL and in the shareholders' funds note (in the year the prior period adjustment is made).

Future developments

14.320 The UITF issued Information Sheet 36, 23 March 2000 including a draft abstract which goes beyond the scope of FRS 15 and seeks to require the expensing of certain types of initial costs, rather than treating them as prepayments, whereas FRS 15 only seeks to ensure that they should not be capitalised.

14.321 The text of the proposed consensus is as follows:

'The UITF reached a consensus that start-up costs that do not meet the criteria for recognition as fixed assets set out in FRS 15 'Tangible Fixed Assets', FRS 10 'Goodwill and Intangible Assets' or SSAP 13 'Accounting for research and development' should be recognised as an expense when they are incurred. They should not be carried forward as prepayments, deferred expenditure or other kinds of asset.

Examples of expenditure that should be recognised as an expense when incurred include the costs of establishing a new entity, costs of starting new operations or launching new products or processes (including expenditure on training, advertising and promotion), and costs of relocating or reorganising part or all of an enterprise.'

14.322 References to this development have been incorporated into the text of the manual where relevant. At this point, it is not clear whether or not this proposal will be modified before adoption.

15 Fixed asset investments

15 Fixed asset investments

Disclosure requirements

Statutory headings

15.1 'Investments' is a main heading which should appear on the face of the balance sheet. It appears twice: under fixed assets and under current assets. The following subheadings are required, but may be shown either on the face of the balance sheet or in the notes.

Fixed assets	Current assets

Shares in group undertakings
Loans to group undertakings
Participating interests
Loans to undertakings in which
  the company has a participating
  interest
Other investments other than loans
Other loans
Own shares
	Shares in group undertakings
	Own shares
	Other investments

15.2 Shares in group undertakings are normally fixed assets of the parent company (FRS 9 paragraph 26, in respect of associates) and would only appear as current assets in the exceptional circumstance where they have been acquired with the intention of resale. If a company holds (legitimately or otherwise) any of its own shares, these should be separately disclosed (see **15.47** to **15.50** below) in either fixed or current assets.

15.3 In normal circumstances, the only investments to be classified as current assets will be 'other investments', consisting of the investment of a company's surplus funds on a relatively short-term basis.

15.4 The disclosures listed in **15.5** to **15.28** below are all required in respect of fixed asset investments. Some of them apply also to current asset investments, and this fact is mentioned in respect of each disclosure where it applies.

Movements

15.5 For each subheading there should be shown:
[Sch 4: 42]

(a) in respect of the gross valuation (whether on cost or other valuation basis):

(i) the balances at the beginning and end of the year;
(ii) any revision arising from a revaluation made during the year;
(iii) acquisitions and disposals during the year; and
(iv) transfers of assets to or from fixed asset investments;

(b) in respect of provisions made for diminution in value:

(i) the balances at the beginning and end of the year;
(ii) provisions made during the year;
(iii) adjustments of provisions arising from disposals; and
(iv) any other adjustment made in respect of such provisions during the year.

Comparative figures for the preceding year are not required.

Information on valuation bases

15.6 Where fixed asset investments are valued in accordance with the alternative valuation rules of Sch 4 (see **15.32** below), the following information is to be given in the notes to the accounts:

(a) the investments affected (fixed and current) and the basis of valuation; [Sch 4: 33(2)]

(b) in respect of fixed asset investments other than listed investments, the year of valuation and the values; also in the year of valuation, the name of the valuers (or particulars of their qualifications) and basis of valuation. [Sch 4: 43] Where any basis other than market value is used, the reasons for adopting the alternative basis is to be disclosed; [Sch 4: 31(3)] and

(c) in respect of both fixed and current asset investments, the comparable historical cost amount for both cost and provision for diminution in value, or the difference between these amounts and the alternative valuation. [Sch 4: 33(3)]

Listed investments

15.7 The following additional information about listed investments (both fixed and current) should be given:
[Sch 4: 45]

(a) the amounts of listed investments included in each subheading;

(b) for each subheading, the aggregate market value of listed investments, where this differs from the amount at which it is stated in the financial statements; and

(c) where the market value of any listed investments is used for the purposes of the financial statements and this value is higher than the stock exchange value, both the market value and the stock exchange value should be stated.

15.8
> The circumstances under which market value may differ from the stock exchange value include those where there is an intention to dispose of a large tranche of shares in the near future, with the likelihood that they will need to be placed at below the unit value on the stock exchange. This would not include sale of a controlling tranche, which would probably command a premium, but the outcome would be too unpredictable to justify disclosure of that premium under this requirement. Disclosure under this heading may therefore arise in respect of current assets, but is unlikely in respect of fixed asset listed investments.

15.9   The definition of a listed investment under the Act includes those investments listed on a recognised investment exchange and those listed on any stock exchange of repute outside Great Britain.

15.10 A 'recognised investment exchange' as defined by s207 Financial Services Act 1986 is one which is so declared by an order of the Secretary of State. The following investment exchanges in Great Britain have been recognised under this Act.

The London Stock Exchange	The International Petroleum Exchange of London Ltd
The London Securities and Derivatives Exchange Ltd	The London International Financial Futures and Options Exchange (LIFFE)
The London Metal Exchange	Tradepoint Stock Exchange

15.11 References within the Act's definition of listed investments to 'any stock exchange of repute outside Great Britain' may be taken to include, but not necessarily be limited to, the following stock exchanges currently listed by the London Stock Exchange as 'approved organisations'. All official exchanges in the following countries:

Austria	Japan
Belgium	Luxembourg
Denmark	Netherlands
Finland	Norway
France	Portugal
Germany	Spain
Greece	Sweden
Ireland	Switzerland
Italy	USA

and the following specific investment exchanges:

Alberta Stock Exchange	New Zealand Stock Exchange
Australian Stock Exchange	Securities Exchange of Thailand
Budapest Stock Exchange	Singapore Stock Exchange
Cayman Islands Stock Exchange	
Hong Kong Stock Exchange	Toronto Stock Exchange
Johannesburg Stock Exchange	Tradepoint Investment Exchange
Kuala Lumpur Stock Exchange	Vancouver Stock Exchange
Mexican Stock Exchange	Zagreb Stock Exchange

For the purposes of the gilt-edged and sterling bond market, the list of approved organisations includes the International Securities Market Association Ltd (ISMA).

Companies dealt with on AIM are not listed companies for this purpose.

Holdings of 20 per cent or more (up to and including subsidiaries)

15.12   Where the nominal value of the holding in an undertaking is 20 per cent or more of any class of shares, or the value of the holding as shown in the investing company's accounts exceeds 20 per cent of the assets of the investing company, the following information in respect of each holding is to be given in the notes to the accounts (including any situation in which such a holding is held in current assets): [Sch 5: 1, 2, 7, 8, 15, 16, 22, 23, 24, 26 and 27]

(a)   the name of each company;

(b)   if it is incorporated outside Great Britain, the country of incorporation;

(c)   if it is unincorporated, the address of its principal place of business; and

(d)   the identity and proportion of the nominal value of each class of shares held.

15.13   In addition, FRS 2 requires, in respect of each subsidiary company whose results or financial position principally affect the figures in the consolidated financial statements, both an indication of the nature of its business and the proportion of voting rights held by the parent and its subsidiaries.

15.14   Corresponding information for the preceding year need not be given.

15.15   In addition to the above, holdings in subsidiary and associated undertakings should distinguish separately holdings by the parent company and by the group (if different); where group accounts are not required to be prepared, separate disclosure of holdings in subsidiary undertakings held respectively by the parent company and by its subsidiary undertakings is to be given.

15.16   If the undertakings referred to above are too numerous, the directors need only give the information for undertakings which principally affect the figures shown in the individual or group accounts and undertakings which have been excluded from consolidation. They should then include a statement to this effect and give the balance of the information annexed to the next annual return. [s231(5) and (6)]

15.17   Information in respect of any undertaking established, or carrying on business, abroad need not be given if, in the opinion of the directors, disclosure would be seriously prejudicial to the business and the Secretary of State agrees to the exclusion. Where advantage is taken of this section, this fact should be stated in the notes to the accounts. [s231(3) and (4)]

15.18   Application to the Secretary of State to gain his agreement, although a formal procedure, is not one for which guidance is available from the DTI. A letter is necessary, explaining why the directors believe disclosure would be seriously prejudicial, and experience suggests that the reasons given should be seen to have real substance. The criteria applied by the Secretary of State tend to vary from country to country and from time to time.

Investment in shares not consolidated or accounted for by the equity method

15.19 The following additional information should be given about each undertaking in which the shares held by the company or the group represent 20 per cent or more of the nominal value of shares in the undertaking [Sch 5: 3, 9, 17, 25 and 28] (including any situation in which such a holding is held in current assets):

(a) the total of its share capital and reserves as at the end of its financial year ending with or last before the financial year of the parent company; and

(b) its profit or loss for that financial year.

15.20 Most investments are excluded from this requirement by virtue of the following exemptions:

(a) the undertaking is consolidated; or

(b) the undertaking is included in the accounts by way of the equity method of valuation; or

(c) the holding relates to subsidiary undertakings and the company is exempt from the requirement to prepare group accounts by virtue of s228 (company included in accounts of larger group) (see **23.7** below); or

(d) the company is exempt from the requirement to prepare group accounts by virtue of s228 (parent company included in accounts of larger group) and the investments in 20 per cent or more undertakings are shown, in aggregate, in the notes by way of the equity method of valuation; or

(e) the subsidiary undertaking is not required by the Act to deliver a copy of its balance sheet and does not otherwise publish it, and the company holds less than 50 per cent of the nominal value of the shares in the undertaking; or

(f) in respect of minor companies, the company has taken advantage of the concession given in the Act and has limited the disclosure of particulars to principal investments. The information about such minor companies should be annexed to the next annual return (see **15.16** above); or

(g) the holding is not material.

Associates where no consolidated accounts are prepared

15.21 Where an investing entity does not prepare consolidated financial statements, but owns stakes which would be accounted for as associates or joint ventures if it did do so (i.e., where it has no qualifying subsidiaries), it should present the relevant amounts for associates and joint ventures, as appropriate, by preparing a separate set of financial statements or by showing the relevant amounts, together with the effects of including them, as additional information to its own financial statements. However, investing entities that are exempt from preparing consolidated financial statements, or would be exempt if they had subsidiaries, are exempt from this requirement. [FRS 9(48)] This requirement also would not apply to any interests held for resale as current assets, as they would not constitute an interest in an associate or joint venture. (See chapter 25 for disclosure requirements in respect of associates and joint ventures where consolidated financial statements are prepared.)

Qualifying undertakings

15.22 The Partnerships and Unlimited Companies (Accounts) Regulations 1993 (SI 1993 No 1820) introduced disclosure requirements in respect of interests in 'qualifying undertakings' (i.e., 'qualifying companies' and 'qualifying partnerships'). (These would apply whether such investments were held as fixed assets or as current assets.)

15.23 A 'qualifying company' is an unlimited company each of whose members is:
[SI 1993 No 1820 reg 9]

(a)   a limited company; or

(b)   another unlimited company, or a Scottish firm, each of whose members is a limited company.

15.24 A 'qualifying partnership' is a partnership governed by the laws of any part of Great Britain each of whose members is:
[SI 1993 No 1820 reg 3]

(a)   a limited company; or

(b)   an unlimited company, or a Scottish firm, each of whose members is a limited company.

15.25 In **15.23** and **15.24** above, references to limited companies, unlimited companies or a Scottish firm include comparable undertakings incorporated or formed outside Great Britain.

15.26 Where a company or group holds a material interest in a qualifying undertaking at the end of the financial year, the notes to the accounts of the company or group should disclose:

(a)   the name and legal form of the undertaking; and

(b)   the address of the undertaking's registered office or, if it does not have such an office, its head office.

> ### *Example 15.26*
>
> Delto PLC has a 45 per cent interest in 'Vector/Delto Joint Venture', a partnership governed by English law. Vector/Delto Joint Venture's head office is: Thrift House, Cheapside, London.

15.27   Where the undertaking is a qualifying partnership there shall also be stated either:

(a)   that a copy of the latest accounts of the undertaking has been or is to be appended to the copy of the company's accounts sent to the Registrar of Companies under s242;

> ### *Example 15.27.1*
>
> A copy of the latest accounts of 'Vector/Delto Joint Venture' will be appended to the copy of these financial statements to be filed with the Registrar of Companies under s242 Companies Act 1985.

or

(b)   the name of at least one body corporate (which may be the company) in whose group accounts the undertaking has been or is to be dealt with on a consolidated basis.

> ### *Example 15.27.2*
>
> The results and financial position of 'Vector/Delto Joint Venture' are included on a consolidated basis in the financial statements of Vector Group plc, a company registered in England and Wales.

15.28   The disclosures set out in **15.27** above are not required if the qualifying partnership is not required to prepare accounts and reports (see **4.117** to **4.132** above) and disclosure is made of the fact that advantage has been taken of the exemption conferred by SI 1993 No 1820 reg 7.

> ### *Example 15.28*
>
> Regulation 7 of The Partnerships and Unlimited Companies (Accounts) Regulations 1993 provides exemptions for the members of 'Vector/Delto Joint Venture' from the requirements of regs 4 to 6 of those Regulations.

Basis of valuation

Historical cost convention

15.29   Under the historical cost accounting rules, investments classified as fixed assets are valued at cost, but:

    (a)   provision should be made for any diminution in value which is expected to be permanent [Sch 4: 19(2)]; and

    (b)   provision may be made for a diminution in value even if it is not expected to be permanent [Sch 4: 19(1)].

15.30   Where the reasons for making any such provisions no longer apply to any extent, they should be written back to the extent that they are no longer necessary. [Sch 4: 19(3)]

15.31   The Act requires that any such provisions made or written back which are not shown in the profit and loss account shall be disclosed (either separately or in aggregate) in a note to the accounts. This is generally interpreted as a requirement that such provisions charged or written back shall be debited/credited to the profit and loss account for the period, and shown either on the face of the profit and loss account or in the notes.

Alternative valuation bases

15.32   Under the alternative valuation rules investments classified as fixed assets may be valued either:
[Sch 4: 31(3)]

    (a)   at market value as at the date of their last valuation; or

    (b)   at a value determined on any basis which the directors consider appropriate in the circumstances.

15.33   Schedule 4 para 19 (see **14.237** et seq. above) also applies to the determination of the value for the year's accounts under the alternative accounting rules. The question of whether and the extent to which any provision for diminution in value should be passed to the profit and loss account for the year is considered in **14.282** to **14.283** above.

Shares in group undertakings

15.34   Shares in group undertakings held as fixed assets are usually included in an investing company's balance sheet at cost less provision for any permanent diminution in value. The problem of determining the 'cost' of shares acquired by share exchange is discussed in **15.38** below.

15.35

An alternative treatment, which is sometimes adopted, is for the carrying value of investments in subsidiaries in the books of the parent company to be adjusted, using the alternative valuation rules, to the amounts of the net assets shown in the historical cost balance sheets of the individual subsidiaries. The principal reason normally given for doing this is to make the total reserves shown in the parent company's own balance sheet identical to those shown in the group balance sheet. However, it should be noted that this effect can only be achieved where the fair value exercise on acquisition established fair values of net assets that were not materially different from the existing carrying values in the subsidiary undertaking. The write-down is allowable because, under the alternative accounting rules, fixed asset investments may be included 'at a value determined on any basis which appears to the directors to be appropriate in the circumstances of the company', i.e., any number they choose, provided it does not overstate value to the business. Unless it is apparent that there has been a permanent diminution in value (not a part of this scenario), the debit will be to the revaluation reserve. If there is no adequate credit balance standing to the credit of the revaluation reserve, this results in a negative reserve; although unusual, this is not precluded.

15.36

A situation that can arise on group reorganisations is the transfer of businesses between subsidiaries. Where consideration for such transfers is inadequate, the value of the investment in the subsidiary which has not been recompensed for the loss of its assets will be impaired, and that impairment may constitute a permanent diminution of the value of the asset below the cost or value at which it is being carried in the parent company's balance sheet. Normally, it will be necessary for the parent to make provision in its profit and loss account accordingly. However, where a major part of the business of one subsidiary has been transferred to another, it is reasonable to treat this as the transfer of that part of the investment into a different shell and allow the cost of the investment to follow the business which constitutes it. The investing company will adjust its cost of each investment so that the transferee company is recorded as having cost all or most of the sum of both investments, and the transferor (the entity losing its business) will be recorded at nil or at a substantially reduced cost. Consequently, no gain or loss falls to be recorded in the investing company, which accurately reflects the fact that its control over net assets has not changed.

15.37 A variant of this situation arises when the intra-group transfer involves hiving the business of a subsidiary up into the parent without compensating the subsidiary. The same logic applies: the cost of the business to the parent ceases to be the cost of the shares in the subsidiary and becomes the cost of an unincorporated business. To the extent that the cost exceeds the fair value of the relevant net assets, that excess is now purchased goodwill and should thereafter be accounted for accordingly. In place of an investment at cost, the parent records net assets at their fair value plus goodwill, to a total precisely equalling the cost of the investment (see **24.181** below).

15.38 Another special situation arises where a subsidiary is acquired entirely or partly by share exchange and chooses to take advantage of s131 of the Companies Act by claiming merger relief. Under these circumstances, the acquiring company is not obliged to fair value the share element of the consideration given to acquire the subsidiary, but may choose to do so if it wishes. The consequence is that, apart from the impact that this choice has on any group accounts that it prepares, it also offers alternative ways of accounting for the cost of the investment in its entity balance sheet. The cost to the entity will consist of the fair value of any consideration given in addition to its share issue, together with either the nominal value of the shares issued or alternatively their fair value [s133(1)]. The choice should be consistent with that made for the group accounts (see **24.26** below).

Participating interests and associated undertakings

15.39 The Act defines a participating interest as an interest in the shares of another undertaking held on a long-term basis for the purpose of securing a contribution to its activities by the exercise of control or influence arising from that interest. [s260] A holding of 20 per cent or more of the shares of an undertaking is presumed to be a participating interest unless the contrary is shown. An interest for this purpose includes convertible rights and options, interests held by subsidiaries and interests held on behalf of the company. The term 'shares' is broadly defined to include interests in partnerships and joint ventures.

15.40 The amounts to be included in the balance sheet heading 'Participating interests' exclude group undertakings. It will include interests defined in the Act as 'associated undertakings', the definition of which is very similar to the definition of an associate in FRS 9 (see **25.8** below).

15.41 Participating interests are normally carried in the investing company's own balance sheet at cost less provision for any permanent diminution in value. In group accounts, associated undertakings are usually accounted for using the equity method of accounting (see **25.49** below). Where no consolidated accounts are prepared, FRS 9 requires extensive additional disclosure to give the information that would have been given had they been prepared (see **25.69** below).

Investments in partnerships, joint ventures and joint arrangements that are not entities

15.42 These are considered in more depth in chapter 25. Although that chapter considers them principally in the context of the preparation of consolidated accounts, they will sometimes fall to be accounted for by the same method in the owning entity's own accounts as in consolidated accounts, rather than simply at cost (or value). For considerations affecting accounting and disclosure for this group of entities/arrangements, please refer to:

- associates – see **25.49**;

- joint ventures – see **25.81**;

- joint arrangements that are not entities – see **25.123**;

- partnerships – see **25.43**.

Other investments

15.43 This category will comprise all investments, other than group undertakings and participating interests, and will include:

- listed and unlisted securities;

- building society deposits;

- time deposits with banks; and

- life insurance policies.

These investments should be classified under either fixed or current assets, according to the definition contained in s262 (see **12.11** above).

15.44 In practice, investments which are not intended for use on a continuing basis in the company's activities are likely to be restricted to those representing the investment of surplus funds on a relatively short-term basis. Thus, of the above items, interests in partnerships and joint ventures and life assurance policies are normally fixed assets, while building society deposits and time deposits with banks are normally current assets. Listed securities and unlisted securities in which there is a ready market could be either, depending on the nature and purpose of the investment.

Loans

15.45 Loans to third parties should only be treated as fixed assets where they are made for a significant period, normally exceeding 12 months, and for a purpose clearly connected with the company's activities, such as to establish a trading link with an important customer or supplier. Normally, the loan would be the subject of a formal agreement as to repayment arrangements and interest would be payable. Short-term advances and any which are unconnected with the company's activities should be included under 'Debtors' (with any amount falling due after more than one year being separately disclosed).

15.46 The classification of loans to group and participating undertakings should be determined by reference to the facts in each case. Loans which are in the nature of current accounts and loans that are made on the clear understanding that they will be repaid within a relatively short period should be treated as current assets and shown under debtors. However, many loans between companies in a group are made on an informal basis, with no agreed repayment terms, but, in practice, they are used to meet the capital requirements of the borrower and there is no realistic expectation of early repayment. Such loans are, in effect, investments intended for use on a continuing basis in the lender company's activities and should therefore be classified as fixed assets.

Own shares

15.47 UK legislation permitting the purchase or redemption of own shares requires such shares to be cancelled (see **33.15** below). Consequently, the heading 'own shares' will rarely be used, its application being normally restricted to those cases where shares can legally be held (the bar on companies owning their own shares includes a bar on subsidiaries purchasing/owning shares in their UK parent company). Cases where ownership is permitted include the situations where shares in the parent were acquired by a company before it became a subsidiary of that parent, and where a subsidiary has held such shares since prior to the Companies Act 1948. In the parent's consolidated accounts, such shares should appear under the 'own shares' heading.

15.48
> The heading will also be used where shares have been acquired by a trust under an ESOP and the trust vehicle is in a form which requires that it should be included on the balance sheet.

15.49 UITF Abstract 13 *Accounting for ESOP trusts* is dealt with in **28.103** to **28.116** below.

15.50 Where such shares are held, there is a requirement to disclose their nominal values in addition to their carrying cost or value. [Sch 4: Note 4 on the balance sheet formats]

16 Current assets

16 Current assets

Stocks (including long-term contracts)

Disclosure requirements

Statutory headings

16.1 Stocks is a main heading which should appear on the face of the balance sheet. The subheadings required, which may be shown either on the face of the balance sheet or in the notes to the accounts, are:

(a) Raw materials and consumables;

(b) Work in progress;

(c) Finished goods and goods for resale;

(d) Payments on account.

16.2 There is an overriding requirement that the directors should adapt the arrangement and headings in any case where the special nature of the company's business requires such adaptation. [Sch 4: 3(3)] An example of an adaptation that might be appropriate for a contracting and property development company is as follows.

Example 16.2		
	£'000	*£'000*
Raw materials and consumables		597
Land held for development		2,724
Work in progress:		
Contracting, less payments on account of £200,000	700	
Commercial developments	1,400	
Housing	928	
		3,028
Completed developments and houses for sale		3,500
		9,849

Accounting policies

16.3 There is a statutory requirement for the disclosure of the accounting policies adopted in determining the amounts to be included in respect of the items shown in the balance sheet. [Sch 4: 36] The accounting policies that have been applied to stocks and long-term contracts and, in particular, the method of ascertaining turnover and attributable profit, should be stated and applied consistently within the business and from year to year. [SSAP 9(32)]

16.4 The description of the accounting policies should be as brief as possible, while making clear to the reader which of the different policies permissible under the Act have been adopted. The following is an example of a form of disclosure which would be acceptable in a simple situation.

> **Example 16.4**
>
> Stocks and work in progress are stated at the lower of cost and net realisable value. Cost represents direct materials and labour and production overheads.

16.5 An example of an accounting policy note dealing with long-term contracts which meets the requirements of SSAP 9 is as follows.

> **Example 16.5**
>
> Long-term contract balances represent costs incurred on specific contracts, net of amounts transferred to cost of sales in respect of work recorded as turnover, less foreseeable losses and payments on account not matched with turnover. Contract work in progress is recorded as turnover on the following bases: on contracts which provide for delivery of own manufactured units or components, turnover is recorded when deliveries are made to customers; on other contracts and in respect of the installation phase of delivery type contracts, turnover is determined by reference to the value of work carried out to date. No profit is recognised until the contract has advanced to a stage (normally, when work exceeds 25 per cent completion) where the total profit can be assessed with reasonable certainty. Provision is made for the full amount of foreseeable losses on contracts. Income arising from settlement of contract claims is recorded when final negotiations have been completed and the amount of the settlement is considered to be collectable.

Disclosure of replacement cost or most recent cost

16.6 Where stocks are determined by one of the acceptable methods other than the ascertainment of actual cost (LIFO, FIFO, etc. – see **16.32** below), the difference between the amount determined by that method and the 'relative alternative amount' should be disclosed in a note to the accounts if the difference is material. [Sch 4: 27]

16.7 The 'relative alternative amount' is the replacement cost of the stock at the balance sheet date or the amount determined by reference to the most recent actual purchase price or production cost before the balance sheet date if this appears to the directors to constitute a more appropriate standard of comparison in the circumstances.

16.8 Only the difference between the carrying value and the 'relative alternative amount' of those stock items valued at FIFO, LIFO, weighted average or any other similar method need be disclosed. There is no requirement to disclose the amount of stock actually carried on any particular basis. An appropriate wording for the disclosure in such a situation would be as follows.

> ### Example 16.8
>
> Included in the amount shown above for stocks of raw materials and consumables are items valued at cost calculated on a first in, first out basis. The replacement cost of these items at 31 March 2000 was £143,000 greater (1999 – £128,000 greater) than the amount at which they are included in the accounts.

16.9 Although determination of the value of stock on the basis of actual cost is rare, there are very few examples in practice of published financial statements including this disclosure. Presumably, it has been omitted on the grounds that it is not material. It is difficult to determine what is material in this context, since it is difficult to identify the possible usefulness of the information to readers of financial statements. It is suggested that, in most circumstances, a difference which is less than 10 per cent of the total amount of stocks can reasonably be regarded as not material.

Interest capitalised

16.10 The amount of interest capitalised in the cost of stocks is required to be disclosed in a note to the accounts. [Sch 4: 26(3)] The total cost of finance capitalised in the cost of stocks (see **16.27** below) may include, in addition to interest, for example, the amortisation of the issue costs and/or any premium on redemption of the borrowing instrument(s). However, the disclosure required under Sch 4 is limited to the interest element alone. [Sch 4: 26(3)]

Long-term contract work in progress

16.11 The special disclosure requirements applicable to long-term contracts are discussed in **16.43** to **16.57** below.

Basis of valuation

Historical cost rules

16.12 Stocks should be valued at their purchase price or production cost, unless their net realisable value is lower; in which case, the latter basis should be used. [Sch 4: 22 and 23] The comparison of net realisable value with cost should, in principle, be carried out on an item by item basis but, if this is impracticable, groups of similar items may be considered together. It is unacceptable to compare the total net realisable value of all stocks with their total purchase price or production cost. Where the reasons for making a provision in a previous year to write down stocks to net realisable value have ceased to apply to any extent, the Act requires that provision to be written back to the extent that it is no longer necessary. [Sch 4: 23(2)]

16.13 The purchase price of stocks is to be determined by adding to the actual price paid any expenses incidental to their acquisition. [Sch 4: 26(1)]

16.14 Production cost is to be determined by adding to the purchase price of raw materials and consumables used the amount of the costs incurred by the company which are directly attributable to the production of the stock. In addition, there may be included a reasonable proportion of the costs which are only indirectly attributable to the production of the stock, but only to the extent that they relate to the period of production, and interest on capital borrowed to finance the production of stock. [Sch 4: 26(2) and (3)]

16.15 SSAP 9 defines cost as that expenditure which has been incurred in the normal course of business in bringing the product or service to its present location and condition. [SSAP 9(17)] It includes both the cost of purchase (discussed in **16.19** and **16.20** below) and costs of conversion. Costs of conversion include direct costs, production overheads and other overheads 'attributable in the particular circumstances of the business to bringing the product or service to its present location and condition'.

16.16 Net realisable value is defined by SSAP 9 as the actual or estimated selling price (net of trade but before settlement discounts) and after deduction of all further costs to completion and of costs of marketing, selling and distribution. [SSAP 9(21)]

Alternative valuation rules

16.17 Schedule 4 permits stocks to be valued at current cost (normally, replacement cost). This basis is rarely used and then only in the context of accounts prepared wholly under the current cost convention. Very few organisations use current cost accounting except, as in the water industry, in a regulatory context, not as main statutory accounts.

Elements of cost

16.18 The various elements of cost to be included in the value of stock are discussed under the headings below.

Material costs

16.19   Normally, these will consist of the actual invoice price of the material, together with the ancillary costs of purchase, such as import duties, transport and handling costs, and any other directly attributable costs. Trade discounts, rebates and subsidies should be deducted.

16.20   Where raw material is unavoidably subject to wastage and spoilage during production, it may be convenient to include the cost of such normal scrapping and wastage as part of the material cost of the product. Alternatively, the costs of material scrapped or wasted may be included in overheads.

Direct labour costs

16.21   The cost of wages of employees directly engaged in production should be allocated to production on the basis of normal operating conditions. Labour costs which are the result of operating inefficiencies, such as abnormal idle capacity or abnormal rectification work, should not be included in the stock valuation. This will require the costs of these abnormal inefficiencies to be capable of identification in the company's accounting records.

Overhead costs

16.22   SSAP 9 requires that all production overheads should be included in stock valuations. [SSAP 9(19)] The practice of omitting some or all overheads from valuation on the grounds of prudence is not acceptable. Equally, the valuation of stocks on a 'marginal costing' basis, whereby only costs which vary directly with volume of output are included and costs which accrue on a time basis are excluded, is not acceptable.

16.23   Overheads other than production overheads should only be included in stock valuation where this is justified by exceptional circumstances: those which are properly classified as selling or administrative overheads should not be included. An exception is made in circumstances where firm sales contracts have been entered into for the provision of goods or services to customer specification; in these circumstances, overheads relating to design, and marketing and selling costs incurred before manufacture, may be included in arriving at cost.

16.24 The problem of determining the amount of overheads to be carried forward in stocks may be considered under two headings: identifying the overheads to be included and applying these overheads to production in a logical manner. It is necessary first to analyse overheads by function between production, marketing and distribution and administration. There are practical problems in making this analysis. For example, management salaries may include an element of supervision of production, as well as of administration, and pension costs are likely to cover employees in the production sphere, as well as those in sales and general administration departments. Central services departments, such as accounts, may provide identifiable services for production. Costs should be allocated over the functions on a reasonable basis which should be consistently applied.

16.25 The method of applying overheads to production should be one that is appropriate to the nature of the product and the method of production. The most popular methods of applying overheads are:

(a)   by way of a labour hour or machine hour rate;

(b)   in proportion to direct labour costs;

(c)   in proportion to material costs;

(d)   in proportion to prime cost; and

(e)   equally to each unit of production (this is only appropriate where a single product is being produced in a given cost centre).

16.26 Whichever method of applying overheads is adopted, the overheads should be applied on the basis of the company's normal level of activity. Overhead costs which are the result of operating inefficiencies, such as abnormal idle capacity or abnormal rectification work, should not be included in the stock valuation.

Interest

16.27 The inclusion in the valuation of stock of interest on capital borrowed to finance its production is permitted to the extent that the interest accrues in respect of the period of production. If this is done, the amount of interest included should be disclosed in a note to the accounts. [Sch 4: 26(3)]

16.28 Interest has not generally been included in stock valuations, since capital is borrowed to finance the activities of the business as a whole and not specifically to finance stocks during the period of production. Appendix 1 to SSAP 9 indicates that, in ascertaining the cost of long-term contract work in progress, it is not normally appropriate to include interest payable on borrowed money, but that this may be acceptable in circumstances where sums borrowed can be identified as financing specific long-term contracts. However, there is no reason in principle why the interest capitalisation rules applicable to long-term contract work in progress should be different from those applicable to tangible fixed assets. FRS 15 has codified those rules for tangible fixed assets (see **14.42** to **14.54** above), so that it may now be appropriate under certain circumstances to capitalise interest calculated at a weighted average cost of general borrowings rather than limiting it to that on specific borrowings.

16.29 An exception to the general rule that interest should not be included in stock valuations arises when a company holds significant quantities of maturing stocks such as whisky. The maturing period is clearly part of the period of production and the addition of interest is therefore permissible under Sch 4. Similarly, interest incurred is clearly attributable to bringing the product to its existing condition and should therefore be included under SSAP 9. Provided that it can be demonstrated that the whole, or at least a large proportion, of the company's borrowings is invested in maturing stocks, it is appropriate to include the whole or an appropriate proportion of the company's interest charges in the value of such stocks. The interest included in stocks should be the appropriate proportion of the company's actual interest expense incurred; a 'notional' charge for interest on capital should not be added.

16.30 It is sometimes difficult to determine when the 'period of production' ends, i.e., when stocks are being held for sale as opposed to being held for maturing. For example, stocks of whisky 'mature' after three years but go on improving with age for many more years. It is considered acceptable to continue adding interest to the value of maturing stocks for as long as it can be demonstrated that the particular stock item continues to increase in value solely on account of age rather than because of market fluctuations or inflation. This increase in value should be greater than the interest cost incurred to achieve it. If this cannot be demonstrated, then the stocks should be regarded as held for sale and no further interest should be added.

Transfer price

16.31

> Where the manufacturing process involves the transfer of work from one department to another, the transfer may be made at a price different from the cost incurred by the transferring department, either for reasons of convenience in accounting or as part of the system of management control. Where this takes place, it is necessary for the purpose of valuing closing stocks to adjust the valuations to actual cost by eliminating any profits or losses arising at the separate department levels.

Methods of determining cost

16.32 Stocks should be valued wherever possible by attributing costs directly to specific items. This requires the identification of each item in stock with a particular purchase invoice or specific costs of production. In the vast majority of cases, such specific identification is not practicable and Sch 4 permits cost to be determined by any one of the following methods:
[Sch 4: 27(2)]

- first in, first out (FIFO);

- last in, first out (LIFO);

- weighted average price;

- any other method similar to these.

16.33 The Act specifically permits the use of the LIFO basis of valuation and the Act can be interpreted to permit the use of the 'base stock' method on the basis that it is similar in concept to the LIFO method. However, SSAP 9 advises that methods such as LIFO and base stock are not usually appropriate, because they often result in stocks being stated at amounts which bear little relation to recent cost levels. [SSAP 9(39)]

16.34

> Generally, the methods which will be acceptable are:
>
> (a) FIFO, which is based on the assumption that the earliest purchased stock is the first to be disposed of, and the stock on hand, therefore, represents the most recent purchase or production; or
>
> (b) weighted average price, which is determined by dividing the total cost of units by their number to arrive at a weighted average price. This average price may be arrived at by a continuous calculation, a periodic calculation, or a moving average.

16.35 Many companies use predetermined estimates of costs in advance of production, based on expected levels of costs, efficiency and operational activity. These estimates, usually referred to as 'standard costs', are used for internal management accounting purposes and sometimes also as a basis for year end stock valuation. Standard costs should only be used for year end stock valuation purposes if they bear a reasonable relation to actual costs obtained during the period. This can be achieved by frequent updating of standards or by adjusting for the recorded variances (differences between actual cost and standard arising from price, volume and other factors) which have arisen during the stockholding period.

16.36 Other methods of valuation which are sometimes adopted include:

- latest invoice price;

- retail method;

- fixed amount.

16.37 SSAP 9 states that the 'latest invoice price' method (under which the latest invoice price is applied to the total volume of stocks held) is not acceptable in principle, since the result does not normally represent cost; it may only be accepted where it can be demonstrated that price fluctuations during the stock holding period have been so insignificant that the result is a reasonable approximation of cost.

16.38 The 'retail method' is frequently adopted by retail establishments. The total stock on hand is valued at current selling price and then reduced to approximate cost by deducting the normal gross margin.

16.39 This method results in a valuation of stocks that approximates to average price and is, therefore, acceptable subject to certain constraints. The method only works satisfactorily for an entire department or shop if all the lines held are expected to generate a similar profit margin. For example, the stocks of a newsagent and confectioner normally include lines of widely differing profit margins and, to arrive at an acceptable stock figure by the retail method, it is necessary to divide the stocks into categories according to the profit margin achieved. A further problem with the retail method arises if the selling price on slow moving items has been marked down. If the normal gross profit percentage is then deducted from such items, this will result in their being valued below cost, giving a result that may well be excessively prudent. It is therefore necessary to ensure that the volume of marked down items is insignificant

> or, alternatively, they should be segregated and valued separately. Sometimes, the margin that is deducted from selling price is the net rather than the gross margin. This would only be acceptable where the difference between the two is too small to make a material difference.

16.40 The Act permits certain items to be included in stocks of raw materials and consumables at a fixed quantity and value ('fixed amount'). [Sch 4: 25] This treatment is acceptable, provided that:

(a) their overall value is not material to assessing the state of the company's affairs; and

(b) their quantity, value and composition are not subject to material variation.

Payments on account

16.41 One of the statutory subheadings of stocks is 'Payments on account'. Identical subheadings are included under both tangible and intangible fixed assets, while the subheading 'Payments received on account' appears under creditors. It therefore appears that this subheading relates to payments made, not to payments received, and it would only be used in the rare circumstance where payments have been made in advance in respect of items ordered for stock but not yet delivered.

16.42 However, the Act permits and SSAP 9 requires payments received on account to be shown as deductions from long-term contract balances within the heading 'Stocks'. [Sch 4: Note 8 on the balance sheet formats and SSAP 9(30)]

Long-term contracts

16.43 Generally, the principal requirement before turnover and profit can be recognised in accounts is the full performance by the seller of the terms of a contract. However, in the case of long-term contracts, a required exception to this rule is laid down in SSAP 9 paragraph 29 on the grounds that, owing to the length of time to complete such contracts, the taking of profit in this way could result in the profit and loss account reflecting the results of those contracts which happen to be completed in the year, rather than showing a fair view of the results of the activities during the year. [SSAP 9(7)] Consequently, SSAP 9 sets out a different basis for recognition of turnover on long-term contracts. The sections below discuss the requirements of SSAP 9 in respect of the accounting treatment of long-term contracts.

Accounting for turnover and profit

16.44 Where the outcome of a long-term contract can be assessed with reasonable certainty before its conclusion, the attributable profit (see **16.52** to **16.55** below) should be recognised in the profit and loss account on a prudent basis. This is achieved by including in turnover a proportion of the total contract value in a manner appropriate to the stage of completion and the business and industry in which the company operates, and by transferring from contract work in progress to cost of sales those costs incurred in reaching the stage of completion reported as turnover.

16.45 Where the outcome cannot be assessed with reasonable certainty, no profit should be included in the accounts. In such cases, it may be appropriate to show as turnover a proportion of the total contract value, using a zero estimate of profit.

16.46 Paragraph 24 of appendix 1 to SSAP 9 suggests that it is necessary to define for each contract the earliest point before which no profit is taken up. While some companies establish a minimum percentage to measure the stage from which profit is taken, this seems to be an unnecessarily rigid approach. Progress on contracts subsequent to the accounting period may provide sufficiently reliable evidence of the ultimate outcome of a contract to permit profit to be taken up, even if a pre-established minimum percentage of completion had not been reached at the balance sheet date.

16.47 Where an overall loss is foreseen on a contract as a whole, the full loss should be recognised immediately in accordance with the prudence concept (see **16.56** below).

16.48 The example given in **16.51** below illustrates the application of these principles.

Definition of long-term contract

16.49 SSAP 9 defines a long-term contract as a contract entered into for the design, manufacture or construction of a single substantial asset or the provision of a service (or a combination of assets or services which together constitute a single project) where the time taken substantially to complete the contract is such that the contract activity falls into different accounting periods. [SSAP 9(22)] This definition allows contracts with a duration of less than one year to be accounted for as long-term contracts if they are sufficiently material to the activities of the period that failure to record turnover and profit on them would result in the accounts not giving a true and fair view.

16.50

> The principal determinant of classification as a long-term contract is not the duration of each contract but the materiality of all the relevant contracts taken together. Even if all of a contracting company's contracts are of less than one year, nonetheless they should in aggregate be material to the period's activities, in terms of both turnover and profit. It follows therefore that all contracts should be treated as long-term contracts if to do so has a material effect upon the period's results; conversely, the only contracts not to be treated as long-term are those which, in aggregate, are immaterial.

16.51   Example of application of the principles set out in SSAP 9 on long-term contracts.

Example 16.51

Assume the following transactions:

1.   Contract costs of £280,000, £740,000 and £450,000 for Jobs A, B and C, respectively, were incurred by payments of £600,000 in cash and purchases of £870,000.

2.   Invoices requesting stage payments were sent to customer A for £100,000, customer B for £1,060,000 and customer C for £400,000.

3.   Cash of £1,100,000 was collected from customers and payments of £400,000 were made to creditors.

4.   Value of work done to date has been assessed at £220,000 for Job A, £960,000 for Job B and £380,000 for Job C, based on progress milestones (e.g., units delivered, production stage reached).

5.   Costs of £240,000, £680,000 and £350,000 relate to the work recorded as turnover on Jobs A, B and C, respectively, and are transferred to cost of sales; the remainder of costs relate to costs on stages of work on which profit has not yet been earned.

6.   A further loss to completion of Job A of £70,000 is foreseen. This loss is recognised by writing down the remaining cost of work in progress by £40,000 to net realisable value (nil value) and the balance of £30,000 is recognised by establishing a loss provision.

7.   As Job A has no work in progress, payments on account of £100,000 is set off against the amounts recoverable on that contract. Of the payments on account for Job B of £1,060,000, £960,000 is first applied against amounts recoverable on that contract, £60,000 is applied to reduce work in progress to nil value, leaving a balance of £40,000 to be shown separately under creditors as 'payments on account' in the balance sheet. For Job C, payments on account are first applied against amounts recoverable on that contract, and the balance of £20,000 is applied to reduce work in progress to £80,000.

The table below illustrates the appropriate journal entries to record these transactions. See also **16.57** below on presentation in the financial statements.

Transactions	Job A	Job B	Job C	Trade debtors	Job A	Job B	Job C	Cash	Creditors/ Provisions	Job A	Job B	Job C	Profit and loss account
	£'000	£'000	£'000	£'000	£'000	£'000	£'000	£'000	£'000	£'000	£'000	£'000	£'000
1. Contract costs incurred	280	740	450	–	–	–	–	(600)	(870)	–	–	–	–
2. Request for stage payments	–	–	–	1,560	–	–	–	–	–	(100)	(1,060)	(400)	–
3. Cash collected and paid out	–	–	–	(1,100)	–	–	–	700	400	–	–	–	–
4. Value of work done, recorded as turnover	–	–	–	–	220	960	380	–	–	–	–	–	(1,560)
5. Transfer of work in progress to cost of sales	(240)	(680)	(350)	–	–	–	–	–	–	–	–	–	1,270
6. Provision for foreseeable losses	(40)	–	–	–	–	–	–	–	(30)	–	–	–	70
	–	60	100	460	220	960	380	100	(500)	(100)	(1,060)	(400)	(220)
7. Allocation of payments on account													
Job A	–	–	–	–	(100)	–	–	–	–	100	–	–	–
Job B	–	(60)	–	–	–	(960)	–	–	–	–	1,020	–	–
Job C	–	–	(20)	–	–	–	(380)	–	–	–	–	(400)	–
FINAL ACCOUNT BALANCES	–	–	80	460	120	–	–	100	(500)	–	(40)	–	(220)

The balance sheet note on stocks should disclose separately the gross work in progress of £160,000 and the applicable payments on account of £80,000.

Attributable profit

16.52 Attributable profit is defined by SSAP 9 as 'that part of the total profit currently estimated to arise over the duration of the contract, after allowing for estimated remedial and maintenance costs and increases in costs so far as not recoverable under the terms of the contract, that fairly reflects the profit attributable to that part of the work performed at the accounting date'. [SSAP 9(23)]

16.53

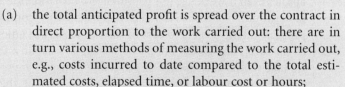

There are two principal approaches to the determination of attributable profit:

(a)   the total anticipated profit is spread over the contract in direct proportion to the work carried out: there are in turn various methods of measuring the work carried out, e.g., costs incurred to date compared to the total estimated costs, elapsed time, or labour cost or hours;

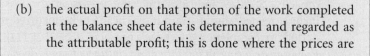

(b)   the actual profit on that portion of the work completed at the balance sheet date is determined and regarded as the attributable profit; this is done where the prices are determined and invoiced according to separate parts of the contract (either as units are delivered or definable stages are reached).

16.54 Both methods are used, but the first is preferable, provided the method of measuring the work carried out is appropriate. A problem with the second method, particularly in the construction and civil engineering industries, is that tenders are often 'front-end loaded', i.e., while the total price is competitive, items for completion early in the contract are priced more highly than those to be completed later on. This improves the rate of cash flow from the contract. However, if the tender prices are used to measure profit, the contract will appear to be very much more profitable in the early stages than on completion. Indeed, an apparent loss may be sustained on later work in some cases. SSAP 9 states that profit taken up should take account of any known inequalities of profitability in the various stages of the contract. [SSAP 9(9)]

16.55 It is important that prudence should be exercised in estimating both the total anticipated profit on the contract and the proportion thereof attributable to the work completed during the period. For example, claims for additional work or losses caused by the customer should not be accrued unless they have been agreed or established; claims against the company by the customer for penalties, and estimated future work such as rectification work, should be accrued where it is likely that such costs will be incurred. Estimated costs to complete should take account of likely inflationary increases in costs which are not recoverable from the customer under the terms of the contract. (Some guidance on these points is given in appendix 1 to SSAP 9, paragraphs 25 to 27.)

Loss-making contracts

16.56 All foreseeable (and unavoidable) losses on contracts entered into before the balance sheet date should be provided in full and this applies even if work has not commenced. Provision for a foreseeable loss should be deducted from the balance of contract work in progress after transfers to cost of sales in respect of amounts treated as turnover; any excess should be shown as a liability. In the exceptional circumstances where unprofitable contracts are such that they can be expected to utilise a considerable part of the company's capacity, SSAP 9 indicates that the provision for losses should include related administration overheads to be incurred during the period to completion of those contracts. [SSAP 9(11)] (FRS 12, *Provisions, contingent liabilities and contingent assets* does not impact upon contracts because SSAP 9 is the more specific standard. However, there is no apparent clash between the two standards. FRS 12 acts as a useful reminder that foreseeable losses under SSAP 9 should not include provision for any element of loss that is avoidable by action that it is open to the company to take.)

Presentation in the financial statements

16.57 The various elements of long-term contracts should be disclosed in the balance sheet as follows:
[SSAP 9(30)]

(a) *amounts recoverable on contracts*: the excess of recorded turnover over payments on account should be classified as 'amounts recoverable on contracts' and separately disclosed within debtors. Like most debtors, it constitutes a 'financial asset' within the meaning of FRS 13 and will fall to be taken into account in making the disclosures required under that standard (see chapter 21);

(b) *long-term contract balances*: the costs incurred on long-term contracts, net of amounts transferred to cost of sales, less foreseeable losses and payments on account not matched with turnover, should be classified as 'long-term contract balances' and separately disclosed with the heading 'Stocks'. The notes should disclose separately the balances of:

(i)   net cost less foreseeable losses; and
(ii) applicable payments on account.

> As amounts will be transferred from long-term contract balances to cost of sales as work progresses, all that will remain in this category will be those items which have not yet reached a stage to be included in turnover, such as unworked materials;

(c) *invoiced amounts*: requests for stage payments, including retentions, which remain uncollected should be classified under the heading 'Trade debtors';

(d) *payments on account*: the balance of payments on account in excess of amounts offset against 'amounts recoverable on contracts' and 'long-term contract balances' should be classified under the heading 'Payments received on account' and separately disclosed within creditors;

(e) *provision for foreseeable losses*: the provision for foreseeable losses in excess of the costs incurred (after transfers to cost of sales) should be included within either 'Provisions for liabilities and charges' or creditors, as appropriate (see **17.9** below).

Debtors

Disclosure requirements

16.58   General requirements are discussed in **16.59** and **16.60** below. Additional disclosures for particular items are discussed below in respect of each relevant subheading. The additional disclosure requirements of FRS 13 *Derivatives and other financial instruments*, which apply to most debtors as financial assets, are separately dealt with in chapter 21.

Statutory headings

16.59   'Debtors' is a main heading which should appear on the face of the balance sheet. The subheadings required by the Sch 4 formats, which may be disclosed on the face of the balance sheet or in the notes, are:

- Trade debtors;

- Amounts owed by group undertakings;

- Amounts owed by undertakings in which the company has a participating interest;

- Other debtors;

- Called up share capital not paid;

- Prepayments and accrued income.

Amounts falling due after more than one year

16.60   Any amounts which fall due after more than one year should be shown separately for each subheading. [Sch 4: Note 5 on the balance sheet formats] In addition, in those instances where the amount involved is so material in the context of the total net current assets that, in the absence of disclosure of debtors due after more than one year on the face of the balance sheet, readers may misinterpret the accounts, then the amount should be disclosed on the face of the balance sheet. [UITF Abstract 4] Examples of items which may meet this criterion include prepayments arising out of pension fund surpluses, the trade debtors of lessors and deferred consideration in respect of the disposal of fixed assets. Certain such items may be expected to last for several years – pension fund surpluses may extend for many years ahead – and this challenges the broad popular assumption that current assets have a short life, generally less than one year, and can lead to misinterpretation of this heading unless attention is drawn to the extent of the longer-term element.

Trade debtors

16.61   This item generally includes amounts invoiced to customers, accrued sales for goods delivered but not billed, contract retentions, suppliers' debit balances, less provision for bad debts and credits for returns, allowances, cash discounts and rebates. Amounts owed by group and related undertakings should not be included in this category.

Amounts owed by group undertakings

16.62 This item includes all amounts owed by group undertakings (i.e., parent, subsidiary or fellow subsidiary undertakings), e.g., loans, current accounts and dividends receivable, but with the exception of loans which are recorded as fixed assets (see chapter 15).

16.63 The netting of inter-company balances due from one group undertaking against inter-company balances due to another group undertaking is not permitted. [Sch 4: 5] Even where such debit and credit balances are with the same company, the principle remains the same: netting is only permissible where it is clear that a legal right of offset exists.

Amounts owed by participating interests

16.64 The subheading 'Amounts owed by undertakings in which the company has a participating interest' is fortunately a heading which the Act permits to be modified. A much shorter heading, such as 'Amounts owed by associated undertakings', will be appropriate in the majority of cases where the significant participating interests represent associated undertakings. FRS 9 has introduced a requirement that any amount meeting this description should be analysed (where necessary) between amounts relating to loans and amounts relating to trading balances. [FRS 9(55)] In practice, this distinction may well coincide with the categorisation of the loans as fixed assets and the trading balances as current. FRS 9 points out that this disclosure may be combined with related party disclosures required by FRS 8.

Other debtors

16.65 This heading generally includes debtors resulting from non-trading activities, such as amounts due from the sale of fixed assets, loans not included under other headings, insurance claims, and refundable deposits. Advances or partial payments (not to be confused with deposits which are to be refunded) made towards the purchase or construction of fixed assets or stocks are more appropriately included under those captions. Note the possible separate disclosure requirements in respect of amounts due after more than one year (see **16.60**) above. [UITF Abstract 4]

16.66 No amount which includes an unearned interest element should appear as a debtor. The unearned interest element should be stripped out, leaving the principal balance, because the interest cannot be an asset until it has been earned by the passage of time. The treatment of debtors under lease or hire-purchase contracts is discussed in **29.78** to **29.87** below.

16.67 Where amounts are due from directors and officers of the company or its holding company or from other related parties, disclosure may be necessary to meet specific requirements of statute and FRS 8 or the general requirement for the accounts to show a true and fair view. This subject is dealt with in chapter 32.

Loans to finance acquisition of own shares

16.68 Where a company has any loans outstanding at the balance sheet date arising from:

(a) the provision of financial assistance for the purpose of an employee share scheme or to enable or facilitate transactions in the company's shares between employees or former employees or their spouses, widow(ers), infant children or stepchildren; or

(b) loans made to bona fide employees (not directors) to enable them to purchase shares in the company or its holding company to be held by them by way of beneficial ownership; or

(c) loans made by a private company for the purpose of the acquisition of its shares or those of its holding company or for the purpose of reducing or discharging any liability incurred in the acquisition of such shares,

the aggregate amount of those loans should be disclosed in the notes to the accounts. [Sch 4: 51(2)]

16.69 The restrictions on the ability of a company to provide financial assistance for the purchase of its own shares are discussed in **33.28** to **33.35** below.

Called up share capital not paid

16.70 The unpaid balance of a call should be shown separately either as a subheading under 'Debtors' (which will normally be the more appropriate) or as a main heading.

Prepayments and accrued income

16.71 'Prepayments and accrued income' should be shown as a separate item either as a subheading under 'Debtors' or as a main heading. It is unlikely that the total of this item will be of sufficient size or importance to deserve the prominence which a main heading would give to it. Often, the separate subheading is not used, since the amount concerned is not material and it can be combined with another subheading, such as trade debtors or other debtors. However, the use of a main heading may well be particularly appropriate where the amount involved is material and is due after more than one year, if it assists in meeting the UITF Abstract 4 requirement for separate disclosure on the face of the balance sheet (see **16.60** above). Note that, unlike other categories falling within the 'Debtors' heading, prepayments will not normally be classified as financial assets within the FRS 13 definition and, therefore, do not fall to be taken into account in making the disclosures required under that standard; accrued income, on the other hand, is a financial asset within the meaning of that standard (see chapter 21).

Prepayments

16.72   In accordance with the fundamental accounting concept of matching revenue with the expenditure incurred to earn it, it is appropriate in certain circumstances and with certain safeguards for expenditure to be carried forward and charged in the profit and loss account in the period in which the related benefits are received.

16.73   The following principles should be considered:

(a)   no expenditure should be carried forward unless it can be shown that:

(i)   the expenditure does not relate to any revenue already brought into the profit and loss account but to revenue which it is anticipated will be earned in the future; and

(ii)   the expenditure will directly generate, in the future, profits which will amply cover the amortisation of the expenditure over the period during which benefits will be received. Alternatively, the expenditure carried forward has an intrinsic realisable value of its own which will at least equal the cost;

(b)   the period of amortisation should be short enough to allow a reasonable certainty of recovery of such costs;

(c)   the unamortised balance of expenditure should be kept under continuous review and written off immediately to the extent that its recoverability becomes open to doubt.

16.74   Two particular problem areas are:

(a) *Advertising costs*: these usually cannot be identified with specific revenue and thus these expenses should not normally be carried forward. An exception to this might be advertising expenditure directly related to the launching of a new product, but there would need to be powerful evidence of future benefits and the period of write-off should be short. The cost of tangible promotional materials, such as brochures relating specifically to next season's goods or services, may normally be carried forward. Catalogues and show cards might be regarded as a part of stock, provided the material is not out of date and quantities are not excessive in relation to expected consumption. It is worth noting that, as this manual goes to press, UITF has issued (Information Sheet 36, 23 March 2000) a draft abstract (see **14.322**) which seeks to preclude the treatment as prepayments of start-up costs such as advertising, training and promotion costs relating to the costs of establishing a new entity, of starting new operations, of launching new products or processes or of relocating or reorganising part or all of an enterprise. It seeks to ensure that such costs are expensed immediately;

(b) *Contract cancellation costs*: expenditure incurred to cancel an onerous contract, even when apparently linked to the obtaining of another profitable contract, should not be carried forward, because the purpose of the expenditure is not directly related to the generation of future profits.

16.75 Prepayments will include amounts paid in advance of benefits to be received (e.g., unexpired portion of rents, insurance, interest and advertising costs, paid in advance of the campaign commencing).

Discount of loans

16.76 Schedule 4 provides that, where the amount repayable on a debt is greater than the value of the consideration received, the difference may be treated as an asset. [Sch 4: 24] The Act does not specify the heading under which this 'asset' is to be shown and, prior to the introduction of FRS 4, it was often shown as 'Prepayments and accrued income'. However, since the introduction of FRS 4, the treatment of such a discount as an asset is no longer allowed (see **17.18** below).

Accrued income

16.77 Accrued income includes amounts earned at the balance sheet date but which the company is not yet entitled to bill or receive, e.g., interest and rental income.

16.78   Accrued income should normally exclude sales accruals for goods shipped but not invoiced, which should be shown as trade debtors, since these usually arise from delays in invoicing or premature closing of the sales journal; they represent amounts which the company is legally entitled to bill to the customer.

Amounts recoverable on contracts

16.79   In the case of long-term contracts (see **16.57** above), SSAP 9 requires the excess of recorded turnover over payments on account (i.e., both amounts received and receivable) to be classified as 'amounts recoverable on contracts' and separately disclosed within debtors. If they are material, it will not be appropriate to include these amounts under the headings of 'trade debtors' or 'other debtors', so they will require a separate heading. The amounts invoiced to customers (including requests for progress payments allowed under the contract and retentions) which remain unpaid should be included in trade debtors.

Investments

Disclosure requirements

16.80   The classification of investments between fixed assets and current assets is discussed in **15.1** to **15.4** above. Investments classified as current assets will normally consist either of deposits or short-term loans to institutions, such as building societies or banks, or of marketable shares or securities.

16.81   With the exception of investments in subsidiary, quasi-subsidiary and associated undertakings, partnerships and joint ventures, all equity instruments of other entities held by the reporting entity will normally fall to be classified as financial assets within the FRS 13 definition and therefore should be taken into account in making any additional disclosures required under that standard (see chapter 21).

16.82   The amount of listed investments should be disclosed separately, together with their market value at the balance sheet date. [Sch 4: 45] The precise requirements are detailed in **15.7** to **15.11** above.

16.83   Under the historical cost accounting rules, each separate investment held should be valued at the lower of cost and net realisable value. Any provision for diminution in value should be charged to the profit and loss account.

'Marked to market' treatment

16.84

Some companies adopt a different treatment for listed investments in which there is a ready and active market, which is to carry the shares at their market value ('marked to market'). Where some or all of the shares have a market value which is above cost at the balance sheet date, it is argued that the excess of market value over cost is a realised profit in accordance with generally accepted accounting principles. This is because the existence of the active market makes the investment equivalent to cash. Under this view, the profit may be recognised in the profit and loss account. However, the historical cost accounting rules apparently prohibit adding the excess of market value over cost to the amount at which the investment is shown in the balance sheet. One approach is to include the excess over cost under the heading 'Prepayments and accrued income', but there is a serious danger of this treatment being misleading because of the separate requirement to disclose the market value of the investment. A reader of the financial statements might compare market value to cost without appreciating that the difference had already been recognised and therefore draw an incorrect conclusion. Consequently, it will be necessary to explain clearly the treatment adopted, preferably in the note disclosing market value.

Example 16.84

The market value of the listed investments was £150,000 and the excess of this amount over cost of £30,000 is included in the balance sheet under 'Prepayments and accrued income'.

16.85

The ASC reached the conclusion that the practice of marking to market does not comply with the provisions of the Act and has to be justified by claiming the need to override those provisions in order to show a true and fair view. [ED 55(1.17) and (1.18)] Nonetheless, ED 55 supported the need to include readily marketable investments at market value, disclosing the fact that the true and fair override has been invoked. A number of companies choose to follow this route. It remains contentious because of the DTI's view that the true and fair override should not be invoked except where the individual company can claim the existence of special circumstances affecting themselves in particular, i.e., the override does not have a generic application.

16.86 Another argument has been advanced, and this may account for the fact that many companies which actively trade as market-makers, such as in commodities, mark to market but do not disclose the use of a true and fair override. The argument is that the investments are revalued at the year end, and the gain is taken to Revaluation Reserve and immediately released to the profit and loss account as permitted by Sch 4: 34(3)(a) on the grounds that it represents a realised profit. A weakness of this argument is that, if this route has been followed, FRS 3 would appear to require that the gain passing to Revaluation Reserve should pass through the STRGL, in which case its release from there is merely a movement on reserves and should not appear in the profit and loss account for the period. Against that is the claim that, where both the debit and the credit in compliance with Schedule 4 take place simultaneously, the period end accounts (full year or interim) should take account of the outcome, not the successive steps, in order to comply with FRS 3. This remains an unresolved and potentially contentious issue.

Interest in business or entity held exclusively for resale

16.87 If an entity or business is acquired exclusively with a view to subsequent resale (e.g., as an unwanted component of a larger acquisition), the interest in that business or the assets of that business should be fair valued at estimated proceeds of sale and included in current assets under the heading of 'Investments'. [FRS 7(17)] Unlike other interests in subsidiaries, associates and joint ventures, such an interest is not exempted from the scope of FRS 13 and therefore falls to be regarded as a financial asset for the purposes of the required disclosures under that standard (see chapter 21). [FRS 13(5a)]

Disclosure requirements in respect of substantial investments

16.88 There are additional disclosure requirements in respect of substantial investments, i.e., investments which represent more than 20 per cent in nominal value of a company's allotted share capital or of any class of its equity capital or whose value in the investing company's accounts exceeds 20 per cent of the investing company's assets. The detailed requirements in such circumstances are described in **15.12** to **15.18** above. Note that FRS 9 precludes the carrying of interests in associates as current asset investments. [FRS 9(26)]

16.89 Shares in group undertakings will only appear under current assets in very exceptional circumstances (see **15.2** above) but, if they do, then they should be subdivided between shares in a holding or fellow subsidiary undertaking and shares in subsidiary undertakings.

Cash at bank and in hand

Definition

16.90   In addition to legal tender and amounts due by banks, items such as cheques, postal orders and bank credit card vouchers held in the ordinary course of collection should be included under this heading.

16.91   Demand deposits and deposits on up to seven-day call with banks and similar institutions, including building societies, should be included. Note that the definition of cash at bank and in hand for the purposes of the format of the balance sheet is different from the definition of cash for the purposes of FRS 1 *Cash flow statements* (see **19.52** below).

16.92   Advances to employees on account of expenditure should be included in 'Other debtors' and not cash.

16.93   Normally, the amounts to be shown under the heading of 'Cash at bank and in hand' should be the amounts recorded in the company's accounting records, i.e., amounts should be treated as withdrawn from the bank when cheques are drawn rather than when they are presented.

16.94   Some companies show the amount in the bank statement at the year end as the balance sheet figure; cheques drawn and not presented are added back to creditors and unbanked receivables are included in debtors. One reason advanced for this treatment is that, in the event of a liquidation, all movements on bank accounts would be frozen, but this seems inconsistent with the fundamental accounting principle that the company should be presumed to be carrying on the business as a going concern. Accordingly, this treatment is not recommended.

16.95   However, the practice is sometimes encountered whereby cheques are drawn in settlement of liabilities but these cheques are not released to the creditors until a later date. In such circumstances, if the amounts are material, it is necessary to reverse the entries recording payment.

16.96   If any funds are held in specially designated bank accounts which may only be used for certain restricted purposes, it is good practice to disclose these amounts separately from the unrestricted funds. Restrictions may be imposed by statute, by the rules of a professional body or trade association, by the Articles or by an agreement, such as a loan agreement.

16.97   All items classified as cash fall to be classified as financial assets within the FRS 13 definition and therefore should be taken into account in making any additional disclosures required under that standard (see chapter 21).

16.98   If bank accounts with both debit and credit balances are maintained at the same bank and there is a right of set-off, the net amount should be shown under current assets or liabilities as appropriate. Where the right of set-off does not exist, the assets and liabilities should both be shown at their full amount in the balance sheet, regardless of whether the balances are with the same bank or different banks. Set-off is examined further as part of the requirements of FRS 5 *Reporting the substance of transactions*, which are discussed in chapter 28.

16.99   A common situation found in groups of companies is that one company in the group controls the treasury function. This can give more efficient use of finance for the group as a whole and often means that finance can be obtained at a lower rate than individual companies within the group could achieve. All companies within the group use this 'treasury' company in the same way as a bank, all their cash positions are held with this company. Balances with such a 'treasury' company should be disclosed as amounts owed by/to group undertakings, not as cash at bank/bank loans and overdrafts.

17   Liabilities, provisions and contingencies

17 Liabilities, provisions and contingencies

Introduction

Sources of accounting requirements

17.1 The requirements on presentation and disclosure of liabilities, provisions and contingencies come from four sources: the Act, FRS 4 *Capital instruments*, FRS 12 *Provisions, contingent liabilities and contingent assets* and the UK Listing Authority Listing Rules.

17.2 This chapter considers the disclosure and measurement of liabilities and provisions and of the capital instruments that are reported under those format headings. It also considers the accounting and disclosure requirements for contingencies, both losses and gains.

Definitions

17.3 In chapter 4 of the ASB's Statement of Principles, liabilities are defined as being 'obligations of an entity to transfer economic benefits as a result of past transactions or events'. These do not necessarily have to be legal obligations, e.g., where an entity has demonstrably committed itself to discontinuing an operation under FRS 3 and FRS 12, it should make provisions for future costs even though they are not necessarily legal obligations.

17.4 Capital instruments are defined by FRS 4 as being all instruments issued by reporting entities which are a means of raising finance. [FRS 4(2)] These include shares, debentures, loans, other debt instruments and options and warrants which give the holder the right to subscribe for, or obtain, capital instruments. In the case of consolidated financial statements, the term includes capital instruments issued by subsidiaries, except those which are held by another member of the group included in the consolidation.

17.5 Capital instruments (other than shares) should be classified as liabilities if they contain an obligation or contingent obligation to transfer economic benefits. [FRS 4(24)] This extends the definition of liabilities contained in chapter 4 of the ASB's Statement of Principles to include instruments that contain contingent obligations to transfer economic benefits.

17.6 A common example of an obligation to transfer economic benefits is the requirement to make cash payments to the holder of debt or other liability either by way of interest payments or amounts payable on redemption. The obligation to transfer economic benefits is not restricted to a requirement to make cash payments; the payment could be in the form of a transfer of assets such as property.

17.7 An instrument that does not include an obligation or contingent obligation to transfer economic benefits should be reported as part of shareholders' funds, even if the instrument is termed 'debt'.

17.8 The definition of a liability does not apply to shares issued by the reporting entity, but, for the purpose of consolidated financial statements, it may apply to shares issued by subsidiary undertakings. If the terms attaching to the subsidiary undertaking's shares are such that the group as a whole has an obligation to transfer economic benefit, then these shares will be accounted for as liabilities in the consolidated financial statements. [FRS 4(49)] Shares issued by subsidiaries are dealt with further in **17.61** to **17.66** below.

17.9 The Act defines 'Provisions for liabilities and charges' as 'any amount retained as reasonably necessary for the purpose of providing for any liability or loss which is either likely to be incurred, or certain to be incurred but uncertain as to amount or as to the date on which it will arise'. [Sch 4: 89]

17.10 Consistent with the Act, FRS 12 defines a provision as a subset of liabilities, i.e., 'a liability of uncertain timing or amount'. FRS 12 repeats the definition of a liability found in the Statement of Principles and applied in FRS 5 *Reporting the substance of transactions* as 'obligations of an entity to transfer economic benefits as a result of past transactions or events'. From this, the definition of a provision is derived as having three components:
[FRS 12(2)]

(a)   a present obligation resulting from a past event; and

(b)   an outflow of economic benefits is probable; and

(c)   ability to measure the outflow.

17.11 Previously, contingent assets and liabilities were dealt with by SSAP 18 *Accounting for contingencies*. That standard defined a contingency, rather than a contingent asset or liability as such. The definition of a contingency was 'a condition which exists at the balance sheet date, where the outcome will be confirmed only on the occurrence or non-occurrence of one or more uncertain future events'.

17.12   FRS 12 supersedes SSAP 18 and contains separate definitions of a contingent asset and a contingent liability. The definition of contingent liability is wider than before and includes three scenarios where the definition of a provision is not met:
[FRS 12(2)]

(a)   where the obligation is only possible rather than certain; or

(b)   a present obligation exists but:

    (i)   an outflow of economic benefits is not probable; or
    (ii)   the probable outflow cannot be reliably measured.

FRS 4 *Capital instruments*

Introduction

17.13   FRS 4 applies to all transactions and instruments, irrespective of the date on which they were issued. It addresses only accounting for capital instruments by those who issue them; it does not address the accounting by those who hold them as investments.

17.14   FRS 4 does not, however, apply to the following types of capital instruments:
[FRS 4(21)]

(a)   warrants issued to employees under employee share schemes;

(b)   leases which are accounted for in accordance with SSAP 21; and

(c)   equity shares issued as part of a business combination which is accounted for as a merger.

17.15   The definition of capital instruments is dealt with in **17.4** to **17.8** above.

Identification of distinct capital instruments

17.16   When two or more capital instruments are issued at the same time, it is necessary to determine whether the instruments should be accounted for individually or whether they are part of a composite transaction and should be considered together as one instrument in applying the requirements of the FRS. The instruments will be accounted for as a single composite instrument, unless the individual component instruments are capable of being transferred, cancelled or redeemed independently of each other. [FRS 4(22)] Where, for example, debt is issued with warrants, if the warrants are detachable and could be transferred as separate instruments, the two components should be accounted for separately. In this case, the proceeds will have to be apportioned between the two instruments and each accounted for appropriately.

Carrying amount

17.17 Immediately after issue, a capital instrument should be recorded at the net proceeds of the issue. Net proceeds are defined as 'the fair value of the consideration received on the issue of the instrument after deduction of issue costs'. Issue costs are considered in **17.22** to **17.32** below. It should be noted that this may differ from the acquisition cost for FRS 7 purposes (see **24.7** below). This is discussed in FRS 7, Appendix I (6) where it is noted that any such difference would be recorded as a separate element of consolidated reserves and does not form part of goodwill.

17.18 Deep discount bonds or zero coupon bonds (i.e., those which carry a low or zero nominal rate of interest and are issued at a discount to the value at which they will be redeemed) will be recorded at the net amount of proceeds received on the issue. FRS 4 does not allow the discount on issue to be treated as an asset within 'prepayments and accrued income', even though such a treatment is permitted by Sch 4 (see **16.76** above), because the discount does not give rise to future economic benefits and thus does not meet the definition of an asset in the ASB's Statement of Principles. Recording the debt at net proceeds does not, therefore, contravene the offsetting rule in the Act. In subsequent periods, the carrying amount of debt will be increased by the finance charge for the period (see **17.33** to **17.50** below) and reduced by any amounts paid in the period.

Example 17.18

A company issues convertible debt on 1 January 1999 for £100,000, which is redeemable on 31 December 2008 for £150,000. It carries an interest charge of £3,410 per annum for the first five years, after which the charge increases to £9,000 per annum for the remaining period of the instrument.

In order to comply with the requirement to allocate the finance costs on a constant rate on the carrying amount, a rate of nine per cent will have to be used. The movements over the period of the debt would then be as follows:

Year ending	Balance at beginning of year	Finance cost	Cash paid	Balance at end of year
	£	£	£	£
31.12.99	100,000	9,000	3,410	105,590
31.12.00	105,590	9,412	3,410	111,592
31.12.01	111,592	9,894	3,410	118,076
31.12.02	118,076	10,458	3,410	125,124
31.12.03	125,124	11,117	3,410	132,831
31.12.04	132,831	11,890	9,000	135,721

31.12.05	135,721	12,119	9,000	138,840
31.12.06	138,840	12,388	9,000	142,228
31.12.07	142,228	12,702	9,000	145,930
31.12.08	145,930	13,070	159,000	0
		112,050		

The total finance cost of the debt is the payments made, five years at £3,410 plus five years at £9,000, plus the premium on redemption of £50,000. The total of £112,050 has been allocated at a constant rate on the opening balance each year.

17.19 In the circumstances where the accrued finance cost will be paid in cash in the next period, the FRS allows the accrued finance charge to be shown in accruals rather than included in the carrying amount of the debt. [FRS 4(30)]

17.20 This presentation can be demonstrated by considering a very straightforward example of redeemable debt with a fixed nominal yield and a premium payable on redemption. The nominal yield is normally paid in the two months following the year end. In this example, it would be appropriate for the nominal yield portion of the finance charge recognised for the year to be shown within accruals rather than as an adjustment to carrying value. The carrying amount of the debt will be increased only for the proportion of the finance charge related to the accrued premium on redemption. In other words, in these simple cases, the carrying amount of the debt will reflect the accrual of the discount on issue or premium on redemption, but not the nominal interest payable each year.

Example 17.20

Following the example in **17.18** above, assume that the interest for each year is payable on 15 January in the following year. (For the purpose of illustration, ignore the effect the change of payment date will have on the allocation of the overall charge between years.)

In the financial statements to 31 December 2001, the entries in respect of the debt would be:

Dr: Interest payable and similar charges   £9,894
(profit and loss account)

Cr: Accruals and deferred income   £3,410
(interest payable in 15 days)

Cr: Debenture loans, loan stock and other loans   £6,484

17.21

> The FRS states that whether or not the accrued finance cost is shown in accruals, it should always be included in the carrying amount of the debt for the purposes of allocating the finance cost at a constant rate on the carrying amount. In practice, if the nominal yield amount is payable soon after the year end, excluding the amount shown in accruals from the calculation will probably have an immaterial effect on the allocation of the finance charge and can be ignored.

Issue costs

17.22 The net proceeds of the issue are defined as 'the fair value of the consideration received on the issue of a capital instrument after deduction of issue costs'. [FRS 4(11)]

17.23 FRS 4 defines issue costs as the costs which are incurred directly in connection with the issue of a capital instrument and which would not have been incurred had the specific instrument in question not been issued. Costs which do not qualify as issue costs should be written off to the profit and loss account as incurred.

17.24 This definition should be interpreted quite narrowly, so as not to overstate the finance charge being included in respect of the instrument.

17.25 The type of costs which would be excluded from the definition would be:
[FRS 4(96)]

  (a) costs of researching and determining feasibility of particular sources of finance;

  (b) costs of negotiating sources of financing;

  (c) internal costs for items such as management time associated with the negotiations;

  (d) costs of renegotiating or restructuring financing.

17.26

> In the case of a private company, the costs of issuing shares or debt will normally only include such items as legal fees and printing costs.

17.27

> Public companies issuing listed shares or debt instruments must comply with the requirements of the UK Listing Authority Listing Rules. The issue costs for listed shares and debt will therefore include underwriting fees from merchant banks and legal and accountancy fees in connection with the circular. Care should be taken to ensure that fees related to the

items listed in **17.25** above are not included in the costs from any of these parties.

17.28 Often, the issue of listed shares or debt instruments is a linked transaction with either an acquisition or flotation. In these cases, it is necessary to split the costs between the two parts of the transaction. Splitting these costs is a matter of judgement and it may be difficult to estimate what proportion should be allocated to issue costs. The proportion allocated should certainly not result in a level of issue costs above that which would have been incurred if the transaction had been an issue only.

17.29 In respect of debt instruments, it is not anticipated that there will be any difference between the costs that it is deemed appropriate to take to the share premium account and the costs which will be treated as issue costs for the purposes of applying FRS 4. (For shares, see **18.83** below.)

17.30 Issue costs in respect of debt instruments which have a finite term are deducted from the proceeds of the issue and charged to the profit and loss account as part of the finance costs at a constant rate on the carrying amount over the term of the instrument. The Act permits issue costs on debentures to be written off to the share premium account and the FRS does not restrict this. So, the amount of the finance charge recognised in the profit and loss account each year relating to issue costs can be taken to the share premium account, if sufficient balance exists on that account, by means of a reserve transfer.

17.31 It appears appropriate to interpret the Act as allowing the assessment of whether sufficient balance exists in the share premium account to be made at the date at which each tranche of issue costs is written off through the profit and loss account, even if the balance against which the issue costs are taken was created subsequent to the issue of the debt.

17.32 Issue costs in respect of capital instruments which have an indeterminate life, such as perpetual debt, should not be taken to the profit and loss account until the instrument is redeemed or cancelled. [FRS 4(95)]

Finance costs

17.33 Finance costs are the difference between the net proceeds of an instrument and the total amount of the payments (or other transfers of economic benefits) which the issuer may be required to make in respect of the instrument. [FRS 4(8)]

17.34

> Applying the definition of finance costs to debt instruments
> means that the finance cost will include interest payments plus
> any premiums payable on repayment plus issue costs. Where
> debt is issued at a discount, it is likely that it will carry a lower
> rate of interest than would apply had it been issued at par. The
> debt will be recorded at the net amount of the proceeds result-
> ing in the discount being treated as part of the finance charge
> amortised to the profit and loss account over the term of the
> finance.

17.35   Finance costs should be allocated to the profit and loss account over
the term of the debt at a constant rate of return on the carrying
amount. [FRS 4(28)]

17.36

> It would seem acceptable to base the finance charge on the
> average amount outstanding during the year, as this would
> most accurately reflect the finance charge during the year.

17.37   The finance charge on debt instruments should be included within
the interest payable caption of the profit and loss account.

17.38   Where the amount of the payments required by a debt instrument
are contingent on uncertain future events, the finance charge and
carrying amount of the debt should reflect the circumstances at the
balance sheet date.

17.39   For example, if the premium on redemption is dependent upon an
index, such as the FT-SE 100, the carrying amount of the debt should
be adjusted at the balance sheet date to reflect the amount payable calculated with reference to the FT-SE 100 index at that date. Any adjustment to the estimated premium or nominal yield should be
recognised in the finance charge for that period. The application notes
to FRS 4 include an example of accounting for index-linked loans.

17.40   The simplest example of an instrument with payment contingent on
an uncertain future event is a floating interest rate loan. For this type
of loan, the interest rate is normally expressed as London Inter-Bank
Offer Rate (LIBOR) plus a percentage. The finance charge each year
will be determined by LIBOR in that year, just as it was prior to
FRS 4.

17.41

> Some loans are negotiated which carry a fixed rate of interest
> for an initial period, followed by a floating rate of interest
> beyond that period. Where the fixed rate is comparable to the
> market rate that could be obtained for a purely fixed-rate loan
> at the date the loan is issued, it is appropriate to treat the debt
> as effectively two separate loans. The finance charge will simply
> be the fixed rate in the initial period and the actual rate paid
> when the loan becomes floating rate.

Example 17.41

A company negotiates a loan for £1 million at a fixed interest rate of seven per cent for three years and a floating rate of LIBOR plus one per cent thereafter. Both the fixed seven per cent and the LIBOR plus one per cent appear to be reasonable market rates in their own right and it is appropriate for the finance charge to equal the actual interest charge each year.

17.42 Where the fixed rate of interest on the initial term is not at a market rate and has been negotiated only on the basis of the rate to be paid on the subsequent term of the loan, the loan cannot simply be treated as two separate loans. This situation will normally be evidenced by the existence of early repayment penalties.

17.43 In this case, FRS 4 requires spreading of the finance charge over the whole period of the loan. There appears to be only one practical method to achieve this. The early repayment penalties should be reviewed to establish the effective rate of return being achieved by the lender. This can be used to establish effective rates as if the loan had been a fixed rate loan followed by a floating rate loan.

Example 17.43

At 1 January 2000, a company negotiates a loan of £1 million at a fixed rate of two per cent until December 2003 and a floating rate of LIBOR plus 8.5 per cent until December 2007. If the loan is repaid prior to December 2007, this gives rise to additional premiums of £50,000 in 2000, rising to £220,000 in 2003 then reducing to £60,000 in 2006.

Clearly, in this case, neither the two per cent nor the LIBOR plus 8.5 per cent individually are market rates. Looking at the additional amounts payable on early repayment, these equate to the lender seeking an additional five per cent return for years 2000 to 2003. This equates to an effective return of seven per cent in the initial years followed by LIBOR plus two per cent for the remaining years.

The finance charge should reflect that the loan is equivalent to two loans, a fixed loan followed by a floating loan, at the effective market rates.

Negative finance charge

17.44 The instances where a negative finance charge will arise are rare, but one situation where it might occur is where a company issues convertible debt with a redemption option. The debt is issued at a premium and redeemable at a value below the issue price if the conversion option is not exercised. Under the standard, the finance costs are calculated on the assumption that conversion will not take place. In this case, the negative finance costs will be recognised as credits to the profit and loss account over the term of the debt.

Investment companies

17.45 Investment companies may include finance costs, to the extent that they relate to capital, in the statement of total recognised gains and losses rather than in the profit and loss account. Where this is the case, the amount so treated should be disclosed in the statement of total recognised gains and losses. The accounting policy for determining the allocation of finance costs between revenue and capital should be disclosed. [FRS 4(52)]

Calculation of constant rate of return on carrying value

17.46 The ease with which the rate that will give a constant rate of return on the carrying amount can be calculated depends on the amounts and timing of the various cash flows associated with the instrument.

17.47 In the explanatory notes, the FRS states that, in some instances, the nominal yield on the debt will not be materially different from the amount required by the FRS to be recognised. In these circumstances, it is acceptable not to perform exact calculations of the finance amount to be recognised in each period. An example of the sort of circumstances where it may be possible to use an approximate figure is where an instrument carries a constant nominal yield and the premium payable on redemption and the issue costs taken together are not material. In these cases, recognising the premium and issue costs on a straight-line basis together with the nominal amount each year would not give a materially different finance cost from the strict requirements of the standard.

17.48 A simple formula can be used to calculate the rate of return on an instrument on which no payments are made during the term of the instrument, e.g., a zero coupon bond.

17.49 The general formula for expressing the relationship between a monetary amount at one date (terminal value) and an earlier date (present value) is:

Present value (£) = Terminal value (£) × Discount factor

For a single sum, the discount factor will be:

Discount factor = $(1 + i)^{-n}$

where:

i = periodic rate of interest; and
n = the number of periods between the present and terminal dates.

> ### *Example 17.49*
>
> £1 bonds (with no interest coupon) are issued at a discount of 30 per cent (i.e., at 70p) and are redeemable in six years from the issue date at par.
>
> The general formula is applied as follows:
>
> $0.7 = 1 \times (1 + i)^{-6}$
> $(1 + i)^6 = {}^1/_{0.7} = 1.43$
> $1 + i = 1.43^{1/6} = 1.0614$
> $i = 0.0614$
>
> The total annual rate of return is 6.14 per cent.

17.50   If the calculations become more complex, e.g., the coupon rate is stepped, there is no simple method of calculating the constant rate of charge. It involves an iterative trial process to find the nearest approximate figure. In these cases, most computer spreadsheet packages have a function which can calculate the rate, termed the internal rate of return (IRR), of a pattern of cash flows.

Term of debt

17.51   The term of a capital instrument should be taken to be the earliest date under which the lender can demand repayment. For debt, this will usually be self-evident. The effects of 'material adverse change' clauses are discussed in **17.130** below.

17.52   FRS 4 states that where options for early redemption are available to either party, the term of the instrument will usually be taken to be the earliest date at which the option can be exercised. Similarly, the term should not include any periods for which the instrument may be extended, unless such an extension is certain at the time the instrument is issued, i.e., there is no genuine commercial possibility that it will not be extended. [FRS 4(16) and (73)]

17.53   Options contained in capital instruments should be evaluated carefully.

Holder call options

17.54   Where an instrument contains an option by the holder to redeem early, then the term of the debt will normally be taken to be to the earliest exercise date of the option. An exception to this general rule will be where there is no commercial possibility that this will occur, e.g., an instrument containing an option for the lender to redeem early where the lender would receive a disproportionately small fraction of the redemption value on exercise of the option. In this case, it would be considered that there would be no commercial reason for the option to be exercised and it would be ignored for the purpose of determining the term of the debt. [FRS 4(73) and (74)]

Issuer call options

17.55 The UITF has issued UITF Abstract 11, entitled *Capital instruments: issuer call options*. This addresses the situation where an instrument is issued with an option for the issuer to redeem it before the normal redemption date, usually with the payment of a premium.

17.56 UITF Abstract 11 confirms the general requirement in FRS 4 (see **17.52** above) that, in the case of an instrument with an issuer call option, exercise of which is uncertain, the term of the instrument, as defined in FRS 4 (16), would end on the date that the option was exercisable.

17.57 The finance costs of a capital instrument are defined by FRS 4 as the difference between the net proceeds and the payments that the issuer may be required to make. [FRS 4(8)] The premium on early redemption under an issuer call option is not a payment that the issuer may be required to make; it is up to the issuer to decide whether or not to pay the premium and, therefore, UITF Abstract 11 concludes that it is inappropriate to account for a premium which the issuer can elect not to make. It also concludes that premiums payable as a result of the exercise of an issuer call option should not be reflected in the finance charge, but reflected as a gain or loss arising on early settlement if and when the option is exercised.

Example 17.57

One million £1 bonds are issued at par and are redeemable in 10 years from the issue date, also at par. Interest is payable at 10 per cent per annum. The issuer has the option to redeem the bonds after six years at a premium of 20p.

Applying UITF Abstract 11, the term of the bonds will be six years (i.e., to the date on which the issuer may redeem them). The finance costs to be allocated over this period will consist only of the interest charges for that period at 10 per cent. Accordingly, the interest charged in the financial statements for the first six years will be the same as that paid, i.e., £100,000 per annum.

If the issuer elects to redeem the bonds after six years, the premium of £200,000 will represent a loss on exercise.

17.58 UITF Abstract 11 does not apply to those cases where the effective rate of interest (or the margin above a base rate by which interest is calculated) increases after the date on which the option is exercisable. In these cases, the issuer's exercise price may be deemed to compensate the investor for forgoing such increased interest and, accordingly, the premium payable on exercise of the option should be included as part of the finance costs.

17.59 In **17.58** above, the reference to increased interest after the date on which the option is exercisable should be treated as including any premium payable on the redemption of the capital instrument on a date later than the option exercise date. Failure to take account of such a premium would result in a distortion of the finance charge.

17.60 UITF Abstract 11 applies only to genuine options. An issuer call option would not be considered genuine if it is clear that in all conceivable circumstances the issuer would be commercially obliged to exercise its call option. In these cases, the accounting would reflect the premium payable and the early repayment date.

Shares issued by subsidiaries

17.61 Shares of subsidiary undertakings which are not held by other group companies are usually reported as part of minority interests in the consolidated financial statements. FRS 4, however, requires some of these to be shown within liabilities.

17.62 In consolidated financial statements, shares issued by subsidiaries, other than those held by other group companies, should be reported as liabilities if any member of the group has an obligation to transfer economic benefits in connection with those shares.

17.63 An obligation to a third party in these circumstances is likely to be in the form of:

(a) guarantees of future dividends;

(b) agreements to purchase the shares of the minority;

(c) guaranteed redemption proceeds in the case of redeemable shares; or

(d) a subsidiary incorporated in a jurisdiction where it cannot avoid paying dividends, but where there are insufficient distributable profits such that the funds would have to be provided by other group companies.

17.64 The balance shown as a liability within the consolidated financial statements would appear to be the full value of the minority interest rather than the value of the guarantee provided by other group companies. This is because FRS 4 states that 'shares issued by subsidiaries should be accounted for in consolidated financial statement as liabilities'. [FRS 4(49)]

> Therefore, no attempt should be made to split the proceeds of the shares between a liability and any other element; the total carrying value determined by FRS 4 will be shown within liabilities.

Extract 17.64

MEPC plc

Year ended 30 September 1998

Subsidiary undertakings' preference shares and non-equity minority interests

At 30 September 1997 the Group had public US$ denominated share issues made by five subsidiary undertakings.

During the year four of these issues were redeemed and the US$215m Cumulative Guaranteed Quarterly Income Preferred Securities (QUIPS) remains in issue.

The QUIPS were issued in September 1995 through MEPC International Capital, L.P., a special purpose limited partnership which is not credit-supported. They have been structured to provide a guarantee by MEPC plc such that the holders are effectively in the same position as the holders of MEPC's preference shares with respect to payment of dividends and amounts upon liquidation, dissolution and winding-up. The capital outstanding and the dividends payable are, therefore, classified as non-equity minority interests in both the balance sheet and the profit and loss account since there is a guarantee such that the subsidiary's preference shareholders rank pari passu with MEPC plc's preference shareholders. For the purposes of the financial statements as regards the issues redeemed during the year, the 1997 balance sheet classifications and the profit and loss classifications to redemption have been determined on the following basis:

(i)   The capital outstanding is classified as subsidiary undertakings' preferences shares within creditors in the balance sheet, and the dividends payable included in finance costs in the profit and loss account where the parent undertaking or a Group company has a contingent obligation under guarantees either directly or in respect of letters of credit supporting the issue.

(ii)   The capital outstanding and the dividends payable are classified as non-equity minority interests in the balance sheet and profit and loss account, respectively, where the issue does not represent a contingent obligation on the parent undertaking or a Group company under guarantees in respect of letters of credit supporting the issue.

17.65   The liability will only be in respect of the consolidated financial statements. In the financial statements of the parent company, the guarantee made in respect of the subsidiary's share will be accounted for and disclosed in accordance with the requirements of FRS 12.

Example 17.65

On 1 January 2000, B Ltd, a subsidiary of A Ltd, issued 10,000 nine per cent redeemable convertible preference shares for £5 per share. The shares are convertible into ordinary shares of A Ltd after 1 January 2005. If the shares are not converted by 31 December 2009, they will be redeemed at £10. Payment of both the coupons and the redemption amount are guaranteed by A Ltd. The shareholders may, however, redeem the shares on 31 December 2004 at £8 per share.

The amount of the liability shown in the consolidated financial statements will be the proceeds received on the issue of the preference shares, i.e., £50,000 (assuming no issue costs), plus the accrued finance charge calculated on a constant rate of return on the carrying amount in order to build the value of the liability up to the potential redemption proceeds at the earliest date at which they can be redeemed.

Year ended	Value at 1 January £	Accrued Finance Charge £	Value at 31 December £
31.12.00	50,000	4,928	54,928
31.12.01	54,928	5,414	60,342
31.12.02	60,342	5,947	66,289
31.12.03	66,289	6,533	72,822
31.12.04	72,822	7,178	80,000

If the holder of the preference shares does not elect to convert at 31 December 2004, the liability will be built up in the same way over the remaining five years such that the liability will equal £100,000 by the end of its term.

The above example assumes that the nine per cent dividend is paid each year.

17.66 In the above example, as in most cases, the liability will be converted into shares at which point the balance sheet liability will be taken to be the issue proceeds, with any excess over nominal value being taken to the share premium account (see **18.62** below). This will also apply if the liability is convertible into shares of the subsidiary which are immediately exchanged for shares of the parent.

Examples of capital instruments

Introduction

17.67　The following examples reflect the application of FRS 4 to various capital instruments.

Stepped bonds

17.68　The term 'stepped bonds' describes an issue with interest increasing by fixed steps over the life of the issue (e.g., three per cent in the first two years, five per cent in the next two years, increasing in steps to 15 per cent for the last years). It is inappropriate for the earlier years to benefit from the lower rates. The FRS requires the effective finance rate computed over the anticipated life of the bond to be charged to the profit and loss account in each period, irrespective of the interest paid in each year. [FRS 4(28) and FRS 4 (Application note: Stepped interest bonds)]

Bonds with variable redemption payments

17.69　Where a loan is repayable at a rate adjusted by the RPI or some other index, FRS 4 suggests that a charge (or credit) against profits should be made to reflect the change in the liability caused by the movement in the relevant index during the period, even though the liability to repay has not yet arisen.

Bonds with share warrants attached

17.70　Where bonds are issued with detachable warrants giving the holder the option to subscribe for equity shares, the holder may sell the bonds and warrants independently of each other. The proceeds of this type of issue should be split between the constituents and accounted for separately. No guidance is given in FRS 4 as to how the split is to be calculated.

17.71　　The following approach is recommended:

　　(a)　if the coupon rate is equal to the market rate for comparable bonds without warrants, the excess of the gross proceeds over the face amount of the bonds should be attributed to the value of the warrants;

　　(b)　if the coupon rate is less than the market rate, the gross proceeds should be apportioned based on the respective market values of the bonds and warrants on the first day on which they are traded;

　　(c)　if the instruments are not freely traded some value should be ascribed to the warrants to take into account the conversion price in relation to the value of the equity shares and the time to expiry of the warrants.

Interest rate swaps

17.72 An interest-rate swap agreement is a contract with another party, usually a financial institution or another corporate borrower, whereby each agrees to exchange an interest obligation over an agreed period of time with that of the other party. Such contracts can be used to hedge a floating interest-rate obligation by effectively substituting it for a fixed-rate obligation from a party that is prepared to take on the speculative risks and rewards of a floating-rate obligation.

17.73 The swap agreement does not change the existing loan obligation, but the company should record as the interest cost of the loan an amount, including the effect of the swap. Usually, the swap agreement provides that only the interest differential is payable to the other party.

> ### Example 17.73
>
> Assume Company A with a floating interest-rate obligation of LIBOR plus $\frac{1}{2}$ per cent swaps it to pay a fixed rate of 15 per cent and, during the first period of the swap to the balance sheet date, the floating rate is 14 per cent. Company A ultimately has an obligation to pay the additional one per cent under the swap agreement and should accrue the additional one per cent interest cost.

17.74 FRS 4 requires a description of the legal nature of debt where this is different from that normally associated with debt. It is suggested, therefore, that there should be full disclosure of the arrangement in the notes to the accounts, so that the commercial effect on the whole transaction, including any possible risk of exposure in the event of the failure of the counterparty, is explained clearly. See also chapter 21 as regards the requirements of FRS 13 *Derivatives and other financial instruments: disclosures*.

Subordinated debt

17.75 There are various forms of subordination that debt can take. However, the basic feature of subordinated debt is that the right to repayment is subordinate to the right of other creditors. This does not mean that the lender has forgone the right to repayment and therefore subordinated debt represents an obligation or contingent obligation to transfer economic benefits and subordinated debt should be shown within liabilities.

Repackaged perpetual debt

17.76 The basic feature of repackaged perpetual debt is that the 'principal' amount of the debt is perpetual, i.e., never becomes payable. The debt carries a high coupon rate for a number of years, the primary period, and then a nominal or nil amount thereafter. The substance is that, at the end of the primary period, the entity ceases to have a liability, as there remains no obligation, contingent or otherwise, to transfer economic benefits. The substance of the transaction is that the debt has been repaid over the primary period. The payments made represent repayment of principal and finance charge. The finance charge, being the difference between net proceeds and the total payments made, will be allocated over the primary period at a constant rate on the outstanding liability.

Creditors

Statutory headings

17.77 Schedule 4 permits two alternative formats for the balance sheet. In format 1, there are two separate main headings: 'Creditors: amounts falling due within one year' and 'Creditors: amounts falling due after more than one year'. In format 2, there is only one main heading, 'Creditors', but the amounts falling due within one year and after one year should be shown separately for each subheading and totals should be shown for amounts falling due within one year and after one year.

17.78 The subheadings that are required, which may be shown separately on the face of the balance sheet or in the notes to the accounts, are:

- Debenture loans;

- Bank loans and overdrafts;

- Payments received on account;

- Trade creditors;

- Bills of exchange payable;

- Amounts owed to group undertakings;

- Amounts owed to undertakings in which the company has a participating interest;

- Other creditors, including taxation and social security;

- Accruals and deferred income.

The directors may adapt these subheadings in any case where the special nature of the company's business requires such adaptation. In addition, subheadings may be combined if their individual amounts are not material.

17.79 As an alternative, 'Accruals and deferred income' may be shown as a separate main heading, rather than as a subheading of creditors, but this alternative is rarely followed.

Dividends

17.80 The aggregate amount of any dividends proposed should be shown either on the face of the profit and loss account or in the notes to the accounts. [Sch 4: 3(7)] A proposed dividend is not strictly a liability in law until it has been declared and therefore it is not appropriate to include it under any of the items listed in the balance sheet formats. Instead, it should be shown as an additional item under the heading 'Creditors: amounts falling due within one year' as permitted by Sch 4. [Sch 4: 3(2)] Dividends declared but unpaid at the balance sheet date could be included under the item 'Other creditors including taxation and social security'. Many companies, however, will probably choose also to show these separately.

17.81 Cumulative dividends accrued (but not yet declared) under the requirements of FRS 4, i.e., where the dividend entitlement on non-equity shares is calculated by reference to time, are normally included in other reserves, not shown as a creditor. [FRS 4(43)] In most cases, such dividends which remain unpaid become payable as an 'additional premium' on redemption and therefore identical treatment with other premiums payable on redemption seems appropriate (see **18.68** below).

Disclosure requirements

17.82 An analysis of the maturity of total debt should be given (either on the face of the balance sheet or in the notes to the accounts) showing amounts falling due:
[FRS 4(33)]

   (a)   in one year or less, or on demand;

   (b)   in more than one year but not more than two years;

   (c)   in more than two years but not more than five years; and

   (d)   in more than five years.

17.83 FRS 13 requires a similar maturity analysis to be disclosed for all financial liabilities [FRS 13(38)]. For entities that fall within the scope of FRS 13 it suggests that the required FRS 4 analysis and the SSAP 21 analysis of finance leases could be combined and extended to meet the FRS 13 requirement. [FRS 13(39)] See **21.66** to **21.70** below.

17.84 For each item shown under creditors, there should be stated the aggregate of:
[Sch 4: 48]

   (a)   debts which fall due after five years from the balance sheet date and which are payable otherwise than by instalments; and

(b) in the case of debts payable by instalments, the amount of instalments which fall due after five years.

For each debt included here, the terms of payment and rates of interest payable should be shown. However, where the number of debts is large, a general indication of the terms of payment and rates of interest payable is sufficient.

17.85 The amount of any convertible loans should be shown separately. [Sch 4: Note 7 on the balance sheet formats] FRS 4 requires convertible debt to be reported separately on the face of the balance sheet within liabilities, unless the amount is not material; in which case, disclosure may be made in the notes to the accounts, but the relevant caption on the face of the balance sheet should state that convertible debt is included.

Example 17.85

Creditors: amounts falling due within one year

	Note	2000 £'000	1999 £'000
Debenture loans (including convertible loans)	x	120	110
Trade creditors		453	483
Other creditors including taxation and social security		86	76
Accruals and deferred income		99	72
		758	741

17.86 For each subheading of creditors, the aggregate amount of debts for which any security has been given by the company and an indication of the nature of that security should be disclosed. [Sch 4: 48(4)]

17.87 In consolidated financial statements, the nature of the securities given by all group undertakings and the consolidated amount of debt so secured should be disclosed.

17.88

A guarantee or other security given by a director to secure a loan made to his company is not required to be disclosed under this provision, but it will need to be disclosed under the requirements of FRS 8 (see **32.62** below). Any security given by group undertakings to secure the debts of another member of the group need not be disclosed in the financial statements of that other member under the Act and is also likely to fall within the exemptions of FRS 8.

17.89 Reference should be made to **17.315** and **17.317** below for further disclosures to be given in respect of guarantees and charges on company assets made to secure obligations of other parties.

17.90 An example of an appropriate note to the accounts which meets the requirements as they affect creditors falling due after more than one year is given below.

Example 17.90

Creditors: amounts falling due after more than one year

	2000 £'000	1999 £'000
Debenture loans:		
8% loan stock 1990/2011,		
(repayable £140,000 annually)	1,455	1,595
12% loan stock 1997/2018,		
(repayable £136,000 annually)	2,312	2,448
	3,767	4,043
Bank loans:		
Repayable 2007, interest at 1½% above		
the bank's base lending rate	800	800
Other	300	380
	1,100	1,180
Other loans:		
Obligations under finance leases and		
hire purchase contracts	230	195
Other loans	392	304
	622	499
Total loans	5,489	5,722
Analysis of loan repayments:		
In one year or less or on demand	588	576
In more than one year but not	546	535
more than two years		
In more than two years but not	1,535	1,443
more than five years		
In more than five years	3,408	3,744
	6,077	6,298
Amounts payable wholly or partly after five years:		
Debenture loans	2,608	2,884
Bank loans	800	860

The debenture loans of £3,767,000 are secured by a floating charge on all the assets of the group. Bank loans are secured by first mortgages on all the group's freehold and leasehold properties in Crewe and by guarantees given by all companies in the group. Lease obligations are secured by retention of title to the relevant plant and machinery.

17.91

The example note in **17.90** above discloses repayment terms and interest rates only on those loans any part of which fall due after five years, as required by the Act. Similar disclosure for other loans is encouraged. Entities which fall within the scope of FRS 13 are required to provide further maturity and interest rate information (see chapter 21).

17.92 There is a presumption that amounts included in debt represent unconditional contractual obligations which, on a winding-up, would give rise to a claim for an amount similar to that shown in the financial statements. Where this is not the case, the following should be disclosed:

(a) a brief description of the legal nature of the debt; and

(b) the amount of any claim on a winding-up.

These details need not be given for each individual instrument, but may be presented in a summarised form. [FRS 4(63)]

17.93 This disclosure will usually be necessary, for example, where shares issued by subsidiary undertakings have been classified as debt or if the entity has subordinated or non-recourse debt.

Example 17.93

Note 19. Creditors: amounts falling due after more than one year

	Group		Company	
	2000	*1999*	*2000*	*1999*
	£'000	*£'000*	*£'000*	*£'000*
Debenture loans,				
loan stock and other loans	304	304	20	20
Bank loans	426	387	–	–
Other creditors	27	33	–	–
Accruals and deferred income	109	95	–	–
	866	819	20	20
Guaranteed redeemable				
convertible preference shares	1,030	1,010		
	1,896	1,829		

Note 20. Guaranteed redeemable convertible preference shares

On 30 June 1999, Distribution Finance, a subsidiary company incorporated in the Cayman Islands, issued 100,000 8.2 per cent guaranteed redeemable convertible preference shares with a paid up value of £10 per share. Distribution Holdings plc have guaranteed the shares on a subordinated basis and they are convertible into ordinary shares of Distribution Holdings plc at a price of 250p per share at any time between 1 July 2009 and 30 June 2014. The shares outstanding at

---

30 June 2014 will be redeemed on 15 July 2014 at their issue price or in specified circumstances on earlier revocation of the guarantee. The shares may be redeemed on 1 July 2009 at the preference shareholders' option at a redemption price of 120 per cent of the paid-up value of the shares. Provision is made for the possible premium on redemption and included within the carrying amount of the shares. At 31 December 2000, the amount accrued was £30,000 (1999 – £10,000).

17.94 Where the market value of a class of debt security is readily available, it should be considered best practice to disclose the market value at the balance sheet date and the carrying amount. [FRS 4(102)]

Creditors: subheadings

Debenture loans

Definition

17.95 The Act's definition of the term 'debenture' includes debenture stock, bonds and any other securities of a company, whether constituting a charge on the assets of the company or not. [s744]

17.96 As this is not a particularly helpful definition, any liability that is formally recognised in a written instrument is usually taken to be a debenture.

Disclosure

17.97 Disclosure is required of the following particulars of debentures issued during the financial year in the notes to the accounts: [Sch 4: 41(1)]

(a)   the classes of debentures issued; and

(b)   as respects each class of debentures, the amount issued and the consideration received.

17.98 Some loan agreements include clauses which restrict the activities of the company. In such cases, the notes to the accounts should disclose the significant restrictions, such as those which limit the payment of dividends or establish minimum working capital.

Convertible debt

Accounting for convertible bonds

17.99 Any redemption option carried by a convertible debt represents a contingent liability to transfer economic benefits. The possibility of conversion should not be anticipated, so the probability that the liability will not materialise does not influence the classification. The instrument should be reported within liabilities. The associated finance cost should also be calculated on the assumption that the debt will not be converted. [FRS 4(25)]

17.100 Convertible bonds are usually issued with a lower coupon than the market rate for similar non-convertible debt. Some convertible bonds allow the holder to elect at some point during the life of the bond to give up the conversion rights and receive instead a premium on redemption or a higher rate of interest backdated to the issue date. The difference between the coupon and the higher rate of interest is referred to as supplemental interest.

17.101 Accounting for these supplemental interest premiums is covered by FRS 4. Under the definition of finance costs, the finance costs of a convertible bond will include any premiums that may be payable on redemption. The total finance costs, including the supplemental interest amount, must be charged to the profit and loss account over the term of the debt at a constant rate on the carrying amount.

Disclosure

17.102 The Act requires the amount of any convertible loans (which will almost invariably fall within the definition of debentures) to be shown separately. [Sch 4: Note 7 on the balance sheet formats] FRS 4 states that convertible debt should be reported separately on the face of the balance sheet within liabilities. If the amount of convertible debt is not material, disclosure may be made in the notes to the accounts, but the relevant caption on the face of the balance sheet should state that convertible debt is included.

17.103 The following disclosures should be made in the notes to the accounts in respect of convertible debt:

(a) details of the date of redemption and the amount payable on redemption [FRS 4(62)];

(b) the number, description and class of shares into which the debt may be converted and the date at, or the period within which, conversion may take place [Sch 4: 40 and FRS 4(62)]; and

(c) whether conversion is at the option of the issuer or holder [FRS 4(62)].

Example 17.103

The convertible unsecured loan stock may be converted at a holder's option into fully paid ordinary shares of £1 each in any year up to 2002 at the rate of one ordinary share for every £2.50 of convertible

---

> loan stock. Full conversion of the outstanding rights will result in the issue of 5,250,000 ordinary shares. If the conversion option is not exercised, the loan stock will be redeemed on 1 January 2003 at a premium of 10 per cent.
>
> The finance cost charged in the profit and loss account comprises the aggregate of the coupon on the loan stock and the proportion of the premium on redemption that relates to the financial year.

Bank loans and overdrafts

17.104 As noted in **17.135** below, many bank loans give the bank an unconditional right to demand payment; in which case, they should be classified as creditors falling due within one year.

17.105 If bank accounts with both debit and credit balances are maintained at the same bank and there is a right of set-off, the net amount should be shown under current assets or liabilities as appropriate. Where the right of set-off does not exist, the assets and liabilities should both be shown at their full amount in the balance sheet, regardless of whether the balances are with the same bank or different banks. Set-off is examined further as part of the requirements of FRS 5 *Reporting the substance of transactions,* which are discussed in **28.52** to **28.59** below.

17.106   A common situation found in groups of companies is that one company in the group controls the treasury function. This can give more efficient use of finance for the group as a whole and often means that finance can be obtained at a lower rate than individual companies within the group could achieve. All companies within the group use this 'treasury' company in the same way as a bank, all their cash positions are held with this company. Balances with such a 'treasury' company should be disclosed as amounts owed by/to group undertakings not as cash at bank/bank loans and overdrafts.

Payments received on account

17.107 Payments received (and receivable) on account of orders (e.g., progress payments on contracts) should first be set off against amounts recoverable on the same contract included in debtors, then against any balance included in stocks relating to the same contract. Any balance remaining should be shown under this heading (see **16.57** above). [Sch 4: Note 8 on the balance sheet formats]

Trade creditors

17.108 Although bills of exchange payable and accruals are separate sub-headings, their amounts are often insufficiently material to justify separate disclosure. When this arises, they are usually included with trade creditors. Debit balances on suppliers' accounts, if the aggregate amount is significant, should be included in debtors.

Disclosure

17.109 Public limited companies and their large private subsidiaries must include in their directors' report a statement of the company's creditor payment policy and the number of days represented by trade creditors at the year end. [Sch 7: 12] This is discussed in **6.72** to **6.75** above.

Reservation of title clauses

17.110 Suppliers of goods sometimes seek to protect their position on the insolvency of a customer by inserting 'reservation of title' clauses into their terms of trade. These clauses which aim to establish that the goods remain the property of the seller until they are paid for, have no practical effect except in the event of the insolvency of the debtor. Even on insolvency, legal cases arising since the *Romalpa* judgment of 1976 have indicated that, the legal effect of such clauses is not always clear.

17.111 Accordingly, goods purchased subject to a reservation of title clause should be accounted for in precisely the same way as goods purchased without such a clause, i.e., the goods should be recorded as being the property of the company and the amount payable recorded as a trade creditor.

17.112 The above treatment was recommended in a guidance statement issued by the accountancy bodies in 1976. The same statement also recommended that:

(a) where accounts are materially affected by adopting this accounting treatment, it should be disclosed; and

(b) the fact that liability to suppliers may be secured in this way should also be disclosed.

17.113 In spite of the use of these clauses being now widespread, disclosures of the type suggested in the guidance statement are almost never seen in published financial statements. This is not surprising, since the suggested disclosures are usually unnecessary and frequently impracticable. Financial statements prepared on a going concern basis are not in general required to

> disclose matters which are only relevant in the event of insolvency. It is common in routine commercial dealings for the precise contractual terms between the parties to be uncertain, since they only become significant in the event of a dispute or other difficulty; most managements of commercial entities neither know nor care whether the goods which they purchase are subject to valid reservation of title.

Bills of exchange payable

17.114 Bills of exchange are negotiable instruments usually entered into to obtain longer than normal credit terms or to facilitate transactions with overseas suppliers. Such bills, if material, should be distinguished separately from other trade creditors in the balance sheet or in the notes.

Amounts owed to group undertakings

17.115 As indicated in **17.136** below, all amounts owed to group undertakings should be treated as due within one year, unless there is a formal agreement which restricts the creditor company's right to demand repayment.

Amounts owed to associated undertakings and joint ventures

17.116 The subheading 'Amounts owed to undertakings in which the company has a participating interest' can, in most cases, be shortened to 'Amounts owed to associated undertakings' where the only significant participating interests represent associated undertakings.

17.117 FRS 9 has introduced a requirement that any amount shown under this heading should be analysed (where necessary) between amounts relating to loans and amounts relating to trading balances. [FRS 9(55)]

Other creditors including taxation and social security

17.118 'Other creditors including taxation and social security' is an all-inclusive heading for all liabilities that do not come under any other subheading.

17.119 The amount included in respect of taxation and social security should be disclosed separately from the amount for other creditors. [Sch 4: Note 9 on the balance sheet formats] This requirement is usually met by disclosing in the notes to the accounts one figure representing the total amount due to central governments by the company: thus, it would include corporation tax, income tax, VAT, PAYE and NI contributions and any similar liabilities to foreign governments. It is not necessary to subdivide these items in any way.

17.120 Loans, other than debenture loans and bank loans which should be included under separate subheadings, may be included in other creditors. Given the wide scope of debenture loans (see **17.95** above), it is likely that few loans will fall into this category. Details of loans from directors should be separately disclosed (see **32.14** below).

Accruals and deferred income

17.121 Accruals and deferred income may be shown either under creditors or as a separate heading. Where the total of these items is not material, they may be included in another category of creditors, such as 'Trade creditors' or 'Other creditors, including taxation and social security'.

Accruals

17.122 An accrual, as distinguished from a liability shown under trade creditors, is an estimate of an actual liability which at the time the financial statements are prepared is not supported by an invoice or other request for payment. Examples of accruals which might be included under this heading are unpaid salaries, pension costs, vacation pay, rents, royalties and interest. Accruals relating to taxation liabilities should be included under the heading 'Other creditors, including taxation and social security'.

17.123 Under FRS 4, finance costs accrued in respect of capital instruments which will be paid in cash in the next period can be shown in accruals, rather than added to the carrying value of the debt (see **17.19** above).

Deferred income

17.124 Income, such as rents and interest, may be received in advance of the period to which it relates. The portion of such income relating to periods after the balance sheet date should be deferred and included under this heading.

Maturity of debt

Introduction

17.125 The provisions of the Act state that, for the purpose of complying with the statutory disclosure requirements, loans are to be regarded as due for repayment on the earliest date on which the lender could require repayment if he exercised all options and rights available to him. [Sch 4: 85]

17.126 FRS 4 contains further provisions that would apply to all forms of debt, not just loans. Under FRS 4, the maturity of debt should be analysed according to the earliest date on which the lender can demand repayment, which is in line with the statutory requirements, but the FRS goes on to explain the considerations which apply in determining the earliest repayment date where early repayment or refinancing options exist. [FRS 4(34)]

17.127 If the lender has the right to require early redemption, but, under such an agreement, would receive substantially less than the full redemption value, it can be assumed that the lender would not exercise the option unless the creditworthiness of the issuer was called into question. The term of the debt would then be classified as extending to its final maturity. [FRS 4(74)] This does not appear to conflict with the legal requirements, as the earliest date on which the lender could demand repayment can be taken to be that date at which he can demand repayment without penalty.

17.128 Where there is a committed facility at the balance sheet date which permits the refinancing of debt for a period beyond its maturity, the earliest date on which the lender has the right to demand repayment should be taken to be the end of the permitted refinancing, but only where all the following conditions are met: [FRS 4(35)]

    (a)   the debt and facility are under a single agreement or course of dealing with the same lender or group of lenders;

    (b)   the finance costs of the new debt are on a basis that is not significantly higher than that of the existing debt;

    (c)   the obligations of the lender (or group of lenders) are firm; the lender is not able legally to refrain from providing funds except in circumstances the possibility of which can be demonstrated to be remote;

    (d)   the lender (or group of lenders) is expected to be able to fulfil its obligations under the facility.

17.129 The explanatory notes state that for determining whether the price of debt is significantly higher than the original debt, it is not referring to the absolute costs of finance but the basis of the finance charge. If, for example, the cost of finance is linked to a base rate such as LIBOR, an increase in that base rate would not constitute an increase in the level of finance cost for the purpose of meeting this condition.

17.130 For the purpose of determining whether the obligation is firm, if the facility agreement includes a clause which states that the facility may be withheld if there is a 'material adverse change' in the company's circumstances and 'material adverse change' is not defined, then what defines a breach of this condition cannot be said to be objectively ascertainable. It would be inappropriate to rely on the facility not being withheld under this clause and therefore the possibility of refinancing should not be taken into account in determining the maturity of existing debt. [FRS 4(81)] By contrast, where a 'material adverse change' clause gives a lender the right to require early repayment of existing debt, in the absence of any apparent material adverse change, it may be possible to regard the likelihood of such repayment as remote (see **17.35** below).

17.131 The FRS 4 conditions for determining whether reference can be made to refinancing facilities appear to be more stringent than the requirements that have generally been applied in the past. In particular, the explanatory notes state that, while the facilities should be reviewed in the light of post balance sheet events, the condition that the obligations of the lender must be firm must have existed at the balance sheet date. [FRS 4(80)]

17.132 If funding arrangements have been made between the date of the balance sheet and the date of approval of the financial statements, this fact can be disclosed by a note to the accounts.

Disclosure

17.133 Where the maturity of debt is assessed by reference to the refinancing period permitted by a facility as described above, the date on which the lender could have demanded repayment in the absence of that facility should be disclosed. [FRS 4(36)]

17.134 The appropriate treatment of various situations is discussed below.

Bank loans

17.135 It is not uncommon to find that, although arrangements are made for a bank loan to be repaid by a regular schedule of periodic repayments over a period of years, the agreement gives the bank the right to demand repayment at any time. Where this is the case, the loans should be shown as repayable within one year. Where the right to demand repayment is conditional on the company suffering an adverse change in circumstances, it is appropriate to review the situation at the balance sheet date and up to the date of signing the financial statements. If the situation is that under reasonable circumstances the likelihood of the clause being invoked is remote, then presentation will reflect that the loan is repayable under the agreed schedule.

Balances with group companies

17.136 Frequently, large balances are built up between one group company and another, with no likelihood of them being repaid; unless there is a formal agreement between the two companies which restricts the creditor company's right to demand repayment, the amount should be shown as due within one year in the balance sheet of the debtor company.

Default

17.137 Where a company has defaulted on the terms of a loan, e.g., due to a breach of covenants, the creditor is normally entitled to demand immediate repayment and, in these circumstances, the whole of the outstanding loan should be classified as falling due within one year.

17.138 It is thought that this is not necessary if, before the balance sheet date, the default has been cured and the creditor's rights arising from the default either have been waived or have lapsed.

Refinancing of long-term loans

17.139 Where a long-term loan is within 12 months of its maturity date, it should, according to the rules of Sch 4, be included as a creditor falling due within one year.

17.140 Often, the company will make arrangements to refinance this loan on a medium or long-term basis. Unless the four requirements of FRS 4 given in **17.128** above are met by the balance sheet date, such loans are required to be disclosed as short term. In the past, where refinancing has been arranged with the same lender after the balance sheet date but prior to the due date so that no cash settlement has been required, the true and fair override has been invoked and the loan disclosed as long term. This treatment is no longer allowed under the requirements of FRS 4.

Multi-option facilities

17.141 Multi-option facilities exist when a lender or group of lenders provide a range of facilities under which the borrower can draw down in a variety of different currencies, forms and maturity dates during the period of the facility.

17.142 Where such a long-term facility from one or more banks is obtained which commits participating banks to lend to the borrower a stipulated maximum sum, any short-term bank financing included under the umbrella of the facility can be shown as long-term debt, provided that the arrangements and

> the treatment adopted are disclosed in a note to the accounts. There would be no need in this case to use the true and fair override, because, under the Act and the requirements of FRS 4, the earliest date on which the lender, being the group of banks which are parties to the arrangement, could demand repayment would be the end of the committed line of credit. This classification is appropriate, because the substance of the arrangement is that, although the present lending banks may not renew the borrowings throughout the period of the facility, they can always be replaced by borrowing under the committed line of credit from another member of the group. For the purpose of satisfying the first FRS 4 condition (see **17.128** above), the lenders are considered as part of the same group, even if it is not always the same members of the group who participate in individual financings.

Commercial paper arrangements

17.143 Under commercial paper arrangements, funds are raised from lenders who are not parties to an agreement that provides for finance beyond the existing maturity date. Therefore, the 'roll over' of commercial paper cannot be taken into account when determining its maturity date. [FRS 4(78)]

Repurchase of own debt

Gain or loss on repurchase or early settlement of debt

17.144 FRS 4 contains a general requirement that on early settlement or repurchase of debt any gain or loss arising should be recognised in the profit and loss account in the period in which the repurchase or early settlement takes place [FRS 4(32)].

17.145 Where the difference on repurchase is material and has been taken to the profit and loss account, it is most appropriate to disclose it as a separate item on the face of the profit and loss account, adjacent to 'interest payable and similar charges' [FRS 4(64)].

17.146 This requirement supersedes UITF Abstract 8 *Repurchase of own debt* which stated two exceptions to this general rule of immediate recognition, requiring the difference on repurchase to be deferred and amortised over the period of the original debt where:

(a) the replacement borrowing gives the same effective economic result as the original borrowing; or

(b) the overall finance costs of the replacement borrowing are significantly different from market rates.

17.147 For the new finance to be treated as giving the same effective economic result as the original borrowings, UITF Abstract 8 required as a minimum the following conditions to be met:

(a) the replacement borrowing and the original borrowing are both fixed rate;

(b) the replacement borrowing is of a comparable amount to the original borrowing;

(c) the maturity of the replacement borrowing is not materially different from the remaining maturity of the original borrowing;

(d) the covenants of the replacement borrowing are not materially different from those of the original borrowing.

17.148 The replacement borrowing could be considered to be of a comparable amount to the original borrowing if the net present value of the cash flows for the new loan is similar to that of the original loan.

17.149 The FRS has not repeated these exemptions contained in UITF Abstract 8. However, under the requirements of FRS 5, if a transaction has resulted in no change in economic substance, then no change will be recorded in assets and liabilities. It does not appear appropriate for the purposes of showing a true and fair view to recognise a gain or loss on repurchase of debt in cases where the substance of the transaction is that the entity is in substantially the same position before and after the transaction. In establishing whether a change in economic sub stance has occurred or not, it is still appropriate to use UITF Abstract 8 as guidance.

17.150 Where the difference is deferred and amortised, the circumstances should be disclosed, together with the method of accounting adopted and the principal terms of the original and replacement borrowing.

Investment companies

17.151 Investment companies may recognise the difference arising on the repurchase of debt in the statement of total recognised gains and losses rather than in the profit and loss account to the extent that it relates to capital. This is in line with the exemption proposed by FRS 4 for finance costs incurred by investment companies. [FRS 4(52)] Any amounts treated in this way should be disclosed separately in the statement of total recognised gains and losses. The policy for determining the allocation between revenue and capital should also be stated. [FRS 4(52)]

Limited recourse loans

17.152 Some debt refinancing arrangements result in an agreement whereby the lender has recourse limited to certain assets and the income from those assets. Such an arrangement means that the loan and interest on the loan will be paid from the income stream and any sale proceeds generated by the asset; the lender will have no further claim over any other assets of the entity to make good any shortfall. In such situations, at the time of the agreement the asset is normally valued at less than the full amount of the liability. The question which arises is 'at what value should the asset and liability be recorded?'

17.153 Because the liability can only be paid from amounts generated by a specific asset, without recourse to other assets held by the entity, the recorded amount of the asset and loan should be same. One option is to show the liability at the value of the asset. Under this option the full amount of the legal liability would be disclosed in the notes. Often investment properties, which are included in the financial statements at open market value, are the subject of such an arrangement. If this is the case then the disadvantage of recording the liability at the asset value is that this will change each year. The recommended approach is to show the asset at the value of the gross legal liability; this represents the asset's economic value to the entity as it can be used to settle the whole liability. Subsequent remeasurement will only occur when the market value of the asset rises above the full amount of the liability.

FRS 12 *Provisions, contingent liabilities and contingent assets*

The requirements of FRS 12

17.154 FRS 12 seeks to ensure that appropriate recognition criteria and measurement bases are applied to provisions, contingent liabilities and contingent assets and that sufficient information is disclosed in the notes to the accounts to enable users to understand their nature, timing and amount.

17.155 It sets out clear definitions of provisions, contingent assets and contingent liabilities, discussed in **17.10** to **17.12** above, making it a requirement to justify the existence of a liability at the balance sheet date to support recognition in the financial statements. The recognition criteria are considered in **17.167** to **17.217** below.

17.156 In terms of measurement, FRS 12 specifies the methods to be used and the costs which can be included in calculating the amount of a provision. The overall rule is that a provision should be the best estimate of the amount required to settle the obligation; costs which relate to ongoing activities of an entity are excluded. Provisions must be reviewed annually and revised or completely reversed if appropriate. Measurement is considered in **17.221** to **17.258** below.

17.157   FRS 12 introduced a complete framework of disclosure requirements for provisions, contingent assets and contingent liabilities covering both narrative and numerical information. The disclosures will enable users to make judgements about the significance of a provision and any changes in it during the year and show how provisions have been used as expenditure occurs. Disclosure is described in **17.291** to **17.301** below.

Scope

17.158   FRS 12 applies to all financial statements that are intended to give a true and fair view, other than financial statements of reporting entities applying the FRSSE. [FRS 12(3) and (4)]

Exemptions and exclusions

17.159   The requirements of the FRS apply to all provisions, contingent liabilities and contingent assets other than those:

(a)   resulting from financial instruments that are carried at fair value;

(b)   resulting from executory contracts, except where the contract is onerous;

(c)   arising in insurance entities from contracts with policy holders; or

(d)   covered by another FRS or a SSAP. [FRS 12(3)]

17.160   Those resulting from financial instruments that are not carried at fair value (such as guarantees for example) do come within the scope of the standard. [FRS 12(5)]

17.161   An executory contract is not strictly defined in the standard, but an explanation is given: 'Executory contracts are contracts under which neither party has performed any of its obligations or both parties have partially performed their obligations to an equal extent'. [FRS 12(6)] This exemption covers contracts such as:

(a)   employee contracts in respect of continuing employment;

(b)   contracts for future delivery of services such as gas and electricity;

(c) obligations to pay council tax and similar levies; and

(d) most purchase orders.

17.162 An onerous contract, on the other hand, is defined as 'a contract in which the unavoidable costs of meeting the obligations under it exceed the economic benefits expected to be received under it'. [FRS 12(2)] FRS 12 does not apply to executory contracts unless they are onerous. Executory contracts are considered further in **17.302** below.

17.163 The rules of the standard do apply to provisions, contingent liabilities and contingent assets of insurance entities, other than those arising from contracts with policyholders. [FRS 12(7)]

17.164 There will be occasions where another FRS or SSAP deals with a specific type of provision, contingent liability or contingent asset. Examples might be long-term service contracts falling under SSAP 9 (see the examples in **17.276** and **17.277** below), tax falling under SSAP 15, pension costs falling under SSAP 24 or leases falling under SSAP 21. Where these circumstances arise, then the entity applies that standard instead of FRS 12. [FRS 12(8)]

17.165 Use of the term 'provision' is restricted to items that are disclosed in a balance sheet under headings for liabilities. It does not cover adjustments to assets, such as depreciation, impairment and bad debts, which may be popularly referred to as 'provisions'. [FRS 12(9)]

Transitional arrangements

17.166 FRS 12 is mandatory for accounting periods ending on or after 23 March 1999. FRS 12 is a little unusual, in that it contains no stated transitional arrangements. The standard explains how the accounting treatment should work on implementation and the details of these requirements are set out in **17.318** to **17.322** below. [FRS 12(101) and (102)]

Recognition of provisions, contingent liabilities and contingent assets

17.167 The recognition conditions for a provision cover two elements: the existence of a liability and measurement of that liability.

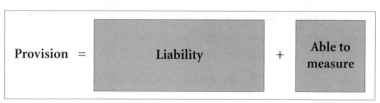

17.168 The existence element is further subdivided by FRS 12 into two conditions.

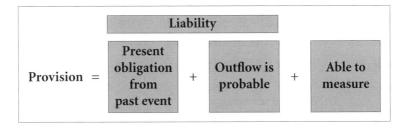

17.169 A contingent liability, which is not recognised but disclosed by way of note, results when one or more of the three recognition conditions for a provision is not met.

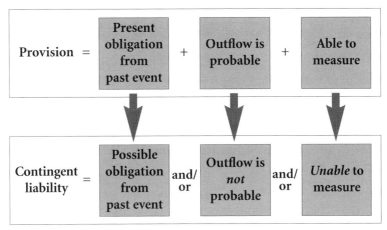

17.170 A contingent asset is not recognised but disclosed by way of note.

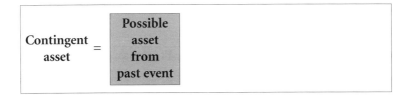

Distinguishing provisions from other liabilities

17.171 Provisions can be distinguished from other types of liability, including those which involve uncertain amounts, by considering the events which give rise to the obligation and also the degree of certainty over the amount. [FRS 12(11)] In each case, the definition of a liability will be met through the existence of a present obligation arising from a past event.

Example	Classification	Degree of uncertainty
Goods or services received and invoiced	Trade creditor	None
Goods or services received, but not invoiced	Accrual	Some
Legal claim from supplier for breach of exclusive supply agreement	Provision (if conditions met)	Significant

Recognition criteria for provisions

17.172 The FRS sets out three criteria which must all be present in order to recognise a provision:

(a) an entity has a present obligation (legal or constructive) as a result of a past event;

(b) it is probable that a transfer of economic benefits will be required to settle the obligation; and

(c) a reliable estimate can be made of the amount of the obligation. [FRS 12(14)]

17.173 The first two of these criteria derive from the definition of a liability (see **17.3** above). The third derives from the conditions for recognising a liability.

17.174 The table below aims to illustrate the application of these criteria.

Situation	Provision?	Action
Past event has occurred, resulting in a *possible* obligation for which a transfer of benefits is possible but not probable.	✗	Disclose a contingent liability.
Past event has occurred, resulting in a present obligation for which there may *possibly* be a transfer of benefits, but there probably will not.	✗	Unless the possibility of a transfer of benefits is remote, disclose a contingent liability.

Past event has occurred, resulting in a present obligation for which it is likely there will be a transfer of benefits, but a *reliable estimate cannot be made* of the amount of the obligation.	✗	Disclose a contingent liability. (N.B. This situation is likely to be very rare – see **17.190** below.)
Past event has occurred, resulting in a present obligation for which it is likely there will be a transfer of benefits; a reliable estimate can be made of the amount of the obligation.	✓	Disclosures are required in respect of the provision.
An obligating *event has not taken place by the balance sheet date*, but it takes place after the balance sheet date, resulting in an obligation for which it is likely there will be a transfer of benefits; a reliable estimate can be made of the amount of the obligation.	✗	Consider whether the requirements of SSAP 17 *Accounting for post balance sheet events* require the disclosure of the non-adjusting event which has arisen.

Present obligations and past events

17.175 As will be clear from the above table, a present obligation and a past event are key considerations when trying to determine whether a provision or a contingent liability is appropriate. The terms 'present obligation' and 'past obligating event' are not actually defined in the standard, but there is a considerable amount of narrative devoted to explaining the concepts. [FRS 12(15)–(22)]

17.176 In order for there to be a present obligation, the FRS requires that an obligating event has taken place. An obligating event means that the entity has no realistic alternative but to settle the obligation created by the event. Such obligations will be either:

(a) a legal obligation, i.e., enforceable by law; or

(b) a constructive obligation, i.e., the event creates a valid expectation in another party such that the entity has no realistic alternative to settling that obligation.

17.177 It may be that an event which happens does not immediately give rise to an obligation. However, where a subsequent obligation arises, which can be traced back to the event, then the event becomes an obligating event. For example, an unexpected legal claim is received after the balance sheet date in respect of damage alleged to have occurred before the balance sheet date.

Implications relating to present obligations and past events

Events before the balance sheet date

17.178 Financial statements deal with the financial position of an entity at the end of its reporting period and not its possible position in the future. The only liabilities recognised in an entity's balance sheet are those that exist at the balance sheet date. Therefore, no provision is recognised for costs that need to be incurred to operate in the future, notwithstanding that such costs may be necessary to continue as a going concern. [FRS 12(18)]

Future actions

17.179 It is only obligations which exist independently of the entity's future actions which fall to be recognised as provisions. One example where a provision is recognised might be clean-up costs for environmental damage. Even if the entity changed its future business, it would still incur the expenses relating to cleaning up, because of its past activities. In contrast, if an airline was legally required to service its planes every 2,000 flying hours, in theory, it could stop flying planes, or stop flying that particular plane, and therefore no present obligation exists. [FRS 12(19)]

Role of third parties

17.180 An obligation always involves a commitment to another party. Sometimes, the identity of the party will not be known or it may be the public at large. [FRS 12(20)]

Management decisions

17.181 It is because of the requirement for a clear commitment to another party that a decision made by management before the balance sheet date does not of itself give rise to a present obligation, unless it is communicated to those affected by it in a sufficiently specific manner to raise a valid expectation in them that the entity will discharge its responsibilities. [FRS 12(20)]

New legislation

17.182 Where details of new legislation have yet to be finalised, an obligation arises only when the legislation is virtually certain to be enacted as drafted. Under FRS 12, such expectation is treated as a legal obligation. [FRS 12(22)]

Smoothing of results

17.183 FRS 12 seeks to prevent artificial 'smoothing' of results. Through basing the recognition of a provision on the existence of a present obligation, it rules out the recognition of any provision made simply to allocate results over more than one period or otherwise to smooth the results reported. For example, companies cannot provide in advance for items such as future repairs. The cost will instead be charged to the profit and loss account when it is actually incurred, i.e., when the work is done.

17.184 An entity may be aware of some future commitment to spend money, and may even feel less well off at the prospect of the expense, but future expenditure, however necessary, does not justify the recognition of a provision unless a liability exists at the period end.

Repairs and maintenance

17.185 Example 11A from FRS 12 appendix 3 (see **17.265** below) illustrates the application of the FRS to repairs and maintenance for fixed assets. Because future repairs and maintenance are not present obligations of the entity resulting from past events, no provision should be made for them, even if they are required by legislation if the asset is to continue to be used. There are no grounds for recognising a provision for future repairs and maintenance expenditures, because these relate to the future operation of the business and the restoration of service potential and are therefore either to be capitalised as assets or written off as operating expenses when incurred. Where a part of the asset can be identified as declining in service potential because of the need for repairs or maintenance, it should be depreciated to show the declining service potential. Subsequent expenditure on repairs and maintenance should then be capitalised to show the restoration of service potential (see **17.259** below).

17.186 There is an exception to this general rule prohibiting provision of maintenance costs where an asset is held under a lease and the lease terms include a requirement for the asset to be made good at whatever stage of the lease it is returned. See **17.270** to **17.275** below.

Situations of uncertainty regarding present obligations

17.187 FRS 12 states that there will, on rare occasions, be circumstances where it is unclear whether a present obligation has arisen. In order to determine whether a present obligation exists under such rare circumstances, the standard advises that account be taken of all available evidence. Such evidence may include, by way of example, the opinion of experts. When examining evidence, events occurring after the balance sheet date should also be taken into consideration. The advice contained in the standard is to look at all the available evidence and come to a reasoned judgement on whether or not there is a present obligation. If there is, then a provision is recognised; if not, a contingent liability is disclosed, unless the possibility of any transfer of economic benefits in settlement is remote. [FRS 12(15) and (16)]

Transfer of economic benefits

17.188   An essential part of the definition of a liability is the existence of an obligation to transfer economic benefits. Recognition of a provision is conditional on the transfer of economic benefits being 'probable'. The interpretation which FRS 12 adopts for the meaning of probable is more likely than not to occur. [FRS 12(23)]

17.189   Where a number of similar obligations exist (e.g., product warranties) the overall probability that a transfer of economic benefits will be made is determined by looking at the class of obligations as a whole. A typical situation will be that, despite the likelihood of an outflow of resources for any one item being small, it may well be probable that a transfer of some economic benefits will be needed to settle the class of obligations as a whole. Where this is the case, assuming that the other recognition criteria apply, then a provision is recognised (see **17.223** below). [FRS 12(24)]

Reliable estimate

17.190   The use of estimates is an inherent part of preparing financial statements. Provisions are clearly uncertain by nature, but FRS 12 emphasises that it should not be impossible to determine a range of possible outcomes and, from this range, to reach an appropriate conclusion which is sufficiently reliable for the provision to be recognised. [FRS 12(25) and (26)]

17.191   Despite this optimistic view, it is likely that this area will be open to vigorous debate between auditors and their clients. FRS 12 does allow for the possibility that a reliable estimate may not be able to be made. In this instance, because the three general criteria are not met, it falls to be disclosed as a contingent liability.

Application of criteria – future operating losses

17.192   FRS 12 contains two prohibitions on the recognition of provisions for future operating losses:

   (a)   a general prohibition, on grounds that there is no present obligation and thus no liability (however, it may indicate a need to test whether assets have been impaired under FRS 11) [FRS 12(68)–(70)]; and

(b)   a specific prohibition in respect of future operating losses up to the date of a restructuring, again on grounds that there is no present obligation, unless the losses relate to an onerous contract (see **17.197** to **17.200** below) [FRS 12(87)].

17.193   In both cases, future operating losses relate to an activity which will continue, albeit in a restructured form, and are presumed to be avoidable (e.g., by an immediate closure of the loss-making activities). They are therefore appropriately recognised as the activity occurs.

17.194   A different conclusion is required by FRS 3 regarding future operating losses in respect of a sale or termination of an operation. FRS 3(18), as amended by FRS 12, states:

'If a decision has been made to sell or terminate an operation, any consequential provisions should reflect the extent to which obligations have been incurred that are not expected to be covered by the future profits of the operation. This principle requires that the reporting entity should be demonstrably committed to the sale or termination. … The provision should cover only (a) the direct costs of the sale or termination and (b) any operating losses of the operation up to the date of sale or termination, in both cases, after taking into account the aggregate profit, if any, to be recognised in the profit and loss account from the future profits of the operation.'

17.195   Distinctions that may be drawn between the FRS 3 scenario and the cases covered by the prohibitions on providing for future operating losses in FRS 12 are that, under FRS 3:

(a)   there is total cessation of activity (by sale or termination); and

(b)   it is assumed that sale or termination will happen at the earliest achievable date. Thus, the operating losses up to the date of sale or termination are unavoidable and therefore are of the same nature as losses under an onerous contract.

17.196   This second difference is crucial to justifying the existence of a present obligation. In the event that the date of sale or termination is not scheduled at the earliest possible time, then there is a degree of management choice. To the extent that operating losses are avoidable, there is no present obligation and a provision for future operating losses is not justified. The requirements of FRS 3(18) are dealt with in detail in **9.164** to **9.180** above.

Application of criteria – onerous contracts

17.197 Provision is required for the present obligation under an onerous contract. However, where assets dedicated to a contract are involved, a separate provision is recognised only after any impairment loss has been recognised on those assets. [FRS 12(71)–(74)]

17.198 An onerous contract is defined as 'a contract in which the unavoidable costs of meeting the obligations under it exceed the economic benefits expected to be received under it'. The unavoidable costs under a contract reflect the least net cost of exiting from the contract, i.e., the lower of:

(a) the cost of fulfilling the contract; and

(b) any compensation or penalties arising from failure to fulfil the contract.

Example 17.198.1

Long-term supply contract

Long-term contracts for the supply of goods or services where costs have risen or current market prices have fallen are onerous, and a provision is recognised, to the extent that future supplies must be made at a loss. No provision is recognised under a contract for the supply of goods which is profitable, but at a reduced margin compared to other contracts, since there is no probable net transfer of economic benefits by the entity.

Example 17.198.2

Vacated property

A lease for property which has been vacated is onerous, and a provision recognised, to the extent that rentals continue which are not recoverable from subleasing the property. The provision should represent the best estimate of the expenditure required to settle the obligation at the balance sheet date, which, in this case, might be the amount the landlord would accept to terminate the lease.

17.199 Examples of contracts which do not meet the criteria for recognition of a provision are:

(a) routine purchase orders, and similar contracts, which realistically could be cancelled by agreement with the vendor without paying compensation; and

(b) purchase orders where the future benefits from use of the asset exceed its cost, notwithstanding that compensation must be paid if the order is cancelled.

17.200 Executory contracts, i.e., contracts under which neither party has performed any of its obligations or both parties have performed their obligations to an equal extent, which are not onerous are excluded from the scope of FRS 12. This exemption covers contracts such as:

(a)   employee contracts in respect of continuing employment;

(b)   contracts for future delivery of services such as gas and electricity;

(c)   obligations to pay council tax and similar levies; and

(d)   most purchase orders.

See **17.302** to **17.305** below regarding the accounting treatment of executory contracts.

Application of criteria – restructuring

17.201   FRS 12 provides specific guidance on how the general recognition criteria for provisions apply to restructurings. [FRS 12(75) – (88)]

17.202   Restructuring in FRS 12 is used in a wider set of circumstances than the word would suggest and includes events such as:
[FRS 12(75)]

(a)   sale or termination of a line of business;

(b)   the closure of business locations in a country or region or the relocation of business activities from one country or region to another;

(c)   changes in management structure, e.g., eliminating a layer of management; and

(d)   fundamental reorganisations that have a material effect on the nature and focus of the entity's operations.

17.203   Although a restructuring may encompass both closure of an operation and the opening of a new operation, the effect of FRS 12 will be to allow provision only for the closure element. [FRS 12(85)(b)] This is discussed in **17.214** to **17.216** below.

17.204   The two principal requirements for recognition of a provision in respect of a restructuring are:
[FRS 12(77)]

(a)   a detailed plan; and

(b)   a valid expectation that the plan will be implemented.

17.205   The detailed plan must specify:

(a)   the business or part of a business concerned;

(b)   the principal locations affected;

(c)   the location, function, and approximate number of employees who will be compensated for terminating their services;

(d)   the expenditures that will be undertaken; and

(e)   when the plan will be implemented.

17.206   In order to give rise to a constructive obligation when it is communicated to those affected by it, implementation of the plan should commence as soon as possible and be completed within a timeframe that makes significant change to the plan unlikely. Where either there is a long delay before commencement or execution of the plan will take a long time, the timeframe allows opportunities for the plan to be changed. Thus, it is unlikely that the entity has raised a valid expectation that it is presently committed to the restructuring.

17.207   FRS 12 requires that the entity has raised a valid expectation in those affected that it will carry out the restructuring by:

(a)   actually starting to implement that plan; or

(b)   announcing its main features to those affected by it.

17.208   The existence of a valid expectation in those affected relates to the situation at the balance sheet date. The fact that implementation has commenced by the date financial statements are approved does not give rise to a present obligation at the balance sheet date, unless some other event gave rise to a valid expectation at that earlier date. Actually starting to implement the plan at the balance sheet date would be evidenced by, e.g., dismantling plant, the sale of assets or a public announcement. To constitute a constructive obligation, a public announcement must be made in such a way and in sufficient detail that it gives rise to valid expectations in other parties such as customers, suppliers and employees (or their representatives) that the entity will carry out the restructuring.

17.209   A management or board decision to go ahead with its plan will not, by itself, constitute a constructive obligation, unless it is accompanied by a valid expectation (see **17.207** above) in those affected by either (a) or (b) above, i.e., commencement of the plan or a suitable announcement. Similarly, events involving third parties which occur before a board decision is taken or approval given to a detailed plan, e.g., negotiations with employee representatives for termination payments or with purchasers for the sale of an operation, do not amount to a constructive obligation without a valid expectation in those affected. However, a constructive obligation could arise where, as happens in some countries, a board includes non-management representatives such as employees, with the effect that notification to those affected and approval by the board of a detailed plan satisfies the requirement for a valid expectation being raised with those employees affected.

17.210 A valid expectation is unlikely to exist in the following cases:

(a) management has developed a detailed plan, but has not notified those affected by it, even though it can point to previous instances where it has proceeded with a plan; and

(b) management has developed a plan which involves closure of one of two possible sites. It has made general indications to employees that one site will close, but has not communicated which of the two sites will close, in order to avoid alienation of employees at that site before implementation commences.

Sale of an operation

17.211 FRS 12 specifies that an obligation does not exist for the sale of an operation until the entity is committed to the sale, i.e., there is a binding sale agreement. Until there is such an agreement, the entity will be able to change its mind and, indeed, will have to take another course of action if a purchaser cannot be found on acceptable terms. [FRS 12(83) and (84)]

17.212 When a sale is only part of a restructuring, a constructive obligation can arise for the other parts of the restructuring before a binding sale agreement exists. In this case, the assets of the operation are reviewed for impairment, under FRS 11.

17.213 Where, at the year end, an entity had signed heads of agreement to dispose of a loss-making part of its business, but a binding sale agreement was not signed until a month later, no provision may be made under FRS 12 at the balance sheet date. However, an impairment review should be carried out and this may cover much of the provision which would otherwise have been made. Also, consideration should be given to whether the business has onerous contracts for which provision should be made.

Amounts included in a restructuring provision

17.214 FRS 12 restricts a restructuring provision to the direct expenditures arising from the restructuring, which are those that are both: [FRS 12(85)–(88)]

   (a)   necessarily entailed by the restructuring; and

   (b)   not associated with the ongoing activities of the entity.

17.215 Specific items which are excluded by the standard on the basis that they relate to the ongoing activities of the business are:

   (a)   retraining or relocating continuing staff;

   (b)   marketing; or

   (c)   investment in new systems and distribution networks.

17.216

> A practical test is that a liability exists only for those costs that arise if there was only a closure and there was no continuation.

Restructuring provision flowchart

17.217 The flowchart opposite sets out the steps to consider in deciding whether or not a restructuring provision should be made.

Contingent liabilities and contingent assets

17.218 To a degree, all provisions are contingent, because there is uncertainty over the timing or amount of settlement. However, in FRS 12, the term 'contingency' is reserved for those items where their existence will be confirmed by the occurrence of one or more uncertain future events which are not within the entity's control. In addition, FRS 12 uses the term 'contingent liability' for liabilities which do not meet the criteria for recognition as a provision, either because a payment is not probable or because no reliable estimate of the amount can be made. [FRS 12(12)]

Contingent liabilities

17.219 A contingent liability is defined as either:
[FRS 12(2)]

   (a)   a possible obligation that arises from past events and whose existence will be confirmed only by the occurrence of one or more uncertain future events not wholly within the entity's control; or

   (b)   a present obligation that arises from past events but is not recognised because:

      (i)   it is not probable that a transfer of economic benefits will be required to settle the obligation; or

      (ii)   the amount of the obligation cannot be measured with sufficient reliability.

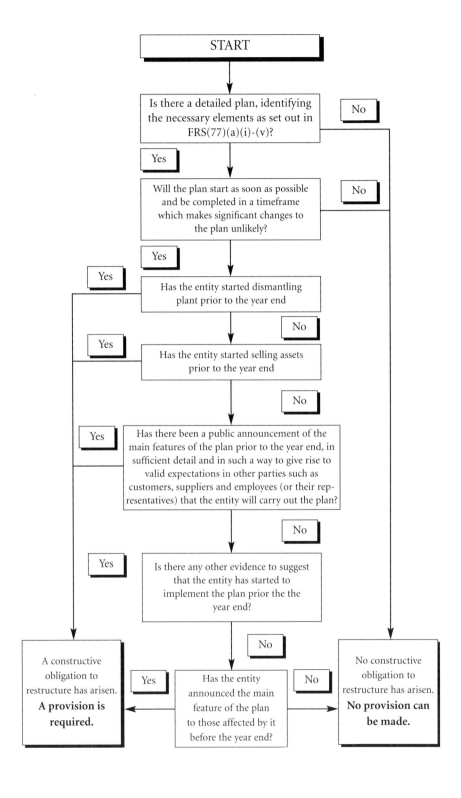

Contingent assets

17.220 A contingent asset is a possible asset that arises from past events and whose existence will be confirmed only by the occurrence of one or more uncertain future events not wholly within the entity's control. [FRS 12(2)] Contingent assets are not recognised as assets because it could result in the recognition of profit that may never be realised. However, when the realisation of the profit is virtually certain, then the related asset is not a contingent asset and its recognition is appropriate. [FRS 12(33)]

Measurement of provisions

Best estimate

17.221 The measurement principle of FRS 12 is the familiar 'best estimate' of expenditure required to settle the present obligation at the balance sheet date. The reference to balance sheet date does not preclude use of later additional evidence or better information, but indicates that the best estimate will be the amount that an entity would rationally pay to have the obligation go away – by settlement or by transfer to a third party. The addition of 'rationally' in FRS 12(37) suggests that, although it may be difficult to arrange settlement or transfer, there is nevertheless a point of balance and thus a price at which management would be willing to settle. [FRS 12(36)–(38)]

17.222 Ultimately, judgement will be that of management and will reflect experience of similar transactions. In reaching their judgement, reports of independent experts may be required. Examples of relevant independent experts are:

- solicitors and barristers;
- surveyors and valuers;
- loss adjusters;
- actuaries; and
- technical experts (e.g., regarding a decommissioning process).

Use of expected value

17.223 Where the provision relates to a large population of items, it is valid to use an 'expected value'. This is the amount that takes account of all possible outcomes, using probabilities to weight the outcomes. Expected value as a method of estimation has a number of desirable features. The method provides an estimate that reflects the entire probability distribution, i.e., all the possible outcomes weighted by their probabilities. For a given assessed distribution, the method has the advantage of objectivity in that different measurers would calculate the same estimate. Furthermore, expected value is additive (i.e., the expected value of a number of items is the sum of the expected values of the individual items).

> **Example 17.223**
>
> An entity faces 100 legal claims, each with a 40 per cent likelihood of success with no cost and a 60 per cent likelihood of failure with a cost of each claim of £1 million.
>
> Using expected value, the statistical likelihood is that 60 per cent of claims will result in a cost of £1 million, thus the provision should be 60 per cent of 100 × £1 million = £60 million.

17.224 Where the provision relates to a single event, or a small number of events, expected value is not a valid technique.

> **Example 17.224**
>
> An entity faces a single legal claim, with a 40 per cent likelihood of success with no cost and a 60 per cent likelihood of failure with a cost of £1 million.
>
> Expected value is not valid in this case, since the outcome will never be a cost of £600,000 (60 per cent of £1 million). It will either be nil or £1 million. FRS 12(40) states that the provision should represent whichever is the most likely of these two outcomes. In this example, it is more likely that a cost of £1 million will result and therefore full provision would be made.

17.225 As a general rule of thumb, where the most likely outcome is close to expected value, it will be appropriate to provide the most likely outcome, since expected value provides evidence of the probable outflow of benefits.

> **Example 17.225**
>
> An entity is required to replace a major component in an asset under a warranty. Each replacement costs £1 million. From experience, there is a 30 per cent chance of a single failure, 50 per cent chance of two failures, and a 20 per cent chance of three failures.
>
> The most likely outcome is two failures, costing £2 million. The expected value is £1.9 million (30 per cent of £1 million + 50 per cent of £2 million + 20 per cent of £3 million). The expected value supports the provision for the most likely outcome of £2 million.

17.226 A second rule of thumb, implied by FRS 12, is that where most likely outcome and expected value are not close together, it will often be appropriate to provide for whichever possible outcome is nearest to the expected value. [FRS 12(40)]

> ### *Example 17.226*
>
> An entity is required to replace a major component in an asset under a warranty. Each replacement costs £1 million. From experience, there is a 40 per cent chance of a single failure, 30 per cent chance of two failures, and a 30 per cent chance of three failures.
>
> The most likely outcome is a single failure, costing £1 million. The expected value is £1.9 million (40 per cent × £1 million + 30 per cent × £2 million + 30 per cent × £3 million). In this case, the most likely outcome of £1 million has only a 40 per cent probability. There is a 60 per cent probability that the cost will be higher. The outcome closest to expected value is £2 million, i.e., two failures.

Tax

17.227 Under FRS 12, provisions are measured before tax. The tax consequences of the provision, and of changes in the provision, are dealt with under SSAP 15 *Accounting for deferred tax* (see chapter 27).

Risks and uncertainties

17.228 FRS 12 contains a rather vague requirement that 'risks and uncertainties that inevitably surround many events and circumstances should be taken into account in reaching the best estimate of a provision'. The explanatory guidance suggests that a balance needs to be struck between, on the one hand, being imprudent (resulting in overstated assets or profits or understated liabilities or expenses) and, on the other hand, being over-prudent (resulting in excessive provisions or overstated liabilities). Also, adjustment for risk and uncertainty should not be double-counted. The most obvious situation when this may happen is when risk is reflected both in estimated future cash flows and in the discount rate (see **17.238** to **17.245** below). Disclosures concerning uncertainty required by FRS 12(90)(b) would act as a safeguard against obvious error. [FRS 12(42)–(44)]

Future events – changes in technology

17.229 In many cases, future events do not represent present obligations and therefore provision is not generally made. However, future events may affect the measurement of a present obligation. A common example cited in FRS 12 is the impact of future technology changes on site clean-up costs at the end of the site's life. A similar example would be decommissioning. FRS 12 requires the current provision to reflect reduced costs of technology expected to be available at the time of a future clean-up. [FRS 12(51) and (52)] This allows cost reductions to be recognised for:

(a)   increased experience in applying existing technology; and

(b) applying existing technology to a larger or more complex clean-up operation than has been carried out to date.

17.230 However, a completely new technology should only be assumed where there is sufficient objective evidence that it will be available and will be effective for the claimed cost.

Future events – changes in legislation

17.231 New legislation should be reflected in the measurement of a provision for an existing obligation when there is sufficient objective evidence that the legislation is virtually certain to be exercised. FRS 12 specifies that this will include evidence:
[FRS 12(53)]

(a) of what the legislation will demand; and

(b) that the legislation will be enacted and implemented.

17.232 In practice, there is no single event in the passage of new legislation prior to enactment which provides a general trigger point.

17.233 Enactment of new tax rates is a common example of a future change in legislation affecting a provision for taxation. FRS 16 states that current tax should be measured using tax rates and laws that have been enacted or substantively enacted by the balance sheet date. It is generally held that announcement of tax rates in a formal Budget presentation routinely leads to enactment and such rates can be considered as 'substantively enacted' for the purpose of measuring accounting provisions for tax, provided the budget occurs before the balance sheet date. Moreover, a formal Budget will be accompanied by a resolution under the Provisional Collection of Taxes Act 1968 to enable taxes to be collected at the new rate. However, announcement in a 'green Budget' is not considered 'substantively enacted', since it is seen more as a statement of policy and not draft legislation.

Discounting and materiality

17.234 FRS 12 requires provisions to be discounted to present value when the time value of money is material. [FRS 12(45) and (46)]

17.235 Quantifying materiality will depend on a range of factors, e.g., the size of the provision relative to other items in the balance sheet, the impact of any adjustment on profit for the year, etc. The following table summarises the impact of discounting a single future cash flow for a range of future dates and for a range of possible discount rates. The table indicates that discounting reduces an amount by around 10 per cent over a one- to two-year period. However, over a 40-year period, discounting reduces an amount to less than 10 per cent of its nominal amount (with the effect that most of the charge would be recognised through the unwinding of the discount).

	Discount rate		
	5%	7.5%	10%
Cash flow of 100 after:			
1 year	95	93	91
2 years	91	87	83
3 years	86	80	75
4 years	82	75	68
5 years	78	70	62
10 years	61	49	39
15 years	48	34	24
20 years	38	24	15
40 years	14	6	2

Choice of discount rate

17.236 Discount rate (or rates) should:
[FRS 12(47)]

(a) be pre tax;

(b) reflect current market assessments of the time value of money; and

(c) reflect risks specific to the liability.

17.237 Further detailed guidance on the selection of discount rates, and the calculations required for present value, are contained in Appendices X and XI.

Adjustment for risk

17.238 Under FRS 12, it is acceptable to reflect risk either in estimation of cash flows or by adjusting the discount rate. FRS 12 states that use of an adjusted discount rate will normally be the easiest method. [FRS 12(49)] However, practical experience of estimating discount rates for use in impairment tests suggests that it is a most imprecise science. There is therefore a good case, on grounds of simplicity and avoiding spurious accuracy, for dealing with risk through a detailed estimation of cash flows to include the impact of risk. Whichever method is used, care should be taken to avoid double-counting the effect of risk.

17.239   It follows that where risk is reflected in estimates of cash flows, the appropriate discount rate will be a pre-tax risk-free rate such as a current government bond rate.

17.240

> The following is a general guide:
>
> (a)   a risk-free rate, based on government bond rates, reflects the discount that a creditor will accept to receive a risk-free cash flow now rather than at the due date;
>
> (b)   a risk-adjusted rate, based on a general corporate bond rate, will reflect general corporate credit risk and will be appropriate for 'blue-chip' entities;
>
> (c)   a risk-adjusted rate, based on an entity-specific corporate bond rate or weighted average cost of capital (adjusted to a gross tax basis), will reflect risk factors specific to an entity and will be appropriate for most entities where risk is not specifically considered in the estimation of cash flows.

Example 17.240.1

Risk-free rate

An entity sells goods subject to a warranty. A provision is calculated for warranty claims, based on detailed records of past faults in products. Since the estimation of cash flows takes account of entity-specific risks, the appropriate discount rate will be a risk-free rate, e.g., a government bond rate.

Example 17.240.2

Risk-adjusted rate

An entity vacates a leased property and identifies a liability in respect of continuing rentals due. Estimated cash flows are lease rentals stipulated in the lease and, as such, do not reflect risk. The appropriate discount rate is a rate which reflects the credit risk of the entity, such as a rate derived from weighted average cost of capital (grossed up for tax).

Pre-tax rates calculated from post-tax rates

17.241   Care should be taken in determining a pre-tax discount rate by adjusting a post-tax rate. Because the tax consequences of different cash flows may be different, the pre-tax rate of return is not always the post-tax rate of return grossed up by the standard rate of tax.

Impact of inflation

17.242 Where estimated cash flows are expressed in current prices, a real discount rate (i.e., reduced for the impact of future inflation) will be used. Where, alternatively, cash flows are expressed in expected future prices (normally higher than current prices), a nominal discount rate will be used. The effects of inflation on the present value will be the same, provided one of these methods is used:

(a)   current (lower) prices – real (lower) discount rate; or

(b)   future (higher) prices – nominal (higher) discount rate.

Unwinding of a discount

17.243 In balance sheets for years following the initial measurement of a provision at a present value, the present value will be restated to reflect estimated cash flows being closer to the measurement date. This unwinding of the discount should be disclosed (normally, it is a charge) as part of the financial items in the profit and loss account. This may be achieved by including the charge within (or adjacent to) interest payable, with separate disclosure either on the face of the profit and loss account or in a note. [FRS 12(48)] The effect of revising estimates of cash flows is not part of this unwinding and should be dealt with as part of any adjustment to previous provisions.

17.244 Since FRS 12 requires provisions to be remeasured using a current market assessment of the time value of money, the revision to a new present value will have three components:

(a)   revision of future cash flow;

(b)   discount rate – unwinding of the original time value of money discount; and

(c)   discount rate – any change in market interest rates.

17.245 Although the second and third items both arise from changes in the discount rate, there is a theoretical case for distinguishing these two and disclosing the second part (i.e., **17.244**(c)) as an adjustment to provisions, not as a financial item. However, the disclosure of the unwinding required by FRS 12 suggests they will both be regarded as financial items. [FRS 12(89)(e)]

Expected disposal of assets

17.246 Gains from the expected disposal of assets should not be taken into account in measuring a provision. [FRS 12(54) and (55)] This represents a change to the practice previously required by FRS 3(18), which is amended accordingly.

Example 17.246

At the end of year one, an entity is demonstrably committed to clo-sures of some facilities, having drawn up a detailed plan and made announcements. The plan shows the effects to be:

	Year 1 £ million	Year 2 £ million	Year 3 £ million
Direct costs	10	100	
Gain from sale of property			– 20

Prior to FRS 12, a provision at the end of year one would be made for £80 million (being 100 – 20). In practice, this treatment would result in the balance sheet at the end of year two recognising as an asset the £20 million expected gain on sale, irrespective of whether this quali-fied for recognition.

Under FRS 12, the provision at the end of year one is £100 million. The gain on sale of the property is dealt with separately under the principles of asset recognition.

17.247 The treatment of estimated operating future losses in a closure pro-vision is considered in **17.192** to **17.196** above.

Reimbursements

17.248 An entity with a present obligation requiring a provision to be recog-nised may be able to seek reimbursement of part or all of the expen-diture from another party. For example:

(a) an insurance contract arranged to cover a risk;

(b) an indemnity clause in a contract; and

(c) a warranty provided by a supplier.

17.249 Recognition of a reimbursement is on the basis that any asset arising is separate from the related obligation. Consequently, such a reimburse-ment should be recognised only when it is virtually certain that it will be received consequent upon the settlement of the obligation. [FRS 12(56)] This treatment is also consistent with guidance on con-tingent assets. When a provision has been recognised it is taken to be a certain payment for the purposes of assessing the probability of receiv-ing reimbursement and judging whether that is virtually certain.

17.250 Reporting of a reimbursement is as follows:

(a) in the balance sheet, a separate asset is recognised (which must not exceed the amount of the provision); and

(b) in the profit and loss account, a net amount may be presented being a provision for the obligation less the reimbursement.

17.251 Offset of a provision and related reimbursement is only appropriate where an entity can avoid making payment in respect of its obligation such that it has no liability. This is consistent with the rules of offset in FRS 5. [FRS 5(29)]

17.252 Where an entity is jointly and severally liable for an obligation, it should provide for that part of the obligation for which payment by it is probable. [FRS 12(29)] The remainder, which is expected to be paid by other parties, is a contingent liability. [FRS 12(61)]

17.253

> If an entity has a provision and a matching reimbursement, and the time value of money is material to both, the question arises whether both should be discounted. In principle, both the asset and the liability should be discounted. If there will be a significant interval between the cash outflows and receiving the reimbursement, the reimbursement will be more heavily discounted – so, on initial recognition, there will be a net cost. If (presumably rarely) the reimbursement will be received first, FRS 12 will restrict the discounted amount of the reimbursement so that it does not exceed the discounted amount of the provision. [FRS 12(56)] In the profit and loss account, the unwinding of the discount on the reimbursement may be offset against that on the provision.

Changes in provisions

17.254 Provisions should be reviewed at each balance sheet date and adjusted to reflect current best estimate. [FRS 12(62) and (63)]

17.255 Adjustments arise from three sources:

(a) revision to estimated cash flows (both amount and likelihood);

(b) change to present value due to the passage of time (unwinding of discount); and

(c) revision of discount rate to prevailing current market conditions.

17.256 Where a provision has resulted in recognition of an asset, see **17.261** below, changes in the provision arising from a revision to estimated cash flows essentially represent a change in the consideration for that asset and therefore result in an adjustment to the asset value.

17.257 Where a provision is no longer required, e.g., if it is no longer probable that a transfer of economic benefits will be required to settle the obligation, the provision should be reversed.

17.258 Disclosure of changes in provisions is dealt with in **17.291** to **17.294** below.

Use of provisions

17.259 One of the objectives of FRS 12 was to increase the transparency of accounting for provisions and, in particular, prevent the use of an existing provision to meet a different undisclosed obligation. Accordingly, the standard requires provisions to be used only for expenditures for which the provision was originally recognised. [FRS 12(64) and (65)]

17.260 The disclosure requirements (see **17.291** to **17.301** below), especially the requirement to identify movements on each class of provision, are intended to reinforce this objective.

Recognising an asset when recognising a provision

17.261 Where a provision or a change in a provision is recognised, an asset should be recognised when, and only when, the incurring of the present obligation recognised as a provision gives access to future economic benefits. In other cases, a provision should be charged immediately to the profit and loss account. [FRS 12(66) and (67)]

> ### Example 17.261
>
> **Decommissioning an oil rig**
>
> Commissioning of a new oil rig creates an obligation to incur costs of decommissioning in the future, but also gives access to future economic benefits from oil reserves. Provision for the present value of costs of decommissioning should be recognised at the time of commissioning and added to the cost of the oil rig. The aggregate cost is amortised over the life of the rig.

17.262 It is sometimes the case that the initial incurring of an obligation gives rise to recognition of an asset but subsequent increases in the obligation do not give increased future economic benefits, but relate to benefits received in the period. In this case the additional provision recognised in the period is charged directly to the profit and loss account and does not result in a change to the asset recorded.

> ### Example 17.262.1
>
> **Decommissioning a quarry or opencast mine**
>
> Costs incurred at the end of a quarry's life are of two types: removal of plant and other site preparation work which was installed at the time of commissioning and restoration of site damage which has been progressively created as material is extracted from the quarry. An obligation in respect of the first type, i.e., removal of initial plant and

restoration of site preparation, is created by commissioning the quarry: provision for the present value of costs should be made at the time of commissioning and recognised as an asset. An obligation for restoration of subsequent damage is only created as the quarry is used: provision should be recognised as extraction progresses charged immediately to the profit and loss account.

Example 17.262.2

Major refit and repair costs

Ships and aircraft are required to undergo major work at regular intervals, e.g., a ship may be required to undergo a dry dock overhaul every five years. No present obligation exists in respect of the cost of future overhauls and thus no provision should be recognised. However, the cost of an overhaul gives rise to benefits over the following five years and will usually be capitalised and amortised over the period to the next overhaul. Treatment of such costs in an initial or final period of an asset's useful life is considered further in **17.270** to **17.275** below.

17.263 Where a provision has been discounted, the amount capitalised will be the discounted amount only. The unwinding of the discount will then be charged as a financial cost and not as depreciation.

17.264   In the case of long-lived assets such as oil wells, the impact of discounting may be very material. For example, the table in **17.235** above shows that a cash flow of 100 after 40 years, discounted at 10 per cent, has a present value of two. Thus, almost all the charge will be the unwinding of the discount.

Examples

17.265 The tables that follow provide a summary of:

(a)   examples introduced and discussed in **17.268** to **17.290**; and

(b)   examples from FRS 12 appendix 3.

The tables identify reasons for particular items meeting, or not meeting, the definition of a provision. In all cases, it is assumed that a reliable estimate can be made.

Examples discussed in 17.268 to 17.283

Type of risk or cost	Present obligation as a result of a past event?	Probable transfer?	Conclusion
Regulated industry – adjustment to sales price. Consumers are to be compensated for high profits being achieved via lower price increases in a future year.	✗		No obligation – a restriction on profits in future periods.
Partnership profit share. Partnership charge for future annuity payments to retired partners.	✗		No present obligation.
Repairs under lease (1). Terms of lease do not require maintenance check prior to return of asset.	✗		No present obligation.
Repairs under lease (2). Terms of lease specify lessee must make pro-portional payment for maintenance check on return of asset.	✓	✓	Provide for proportionate cost of maintenance.
Loyalty schemes. Vouchers awarded giving future discounts on products.	✓	✗	Items sold at reduced profit – no transfer of economic benefits.
Directors' bonuses. Annual bonuses routinely paid, amount confirmed when accounts drawn up.	✓	✓	Provide for constructive obligation.

Examples from FRS 12 Appendix 3

Type of risk or cost	Present obligation as a result of a past event?	Probable transfer?	Conclusion
Warranty Example 1: Warranty given by a manufacturer under the terms of a contract for sale. Past experience shows claims will be received.	✓	✓	Provide at date of sale for legal obligation.
Contaminated land (1) Example 2A: Contaminated land – entity cleans up only to meet legal requirements, which are virtually certain to be enacted soon after the year end.	✓	✓	Provide for expected legal obligation.
Contaminated land (2) Example 2B: Contaminated land – entity has no legal obligation, but meets widely published clean-up policy.	✓	✓	Provide for constructive obligation.
Decommissioning Example 3: Decommissioning – terms of a licence impose a legal obligation to remove an oil rig at the end of its life.	✓	✓	Provide on commissioning of asset and include in cost.
Refunds Example 4: Refunds – retail store follows a published policy of providing refunds, even though there is no legal obligation.	✓	✓	Provide for constructive obligation.
Closure of a division (1) Example 5A: Closure of a division – board decision taken before the balance sheet date, but not communicated to those affected and plan not commenced.	✗		No obligating event before the balance sheet date.

Closure of a division (2) Example 5B: Closure of a division – board decision, detailed plan completed, staff and customers notified before the balance sheet date.	✓	✓	Provide for expected costs of closure.
Installation of new equipment Example 6: Installation of new equipment – legal requirement to fit smoke filters within six months of balance sheet date.	✗		No obligating event until filters fitted. Capitalise cost when incurred.
Staff retraining Example 7: Staff retraining – need to retrain staff to meet new system requirements imposed by change in the law.	✗		No obligating event until training occurs.
Onerous contract Example 8: Onerous contract – operating lease rental payments on vacated property.	✓	✓	Provide for unavoidable lease payments.
Guarantee (1) Example 9(a): Guarantee – guarantee provided for another entity's borrowings and that entity is in a sound financial condition.	✓	✗	No transfer of benefits is probable.
Guarantee (2) Example 9(b): Guarantee – guarantee provided for another entity's borrowings and that entity has filed for protection from creditors.	✓	✓	Provide for estimated call on guarantee.
Court case (1) Example 10(a): Court case – unsettled case where lawyers advise that no liability will be proved.	✗		No obligation exists based on evidence.

Court case (2) Example 10(b): Court case – unsettled case where lawyers advise that liability will be proved.	✓	✓	Provide for estimated settlement.
Repairs and maintenance Example 11A: Repairs and maintenance – a furnace has a lining that needs to be replaced every five years for technical reasons. At the balance sheet date, the lining has been in use for three years.	✗		No obligation exists independently of future actions. Expenditure capitalised and depreciated.
Refurbishment costs Example 11B: Refurbishment costs – legislative requirement – an airline is required by law to overhaul its aircraft once every three years.	✗		No obligation exists. Expenditure capitalised and depreciated.
Self-insurance Example 12: Self-insurance – entity accepts risk of previously insured liability and can estimate 'normal' long-term annual cost.	✗		No obligation exists to third parties (see also **17.278** below).

Going concern obligations

17.266 On the grounds of prudence, management may believe in making provision for items that relate to the entity's ability to continue as a going concern. An example of such an expense is the expected cost of overhauling an aircraft. The legal requirement is to overhaul the aircraft after a certain number of flying hours. Since there is no obligation to incur this maintenance expenditure, no provision is justified.

17.267 Similarly, by basing the recognition of a provision on the existence of a present obligation, the FRS rules out the recognition of any provision made simply to allocate results over more than one period or otherwise to smooth the results reported. Two examples where this occurs are adjustment of future sales prices in regulated industries (see **17.268** below) and partnerships (see **17.269** below).

Adjustment of future sales prices in regulated industries

17.268 In a regulated industry, the results achieved in the current period may cause the pricing structure in future periods to be adjusted, e.g., the higher the profits in this year, the lower the prices permitted for next year in order to compensate customers. Appendix VII to FRS 12 sites this as a scenario where companies may try to smooth results by making provision in the year of higher profits. It states that there is no justification under the standard for a provision to be recognised in such circumstances. This has been reconfirmed in UITF information sheet 35.

Partnerships

17.269 In addition to the normal fundamental principles of accounting, partnerships also need to consider equity between partners. This may lead to circumstances where current partners bear a charge against profits available for distribution in order to meet payments due in the future. Under FRS 12, however, there is no present obligation to transfer economic benefits; hence, any amount carried forward is an appropriation of profits to be held as a reserve within partners' interests and not as a provision within liabilities. For example, retired partners receive an annuity based on future profits. Since the amount is dependent on future profits, there is no present obligation falling on the partnership. Any reduction in profits available to current partners is an appropriation of profits to a reserve and not a provision for a liability.

Repairs and maintenance obligations under leases

17.270 In some operating leases the lessee is required to incur periodic charges for maintenance of the leased asset or to make good dilapidations or other damage occurring during the rental period. Since the lease is a legal contract, it may give rise to legal obligations. Accordingly, the principles of FRS 12 which preclude the recognition of provisions for repairs and maintenance generally do not preclude the recognition of such liabilities in a lease once the event giving rise to the obligation under the lease has occurred. This would include provision for rental payments for a lease where the property has been vacated by the lessee. In assessing the best estimate of the provision, a judgement would be made of the period for which rentals will be paid which will not be covered by rentals received from a sublease.

17.271 Aircraft leases provide a useful source of examples to examine circumstances when an obligation under the lease has arisen. For example, an entity leases an aircraft under an operating lease. The aircraft has to undergo an expensive 'C check' after every 2,400 flying hours. Should provision be made for the cost of these checks?

17.272 The requirement to perform a 'C check' does not give rise to a present obligation at the time the lease is signed, because, until 2,400 hours have been flown, there is no obligation which exists independently of the entity's future actions. Even the intention to incur the cost of a 'C check' depends on the entity deciding to continue flying the aircraft. The cost of each successive 'C check' will therefore be capitalised as it is incurred, and amortised over the period to the next 'C check'.

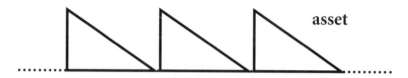

17.273 This leaves the question of the condition in which the aircraft must be returned to the lessor at the end of the lease and of whether this creates a present obligation, thus a provision, at the time the lease is signed. The answer depends on what the lease terms state will happen when the aircraft is returned at the end of the lease. If no final 'C check' is required (i.e., in the final period, the client can use the aircraft for up to 2,399 flying hours and then return it without bearing any cost), no provision should be made, since there is no legal obligation. Since the profit and loss account will first be charged with amortisation of costs after the first 'C check', this will mean the first 2,400 flying hours are effectively a 'free period'. (Note: in this scenario, consider whether the operating lease costs should be recognised on a non-straight line basis under SSAP 21 paragraph 37.)

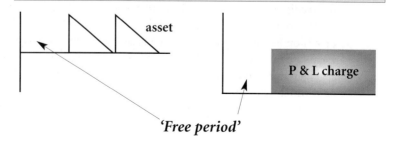

'*Free period*'

17.274 If a 'C check' is required at the end of the lease, irrespective of how many hours have been flown, full provision for the cost should be made at the start of the lease. The costs should be carried forward and written off over the shorter of the next 2,400 flying hours and the number of flying hours to the end of the lease – and similarly each time a 'C check' is carried out. (This will fill the 'free period' above.)

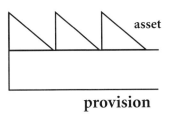

provision

P & L charge

17.275 If, on returning the aircraft, the client must make a payment towards the 'C check' which is in proportion to the number of hours flown (e.g., 75 per cent of the cost of a 'C check' for 1,800 hours flown), then an obligation is created as the aircraft is used. It will be appropriate to build up a provision based on the number of hours flown.

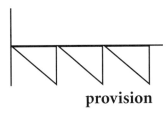

provision

P & L charge

Long-term service contracts

17.276 Long-term service contracts often involve a difference in the pattern of income received and the costs incurred. For example, under a service contract, an entity receives income of £10 per annum for three years. However, the expected pattern of costs of meeting the contract is £6 in year one, £9 in year two, and £12 in year three, leaving an expected profit of £3 over the three years. In the past, the entity may have recognised income as received, but used a provision for future costs in order to achieve a reasonable matching. The question may arise whether such a provision is allowed under FRS 12.

17.277

The service contract would appear to be a long-term contract falling under SSAP 9. Consequently, FRS 12 requires that the more specific standard should be applied. [FRS 12(8)] Under SSAP 9, one option is to defer and allocate revenue on a systematic basis, e.g., a pattern which matched the expected pattern of costs. This method would avoid any provision being created. Alternatively, other methods allowed by SSAP 9 which allocate costs may give rise to provisions. This treatment is not prohibited by FRS 12 on the basis that SSAP 9 is a more specific standard.

Self-insurance – cost of accidents

17.278

Example 12 in appendix III to FRS 12 (see **17.265** above) indicates that no provision can be made in respect of self-insurance. However, a company which self-insures should provide each year for the costs of accidents which have occurred prior to the balance sheet date. What the example seeks to prohibit is making provision for the excess of the 'normal annual cost' over the cost of actual accidents in that year. In other words, it prevents a self-insuring company from 'smoothing' the cost of accidents by making a 'buffer' provision in a year when actual costs are low.

Loyalty schemes

17.279

An entity may operate a range of loyalty schemes, e.g., it may award loyalty points which can be exchanged, within a set period, for vouchers giving discounts on both the entity's products and third parties' products.

17.280 Applying the recognition criteria from FRS 12:

(a) is there a present obligation? Generally, the answer will be yes, but if the entity reserves the right to terminate the scheme at any time, thus invalidating existing vouchers, then there may or may not be a constructive obligation, depending on past behaviour which may have influenced the legitimate expectations of employees and other third parties;

(b) is it probable that economic benefits will be transferred? If, after vouchers are deducted, the entity's products are still being sold at a profit, the answer will be no – therefore no provision will be made. To the extent that products will be sold at a loss, however, or that a third party will be reimbursed for discounts, there will be a transfer of economic benefits;

(c) can a reliable estimate be made? The answer here will almost always be yes, but in making the estimate the entity should consider how likely the vouchers are to be used – so a range of answers may be acceptable.

17.281   In summary, if the criteria are met, provision should be made for the likely cost to the entity (which may not be the 'face value' of the discounts). The entity will need to form a view as to how many vouchers are likely to be used and should also consider whether discounting is appropriate.

Directors' bonuses

17.282   Many companies pay directors' bonuses where the amount to be paid is not finalised until after the year end. For owner managed businesses (where the directors are the shareholders), both directors' bonuses and dividends may be paid, determining the balance between the two on the basis of (among other things) the draft audited financial statements.

17.283   FRS 12 may not prohibit a provision for such bonuses. The fact that the amount is not finalised until after the year end is not inherently a problem, for provision would still be made if there is a constructive obligation to pay the bonuses. A constructive obligation might be supported by the pattern of past practice, but it might also be a good idea for the entity to distinguish this from mere board intention by writing to individual directors prior to the year end to indicate that a bonus will be paid, of an amount yet to be determined.

Provisions for taxation

17.284   Two questions may arise in respect of taxation. Firstly, to what extent do the disclosure requirements of FRS 12 apply to corporation tax? Secondly, if an entity adopts a 'tax scheme' which might be challenged by the Inland Revenue, does any unprovided tax 'at risk' have to be disclosed as a contingent liability?

17.285   In general, the answer to both questions will be no, for the following reasons:

(a) FRS 12 does not apply to *all* liabilities: it applies to contingencies (i.e., obligations which are not recognised) and to provisions (as defined in the standard). Each is considered below;

(b) it notes that 'provisions can be distinguished from other liabilities, such as trade creditors and accruals' where 'the uncertainty is generally much less than for provisions'. Although there is often some uncertainty associated with a tax liability, it would appear to fall into the 'other liabilities' category. Provisions for the purposes of FRS 12 will usually be items which would be categorised as 'provisions for liabilities and charges' in a company's balance sheet, unlike trade creditors, accruals and corporation tax. Accordingly, a tax 'provision' will not usually be within the scope of FRS 12;

(c) where the amount of tax payable by an entity is uncertain (e.g., as a result of a tax scheme), any potential amount payable over that provided is *not* a contingent liability, because it is not a separate liability. It is simply part of the range of uncertainty associated with the liability which has already been recognised.

17.286 One exception is where it is uncertain whether or not a company (a charity, for example) falls within the scope of corporation tax. In these circumstances, the amounts of tax which may be payable (whether provided or not) will fall within the scope of FRS 12.

17.287 A further situation where the logic of FRS 12 is helpful relates to the reopening of a prior year by the Inland Revenue. Even though the arguments outlined above would support a view that this is outside the scope of FRS 12, there may be a need to disclose the uncertainties surrounding the outcome which are similar to the disclosures for a contingent liability.

17.288 On the separate question of deferred tax, FRS 12 notes that a more specific standard applies instead, i.e., SSAP 15. [FRS 12(8)]

Holiday pay

17.289 For many UK entities, staff take holidays at a range of dates such that production and staff activity continue throughout the year and accordingly, recognition of accrued holiday pay is not an issue in these circumstances.

17.290 However, in certain industries and particular countries abroad, it is more common for staff to take holiday at the same time, with the effect that the entity's business shuts down for a period, e.g., the month of August. Since the entity has no revenue in this period, the cost of paying staff during the holiday may be accrued and spread over the 11 months when activity occurs. Such a basis is not prohibited by FRS 12 and should be disclosed as an accrual. [FRS 12(11)]

Disclosure requirements

17.291 The objective of FRS 12 with respect to disclosure is to ensure that sufficient information is disclosed in the notes to the financial statements to enable users to understand the nature, timing and amount of provisions, contingent liabilities and contingent assets. By the issue of FRS 12, the ASB has taken the opportunity to develop a complete framework of disclosure requirements. The FRS sets out the disclosure requirements for contingent liabilities and contingent assets alongside those for provisions, making clear the consistent basis for the requirements.

17.292 With respect to provisions, the thinking behind the requirements is to supply information about their significance, any changes during the year and an explanation of how a provision has been used as expenditure is incurred during the year.

17.293 The general requirements are set out in the following paragraphs.

Disclosure for provisions

17.294 For each class of provision there should be disclosed:
[FRS 12(89) and (90)]

    (a)   brought and carried forward balances;

    (b)   changes during the period (showing separately additional provisions made, amounts incurred and charged against the provision and unused amounts reversed);

    (c)   increase during the period in the discounted amount arising from the passage of time and the effect of any change in the discount rate;

    (d)   the nature of the obligation and expected timing of payments;

    (e)   uncertainties surrounding the amount or timing of payments;

    (f)   major assumptions concerning future events (if considered necessary to provide adequate information); and

    (g)   expected reimbursement, including amount of any asset recognised for that reimbursement.

Extract 17.294

BG plc

Year ended 31 December 1998

Provisions for liabilities and charges (extracts)

	As at 1 January 1998 (as restated) £m	Profit and loss charge/ (credit) £m	Paid £m	Transfers and other adjust- ments(i) £m	As at 31 December 1998 £m
Group					
Decommissioning costs	197	–	–	8	205
Pension costs	589	(45)	(25)	–	519
Environmental costs	342	–	(49)	20	313
Property restructuring costs	101	–	(18)	–	83
Long-term gas sales contract loss provisions	205	–	(5)	22	222
Deferred petroleum revenue tax	72	4	–	–	76
Deferred corporation tax	110	33	–	–	143
Other	43	12	–	3	58
	1,659	4	(97)	53	1,619

(i)   Includes unwinding of discount added to net interest in respect of the Group amounting to £56m (see note 7, page 59), of which £44m relates to the Company.

A brief description of each provision together with estimates of the timing of expenditure is given below.

Decommissioning costs

The estimated cost of decommissioning at the end of the producing lives of fields is based on engineering estimates and reports from independent experts. Provision is made for the estimated cost of decommissioning at the balance sheet date. The payment dates of total expected future decommissioning costs is uncertain, but are currently anticipated to be between 2000 and 2019.

Pension costs

These represent the difference between the charge or credit to the profit and loss account in respect of pension costs and the contributions to the pension schemes (see Principal accounting policies, page 44 and note 26, page 77).

Environmental costs

The undiscounted provision of £409m for statutory decontamination costs of old gas manufacturing sites is determined by periodic assessments undertaken by environmental specialists employed by the Group and has been discounted at 6 per cent. The expected payment dates for statutory decontamination remain uncertain, but it is anticipated that most expenditure will take place between 1999 and 2005.

Non-statutory decontamination costs are included within the valuation of land and buildings (see Principal accounting policies, page 44).

Property restructuring costs

Consists primarily of provision of disposal of surplus leasehold interests and rent and rates payable on surplus properties.

Long-term gas sales contract loss provisions

These represent forecast future losses under certain gas purchase and supply sales contracts assigned to BG on demerger in 1997. The contracts terminate in years 2001 and 2008. The estimated net losses have been discounted and are dependent upon factors such as prices, which vary with a basket of indices, and supply and demand volumes.

Disclosure for contingent liabilities

17.295   For each class of contingent liability (unless possibility of settlement is remote) there should be disclosed:
[FRS 12(91)]

(a)   estimate of the financial effect;

(b)   uncertainties relating to the amount or timing of any outflow; and

(c)   the possibility of any reimbursement.

17.296   Where an inflow of economic benefits is probable, a brief description of the nature of the contingent assets and, where practicable, their estimated financial effect should be given, taking care to avoid giving misleading indications of the likelihood of a profit arising. [FRS 12(94) and (95)]

17.297   There may be confusion about whether a group of provisions or contingent liabilities may be aggregated to form a class. Under these circumstances, it is necessary to consider whether the nature of the items is sufficiently similar for a single statement about them to fulfil the requirements outlined above with respect to nature and uncertainties. [FRS 12(92)]

17.298   One important point to note is that where a provision and contingent liability arise from the same set of circumstances, an entity should make the disclosure so that it clearly shows the link between the provision and the contingent liability. [FRS 12(93)]

Comparative information

17.299 Comparative information is not required for the numerical disclosures which relate to provisions (i.e., (a) to (c) in **17.294** above). [FRS 12(89)]

Exemptions applying to disclosure of contingent liabilities and contingent assets

17.300 Where any of the information required in respect of contingent liabilities and contingent assets above is not disclosed because it is not practicable to do so, then this fact should be stated. [FRS 12(96)]

Exemptions applying to all disclosures

17.301 In extremely rare cases, it is conceivable that some or all of the disclosures required can be expected to prejudice seriously the position of the entity in a dispute with other parties on the subject matter of the provision, contingent liability or contingent asset. In such cases, an entity need not disclose the information, unless its disclosure is required by law, but it should disclose the general nature of the dispute, together with the fact that the information has not been disclosed and the reason for this. [FRS 12(97)]

Executory contracts

17.302

FRS 12 does not apply to executory contracts, except where the contract is onerous. As discussed in **17.161** above, executory contracts are not strictly defined. The discussion paper issued by the ASB on leases, although it recommends that executory contracts be scoped out, provides further assistance. It confirms the explanation given in FRS 12. It states that the term 'executory contract' is generally used to refer to contracts under which both parties are still to perform to an equal degree the actions promised by and required of them under the contract. It goes on to say that an obvious example of an executory contract is a contract under which neither party has performed any of the promises it made in the contract, but that a contract may also be equally proportionately unperformed at various stages during the period to completion of the contract.

17.303 The discussion about the point at which assets and liabilities in respect of a lease should be recognised, appears to be equally valid for executory contracts generally. It suggests that for leases various events could be considered as the point of recognition, including:

(a) signing the lease;

(b) delivery of the physical property/assignment of rights of an intangible asset;

(c) rental payments falling due.

It concludes that the most significant act of performance and the point at which recognition should occur for lease assets and liabilities is the point of delivery.

17.304 One of the features of most executory contracts is that neither party to them could enforce the contract. Consider the example of a take or pay contract. Under such a contract, even if the purchaser decides not to take the asset or service which is the subject of the contract, payment must be made. Some would argue that an obligation should therefore be recognised by the purchaser at the point of signing the contract. However, if an obligation were to be recorded, the question arising is 'what asset would it represent?' It could represent at most a receivable. However, the vendor controls the right to the related asset and can decide whether or not to deliver. Delivery cannot be enforced and if it did not occur no obligation would exist.

17.305 It appears appropriate, therefore, to take the same approach as proposed for leases, that is to consider the delivery of the asset or service to be the significant act of performance. It follows then that under executory contracts no provisions should be made until the asset or service has been received. Circumstances where an asset is used to provide a service should be analysed under FRS 5 Application Note F. See chapter 28.

Requirements of the Companies Act 1985

17.306 The main requirements that are relevant come from Schs 4 and 4A. Schedule 4 requires that all liabilities and losses which have arisen, or are likely to arise, in respect of the accounting period or a previous financial year, shall be taken into account.

17.307 'Provisions for liabilities and charges' is a main heading which should appear on the face of the balance sheet. The following subheadings are required, but may be shown either on the face of the balance sheet or in a note to the accounts:

- Pensions and similar obligations;

- Taxation, including deferred taxation;

- Other provisions.

17.308 The directors may adapt these subheadings in any case where the special nature of the company's business requires such adaptation. In addition, subheadings may be combined if their individual amounts are not material.

17.309 Where a transfer has been made to any provision for liabilities and charges, or from such a provision for a purpose other than that for which the provision was established, the following information is required by Sch 4 to be given by way of note:
[Sch 4: 46]

(a) opening and closing balances;

(b) amounts transferred to or from the provision during the year; and

(c) the source and application, as appropriate, of the amounts so transferred.

17.310 Comparative amounts for the preceding year do not have to be shown. [Sch 4: 58]

17.311 Schedule 4 requires separate disclosure in the notes of the amount of any provision for deferred taxation and the amount of any provision for other taxation. [Sch 4: 47]

17.312 Taxation is dealt with in chapter 27.

17.313 Particulars of any pension commitments included under provisions, together with separate particulars of any such commitments relating to pensions payable to past directors of the company, should be given. [Sch 4: 50(4)] Pension accounting and related disclosures are further discussed in chapter 30. Directors' remuneration is discussed in chapter 8.

17.314 Particulars of any material provision included in 'Other provisions' are required to be stated. [Sch 4: 46(3)]

17.315 With respect to contingencies, Sch 4 requires disclosure of the amount or estimated amount of any contingent liability, its legal nature and whether any security has been provided by the company in connection with it and, if so, then what that security is. [Sch 4: 50(2)]

17.316 There is a further requirement for particulars to be given of any charge on the assets of the company to secure the liabilities of any other person, including, when practicable, the amount secured. [Sch 4: 50(1)] This requirement may be superfluous where the existence of the charge creates a contingent liability requiring disclosure in any event. However, when the likelihood of the charge being exercised would be so remote as not to require disclosure as a contingency, the charge will still need to be disclosed as specifically required by the Act.

17.317 Within the individual financial statements of a company, contingencies and charges on the assets of a company to secure the liabilities of any other person which arise from undertakings entered into on behalf of or for the benefit of other group companies (e.g., guarantees or bills discounted), should be disclosed separately, subdivided between those benefiting: parent and fellow subsidiary undertakings and subsidiary undertakings. [Sch 4: 59A]

Transitional requirements

17.318 On the initial application of FRS 12, it is necessary to identify whether adjustments represent a change in accounting policy or revisions of estimates.

Change of accounting policy

17.319 A change of accounting policy occurs where either: [FRS 12(101) and (102)]

   (a) a provision previously recognised does not qualify as a provision under FRS 12. For example, in the past, management have made provision for reorganisation at the time of a board decision; or

   (b) a provision required by FRS 12 has not previously been recognised. For example, in the past, no provision has been recognised for decommissioning costs.

17.320 A change of accounting policy is accounted for as a prior year adjustment in accordance with FRS 3.

Revision of an accounting estimate

17.321 A revision of an accounting estimate occurs where an entity already provides for an item, but FRS 12 results in the provision being measured at a different amount.

17.322 Accounting for a change in accounting estimate is a current year profit and loss account item.

Comparison with international standards

17.323 Appendix VI to FRS 12 deals with compliance with IASs. It makes clear that, as a result of FRS 12 being developed in parallel with the new IAS 37 *Provisions, contingent liabilities and contingent assets,* all the requirements of the IAS are included in the FRS and there are no differences of substance between the common requirements. The FRS has some additional material within it which deals with the circumstances under which an asset should be recognised when a provision is recognised and gives more guidance than the IAS on the discount rate to be used in the present value calculation.

17.324 The IAS was published in September 1998 and became operative for annual financial statements covering periods beginning on or after 1 July 1999.

18   Share capital and reserves

18 Share capital and reserves

Introduction

The Act and FRS 4 Capital instruments

18.1   The Act lays down, in the Sch 4 balance sheet formats, the headings which should be shown on the face of the balance sheet under share capital and reserves. Schedule 4 also sets out a number of disclosure requirements.

18.2   The provisions of the Act refer to shares and debentures. Many companies now issue capital instruments, which have many of the features of debt, but are legally shares, or debt instruments, which can be converted into shares. FRS 4 aims to ensure a consistent treatment of capital instruments and to ensure that financial statements provide relevant information concerning the nature and amount of the entity's sources of finance. To this end, FRS 4 specifies which capital instruments should be reported as part of shareholders' funds and sets out some additional disclosure requirements.

18.3   FRS 4 requires any instrument which does not fall under the definition of a liability (i.e., any instrument, other than shares, which contains an obligation or contingent obligation to transfer economic benefits) to be shown within shareholders' funds.

18.4   Warrants and options requiring the issue of shares do not contain an obligation to transfer economic benefits and therefore are not liabilities and should be included in shareholders' funds. [FRS 4(37)]

18.5   Although many shares have features which make them economically similar to debt, because of their legal status, the FRS requires them to be classified as shares under the balance sheet formats prescribed by the Act. So, although shares may contain rights which mean that the company has obligations to transfer economic benefits, shares are excluded from this definition of a liability and must be reported within shareholders' funds.

18.6   The Act contains provisions, to ensure the maintenance of capital, which place restrictions on the ability to redeem or repurchase shares.

18.7   While this categorisation reflects the legal form of the instruments, the FRS requires additional analysis on the face of the balance sheet to reflect economic substance.

Called up share capital

Introduction

18.8   The amount of 'Called up share capital' should be shown on the face of the balance sheet under the heading 'Capital and reserves'.

Disclosure requirements

Companies Act

18.9   The following should be stated in the notes to the accounts:

(a)   the amount of the authorised share capital [Sch 4: 38];

(b)   the amount of the allotted share capital and the amount of called up share capital which has been paid should be shown separately. [Sch 4: Note 12 on the balance sheet formats] Since partly paid shares are rare in the UK, this provision has little significance and the requirement can normally be met by using the words 'allotted and fully paid' after the heading;

(c)   where more than one class of shares has been allotted, the number and aggregate nominal value of shares of each class [Sch 4: 38];

(d)   if the allotted capital includes redeemable shares:
[Sch 4: 38]

  (i)   the earliest and latest dates on which the company has power to redeem these shares;
  (ii)   whether those shares must be redeemed in any event or may be redeemed at the option of the company or of the shareholder; and
  (iii) whether any (and, if so, what) premium is payable on redemption;

(e)   if any shares have been allotted during the year:
[Sch 4: 39]

  (i)   the classes of shares allotted; and
  (ii)   regarding each class of shares, the number allotted, their aggregate nominal value, and the consideration received;

(f)   if there are any options to subscribe for shares or any other rights to require the allotment of shares to any person (including conversion rights of other securities):

[Sch 4: 40]

(i)   the number, description and amount of shares in relation to which the right is exercisable;

(ii) the period during which the right is exercisable; and

(iii) the price to be paid for the shares;

(g) if fixed cumulative dividends are in arrears, the amount and
period of arrears for each class of shares [Sch 4: 49];

(h) the number, description and amount of shares in the company
held by its subsidiary undertakings [Sch 5: 6].

Extract 18.9

Coats Viyella plc 1998

22 Called up share capital

	Number of shares	1998 £m	Number of shares	1997 £m
Authorised:				
Ordinary shares of 20p each	876,952,750	175.4	876,952,750	175.4
4.9% Cumulative preference shares of £1 each – non-equity shares	14,609,450	14.6	14,609,450	14.6
		190.0		190.0
Allotted and fully paid:				
Ordinary shares of 20p each	703,623,098	140.7	703,623,098	140.7
4.9% Cumulative preference shares of £1 each – non-equity shares	14,609,449	14.6	14,609,449	14.6
		155.3		155.3

The 4.9% Cumulative Preference Shares of £1 each confer on the
holders thereof the right to receive a cumulative preferential dividend
at the rate of 4.9% on the capital for the time being paid up thereon
and the right on a winding up or repayment of capital to a return of
the capital paid thereon (together with a premium calculated at the
rate of £0.125 for every £1 of such capital) and a sum equal to any
arrears or deficiency of the fixed dividend thereon calculated down to
the date of the return of capital subject to such taxes as shall be in
force at that date and to be payable whether such dividend has been
declared or earned or not in priority to any payment to the holders of
the ordinary shares, but the Preference Shares shall not entitle the
holders to any further or other participation in the profits or assets of
Coats Viyella.

The Preference Shares shall not entitle the holders thereof to attend or
vote at any general meeting unless either:

(i)   at the date of the meeting, the fixed dividend on the Preference
Shares is six months in arrears, and so that for this purpose such

---

dividend shall be deemed to be payable half-yearly on the 31st day of March and the 30th day of September in every year; or

(ii) the business of the meeting includes the consideration of a resolution for winding up or reducing the Capital of Coats Viyella or directly and adversely affecting any of the special rights or privileges for the time being attached to the Preference Shares.

The Preference Shares shall nevertheless entitle the holders thereof to receive notice of every general meeting. At a general meeting at which the holders of Preference Shares are entitled to attend and vote the Preference Shares shall, in voting upon a poll, entitle a holder thereof or his proxy to one vote only for every Preference Share held by him.

The conversion rights attaching to the £65.229 6.25% Senior Convertible Bonds issued by Coats Viyella Plc are detailed in note 18.

Options granted for ordinary shares but not exercised are as follows:

	Options granted	Price per share	Period of option	Number of shares
1984 Executive Share Option Scheme	1989 to 1994	103.57p to 256.08p	1999 to 2004	2,671,721
Overseas Executive Share Option Scheme	1989 to 1994	103.57p to 256.08p	1999 to 2004	2,360,901
1994 Executive Share Option Scheme	1994 to 1998	33.75p to 214.5p	1999 to 2008	14,837,350
Savings Related Share Option Scheme	1992 to 1993	168.18p to 190.86p	1999 to 2000	696,142
Sharesave Scheme	1994 to 1997	110p to 183p	1999 to 2002	6,565,579
Total Group Executive Share Option Scheme	1990	150.91p	1999 to 2000	116,181
				27,247,874
Shares issued during the year: Options exercised during the year were: Savings Related Share Option Scheme				308,414

The consideration for the issue for option shares was £0.3m.

FRS 4

18.10 An analysis should be given in the notes to the accounts of the total amount of non-equity interests in shareholders' funds relating to each class of non-equity shares and series of warrants for non-equity shares.

18.11 A brief summary of the rights of each class of shares should be given. This should include the following:

(a)   the rights to dividends;

(b)   the date at which redeemable and the amounts payable in respect of redemption;

(c)   priority and amount receivable on a winding-up;

(d)   voting rights.

18.12   The above disclosure will usually make it clear why a class of share has been classified as equity or non-equity, but, if necessary, additional information should be given to explain the classification.

18.13   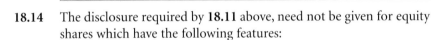 For example, participating preference shares are preference shares which are entitled, in addition to the fixed dividend for each period, to a percentage of the dividends paid on the ordinary shares. Under FRS 4, they are non-equity shares (because they have a right to receive a fixed dividend not dependent upon profits or assets), but their dividend entitlement would need to be explained, so as not to give a misleading impression of the funds available for distribution to the equity shareholders.

18.14   The disclosure required by **18.11** above, need not be given for equity shares which have the following features:

(a)   no right to dividends other than those which may be recommended by the directors;

(b)   no redemption rights;

(c)   unlimited right to share in the surplus remaining on a winding-up after all liabilities and participation rights of other classes of shares have been satisfied; and

(d)   one vote per share.

18.15   Where, in rare circumstances, equity shares under the Act fall to be treated as non-equity shares under FRS 4, fuller explanations should be given in order to avoid the financial statements being confusing or misleading.

18.16   The Act defines an equity share as one which carries rights to participate in the company beyond a specified amount in a distribution. This is a much wider definition than that contained in FRS 4. Consider, for example, participating preference shares which carry a right to a proportion of the distribution paid on ordinary shares and, in addition, a fixed dividend for the period. Under FRS 4, the entitlement to the fixed dividend means the shares fall under the definition of non-equity shares. Under the Act, however, the entitlement to participate in a

> proportion of the distribution on ordinary shares is not limited to a specified amount, with the result that the shares would be classified as equity shares. As there are no accounting or disclosure requirements in the Act regarding this definition, there is no need to use the true and fair override. Furthermore, as the FRS requires all necessary information to explain the classification between equity and non-equity to be given, it is difficult to see how the users of the financial statements could be misled.

18.17 Where warrants or convertible debt are in issue which may require the company to issue shares of a class which is not currently in issue, the information set out in **18.11** above should be given in respect of that class. [FRS 4(58)]

Example 18.17

The class 1 warrants entitle the holders to receive one class 'C' share.

Class 'C' shares when issued will have the following rights attached:

(a)   one vote per share;

(b)   10 per cent fixed cumulative dividend;

(c)   ranking after class B shares in a winding-up, with an entitlement to receive up to £1.50 per share.

UK Listing Authority Listing Rules

18.18 Where a listed company, without the specific authorisation by the company's shareholders, issues for cash securities with an equity element otherwise than to the equity shareholders in proportion to their equity interest, its annual report and accounts should disclose: [Listing Rules 12.43(o)]

(a)   the names of the allottees, if less than six in number; in the case of six or more, also a brief generic description of them; and

(b)   the market price of the securities concerned on the date on which the terms of the issue were fixed.

Directors' interests in shares and debentures

18.19 The particulars of directors' interests in shares and debentures may be given by way of note to the accounts instead of in the directors' report. [Sch 7: 2(1)] These particulars are discussed in **6.41** to **6.51** above.

Non-equity minority interests

18.20   Where there are non-equity minority interests, a description should be given of any rights of holders of the shares against other group companies, e.g., in respect of convertible preference shares. Where this right is in the form of a guarantee, the non-equity minority interest will be classified as a liability (see **17.61** to **17.66** above).

18.21   Where non-equity interests in minority interests are disclosed in the notes to the accounts rather than on the face of the balance sheet on the grounds that they are not material, the relevant caption on the face of the balance sheet should state that non-equity interests are included.

Reserves

Statutory disclosure requirements

18.22   Reserves represent the excess of assets over liabilities of a company after deducting its called up share capital. The following reserves should be shown on the face of the balance sheet:

- Share premium account;

- Revaluation reserve (but a title other than this may be used);

- Other reserves;

- Profit and loss account.

18.23   The main heading 'Other reserves' has the following subheadings which should be shown either on the face of the balance sheet or in a note to the accounts:

- Capital redemption reserve;

- Reserve for own shares;

- Reserves provided for by the Articles of Association;

- Other reserves.

18.24   Where any amount is transferred to or from any reserves, the following should be shown in respect of each reserve affected:
[Sch 4: 46]

(a)   opening and closing balances;

(b)   amounts transferred to or from the reserves during the year; and

(c)   the source and application, respectively, of the amounts so transferred.

Comparative amounts for the preceding year do not have to be shown.

18.25 The requirements of the Act and accounting standards in respect of share premium accounts, revaluation reserves, capital redemption reserves and other reserves are dealt with in **18.81** to **18.122** below.

Statement of movements on reserves

18.26 Unlike its predecessor standard (SSAP 6), FRS 3 does not include a requirement to include a statement of movements on reserves. This omission will not affect companies, as they are required by the Act to reconcile the opening and closing balances of individual reserves in their financial statements. In situations where the reserve structure is complex, the statement of movements on reserves gives useful information and, accordingly, such a statement should be produced, unless the relevant information is disclosed elsewhere in the financial statements.

18.27 If the statement of movements on reserves does not immediately follow the profit and loss account, there is no longer any requirement to make reference to it on the face of the profit and loss account.

18.28 Although not mentioned in the body of the standard, the illustrative examples accompanying FRS 3 do include a statement of movements on reserves. The following is based upon those examples.

Example 18.28

Statement of movements on reserves

	Share premium account £ million	Revaluation reserve £ million	Profit and loss account £ million	Total £ million
At beginning of the year	40	147	49	236
Deficit on revaluation of investment properties		(3)		(3)
Decrease in value of trade investment		(4)		(4)
Foreign exchange translation differences on foreign currency net investment in subsidiaries			(2)	(2)
Transfer of realised profits		(6)	6	–
Profit retained for the year	–	–	8	8
At end of the year	40	134	61	235

Distributable reserves

18.29 FRS 2 requires, in relation to group accounts, that if there are significant statutory, contractual or exchange control restrictions on the ability of the subsidiary undertakings to distribute their retained profits (other than those shown as non-distributable), the nature and extent of the restrictions should be indicated. [FRS 2(53)]

18.30 > Clearly, similar information should also be given if the retained profits of a single company are subject to such restrictions.

18.31 The Act imposes restrictions on the amounts which may legally be distributed by a company by way of dividend or otherwise; these restrictions are described in **33.36** to **33.83**.

18.32 > There is no requirement to disclose the actual amount of a company's reserves which are legally available for distribution and it is not normally meaningful to do so in the case of a group. However, where there is a significant difference between retained profits as shown in a company's own accounts and distributable profits for that company, best practice would require the amount of reserves legally available for distribution to be disclosed.

Items charged or credited direct to reserves

18.33 As indicated in **9.3**, items should only be charged or credited to reserves without being included in the profit and loss account in exceptional circumstances. In many circumstances, items that would previously have bypassed the profit and loss account will now be reported in the statement of total recognised gains and losses. The following items have been identified as being taken directly to the reconciliation of movements in shareholders' funds:

(a) items charged direct against share premium account (see **18.83** below);

(b) capital contributions from a parent which are deemed to be contributions from owners (see **18.54** and **18.55** below); and

(c) the immediate elimination of purchased goodwill (not permitted after adoption of FRS 10).

18.34 > Charges direct to the share premium account may not be made in respect of capital instruments classified as debt and accounted for under FRS 4. These costs will have to pass

> through the profit and loss account first and can only be written off to the share premium account as a reserve transfer from the profit and loss account reserve. Issue costs on equity and non-equity shares can still be taken directly to the share premium account, although the issue costs in respect of non-equity shares will be taken into account in determining the annual finance costs (see 18.64 to 18.73 below).

Shareholders' funds

Analysis on the face of the balance sheet

18.35   FRS 4 requires shareholders' funds to be analysed on the face of the balance sheet between those attributable to equity and those attributable to non-equity shares. [FRS 4(40)]

18.36   Minority interests should also be analysed on the face of the balance sheet between the aggregate amount attributable to equity interests and the amounts attributable to non-equity interests. [FRS 4(50)]

18.37   If the amount attributable to non-equity interests of either shareholders' funds or minority interests is not material, the disclosure of non-equity amounts may be made in the notes to the accounts, but the fact that non-equity interests are included should be stated on the face of the balance sheet. [FRS 4(100)]

> ### *Example 18.37*
>
> | | Note | 2000 £'000 | 1999 £'000 |
> |---|---|---|---|
> | Shareholders' funds (including non-equity interests) | 23 | 4,275 | 4,032 |

18.38   In requiring an analysis of shareholders' funds, the FRS does not require that each statutory heading be analysed. Companies have the option of choosing to show the analysis for each heading, but this could be quite voluminous; it is likely that most companies will choose to show the split just for the total of shareholders' funds.

18.39   The following example illustrates one way in which the analysis of shareholders' funds and minority interests on the face of the balance sheet could be shown.

Example 18.39

	£'000	£'000
Called up share capital	536	
Share premium account	123	
Revaluation reserve	118	
Profit and loss account	2,210	
	2,987	
Equity shareholders' funds		2,826
Non-equity shareholders' funds		161
Total shareholders' funds		2,987
Minority interests		
Equity minority interests	339	
Non-equity minority interests	81	
		420
Total capital employed		3,407

18.40 An alternative where there are no minority interests is as follows.

Example 18.40

	£'000
Called up share capital	536
Share premium account	123
Revaluation reserve	118
Profit and loss account	2,210
Total shareholders' funds	2,987
Shareholders' funds are attributable to:	
Equity shareholders' funds	2,826
Non-equity shareholders' funds	161
	2,987

18.41 The amount attributable to non-equity shareholders' funds will be the carrying value of the instruments, as discussed in **18.57** to **18.61** below.

18.42 Where an entity has:

(a) net liabilities; or

(b) non-equity shareholders' funds exceed the total shareholders' funds,

this will result in showing a negative amount attributable to equity interests.

Classification of shares as equity or non-equity

18.43   Equity shares are defined as all shares other than non-equity shares.

18.44   Non-equity shares are defined as those possessing any of the following characteristics:

(a)   any of the rights of the shares to receive payments (whether in respect of dividends, in respect of redemption or otherwise) are for a limited amount that is not calculated by reference to the company's assets or profits or the dividends on any class of equity share;

(b)   any of their rights to participate in a surplus in a winding-up are limited to a specific amount that is not calculated by reference to the company's assets or profits and such limitation had a commercial effect in practice at the time the shares were issued or, if later, at the time the limitation was introduced;

(c)   the shares are redeemable, either according to their terms or because the holder, or any party other than the issuer, can require their redemption.

18.45

The limitation on rights to participate in a winding-up should only be taken into account in determining the classification between equity and non-equity when it has a commercial effect in practice. The FRS examines this further in the explanatory notes. In general, financial statements are drawn up on a going concern basis; in such a case, the rights attaching to shares on a winding-up usually have no commercial effect. However, in some situations, shares are issued for a predetermined life. This might arise where a joint venture company is established to develop a property, where the company will be wound up when the property has been completed and sold. In these circumstances, the rights to participation on winding-up do have a commercial effect in practice.

18.46   The determination of whether the limitation has a commercial effect in practice should take place when the shares are first issued or when the limitation is introduced on a subsequent alteration of the rights attaching to the shares. If, on issue, it is determined that the limitations on winding-up have no commercial effect and subsequently the company ceases to be a going concern, the shares should not be reclassified as non-equity at that stage.

18.47   Warrants and options will usually be classified as equity or non-equity shareholders' funds, depending upon the rights of the shares to be issued on the exercise of the warrants.

Reconciliation of movements in shareholders' funds

18.48 FRS 3 requires the presentation of a note to reconcile the opening and closing totals of shareholders' funds for the period. [FRS 3(28)] The purpose of the reconciliation is to highlight those items that do not appear in the profit and loss account or the statement of total recognised gains and losses, but which can be important for an understanding of the change in financial position of an entity. [FRS 3(59)]

18.49 The standard does not specify what items should appear in the reconciliation other than to say that it will highlight those not shown in the profit and loss account or the statement of total recognised gains and losses. Such items would include:

(a)   the proceeds of a share issue;

(b)   redemption or purchase of own shares; and

(c)   purchased goodwill immediately eliminated against reserves (not permitted after adoption of FRS 10).

18.50 The standard does not stipulate a format for the reconciliation. The example below is based upon the illustrative examples which accompany FRS 3.

Example 18.50

Reconciliation of movements in shareholders' funds

	2000	1999
	£ million	£ million
Profit attributable to members of the company	15	10
Dividends	(7)	(6)
	8	4
Other recognised gains and losses for the year (net)	(9)	17
Capital subscribed	–	8
Net (reduction)/addition to shareholders' funds	(1)	29
Opening shareholders' funds	259	230
Closing shareholders' funds	258	259

18.51 The reconciliation should be shown separately from the statement of total recognised gains and losses, so as not to divert attention from the components of performance of the total recognised gains and losses for the period. [FRS 3(59) and 'The development of the standard' (xii)]

18.52 FRS 3 does not discuss what should be disclosed if there has been no movement in shareholders' funds other than the total of recognised gains and losses for the period. The reconciliation may be omitted if there are no movements in shareholders' funds other than the recognised gains and losses for the period in both the current and prior period and a statement to that effect is given at the base of the statement of total recognised gains and losses.

18.53 Companies with few movements on reserves may be able to combine the statement of movements in shareholders' funds with the statement of movements on reserves.

Example 18.53

Combined statement of movements in shareholders' funds and statement of movements on reserves

	Issued share capital	Share premium account	Revalu- ation reserve	Profit and loss account	Total	Total
					2000	1999
	£ million	£ million	£ million	£ million	£ million	£ million
At beginning of the year	23	40	147	49	259	230
Profit attributable to members of the company	–	–	–	15	15	10
Dividends	–	–	–	(7)	(7)	(6)
(Deficit)/Surplus on revaluation of investment properties	–	–	(3)	–	(3)	6
Decrease in value of trade investment	–	–	(4)	–	(4)	6
Foreign exchange translation differences on foreign currency net investment in subsidiaries	–	–	–	(2)	(2)	5
Capital subscribed	–	–	–	–	–	8
Transfer of realised profits	–	–	(6)	6	–	–
At end of the year	23	40	134	61	258	259

Capital contributions

18.54 Capital contributions are a means sometimes used by a parent company to increase 'capital' in a subsidiary. The parent passes funds to the subsidiary in the form of a non-returnable gift. Because the subsidiary that receives the contribution does not have an obligation to transfer economic benefits, FRS 4 requires the capital contribution to be taken directly to shareholders' funds and shown in the reconciliation of movements in shareholders' funds. Capital contributions are the subject of an application note to FRS 4.

18.55   The FRS does not state where within shareholders' funds a capital contribution should be shown. There appear to be no legal restrictions on the distribution of contributions made in this way, unless imposed by the Articles of Association, and therefore they can be taken to the profit and loss account or an 'other reserve' as the company wishes.

Share issue expenses

18.56   See **17.22** to **17.32** for a discussion of the costs that can be treated as issue costs. FRS 4 states that, in respect of shares, the issue costs are to be treated as an integral part of the transaction with owners. The FRS requires that, on the initial recording of the shares, these issue costs be taken into account in determining the net proceeds of the issue and reported in the reconciliation of movements in shareholders' funds. Issue costs should not be disclosed in the statement of total recognised gains and losses. [FRS 4(93)] Subsequently, for non-equity shares, the total finance costs recognised in the profit and loss account over the term of the shares include the amount in respect of issue costs (see **18.64** to **18.70** below).

Carrying amounts

Amount recorded on issue

18.57   All shares will initially be reported in the reconciliation of shareholders' funds at the net proceeds of the issue, being the consideration received less costs of issue. [FRS 4(37)]

18.58   The standard does not specify which accounts within shareholders' funds should be used to record the net proceeds. However, the Act requires the nominal value of shares be shown as share capital and, in most cases, any premium on issue to be taken to the share premium account. Additionally, under the Act, any amount in the share premium account may be used to write off the expenses of issues of shares.

Example 18.58

Assume 1,000 £1 shares are issued at £1.50, with issue costs of £100.

The entries will be:

Cr Share capital (nominal amount)		1,000
Cr Share premium (the premium)		500
Dr Share premium (issue costs)	100	

The shareholders' funds will have been increased by the net proceeds of £1,400.

18.59   If there is an insufficient premium on issue or balance on the share premium account against which to offset the issue costs, the costs can either be taken to an 'other' reserve or to the profit and loss account reserve. It is preferable to take the issue costs to an 'other' reserve for two reasons:

(a)   because the issue costs are not a realised loss. Debiting the profit and loss reserves may give a misleading impression of the profits legally available for distribution. It will also mean that, for the purposes of establishing legally distributable reserves, a memorandum will have to be kept which records the amount of unrealised loss included within profit and loss reserves; and

(b)   because it provides a clear record of the net proceeds both for the reader of the accounts and for the company.

Adjustments to carrying amount subsequent to issue

Equity shares

18.60   For equity shares, there will be no subsequent adjustments to the initial amount recorded to reflect any changes in value of the shares. [FRS 4(45)]

Non-equity shares

18.61   For non-equity shares, at each subsequent balance sheet date the carrying value will be increased by the amount of the finance charge for the period and reduced by the amount of any dividend or other payment made during the period. [FRS 4(41)] Finance charges associated with non-equity shares are dealt with in **18.64** to **18.70** below.

Conversion of debt or non-equity shares

18.62   When a conversion option within convertible debt is exercised, the amount which will be recorded within shareholders' funds for the shares issued will be the carrying amount of the debt at the date of conversion. No gain or loss will be recognised. [FRS 4(26)]

18.63   Similarly, if non-equity shares are converted to equity shares, no gain or loss is recognised. Conversion can be legally effected in a number of ways. In essence, either the original shares can be cancelled and new shares issued or the rights attaching to the shares can be altered. While neither route will impact on the total reserves, individual reserves may be affected. If the conversion is effected by cancellation and new issue, the carrying amount of the original shares is considered to be the net proceeds of the new issue and will be posted to share capital and share premium in the normal way (see the example below). If the conversion is effected by a change of rights attaching to the shares, the only entry normally required is to transfer any accrued finance charges from 'Other reserves' to profit and loss reserves.

Example 18.63

One thousand £1 eight per cent redeemable convertible preference shares were issued at £1.30. They can be redeemed for 125 per cent of par in five years' time, but are convertible into two 25p ordinary shares for each preference share held at the option of the holder at any time after the first two years. The company incurred costs of £220 directly in relation to the issue. The finance costs will have to be apportioned at a rate of 10 per cent on the carrying amount.

Year	At beginning of year	Finance charge	Payments	At end of year
1	1,080	108	80	1,108
2	1,108	110	80	1,138
3	1,138	114	80	1,172
4	1,172	117	80	1,209
5	1,209	121	80+1,250	0

The net proceeds of the issue, £1,080, will be recorded as £1,000 share capital and £80 share premium (premium of £300 less issue costs of £220).

The annual finance costs in excess of the dividends paid should preferably be taken to a separate reserve. In the first year, the amount transferred will be £28 (i.e., 108 - 80), in the second year £30 (i.e., 110 - 80), and so on.

Over five years, the carrying amount of non-equity shareholders' funds will build up to equal the redemption proceeds at the end of the instrument i.e., £1,250. If the shares have not been converted at the end of five years, they will be redeemed.

If the shares are converted at any time before their redemption date, the proceeds of the ordinary shares issued would be the carrying value of the non-equity shares in the balance sheet i.e., the total of the nominal value of the shares, the other reserve and the share premium account.

Therefore, if all 1,000 of the preference shares were converted (into 2,000 25p ordinary shares) at the end of year two, the following entries would be made:

DR Preference share capital	1,000	
DR Preference share premium	80	
DR Reserve for redemption premium	58	
CR Ordinary share capital		500
CR Ordinary share premium		638

Finance costs associated with non-equity shares

General requirements

18.64 Finance costs are defined as the difference between the net proceeds of an instrument and the total amount of payments that the issuer may be required to make in respect of the instrument.

18.65 Applying this definition to non-equity shares, we see that the finance charge will include all dividend payments, any premium on redemption and any amounts treated as issue costs. The allocation of the finance charge for non-equity shares is the same as for debt instruments, i.e., it should be allocated over the term of the shares at a constant rate on the carrying amount. [FRS 4(42)] See chapter 17 for a discussion of the calculation of a constant rate on the carrying amount.

18.66 Where the finance charge for the period in respect of a non-equity share differs from the dividend paid and/or proposed, the difference will be shown with the appropriations of profit on the face of the profit and loss account. A suitable caption might be 'Difference between non-equity finance costs and the related dividends' (see **9.94** above for an example of disclosure).

18.67

> The FRS does not specify where within shareholders' funds the amounts accrued in excess of dividends (or deferred if dividends exceed the finance costs) should be shown. These amounts will normally be credited (or debited) to an 'other' reserve, which could be given a caption such as 'Reserve for redemption premium'.

Example 18.67

A company has 10,000 £1 class B non-equity shares. These carry a fixed dividend of eight per cent. In addition, on repayment after 10 years, a premium is payable, with the result that the finance costs to be charged in the profit and loss account equate to a constant rate of 9.84 per cent.

In year one, the dividend payment will be £800 and the additional finance charge to be accrued is £184.

The profit and loss account would show:	£
Profit for the financial year	8,000
Dividends paid and proposed	800
Other finance charges in respect of non-equity shares	184
Retained profit for the financial year	7,016

> This additional finance charge represents the accrual of the premium on redemption. This amount will normally be shown under the 'Other reserves' heading and could be entitled 'Reserve for redemption premium'.

18.68 Where the entitlement to dividends on non-equity shares is calculated by reference to time, they should be accounted for on an accruals basis. If preference shares are cumulative, even though there may be insufficient distributable reserves to pay the dividend, the appropriate finance costs should be accrued in the normal way. There is an exception to this rule which allows non-accrual of the dividends where the circumstances are such that the payment of the dividend is remote. [FRS 4(43)]

18.69 As long as a company is a going concern, it is assumed that profits will be generated in the future and therefore ultimate payment of arrears of cumulative dividends, whether made by way of a dividend or by way of an extra premium at the date of redemption, cannot be considered to be remote. The standard does not indicate what form payment of dividend has to take. If the arrears of dividends are to be satisfied by way of an issue of additional shares or otherwise taken into account in a restructuring arrangement, this will still constitute a means of payment and the arrears should still be accrued. One situation which would indicate payment is remote and an accrual not needed is if there has been a legal waiver of the right to the arrears.

18.70 It is appropriate to take the cumulative dividends accrued to an 'other' reserve until such time as the company has sufficient distributable reserves and the intention to pay the dividend when they can be transferred to current liabilities.

The term of equity and non-equity instruments

18.71 The total finance costs of non-equity shares should be spread over the term of the instrument. The term of a capital instrument should be taken to be the earliest date under which the provider of finance can demand repayment. For non-equity interests, this will usually be self-evident.

18.72 Where options for early redemption are available, these options should be carefully evaluated. The term of the instrument will usually be taken to be the earliest date at which the option can be exercised, unless there is no genuine commercial possibility that this will occur, e.g., where the provider of finance would receive only a fraction of the redemption value on exercise of the option. See chapter 17 for further discussion.

18.73 Similarly, the term should not include any periods for which the instrument may be extended, unless such an extension is certain at the time the instrument is issued i.e., there is no genuine commercial possibility it will not be extended.

Warrants and options

18.74 The identification of distinct capital instruments is discussed in chapter 17. Any instrument which is capable of being separately transferred or redeemed should be separately accounted for. For example, if a debt instrument is issued with warrants and the warrants are capable of being separately transferred, a value should be allocated to the warrants and reported within shareholders' funds. This applies even if the debt with warrants is issued at par, so that allocating a value to the warrants results in the debt being recorded at a discount.

18.75 A company may issue options which allow their holders to purchase shares in the company over a period of time. Where the company charges the option holder for this right, the proceeds should be treated as capital.

18.76 The FRS does not specify where amounts received in respect of warrants and options should be disclosed. The only appropriate location appears to be as an 'other' reserve.

18.77 When a warrant is exercised, the amount previously recorded for the warrant will be included in the net proceeds of the issue of the shares. The amount initially attributed to the warrants will be transferred from 'Other reserves' to the share capital account and share premium account as appropriate.

18.78 If a warrant lapses unexercised, FRS 4 requires the amount previously recorded in respect of the warrant to be reported as a gain in the period in the statement of total recognised gains and losses. [FRS 4(47)]

18.79 If a warrant lapses unexercised, the company has, in effect, received a gift of the amount originally received for the warrant. The requirement for this to be reported as a gain in the statement of total recognised gains and losses appears to be at odds with the rules that normally apply to reporting a gift. Under normal principles, if the warrants were originally issued to shareholders, the gift would be termed a capital contribution from shareholders and, as such, under FRS 4, be reported as a movement in shareholders' funds; a gift from any other party would be recognised in the profit and loss account.

18.80   Where warrants or convertible debt are in issue which may require the company to issue shares of a class which is not currently in issue, the rights, as set out in **18.11** above, which will attach to those shares should be disclosed (see **18.17** above for an example of appropriate disclosure).

Share premium account

Statutory requirements

18.81   Where a company issues shares (whether for cash or otherwise) for a consideration in excess of their par value, the excess is to be placed in a share premium account. [s130(1)]

18.82   Exceptions to this rule are discussed in **24.26** and **24.104** et seq. below.

18.83   The share premium account can be used for the following purposes: [s130(2)]

(a)   to issue fully paid bonus shares (scrip issue);

(b)   to write off the preliminary expenses of the company;

(c)   to write off the expenses, commission or discount, on any issue of shares or debentures of the company; and

(d)   to provide for any premium payable on the redemption of debentures of the company.

The Act allows these items to be taken directly to reserves.

18.84   Issue costs which may be charged against the share premium account fall into three categories, only one of which may be charged directly against the share premium account without first passing through the profit and loss account for the period:

(a)   costs of issuing shares in order to raise finance: these costs should be charged directly to the share premium account, or to another appropriate reserve, in the absence of a share premium account. (Note that, where non-equity shares have a redemption date, the profit and loss account for the period will still suffer an annual appropriation, as a part of the 'finance charge'. In effect, the debit is on the face of the period's profit and loss account, while the credit passes through the statement of movements of reserves);

(b)   costs of issuing debentures: these are a part of finance charges as defined under FRS 4 and should be deducted initially from proceeds and expensed to profit and loss account over the life of the instrument, with a matching transfer from share premium account to profit and loss reserve each year (FRS 4 has no other impact on the timing or amounts permitted to be taken to the share premium account). If the life of the debentures is indeterminate, the issue costs will not be charged to the profit and loss account, and no matching transfer to share premium account made, until the debentures are redeemed or cancelled [FRS 4(95)];

(c) costs of issuing shares in order to effect a reconstruction/merger, e.g., where shares are issued in exchange for other shares: the guidance in FRS 6, indicates that these costs should be expensed to the period's profit and loss account and shown as an exceptional item [FRS 6(51)] (see **9.49**), with a matching transfer from share premium account to profit and loss reserve.

18.85

In respect of the costs of issue of either shares or debentures, for most practical purposes, it is reasonable to assume that the definition of issue costs in FRS 4 coincides with that in the Act. [s130(2)] However, in material cases where doubt arises over whether particular costs qualify as 'expenses of issue' for the purposes of writing off against the share premium account, informed legal advice should be sought.

18.86 The share premium account may also be used in the special circumstances described in **33.20** below to write off the excess of the 'permissible capital payment' over the nominal value of shares redeemed or purchased by a private limited company. [s171(5)]

18.87 Where a company redeems or purchases its own shares which were issued at a premium, any premium payable on redemption or purchase may be paid out of the proceeds of a fresh issue of shares made for the purpose up to an amount equal to the lesser of the premium received by the company on the issue of the shares being redeemed or purchased and the current amount of the company's share premium account. [ss160(2) and 162] The practical effect of these sections is to permit the reduction of the share premium account under these circumstances (see **33.17** et seq.).

18.88 In October 1999, the Company Law Steering Committee issued consultation document *Company Formation and Capital* as part of the large scale company law reform. It includes a proposal to move to no par value shares. Under this proposal, the net proceeds on issue of shares would go to a single undistributable reserve, subscribed share capital, which will have combined characteristics of share premium and share capital accounts. See chapter 2 for a discussion of other proposals for changes in the company law.

Revaluation reserve

Introduction

18.89   The revaluation reserve is the only balance sheet heading with a Roman numeral designation in the Sch 4 formats which may be given another name. [Sch 4: 34(2)]

18.90   Schedule 4 paragraph 34 requires the amount of the profit or loss arising from the valuation of any asset by any of the alternative methods prescribed by Sch 4 to be credited or debited to the revaluation reserve. An exception is made in the case of an investment company; any profit or loss arising from a revaluation of investments in the accounts of an investment company need not be transferred to the revaluation reserve. [Sch 4: 71(1)] The balance on the revaluation reserve represents an unrealised surplus and hence it is not a distributable balance.

18.91   The only circumstances under which an amount may be transferred from the revaluation reserve are:
[Sch 4: 34(3)]

   (a)   transfers to the profit and loss account of amounts previously charged to that account or amounts representing realised profits;

   (b)   capitalisation (such as a bonus or scrip issue);

   (c)   taxation relating to any profit or loss credited or debited to the reserve; or

   (d)   amounts which are no longer necessary for the purposes of the valuation method used.

18.92   Asset write-offs which are not valuation adjustments, such as impairment of goodwill and other impairments below depreciated historic cost, cannot therefore be charged against the revaluation reserve (see **18.101** below).

18.93   The appropriate treatment of the various items which may be dealt with in the revaluation reserve is discussed below.

18.94   Where amounts have been transferred from the revaluation reserve, such as with a bonus issue of shares, and the assets to which the original revaluation related are subsequently sold, the balance to be transferred to the profit and loss account will be limited to the balance remaining on the revaluation reserve rather than the whole of the original revaluation surplus.

18.95 If the revaluation surplus is related to more than one asset, then it is usual for the surplus to be released on the sale of each asset until it is exhausted, when no further transfers will be made. However, there does not appear to be anything to prevent the bonus issue from being apportioned to each of the assets previously revalued.

18.96 Similarly, any amount so used will no longer be available for transfer to the profit and loss account, e.g., to offset depreciation. Accordingly, once the balance on the reserve has been reduced to nil, such transfers should no longer be made.

Initial surplus on revaluation

18.97 Any surplus arising from the use of the alternative methods of valuation which does not reverse a previous impairment loss recognised on the same asset (see **18.103**) should be credited to a separate revaluation reserve. [Sch 4: 34(1)] It should also be included in the FRS 3 statement of total recognised gains and losses.

18.98 The revaluation surplus will represent the revalued amount less the previous carrying amount of the asset in the balance sheet, i.e., after deduction of accumulated depreciation from the historical cost of the asset. Where, for example, a fixed asset costing £100,000 and having £20,000 accumulated depreciation based on cost (i.e., a net book value of £80,000) is revalued to £110,000, the surplus of £30,000 (£110,000 - £80,000) is to be credited to the revaluation reserve.

Initial impairment loss

18.99 Schedule 4 only requires a provision for the diminution in value of a fixed asset if the diminution is considered to be permanent, rather than temporary. [Sch 4: 19] However, as no guidance was given on the meaning of permanent, prior to the issuance of FRS 11, there was considerable debate over what constituted a permanent diminution. FRS 11 refers to impairment rather than permanent diminutions in value. Nevertheless, the distinction between permanent and temporary diminutions in value is effectively resolved by the FRS. A principle is established that impairment is measured by comparing carrying value with 'recoverable amount', which is the higher of net realisable value and value in use, i.e., respectively, what you could sell the asset for and what you could make it earn for you over its useful economic life. As those two values cover between them all possible outcomes, based on the best estimates currently available, any impairment so measured must logically be regarded as a permanent diminution.

18.100 See **14.240** to **14.244** above for a description of the process for measurement of an impairment loss in accordance with FRS 11. Once it has been determined that an impairment has occurred, if the asset has not been revalued upwards in the past, the impairment loss is recognised in the profit and loss account. See **9.203** to **9.212** above for a discussion of where within the profit and loss account impairment losses should be shown.

Impairment of revalued fixed assets

18.101 If an impairment loss is recognised related to an asset which has previously been revalued upwards, the loss is either:

(a) recognised in the profit and loss account if it is caused by a clear consumption of economic benefits; or

(b) recognised in the statement of total recognised gains and losses until the carrying amount of the asset reaches its depreciated historical cost and thereafter in the profit and loss account.

See **14.265** to **14.272** above for a discussion of this distinction.

18.102 If it is determined that option (b) above is appropriate, the impairment loss is recognised in the statement of total recognised gains and losses only until the carrying amount of the asset is reduced to its depreciated historical cost. Any remaining impairment loss is taken to the profit and loss account, as discussed in **9.203** to **9.212** above.

Example 18.102

An asset costing £10,000 is revalued on 31 December 1997 to £15,000, when its book value is £8,000. At that date, it is envisaged that the asset will have a further useful life of 10 years. In January 2000, the asset is deemed to have suffered an impairment (see **18.99** above) and its carrying value is reduced to £3,000.

	£
At 31 December 1997, the revaluation surplus transferred to the revaluation reserve	7,000
The excess annual depreciation charge transferred to the profit and loss account of £700 for two years	1,400
Balance on revaluation reserve	5,600
Carrying value of the asset at the date the impairment is deemed to have occurred	12,000
Transfer from the revaluation reserve	5,600
Impairment loss recognised in the profit and loss account	3,400
Residual value	3,000

> The £3,400 taken to the profit and loss account represents the impairment loss that would have arisen if the asset had been carried at depreciated historical cost. For the purpose of this example it is assumed that the loss in value is not caused by a clear consumption of economic benefits – see **18.101** above.

Reversal of an impairment loss

18.103 If, after an impairment loss has been recognised, the recoverable amount of an intangible fixed asset or investment increases because of a change:

(a)   in economic conditions; or

(b)   in the expected use of the asset,

the resulting reversal of the impairment loss should be recognised in the current period to the extent that it increases the carrying amount of the fixed asset up to the amount that it would have been (adjusted for subsequent depreciation) had the original impairment not occurred. [FRS 11(56)]

The reversal of the impairment loss should be recognised in the profit and loss account in the same line as the impairment loss was recognised. However, if the reversal arises on a previously revalued fixed asset, it should be recognised in the profit and loss account only to the extent that the original impairment loss (adjusted for depreciation that would have been charged on unimpaired cost) was recognised in the profit and loss account. Any remaining balance of the reversal of an impairment should be recognised in the statement of total recognised gains and losses. [FRS 11(66)] (See **14.284** above for a discussion of when the above two criteria are met.)

18.104 The following table broadly summarises where impairment losses and revaluation surpluses are presented.

Event	Recognition in profit and loss account	Recognition in statement of total recognised gains and losses
Impairment loss on historical cost carrying amount	✓	
Impairment loss reversing previous upwards valuation	✓ (excess over previous revaluation surplus)	✓ (to extent of previous revaluation surplus)
Revaluation surplus		✓

Reversal of impairment loss	✓ (to extent previous loss less implied depreciation was recognised in the profit and loss account)	✓ (excess over reversal recognised in the profit and loss account)

Adjustment of depreciation

18.105 As indicated in **14.184**, the depreciation to be charged in the profit and loss account in respect of an asset which has been revalued should be based on the revalued amount. However, to the extent that depreciation on the revalued amount exceeds the corresponding depreciation based on historical cost, the revaluation represents a realised profit. [s275(2)] Therefore, an amount equal to the excess of the depreciation charged over the depreciation based on historical cost should be transferred annually from the revaluation reserve to the profit and loss account. The examples which accompany FRS 3 show this as being done as a movement in reserves and reported in the statement of historical cost profits and losses.

18.106 In rare circumstances, a depreciable asset may be revalued at an amount below its carrying amount as a 'temporary' diminution in value, i.e., no impairment falls to be recognised under FRS 11. In the normal application of the FRS 15 rules, the annual depreciation charge will be based on the revalued amount. Where this occurs, the charge for depreciation based on the revalued amount would be insufficient to amortise the balance of the historical cost over its remaining useful life and a transfer should be made from profit and loss account to revaluation reserve of an amount equal to the difference between the depreciation charged and the depreciation based on historical cost.

Sale of revalued assets

18.107 Under the requirements of FRS 3, where an asset is sold which has been previously revalued, the gain or loss recorded in the profit and loss account will be based on the net carrying amount rather than the historical cost. Any previously revalued amounts will be transferred to the profit and loss account as a reserve movement, as they have now become realised. This is discussed in more detail in **9.54** above.

18.108 In very limited situations, it appears possible for a company to revalue the asset prior to the sale. This is outlined in more detail in **9.55** to **9.58**.

18.109 If any provision had been made for deferred tax out of the revaluation reserve in respect of the asset being sold, this provision should be reversed on sale. To the extent that this provision differs from the actual tax attributable to the revaluation gain (or loss), that has been recognised in the statement of total recognised gains and losses, that difference will be recognised in the statement of total recognised gains and losses in line with FRS 16 (see **18.110** below).

18.110 A company that has revalued an asset without providing for deferred tax may find that on disposal the tax arising is out of all proportion to the gain recognised in the profit and loss account because a proportion of the tax relates to the gains previously recorded in the revaluation reserve. In extreme cases, there may even be an accounting loss but a taxable gain. FRS 16(6) (effective for periods ending on or after 23 March 2000 – see chapter 27) requires that where a gain or loss is or has been recognised in the statement of total recognised gains and losses the attributable tax should also be recognised directly in the statement of total recognised gains and losses (see **27.44** to **27.48** below).

Investment properties

18.111 SSAP 19 requires that investment properties should be included in the balance sheet at their open market value (see **14.170** to **14.174** above) and that changes in value should be dealt with in an 'investment revaluation reserve' via the statement of total recognised gains and losses. This heading should appear in the balance sheet if the only revalued assets are investment properties. However, if other assets have also been revalued in the financial statements so that the amount in the revaluation reserve does not relate solely to investment properties, then it is preferable to show the revaluation reserve as one amount in the balance sheet and the subdivision between the investment revaluation reserve and the rest in a note to the accounts.

18.112 Amendment to SSAP 19 *Accounting for investment properties*, issued by the ASB in July 1994, removed the apparent contradiction between the previous requirement of SSAP 19 (i.e., that changes in value of investment properties be taken to the investment revaluation reserve, unless this creates an overall deficit; in which case, the deficit should be taken to the profit and loss account) and the Act. The amended SSAP 19 requires all changes in the market value of investment properties to be taken to the investment revaluation reserve even if this creates an overall deficit, unless a deficit on an individual investment property is expected to be permanent; in which case, it should be charged to the profit and loss account in the period. (This is not affected by the issue of FRS 11 or impairment, as investment properties are excepted from its scope.)

18.113 There are two alternative views on how the term 'deficit' should be defined. The omission of a definition of the term in the amendment appears to have been deliberate. The long-standing interpretation of the Act is that only a permanent deficit below historical cost needs to be debited to the profit and loss account. The alternative view is that 'deficit' means any permanent fall below revalued carrying amount. Until the ASB rejects the use of one or other of these definitions, the use of either interpretation is acceptable as long as it is applied consistently.

18.114 In the past, it has generally been the case that investment properties were held at least as much for capital appreciation as for rental income and thus it was unlikely that an investment property would continue to be held if it was no longer expected to increase in value. Falls in value of investment properties could usually reasonably be regarded as temporary in nature, due to fluctuations in the property market generally or in relation to the particular location and nature of the property concerned. Since the property market crash, the circumstances where an investment property has fallen in value below cost and the reduction in value is expected to be permanent have increased.

18.115 SSAP 19 is silent as to how gains and losses arising from the realisation of investment properties should be accounted for. The treatment of the sale of a revalued asset is discussed in **18.107** to **18.110** above.

Taxation

18.116 The treatment for taxation purposes of amounts credited or debited to the revaluation reserve should be disclosed in a note to the accounts. [Sch 4: 34(4)] The appropriate treatment is discussed in chapter 27.

Other reserves

Capital redemption reserve

18.117 The capital redemption reserve is a subheading under 'Other reserves' in the balance sheet formats and may be shown either on the face of the balance sheet or in the notes.

18.118 The provisions of s170 require the amount by which the issued share capital of the company is diminished through the purchase or redemption of its own shares, otherwise than out of capital or out of the proceeds of a new issue made for that purpose, to be credited to the capital redemption reserve (see **33.16** and **33.22** to **33.25** below).

18.119 The Act does not allow this reserve to be used for any purpose other than to pay up fully paid bonus shares. [s170(4)]

Reserves provided for by the Articles of Association

18.120 This reserve should be confined to amounts required specifically by the company's Articles of Association to be set aside. These will include, for example, the profits on sale of investments which are required by the Articles of many investment trusts to be transferred to a non-distributable 'capital' reserve.

Other reserves

18.121 Prior to FRS 4, the only items which might have appeared in other reserves would have been translation differences arising on the consolidation of foreign subsidiaries (which are dealt with in chapter 26) and reserves relating to write-off of goodwill (which are no longer allowed under FRS 10).

18.122 FRS 4 now requires finance costs in respect of non-equity shares to be accrued over the term of the shares. Amounts accrued under this requirement will normally be shown as an 'other' reserve. The Act allows a more appropriate title to be given to such reserves. An appropriate title might be 'Reserve for premium on redemption'.

Scrip dividends

Introduction

18.123 Where shares are issued as an alternative to a cash dividend, this is termed a 'scrip dividend'. Where the dividend is structured such that it is probable that most of the shareholders will decide to take the shares, because the market value of the share alternative is above the cash alternative and because it is tax beneficial, the dividend is referred to as an enhanced scrip dividend.

Accounting requirements

18.124 Prior to FRS 4, there was no authoritative guidance issued on how to account for scrip dividends.

18.125 FRS 4 now requires that where shares are issued as an alternative to cash dividends, the value attributed to those shares should be the amount of the cash alternative. This represents the benefit the company has received from the shareholder by the shareholder taking the dividend instead of the cash.

18.126 If, at the date of approval of the balance sheet, it is uncertain how many shareholders will choose to receive the shares, even if an estimate could be made, the whole amount should be treated as a liability to pay the cash alternative. [FRS 4(48)]

18.127　When the actual dividend is paid or the shares are issued, there are two methods of accounting that can be used: the capitalisation method or the reinvestment method (both explained below). The FRS requires that where the scrip dividend takes the legal form of a bonus issue of shares, the appropriation should be written back as a reserve movement and appropriate amounts transferred between reserves and share capital to reflect the capitalisation of reserves; in other words, the capitalisation method. [FRS 4(99)] The details of each scrip dividend proposal should be reviewed to determine whether it legally constitutes a bonus issue necessitating the use of the capitalisation method or whether the reinvestment method is an option. The Articles of Association should also be reviewed, as they may also contain restrictions which will determine whether the company is permitted to issue bonus shares.

The capitalisation method

18.128　Under this method, the scrip dividend is treated as a bonus issue of shares, such that the nominal value of the shares issued is credited to share capital and debited to any reserve which can fund a bonus issue, such as the share premium account. This treatment is usually favoured, as it has a beneficial effect on the distributable reserves of the company.

18.129　FRS 4 implies that the full amount of the dividend should be shown on the face of the profit and loss account. [FRS 4(99)] The FRS requires that where the scrip dividend takes the legal form of a bonus issue, the amount of the appropriation equal to the difference between the cash alternative taken and the full dividend amount be written back as a reserve movement. An appropriate transfer must be made between the share premium account or other reserve available and the share capital account to reflect the capitalisation. This treatment should be adopted whether or not the dividend is paid in the same period in which it is proposed.

Example 18.129

ABC plc proposes a final dividend of 8p per share for the year ended 31 March 2000. There is a scrip alternative, which is one £1 ordinary share for every 18 already held. The market price of the shares is £1.44. The company has a share capital of £50 million and holders of 12 million shares take the scrip alternative.

The profit and loss account would show a dividend of £4 million as an appropriation of profit and a corresponding creditor would be set up. When it is paid, the following journal entries will be made:

Dr Creditors	4,000,000	
Cr Cash		3,040,000
Cr Profit and loss reserve		960,000
Dr Suitable reserve	666,667	
Cr Share capital		666,667

The reinvestment method

18.130 Under this method, the scrip dividend is treated as a cash payment which is simultaneously reinvested by the shareholders that have elected for the scrip alternative.

18.131

The excess of the scrip amount over the nominal value of the shares is taken to the share premium account just as it is for any other issue of shares.

> **Example 18.131**
>
> Using the above example, the accounting entries are the same when the dividend is proposed. When the dividend is paid, accounting entries will be:
>
> | | | |
> |---|---|---|
> | Dr Creditors | 4,000,000 | |
> | Cr Cash | | 3,040,000 |
> | Cr Share capital | | 666,667 |
> | Cr Share premium | | 293,333 |

18.132 The above example assumes that the election for the scrip alternative is not known until after the accounts are signed. An estimation of the take-up of the scrip alternative based upon past experience should not be made, even if it is relatively certain that one or other of the alternatives will be chosen, e.g., in the case of enhanced scrip alternatives.

Enhanced scrip dividends

18.133

There appears to be no difference in the way in which such issues should be accounted for and thus one of the methods outlined above would be used, but the policy adopted should be the same for both normal and enhanced scrip dividends (see **18.123** above for a definition of enhanced scrip dividend).

Future developments

Company law reform

18.134 As part of the government's company law review and other initiatives, a number of proposals were made to change current rules relating to the capital maintenance, redenomination of share capital into different currency, share buybacks and holding of treasury shares, etc. One of the proposed changes is to move to no par value shares for private companies and, possibly, for public companies, the latter being conditional on amending the second EC directive. See **33.89** below for further details. See also chapter 2 for a general overview of the company law review proposals.

19   Cash flow statements

19 Cash flow statements

General requirements

Introduction

19.1 There is no statutory requirement for companies to produce a cash flow statement. However, FRS 1 (revised) *Cash flow statements* requires financial statements intended to give a true and fair view of the reporting entity's financial position and profit or loss to include such a statement and related notes, unless the entity is specifically exempted from producing a cash flow statement by the standard. [FRS 1(4)] Such exemptions are dealt with in **19.9** below. Also, the Statement of Principles includes a cash flow statement within the set of primary statements. [SoP7.3]

19.2 FRS 1 (revised) is mandatory for financial statements in respect of accounting periods ending on or after 23 March 1997.

19.3 For accounting periods ending on or after 23 June 1998, FRS 1 (revised) has been amended by FRS 9 in respect of the treatment of dividends received from associates and joint ventures.

19.4 This chapter deals only with the requirements of FRS 1 (revised) as amended by FRS 9. References to FRS 1 are to the amended revised version of the standard.

Form of cash flow statement

19.5 Where an entity prepares only individual accounts, the cash flow statement will be for the individual entity. Where consolidated accounts are prepared, a consolidated cash flow statement will be prepared.

19.6 FRS 1 states the requirement to provide a cash flow statement in terms of 'reporting entities'. Therefore, although the standard does not specifically state that consolidated financial statements do not need to include a cash flow statement for the parent undertaking, there does not appear to be a requirement to include one, because the reporting entity in such circumstances is the group and not the parent undertaking.

19.7 Comparative figures for the preceding period should be given. This requirement extends to the notes to the cash flow statement, other than the note analysing changes in the balance sheet amounts making up net debt (see **19.61** below) and the note on material effects of acquisitions and disposals of subsidiary undertakings on each of the standard headings (see **19.70** below). [FRS 1(48)]

Banks and insurance companies

19.8 There are special rules for the cash flow statements of banks and insurance companies, which are set out in FRS 1. [FRS 1(34) and (36)]. Also, the appendix to FRS 1 includes illustrative examples of a cash flow statement for a bank and an insurance group.

Exemptions

19.9 The following entities are outside the scope of FRS 1: [FRS 1(5)]

(a) companies incorporated under companies legislation and entitled to the exemptions available in the legislation for small companies when filing accounts with the Registrar of Companies and entities that would have been entitled to those small company exemptions if they had been companies incorporated under companies legislation;

(b) subsidiary undertakings where 90 per cent or more of the voting rights are controlled within the group, provided that consolidated financial statements in which the subsidiary undertakings are included are publicly available;

(c) mutual life assurance companies;

(d) pension funds;

(e) open-ended investment funds that meet all the following conditions:

(i) substantially all of the entity's investments are highly liquid,

(ii) substantially all of the entity's investments are carried at market value, and

(iii) the entity provides a statement of changes in net assets;

(f) building societies that prepare, as required by law, a statement of source and application of funds in a prescribed format. This exemption applies only for two years from the effective date of the FRS (i.e., from 23 March 1997). Note that the statutory requirement for building societies to publish a statement of source and application of funds has been repealed for financial years ending on or after 23 March 1999. From that date, building societies are required, by FRS 1, to provide a cash flow statement.

19.10   The qualifying conditions (set out in ss246 and 247 of the Act) for a company to be treated as a small company for this purpose are dealt with in chapter 34.

19.11
> Although the small entities exemption does not seem to extend to small groups (as groups cannot file abbreviated group accounts), in practice, as the parent company of a small group is likely to qualify as a small company in its own right and as the exemption is based principally on size, a small group does not need to provide a cash flow statement.

Format and content of the statement

Classification of cash flows

19.12   FRS 1 requires the cash flow statement to include all of the reporting entity's inflows and outflows of cash (the definition of cash used in the standard is examined further in **19.52** to **19.55** below), classified under the following standard headings:
[FRS 1(6) and (7)]

- Operating activities;

- Dividends from joint ventures and associates;

- Returns on investments and servicing of finance;

- Taxation;

- Capital expenditure and financial investment;

- Acquisitions and disposals;

- Equity dividends paid;

- Management of liquid resources;

- Financing.

The first seven headings should be in the sequence set out above.

19.13   The basis for the classification of each cash flow should be the substance of the transaction giving rise to it. [FRS 1(10)] The FRS, however, makes an exception to this general rule for cash flows relating to interest paid. Such cash flows should always be classified under 'Returns on investments and servicing of finance', even if the interest is capitalised as part of the cost of an asset.

19.14   The heading 'Capital expenditure and financial investment' may be changed to 'Capital investment' if there are no cash flows relating to financial investment. [FRS 1(19)]

19.15 The cash flows relating to the management of liquid resources and financing may be combined under a single heading, provided that the cash flows relating to each are shown separately and separate subtotals are given. [FRS 1(7)]

19.16 Because the FRS calls the headings 'standard headings' the wording should only be altered (other than as set out in **19.14** above) to suit individual circumstances if the use of the standard wording is likely to mislead readers of the financial statements.

19.17 A total should be shown for each of the standard headings used.

19.18 Individual categories of cash inflow and outflow should be separately disclosed (i.e., not netted) in the cash flow statement or in a note, unless they relate to operating activities or they relate to management of liquid resources or financing and one of the following conditions is met:
[FRS 1(8)–(10)]

(a) the cash flows relate in substance to a single financing transaction (i.e, one that fulfils the conditions in FRS 4 – see **17.128** above); [FRS 4(35)] or

(b) the cash flows arise from the rollover or reissue of short maturity, high turnover instruments (e.g., short-term deposits or a commercial paper programme).

19.19 The standard headings are discussed in more detail in **19.21** to **19.51** below.

19.20 The appendix to FRS 1 contains illustrative examples of a cash flow statement for:

- an individual company;
- a group;
- a bank; and
- an insurance group.

Operating activities

19.21 Generally, cash flows from operating activities are the cash effects of transactions or other events relating to operating or trading activities. Cash flows from operating activities may be shown net in the cash flow statement, but a reconciliation between the operating profit reported in the profit and loss account and the net cash flow from operating activities should be given either adjoining the cash flow statement or as a note (see **19.56** and **19.57** below).

19.22 Net cash flow from operating activities includes:
[FRS 1(11) and (58)]

(a) the net increase or decrease in cash resulting from the operations included in the profit and loss account in arriving at
operating profit; and

(b) cash flows in respect of operating items set against provisions,
whether or not the provision was established by way of a charge
against operating profit. This includes, for example, cash flows
resulting from a termination of an operation or a reorganisation or restructuring treated in accordance with FRS 3
(i.e., charged after operating profit) and cash flows resulting
from the utilisation of provisions set up as part of a fair value
on acquisition exercise [FRS 3(20a and b)].

19.23 A company may choose to add the information given by the so-
called 'direct method'. [FRS 1(7)] The direct method reports gross
operating receipts and payments including, for example, cash
receipts from customers, cash payments to suppliers and cash paid to
employees.

Example 19.23

	£'000
Operating activities	
Cash received from customers	6,878
Cash payments to suppliers	(5,103)
Cash paid to and on behalf of employees	(974)
Other operating cash payments	(72)
Net cash inflow from operating activities	729

Discontinued operations

19.24 The explanation section of the FRS notes that, in circumstances in
which a reporting entity has discontinued operations reported in the
profit and loss account under FRS 3, it may be useful to users of the
financial statements to provide a division of cash flows from operating activities into those relating to continuing and discontinued
operations. [FRS 1(56)]

Example 19.24

	£'000
Operating activities	
Net cash inflow from continuing operating activities	17,012
Net cash outflow in respect of discontinued activities and reorganisation costs	(990)
Net cash inflow from operating activities	16,022

19.25 An example of how discontinued operations can be disclosed in the reconciliation of operating profit to net cash flows from operating activities is illustrated in **19.57** below.

Dividends from joint ventures and associates

19.26 Receipts of dividends from joint ventures and associates should be included under the heading 'Dividends from joint ventures and associates'.

19.27 Frequently, joint ventures and associates are financed by long-term loan capital from the equity participants rather than by equity. In such circumstances, it seems appropriate to regard any interest received on such long-term loan capital as an 'equity return' and thus include the cash inflow under the same heading as dividends, i.e., 'Dividends from joint ventures and associates', as illustrated below.

Example 19.27

	£'000
Dividends from joint ventures and associates	
Dividends received from associated undertaking	36
Interest received from joint venture in respect of long-term financing loan	10
Cash inflow from dividends from joint ventures and associates	46

Returns on investments and servicing of finance

19.28 Receipts resulting from the ownership of an investment (e.g., interest and dividends received) and payments to providers of finance (e.g., interest and preference dividends paid) should, unless they are required to be included under another heading, be classified under the heading 'Returns on investments and servicing of finance'. [FRS 1(13)] These amounts will include all cash flows that are treated as non-equity finance costs under FRS 4, e.g., issue costs on debt and non-equity share capital.

19.29 The example below illustrates the types of cash flows that should be shown under the heading 'returns on investments and servicing of finance'.

Example 19.29	
	£'000
Returns on investments and servicing of finance	
Interest received	626
Interest paid	(1,785)
Dividends paid to minority shareholders in subsidiary undertaking	(37)
Interest element of finance lease payments	(83)
Net cash outflow from returns on investments and servicing of finance	(1,279)

Taxation

19.30 The cash flows to be included under the heading 'Taxation' are cash flows to or from taxation authorities in respect of the reporting entity's revenue and capital profits. If the reporting entity is a subsidiary undertaking, any receipts or payments in respect of group relief should also be included under this heading. [FRS 1(16)–(18)]

19.31 As far as VAT and other sales taxes are concerned, cash flows should be shown net of such taxes, unless the tax is irrecoverable by the reporting entity, and the net payment to (or receipt from) Customs & Excise should normally be classified under operating activities. If the tax is irrecoverable, then it should be included as part of the cash flow relating to the expenditure concerned. [FRS 1(39)]

19.32 Other forms of taxation are included under the heading to which the related cash flow belongs. [FRS 1(40)] For example, income tax paid on behalf of employees should be included under operating activities.

19.33 The example below illustrates the types of cash flows that should be shown under the heading 'Taxation'.

Example 19.33	
	£'000
Taxation	
UK corporation tax paid (including advance corporation tax)	(1,309)
Overseas tax paid	(14)
Return of overpayment	32
Purchase of certificate of tax deposit	(100)
Total tax paid	(1,391)

Capital expenditure and financial investment

19.34 The cash flows to be included under the heading 'Capital expenditure and financial investment' are cash flows related to the acquisition or disposal of:
[FRS 1(19)]

(a) any fixed asset, other than one required to be disclosed under 'Acquisitions and disposals'; and

(b) any current asset investment not included in liquid resources.

19.35 The example below illustrates the type of cash flows to be classified under 'Capital expenditure and financial investment'.

Example 19.35

	£'000
Capital expenditure and financial investment	
Payments to acquire tangible fixed assets	(221)
Receipts from sales of tangible fixed assets	718
Sale of trade investment	106
Net cash inflow from capital expenditure and financial investment	603

19.36 The heading 'Capital expenditure and financial investment' may be changed to 'Capital expenditure' if there are no cash flows relating to financial investment. [FRS 1(19)]

Acquisitions and disposals

19.37 The cash flows to be included under the heading 'Acquisitions and disposals' are cash flows related to the acquisition or disposal of any trade or business or of an investment in an entity that is or, as a result of the transaction, becomes or ceases to be either an associate, a joint venture or a subsidiary undertaking. [FRS 1(22)] The example below illustrates the type of cash flows to be classified under 'Acquisitions and disposals'.

Example 19.37

	£'000
Acquisitions and disposals	
Payments to acquire subsidiary undertaking *	(9,545)
Receipts from sale of investment in associated undertaking	824
Payment to acquire unincorporated business	(718)
Net cash outflow from investing activities	(9,439)

NB: The example in **19.70** below illustrates the full disclosure required by FRS 1 in respect of acquisitions.

19.38 In addition to cash flows related to acquisition and disposal transactions, there are other cash flows that it is appropriate to report under the heading 'Acquisitions and disposals'. Such cash flows include those resulting from:

(a) taking up shares as a result of a rights issue by a subsidiary; and

(b) making a capital contribution to a subsidiary.

(The receipt of capital contributions by a subsidiary is considered in **19.49** below.)

Equity dividends paid

19.39 The cash outflows included in 'Equity dividends paid' are dividends paid on the reporting entity's, or, in a group, the parent's, equity shares. [FRS 1(25)] See **19.28** above as regards preference dividends and dividends paid to a minority interest.

Management of liquid resources

19.40 The 'Management of liquid resources' section of the statement should include cash flows in respect of increases or decreases in liquid resources. Certain cash flows relating to management of liquid resources may be netted against each other (see **19.18** above).

19.41 The FRS defines liquid resources as 'current asset investments held as readily disposable stores of value'. [FRS 1(2)] A readily disposable investment is one that is disposable by the reporting entity without curtailing or disrupting its business and is either:

(a) readily convertible into known amounts of cash at or close to its carrying amount; or

(b) traded in an active market.

19.42 The definition of liquid resources is reasonably flexible, with the result that different reporting entities will include different assets within the category. Assets which a reporting entity may regard as liquid resources include:
[FRS 1(52)]

- government securities;

- loan stock;

- equities; and

- derivatives.

Term deposits could also fall within the definition if they are readily convertible into known amounts of cash at, or close to, their carrying amounts. The FRS states that this requirement would tend to exclude any that are more than one year from maturity on acquisition. [FRS 1(52)]

19.43 Reporting entities should disclose their policy on liquid resources. [FRS 1(52)]

19.44 The cash flows included under 'Management of liquid resources' may be shown in a single section with those under the 'Financing' section, provided that separate subtotals for each are given. [FRS 1(26)]

Financing

19.45 Financing cash flows include receipts from, or repayments to, external providers of finance in respect of principal amounts of finance. [FRS 1(29)] Certain cash flows relating to financing may be netted against each other (see **19.18** above).

19.46 The example below illustrates the types of cash flows to be classified under this heading.

Example 19.46

	£'000
Financing	
Issue of ordinary share capital	1,671
Expenses of issue of ordinary share capital	(38)
Redemption of preference share capital	(1,111)
Issue of debentures 2008	649
Medium-term bank loans	275
Capital element of finance lease payments	(238)
Net cash inflow from financing	1,208

19.47 The cash flows included under 'Financing' may be shown in a single section with those under the 'Management of liquid resources' section, provided that separate subtotals for each are given. [FRS 1(26)]

19.48 For more complicated capital instruments, it is important not to confuse principal amounts of finance with the nominal amounts of the instruments concerned. The principal amount of a financing arrangement is the amount borrowed at the beginning of an arrangement; it is not the nominal value of the financial instrument. This is necessary to ensure that cash flows relating to finance costs are reported under 'Returns on investments and servicing of finance' as required by the FRS (see **19.28** above).

Example 19.48

A bond with a nominal value of £100,000 is issued for cash of £90,000 on 1 January 1997. It pays interest of 6 per cent (on 31 December in each year) on its nominal amount and is repayable on 31 December 2001 at par (i.e., £100,000).

The example assumes that there are no issue costs.

The cash flows and profit and loss account charges are as follows:

Date	Cash flows £	Profit and loss charge £
1/1/97	90,000	–
31/12/97	(6,000)	7,686
31/12/98	(6,000)	7,830
31/12/99	(6,000)	7,987
31/12/00	(6,000)	8,156
31/12/01	(106,000)	8,341
		40,000

The cash flow statement would report this as follows:

Year	Returns on investments and servicing of finance £	Finance £
1997	(6,000)	90,000
1998	(6,000)	–
1999	(6,000)	–
2000	(6,000)	–
2001	(16,000)	(90,000)
	(40,000)	–

The points to note are as follows.

(a)   The principal amount of finance is the amount borrowed, i.e., the amount of cash received initially.

(b)   The principal amount of finance repaid is the same as the amount borrowed.

(c)   The total amount shown under 'Returns on investments and servicing of finance' over the whole period of the borrowing is the same as the total charge to the profit and loss account over that period.

Capital contributions

19.49 Capital contributions are a means sometimes used by a parent company to increase 'capital' in a subsidiary. Quite simply, the parent passes funds to the subsidiary in the form of a non-returnable gift. FRS 1 does not indicate how such contributions from shareholders should be treated, but, as they are a form of capital financing, they should be treated as inflows within the 'Financing' section of the statement. The treatment in the cash flow statement of the parent company is considered in **19.38** above.

Exceptional and extraordinary items

19.50 Cash flows relating to items that are classified as exceptional or extraordinary in the profit and loss account are required to be shown in the cash flow statement under the standard heading according to the nature of each item. They should be identified in the cash flow statement or in a note and the relationship between them and the related exceptional or extraordinary item should be explained. [FRS 1(37)]

19.51 Sufficient disclosure to explain the cause and nature of any cash flows that are themselves exceptional (because of their size or incidence), but not related to items that are treated as exceptional or extraordinary in the profit and loss account (i.e., not covered by **19.50** above), should be given. [FRS 1(38)] The FRS uses as an example of this situation a large prepayment against a pension liability. [FRS 1(63)]

Definition of cash and cash flow

19.52 The FRS defines cash as:
[FRS 1(2)]

> 'Cash in hand and deposits repayable on demand with any qualifying financial institution, less overdrafts from any qualifying financial institution repayable on demand. Deposits are repayable on demand if they can be withdrawn at any time without notice and without penalty or if a maturity or period of notice of not more than 24 hours or one working day has been agreed. Cash includes cash in hand and deposits denominated in foreign currencies.'

It should be noted that this definition is not necessarily the same as the definition for balance sheet purposes (see **16.91** above).

19.53 The FRS defines an overdraft as: 'A borrowing facility repayable on demand that is used by drawing on a current account with a qualifying financial institution'. [FRS 1(2)]

19.54 The FRS defines a qualifying financial institution as: 'An entity that as part of its business receives deposits or other repayable funds and grants credits for its own account'. [FRS 1(2)]

19.55 A cash flow is defined as: 'An increase or decrease in an amount of cash'. [FRS 1(2)]

Operating profit reconciliation

19.56 A reconciliation between the operating profit reported in the profit and loss account and the net cash flow from operating activities should be given either adjoining the cash flow statement or as a note. This reconciliation should disclose separately the movements in stocks, debtors and creditors related to operating activities and other differences between cash flows and profits. The reconciliation should not be shown as part of the cash flow statement. [FRS 1(12)]

Example 19.56

Reconciliation of operating profit to net cash inflow from operating activities

	£'000
Operating profit	6,022
Depreciation	899
Increase in stocks	(194)
Increase in debtors	(72)
Increase in creditors	234
Net cash inflow from operating activities	6,889

Discontinued operations

19.57 The explanation section of the FRS notes that, in circumstances in which a reporting entity has discontinued operations reported in the profit and loss account, it may be useful to users of the financial statements to provide a division of cash flows from operating activities into those relating to continuing and discontinued operations. [FRS 1(56)] The illustrative example for a group in the appendix to the FRS gives an example of how discontinued operations could be shown in the operating profit reconciliation. This is reproduced in the following example.

Example 19.57

Reconciliation of operating profit to net cash inflow from operating activities

	Continuing operations £'000	Discontinued operations £'000	Total £'000
Operating profit/(loss)	18,829	(1,616)	17,213
Depreciation charges	3,108	380	3,488
Cash flow relating to previous year restructuring provision	–	(560)	(560)
Increase in stocks	(11,193)	(87)	(11,280)
Increase in debtors	(3,754)	(20)	(3,774)
Increase in creditors	9,672	913	10,585
Net cash inflow from continuing activities	16,662	–	–
Net cash outflow in respect of discontinued activities	–	(990)	–
Net cash inflow from operating activities			15,672

Reconciliation to net debt

19.58 FRS 1 requires the financial statements to include a statement reconciling the movement of cash in the period with the movement in net debt. Such a statement should not form part of the cash flow statement, but it may be given adjoining the cash flow statement; alternatively, it may be shown as a note to the accounts. Because the reconciliation is not part of the cash flow statement, if it is presented adjoining the cash flow statement, it should be clearly labelled and kept separate. [FRS 1(33)]

19.59 The standard defines net debt as:
[FRS 1(2)]

> 'The borrowings of the reporting entity (comprising debt as defined in FRS 4 "Capital Instruments" (paragraph 6), together with related derivatives, and obligations under finance leases) less cash and liquid resources.'

Where cash and liquid resources exceed the borrowings of the entity, reference should be to 'net funds' rather than to 'net debt'.

19.60 The following examples provide illustrations of reconciliations of net cash flows to movements in net debt. The first example is reasonably straightforward; all of the changes in net debt are cash flows.

The second example is more complicated, involving non-cash changes in net debt.

Example 19.60.1

Reconciliation of net cash flow to movement in net debt

	£'000
Increase in cash in the period	2,631
Cash to repurchase debenture	149
Cash used to increase liquid resources	450
Change in net debt	3,230
Net debt at 1 January 1999	(2,903)
Net funds at 31 December 1999	327

Example 19.60.2

Reconciliation of net cash flow to movement in net debt

	£'000	£'000
Decrease in cash in the period	(6,752)	
Cash inflow from increase in debt and lease financing	(2,347)	
Cash inflow from decrease in liquid resources	(700)	
Change in net debt resulting from cash flows		(9,799)
Loans and finance leases acquired with subsidiary		(3,817)
New finance leases		(2,845)
Translation difference		643
Movement in net debt in the period		(15,818)
Net debt at 1 January 1999		(15,215)
Net debt at 31 December 1999		(31,033)

19.61 The FRS also states that 'the changes in net debt should be analysed from the opening to the closing component amounts, showing separately, where material changes resulting from:

(a)   the cash flows of the entity;

(b   the acquisition or disposal of subsidiary undertakings;

(c)   other non-cash changes; and

743

(d) the recognition of changes in market value and exchange rate movements'. [FRS 1(33)]

FRS 1 goes on to state that where several balance sheet amounts or parts thereof have to be combined to form the components of opening and closing net debt, sufficient detail should be shown to enable the cash and other components of net debt to be respectively traced back to the amounts shown in the balance sheet. [FRS 1(33)]

19.62 Although it is not entirely clear what is required by the provisions set out in **19.61** above, the following examples are based on the examples included in the appendix to FRS 1.

Example 19.62.1

Analysis of changes in net debt

	At 1 Jan 1999 £'000	Cash flows £'000	Other changes £'000	At 31 Dec 1999 £'000
Cash at bank and in hand	42	847	–	889
Overdrafts	(1,784)	1,784	–	–
		2,631		
Debt due within one year	(149)	149	(230)	(230)
Debt due after one year	(1,262)	–	230	(1,032)
Current asset investments	250	450	–	700
TOTAL	(2,903)	3,230	–	327

Example 19.62.2

Analysis of changes in net debt

	At 1 Jan 1999 £'000	Cash flows £'000	Acquisition (exc. cash and overdrafts) £'000	Other non-cash changes £'000	Foreign exchanges movements £'000	At 31 Dec 1999 £'000
Cash at bank and in hand	235	(1,250)	–	–	1,392	377
Overdrafts	(2,528)	(5,502)	–	–	(1,422)	(9,452)
		(6,752)				
Debt due after one year	(9,640)	(2,533)	(1,749)	2,560	(792)	(12,154)
Debt due within one year	(352)	(1,156)	(837)	(2,560)	1,465	(3,440)
Finance leases	(4,170)	1,342	(1,231)	(2,845)	–	(6,904)
		(2,347)				
Current asset investments	1,240	(700)	–	–	–	540
TOTAL	(15,215)	(9,799)	(3,817)	(2,845)	643	(31,033)

Other disclosures

Introduction

19.63 In addition to the cash flow statement itself, the operating profit reconciliation and the reconciliation to net debt, FRS 1 requires a number of explanatory notes to be included within the financial statements. These are explained in the following paragraphs.

Non-cash transactions

19.64 Since the purpose of a cash flow statement is to report cash flows, the ASB considers that it is not appropriate to include non-cash transactions in the statement. However, in order to obtain a fuller understanding of the changes in financial position of the reporting entity, separate disclosure of material non-cash transactions is required to be given. [FRS 1(46)] Such transactions may include the inception of a finance lease contract, the exchange of assets for non-cash consideration and shares issued for the acquisition of a subsidiary.

19.65   The inception of a finance lease contract is one of the most commonly encountered non-cash transactions. Such a transaction, although reflected in the balance sheet by recording an asset and a matching liability, should not be reflected in the cash flow statement because the reporting company neither pays nor receives cash. The practice sometimes seen of showing a cash outflow in respect of an asset purchase and the drawdown of a loan does not seem to be in accordance with the standard.

Restrictions on remitability

19.66 A note to the cash flow statement should identify the amounts and explain the circumstances where restrictions prevent the transfer of cash from one part of the business or group to another. [FRS 1(47)]

19.67 The note should refer only to circumstances where access is severely restricted by external factors such as strict exchange control, rather than where the sole constraint is a special purpose designated by the reporting entity itself. Examples of such severe restrictions may be cash balances:
[FRS 1(68)]

(a)   in escrow;

(b)   deposited with a regulator;

(c)   held within an employee share ownership trust.

Example 19.67

Cash at bank and in hand

Cash at bank and in hand includes an amount of £245,000 (1997 – £250,000) deposited with banks in Zambia. This cash cannot currently be transferred outside Zambia due to exchange control restrictions.

Consolidated cash flow statements

Intra-group cash flows

19.68   Cash flows between members of a group should be eliminated in the same way that intra-group sales and purchases are eliminated from the consolidated profit and loss account. [FRS 1(43)]

Acquisitions and disposals

19.69   The amount of cash paid in respect of acquisitions, and received in respect of disposals, should be included in the cash flow statement under the heading 'Acquisitions and disposals'; any balances of cash and overdrafts transferred should be shown separately. [FRS 1(23)]

Example 19.69

Acquisitions and disposals

	£ million	£ million
Acquisition of subsidiary	(330.4)	
Net cash acquired with subsidiary	16.9	
		(313.5)

19.70   The notes to the cash flow statement should show a summary of the effects of acquisitions and disposals, indicating how much of the consideration comprised cash. Material effects on amounts reported under each of the standard headings reflecting the cash flows of the subsidiary undertaking acquired or disposed of should be disclosed, as far as is practicable. [FRS 1(45)]

Example 19.70

Purchase of subsidiary undertaking

	£'000
Net assets acquired:	
Tangible fixed assets	4,873
Stocks	351
Debtors	408
Investments	92
Cash at bank and in hand	711
Creditors	(614)
Bank overdraft	(196)
Deferred taxation	(83)
	5,542
Goodwill	10,836
	16,378
Satisfied by:	
Shares allotted	6,318
Cash	10,060
	16,378

The subsidiary undertaking acquired during the year contributed £765,000 to the group's net operating cash flows, paid £315,000 in respect of interest, paid £298,000 in respect of taxation and utilised £392,000 for capital expenditure.

19.71 The cash flows of a subsidiary undertaking acquired or sold part way through the year should be included in the group cash flow statement for the same period as the results are included in the group profit and loss account. [FRS 1(43)]

Associates and other equity accounted investments

19.72 Only actual cash flows between the group and an entity that is equity accounted, e.g., an associated undertaking or unconsolidated subsidiary, should be included in the cash flow statement. [FRS 1(44)]

19.73 In practice, this will usually be limited to transactions with associates and joint ventures; dividends received being shown under 'Dividends from joint ventures and associates', loans advanced or repaid being shown under 'Capital expenditure and financial investment' and interest on loans being shown under either 'Dividends from joint ventures and associates' or 'Returns on investments and servicing of finance' as appropriate (see **19.27** above).

Joint arrangements that are not entities

19.74 The group's share of cash flows of joint arrangements that are not entities (as defined by FRS 9 paragraph 4) should be included in the cash flow statement and notes on a line-by-line basis. Thus, the relevant percentage of each of the joint arrangement's cash flows is aggregated with the corresponding cash flows of the group. Similarly, the opening and closing group cash and net debt balances will include the relevant percentage of the joint arrangement's balances.

Minority interests

19.75 Dividends paid to minority shareholders should be reported under 'Returns on investments and servicing of finance' and should be disclosed separately. [FRS 1(15)]

Foreign currency

Requirements and guidance within FRS 1

19.76 FRS 1 is surprisingly brief in its guidance on how to deal with the effects of foreign currency in a cash flow statement. For a company with direct transactions in foreign currencies, it is necessary to consider the basic components of each transaction in order to determine the relevant cash flows. Where a portion of a company's business is undertaken through a foreign entity, then the cash flows of that entity should be translated into sterling for inclusion in the group cash flow statement on the same basis that has been used to translate the results included in the profit and loss account, i.e., at either the closing rate or an average rate. [FRS 1(41)]

19.77 In relation to hedging transactions, when a futures contract, forward contract, option contract or swap contract is accounted for as a hedge, the cash flows of the contract should be reported under the same standard heading as the transaction that is the subject of the hedge. [FRS 1(42)]

Settled foreign currency transactions forming part of operations

19.78 Where a company has completed a foreign currency transaction related to operations, e.g., a purchase or sale of trading stock in a foreign currency or the settlement of a foreign currency trade creditor, it follows that any profit or loss arising on conversion to sterling will be reflected in the profit and loss account as part of operating profit. Since any exchange difference will form part of the overall operating cash flows, the entire transaction will be included in the cash flow statement as part of the total 'Net cash flow from operating activities'. When preparing the cash flow statement, no special adjustment is necessary to achieve this result.

Settled foreign currency transactions falling outside operations

19.79 Where an exchange difference is included in the profit and loss account, but falls outside operating profit, e.g., a dividend received from a foreign investment or arising from the repayment of foreign currency debt, then the profit or loss should be matched and included as part of the cash flow arising from the related transaction.

19.80 In the case of a dividend received, it is the cash flow received (including any profit or loss on conversion to sterling) that is included under 'Returns on investments and servicing of finance' or 'Dividends from joint ventures and associates'.

19.81 Where foreign debt is repaid, it is the sterling equivalent of the capital repayment that is included under 'Financing'; any profit or loss that is included in the profit and loss account representing the effects of currency movements up to the date of repayment should not appear separately in the cash flow statement, but will be shown in the reconciliation of net debt. In addition, to the extent that a profit or loss was included in operating profit, it will need to be adjusted for in the note that reconciles operating profit to 'Net cash flow from operating activities'.

Unsettled foreign currency transactions

19.82 Where, at the balance sheet date, monetary assets and liabilities denominated in a foreign currency, such as cash and bank balances, debtors, creditors and loans, are retranslated to the rate ruling at the balance sheet date, the differences arising will generally be included in the profit and loss account.

19.83 Where these relate to short-term working capital items such as debtors and creditors, no adjustment is required in preparing the cash flow statement. The exchange difference arising forms part of 'Operating profit'. Similarly, increases and decreases in the debtor and creditor balances will automatically include the impact of translation to the closing rate.

749

Example 19.83

An item of stock was purchased during the year for US$600, when the US$/£ exchange rate was 2:1.

The stock and the associated creditor were recorded in the books at £300.

The stock was sold before the year end for £500; other expenses of £50 being incurred, all of which were paid during the year.

At the year end, the creditor of US$600 was still outstanding and the US$/£ exchange rate was 1.5:1. The retranslation of the creditor to £400 gives rise to an exchange loss of £100.

Profit and loss account

	£
Sales	500
Cost of stock	(300)
Other costs	(50)
Foreign exchange loss	(100)
Operating profit	50

Cash flow statement

	£
Sales receipts	500
Payments for stock	–
Other payments	(50)
Net cash flow from operations	450

Reconciliation of operating profit to net cash flow from operations

	£
Operating profit	50
Increase in creditors	400
Net cash flow from operations	450

19.84 Exchange differences arising from translation of cash and bank balances, and other items falling within the definition of cash, do not appear in the cash flow statement, since they do not form part of the 'Increase/Decrease in cash'. They do, however, form part of the reconciliation of opening to closing balances and therefore will appear in the 'Reconciliation to net debt'.

19.85 Where differences included in the profit and loss account relate to items classified as 'Financing' in the cash flow statement, e.g., long-term loans, then the translation differences will appear in the 'Reconciliation to net debt'.

> **Example 19.85**
>
> A company financed its activities by loans amounting to US$300,000. At 1 January, the US$/£ exchange rate was 2:1. No repayments of principal were made during the year and at 31 December, the company's year end, the US$/£ exchange rate was 1.5:1.
>
> This would be reported in the reconciliation to net debt as follows.
>
> | | Loan capital |
> | --- | ---: |
> | | £'000 |
> | Balance at 1 January | 150 |
> | Effect of foreign exchange rate changes | 50 |
> | Balance at 31 December | 200 |
>
> Note: The amount of £50,000 represents the exchange movement on the loan capital outstanding from the opening balance sheet date to the closing balance sheet date. It does not appear on the face of the cash flow statement.

19.86 To the extent that differences are included in operating profit, then the translation differences will also appear in the 'Reconciliation of operating profit to net cash inflow from operating activities'.

Foreign exchange contracts which match trading transactions

19.87 Where a foreign exchange contract has been arranged for the settlement of a trading transaction, the transaction may be recorded at the contracted rate. It follows that any exchange difference arising has already been accrued and reflected in the period in which the transaction occurred. Consequently, to the extent that turnover or cost of sales reflect such differences, they will remain within the 'Net cash inflow from operating activities' without adjustment. Similarly, to the extent that debtors and creditors in the balance sheet reflect future contracted rates of exchange, these inclusive amounts will be used to compute increases and decreases in debtors and creditors.

Foreign currency borrowings used as hedges

19.88 Where a group has used foreign currency borrowings to hedge group equity investments, differences arising will have been offset as reserve movements against exchange differences arising on the retranslation of the net investment. [SSAP 20(57)]

Since no cash flow will have occurred, the difference will form part of the explanatory note reconciling opening and closing net debt.

Preparation of a consolidated cash flow statement including overseas subsidiaries

19.89 FRS 1 requires the cash flows of a foreign subsidiary to be included in the consolidated cash flow statement on the basis used for translating the results of the subsidiary in the consolidated profit and loss account, i.e., either at the closing rate or the average rate for the period.

Net investment method

19.90 For a parent dealing with a subsidiary under the net investment basis, this would be most easily done by:

(a) preparing a cash flow statement for the foreign entity in its own reporting currency, together with appropriate supporting notes;

(b) translating this cash flow statement to sterling at closing rate or at average rate, whichever is used for profit and loss account translation (alternatively, groups of foreign entities with the same reporting currency could be translated together);

(c) the resulting sterling cash flow statement is consolidated with that of the parent entity, with appropriate elimination of intra-group items such as dividend payments, loans and other capital transactions, sales of assets and trading transactions.

The resulting consolidated cash flow statement will thus present only cash flows between the group and the outside world.

19.91 The difference that arises between the resulting sterling equivalent of 'Increase/Decrease in cash' and the actual movement between the foreign entity's cash resources, as included in the consolidated balance sheet, will form part of the changes in net debt. This difference can be explained as the impact on opening cash balances of movements in the exchange rate from the opening balance sheet date to the closing rate; plus, where the average rate is used for translation, the change in foreign currency cash and cash equivalents from the average rate to the closing rate. There will be similar differences arising on the other elements of a foreign entity's net debt.

Temporal method

19.92

> Where a foreign subsidiary or branch is translated using the temporal method, the accounting approach is to include the transactions of the foreign entity as if they had been entered into by the investing company itself in its own currency. To incorporate such a foreign entity within the parent's cash flow statement, the most straightforward approach is first to translate the individual entity's foreign currency results and balances to sterling (using actual rates or possibly average rates as an approximation) and consolidate with the parent's results (alternatively, groups of foreign entities with the same reporting currency could be translated together). A consolidated cash flow statement may then be produced from the resulting sterling financial statements.

Extract 19.92

WHSmith

12 months to 31 August 1999

GROUP CASH FLOW STATEMENT

For the 12 months to 31 August 1999

	Note	12 months to 31 Aug 1999 £m	Proforma 15 months to 31 Aug 1998 £m	15 months to 31 Aug 1998 £m
Cash flow from operating activities	23	145	179	180
Returns on investment andservicing of finance		14	7	6
Taxation		(37)	(5)	(15)
Purchase of fixed assets		(60)	(56)	(70)
Disposal of tangible fixed assets		54	8	14
Cash flow from capital expenditure and financial investment		(6)	(48)	(56)
Proceeds on disposal of operations		–	465	465
Acquisitions		(171)	(80)	(80)
Cash flow for acquisitions and disposals		(171)	385	385
Equity dividends paid		(55)	(44)	(44)

	Note	12 months to 31 Aug 1999 £m	Proforma 31 Aug 1998 £m	15 months to 31 Aug 1998 £m
Cash flow before use of liquid resources and financing		(110)	474	456
Issue of shares		5	6	7
Repurchase of shares	21	(24)	(167)	(167)
Decrease in debt	17	(63)	(20)	(70)
Cash flow from financing		(82)	(181)	(230)
(Decrease)/Increase in cash		(192)	293	226

MEMORANDUM – ANALYSIS OF FREE CASH FLOW

	Note	12 months to 31 Aug 1999 £m	Proforma 31 Aug 1998 £m	15 months to 31 Aug 1998 £m
Profit before tax and beforeexceptional items		134	142	145
Depreciation/amortisation of goodwill				
– continuing		43	40	49
– discontinued		–	16	22
Movement in working capital				
– continuing		(9)	25	–
– discontinued		–	(24)	(15)
Capital expenditure on fixed assets				
– continuing		(60)	(40)	(47)
– discontinued		–	(16)	(23)
Proceeds on disposal of tangible fixed assets		8	8	14
Tax paid		(29)	(5)	(15)
Cash spend against provisions	20	(9)	(13)	(15)
Free cash flow		78	133	115
Dividends	9	(55)	(44)	(44)
Issue of shares		5	6	7
Proceeds on disposal of businesses Acquisitions		–	465	465
– cash paid	13	(171)	(80)	(80)
– issue of loan notes		(27)	–	–
Sale and leaseback of freehold properties		46	–	–

	Note	12 months to 31 Aug 1999 £m	Proforma 31 Aug 1998 £m	15 months to 31 Aug 1998 £m
Repurchase of shares and ACT on repurchases	21	(32)	(167)	(167)
Cash movement in debt		(156)	313	296
Opening net cash/(debt)		266	(48)	(31)
Hodder Headline debt acquired		(5)	–	–
Exchange movement		–	1	1
Closing net cash		105	266	266

1 The example in **17.70** below illustrates the full disclosure required by FRS 1 in respect of acquisitions.

2 Returns on investments and servicing of finance.

20 Segmental information

20   Segmental information

General requirements

Introduction

20.1   The requirements to provide segmental information come from two sources: the Companies Act 1985 and SSAP 25 *Segmental reporting*. SSAP 25 basically repeats the statutory disclosures and then adds some more disclosures which are required to be given by certain companies (see **20.11** below) and are encouraged to be given by all other entities.

20.2   The table below provides a brief summary of the requirements, which are considered in detail in the sections that follow.

Disclosure required:	Companies Act	SSAP 25
Turnover by:		
(a) Class of business	✓	✓ (see 1 below)
(b) Geographical market:		
– destination	✓	✓ (see 2 below)
– origin		✓ (see 1 below)
Profit/loss before tax:		(see 3 below)
(a) Class of business		✓
(b) Geographical market		✓
Net assets:		(see 3 below)
(a) Class of business		✓
(b) Geographical market		✓
Segmental associate information		✓

1   Split between external and other segments.

2   External only.

3   Normally by origin (see **20.33** below).

20.3 The purpose of segmental information is to provide information to assist the users of financial statements:

(a) to appreciate more thoroughly the results and financial position of the entity by permitting a better understanding of the entity's past performance and thus a better assessment of its future prospects; and

(b) to be aware of the impact that changes in significant components of a business may have on the business as a whole.

This information is becoming increasingly important as more and more companies trade globally and carry on numerous classes of business. Without segmental information, it is very difficult for users to assess different profitability rates, opportunities for growth, and different degrees of risk [SSAP 25(1)].

20.4 However, care should be exercised when analysing segmental information due to the fact that the basis for reportable segments, the treatment of common assets and costs, and changes in accounting policies can all affect the comparisons made between different companies and even between different years.

The Companies Act

Disclosure requirements

20.5 The Act requires that where the company has operated in classes of business or supplied markets, which, in the opinion of the directors, differ substantially from each other, the notes to the accounts should disclose turnover attributable to classes of business and to markets. [Sch 4:55] The disclosure requirements for small company's that are applying Sch 8 are discussed in **34.33** below.

20.6 Only those classes of business or markets which contribute materially need be disclosed. The amounts which are not material may be included in amounts stated in respect of another class or market or combined together and shown as 'other'.

20.7 The Companies Act reference to 'where the company has supplied markets' indicates that the amounts to be disclosed in each geographical market is the amount of turnover that is actually made to that country (i.e., turnover by destination, not turnover by origin – see **20.33** below for further discussion).

20.8 The Act gives little guidance for determining classes of business, but suggests that the directors should have regard to the manner in which the company's activities are organised. It is suggested that this term might reasonably be regarded as equivalent to the 'principal activities' of the company which should be disclosed in the directors' report (see **6.10** above). Similarly, for markets, it states that a market means a geographical market, but it gives no further criteria for determining when markets differ substantially from each other.

20.9   Additional guidance in relation to these requirements is provided by SSAP 25. This is discussed below.

Exemption

20.10   The requirements of the Act are subject to the proviso that where, in the opinion of the directors, disclosure of this information would be seriously prejudicial to the interests of the company, it need not be given, but the fact that the information has not been disclosed must be given.

SSAP 25 *Segmental reporting*

Scope

20.11   SSAP 25 does two things: it gives guidance on interpreting the statutory requirements and also requires additional disclosure for some specified entities. The additional requirements apply to any entity which:

(a)   is a public limited company or has a subsidiary which is a public limited company; or

(b)   is a banking or insurance company or group (as defined in the Act); or

(c)   exceeds the criteria (i.e., two of: turnover, balance sheet total or average number of employees), multiplied in each case by 10, for defining a medium-sized company (see **34.47** below).

20.12   The third category in **20.11** above refers to *exceeding* the criteria for defining a medium-sized company, not *qualifying* as a medium-sized company. It would seem appropriate to interpret these words strictly. Therefore, if, having previously exceeded the criteria, a company falls below them in a current period, it would not be deemed to exceed the criteria for the period and the company would not have to give the additional SSAP 25 disclosures nor disclose the comparative figures. (If the requirement referred to qualifying as a medium-sized company, then the company would only qualify if it fell below the criteria for two consecutive years.) In subsequent periods, if the company again exceeds the criteria, the disclosures will have to be given for that year along with comparative figures,

> even if those figures had not been disclosed in the previous year. This is because SSAP 25 only permits comparatives not to be given on the first occasion of compliance with the standard, presumably because the necessary information would not be readily available.

20.13 Even though entities not falling within the categories in **20.11** above do not need to provide additional disclosure, SSAP 25 encourages all entities to apply the provisions of the standard.

Exemption

20.14 An exemption is given from the provisions of the SSAP for a subsidiary which exceeds the medium-sized company criteria but is neither a public, banking nor insurance company, on condition that its parent provides segmental disclosures in accordance with SSAP 25 [SSAP 25(4)].

20.15 This exemption presumably applies only when the parent is preparing consolidated accounts and has included the subsidiary's information in the disclosures. If the parent does not prepare group accounts, or does not include the subsidiary in their disclosures, then it seems logical for the subsidiary to give the disclosures.

Example 20.15

Whether a UK subsidiary (which exceeds the size criteria given in **20.11** above and therefore falls within the scope of SSAP 25) gives the disclosures required by SSAP 25 will depend on whether its parent provides the appropriate information. Scenarios could be as follows:

1. If the UK subsidiary has a UK parent which gives the disclosures in accordance with SSAP 25, then *no* disclosure needs to be given in the subsidiary's accounts.

2. If the UK subsidiary has a UK parent which is exempt from preparing group accounts, then the subsidiary:

   (a) *must give* the disclosure if its ultimate parent does not give the disclosure (i.e., no group accounts are prepared which include the subsidiary's segmental information); or

   (b) *does not need* to give the disclosure if its ultimate parent discloses SSAP 25 information.

3. If the UK subsidiary has a non-UK parent which does not give the disclosures required by SSAP 25, then the subsidiary *must* give the disclosure.

> N.B. If the non-UK parent gives the information required by SSAP 25 in its group accounts (or information that is equivalent), then this can be taken as meeting the standards requirements and therefore *no* disclosure is needed in the UK subsidiary's accounts.

Guidance on determining reportable segments

20.16 The SSAP does not seek to change the requirement of the Act to report segments which differ substantially from each other, but rather seeks to provide guidance to assist the directors in determining what is 'substantially different'.

20.17 It is the directors who make the decisions as to what defines a reportable segment. Those definitions, once made, should be reviewed annually and redefined as appropriate. If a change is made to the definitions of the segments or to the accounting policies that are adopted for reporting segmental information, the nature, reason for and the effect of the change should be disclosed. Comparatives should be restated in accordance with the newly defined segments.

20.18 In identifying a reportable segment, the SSAP requires that directors have regard to the overall purpose of giving segmental disclosure, which is to provide information that will allow a more thorough understanding of the results and financial position of a reporting entity and highlight the impact of changes on material components of the business.

20.19 Classes of business or geographical segments should be identified if they are significant to the entity as a whole. A segment is normally considered significant if it accounts for 10 per cent or more of the total turnover, results or net assets.

20.20 The standard lists some general criteria which should be taken into consideration in identifying reportable segments, i.e., differing rates of return, degrees of risk, growth rates and potential for development. It also provides the following criteria specific to determining classes of business and geographical segments.

Class of business

20.21 A class of business is defined as being 'a distinguishable component of an entity that provides a separate product or service or a separate group of related products or services' [SSAP 25(11)].

20.22 The determination of classes of business depends on the judgement of the directors and there is no single set of characteristics that can be universally applied to differentiate classes of business, but the following factors should be taken into account:

[SSAP 25(12)]

(a) the nature of the products or services;

(b) the nature of the production process;

(c) the markets in which the products or services are sold;

(d) the distribution channels for the products;

(e) the manner in which the entity's activities are organised; and

(f) any separate legislative framework relating to part of the business, e.g., a bank or an insurance company.

Geographical segment

20.23 A geographical segment is defined as a geographical area comprising an individual country or a group of countries in which an entity operates or to which it supplies products or services [SSAP 25 (14)].

20.24 A geographical analysis should help the user to assess the extent to which an entity's operations are subject to such factors as:
[SSAP 25(15)]

• expansionist or restrictive economic climates;

• stable or unstable political regimes;

• exchange control regulations; and

• exchange rate fluctuations.

20.25 Entities normally find determination of classes of business relatively straightforward; more questions arise over the determination of geographical segments. In the past, some entities looked to the suggestion in the old Listing Rules (now deleted) of providing an analysis by continent. Normally, this is unlikely to satisfy the requirements of the SSAP. Following the guidance in the SSAP, it would normally be more appropriate for geographical segments to be countries or perhaps groups of countries with closely linked economies, e.g., those that have the euro as currency.

20.26 There may be industries, e.g., international securities trading, where an entity could justify that it deals in a single global market, where the allocation to geographical segments may be of limited use or possibly arbitrary, e.g., a trader based in London matches a dollar denominated transaction for a buyer in Japan and a seller in Germany.

Required disclosures

20.27 The SSAP requires various disclosures where an entity has carried on business in two or more business classes or geographical areas which differ substantially from each other. These are as follows.

1. Definition of each reported class of business and geographical segment [SSAP 25(17)].	
2. For each class of business or geographical segment, disclose:	
(a) turnover by origin (distinguishing between that derived from external customers and that derived from other segments);	Section **20.32** to **20.35** below
(b) results, before accounting for taxation, minority interests and extraordinary items (normally by origin but can be by destination if more appropriate); and	Section **20.36** to **20.40** below
(c) net assets by origin.	Section **20.41** to **20.44** below
3. In addition, for each geographical segment, disclose turnover by destination only when materially different to turnover by origin (external customers only).	Section **20.32** to **20.35** below.
4. Where associated undertakings are significant, disclose, for each reported class of business and geographical segment, the reporting entity's share of:	Section **20.45** to **20.50** below.
(a) the profits or losses of associated undertakings before accounting for taxation, minority interests and extraordinary items; and	
(b) the net assets of associated undertakings (including goodwill to the extent that it has not been written off).	
5. Reconciliations need to be made where the total amount reported in the financial statements differs to the total of the segments.	
6. Comparative figures need to be given.	

Exemption

20.28   SSAP 25(6) repeats the proviso contained in the Act that where the directors believe the provision of this information to be seriously prejudicial to the interests of the entity, it need not be disclosed.

20.29   The following factors are relevant in considering the directors' use of this proviso.

(a)   This segmental information is required and presented by the majority of UK companies. It is therefore unlikely that it could be demonstrated as being prejudicial for a particular company to disclose this information, unless it could show that direct competitors are not providing similar information.

(b)   With respect to the geographical analysis, it would appear that a geographical analysis of turnover is unlikely to be prejudicial. However, where companies are operating in countries in which competitors are not required to provide segmental analyses, there may again be a case for not presenting the geographical analyses of results and net assets.

Example from published accounts

20.30   The following extract is an example of an exemption on the grounds of 'seriously prejudicial'.

Extract 20.30

Dawson Holdings plc

53 weeks ended 2 October 1999

Segmental analysis

An analysis of turnover, operating profit and net assets by geographical segment has not been included as the directors believe that to do so would be seriously prejudicial to the interests of the group. For the same reason, an analysis of net assets by class of business has also been omitted.

Group accounts

20.31   When both parent and consolidated financial statements are presented, segmental information should be presented on the basis of the consolidated financial statements.

Turnover

20.32   Turnover needs to be disclosed by class of business and by geographical segment.

20.33   The disclosure of segment results and net assets will generally be based on the location of operations (i.e., the origin). It is therefore appropriate that the geographical analysis of turnover should be provided according to location of operations, i.e., the geographical area from which products or services are supplied. This is known as 'turnover by origin'. However, the factors which affect the geographical areas of the business are equally as applicable to the location of markets supplied as to the location of operations. Therefore, where it is materially different from the analysis of turnover by origin, the SSAP also requires an analysis of turnover by destination, i.e., the geographical area to which products or services are supplied. [SSAP 25(34)] If these two analyses are not materially different, a note to this effect should be included.

20.34   Additionally, the standard requires turnover by origin to be separated into total turnover and turnover which has been made to other (internal) segments [SSAP 25(34)]. This then highlights the amount of turnover that has been made to external customers. Turnover by destination is not required to be broken down into these categories as the breakdown has little or no value to users. Therefore, turnover by destination is shown as amounts to external customers only.

Example 20.34

Transactions between a UK company, its US subsidiary and their customers are as follows:

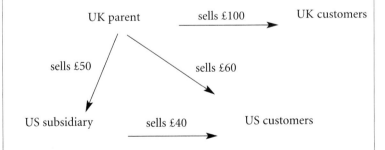

Disclosures for turnover by geographical origin:

		£	
UK	– total	210	(100 + 50 + 60)
	– other segments	(50)	
	– external	160	

US – external	40
Total	200

Disclosures for turnover by geographical destination:

	£
UK – external	100
US – external	100 (60 + 40)
Total	200

Example from published accounts

20.35 The following extracts are examples of disclosures of segmental information relating to turnover.

Extract 20.35.1

P & O Ferries plc

Year end 31/12/98	Group 1998 £m	Joint Venture 1998 £m	Total 1998 £m
Turnover			
By division:			
Continuing operations			
Cruises	1,141.1	–	1,141.1
Ferries	472.2	219.6	691.8
Ports and logistics	1,525.8	47.5	1,573.3
Cargo shipping	44.9	1,207.4	1,252.3
Property and related businesses	2,727.7	48.2	2,775.9
	5,911.7	1,522.7	7,434.4

	1998 £m	1998 £m	1998 £m
By geographical area of origin:			
Continuing operations			
UK and the Republic of Ireland	2,161.7	292.6	2,454.3
Continental Europe	722.4	356.2	1,078.6
USA and Canada	2,295.9	150.7	2,446.6
Australia, Far East and Pacific	662.3	691.8	1,354.1
Other Areas	69.4	31.4	100.8
	5,911.7	1,522.7	7,434.4

Turnover by destination is not materially different from turnover by origin.

N.B. 1997 comparatives for all the above were also given. These have not been repeated here.

> **Extract 20.35.2**
>
> The Body Shop plc
>
> 52 Weeks ended 27/02/99
>
> Turnover and operating profit relate principally to the main activity of the sale of skin and hair products, and are attributable to the continuing operations of the group.
>
> The comparative figures have been restated to reflect the new regional structure for the group.
>
> | | Total Sales £m | Intra Group £m | 1999 Third Party £m |
> |---|---|---|---|
> | Turnover by Origin | | | |
> | UK | 221.4 | (16.8) | 204.6 |
> | Americas | 86.6 | – | 86.6 |
> | Europe and Middle East | 6.9 | – | 6.9 |
> | Asia Pacific | 5.6 | – | 5.6 |
> | | 320.5 | (16.8) | 303.7 |
>
> N.B. 1998 comparatives for all the above were also given. These have not been repeated here.
>
> Turnover by destination was also given.

Results

20.36   Results, before accounting for taxation, minority interests and extraordinary items need to be disclosed by class of business and by geographical segment.

20.37   The disclosure of segment results will normally be based on the location of operations (i.e., the origin). However, it is possible to disclose results based on the geographical area to which products or services are supplied (i.e., the destination). Reference should be made of the basis used in the latter case.

20.38   As interest is normally a result of the company's financial policy rather than individual segments' policy, it is normally excluded from the segments' results as it would lead to a meaningless allocation between segments. Where interest income or expense is central to the business, interest should normally be included in arriving at the segment result (see **20.42** below).

20.39   A problem arises where costs are incurred which are common to more than one segment. The SSAP gives some guidance on this and suggests that entities may apportion common costs to segments in a way that the directors deem appropriate, as long as the apportionment would not be misleading. Any common costs not apportioned should be deducted from the total of the segment results [SSAP 25(23)]. This is in line with the general practice that has developed.

Example 20.39

Unallocated common costs

Profits per class of business (based on origin)

	2000 £'000	%	1999 £'000	%
Agricultural services	1,200	(39)	1,350	(77)
Building materials	475	(15)	360	(21)
Property development	1,800	(58)	488	(28)
Subtotal	3,475	(112)	2,198	(126)
Interest and parent company expenses *less* other income	(390)	(12)	(456)	(26)
Group profit before taxation	3,085	(100)	1,742	(100)

Examples from published financial statement

20.40 The following extracts from financial statements give examples of profit analysed by origin and by destination.

Extract 20.40.1

Imperial Tobacco Group plc

52 weeks ended 26/09/1998

Operating profit	1998	1997
By destination:		
UK	319	312
International trading operations	117	79
	436	391
By origin:		
UK	387	371
International trading operations	49	20
	436	391

Extract 20.40.2

P&O Ferries plc

Year end 31/12/98

Operating profit	Group 1998 £m	Joint Ventures 1998 £m	Associates 1998 £m	Total 1998 £m
By division:				
Continuing operations				
Cruises	216.1	–	–	216.1
Ferries	35.7	45.3	–	81.0
Ports and logistics	61.1	13.7	5.2	80.0
Cargo shipping	(9.8)	18.0	–	8.2
Property and related businesses	173.8	17.3	2.5	193.6
Less: reorganisation costs	(3.3)	(15.1)	–	(18.4)
	473.6	79.2	7.7	560.5

	1998 £m	1998 £m	1998 £m	1998 £m
By geographical area of origin:				
Continuing operations				
UK and the Republic of Ireland	181.9	40.2	1.7	223.8
Continental Europe	25.1	18.2	1.1	44.4
USA and Canada	239.5	14.0	(0.4)	253.1
Australia, Far East and Pacific	33.4	17.1	5.3	55.8
Other areas	(3.0)	4.8	–	1.8
Less: reorganisation costs	(3.3)	(15.1)	–	(18.4)
	473.6	79.2	7.7	560.5

N.B. 1997 comparatives for all the above were also given. These have not been repeated here.

Net assets

20.41 Net assets need to be disclosed by class of business and by geographical segment.

20.42 In most cases, the net assets of each reportable segment will be the non-interest bearing operating assets less the non-interest bearing operating liabilities. Interest bearing assets and liabilities will only be included if the segmental results include interest because the entity's business is to earn and incur interest (see **20.38** above).

20.43 Where assets or liabilities do not relate exclusively to one segment (i.e., common assets), they should be allocated to segments on a reasonable basis. The total of any assets or liabilities not allocated to segments should be shown as an item reconciling the segment net assets to the total balance sheet net assets.

Examples from published financial statements

20.44 The following extracts from financial statements give examples of net assets, analysed by class of business and geographical segment.

Extract 20.44.1

The Body Shop

52 weeks ended 27/02/99

Net operating assets by location of company	1999 £m	1998 £m
UK	78.2	82.6
Americas	23.2	37.9
Europe and Middle East	7.3	2.4
Asia Pacific	0.5	0.6
	109.2	123.5
Net cash	5.1	6.8
Total net assets of Group	114.3	130.3

Extract 20.44.2

J. Sainsbury plc

56 weeks ended 03/04/99

	1999 Net Assets £m
Food retailing – UK	4,595
Food retailing – US	505
DIY retailing – UK	452
Banking – UK	100
Property development – UK	130
Other – UK	10
	5,792
Associated undertakings	38
Non-operating assets and liabilities	(437)
Net borrowing	(704)
Total net assets	4,689

Associated undertakings

20.45   SSAP 25 states that if associated undertakings are significant, then the reporting entity's share of the aggregate results and net assets of associated undertakings should be disclosed for each class of business and geographical segment. Significant is defined as being 20 per cent or more of the total results or net assets of the reporting entity. [SSAP 25(36)]

20.46   FRS 9 introduced joint ventures as a separate type of investment to be accounted for under the gross equity method and shown separately in consolidated financial statements. FRS 9 is largely silent on the segmental analysis of associates and joint ventures, except that it states that, in the segmental analysis, the share of joint ventures' turnover should be clearly distinguished from the turnover for the group itself. This is normally done by showing turnover of joint ventures separately on the face of the profit and loss account (see **25.83** below).

20.47   On the basis that, prior to FRS 9, incorporated joint ventures would have been accounted for as associates, it appears that post-FRS 9, it is permissible to apply the reference in SSAP 25 to associate undertakings as meaning joint ventures and associates in aggregate. So, in aggregate, if joint ventures and associate undertakings account for 20 per cent or more of total results or net assets of the reporting entity, then the aggregate results and net assets of joint ventures and associates should be disclosed segmentally. If separately, joint ventures or associate undertakings account for 20 per cent or more of the aggregate results or net assets of the reporting entity, this separate segmental analysis could additionally be given for each category.

20.48   This segmental information is in addition to the information required for significant interests in associates and joint ventures (see **25.131** to **25.134** below). [FRS 9(57) and (58)]

20.49   If this associated undertaking information is unobtainable or publication is prejudicial to the associate's business, it need not be disclosed, but the reason for non-disclosure should be stated together with a brief description of the omitted business. [SSAP 25(36)]

Examples of published financial statements

20.50   In addition to the method set out in extract **20.35.1** above, the following extract reflects another way to disclose information regarding associates and joint ventures.

Extract 20.50

Vodafone plc

Year end 31/3/99

1. Segmental analysis

The Group's share of profit on ordinary activities before interest and share of net assets of associated undertakings by geographical region are as follows:

Share of profit on ordinary activities before interest	1999 £m	1998 £m
United Kingdom	4.0	2.4
Continental Europe	58.2	11.3
Pacific Rim	2.9	15.8
Rest of the World	53.0	43.7
	118.1	73.2

Share of net assets and attributable goodwill	1999 £m	1998 £m
United Kingdom	(5.3)	(7.4)
Continental Europe	113.8	52.3
Pacific Rim	13.5	12.2
Rest of the World	147.5	73.2
	269.5	130.3

Consolidated accounts

20.51   When both parent and consolidated financial statements are presented, segmental information should be presented on the basis of the consolidated financial statements.

20.52   FRS 2(94) encourages parent undertakings to consider the disclosure requirements of SSAP 25 as a minimum rather than a limit. It suggests two areas where supplemental segmental information could be given:

(a)   where subsidiaries engage in different activities or are subject to restrictions but still fall to be consolidated; and

(b)   minority interests in different group segments.

Acquisition, sale or termination

20.53   FRS 3 stresses the need to take into consideration the general purpose of providing segmental information, i.e., of highlighting the impact of changes on material components of the business to allow a thorough understanding of the results and financial position of a reporting entity. It imposes an additional segmental disclosure requirement that where an acquisition, sale, or termination has a material impact on a major business segment, this should be disclosed and explained. [FRS 3(15)] No guidance is given in FRS 3 as to the format of such a disclosure, although FRS 6 repeats this requirement and states that the segmental information should be given for each material acquisition and for other acquisitions in aggregate [FRS 6(23 and 28)].

20.54

Given FRS 3's requirement to show, as a minimum, turnover and operating profit relating to discontinued and acquired activities, an appropriate interpretation of FRS 3 would be to extend these disclosures into segmental information. Additionally, although the requirement is to disclose information per business segment, given its relevance it is advisable to give the information per geographical segment as well. This has been done in example **20.54** below.

Example 20.54

Example of how FRS 3 segmental disclosures could be made

A company sells three products in the UK, USA and Australia. Turnover by origin is as follows:

	£'000 UK	£'000 USA	£'000 Australia	£'000 Total
Product 1	40	30	20	90
Product 2	40	30	20	90
Product 3	35	25	15	75
	115	85	55	255

(a) If the company decides to discontinue activities in the USA, disclosures could be:

Profit and loss extract	Continuing £'000	Discontinuing £'000	Total £'000
Turnover	170 (115 + 55)	85	255

Segmental analysis *Turnover by origin*	£'000 UK	£'000 USA	£'000 Australia	£'000 Total
Continuing	115	–	55	170
Discontinuing		85		85
				255

	£'000	£'000	£'000	£'000
Class of business	**Product 1**	**Product 2**	**Product 3**	**Total**
Continuing	60	60	50	170
Discontinuing	30	30	25	85
				255

N.B. Turnover by origin is not materially different from turnover by destination.

(b) If the company decides to discontinue product 3, disclosures could be:

Profit and loss extract	**Continuing**	**Discontinuing**	**Total**
	£'000	**£'000**	**£'000**
Turnover	180	75	255
	(90 + 90)		

Segmental analysis	£'000	£'000	£'000	£'000
Turnover by origin	**UK**	**USA**	**Australia**	**Total**
Continuing	80	60	40	180
Discontinuing	35	25	15	75
	115	85	55	255

	£'000	£'000	£'000	£'000
Class of business	**Product 1**	**Product 2**	**Product 3**	**Total**
Continuing	90	90	–	180
Discontinuing	–	–	75	75
	90	90	75	255

N.B. Turnover by origin is not materially different from turnover by destination

21 Other disclosure requirements, including derivatives

21 Other disclosure requirements, including derivatives

Summary of changes since the previous issue of this publication

Para.	Topic	Summary
21.104	Consultation document *Developing the Framework*	Issued by company law review in March 2000. The paper addresses a number of topics including reporting and accounting.
21.106	FRED 21 *Accounting policies*	Issued by the ASB in December 1999, it proposes an update on the guidance on accounting policies contained in SSAP 2, to be consistent with the Statement of Principles and other recent pronouncements, including FRS 12 (*Provisions*) and FRS 5 (*Substance of transactions*).

Accounting policies

Introduction

21.1   The Act prescribes certain fundamental accounting principles to be followed in the preparation of a company's financial statements and these are discussed in **5.14** to **5.31** above. Within the framework of these fundamental principles, there is room for some measure of choice in regard to the specific accounting policies to be applied, though this choice is significantly reduced by the statutory valuation rules, accounting standards and UITF Abstracts. The effect of these rules and standards is discussed under the appropriate headings throughout this volume.

21.2   Accounting policies are the specific accounting bases selected and consistently followed by a reporting entity (not necessarily a company) for the purpose of financial statements; in particular, for determining the accounting periods in which revenue and costs should be recognised in the profit and loss account and for determining the amounts at which material items should be stated in the balance sheet.

Disclosure of accounting policies

21.3 SSAP 2 states that the accounting policies followed for dealing with items which are judged material or critical in determining profit or loss for the year and in stating financial position should be disclosed. This requirement is similar to the legal requirement in Sch 4 to disclose accounting policies adopted by the company. [Sch 4: 36]

21.4 It is recommended that the accounting policies used should be identified in the first note to the accounts. An alternative presentation which is often found is to have a separate statement of accounting policies, possibly inserted before the primary statements. A further approach is to state the policies applicable to individual items in the notes on each item along with other required information. If the latter approach is adopted, it is advisable to explain this in the first note.

> ### Example 21.4
>
> The accounting policies adopted are disclosed in the appropriate notes below.

21.5 It should be borne in mind that a policy which is not significant in one company (or industry) may be highly significant in another company (or industry). For example, the method of accounting for investments will normally not be significant in a manufacturing company, but would be significant in an investment company.

21.6 In a large group or complicated situation, the explanations of accounting policies may have to be greatly enlarged. However, SSAP 2 specifies that the explanations should be clear, fair and as brief as possible. Policy notes should deal solely with policy matters; they should not deal with information concerning the make-up of amounts dealt with in the financial statements.

21.7 Accounting standards specifically require disclosure of accounting policies regarding the following, where they have a material effect on reported results and financial position:

(a) depreciation method and useful lives or depreciation rates used for each class of depreciable asset;*

(b) translation method and treatment of foreign currency

balances* (including the policy adopted to eliminate the distortions on group results of operations in areas of hyperinflation);

(c)   stocks and long-term contracts; in particular, the method of ascertaining turnover and attributable profit;

(d)   research and development;

(e)   goodwill and intangible assets;

(f)   government grants;

(g)   operating and finance leases;

(h)   recognition of finance lease income;

(i)   pension costs (and the funding policy for defined benefit schemes if different from the accounting policy);

(j)   post-retirement benefits other than pensions; and

(k)   deferred tax on pensions and other post-retirement benefits.

Note: Items marked '*' are also specifically required to be disclosed by Sch 4.

21.8   Examples of other policies which will often have a material effect on reported results and financial position include the treatment of the following:

- income recognition;

- warranties for products or services;

- capitalisation of interest;

- property development transactions;

- valuation of investments;

- valuation of tangible fixed assets;

- investment properties;

- financial instruments, including derivatives;

- deferred taxation;

- consolidation principles; and

- associates and joint ventures.

21.9   Reference should be made to the policy note in the model financial statements of Delto PLC for examples of wording (see chapter 46).

Compliance with accounting standards

21.10   The Act requires companies and groups which are not small or medium-sized to disclose whether the accounts have been prepared in accordance with applicable accounting standards, together with particulars of and reasons for any material departure from them. [Sch 4: 36A] For this purpose, accounting standards are statements of standard accounting practice issued by such body or bodies as prescribed by regulation. So far, the ASB is the only body to have been prescribed as a standard setting body.

21.11   In addition to the statutory requirements, the *Foreword to accounting standards* requires disclosure of particulars of, reasons for and financial effects of any material departure and that such disclosures should be equivalent to that given in respect of departures from specific accounting provisions of companies legislation (see **21.17** below).

21.12   Although small and medium-sized companies/groups are exempt from the requirement of Sch 4 para 36A, the *Foreword to accounting standards* does not give an exemption to such companies/groups. Therefore, small and medium-sized companies/groups still have to disclose any material departure from accounting standards, though they are not required to give a statement of compliance if they have complied with applicable accounting standards.

21.13   An example of appropriate disclosure is contained in the accounting policy note of the model financial statements of Delto PLC (see chapter 46).

21.14   Small companies which are entitled to the exemptions available in the legislation when filing accounts with the Registrar of Companies can choose to adopt the FRSSE. Where they do so, small companies should state that their financial statements have been prepared in accordance with FRSSE (see **34.69** below).

21.15   Eligibility of companies to adopt FRSSE and the requirements of that standard are dealt with in chapter 34.

Accounting convention

21.16   Although there is no accounting standard or legal requirement to do so, it is customary to disclose in the accounting policy note or separately the particular accounting convention used in preparing the financial statements.

> ### *Example 21.16*
>
> The financial statements have been prepared under the historical cost convention as modified by the revaluation of land and buildings.

Departures from requirements of the Act in order to show a true and fair view

21.17　As discussed in **5.10** above, in rare circumstances, it may be necessary to depart from the requirements of the Act for the financial statements to give a true and fair view. If such a departure is necessary, the Act requires that the particulars of the departure, the reasons for it and its effect are given in a note to the accounts. [ss226(5) and 227(6)] UITF Abstract 7 states that these statutory disclosure requirements should be interpreted as follows:

> '"Particulars of any such departure" means a statement of the treatment which the Act would normally require in the circumstances and a description of the treatment actually adopted;
>
> "the reasons for it" means a statement as to why the treatment prescribed would not give a true and fair view;
>
> "its effects" means a description of how the position shown in the accounts is different as a result of the departure, normally with quantification. Whenever the effect cannot reasonably be quantified, the directors should explain the circumstances.'

21.18　In practice, it is often not practicable to quantify the effect of the departure, as in the following example.

> ### *Example 21.18*
>
> **Accounting policy – investment properties**
>
> In accordance with SSAP 19, investment properties are revalued annually and the aggregate surplus or deficit is transferred to revaluation reserve. No depreciation is provided in respect of investment properties.
>
> The Companies Act 1985 requires all properties to be depreciated. However, this requirement conflicts with the generally accepted accounting principle set out in SSAP 21. The directors consider that, because these properties are not held for consumption, but for their investment potential, to depreciate them would not give a true and fair view and that it is necessary to adopt SSAP 19 in order to give a true and fair view.
>
> If this departure from the Act had not been made, the profit for the financial year would have been reduced by depreciation. However, the

---

> amount of depreciation cannot reasonably be quantified, because depreciation is only one of many factors reflected in the annual valuation and the amount which might otherwise have been shown cannot be separately identified or quantified.

21.19 UITF Abstract 7 also states that the required disclosures (as discussed in **21.17** above) should either be included, or cross-referenced, in the note required under Sch 4 para 36A (i.e., the note on compliance with applicable accounting standards, as discussed in **21.10** above). An example of the latter approach is given below.

> ### Example 21.19
>
> . . . Compliance with SSAP 19 *Accounting for investment properties* requires departure from the requirements of the Companies Act 1985 relating to depreciation and an explanation of the departure is given in note (x) below.

Compliance with UITF Abstracts

21.20 *The Foreword to UITF Abstracts* states that UITF Abstracts should be read in conjunction with accounting standards and should be regarded as part of the corpus of practices forming the basis for determining what constitutes a true and fair view. It also states that any significant departures from UITF Abstracts found to be necessary should be adequately disclosed and explained in the financial statements. Particulars of the departure, the reasons for it and its financial effects should be disclosed. These disclosures should be equivalent to that given in respect of departures from specific accounting provisions of companies legislation (see **21.17** above). [UITF *Foreword* (16)]

Change in accounting policy

21.21 As discussed in **5.19** above, a change in accounting policy is allowed only if the new policy is preferable to the one it replaces because it will give a fairer presentation of the result and financial position. In the year in which an accounting policy has been changed, the accounting policy note should disclose the nature of the change from the policy previously adopted and that the preceding year's figures have been restated in accordance with the new policy. The Act requires that the particulars of any departure from the principle of consistency, the reasons for it and the effect shall be given in a note to the accounts. Furthermore, FRS 3 requires the effect on the results for the preceding period to be disclosed where practicable. UITF Abstract 14 clarifies the requirements of the Act to disclose the 'effect'. UITF Abstract 14 requires the disclosures to include, in addition to the FRS 3 requirement, an indication of the effect on the current year's results. Where this is not practicable, that fact, together with the reasons for it, should be stated.

21.22 Prior period adjustments are dealt with further in **9.251** to **9.263** above.

Financial commitments

Introduction

21.23 Particulars of the following financial commitments should be disclosed in the notes to the accounts: [Sch 4: 50]

(a) capital commitments;

(b) pension commitments; and

(c) other financial commitments.

Capital commitments

21.24 The Act requires the aggregate amount of capital expenditure contracted for at the balance sheet date, to the extent that this amount has not been provided in the accounts to be disclosed. [Sch 4: 50(3)]

21.25 An example of appropriate disclosure is given in the model financial statements of Delto PLC (see chapter 46).

21.26 Disclosure of leasing commitments is required by SSAP 21. These are dealt with in chapter 29.

Pension commitments

21.27 Pension accounting and related disclosures are discussed in chapter 30. Particulars of any pension commitments which are provided in the balance sheet and any such commitments for which no provision has been made should be disclosed. [Sch 4: 50(4)]

21.28 Separate particulars should be given where any of these commitments relate to past directors of the company.

Other financial commitments

21.29 Particulars of other financial commitments which have not been provided for in the financial statements and are relevant to assessing the company's state of affairs are also to be disclosed. [Sch 4: 50(5)] These might include:

(a) purchase commitments in excess of normal requirements (especially speculative positions); however, to the extent that such commitments are covered by hedging agreements, they are unlikely to be relevant to assessing the company's state of affairs and so would not require disclosure;

(b) exposed foreign currency positions; and

(c) commitments to lend money or to guarantee future loans to third parties by companies which do not customarily provide financial services.

21.30 Schedule 4 para 59A requires separate disclosure of guarantees and financial commitments within any of the subparagraphs of Sch 4 para 50 (i.e., in addition to the disclosures in respect of charges on assets and contingent liabilities discussed in **17.317** above, sub-analysis is required in respect of items covered in **21.24**, **21.27** and **21.29** above) undertaken on behalf of or for the benefit of:

(a) any parent or fellow subsidiary undertakings; and

(b) subsidiary undertakings.

Year 2000 and the euro

21.31 Disclosures of the following commitments at the balance sheet date should be given in financial statements:

(a) in respect of year 2000 software modification costs (whether to be treated as capital or revenue) where they are relevant to assessing the entity's state of affairs [UITF Abstract 20]; and

(b) in respect of costs associated with the introduction of the euro (whether to be treated as capital or revenue) where they are relevant to assessing the entity's state of affairs [UITF Abstract 21].

21.32 Other disclosure requirements relating to year 2000 and the euro are dealt with in **6.77** to **6.85** above.

Participation of parent undertaking in vendor placing

Listing Rules requirements

21.33 If a listed company is a subsidiary undertaking of another company, the Listing Rules require disclosure of particulars of the participation by the parent undertaking in any placing made during the period under review. [Listing Rules (12.43(p))] 'Company' is defined by the Listing Rules as a body corporate wherever incorporated.

21.34

> This situation may arise where a listed company acquires assets in exchange for the issue of its own shares to vendors who, under a prior arrangement, then place the shares with selected investors (one of which may be the parent company) for cash.

Particulars of advisers

Alternative investment market companies

21.35 The published accounts of companies that have securities which have been admitted to trading on AIM should include the name and address of both the nominated adviser and the nominated broker.

Financial instruments

Background

21.36 In July 1996, the ASB issued a discussion paper setting out proposals for recognition and measurement, including hedge accounting, and disclosure of derivatives and other financial instruments. The proposals on recognition and measurement, including hedge accounting, are discussed in chapter 26. The ASB argued that an improvement in disclosure alone will not address all the problems in the area of accounting for derivatives and other financial instruments. Yet, since there is an obvious need for an urgent solution, it was decided to split the project into two parts and introduce a disclosure standard first, as a temporary solution, and thus allow more time to consider the conceptual issues of measurement, recognition and hedging. FRS 13 *Derivatives and other financial instruments: disclosures* was published in September 1998 and is effective for accounting periods ending on or after 23 March 1999.

Scope of FRS 13

21.37 The standard applies to all entities, other than insurance companies, which have one or more of their capital instruments listed or publicly traded on a stock exchange or market, and all banks and similar institutions [FRS 13(3) and (82)]. The scope is wide and, in addition to companies with listed shares traded on the London Stock Exchange, covers:

(a) entities with listed instruments other than shares, e.g., those with listed debt;

(b) all banks, irrespective of size;

(c) building societies and credit unions;

(d) entities traded on AIM, EASDAQ, NASDAQ and other markets.

Disclosures need not be provided in the parent company's own financial statements when these are presented with the consolidated financial statements.

All financial assets and liabilities except those specifically excluded (see **21.46** below) are to be dealt with in the disclosures.

21.38

> The standard does not define what 'traded on other markets' is, but it would appear from the explanations provided throughout the development of the FRS and in FRS 13(4) that the definition is intended to be wide and covers, for example, companies traded on OFEX. OFEX is an off-exchange share matching and trading facility established by J P Jenkins Limited to enable London Stock Exchange member firms to deal in the securities of unlisted and unquoted companies. Though OFEX is not a Recognised Investment Exchange, a member of the public can buy shares of the OFEX participants, and hence such shares are "publicly traded" for the purposes of FRS 13.

Instruments included

21.39 A financial asset is defined as any asset that is:

(a)   cash;

(b)   a contractual right to receive cash or another financial asset from another entity;

(c)   a contractual right to exchange financial instruments with another entity under conditions that are potentially favourable; or

(d)   an equity instrument of another entity.

A financial liability is defined as a contractual obligation:

(a)   to deliver cash or another financial asset to another entity; or

(b)   to exchange financial instruments with another entity under conditions that are potentially unfavourable.

An equity instrument is a residual interest in the assets of the entity after deducting all of its liabilities. [FRS 13(2)]

21.40 A financial instrument is defined as a contract that gives rise to a financial asset of one entity and a financial liability or equity instrument of another entity [FRS 13(2)]. A financial instrument is therefore effectively a contract which will ultimately lead to the receipt or payment of cash or to the acquisition or issue of shares.

21.41 Examples of financial instruments include:

(a) deposits with banks;

(b) trade debtors and creditors;

(c) shares;

(d) loans;

(e) bank overdrafts; and

(f) derivative instruments such as forwards, futures, options, swaps, etc.

21.42 Examples of items that do not meet this definition of financial instrument include tax liabilities (these arise from a statutory obligation rather than as a result of a contract), prepayments (unless it represents a prepayment in respect of a financial liability like interest expense) and deferred revenue.

21.43 Cash-settled commodity contracts, though strictly not financial assets and liabilities, are included on the grounds of their similarity with other financial instruments.

21.44 Short-term debtors and creditors are normally financial instruments. FRS 13 allows the preparer either to include them in all disclosures or to exclude them from all disclosures other than currency disclosures (see **21.71** below). [FRS 13(6)] An explanation of how such items have been dealt with should be provided. Short-term debtors and creditors are defined as non-derivative financial instruments included under certain balance sheet headings (debtors, prepayments, creditors within one year, accruals and provisions for liabilities and charges) and which mature or become payable within 12 months of the balance sheet date. [FRS 13(2)]

21.45 Non-equity shares should be dealt with in the same way as financial liabilities, but should be disclosed separately.

Exemptions

21.46 The following financial assets and financial liabilities are to be excluded from all the disclosures other than currency disclosures (see **21.71** below). [FRS 13(5)]

(a) interests in subsidiary, quasi-subsidiary and associated undertakings, partnerships and joint ventures which fall within the relevant FRS concerned with such interests, other than an interest in such entities that is held exclusively with a view to subsequent resale;

(b) employers' obligations to employees under employee share option and employee share schemes and any shares held in order to fulfil such obligations;

789

(c) pensions and other post-retirement benefit assets and liabilities which fall within the scope of SSAP 24 and UITF Abstract 6 ;

(d) rights and obligations under operating leases;

(e) entity's own equity shares and warrants and options on them, other than those that are held with a view to a subsequent resale;

(f) financial assets, financial liabilities and cash-settled commodity contracts of an insurance company or group.

Approach in FRS 13

21.47 The standard differentiates between three types of entity:

(a) 'normal corporate';

(b) bank or similar institution; and

(c) non-bank financial institution.

21.48 The distinction between the banks and 'normal corporates', reflects the fact that derivatives play an integral part in the wealth-generating activities of a bank and are often the primary source of a bank's net income, while, for a 'normal corporate', they are a 'by-product' of its operating activities or a result of the financing arrangements. The recognition of the third type of entity represents the ASB's acceptance that some non-bank financial institutions handle financial instruments in the same way as banks, so, under FRS 13, such entities can provide the disclosures in the form that best suits their circumstances, i.e., either the 'banking set' (with minor modifications – see **21.103** below) or the 'normal corporates' set.

21.49

A 'normal corporate' with a material banking subsidiary will need to consider whether to provide two sets of disclosures – a banking set in addition to the 'normal corporate' set. Even if the 'numbers' appear immaterial, some narrative disclosure might be appropriate as the risks involved and the way these are managed in the subsidiary will be materially different to the rest of the group.

21.50 All entities are required to provide both narrative and numerical disclosures: the former will explain the entity's chosen risk profile and its risk management policies, while the latter will show how these policies were implemented in the period and will give sufficient information to enable the reader of the accounts to evaluate any significant exposures. Narrative disclosures can be given in the operating and financial review (or similar statement), provided they are incorporated into the financial statements by means of a clear cross-reference. [FRS 13(23)] This cross-reference will make narrative disclosures subject to audit, irrespective of their location in the financial statements.

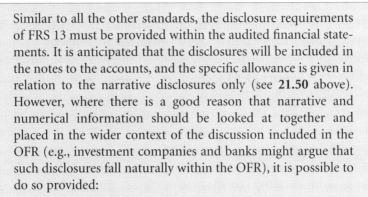

21.51   Similar to all the other standards, the disclosure requirements of FRS 13 must be provided within the audited financial statements. It is anticipated that the disclosures will be included in the notes to the accounts, and the specific allowance is given in relation to the narrative disclosures only (see **21.50** above). However, where there is a good reason that narrative and numerical information should be looked at together and placed in the wider context of the discussion included in the OFR (e.g., investment companies and banks might argue that such disclosures fall naturally within the OFR), it is possible to do so provided:

(a)   there is a clear cross-reference from the notes; and

(b)   the section of the OFR containing the required disclosures is clearly identified as comprising a note to the accounts (both in the heading of the section and in the contents page).

Where companies are intending to follow this approach, they should consider the balance between the danger of being accused of undermining the standard and the benefit of the presentation they want to achieve.

Narrative disclosures

21.52   The role that financial instruments have had during the period, in creating or changing the risks the entity faces in its activities, should be explained. [FRS 13(13 to 22)] The disclosures will deal *inter alia* with the entity's objectives and policies in respect of financial instruments and the strategies it has adopted for achieving these objectives. Though the focus of the disclosures is on risks arising from financial instruments, the standard envisages that such risks would be discussed in the context of the financial risk profile of the entity as a whole.

21.53   The narrative disclosures are meant to set the scene for the numerical information and to explain how the year-end figures reflect the agreed objectives and policies. Where the year-end figures are unrepresentative of the position during the year, the extent to which this is the case should be explained. [FRS 13(20)] Similarly, any changes to objectives, policies or risks from one period to another will need to be explained, so that a meaningful comparison can be made between the periods. [FRS 13(16)]

21.54   Narrative disclosures are subject to audit irrespective of their location in the financial statements (see **21.50** above). It is important, therefore, that the disclosures should be entirely factual, i.e, should not contain any statements of mere intent. [FRS 13 Appendix VII(26)]

21.55   The following extract illustrates the narrative disclosures. It includes a sensitivity analysis (see **21.98** and **21.99** below).

Extract 21.55

Diageo

30 June 1999

Risk management

The group's funding, liquidity and exposure to interest rate and foreign exchange rate risks are managed by the group's treasury department. Treasury operations are conducted within a framework of policies and guidelines authorised by the board, and are reported bimonthly to the board. This framework provides flexibility for the best execution of board approved strategies. The group uses derivative instruments for risk management purposes only, and these are transacted by specialist treasury personnel. The internal control environment is reviewed regularly.

Currency risk: the group publishes its financial statements in pounds sterling and conducts businesses in many foreign currencies. As a result, it is subject to foreign currency exchange risk due to exchange rate movements which will affect the group's transaction costs and the translation of the results and underlying net assets of its foreign subsidiaries.

The group hedges a substantial portion of its exposure to fluctuations on the translation into pounds sterling of its foreign currency net assets by holding net borrowings in foreign currencies and by using foreign currency swaps and cross-currency interest rate swaps. The group's current policy is to hedge currency exposure on its net assets before net borrowings at approximately the following percentages – 75 per cent for US dollars, 90 per cent for European currencies and 50 per cent for other significant currencies. Although this leaves the remaining part of the group's net assets subject to currency movements, this policy reduces the volatility of interest charge, interest cover, gearing and absolute debt levels. Exchange differences arising on the retranslation of foreign currency net borrowings and foreign exchange swaps are recognised in the statement of total recognised gains and losses to match exchange differences on foreign equity investments, in accordance with SSAP 20.

The group hedges, on a rolling 12 months basis, the translation of a proportion of its forecast future profits denominated in US dollars and European currencies, primarily with currency option cylinders (which consist of separate put and call options). This limits in part the translation exposure of the group's profit to movements in the

---

exchange rates. For the profits hedged with currency options cylinders, the group is only exposed to exchange rate movements within a specified range. The impact of exchange rate movements outside that range is taken by the counterparty to the hedge. Gains and losses on option cylinders are recognised in the underlying hedged periods.

For currencies in which there is an active market, the group hedges between 80 per cent and 100 per cent of transactional foreign exchange rate risk, up to 18 months forward, using forward exchange contracts. The gain or loss on the hedge is recognised at the same time as the underlying transaction.

Interest rate risk: the group has an exposure to interest rate risk and within this category of market risk is most vulnerable to changes in US dollar, sterling and euro interest rates. To manage interest rate risk, the group manages its proportion of fixed to variable rate borrowings within limits approved by the board, primarily through issuing long-term fixed rate bonds, medium-term notes and floating rate commercial paper, and by utilising interest rate swaps, cross-currency interest rate swaps and swaptions. The profile of fixed rate to floating rate net borrowings is maintained such that projected net borrowings are fully floating after five years, and are approximately 50 per cent fixed and 50 per cent floating within five years. The floating element of US dollar net borrowings within five years is partly protected using interest rate collars. In addition, where appropriate, the group uses forward rate agreements to manage short-term interest rate exposures. Swaps, swaptions, forward rate agreements and collars are accounted for as hedges.

Such management serves to increase the accuracy of the business planning process and to help manage the interest cover ratio, which the group currently aims to maintain at a minimum level of five times over the long term. The group's interest cover ratio may, however, go below such minimum level in the short term.

Liquidity risk: the group's strategy with regard to the maturity profile of borrowings is to maintain the proportion of borrowings maturing within one year at below 60 per cent of total borrowings, and to maintain the level of commercial paper at below 50 per cent of total borrowings. In addition, it is group policy to maintain backstop facility terms from relationship banks to support commercial paper obligations.

Credit risk: a large number of major international financial institutions are counterparties to the interest rate swaps, foreign exchange contracts and deposits transacted by the group. The group continually monitors its position and the credit ratings of its counterparties and credit exposure to each counterparty. The group is exposed only to counterparties which have a long-term credit rating of A − or better.

Commodity price risk: the group uses commodity futures and options to hedge against price risk in certain major agricultural commodities purchased by the Packaged Food business. All commodity futures and options contracts hedge a projected future purchase of raw material. Commodity futures are then either sold at the time the raw material is purchased or they are exchanged with the company manufacturing the raw material to determine the contract price. Commodity contracts are held in the balance sheet at fair value, but any gains and losses are deferred until the contracts are sold or exchanged. Open contracts at 30 June 1999 and gains and losses realised in the period or deferred at the balance sheet date were not significant.

Employee share schemes: during the year, the group changed its policy regarding the satisfaction of its obligations under the various employee share schemes. All further awards granted under such schemes will be satisfied by the transfer of existing shares. Previously, awards under certain schemes were satisfied by the issue of new equity. In general, awards made under equity schemes, including the LTIP, are hedged through the purchase of shares, while option grants, including those to be granted under the forthcoming SAYE schemes, are hedged through the purchase of call options. As an exception to this, resulting from the change in policy, options already granted under past SAYE schemes have been hedged through the purchase of shares.

Sensitivity analysis

For financial instruments held, the group has used a sensitivity analysis technique that measures the change in the fair value of the group's financial instruments from hypothetical changes in market rates.

The amounts generated from the sensitivity analysis are forward-looking estimates of market risk assuming certain adverse market conditions occur. Actual results in the future may differ materially from those projected results due to developments in the global financial markets which may cause fluctuations in interest and exchange rates to vary from the hypothetical amounts disclosed in the table below, which therefore should not be considered a projection of likely future events and losses.

The estimated changes in the fair values of borrowings, the guaranteed preferred securities and the associated derivative financial instruments at 30 June 1999 are set out in the table below. The basis of the estimated fair values is set out in note 18 to the financial statements.

The estimated changes in fair values for interest rate movements are based on an instantaneous decrease of 1 per cent (100 basis points) in the specific rate of interest applicable to each class of financial instruments from the levels effective at 30 June 1999, with all other variables remaining constant. The estimated changes in the fair value for foreign exchange rates are based on an instantaneous 10 per cent weakening in sterling against all other currencies from the levels applicable at 30 June 1999, with all other variables remaining constant. Such analysis is for illustrative purposes only – in practice market rates rarely change in isolation.

Sensitivity analysis table at 30 June 1999			
		Fair value changes arising from:	
	Estimated fair value	**1% decrease in interest rates**	**10% weakening in sterling**
	£m	**£m**	**£m**
Borrowings	(7,433)	(180)	(771)
Interest rate contracts	215	96	22
Foreign exchange contracts:			
Transaction	(22)	–	(134)
Balance sheet translation	11	–	3
Foreign exchange options:			
Profit translation	(6)	–	(84)
Guaranteed preferred Securities	(429)	(18)	(48)
Other financial net assets	103	8	10

Numerical disclosures

21.56 As explained in **21.47** and **21.48** above, FRS 13 differentiates between three types of entity and allows non-bank financial institutions to choose which set of disclosures is most suitable in their circumstances. Appendix II contains a full disclosure checklist for 'normal corporates'. A summary of the requirements for banks is included at the end of this chapter (see **21.102** below).

Interest rate risk disclosures

21.57 The FRS requires all financial liabilities and any significant financial assets to be analysed by principal currency and, within that, by reference to their interest rate profile. This analysis should reflect the effect of any non-option derivatives. For example, floating rate borrowing with a swap converting this borrowing from floating to fixed will be included under fixed rate liabilities. Where an instrument cannot be adequately reflected in the analysis it should be excluded and its effect explained. For example, where interest rates are capped, an explanation of the effect of capping will include how much is covered by the cap, how long the cap operates for, and the rate at which the cap is set.

21.58 The standard defines floating rate assets and liabilities as those where interest resets at least once a year. [FRS 13(2)] Hence, for the purposes of FRS 13, cash held on term deposits (3 months, 6 months and one year) is not a financial asset earning interest at fixed rates. For the purposes of FRS 13, financial assets and financial liabilities that have their interest rate reset less frequently than once a year are to be treated as fixed rate financial assets and financial liabilities. [FRS 13(2)]

21.59   Borrowings that have an interest rate that is fixed throughout their term, but are within 12 months of maturity, could be argued to be similar to floating rate liabilities in terms of the risks to which they expose the entity. In fact, the exposure draft that preceded FRS 13 (FRED 13) suggested that such borrowings should be reclassified into floating rate liabilities. This proposal has not been carried through into FRS 13 and, as a result, following the definition of fixed rate assets and liabilities (see **21.58** above), fixed rate borrowing within 12 months of maturity will continue to be presented as fixed rate financial liabilities.

21.60   The benchmark rate for determining interest payments for the floating rate financial liabilities and the benchmark rate for determining the interest return earned on floating rate financial assets should be disclosed. [FRS 13(30) and (32)] The standard does not require disclosure of the actual margin above or below the benchmark rate, but such disclosure might be necessary in order to comply with the Companies Act 1985. [Sch 4: 48(2) and (3)]

21.61   For fixed rate liabilities the weighted average interest rate and the weighted average period for which the rate is fixed should be disclosed. The disclosure is required to be given by reference to principal currency. The disclosure is also required for fixed rate financial assets (see **21.57** above). [FRS 13(30) and (32)]

21.62   The weighted average period until maturity for financial liabilities on which no interest is paid should be disclosed, analysed by principal currency. The disclosure is also required for fixed rate financial assets (see **21.57** above). [FRS 13(30) and (32)]

21.63   Financial liabilities where an interest cost is imputed and allocated in accordance with FRS 4, e.g., a zero coupon bond, should be treated as interest bearing. Financial assets accounted for in a similar way should be treated as interest bearing. [FRS 13(27)]

21.64   The standard does not address the issue of whether a non-interest bearing long-term liability (e.g., a provision or a long-term creditor) recorded at a discounted amount (with the discount unwound through the interest line) should be classified as financial liability on which no interest is paid. Discounting recognises the time value of money which is a real cost to the business. This is well understood where the transaction terms reflect the time value of money (e.g., deferred consideration): at the time of the transaction both parties to it agree that the amount of the deferred payment should be calculated by taking into account the time value of money, hence imputing an interest cost. Here an analogy with a zero-coupon bond can be seen easily and, per FRS 13(27) (see **21.63** above), such a liability will be treated as interest bearing. It is more difficult to see this analogy where discounting relates to a provision for a future liability (e.g., an onerous contract to pay rentals on a vacant property). But, nevertheless, it is still the same analogy: here the entity itself recognises that the amount of cash it needs to 'reserve' today is less, but that the interest earned on that cash will also have to be 'reserved' and will not be available for anything else in the business (similar to interest accruing to the zero-coupon bond holder). However, due to the lack of definitive guidance in the standard as to how such items should be treated and the lack of definitive guidance on discounting, other interpretations are possible and, therefore, if the terms of an instrument cannot be reflected adequately in the required tabular disclosure, further explanation should be given.

21.65 The following extract illustrates the numerical interest disclosure.

Extract 21.65

Diageo

30 June 1999

Interest risk management

At 30 June 1999, after taking account of interest rate swaps, cross currency interest rate swaps and forward rate agreements, the currency and interest rate profile of the financial liabilities and assets of the group was as follows:

	Floating rate £m	Fixed rate £m	Financial (liabilities)/ assets on which no interest is paid £m	Total £m	Weighted average fixed interest rate %	Weighted average period for which rate is fixed Years
Financial liabilities:						
US dollar	(2,136)	(1,895)	(115)	(4,146)	7.5	2.6
Euro	(1,124)	(690)	(3)	(1,817)	4.2	2.1
Sterling	(538)	(374)	(91)	(1,003)	7.4	1.5
Other	(301)	(53)	–	(354)	15.2	1.0
	(4,099)	(3,012)	(209)	(7,320)	6.9	2.3
Guaranteed preferred securities	–	(388)	–	(388)	9.3	5.5
Financial assets:						
US dollar	244	129	116	489	6.9	9.4
Euro	362	–	24	386	–	–
Sterling	258	40	17	315	5.5	3.7
Other	235	–	4	239	–	–
	1,099	169	161	1,429	6.6	8.1
Net financial liabilities	(3,000)	(3,231)	(48)	(6,279)	7.2	2.4

> Floating rate financial liabilities bear interest based on short-term interbank rates (predominantly six months LIBOR) and commercial paper rates.
>
> Interest bearing financial liabilities comprise bonds, medium-term notes, commercial paper issued, money market loans, forward rate agreements, net obligations under finance leases and bank overdrafts. Financial liabilities on which no interest is paid consist of provisions for liabilities and charges payable after one year in respect of vacant properties, employees incentive plans and disposals of £88 million; long-term creditors of £60 million; recourse in respect of franchisee loans of £38 million; and derivatives financial instruments of £23 million. Interest bearing financial assets comprise cash, money market deposits and certain fixed asset investments, loans and debtors. Financial assets on which no interest is paid include certain fixed asset investments, loans and debtors.
>
> In addition to the interest rate and currency swaps reflected in the table above, the group has £1,930 million notional principal of US dollar interest rate collars which mature between 31 December 1999 and 30 June 2003 and which have a floor of 5.03% and a cap of 7.30%.

Liquidity

21.66 A maturity analysis is required for all financial liabilities. Companies are already required to analyse their borrowings and lease obligations by the Companies Act 1985, FRS 4 and SSAP 21. FRS 13 extended the requirement to all financial liabilities and almost imperceptibly amended the FRS 4 time bands for all reporting entities so that all maturity disclosures can be presented in one note. The effect of the amendment is that the treatment of the amounts falling due exactly two years and five years after the balance sheet date is now unambiguous. For example, an amount due in exactly five years falls within the time band 'in more than 2 years but no more than 5 years'; previously it could have been included within the next time band. The new bands are:

(a) in one year or less, or on demand;

(b) in more than one year but no more than two years;

(c) in more than two years but no more than five years; and

(d) in more than five years.

21.67 The maturity profile is determined in the same way as in FRS 4, by reference to the earliest date on which payment can be required or on which the liability falls due. [FRS 13(38)] The amount analysed is the carrying amount, i.e., not necessarily the amount which will be paid on maturity. [FRS 13(39)]

21.68 The ASB's Statement '*Operating and Financial Review*' encouraged companies to provide the maturity profile of the committed borrowing facilities. This is a requirement under FRS 13: any material undrawn committed borrowing facilities should be analysed between those expiring within one year or less, in more than one year but not more than two years, and in more than two years. [FRS 13(40)] Where, in accordance with FRS 4, committed facilities have been taken into account in determining maturity of borrowings, they should be excluded from the analysis of the undrawn facilities. [FRS 13(41)]

21.69 The fact that a facility is subject to an annual review does not necessarily mean that it should be disclosed as that expiring within one year or less. If the annual review is there to establish whether the facility is available at all, the expiry date is within one year: there is no certainty that it will be renewed in one year's time. Where it is only certain terms (e.g., pattern of draw-down) that are subject to an annual review, the expiry date is the date specified in the agreement. In the latter case the extent to which the facility is subject to an annual review should be disclosed.

21.70 The extract below shows how these disclosures might be met.

Extract 21.70

The EMI Group

31 March 1999

Maturity of financial liabilities

The maturity profile of the Group's financial liabilities, other than short-term creditors such as trade creditors and accruals, at 31 March 1999 was as follows.

	£m
In one year or less, or on demand	848.3
In more than one year but not more than two years	8.6
In more than two years but not more than five years	72.0
In more than five years	11.2
	940.1

Undrawn facilities
The Group has various borrowing facilities available to it. The undrawn committed facilities available at 31 March 1999 in respect of which all conditions precedent had been met at that date were as follows.

	£m
Expiring in one year or less	505.1
Expiring in more than one year but not more than two years	18.5
Expiring in more than two years	69.1
	592.7

Currency risk

21.71   FRS 13 requires entities to provide an analysis of the net amount of monetary assets and liabilities by reference to the principal functional currencies of its operations. The short-term debtors and creditors exemption is not available in respect of this disclosure, i.e., all monetary assets and liabilities need to be considered. The analysis should only deal with assets and liabilities giving rise to exchange gains and losses in the profit and loss account (unmatched assets and liabilities). It should exclude foreign currency borrowings which qualify as hedges of foreign equity investments where, under SSAP 20, gains and losses on these are taken to the statement of total recognised gains and losses.

21.72   As with interest rate risk disclosures, the effect of non-option derivatives should be taken into account, while the effect of those instruments that cannot be adequately reflected in the analysis should be disclosed separately. For example, where an entity enters into a forward contract to sell US dollars for sterling, in order to hedge a debtor balance denominated in US dollars, the debtor balance should be viewed as if it were denominated in sterling.

21.73

> The standard does not address the question as to whether the table should include a loan denominated in the functional currency of the parent company where that loan is given to a foreign subsidiary (assuming the loan is not treated as a permanent equity stake in that subsidiary). The argument for inclusion could be built as follows: the loan is recorded as a foreign currency loan in the books of the subsidiary; it is retranslated at the year end with a resulting foreign exchange gain or loss; this gain or loss is not reversed on consolidation and no consolidation adjustment is made; hence, there is an impact on the group profit and loss account. The counter-argument is that the required disclosure is about the exposures of the group as a whole, and on that basis it would be misleading to overstate the exposures by including an intra-group item. Both answers are acceptable, provided the treatment of the loan is explained.

21.74   The extract below shows how these disclosures might be met.

> ### Extract 21.74
>
> The EMI Group
>
> 31 March 1999
>
> **Currency exposures**
>
> As explained on page 36 in the Operating and financial review, the Group's objectives in managing currency exposures arising from its

net investments overseas (its structural currency exposures) are to maintain appropriate levels of borrowings by currency to hedge partially against currency depreciation. Gains and losses arising from these structural exposures are recognised in the statement of total recognised gains and losses.

The table below shows the Group's currency exposures, being those trading assets and liabilities (or non-structural exposures) that give rise to the net currency gains and losses recognised in the profit and loss account. Such exposures comprise the monetary assets and monetary liabilities of the Group that are not denominated in the operating (or 'functional') currency of the operating unit involved, other than certain non-sterling borrowings treated as hedges of net investments in overseas operations.

At 31 March 1999, these exposures were as follows.

Functional currency of Group operation	Net foreign currency monetary assets (liabilities)				
	Sterling £m	US dollar £m	Yen £m	Euro £m	Other £m
Sterling	n/a	13.0	1.8	(1.1)	7.5
US dollar	(5.5)	n/a	–	0.1	(0.1)
Yen	(0.2)	(0.1)	n/a	–	0.1
Euro	4.2	(1.9)	–	n/a	1.6
Other	(2.6)	(6.7)	0.5	0.1	0.8
Total	(4.1)	4.3	2.3	(0.9)	9.9

21.75 The exposure draft of FRS 13 suggested a further requirement in relation to foreign currency risk: an analysis of structural exposures, i.e., an analysis showing the extent to which foreign net assets are matched by foreign borrowings. This proposal was not carried through into the standard, but later resurfaced as an exposure draft amendment to SSAP 20 which again got withdrawn (see **26.95** below). However, some companies still choose to provide this information: Unigate PLC (see below) shows its matched exposures and states that it has no unmatched ones.

Extract 21.75

Unigate PLC

31 March 1999

Currency analysis of net assets

In accordance with the Group's policy to hedge all contractual commitments, all of the Group's monetary assets and liabilities are denominated in, or are hedged to, the functional currency of the subsidiary concerned.

The Group's net assets by currency at 31 March 1999 were as follows.

	Sterling £m	Euro £m	US$ £m	Total £m
Net cash/(borrowings) by currency	163.3	118.1	(94.5)	186.9
Currency swaps	30.7	(124.2)	93.5	–
Net cash position	194.0	(6.1)	(1.0)	186.9
Other net assets	423.2	37.1	(1.6)	458.7
Total net assets	617.2	31.0	(2.6)	645.6

Net assets includes minority interests. No gain or loss arises in the profit and loss account in respect of any of the above foreign currency assets and liabilities because such foreign currency assets and liabilities are either denominated in the currency of the Group operation to which they belong (the functional currency), or they provide a hedge against a foreign equity investment.

Fair values

21.76 FRS 13 requires companies to disclose aggregate fair values, together with the carrying amount, for each category of financial assets and liabilities. Entities can choose whether to disclose a single net figure for each category of financial assets and liabilities or to disclose two 'gross' figures – one for the items with a positive fair value and one for the items with a negative fair value. Where fair value is not materially different from the carrying amount, the carrying amount can be used as an approximation. The methods used to calculate fair values should be disclosed.

21.77 In limited circumstances where it is not practicable to determine fair value of a non-traded instrument, reasons for this should be disclosed together with information about the principal characteristics of the underlying financial asset or liability. The standard does emphasise that the exemption is only available in extreme circumstances and that the following factors would normally be present for it to apply: the instrument is unique; the cash flows cannot be predicted reliably; and a reliable valuation model is not available from either internal or external sources.

21.78 It should not be assumed that where an asset or liability is short-term and/or at floating rate (e.g. cash, bank overdraft, floating rate loan), the fair value will always approximate carrying amount. For example, floating rate debt that does not re-price to market frequently can change in value if the credit rating of a company deteriorates or improves. Such a change can be material.

21.79 Financial instruments should be divided into "appropriate categories" for the purpose of the fair value disclosures. What constitutes such a category is not defined in FRS 13, though the guidance in FRS 13(46) suggests that the purpose for which assets and liabilities are held can be used in determining a category. FRS 13(47) goes on to state that if the item is a hedge, it may be useful to indicate the link between the hedge and the hedged item. Hence, it is possible to have a disclosure along the following lines:

	Fair value	Carrying amount
Financial liability x	'...'	'...'
Interest rate swaps used to hedge it	'...'	'...'
Financial liability y	'...'	'...'
Interest rate swaps used to hedge it	'...'	'...'

21.80   The extract below shows how the fair value disclosure requirements might be met.

Extract 21.80

Scottish Power Plc

31 March 1999

Current value of financial instruments	At 31 March 1999		At 31 March 1998	
	Book amount £m	Current value £m	Book amount £m	Current value £m
Short-term debt and current portion of long-term debt	843.6	843.6	1,035.7	1,035.7
Long-term debt	1,684.5	1,829.3	1,032.4	1,101.4
Total debt	2,528.1	2,672.9	2,068.1	2,137.1
Interest rate swaps	–	8.0	–	51.7
Interest rate caps	(3.4)	(0.6)	(4.7)	(3.0)
Cross currency interest rate swaps	–	1.6	–	3.1
Total financial instruments	2,524.7	2,753.9	2,063.4	2,198.9

The assumptions used to estimate current fair values of debt and other financial instruments are summarised below.

(i)   For cash, short-term deposits and short-term borrowings (uncommitted borrowing, commercial paper, and short-term borrowings under the committed facilities) the book value approximates to fair value because of their short maturities.

(ii)   The fair values of all quoted euro bonds are based on their closing clean market price converted at the spot rate of exchange as appropriate.

> (iii)   The fair values of the sterling bond 2001 and the European Investment Bank loans have been calculated by discounting their future cash flows at market rates adjusted to reflect the redemption adjustments allowed under each agreement.
>
> (iv)   The fair values of the sterling interest rate swaps and sterling interest rate caps have been estimated by calculating the present value of estimated cash flows.
>
> (v)   The fair values of the cross currency interest rate swaps have been estimated by adding the present values of the two sides of each swap. The present value of each side of the swap is calculated by discounting the estimated future cash flows for that side, using the appropriate market discount rates for that currency in effect at the balance sheet date.
>
> (vi)   The fair values of unquoted debt have been calculated by discounting the estimated cash flows for each instrument at the appropriate market discount rate in the currency of issue in effect at the balance sheet date.

Hedging disclosures

21.81   These disclosures are required for all hedges and aim to make the effects of hedge accounting transparent: hedge accounting involves matching of gains and losses on the hedge with those on the item being hedged. Hence, the disclosures deal with the timing of recognition of hedging gains and losses. The amounts required to be disclosed are as follows:

(a)   the cumulative aggregate gains and losses that are unrecognised at the balance sheet date. If an item's fair value is not disclosed under the standard, any gain or loss on that item need not be included in this disclosure;

(b)   the cumulative aggregate gains and losses carried forward in the balance sheet at the balance sheet date, pending their recognition in the profit and loss account;

(c)   the extent to which the gains and losses disclosed under (a) and (b) are expected to be recognised in the profit and loss account in the next year;

(d)   the amounts of gains and losses included in this year's profit and loss account that arose in previous years and were brought forward at the start of the current year, either as unrecognised or included in the balance sheet. [FRS 13(59)]

21.82   A 'hedge' is not defined, though there is an explanation within the narrative disclosure requirements: it is "an instrument that individually, or with other instruments, has a value or cash flow that is expected, wholly or partly, to move inversely with changes in the value or cash flows of the position being hedged". [FRS 13(22)]

21.83 It is often argued that it is not meaningful to disclose hedging gains and losses where a company hedges all of its trading transactions denominated in foreign currencies, i.e., where effectively the decision to hedge forms part of a larger decision whether to enter into a transaction in the first instance. The ASB argued that the relevance of these gains and losses to the user of the accounts is quite apparent – they show whether the adopted hedging strategy left shareholders better or worse off.

21.84 There is then a question at to whether there is a gain or loss to be disclosed once a foreign exchange item has been recorded at the contracted rate (i.e., a rate specified in a forward foreign exchange contract taken out to hedge that item). The answer depends on what item is involved. Below, we consider a fixed asset; an asset purchased with a view to resale; stock and a debtor.

(a) *Fixed asset.* FRS 13(60) and (61) specifically address this situation and state that no disclosure is required on pragmatic grounds – the recognition of a gain or loss deferred as a result of adjusting the carrying amount of a fixed asset will be through the depreciation of that asset. Hence, the required record-keeping is admitted to be too onerous to insist on such disclosure.

(b) *Asset for resale.* The argument above does not apply if the asset is purchased with a view to subsequent resale – disclosures are required. The gain or loss deferred should be calculated by retranslating the asset at the spot rate at the time of the transaction and comparing the result to its carrying amount. The deferred gain or loss will be recognised simultaneously with the disposal of the asset.

(c) *Stock.* An exemption on pragmatic grounds could be argued for stock items as successfully as it has been for fixed assets, but the standard does not give such an exemption – disclosures are required. The gain or loss deferred should be calculated by retranslating the stock at the spot rate at the time of the transaction and comparing the result to its carrying amount. The time of recognition of the deferred gain or loss will be in line with stock utilisation in production or its subsequent resale, whichever is appropriate.

(d) *Debtor.* The argument for fixed assets does not apply – disclosures are required. The gain or loss deferred should be calculated by retranslating the debtor at the spot rate at the year end and comparing the result to its carrying amount. The time of recognition of the deferred gain or loss will be when the debtor pays.

21.85 Another contentious issue is that the required disclosure is one-sided, since the matching losses and gains are not shown, and hence, can be seen as misleading. This issue was looked at by the UITF in order to determine the exact requirement of FRS 13(59). The words of the standard are not very clear, especially where an entity uses a financial instrument to hedge another financial instrument. Close reading of FRS 13 suggests that it is only disclosure of the gain or loss arising on the hedging instrument that is requried, hence the UITF did not issue a pronouncement on the subject (see UITF Information Sheet 33). Clearly, if a company wants to give a more balanced picture, FRS 13 does not preclude it from doing so, provided the requirements are met and the additional information is properly described.

21.86 There are some practical problems in estimating the amount of gain or loss that will be recognised in the next year's profit and loss account in respect of an instrument (e.g., an interest rate swap) that has more than one year to its maturity. There is no guidance in FRS 13, but it would appear sensible to assume that the recognition should reflect the valuation model used. For example, an interest rate swap is valued by using a 'bond model' of valuation, i.e., by discounting the cash flows associated with the two 'legs' of the swap. The amount expected to be recognised in the next year is the next year's discounted cash flow using the current interest yield curve. It is worth noting, however, that the amount calculated is unlikely to be the actual gain or loss that will be recognised in the next year due to changes in yield curves and the time value adjustment to the remaining future cash flows associated with the swap. Where a company does not have an in-house capability to value its instruments, any reasonable approximation to that amount will normally be acceptable.

21.87 Similarly, there is a question as to the timing of recognition of the gain or loss on an option. If it is a 'european option', i.e., an option that can only be exercised on a specified date, then that date should probably be taken as the date for recognition. If it is an 'American option', i.e., an option that can be exercised at any point up to and including the specified date, the expected exercise date could be taken to be the recognition date.

21.88 Where an instrument, previously accounted for as a hedge, is reclassified during the period and no longer accounted for as a hedge and, as a result, a gain or a loss that arose in previous years is recognised in the profit and loss account, the amount of any such gain or loss should be disclosed. [FRS 13(62)]

21.89 The requirement in the paragraph above does not apply to a situation where an instrument is terminated but the underlying exposure is still in place, and on that basis a company chooses to spread the termination payment or receipt (which represents a loss or a gain respectively) over the remaining life of the underlying exposure. The amount deferred will need to be disclosed per **21.80** above as it represents a gain or a loss carried forward in the balance sheet at the balance sheet date, pending its recognition in the profit and loss account.

21.90 The extract below shows how these disclosures might be met.

Extract 21.90

Scottish Power Plc

31 March 1999

The group's policy is to hedge the following exposures:

(a) interest rate using interest swaps, both sterling and cross currency, caps, collars and forward foreign currency contracts;

(b) currency exposures on foreign denominated debt and future purchases/sales using currency swaps and forwards and spot foreign currency contracts.

Gains and losses on instruments used for hedging are not recognised until the exposure that is being hedged is itself recognised. Unrecognised gains and losses on instruments used for hedging, and the movements therein, are as follows.

	Gains £m	Losses £m	Total net gains/ losses £m
Unrecognised (losses) on hedges at 1 April 1998	(1.6)	(60.2)	(61.8)
Losses arising in previous years that were recognised in 1998-99	9.7	6.5	16.2
Gains and (losses) arising before 1 April 1998 that were not recognised in 1998-99	8.1	(53.7)	(45.6)
Gains and (losses) arising in 1998-99 that were not recognised in 1998-99	2.6	(38.0)	(35.4)
Unrecognised gains and (losses) on hedges at 31 March 1999	10.7	(91.7)	(81.0)

Gains and (losses) expected to be recognised in 1999-2000	(4.6)	(23.6)	(28.2)
Gains and (losses) expected to be recognised in 2000-01 or later	15.3	(68.1)	(52.8)

The total net unrecognised loss of £81.0 million principally represents the opportunity cost of protecting the group's interest charge against movements in interest rates at a time when interest rates were higher than at 31 March 1999.

Instruments held or issued for trading

21.91 Often within a 'normal corporate', instruments held for trading result from speculative transactions, so the risk associated with them is different from that associated with other financial assets and liabilities. FRS 13 requires such instruments to be disclosed separately from those used for risk management purposes.

21.92 Period-end fair values of financial assets and, separately, of financial liabilities held or issued for trading are required, supplemented by the average fair values over the period where the period-end position is unrepresentative of the entity's typical position during the year. The average is to be calculated by reference to the daily figures, or where these are not used, by reference to the most frequent interval that the entity's systems generate for management purposes. [FRS 13(57)]

21.93 The net gain or loss from trading included in the profit and loss account is also required to be disclosed, analysed by type of financial instrument, business activity, risk or in any other way consistent with the entity's management of this activity. If the net gain or loss from trading is analysed other than by type of instrument, then a description of the instruments involved should be given for each line in the analysis. [FRS 13(57)]

21.94 The disclosures in the extract below are pre-FRS 13 and would be fully compliant with the requirements explained in the paragraphs above, provided that either commodity swaps/options are argued to be materially one type of financial instrument, or the net trading gain of $25 million included in 1998 income was analysed between commodity swaps and commodity options.

> **Extract 21.94**
>
> Royal Dutch/Shell Group of Companies
>
> 31 December 1998
>
> Some Group companies operate as traders in crude oil, natural gas and oil products. These companies use commodity swaps and options in the management of their price and timing risks. In addition, some other Group companies use commodity swaps and options to hedge

the price and timing risks on underlying business transactions. The effects of transactions in these instruments are reflected in sales and purchase costs.

The total contract/notional amounts and estimated fair values of Group companies' commodity swaps/options at December 31 are given in the table below.

	1998		1997	$million
	Contract/ notional amount	Estimated fair value	Contract/ notional amount	Estimated fair value
Trading purposes				
Assets	658	67	610	58
Liabilities	957	(79)	626	(77)
Not for trading purposes	671	(25)	25	1

The average fair values of commodity swaps/options used for trading purposes during 1998 were: assets of $80 million (1997: $31 million) and liabilities of $65 million (1997: $36 million). Trading gains of $25 million arising on commodity swaps/options were included in 1998 income (1997: gains of $40 million).

Group companies also enter into forward sales and purchase contracts for commodities which may be settled by the physical delivery or receipt of the commodity. These contracts are not included in the above amounts.

Commodity contracts

21.95 Cash-settled commodity contracts, though strictly not financial assets and liabilities, are included in the scope of the standard on the grounds of their similarity with other financial instruments. 'Cash-settled' covers contracts which are normally extinguished other than by physical delivery in accordance with general market practice. [FRS 13(2)]

21.96 The use of such contracts needs to be explained in the narrative and their fair values should be disclosed. In addition, they should be included in the disclosures about instruments used for hedging and those used for trading, as appropriate (see **21.80** to **21.93** above). [FRS 13(64)]

21.97 In exceptional circumstances an exemption from these disclosures can be claimed on 'seriously prejudicial' grounds. This would apply where the commodity market in which an entity operates is illiquid and dominated by very few participants, so that the disclosure would move the market significantly. If this exemption is taken, an entity is required to state this fact and also, to explain the reasons for its decision not to disclose information. [FRS 13(65)]

21.98   The example below shows how United Utilities deals with the disclosure of fair value of contracts for differences, the cash-settled commodity contracts in which it deals.

Extract 21.98

United Utilities Plc

31 March 1999

Contracts for differences

The fair value of outstanding CfDs at 31 March 1999 was £(258.2) million (1998 – £(299.6) million). The approximate effect on the fair value of CfDs from a 10 per cent increase in average pool purchase price is £104.3 million (1998 – £112.7 million). The approximate effect on the fair value of CfDs from a 10 per cent decrease in average pool purchase price is £(104.3) million (1998 – £(112.7) million). The movement in fair values of CfDs will not result in any immediate changes to the group's financial statements since fair values are not recognised on the group's balance sheet.

The fair values of outstanding CfDs were based on the difference between projected Pool prices and agreed contract prices, discounted at an appropriate cost of capital. The calculation of fair value takes into account a number of complex factors, including future Pool prices, plant availability, plant operating costs and inflation indices. The principal influence on the fair value is the projected Pool price. For the purposes of these calculations the projected Pool price is based on historic data.

Market price risk

21.99   Disclosure of market price risk is encouraged but not required by FRS 13. But where an entity chooses to disclose market price risk it should do so in a way that reflects its exposures and how they are managed. This could be either by giving comprehensive disclosure of its positions at the balance sheet date, or by disclosure of risk based on an appropriate risk management methodology, or by a combination of methodologies, e.g., sensitivity analysis, 'gap' analysis, 'duration' of instruments, value at risk. Whatever method is chosen, the entity should disclose the methodology used and its objectives and limitations. [FRS 13(66)]

21.100   Some companies disclosed their market price risk prior to FRS 13 becoming mandatory. Reuters Holdings PLC and BP referred to value at risk: the former used it to assess the potential impact of exchange rate volatility on reported earnings, while the latter did so to estimate the exposure on its trading activity. Diageo, in extract **21.55** above, explains the use of sensitivity analysis to measure the change in the fair value of the group's financial instruments from hypothetical changes in market rates.

Accounting policies

21.101   SSAP 2 *Disclosure of accounting policies* requires financial statements to include clear, fair and concise explanations of all material or critical accounting policies adopted.

21.102   FRS 13 does not contain any new requirements on this but emphasises that in relation to financial instruments such disclosure is of particular importance since entities can currently adopt a wide variety of accounting treatments. The standard goes on to give a list of matters that might require disclosure. The list is lengthy and goes far beyond the level of detail that companies have been used to prior to FRS 13. [FRS 13(74–76)]

Extract 21.102

Scottish Power Plc

31 March 1999

Financial instruments

Debt instruments

All borrowings are stated at the fair value of consideration received after deduction of issue costs. The issue costs and interest payable on bonds are charged to the profit and loss account at a constant rate over the life of the bond.

Interest rate swaps

Interest rate swap agreements are used to manage interest rate exposures and are accounted for using hedge accounting. In order to qualify for hedge accounting, the company's notional amount of interest rate swaps and caps must be less than or equal to existing variable rate debt. Amounts payable or receivable in respect of these agreements are recognised as adjustments to interest expense over the period of the contracts. The cash flows from interest rate swaps and gains and losses arising on terminations of interest rate swaps are recognised as returns on investments and servicing of finance. Where associated debt is not retired in conjunction with the termination of an interest swap, gains and losses are deferred and are amortised to interest expense over the remaining life of the associated debt to the extent that such debt remains outstanding.

Interest rate caps

Interest rate caps are used to limit interest rate exposures. The premiums on these contracts are amortised over the period of the contracts and are disclosed as interest expense.

Forward contracts

The company enters into forward contracts for the purchase and/or sale of foreign currencies in order to manage its exposure to fluctuations in currency rates. Unrealised gains and losses on contracts are

---

> not accounted for until the maturity of the contract. The cash flows from forward purchase contracts are classified in a manner consistent with the underlying nature of the hedged transaction.
>
> *Premiums and discounts*
>
> Premiums and discounts arising on the early repayment of borrowings are written off to the profit and loss account as incurred.
>
> *Contracts for Differences (CfDs)*
>
> The company uses CfDs to minimise exposure to Pool price variations. The cost or the income attributable to CfDs is recorded in the accounting records when settlement is made. Where delivery under the CfD has taken place prior to the period end, adjustments are made to account for the known variances between the contract strike price and the Pool price on the date of delivery.

Banks and similar institutions

21.103 As explained in **21.47** above, the standard differentiates between three types of entity. Banks and similar institutions form one of the three types. There is a separate set of disclosure requirements contained in part B of FRS 13. Other financial institutions can opt to adopt the 'banking set' of disclosures (part C of FRS 13). The table below compares the requirements for banks to those for 'normal corporates'.

'Normal corporates'. [FRS 13(26)–(76)]	Banks and similar institutions. [FRS 13(86)–(116)] Modifications for non-bank financial institutions are noted. [FRS 13(123)–(133)].
Interest-rate risk	
Financial liabilities (and any significant financial assets) should be analysed by principal currency and, within that, by reference to their interest-rate profile. This analysis should reflect the effect of any non-optional derivatives, e.g., floating-rate borrowing with a swap converting this borrowing from floating to fixed will be included under fixed-rate liabilities.	An interest-rate sensitivity gap table is required for assets and liabilities in the non-trading book. The table will show the net position for each time band after taking account of non-optional derivatives which alter the interest basis of the assets and liabilities in the non-trading book. The allocation to time bands should be by reference to the earlier of the next interest-rate repricing date and the maturity date.

Currency risk	
Net amount of monetary assets and liabilities should be analysed by reference to principal functional currencies of operations involved. This analysis will only deal with assets and liabilities giving rise to exchange gains and losses in the profit and loss account, i.e., with 'unmatched assets and liabilities'. Foreign currency borrowings which qualify as hedges of foreign equity investments should be excluded from the analysis, since gains and losses on these under SSAP 20 are taken to the statement of total recognised gains and losses.	Same disclosures as for 'normal corporates' should be given in respect of the monetary assets and liabilities in the non-trading book. In addition, banks should disclose details of their structural currency exposures, since, in a bank, these arise primarily from financial instruments.
Liquidity	
A maturity analysis is required for all financial liabilities and, if any, material undrawn committed borrowing facilities. Companies were already required to analyse their borrowings and lease obligations by Sch 4 Companies Act 1985, FRS 4 and SSAP 21. FRS 13 extends the requirement to *all* financial liabilities and, in order to enable the preparer to combine all maturity disclosures in one note, it amends the FRS 4 time bands.	Not addressed in FRS 13, but extensive disclosures are already required by Sch 9 Companies Act 1985. Non-bank financial institutions are required to provide this disclosure.
Fair values	
Aggregate fair values should be disclosed, together with the carrying amount, for each category of financial assets and liabilities. Entities can choose whether to disclose a single net figure for each category of financial assets and liabilities or to disclose two 'gross' figures: one for the items with a positive fair value and one for the items with a negative fair value.	Same disclosures as for 'normal corporates' should be given in respect of all financial assets and liabilities in the trading book and for the following financial assets and liabilities in the non-trading book: (a) all derivatives; (b) listed/publicly traded securities; (c) other items for which a liquid and active market exists.

In limited circumstances where it is not practicable to determine fair value of a non-traded instrument, reasons for this should be disclosed, together with information about the principal characteristics of the underlying financial asset or liability.	For non-bank financial institutions, the requirements are the same as for 'normal corporates'.
Instruments held for trading	
Often, within a 'normal corporate', these result from speculative transactions, so risk associated with them is different from that associated with other financial assets and liabilities. Such instruments will need to be disclosed separately and some additional disclosures might be required.	Banks are required to disclose the highest, lowest and average exposure of their trading book, using value at risk or any other market price risk measure used for market price risk management and approved by the regulator. Such measures are deemed most appropriate for the trading book in view of the short-term nature of the risks and the rapid changes in the types of risk held in it.
Hedges	
These disclosures are required for all hedges and aim to make the effects of hedge accounting transparent: hedge accounting involves matching of gains and losses on the hedge with those on the item being hedged, i.e., deferral of gains and losses, so the disclosures deal with the timing of recognition of hedging gains and losses.	Same as for 'normal corporates'.
Market price rise	
This disclosure is encouraged but not required. However, if an entity chooses to provide this information, it should also disclose the method used in the calculations, together with its objectives and limitations. Any significant assumptions made should also be disclosed.	Same as for 'normal corporates'.

Future developments

Company law review

21.104 The consultation document published by the company law review Steering Group in March 2000 considered relative roles of statute and standard-setting bodies in setting the form and content of company accounts and reports. Currently, there is a considerable overlap between statute and accounting standards. Under the proposals, only the overall framework and purpose of the accounting and reporting documents will be dealt with by statute; the power to set all the detailed rules on accounting treatments and disclosures will be delegated to an appropriate standard-setting body. As a result, the rules relating to the disclosure of accounting policies, explained in **21.3** to **21.9** and **21.21** above, and to disclosure of financial commitments (**21.23** to **21.30** above) would fall within the ambit of accounting standards.

21.105 The proposed split of responsibilities will be accompanied by a statutory requirement on companies to prepare accounts in accordance with applicable accounting standards set by a prescribed body. This is different to the current position whereby companies have to state whether accounts have been prepared in accordance with applicable accounting standards (see **21.10** above). Departure from the requirements of the Act, explained in **5.10** and **21.17** above, will remain possible.

FRED 21 Accounting policies

21.106 In addition to the above developments, the issue by the ASB of the Statement of principles for financial reporting prompted a review of SSAP 2. FRED 21 Accounting policies (see also **5.54** to **5.58** above) distinguished between accounting policies and estimation techniques. The former are applied by an entity to reflect the effect of transactions through recognition, measurement and presentation, while the latter are the methods of arriving at values at which transactions are then recorded. The disclosures proposed by the FRED cover:

(a) a description of material accounting policies and estimation techniques;

(b) details of any change to an existing accounting policy, together with the reason for the change and its resulting effect on both current and prior periods (by contrast, disclosure of a change to an estimation technique will only be required where the effect of a change to a technique is material);

(c)   where this is the case, a statement of the fact that financial statements have been prepared on the basis of assumptions that differ from either the going concern assumption or the accruals concept;

(d)   any material departure from the requirements of the Companies Act, the resons for it and its effect (consistent with UITF 7 – see **21.17**)

22   Post balance sheet events

22 Post balance sheet events

Introduction

22.1 The Act requires that all liabilities and losses which have arisen or are likely to arise relating to a period prior to the balance sheet date should be taken into account, including those which only become apparent between the balance sheet date and the date on which it is signed on behalf of the board of directors. [Sch 4: 12] This requirement does no more than give statutory authority to part of the standard practice required under SSAP 17.

22.2 Post balance sheet events are defined by SSAP 17 as those which occur between the balance sheet date and the date on which the financial statements are approved by the board of directors. A distinction is made between two principal types of post balance sheet events:

(a) adjusting events, being those that require adjustment of the financial statements and,

(b) non-adjusting events, being those that may require disclosure but do not require adjustment of the financial statements.

The statement also discusses the treatment of 'window dressing' transactions.

Adjusting events

22.3 Adjusting events are defined in SSAP 17 as post balance sheet events which provide additional evidence of conditions that existed at the balance sheet date. The financial statements should be changed to take account of the additional evidence provided by such events. [SSAP 17(19)]

22.4 Examples of adjusting events are:

(a) the renegotiation of amounts owing by debtors, or the insolvency of a debtor;

(b) a fall in selling price of a product, causing the net realisable value of stocks to fall below cost;

(c)   the settlement of litigation arising from events which took place prior to the year end; and

(d)   changes in rates of taxation based on profits taken up in the financial statements.

Other examples of adjusting events are contained in the appendix to SSAP 17.

22.5   Special consideration should be given to post balance sheet events such as a deterioration in operating results and in the financial position of the company which, although they do not provide direct evidence of conditions existing at the balance sheet date, may raise doubts as to whether the accounts can properly be prepared under the going concern concept. SSAP 17 requires that financial statements should be changed if post balance sheet events indicate that application of the going concern concept to the whole or a material part of the company is not appropriate.

Non-adjusting events

22.6   Non-adjusting events are defined in SSAP 17 as post balance sheet events which concern conditions which did not exist at the balance sheet date. They do not create a need for changes in the financial statements, but should be disclosed if they are so material that non-disclosure would affect the ability of users of the financial statements to reach a proper understanding of the financial position. [SSAP 17(20)]

22.7   Examples of non-adjusting events are:

(a)   a change in exchange rates;

(b)   a fall in value of property or investments which has occurred after the year end;

(c)   the acquisition or disposal of a business; and

(d)   the issue of shares or loan capital.

Other examples are contained in the appendix to SSAP 17.

22.8

Although these events are listed as non-adjusting, the circumstances surrounding some of the events may alter their classification and require adjustment of the financial statements. For example, the sale of an investment after the year end is normally a non-adjusting event. However, if no information as to the market value (or other basis of valuation) at the balance sheet date was available, the sale price might provide valid

> evidence of the net realisable value of the investment at the year end. It might be appropriate to adjust the carrying value of the investment to net realisable value, if lower than its book value, in such circumstances.

Disclosure requirements

22.9   SSAP 17 requires disclosure by way of note of the nature of a non-adjusting event and an estimate of the financial effect before taxation or a statement that it is not practicable to make such an estimate. The tax implications should be explained if necessary for a proper understanding of the financial statements. [SSAP 17(23), (24) and (25)]

22.10   The Act also requires disclosure in the directors' report of particulars of important events affecting the company and its subsidiaries which have occurred after the end of the year (see **6.27** above). [Sch 7: 6(a)]

Window dressing

22.11   'Window dressing' is the term used to describe transactions whose primary purpose is to alter the appearance of the balance sheet. The 'window dressing' transaction is the one entered into before the balance sheet date, while the post balance sheet transaction reverses it.

22.12   Window dressing transactions include legitimate transactions entered into before the year end which are reversed after the year end. For example, a loan to a related party may be paid back a few days prior to the year end but lent back again to the same party in the first days of the new financial year, the result being to hide the existence of the loan and to increase cash at bank.

22.13   SSAP 17 includes in the definition of non-adjusting events a material post balance sheet event which is the reversal or maturity after the year end of a transaction entered into before the year end whose substance was primarily to alter the appearance of the balance sheet. In consequence, the nature of such a transaction and its financial effect should be disclosed in the notes. [SSAP 17(23)(b)]

22.14   It is important to distinguish between a window dressing transaction, which only affects the balance sheet, and a transaction, which also affects the profit and loss account. The latter will almost certainly be an adjusting event. For example, the reversal in the post balance sheet period of significant sales recorded prior to the balance sheet date should be treated as an adjusting event; the sales and debtors at the balance sheet date should be reduced and stocks increased appropriately.

22.15 The requirements of FRS 5 *Reporting the substance of transactions* may also be relevant to certain 'window dressing' transactions. FRS 5 is discussed in chapter 28.

23 Group accounts

23   Group accounts

Requirements to prepare group accounts

General requirements

23.1   The Act requires that 'if at the end of a financial year a company is a parent company the directors shall, as well as preparing individual accounts for the year, prepare group accounts'. [s227(1)] It follows from this that the assessment of whether group accounts are required depends on the situation at the balance sheet date; where a parent has held subsidiaries during a period, but at its balance sheet date no longer has any subsidiaries, then group accounts are not required. The Act also requires group accounts to be presented as consolidated accounts.

23.2   FRS 2 extends the requirement for consolidated financial statements beyond parent companies to all types of parent undertaking that prepare financial statements intended to give a true and fair view.

Exemptions

23.3   A parent undertaking is exempt from preparing consolidated financial statements for its group on any one of the grounds described in **23.4** to **23.10** below.

Small and medium-sized groups

23.4   Both the Act and FRS 2 exempt a group which is small or medium-sized and which is not an ineligible group from preparing consolidated financial statements. [s2 and FRS 2(21)(a)] A group is ineligible if any of its members is a public company, a banking institution, an insurance company or an authorised person under the Financial Services Act 1986. In addition, if a parent undertaking is a company reporting under the Companies Act 1985, a group will also be ineligible if any of its members is a body corporate which has power under its constitution to offer its shares or debentures to the public and may lawfully exercise that power. The qualifying size criteria for classification as small or medium-sized are set out in s249 (see chapter 34).

23.5   For accounting periods ending on or after 2 February 1996, auditors are no longer required to make a positive statement that the directors are entitled to the exemption given by s248. [SI 1996 No 189] However, if the directors have taken advantage of the exemption and, in the auditors' opinion, they were not entitled to do so, the auditors are required to state that fact in their audit report on the company's individual financial statements. (see **39.98** below). [s237(4A)]

23.6

> Parents which report under FRS 2 but do not report under the Act, e.g., a partnership preparing 'true and fair view accounts', would be entitled to the same exemption if they were able to meet equivalent size criteria. Similar logic may be applied to the few instances of a pension fund which has a subsidiary undertaking. However, the SORP *Accounting by charities* requires that 'charities – whether incorporated or not – which use non-charitable subsidiary undertakings to carry out their charitable purposes should prepare consolidated accounts for the charity and such subsidiary undertakings, regardless of the size of the charity group'. [SORP (54)] In addition, the SORP states that: 'A charity may have a number of subsidiary undertakings whose activities are not of a charitable nature. Typically, such subsidiary undertakings conduct a trade and pass any profits up to the parent charity. Consolidated accounts should be prepared in all cases – regardless of the size of the charity group – as set out in Financial Reporting Standard No. 2, subject to paragraphs 62 to 66 below.' [SORP (55)] In addition, FRS 2 clarifies that a not-for-profit organisation is not permitted to exclude a subsidiary undertaking from consolidation solely on the grounds that the subsidiary is a trading subsidiary (see **23.81** and **23.17** below). [FRS 2(78)(e)]

Parents included in accounts of larger groups

23.7 Both the Act and FRS 2 exempt a parent undertaking, which is itself a subsidiary undertaking and whose immediate parent undertaking is established under the law of a Member State of the EU, from the requirement to prepare group accounts providing certain conditions are met. [s228 and FRS 2(21)(b) and (c)]

23.8 The conditions for this exemption to apply are:

(a) the UK parent claiming the exemption does not have any securities listed on an EU stock exchange (this condition applies to any UK parent that is a company reporting under the Companies Act 1985 and to any other UK parent that is wholly owned by its immediate parent);

(b) the UK parent is either wholly owned, or majority owned ('more than 50 per cent of the shares') by the immediate parent (which is established under the law of a Member State of the EU);

(c) in the event that it is majority (rather than wholly) owned, minority shareholders holding in aggregate either more than half the remaining shares or five per cent of the total shares have not requested group accounts. Such notice must be served (the onus being on the minority shareholders) not later than six months after the end of the previous financial year, i.e., normally within six months of the beginning of the financial year to which it relates; and

(d) the UK parent is included in consolidated financial statements (not necessarily those of its immediate parent) which are:

   (i) prepared by a parent undertaking established under the law of a Member State of the EU;
   (ii) in English (or if not in English, accompanied by a certified translation into English);
   (iii) drawn up to the same date, or an earlier date in the same financial year, as the UK parent;
   (iv) prepared in accordance with law based on the EU Seventh Directive on company law;
   (v) audited;
   (vi) filed with the UK Registrar of Companies, together with the UK parent's individual accounts (which must contain various additional disclosures).

Exclusion from consolidation of all subsidiaries

23.9   Both the Act and FRS 2 recognise that a parent undertaking is effectively relieved from preparing consolidated financial statements if each of its subsidiaries is individually excluded from consolidation under s229. [s229(5) and FRS 2(21)(d)] The conditions which have to be satisfied for a subsidiary to be excluded under s229 are discussed in **23.58** to **23.83** below. In such cases, comparative figures will be for the individual company only and not consolidated financial statements. Conversely, in a period where total exemption ceases and consolidated financial statements are prepared, comparative figures will be on a consolidated basis.

23.10   Disclosures for exempt groups are detailed in **23.164** to **26.168** below.

Definition of parent and subsidiary relationship

Introduction

23.11   Under s258 and FRS 2, an undertaking is the parent undertaking of another undertaking (a subsidiary undertaking) if any of the following apply:

(a) it holds a majority of the voting rights in the undertaking [s258(2)(a)];

(b) it is a member of the undertaking and has the right to appoint or remove directors holding a majority of the voting rights at meetings of the board on all, or substantially all, matters [s258(2)(b) and Sch 10A: 3(1)];

(c) it has the right to exercise a dominant influence over the undertaking:

    (i) by virtue of provisions contained in the undertaking's Memorandum or Articles; or

    (ii) by virtue of a control contract. The control contract must be in writing, and of a kind authorised by the Memorandum or Articles of the controlled undertaking. It must also be permitted by the law under which that undertaking is established [s258(2)(c) and Sch 10A: 4(2)];

(d) it is a member of the undertaking and controls alone, pursuant to an agreement with other shareholders or members, a majority of the voting rights in the undertaking [s258(2)(d)];

(e) it has a participating interest in the undertaking and: [s258(4)]

    (i) it actually exercises a dominant influence over the undertaking; or

    (ii) it and the undertaking are managed on a unified basis.

The various expressions used in the above definition are further defined and explained elsewhere in the Act and in FRS 2 (see **23.12** to **23.42** below).

Parent undertakings

23.12   Both the Act and FRS 2 define an undertaking as 'a body corporate or partnership, or an unincorporated association carrying on a trade or business with or without a view to profit'. Thus, while the Act (which applies only to companies) requires only parent companies to prepare group accounts, FRS 2 extends the requirement to embrace all entities which have subsidiaries and which prepare financial statements that are intended to give a true and fair view.

23.13   As a result, organisations such as charitable trusts and pension funds that control economic resources and/or operate trading activities through subsidiaries, and who had, prior to FRS 2, avoided consolidation of such subsidiaries, are now required to prepare consolidated group financial statements in order to give a true and fair view.

23.14 Specifically, charities may historically have invoked the superseded SORP 2 *Accounting by charities* to justify exclusion of trading subsidiaries on the grounds that their activities are fundamentally different from those of the charity. This is no longer acceptable under FRS 2, the wording of which goes considerably beyond the old wording of SSAP 14. The SORP *Accounting by charities* issued in October 1995 confirms the 'all-inclusive' basis of FRS 2, although the SORP allows some variation in the detailed method of consolidated presentation. [SORP (54)–(66)]

23.15 FRS 2 makes specific reference to parent undertakings that do not report under the Act and states that they 'should comply with the requirements of the FRS, and of the Act where referred to in the FRS, except to the extent that these requirements are not permitted by any statutory framework under which such undertakings report'. [FRS 2(19)] Such parent undertakings will not be able to take advantage of this proviso where their constitution, e.g., a Royal Charter or some alternative legislation under which they operate, is silent on the matter. It will be necessary to demonstrate an actual infringement of some statutory requirement.

23.16 A parent undertaking is also treated as the parent undertaking of the subsidiary undertakings of its subsidiary undertakings. [s258(5)]

Subsidiary undertakings

23.17 The definition of 'undertaking' serves to require unincorporated subsidiary undertakings to be included within consolidated financial statements.

Use of trusts

23.18 Some organisations may attempt to argue that, because they do not 'own' a particular undertaking, such as a trust, it is inappropriate for it to be consolidated. FRS 2 not only requires consolidation of companies, but requires consolidation of undertakings (meeting the definition). Accordingly, following the Companies Act 1989 and FRS 2, it has become more difficult to argue that something should not be consolidated. However, trusts are not included in either the Act's or FRS 2's definition of 'undertaking'. Accordingly, they will not meet the definition of subsidiary undertaking. However, trusts may now fall to be consolidated as quasi-subsidiaries under FRS 5.

23.19 Where a trust is entitled to the benefits of a fellow trust, but has no control over the flow of the benefits (i.e., the trustees normally transfer the income of their trust, but the trust deed does not require it), then the 'parent' trust is not, under FRS 2, required to consolidate the fellow trust. However, it is possible that the trust may be a 'quasi-subsidiary' requiring consolidation under FRS 5 (see **23.44** to **23.48** below), e.g., this may occur when the settlor and beneficiary of the trust is the same, such that predetermined control exists.

Horizontal groups

23.20 The term 'horizontal group' is sometimes used to describe the situation where two or more undertakings are controlled by a common 'parent', such as a private individual who is not an undertaking within the meaning either of the Act or FRS 2. Since the common parent is not subject to a requirement to prepare financial statements (or is subject, but does not prepare financial statements intended to give a true and fair view), there is no mechanism, either legal or professional, by which consolidated financial statements can be required. The ASB has, however, issued FRS 8 *Related party disclosures*, which requires transactions between entities that are under common control to be disclosed (see chapter 32).

Voting rights in the undertaking

23.21 'Voting rights' means the rights conferred on shareholders in respect of their shares or, in the case of an undertaking not having a share capital, on members, to vote at general meetings of the undertaking on all, or substantially all, matters. [Sch 10A: 2(1)]

23.22 Where an undertaking does not have general meetings, a 'majority of voting rights' means the right to direct the overall policy of the undertaking or to alter its constitution. [Sch 10A: 2(2)] The voting rights in an undertaking are to be reduced by any rights held by the undertaking itself. [Sch 10A: 10]

Rights

23.23 The following rules apply in determining whether an undertaking holds a right in another undertaking for purposes of s258:
[Sch 10A: 5 to 10]

(a) rights which are exercisable only in certain circumstances are to be taken into account only when the circumstances have arisen and for so long as they continue to obtain, or when the circumstances are within the control of the person having the rights;

(b) rights which are normally exercisable but are temporarily incapable of exercise shall continue to be taken into account;

(c) rights held by a person in a fiduciary capacity or as nominee for another are to be disregarded;

(d) rights attached to shares held by way of security are to be treated as held by the person giving the security where, apart from the right to preserve the value of the security or of realising it, the rights are exercisable in accordance with his instructions or in his interest;

(e) rights held by a subsidiary undertaking are to be treated as held by the parent undertaking;

(f) the voting rights in an undertaking are to be reduced by any rights held by the undertaking itself.

Member of an undertaking

23.24 For the purpose of the definition in **23.11** above, an undertaking shall be treated as a member of another undertaking if: [s258(3)]

(a) any of its subsidiary undertakings is a member of that undertaking; or

(b) any shares in that other undertaking are held by a person acting on behalf of it or any of its subsidiary undertakings.

23.25 This clause makes clear that any shares held by another on behalf of the parent are equivalent to direct holdings of the parent in that undertaking.

Unincorporated bodies

23.26 Although some parts of the Act refer only to 'subsidiary' or 'subsidiaries', the sections dealing with the preparation of consolidated financial statements refer instead to 'subsidiary undertakings'. The definitions of the two terms differ and something that meets the definition of subsidiary undertaking might not meet the definition of a subsidiary (see CA 1985 s736). An important distinction is that, to be a subsidiary, an entity must be a company or other body corporate. However, subsidiary undertaking is defined more widely and applies to undertakings. An undertaking is defined as 'a body corporate or partnership, or an unincorporated association carrying on a trade or business, with or without a view to profit'. The Act's reference to 'a member of an undertaking' means that the parent has shares in that undertaking. Since there are no shares in partnerships and unincorporated associations, the Act clarifies what is actually meant by shares. It states that references to 'shares' in relation to an undertaking:

[s259 (2)]

(a)   with share capital, are to alloted shares;

(b)   with capital but no share capital, are to rights to share in the capital of the undertaking; and

(c)   without capital, are to interests:

    (i)   conferring any right to share in the profits or liability to contribute to the losses of the undertaking, or

    (ii)   giving rise to an obligation to contribute to the debts or expenses of the undertaking in the event of a winding up.

The definition of voting rights is set out in **23.21** and **23.22** above.

Dominant influence

23.27   FRS 2 defines 'dominant influence' as influence that can be exercised to achieve the operating and financial policies desired by the holder of the influence, notwithstanding the rights or influence of any other party.

Right to exercise a dominant influence

23.28   The 'right to exercise a dominant influence' means that the holder has a right to give directions with respect to the operating and financial policies of another undertaking with which its directors are obliged to comply, whether or not they are for the benefit of that undertaking. [Sch 10A: 4(1)]

23.29   The Act specifically covers the situation in which such a right is formally expressed, either within the Memorandum or Articles of the company or within a separate written control contract. Such a contract must be both authorised by the Memorandum or Articles and permitted by the law under which the subsidiary undertaking is established. [Sch 10A: 4(2)] While it is understood that such arrangements are found in continental European countries and, because of this, were included within the EU Seventh Directive on company law, the explanatory paragraphs of FRS 2 state that 'in the United Kingdom directors are bound by a common law duty to act in the best interests of their company. For this reason there may, in some cases, be a risk that accepting a right to exercise dominant influence, as here defined, would be in breach of the above duty'. [FRS 2(70)] The potential problem is thus with the directors of the subsidiary, in that they are party to others having rights over matters for which they have a common law responsibility. The conclusion, therefore, is that a control contract is only likely to be effective where it has been specifically drafted to meet the requirements of UK law (or the law of the country of a foreign subsidiary's incorporation).

This test is therefore unlikely to catch UK companies which were not intended to be subsidiaries, although it may well apply to other forms of entities.

Actual exercise of dominant influence

23.30   FRS 2 defines 'the actual exercise of dominant influence' as 'the exercise of an influence that achieves the result that the operating and financial policies of the undertaking influenced are set in accordance with the wishes of the holder of the influence and for the holder's benefit whether or not those wishes are explicit. The actual exercise of dominant influence is identified by its effect in practice rather than by the way in which it is exercised'. This definition focuses upon the influencer's impact on the influencee's operating and financial policies. The first sentence of the definition appears to imply a total ability to control what policies are set; the latter sentence, however, makes judgement subjective, since the assessment is of the behaviour of the influenced management and of why they have adopted particular operating and financial policies.

23.31   The explanation section to FRS 2 adds the following guidance to assist in determining whether there is actual exercise of dominant influence:
[FRS 2(72) and (73)]

(a)   the effect of formal and informal agreements are relevant;

(b)   influence may be in an interventionist or non-interventionist way. Thus, influence may be through the setting of targets without involvement on a day-to-day basis or of continuous intervention. Sufficient evidence might be provided by a rare intervention on a critical matter;

(c)   once evidence of actual exercise of dominant influence is shown to exist, it should be presumed to continue until the contrary is shown. Nevertheless, an annual review should be undertaken to assess whether there is evidence of change;

(d)   a power of veto, or any other reserve power that has similar effect in practice, can form the basis whereby one undertaking actually exercises a dominant influence over another. However, such powers are likely to lead to the holder actually exercising a dominant influence over an undertaking only if they are held in conjunction with other rights or powers or they relate to the ordinary activities of that undertaking and no similar veto is held by other, unconnected, parties;

(e)   commercial relationships such as that of supplier, customer or lender do not by themselves imply actual exercise of dominant influence.

23.32

> Operating and financial policies are not defined in either the Act or in FRS 2. They are not the decisions taken by management on a day-to-day basis, but are the strategic decisions (e.g., should the group expand into a particular area? Should the group pull out of an area? How does the group finance a particular project or expansion plan? At what level should the debt-equity ratio be set? What level of earnings are to be retained and what level are to be paid out as dividends?) Further guidance may be found in the FRS 5 definition of a quasi-subsidiary which uses similar language. In particular, 'control of an entity' requires both control of operating and financial policies and an economic benefit derived from such control. Where there is no economic benefit, it is unlikely that actual exercise of a dominant influence will exist.

Common control

23.33 A problem may arise where control flows from a common third party.

Example 23.33

For example, two companies, A and B, may have the same directors and A may hold a minority shareholding in B, but with the remaining shares in B, and a controlling interest in A, held by a third party, say Mr C. Treatment of B as a subsidiary undertaking of A involves a demonstration that B is influenced through (and thus by) A. The fact that both are influenced in the same way by Mr C does not necessarily imply that B is influenced by A.

Control and benefits of control with different parties

23.34

> Similarly, a problem may arise where one party has the power of control over an entity but the benefits of that control flow totally to another party. This may arise in the securitisation industry, e.g., where the originator participates in residual profits of the securitisation vehicle through deferred consideration, performance-related service fee, dividends or super-interest from the vehicle or through payments from a reserve fund.

23.35

> In such an arrangement, the legal owner of the securitisation vehicle, usually a charitable trust, although having the ability to make certain operating and financial decisions, does not derive any benefit from those decisions. Under the rules in both the Act and FRS 2, the originator is not the parent of the vehicle,

> because it does not have any ownership interest in it nor does it exercise dominant influence over it. However, under FRS 5, the vehicle will usually be a quasi-subsidiary of the originator (see **23.44** to **23.48** and **28.61** to **28.72** below).

Limited partnerships

23.36 In the case of limited partnerships, situations may arise where the limited partners are the majority equity interest holders. By definition, limited partners do not have any involvement in the management of the partnership and are therefore not the parent of the partnerships. The general partners, despite holding minority equity interests, usually exercise dominant influence over the partnerships and, if so, this would make them the parent undertakings under both the Act and FRS 2. However, in the unlikely event that the general partner has no equity interest at all, it will not fall under the definition of FRSs 2 and 5. This may result in the partnership not being consolidated by anyone.

Meaning of participating interest

23.37 A participating interest is an interest held by an undertaking in the shares of another undertaking which it holds on a long-term basis for the purpose of securing a contribution to its activities by the exercise of control or influence arising from or related to that interest. [s260(1)]

23.38 A holding of 20 per cent or more of the shares of an undertaking shall be presumed to be a participating interest unless the contrary is shown. [s260(2)]

23.39 An interest in shares includes an interest which is convertible into an interest in shares and includes an option to acquire shares or any interest which is convertible into shares. [s260(3)]

23.40 An interest held on behalf of an undertaking shall be treated as held by that undertaking. [s260(4)]

Managed on a unified basis

23.41 Two or more undertakings are managed on a unified basis if the whole of the operations of the undertakings are integrated and they are managed as a single unit. Unified management does not arise solely because one undertaking manages another, because this may not fulfil the condition that the operations of the undertakings are integrated. [FRS 2(12) and (74)]

23.42

> The phrase 'managed on a unified basis' is not expected to have much impact in practice, because instances of unified management are expected to be relatively few and, even in cases where unified management exists, there will usually be the existence of dominant influence as well. Hence, the existence of control could be established on the basis of dominant influence itself. In addition, where one entity holds a majority equity interest in another, a parent/subsidiary relationship will be established through other tests. Where one entity holds an interest in 20 to 50 per cent of the shares in another and does not actually exercise dominant influence, it is unlikely that the two entities will have integrated operations or be 'managed as a single unit'.

Investment managers

23.43

> Where an investment manager has discretion over the investment decisions of a fund, it might be argued that the manager either exercises a dominant influence over the fund, or manages the fund together with its own business on a unified basis, and should therefore consolidate the fund with its own activities. Against this, it may be argued that the nature of the manager's business is the provision of expertise for a fee, with the benefit of investment returns accruing to investors in the fund. The manager's business is thus different from that of the fund. This view is reinforced in FRS 5(54) which states that control can be distinguished from management. Provided that the manager does not take a significant equity stake in the fund, the fund is unlikely to represent a subsidiary, since the manager's interest will not fall within the meaning of 'participating interest'. Where, alternatively, the manager does hold a significant equity interest in the capital and income of the fund, it may be able to justify that the two businesses are not managed on a unified basis, but the manager will have more difficulty demonstrating that it does not actually exercise a dominant influence. One way of demonstrating that it does not actually exercise a dominant influence would be by demonstrating that the manager, despite its equity holding, could be removed from the role of manager of the fund by the other equity holders.

Problem areas in identification of subsidiaries

Quasi-subsidiaries

23.44   A quasi-subsidiary of a reporting entity is a 'company, trust, partnership or other vehicle that, though not fulfilling the definition of a subsidiary, is directly or indirectly controlled by the reporting entity and gives rise to benefits for that entity that are in substance no different from those that would arise were the vehicle a subsidiary'. [FRS 5(7)] FRS 5 uses the term 'subsidiary' to mean 'subsidiary undertaking'. [FRS 5(9)]

23.45   The replacement of the term 'subsidiary' with the term 'subsidiary undertaking' by the Companies Act 1989 went a long way towards reducing the incidence of quasi-subsidiaries. However, there still remain instances in practice. For example, an entity may arrange for a nominally capitalised company to be formed, legally owned by a trust, which will be used to raise finance for the 'parent' or hold legal title to property previously owned by the 'parent'. The arrangement may be such that all significant economic benefits and risks accrue to the 'parent'. Devices used to ensure that such risks and rewards of ownership lie with the 'parent', and not with the legal owner, include the use of non-voting shares, options and guarantees.

23.46   Under FRS 5, quasi-subsidiaries are required to be presented in the consolidated accounts as if they were legal subsidiaries.

23.47   The requirements of FRS 5 on accounting and disclosures for quasi-subsidiaries are discussed in **28.61** to **28.72** below.

23.48   One problem introduced by the definition of quasi-subsidiary involves the possible consolidation of various funds under the control of a company, e.g., an ESOP and an employee pension fund. Such funds typically have directors of the company forming a majority of the trustees of the fund. The position of ESOPs was clarified by the issue of UITF Abstract 13 (see **28.103** to **28.116** below) which concludes in favour of shares and other assets held in an ESOP trust being, in many cases, assets of the sponsoring company. Whether the trust is a quasi-subsidiary is therefore not an issue. The question arises as to whether a pension fund is, in principle, any different from an ESOP trust. The appendix to UITF Abstract 13 notes that 'the substance of ESOP trusts is different from that of pension schemes (where, under the requirements of SSAP 24, the gross assets and liabilities of the scheme are not required to be included in the balance sheet) in that pension schemes have a longer time-frame and are wider in scope with the result that the obligations imposed by trust law and statute have a much greater commercial effect in practice'. Apart from the existence of a more specific standard, SSAP 24, the arguments against consolidation of pension funds seem less than convincing. Perhaps the most effective argument is that, given the materiality of pension fund assets, consolidation would result in the combined financial statements ceasing to give a clear picture of the sponsoring company's underlying business. This issue will be removed if FRED 20 becomes a standard (see **30.67** to **30.85** below).

More than one parent undertaking

23.49 An undertaking may qualify as a subsidiary undertaking of more than one parent. For instance, one undertaking may qualify as a parent because it holds a majority of the voting rights in an undertaking, while another undertaking may also qualify as a parent of the same undertaking because it has a participating interest and actually exercises a dominant influence. FRS 2 does not deal specifically with this issue. It is possible that, in such circumstances, one of the parents should exclude the subsidiary from consolidation on the grounds of severe long-term restrictions (see **23.65** to **23.70** below).

Venture capital companies

23.50 With the publication of FRS 9, the ASB has made a very large and important u-turn in this area in relation to the treatment of associates and joint ventures.

23.51 Prior to the publication of FRS 2, the ASB issued its *Interim Statement: Consolidated Accounts* to provide immediate guidance on the changes in the definitions of parent and subsidiary undertakings and reasons for exclusion from consolidation introduced by the Companies Act 1989. It included a specific reference to venture capital companies. Representations had been received by the ASB from venture capitalists that their interest in their investments is so different from that of other investors in companies that their investments should be treated differently from other companies. Specifically, such companies wished to continue their practice of including, in their balance sheets, subsidiaries and associates on the basis of a directors' valuation. The Interim Statement included the ASB's conclusion that no exemption was justified.

23.52 FRS 2 makes no reference to venture capital companies. The relevant paragraph of the Interim Statement, which dealt with subsidiaries and associates, was superseded by FRS 2. Accordingly, there was no longer any remaining reference to venture capital companies in the Interim Statement. However, in remaining silent on the matter, the ASB had not granted any exemption to venture capital companies in respect of their investments meeting the definition of subsidiary or associate. Therefore, all investments which fall to be treated as subsidiaries under FRS 2 should be consolidated as normal. This could lead to inconsistencies in the accounting treatment between different investments in a portfolio, some of which are subsidiaries (and are therefore consolidated) and some of which fall under FRS 9 (the accounting treatment of which is described in **23.53** to **23.57** below).

23.53 Prior to FRS 9, therefore, venture capitalists were required to comply with the Act, FRS 2 and SSAP 1 in accounting for their investments and thus were required to:

(a)   consolidate the accounts of subsidiary undertakings;

(b)   treat as associates those undertakings in which the group has both active general management involvement and more than 20 per cent of the equity and those whose business is similar to that of the group and in which the holdings are intended to be retained as long-term investments; and

(c)   treat as simple investments any other equity share investments, i.e., those where the role of the group is that of a passive investor.

23.54   In practice, however, it is possible that a venture capitalist holding a large portfolio of equity share investments as a passive investor may have a small number of investments which fall within the definitions of associates or subsidiaries. Some have argued that it is impractical to determine which of the investments fall within the definitions at a particular point in time (i.e., at the year end date). Moreover, they have argued that it is appropriate to apply the true and fair override in such circumstances, on the grounds that equity accounting or consolidation of passive investments would not give a true and fair view of the income from the investment activities of the group, since this is better measured by the inclusion of dividend and interest income, and that they should treat all investments on the same basis which reflects their value to the investor. Accordingly, in practice, not all investments meeting the definition of subsidiary undertaking have been consolidated.

23.55   The publication of FRS 9, however, heralded a u-turn by the ASB in relation to associates and joint ventures. In FRS 9 the ASB states that: 'Investment funds, such as those in the venture capital and investment trust industry, should include all investments that are held as part of their investment portfolio in the same way (i.e., at cost or market value), even those over which the investor has significant influence or joint control.' [FRS 9(49)] The ASB explains that 'Investments are held as part of an investment portfolio if their value to the investor is through their marketable value as part of a basket of investments rather than as media through which the investor carries out its business'.

23.56   In FRS 9, the ASB explains that the investor's relationship to its investment tends to be that of portfolio investor and, for consistency, the investment should therefore be accounted for in the same way as the other investments in the portfolio. [FRS 9(50)] Where venture capital funds and investment trusts hold

> investments outside their portfolio that qualify as associates or joint ventures, FRS 9 requires them to be accounted for using the equity or gross equity method as appropriate. [FRS 9(50)]

23.57   FRS 9's scope does not extend to subsidiary undertakings. Even though, with respect to associates and joint ventures, the ASB has clearly reversed the decision it took in its Interim Statement of 1990 (see **23.51** above) this does not change the position relating to investments which fall to be treated as subsidiaries under FRS 2 (see **23.52** above). Therefore, the normal treatment of investments falling within the definition of a subsidiary under FRS 2 is to consolidate (see **25.80** below). In rare situations, departure from this treatment may be necessary to show a true and fair view.

Exclusion from consolidation

Bases for exclusion

23.58   Both the Act and FRS 2 deal with the circumstances where it is appropriate to exclude subsidiaries from consolidated financial statements. Paragraph **23.9** above deals with the situation where all subsidiary undertakings are individually excluded. The circumstances which justify exclusion from consolidation of an individual subsidiary undertaking are as follows:

(a)   Immateriality (see **23.59** below);

(b)   Expense and delay (see **23.60** to **23.64** below);

(c)   Severe long-term restrictions (see **23.65** to **23.70** below);

(d)   Temporary control (see **23.71** to **23.78** below); and

(e)   Different activities (see **23.79** to **23.83** below).

Immateriality

23.59   Since the definition of a subsidiary undertaking covers all relevant entities irrespective of materiality, the Act includes a specific exclusion for subsidiaries on grounds of immateriality. The Act permits an individual subsidiary to be excluded from consolidation 'if its inclusion is not material for the purpose of giving a true and fair view'. [s229(2)] However, the exclusion is then qualified in respect of multiple exclusions by stating 'but two or more undertakings may be excluded only if they are not material taken together'. Similarly, FRS 2 states that 'the FRS deals only with material items. Thus, this ground for exclusion requires no special mention in the FRS'. [FRS 2(78)(a)]

Expense and delay

23.60 The Act permits subsidiary undertakings to be excluded from consolidation if the information necessary for preparing consolidated accounts cannot be obtained without disproportionate expense or undue delay. [s229(3)(b)]

23.61 Prior to the Companies Act 1989, companies legislation allowed exclusion from consolidation if it was impracticable, or would be of no real value to members of the company, in view of the significant amounts involved, or would involve expense or delay out of proportion to the value to members of the company.

23.62 It is noteworthy that the 1989 Act has omitted the words 'to members' and refers to obtaining information. Therefore, the most appropriate interpretation of 'disproportionate' in the above context is disproportionate to the value to a reader of the accounts of inclusion of that subsidiary undertaking in the consolidation. This means that if the subsidiary is material, the exclusion will apply only where very significant expense or delay will result from the inclusion of the subsidiary.

23.63 However, FRS 2 seeks to remove the exclusion completely. The FRS reduces the exclusion to a test of materiality by stating 'neither disproportionate expense nor undue delay in obtaining the information necessary for the preparation of consolidated financial statements can justify excluding from consolidation subsidiary undertakings that are individually or collectively material in the context of the group'. [FRS 2(24)]

23.64 It is, however, noteworthy that the explanatory section of FRS 2 takes a significantly weaker position by adding two words to the main guidance: 'In principle neither expense nor delay ...'. [FRS 2(78)(b)] Although no general exclusion appears to exist, individual cases may need to be examined further to identify whether departure from the 'principle' is justified. It is, however, recommended that legal advice be sought on such cases on an individual basis, to ensure that they meet the tests in the Act as well as the FRS.

Severe long-term restrictions

23.65 The Act allows a subsidiary undertaking to be excluded from consolidation where 'severe long-term restrictions substantially hinder the exercise of the rights of the parent company over the assets or management of that undertaking'. [s229(3)(a)] FRS 2 toughens this from a permissible exclusion to a required exclusion by stating that the subsidiary undertaking *should* be excluded from consolidation. [FRS 2(25)(a)] The argument presented is that exclusion from consolidation for this reason is justified only where the effect of the restrictions is to prevent the parent from controlling the subsidiary undertaking.

23.66

The rights referred to must be those that result in the undertaking being a subsidiary undertaking (under s258) and, without which, it would not be a subsidiary undertaking. Since control is most commonly achieved through the exercise of votes in general meeting, restrictions justifying exclusion would normally involve the parent being rendered unable to exercise those votes. Similarly, if the definition of subsidiary undertaking is met by another of the s258 clauses, e.g., control of votes in the management body, or actual exercise of dominant influence, it would need to be demonstrated that this essential aspect of control had been removed or restricted to the point where control no longer exists. The FRS also states that it is not enough that restrictions are threatened or another party has the power to impose them. It is required that there is a severe and restricting effect in practice. It should be noted that, whereas SSAP 14 required that restrictions be in place 'for the foreseeable future', FRS 2 does not make any equivalent statement. As a minimum, it is suggested that there should be an expectation of continuation of restrictions beyond one year.

23.67

An example of where the use of this exclusion may be seen is cited by FRS 2, i.e., when a subsidiary is made the subject of a UK insolvency procedure, control may pass to the administrator, administrative receiver or liquidator. A voluntary arrangement does not necessarily lead to loss of control. [FRS 2(78)(c)] Similarly, insolvency procedures in overseas jurisdictions may not lead to loss of control.

23.68

It should be noted that, though a liquidation implies severe long-term restrictions, a receivership or administration order does not give rise to severe long-term restrictions if the subsidiary is expected to come out of receivership or administration in due course.

23.69

Where a subsidiary is made the subject of an insolvency procedure soon after the year end, the issue arises as to whether that subsidiary can be excluded from consolidation. As stated in **23.1** above, the assessment of whether group accounts are required depends on the situation at the balance sheet date. As the administrator, administrative receiver or liquidator is appointed after the year end, there are no severe long-term restrictions at the balance sheet date and therefore the subsidiary should be included in the group accounts. If material, this should be disclosed in the notes to the accounts as a non-adjusting post balance sheet event.

23.70 Restrictions on cash flows from a subsidiary undertaking, perhaps because it is located in a foreign jurisdiction, do not normally amount to a severe restriction of rights. The fact that a parent may not be able to remit dividends from the subsidiary or use the funds for other parts of the group outside the country of operation does not by itself indicate that the parent no longer has control over the operating and financial policies of that subsidiary. Indeed, subsidiaries are often set up in the face of such restrictions and are, presumably, expected to be beneficial to the parent.

Temporary control

23.71 The Act permits exclusion where 'the interest of the parent is held exclusively with a view to subsequent resale and the undertaking has not previously been included in consolidated group accounts prepared by the parent company'. [s229(3)(c)] FRS 2 repeats the same wording, but requires, rather than permits, such a subsidiary to be excluded. [FRS 2(25)(b)]

23.72 Where a business combination involves the acquisition of a number of operations, one of which is, or is expected to be, sold as a single unit within approximately one year of the acquisition, the investment in this business should be fair valued as a single asset. The asset that the group acquires is effectively an investment in the business operation, rather than in individual assets and liabilities. Accordingly, the most appropriate fair value is the actual net realised value or an estimate of that amount. See **23.87** to **23.96** below for a fuller discussion on the accounting treatment.

23.73 FRS 2 further restricts the use of this exemption by defining an 'interest held exclusively with a view to subsequent resale' as: [FRS 2(11)]

(a) an interest for which a purchaser has been identified or is being sought and which is reasonably expected to be disposed of within approximately one year of its date of acquisition; or

(b) an interest that was acquired as a result of the enforcement of a security, unless the interest has become part of the continuing activities of the group or the holder acts as if it intends the interest to become so.

23.74 The first condition (in **23.73** above) depends both on an immediate intention to sell and the expectation of a sale within approximately one year of acquisition. FRS 7 requires that where the subsidiary undertaking has not been sold within approximately one year of the acquisition, it should be consolidated normally with fair values attributed to the individual assets and liabilities as at the date of acquisition, with corresponding adjustments to goodwill. [FRS 7(18)] The inclusion of the words 'approximately one year' means that where at the end of that year disposal has not been completed, it will be acceptable to continue to exclude the subsidiary from consolidation provided that, at the date the accounts are signed, the terms of the sale have been agreed, the process of disposing of the interest is substantially complete and the disposal is expected to be completed. [FRS 2(79)(b)]

23.75   The second condition (in **23.73** above) depends on the method of acquiring the interest: the enforcement of a security. However, if the group has taken the interest (acquired by enforcing a security) into the continuing activities of the business, or it acts as though it intends that interest to become so, the undertaking should be consolidated.

23.76   The condition also applies to transactions that are, in substance, an acquisition of interest by the enforcement of a security. For instance, an entity may have initially lent money on the security of a property. The borrower subsequently defaults on the loan and enters into a financial restructuring whereby the lender receives a majority of shares in the borrower. The lender should exclude the subsidiary from consolidation on the ground that effectively it was acquired as a result of the enforcement of a security, unless, of course, the interest has, or is to, become part of the investor's continuing activities.

23.77   FRS 7 requires these principles to apply not only to disposals of subsidiary undertakings but also to disposals of other business operations, e.g., the assets of a division held for resale would be shown as a single separately described current asset.

23.78   Where an interest in an associated undertaking is acquired with the intention of subsequent resale, it should also be accounted for in the same manner as for subsidiary undertakings (i.e., as a single asset and not equity accounted).

Different activities

23.79   The Act requires exclusion on grounds of dissimilar activities, which is the only required exclusion within the Act. The wording is very strict, basing the test on failure to give a true and fair view: 'Where the activities of one or more subsidiary undertakings are so different from those of other undertakings to be included in the consolidation that their inclusion would be incompatible with the obligation to give a true and fair view, those undertakings shall be excluded from consolidation'. [s229(4)]

23.80 The Act further states that this exclusion does not apply merely because some of the undertakings are industrial, some commercial and some provide services or because they carry on industrial or commercial activities involving different products or provide different services.

23.81 FRS 2 repeats the wording of the Act, but also introduces a major change to past practice by stating that 'it is exceptional for such circumstances to arise'. [FRS 2(25)(c)] Also, the FRS states that it has not been possible for the ASB to identify any particular contrast of activities the consolidation of which would be incompatible with giving a true and fair view. The explanatory section of the FRS 2 confirms this restrictive interpretation of the exclusion by making clear the ASB's unwillingness to provide any examples; to do so would result in automatic exclusion in practice of all similar circumstances. [FRS 2(78)(e)] Specifically, two instances where non-consolidation is not justified are:

(a) the contrast of Schs 9 and 9A companies (banking and insurance companies) and other companies that comply with Sch 4; and

(b) profit and not-for-profit undertakings. (This reference is a further instance of FRS 2 extending its requirements to charities and pension funds, some of whom have in the past not consolidated trading subsidiaries.)

23.82 This approach adopted in FRS 2 is in contrast to that in ED 50 *Consolidated accounts,* which preceded the issue of FRS 2. The ED specifically mentioned banking and insurance companies as the only circumstance where such incompatibility may be considered to arise.

23.83 Rather than exclude such subsidiaries from consolidation, it is stated that the presentation of segmental information, presumably in accordance with SSAP 25 *Segmental reporting* (see chapter 20), is the best way of disclosing different activities. This restrictive approach brings UK practice in line with the USA and IASs, which do not have an exclusion on the grounds of dissimilar activities. In fact, IAS 27(14) states that better information is provided by consolidating such subsidiaries and disclosing additional information about the different business activities of subsidiaries.

Accounting for excluded subsidiary undertakings

23.84 The following table sets out a summary of the rules for accounting for excluded subsidiary undertakings. The detailed requirements are set out in the following sections.

Reason for exclusion	Classification	Basis of accounting
Severe long-term restrictions without significant influence (see **23.85** to **23.86** below)	Fixed asset investment	'Cost' basis – carried initially at a fixed amount
Severe long-term restrictions with significant influence (see **23.85** to **23.86** below)	Fixed asset investment	Equity method
Held exclusively with a view to resale (see **23.87** to **23.96** below)	Current asset investment	'Cost' basis – valued at actual or estimated net proceeds
Different activities (see **23.97** to **23.99** below)	Fixed asset investment	Equity method (and separate accounts)

Severe long-term restrictions

23.85   Accounting for a subsidiary undertaking which is the subject of severe long-term restrictions depends on when the restrictions came into place. The most common occurrence is that restrictions are imposed some time after control was acquired. In such circumstances:

(a)   the subsidiary should be consolidated to the date that the restrictions come into force;

(b)   at that date, the subsidiary should cease to be consolidated and should be transferred to fixed asset investments at an amount calculated using the equity method. Neither profit nor loss should arise as a result of this reclassification;

(c)   the fixed asset investment should, for the duration of the restrictions, be carried at a fixed amount, subject to any impairment in value which should be charged to the consolidated profit and loss account. An impairment test should be performed for each subsidiary individually and should extend to intra-group balances;

or

(as an alternative to this step, it is possible that control is lost but significant influence is retained during the period of the restrictions. In such circumstances, the subsidiary should be treated as an associate using the equity method. It should be noted that the implications of equity accounting for a

subsidiary will normally result in the same figure for consolidated profit or loss on ordinary activities after taxation and
after minority interests as if the subsidiary had been consolidated. Clearly, there will need to be careful analysis of whether
significant influence genuinely exists);

(d) on removal of the restrictions, and the parent regaining control
by restoration of its rights, the amount of unrecognised profit
or loss that has accrued during the period of the restrictions
should be separately disclosed in the consolidated profit and
loss account of the period when control is resumed. Such an
item normally will be shown as an exceptional item. Similarly,
any impairment that needs to be written back now that the
restrictions have ceased should also be separately disclosed.
[FRS 2(28)]

> It is also possible that the parent could regain significant
> influence, but not control, through a partial lifting of
> restrictions. Although FRS 2 is silent on the matter, it fol-
> lows that the subsidiary undertaking should commence
> being accounted for under the equity method. The profit
> or loss accrued through the period of restrictions would
> similarly be disclosed in the period that the significant
> influence was obtained and accounted for as an excep-
> tional item.

23.86 In the event that a subsidiary undertaking is acquired subject to
restrictions, FRS 2 requires that the subsidiary should be carried initially at cost as a fixed asset investment. [FRS 2(27)] While the
restrictions are in force, no further accruals should be made for the
profits or losses of that subsidiary, unless the parent undertaking
exercises a significant influence; in which case, it should treat the
subsidiary as an associated undertaking and use the equity method.

Held exclusively for resale

23.87 FRS 2 requires a subsidiary undertaking that is excluded from consolidation on the grounds that it is held exclusively with a view to
subsequent resale (and the subsidiary undertaking has not previously been consolidated in group accounts prepared by the parent
undertaking) to be recorded in the consolidated financial statements
as a current asset. [FRS 2(29)] FRS 7 requires that the fair value at the
date of acquisition (i.e., the cost to the group) be based on the net
proceeds of the sale, or the estimated net proceeds if the sale has not
been completed. [FRS 7(16)] No goodwill arises on this part of the
acquisition as the (estimated) net proceeds of the sale are deemed to
be equivalent to the consideration paid. The net proceeds of sale
should be adjusted for the fair value of any assets or liabilities

transferred into or out of the business, unless such adjusted net proceeds are demonstrably different from the fair value at the date of acquisition as a result of a post-acquisition event. The results of its operations during the holding period should be excluded from the profit and loss account of the acquiring group. [FRS 7(67)]

23.88 If the interest has not been sold by the time of approval of the first financial statements after the date of acquisition, the interest is included based on estimated net proceeds.

23.89 Where the investment, recorded in the first post-acquisition balance sheet at estimated net proceeds, is sold for a different amount, the difference is used to adjust the original consideration allocated to the remaining parts of the acquisition that were not acquired with a view to resale, with a corresponding adjustment to goodwill. FRS 7 requires this treatment no matter why the difference arose. [FRS 7(17)] However, if the difference arose due to an obvious post-acquisition event, it would appear appropriate to take that difference to the profit and loss account (despite FRS 7's requirements).

23.90 If:

(a) the acquirer makes material changes to the acquired business before disposal;

(b) specific post-acquisition events occur during the holding period that materially change the fair value of the business from the fair value estimated at the date of acquisition; or

(c) the disposal is completed at a reduced price for a quick sale,

it would be appropriate to estimate separately fair values at the acquisition date and to record a post-acquisition profit or loss on disposal. [FRS 7(69)]

23.91 One effect of this treatment is that goodwill is effectively apportioned between the part of the acquired group that is to be kept and the part that is sold, with the result that no further adjustment to write off the goodwill relating to the business disposed of, to comply with FRS 2 and FRS 10, would be necessary. [FRS 7(65)]

23.92

Where a subsidiary undertaking was originally recorded as a current asset held for resale but is subsequently consolidated on a line-by-line basis (because the interest was not sold within approximately one year of the acquisition), the question arises of how to account for the group's share of the subsidiary's profit that arose in the previous year (when it was being held as a current asset): should the prior year figures be adjusted or should the amount be recorded in the current year's profit and loss account? For example, on 1 July 1999, company A acquired the B group. Company A intended at the outset to dispose of one of B's subsidiaries, Z Limited. In preparing A's financial statements for the year to 31 December 1999, the investment in Z was included as a current asset, as negotiations were taking place within a potential purchaser. Accordingly, Z's post-acquisition profit of £500,000 (from acquisition to 31 December 1999) was not included in the consolidated profit and loss account. The sale negotiations fell through in mid-2000 and sale terms had not been agreed with any party at the date of signing the 2000 financial statements, so Z was included in those financial statements consolidated on a line-by-line basis.

23.93   Including the £500,000 in the 2000 profit and loss account is consistent with:

(a)   the treatment of a subsidiary previously excluded from consolidation on the grounds of severe restrictions and for which the restrictions were lifted in the current year (see **23.85**(d) above); and

(b)   accounting for a change in estimate where the decision taken in preparing the previous year's financial statements is still the correct decision at that date.

Restating the 1999 figures to include the £500,000 in its consolidated profit and loss account is consistent with a prior year adjustment.

23.94   On balance, it is suggested that the previous year's result is included in the current year's profit and loss account. A subsidiary question is whether the result is included on a line-by-line basis or as a one-line entry. In keeping with a subsidiary where restrictions are lifted, it is suggested that the result is included as a one-line entry for operating profit and loss, plus separate line-by-line entries for subsequent entries such as interest, tax and minority interest.

23.95   FRS 7 requires these principles to apply not only to disposals of subsidiary undertakings but also to disposals of other business operations, e.g., the assets of a division held for resale would be shown as a single separately described current asset.

23.96   Where an interest in an associated undertaking is acquired with the intention of subsequent resale, it should also be accounted for in the same manner as for subsidiary undertakings (i.e., as a single asset and not equity accounted). It is possible that an interest is acquired with the intention of retaining

> part and disposing of the balance. For example, a 75 per cent interest is acquired with the intention of selling 45 per cent and retaining 30 per cent. In genuine cases, it will be acceptable to treat the 30 per cent stake as an associate and the 45 per cent stake as held for disposal.

Different activities

23.97 Both FRS 2 and the Act require that a subsidiary excluded on the grounds of different activities (i.e., inclusion is incompatible with the obligation to show a true and fair view) should be recorded in the consolidated financial statements, using the equity method. [FRS 2(30) and Sch 4A: 18] FRS 2 justifies this on the basis that the excluded subsidiary contributes to the wealth and performance of the group and therefore its net assets and results should be included; since consolidation is inappropriate, the equity method provides the only alternative that achieves this objective. [FRS 2(79)(c)] In addition, in order that the information about the group is complete, and reflects fully the different sorts of assets and liabilities used in the activities of the group as a whole, the separate financial statements of those subsidiaries excluded on the grounds of different activities should accompany the consolidated financial statements.

23.98 In presenting such separate financial statements, FRS 2 permits summarised information to be given for undertakings that individually, or combined with those with similar operations, do not account for more than 20 per cent of any one or more of operating profit, turnover or net assets of the group. [FRS 2(31)(d)] The group amounts should be measured by including all excluded subsidiary undertakings.

23.99 Unhelpfully, FRS 2 gives no indication of what is meant by summarised information; a reasonable precedent would involve the same information as required in the statutory regulations for summary financial statements (see chapter 36).

23.100 Disclosures in respect of excluded subsidiaries are shown in **23.169** to **23.173** below.

Form and content of group accounts

General rules

23.101 The Act provides that group accounts shall be consolidated accounts, comprising a consolidated balance sheet and a consolidated profit and loss account. [s227(2)] Alternative forms of group accounts previously permitted under the Act are prohibited following the amendments to the Act made by the Companies Act 1989.

23.102 Consolidated financial statements should combine the financial information contained in the individual financial statements of a parent company and its subsidiary undertakings, subject to adjustments required by Sch 4A (elimination of group transactions, value adjustments to accord with rules used for group accounts, acquisition and merger accounting rules and minority interests) and other adjustments as may be appropriate in accordance with generally accepted accounting principles. [Sch 4A: 2]

23.103 The consolidated financial statements should also comply, as far as practicable, with the requirements of Sch 4, and with the disclosure of auditors' remuneration required by s390A(3), as if the group were a single company. [Sch 4A: 1]

23.104 However, as the following items derive from Sch 6 rather than Sch 4, they apply only to the parent company's individual accounts rather than to the consolidated accounts:

(a) particulars of directors' remuneration should deal with directors of the parent company only [Sch 6: Part I];

(b) loans to, and transactions with, directors and officers should deal with parent company directors and officers only [Sch 6: Part II].

23.105 Consolidated financial statements may deal with an investment by way of the equity method of accounting in appropriate circumstances. Some such circumstances are referred to in **23.84** above in relation to undertakings excluded from consolidation; other appropriate circumstances and the application of the method are discussed in chapter 25. Joint ventures dealt with in the consolidation by the gross equity method are also discussed in chapter 25.

Elimination of intra-group transactions

23.106 In order to produce group accounts which achieve the objective of showing a true and fair view of the state of affairs and profit or loss of the group as though it was a single company, certain adjustments are usually necessary. In particular, the effect of transactions between group undertakings should be eliminated; liabilities due to one group company by another should be set off against the corresponding asset in the other company's accounts; sales made by one group company to another should be excluded both from turnover and from cost of sales or appropriate expense heading in the group profit and loss account. Some other consolidation adjustments that are frequently required are discussed in **23.112** to **23.116** below (but the list is not exhaustive).

Requirements of the Act

23.107 Schedule 4A requires the elimination of group transactions in the preparation of group accounts. In particular:
[Sch 4A: 6]

    (a)   the elimination of 'debts and claims' and 'income and expenditure' relating to transactions between undertakings included in the consolidation; and

    (b)   the elimination of 'profits and losses' on such transactions to the extent that they are 'included in the book value of assets'. This elimination is specifically permitted to be in proportion to the group's interest in the shares of the undertakings.

23.108 It is noteworthy that the required eliminations are only in respect of undertakings included in the consolidation. It is not extended to subsidiaries excluded from consolidation. Also, elimination is not required where the amounts are not material for the purpose of giving a true and fair view.

23.109 Although elimination is not required for excluded subsidiaries, it is an integral part of the process of equity accounting. Consequently, where an excluded subsidiary is equity accounted, elimination should be carried out in the same way as if the subsidiary were an associate (see **23.84** above and **23.117** and **25.101** below).

Requirements of FRS 2

23.110 FRS 2 qualifies the Act's requirements in two respects. [FRS 2(39)] The first relates to the amount eliminated: 'profits and losses on any intra-group transactions should be eliminated in full'. The second relates to the way in which the elimination is allocated: the elimination shall be 'set against the interests held by the group and the minority interest in respective proportion to their holdings in the undertaking whose individual financial statements recorded the eliminated profits or losses'. The following points are relevant:

    (a)   arm's-length transactions are not exempt. In the past, there used to be an acceptance that where, e.g., a subsidiary, whose business is property development, supplied a property to another group company at an arm's-length price that included a profit, that profit need not be eliminated on consolidation but could be included within the cost of property in the consolidated balance sheet. There is no reason for such a situation being interpreted as exempt from the requirements of either the law or FRS 2 (other than on grounds of immateriality) and, consequently, such profits should be fully eliminated;

    (b)   the method known as 'proportional elimination', whereby only the group's share of profit is eliminated from the asset (leaving minority interests unchanged), is not acceptable under FRS 2; and

(c) where the asset was sold by a subsidiary undertaking in which there is a minority interest, the double entry for elimination of unrealised profit in the balance sheet will be:

Dr Consolidated profit and loss   (Group's share of profit)
account

Dr Minority interests   (Minority's share of profit)

Cr Asset   (Full profit)

with the minority interest being based on the minority share-holding in the selling company.

Example 23.110

A has two subsidiaries: B, in which it has an 80 per cent interest; and C, in which it has a 75 per cent interest. During the accounting period, B sold goods to C for £100,000. The goods had been manu-factured by B at a cost of £70,000. Of these goods, C had sold one half by the balance sheet date.

In the preparation of A's consolidated financial statements, there will be elimination of the unrealised profit remaining in stock still held by C. This has a transfer value of £50,000 and a cost to the group of £35,000. The amount eliminated is by reference to shareholdings in the selling company, B, in which A owns 80 per cent, and minority interests own 20 per cent. The consolidation adjustment for the bal-ance sheet items is thus:

Dr Consolidated profit and loss account   £12,000
Dr Minority interests   £3,000
Cr Stocks   £15,000

Alternatively, by eliminating £100,000 from turnover (being B's turnover on the transaction) and £85,000 from cost of sales (being £35,000 of B's cost of sales still in C's stock and £50,000 of C's cost of sales), the net adjustment to gross profit is £15,000 (being the intra-group profit still in C's stock). The other side of this adjustment is to stock, to eliminate the intra-group profit. The minority's share of group profit is thus lower by 20 per cent of the £15,000 (i.e., £3,000) than if the adjustments to turnover and cost of sales were not made and thus the group profit retained in reserves is lower by the required £12,000.

23.111 This approach may result in some anomalies. Nevertheless, the ASB has not considered any particular circumstance as warranting an exemption from the general principle of full elimination.

Application of the rules

23.112 The following rules for eliminating group transactions in the consolidation comply with both Sch 4A para 6 and FRS 2.

23.113 Current assets should be recorded in historical cost financial statements at cost to the group (or net realisable value if this is lower than cost). As a consequence of this valuation rule, any unrealised profit included in the book value of an asset arising from trading transactions between group undertakings should be eliminated from the consolidated financial statements. Similarly, unrealised inter-company profits arising from intra-group construction of fixed assets and from transfers of assets between group undertakings should be eliminated.

23.114 Consideration needs to be given to the effect of consolidation adjustments on the deferred tax balance to be shown in the consolidated accounts. The intra-group elimination is made as a consolidation adjustment and not in the financial statements of any individual company. Since UK tax is charged on the results of individual companies and not on the group, the elimination will result in a timing difference, as far as the group is concerned, between income recognised for financial statements purposes and income recognised for taxation purposes (see **27.81** below). This will require an adjustment to deferred tax in the consolidated financial statements if it is probable that a liability or asset will crystallise.

23.115 Special considerations should be borne in mind if a construction or contracting company is a member of a group and carries out work for other group companies:

(a) if the building or other asset being constructed will, on completion, be a fixed asset of another group company (e.g., a new factory or an investment property) then, as indicated above, any profit made by the construction company should be eliminated on consolidation. However, if the asset being constructed will become a current asset of the other group company for which there is a contract for sale to a third party, then any profit made by the construction company need not be eliminated, provided it is measured in accordance with the rules governing the recognition of profit on contract work in progress based on that contract with the third party;

(b) if the construction company includes interest in the cost of construction, any interest should be a genuine charge as far as the group is concerned. This point is significant if finance for the project is being provided by another group company which is charging interest, since the interest charged may not represent interest paid by the group on money borrowed to finance the project.

23.116 The measurement of unrealised profits on intra-group transactions often involves difficult practical problems in identifying intra-group purchases held as stock and complex calculations to determine the amount of unrealised profit; usually, the amounts involved are not large. Consequently, it is common for such adjustments not to be made other than in circumstances where a large volume of assets purchased intra-group and held at the balance sheet date makes the element of unrealised profit material.

Excluded subsidiaries

23.117 In addition, FRS 2 requires elimination of transactions with a subsidiary that is excluded from consolidation on grounds of dissimilar activities. In view of guidance elsewhere in FRS 2, this situation is likely to be rare. Of more immediate relevance are subsidiaries excluded for other reasons, e.g., severe long-term restrictions and temporary control. The core standard paragraphs of FRS 2 are silent on this issue. The explanatory paragraphs, however, state that such profits and losses 'need not be eliminated, except to the extent appropriate where significant influence is retained and the subsidiary undertaking is treated as an associated undertaking. However, it is important to consider whether it is prudent to record any profit arising from transactions with subsidiary undertakings excluded on these grounds' (see **23.109** above). [FRS 2(83)]

Uniform accounting policies

23.118 Where group accounting policies are not adopted in the individual financial statements of a subsidiary undertaking, appropriate adjustments should be made in the consolidated financial statements to accord with the rules used for the group accounts. [Sch 4A: 3(1)] Two exceptions to this rule are permitted under the Act:

(a) in the judgement of the parent company directors, there are special reasons for using differing bases, provided the policies adopted are generally accepted and disclosure is made of:

(i) the different accounting policies used;

(ii) an indication of the amounts of assets and liabilities involved and, where practicable, of the effect on results and net assets of the adoption of the differing policies; and

(iii) the reasons for the different treatment;

(c) any adjustments are not material for the purpose of giving a true and fair view.

23.119 FRS 2 does not alter the general thrust of the Act, but the exception allowing the use of different accounting policies is further restricted beyond the Act's 'special reasons' to be 'in exceptional cases'.

[FRS 2(41)] Neither the Act nor FRS 2 give any assistance in interpreting or illustrating the meaning of these terms.

Individual accounts

23.120 It is relevant to note that neither the Act nor FRS 2 require the use of uniform accounting policies by members of a group in their individual accounts. In practice, uniform policies are generally adopted in order to provide consistent bases for reporting management information and also to minimise the level of consolidation adjustments necessary.

23.121

The following are examples of circumstances where it is impracticable or inappropriate to adopt uniform accounting policies in the individual financial statements of each undertaking in the group, i.e. the policy:

(a) is prohibited by legislation in another country;

(b) is contrary to generally accepted accounting principles in the relevant country; and

(c) would result in serious adverse tax consequences.

23.122 Also, neither the Act nor FRS 2 require a parent to use the same accounting policies in its own individual accounts and the group accounts. However, where different policies are used, the Act requires the consolidated accounts to disclose any differences of accounting rules as between the parent company's individual accounts and the consolidated accounts and the reasons for the differences. [Sch 4A: 4]

Accounting periods and dates

23.123 The Act requires the directors of a parent company to 'secure that, except where in their opinion there are good reasons against it, the financial year of each of its subsidiary undertakings coincides with the company's own financial year'. [s223(5)]

23.124 FRS 2 does not dictate when the financial year of the subsidiary undertakings should end, but, for the purposes of preparing consolidated financial statements, it requires that the financial statements of all subsidiary undertakings to be used in preparing the consolidated financial statements should, 'wherever practicable' be prepared to the same financial year end and for the same accounting period as those of the parent of the group. [FRS 2(42)]

23.125

There are circumstances, however, which make it necessary or appropriate to have different dates. Some reasons which may be justifiable are:

(a) companies in remote territories may be unable to comply with the parent company's timetable for preparing annual financial statements, which will usually be framed with a view to avoiding undue delay in publication. This may result in some foreign subsidiaries closing their accounts one or two months earlier than the parent, in order to allow time to complete and transmit information for consolidation;

(b) legislation in certain countries requires financial statements to be prepared to a specified date;

(c) the normal trading cycle in certain trades (e.g., agriculture) may make it desirable for subsidiaries to have financial years which end at a particular time of the year (e.g., when crops have been harvested). In addition, subsidiaries with cyclical trade such as retail businesses may wish to avoid a year end routine during busy pre-Christmas trading when stock levels are high; and

(d) a change in accounting date may have serious adverse tax consequences or significant tax advantages may arise from having a different accounting date.

23.126 Where a subsidiary undertaking's financial year does not end on the same date as its parent's year end, Sch 4A permits two alternatives for the purpose of producing the consolidated financial statements. These are to allow consolidation of either:
[Sch 4A: 2(2)]

(a) statutory accounts of the subsidiary for the period last ending before the end of the parent's financial year, provided that year end is no more than three months before that of the parent; or

(b) interim accounts for the subsidiary specially prepared to the parent's year end. For example, where the group's financial year end is 31 December 2000 and a subsidiary's financial year end is 31 July, that subsidiary's results would be based on the interim accounts for the year to 31 December 2000.

23.127 FRS 2 does not alter the principles of the Act, but introduces a set priority:

(a) a positive statement is made (absent in the Act) that the financial statements of subsidiaries to be used in preparing consolidated financial statements should 'wherever practicable' be prepared to the same financial year end and for the same accounting period as those of the parent of the group;

(b) where the subsidiary's financial year is not the same as that of the parent, this is achieved by the use of interim accounts prepared to the same date as those of the parent;

(c)   only where this is not practicable, latest statutory accounts (subject to the three-month gap limit) should be used, provided that adjustments are made on consolidation to reflect any changes that have taken place in the intervening period that materially affect the view given by the group's financial statements.

> Since material adjustments occurring after the subsidiary's year end and before the parent's year end have to be made, these would similarly have to be adjusted out of the following year's accounts. Accordingly, there seems to be no difference in practice between interim accounts and the subsidiary's adjusted latest accounts.

23.128   In respect of matching lengths of accounting periods, there is unlikely to be any good reason for adopting a different length of period to the parent other than in a year when a subsidiary is acquired or formed, or where a subsidiary is changing its accounting year end to coincide with that of the parent and the effect of not using a 12-month period for the subsidiary is not material.

23.129   Where disclosure of an excluded subsidiary undertaking's capital and reserves, and profit or loss for the year, is required by Sch 5 para 17(1) (but note exemptions from disclosure in Sch 5 para 17(2) and (3)) and that subsidiary undertaking's financial year does not end with that of the parent undertaking, its financial year which last ended before the parent is to be used. [Sch 5: 17(4)]

23.130   FRS 2 goes further than the requirements of the Act by requiring the following information to be given for each material subsidiary which is included in the consolidated financial statements on the basis of information prepared for a different date or for a different accounting period from that of the parent:
[FRS 2(44)]

(a)   the name of the subsidiary;

(b)   the accounting date or period of the subsidiary; and

(c)   the reason for using a different accounting date or period for the subsidiary.

Individual profit and loss account of the parent

23.131   Where a parent company is required to prepare and does prepare group accounts, the Act allows the individual profit and loss account of the parent company to be omitted from the annual accounts. This exemption is normally taken and is conditional upon the following:
[s230]

(a) a note to the parent's individual balance sheet indicates the parent's profit or loss for the financial year;

(b) there is disclosure of the use of this exemption; and

(c) the parent's individual profit and loss account is nevertheless prepared and is approved by the board of directors.

Small and medium-sized groups

23.132 A question has arisen regarding small and medium-sized groups which are entitled to an exemption from the requirement to prepare group accounts, but choose not to use the exemption, e.g., where a provider of finance requests group accounts. [s248] A strict reading of the Act may appear to lead to the conclusion that the condition of s230 in **23.131** above ('is required to prepare and does prepare group accounts') is not met, since the parent is not required to prepare group accounts. This would imply that the parent's individual profit and loss account should be included in the annual accounts. It is hoped that a future amendment to the Companies Act will remove this anomaly.

Wholly owned subsidiaries

23.133 Similar considerations to those in **23.132** above apply to a wholly owned, or majority owned, subsidiary that wishes to prepare group accounts, although entitled to an exemption. In this case, however, exemption from preparing group accounts is conditional on compliance with the conditions set out in the Act (see **23.8** above). [s228(2)] Failure to meet any of these conditions would result in a requirement to prepare group accounts. Accordingly, the parent may dispense with publishing an individual profit and loss account.

Acquisitions and disposals

Dates of acquisition and disposal

23.134 Under FRS 2, the date of acquisition of a subsidiary undertaking is the date on which control of that undertaking passes to its new parent undertaking. [FRS 2(45)] Similarly, the date of disposal of a subsidiary undertaking is the date on which its former parent undertaking relinquishes its control over that undertaking. This follows directly from the definition of a subsidiary undertaking which is based on the existence of control (see **23.11** above).

23.135 FRS 2 states that the date that control passes is a matter of fact. [FRS 2(84)] It cannot be artificially altered, e.g., by indicating in the purchase agreement some other date: 'The date on which the consideration for the transfer of control is paid is often an important indication of the date on which a subsidiary undertaking is acquired or disposed of. However, the date the consideration passes is not conclusive evidence of the date of the transfer of control because this date can be set to fall on a date other than that on which control is transferred, with compensation for any lead or lag included in the consideration. Consideration may also be paid in instalments'. [FRS 2(85)] Where profits continue to accrue to the vendor under an earn-out arrangement, or consideration is payable in instalments, the date of acquisition/disposal is not usually thereby deferred. It is important to consider all the circumstances in order to determine when control passes. For example, in an acquisition, if the deferred consideration represented all of a subsidiary undertaking's profits (rather than a portion of them), this might be indicative that control of the subsidiary had not passed. This would align with the recognition criteria under FRS 5. For practical purposes, determining the exact date when control passed will depend on the form of consideration. The following guidance (see **23.136** to **23.141** below) is based on FRS 2 paragraph 85.

Public offer of shares

23.136 Where a public offer of shares is made, the date that control is transferred is the date when the offer becomes unconditional. This is usually the date that the number of acceptances passes a predetermined threshold. In the absence of such a threshold, it is the date the offer is declared unconditional.

Private treaty

23.137 For a private treaty, the date that control passes will be the date that an unconditional offer is accepted.

Other share issue or cancellation

23.138 Where control passes by virtue of some other form of share transaction, e.g., new shares issued to minority shareholders or existing shares repurchased from a majority shareholder, the relevant date will be the date of share issue or cancellation. For an issue of shares, this is generally the date that shares are allotted and thus qualify to be recorded as called up share capital in the issuer's balance sheet.

Other forms of consideration

23.139 A number of dates are possible, including:

(a) the date that the acquirer commences direction of operating and financial policies;

(b) the date from which the flow of economic benefits changes; or

(c) the date that consideration passes (although this is not conclusive, since it is capable of being adjusted either forwards or backwards or settled in instalments – see **23.135** above).

In practice, the date adopted should reflect all the various circumstances surrounding the transfer of control.

23.140 The consolidated profit and loss account should only include the results of subsidiaries from the effective date of acquisition, even though the buyer, under the purchase agreement, may share in the profits of the acquired business from an earlier date.

23.141 Often, financial statements drawn up to the effective date are not available. An acceptable approximation may be obtained by apportioning the results on a time, turnover or other appropriate basis, based on the audited financial statements or latest audited financial statements drawn up to a date sufficiently near the effective date.

Disclosures in respect of subsidiaries acquired

Requirements of the Act

23.142 The following disclosures are required by Sch 4A in respect of each acquisition during the financial year:
[Sch 4A: 13]

(a) the name of the undertaking or, if a group was acquired, the name of the parent undertaking; and

(b) whether the acquisition has been accounted for by the acquisition or merger method.

In addition, if the acquisition significantly affects the figures shown in the group accounts, the following further information is to be given:

(a) the composition and fair value of the consideration given for the acquisition;

(b) where acquisition accounting has been adopted, a table showing the book values and fair values at the time of acquisition of each class of assets and liabilities of the undertaking or group acquired, including the amount of any goodwill or negative goodwill arising, together with an explanation of any significant adjustments made (see **13.72** and **13.74** above, which give an example of a tabular format which meets this requirement);

(c) where merger accounting has been adopted, an explanation of any significant adjustments made in relation to the amounts of the assets and liabilities of the undertaking or group acquired and a statement of any resulting adjustments to the consolidated reserves (including the restatement of opening reserves).

23.143 The information required above need not be given with respect to an undertaking which is established under the law of a country outside the UK or carries on business outside the UK if the Secretary of State is satisfied that disclosure would be seriously prejudicial to the business of that undertaking or of the group.

Requirements of accounting standards

23.144 The disclosure requirements in respect of acquisitions are set out in FRS 6, which supplements the requirements of the Act. In producing FRS 6, the ASB took the opportunity to pull together the various disclosure requirements in respect of acquisitions that previously had appeared in a number of accounting standards. In addition, however, FRS 6 substantially increased the volume of disclosure required in respect of acquisitions.

23.145 FRS 6 states that for all business combinations occurring in the financial year the following should be disclosed:
[FRS 6(24)]

(a) the names of the combining entities (other than the reporting entity);

(b) whether the combination has been accounted for as an acquisition or a merger;

(c) the date of the combination.

This requirement is very similar to the requirements of the Act (as explained in **23.142** above), but with the addition of the requirement to disclose the date of the combination.

23.146 FRS 2 requires disclosure of the circumstances where an undertaking has become a subsidiary other than as a result of a purchase or exchange of shares.
[FRS 2(49)]

Combinations accounted for as acquisitions

23.147 As far as combinations accounted for by the acquisition method are concerned, FRS 6 requires additional disclosures to be made if an acquisition is:

(a) material (see **23.149** to **23.155** below); or

(b)   substantial (see **23.156** to **23.158** below); or

(c)   other: give the information required for material acquisitions, with the exception of the details of pre-acquisition profits of the acquired entities, for all other acquisitions in aggregate.

23.148   The FRS does not define material acquisitions, but substantial acquisitions are defined as those that:

(a)   for listed companies, the combination would meet the criteria for a Class 1 transaction (previously 'superclass' but changed by Amendment 13) under the Listing Rules, but with the appropriate ratios based on a 15 per cent threshold, and not a 25 per cent threshold [UITF Abstract 15 (revised 1999)];

(b)   for other entities, either:

(i)   the net assets or operating profits of the acquired entity exceed 15 per cent of those of the acquiring entity; or

(ii)   the fair value of the consideration given exceeds 15 per cent of the net assets of the acquiring entity;

(c)   although not meeting the above criteria, are of such significance that the disclosure is necessary in order to give a true and fair view.

For the purposes of (b) above, net assets and profits should be those shown in the financial statements for the last financial year before the date of the acquisition. When considering the amount of the net assets, any purchased goodwill eliminated against reserves as a matter of accounting policy and not charged to the profit and loss account should be added back.

Material acquisitions

23.149   For each material acquisition, the following should be disclosed:

(a)   the composition and fair value of the consideration given by the acquiring entity and its subsidiary undertakings [FRS 6(24)];

(b)   the nature of any deferred or contingent purchase consideration, including, for contingent consideration, the range of possible outcomes and the principal factors that affect the outcome [FRS 6(24)];

(c)   a table showing the amount of purchased goodwill or negative goodwill arising on the acquisition and for each class of assets and liabilities of the acquired entity [FRS 6(25)]:

(i)   the book values, as recorded in the acquired entity's books immediately before the acquisition and before any fair value adjustments;

(ii)   the fair value adjustments, analysed into: revaluations; adjustments to achieve consistency of accounting policies; any other significant adjustments, giving the reasons for the adjustments; and

(iii) the fair values at the date of acquisition;

(d) provisions for reorganisation and restructuring costs that are included in the liabilities of the acquired entity, and related asset write-downs, made in the 12 months up to the date of acquisition (such items should be identified separately in the 'fair value' table referred to above) [FRS 6(26)];

(e) the fact that the fair values of the identifiable assets or liabilities, or the purchase consideration, have been determined on a provisional basis at the end of the accounting period in which the acquisition took place (if this is the case) together with reasons for this being the case [FRS 6(27)];

(f) the profit after taxation and minority interests of the acquired entity for:

(i)   the period from the beginning of the acquired entity's financial year to the date of acquisition giving the date on which this period began; and

(ii)   its previous financial year.

23.150   In the period of acquisition, the post-acquisition results of the acquired entity should be shown as a component of continuing operations in the profit and loss account, other than those that are also discontinued in the same period. [FRS 3(14) and FRS 6(28)] FRS 6 and FRS 3 further require that where an acquisition has a material impact on a major business segment, this should be disclosed and explained. [FRS 6(28) and FRS 3(15)] The effect of FRS 6 is that these disclosures are required for each material acquisition. [FRS 6(23)(a)] Clearly, this will not be on the face of the profit and loss account, but as added analysis within the notes.

23.151   Where it is not practicable to determine the post-acquisition results of an operation to the end of the period of acquisition, an indication should be given of the contribution of the acquired entity to the turnover and operating profit of the continuing operations. If an indication of the contribution of an acquired entity to the results of the period cannot be given, this fact and the reason should be explained. [FRS 3(16) and FRS 6(29)] Again, the effect of FRS 6 is that these disclosures are required for each material acquisition. [FRS 6(23)(a)]

23.152   The consolidated cash flow statement should show the payments made to acquire the subsidiary undertaking, showing separately any balances of cash and overdrafts acquired. Again, the effect of FRS 6 is that these disclosures are required for each material acquisition. [FRS 6(23)(a)] In addition, a note to the cash flow statement should show a summary of the effects of acquisitions of subsidiary undertakings, indicating how much of the consideration comprised cash. [FRS 1(24), FRS 1(45) and FRS 6(33)]

23.153 Material effects on amounts reported under each of the standard headings reflecting the cash flows of the entity acquired in the period should be disclosed, as far as practicable. This information need be given only in the financial statements for the period in which the acquisition occurs. [FRS 1(45) and FRS 6(34)]

23.154 Subsequent to a material acquisition, the following should be disclosed, if applicable:

(a) any material adjustments to provisional fair values, with corresponding adjustments to goodwill, together with an explanation of the adjustments [FRS 6(27)];

(b) any exceptional profit or loss that is determined using the fair values recognised on acquisition. Such profit or loss should be identified as relating to the acquisition [FRS 6(30)];

(c) costs incurred in reorganising, restructuring and integrating the acquisition. [FRS 6(31)] Such costs are those that:

(i) would not have been incurred had the acquisition not taken place; and

(ii) relate to a project identified and controlled by management as part of a reorganisation or integration programme set up at the time of acquisition or as a direct consequence of an immediate post-acquisition review;

(d) movements on provisions or accruals for costs related to an acquisition, analysed between the amounts used for the specific purpose for which they were created and the amounts released unused [FRS 6(32)].

Again, the effect of FRS 6 is that these disclosures are required for each material acquisition. [FRS 6(23)(a)]

23.155 Some examples of published disclosures are as follows:

Extract 23.155.1

Logica plc Annual Report

Year ended 30 June 1999

All acquisitions have been accounted for under the acquisition method of accounting.

Quaestor retail banking product suite

The acquisition of the Quaestor retail banking solutions product suite and certain other assets from the Synectics group was completed on 13 August 1998. Following the acquisition the employment contracts of the development team, based in Bangalore in India, were assigned to Logica.

The consideration paid or payable is as follows:

(i)   an initial consideration of £8.1 million has been paid;

(ii) further consideration of £22.0 million will be payable before the end of 1999 following the achievement of certain profitability targets;

(iii) a further £0.7 million is due in September 2000.

The provisional fair value to the group is shown below:

	Book value of assets acquired £'000	Revaluation adjustments £'000	Provisional fair value to the group £'000
Tangible fixed assets	282	(17)	265
Net assets acquired	282	(17)	265
Goodwill			29,223
			29,488

Satisfied by:

Initial cash consideration (including costs of the acquisition of £84,000)	8,084
Contingent consideration	22,000
Deferred consideration	702
Discount re contingent and deferred consideration	(1,298)
	29,488

Carnegie Group Inc.

The acquisition of Carnegie Group Inc. was completed on 5 November 1998 following a successful tender offer for this NAS-DAQ-listed company. The total consideration payable was US$36.8 million (£22.3 million).

In its last financial year, prior to acquisition, to 31 December 1997, Carnegie Group Inc. made a profit after taxation of US$0.1 million.

For the period since that date to the date of acquisition, Carnegie Group Inc. made a loss after tax of US$2.5 million (this includes amortisation of goodwill of US$2.4 million).

The provisional fair value to the group is shown below:

	Book value of assets acquired £'000	Revaluation adjustments £'000	Accounting policy adjustments £'000	Provisional fair value to the group £'000
Tangible fixed assets	1,483	–	188	1,671
Debtors	12,074	(375)	(4,739)	6,960
Cash at bank and in hand	2,750	–	–	2,750
Creditors	(3,280)	(1,971)	96	(5,155)
Net assets acquired	**13,027**	**(2,346)**	**(4,455)**	**6,226**
Goodwill				16,095
				22,321

Satisfied by:	
Cash (including costs of the acquisition of £1,163,000)	21,045
Options payment	1,276
	22,321

The main adjustments are:

Tangible fixed assets

The net book value of fixed assets has been adjusted by £0.2 million to align Carnegie fixed assets with Logica depreciation policies.

Debtors

Specific provisions of £0.7 million have been made for doubtful debtors at the date of acquisition.

Pre-paid sale related expenses of £0.2 million have been written off.

Goodwill of £1.8 million on previous acquisitions made by Carnegie has been written off.

A deferred tax asset of £2.3 million has been written off in line with Logica's accounting policy.

Creditors

Carnegie advisors' transaction costs of £0.6 million have been provided for.

Provisions in respect of pre-acquisition project losses of £0.7 million and vacant property of £0.6 million have been made.

Extract 23.155.2

FirstGroup plc Annual Report

Year ended 31 March 1999

Summary of purchase of subsidiary undertakings and businesses	Capital Citybus	Mainline	Other Acq'ns	Total 1999	Total 1998
	£m	£m	£m	£m	£m
Fair value of net assets acquired:					
Tangible fixed assets	11.5	21.3	1.4	**34.2**	28.1
Fixed asset investments	–	3.7	–	**3.7**	(0.4)
Current asset investments	–	–	–	–	33.3
Other current assets	1.3	3.8	–	**5.1**	67.1
Cash at bank and in hand	0.2	1.4	–	**1.6**	57.8
Bank overdrafts	–	–	–	–	(0.3)
Bank loans and other loans	(5.5)	–	–	**(5.5)**	(0.3)
Obligations under hire purchase contracts and finance leases	(4.4)	(13.1)	(1.4)	**(18.9)**	(3.0)
Pension fund creditors	–	(2.0)	–	**(2.0)**	(6.0)
Other creditors	(5.9)	(15.9)	1.0	**(20.8)**	(191.0)
Deferred taxation	0.5	0.8	(0.8)	**0.5**	3.6
Other provisions		(6.7)	0.36	**(6.1)**	–
Minority interest			(0.1)	**(0.1)**	(4.6)
	(2.3)	(6.7)	0.7	**(8.3)**	(15.7)
Goodwill	16.9	56.1	1.8	**74.8**	182.8
	14.6	49.4	2.5	**66.5**	167.1
Satisfied by:					
Shares including premium	2.5	24.7	–	**27.2**	65.4
Cash paid and payable	12.1	22.0	2.5	**36.6**	69.0
Loan notes	–	–	–	–	38.0
Existing investment	–	2.7	–	**2.7**	4.7
	14.6	49.4	2.5	**66.5**	167.1

Substantial acquisitions

23.156 For substantial acquisitions, the following information should be given in the financial statements for the period in which the acquisition took place, in addition to that required for material acquisitions: [FRS 6(36)]

(a) summarised profit and loss account and statement of total recognised gains and losses of the acquired entity for the period from the beginning of its financial year to the effective date of acquisition, giving the date on which this period began. This summarised profit and loss account should show as a minimum:

   (i) turnover;
   (ii) operating profit;
   (iii) those exceptional items falling within FRS 3 [FRS 3(20)];

(iv) profit before taxation;
(v) taxation;
(vi) minority interests; and
(vii) extraordinary items;

(b) the profit after tax and minority interests for the acquired entity's previous financial year.

23.157 The information above (see **23.156**) should be shown on the basis of the acquired entity's accounting policies prior to the acquisition.

23.158 An example of published disclosure is as follows.

Extract 23.158

Firth Rixson plc

Annual report 30 September 1999

Summarised profit and loss accounts of the Aurora group* for the year ended 30 June 1999 and the period ended 27 August 1999 are set out below.

	Year to 30 June 1999	Period to 27 August 1999
	£m	£m
Turnover	100	11.8
Operating profit	6.9	(0.2)
Restructuring costs	(1.0)	–
Profit/(loss) on ordinary activities before interest	5.9	(0.2)
Net interest payable	(0.1)	–
Profit/(loss) on ordinary activities before taxation	5.8	(0.2)
Taxation on ordinary activities	(2.0)	(0.2)
Profit/(loss) on ordinary activities after taxation	3.8	0.4

Operating profit/(loss) for the year to 30 June 1999 and the period to 27 August 1999 is stated after charging exceptional operating costs and other non-recurring costs of £1.0m and £0.3m in the respective periods. Operating profits before exceptional operating costs and other non-recurring costs for the year to 30 June 1999 of £7.9m is in line with the profit estimate for Aurora disclosed in the circular to shareholders dated 3 August 1999.

There were no material recognised gains and losses in the period to 27 August 1999 other than the loss on ordinary activities after taxation.

* acquired on 27 August 1999

N.B. This information was given in addition to the material acquisition disclosures as detailed in **23.149–23.155** above.

Combinations accounted for as mergers

23.159 In respect of each business combination accounted for as a merger (other than group reconstructions – see **24.171** to **24.181** below) the following information should be disclosed in the financial statements of the combined entity for the period in which the merger took place:
[FRS 6(22)]

(a) an analysis of turnover, operating profit and exceptional items (each split between continuing operations, discontinued operations and acquisitions), profit before taxation, taxation, minority interests and extraordinary items relating to the current year into:

    (i) amounts relating to the merged entity for the period after the date of the merger; and

    (ii) for each party to the merger, amounts relating to that party for the period up to the date of the merger;

(b) an analysis of the principal components of the current year's statement of total recognised gains and losses into:

    (i) amounts relating to the merged entity for the period after the date of the merger; and

    (ii) for each party to the merger, amounts relating to that party for the period up to the date of the merger;

(c) an analysis between the parties to the merger of the turnover, operating profit and exceptional items (each split between continuing operations, discontinued operations and acquisitions), profit before taxation, taxation, minority interests and extraordinary items for the previous financial year;

(d) an analysis between the parties to the merger of the principal components of the statement of total recognised gains and losses for the previous financial year;

(e) the composition and fair value of the consideration given by the issuing company and its subsidiary undertakings;

(f) the aggregate book value of the net assets of each party to the merger at the date of the merger;

(g) the nature and amount of any significant accounting adjustments made to the net assets of any party to the merger to achieve consistency of accounting policies, and an explanation of any other significant adjustments made to the net assets of any party to the merger as a consequence of the merger; and

(h) a statement of the adjustments to the consolidated reserves resulting from the merger.

Disclosures in respect of subsidiaries disposed of

Requirements of the Act

23.160 The following disclosures are required by Sch 4A in respect of each disposal of an undertaking or group which significantly affects the figures shown in the group accounts:
[Sch 4A: 15]

(a) the name of the undertaking or of the relevant parent undertaking where the disposal is of a group; and

(b) the extent to which the profit or loss in the group accounts is attributable to the profit or loss of the undertaking or group disposed of. As this disclosure does not fall within the exemption given by Sch 4 from the requirement to show comparative figures (see **5.41** above), both the current and preceding year's results should be disclosed [Sch 4: 58(3)].

23.161 The information required above need not be given with respect to an undertaking which is established under the law of a country outside the UK or carries on business outside the UK if the Secretary of State is satisfied that disclosure would be seriously prejudicial to the business of that undertaking or of the group.

Requirements of FRS 2

23.162 FRS 2 requires disclosure of the following:

(a) where a material undertaking has ceased to be a subsidiary during the period [FRS 2(48)]:

(i)   the name of the undertaking;
(ii) any ownership interest retained; and
(iii) where it ceased to be a subsidiary other than by disposal of at least part of the interest held by the group, an explanation of the circumstances;

(b) the circumstances where an undertaking has ceased to be a subsidiary other than as a result of a purchase or exchange of shares [FRS 2(49)].

Requirements of FRS 1

23.163 FRS 1 requires disclosure of a summary of the effects of disposals of subsidiary undertakings, indicating how much of the consideration comprised cash. [FRS 1(45)] In addition, where the cash flows of the subsidiary undertaking disposed of have a material effect on the amounts reported under any of the standard headings, those effects shall be disclosed where practicable. The latter information can be given by dividing cash flows between continuing and discontinued operations and acquisitions.

Disclosure by exempt groups

Requirements of the Act and Standards

23.164 When group accounts are not prepared, the Act requires disclosure of the name of each subsidiary undertaking and the reason that the parent company is not required to prepare group accounts. [Sch 5: 1(2) and (4)]

23.165 A parent undertaking which is exempt because it is itself a subsidiary undertaking (see **23.7** and **23.8** above) should also disclose the following in its individual accounts:
[s228(2)]

(a) a statement that it is exempt from the obligation to prepare and deliver group accounts; and

(b) the name of the parent undertaking which draws up the group accounts referred to in **23.8** above and its country of incorporation if outside Great Britain or, if unincorporated, the address of its principal place of business.

23.166 In addition to the requirements of the Act, FRS 2 requires a statement by the parent undertaking that its financial statements present information about it as an individual undertaking and not about its group. [FRS 2(22)] This statement should include or refer to the note required by Sch 5, giving the grounds on which the parent is exempt from preparing consolidated financial statements. [Sch 5: 1(4)]

23.167 Where the reason for not preparing group accounts is that all subsidiary undertakings fall within the exclusions permitted by the Act (see **23.9** above), the parent's individual accounts must state which of the exclusions applies in respect of each subsidiary. [Sch 5: 1(4) and (5)] Disclosure of qualifications in the audit reports of subsidiary undertakings is not required for accounting periods ending on or after 2 February 1996. [SI 1996 No 189]

23.168 Although the disclosures in **23.164** to **23.167** above are required by the Act, FRS 2 requires them to be disclosed by other parent undertakings not preparing consolidated financial statements. [FRS 2(22)]

Disclosures in respect of excluded subsidiaries

23.169 Where a subsidiary undertaking is excluded from consolidation, the following information is required by the Act and FRS 2 paragraph 31 to be given in the notes to the accounts:

(a) the reasons for excluding the undertaking from consolidation [Sch 5: 15(4)];

(b)   the aggregate amount of the capital and reserves of the excluded subsidiary undertaking at the end of its financial year and its profit or loss for the year. This information need not be given if:

   (i)   the investment in that undertaking is accounted for by way of the equity method; or

   (ii)   the subsidiary is not required by the Act to deliver a copy of its balance sheet and does not otherwise publish that balance sheet in Great Britain or elsewhere and the holding of the group is less than 50 per cent of the nominal value of the shares in the undertaking; or

   (iii) the information is not material [Sch 5: 17].

23.170 Application can be made to the Secretary of State for exemption from the above requirements in respect of overseas businesses where it can be shown that the disclosures are seriously prejudicial to the business of the company or the group.

23.171 The following additional information is required by FRS 2 to be disclosed in respect of subsidiaries excluded from consolidation:

(a)   particulars of the balances between the excluded subsidiary undertakings and the rest of the group;

(b)   the nature and extent of transactions of the excluded subsidiary undertakings with the rest of the group;

(c)   for an excluded subsidiary undertaking carried other than by the equity method, any amounts included in the consolidated financial statements in respect of:

   (i)   dividends received and receivable from that undertaking; and

   (ii)   any write-down in the period in respect of the investment in that undertaking or amounts due from that undertaking.

23.172 The disclosures required by FRS 2 may be made on an aggregate basis, grouping together subsidiaries which have been excluded for the same reason, where such information is more appropriately presented on this basis. However, individual disclosure is required where any one such subsidiary (including subsidiaries of that subsidiary) accounts for more than 20 per cent of any one or more of operating profit, turnover or net assets of the group. The group amounts should be measured by including all excluded subsidiary undertakings. [FRS 2(32)]

23.173 FRS 2 requires disclosure of guarantees in respect of subsidiaries excluded from consolidation in the same way as guarantees given by members of the group to third parties. [FRS 2(79)(d)]

Other disclosures

23.174 Other information regarding the company's subsidiary undertakings which is required to be given is described in **15.12** to **15.20** above.

24 Consolidation techniques

24 Consolidation techniques

Accounting for the purchase of subsidiary undertakings

Methods used

24.1 Where an undertaking becomes a subsidiary undertaking (see chapter 23), the Act describes two possible methods of accounting for the combination: acquisition accounting; or merger accounting. Relevant rules are set down in Sch 4A paras 7 to 16, FRS 2 *Accounting for subsidiary undertakings,* FRS 6 *Acquisitions and mergers,* FRS 7 *Fair values in acquisition accounting* and FRS 10 *Goodwill and intangible assets.* Chapter 23 explains when group accounts are needed and also the form , content and disclosures required to meet the various rules.

24.2 The Act allows acquisition accounting to be used for any business combination, but if directors wish to use merger accounting then there are a number of conditions which must be met first. [Sch 4A: 8] These conditions are considered in **24.75** to **24.79** below.

24.3 FRS 6, however, requires merger accounting to be used for a business combination if five criteria are met. The five criteria (which are dealt with in more detail in **24.80** to **24.103** below) relate to:

(a) the way the roles of each party to the combination are portrayed and, in particular, whether any party to the combination is portrayed as either acquirer or acquired;

(b) the involvement of each party in the selection of management;

(c) the relative sizes of the parties to the combination;

(d) whether the form of consideration included any payment other than equity shares, taking into account for this purpose any purchase of shares in the previous two years; and

(e) whether shareholders of the combining entities retain an interest in the performance of part only of the combined entity.

The effect of this is that merger accounting is required for those business combinations that are true mergers when the use of acquisition accounting would not properly reflect the true nature of the combination. There are likely to be a relatively small number of business combinations that fall to be treated as merger.

24.4   FRS 6 also allows the use of merger accounting to account for certain business combinations that are related to group reconstructions. The logic for this is that it is inappropriate to use acquisition accounting, which requires restatement at fair value of the net assets and recognition of goodwill, for a transaction that does not alter the relative rights of the ultimate shareholders. Group reconstructions are dealt with further in **24.171** to **24.181** below.

Acquisition accounting

Introduction

24.5   The objective of consolidated financial statements is to present the financial position and results of the parent and its subsidiary undertakings as if they were those of a single company from the point of view of the members of the parent. This generally implies that when a new subsidiary undertaking is purchased by the group, for the purpose of the consolidated financial statements, the holding company is treated as having acquired the assets and liabilities as they existed at the date of acquisition at their fair values at that date; consequently, any profits earned by the subsidiary prior to the date of acquisition are included in the value of the net assets acquired and only income and expenditure of the subsidiary subsequent to the date of acquisition is included in the consolidated profit and loss account. This approach, known as 'acquisition accounting', is required to be followed by FRS 6, unless the conditions for accounting for a business combination as a merger are met (see **24.75** to **24.103** below).

24.6   In the consolidation process, it is necessary to set off against the cost of the investment in a subsidiary the identifiable assets and liabilities of the subsidiary at the date of acquisition. 'Identifiable' assets and liabilities are those which are capable of being disposed of or discharged separately, without disposing of a business of the undertaking. Sch 4A para 9 and FRS 7 require the purchase consideration to be allocated between the identifiable assets and liabilities on the basis of their fair values as at the date of acquisition. The difference between the aggregate fair values and the purchase consideration represents a premium or discount on acquisition (i.e., goodwill or negative goodwill respectively). The goodwill or negative goodwill should be accounted for in accordance with FRS 10 (see chapter 13).

Calculation should be as follows:

Cost of acquisition (see **24.7** to **24.26** below)	£x
Less fair value of net assets at acquisition date (see **24.27** to **24.51** below)	(£x)
= Goodwill – positive/(negative) (see chapter 13)	£x

Determination of the cost of acquisition

24.7 The cost of an acquisition is the aggregate of:
[FRS 7(26)]

(a) the amount of cash paid;

(b) the fair value of other purchase consideration given by the acquirer; and

(c) the expenses of the acquisition (see **24.22** to **24.25** below).

24.8 When assets other than cash are given as part of the consideration for the purchase of shares in another entity, it is necessary to ascertain the fair value of these assets in order to determine the value of the total consideration given.

24.9 FRS 7 gives guidance on how to determine the fair value of purchase consideration. The following table sets out the bases to be used:

Consideration given	Fair value basis
Cash and other monetary consideration (e.g., monetary assets given or liabilities assumed)	The amount paid or payable in respect of the item. When settlement of cash consideration is deferred, fair values are obtained by discounting the expected cash flows to their present values (using the rate at which the acquirer could obtain a similar borrowing) (see **24.11** to **24.21** below).
Capital instruments – quoted on a ready market	The market price of the security on the date of acquisition (for a public offer, the date on which the successful offer becomes unconditional). Where, owing to unusual fluctuations, the market price on one particular date is an unreliable measure of fair value, market prices for a reasonable period before the date of acquisition, during which acceptances could be made, would need to be considered. (For example, an average of prices over 10 days could be used to eliminate short-term fluctuations.)
Capital instruments – unquoted (or quoted, but the market price is unreliable due to, say, the lack of an active market in the quantities involved)	Estimated by reference to items such as the value of similar securities that are quoted, the present value of the future cash flows of the instrument issued, any cash alternative to the issue of securities and the value of any underlying security into which there is an option to convert.

	Where it is not possible to value the consideration given by any of the above methods, the best estimate of its value may be given by valuing the entity acquired.
Non-monetary consideration	Estimated by reference to market prices, estimated realisable values, independent valuations or other available evidence.

24.10 Acquisition agreements may require payments to be made in various forms, e.g., as non-competition payments or as bonuses to the vendors who continue to work for the acquired company. In such circumstances, it is necessary to determine whether the substance of the agreement is payment for the business acquired or an expense such as compensation for services or profit sharing. In the first case, the payments would be accounted for as purchase consideration; in the other case, the payments would be treated as expenses of the period to which they relate. [FRS 7(84)]

Deferred and contingent purchase consideration

24.11 Some acquisition agreements provide for part of the purchase consideration to be deferred to a future date (deferred consideration) or to be contingent upon the occurrence of some future event (contingent consideration). An acquisition agreement providing for the payment of an agreed sum upon signing of the agreement plus an additional amount if the future earnings of the acquired company exceed a stipulated amount is a commonly encountered example of contingent consideration.

24.12 FRS 7 requires the cost of acquisition to include the fair value of deferred consideration. Such fair value should be obtained by discounting the estimated cash flows to their present values using the rate at which the acquirer could obtain a similar borrowing, taking into account its credit standing and any security given. [FRS 7(77)]

24.13 The borrowing rate referred to in **24.12** above should normally be the rate for fixed interest borrowing over the period to the date on which the deferred consideration is due to be paid and the 'unwinding' of the discount should be charged through the profit and loss account within 'Interest payable and similar charges' and be separately disclosed in the notes. No adjustments should be made to goodwill, even if interest rates change prior to the deferred consideration being paid.

24.14   FRS 7 requires the cost of acquisition to include a reasonable estimate of the fair value of the amounts of contingent consideration
expected to be payable in the future. [FRS 7(27)] These estimates
should be reviewed and adjusted, if necessary, at each balance sheet
date subsequent to acquisition, with consequential corresponding
adjustments to goodwill. Such subsequent adjustments should continue to be made until the ultimate amount is known. There is no
time limit for these adjustments, unlike the one year time limit
placed on adjustments to fair values of assets and liabilities acquired
(see **24.29** below).

24.15

> In most circumstances, contingent consideration is deferred to
> a future date, normally until such time as the future event
> determining the contingent element has occurred. Accordingly,
> it may be appropriate to discount the estimates of the future
> cash flows in the same manner as other deferred consideration.
> In such circumstances, it would normally be appropriate to
> charge the 'unwinding' of the discount in the profit and loss
> account within 'Interest payable and similar charges' and to
> disclose it separately in the notes.

24.16   Where the deferred or contingent consideration is to be satisfied by
the payment of cash or the issue of debt instruments, it should be
provided as a liability in the balance sheet at the time of acquisition.

> It is not clear where in the balance sheet the liability should be
> shown. Some companies, following the issue of FRS 12, may
> wish to show the balance within provisions. Others may
> include it within creditors. Companies should note that if dis-
> closed within provisions, various Companies Act disclosure
> requirements apply (see chapter 17 above). A point to consider
> when deciding where to disclose the liability is whether, in
> situations where an estimate has been used to calculate the lia-
> bility, it may give a misleading impression to users to include it
> within creditors.

24.17   Where the deferred or contingent consideration is to be satisfied by
the issue of shares, there is no obligation to transfer economic benefits and, accordingly, amounts recognised should be reported in the
balance sheet as part of shareholders' funds, e.g., as a separate caption representing shares to be issued. In the analysis of shareholders'
funds, amounts should be attributed to equity and non-equity
interests, depending on the nature of the shares to be issued, in
accordance with FRS 4 (see **18.35** above). When the shares are issued,
appropriate transfers should be made between any amounts then
held in shareholders' funds in respect of their issue and called up
share capital and share premium. [FRS 7(82)]

24.18   If the acquirer can satisfy part of the consideration by the issue of shares or the payment of cash at its option, this part of the future consideration is not a liability, because there is no obligation to transfer economic benefits. Consequently, the expected future consideration should be accounted for as a credit to shareholders' funds (as explained in **24.17** above) until an irrevocable decision regarding the form of consideration has been taken. If, however, the vendor has the right to demand cash or shares, the expected future consideration represents an obligation to the vendor and would be accounted for as a liability until the shares are issued or the cash is paid. [FRS 7(83)]

24.19

In circumstances in which the additional consideration is to be (or may be, at the option of the acquirer) satisfied by the issue of additional shares at some future date, a note to the accounts should explain that the consideration is to be satisfied by the issue of shares giving rise to additional share capital and share premium account and also indicate the contingent factors surrounding the number of shares to be issued and the effect on goodwill.

24.20   The number of such shares which it is expected will be issued should be taken into account in calculating fully diluted earnings per share (see **10.180** and **10.181** above).

24.21   Paragraph (h) of the summary to FRS 7 explains that 'where the payment of consideration for an acquisition is to be made after the date of acquisition, reasonable estimates of the amounts expected to be paid should be included in the cost of acquisition at their present values'. This implies that any consideration paid post-acquisition, whether in the form of cash, shares or other assets, should be discounted. However, FRS 7 itself only discusses discounting in the context of consideration in the form of cash and other monetary assets and requires such consideration, when it is to be deferred, to be discounted. The question therefore arises whether deferred and contingent consideration in the form of shares should be discounted. Where the number of shares to be issued is determined by dividing a fixed monetary amount by the share price on the day the shares are issued, the fixed monetary amount should be discounted. Where the deferred/contingent consideration is to be settled as either cash or shares, at the option of the vendor, it is likely that the number of shares will be determined by dividing the cash consideration by the share price at the date of issue of shares; if so, again, the deferred/contingent consideration should be discounted. Where, however, the deferred/

> contingent consideration is to be settled solely in shares, it can be more difficult. As discussed, deferred/contingent consideration takes many forms; at one end of the spectrum is cash, which should be discounted, and at the other end of the spectrum are shares, where it is agreed that no dividend will be declared on any of the shares in that class between the date of acquisition and the date the additional shares are issued to the vendor. In this case, the vendor will get the benefit (via later dividends or capital value) of the post-acquisition profits or losses and the delay in issuing the shares is partly in order to establish a more accurate valuation of the acquired company in order to give the vendor an appropriate proportion of the combined group. Here, it would be inappropriate to discount. The situation of settling deferred/contingent consideration in the form of shares, but where dividends are declared in the meantime, is not so clear. On balance it is suggested that such consideration is not discounted.

Acquisition costs

24.22   As stated in **24.7** above, the cost of an acquisition should include the expenses of the acquisition. [FRS 7(28)] Such expenses should be limited to those incurred directly in making the acquisition. They will not include the issue costs of shares or other securities that are required by FRS 4 to be accounted for as a reduction in the proceeds of a capital instrument. [FRS 7(28)] The UITF were asked to consider whether costs such as arrangement fees for bridging finance, participation fees and costs of researching alternative financing arrangements for a takeover could be included in the cost of an acquisition (and thus effect goodwill). UITF Information Sheet No 35 stated that 'Incremental financing costs that do not themselves fall to be accounted for under FRS 4 are not incremental costs incurred directly in making an acquisition and therefore should not be included as part of the cost of the acquisition, but should be written off immediately.'

24.23   The expenses included as part of the cost of an acquisition should not include any allocation of costs that would have been incurred had the acquisition not been entered into, e.g., the costs of maintaining an acquisitions department or management remuneration. Such costs should be charged to the profit and loss account as incurred. [FRS 7(85)]

24.24   It is suggested that the cost of a due diligence report prepared by an external party on the acquiree can be capitalised as part of the cost of acquisition. Similarly, travel and other direct costs

> incurred by the acquirer's own employees in connection with the acquisition could be capitalised, although the salary of those employees could not be capitalised (being a cost that would have been incurred had the acquisition not been completed). However, if the acquirer employed some temporary staff to carry out various investigations into the target acquiree, the cost of the staff could be capitalised if the acquisition goes ahead, being a direct cost incurred.

24.25 Costs that do not relate directly to the making of the acquisition, e.g., post-acquisition reorganisation costs, do not form part of the acquisition cost.

Merger relief

24.26 As stated in **24.104** below, a company which issues shares to acquire the equity shares of another company may, in certain circumstances, obtain relief from the requirement to transfer to a share premium account any premium arising from the issue. [s131] Although the relief given is intended to facilitate the use of merger accounting, the business combination may not meet the conditions which would permit such a treatment; nevertheless, the acquisition may still be recorded in the parent company's books at the nominal value of the shares issued. Where this is done and acquisition accounting is to be used, on consolidation, the excess of the fair value of the shares issued over their nominal value should be set up and credited to another reserve, often designated as a 'merger reserve'. This reserve is not distributable at this stage. Where the conditions of s131 are met, then merger relief must be taken. This means that where a decision is made to record an investment at more than the nominal value of shares issued, any premium recorded is not share premium within the meaning of s130 CA 1985.

Example 24.26

Merger relief s131

Company X acquires 100% of company Y by issuing 100,000 £1 nominal value shares. Company X shares are valued at £1.50. The entries following the acquisition in company X could be as follows:

If shares are recorded at fair value:

Dr Investment	£150,000
Cr Share capital	£100,000
Cr Share premium	£50,000

If shares are recorded at nominal value:

Dr Investment	£100,000
Cr Share capital	£100,000

> Plus on consolidation, entries needed are:
> Dr Investment   £50,000
> Cr Other reserve*   £50,000
>
> *This reserve could be named merger reserve

Fair value of identifiable assets and liabilities

24.27 The Act requires that, where the acquisition method of accounting is used, the identifiable assets and liabilities of the acquired undertaking are included in the consolidation at their fair values as at the date of acquisition. [Sch 4A: 9(1)] This fair value process is an exercise in determining cost, not a valuation exercise, from the point of view of the acquirer, because the assignment of fair values in acquisition accounting results in allocation of the purchase consideration paid by the acquirer. Therefore, the fair value of the acquired undertaking's assets and liabilities represents cost to the acquirer.

24.28 FRS 7 provides guidance on applying the above requirement of the Act. The FRS states that the identifiable assets and liabilities to be fair valued are those of the acquired entity that existed at acquisition date. [FRS 7(5)] The fair value exercise should:

(a) reflect the conditions at the date of acquisition [FRS 7(6)];

(b) not reflect any changes resulting from the acquirer's intentions or its actions subsequent to the date of acquisition [FRS 7(7)(a)];

(c) not reflect any impairments, or other changes, resulting from events subsequent to the acquisition [FRS 7(7)(b)];

(d) not include provisions or accruals for future operating losses [FRS 7(7)(c)];

(e) not include provisions or accruals for reorganisation and integration costs expected to be incurred, whether relating to the acquired or acquiring entities [FRS 7(7)(c)].

The fair values should be identified and valued using the acquirer's accounting policies [FRS 7(8)].

24.29 FRS 7 states that the recognition and measurement of the assets and liabilities acquired should be completed, if possible, by the date on which the first post-acquisition financial statements of the acquirer are approved by the directors. [FRS 7(23)] However, if it is not possible to complete the investigation for determining fair values by the date on which the first post-acquisition financial statements are approved, provisional valuations should be made. These provisional valuations should be amended, if necessary, in the next financial statements, with a corresponding adjustment to goodwill. [FRS 7(24)] Thereafter, any adjustments, except for the correction of fundamental errors, which should be accounted for as prior period adjustments, should be recognised as profits or losses when they are identified. [FRS 7(25)]

Published example

24.30   As stated in **23.154** below if, subsequent to a material acquisition, any material adjustments are made to provisional fair values (which then impact on goodwill arising on acquisition) these should be disclosed and explained. An extract from a published annual report showing these disclosures is as follows.

Extract 24.30

Logica plc annual report

Year ended 30 June 1999

(disclosure within the acquisitions note for 1998/99)

1997/98 acquisitions

Aldiscon Limited

The fair value of the net assets acquired has been revised from £7,132,000 to £7,591,000. This is due to the reversal of unrequired debtor provisions of £394,000 and the reversal of the unused balance of the US office relocation provision of £65,000. Hence goodwill is now calculated to be £43,606,000.

Delog Conseil SA

No adjustments to the original fair value provisions have been made as of 30 June 1999.

Administra-CIM/Hardi SA/NV

The fair value of the net assets acquired has been revised from £1,279,000 to net liabilities of £575,000. This is principally due to provision for corporation tax and pension scheme liabilities.

24.31   The following table sets out the bases that should be used for determining the fair value of identifiable assets and liabilities acquired. [FRS 7(9)–(25)]

Asset/liability	Fair value/recognition basis
Tangible fixed assets	Lower of: (a) the recoverable amount of the asset; and (b) its depreciated replacement cost (reflecting the acquired business's normal buying process and the sources of supply and prices available to it) or, if assets similar in type and condition are bought and sold on an open market, its market value.
Intangible fixed assets	Replacement cost (normally estimated market value).
Stocks and work in progress	Commodity or traded stocks: current market prices. Other stocks: lower of replacement cost and net realisable value. Replacement cost is the cost at which the stocks would have been replaced by the *acquired* entity, reflecting its normal buying process and the sources of supply and prices available to it.
Quoted investments	Market price (adjusted if necessary for unusual price fluctuations or for the size of holding).
Monetary assets and liabilities	The fair value of monetary assets and liabilities, including accruals and provisions, should take into account the amounts expected to be received or paid and their timing. Fair value should be determined by reference to market prices, where available, by reference to the current price at which the business could acquire similar assets or enter into similar obligations, or by discounting to present value.
Contingent assets and liabilities	Reasonable estimate of expected outcome. Contingent assets and liabilities that crystallise as a result of the acquisition should be recognised, provided that the underlying contingency was in existence before the acquisition.
Businesses sold or acquired exclusively with a view to subsequent resale	Net proceeds of the sale or, if the sale has not yet occurred, estimated net proceeds of sale: treated as a single asset within current assets (see **24.36** to **24.38** below and **23.71** to **23.78** above).

Pensions and other post-retirement benefits	Funded schemes: amount of the surplus or deficiency should be recognised as assets (but only if reasonably expected to be realised) or liabilities respectively. Unfunded schemes: valuation of accrued obligations should be recognised as liabilities. (See **24.43** to **24.47** below.)
Deferred taxation	Deferred tax assets and liabilities recognised in the fair value exercise should be determined by considering the enlarged group as a whole. Tax losses attributable to the acquired entity should be recognised in accordance with the requirements of the accounting standard concerned with deferred tax (i.e., recognised as an asset if the losses have a value that can be measured reliably). (See **24.48** to **24.51** below.)

24.32   It should be noted that values attached to specific assets and liabilities in a vending agreement or in negotiating positions are not necessarily conclusive as to the fair value.

24.33   The identifiable assets and liabilities fair valued in accordance with the guidelines set out in **24.31** above may include items that were not previously recognised in the financial statements of the acquired entity. These include assets and liabilities that are not normally recognised in financial statements where no acquisition is involved, because other accounting standards preclude their immediate recognition. Examples include:

(a)   contingent assets that may be assigned a value on acquisition, but cannot otherwise be recognised in financial statements because FRS 12 precludes the recognition of a contingent gain until realisation becomes virtually certain; and

(b)   pension surpluses or deficiencies identified on an acquisition that are otherwise recognised over several financial years in an entity's financial statements, in accordance with the requirements of SSAP 24.

24.34   These identifiable assets and liabilities are recognised on acquisition, because, if this is not done, the reporting of post-acquisition performance is distorted by changes in assets and liabilities not being recognised in the correct period. The usual accounting practice, e.g., of deferring recognition of contingent assets, does not apply, because the recognition of an acquired asset represents the expectation that the amounts expended on its acquisition will be recovered; it does not anticipate a future gain. It is, however, necessary to review the recoverable amounts of such assets to ensure that provision is made for any probable losses. [FRS 7(36)]

24.35   Paragraphs **24.36** to **24.51** below set out guidance on specific areas.

Business sold or held exclusively with a view to subsequent resale

24.36   An operation should not be treated as held for resale and valued at estimated sales proceeds unless:
[FRS 7(17)]

(a)   a purchaser has been identified or is being sought; and

(b)   the disposal is reasonably expected to occur within approximately one year of the date of the acquisition.

24.37   If an operation is not, in fact, sold within approximately one year of the acquisition, in subsequent financial statements, it should be consolidated normally, with fair values attributed to the individual assets and liabilities as at the date of acquisition and with corresponding adjustments to goodwill.

24.38   More detailed guidance on accounting for a business sold or held exclusively with a view to subsequent resale is contained in **23.71** to **23.78** above.

Reconstructions and closures of operations

24.39   If the acquired entity was demonstrably committed (within the terms of FRS 3 paragraph 18) to a reconstruction or closure of an operation at the date of acquisition, then any provisions arising as a result of the reconstruction or closure should be regarded as pre-acquisition and treated as identifiable liabilities. [FRS 7(38)] All other reorganisation costs and provisions for future losses should be charged in the post-acquisition profit and loss account of the combined entity. [FRS 7(39)]

Onerous contracts

24.40   If the acquired entity has onerous contracts or commitments at the date of acquisition, the corresponding obligations should be recognised as liabilities when carrying out the fair value exercise, whether or not those obligations were recorded in the financial statements of the acquired entity.

24.41 Examples of items which may qualify are:

(a) finance and operating leases where the rental is at above market value (equally, where rental is below market value, then an asset should be recognised); and

(b) contracts for the supply of materials or the sale of output at significantly uncompetitive rates which existed at the time of acquisition and which cannot be renegotiated or terminated.

24.42 Examples of items which do not qualify are:

(a) contracts for supply of materials or sale of output at uncompetitive rates which are negotiated during the acquisition; and

(b) the cost of reducing or replacing staff of the acquired entity on grounds of overmanning or overpayment.

Both these items fail because there was no commitment existing at the date of acquisition. In particular, costs that arise from a decision to reduce staff levels or salaries only exist as a result of that decision and not otherwise. It is therefore clearly a change 'resulting from the acquirer's intentions'. [FRS 7(7)(a)]

Pensions and other post-retirement benefits

24.43 FRS 7 requires that fair values should be attributed to deficiencies in funded pension and other post-retirement benefits scheme and, to the extent that they are reasonably expected to be realised, to surpluses in such schemes. [FRS 7(19)] For unfunded schemes, the accrued obligations should be recognised as liabilities of the acquiring group. These assets or liabilities are in substitution for existing prepayments or provisions that have accumulated in the accounts of the acquired entity under the requirements of SSAP 24 (see chapter 27).

24.44 The fair value attributed to a surplus in a funded scheme would be determined by taking into account not only the actuarial surplus of the fund, but also the extent to which the surplus could be realised in cash terms, by way of reduction of future contributions or otherwise and the timescale of such potential realisations. [FRS 7(71)]

24.45 The treatment required by FRS 7 differs from the normal requirements of SSAP 24, which, in many circumstances, do not permit the immediate recognition of assets and liabilities in respect of surpluses or deficiencies, but require them to be recognised systematically over the average remaining service lives of the employees in the scheme. While SSAP 24 is primarily concerned with the allocation of pension costs to a company's profit and loss account on a continuing basis over several financial years, accounting for an acquisition transaction necessitates the recognition in the acquirer's group accounts of all assets and liabilities of the acquired entity identified at the date of acquisition. A pension asset, however, would be recognised only insofar as the acquired entity or the acquirer was able to benefit from the existing surplus. [FRS 7(72)]

24.46 FRS 7 requires changes in pension or other post-retirement arrangements following an acquisition to be accounted for as post-acquisition items. [FRS 7(20)]

24.47 An example of a post-acquisition change to a scheme is a change to the benefits granted to members of the acquired scheme as part of a policy of harmonising remuneration packages in the enlarged group. The cost of post-acquisition changes to pension and other post-retirement arrangements would be dealt with in accordance with the requirements of SSAP 24 relating to variations in pension cost.

Deferred taxation

24.48 FRS 7 states that the deferred tax assets and liabilities recognised in the fair value exercise should be determined by considering the enlarged group as a whole. [FRS 7(24)]

24.49 At the end of the accounting period in which the acquisition occurred, the enlarged group's deferred tax provision should be calculated as a single amount using assumptions applicable to the group. The deferred tax relating to the acquired company at the date of acquisition should be calculated using the same assumptions, with the result that the post-acquisition profit and loss account will reflect only real changes in the circumstances of the group and not any effects of changing from one set of assumptions to another.

24.50 The benefit to the group of any tax losses in an entity at the date of its acquisition should be recognised in accordance with the requirements of SSAP 15 *Accounting for deferred tax*. The losses should, therefore, be treated as timing differences and recognised as reductions in deferred tax liabilities (if any), with any remainder recognised as deferred tax assets provided that the criteria for recognition specified in SSAP 15 are met.

24.51 If the criteria for the recognition of the benefits of tax losses in the group financial statements are not met as at the date of acquisition or within the permitted period for completing the fair value exercise (see **24.29** above), the benefits (if any) will be recognised in post-acquisition periods when the criteria are met. In such periods, the notes to the accounts should disclose any special circumstances affecting the tax charge, if material (see **27.142** below). [FRS 7(75) and FRS 3(23)]

Negative goodwill

24.52   Where the initial determination of fair values of the identifiable net assets appears to give rise to negative goodwill, FRS 10 requires the fair values of the acquired assets to be tested for impairment and the fair values of the acquired liabilities checked carefully to ensure that none have been omitted or understated. [FRS 10(48)]

24.53   In these instances, further consideration should also be given to the basis used to determine fair value; in particular, depreciated replacement cost may not provide a fair value for fixed assets being used in a business which is presently insufficiently profitable. Net realisable value may be a more appropriate basis in such circumstances.

Changes in stake – piecemeal acquisitions

24.54   There are different bases of accounting for an interest in shares: investment (for passive holdings), equity accounting (for associated undertakings), gross equity accounting (for joint ventures), each investor accounting for its own assets, liabilities, cash flows and share of shared items (for joint arrangements that are not entities) and consolidation (for subsidiary undertakings). A change in the basis of accounting will be triggered by a change in circumstances, e.g., an acquisition or disposal, that results in the interest qualifying under a different definition.

24.55   In addition to the change in basis of accounting, further issues arise on a change in shareholding:

(a)   the need for, and amount of, fair value adjustments to assets and liabilities of the subsidiary;

(b)   the resulting calculation of goodwill; and

(c)   the measurement of minority interests.

Piecemeal acquisitions – one-stage calculation of goodwill

24.56   In describing the acquisition method of accounting, the Act requires identifiable assets and liabilities of the undertaking acquired to be included in the consolidated balance sheet at their fair value as at the date of acquisition, i.e., the date of becoming a subsidiary. [Sch 4A: 9] Goodwill is to be calculated based on these fair values. Where an acquisition occurs through two or more purchases of shares, the effect of the Act is to require the calculation of goodwill to be performed once, at the date that control passes. It follows that, under this method of calculation, the fair value of net assets on the dates that earlier purchases of shares were made will not be relevant.

Example 24.56

X acquired shares in Y as follows:

(a) 10 per cent at a cost of £15 million, when Y's net assets had a fair value of £100 million;

(b) a further five per cent at a cost of £10 million, when Y's net assets had a fair value of £120 million;

(c) the balance of 85 per cent at a cost of £150 million, when Y's net assets had a fair value of £130 million.

Y became a subsidiary of X only on the third purchase of shares. Thus, goodwill of £45 million is found by comparing the aggregate cost of shares of £175 million (£15 million + £10 million + £150 million) with the fair value of net assets on the date control passes – £130 million. The fair value of net assets when the 10 per cent and five per cent purchases of shares were made are not considered in calculating goodwill on Y becoming a subsidiary.

Associate (or joint venture) becoming a subsidiary

24.57 An exception to the one-stage goodwill calculation occurs where, prior to becoming a subsidiary, earlier purchases of shares resulted in an associate or joint venture that was accounted for under the equity or gross equity method (see chapter 25). Under the requirements of FRS 9 *Associates and joint ventures*:

(a) the associate's/joint venture's net assets are fair valued at the date it became an associate/joint venture and the investor's share of net assets is determined accordingly [FRS 9(31)(a)];

(b) goodwill is calculated based on those fair values in the same way that goodwill is calculated on a subsidiary [FRS 9(31)(a)]; and

(c) subsequent changes in the associate's/joint venture's net assets are reflected in the investor's consolidated financial statements. [FRS 9(4)] For example, the investor's share of increases in net assets representing profits are reflected in the investor's consolidated profit and loss account [FRS 9(27)].

24.58 On a further purchase of shares that results in the associate/joint venture becoming a subsidiary undertaking, the Act's one-stage method of calculating goodwill would result in two problems:

(a) profits already included in the investor's consolidated profit and loss account (and any other changes in the associate's/joint venture's net assets) would form part of the fair value of the subsidiary's net assets acquired. The effect would be that the group's share of profits or losses and reserve movements of the associate/joint venture would become reclassified as goodwill; and

(b) since the aggregate cost of shares in the subsidiary is a mixture of earlier and new costs, but the fair value of the subsidiary's net assets is measured at a single recent date, the resulting goodwill may be negative. This would, in part, represent a revaluation of net assets between the dates of becoming an associate/joint venture and a subsidiary.

24.59 The explanation section of FRS 2 offers a solution to the above problem. [FRS 2(89)] It suggests that this situation may represent special circumstances where compliance with the Act would be misleading and thus the use of the true and fair view override is justified. Specifically, it suggests that it will be appropriate to calculate goodwill on a piecemeal basis taking, for each parcel of shares acquired, the cost of that parcel compared with the related share of net assets at fair value when acquired. The difference between the resulting goodwill amount and that calculated on the method provided by the Act is to be 'shown in reserves' (see Example 24.59 below). It follows that the subsidiary's net assets will be included in the consolidated balance sheet at fair value at the date of acquisition.

Example 24.59

X acquired a 70 per cent interest in Y as follows:

(a) 30 per cent at a cost of £40 million, when Y's net assets had a fair value of £90 million; and

(b) a further 40 per cent at a cost of £90 million, when Y's net assets had a fair value of £200 million.

On the first acquisition, goodwill of £13 million (cost £40 million less share of net assets £27 million) was capitalised and deemed to have an indefinite life. The increase of £110 million in net assets between the two acquisitions was due in part to £40 million trading profits for which X had accounted for its share in its consolidated profit and loss account under the equity method (30 per cent x £40 million = £12 million) and £70 million increase in land and buildings values which had not been reflected in Y's accounts and, consequently, X had not accounted for its share of the increase.

GAAP 2001: Not just another book more a way of working

Keep up to date with additional *GAAP 2001* services by registering as a *GAAP 2001* user. Simply complete the section below and return this card to ABG Professional Information – no stamp is required as this card is postage paid.

All registered users will receive FREE the *GAAP 2001* newsletter providing full coverage and commentary on all the very latest developments in the financial reporting regime.

You will be kept up to date with news of *GAAP Xtra*, the quarterly CD-ROM service which provides you with a unique and comprehensive financial reporting service.

Further *GAAP 2001* developments will also be sent to you, including of course news of *GAAP 2002* publishing in early summer 2001.

☐ Please register my details for further *GAAP 2001* services

Name (Mr/Mrs/Ms/Miss): _____

Company/firm: _____

Address: _____

_____

_____

_____ Postcode: _____

Tel: _____ Fax: _____

E-mail: _____

ICAEW no. (if applicable): _____

How did you first hear of GAAP 2001? (Delete as appropriate):
Accountancy magazine/other magazine advertising/colleague/course/ bookshop/direct mail/other (please state) _____

ABG Professional Information, 40 Bernard Street, London WC1N 1LD
Telephone: 0207 920 8991 Fax: 0207 920 8992
E-mail: info@abgpublications.co.uk
Website: www.abgweb.com

abg
professional
information

ABG Professional Information
FREEPOST LON 14282
LONDON
WC1N 1BR

Position prior to becoming a subsidiary

	Company £ million	Consolidated £ million
Carrying value of investment in Y:		
– at cost	40	–
– equity method (30% × £130 million[1])	–	39
– goodwill (£40 million –		
(30% × £90 million))		13
Reserves:		
– profit and loss account (30% × £40 million)	–	(12)

Prior to the second purchase, the £39 million investment in Y represents 30 per cent of Y's net assets of £130 million (£90 million at acquisition + £40 million increase from profits while an associate). X's share of this £40 million post-acquisition profit is included in the consolidated profit and loss account.

Goodwill on becoming a subsidiary

Under the Act:

	£ million
Aggregate cost of shares (£40 million + £90 million)	130
Share of net assets (70% × £200 million)	(140)
Goodwill (negative)	(10)

Under FRS 2:

	£ million	£ million
Goodwill on first purchase (positive goodwill)		13
Second purchase:		
Cost	90	
Share of net assets (40% × £200 million)	(80)	10
Goodwill (positive)		23

Goodwill difference between two methods   £33 million[2]

Position after becoming a subsidiary using the FRS 2 method

	Company £ million	Consolidated £ million
Carrying value of investment in Y:		
– at cost (£40 million + £90 million)	130	
Goodwill		23
Net assets (at fair value)		200
Minority interests (30% × £200 million)	–	(60)
	130	163
Reserves:		
– profit and loss account (unchanged)		(12)
– other reserve arising on consolidation	–	(21)
	–	(33)

> The credit balance 'other reserve arising on consolidation' appearing in the consolidated balance sheet of £21 million represents the group's share of the increase in Y's land and buildings between the date it became an associate and the date it became a subsidiary, to the extent that this had not been equity accounted (30% × £70 million). This should be reflected in the consolidated statement of total recognised gains and losses in the year.
>
> Notes
>
> 1   £130 million = £90 million net assets + £40 million post-acquisition profits.
>
> 2   The £33 million difference between goodwill under the Act's method and that under FRS 2's method is the aggregate of the revaluation change of £21 million and the amount already included within the consolidated profit and loss account of £12 million.

24.60   The treatment discussed in **24.59** above also applies in extreme situations where the group has substantially restated its investment in an undertaking prior to it becoming a subsidiary, even where the investment was not an associate or joint venture. For example, as cited in FRS 2, where a provision has been made against such an investment for a permanent diminution in value (or an impairment as per FRS 11), the effect of applying the method provided by the Act (as described in **24.56** above) would be to increase reserves and create an asset (goodwill) and hence give a misleading goodwill figure. [FRS 2(89)]

Increasing an interest in an existing subsidiary undertaking

24.61   When further shares are purchased in an undertaking that is already a subsidiary included in the consolidation, FRS 2 requires that the identifiable assets and liabilities of the subsidiary undertaking be revalued to fair value at the date of the later purchase (current fair value). [FRS 2(51)] This revaluation is not required if the difference between net fair values and the carrying amounts of the assets and liabilities attributable to the increase in stake is not material.

24.62   The objective of the revaluation exercise required by FRS 2 is to calculate goodwill properly, and particularly to avoid including revaluation changes within goodwill. [FRS 2(51)] The procedures on such an increase in stake are:

(a)   within the consolidated financial statements, revalue the net identifiable assets and liabilities of the subsidiary undertaking to their current fair value;

(b)   allocate the revaluation difference arising on the subsequent purchase between the group's revaluation reserve (based on group's share before the increase in interest) and the minority interest. However, it should be noted that it may be necessary to charge the profit and loss account for increases in provisions and asset write-downs of current assets (see interpretation in **24.65** below); and

(c) calculate goodwill arising on the second acquisition as the difference between the cost of additional shares acquired and the increase in group's interest (based on the current fair value of net assets). The minority interest will be reduced by this latter amount.

24.63 In prescribing the above method, FRS 2 has rejected two other possible methods of accounting for increasing an interest in a subsidiary. One method is not to revalue the identifiable assets and liabilities, which would result in a goodwill figure which incorrectly includes revaluation changes.

24.64 The other method is to calculate goodwill arising as in **24.62** (c) above, but to recognise in the consolidated balance sheet only the proportion of the revaluation difference that is attributable to the increase in group's interest. This method gives the correct goodwill figure, but less meaningful carrying values of assets and liabilities.

24.65 It should be noted that the FRS 2 requirement to revalue assets and liabilities to their fair values on a subsequent purchase of shares in a subsidiary (as discussed in **24.59** above) does not mean that all revaluation adjustments can be taken directly to reserves. As part of the revaluation exercise, the parent undertaking may wish to revise fair value provisions made at the time that the subsidiary was acquired. Unless this occurs within a reasonable hindsight period of the original acquisition (see **24.29** above for FRS 7's rules in this respect), it will be necessary to deal with a revision to provisions in accordance with normal rules, i.e., by making a charge through the profit and loss account, with an appropriate percentage being allocated to the minority shareholders. The appropriate minority percentage would be that existing before the further purchase of shares. Similar considerations apply to amounts written off current assets or to an impairment in a fixed asset.

Deemed acquisitions

24.66 A deemed acquisition arises when a group increases its interest in a subsidiary without purchasing further shares in the subsidiary. For example, it may arise when the subsidiary repurchases or redeems its own shares from the minority shareholders. If the repurchase or redemption price is below the subsidiary's net asset value per share, a gain arises in the group accounts; if it is above the subsidiary's net asset value per share, a loss would arise.

24.67

> If FRS 2 were applied to a deemed acquisition, it would be necessary to revalue assets and liabilities to fair value at the date of the deemed acquisition and recognise goodwill (positive or negative). [FRS 2(51)] However, since no further shares have been purchased directly, it is possible to argue that the group has not increased its interest, and therefore no fair value exercise is required.

24.68

> Nevertheless, the deemed acquisition will result in a change to the net assets of the subsidiary and a change to the group's attributable percentage interest. Since it predates FRS 3, FRS 2 does not make reference to whether the gain or loss should be dealt with in the profit and loss account or the statement of total recognised gains and losses. Since the group is not involved directly in the transaction, it seems logical that the difference should be dealt with in the statement of total recognised gains and losses. However, once the group has decided its policy on which performance statement to recognise gains and losses on deemed acquisitions/disposals, it should apply that policy consistently.

Dividends received from pre-acquisition profits

24.69 Prior to the Companies Act 1981, any profits earned by a subsidiary up to the date of acquisition were considered capital in nature so far as the new parent company was concerned. Consequently, the receipt of a dividend paid by a subsidiary from such profits was considered a partial return of the investment in the subsidiary; the parent company would account for the dividend by reducing the carrying value of the investment, rather than including the dividend in its profit and loss account.

24.70 The present Act no longer contains such a rule. Paragraph 16 of appendix 1 to FRS 6 summarises the current position as follows:

> 'Where a dividend is paid to the acquiring or issuing company out of pre-combination profits, it would appear that it need not necessarily be applied as a reduction in the carrying value of the investment in the subsidiary undertaking. Such a dividend received should be applied to reduce the carrying value of the investment to the extent necessary to provide for a diminution in value of the investment in the subsidiary undertaking as stated in the accounts of the parent company. To the extent that this is not necessary, it appears that the amount received will be a realised profit in the hands of the parent company.'

> ### *Example 24.70*
>
> H Plc acquired all of the share capital of S Ltd in exchange for 60,000
> £1 ordinary shares with an aggregate fair value of £520,000. At a sub-
> sequent date, S Ltd paid a dividend of £50,000 to H Plc. The directors
> consider that, following the dividend payment, the value of its invest-
> ment in S Ltd is £500,000.
>
> As this transaction qualifies for merger relief under s131 (see **24.26**
> above), the holding company has the option of recording the invest-
> ment, in its own balance sheet, at either fair value or nominal value of
> the shares issued.
>
> If H Plc recorded the investment in S Ltd at fair value of £520,000,
> then, on receipt of the dividend, the investment should be written
> down to £500,000 to reflect the diminution in its value. The double
> entry for the receipt by H Plc will therefore be:
>
> | | | |
> |---|---|---|
> | Dr Cash | £50,000 | |
> | Cr Investment in subsidiary | | £20,000 |
> | Cr Profit and loss account | | £30,000 |
>
> If H Plc recorded the investment in S Ltd at nominal value of shares
> issued of £60,000, then, on receipt of the dividend, the investment
> shows no diminution in value below its book amount. The double
> entry for the receipt by H Plc will therefore be:
>
> | | | |
> |---|---|---|
> | Dr Cash | £50,000 | |
> | Cr Profit and loss account | | £50,000 |
>
> To maintain parity in distributable profits, the following further entry
> may be made to reserves in the first scenario. This represents a partial
> realisation of the merger reserve, due to a linked asset (investment)
> being written down through the profit and loss account:
>
> | | | |
> |---|---|---|
> | Dr Merger reserve | £20,000 | |
> | Cr Profit and loss account | | £20,000 |

Merger accounting

Introduction

24.71   A merger occurs when two or more companies are combined to
form one group on terms that the equity shareholders in each company become the equity shareholders in the combined entity. The
substance of the transaction is that the shareholders have pooled
their interests in their respective companies, even though the form
may be an acquisition of one by the other. An essential feature of a
merger is that the net assets of the combined companies are substantially the same as the net assets of the individual companies prior
to the merger, i.e., no significant resources leave the group, in cash or

otherwise, as a result of the merger. This is usually achieved by structuring the deal substantially by means of a share-for-share exchange. The most appropriate way of accounting for a merger under such circumstances is to prepare accounts as if the companies had always been one. The conditions for merger accounting are dealt with in **24.75** to **24.103** below. Chapter 23 deals with the form, content and disclosures of consolidated accounts.

24.72   The practical effects of the merger approach are that:

(a)   the new shares issued as consideration for the merger, and therefore the investment in the acquired company, are recorded at their nominal amount in the books of the acquiring company (their fair value being ignored);

(b)   the net assets of the two companies are combined using existing book values; and

(c)   no amount is recognised as consideration for goodwill or negative goodwill.

24.73   The consolidated profit and loss account includes the profits of each company for the entire period, regardless of the date of the merger, and the comparative amounts in the consolidated accounts are restated to the aggregate of the amounts recorded by the two companies. The only exception is the disclosure of directors' remuneration (see **24.122** below). [Sch 4A: 11 and FRS 6(16)–(19)]

24.74   A merger usually takes the form of an issue by one company of its own equity shares, as consideration for the acquisition of the equity capital of the other, but it may also take other forms, such as the creation of a new holding company which issues its own equity shares in exchange for the *equity* shares of two or more other companies.

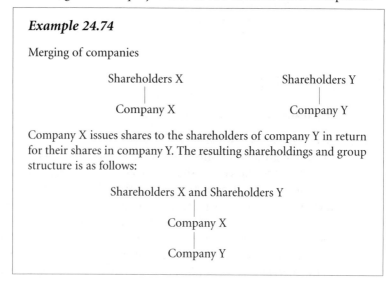

Example 24.74

Merging of companies

Shareholders X   Shareholders Y

Company X   Company Y

Company X issues shares to the shareholders of company Y in return for their shares in company Y. The resulting shareholdings and group structure is as follows:

Shareholders X and Shareholders Y

Company X

Company Y

Conditions for merger accounting

Conditions in the Act

24.75 The Act states that merger accounting may be used only if all of the following conditions are met:
[Sch 4A: 10]

(a) at least 90 per cent of the nominal value of the relevant shares in the undertaking acquired is held by or on behalf of the parent and its subsidiary undertakings;

(b) the proportion referred to in (a) above was attained pursuant to an arrangement providing for the issue of equity shares by the parent or its subsidiary undertakings;

(c) the fair value of any consideration other than the issue of equity shares given pursuant to the arrangement by the parent and its subsidiary undertakings did not exceed 10 per cent of the nominal value of the equity shares issued; and

(d) the merger method adopted accords with generally accepted accounting principles or practice.

24.76 Condition (d) of the Act (see **24.75** above) brings in requirements established by generally accepted accounting principles and practices, such as those contained in FRS 6. These are dealt with in **24.80** to **24.103** below.

24.77 Where the nominal value of a company's equity share capital is small in relation to its market value, the legal requirement to measure the non-equity element of the consideration by reference to the nominal value of the shares issued (see **24.75**(c) above) may possibly deny merger accounting treatment, even when the non-equity portion of the consideration is quite small.

24.78 In **24.75** above:

(a) the term 'arrangement' can include a number of separate transactions which constitute in substance a composite transaction. It is not possible to place any time limit upon the intervals between the separate transactions which allows a series of transactions to be considered as a single arrangement or offer;

(b) 'relevant shares' are those carrying unrestricted rights to participate both in distributions and in the assets of the undertaking upon liquidation;

(c) the term 'equity shares' is defined in s744 as excluding any shares which neither as respects dividends nor as respects capital carry any rights to participate beyond a specified amount in a distribution.

24.79 The following table sets out the permutations for classifying relevant and equity shares.

Capital distribution (liquidation)	Revenue distribution (dividend)	Participation restricted to specified amount (e.g., fixed rate)	Participation not restricted
Participation restricted to specified amount (e.g., to nominal value)		Neither relevant nor equity	Equity but not relevant
Participation not restricted		Equity but not relevant	Both relevant and equity

Conditions in FRS 6

24.80 FRS 6 states that merger accounting must be used if:
[FRS 6(5)]

(a) the use of merger accounting for the combination is not pro-hibited by companies legislation [Sch 4A: 10]; and

(b) the combination meets all the specific criteria set out in paras 6 to 11 of FRS 6 and explained further in paras 60 to 77 of FRS 6. These criteria are dealt with in **24.82** to **24.103** below.

24.81 The criteria in FRS 6 (see **24.82** to **24.103** below) refer to equity and non-equity shares. The definitions of these terms in FRS 6 are the same as those in FRS 4 (see **18.43** and **18.44** above). [FRS 6(2) and FRS 4(7) and (12)] However, for the purposes of the FRS 6 criteria, any convertible share or loan stock should be regarded as equity, to the extent that it is converted into equity as a result of the business combination. It should be noted that the Act's definitions of equity and non-equity are not the same as those in FRS 4; the relationship between the two is discussed in **18.16** above.

Role of the parties – criterion 1

24.82 A key feature of a merger is that it represents a combining of the interests of two (or more) parties. Accordingly, FRS 6 states that a combination cannot be accounted for as a merger if one party to the combination is portrayed as either acquirer or acquired, either by its own board or management or by that of another party to the com-bination. [FRS 6(6)]

24.83 When considering whether or not a combination represents a gen-uine combination of interests, the circumstances surrounding the transaction as a whole should be considered. The following, while not individually conclusive, should be considered:
[FRS 6(62)]

(a) the form by which the combination was achieved;

(b) the plans for the combined entity's future operations (e.g., whether any closures or disposals relate more to one party than another); and

(c) the proposed corporate image (such as the name, logo and the location of the headquarters and principal operations).

24.84 If the terms of the combination of interests result in one party paying a premium over the market value of the shares in the other party, the FRS regards this as evidence that that party has taken the role of an acquirer, unless there is a clear explanation for this apparent premium other than its being a premium paid to acquire control. [FRS 6(61)]

24.85 Where a publicly quoted company is a party to a business combination, the content of communications with its shareholders is likely to be relevant in determining the substance of the transaction. [FRS 6(62)]

Dominance of management – criterion 2

24.86 A key feature of a genuine merger is that all parties to the combination are involved in determining the management of the combined entity and reach a consensus on the appropriate structure and personnel. Thus, for a combination to be accounted for as a merger, FRS 6 requires that all parties to the combination, as represented by the boards of directors or their appointees, participate in establishing the management structure for the combined entity and in selecting the management personnel, and such decisions are made on the basis of a consensus between the parties to the combination rather than purely by exercise of voting rights. [FRS 6(7)]

24.87 If decisions can be reached only by the exercise of majority voting rights against the wishes of one of the parties to the merger, or if one party clearly dominates this process, this indicates that the combination is not a genuine pooling of interests.

24.88 In a genuine merger, the management of the combined entity is likely to include representatives of each of the combining parties, but this need not be the case, provided that it is clear that all the parties to the merger genuinely participated in the decision. Thus, it is possible that all, or most, of the management team of the combined entity come from only one of the parties, provided that this clearly reflects the wishes of the others.

24.89 When considering this criterion, it is necessary to consider not only the formal management structure of the combined entity, but also the identity of all persons involved in the main financial and operating decisions and the way in which the decision-making process operates in practice within the combined entity.

24.90 It is also necessary to consider not only the decisions made in the period of initial integration and restructuring at the time of the combination, but both the short-term effects and the expected long-term consequences of those decisions. [FRS 6(66)]

Relative size of the parties – criterion 3

24.91 FRS 6 states that a combination should not be accounted for as a merger if the relative sizes of the combining entities are so disparate that one party dominates the combined entity by virtue of its relative size. [FRS 6(8)]

24.92 For the purposes of this criterion, a party is presumed to dominate if it is more than 50 per cent larger than each of the other parties to the combination, judged by reference to the ownership interests, i.e., by considering the proportion of the equity of the combined entity attributable to the shareholders of each of the combining parties. However, this presumption may be rebutted if it can be clearly shown that there is no such dominance. Where the presumption is rebutted, the circumstances and an explanation must be disclosed. [FRS 6(68)]

Non-equity consideration – criterion 4

24.93 This criterion is concerned with the extent to which equity shareholders of the combining entities receive any consideration other than equity shares (e.g., cash, other assets, loan stock and preference shares) in the combined entity.

24.94 FRS 6 states that, for a combination to be accounted for as a merger, the consideration received by the equity shareholders of each party to the combination (in respect of their equity shareholdings) should comprise primarily equity shares in the combined entity. [FRS 6(9)] Any non-equity consideration, or equity shares carrying substantially reduced voting or distribution rights, should represent an immaterial proportion of the fair value of the consideration received by the equity shareholders of that party.

24.95 Some adjustment to the rights attaching to the shares held by the non-issuing entities' shareholders may be compatible with the combination being a merger, as business combinations result from a negotiating process where different pre-existing rights have to be reconciled. Whether any change in the rights of one group of shareholders is sufficient to prevent that business combination being treated as a merger will depend on the facts in any individual case, taking into account such matters as:

(a) the rights the shareholders had before the combination;

(b) the total arrangement negotiated;

(c) time limits; and

(d) whether any new restrictions apply equally to all sets of share-holders.

In determining whether equity shares with reduced rights have been issued, both rights to vote and rights to distributions attaching to the shares would need to be taken into account. If any of these individual rights were significantly reduced or circumscribed, the combination would fail to fulfil this condition. [FRS 6(72)]

24.96 If one entity has acquired an interest in another of the combining entities in exchange for non-equity consideration, or equity shares with significantly reduced rights, within the two years before those entities combined, such consideration should be regarded as part of the consideration for the combination for the purpose of determining whether this criterion is met. [FRS 6(9)]

24.97 FRS 6 requires all arrangements made in conjunction with the combination to be taken into account. Equity shareholders will be considered to have disposed of their shareholding for cash where any arrangement is made in connection with the combination that enabled them to exchange or redeem the shares they received in the combination for cash (or other non-equity consideration). For example, a vendor placing or similar arrangement should be treated as giving rise to non-equity consideration, but a normal market selling transaction, or privately arranged sale, entered into by a shareholder is not made in conjunction with the combination and does not prevent the criterion being met. [FRS 6(71)]

24.98 If a peripheral part of the business (i.e., a part of the business that can be disposed of without having a material effect on the nature and focus of the entity's operations) of one of the parties to the combination is disposed of as part of the arrangements surrounding a combination, the distribution to shareholders of:

(a) an interest in that part of the business, which does not form part of the combined entity; or

(b) the proceeds of the sale of such a business, or loan stock representing such proceeds,

does not, of itself, breach this FRS 6 criterion. [FRS 6(10)]

Minorities, etc. – criterion 5

24.99 This criterion is concerned with a party retaining an interest in only part of the combined entity. The concept of a merger is that the participants share the risks and rewards of the whole of the new entity. This concept is incompatible with certain participants having a preferential interest in one part of the combined entity.

24.100 Therefore, FRS 6 states that merger accounting can be used for a combination only when no equity shareholders of any of the combining entities retain any material interest in the future performance of only part of the combined entity. [FRS 6(11)]

24.101 The criterion would not, therefore, be met if the share of the equity in the combined entity allocated to the shareholders of one of the parties to the combination depended to any material extent on the post-combination performance of the business, or any part of it, formerly controlled by that party. [FRS 6(75)]

24.102 Similarly, the criterion would not be met where earn-outs or similar performance-related schemes are included in the arrangements to effect the combination. The test is also failed if there is any material minority (defined by companies legislation as 10 per cent) of shareholders left in one of the combining parties that have not accepted the terms of the combination offer. [FRS 6(76)]

24.103 However, the criterion would not necessarily be invalidated by an arrangement whereby the allocation of consideration between the shareholders of the combining parties depended on the determination of the eventual value of a specific liability or asset contributed by one of the parties (such as the eventual outcome of a claim against one of the parties, or the eventual sales value of a specific asset owned by one of the parties) as opposed to the future operating performance of that party. [FRS 6(77)]

Merger relief

24.104 The Act contains measures to facilitate merger accounting. [s131] Briefly, relief is given from the normal requirement to transfer to the share premium account any premium arising on shares issued. The relief is normally only available on the issue of equity shares.

24.105 The relief is given if equity shares are issued as part of an arrangement for the acquisition of another company and:

(a) the issuing company has secured at least a 90 per cent equity holding in the other company; and

(b) the consideration for the new shares allotted is provided by the issue or transfer to the issuing company of equity shares in the other company (or by the cancellation of any such shares not held by the issuing company).

The amount of the premium that would otherwise have to be transferred to the share premium account may also be disregarded for the purpose of determining the carrying amount of the investment in the company's balance sheet. [s133(1) CA 1985] Where the conditions of s131 are met, then merger relief must be taken. This means that where a decision is made to record an investment at more than the nominal value of shares issued, any premium recorded is not share premium within the meaning of s130 CA 1985.

24.106 If the acquired company's equity share capital is divided into different classes of shares, the requirements in **24.105** above are satisfied in relation to each of the classes of shares taken separately.

24.107 Although the relief is normally only available on the issue of equity shares, the relief extends to any other shares allotted by the issuing company as part of the same arrangement, provided that the consideration for the newly allotted shares is the issue or transfer to the issuing company of non-equity shares in the other company (or by the cancellation of any such shares not held by the issuing company).

24.108 The definitions of equity shares and non-equity shares, for the purposes of merger relief, are not the same as the definitions in FRS 4. For the purposes of merger relief, equity shares are a company's issued shares excluding any which, neither as respects dividends nor as respects capital, carry any right to participate beyond a specified amount in a distribution. [s744] Non-equity shares are any shares not meeting the definition of equity shares. [s131(7)(b)]

24.109 A preference share with a nominal value of £1, an annual dividend of 10 per cent of the nominal value, being redeemable at £1 and entitling the owner, on a winding-up of the company, to £1 plus any accrued dividend would thus not meet the definition of equity shares and would, accordingly, be a non-equity share. If, instead of a dividend equal to 10 per cent of the nominal value, the dividend entitlement were four per cent of the nominal value plus 20 per cent of the dividend declared on the company's £1 ordinary shares, then the preference shares would be classified as equity shares for the purposes of merger relief, even though the shares would be classed as non-equity under FRS 4.

24.110 In order to obtain the relief, it is not necessary for the issuing company to go from a stake of nil to an equity stake of 90 per cent or more in one transaction. [s131(4)] Consider the following example.

> ### Example 24.110
>
> Company B's share capital comprises 100,000 £1 ordinary shares.
>
> In 19X1, company A acquires 30,000 of the shares in B for £75,000, the consideration being satisfied by the issue of £1 ordinary shares in

company A. In 19X3, company A issues 32,000 shares in order to acquire a further 40,000 of B's shares valued at £120,000. The remaining 30,000 shares in B are acquired by A for £110,000 in 19X5, the consideration being satisfied by the issue of 20,000 £1 ordinary shares in A.

It is only the third and final acquisition of shares that takes A's holding of B's equity shares above 90 per cent. Therefore, the merger relief would not be available to company A with respect to the allotment in 19X1 of 25,000 shares and the allotment in 19X3 of 32,000 shares.

However, the relief would be available in 19X5 on the issue of 20,000 shares. Accordingly, the company's share capital account would be credited with the £20,000 nominal value and company A could choose either not to record the premium of £90,000 at all or to credit a merger reserve with the £90,000 premium.

If the acquisitions of shares in 19X1 and 19X3 had been for cash (rather than in a share-for-share exchange), the merger relief would still have been available in 19X5, because that was the acquisition that took A's holding over 90 per cent and was an equity share for equity share exchange.

24.111 Although these measures are primarily intended to make merger accounting possible, they may be adopted in the accounts of the acquiring company whether or not merger accounting is to be used for the consolidation (see **24.26** above).

Special considerations in merger accounting

Uniform accounting policies

24.112 As indicated in **23.118** to **23.122** above, it is desirable that all undertakings in the group should follow uniform accounting policies and, where this is not the case, appropriate adjustments should be made in the consolidated financial statements to achieve uniformity. This requirement is equally applicable whether acquisition or merger accounting is adopted. Thus, although book amounts rather than fair values of the net assets of the merged subsidiary are used for the purpose of consolidation, these book amounts should first be adjusted to the extent necessary to achieve uniformity in accounting policies. [FRS 6(16)]

Restatement of comparative figures

24.113 As noted in **24.73** above, the comparative amounts in the consolidated accounts should be restated as if the entities had been combined throughout the previous period and at the previous balance sheet date. This requires a restatement of the comparative figures to include the results for all the combining entities for the previous period and their balance sheets for the previous balance sheet date. Adjustments should be made as necessary to achieve uniformity of accounting policies. [FRS 6(17)]

24.114 The called up share capital should be restated at the preceding balance sheet date to reflect the nominal value of the new shares subsequently issued to acquire the merged company. If there is any cash or other non-share element in the consideration, this should also be reflected in the preceding balance sheet; it is suggested that this is shown on a separate line under liabilities or, alternatively, as a reduction in cash at bank or increase in overdrafts or other liabilities, as appropriate.

Statement of reserves

24.115 The reserves at the beginning of the year should be adjusted to include the reserves of the merged companies. A further adjustment is necessary to take account of any difference between the carrying value of the investment in the accounts of the parent company (i.e., the nominal value of the shares issued to acquire the subsidiary for which merger relief has been applied together with the fair value of any other consideration given) and the nominal value of the shares acquired. Schedule 4A requires the resulting difference to be shown as an adjustment to consolidated reserves. [Sch 4A: 11(6)]

24.116 The Act is silent on which reserves are available for purposes of absorbing any difference. However, FRS 6 states that the difference, if any, between the nominal value of the shares issued plus the fair value of any other consideration given and the nominal value of the shares received in exchange should be shown as a movement on other reserves in the consolidated financial statements. [FRS 6(18)] Also, any existing balance on the share premium account or capital redemption reserve of the new subsidiary undertaking should be brought in by being shown as a movement on other reserves. These movements should be shown in the reconciliation of movements in shareholders' funds.

24.117 Terms such as 'merger reserve' or 'merger capital reserve' are appropriate for this 'other reserve'.

24.118 If the 'other reserve' that arises as a result of the application of FRS 6 (see **24.116** above) is a debit balance, a question arises as to whether it may remain as a separate negative reserve. [FRS 6(18)] Since the difference arises only on consolidation, it cannot be deemed a realised loss which would require elimination against the profit and loss account over its useful life; consequently, there does not appear to be any barrier to the treatment as a negative reserve. An alternative to having a negative reserve would be to write it off against the balance on the profit and loss account reserve.

24.119 An example of a suitable statement of reserves following a merger is given below.

> **Example 24.119**
>
> | | Profit and loss account £'000 | Revaluation reserve £'000 | Other reserves £'000 |
> |---|---|---|---|
> | Balance at beginning of year: | | | |
> | As previously reported | 13,450 | 1,283 | – |
> | Excess of par value of shares issued over par value of shares of merged company acquired (assuming transfer to a separate reserve) | – | – | (1,832) |
> | Reserves of merged company | 5,991 | 588 | 250 |
> | As restated | 19,441 | 1,871 | (1,582) |
> | Profit retained for the year | 2,595 | – | – |
> | Balance at end of year | 22,036 | 1,871 | (1,582) |

24.120 The above example assumes that there is no share premium balance in either of the two combining companies. Had there been a balance on the share premium account of the acquired company, this would also need to be eliminated. It is suggested that this is eliminated to the same 'other reserve' as the difference in share nominal values.

Expenses connected with the merger

24.121 FRS 6 states that merger expenses should be charged to the profit and loss account of the combined entity at the effective date of the merger, as reorganisation or restructuring expenses, in accordance with FRS 3 (i.e., as costs of a fundamental reorganisation or restructuring that has a material effect on the nature and focus of the reporting entity's operations). [FRS 6(19) and FRS 3(20)]

Remuneration of directors

24.122 In determining the disclosures to be made in the group accounts in relation to the remuneration of directors, only directors of the parent company and only their remuneration during the period when they had that status should be considered. For example, if a director of the acquired company becomes a director of the acquiring company on the merger, the emoluments to be reported should be restricted to those which he received following the merger. (The full remuneration for the financial year in respect of directorships of the acquired company and its subsidiaries will, of course, be reported in the acquired company's own financial statements.) As described in more detail in **8.109** above, companies may wish to present proforma financial results for 12 months (plus comparatives) which include the directors' previous emoluments.

24.123 If an off-the-shelf company is acquired to purchase the issued shares of the merging companies in exchange for the issue of new shares in itself, there will have been one or more directors appointed prior to the change in ownership. If the change in ownership occurred during the financial year in which the merger took place, the remuneration of the earlier director(s) will have to be taken into account in the disclosures. However, in practice, such remuneration is likely to be nil and, if so, there will be no disclosure impact.

Accounting period covered by a newly formed parent company

24.124 When a merger is effected by setting up a new parent company which acquires the issued shares of the merging companies in exchange for the issue of its own shares, it frequently happens that the first accounting reference period of the new company will be a period of less than a year, ending on the accounting reference date chosen for the group. This will normally be the existing accounting reference date of one or more of the merged companies.

24.125 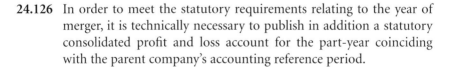 Frequently, the date of formation will be arbitrary and will not coincide with the group's accounting periods. Strictly, the Act requires the consolidated financial statements to cover the accounting period of the parent company; this may imply that there could be no comparative figures at all. In substance, however, where the group is continuing to trade as before, but with a new legal parent company, it will be appropriate to prepare consolidated accounts as if the parent company had been in existence throughout the reported periods, but with a prominent footnote explaining the basis on which financial statements are presented.

24.126 In order to meet the statutory requirements relating to the year of merger, it is technically necessary to publish in addition a statutory consolidated profit and loss account for the part-year coinciding with the parent company's accounting reference period.

24.127 The DTI had earlier announced its intention to amend this part of the law and thus allow consolidated financial statements to be prepared on a merger basis, notwithstanding that this would cover a longer period than the financial statements of the legal parent. However, the DTI did not enact the change when it subsequently legislated in 1996.

Comparison of merger accounting and acquisition accounting

24.128 The difference between merger accounting and acquisition accounting is best illustrated by an example.

Introduction to example

24.129 Upper Ltd makes an offer for the shares of Lower Ltd, which is accepted on 31 December 1999, the year end of both companies. The combined group is to be known as Midway Ltd. On 31 December 1999, the summarised accounts of the two companies were as follows.

Example 24.129

Balance sheets at 31 December 1999

	Upper Ltd £'000	Lower Ltd £'000
Tangible net assets	350	300
Share capital (shares of £1 each)	120	50
Profit and loss account	230	250
	350	300
Profit for the financial year		
1999	70	30
1998	60	80

24.130 Under the offer, Upper Ltd issues 100,000 shares in exchange for all of the 50,000 shares of Lower Ltd. Assume a fair value of £3.50 for each Upper Ltd share and a fair value of the net tangible assets of Lower Ltd of £320,000.

Merger accounting

24.131 Using merger accounting, Upper Ltd would record the investment in the subsidiary in its books at £100,000 (i.e., the nominal value of the 100,000 shares issued by Upper Ltd) and the only difference to be eliminated on consolidation is the difference between the nominal value of the issued capital of Lower Ltd of £50,000 and the nominal value of the shares in Upper Ltd issued to acquire it. This difference is adjusted on the group reserves. With this exception, the consolidated accounts are simply the aggregation of the accounts of the two separate companies.

Acquisition accounting

24.132 Under acquisition accounting, Upper Ltd would, for consolidation purposes, record the investment in the subsidiary (i.e., the 50,000 shares of Lower Ltd acquired) at the fair value of the consideration given for the shares, i.e., £350,000 (100,000 x £3.50), although in its own books, Upper Ltd would probably take advantage of the merger

relief provisions of the Act to record the investment at £100,000, the
nominal value of the shares issued. The excess of £350,000 over the
£100,000 nominal value of the shares issued must be credited in the
consolidated balance sheet to a separate (merger) reserve. On consolidation, the excess of the investment (£350,000) over the fair value
of the tangible net assets of Lower Ltd (£320,000) would be treated
as goodwill on consolidation.

The effects

24.133 The respective consolidated balance sheets at 31 December 1999
would be as follows.

Example 24.133

	Merger accounting		Acquisition accounting	
	£'000		£'000	
Tangible net assets	650		670	(a)
Goodwill	–		30	(b)
	650		700	
Share capital	220		220	
Merger reserve	–		250	(c)
Profit and loss account	430	(d)	230	
	650		700	
Group profit for 1999	100		70	(e)
Corresponding amount for 1998	140	(f)	60	

Notes

(a) Under acquisition accounting the net assets of Lower Ltd are
included at their fair value at the date of acquisition (£320,000).
Under merger accounting, they are included at their book
amount of £300,000.

(b) The goodwill should be accounted for in accordance with
FRS 10.

(c) The merger reserve represents the excess of the fair value of the
shares issued over their par value (£250,000). If merger relief was
not available under the Act (see **24.104** above), the excess of
£250,000 would have been credited to the share premium
account.

(d) The consolidated profit and loss account under merger accounting is the aggregate of the profit and loss accounts of the
individual companies (£480,000) less the difference between the
nominal value of the shares issued and the nominal value of the
shares acquired (£50,000).

(e) Since the acquisition took place at 31 December 1999, all the
profits of Lower Ltd prior to that date are pre-acquisition and are
excluded from group reserves under acquisition accounting.

(f) Under merger accounting, corresponding amounts are restated
to include the profits of Lower Ltd for 1998.

Accounting for disposals

Introduction

24.134 FRS 2 includes specific guidance on the accounting treatment following an undertaking ceasing to be a subsidiary undertaking. A distinction is drawn between:

(a) disposal, which involves a reduction in the share of a subsidiary's net assets attributable to the parent (resulting from a reduced shareholding); and

(b) loss of rights, where the parent loses control but without any reduction in its shareholding.

24.135 Disposal may be further subdivided into 'direct disposal', involving the receipt of proceeds of shares sold (see **24.137** to **24.141** below), and 'deemed disposal' where no proceeds are received (see **24.142** to **24.146** below).

24.136 In addition, although not discussed in FRS 2, it is possible that an undertaking may cease to be a subsidiary undertaking through a demerger, whereby shares in the subsidiary are distributed *in specie* to members of the parent (see **24.182** to **24.188** below).

Direct disposals

24.137 Direct disposals have two effects: the investing company's entity profit and loss account will show a gain or loss on disposal (and maybe some adjustments to revaluation reserve if the investment had been carried at a valuation higher than cost) (see **24.138** below); and the group accounts will consolidate, in the group profit and loss account, the disposed of subsidiary up to the date of disposal (assuming that group accounts are being prepared (see **23.1** above) and reflect a gain or loss on disposal (see **24.139** below).

Individual company

24.138 In the individual company financial statements of the investing company in the year that a direct disposal occurs, the profit or loss on sale will be the difference between the carrying amount of the investment and the proceeds of sale.

> ### Example 24.138.1
>
> Assume the following:
>
> (a) A purchased the whole of the issued capital of B for £100,000 (assume no goodwill arose on consolidation and no assets have been revalued).

(b) The undistributed post-acquisition profits of B at 31 December 1999 amounted to £120,000.

(c) The profit after tax of B for the six months to 30 June 2000 is estimated at £30,000.

(d) A sold the whole share capital of B on 30 June 2000 for £300,000.

In A's own accounts, the transaction results in a profit of £200,000 (sale price of £300,000 less cost of £100,000). Of this amount:

(a) £120,000, being the undistributed post-acquisition profit, is already included in the group accounts as part of the balance of the consolidated profit and loss account;

(b) £30,000 represents the trading profit to the date of sale which should be included in the consolidated profit and loss account in the current year; and

(c) £50,000 is the balance to be recognised in the consolidated profit and loss account as the profit on sale of the subsidiary (see **24.140** below).

Example 24.138.2

Following on from Example **24.138.1** above, if the investment had been revalued in the investing company's books by £35,000 to £135,000, then the transaction results in a profit of £165,000 (sale price of £300,000 less carrying amount of £135,000). On sale, £35,000 is transferred from the revaluation reserve to the profit and loss reserve, which results in a total increase to the profit and loss reserve of £200,000. This is reconciled as shown in Example **24.138.1** above.

Group accounts

24.139 In the consolidated financial statements, FRS 2 requires the following items to be included in the consolidated financial statements: [FRS 2(46)]

(a) the results of the subsidiary undertaking up to the date of its ceasing to be a subsidiary; and

(b) any gain or loss from the disposal.

This assumes that, at the end of the year, a group still exists (i.e., the parent controls another subsidiary and prepares group accounts as required by FRS 2 (see **23.1** above). If any assets of the subsidiary have been revalued, then any balance on the group revaluation reserve in respect of the subsidiary should be released at the date of sale; the amount released should be treated in the same way as for any other disposal of a revalued asset.

24.140 FRS 2 also describes the general principle for calculating the gain or loss as a comparison of the carrying amount of net assets attributable before the disposal with the carrying amount of net assets attributable after the disposal. FRS 2 requires that the gain or loss should reflect any related goodwill (positive or negative) that has previously not been charged in the consolidated profit and loss account. [FRS 2(47)] FRS 10 contains a similar provision. Thus, the calculation will be:

	£
Proceeds	(X)
Less: reduction in the group's share of subsidiary net assets	(X)
Less: related goodwill not previously charged in the profit and loss account	X
Gain/Loss	X

Tying this in to Example **24.138.1** above, the gain of £50,000 is represented by:

	£
Proceeds	300,000
Less: reduction in the group's share of subsidiary net assets	
– had 100% of £250,000 (100 + 120 + 30)	
– now have 0%	
– *net assets disposed of*	(250,000)
Gain/Loss	50,000

Example 24.140

X acquired 100 per cent of Y for £100 million when Y's net assets were £40 million. The resulting £60 million of goodwill was eliminated against consolidated reserves and was not reinstated as an asset on the adoption of FRS 10. At the beginning of the current year, Y's net assets stood at £65 million. During the year, X disposed of all the shares in Y for net proceeds of £90 million. From the beginning of the year to the date of disposal, Y's net assets increased through trading to £68 million.

The accounting treatment will be as follows:

(a) consolidated revenue and expense headings will each reflect amounts relating to Y to the date of disposal resulting in a net profit included of £3 million (£68 million – £65 million);

(b) on disposal, the consolidated profit and loss account will show a loss calculated as:

	£ million	£ million
Proceeds		90
Less:		
Net assets of Y at date of disposal (100%)	68	
Goodwill written off to reserves		
immediately on acquisition (100%)	60	
		128
Loss		38

The credit entry for the goodwill adjustment is made in the reserve used to write off goodwill initially. This will be disclosed in the group's reconciliation of shareholders' funds and reserve notes.

24.141   The rule in FRS 2 and FRS 10 (discussed in **24.140** above) is necessary in order to prevent purchased goodwill which has been eliminated against reserves from bypassing the profit and loss account completely. [FRS 2(47) and FRS 10(71)(c)] The following example illustrates the impact of this rule.

Example 24.141

Suppose that X in Example **24.140** above had, in respect of the goodwill arising on the acquisition of Y, adopted the accounting policy of amortising purchased goodwill instead of immediate write-off and that the balance in the accumulated amortisation account at the date of disposal was £40 million. The profit on disposal is calculated as:

	£ million	£ million
Proceeds		90
Less:		
Net assets of Y at date of disposal	68	
Goodwill not yet charged through the		
profit and loss account (£60−£40)	20	
		88
Profit		2

In this example, the consolidated financial statements show a profit on disposal of £2 million, as opposed to a loss of £38 million in the previous example where goodwill was written off to reserves immediately on acquisition. The difference is attributable to the fact that, in this example, £40 million has already been charged through the consolidated profit and loss account in previous years as amortisation of goodwill.

The entries for the goodwill adjustment will be to remove the goodwill cost and accumulated amortisation from the accounts (i.e., Cr Cost £60m, Dr Accumulated amortisation £40m).

In addition, in this example, it is irrelevant for the purposes of calculating the profit or loss on disposal whether the £40 million balance

---

in the accumulated amortisation account arose through regular amortisation of goodwill or included write-offs for impairment. This is because, in both cases, the write-offs would have been charged through the profit and loss account and therefore need not be taken into account in the calculation of profit or loss on disposal.

Deemed disposals

24.142 A deemed disposal may arise through (not an exhaustive list):

(a) the parent not taking up its full entitlement in a rights issue;

(b) the payment of scrip dividends not taken up by the parent;

(c) the issue of shares to minority shareholders; or

(d) the exercise of options or warrants granted to another party.

Although the number of shares that the parent holds does not alter, the effect will be that the parent's attributable shareholding interest will be reduced and the net assets of the subsidiary may be increased. There are three possible outcomes: the residual interest still qualifies as a subsidiary undertaking or is reduced to either an associated undertaking, or a passive investment.

24.143 Where the subsidiary continues to be a subsidiary, the difference in the group's share of net assets before and after the deemed disposal should be dealt with in the statement of total recognised gains and losses (see also **24.148** below for further discussion).

24.144 Where the subsidiary ceases to be a subsidiary, then FRS 2 requirements described in **24.139** above will apply. [FRS 2(46)] The calculation of the gain or loss will be, in principle, the same as above for a direct disposal.

24.145 Following the date of disposal, shares that the former parent continues to hold will now represent either:

(a) an associated company to be accounted for under the equity method. This is dealt with in **24.149** below under partial disposals; or

(b) an investment to be accounted for on a 'cost basis'. The initial cost of the investment will be determined as the group's residual share of net assets in its former subsidiary. It follows that the residual share of original purchased goodwill may also be added to the 'cost' of the investment, although there seems no requirement to do this. Subsequently, the group will account for dividends only.

24.146	The option described in **24.145**(b) above, concerning inclusion of the residual share of purchased goodwill in the 'cost' of the investment, is available even if the goodwill has been written off to reserves immediately on acquisition. In such cases, it is appropriate to debit investments and credit reserves in the consolidated balance sheet.

Loss of rights

24.147 Just as an undertaking may be a subsidiary undertaking even though the parent has only a minority holding of shares, e.g., through rights that enable the actual exercise of a dominant influence, the loss of such rights may result in an undertaking ceasing to be a subsidiary, even though there is no reduction in the share of net assets attributable to the former parent. Similarly, loss of subsidiary status may follow from changes in the rights of shares held by another party or from a reversal of other arrangements that gave the parent control without increasing its shareholding. In such circumstances:

(a) no gain or loss accrues, unless a payment has been made for the transfer of control, since there is no change in the group's share of attributable net assets;

(b) no further consolidation of results or net assets should occur;

(c) the group's share of net assets should be dealt with as an interest in an associated company (if the associated company definition is met) or (if not met) as an investment;

(d) subsequent accounting will be on an equity basis or investment basis respectively;

(e) on the latter basis, in determining the appropriate investment carrying value, the goodwill attributable to the group's interest may be added to the investment. This involves a transfer of the goodwill from the goodwill account to the investment account (if goodwill is carried as an intangible fixed asset) or a transfer from reserves to the investment account (if goodwill has been written off to reserves immediately on acquisition – see **24.146** above).

Partial disposals

Reducing interest but retaining a subsidiary undertaking

24.148 Where a group reduces its interest in a subsidiary as a result of a disposal or a deemed disposal, but the undertaking remains a subsidiary:

(a) there is no adjustment to the carrying value of the subsidiary's net assets included in the consolidation apart from the effect of the transaction e.g., the proceeds of shares issued to outside shareholders;

(b) the minority interest's share of net assets in the consolidated balance sheet increases;

(c) a profit or loss on the disposal arises as follows:

    (i) for a direct disposal, the calculation will be the same as under **24.140** above, except that the subsidiary net assets and goodwill taken into the calculation will be a percentage only reflecting the interest sold to minority shareholders; the profit or loss should be reported in the consolidated profit and loss account;

    (ii) for a deemed disposal, a comparison is made between the respective group share of attributable subsidiary net assets before and after the disposal (including goodwill). Since it predates FRS 3, FRS 2 does not make reference to whether the gain or loss should be dealt with in the profit and loss account or the statement of total recognised gains and losses. Since the group is not involved directly in the transaction, it seems logical that the difference should be dealt with in the statement of total recognised gains and losses (although FRS 2 does not appear to prohibit inclusion in the profit and loss account). However, once the group has decided its policy on which performance statement to recognise gains and losses on deemed acquisitions/disposals, it should apply that policy consistently. In addition, the 'gain' arising on some deemed disposals is capital in nature (see Example **24.148** below) and is more appropriately dealt with in the statement of total recognised gains and losses. Where, following a group's chosen policy, such a gain is taken to the profit and loss account, it would be necessary to make a transfer out of the profit and loss reserve to a capital reserve;

(d) no goodwill is attributed to the minority; goodwill relating to the interest sold or to the interest deemed to have been disposed of is taken into the calculation of gain or loss on disposal (see (c)(i) above).

Example 24.148

X acquired 100 per cent of Y for £1,000 million when Y's net assets were £400 million. The resulting £600 million of goodwill was eliminated against consolidated reserves and was not reinstated as an asset on the adoption of FRS 10. At the beginning of the current year, Y's net assets stood at £650 million. During the year, at a date when Y's net assets have increased to £680 million due to trading, warrants to subscribe for new shares were exercised by a third party, resulting in the third party holding 20 per cent of total ordinary shares. The warrant holders paid Y £450 million on exercise of the warrants. As a result, Y's net assets increased to £1,130 million (= £680 million + £450 million). Net assets at the year end were £1,200 million.

The deemed disposal is accounted for as follows:

(a)   consolidated revenue and expense headings will each reflect amounts relating to Y's trading throughout the period. In addition, a minority share of profits of £14 million will be deducted, reflecting their share of profits following the deemed disposal by the group calculated as 20 per cent x (£1,200 million – £1,130 million);

(b)   arising from the deemed disposal, the consolidated statement of total recognised gains and losses (or, alternatively, the consolidated profit and loss account) will show a profit calculated as:

	£ million	£ million
Share of net assets before disposal		
(100 percent × £680 million)	680	
Goodwill	600	
		1,280
Share of net assets after disposal		
(80 per cent × £1,130 million)	904	
Goodwill (80 per cent × £600 million)	480	
		1,384
Gain		104

An alternative calculation of the gain would be:

	£ million	£ million
Share of proceeds accruing to the group		
(80 per cent × £450 million)		360
Less:		
Share of net assets transferred to minority		
(20 per cent × £680 million)	136	
Share of goodwill (20 per cent × £600m)	120	
		256
Gain		104

Consider now the balance sheets. In order to make the changes clearer, the goodwill written off to reserves has been shown as a separate reserve, although under FRS 10 this would not be allowed. Assume that the balance sheet of X and Y together with the consolidated balance sheet immediately before the warrants were exercised were as follows:

	X	Y	Consol'd
	£ million	£ million	£ million
Investment in Y	1,000	–	–
Other net assets	5,750	680	6,430
	6,750	680	6,430
Share capital	1,000	200	1,000
Share premium	1,000	–	1,000
Profit and loss account	4,750	480	5,030[1]
Goodwill	–	–	(600)
	6,750	680	6,430

The same balance sheets immediately after the warrants were exercised are:

	X	Y	Consol'd
	£ million	£ million	£ million
Investment in Y	1,000	–	–
Other net assets	5,750	1,130	6,880
Minority interests	–	–	(226)
	6,750	1,130	6,654
Share capital	1,000	250	1,000
Share premium	1,000	400	1,000
Capital reserve	–	–	160[2]
Profit and loss account	4,750	480	4,974[3]
Goodwill	–	–	(480)
	6,750	1,130	6,654

From the capital and reserves section of the consolidated balance sheets, it can be seen that, as a result of the transaction, there has been a reduction in the balance on the profit and loss account reserve by £56 million and the creation of a capital reserve of £160 million; these two net to give an overall gain of £104 million (which agrees with the profit on deemed disposal calculation above). The capital reserve represents the group's share (80 per cent) of the share capital and share premium raised by the subsidiary post-acquisition less 20 per cent of the original cost of investment. It has been put to a capital reserve because the share capital and premium (which it represents) is a non-distributable reserve, in the subsidiary. Because the transaction creates a non-distributable reserve it appears to be more appropriate to include the gain arising on the deemed disposal in the statement of total recognised gains and losses rather than including it in the profit and loss account. However, it would still necessitate a transfer out of the profit and loss reserve to the capital reserve of the additional £56 million. Where a company chooses to record the gain of £104 million in the profit and loss account (see **24.148**(c)(ii) above), it will be necessary to transfer £160 million (£104 million + £56 million) out of the profit and loss reserve into the capital reserve.

Notes

1   £5,030 = £4,750 + £(480 − (400 − 200))
2   £160 = 80 per cent of £450 (being the share capital and share premium raised by the subsidiary post-acquisition) less £200 (being 20 per cent of the original cost of investment − this adjustment is needed because X is deemed to have disposed of 20 per cent of its goodwill)
3   £4,974 = £4,750 + 80 per cent of £(480 − (400 − 200))

Reducing interest but retaining an associate undertaking

24.149 Where a disposal results in the subsidiary ceasing to be a subsidiary undertaking, but the residual holding meets the definition of an associated undertaking:

(a)   the subsidiary will be consolidated for the period from the beginning of the period until it ceased to be a subsidiary;

(b)   a gain or loss on the disposal, calculated in **24.140** above, will be recorded;

(c)   thereafter, the associated company will be accounted for under the equity method. Initially, the group's residual share of net assets will be transferred to the appropriate balance sheet fixed asset investment heading as 'Investment in associated undertaking'. Any residual share of original purchased goodwill related to the retained interest will remain without adjustment (e.g., if goodwill had been eliminated, then the residual share of goodwill will remain as eliminated goodwill). Subsequently, the group will equity account for its residual share of net profits and losses and for changes in net assets of the associate (see chapter 25 for equity accounting).

Minority interests

Introduction

24.150 As indicated in previous sections, the basic consolidation process involves the aggregation of the assets, liabilities, income and expenditure of the individual group undertakings. Therefore, where the group does not hold the whole of the share capital of a subsidiary, an adjustment is necessary to take account of the interests of the outside shareholders. Their interests in the capital and reserves of the subsidiary need to be recognised in the group balance sheet and their share of the subsidiary's profit or loss for the year needs to be taken into account in arriving at the group profit or loss.

24.151 The term 'minority interests' denotes the element of subsidiary profit or losses, and capital and reserves, that are attributable to shareholders in subsidiaries, other than group undertakings. This term is now enshrined within the Act's prescribed formats.

24.152 As a result of the changes within the Companies Act 1989, and the possibility of a parent having control without majority ownership of shares, there is no upper limit to the proportion of net assets and profits or losses that may be attributable to 'minority' shareholders. While the term 'outside shareholders interests' may have been more appropriate to certain situations, the term 'minority interests' is required by the Act.

Balance sheet presentation

24.153 In certain instances, minority interests should be included in the consolidated balance sheet as a liability (see **17.61** to **17.66** above for details). Where they are not being included as a liability, the balance sheet formats provide a heading for minority interests. This heading should appear as a separate item in the consolidated balance sheet either after 'Provisions for liabilities and charges' or after 'Share capital and reserves'. Minority interests should not be shown as part of the total of capital and reserves, as the consolidated balance sheet is intended to show the financial position of the group so far as concerns members of the parent company only. FRS 4 requires the amount of minority interests shown in the balance sheet to be analysed between the aggregate amount attributable to equity interests and amounts attributable to non-equity interests. [FRS 4(50)] The amounts attributed to non-equity minority interests and their associated finance costs should be calculated in the same manner as those for non-equity shares.

24.154 Dividends payable to minority interests should be included under 'Other creditors, including taxation and social security'.

Profit and loss account presentation

24.155 Where minority interests are classified as liabilities in the balance sheet, the profit and loss account charge will be classified as interest. For other minority interests, the profit and loss formats require minority interests in the profit or loss on ordinary activities to be shown immediately below the heading 'Profit or loss on ordinary activities after taxation'. The minority interest in respect of extraordinary items is required by the Act to be shown as a separate line below 'Tax on extraordinary profit or loss'. The amount to be included in the minority interests line in the profit and loss account for non-equity minority interests is the finance cost (per FRS 4) associated with the interest.

24.156 FRS 4 requires the minority interests charge in the profit and loss account to be analysed between equity and non-equity interests. [FRS 4(60)]

24.157 Where there are non-equity minority interests, a description should be given of any rights of holders of the shares against other group companies, e.g., in respect of convertible preference shares. Where this right is in the form of a guarantee, the non-equity minority interest will be classified as a liability (see **17.61** to **17.66** above).

24.158 Where non-equity minority interests are disclosed in the notes to the accounts rather than on the face of the balance sheet on the grounds that they are not material, the relevant caption on the face of the balance sheet should state that non-equity interests are included.

Determination of minority interests at the date of acquisition

24.159 On acquisition of a subsidiary undertaking, two issues arise relating to the measurement of minority interests. The first issue is whether minority interests are based on original net book values as disclosed in the subsidiary's books or on values used for consolidation purposes. The second issue is whether any goodwill should be attributed to minority interests.

24.160 In respect of the first issue, FRS 2 requires minority interests to be based on the attributable share of adjusted values as used for consolidation purposes. [FRS 2(38)] Under acquisition accounting, this will be the fair value of a subsidiary's net assets. Under merger accounting, it will be the amounts at which they stand in the subsidiary's books subject to adjustments permitted by the Act (e.g., for accounting policy changes). The treatment under acquisition accounting differs from international accounting standards. IAS 22 (revised 1993) requires, as its benchmark treatment, that when an entity becomes a subsidiary, the minority interests should be measured at the appropriate proportion of the pre-acquisition carrying amounts as recorded in the subsidiary's books. The treatment required under FRS 2 is permitted, but only as an allowed alternative.

24.161 In respect of the second issue, FRS 2 requires that no amount of goodwill should be attributed to minority interests. [FRS 2(38)] To do so would require a hypothetical extrapolation of purchase cost.

> ### *Example 24.161*
>
> A acquires 60 per cent of B for £360 and the fair value of B's net assets at the time of acquisition was £500. Under FRS 2, this acquisition gives rise to goodwill of £60 (being £360 minus 60 per cent of £500).

> Under the alternative that FRS 2 rejects, goodwill would be extrapolated to the amount that might arise if 100 per cent of the shares had been purchased, i.e., £100, with the additional £40 of goodwill being adjusted against minority interests.

Ongoing accounting for minority interests

24.162 After becoming a subsidiary, FRS 2 requires profits or losses arising to be apportioned between the controlling and minority interests in proportion to their respective interests held over the period in which the profit or loss arose. [FRS 2(37)] It follows that a minority interest should be disclosed from the date of acquisition through to the date of disposal.

24.163 Where there is a change in the respective interests of the group and the minority, it is necessary to apportion the subsidiary's profits or losses arising in the accounting period between the periods which have different minority interests before apportioning the resulting profits or losses for each period between the controlling and minority interests, as described in **24.162** above.

24.164 For non-equity minority interests, the charge to the profit and loss account is the finance cost (calculated in the same way as for non-equity shares) associated with the interest.

Two classes of shares

24.165 A practical problem may arise where there is more than one class of share, each having differing rights to profits or assets, and in which the group and minority hold different proportions of each class. The following guidelines may assist in such circumstances:

(a) where a subsidiary has in issue both ordinary and preference shares, it will be necessary to consider first the element of profit used to pay preference dividends and, secondly, the residual element (profit or loss) attributable to ordinary shareholders. Where there is insufficient profit to pay preference dividends, the preference share allocation should nevertheless be provided, unless there is clear evidence not only that directors are not under any obligation to pay preference dividends, but also that it is unlikely that they will do so;

(b) since accounts are drawn up on a going concern assumption, the basis used to allocate equity interests should give precedence to the distribution of revenue profits, rather

> than rights to capital distributions which could arise under a liquidation, unless some other basis is more appropriate.

Debit balances

24.166 Where a subsidiary included in the consolidation reports losses, the requirements of FRS 2 (described in **24.162** above) mean that the minority interests within the consolidated profit and loss account must reflect the appropriate share of those losses. [FRS 2(37)] This FRS 2 requirement has to be followed even in cases where losses result in a subsidiary having net liabilities; in which case, the recognition of the minority share of such losses results in a debit balance for minority interests in the consolidated balance sheet. However, in such a situation, it is necessary to consider whether the debit balance may be carried or whether a provision has to be made.

24.167 FRS 2 requires provision to be made to the extent that the group has a commercial or legal obligation, whether formally expressed or informally implied, to provide finance that may not be recoverable in respect of the accumulated losses attributable to the minority. [FRS 2(37)] Such an obligation will exist if, for example, the parent has given guarantees that could be held to cover the minority share of liabilities or where the group is likely in practice to settle such liabilities.

24.168 Where such a provision is made, FRS 2 allows it to be set directly against the minority interests amount in the consolidated profit and loss account and balance sheet. [FRS 2(81)]

24.169 FRS 2 does not specify how the above provision is to be presented in the consolidated accounts, other than that it should be set directly against the minority interest. As the separate disclosure of the minority interest before any set-off and the provision would not seem to provide any useful additional information, it is suggested that only the net figure for minority interests be shown in the consolidated profit and loss account and balance sheet. If material, the amounts of provision that have been set directly against minority interests should be disclosed separately in the notes to the accounts.

24.170 The wording of FRS 2 on this issue appears to represent a change from prior practice, which focused to a greater extent on whether the minority shareholders were under an obligation to make good losses of the subsidiary. FRS 2 switches emphasis away from whether the group can obtain support for the subsidiaries from the minority shareholders onto whether the group has an enforceable obligation against it in respect of losses attributable to the minority interest.

Group reconstructions

Definition

24.171 FRS 6 defines a group reconstruction as any of the following arrangements:
[FRS 6(2)]

(a) the transfer of a shareholding in a subsidiary undertaking from one group company to another;

(b) the addition of a new parent company to a group;

(c) the transfer of shares in one or more subsidiary undertakings of a group to a new company that is not a group company, but whose shareholders are the same as those of the group's parent;

(d) the combination into a group of two or more companies that, before the combination, had the same shareholders.

Such reconstructions also include the splitting off of one or more subsidiary undertakings, as in some demergers, where a separate group is formed. [FRS 6(78)] Demergers are explained further in **24.182** to **24.188** below.

24.172 Where a minority interest exists, merger accounting is permitted only for those group reconstructions that do not change the interest of the minority in the net assets of the group. Thus, the transfer of a subsidiary undertaking within a sub-group that has a minority shareholder may qualify for merger accounting, but acquisition accounting must be used for the transfer of a subsidiary undertaking out of, or into, such a sub-group. If a minority has effectively acquired, or disposed of, rights to part of the net assets of the group, FRS 6 requires the transfer to be accounted for by using acquisition accounting rather than merger accounting. [FRS 6(79)]

24.173 Where a group reconstruction involves inserting a new shell holding company, the accounting treatment depends on the substance of the business combination being effected, i.e., whether a combination of the entities other than the new parent company would have been an acquisition or a merger. If the combination would have been an acquisition, one entity can be identified as having the role of an acquirer. This acquirer and the new parent company should first be combined by using merger accounting, then the other parties to the business combination should be treated as acquired by this combined company, by using the acquisition method of accounting. On the other hand, where the substance of the business combination effected by a new parent company is a merger, the new parent company and the other parties should all be combined by using merger accounting. [FRS 6(14)]

Accounting methods

24.174 Merger accounting is often appropriate for a group reconstruction. The use of acquisition accounting would require the restatement, at fair value, of the assets and liabilities of the company transferred, and the recognition of goodwill, which is likely to be inappropriate in the case of a transaction that is wholly internal to the group and does not alter the relative rights of the ultimate shareholders. In addition, under acquisition accounting, the comparatives would not reflect the new combination.

24.175 A group reconstruction may be accounted for by using merger accounting, even though there is no business combination meeting the definition of a merger, provided:
[FRS 6(13)]

(a) the use of merger accounting is not prohibited by companies legislation [Sch 4A(10)];

(b) the ultimate shareholders remain the same and the rights of each such shareholder, relative to the others, are unchanged; and

(c) no minority's interest in the net assets of the group is altered by the transfer.

Although neither the Act nor FRS 6 expressly forbids the use of acquisition accounting for group reorganisations, it is unlikely to give a true and fair view. Although FRS 6 refers to merger accounting, for a group reconstruction it is more likely that hybrid accounting results. This could be as follows:

(a) assets and liabilities are retained at previous book value;

(b) no goodwill is recognised; and

(c) comparative amounts are not restated.

Disclosure requirements

24.176 The normal disclosure requirements of FRS 6 do not apply to group reconstructions that are accounted for by using merger accounting. [FRS 6(22)] However, there is no similar exemption from the disclosure requirements of the Act.

Relief available under the Act

24.177 The Act deals specifically with group reconstructions and provides that, where shares are issued at a premium, relief is given from the requirement of s130 to transfer all of the premium to the share premium account. [s132] As a result, in certain group reconstructions, the share premium recorded can be restricted to a defined minimum (the minimum premium value – see **24.180** below). The intention is to maintain capital at the same level as existed before the reconstruction.

24.178 The following conditions must exist to obtain relief:

(a)   the company issuing the shares is a wholly owned subsidiary of another company;

(b)   the shares are allotted to the issuing company's parent company or to another wholly owned subsidiary of that parent company; and

(c)   the consideration received for the shares allotted is assets, other than cash, of either the parent company or another wholly owned subsidiary of that parent company.

24.179 The most obvious occurrence of these events is where shares are issued as consideration for an investment of shares held in another group company. However, the relief is not restricted to a share exchange, but is available for the transfer of any non-cash asset.

24.180 The minimum premium value is determined as follows:

(a)   the lower of the original cost to the transferor and the book value immediately prior to transfer of assets transferred by the transferor company;

less

(b)   the book value immediately prior to transfer of liabilities transferred by the transferor company;

less

(c)   the nominal value of shares issued by the transferee company.

The issuing company (the transferee company) can choose to record the net assets it receives at either their fair value or at the value used in the calculation of the minimum premium value. [s133]

Example 24.180.1

A owns 100% of B and C directly. B (the transferee) issues 45 £1 shares to A (the transferor) in return for shares in C. (The resulting structure would be A owning 100% of B which owns 100% of C.)

A's investment in C was £100 (original cost and current carrying value).

C's balance sheet is:

	Carrying value	Fair value
Gross assets (original cost = £350)	£300	£550
Liabilities	(£50)	(£50)
Net assets	£250	£500

The share for share transfer could be recorded as follows:

(a) Recording the minimum premium permissible:

the lower of the original cost to the transferor (£100) and the book value immediately prior to transfer of assets transferred by the transferor company (£100)	£100

less

the book value immediately prior to transfer of liabilities transferred by the transferor	£nil (as no individual company liabilities were transferred)

less

the nominal value of shares issued by the transferee	(£45)

The minimum premium to be recognised =	£55

Entries would be:

In B's (the transferee's) accounts

Dr Investment (bal. fig.) 100

Cr Share capital   45

Cr Share premium   55

A has simply swapped a £100 investment in C for a £100 investment in B.

(b) Per ss132 and 133, recording the net assets acquired at their fair value:

In B's (the transferee's) accounts

Dr Investment   500

Cr Share capital   45

Cr Share premium   55

Cr Merger reserve   400

Under s133, the company has a choice whether to record the assets transferred in at book or fair value. In this example, the company has chosen to record the premium above the minimum premium required. The fair value of the shares in C is assumed to be the same as the fair value of C's underlying net assets (i.e., £500).

Example 24.180.2

Following on from Example **24.180.1** above, if B issues 45 £1 shares to C in return for the net assets of C. (The resulting structure would be A owning 100% of C and both A and C owning together 100% of B. C is a shell company as all of its trade has been transferred to B.)

The transfer could be done as follows:

(a) Recording the minimum premium permissible (following ss132 and 133):

the lower of the original cost to the   £300
transferor (£350) and the book value
immediately prior to transfer of assets
transferred by the transferor company (£300)

less

the book value immediately prior to transfer of
liabilities transferred by the transferor   £50 (as the individ-
                                           ual company liabili-
                                           ties were transferred)

less

the nominal value of shares issued by the
transferee   (£45)

The minimum premium to be recognised =   £205

Entries would be:

In B's (the transferee's) accounts

Dr Assets   300

Cr Liabilities   50

Cr Share capital   45

Cr Share premium   205

(b) Per ss132 and 133, recording the net assets acquired at their fair value:

In B's (the transferee's) accounts

Dr Assets	550
Cr Liabilities	50
Cr Share capital	45
Cr Share premium	205
Cr Merger reserve	250

Under s133, the company has a choice whether to record the assets transferred in at book or fair value. In this example, the company has chosen to record the premium above the minimum premium required.

Transfer of business (hive up)

24.181 Where, following an acquisition, a group reorganisation transfers business and goodwill from one company to another, it is necessary to consider the effect on the investment's carrying values. In particular, when goodwill is transferred up but no consideration is paid, it may be necessary to reallocate part of the investment's carrying value to goodwill.

Example 24.181

A acquired all the share capital of B for £100 when the net assets of B were valued at £60. Goodwill arising on acquisition was £40. B then transfers its business and net assets to A for their fair value of £60. Entries to record the transaction would be:

| In B's accounts: | Dr Intercompany | 60 |
| | Cr Net assets | 60 |

In A's accounts:	Dr Net assets	60
	Cr Intercompany	60
	Plus	
	Dr Goodwill	40
	Cr Investment	40

In A, the investment appears to have been 'impaired' by £40 (as the value of B is now equal to the value of the intercompany balance of £60). However, this £40 reflects the goodwill related to the business that has been hived up and so it is acceptable to reflect the goodwill in A's entity accounts as a reclassification of the original cost of investment, and not just on consolidation.

Demergers

Definition of demerger

24.182 The term 'demerger' describes the procedure whereby a company divests itself of a segment of the group's business activities to its shareholders by way of dividend in kind, consisting of the shares or trade of the company or companies being disposed of.

24.183 A number of demergers have occurred in the UK since the enactment of the Finance Act 1980, which made it attractive, from a taxation point of view, to transfer trades or subsidiaries to shareholders under conditions laid down in that Act.

Accounting for demergers

24.184 Although there is no accounting requirement dealing specifically with demergers, both FRS 2 and the Act cover the treatment of disposals of subsidiaries, which is relevant to demergers. FRS 6 notes that, although the FRS does not deal with the issues that arise on a demerger, the restructuring that takes place on a demerger may fall within the group restructuring provisions of the FRS (see **24.171** to **24.181** above). The general principles set out in the following paragraphs are suggested.

24.185 Shares (and other assets) distributed to shareholders *in specie* will represent a distribution of available profits of the company making the distribution. The amount of the distribution will equal, for accounting purposes, the book value of assets transferred. In the parent's books, this will be the carrying value of shares held in the subsidiary. In the consolidated books, it will be the group's share of subsidiary net assets at the date of demerger.

24.186

> Under FRS 2's rules, the results of the demerged business should be included in the consolidated financial statements up to the date of demerger. However, an additional viewpoint is that, just as the use of merger accounting supports full restatement of comparatives to include a merging business, an equivalent treatment for a demerger would exclude the demerged business completely from both the current and comparative periods. The directors could give this additional presentation as pro forma information if they choose. (see **24.188** below)

24.187 In the statutory accounts, the information that includes the demerged business to the date of demerger should include the amount of the distribution *in specie* as a dividend, disclosed on the face of the profit and loss account (this follows from Sch 4 para 3(7)(b)). As indicated in **24.185** above, the amount of the dividend appearing in the parent and consolidated profit and loss accounts may differ.

24.188 The treatment in the pro forma accounts, if they are to be given, is as follows:

(a) the consolidated profit and loss account of the period in which the demerger takes place and the consolidated balance sheet and profit and loss account of the prior year should exclude the demerged undertaking;

(b)   the costs associated with the demerger should be charged through the profit and loss account, in symmetry with the treatment of merger costs (see **24.121** above);

(c)   while the Act requires dividends paid and proposed to be shown on the face of the profit and loss account, this requirement cannot effectively be met in the pro forma accounts in respect of the dividend paid in kind, since the net assets of the demerged company will not be reflected in the accounts. Therefore, the dividend should be shown as a movement of previously reported reserves as at the beginning of the year.

Other matters

Disclosure of restrictions on, and reserves available for, distribution

24.189   The purpose of consolidated financial statements is explained in FRS 2. [FRS 2(59)] It states that when undertakings choose to conduct their activities through several undertakings under the control of the parent rather than through a single legal entity, the financial statements of a parent undertaking by itself do not present a full picture of its economic activities or financial position. Hence, consolidated financial statements are required in order to reflect the extended business unit that conducts activities under the control of the parent.

24.190   In the consolidated financial statements, the group is effectively treated as though it were a separate single entity with only one group of shareholders. As discussed in **23.106** above, all intra-group balances and transactions are eliminated. This means that the consolidated profit and loss account discloses the aggregate of the parent's and its subsidiaries' profits for the year arising from transactions with third parties, and the consolidated balance sheet discloses the aggregate of the net assets of the parent and its subsidiaries. It also means that the retained profit shown in the consolidated balance sheet does not purport to show the total of the distributable profits of the parent and its subsidiaries. Distributable profits of each subsidiary are determined on the basis of rules in their country's legislation or other regulations. In addition, there may be significant restrictions on the ability of the subsidiaries to distribute their distributable profits to the parent. Such restrictions can arise in many ways, for example:

(a)   as a result of contractual undertakings, such as sometimes arise in loan agreements or agreements for the acquisition of a subsidiary;

(b)   statutory or exchange control restrictions in a foreign country;

(c)   additions to consolidated reserves arising from the adjustment of a subsidiary's accounts to group accounting policies;

(d)   post-acquisition profits of a subsidiary company which have to be applied against pre-acquisition losses; and

(e)   post-acquisition profits of a subsidiary which have been capitalised.

24.191

> The existence of such restrictions is clearly of importance to shareholders and other users of financial statements and should therefore be disclosed in a note to the accounts. The most significant matter which should be disclosed is the extent to which the retained profits of the year cannot be distributed. Readers of financial statements are interested in the extent to which the profits after tax cover the dividends and may be mis-led if a significant proportion of the retained profits is not available for payment of dividends and this fact is not clearly disclosed.

24.192   Although restrictions on the group's ability to distribute the retained profits of prior years are usually of less significance, FRS 2 requires disclosure of the nature and extent of restrictions in cases where significant statutory, contractual or exchange control restrictions on distributions by subsidiary undertakings materially limit the parent undertaking's access to distributable profits. [FRS 2(53)] Accordingly, disclosure should be made if a large proportion of the accumulated retained profits cannot be distributed for such reasons. A general indication of the extent of the restrictions is sufficient; it is usually unnecessary and often impracticable to define precisely the amount of profits affected.

Segmental information

24.193   Although it appears only at the very end of the explanation section, FRS 2 devotes considerable space to the importance of segmental information, setting out its merits and encouraging parents to consider SSAP 25 as a minimum rather than a limit to disclosure. Two examples suggested by FRS 2 where supplementary segmental information could be given are:
[FRS 2(94)]

(a)   segmentation as a preferred alternative to exclusion from consolidation, e.g., where subsidiaries engage in different activities; and

(b)   minority interests, as they affect group segmental information.

Section 231 exemptions

24.194 Section 231 allows certain exemptions from disclosures, conditional upon permission being sought from the Secretary of State [s231(3)] or inclusion of information within the parent's next annual return. [s231(6)] Where FRS 2 refers to s231, and therefore its conditions and exemptions, it is assumed that if a company complies with the s231 exemption criteria, the information required by FRS 2 may also be excluded without any Secretary of State approval or inclusion within the annual return.

Disclosure

24.195 Although this chapter gives details of the disclosures required when an entity acquires or disposes of a subsidiary undertaking, it does not attempt to detail all the other disclosures, required annually, in consolidated financial statements.

Future developments

24.196 In December 1998, the ASB issued a discussion document based on proposals put forward in the FASB's position paper *Business Combinations*. The paper reflects the view of the US Securities and Exchange Commission that a single method of accounting for business combinations is desirable. The proposals are to either restrict the use of merger accounting by tightening up the existing criteria in FRS 6 paragraph 6.11 or to abolish merger accounting all together. In the latter case, this may mean that 'true mergers' will either have to be acquisition accounted or the 'true and fair' override applied in order to merger account. It is unlikely that any revision to FRS 6 or abolition will occur in 2000.

25 Associates and joint ventures

25　Associates and joint ventures

Summary of FRS 9

Summary of FRS 9 Classification and accounting

25.1　The following table sets out the types of investment that one entity may hold in another entity together with a summary of the appropriate accounting treatments.

Type of investment	Nature of relationship	Key elements of the relationship and key definitions	Accounting treatment
Subsidiary	Investor controls investee	Ability to direct the operating and financial policies of the investee with a view to gaining economic benefits from its activities *Key definitions:* *Control*	Consolidation (see FRS 2 in chapter 23)
Joint arrangement that is not an entity (JANE)	Joint control of assets or operations which do not amount to a separate entity	Investor extends its own trade through the joint arrangement *Key definitions:* *Joint control, Entity*	Each investor accounts for its own assets, liabilities and cash flows, and its share of shared items
Joint venture	Joint control of an entity	Under a contractual arrangement, two or more investors together control a venture which is a separate business in its own right *Key definitions:* *Joint control, Entity*	Gross equity method
Associate	Participating interest plus actual exercise of a significant influence	A long-term substantial minority shareholding which enables the investor to be actively involved, and influential, in policy decisions *Key definitions:* *Participating interest, Significant influence*	No equity method

F R S 9

| Simple investment | Passive | An insubstantial interest giving the investor limited influence, or a short-term interest, in an investee | Cost or valuation (see accounting for investments in chapter 15) |

Objective of FRS 9

25.2 FRS 9 *Associates and joint ventures* was issued in November 1997 and applies to accounting periods ending on or after 23 June 1998. The FRS deals with accounting for the range of interests above a simple passive investment, but less than a controlled subsidiary undertaking (dealt with by FRS 2 *Accounting for subsidiary undertakings*). FRS 9 classifies these interests into three types:

- associates;

- joint ventures; and

- joint arrangements that are not entities.

Although the requirements of Sch 4A paras 19 to 22 remain in force, the requirements of FRS 9 are more detailed and thus provide a one-stop source of rules and guidance.

Scope of FRS 9

25.3 FRS 9 applies, with the exception below, to all financial statements intended to give a true and fair view.

25.4 Reporting entities applying the FRSSE are exempt from the FRS, unless preparing consolidated financial statements. FRS 9 thus applies to any reporting entity which is reporting under the FRSSE but, with one or more subsidiaries, is required to prepare, or prepares on a voluntary basis, consolidated financial statements. FRS 9 does not apply to a reporting entity which is reporting under the FRSSE and which has an associate or joint venture, but does not have any subsidiaries.

Background to FRS 9

25.5 FRS 9 supersedes both SSAP 1 *Accounting for associated companies* and the remaining paragraphs of the *Interim Statement: Consolidated Accounts* which was issued following the Companies Act 1989 in order to give interim guidance on joint ventures. SSAP 1 was regarded by the ASB as suffering from a number of defects:

(a) *definition of an associate*: the boundary between a passive investment and an associate was established in SSAP 1, based on the point at which significant influence started to be exercised by the investor. This was presumed to align with an equity shareholding threshold of 20 per cent. In the ASB's view, too much emphasis was placed on the level of shareholding and too little on other factors which indicated the existence of a significant influence in practice. This could result in simple investments being inappropriately classified as associates;

(b) *joint ventures*: SSAP 1 included only a brief reference to a joint venture, by including an investor's interest as 'a partner in a joint venture or consortium' within the definition of an associate. Since that time, the forms and number of joint arrangements have increased. For example:

   (i) arrangements between companies with complementary skills, e.g., a private finance initiative consortium involving a construction company, project manager, financier and service provider;

   (ii) a UK company combining with a foreign company to gain access to that foreign company's market;

   (iii) merging similar interests to form a single large company in order to meet the cost of developing new products, increase ability to compete against larger competitors or as protection against predators; and

   (iv) securing a strategic stake in a foreign raw materials supplier, or distribution network.

   There was thus a need to update guidance on accounting for joint ventures to take account of current commercial practice. Such guidance would also need to take account of the references to joint ventures introduced into the Act as a result of the enactment of the EU Seventh Directive on company law (consolidated accounts);

(c) *disclosure of significant interests*: although SSAP 1 included a general requirement in respect of associates to give more detailed information (e.g., turnover and depreciation in the profit and loss account, and tangible and intangible assets and liabilities in the balance sheet) if this 'would assist in giving a true and fair view', there were, in practice, few situations where additional disclosure was given. As noted above, this is during a period when the significance of joint arrangements has increased. It is also interesting to note that SSAP 1 referred only to disclosure of turnover and depreciation in respect of profit and loss account items; this may have been because, at the time of issue of the original SSAP 1 in 1971, the statutory format for a profit and loss account was based on the Companies Act 1967, which did not require disclosure of items between turnover and profit before tax; depreciation would be disclosed by way of note as an item charged in arriving at profit before tax. Moreover, since disclosure of operating costs and operating profit was only added in the Companies Act 1981, investors have adopted different practice for:

(i) regarding the investor's share of associate results as being either a proportion of the associate's operating profit or profit before tax; and

(ii) reporting the investor's share of this result either before, or after, the investor's operating profit.

There was thus a need both to standardise requirements for additional disclosures and to specify how associates and joint ventures should be reported within the current statutory accounts formats.

Proportional consolidation

25.6   Since the Companies Act 1989, accounting for joint ventures has been largely determined by each particular venture's legal form. This is because that Act (which amended the Companies Act 1985) restricted use of proportional consolidation to unincorporated joint ventures such as partnerships. [Sch 4A: 19(1)] Incorporated joint ventures were therefore required to be dealt with on an equity basis. Under FRS 9, no reference is found to proportional consolidation within the text. However, an explanation of the ASB's continued opposition to the method is given with FRS 9 appendix 3 'The development of the FRS'. The effect is that:

(a) joint arrangements that qualify as entities in their own right (within the meaning of FRS 9) are required to be dealt with using a version of the equity method (the 'gross' equity method – see **25.81** below);

(b) joint arrangements that do not qualify as entities in their own right (within the meaning of FRS 9), irrespective of whether they are legal or unincorporated entities, are dealt with by each investor accounting for its own assets and liabilities and a share of joint assets and liabilities (see **25.123** below). Where assets and liabilities are shared, this basis may produce an effect which is similar to proportional consolidation.

Classification and definitions

25.7   Classification of investments is based on the application of definitions within FRS 9 and, where relevant, FRS 2 *Accounting for subsidiary undertakings*. The following table is a summary of the relevant stages of analysis, with cross-references to the full definitions and relevant guidance.

Stage of analysis	Definitions and guidance	Outcome of analysis
Test for the existence of a *long-term significant influence*.	Participating interest (see **25.12** below). Significant influence (see **25.20** below).	No long-term significant influence exists → *passive investment*. At least a significant influence exists → go to next stage.
Test whether the investor has *sole control*.	Actual exercise of a dominant influence. (FRS 2(7(b))	Investor controls investee alone → *subsidiary undertaking*. Investor has significant influence, but not control → go to next stage.
Test whether the investor exercises *joint control* with another investor.	Joint control (see **25.29** below).	Investor holds a substantial minority stake and exercises significant influence → *associate*. Investor exercises joint control with other investor(s) → go to next stage.
Test whether the investee is an *entity*.	Joint arrangement that is not an entity (see **25.34** below). Entity (see **25.36** below). Application to examples (see **25.41** below).	Investor shares joint control of an entity → *joint venture*. Investor extends own business through jointly controlled arrangement → *joint arrangement not an entity*.

In the paragraphs which follow, boxed paragraphs reproduce the definitions that appear in FRS 9 paragraph 4. Expressions appearing in **bold italics** are themselves defined terms.

Associate

25.8   *Associate*: an *entity* (other than a subsidiary) in which another entity (the investor) has a *participating interest* and over whose operating and financial policies the investor *exercises a significant influence*.

25.9   This definition of associate is consistent with the definition of an associated undertaking included in the Act.[Sch 4A: 20]

25.10 *Entity*: a body corporate, partnership or unincorporated association carrying on a trade or business with or without a view to profit. The reference to carrying on a trade or business means a trade or business of its own and not just part of the trades or businesses of entities that have interests in it.

25.11 This definition extends the scope of an associate to include unincorporated and not-for-profit bodies. The elements of the definition dealing with 'a trade or business of its own' are most relevant in the determination of joint ventures and joint arrangements and are therefore dealt with in **25.37** below.

25.12 *Participating interest*: an **interest held** in the shares of another entity **on a long-term basis** for the purpose of securing a contribution to the investor's activities by the exercise of control or influence arising from or related to that interest. The investor's interest must, therefore, be a beneficial one and the benefits expected to arise must be linked to the exercise of its significant influence over the investee's operating and financial policies. An interest in the shares of another entity includes an interest convertible into an interest in shares or an option to acquire shares. Companies legislation provides that a holding of 20 per cent or more of the shares of an entity is to be presumed to be a participating interest unless the contrary is shown. The presumption is rebutted if the interest is either not long term or not beneficial.

25.13 *Equivalent rights*: the reference to shares should be applied to instruments carrying equivalent rights in entities without a share capital:

(a)   for an entity with capital, it is to rights to share in the capital;

(b)   for an entity without capital, it is to rights to share in profits (or imposing a liability to contribute to losses, or an obligation to contribute to debts or expenses in a winding-up).

25.14 *Beneficial interest*: the reference to benefits is not restricted to dividends, but extends to other methods of extracting benefits that are equivalent to the return normally associated with an equity holding.

25.15 *Start-up situations*: the inclusion of 'an interest convertible into an interest in shares or an option to acquire shares' has the effect of including within the definition of an associate situations where an investor initially avoids owning shares, but has an involvement in the strategic financial and operating policy decisions, together with an option to acquire shares in the future. Such an arrangement may have been devised with the intention of avoiding reporting the investor's share of losses in a start-up or development phase of a new business.

25.16 *Interest held on a long-term basis*: an interest that is held other than exclusively with a view to subsequent resale. An interest held exclusively with a view to subsequent resale is:

(a) an interest for which a purchaser has been identified or is being sought and which is reasonably expected to be disposed of within approximately one year of its date of acquisition; or

(b) an interest that was acquired as a result of the enforcement of a security, unless the interest has become part of the continuing activities of the group or the holder acts as if it intends the interest to become so.

25.17 *Intention to dispose*: the conditions relating to seeking a purchaser, and expectation of sale within a year, are similar to the requirements contained in FRS 7 for the fair valuation as a single asset of a business acquired for resale. These conditions are unlikely to be met unless the investor recognises its intention to dispose at the time of acquisition and is actively involved in seeking a purchaser from that date. Where an investor decides some time after an acquisition that it will dispose of an investment, it may in practice prove difficult to show that disposal will be achieved within one year of the acquisition.

Retention of only part of a holding: an investor may acquire a shareholding as part of a larger acquisition with the intention of retaining part, and disposing of part, e.g., in acquiring a group of companies, an investor acquires a 60 per cent holding in an entity; it is the investor's intention to retain a 35 per cent holding but immediately seek a buyer for the remaining 25 per cent. Where the FRS 7 conditions relating to seeking a buyer are met in relation to the 25 per cent stake, the investor should account for the 35 per cent long-term interest as an associate, but the 25 per cent temporary interest as a single current asset investment held for sale.

25.18 *Cessation of long-term relationship*: since qualification as an associate or joint venture is based on long-term factors, minor or temporary changes in the relationship should not affect its status unless the long-term relationship has changed, e.g., that significant influence has ceased to be exercised permanently. [FRS 9(7)] This is likely to be at the date of actual disposal of the participating interest. Examples of changes that should not affect classification as an associate or joint venture are:

(a) the associate or joint venture moves from profitable trading to loss making;

(b) the associate or joint venture has net liabilities;

(c) a decision is made to sell the associate or joint venture.

25.19

> *Reclassification following a decision to sell:* when an investor decides to dispose of an existing associate, the question is sometimes asked whether the investment should be reclassified as a current asset. In general, such a reclassification is both problematic and unnecessary. Two problems are the need to restate current assets to a cost basis and the difficulty of applying the equity basis to an investment which is carried at cost. Consistency with FRS 9 is achieved by continuing to show the associate as a fixed asset, and applying the equity basis of accounting, until the date of disposal.

25.20 *Exercise of significant influence:* the investor is actively involved and is influential in the direction of its investee through its participation in policy decisions covering aspects of policy relevant to the investor, including decisions on strategic issues such as:

(a) the expansion or contraction of the business, participation in other entities or changes in products, markets and activities of its investee; and

(b) determining the balance between dividend and reinvestment.

Companies legislation provides that an entity holding 20 per cent or more of the voting rights in another entity should be presumed to exercise a significant influence over that other entity, unless the contrary is shown. For the purpose of applying this presumption, the shares held by the parent and its subsidiaries in that entity should be aggregated. The presumption is rebutted if the investor does not fulfil the criteria for the exercise of significant influence set out above.

25.21 *Actual exercise of a significant influence:* an investor exercising significant influence will be directly involved in the operating and financial policies of its associate. This relationship requires a basis for reaching agreement or understanding, which may be formal or informal. The investor will use the associate as a medium through which it pursues a part of its own strategy (which may or may not be in the same business as the investor). Over time, the associate will implement policies that are consistent, and avoid implementing policies which are inconsistent, with the strategy of the investor. Evidence that an investee persistently implements policies which are inconsistent with its investor's strategy indicates that the investor does not exercise significant influence. [FRS 9(14)]

25.22 *Dividends and reinvestment:* the investor's participation in policy decisions of an associate is stated to be with a view to gaining economic benefits from the associate's activities (and thus exposure to risk relating to the associate's activities, including the possibility of losses). Such benefits are not limited to payment of dividends, but include capital growth and trading transactions. Accordingly, the investor will not always seek the highest level of dividends, but rather that it is involved in decisions such as the balance between dividend and reinvestment. [FRS 9(15)]

25.23   *Board membership and 20 per cent rebuttable presumption*: involvement in an associate requires the investor to be actively involved in policy-making decisions. This is usually achieved through board representation (or representation on an equivalent management body), but may be achieved through other forms of arrangement which give access to the decision-making process. Similarly, the exercise of influence will generally require a substantial basis of voting power. While a holding of 20 per cent in the voting rights often coincides with access to the decision-making process, it is not of itself conclusive evidence. [FRS 9(16)]

25.24   *Initial assessment and subsequent events*: determination of whether there is exercise of a significant influence in practice depends on the pattern of behaviour. Initially, following an acquisition, an assessment may need to be made on apparent arrangements such as the board presentation and the proposed decision-making process. As subsequent evidence of the actual relationship becomes available, this initial assessment should be verified or amended. Once it is established that significant influence is being exercised, it should be regarded as continuing until an event or transaction removes the investor's ability to do so. [FRS 9(17)] A decision to dispose of an associate will not, of itself, amount to such an event or transaction.

25.25   *Investee which is both a subsidiary and an associate*: an investor may hold, say, a 30 per cent shareholding in an investee which is a subsidiary undertaking of another entity (which is unrelated to the investor). The question arises whether the investee can be both a subsidiary of one entity and an associate of another at the same time. The obvious assumption is that, since a subsidiary undertaking is controlled by its parent undertaking, there is no scope for another investor to be in a position to exercise a significant influence. This assumption may be rebutted if it can be demonstrated that the parent undertaking has allowed the investor some degree of influence. This could be achieved by a shareholder agreement which amounts to an arrangement for joint control (see **25.29** below). In such cases, the parent undertaking may need to consider excluding its subsidiary undertaking from consolidation, on grounds that the shareholder agreement represents a severe long-term restriction which impairs control (see FRS 2, dealt with in **23.65** above), and is instead accounted for as a joint venture.

Joint ventures and joint arrangements

25.26   FRS 9 describes two forms of arrangement which involve joint control, but which result in fundamentally different accounting treatments:

(a)   joint venture: this is a jointly controlled entity (entity meaning a venture with a trade or business of its own, which may or may not be a legal entity);

(b)   joint arrangement that is not an entity (JANE): this is a jointly controlled asset, operation or legal entity which amounts to an extension of the investor's own trade.

The distinction between these two forms of arrangement will often require an analysis of whether the arrangement amounts to an entity within the meaning given by FRS 9.

25.27   *Joint venture*: an entity in which the reporting entity holds an interest on a long-term basis and is *jointly controlled* by the reporting entity and one or more other venturers under a contractual arrangement.

25.28   The simplest form of joint venture would involve two investors with an equal share of control and ownership. Three or more investors may similarly share control. However, as the number of investors increases, the ability of all to participate meaningfully in the process of shared control is reduced. For example, it is difficult to see how 10 or more investors, each with a power of veto, could each be involved in an effective decision-making process. In reality, it is likely that active control will be shared by only some of the investors. Similarly, where the interests of investors are unequal, it is necessary to restrict the classification as a joint venture to those who share control. Other investors who do not share control should account for their interest as a simple investment. [FRS 9(10)]

25.29   *Joint control*: a reporting entity jointly controls a venture with one or more other entities if none of the entities alone can control that entity, but all together can do so and decisions on financial and operating policy essential to the activities, economic performance and financial position of that venture require each venturer's consent.

25.30   *Contractual arrangement and power of veto*: the key test of whether joint control exists is whether strategic decisions require each venturer's consent, (i.e., that each venturer has a power of veto). Equal shareholders operating under normal company law provisions are unlikely to be in this position. Joint control requires some additional contractual arrangement, such as a shareholder agreement or Articles of Association which include non-standard clauses, which provide for each venturer that shares control to play an active role in setting the operating and financial policies of the joint venture, at least at a general strategy level. This does not preclude the delegation of management to one of the venturers, provided that the principal policies are collectively agreed, and each venturer has the power to ensure those polices are followed. [FRS 9(11) – (12)]

25.31   *Beneficial interest*: consistent with the definitions of control in FRSs 2 and 5, the exercise of control or shared control is with a view to gaining economic benefits. In most cases, ownership of equity shares conveys such a beneficial interest. FRS 5 describes a circumstance where financial and operating policies are not set by the shareholders, but are predetermined such that the benefits arising from the net assets accrues to another party, which is deemed to have control. [FRS 5(34)] In this latter case, the definition of a joint arrangement that is not an entity (see **25.34** below) suggests that the venture will not be a separate entity within the meaning of FRS 9, and therefore not a joint venture, since the venturers are not active in exercising control.

25.32   *Interest qualifying as a subsidiary undertaking*: where interests of venturers are unequal, the joint venture may meet the definition of a subsidiary undertaking to one of the venturers, e.g., where that venturer owns a majority of voting rights. Nevertheless, contractual arrangements may mean that control is shared. In such a case, the parent undertaking would exclude its subsidiary undertaking from consolidation on grounds of 'severe long-term restrictions' (see FRS 2 paragraph 25, dealt with in **23.65** above) and deal with it under FRS 9 as a joint venture.

25.33   The following table sets out the key test and two supplementary tests for determining whether joint control exists.

Determining whether joint control exists		
Key test: Joint control exists when each investor has a power of veto over high level strategic decisions		
Supplementary tests	**Evidence that joint control does not exist**	**Evidence of joint control**
1. Shareholder agreement which provides for investors to consent to major decisions.	No agreement exists beyond normal shareholder rights and procedures.	Separate agreement exists, or Articles of Association go further than Table A.

2. Basis of strategic financial and operating decisions.	Large number of investors makes joint decisions impractical; investor is a single substantial minority shareholder who could be outvoted by majority.	Small number of investors who each give consent to major policy decisions; control is exercised together, but no single investor able to control.

25.34 *Joint arrangement that is not an entity*: a contractual arrangement under which the participants engage in joint activities that do not create an **entity** because it would not be carrying on a trade or business of its own. A contractual arrangement where all significant matters of operating and financial policy are predetermined does not create an **entity** because the policies are those of its participants, not of a separate entity.

25.35 *Predetermined control*: **25.31** above, which deals with beneficial interest, refers to circumstances where benefits accrue to parties other than shareholders, e.g., a joint special purpose vehicle created to undertake securitisation transactions for two or more originators. In such cases of predetermined control, the shareholders will not be in a position to exercise active control and the special purpose vehicle will not meet the definition of an entity. The special purpose vehicle will, in substance, be a form of quasi joint arrangement undertaking transactions which are an extension of the originators' own trade and therefore subject to accounting within the originators' own or consolidated accounts in accordance with FRS 5.

25.36 *Entity*: a body corporate, partnership or unincorporated association carrying on a trade or business with or without a view to profit. The reference to carrying on a trade or business means a trade or business of its own and not just part of the trades or businesses of entities that have interests in it.

25.37 *Key test*: the key test of an entity is whether it is carrying on a trade or business of its own or, alternatively, is an extension of the trade of its investors. Guidance based on FRS 9 paragraphs 8 and 9 is presented in the table in **25.39** below.

25.38 *Supplementary tests*: the table in **25.39** below provides a summary of the factors discussed in FRS 9 paragraphs 8 and 9 and examples of arrangements which meet the tests. In applying the tests, regard should be given to the key test in **25.37** above. In practice, it is unlikely that all four tests will be directly relevant in all cases. It is more likely that one or two tests will be directly applicable and give useful evidence, while other tests are less relevant.

25.39 The following table sets out the key test and four supplementary tests for determining whether a venture is an entity.

Determining whether a venture is an entity

Key test: An entity has a trade or business of its own, and is not an extension of the investors' own businesses.

Supplementary tests	Evidence of an entity	Evidence of not an entity
1. Examine the degree to which the investor is actively involved in the venture.	Active involvement of investor has ceased; investor's interest is capable of sale or transfer without affecting the venture; venture's trade differs to that of investors.	Investor is actively involved throughout the venture's life through provision of operational staff and support services.
2. Examine the relationship between investor and venture.	Significant trade occurs with third parties; the venture trades using its own name, staff and support systems; trade with investors is at market rates; venture competes with investors; venture's trade different to that of investors.	Investors account for substantially all the venture's inputs *or* outputs; venture is a cost- or risk-sharing means of carrying out a process.
3. Examine the source of strategic operating and financial policy decisions.	Policies are determined by the venturer's own management; management includes independently appointed members; remuneration may include incentives linked to the venture's performance.	Policies are those of the investors; management is exclusively and continuously appointed by investors; policies may be predetermined by investors; funding or projects provided or arranged by investors.
4. Examine the extent to which risks are shared.	Investors receive main return through distributions from net profits; profits may be retained by the entity for reinvestment.	Able to identify significant risks which are borne by each separate investor; investors receive little or no return through distribution of net profits.

25.40   *Repetition of activity*: one test which appears in FRS 9, but which does not appear to be totally reliable, and is therefore excluded from the guidance presented in **25.39** above, is whether the venture exists to undertake a single project (evidence that it is not an entity) or contains repetition in the buying and selling activities (evidence of an entity). [FRS 9(9)] The implication is that construction industry projects, which are typically single project ventures, will generally not be entities. However, the decision to use a venture to undertake a series of projects, or to place each project in a separate venture,

> is likely to be based on a number of factors, e.g., taxation and exposure to legal liabilities. Moreover, other tests relating to the relationship and active involvement are likely to provide sufficient evidence for an assessment of entity or non-entity status to be made.

25.41 *Application to examples:* the table in **25.42** below identifies a range of common joint activities and considers whether these are generally more likely to indicate an 'entity' or 'not an entity'. Also shown are the tests identified in the table in **25.39** above, which are more likely to provide clear evidence using the factors:

- active involvement;
- relationship;
- policy decisions;
- risk sharing.

25.42 The following table sets out examples of 'entity' and 'not an entity'.

Examples of 'entity' and 'not an entity'						
Example	Entity	Not an entity	Factors providing useful evidence (see table in 25.39 above)			
			1.	2.	3.	4.
Construction contract using own labour	✓		●			
Construction company interest in completed asset (e.g., hotel)	✓		●			●
Interest in private finance initiative joint venture consortium	✓		●			●
Property investment trust – open ended	✓				●	●
Property development – single property with outcome determined		✓			●	●
Upstream oil industry, e.g., oil field, pipeline carrying own oil		✓		●		

Downstream oil industry, e.g., jointly-owned refinery serving third parties	✓			●	●
Distribution network without third-party customers		✓		●	
Production consortium with each venturer manufacturing one part of product, e.g., aircraft		✓		●	
Special purpose finance, e.g., providing consignment stock finance to manufacturer		✓		●	●

Partnerships

25.43 Partnerships are not separately considered in FRS 9. Prior to FRS 9, unincorporated structures such as partnerships would be dealt with on a proportionate basis in both the investing entity's own and consolidated financial statements. This treatment was specifically permitted by the Companies Act for the investor's consolidated financial statements and it followed logically that it would also be appropriate for individual financial statements since, in substance, each partner owned a proportion of assets and liabilities. Moreover, inclusion of a share of partnership assets and liabilities in the investor's accounts also enabled a share of partnership profits to be recorded. However, since the Act permitted, but did not require, proportional consolidation, use of the equity method for a partnership was also possible.

25.44 Under FRS 9, the legal status of an investee is not a primary consideration. Rather, it is necessary to subject a partnership to the classification rules discussed above; in particular, whether it is an entity to be equity (or gross equity) accounted (see **25.49** and **25.81** below), or not an entity, to be dealt with on a proportionate basis (see **25.123** below).

25.45 *Investor's individual financial statements*: where it is determined that an investee is an entity within the meaning of FRS 9, FRS 9 requires the investing entity's individual financial statements to deal with the investee as a fixed asset investment shown at cost (or a revalued amount). [FRS 9(20) and (26)] While this seems appropriate for an investee which is a legal entity, it is less suitable for an unincorporated entity such as a partnership, since it results in only drawings being included in the investor's profit and loss account. Thus, the investor's share

955

> of partnership profits which are retained in the partnership, but which in law 'belong' to the partners and on which the partner is taxed, would be excluded from the investor's individual profit and loss account. Accordingly, it is usually appropriate to follow the legal relationship and allow an investing entity to record its share of a partnership's profits within its own profit and loss account and regard it as a realised profit, and also to include in the investor's balance sheet the investing entity's share of the partnership's assets and liabilities on either an equity basis or by proportional consolidation.

Date of acquisition and disposal of associates and joint ventures

25.46   The classification of investments under FRS 9 is based on long-term factors. [FRS 9(7)] Consistent with this principle, the date on which an investment commences or ceases to be an associate or joint venture will be the date on which the essential components of the definitions are met or cease to be met.

25.47   For an associate, acquisition occurs when both a *participating interest* and *exercise of significant influence* exist. Disposal occurs when one of the conditions ceases to be met permanently, such that the long-term relationship has changed. Temporary or minor changes, such as a period during which an associate makes losses, do not of themselves result in any change to the long-term relationship. [FRS 9(40)]

25.48   For a joint venture, acquisition occurs when an interest is long term and *joint control* is exercised. Disposal occurs when joint control ceases to be exercised. [FRS 9(40)] This is likely to be the date on which contractual arrangements are terminated.

> ### Extract 25.48
>
> BG plc Annual Report and Accounts 1998
>
> 'Basis of consolidation. The Group accounts comprise a consolidation of the accounts of the Company and its subsidiary undertakings and incorporate the results of its share of joint ventures and associated undertakings. The results of undertakings acquired or disposed of are consolidated from or to the date when control passes to or from the Company. Most of the Group's exploration and production activity is conducted through joint arrangements. The Group accounts for its own share of the assets, liabilities and cash flows associated with these joint arrangements.'

Accounting for associates – applying the net equity basis

Background and summary

25.49   In summary, associates are accounted for as follows.

(a)   In an investor's consolidated accounts – **on an equity basis**:

Consolidated profit and loss account	Share of associate items, separately disclosed, commencing with share of operating result.
Consolidated statement of total recognised gains and losses	Share of associate items, separately disclosed.
Consolidated balance sheet	As a fixed asset investment, share of associate net assets, separately disclosed, together with goodwill (less amortisation) on acquisition of the associate.
Consolidated cash flow statement	Dividends received, as a separate item. Other cash flows between investor and associate under appropriate headings.

(b)   In the investor's individual financial statements (assuming con-solidated financial statements are prepared) – **on a cost basis (which may be revalued)**.

(c)   Where an investor does not prepare consolidated accounts (e.g., because it has no subsidiaries) – **provide equity-based information**, either in a separate set of financial statements or as additional information to its own financial statements.

(d)   Where an investor is exempt from preparing consolidated accounts (e.g., it is a small group or would be a small group if it had subsidiaries) – **no equity-based information is required**. (However, certain information is required by Sch 5 – see **25.135** below.)

(e)   In an investment fund (e.g., venture capital company) holding an interest as part of an investment portfolio – use the same basis (**cost or market value**) as for other investments.

25.50   *Comparison with consolidation*: the objective of the equity basis flows from the relationship between investor and associate. This is that the investor has participated in the activities and operations of the asso-ciate. That effect on bottom-line net income (and hence earnings per share) and net assets is similar to consolidation of a majority inter-est in a subsidiary: the associate is reflected in the profit and loss account by reporting earnings rather than dividends, and in the balance sheet by including information based on net assets rather than the cost or market value of the investment in shares. However, the equity method can be clearly differentiated from consolidation: the lack of control of an associate is evident from the balance sheet (where the associate is included as a single asset wholly within the fixed asset investment category) and the cash flow statement (which reflects purely cash flows between investor and associate and not underlying profits and net assets).

25.51 *Comparison with gross equity basis*: the net equity basis (used for associates) can be differentiated from the gross equity basis (used for joint ventures). The basic accounting is the same, but the gross equity basis presents additional information on the face of the primary statements. This is described in **25.81** below.

Treatment in consolidated profit and loss account

25.52 The requirements of FRS 9 for including an associate on an equity basis are:

    (a)   the investor's share of associate operating result should be included immediately after group operating result (but after any share of results of joint ventures) [FRS 9(27)];

    (b)   any amortisation of goodwill arising on the acquisition of the associate should be included at this point and disclosed [FRS 9(27)];

    (c)   the investor's share of any associate exceptional items shown below operating result (under FRS 3) should be shown with similar group items, but shown separately [FRS 3(20) and FRS 9(27)] ;

    (d)   the investor's share of any associate interest (or similar items) should be shown with similar group items, but shown separately [FRS 9(27)];

    (e)   the investor's share of associate items below this level (i.e., at and below profit before tax) should be included within amounts for the group [FRS 9(27)];

    (f)   the investor's share of associate tax should be separately disclosed [FRS 9(27)];

    (g)   a total combining group turnover and the investor's share of associate turnover may be shown as a memorandum item, provided that the share of associate's turnover is clearly distinguished from group turnover [FRS 9(27)];

    (h)   similarly, the segmental analysis of turnover and operating result (if given) should clearly distinguish between group and associate [FRS 9(27)];

(i) further guidance is included on acquisitions and changes in stake, unrealised gains and losses, accounting policies, non-coterminous year ends, associates with their own subsidiaries and associates, options and similar instruments, and loss-making associates (see **25.98** to **25.122** below).

25.53 *Exceptional items*: the normal basis of including a share of associate exceptional items below operating result on the investor's consolidated profit and loss account will be that they are classified as falling within FRS 3 exceptional items in the associate's own profit and loss account. [FRS 3(20)] Through the combination of taking a share of these items only, and including them within consolidated accounts of a larger reporting entity, such items may appear to be immaterial. For consistency, such items should normally continue to be disclosed as exceptional items, even if this results in items appearing to be less material than other group exceptional items.

25.54 *Information on the face of the consolidated profit and loss account*: the wording of FRS 9 is not completely clear on what items must appear on the face of the consolidated profit and loss account and what can be analysed in notes. The following guidance may assist.

Item	Requirements	Reason
Share of turnover	Face or Notes or No disclosure	Optional disclosure
Share of operating result	Face (but may be combined with share of joint venture and amortisation of goodwill)	FRS 9(27) and Companies Act formats
Amortisation of goodwill	Face or Notes	Not expressly required on the face
Share of post-operating exceptional items	Face (for material exceptional item) Notes (if combined with group exceptional item of the same class, or with other associate exceptional items, on grounds of materiality)	FRS 3
Share of interest	Face or Notes	Not expressly required on the face (FRS 9(27)
Share of tax	Notes	FRS 9(27)

25.55 The following example reflects the requirements of FRS 9 in respect of consolidated profit and loss account presentation, assuming options to include information on the face of the profit and loss account are taken.

Example 25.55

Consolidated profit and loss account

	£ million	£ million	Notes
Turnover: Group and share of associate – continuing activities	320		1
Less: Share of associate	(120)		
Group turnover – continuing activities		200	
Cost of sales		(120)	
Gross profit		(80)	
Administrative expenses		40	
Group operating profit		40	
Share of operating profit in associate	24		2
Amortisation of goodwill arising on acquisition of associate	(7)		3
		17	
		57	
Exceptional items – continuing activities			
Group – gain on sale of an operation	20		
Share of associate – costs of fundamental reorganisation	(8)		4
		12	
Interest payable:			
Group	(26)		
Share of associate	(12)		4
		(38)	
Profit on ordinary activities before taxation		31	
Tax on profit on ordinary activities		(11)	5
Profit on ordinary activities after taxation		20	

Notes:
1. Optional – memorandum combined disclosure.
2. Must follow group operating result.
3. Shown following associate operating result.
4. Share of associate shown separately.
5. Share of associate disclosed within notes to accounts.

Treatment in consolidated statement of recognised gains and losses

25.56 The investor's share of associate items (e.g., revaluation gains and losses and foreign exchange differences) should be included within equivalent group headings. If the amounts included are material, separate disclosure of the associate amounts is required either on the face of the statement or in a note that is referred to in the statement. [FRS 9(28)]

25.57 The following example reflects the requirements of FRS 9 in respect of consolidated statement of total recognised gains and losses presentation.

Example 25.57

Consolidated statement of total recognised gains and losses

	£ million	£ million
Profit for the financial year		20
Revaluation of properties:		
Group	40	
Share of associate	8	
		48
Foreign exchange translation differences:		
Group	(15)	
Share of associate	(7)	
		(22)
Total recognised gains and losses for the year		46

Notes: Separate analysis of associate amounts is required if the amounts are material. The analysis may be given in a note to the financial statements.

Treatment in consolidated balance sheet

25.58 The requirements of FRS 9 are:

(a) the investor's share of the associate's net assets should be included as a separate item within fixed asset investments [FRS 9(29)];

(b) goodwill arising on the investor's acquisition of the associate, less any amortisation or write-down, should be included within the carrying amount for the associate, but separately disclosed [FRS 9(29)];

(c)   where there has been an impairment in any goodwill attributable to an associate, the goodwill should be written down and the amount written off in the period disclosed [FRS 9(38)];

(d)   where an associate has net liabilities, the investor's share is shown within provisions or liabilities [FRS 9(45)].

25.59   Where loans to associates form part of the long-term funding for the associate, the loan should be included in the carrying value of the associate in fixed asset investments, but separately disclosed (per Companies Act 1985 balance sheet format item B III 4). Where, alternatively, a short-term loan or current account trading balance is expected to be repaid, it may be more appropriately included within debtors (per Companies Act 1985 balance sheet format item C II 3).

25.60   The FRS requires that goodwill arising on the investor's acquisition of the associate, less any amortisation or write-down, should be included within the carrying amount for the associate, but separately disclosed. Where an associate itself has subsidiaries or associates that give rise to goodwill in its own consolidated accounts, this goodwill should be excluded from the fair value of the associate's net assets that are used to calculate goodwill arising on the acquisition of the associate. [FRS 9(31)(a)] The effect is that goodwill arising on the acquisition of the associate will include goodwill previously recorded by the associate arising from its own acquisitions. The amount of this goodwill calculated by the investor may differ from the amount originally calculated by the associate at the time of its acquisition to the extent that the investor's assessment of fair values is different. However, this will not be apparent, since FRS 9 does not require separate disclosure of the components of goodwill arising from an associate.

25.61   Where an investor's share of an associate's net liabilities is disclosed within provisions, the question arises of whether any goodwill (less amortisation) should continue to be shown within fixed asset investments or shown together with the provision. It seems appropriate to continue to show the goodwill within fixed asset investments in order to provide consistency of goodwill treatment irrespective of whether the associate has net assets or net liabilities. Also, it is assumed that, in the future, the associate will return to a net asset position and be reclassified as a fixed asset investment. However, the alternative treatment is not prohibited by the FRS.

25.62   FRS 9 does not refer to the presentation of the investor's share of associate retained reserves, e.g., post-acquisition revaluation reserve, profit and loss account and other reserves. In practice, it will therefore be acceptable to include either:

> (a)   a share of associate items within group reserve headings; or
>
> (b)   all associate items together as a separate 'other reserve'.

25.63   The following example reflects the requirements of FRS 9 in respect of consolidated balance sheet presentation.

Example 25.63

Notes to consolidated balance sheet

Note X – Investments in associates:

	£ million
Share of net assets	60
Loans to associates	20
Goodwill arising on acquisition less amortisation	15
	95

Notes:

Loans are shown separately from interests in shares. Separate disclosure of amounts relating to trading balances is required.

Goodwill is shown separately. Further disclosures are required by FRS 10 (see **13.5** above).

Treatment in consolidated cash flow statement

25.64   The requirements of FRS 9 are:

(a)   dividends received from associates should be included as a separate item after cash flow from group operating activities, but before returns on investments and servicing of finance [FRS 9(30)];

(b)   any other cash flows between the investor and the associate are included within the appropriate heading, e.g., acquisition and disposal of shares, advance and repayment of loans, interest on loans [FRS 9(30)].

The following items do not appear in the cash flow statement:

(a)   group share of any items included on an equity basis, e.g., operating result, exceptional items, interest payable, tax, change in net assets;

(b)   amortisation of goodwill on acquisition of an associate.

25.65

> Following the requirements of FRS 9 would suggest that interest paid by associates on loans from an investor would be included within 'returns on investments and servicing of finance', and not under 'dividends received from associates'. [FRS 9(30)] In practice, there may be circumstances where a significant part of an investment in an associate is through loan finance rather than shares, such that the investor receives a significant part of its return from interest receipts as an alternative to dividends. In such cases, there may be a case for including interest within the heading 'Dividends received from associates', provided that the heading is appropriately adapted and the interest is separately disclosed.

25.66 The following example reflects the requirements of FRS 9 in respect of consolidated cash flow statements presentation.

Example 25.66

Consolidated cash flow statement

	£ million	Notes
Cash flow from operating activities	70	1
Dividends received from associate	20	2
Returns on investments and servicing of finance	(22)	3
Taxation	(10)	4
Capital expenditure and financial investment	(40)	5
Acquisitions and disposals	35	6
Equity dividends paid	(15)	
Cash outflow before use of liquid resources and financing	38	
Management of liquid resources	5	
Financing	(25)	
Increase in cash in the period	18	

Notes:
1. Group only, excluding associate.
2. May be combined with joint ventures.
3. Includes interest on loans to associate.
4. Excludes associate.
5. Includes loans advanced to/repaid from associate.
6. Includes purchase or sale of shares in associate.

Extract 25.66

Rank Group plc

Year ended 31 December 1998

The principal change arising from the adoption of FRS 9 is that the Group's share of the profit before tax from associates and joint

---

ventures is now analysed between share of operating profit and share of interest on the face of the profit and loss account.

GROUP PROFIT AND LOSS ACCOUNT (Extract)

FOR THE YEAR ENDED 31 DECEMBER 1998

	Note	Before exceptional items £m	Exceptional items £m	1998 Total £m
Turnover				
Continuing operations		2,025	–	2,025
Acquisitions		32	–	32
	1,2	2,057	–	2,057
Discontinued operations	1,2	–	–	–
	1,2	2,057	–	2,057
Operating profit				
Continuing operations		275	(98)	177
Acquisitions		5	–	5
	1,2	280	(98)	182
Discontinued operations	1,2	–	–	–
Group operating profit	1,2	280	(98)	182
Share of operating profit in joint ventures and associates				
Joint ventures	12	4	–	4
Associated undertakings	13	27	–	27
		311	(98)	213
Non-operating items				
Loss on disposal of continuing operations' properties	3	–	(55)	(55)
Loss on disposal of continuing operations	3	–	(153)	(153)
Loss on disposal of investment	3	–	–	–
Profit on disposal of discontinued operations	3	–	–	–
Income from fixed asset investment				
Rank Xerox dividends receivable		–	–	–
Profit (loss) before interest		311	(306)	5
Net interest payable and other similar charges				
Group	4	(48)	–	(48)
Joint ventures	12	(3)	–	(3)
Associated undertakings	13	(5)	–	(5)
		(56)	–	(56)
Profit (loss) on ordinary activities before tax		255	(306)	(51)

Treatment in investor's individual financial statements

25.67   Where an investor prepares consolidated financial statements, the requirement to equity account is fulfilled in those financial statements. Consequently, in the investor's individual financial statements, its interests in associates should be treated as fixed asset investments and shown either at cost, less amounts written off, or at a valuation. [FRS 9(26)]

25.68

> Where an investor chooses to adopt a valuation policy, this will be subject to the alternative valuation rules of the Companies Act 1985. [Sch 4: 31] This would allow valuation on a net asset basis, such that the carrying value equates to that appearing in the consolidated balance sheet. However, gains and losses arising would be dealt with as revaluation surpluses and deficits. In practice, such a basis of valuation does not provide any significant benefit and is not recommended.

An investor that does not prepare consolidated financial statements

25.69   Consolidated financial statements are not required in two circumstances:

(a)   the investor is exempt by virtue of being a small group; or

(b)   the investor does not have subsidiaries.

Investor is exempt from preparing consolidated financial statements

25.70   Where an investor is exempt from preparing consolidated financial statements, it is also exempt from the FRS 9 requirement to present equity-based information. This exemption extends to an investor which has no subsidiaries, but which would be exempt from preparing consolidated financial statements if it did have subsidiaries. [FRS 9(48)]

25.71

> It is not clear from FRS 9 whether the exemption is intended to extend to disclosures set out in FRS 9 paragraphs 51 to 58 (see **25.130** to **25.134** below). On the basis that these disclosures supplement the information given in the primary statements, it is reasonable to take the view that these disclosures are not required.

25.72   However, an investor will be required to meet the normal disclosure requirements (subject to exemptions) of Sch 5 relating to holdings in excess of 20 per cent of any class of an investee's shares (see **15.19** above).

Investor with no subsidiaries

25.73 An investor without subsidiaries (and who would not be entitled to exemption from preparing consolidated financial statements if it did have subsidiaries) is required to present the information required by FRS 9 either:

(a) by preparing a separate set of financial statements; or

(b) by showing the relevant amounts, together with the effects of including them, as additional information to its own financial statements. [FRS 9(48)]

The information required would include the detailed disclosures specified in FRS 9. [FRS 9(51)–(58)]

25.74 A separate set of financial statements is equivalent, in effect, to the preparation of consolidated accounts. Most commonly, such accounts are presented in separate columns alongside the individual company financial statements.

25.75 The second option of showing additional information may be achieved:

(a) in the company profit and loss account, by introducing the investor's share of associate items in accordance with normal rules for a consolidated profit and loss account, but deducting the resulting share of associate profit after tax before the subtotal 'Profit for the financial year';

(b) in the company statement of total recognised gains and losses, by introducing a share of associate items, but distinguishing them separately from the company (subject to the need to reconcile the eventual carrying value to the amount determined under (c) below);

(c) in the company balance sheet, by valuing the investment in the associate on a net asset basis;

(d) in the company cash flow statement, by using the same basis as for a consolidated cash flow statement (see **25.64** to **25.66**).

25.76 A third acceptable approach would be to present information by way of notes to the company financial statements.

Investment funds

25.77 Where an investor, such as a venture capital company or investment trust, holds investments as part of an investment portfolio, FRS 9 recognises that all investments should be carried on a consistent basis, cost or market value, even though the investor may have a significant influence or joint control. Investments are held as part of an investment portfolio if their value to the investor is through their marketable value as part of a basket of investments, rather than as an extension of the investor's trade or business. [FRS 9(49)]

25.78   Other investments which are held outside the investment portfolio, and which meet the definition of an associate or joint venture, should be dealt with under the equity or gross equity basis as appropriate. For example, a venture capital investor may itself hold a participating interest in another venture capital company or investment trust. Where such an investee operates in a field of activity that is closely related or complementary to that of the investor, it is more likely that the investee will be an associate or joint venture of the investor than part of its investment portfolio. [FRS 9(50)]

Current practice

25.79

This requirement of FRS 9 is consistent with current practice in investment businesses, but represents a change to previous codified requirements. The logic is that an investor holding a portfolio, or providing start-up finance, will look for a return from three sources:

(a)   dividends and interest receipts;

(b)   increases in market value of shares; and

(c)   realisation of holdings through sale or flotation.

It can be argued that equity-based information, i.e., a share of underlying profits and net assets, is only one factor affecting performance and is not, of itself, sufficient information for the users of the investment vehicle's financial statements. This is better provided through the change in market value of the portfolio.

Extension to subsidiary undertakings under FRS 2

25.80

Since FRS 9, which covers only associates and joint ventures, specifically provides for investments which form part of an investment portfolio to be carried on a single basis of cost or value, the question arises as to whether this practice can also be extended to subsidiary undertakings under FRS 2. Two arguments can be developed.

(a)   The argument in support of carrying subsidiary undertakings as part of a portfolio at cost is that prior to the issue of both FRS 2 and FRS 9, the *Interim Statement: Consolidated Accounts* (issued in 1990), at paragraph A12, stated that no exemption from normal associate and subsidiary accounting was available for venture capital companies. Since that paragraph was superseded by FRS 2, it left venture capital companies without either express permission or express prohibition on the treatment of either associates or subsidiaries. Thus the ASB's express requirement relating to associates and joint ventures in FRS 9(49) appears to reverse the view expressed in the Interim Statement.

(b)   The argument against including a subsidiary undertaking within a portfolio at cost is that while a venture capital investor's role as lender is consistent with a significant minority stake, it is inconsistent with a majority stake since, after the venture capital investor has achieved an exit route through sale or flotation, the continuing owners would not have control.

On balance, the argument against extending FRS 9(49) to subsidiary undertakings is deemed the more persuasive. Consequently, the normal treatment of investments falling within the definition of subsidiary undertaking is to consolidate (see **23.50** to **23.57** above).

Extract 25.80

Quester VCT plc

Year ended 31 January 1999

INVESTMENTS

Quoted investments, including fixed interest securities and investments traded on AIM are stated at middle market prices. Unquoted investments are stated at directors' valuation. Investments in unquoted companies are valued in accordance with the British Venture Capital Association (BVCA) guidelines. The directors' policy in valuing unquoted investments is to carry them at cost except in the following circumstances:

(a)   where a company's underperformance against plan indicates a diminution in the value of the investment, provision against cost is made as appropriate in bands of 25 per cent;

(b)   where a company is well established and profitable; the shares may be valued by applying a suitable price-earnings ratio to that company's historic post-tax earnings. The ratio used is

> based on a comparable listed company or sector but discounted to reflect lack of marketability. Unquoted investments will not normally be revalued upwards for a period of at least 12 months from the date of acquisition;
>
> (c) where a value is indicated by a material arms-length transaction by a third party in the shares of a company.
>
> Certain venture capital investments deemed to be associated undertakings are carried at cost or valuation in accordance with the Company's normal accounting policy and Financial Reporting Standard (FRS) 9.
>
> Capital gains and losses on investments, whether realised or unrealised, are dealt with in the capital reserve.

Accounting for joint ventures – applying the gross equity basis

Background and summary

25.81 In summary, joint ventures are accounted for as follows.

(a) In an investor's consolidated accounts – **on a gross equity basis:**

Consolidated profit and loss account	*As for associates*: share of joint venture items, separately disclosed, commencing with share of operating result. *Additionally*: share of turnover shown on the face of the primary statement, but not as part of group turnover.
Consolidated statement of total recognised gains and losses	*As for associates*: share of associate items, separately disclosed. *Additionally*: no additional requirement.
Consolidated balance sheet	*As for associates*: as a fixed asset investment, share of associate net assets, separately disclosed, together with goodwill (less amortisation) on acquisition of the associate. *Additionally*: share of gross assets and liabilities shown on the face of the primary statement as an amplification of the net investment.
Consolidated cash flow statement	*As for associates*: dividends received, as a separate item. Other cash flows between investor and associate under appropriate headings. *Additionally*: no additional requirement.

(b) In the investor's individual financial statements (assuming consolidated financial statements are prepared) – **on a cost basis (which may be revalued)**.

(c) Where an investor does not prepare consolidated accounts (e.g., because it has no subsidiaries) – **provide gross equity-based information** either:

   (i) in a separate set of financial statements; or
   (ii) as additional information to its own financial statements (guidance given in **25.73** above for associates is relevant).

(d) Where an investor is exempt from preparing consolidated accounts (e.g., it is a small group or would be a small group if it had subsidiaries) – **no gross equity-based information is required**. (However, certain information is required by Sch 5 Companies Act 1985 – see **25.135** below.) (Guidance given in **25.70** above for associates is relevant.)

(e) In an investment fund (e.g., venture capital company) holding an interest as part of an investment portfolio – use the same basis (**cost or market value**) as for other investments (guidance given in **25.77** above for associates is relevant).

Treatment in the consolidated profit and loss account

25.82   The requirements of FRS 9 in relation to associates also apply to joint ventures. [FRS 9(21) and (27)] These are:

(a) the investor's share of joint venture operating result should be included immediately after group operating result (i.e., before any share of results of associates) [FRS 9(27)];

(b) any amortisation of goodwill arising on the acquisition of the joint venture should be included at this point and disclosed [FRS 9(27)];

(c) the investor's share of any joint venture exceptional items shown below operating result (under FRS 3) should be shown with similar group items, but shown separately [FRS 3(20) and FRS 9(27)];

(d) the investor's share of any joint venture interest (or similar items) should be shown with similar group items, but shown separately [FRS 9(27)];

(e) the investor's share of joint venture items below this level (i.e., at and below profit before tax) should be included within amounts for the group [FRS 9(27)];

(f) the investor's share of joint venture tax should be separately disclosed [FRS 9(27)].

25.83   Additionally, the investor's share of its joint ventures' turnover should be shown on the face of the primary statement, but separate from the group (i.e., parent and subsidiary undertakings) turnover. In the segmental analysis, the investor's share of its joint venture's turnover should be clearly distinguished from the turnover for the group. [FRS 9(21)]

25.84   The most straightforward method of presenting this information is as memorandum disclosure only.

Example 25.84.1

Consolidated profit and loss account

	£ million
Group turnover	200
(In addition, share of joint venture turnover £100 million)	
Group cost of sales	(120)
etc.	

However, the following example illustrates the presentation in the example given in FRS 9, which is described there as the 'normal' presentation.

Example 25.84.2

Consolidated profit and loss account

	£ million	£ million
Turnover: Group and share of joint venture	300	
Less: Share of joint venture	(100)	
Group turnover		200
Group cost of sales		(120)
etc.		

The following alternative example provided within FRS 9 provides more extensive disclosure in respect of the joint venture, and may be more appropriate where the joint venture accounts for a greater proportion of total activity.

Example 25.84.3

Consolidated profit and loss account

	Group	Share of joint venture	Total
	£ million	£ million	£ million
Turnover	200	100	300
Cost of sales	120	55	175
Gross profit	80	45	125
Administrative expenses	30	18	48
Operating profit	50	27	77
Share of operating profit in:			
– Joint ventures	27		
– Associates	15		
	92		

etc.

A further alternative, which is not shown in FRS 9, but is found in practice, shows only turnover and operating result (followed by items below operating result) on the face of the profit and loss account, with other operating items such as costs of sales, gross profit and administrative expenses shown in a note to the profit and loss account.

Example 25.84.4

Consolidated profit and loss account

	£ million
Turnover:	
Group	200
Share of joint venture	100
Share of associates	80
	380
Operating profit:	
Group	50
Share of joint venture	27
Share of associate	15
	92

etc.

In all cases, other requirements of law and accounting standards must be met, e.g., the division of turnover and operating result into continuing and discontinued activities.

25.85 Where segmental analysis of turnover is given, the share of joint venture turnover should be distinguished from group turnover. [FRS 9(21)]

25.86 Further guidance is included on acquisitions and changes in stake, unrealised gains and losses, accounting policies, non-coterminous year ends, joint ventures with their own subsidiaries, associates and joint ventures, options and similar instruments and loss-making joint ventures (see **25.98** to **25.122** below).

Information on the face of the consolidated profit and loss account

25.87

> The wording of FRS 9 is not completely clear on what items must appear on the face of the consolidated profit and loss account and what can be analysed in notes. The following guidance may assist.

Item	Requirements	Reason
Share of turnover	Face	FRS 9(21)
Share of operating result	Face (but may be combined with share of associate and amortisation of goodwill)	FRS 9(27) and Companies Act formats
Amortisation of goodwill	Face or Notes	Not expressly required on the face
Share of post-operating exceptional items	Face (for material) exceptional item) Notes (if combined with group exceptional item of the same class, or with other joint venture or associate exceptional items, on grounds of materiality)	FRS 3
Share of interest	Face or Notes	Not expressly required on the face
Share of tax	Notes	FRS 9(27)

Exceptional items

25.88

> The normal basis of including a share of joint venture exceptional items below operating result in the investor's consolidated profit and loss account will be that they are classified as falling within FRS 3 exceptional items in the venture's own profit and loss account. [FRS 3(20)] Through the combination of taking a share of these items only, and including them within consolidated accounts of a larger reporting entity, such items may appear to be immaterial. For consistency, such items should normally continue to be disclosed as exceptional items and not included within operating result, even if this results in items appearing to be less material than other group exceptional items. In such cases where associate exceptional items do not appear to be material from a group perspective, it would be acceptable to combine the associate exceptional items on the face of the consolidated profit and loss account and to provide details within notes to the accounts.

Treatment in the consolidated statement of total recognised gains and losses

25.89 The investor's share of joint venture items (e.g., revaluation gains and losses and foreign exchange differences) should be included within equivalent group headings. If the amounts included are material, separate disclosure of the joint venture amounts is required either on the face of the statement or in a note that is referred to in the statement. [FRS 9(28)]

25.90 The following example (which is similar to the example for associates in **25.57** above) reflects the requirements of FRS 9 in respect of the consolidated statement of total recognised gains and losses presentation.

Example 25.90

Consolidated statement of total recognised gains and losses

	£ million	£ million
Profit for the financial year		20
Revaluation of properties:		
Group	40	
Share of joint venture	8	
		48

Foreign exchange translation differences:		
Group	(15)	
Share of joint venture	(7)	
		(22)
Total recognised gains and losses for the year		46

Note: Separate analysis is required if amounts are material. The analysis may be given in a note to the financial statements.

Treatment in the consolidated balance sheet

25.91 The requirements of FRS 9 in relation to associates also apply to joint ventures. [FRS 9(21) and (29)] These are:

(a)   the investor's share of the joint venture's net assets should be included as a separate item within fixed asset investments [FRS 9(29)];

(b)   goodwill arising on the investor's acquisition of the joint venture, less any amortisation or write-down, should be included within the carrying amount of the joint venture, but separately disclosed [FRS 9(29)];

(c)   where there has been an impairment in any goodwill attributable to an associate, the goodwill should be written down and the amount written off in the period disclosed [FRS 9(38)];

(d)   where a joint venture has net liabilities, the investor's share is shown within provisions or liabilities [FRS 9(45)].

25.92 Additionally, the investor's share of the gross assets and liabilities underlying the share of net assets should be shown on the face of the balance sheet as an amplification of the net amount.

25.93 The following example reflects the requirements of FRS 9 in respect of consolidated balance sheet presentation.

Example 25.93

Consolidated balance sheet

	£ million	£ million
Fixed assets		
Tangible assets		520
Investments in joint ventures:		
Share of gross assets	350	
Share of gross liabilities	(160)	
		190
Investments in associates		95
		805

etc.

Disclosure is also required of loans to joint ventures and of goodwill arising on acquisition.

25.94   An alternative example provided within FRS 9 provides more extensive disclosure in respect of the joint venture and may be more appropriate where the joint venture accounts for a greater proportion of total activity.

Example 25.94

Consolidated balance sheet

	Group	Share of joint venture	Total
	£ million	£ million	£ million
Fixed assets			
Tangible assets	520	200	720
Investments in joint ventures:	190	(190)	
Investments in associates	95		95
	805	10	815
Current assets			
Stocks	150	60	210
Debtors	165	70	235
Cash at bank and in hand	35	20	55
	350	150	500
Creditors: amounts falling due within one year	(180)	(70)	(250)
Net current assets	170	80	250
Total assets less current liabilities	975	280	1,065
Creditors: amounts falling due after more than one year	(320)	(90)	(410)
Provisions for liabilities and charges	(50)		(50)
Net assets	605		605

etc.

Extract 25.94

GEC plc

Year ended 31 March 1999

BALANCE SHEETS (Extract)

31 March 1999

	Note	Group 1999 £m	Group 1998 Restated £ m	Company 1999 £m	Company 1998 £m
Fixed assets					
Goodwill	9	3,281	1,781	–	–
Tangible assets	10	982	871	24	23
Investments:					
Shares in Group companies	11			4,069	3,445
Joint ventures				365	365
Share of gross assets		1,439	821		
Share of gross liabilities		(995)	(498)		
Share of net assets		444	323		
Alstom		943	725	943	520
Other associates		32	98	1	58
Other		52	20	49	17
	12	1,471	1,166	1,358	960
		5,734	3,818	5,451	4,428

25.95 FRS 9 does not refer to the presentation of the investor's share of joint venture retained reserves, e.g., post-acquisition revaluation reserve, profit and loss account and other reserves. In practice, it will therefore be acceptable to include either:

(a) a share of joint venture items within group reserve headings; or

(b) all joint venture items together as a separate 'other reserve'.

Treatment in the consolidated cash flow statement

25.96 The requirements of FRS 9 are:

(a) dividends received from joint ventures should be included as a separate item (combined with associates where appropriate) after cash flow from group operating activities, but before returns on investments and servicing of finance [FRS 9(30)];

(b) any other cash flows between the investor and the joint venture are included within the appropriate heading, e.g., acquisition and disposal of shares, advance and repayment of loans, interest on loans [FRS 9(30)].

The following items do not appear in the cash flow statement:

(a) group share of any items included on a gross equity basis, e.g., operating result, exceptional items, interest payable, tax, change in net assets;

(b) amortisation of goodwill on acquisition of a joint venture.

25.97 The following example (which is similar to that for associates in **25.66** above) reflects the requirements of FRS 9 in respect of consolidated cash flow presentation.

Example 25.97

Consolidated cash flow statement

	£ million	Notes
Cash flow from operating activities	70	1
Dividends received from joint ventures	20	2
Returns on investments and servicing of finance	(22)	3
Taxation	(10)	4
Capital expenditure and financial investment	(40)	5
Acquisitions and disposals	35	6
Equity dividends paid	(15)	
Cash outflow before use of liquid resources and financing	38	
Management of liquid resources	(5)	
Financing	(25)	
Increase in cash in the period	8	

Notes:

1. Group only, excluding joint venture.
2. May be combined with associates.
3. Includes interest on loans to joint venture.
4. Excludes joint venture.
5. Includes loans advanced to/repaid from joint venture.
6. Includes purchase or sale of shares in joint venture.

Extract 25.97

GEC plc

Year ended 31 March 1999

CASH FLOW STATEMENT

For the year ended 31 March 1999

	Note	1999 £m	1998 Restated £m
Net cash inflow from operating activities	20	775	853
Dividends and management fees received from joint ventures and associates		438	125
Net cash inflow from returns on investments and servicing of finance	21	25	32
Tax paid	21	(358)	(269)
Net cash outflow from capital expenditure and financial investment	21	(286)	(242)
Net cash inflow/(outflow) from acquisitions and disposals	21	(636)	229
Equity dividends paid to shareholders		(218)	(339)
Cash inflow/(outflow) before use of liquid resources and financing		(260)	389
Net cash inflow/(outflow) from management of liquid resources	21	138	(85)
Net cash inflow/(outflow) from financing:			
Purchases of ordinary shares		(310)	(301)
Other	21	516	(27)
Increase/(decrease) in cash and net bank balances repayable on demand		84	(24)

Accounting adjustments and special situations – associates and joint ventures

Treatment of losses and interests in net liabilities

25.98   FRS 9 states that an investment ceases to be an associate or joint venture only when the long-term factors on which the investor/investee relationship are based have changed permanently. [FRS 9(40)] It follows that an associate or joint venture should continue to be dealt with under the equity method or gross equity method both during a time when the investee makes losses and when the investee has net liabilities, so that there is continuity of reporting both losses and the commencement of profits. The only exception will be where there is sufficient evidence that the relationship between investor and investee has irrevocably changed such that influence or joint control is no longer exercised. [FRS 9(44)] Such evidence could include a demonstrable commitment to disposal or withdrawal, or control of financial and operating policies being assumed by bankers or creditors. [FRS 9(45)] Where an associate or joint venture has net liabilities, the investor's share is shown within provisions or liabilities. [FRS 9(45)]

Accounting policies

25.99   FRS 9 requires that, in arriving at the amounts to be included by the equity method, the same accounting policies as those of the investor should be applied. [FRS 9(31)(c)]

25.100   In practice, restatement of associate and joint venture amounts to reflect the accounting policies of the group will be restricted to items that have a material impact on the consolidated accounts of the investor.

Elimination of unrealised profit and other transactions

Elimination of unrealised profit on stocks and other assets including assets introduced to a joint venture

25.101   Where profits and losses resulting from transactions between the investor and its associate or joint venture are included in the carrying amount of assets in either the investor or investee, the part relating to the investor's share should be eliminated. [FRS 9(31)(b)] The elimination is made only in the investor's consolidated financial statements, but extends to all transfers of assets and liabilities, including an initial stake, e.g., the transfer of an asset representing one venturer's initial contribution to the joint venture. [FRS 9(36)]

25.102   Where a sale is made from investee to investor, the asset will appear in the consolidated balance sheet and the profit will be included in the investee's profit and loss account. The elimination is thus:

- Dr Share of associate/joint venture profit;

- Cr Stocks or other asset;

with the investor's share of the unrealised profit or loss.

Where a sale is made from investor to investee, the asset will appear within the investee's net assets and the profit will be included in the group profit or loss. The elimination is thus:

- Dr Consolidated profit and loss account (normally, cost of sales);

- Cr Share of associate/joint venture net assets (and, in the case of joint ventures, gross assets),

with the investor's share of the unrealised profit or loss. This latter double entry would be appropriate for assets transferred to a joint venture, at a gain, as the investor's contribution to the joint venture. In the case of a fixed asset, the gain is only realised through a lower depreciation charge over the life of the asset.

Transactions within a private finance intitiative consortium

25.103 Private finance initiative (PFI) transactions give rise to profit elimination considerations which are of particular significance. For example, three construction companies, A, B and C, form a consortium company (meeting the definition of a joint venture under FRS 9) to design, build, finance and operate a new road and bridge for which they are paid a unitary charge by the local authority which procures the PFI contract. The consortium company contracts with each of A, B and C for the construction work, which lasts for three years. The operating phase lasts for 25 years. Where, under FRS 5 Application Note F, the road and bridge are classified as assets of the consortium (and not of the procuring local authority), it will be necessary to eliminate a share of construction profit in each of A, B and C's books. No elimination will be necessary in the following circumstances:

(a) profit on construction by a contractor who does not equity account for its interest in the consortium company by virtue of its having neither significant influence nor joint control;

(b) profit on construction where the consortium company, under FRS 5 Application Note F, classifies its interest in the PFI contract as a finance lease or similar monetary debtor. In this case, the road and bridge asset is regarded as sold by the consortium company to the local authority and profit is thus realised;

(c) profit on subsequent work done during the operating phase in respect of maintenance work which is expensed by the consortium company.

25.104 The following arguments, which have been put forward, are not considered acceptable as a basis for avoiding profit elimination in the construction companies:

(a) although the road and bridge asset is classified, under FRS 5 Application Note F, as an asset of the consortium company, the construction companies regard the consortium's asset as an in-substance finance lease. This may be by virtue of risks passed back to maintenance providers under back-to-back contracts or an argument which purports to be based on substance;

(b) the PFI contract is regarded as a long-term contract falling under SSAP 9, such that attributable profit may be taken by the contractors partly during the construction phase and partly during the operating phase.

25.105 Particular care is needed when the consortium company does not meet the definition of a joint venture, but amounts to a joint arrangement that is not an entity. Where a PFI contract is thus divisible into distinct assets, with a contractor being responsible for construction and subsequent operation of a separate asset, it may be necessary to eliminate profit in full. For example, A and B jointly undertake a road and bridge PFI contract, whereby A builds and operates the road and B builds and operates the bridge, effectively as assets with separate risks. Where the consortium is an extension of A and B's separate business, then the respective construction contracts with A and B will effectively amount to a contract with themselves and full profit elimination would follow.

Elimination of inter-company balances

25.106 Because associates and joint ventures are not part of the group, inter-company balances between the group and associates are not eliminated. Unsettled normal trading transactions should be included as current assets or liabilities. [FRS 9(36)]

Elimination of inter-company sales

25.107 Where transactions have taken place between a parent and subsidiary, then, in addition to elimination of unrealised profit, it is usual to eliminate the transaction from turnover and cost of sales. However, FRS 9 is silent on the elimination of turnover on transactions between investors and associates or joint ventures.

25.108 For trading transactions to or from an associate, neither the associate's turnover nor cost of sales is disclosed and therefore elimination of inter-company sales is not usually necessary. Where the investor's share of associate turnover is disclosed as a memorandum item, it will be necessary to state clearly the accounting policy on which the group and associate turnover is based. In any event, in accordance with FRS 8 *Related party disclosures* (see chapter 29), a note to the accounts should indicate the amount of transactions from investor to associate, and from associate to investor, and how these are reflected in the financial statements.

25.109 For trading transactions to or from a joint venture, both group turnover and the investor's share of joint venture turnover will be disclosed. Under the alternative presentation shown in **25.84** above, share of joint venture cost of sales would also be disclosed. Where practicable, the investor's share of turnover and/or cost of sales should be eliminated in order to avoid double-counting in any aggregate disclosures. Where this is not practicable, the financial statements should show clearly the extent to which disclosed turnover is impacted by inter-company transactions.

Example 25.109

Inter-company sales

Investor sells goods costing £100 to its 50 per cent owned joint venture for £120, who sells the goods for £130. The information may be summarised as follows:

	Group	Share of JV	Total
	£	£	£
Turnover	120	65	185
Cost of sales	100	60	160
Profit	20	5	25

While the total profit of £25 is correct, the turnover double counts the sale from the group to the joint venture. One solution is to reduce the share of joint venture turnover by £60, and disclose as follows:

Turnover	125
Less: share of joint venture	(5)
Group turnover	120
Cost of sales	(100)
Group operating profit	20
Share of joint venture operating profit	5
Total operating profit	25

Since this solution puts the full elimination against the share of joint venture turnover, it would be advisable to indicate the treatment adopted as an accounting policy where the impact is material.

Non-coterminous year ends

25.110 The requirements of FRS 9 are broadly consistent with those in FRS 2 dealing with subsidiary undertakings, with the additional consideration that an investee (most likely, an associate) may itself be a listed company. Consequently, disclosure of investee information may amount to the release of price-sensitive information. Where an investee's period end differs from that of the investor, the order of preference is as follows.

(a) Prepare special investee financial statements to coincide with that of the investor.

(b) Where this is not practicable, use financial statements of the investee prepared for a period ending not more than three months before the investor's period end.

(c) Where use of such financial statements would release restricted, price-sensitive information, use financial statements of the investee prepared for a period ending not more that six months before the investor's period end. Alternatively, option (a) or (b) may be adopted and arrangements made for the release of information to all shareholders.

Where either of (b) or (c) is used, adjustment should be made for any changes occurring after the investee's year end, but before that of the investor, that would materially affect the view given by the investor's financial statements. [FRS 9(31)(d)]

Group interests and interests in groups

25.111 Where an investing group holds an indirect interest in an associate or joint venture through a subsidiary undertaking, or another associate or joint venture, then the investor's share (of results and net assets) should be based on the aggregate holdings of the investor and its subsidiaries. Interests held by associates and joint ventures of the group should be disregarded, since the parent is not able to control these shareholdings. [FRS 9(32)]

25.112 However, where an associate or joint venture has its own subsidiaries, associates and joint ventures, the results and net assets to which this share is applied should be those included in the associate or joint venture's consolidated financial statements, i.e., including its share of its own associate and joint venture results and net assets. [FRS 9(32)]

Example 25.112

Consider the following structure:

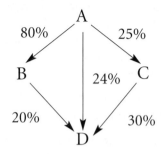

The example illustrates how A accounts for D.

Classification:	Share	
Direct holding	24%	
Indirect holding via B	20%	(Note 1)
Indirect holding via C	0%	(Note 2)
Total share	44%	

Notes:

1. A holds a controlling interest in B and thus is able to control all of B's 20 per cent stake in D (not merely 80 per cent of that stake). B's 20 per cent stake is therefore aggregated in full.

2. A does not hold a controlling interest in C and is not able to control any of C's 25 per cent stake in D. C's stake in D is disregarded in determining whether D is an associate of A.

Accounting:

In A's consolidated financial statements, it will account for:

Share of associate results (operating profit to tax line) and net assets:
– 44% share of D (calculation above)
– 25% share of C (which will include C's 30% share of D).

Minority interests:
– 4% share of D (representing the minority interests in B).

The effect of including C's share of D as part of A's interest in C, and reflecting the minority interest deduction, results in A's bottom line net profit and net assets, including a 47½ per cent share of D (24 per cent direct, 16 per cent indirect via B, 7½ per cent indirect via C).

> *Disclosure of goodwill.* FRS 10 requires goodwill on acquisition of a subsidiary to be shown as a separate item within intangible fixed assets, while FRS 9 requires goodwill relating to joint ventures and associates to be included within the investment in joint venture or associate. Where a group acquires a subsidiary, and that subsidiary has a joint venture, it is necessary to apportion the total goodwill arising between that relating to the subsidiary and that relating to the joint venture or associate and disclose two figures for goodwill separately in accordance with the respective FRSs. This treatment is consistent with the allocation of goodwill to income generating units required by FRS 11(34).Options, convertibles and non-equity shares

Options, convertibles and non-equity shares

25.113 FRS 9 requires that where an investor holds options, convertibles or non-equity shares in an associate or joint venture, these may need to be taken into account in reflecting the investor's interest under the equity or gross equity method. [FRS 9(33)] In such cases, the cost of exercising options, or converting convertibles, or future payments in relation to non-equity shares, should be taken into account. Care should be taken to avoid double-counting for any interest.

Ordinary and preference shares in an associate

25.114 A simple position which gives rise to two possible treatments arises where both equity and non-equity shares are held in an associate. One option is to include the non-equity interest with equity in determining the investor's overall share of associate results. The second option would be to account separately for the non-equity interest as investment income. The choice of option should take into consideration the purpose for which non-equity shares are held. In most cases, this will be an integral part of the investor's long-term interest and thus the first option is generally appropriate.

Example 25.114

A and its wholly owned subsidiaries own 40 per cent of the equity shares in B and 80 per cent of the preference shares. B's profit and loss account shows:

Operating profit	120
Interest payable	(20)
Profit before tax	100
Taxation	(30)
Profit after tax	70
Preference dividends	(35)
Profit attributable to ordinary shares	35

For either option, it is necessary first to allocate the operating profit into equity and non-equity interests. This is achieved by working upwards from the bottom of the profit and loss account:

	Total	Non-equity	Equity
Operating profit	120	50	70
Interest payable	(20)	–	(20)
Profit before tax	100	50	50
Taxation (marginal rate 30%)	(30)	(15)	(15)
Profit after tax	70	35	35
Preference dividends	35	35	
Profit attributable to ordinary shares	35	–	35

N.B.

(1) Interest payable has been allocated wholly to equity.

(2) Tax on the non-equity interest is computed at the marginal rate, with the balance allocated to equity.

Option 1: Include preference dividends in operating result

Share of B's results in A's consolidated profit and loss account would be:

Share of operating profit *(40% × 70) + (80% × 50)*	68
Share of interest payable *(40% × 20)*	(8)
Share of profit before tax	60
Share of taxation *(40% × 15) + (80% × 15)*	(18)
Share of profit after tax	42

Option 2: Include preference dividends as investment income

Share of B's results in A's consolidated profit and loss account would be:

Share of operating profit *(40% × 70)*	28
Share of interest payable *(40% × 20)*	(8)
Investment income *(80% × 35)*	28
Share of profit before tax	48
Share of taxation *(40% × 15)*	(6)
Share of profit after tax	42

N.B. The dividend received has not been grossed up in this example.

Acquisitions, disposals and changes in stake

Acquisitions: fair value adjustments and calculation of goodwill

25.115   FRS 9 requires that, on acquisition of an associate or joint venture, fair values should be attributed to the investee's underlying assets and liabilities, identified using the investor's accounting policies. [FRS 9(31)(a)] The effect is that:

(a)   fair value provides the basis for subsequent depreciation;

(b)   both consideration and fair values of assets and liabilities, and consequently goodwill arising, should be calculated in the same way as on the acquisition of a subsidiary under FRS 7 (see chapter 24, starting at **24.5** above);

(c)   the investee's assets used in the calculation should not include any goodwill arising on the investee's own acquisitions. It follows that goodwill arising on the investee's acquisitions will be included within goodwill arising on acquisition of the investee;

(d)   goodwill arising on acquisition of the investee is subject to the requirements of FRS 10 (see chapter 13, starting at **13.44** above).

Acquisitions: piecemeal and step acquisitions

25.116   Where an investment in an associate or joint venture is acquired in stages, the approach in FRS 9 is the same as for a subsidiary in FRS 2. [FRS 2(50) – (52) and FRS 9(41)] This will mean that:

(a)   the equity method is not applied, and goodwill is not calculated, until the conditions to meet the definition of an associate or joint venture are met;

(b)   once the conditions to meet the definition of an associate or joint venture are met, goodwill is calculated in accordance with **25.115** above;

(c)   further purchases of shares which increase the interest in the associate or joint venture, but do not amount to a subsidiary undertaking, will require goodwill to be calculated based on the additional share acquired, the consideration paid for the subsequent purchase and the fair value of net assets at that date;

(d)   a further acquisition which takes the interest from associate or joint venture to subsidiary is dealt with in essentially the same way, but, to comply with the Act, disclosure is given of goodwill as if subsidiary status was achieved in one transaction (see **24.54** above).

Deemed acquisition: increase in existing interest

25.117 Where an investor's interest changes without a purchase of shares occurring, e.g., due to a redemption of shares from other shareholders (a deemed acquisition), a gain or loss will arise. This is calculated by comparing the investor's share of net assets and goodwill before and after the deemed acquisition. Since there is no transaction, it is suggested that this gain or loss is reported in the statement of total recognised gains and losses.

Deemed acquisition: becoming an associate for the first time

25.118 An investor may hold an interest which is classified as a simple investment carried at cost (or valuation). Subsequently, changes in interests of other investors, or changes in management arrangements, may result in the investor's interest meeting the definition of an associate without any further acquisition of shares taking place. It follows that the date of acquisition will be the date at which the definition of an associate is fulfilled (see also **25.46** above).

Disposals: calculation of gain or loss

25.119 When an interest in an associate or joint venture is disposed of, the profit or loss should take account of goodwill arising on acquisition of the investee, but excluding:

(a) amounts written off through the profit and loss account as a result of amortisation or impairment; and

(b) amounts attributed to prior period amortisation or impairment in applying the transitional arrangements of FRS 10. [FRS 9(40)]

Disposals: piecemeal and partial disposals where associate status continues

25.120 Where shares in an associate or joint venture are disposed of, but the residual interest continues to qualify as an associate or joint venture, then the approach in FRS 9 is the same as for a subsidiary in FRS 2(50) to (52). [FRS 2(50) – (52) and FRS 9(41)] This requires that any profit or loss on sale will be calculated by comparing proceeds with the share of net assets and goodwill relating to the share sold.

Deemed disposal

25.121 | Where an investor's interest changes without a sale of shares occurring, e.g., due to an issue of shares to other shareholders (a deemed disposal), a gain or loss will arise. This is calculated by comparing the investor's share of net assets and goodwill before and after the deemed disposal. Since there is no transaction in which the investor is directly involved, it is suggested that this gain or loss is reported in the statement of total recognised gains and losses.

Disposals: partial disposals where associate status ceases and investment status continues

25.122 A partial disposal (or deemed disposal) which results in a residual interest which has ceased to meet the definition of an associate or joint venture (i.e., the residual interest is a simple investment) gives rise to a gain or loss on disposal calculated in the same way as any other partial disposal (see **25.120** above). An additional consideration is the initial carrying amount of the remaining interest. This will be the aggregate of the residual share of net assets at the date of disposal, together with the residual proportion of goodwill. The resulting investment carrying value is a surrogate cost derived from the former carrying amount and should be described as 'cost'. It should be reviewed and written down, if necessary, to its recoverable amount. [FRS 9(42) – (43)]

Accounting for joint arrangements that are not entities

Requirements of FRS 9

25.123 FRS 9 deals briefly with JANEs. The requirement is that each participant should account for its own assets, liabilities and cash flows, measured according to the terms of the agreement governing the arrangement. [FRS 9(18)]

25.124 | In addition to assets, liabilities and cash flows which are wholly attributable to one participant, there may be shared items. Each participant should account for its share of such shared items. This treatment has an effect which is similar to proportional consolidation.

25.125 | It follows from the principle that participants to a joint arrangement account for their own assets, liabilities and cash flows, that such items are recognised both in the individual entity accounts of the participant, and in its consolidated accounts (if prepared).

25.126 Applying the concept of substance over form, FRS 9 recognises that a joint arrangement may have the appearance of a joint venture (e.g., it is established as a legal entity), but, in substance, is a joint arrangement that does not amount to an entity (e.g., it confers extremely limited commonality of interest between venturers and effectively acts as an agent for each participant to carry on its own business). In such cases, the joint arrangement should be accounted for as a JANE, i.e., each participant accounts for its part of the assets, liabilities and cash flows held within the structure. [FRS 9(24) – (25)]

25.127 The implications of this requirement are potentially far reaching. For example, FRS 9 appears to have the effect that a participating entity:

(a)   is required to include a liability on its balance sheet which legally is a liability of another entity over which it has joint control but not sole control;

(b)   may similarly be required to account for profits which are legally profits of another entity over which it has joint control but not sole control.

Reconciliation to the requirements of the Companies Act

25.128 FRS 9 asserts that its definitions of associate and entity are consistent with the Act. [FRS 9(4) footnote] However, there is one significant difference which is not adequately explained: the Act refers to an 'undertaking', while FRS 9 refers to an 'entity'. An undertaking is defined in the Act as '(a) a body corporate or partnership, or (b) an unincorporated association carrying on a trade or business, with or without a view to profit' [s259(1)] FRS 9 defines an entity purely in terms of a separate trade or business, irrespective of legal separateness. In the case of a body corporate which does not amount to an entity under FRS 9, it would seem that, while the Act requires equity accounting in consolidated accounts as an associate, FRS 9 requires accounting for separate assets, liabilities and cash flows both in investor and consolidated financial statements. FRS 9 identifies the issue and concludes that 'in such cases ... the undertaking acts merely as an agent for the venturers and, therefore, they should account directly for their share of the assets and liabilities'. [FRS 9 appendix 1: 6] However, three issues are open to question:

(a)   *recognition of assets and liabilities by the investing entity*: it is assumed that the principles of FRS 5 would support the treatment required by FRS 9, in that assets and liabilities recognised by the investing entity would meet the

> definitions of asset and liability within FRS 5. Consequently, changes in recognised assets and liabilities would amount to gains and losses in the reporting entity. In individual cases, further consideration may need to be given to whether gains and losses should be regarded as realised or unrealised;
>
> (b) *apparent double-counting*: since there is no legal agency agreement in place, the investee would not be entitled to prepare dormant company accounts and thus assets and liabilities may be accounted for by more than one undertaking (i.e., both investor and investee);
>
> (c) *true and fair view override*: the absence of equity accounting in the investor's consolidated accounts required by the Act would appear to require use of a true and fair view override, so appropriate disclosure should be considered (see **5.11** above).

Examples of joint arrangements

25.129 Four examples are set out below, dealing with construction, a jointly owned pipeline, an aircraft production consortium and property development.

> ### Example 25.129.1
>
> **Construction**
>
> Two construction companies, A and B, set up two joint ventures to bid for a PFI contract to build a bridge and feeder motorway. Joint venture 1 (JV1) is a company, and an entity under FRS 9, which secures the PFI contract on a 25-year concession under which it maintains the bridge and road and receives toll income. Joint venture 2 (JV2), which is not an entity under FRS 9, contracts with JV1 to construct the bridge and road. Company A takes full responsibility for the bridge; and company B for the road.
>
> ***Separate assets, liabilities and cash flows***: construction assets, and work in progress arising from JV2.
>
> ***Shared items***: shared costs related to JV2, e.g., project management expenses. N.B. Assuming JV1 meets the definition of an entity, A and B will each gross equity account for their interest in JV1, subject to elimination of their share of unrealised profit.

Example 25.129.2

Jointly owned pipeline

Two oil companies, with adjacent North Sea oil wells, build and operate a pipeline to transport oil to an on shore refinery which is owned and operated by a third-party oil company. Surplus capacity in the pipeline is used by the third party.

Separate assets, liabilities and cash flows: stocks of oil passing through the pipe.

Shared items: the pipe (asset and decommissioning costs), expenses of maintenance, revenue from use by third party.

Example 25.129.3

Aircraft production consortium

Three aerospace companies, A, B and C, jointly manufacture commercial passenger aircraft for sale and share the revenue in an agreed proportion. A is responsible for manufacture of the fuselage (and assembly of the finished components), B for wings and C for engines. Sales revenue is handled by a jointly owned company.

Separate assets, liabilities and cash flows: manufacturing facilities, supplies and stocks of unused and partly finished goods, labour costs.

Shared items: revenue from sales, expenses of jointly owned company.

Example 25.129.4

Property development

A property development company and a bank form a joint venture to develop residential units. The property development company project manages the venture and owns 'A' shares. The bank provides the majority of finance on a non-recourse basis and owns 'B' shares. Construction work is subcontracted to a construction company. Holders of B shares receive a return of eight per cent on both loan and equity finance, subject to the non-recourse nature of finance. Holders of A shares receive the balance of revenue after meeting payments on loans and B shares.

Separate assets, liabilities and cash flows:

(a) bank: investment (equity and loan) in joint venture, fixed rate income on investment;

(b) property development company: residential units (cost of site and payments to contractors), revenue from sale of units, finance costs paid to bank.

Shared items: none identified.

Disclosure

All associates and joint ventures

25.130 In addition to amounts required to be shown on the face of the primary statements, the following information is required under the equity or gross equity methods.

Summary of disclosure (refer to FRS 9 for detail)	FRS 9 reference	*Commentary*
For each principal associate and joint venture: • its name; • the nature of its business; • proportion of each class of shares held (indicating special rights/constraints); • accounting period, if different to that of the investor.	FRS 9 paragraph 52	*'Principal' is usually interpreted as meaning material.*
Matters which have an impact on an investor, e.g., items within the notes to associate and joint venture financial statements, such as contingent liabilities or capital commitments.	FRS 9 paragraph 53	*This requirement is deliberately vague and therefore broad in its application.*
Restrictions on associate or joint venture distributions, e.g., statutory, contractual or exchange control restrictions.	FRS 9 paragraph 54	*Unless stated otherwise, it is assumed that the investor's share of investee reserves is freely available, subject to arrangements for joint control decisions over use. This disclosure should indicate any circumstances where this assumption is not valid.*
Balances between investor and associate or joint venture, showing separately: • loans; • trading balances.	FRS 9 paragraph 55	*Loans by the investor will usually form part of the fixed asset investment total. Trading balances will usually be current assets or liabilities.*
Circumstances where the 20 per cent rebuttable presumption is rebutted.	FRS 9 paragraph 56	*This will be relevant in any case of a material associate or joint venture where classification does not align with a shareholding above or below 20 per cent.*

Additional disclosures at 15 per cent and 25 per cent thresholds

25.131   Application of the thresholds is as follows. [FRS 9(57)]

Stage 1 **Calculate investor group numbers, excluding associates and joint ventures**	Stage 2 **Compare 15 per cent of investor group with:**	Stage 3 **Compare 25 per cent of investor group with:**
Gross assets (= total fixed + current assets)	Either: (a) gross assets for all associates; or (b) gross assets for all joint ventures	Either: (a) gross assets for individual associates; or (b) gross assets for individual joint ventures
Gross liabilities (= due in less than one year + due in more than one year + provisions)	Either: (a) gross liabilities for all associates; or (b) gross liabilities for all joint ventures	Either: (a) gross liabilities for individual associates; or (b) gross liabilities for individual joint ventures
Turnover	Either: (a) turnover for all associates; or (b) turnover for all joint ventures	Either: (a) turnover for individual associates; or (b) turnover for individual joint ventures
Operating results (on a three-year average)	Either: (a) operating results for all associates; or (b) operating results for all joint ventures	Either: (a) operating results for individual associates; or (b) operating results for individual joint ventures
	↓	↓
Additional disclosures required?	**If any test exceeded, make 15 per cent threshold disclosures for associates or joint ventures in aggregate.**	**If any test exceeded, make 25 per cent threshold disclosures for individual associates or joint ventures.**

25.132 The required disclosures are as follows. [FRS 9(57) and (58)]

Disclosure	Required for 15 per cent threshold: aggregate disclosure	Required for 25 per cent threshold: individual disclosure
Name of the associate or joint venture		●
Turnover (unless already disclosed)	●	●
Profit before tax		●
Taxation		●
Profit after tax		●
Fixed assets	●	●
Current assets	●	●
Liabilities due within one year	●	●
Liabilities due after one year or more	●	●

25.133 Where an individual associate or joint venture accounts for nearly all of the amounts included for that class of investment, then only the aggregate, and not individual, information need be given, provided that this is explained and the associate or joint venture is identified. [FRS 9(58)(c)]

25.134 Further analysis should be given where necessary to understand the nature of the total amounts disclosed, e.g., size and maturity profile of liabilities. [FRS 9(58)] See **20.45** to **20.50** as regards segmental analyses in respect of significant associates.

Requirements of the Companies Act 1985

25.135 The disclosures required by the Act are as follows.

Companies Act requirement	Also required by FRS 9	Not also required by FRS 9
Where, at the end of the year, the company (group) held shares in a subsidiary or had other significant holdings (i.e., exceeded 20 per cent or more of nominal value of any class of shares or the value exceeded 20 per cent of the investing company's (group's) assets, disclose the following: [Sch 5: 7, 22, 23 and 26]		
(a) name of the undertaking [Sch 5: 8, 22, 24 and 27];	●	

(b) country of incorporation or, if unincorporated, the address of its principal place of business [Sch 5: 8, 22, 24 and 27];		●
(c) identity and proportion of the nominal value of each class of shares held. (In group accounts, distinguish holdings in joint ventures and associated companies between direct holdings of the parent and those of the group) [Sch 5: 8, 22, 24 and 27];	●	
(d) the total of its capital and reserves at the end of its financial year [Sch 5: 9, 25 and 29];		●
(e) its profit or loss for that year [Sch 5: 9, 25 and 28].		●
Where the above information is not given because it would be harmful to the business of overseas undertakings and the Secretary of State approves, this fact must be disclosed. [s231(4)]		●
Where the above information is limited to principal undertakings because full disclosure would result in excessive length, this fact must be disclosed and full information annexed to the company's next annual return. [s231(6)]	●	
(Information under (d) and (e) need not be given if the holding is less than 50 per cent and the undertaking is not required to deliver or publish accounts.)		
For each proportionally consolidated joint venture: [Sch 5: 21]		
(a) name of the joint venture;	●	
(b) address of its principal place of business;		●
(c) factors on which joint management is based;		●
(d) proportion of capital of the joint venture held by the group;	●	
(e) for non-coterminous year ends, the joint venture's financial year last ended before the year end of the company.		●

Extract 25.135.1

BG plc

Year ended 31 December 1998

An analysis of the Group's share of turnover and net assets in associated undertakings is shown below:

for the year ended 31 December	1998 £m	1997 £m
Share of turnover	2,254	2,226

as at 31 December	1998 £m	1997 £m
Share of assets		
Share of fixed assets	681	940
Share of current assets	718	396
	1,399	1,336
Share of liabilities		
Liabilities: amounts falling due within one year	(326)	(310)
Liabilities: amounts falling due after more than one year	(819)	(757)
	(1,145)	(1,067)
Share of net assets	254	269

Additional disclosure for Dynegy Inc., an associated undertaking, is given below:

for the year ended 31 December	1998 £m	1997 £m
Share of turnover	2,182	2,073
Share of profit/(loss) before taxation	24	(23)
Share of tax	(8)	10
Share of profit/(loss) after taxation	16	(13)

as at 31 December	1998 £m	1997 £m
Share of assets		
Share of fixed assets	237	319
Share of current assets	509	299
	746	618
Share of liabilities		
Liabilities: amounts falling due within one year	(290)	(260)
Liabilities: amounts falling due after more than one year	(353)	(270)
	(643)	(530)
Share of net assets	103	88

Extract 25.135.2

John Laing plc

Year ended 31 December 1998

Note 28 FRS 9 RESTATEMENT

The effect of introducing FRS 9 on the comparative figures for 1997 is shown below:

	1997 As reported £m	FRS 9 Restatement £m	1997 Restated £m
Summary balance sheet			
Fixed assets	98.0	(10.9)	87.1
Current assets excluding cash	495.0	30.8	525.8
Creditors falling due within one year excluding borrowings	(373.7)	(9.3)	(383.0)
Creditors falling due after one year excluding borrowings	(8.0)	(4.0)	(12.0)
Provisions for liabilities and charges	(22.8)	–	(22.8)
Net cash	26.3	(6.6)	19.7
Net assets	214.8	–	214.8
Summary profit and loss			
Turnover	1,461.4	–	1,461.4
Profit on ordinary activities before interest	32.5	0.7	33.2
Net interest	(0.3)	(0.7)	(1.0)
Profit on ordinary activities before taxation	32.2	–	32.2

Note 12 Investments in Joint Ventures

	W L Homes LLC £m	Other £m	1998 Total £m	1997 Total £m
Turnover	92.6	32.0	125.6	51.2
Profit before tax	4.4	1.2	5.6	2.2
Taxation	–	(1.1)	(1.1)	(0.5)
Profit after tax	4.4	0.1	4.5	1.7
Fixed assets	–	98.6	98.6	48.3
Current assets	123.3	38.7	162.0	21.6
Total liabilities – less than one year	(62.4)	(30.3)	(92.7)	(47.1)
– greater than one year	–	(98.3)	(98.3)	(17.2)
Provisions	(2.9)	(1.8)	(4.7)	–
	58.0	6.9	64.9	5.6

26 Foreign currency transactions

26 Foreign currency transactions

Introduction

Foreign currency transactions and scope of SSAP 20

26.1   A company may enter into foreign currency activities in two main ways:

(a)   it may enter directly into transactions denominated in a foreign currency; and

(b)   it may operate through an investment in a foreign enterprise which maintains its accounting records in a foreign currency.

26.2   SSAP 20 *Foreign currency translation* has standardised the methods of accounting for both of these types of foreign currency transactions.

26.3   Companies can also acquire various foreign currency instruments either for speculative or, more frequently, for hedging purposes. This is an area in which the SSAP is silent. This chapter deals both with the accounting treatments specified in the SSAP for foreign currency transactions and the possible and preferred accounting treatments for other foreign currency instruments.

Preparation of financial statements of individual companies

Initial recording of transactions

26.4   The local currency amount at which transactions denominated in foreign currencies should initially be recorded in the books will be determined by using the exchange rate appropriate to the transaction. Normally, the rate appropriate to the transaction is the rate ruling at the date on which the transaction occurs. As an approximation, an average rate for the period may be used when the rates do not fluctuate significantly. A different rate will be appropriate in the following cases:

(a)   if the contract provides for the transaction to be settled at a specified rate of exchange, then that is the rate appropriate to the transaction; and

(b)   if the rate at which the transaction will be settled has been fixed by entering into a matching forward contract to buy or sell the foreign currency concerned, then the rate established in the forward contract may be used as the rate appropriate to the transaction.

26.5

> It is a common practice among companies which engage in a large number of foreign currency transactions to fix for a period the rate of exchange at which they record those transactions in their accounting records and to disregard day-to-day fluctuations in exchange rates. Where this approach is used, care must be taken to ensure that the carrying value of non-monetary assets, particularly stocks, is not materially different from what it would have been if actual rates had been used for translation. It is suggested that only the actual rate appropriate to the transaction should be used to record large one-off transactions such as the acquisition of fixed assets.

Non-monetary assets

26.6 Non-monetary assets, such as stocks, fixed tangible assets and equity investments, normally remain at the initial recorded amount and are not retranslated, as these balances reflect the historical cost of acquiring the assets. The exception which applies where foreign equity investments are hedged by foreign currency borrowings is described in **26.37** to **26.59** below.

26.7

> For the purpose of assessing the lower of cost and net realisable value of current assets, net realisable value should normally be determined using the rate ruling at the balance sheet date. If any asset is valued in accordance with any of the alternative valuation rules, then the rate to be used for this purpose is that ruling at the date of the valuation.

Monetary assets and liabilities

26.8 All monetary assets and liabilities, such as cash and bank balances, debtors and creditors, which are denominated in foreign currencies should be translated into the local currency using the rates of exchange ruling at the balance sheet date, with one exception. Amounts receivable or payable which represent the settlement of open transactions should be recorded at the rate appropriate to the transaction if the rate is fixed by being specified in the contract. Where the rate was fixed by entering into a matching forward contract, the rate established in the forward contract may be used.

Exchange gains and losses

26.9 Exchange gains and losses arise from exchange rate movements between the time transactions are first recorded in the accounting records (or the beginning of the year in respect of unsettled balances) and when they are settled. They also arise on unsettled transactions when the exchange rate at the balance sheet date differs from the rates at which the transactions are recorded in the accounts.

26.10 Gains and losses arising from trading transactions should normally be included in the profit and loss account in arriving at operating profit and those arising from financing arrangements should be included under 'Other interest receivable and similar income' or 'Interest payable and similar charges'.

Example 26.10

Assume Company A with a year end of 31 December purchased goods abroad on 1 December 1999 when the exchange rate was £1 = $1.60, payment of $24,000 to be made on 26 January 2000. The invoice should be recorded in the bought ledger at £15,000 ($24,000 @ 1.60). If the exchange rate at the year end was £1 = $1.58, the bought ledger balance should be translated into sterling using the year end rate, increasing the liability to £15,190 ($24,000 @ 1.58). The loss of £190 arising from the adverse movement of the dollar between the purchase date and the year end date should be charged as an exchange loss in the profit and loss account for the year ended 31 December 1999. If, at the settlement date of 26 January 2000, sterling had strengthened to £1 = $1.62, the liability would be settled for £14,815 and an exchange gain of £375 (being the difference between the previous translated amount and the settlement) should be credited to the profit and loss account for the year ending 31 December 2000.

26.11 Normally, there is no difference in the treatment of short-term monetary items, i.e., those which fall due within one year of the balance sheet date, and those which are long term, but SSAP 20 does consider one special circumstance. With regard to long-term items only, it is necessary to consider 'the amount of the gain, or the amount by which exchange gains exceed past exchange losses on the same items to be recognised in the profit and loss account'. It states that, in exceptional circumstances, the recognition of this gain should be restricted on the grounds of prudence. The exceptional circumstances arise 'where there are doubts as to the convertibility or marketability of the currency in question'. It is hard to understand what is intended by this requirement and, in particular, why it should apply to long-term items but not to short-term ones. If convertibility or marketability problems exist when the financial statements are being prepared, they affect all monetary items in that currency equally and restricting the recognition of apparent exchange gains is unlikely to be a sufficient response to the problem.

26.12

In SSAP 20, it is stated in the section dealing with legal require-ments in the UK that exchange gains arising on unsettled long-term monetary items are unrealised. This statement is surprising in view of the definition of realised profits in the Act. [s262(3)] Its consequence is that the recognition of such gains in the profit and loss account (which is required by SSAP 20) must be regarded as a departure from one of the account-ing principles prescribed by the Act. Therefore, when material gains on unsettled long-term monetary items are included in the profit and loss account, it is necessary to disclose particu-lars of the departure from the accounting principle, the reasons for it and its effect in a note to the accounts.

Example 26.12

The profit and loss account includes unrealised exchange gains of £243,000 (1999 – £156,000) arising from unsettled long-term mone-tary items. The directors consider this departure from the statutory requirement to include only realised profits in the profit and loss account necessary in order for the financial statements to give a true and fair view.

Translation of financial statements of foreign enterprises

Introduction

26.13 Once a foreign enterprise's own financial statements have been pre-pared in its local currency, they must then be translated into the reporting currency of the investing company or group before they can be incorporated into the investing company's own financial statements or the group's consolidated financial statements.

26.14 SSAP 20 requires one of two translation methods, the closing rate/net investment method (the 'net investment' method) or the temporal method, to be applied to each foreign enterprise, depend-ing upon the economic environment in which that enterprise oper-ates. The net investment method of translation should be applied to the local currency financial statements of those foreign enterprises in the group which operate as separate or quasi-independent entities from that of the investing company. This method recognises that the investment of a company is in the net worth of the foreign enter-prise, rather than in the individual assets and liabilities. The tempo-ral method should be applied to foreign enterprises whose affairs are so closely connected with those of the investing company as to constitute an extension of the economic environment of the invest-ing company. The SSAP recognises that the net investment method will be used in most circumstances. Once adopted, these methods should be applied consistently from period to period, unless the financial and other operational relationships between the enterprise and the investing company change. These methods are described below.

26.15   The translation rules for this purpose set out in SSAP 20 apply to financial statements of foreign subsidiaries, associated companies and branches of the investing company.

Branches

26.16   SSAP 20 defines a foreign branch as 'either a legally constituted enterprise located overseas or a group of assets and liabilities which are accounted for in foreign currencies'.

26.17   When a group of assets and liabilities is identified as a branch, the net investment method of translation can be used for that branch. The most common situations encountered where it may be appropriate to treat a group of assets and liabilities as a branch are where ships or aircraft are purchased in a foreign currency, normally US dollars, and financed by foreign currency loans.

26.18   In determining whether a branch may be accounted for under the net investment method, the factors which need to be considered are those referred to in **26.29** below. It is necessary to look at whether the assets are financed by foreign currency loans and whether the associated revenue and expenses are in the foreign currency. Generally, if at least two of these three, normally the liability and revenue, are in the foreign currency such that the foreign cash flows do not have a day-to-day impact on the company, it may be possible to recognise a foreign branch and use the net investment method of translation.

Closing rate/Net investment method

26.19   Under the net investment method, balance sheet assets and liabilities should be translated using the closing rate of exchange. The objective of the translation is for the translated statements to reflect closely the results and relationships as measured in the foreign currency. In determining what rate should be used to translate the profit and loss account, SSAP 20 states that use of the closing rate is more likely to achieve this objective; however, using the average rate may more fairly reflect the profits or losses and cash flows as they arise to the group. The SSAP therefore allows either the closing rate or the average rate for the period to be used in translating the profit and loss account. The standard does not prescribe the method of calculating the average rate, but any method which appropriately weights the calculation to take account of the volume of transactions during the period generally will be acceptable. For example, a foreign entity which translates monthly accounts into the reporting currency at each month end rate and accumulates these monthly results to produce the full year's results will usually have effectively used an appropriate weighted average rate.

26.20 Exchange differences will arise from the retranslation of:

(a) the opening net investment at the closing rate compared to the exchange rate ruling at the end of the previous year. If there has been a capital injection during the year, a similar difference will arise between the capital injection at the closing rate compared to the exchange rate ruling at the date of such injection. If there has been a reduction in net investment during the year, e.g., due to a dividend payment, the exchange difference arising will be the difference between the opening net investment at the rate ruling at the previous year end compared to the exchange rate ruling on the date of the reduction, plus the exchange difference on the remaining investment at the rate ruling on the date of reduction compared to the closing rate; and

(b) the profit or loss for the financial year at the closing rate compared to the average exchange rate where this rate was used to translate the profit and loss account.

26.21 These exchange differences are dealt with by direct transfer to or from reserves, because they arise from factors unrelated to the trading performance and would distort the results if taken to the profit and loss account. They should be reported in the statement of total recognised gains and losses.

26.22 It is suggested that if foreign exchange translation differences dealt with through reserves constitute in the aggregate a material balance, they should be disclosed as a separate reserve entitled 'Foreign exchange translation'; otherwise, they should be included in the balance of the profit and loss account.

26.23 The introduction of the euro raised a question as to what impact the irrevocable locking of national currencies of participating Member States to the euro has on cumulative translation differences that have been taken to reserves in periods before the introduction of the euro. The UITF considered this issue and concluded that such foreign exchange translation differences should remain in reserves after the introduction of the euro and should not be reported in the profit and loss account. [UITF 21] The reasoning behind this conclusion is that FRS 3 makes it clear that the same gains and losses should not be recognised twice and, since such exchange differences have already been reported in the statement of total recognised gains and losses in accordance with FRS 3, there is no question of reporting them again in the profit and loss account once such differences become permanent. [FRS 3(27)]

26.24   A related question to that discussed in **26.23** above is whether cumulative translation differences that have been taken to reserves in periods before the introduction of the euro became realised with the introduction of the euro. Such differences became irreversible; however, normal realisation principles apply.

Definition of net investment in a subsidiary

26.25   The net investment is defined by SSAP 20 as the company's effective equity stake in the foreign enterprise and comprises its share of the enterprise's net assets. The net investment will be the proportion of share capital and reserves of the enterprise attributable to the investor's holdings, but, in addition, it may include long-term intragroup loans and other deferred balances where these are regarded as equivalent to a permanent equity stake.

26.26   Where loans or other deferred balances are regarded by an investing company as equivalent to a permanent equity stake, then they should be so treated for all purposes. In particular, the investing company should treat the loan or balance as a non-monetary item in its own balance sheet and retain it at historical cost, i.e., assuming that the balance is denominated in the foreign currency (which will normally be most convenient), it should be translated at the rate ruling when it was first recognised as constituting permanent equity.

26.27   If the loan is denominated in the currency of the investing company, it should be treated in the accounts of the enterprise receiving it as a non-monetary item and translated at the rate ruling when it was first recognised as constituting permanent equity. If it is necessary to adopt a different translation policy in order to comply with local regulations, then an adjustment should be made before the accounts are consolidated with those of the investing company.

26.28   In the same way that a loan from the investing company, possibly through another group company, may be considered as constituting permanent equity, a loan to the investing company from the investee, or another group company, may represent a permanent reduction in the equity investment.

Temporal method

26.29   The temporal method should be applied for consolidation purposes to financial statements of a foreign enterprise whose affairs 'are so closely interlinked with those of the investing company that its results may be regarded as being more dependent on the economic environment of the investing company's currency than that of its own reporting currency'. Some of the factors which need to be considered in determining whether the temporal method should be used are given in SSAP 20 as follows:

(a) the extent to which the cash flows of the enterprise have a direct impact upon those of the investing company;

(b) the extent to which the functioning of the enterprise is dependent directly upon the investing company;

(c) the currency in which the majority of the trading transactions are denominated; and

(d) the major currency to which the operation is exposed in its financing structure.

26.30 Situations where the temporal method is appropriate might include foreign enterprises whose principal activities include:

(a) selling of goods received from the investing company, the proceeds of which are remitted back to that company;

(b) manufacturing of components or sub-assemblies to be included in the investing company's own products; and

(c) raising of finance for other companies in the group.

26.31 Under the temporal method, all transactions and balances are treated as if they were directly entered into by the investing company itself, i.e., as described in **26.4** to **26.8** above. Thus, the translation procedures to be applied to the foreign entity's financial statements are as follows.

Items	Exchange rate to be used
Non-monetary items Fixed assets carried at: • historical cost	– historical rate, i.e., the rate ruling at the date the transaction was established.
• valuation	– rate ruling at the date of the valuation.
Stocks and current asset investments carried at: • historical cost • net realisable value	– historical rates. – closing rate.

Monetary items	
All assets and liabilities	– closing rate.
Profit and loss account	
Turnover and cost of sales	– actual rate ruling at date of transaction or average rate.
Opening and closing stocks	– at the rates used for opening and closing balance sheet purposes.
Depreciation	– historical rates, i.e., the same rates as applied to the asset being depreciated.
Impairment charge:	
• those akin to revaluation adjustments and taken through the statement of total recognised gains and losses (per: FRS 11)	– rate ruling at the date of original valuation.
• all other impairments, i.e., those caused by a consumption of economic benefits	– historical rates, i.e., the same rates as applied to the asset being depreciated.
All other income and expense items	– actual rate ruling at date of transaction or average rate.
All differences arising on translation are taken to the profit and loss account.	

Foreign currency enterprise experiencing hyper-inflation

Accounting requirements

26.32   SSAP 20 acknowledges that where a foreign enterprise operates in a country in which there is a very high rate of inflation, it may not be possible to present fairly the financial position of that foreign enterprise simply by applying a translation process to historical cost accounts. It suggests that, in such circumstances, the local currency financial statements should be adjusted where possible to reflect current price levels before the translation process is undertaken.

26.33   More specific requirements are provided by UITF Abstract 9 *Accounting for operations in hyper-inflationary economies*. UITF Abstract 9 requires adjustments where the distortions caused by hyper-inflation are such as to affect the true and fair view given by the group financial statements. In any event, adjustments are required where the cumulative inflation rate over three years is approaching, or exceeds, 100 per cent and the operations in the hyper-inflationary economies are material.

26.34 UITF Abstract 9 recognises two acceptable methods of eliminating the distortions:

(a) adjust the local currency financial statements to reflect current price levels before the translation process is undertaken, as suggested in SSAP 20. Any gain or loss on the net monetary position would pass through the profit and loss account; and

(b) use a relatively stable currency as the functional currency for the relevant foreign operations. Entities in Latin American countries might, e.g., use the US dollar. The transactions of the entity would initially be recorded in the stable currency by applying the temporal method. The stable currency would then be considered the 'local currency' for the purposes of translating for inclusion in the consolidated group accounts. This method is, in effect, using the movement between the original currency and the stable currency to approximate the inflation index.

Disclosure requirements

26.35 The accounting policy adopted with respect to operations in hyper-inflationary economies should be disclosed.

Example 26.35

Transactions, assets and liabilities of subsidiary undertakings that operate in countries with high levels of inflation are reported in a stable currency, in accordance with UITF Abstract 9 *Accounting for operations in hyper-inflationary economies.*

Brazil and Kenya continue to be regarded as high inflation countries. The results and net assets of subsidiary undertakings operating in these two countries are reported using the US dollar as the stable functional currency.

26.36 If neither of the methods set out in **26.34** above is considered appropriate for operations which are material in group terms, alternative methods can be used, but the disclosure should also include reasons for not adopting one of the suggested methods.

Foreign equity investments financed by foreign borrowings

Offset rules applicable to an individual company

26.37   Normally, investments in foreign entities should be treated like other non-monetary items, i.e., they should be carried in the balance sheet at their historical cost, which reflects the exchange rate at which they were purchased.

26.38   An exception to this rule is permitted where a company has borrowed foreign currencies to finance or provide a hedge against its foreign equity investments. In these circumstances, the company may be covered in economic terms against any movement in exchange rates and, in order to recognise the match between the finance, which must be retranslated at the balance sheet rate, and the equity investments, the investments may be denominated in the appropriate foreign currency and the carrying amounts translated each year end at the closing rates of exchange in the individual company's financial statements. Where investments are treated in this way, any exchange differences should be taken to reserves, where they should be offset as a reserve movement by the exchange gains or losses on translating the related foreign currency loans at the closing rates. In order for this treatment to be adopted, SSAP 20 requires the following conditions to be met:

(a)   in any accounting period, exchange gains and losses on the borrowings may be offset only to the extent of the exchange differences arising on the equity investments (as discussed in **26.42** and **26.43** below, UITF Abstract 19 requires this comparison to be undertaken on a net of tax basis);

(b)   the foreign currency borrowings, whose exchange gains or losses are used in the offset process, should not exceed, in the aggregate, the total amount of cash that the investments are expected to generate, whether from profits or otherwise (as discussed in **26.42** below, UITF Abstract 19 requires this comparison to be undertaken on a net of tax basis); and

(c)   the accounting treatment adopted should be applied consistently from period to period.

26.39   Where this treatment is applied to a foreign equity investment which is neither a subsidiary nor an associated company, the same treatment may be applied in the consolidated financial statements.

Offset rules applicable to group companies

26.40   On consolidation under the closing rate/net investment method, the exchange movement on net foreign investments is taken to reserves. Where foreign borrowings have been used to finance group investments in foreign enterprises, the group's economic position is that the exchange risk associated with the investments is matched with that on the borrowings and it may therefore be considered inappropriate to recognise the exchange movement on the borrowings in the profit or loss account. In these cases, the exchange gains or losses arising on the translation of the foreign borrowings may be offset as a reserve movement against the exchange differences arising on the retranslation of the net investments, subject to the following conditions:

(a) the relationships between the investing company and the foreign enterprises concerned justify the use of the closing rate method for consolidation purposes;

(b) in any accounting period, exchange gains and losses arising on foreign currency borrowings may be offset only to the extent of the exchange differences arising on the net investments in foreign enterprises (as discussed in **26.42** and **26.43** below, UITF Abstract 19 requires this comparison to be undertaken on a net of tax basis);

(c) the foreign currency borrowings, whose exchange gains or losses are used in the offset process, should not exceed, in the aggregate, the total amount of cash that the net investments are expected to be able to generate, whether from profits or otherwise (as discussed in **26.42** below, UITF Abstract 19 requires this comparison to be undertaken on a net of tax basis); and

(d) the accounting treatment adopted should be applied consistently from period to period.

Tax on gains and losses on foreign currency borrowings which hedge an investment in a foreign enterprise

26.41 As discussed in **26.38** and **26.40** above, SSAP 20 permits certain gains and losses on foreign currency borrowings which have been used to finance or hedge equity investments in foreign enterprises to be reported in reserves. Additionally, FRS 3 requires these exchange differences to be reported in the statement of total recognised gains and losses. Where these gains and losses are taxable (e.g., where a matching election is not made for tax purposes), there is a potential for a mismatch in the accounting treatment of such exchange differences and the relating tax charge. To prevent occurrence of such a mismatch, UITF Abstract 19 requires tax charges or credits that are directly and solely attributable to such exchange differences also to be taken to reserves and reported in the statement of total recognised gains and losses. The amount of tax charges and credits accounted for in this way should be disclosed, in addition to the gross amount of the exchange differences (which is required by SSAP 20). This treatment of tax charge is now also required by FRS 16 (effective in respect of accounting periods ending on or after 23 March 2000).

26.42   In **26.38** and **26.40** above, reference is made to the conditions which must be met before the offset treatment can be adopted. UITF Abstract 19 specifies that any tax charge or credit directly attributable to the borrowings should be taken into account when applying the restriction on the amount of gains and losses which can be offset in reserves against the exchange differences on the equity investments (in individual accounts) or net investments (in consolidated accounts). Similarly, the comparison of the foreign currency borrowings, whose exchange gains and losses are used for the offset, with the total amount of cash which the investments are expected to be able to generate should be undertaken in after-tax terms.

26.43   The net-of-tax comparison required by UITF Abstract 19 raises a question about how much of the net-of-tax gain/loss can be offset in reserves. The question arises from the wording of SSAP 20, which implies that a net-of-tax gain/loss can be offset in reserves so long as it does not exceed the amount of the exchange loss/gain taken to reserves in respect of the investment. However, this approach, if adopted, would be questionable in view of the justification which SSAP 20 uses to allow the offset treatment: it argues that it would be inappropriate to record an accounting profit or loss when exchange rates change where the company is covered in economic terms against any movements in exchange rates. Therefore, it could be argued that an approach which reflects the economic substance of the transaction should be adopted.

Example 26.43

Company A acquired an equity stake in a German company for DM 600,000, borrowing DM 750,000 to finance the purchase of this investment and also to provide funds for working capital and other purposes. The investment and borrowing would be initially recorded in the accounting records at the rate of exchange then prevailing, say, £1 = DM 2.5, at £240,000 and £300,000 respectively.

If the investment and borrowings remained unchanged at the year end when the exchange rate was, say, £1 = DM 2.45, the investment may be denominated in Deutschmarks and translated at the year end rate (£244,898) with the exchange difference of £4,898 (DM 600,000 @ 2.45 – £240,000) being credited direct to reserves.

A gross exchange loss of £6,122 arises from translating the borrowings at the year end rate (DM 750,000 @ 2.45 – £300,000), but a tax credit of 15 per cent, directly attributable to the exchange loss on retranslation of the borrowing, gives rise to a net-of-tax loss on the borrowing of £5,204.

Under SSAP 20 rules, £4,898 can be offset against the credit arising from the retranslation of the investment and the balance should be charged to the profit and loss account. However, as only £240,000 of the borrowings provide an economic hedge, this does not seem to reflect the economic substance of the transaction.

To reflect the economic substance of the transaction, the amount of loss which it would be appropriate to offset in reserves is (£240,000/£300,000) × £5,204 (i.e., £4,163).

Implementation of the offset rules

26.44   The implementation of the offset rules is discussed below. Although the examples given illustrate their application to an individual company, the approach in group situations is the same.

26.45

There are no restrictions on the application of these rules other than those specified in SSAP 20 and the overall requirement to show a true and fair view. Thus, the period of the loans is not relevant and there is no requirement for them to be in the same currency as the investment. It appears that one loan can be replaced by another in a different currency without invalidating the offset treatment. In view of the flexibility permitted, the requirement for consistency of treatment is extremely important if an unfair presentation is to be avoided.

Determination of borrowings which constitute finance or a hedge

26.46   The following example illustrates the accounting treatment in the case where the borrowing made in the same currency exceeds the related investment.

Example 26.46

Assume Company A acquired a 15 per cent equity stake in a German company for DM 600,000, borrowing DM 750,000 to finance the purchase of this investment and also to provide funds for working capital and other purposes. The investment and borrowing would be initially recorded in the accounting records at the rate of exchange then prevailing, say, £1 = DM 2.5, at £240,000 and £300,000 respectively. If the investment and borrowings remained unchanged at the year end when the exchange rate was say, £1 = DM 2.45, the investment may be denominated in Deutschmarks and translated at the year end rate (£244,898) with the exchange difference of £4,898 (DM 600,000 @ 2.45 – £240,000) being credited direct to reserves.

Of the exchange loss of £6,122 arising from translating the borrowings at the year end rate (DM 750,000 @ 2.45 – £300,000), £4,898 can be offset against the credit arising from the retranslation of the investment and the balance should be charged to the profit and loss account.

Borrowings in different currencies

26.47   It is permissible to apply the offset principle to any foreign currency borrowings to the extent that such borrowings do not exceed the cash expected to be generated from the investment, either from profits or otherwise. Equally, SSAP 20 permits the offset principle to be applied on a pooled basis to a group of investments financed by a variety of different currencies, including those currencies which may have moved in opposite directions during the period.

Cash expected to be generated by investments

26.48   The extent to which foreign currency loans can be offset against net investments in foreign currency is restricted to 'the total amount of cash that the net investments are expected to be able to generate whether from profits or otherwise'. While this restriction seems reasonable in principle, it is hard to see when it will have any practical effect, since no guidance is given either as to how the expectation of cash generation is to be measured or as to the period of profit earning that is to be taken into account. The extent to which offset is possible is, in any case, restricted to the book value of the investment in the case of a single company and the group's share of the book value of the net assets of the enterprise where the net investment method is being used. Accordingly, provided the foreign enterprise is profitable, the additional restriction is unlikely to have any effect, since the cash expected to be generated by future profits is virtually unlimited. If the foreign enterprise is unprofitable or earns negligible profits after taking account of the interest payable on the loan, the expected cash to be generated must be represented by the estimated net realisable value of the investment; if this amount is less than the book values used in the financial statements, then the restriction might apply.

26.49   If the foreign enterprise was subject to stringent exchange control restrictions so that the prospect of significant cash being
generated outside the country was low, it would clearly not be
appropriate to regard a loan in another freely marketable foreign currency as a hedge against that investment. However, in
these circumstances, it may be inappropriate to consolidate by
the net investment method. FRS 2 requires subsidiaries to be
excluded from consolidation if they are subject to severe long-
term restrictions which substantially hinder the exercise of the
rights of the parent over the assets of the subsidiary. [FRS
2(25)] In these circumstances, the investment would (depending on the degree of influence) be shown in the consolidated
accounts at original cost or at a fixed amount calculated using
the equity method at the date restrictions came into force, and
this amount should not be retranslated at the year end.

Partial hedges

26.50   Under SSAP 20, offset rules described in **26.38** to **26.40** above
apply where a company uses foreign currency borrowings to
finance or provide a hedge against foreign equity investment.
However, SSAP 20 does not specify to what extent the investment has to be financed in this way. Therefore, in theory, it
would be possible to retranslate a foreign equity investment in
the parent's own accounts at closing rate where that investment
is 'hedged' to a very low extent, e.g., where an acquisition of a
foreign equity investment was financed by 90 per cent cash and
10 per cent foreign currency loan.

26.51   There also does not appear to be anything to prevent 'split'
accounting, i.e., where part of the investment is translated at
closing rate and part at historic rate. This would reflect the fact
that there is no economic risk on the part of the investment
which is matched by borrowings.

26.52   Both of the above methods, though theoretically acceptable,
could be challenged: the first method on the grounds that it
does not reflect hedging in economic terms and it is economic
hedging that SSAP 20 refers to in the explanation to the standard as the reason for allowing offset; while the second method
could be said to undermine the fact that an entity owns one
asset – a foreign currency asset, rather than two assets – a foreign currency asset and a sterling asset.

26.53   In view of the above arguments, it is recommended that the
closing rate should be used to translate a foreign equity

investment where the investment is 100 per cent or substantially matched by foreign currency borrowings. Where this is not the case, the argument that there is a true economic hedge ought to be challenged and therefore the historic rate would be most appropriate for translating the investment in the parent's own accounts.

Borrowings subsequently reduced

26.54 Borrowings which may have been treated as finance for or a hedge against an equity investment in the preceding year may be substantially reduced or repaid in full during the current financial year. This does not give rise to any change in accounting treatment in group accounts, but, if an equity investment held by an individual company has been translated at the closing rate, that treatment will no longer be appropriate, unless a new foreign currency loan is obtained or there are other foreign currency borrowings available as a hedge for the investment. The investment should be translated at the rate ruling when repayment of the hedging loan takes place. Thereafter, it should be retained at that amount, unless a new hedging loan is arranged.

Example 26.54

Assume, in the example in **26.46** above, that the directors decided to take advantage of the strong pound by repaying the DM 750,000 loan midway through the subsequent year when the exchange rate was £1 = DM 2.60. The rate ruling at the subsequent year end was £1 = DM 2.55.

The exchange gain arising on the settlement of the loan is the difference between the loan balance shown in the opening balance sheet (DM 750,000 @ 2.45 = £306,122) and the loan repayment (DM 750,000 @ 2.60 = £288,462), or £17,660.

The equity investment should be translated using the rate of exchange ruling on the date the borrowing cover ceased, i.e., £1 = DM 2.60, giving rise to a translation debit of £14,129 (£230,769, i.e., DM 600,000 @ 2.60 – £244,898) to be shown as a reserve movement. Therefore, the exchange gain of £17,660 arising on the loan settlement should be applied: £14,129 direct to reserves and £3,531 credited to the profit and loss account. At the year end, the equity investment should continue to be valued at £230,769 (DM 600,000 @ 2.60), subject to any impairment.

Borrowings made before or after the investment

26.55

Sufficient freedom is contained in SSAP 20 to permit the cover approach to be applied to borrowings taken out either before or after the investment is made. However, the standard is not clear as to the appropriate exchange rate to be used in denominating the foreign currency investment where there is a time gap between the date the investment was made and the date of the loan. If the cover method is to make sense, it would appear that the offset of exchange gains or losses on the loans should only be made against the exchange differences arising on the equity investment during the cover period. Accordingly, to achieve this matching, the exchange rates ruling on the first day in which both the investment and loan were held should be used to translate the investment as the starting point in the calculation of the exchange difference available for offset.

Example 26.55

Assume Company B paid $240,000 for an equity investment in an overseas company when the exchange rate was £1 = $2.40, the investment being carried in the books at £100,000. Several years later, the directors considered the investment to be worth at least $600,000 and hedged the investment by obtaining a $600,000 loan the proceeds of which were invested in sterling deposits amounting to £375,000 (£1 = $1.60). At the year end, the exchange rate was £1 = $1.67.

If the purpose is to provide a hedge against the value of the investment, the directors of B should bring it into the accounts at directors' valuation (i.e., $600,000). The investment would be initially valued at £375,000 ($600,000 @ 1.60) and the surplus arising of £275,000 would be credited to the revaluation reserve. As both the investment and loan would be carried at the same amount, the exchange difference arising from retranslating the investment at the closing rate would be fully covered by the opposite difference arising from the retranslation of the loan at the closing rate, leaving no exchange gain or loss to be included in the profit and loss account.

Where the directors of B are not prepared to revalue the investment as suggested above, an alternative approach is to use the historical cost of the investment in dollar terms (i.e., $240,000) as the starting point. This amount would then need to be translated first at the exchange rate at the date the loan was obtained (£1 = $1.60) giving £150,000 and then at the closing rate (£1 = $1.67) giving £143,713. The exchange difference of £50,000 arising from the movement in rates between the purchase of the investment and the date of the loan should be credited direct to reserves, as this represents a revaluation surplus. The movement in rates to the year end produces a further exchange difference of £6,287 (£150,000–£143,713) and it is this exchange difference which should be available to be covered by the exchange gain or loss arising on the loan. In this case, an exchange gain on the loan of £15,719 ($600,000 @ 1.60 – $600,000 @ 1.67) arises, but only £6,287 should be credited direct to reserves, as an off-set to the debit of similar amount arising from the retranslation of the investment and the balance should be credited to the profit and loss account.

Disclosure requirements

26.56 The methods used to translate the financial statements of foreign enterprises and the treatment accorded to exchange differences should be disclosed in the financial statements. Furthermore, the Act requires the basis on which sums originally denominated in foreign currencies have been translated into sterling to be disclosed in the notes to the accounts. [Sch 4: 58(1)] These disclosures are normally given in the accounting policies note.

26.57 An example of a suitable accounting policy note, which should be adapted to fit individual circumstances, might be as follows.

> ### *Example 26.57*
>
> Transactions of UK companies denominated in foreign currencies are translated into sterling at the rates ruling at the dates of the transactions. Amounts receivable and payable in foreign currencies at the balance sheet date are translated at the rates ruling at that date.
>
> The financial statements of overseas subsidiary and associated companies are translated into sterling at the closing rates of exchange and the difference arising from the translation of the opening net investment at the closing rates is taken direct to reserves. Differences arising on the translation of foreign currency loans taken to finance the group's foreign investments are also taken direct to reserves. All other translation differences are dealt with in the profit and loss account.

26.58 SSAP 20 requires all companies to disclose the net movement on reserves arising from exchange differences. It also requires all companies, or groups of companies, which are not exempt companies (i.e., banking and insurance companies and certain companies registered in Northern Ireland and the Republic of Ireland which take advantage of the exemptions from full disclosure given by their companies' legislation) to disclose the net amount of exchange gains and losses on foreign currency borrowings less deposits, identifying separately:

(a) the amount offset in reserves under the rules set out in **26.38** to **26.40** above; and

(b) the net amount charged/credited to the profit and loss account.

26.59 There is no further requirement to disclose the net amount of exchange gains or losses included in the profit and loss account unless the amount involved meets the criteria of an exceptional item.

Goodwill arising on consolidation

26.60 Goodwill may arise on consolidation where a company acquires the equity share capital of a foreign subsidiary. FRS 10 requires positive purchased goodwill to be capitalised and classified as an asset on the balance sheet. The question arises as to whether goodwill should be retranslated at the year end. One approach is to view goodwill as an asset which is measured at a certain point in time and valid only at that point in time in the circumstances then prevailing, i.e., as part of the initial investment. Where this argument is employed, goodwill, irrespective of whether it is capitalised and amortised or written off to reserves, is a sterling asset and should not be retranslated each year end. Alternatively goodwill can be viewed as an asset which resides in the foreign entity's business and generates a foreign income stream, hence retranslation at year end rates is appropriate.

26.61 One advantage of retranslation arises where changes in exchange rates lead to an impairment. Such an impairment would need to be taken through the profit and loss account. Where, however, the investment is hedged, the retranslation difference representing the impairment can be taken through the statement of total recognised gains and losses.

26.62 The decision as to which approach is appropriate should be based on individual circumstances. Management policy on hedging could help in making this decision. Where a company hedges the net assets as they are stated at the time of acquisition, goodwill is likely to be viewed as a sterling asset. On the other hand, if the amount of borrowing used for hedging reflects the future income stream of the foreign subsidiary, e.g., reflects the purchase price where this is calculated by discounting the future income stream, treatment of goodwill as a foreign asset could be more appropriate. In view of this, the accounting policy on retranslation of goodwill could differ from one acquisition to another, though a consistent approach should be adopted when deciding on the accounting treatment.

26.63 Where goodwill arose on acquisitions which took place prior to the introduction of FRS 10, it would seem appropriate to continue with the existing accounting policy on retranslation of goodwill. For example, where goodwill remains written off to reserves, the original policy to translate it each year end at closing rates would mean that the translation differences will continue to be taken through reserves.

Forward exchange contracts

Introduction

26.64 Under a forward exchange contract, a company enters into a binding agreement to buy or sell a specified amount of foreign currency at a specified rate on a given future date. The methods normally used to account for such transactions in year end financial statements depend on whether they are speculative or used for hedging purposes.

Speculative transactions

26.65 Where a forward exchange contract is entered into as a speculative transaction, then it will give rise to a profit or loss, depending on the movement in the exchange rate over the period to maturity. For example, a company contracts to sell $1,000,000 90 days forward at £1 = $1.55. At the end of the 90 days, it must buy $1,000,000 in order to meet its contract; it will thus make a profit if £1 buys more than $1.55 at that time.

26.66 At the year end, it is necessary to determine the profit or loss, if any, which should be recognised in respect of any such contracts which are open at that time. There are two generally accepted methods of doing this:

(a) compare the forward rate in the contract with the corresponding forward rate to maturity at the year end; and

(b) compare the 'spot' rate (i.e., the rate for immediate conversion) at the date the contract is taken out with the spot rate at the balance sheet date and to amortise the contracted forward discount or premium over the period of the contract.

Example 26.66

A company contracts on 1 November 1999 to sell $1,000,000 90 days forward at £1 = $1.55, i.e., on 30 January 2000, it must deliver $1,000,000 in exchange for £645,161. At 1 November 1999, the spot rate was £1 = $1.60 ($1,000,000 = £625,000). At the year end on 31 December 1999, the 30-day forward was £1 = $1.56 ($1,000,000 = £641,026), while the spot rate was £1 = $1.57 ($1,000,000 = £636,943).

Method (a)

	£
Contracted price for delivery of $1,000,000 at 30 January 2000	645,161
Cost of '30 January 2000 dollars' at 31 December 1999 (i.e., 30 days forward)	641,026
Profit earned to 31 December 1999	4,135

Method (b)

	£	£
Spot price of $1,000,000 at 1 November 1999, date of contract		625,000
Spot price of $1,000,000 at 31 December 1999		636,943
		(11,943)
Contracted price at 1 November 1999	645,161	
Spot price of $1,000,000 at same date	625,000	
Premium on contract	20,161	
Proportion accrued to 31 December 1999 − 60/90 of £20,161		13,441
Profit earned at 31 December 1999		1,498

26.67 Another method, adopted by a number of banks, compares the forward rate in the contract with the spot rate at the balance sheet date, on the grounds that the company could crystallise its obligation by buying spot dollars immediately. Thus, in the example in **26.66** above, the profit to be recognised is the difference between the contract amount of £645,161 and the spot price of $1,000,000 at the year end of £636,943, i.e., £8,218. This treatment is not suitable for the majority of companies, because it ignores the cost of holding the dollars for one month, but may be suitable for banks and similar institutions which maintain a level of liquid dollar balances with which to meet such obligations at any time.

Hedging transactions

26.68 Forward exchange contracts are used by companies to hedge the foreign exchange risk on existing positions and on anticipated transactions. Considered below are the appropriate accounting treatments of forward exchange contracts entered into to hedge:

- transactions at the date the transaction takes place;

- future commitments or transactions;

- existing monetary assets or liabilities;

- investments in foreign enterprises; and

- the future results of foreign investments.

Forward exchange contracts entered into at the date of the matched transaction

26.69 The only case dealt with by SSAP 20 is the use of forward exchange contracts to match trading transactions. In this case, the transaction may be recorded by translating at the rate specified in the contract.

26.70 For example, a trader who sells goods for $1,000,000 receivable in 90 days might immediately enter into a forward contract to sell $1,000,000 in 90 days' time, thereby fixing the sterling value of his sale. In such a case, the debt may be converted into sterling at the year end at the rate specified in the forward contract. Normally, no further entries are necessary in respect of the contract.

26.71 An alternative method sometimes used is to record the debtor at the exchange rate ruling at the date of sale and amortise any difference between that rate and the forward contract rate over the period of the contract. If in the example in **26.66** above, the sale had been made on 1 November when the exchange rate was £1 = $1.60 and the three months' forward contract rate was £1 = $1.55, then the debt would be recorded as £625,000, while the sterling amount receivable under the forward contract would be $1,000,000 @ 1.55, i.e., £645,161. At 31 December, two-thirds of the hedging gain of £20,161, i.e., £13,441, would be recognised as profit.

26.72 A third alternative is to look at the two transactions separately. As for an unhedged position, the debtor is translated at the year end rate. If the year end rate is £1 = $1.50, the debtor will be recorded at £666,667 and the profit of £41,667, being the difference between this and amount recorded at 1 November, taken to the profit and loss account. However, accounting for the forward exchange contract as a speculative contract, an equal loss can be recognised to offset this profit. The only profit or loss movement will be the premium on the contract, being the difference between the amount at the spot rate at the date of the contract and the contracted rate, spread over the period of the contract. (See method (b) of accounting for speculative transactions in **26.66** above.)

26.73 Although SSAP 20 suggests using the first of these three methods, it only states that this may be used and therefore does not rule out the use of an alternative method. The first method recognises all the profit or loss relating to the transaction in the year the contract is entered into. The alternative methods seek to allocate the profit or loss over the period of the contract. Both of the alternative methods result in the same movement in the profit and loss account; the difference is that the method in **26.72** above recognises and attributes a value to the forward exchange contract. The use of any of these alternatives is acceptable; the first has the advantage of simplicity, the other two are perhaps more theoretically correct, in that they recognise that the hedge is for the period of the contract.

Forward exchange contracts used to hedge future transactions

26.74 Companies sometimes use forward exchange contracts to hedge future transactions. Consider, e.g., a company which imports goods from the USA. The company knows that at least a certain amount of stock will be purchased in the month after the year end, so enters into a forward exchange contract in anticipation of that debt arising. This is an anticipated transaction. Alternatively, the transaction could be committed, e.g., the company may have contracted to purchase a fixed asset on a future date.

26.75 There are two acceptable methods of accounting for this type of transaction, which are illustrated by the example below.

Example 26.75

The company is importing from the USA stock of $200,000.

The year end is 31 March, at which date the spot rate is £1 = $1.70.

The forward exchange contract for 31 May is taken out at 1 March, when the spot rate is £1 = $1.71, for a contracted rate of £1 = $1.73.

Spot rate at 30 April when stock purchase is recorded is £1 = $1.66.

Spot rate at payment date 31 May is £1 = $1.68.

Method (a)

The first method is exactly the same as for hedges taken out at the time of the transaction. No entries will be made at the year end. At 30 April, the stock purchase is recorded at the contracted rate £1 = $1.73.

Method (b)

The alternative is to consider the two transactions separately. The stock purchase is initially recorded at the rate ruling on that date of the transaction, £1 = $1.66, i.e., £120,482. The profit of £1,434, being the difference between this and the amount at the spot rate on settlement of £119,048, is recognised in the profit and loss account on settlement.

On the forward exchange contract, the exchange difference experienced up to the year end of £688, being £116,959 ($200,000 @ 1.71) less £117,647 ($200,000 @ 1.70), is deferred and will be included in the amount of the asset when it is recognised. Similarly, the difference from the year end to the date of recording the asset of £2,835, being £120,482 ($200,000 @ 1.66) less £117,647, is included in recording the asset. The asset will therefore be recorded at £116,959 (£120,482 − £688 − £2,835), equivalent to the spot rate when the contract was entered into.

After the transaction date, the exchange loss on the contract up to 31 May of £1,434 equals the profit on the movement in the liability to the supplier, reflecting that the position was hedged.

The premium on the contract of £1,352, being the difference in the contracted rate and the spot rate when the contract was taken out, is spread over the period of the contract. One-third will be taken into the profit and loss account at the year end and two-thirds in the following year.

26.76 The second method described is that suggested in SFAS 52 and is to be preferred, although either is acceptable. SFAS 52 is very strict on when a forward contract can be designated as a hedge. It would only allow designation as a hedge of a committed transaction and not for an anticipated transaction as used in the example. SFAS 133, effective for periods commencing 15 June 2001, addresses the accounting for freestanding and certain embedded foreign currency derivatives and, hence, amends SFAS 52. The new standard requires measurement and recognition of derivatives at fair value; on revaluation the resulting gains and losses will be reported in earnings (equivalent to the profit and loss account) unless the derivative qualifies for hedge accounting. SFAS 133 removes the restriction on hedges of forecasted foreign currency transactions, though, other provisions of this new standard mean that hedge accounting will be even more of a 'privilege'. In the UK, the current rules are less strict and will allow designation if the anticipated transaction is reasonable considering the past and budgeted trading.

26.77 The introduction of the euro raised the question of the impact of the event on open forward exchange contracts (and other financial instruments) taken out to hedge future transactions. With the introduction of the euro, the exchange risk between currency units of two participating Member States disappeared and from that date such contracts are no longer required. The UITF considered this issue and concluded that where gains and losses on financial instruments used as anticipatory hedges are deferred and matched with the related income or expense in a future period, the introduction of the euro should not alter this deferral and matching treatment. [UITF Abstract 21] Hence, under method (b) in the example in **26.75** above, if the exchange rate was fixed on 31 March, the exchange difference of £688 experienced on the forward up to that date would remain to be deferred and would be included in the amount of the asset when it is recognised.

26.78

It is less clear, however, whether the conclusion reached by the UITF would equally apply to a company that uses method (a) in the example in **26.75** above. The accounting policy here is not that of deferring gains and losses on anticipatory hedges, i.e., not the situation addressed by the UITF. However, the underlying argument for both accounting treatments is the same: it would be inappropriate to record an accounting profit or loss when the company is covered in economic terms. So, the UITF's conclusion that the introduction of the euro should have no impact on the accounting treatment adopted could be extended to apply to these circumstances and the transaction when it occurs would be recorded at the rate specified in the forward.

Forward exchange contracts taken out to hedge existing monetary assets or liabilities

26.79

Sometimes, forward exchange contracts are entered into to hedge an existing asset or liability.

Example 26.79

The company has a $1,000,000 liability, repayable on 30 June 2000. On 1 January 2000, when the spot rate is £1 = $1.60, to hedge the loan, it enters into a forward exchange contract at a contracted rate of £1 = $1.64. The spot rate at the year end, 31 March 2000, is £1 = $1.70.

There are three generally accepted ways of accounting for this transaction, as follows.

(a) At the year end, translate the loan at the contracted rate of £1 = $1.64, recording it at £609,756. The difference between this and the amount recorded in January £625,000 is taken to the profit and loss account together with any previous exchange differences.

(b) At the year end again, translate the loan at the contracted rate. The difference between this and the amount at which it was recorded in January, £15,244 (£609,756 – £625,000) represents the premium on the contract and should therefore be recognised over the period of the contract; £7,622 is taken to the profit and loss account in the year to 31 March 2000 and £7,622 in the following year.

(c) The third alternative is to look at the two transactions separately. As for an unhedged position, the loan is translated at the year end rate, giving rise to a profit of £36,764 (£625,000 – £588,235) which is taken to the profit and loss account. However, accounting for the forward exchange contract as speculative, an equal loss on the contract can be recognised in the profit and loss account to offset this gain. The only movement in the profit and loss will be the premium on the contract which is spread over the period of the contract. (See method (b) of accounting for speculative contracts in **26.66** above.)

26.80 All of these alternatives are acceptable. The first alternative has the advantage of being the simplest, but the other methods recognise that the balance is being hedged over the period of the contract. The other advantage of the third method is that the translation policy for the asset or liability remains unchanged and the hedge is recognised by the accounting treatment of the exchange contract and is the preferred method.

Forward exchange contracts to hedge investments in foreign enterprises (consolidated accounts)

26.81 SSAP 20 refers to the use of foreign currency borrowings to hedge a foreign investment, but does not consider the use of forward exchange contracts for this purpose. It recognises setting rates using forward contracts for trading transactions only. It could be argued that this silence implies that the contract should not be recognised as a hedge and any premium and exchange difference on the contract would be taken to the profit and loss account.

26.82 This treatment fails to reflect the economic rationale for entering into the contract and thus a second method is recommended. Under this method, the exchange differences on the forward contract are taken to reserves to match with the movement in net investment. The premium on the contract can be taken to the profit and loss account or to reserves. The former treatment is quite logical, in view of the fact that the premium on the contract represents the interest rate differential between the currencies exchanged, i.e., an interest cost. The latter treatment is allowed by SFAS 52 for hedges of net investments. (This will no longer be the case when SFAS 133 becomes effective – see **26.76** above.)

Forward exchange contracts to hedge the future results of foreign investments

26.83 SSAP 20 recognises that companies can fix the translation rate for trading transactions in an individual company, but does not contemplate fixing the rate for foreign subsidiary trading transactions. If a forward exchange contract is taken out to cover the results of a foreign subsidiary, whether the contract extends for the whole year or part of the year, the most appropriate treatment is to translate the profit and loss account of the subsidiary using the closing rate and take any profit or loss on the forward exchange contract to the profit and loss account.

26.84 The result of this, where the contract is for the whole year, will be that the profit and loss account reflects the results of the subsidiary translated at the contracted rate. If the forward exchange contract is for a period less than a year, the profit and loss account will reflect the results covered by the contract at the contracted rate and will also reflect that those results have remained in the subsidiary from the date of maturity of the contract until the year end, i.e., the movement on the results from the contracted rate to the year end rate.

26.85 If the forward exchange contract has not been closed out at the year end, the profit or loss on the contract to date should be recognised in the profit and loss account and the related value of the contract included in the balance sheet.

Disclosure requirements

26.86 Where forward exchange contracts are material, the method adopted should be clearly explained in the accounting policies note. The particulars of significant speculative open forward contracts should be disclosed to comply with the requirements of the Act to disclose financial commitments which are relevant to assessing the company's state of affairs. [Sch 4: 50(5)] Further disclosures as described in chapter 21 are required under FRS 13.

Future developments

ASB discussion paper Derivatives and other financial instruments

Introduction

26.87 In July 1996, the ASB issued a discussion paper, Derivatives and other financial instruments, which contains initial proposals for two new accounting standards. The first, FRS 13, became effective for accounting periods ending on or after 23 March 1999 (see **21.36** et seq. above, which deal with the requirements of the FRS). As regards measurement and hedge accounting, the ASB has now joined a group of other national standard-setters and the IASC, with the aim of developing a common standard, an exposure draft of which is expected in mid-2000.

26.88 The discussion paper defines a financial instrument as a contract for the receipt or payment of cash or of another financial instrument. Unlike a physical asset, a common characteristic of a financial instrument is that its value is independent of either the skill of the owner or the use to which the instrument is put.

26.89 The definition includes non-derivatives (such as debtors, creditors, loans and shares) and derivatives (such as futures, forward foreign exchange contracts, interest rate and currency swaps, and options). It also includes commodity and other non-financial derivatives which are commonly settled in cash or by the purchase of another 'closing out' derivative. It excludes physical assets such as commodities and derivatives contracts that can be settled only by the delivery of a non-financial asset.

Measurement proposals

26.90 The ASB has considered the various options for measurement. The cost basis records only actual transactions and has the benefit of familiarity and reliability. However, its disadvantages are more numerous: many derivatives are omitted from the balance sheet; unrealised items are ignored; the active management of risk is ignored, and accounting does not reflect the actual impact of hedging. The ASB has concluded that cost is unsuitable for a significant proportion of financial instruments.

26.91 Hybrid methods which combine the cost basis for some items and current value for others all suffer from the drawback that they create a dividing line between the two treatments and thus scope for inconsistency in accounting for economically similar positions. For example, if current value was applied only to derivatives, then a company with fixed rate debt would not report any gains and losses when interest rates changed; however, a company in an identical position, but achieved through holding variable rate debt together with an interest rate swap derivative, would report gains and losses as the value of the derivative changed. The ASB has therefore reached the seemingly logical conclusion that no single aspect of financial instruments can be looked at in isolation and that current value should be used for all financial instruments. However, current value will not be applied to the entity's own equity shares (and options or warrants on them), investments in subsidiaries and associates, operating leases, pensions and other post-retirement benefits, and obligations under employee share schemes. It is proposed that insurance companies would be exempt from all the requirements.

26.92 The proposal to use current value for all financial instruments is eased in three respects: firstly, the ASB proposes to apply the measurement basis to only listed and similar public interest companies; secondly, the ASB intends to take several years before a final standard is implemented; thirdly, the ASB proposes to exclude certain gains and losses from the profit and loss account.

Recognition of gains and losses

26.93 FRS 3 sets out principles of reporting financial performance; in particular, that all gains and losses should be reported only once and in one of the recognised statements of performance. It goes on to describe the division of items between the profit and loss account and the statement of total recognised gains and losses. Following these principles, the ASB rejected the alternatives of reporting certain items either as deferred gains or losses in the balance sheet or as adjustments direct to shareholders' equity. However, it also rejected the position that all gains and losses should be reported in the profit and loss account. In particular, the ASB considered it would be desirable that the interest charge in the profit and loss account should continue to be based on FRS 4 and that gains and losses on fixed rate debt due to changes in market interest rates should be excluded from the profit and loss account. The proposed division of gains and losses arising on financial instruments is therefore:

(a)   the statement of total recognised gains and losses should be used to report both realised and unrealised gains and losses from:

   (i)   changes in the value of fixed rate borrowings (and non-equity shares), caused by changes in interest rates;

   (ii)   changes in the value of derivatives, such as interest rate swaps, that are used to convert borrowings from fixed to floating rate and vice versa; and

   (iii)   foreign currency borrowings and derivatives used to hedge a net investment in an overseas operation (this is consistent with practice under SSAP 20);

(b)   the profit and loss account would continue to report:

   (i)   interest expense in accordance with FRS 4, i.e., a yield to maturity based on historical cost;

   (ii)   gains and losses on all other financial instruments, including debtors and creditors, and other derivatives;

(c)   changes in value due to a change in creditworthiness would not be reported at all.

Hedging

26.94   If financial instruments are included in financial statements at current value, many current problems of achieving effective hedge accounting fall away. However, three issues remain:

(a)   hedging of existing items which are not themselves marked to current value (e.g., a forward contract to fix the selling price of an existing asset carried at cost);

(b)   hedging of unrecorded contracted items (e.g., a forward contract to fix foreign currency operating lease rentals); and

(c)   hedging of uncontracted items (e.g., a forward contract to fix expected future sales in a foreign currency).

Where such hedging contracts are included at current value, an effective hedge is only achieved by carrying forward the gain or loss arising as an asset or liability. However, such gains and losses do not meet the ASB's definitions of assets and liabilities. Three alternatives are discussed in the discussion paper:

•   permit no hedging at all;

•   allow (a) and (b); or

•   allow (a), (b) and (c), provided the entity is 'commercially committed' to a hedged future transaction.

The ASB does not state its preference.

Amendment to SSAP 20

26.95   During the development of FRS 13 *Derivatives and other financial instruments: disclosures*, the original proposal (as contained in the discussion paper, referred to in **26.87** above, and later in the draft standard) to disclose structural currency exposures was withdrawn for all entities which fall within the scope of the standard, except for banks and similar institutions. The reason for this was that it was felt that, as far as entities other than financial institutions were concerned, the proposed disclosure did not relate primarily to financial instruments and would be out of place in FRS 13. However, the ASB viewed such exposures as important and stated that an amendment to SSAP 20 would be considered. The draft amendment was published in February 1999 and suggested that companies should provide an analysis which would show the extent to which net investments in foreign entities are matched by foreign currency borrowings financing or hedging them. This analysis would highlight the entity's application of hedge accounting permitted under SSAP 20. The comments received by the ASB did not support this and the proposal was withdrawn. [ASB Press Notice 138]

27 Taxation

27   Taxation

Summary of changes since the previous issue of this publication

Para.	*Topic*	*Summary*
27.26 to 27.32	Self Assessment	The method for taxing UK companies changed from 1 July 1999. Companies are now taxed under the Corporation Tax Self Assessment scheme which means companies should include, on their returns, an assessment of tax which may be enquired into by the Inland Revenue. Additionally, for accounting periods ending on or after 1 July 1999, large companies pay corporation tax in quarterly instalments.
27.54 to 27.72	FRS 16 *Current tax*	Issued in December 1999 and effective for accounting periods ending on or after 23 March 2000. It replaces both SSAP 8 and UITF 16 and requires companies to stop grossing up dividends received for related tax credits and explicitly states the accounting treatment for withholding taxes.
27.118 to 27.136	Advanced corporation tax	ACT was abolished from 6 April 1999. A system of shadow ACT exists that determines relief for surplus ACT existing at 5 April 1999.
27.150 to 27.167	FRED 19 *Deferred tax*	Issued in August 1999, it proposes to move the UK to a full provision basis. No decision has been taken on this at the time of writing.

Introduction

Method of company taxation in the UK

27.1   Companies in the United Kingdom pay corporation tax, in accordance with tax legislation, which is based on their taxable profits. More details are given in **27.21** to **27.32**, but the main features of company taxation in the UK are:

(a)   corporation tax is levied on the company's taxable profit;

(b)   if a company is 'large', it pays corporation tax in quarterly instalments; usually two in the current accounting period and two in the following period (see **27.28** below); otherwise the company pays corporation tax nine months and one day following the ending of an accounting period;

(c)   pre 6 April 1999, advanced corporation tax (ACT) was payable when any dividend was paid. This was abolished on 6 April 1999 (see **27.119** below) and a system of shadow ACT introduced to determine how companies with surplus ACT arising from accounting periods pre 5 April 1999 may utilise it to reduce future corporation tax payments. No ACT is now payable when dividends are made; and

(d)   corporation tax returns should be submitted (see **27.27** below for more details).

27.2   In addition to corporation tax, companies in the UK can suffer tax charges or obtain tax credits under the following headings:

- foreign tax (see **27.33** to **27.36** below);
- double tax relief (see **27.33** to **27.36** below);
- irrecoverable ACT (see **27.130** to **27.132** below);
- adjustments in respect of prior years (see **27.39** below);
- income tax (see **27.37** below);
- withholding tax (see **27.6** and **27.56** to **27.57** below); and
- deferred tax (see **27.73** to **27.117** and from **27.150** to **27.167** below).

Presentation of taxation in financial statements

Profit and loss account and statement of total recognised gains and losses

27.3   Taxation balances can be shown in the profit and loss account (see **27.4** to **27.10** below) and/or the statement of total recognised gains and losses (see **27.11** to **27.12** below).

Profit and loss account

27.4 The Companies Act 1985 requires all profit and loss account formats to disclose the following items relating to taxation:

- tax on profit or loss on ordinary activities (see **27.5** below);

- tax on extraordinary profit or loss (see **27.9** below); and

- other taxes not shown under the above items.

The last heading is provided by the Act but no taxes are generally reported here.

27.5 'Tax on profit or loss on ordinary activities' includes, per the Companies Act:

- UK corporation tax before double tax relief;

- UK corporation tax after double tax relief ;

- income tax; and

- foreign tax.

Various accounting standards add to this list and require the following to be disclosed under 'Tax on profit or loss on ordinary activities':

- deferred taxation (SSAP 15);

- irrecoverable ACT (FRS 16);

- associated companies and joint ventures – tax attributable to group share of profits (FRS 9); and

- adjustments recognised in respect of prior periods, split into corporation tax and foreign tax (FRS 16).

Each of these amounts should be disclosed separately, if material, either on the face of the profit and loss account or in the notes to the accounts.

27.6 If withholding tax has been suffered on income received at source and, as per **27.56** below, if the income received has been grossed up to include the related withholding tax, then FRS 16(9) requires the effect of any withholding tax suffered to be taken into account as part of the tax charge. This will be dealt with within the corporation tax heading and does not need to be separately disclosed.

27.7 Particulars should be given of any special circumstances affecting taxation liabilities in the current year and in future years. [Sch 4: 54(2)] These should be disclosed by way of note to the profit and loss account and their individual effects quantified. Such disclosures should include any special circumstances affecting the tax attributable to the items specified in FRS 3(20). The effects of a fundamental change in the basis of taxation should be included in the tax charge or credit for the period and disclosed separately on the face of the profit and loss account. [FRS 3(23)] See **27.142** to **27.149** below for additional special circumstances.

27.8 FRS 3 also states that, as a minimum, the tax related to FRS 3(20) items should be disclosed in aggregate, but, if the effect of tax differs for the various categories of items, further information should be given. [FRS 3(20)] See **27.52** to **27.53** below.

27.9 Any tax which arises on extraordinary items should be included under the heading 'Tax on extraordinary profit or loss'. In principle, the notes to the accounts should disclose the division of this heading into the same statutory separate elements as in **27.5** above.

Sample tax note disclosures

27.10 There are various ways in which current tax disclosures can be made. Two examples of suitable disclosure of tax on profit on ordinary activities are as follows.

Example 27.10.1

Year end 30 June 2000

Note on tax on profit on ordinary activities

	£'000	£'000
UK corporation tax		
Current tax on income for the period at		
30% (1999 – 30%)	175	
Adjustments in respect of prior periods	(15)	
Irrecoverable ACT written off in the year	10	
	170	
Double taxation relief	(4)	
		166
Foreign tax		
Current tax on income for the period	68	
Adjustments in respect of prior periods	(6)	
		62
Tax on profit on ordinary activities		228

Example 27.10.2

Note on tax on profit on ordinary activities

	UK tax £'000	Foreign tax £'000	Total tax £'000
Current tax on income	175	68	
Adjustments in respect of prior periods	(15)	(6)	
Irrecoverable ACT written off in the year	10	–	
	170	62	
Double taxation relief	(4)	–	
Tax on profit on ordinary activities	166	62	228

Statement of total recognised gains and losses

27.11   FRS 16 requires the current tax balance in the statement of total recognised gains and losses (STRGL) separately to disclose:

- UK corporation tax before double tax relief;

- UK corporation tax after double tax relief;

- foreign tax; and

- adjustments recognised in respect of prior periods, split into corporation tax and foreign tax.

In addition to these disclosures, the taxation balance in the STRGL could include deferred taxation (as per SSAP 15 – see section **27.106** below).

27.12   Pre UITF 19, even though splitting the current tax charge for the year between the profit and loss account and STRGL was not prohibited by FRS 3, it was not seen much in practice. As detailed in **27.40** to **27.43** below, UITF 19 introduced the requirement to split the tax charge between profit and loss account and STRGL. FRS 16 has taken this one step further by explicitly stating that this principle applies, not just to hedged borrowings, but to tax on *any* gain or loss recognised in the STRGL. This will mainly be the effects of revaluation of fixed assets and foreign currency items dealt with in the STRGL. See **27.44** to **27.48** below for a discussion on allocation of tax between the profit and loss account and the STRGL.

Balance sheet

27.13   The headings in the balance sheet formats which include taxation are:

(a) Creditors: other creditors including taxation and social security (subdivided between amounts falling due within one year, and amounts falling due after more than one year); and

(b) Provisions for liabilities and charges: taxation, including deferred taxation.

27.14 It is considered that all amounts due in respect of taxation on the results of the financial year or any previous financial year should be included under creditors, payable either within one year or after more than one year as appropriate. There may be a number of reasons for the exact tax liability not being able to be computed with certainty, including uncertainty over the treatment of particular items or even the tax rate to be applied. This is not a justification for treating the estimated amount payable as a provision rather than as a creditor. This treatment is in line with FRS 12.

27.15 Provisions should normally be restricted to deferred taxation. Provisions for taxation other than deferred taxation only arise on those rare occasions where there is doubt about the existence of a tax liability in respect of particular circumstances or transactions, but it is considered advisable to provide for the possible liability.

27.16 Any amount receivable in respect of repayments of tax should be treated as 'Other debtors'. Any deferred tax carried forward as an asset should be split between current assets less than, and greater than, one year as appropriate.

27.17 The disclosure requirements of the Act are:

(a) the amount in respect of taxation and social security should be shown separately from the amount of other creditors [Sch 4: Note 9 on the balance sheet formats];

(b) the amount of any provisions for deferred taxation should be stated separately from the amount of any provision for other taxation [Sch 4: 47].

27.18 The requirement in **27.17**(a) above is usually interpreted as requiring one amount to be shown to include all liabilities in respect of taxation and social security, i.e., corporation tax, income tax, VAT, PAYE, NI contributions and any foreign equivalents. A further issue arises as to whether the disclosure requirements of FRS 12 extend to taxation. In view of the more specific disclosure requirements of the Act, FRS 16 and SSAP 15, it is not considered that tax falls within the disclosure requirements of FRS 12 (this is discussed in **17.284** to **17.288** above).

27.19   The Listing Rule requirement for companies to indicate whether, so far as the directors are aware, the company is a close company or close investment holding company for taxation purposes no longer exists. This was previously disclosed in the directors' report.

27.20   The treatment of deferred tax, including other disclosure requirements, is dealt with in **27.73** to **27.117** below.

Explanation of tax balances

Corporation tax

General

27.21   Corporation tax should be disclosed in the annual report in accordance with Companies Act 1985 Sch 4(52)(3) and FRS 16(17) (see **27.4** to **27.10** above). The corporation tax charge should be computed using the tax rates and laws that have been enacted or substantively enacted by the balance sheet date (FRS 16(14)). A UK tax rate can be regarded as having been substantively enacted if it is included in either:

(a)   a Bill that has been passed by the House of Commons and is awaiting only passage through the House of Lords and Royal Assent; or

(b)   a resolution having statutory effect that has been passed under the Provisional Collection of Taxes Act 1968. (Such a resolution could be used to collect taxes at a new rate before the rate has been enacted. In practice, corporation tax rates are now set a year ahead in order to avoid having to invoke the Provisional Collection of Taxes Act for the quarterly payment system.) (FRS 16(15))

In the United Kingdom, Bills proposing tax legislation are read three times (with a committee stage before the third reading) in the House of Commons before going through a similar procedure in the House of Lords. Although able to debate the Finance Bill, the House of Lords are not able to propose amendments to it, and so the Bill usually passes through all stages in a single day. Having passed through both the Commons and the Lords, it is transmitted to the Queen for Royal Assent. Following notification of Royal Assent to each House, the Bill becomes an Act. Therefore given this process, it is reasonable to consider that a Bill that has been approved in the House of Commons and is awaiting only passage through the House of Lords and Royal Assent is 'substantively enacted'.

27.22   FRS 16(14) requires the amounts to be calculated on the basis of the rates enacted at the balance sheet date (see **27.21** above). However, should information regarding the rates of taxation at the balance sheet date be received subsequent to the balance sheet date and which affect the year in question, then in accordance with SSAP17, should the effect of the revised tax rates materially change the taxation figures and disclosures in the accounts, the taxation figures should be adjusted in the financial statements.

27.23   Per FRS 16, corporation tax needs to be separated into:

(a)   UK (or Republic of Ireland) tax; and

(b)   Foreign tax.

Additionally, these amounts need to be broken down further into tax for the current period and any adjustments recognised in respect of prior periods.

27.24   The amount of UK (or Republic of Ireland) corporation tax should be disclosed before and after double taxation relief (see examples in **27.10** above).

27.25   There is no requirement in FRS 16 or Companies Act to disclose the rate of tax used. This requirement was in SSAP 8 (see **27.64** and **27.69** below) which has now been superseded. It appears that the requirement to disclose the tax rate used will come from the new deferred tax standard (currently under discussion – see **27.150** below). However, it appears that until that standard is published, there is no requirement to state the tax rate used. This appears to be a timing error and so it is recommended that the tax rate should be given in the tax note (if the comparative is different then this should also be given).

Corporation tax self assessment

27.26   Companies in the UK should now account for corporation tax under the Inland Revenue's Corporation tax self assessment (CTSA) system. The CTSA system applies to all companies within the charge to UK corporation tax and to branches and agencies of non-UK companies. CTSA applies to accounting periods ending on or after 1 July 1999.

27.27   Every entity falling within the CTSA regime should file a corporation tax return for an accounting period by the latest of:

i)   twelve months from the end of the accounting period for which the return is made;

ii)   if the company's relevant period of account is not longer than 18 months, twelve months from the end of that period;

iii) if the company's relevant period of account is longer than 18 months, 30 months from the beginning of that period; or

iv) three months from the date on which the Inland Revenue serve a notice requiring the delivery of a return.

Every return should include an assessment of tax payable which may be queried by the Inland Revenue within 12 months from the filing date. If returns are submitted late or subsequently amended, they may be queried by the quarter date following the first anniversary of filing (quarter dates are 31 January, 30 April, 31 July, 31 October). All claims on the return must be quantified (including quantification of group relief and capital allowance amounts).

27.28   Under CTSA, large companies (see **27.30** below) have to pay corporation tax in quarterly instalments. The due dates for payment of the instalments are six months 14 days, nine months 14 days, twelve months 14 days, and fifteen months 14 days after the start of an accounting period. For non-large companies, corporation tax continues to fall due within 9 months and 1 day of the end of the accounting period.

27.29   Transitional rules apply to the payment of tax in quarterly instalments as the CTSA system is being phased in gradually. In the first year of quarterly instalments, only 60% of the total liability for the year needs to be paid in instalments (the remainder falls due nine months and one day after the end of the accounting period). In the second year of CTSA, the total liability payable in quarterly instalments rises to 72%. The total tax liability payable in quarterly instalments then increases to 88% in the third year and 100% in the fourth and subsequent years.

27.30   In order to determine whether a company is a large company (see **27.28** above) for a specific accounting period it is necessary to estimate the taxable profits for the whole year. The figure is then compared to £1,500,000 divided by the number of group companies. If the taxable profits are greater than this figure, instalments will have to be paid unless either:

(a) in the previous year the taxable profits did not exceed £1,500,000 divided by the number of group companies and in the current year the taxable profits do not exceed £10 million divided by the number of companies in the group; or

(b) the tax liability for the year does not exceed £5,000.

27.31   A company should keep such records as may be needed to enable the company to deliver a complete and correct return. These records should be kept for 6 years from the end of the accounting period. The Inland Revenue has stated that the records needed to be kept to comply with Companies Act requirements will meet their tax requirements.

27.32   Sufficient transfer pricing documentation should be retained in order that a company may demonstrate that its connected party transactions have been undertaken at 'arm's length'.

Foreign taxation and double taxation relief

27.33   The amount of foreign taxation to be disclosed separately is the amount, or estimated amount, of taxation payable by the company or the group in foreign countries in respect of the profits of the financial year. It should include any withholding taxes on incoming foreign dividends, interest or other income receivable but exclude any other taxes, such as attributable tax credits, which are not payable wholly as part of the distribution. In addition to the current period's charge, any adjustments to the foreign tax accounted for in prior periods should be shown separately (Companies Act 1985 Sch 4(52)(3) and FRS 16(17)).

27.34   Double taxation relief is the relief allowed against UK corporation tax on account of foreign taxes suffered.

27.35   Tax which has been deducted at source by an overseas company on payment of a dividend will, under FRS 16, be treated as withholding tax and should be accounted for in the profit and loss account. The amount of the withholding tax suffered on foreign dividends needs to be included in the foreign tax charge (FRS 16(9)) with any relief given for UK corporation tax purposes shown as double taxation relief.

27.36   The following examples explain the tax treatment of foreign dividends received by UK companies. The treatment depends on the amount of control the UK investing company has over the foreign company.

> ### *Example 27.36.1*
>
> A company receives £93 from an investment in an overseas company where the UK company controls less than 10% of the voting rights of the overseas company. The overseas company had tax deducted as follows:
>
> | | £ |
> |---|---|
> | Overseas company profits | 12,000 |
> | Taxation on profits (known as underlying tax) | (2,000) |
> | Profit after tax (to be wholly distributed) | 10,000 |
> | | |
> | Amount received by UK company (assuming a withholding tax rate of 7% and that the UK company owns 1% of the overseas company) | 93 |
>
> The company has received £93. FRS 16 requires withholding tax to be included in the profit and loss account, but excludes any other taxes

not payable wholly on the behalf of the recipient. As the UK company's £20 (1% x £2,000) share of underlying tax is the overseas company's liability to tax (which is not payable wholly on the behalf of the recipient), then this is excluded from the company's income figure.

Assuming that the UK company had no other transactions and is liable to 30% tax, the following disclosure is needed in the UK company accounts:

	£
Income from fixed asset investments (£93/0.93)	100

Tax note

UK corporation taxation	
Current tax on income for the period (£100 x 30%)	30
Double taxation relief	(7)
	23
Foreign taxation	
Current tax on income for the period	7
	30

Double entries are as follows:	£
Dr Cash	93
Cr Income	100
Dr Corporation tax charge	30
Cr Corporation tax liability	23
Dr Foreign tax	7
Cr Double tax relief	7

For the purposes of calculating UK tax payable, the net amount of the dividend received plus the withholding tax will be chargeable to UK corporation tax, but not the underlying tax as the UK company controls less than 10% of the voting rights of the overseas company. Double tax relief would then be given as the lower of foreign tax suffered (i.e. £7) and UK tax payable on the foreign income (i.e. £30).

Example 27.36.2

A company receives £930 from an overseas company where the UK company controls at least 10% of voting rights of the overseas company, but does not have overall control. The overseas company had tax deducted as follows:

	£
Overseas company profits	12,000
Taxation (known as underlying tax)	(2,000)
Profit after tax (to be wholly distributed)	10,000
Amount received by UK company (assuming a withholding tax rate of 7% and that the UK company owns 10% of the overseas company)	930

The company has received £930. FRS 16 requires withholding tax to be included in the profit and loss account, but excludes any other taxes not payable wholly on the behalf of the recipient. As the £200 (10% x £2,000) share of underlying tax is the overseas company's liability to tax (which is not payable wholly on the behalf of the recipient), then this is excluded from the UK company's income figure in the accounts.

Assuming the UK company had no other transactions and is liable to corporation tax at the 30% rate, the following disclosure is needed in the UK company accounts:

	£
Income from fixed asset investments (£930/0.93)	1,000

Tax note

UK corporation taxation	
Current tax on income for the period	
[(£1,000 + £200) x 30%]	360
Double taxation relief [£200 + £70]	(270)
	90
Foreign tax	
Current tax on income for the period	70
	160

Double entries are as follows:	£
Dr Cash	930
Cr Income	1,000
Dr Corporation tax charge	360
Cr Corporation tax liability	90
Dr Foreign tax	70
Cr Double tax relief	270

The UK company will be subject to UK taxation on the net amount of the dividend received plus the withholding tax plus the underlying tax as, in this example, the company controls at least 10% of the overseas company's votes (cf. **27.36.1** above). Double tax relief would then be given as the lower of foreign tax suffered (i.e. £270) and UK tax payable at the UK company's effective rate of UK corporation tax on the gross foreign income (i.e. £360). As in this case the UK company controls at least 10% of the overseas company's votes, when calculating double tax relief and the company's gross foreign income, the underlying tax as well as the withholding tax should be taken into account.

In this situation, the underlying tax relief means that the company will pay less tax than would have been the case if the underlying tax relief was not available (i.e., if no underlying tax relief was available, total tax charge is £1,000 × 30% = £300. With underlying tax relief, total tax charge is £160 – see above for calculation).

Example 27.36.3

A company receives £9,300 from an overseas company which is a 100 per cent owned subsidiary and which had tax deducted as follows:

	£
Overseas subsidiary's profits	12,000
Taxation (underlying tax)	(2,000)
Profit after tax	10,000
Amount received by UK company (assuming a withholding tax rate of 7%)	9,300

The company has received £9,300. How to consolidate the profits of the subsidiary is discussed in chapters 23 and 24 above. FRS 16 requires withholding tax to be included in the profit and loss account, but excludes any other taxes not payable wholly on the behalf of the recipient. As the £2,000 underlying tax is the overseas company's liability to tax (which is not payable wholly on the behalf of the recipient), then this is excluded from the UK company's income figure in the accounts.

Assuming the UK company had no other transactions and is liable to corporation tax at the 30% rate, from a tax perspective the following disclosure is needed in the UK company accounts:

	£
Income from fixed asset investments (£9,300/0.93)	10,000

Tax note to be disclosed in the consolidated accounts

	£
UK corporation taxation	
Current tax on income for the period	
[(£10,000 + £2,000) x 30%]	3,600
Double taxation relief [£2,000 + £700]	(2,700)
	900
Foreign tax	
Tax on income for the period	2,700
	3,600

Double entries are as follows:	£
Dr Cash	9,300
Cr Income	10,000
Dr Corporation tax charge	3,600
Cr Corporation tax liability	900
Cr Foreign tax liability – subsidiary	2,000
Dr Foreign tax – parent	700
Dr Foreign tax – subsidiary	2,000
Cr Double tax relief	2,700

As in Example **27.36.2** above, the UK company controls at least 10% of the overseas company's votes. Therefore, the UK company will be subject to UK taxation on the gross amount of the dividend received (the dividend plus withholding tax plus underlying tax). Double taxation relief is given as the lower of foreign tax suffered (i.e. £2,700) and UK tax payable at the UK company's effective rate of UK corporation tax on the gross income (i.e. £3,600 in this case).

In this example the accounts are consolidated and, therefore, the foreign tax line in the tax note (£2,700) relates to both the parent's withholding tax (£700) and also the actual tax (known as the underlying tax) suffered by the subsidiary (£2,000).

Income tax

27.37 The Act requires the amount of the charge for UK income tax to be disclosed. [Sch 4: 54(3)] However, as the apportionment rules have been abolished under the Finance Act 1989, most companies will never incur a material liability to income tax.

Associated undertakings and joint ventures

27.38 FRS 9(27) requires the amount of tax relating to associated undertakings and joint ventures which has been included in the total for the group's tax to be separately identified (see chapter 25 for further disclosures relating to associates and joint ventures).

Adjustments recognised in respect of prior periods

27.39 Adjustments recognised in respect of prior period liabilities are not normally material. If they are material, the amounts should be disclosed separately in the notes to the accounts. If immaterial, the amounts may be combined with the current year's tax charge. These adjustments arise mainly from the correction of estimates inherent in the accounting process and therefore should not be treated as prior year adjustments in accordance with FRS 3 (see **9.250** above).

Tax effects of exchange differences on foreign currency borrowings

27.40 Where certain conditions are met, SSAP 20 *Foreign currency translation* permits certain gains and losses on foreign currency borrowings, that have been used to finance or provide a hedge against equity investments in foreign enterprises, to be reported in the statement of total recognised gains and losses (see **26.37** to **26.59** above, which set out the rules in detail).

27.41 Where this is done, tax charges or credits that are directly and solely attributable to the exchange differences should also be taken to reserves and reported in the statement of total recognised gains and losses. Although required by UITF 19, this aspect of UITF 19 has been reinforced by FRS 16.

27.42 UITF Abstract 19 also considers the restrictions of SSAP 20 on the gains and losses that are dealt with in the statement of total recognised gains and losses (see **26.38** and **26.40** above). It concludes that the restriction that the gains and losses should not exceed the exchange differences on the equity investments (in individual accounts) or net investments in foreign enterprises (in consolidated accounts) should be applied after taking account of any tax charge or credit relating to the gain or loss on the borrowings. Similarly, it concludes that the comparison with the total amount of cash that the investments are expected to generate and the exposure created by the borrowings should be considered in after-tax terms (see **26.42** above).

27.43 The amount of tax charges and credits accounted for in the STRGL in accordance with UITF Abstract 19 should be disclosed in addition to the gross amount of the exchange differences.

Allocations of tax

Allocations between the profit and loss account and STRGL

27.44 FRS 16 requires current tax to be recognised in the profit and loss account for the period except to the extent that it is attributable to a gain or loss that is or has been recognised directly in the STRGL. The ASB, in FRS 16, explains that where, exceptionally, it is difficult to determine the amount of current tax attributable to gains/losses recognised in the STRGL, a reasonable pro rata allocation, or another more appropriate allocation, should be used. [FRS 16(7)]

27.45 Consider the situation if a company bought a property for £100,000 in 1993. It then revalued the property on 31 December 1997 to £500,000 and sold the property during 1999 for £400,000. A revaluation surplus of £400,000 would have been recorded in the STRGL for 1997 and a loss on disposal of £100,000 recognised in the 1999 profit and loss account. Assuming a tax charge of £90,000 arises in 1999 and that no deferred tax had been provided on the revaluation surplus, the question arises as to how much tax should be recorded in the profit and loss account and how much in the STRGL.

27.46 It could be argued that the £90,000 should go to the 1999 STRGL and nothing to the 1999 profit and loss account – on the grounds that the £90,000 arose on a gain of £300,000 and this gain was all recognised in the STRGL in 1997. Alternatively, tax of £120,000 could be charged in the 1999 STRGL and tax of £30,000 credited in the 1999 profit and loss account.

27.47 | The guidance in FRS 16(7) (pro rata or another more appropriate basis) does not give a categorical answer, although it does appear to favour the second of the above alternatives (£120,000 charge in STRGL and £30,000 credit in profit and loss account). The second alternative is also consistent with the treatment that results if deferred tax is provided when the asset is revalued. If deferred tax is provided, a charge of £120,000 would be made in the STRGL in 1997 (30% of the revaluation surplus of £400,000). At the end of 1999 £90,000 of the £120,000 would be transferred out of deferred tax to current tax liability and the remaining £30,000 would be credited in the profit and loss account.

27.48 | FRED 19 on deferred tax (see **27.150** below), proposes that deferred tax is similarly recognised in the same performance statement (profit and loss account or STRGL) as the underlying item on which the deferred tax is recognised. Although FRED 19 has not yet been finalised as an FRS, it is suggested that (since this is not prohibited by FRS 3 or SSAP 15) this aspect of the FRED is applied by any entity adopting FRS 16.

Allocation of tax to 'non-operating' exceptional items and extraordinary items

27.49 The Act requires that the tax charge for the year is divided between tax on profit or loss on ordinary activities and tax on extraordinary profit or loss. In practice, the total tax charge will be based on the results of ordinary activities and extraordinary items combined.

27.50 FRS 3 states that, as a minimum, the tax related to FRS 3(20) items should be disclosed in aggregate, but, if the effect of tax for each of the various categories differs, further information should be given. [FRS 3(20)]

27.51 FRS 3 sets out the method for allocating the charge between the three elements (i.e., extraordinary items, FRS 3(20) items and other items). Under this method, the tax on the results of ordinary activities is computed as if the extraordinary items and FRS 3(20) items did not exist. This amount should be compared with the actual tax charge on the profit or loss for the financial year and the difference ascribed to extraordinary items and FRS 3(20) items. The tax on any extraordinary items and FRS 3(20) items should be apportioned between the items in relation to their respective amounts, unless a more appropriate basis of apportionment is available. If a more appropriate basis is adopted, the method of apportionment should be disclosed. [FRS 3(26)]

27.52 The following example illustrates the application of the method.

Example 27.52

	£
Operating profit	1,900,000
Costs of factory closure	(400,000)
Profit on sale of building	500,000
Profit on ordinary activities before taxation	2,000,000
Tax on profit on ordinary activities	(609,000)
Extraordinary items	–
Profit on ordinary activities	1,391,000

The tax charge is made up as follows:

The corporation tax charge for the period may be calculated as follows:

	£
Profit on ordinary activities before taxation	2,000,000
Disallowable ordinary expenses	150,000
Capital allowances in excess of depreciation (no deferred tax required)	(200,000)
Disallowable factory closure costs	80,000
Adjusted profit for tax purposes	2,030,000
Tax charge @ 30%	609,000

This calculation assumes that the taxable chargeable gain on the building was also £500,000.

If there had been no non-operating exceptional items, the tax charge would have been £2,030,000 + (£400,000 – £80,000) – £500,000, or £1,850,000, at 30 per cent, i.e., £555,000.

Therefore, it can be seen that the tax charge to be allocated to non-operating exceptional items is £609,000 – £555,000 = £54,000.

In this particular case, because the information is available and its use gives materially different results, it is appropriate to allocate the tax charge more specifically, that is:

	£	£
Tax credit on factory closure costs:		
Costs	400,000	
Disallowable element	(80,000)	
	320,000	
Tax @ 30%		96,000
Tax charge on sale of building:		
Profit on sale	500,000	
Tax @ 30%		(150,000)
		(54,000)

27.53 The circumstances set out in Example **27.52** above could be disclosed in the financial statements, as illustrated below.

Example 27.53

Note 4 – Tax on profit on ordinary activities

	2000
	£
Corporation tax based on the profit for the year at 30%	609,000

Included within the corporation tax charge for the year is a net tax charge of £54,000 in respect of exceptional items shown in the profit and loss account after operating profit (see note (x)). An allocation of this charge to the individual items is set out below:

	2000
	£
Tax credit on factory closure costs	96,000
Tax charge on sale of building	(150,000)
	(54,000)

Current tax

FRS 16

General

27.54 FRS 16 *Current tax*, issued in December 1999, is effective for accounting periods ending on or after 23 March 2000 and replaces SSAP 8 and UITF 16. Early adoption is encouraged. It applies to all true and fair accounts but gives an exemption to companies currently applying the FRSSE. Prompted by the restrictions introduced in respect of the reclaimability of UK tax credits, the ASB considered a limited amendment to SSAP 8. However, before the ASB had finalised the changes, it was announced that ACT was to be abolished. Given that a major part of SSAP 8 deals with ACT, the ASB decided to review SSAP 8 in its entirety. The limited amendment was never made, and, instead, the ASB developed and issued FRED 18 for comment. FRS 16 incorporates the proposals from FRED 18 with little change.

27.55 The main areas covered by FRS 16 are as follows:

(a) Taxation should be shown in the same performance statement as the related income/expense (see **27.44** above);

(b) Dividends, interest and other amounts payable or receivable should be recognised at an amount that:
   (i) includes withholding taxes payable to the tax authorities wholly on behalf of the recipient;

(ii) excludes any other taxes, such as attributable tax credits not payable wholly on behalf of the recipient (see **27.56** to **27.57** below);

(c) Income and expenses should be included in the pre-tax results on the basis of the income or expenses actually receivable or payable (as stated previously in UITF 16) – they should not be adjusted for notional tax (see **27.59** to **27.63** below);

(d) Current tax should be measured using tax rates and laws that have been enacted or substantively enacted by the balance sheet date (see **27.21** above);

(e) Specific disclosures should be made in the annual report (see **27.4** to **27.20** above).

Grossing up of income (including dividends)

27.56 SSAP 8 (see **27.64** to **27.69** below) required dividends received to be grossed up for the related tax credit. It made no mention of withholding taxes. The recent changes in tax legislation prompted the ASB to review the principles in SSAP 8. It debated various options but concluded that dividends (and other amounts payable or receivable) should be shown including withholding taxes but excluding tax credits and other applicable taxes (including underlying taxes). This is the general rule that has been stated in FRS 16(9). The ASB took the view that to show only the net amount of the income received / payment made which was subject to withholding tax failed to reflect the full amount taxable or allowable in the hands of the recipient or payer respectively. The withholding tax amount is included within the corporation tax charge for the year (see Example **27.56** below).

Example 27.56

A UK company with a March 2000 year end, receives the following:

1. £90,000 dividend which has been paid from a UK subsidiary. This has a tax credit of £10,000 attached (10% of the gross dividend); and
2. £385,000 royalty payment that has had income tax at 23% deducted.

Disclosures will be as follows:

Profit and loss extract in the individual company's profit and loss account:

	£
Other operating income (being £385,000/0.77)	500,000
Income from shares in group undertakings	90,000

Tax note:

Corporation tax	150,000

The double entries are as follows: £

Dr Cash	£475,000
Cr Other operating income	£385,000
Cr Income from shares in group undertakings	£90,000
Dr Corporation tax charge	£150,000
Cr Other operating income	£115,000
Cr Corporation tax liability	£35,000

Notes:

Although the dividend has a £10,000 tax credit attached, this should not be included in the receiving company's accounts following adoption of FRS 16.

Dividends from UK group companies are not taxable in the UK recipient company. Therefore, the tax charge is calculated as £500,000 x 30% = £150,000.

The royalty payment has had £115,000 tax paid by the payer to the Inland Revenue on the company's behalf (i.e., withholding tax). The full amount of £500,000 is taxable to the company at the applicable corporate tax rate. As the company does not suffer income tax, it is effectively owed a refund for the £115,000 income tax deducted at source. The Inland Revenue allows companies to net off the corporation tax charge with the income tax refund. In this example, the company owes a further £35,000 tax and this is reflected as a liability at the year end.

In summary, the deducted withholding tax is included in both the income line and the corporation tax charge in the profit and loss account. No separate disclosure of the withholding tax suffered is required by FRS 16.

27.57 A summary of the current position under FRS 16 is shown below:

Summary of grossing up

Taxes	Treatment in P&L account
Tax credit	Exclude from profit and loss account
Other taxes	Exclude from profit and loss account
Withholding tax	Include in profit and loss account as part of item to which it relates

Non-taxpaying entities

27.58 One temporary exemption to the general rule stated in **27.56** above comes from the transitional relief available to certain non-taxpaying entities following the removal of their right to reclaim tax credits. The Inland Revenue has allowed certain non-taxpaying entities (charities, heritage bodies and scientific organisations) to reclaim tax credits, on a reducing scale, up until 5 April 2004. This is known as transitional relief. FRS 16 recognises this relief and allows such entities to gross up the income for the transitional relief (see Example **27.58** and **27.70** below). Where they do so, they must state the nature and amount of the relief.

The transitional relief operates on a sliding scale and is based on the net amount of dividends received. The entities can claim back the following percentage of dividends received:

Tax year	% of net dividend
1999/00	21%
2000/01	17%
2001/02	13%
2002/03	8%
2003/04	4%

Example 27.58

A charity, with a March year end, receives £100 dividends annually. Prior to the change in tax legislation, it would have been able to reclaim the attached tax credit which, pre 6 April 1999, was 20% of the gross dividend (25% of the net dividend).

This would be accounted for as follows:

Dr Cash 100
Dr Debtors 25
Cr Income 125

Given the change in tax legislation and the transitional relief available (see **27.58** above) for accounting periods in 1999/00 tax year, the accounting treatment now should be either:

(a)
Dr Cash 100
Dr Debtors 21 (given that the transitional relief is 21% of net dividend received)
Cr Income 121
(this is the allowed alternative per FRS 16)

OR

(b)

Dr Cash 100

Dr Debtors 21 (given that the transitional relief is 21% of net dividend received)

Cr Income 100

Cr Tax refund 21

Non-standard rates of tax (notional tax grossing-up)

27.59   FRS 16(11) states that, with the exception of taxes discussed in **27.56** above, income and expenses should be included in the pre-tax results on the basis of the income or expenses actually receivable or payable. No adjustment should be made to reflect a notional amount of tax that would have been paid or relieved in respect of the transaction if it had been taxable, or allowable for tax purposes, on a different basis. This embraces the principle in UITF 16 which is superseded by FRS 16.

27.60   Some transactions depend for their overall profitability on some or all of the income or expenditure being either non-taxable or taxable at a lower (or higher) rate than the standard rate. Examples include some leasing transactions, advances and investments made by financial institutions. In some cases, the transaction may, after taking account of the cost of financing, result in a pre-tax loss and an after-tax profit.

27.61   A special accounting treatment has sometimes been adopted for these transactions. This treatment entails increasing the pre-tax profit and the tax charge by the same amount, so that a standard rate of tax is reported. Such an adjustment is sometimes referred to as a 'grossing up' adjustment.

27.62   UITF Abstract 16, and now FRS 16, prohibits this practice of grossing up items of profit before tax and tax charges, which are subject to non-standard rates of tax, on the grounds that such treatment fails to reflect the true nature of the transactions that have occurred in the period.

27.63   SSAP 21 was amended by the ASB in February 1997, such that tax-free grants which are available to a lessor against the purchase price of assets acquired for leasing may no longer be grossed up when the value of the grant is credited to the profit and loss account over the period of the lease (see chapter 29). The only option is therefore to treat the grant as non-taxable income.

SSAP 8

General

27.64 For accounting periods ending before 23 March 2000, and where FRS 16 has not been adopted early, the rules included in SSAP 8 apply.

27.65 SSAP 8 states that dividends received from UK companies should be grossed up for the associated tax credit, the debit side of the entry being made to the tax charge and disclosed in the tax note separately as 'tax attributable to franked investment income'.

Tax credit

27.66 The related tax credit is calculated based on the lower income tax rate. Pre 6 April 1999, this rate was 20% and therefore the associated tax credit is calculated as 20/80 multiplied by the net dividend received. From 6 April 1999, this rate was reduced to 10% and therefore the associated tax credit is calculated as 10/90 multiplied by the net dividend received.

Example 27.66

A company receives dividends as follows:

```
  |-----------|-----------------------------------|
1/1/99      6/4/99                            31/12/99
  |_____|_____|
     £80 received              £90 received
   (tax credit = £20)        (tax credit = £10)
```

The accounting treatment of the dividends depends whether FRS 16 has been adopted.

(a) FRS 16 has not been adopted early:

	£
Income received from investments $[(80 + 20) + (90 + 10)]$	200

Tax note:
– Tax credit on FII $(20 + 10)$	30

(b) FRS 16 has been adopted early:

	£
Income received from investments $(80 + 90)$	170

Two points to note:

(1) Pre 6 April 1999, the tax credit is 20% whilst post 6 April 1999, the tax credit is 10%.

(2) If FRS 16 is adopted early, the dividends are shown in the profit and loss account net of any tax credit (subject to the transitional rules for certain non-taxpaying entities as described in **27.58** above).

Withholding tax

27.67   SSAP 8 does not cover the accounting treatment of withholding tax. Best practice would be to follow FRS 16 as this is the only available guidance. If companies have been accounting for withholding tax in a different way to FRS 16 requirements, then it is possible, on the grounds of consistency, to continue with that other accounting treatment until FRS 16 is adopted. At that stage, it will be necessary to adjust the comparative figures in order to reflect the new accounting treatment.

ACT

27.68   Some companies with year ends before 23 March 2000 may have made payments of ACT in the period up to 5 April 1999 when the system of ACT was abolished. If this is the case, then these payments can be used to reduce the amount of corporation tax payable subject to the maximum set-off permitted by the Inland Revenue. See **27.118** to **27.136** below for full details of the rules regarding ACT and shadow ACT which have been introduced with effect from 6 April 1999.

Additional disclosure

27.69   In addition to the disclosures set out above, SSAP 8 requires the rate of corporation tax used to be disclosed (see **27.25** above).

Transitional arrangements in FRS 16

27.70   Appendix V of FRS 16 states that the application of the standard for the first time will be treated as a change in accounting policy, effective from the start of the accounting period in which the standard was first implemented. Following Companies Act requirements to give comparatives, this means that comparative figures also need to be adjusted and calculated on the same basis as the current figures.

Example 27.70

A company with a year end of 31/8/99 received dividends of £90,000 in May 1999 and included them in the profit and loss account for that year at £100,000, being the net amount received and the tax credit of £10,000 (based on 10% of the gross amount, i.e., 10/90 of the net amount).

In the next accounting period, the company receives dividends of £120,000. As FRS 16 is effective, the profit and loss account reflects the following amounts:

	2000	1999
	£	£
Income from trade investments	120,000	90,000*

*Restated

The 1999 comparative will not reflect the tax credit as it did in 1999. The change in policy should be disclosed in accordance with Companies Act 1985 Sch 4(11) and UITF 14 (see **27.72** below).

27.71   Charities and other entities which, at present, receive a tapering transitional relief following the changes in the tax system that removed their right to reclaim tax credits are allowed, as a concession, to continue to show that particular transitional relief as part of the income to which it relates, rather than as a tax refund (see also **27.58** above). Where a non-tax paying entity is entitled to transitional relief and the entity grosses up its income for this transitional relief, this does not represent a change in accounting policy and thus there is no requirement to restate comparatives. See **27.58** above for disclosure requirements.

Disclosure of change in accounting policy

27.72   Example wording explaining the change in policy on adopting FRS 16 for the first time (as per **27.70** above) could be as follows:

'The company has adopted FRS 16 and has followed the transitional provisions detailed in Appendix V. The main change* results from the exclusion of tax credits, which arise on UK dividends receivable, from both investment income and the tax charge in the profit and loss account. In prior years this tax credit has been included. Following the adoption of FRS 16 the results of prior periods have been restated. There is no effect on either last year's or this year's profit after tax from this change in policy.'

*Amend as appropriate. If the company had been accounting for withholding tax in a way which differs to the required treatment of FRS 16, then this also should be disclosed and the effect on profit for last year and the current year quantified.

Deferred tax

Introduction

27.73   The formats require the provision for deferred taxation to be included in the subheading 'Taxation, including deferred taxation' under the main heading 'Provisions for liabilities and charges'.

27.74 The principles of, and methods of accounting for, deferred taxation are set out in SSAP 15. The requirements of this standard, together with guidance on financial statement presentation, are discussed below.

Definition and principles

27.75 Deferred tax is defined as the tax attributable to timing differences. Timing differences are differences between profits or losses as computed for tax purposes and results as stated in financial statements which arise from the inclusion of items of income and expenditure in tax computations in periods different from those in which they are included in financial statements. Timing differences originate in one period and are capable of reversal in one or more subsequent periods.

27.76 SSAP 15 states that tax deferred or accelerated by the effect of timing differences should be accounted for to the extent that it is probable that an asset or liability will crystallise and should not be accounted for to the extent that it is probable that an asset or liability will not crystallise. An exception to this applies to timing differences in respect of pensions and other post-retirement benefits (see **27.107** and **27.108** below).

27.77 An asset or liability crystallises when the reversal of a timing difference is not replaced by a new timing difference of at least the same tax effect, with the result that there is a decrease or increase in the amount of the taxation liability.

Method of calculation

27.78 SSAP 15 specifies that deferred tax should be computed under the liability method, i.e., the tax is calculated using the corporation tax rate which is expected to apply when the timing differences reverse and a deferred tax asset or liability crystallises. Thus, the amount of the provision for deferred tax should be changed if there is a change in the rate of corporation tax expected to apply.

27.79 The deferral method, whereby the deferred tax is computed using the rate ruling when the provision is set up, and subsequent reversals are made at the same rate, is not acceptable.

Timing differences

27.80 Timing differences arise from five main sources, discussed in **27.81** to **27.86** below.

Use of accruals basis of accounting

27.81 These arise from the use of the accruals basis of accounting in the financial statements and the receipts and payments basis for tax purposes. Normally, these differences reverse in the next accounting period. Examples include non-specific bad debt provisions, provision for future losses on contract work in progress, provision for plant closure or reorganisation costs, and inter-company profits in stocks eliminated on consolidation. Other differences, such as the treatment of a pension surplus as a prepayment, reverse over a longer period. Since 1 April 1996 interest receivable has generally been taxed on an accruals basis and therefore, in most instances, no longer gives rise to a timing difference. See **27.90** below.

Capital allowances

27.82 Timing differences arise when capital allowances exceed the corresponding depreciation charge in the financial statements or, alternatively, where the depreciation charge in the financial statements exceeds the corresponding capital allowances. See **27.91** below.

Revaluation of fixed assets

27.83 To the extent that the valuation exceeds net book value, there is a potential timing difference in that a balancing charge or tax on a chargeable gain may be payable if the asset is sold at its revalued amount. However, no deferred tax should be provided at the time of the valuation if the asset is not expected to be disposed of. Provision should be made out of the revaluation surplus as soon as a liability is foreseen, which, in the absence of rollover relief, will be at the time the company decides in principle to dispose of the asset. Depreciation on the revalued amount in excess of depreciation based on original cost will not have an effect on deferred tax, because this is a permanent difference. See **27.104** to **27.106** below.

Disposal of fixed assets

27.84 Where a fixed asset has been disposed of and the proceeds invested in a replacement asset, tax on the gain may be deferred by the application of rollover relief. Rollover relief can take one of two forms. Where the replacement asset is within one of the prescribed classes, the gain is rolled into the acquisition cost (which is thereby reduced for tax purposes). This relief is called 'rollover relief'. On the other hand, where the replacement asset is a depreciating asset, then the gain is held over for a period of up to 10 years. This relief is called 'holdover relief'. A depreciating asset is defined as an asset which is, or will within 10 years of acquisition become, a wasting asset, i.e., one with a predictable life not exceeding 50 years.

27.85 With holdover relief, the gain will crystallise, unless a further non-depreciating qualifying asset is acquired, on the earliest of:

(a) the date of disposal of the replacement asset; or

(b) the date it ceases to be used for the purposes of the trade; or

(c) ten years after the acquisition of the replacement asset.

With either type of relief, unless the sale of the replacement asset without further rollover relief is likely, crystallisation of the liability cannot be foreseen and it should not be provided.

Losses

27.86 A loss for tax purposes, which is available to relieve future profits from tax, may constitute a timing difference. See **27.92** below.

Assessing the effect of timing differences

27.87 In order to assess the extent to which assets or liabilities arising from timing differences will crystallise, it is necessary to make reasonable assumptions as to future events; in particular, as to the new timing differences which are likely to arise to replace the reversal of existing differences. These assumptions should be based on all relevant information available, including the intentions of management, and ideally will include financial plans and projections covering a future period of years. The appendix to SSAP 15 suggests that a period of three to five years may be sufficient where the pattern of timing differences is expected to be regular, but may need to be longer in other cases. There is little guidance provided for those cases, probably the majority in number, where financial plans and projections for such a period are not available. However, it is stated that a prudent view should be taken, particularly where financial plans or projections are susceptible to a high degree of uncertainty or are not fully developed.

27.88 The combined effect of all timing differences should be considered when attempting to assess whether a tax liability will crystallise, rather than looking at each timing difference separately. This suggests that a potential liability arising from a short-term timing difference, such as the deferral of development costs, should not be provided if, in the period of reversal, substantial capital expenditure can be foreseen which will result in capital allowances in excess of depreciation being such that no net liability will arise. Similarly, the effect of present and forecast future tax losses should be taken into account; clearly, there can be no crystallisation of a deferred tax liability in a future year if there will be no actual liability in that year.

27.89 At least annually or when capital expenditure plans are significantly altered, management should reassess the likelihood of tax liabilities crystallising on the basis of latest information. Often, an acquisition of another company by the group may result in the new group imposing new budgets on capital spend, which will increase or reduce the deferred tax liabilities established prior to the takeover. While the effect of this will result in a change in the deferred taxation balance and give rise to a tax charge or credit to the profit and loss account of the acquired company, the treatment in the consolidated accounts may be different. When assigning fair values to the net assets of the acquired subsidiary accounted for as an acquisition, the deferred tax liability should be assessed on the basis of any revised capital expenditure plans for the acquired company; any change in the deferred tax balance of the acquired subsidiary will impact on the amount of goodwill arising on consolidation and not on the consolidated profit or loss of the group (see also **27.99** and **27.100** below).

Use of accruals basis of accounting

27.90 Generally, assessment of the effect of differences arising from the accruals basis of accounting should be relatively simple. Often, when these timing differences reverse, they are replaced by equivalent new timing differences, so that it is probable that a tax liability or asset will not crystallise. The same considerations apply to annual adjustments such as the elimination of intra-group profits on stocks, assuming that the level of such adjustments will not differ significantly between one year and another. Other differences are likely to be of the 'one-off' variety, which arise in one period and reverse in one or more subsequent periods and for which replacement cannot be foreseen. An exception to the normal rules applies to timing differences in respect of pensions and other post-retirement benefits; such timing differences are dealt with in more detail in **27.107** and **27.108** below.

Capital allowances

27.91 Assessment of the effect of capital allowances requires the making of assumptions as to future levels of capital expenditure and it is in this area that financial plans and projections for some years ahead are most significant. Where adequate plans and projections have been prepared, a comparison between projected depreciation charges and capital allowances will reveal the extent, if any, to which timing differences can be expected to reverse and result in the crystallisation of a liability or asset. Where such plans and projections are not prepared, an assumption should be made on the basis of the best information available, which will normally be restricted to the history of past expenditure and known needs. It is stressed that any assumption based on such limited evidence should be made with prudence, i.e., doubts as to the crystallisation of a deferred tax item should be resolved on the basis that liabilities will crystallise and assets will not.

Losses

27.92 Trading losses constitute timing differences which can be expected to reverse when they are relieved against profits of future years. Therefore, they can be set against other timing differences which are expected to reverse in future and which, on reversal, will form part of the trading profits against which the losses can be relieved. Care should be taken to ensure that the losses will be available for relief, having regard to the timing of the expected reversal of the other differences. Although trading losses can generally be carried forward without limit in the UK, the extent to which carry forward is permitted overseas is often more restricted. Capital losses may constitute timing differences, but they are normally available only to be set off against future capital profits and therefore they can only be expected to crystallise if a future taxable gain against which the loss can be set is identified. They may be set against timing differences which need to be recognised arising from the revaluation of assets (see **27.83** above and **27.104** to **27.106** below), but otherwise can only be recognised if the circumstances justify carrying forward a deferred tax debit balance. These circumstances are discussed in **27.93** to **27.98** below.

Deferred tax debit balances

27.93 Deferred tax debit balances should not be carried forward as assets except to the extent to which they are expected to be recoverable without replacement. The appendix to SSAP 15 uses the rather stronger phrase 'recovery is assured beyond reasonable doubt'.

27.94 With regard to debit balances, other than those arising from losses, SSAP 15 suggests that they should be carried forward only to the extent that:

(a) their recovery without replacement in the following accounting period can be clearly foreseen; or

(b) they are small in amount in relation to the past taxable profits of the company and to the forecast taxable profits in those periods when crystallisation is foreseen.

27.95 The tests which are suggested in the appendix to SSAP 15 to establish that the recovery of deferred tax relating to current trading losses is assured beyond reasonable doubt are:

(a) the loss results from an identifiable and non-recurring cause; and

(b) the enterprise has been consistently profitable over a considerable period, with any past losses being more than offset by
income in subsequent periods; and

(c) it is assured beyond reasonable doubt that future taxable profits will be sufficient to offset the current loss during the carry-
forward period prescribed by tax legislation.

27.96 It is suggested as a general rule that, on grounds of prudence,
sufficient future taxable profits can only be assured beyond
reasonable doubt if they are foreseen to arise in the next
accounting period. Only in exceptional circumstances can
forecasts of profits for longer periods be assured beyond reasonable doubt. Nevertheless, on occasions, such greater certainty may exist and, in principle, carry forward is justified in
these circumstances.

27.97 A question which should be considered is whether the tax
effect of losses of prior years, which has not previously been
recognised as an asset because recovery was not assured
beyond reasonable doubt, may be recognised in the current
year, because, as a result of improved profitability, their recovery can now be foreseen. There is nothing in SSAP 15 to suggest that this is not permissible, but the guidance in the
appendix unhelpfully only refers to current trading losses. It is
suggested that previous losses can properly be taken into
account in determining whether or not it is necessary to recognise a deferred tax liability, but if the tax effect of a loss is not
recognised as an asset in the period in which the loss is
incurred, it should not be recognised subsequently until recovery, in fact, takes place. However, if a case can be presented to
provide evidence that it is very likely that the previous losses
will be utilised in the future (e.g., the company has made profits post-year end against which the losses can be used), then it
is possible, in certain circumstances, to recognise the deferred
tax asset.

27.98 The recovery of deferred tax relating to a capital loss is assured
beyond reasonable doubt only if the taxable gain against which
the capital loss will be relieved can be identified with reasonable certainty. This implies that there is an asset identified for
sale on which a taxable gain can be anticipated; it is suggested
that the sale of the asset should normally be expected to take
place in the next accounting period.

Groups of companies

27.99   Where a company is a member of a group, it should take account of any group relief which is expected to be available and of any charge that would be made for such relief. Assumptions made as to the availability of group relief and payment should therefore be stated. [SSAP 15(43)] (Group relief is discussed in **27.137** to **27.141** below.)

27.100   The deferred tax position of each group company should thus be determined separately and the results aggregated to determine the group position. The only adjustments to the group deferred tax liability or asset which may be necessary are those which arise from consolidation adjustments, such as the elimination of intra-group profits (see also **23.114** and **27.89** above).

Overseas companies

27.101   Where subsidiaries are incorporated overseas, it may not be possible to insist that deferred tax is dealt with in accordance with SSAP 15 in their financial statements. For example, under US accounting principles, full provision for deferred tax must be made. If the effect is material, it will be necessary to restate such financial statements in accordance with SSAP 15 for the purpose of consolidation.

27.102   In many cases, the remittance of earnings of overseas companies results in additional taxation liabilities on those earnings. Thus, to the extent that earnings are not fully remitted, a timing difference may arise which should be dealt with like other timing differences, i.e., the liability should only be recognised to the extent that remittance of past earnings of the overseas subsidiary can be foreseen in the future. To the extent that remittance cannot be foreseen, it may be reasonable to think that it will never take place and to regard the potential liability as a permanent, rather than a timing, difference. Where deferred tax is not provided on earnings retained overseas, this should be stated. [SSAP 15(44)]

27.103   The translation of the financial statements of overseas subsidiaries for the purpose of consolidation does not give rise to any timing differences.

Revaluation

27.104   Timing differences which arise from the revaluation of fixed assets are discussed in **27.83** above.

27.105   No provision is necessary for any deferred tax on any revaluation above net depreciated cost until a liability can be foreseen, which will normally be at the time when the company decides in principle to dispose of the asset in circumstances in which rollover relief is unavailable. This position arises only if there is a significant delay between the decision in principle to sell and actual sale and, in the meantime, the asset continues in use in the company's business, so that it is not reclassified as a current asset (see **14.175** to **14.177** above).

27.106

> If a provision does become necessary under such circum-stances, it should be made by means of a charge in the state-ment of total recognised gains and losses (STRGL) not the profit and loss account. This is in line with the requirement in FRS 16(6) to show tax in the same performance statement as the gain or loss to which it has been attributed (see **27.48** above).

Pensions and other post-retirement benefits

27.107 SSAP 15 (as amended by *Amendment to SSAP 15 'Accounting for deferred tax' – December 1992*) permits preparers of financial state-ments, where they consider it appropriate in their particular circum-stances, to use the same recognition criteria for the deferred tax implications of pensions and other post-retirement benefits as in accounting for the obligations to provide those benefits.

27.108 The 1992 amendment to SSAP 15 was issued on the recommenda-tion of the UITF, following their deliberations over UITF Abstract 6 *Accounting for post-retirement benefits other than pensions*. The amendment was necessary because there are inconsistencies in the approaches adopted by SSAPs 15 and 24. When SSAP 15 was origi-nally issued in 1978 (and, indeed, when it was revised in 1985), the normal practice in accounting for pensions and other post-retirement benefits was to adopt a cash basis; consequently, there were few significant deferred tax implications. Subsequently, SSAP 24 (issued in 1988) and UITF Abstract 6 introduced major changes in the way these long-term and somewhat uncertain obligations are treated in financial statements, with very significant deferred tax implications. Under SSAP 24 and UITF Abstract 6, these long-term obligations are accounted for on a full provision basis, even though, in many cases, it is likely that they will continually roll over (i.e., as one obligation is settled, another will arise) and it has been argued that it is difficult to justify a prohibition, as SSAP 15 previously required, on the related deferred tax being treated on a similar basis if it, too, continually rolls over.

Disclosure requirements in respect of deferred tax

Accounting policy

27.109

> The accounting policy for dealing with deferred tax should be disclosed.

Example 27.109

Deferred taxation is provided at the anticipated tax rates on timing differences arising from the inclusion of items of income and expenditure in taxation computations in periods different from those in which they are included in financial statements to the extent that it is probable that a liability or asset will crystallise in the future.

Profit and loss account

27.110 The following disclosures relating to the profit and loss account are required by the Act and SSAP 15:

(a) deferred tax relating to ordinary activities should be shown as a separate component of tax on ordinary activities;

(b) deferred tax relating to extraordinary items should be shown as a separate component of tax on extraordinary profit or loss;

(c) the amount of any unprovided deferred tax in respect of the period should be disclosed in a note, analysed into its major components. Presumably, the intention is to require the disclosure of any timing differences which arise in the period to the extent that the tax effect is not recognised, but the wording would appear to require offsetting debit and credit items to be separately disclosed.

Example 27.110

The charge to UK corporation tax is reduced by £40,000 by the effect of capital allowances for tax purposes being in excess of depreciation charged in the profit and loss account, and by £30,000 in respect of development expenditure carried forward in the accounts but allowed for corporation tax when incurred.

27.111 Adjustments of deferred tax caused by changes in tax rates and changes in rate of tax allowances should be included as part of the tax charge for the year, but disclosed separately if material.

27.112 The following is an example of disclosure of the details of the tax charge where there has been a change in the rate of tax and the rate change was sufficiently material to necessitate its separate disclosure.

Example 27.112

	2000	1999
	£	£
Tax on profit on ordinary activities		
Corporation tax based on the profit for		
the year at 30% (1999 – 31%)	175,000	240,000
Deferred tax	18,000	(37,000)
Decrease in opening balance of deferred		
tax arising from changes in anticipated		
rates of tax	(14,000)	–
	179,000	203,000

Balance sheet

27.113 Deferred tax provisions should be included in the balance sheet under the heading 'Provisions for liabilities and charges' as part of the provision for 'Taxation, including deferred taxation'. SSAP 15 requires that deferred tax debit balances should be matched with the deferred tax liability against which they will be able to be offset. This is because individual deferred tax debit balances and liabilities which can be offset for tax purposes are not separate items but are elements of an aggregate deferred tax asset or liability. Where any deferred tax is to be carried forward as an asset, this should be included under the heading of 'Prepayments and accrued income' either within 'Current Assets' if it is current, or separately if the amount falls due after more than one year.

27.114 The following additional disclosures relating to the balance sheet are required by SSAP 15:

(a) the amount of the deferred tax account and its major components should be shown in a note (see **27.115** below);

(b) the total amount of unprovided deferred tax should be disclosed in a note, analysed into its major components;

(c) transfers to and from deferred tax;

(d) where amounts of deferred tax arise which relate to movements on reserves (e.g., resulting from the expected disposal of revalued assets), the amounts transferred to or from deferred tax should be shown separately as part of such movements;

(e) if the potential amount of deferred tax arising on the revaluation of an asset or as a result of the receipt of rollover relief is not disclosed because the revaluation does not constitute a timing difference, the fact that it does not constitute a timing difference and that tax has therefore not been quantified should be stated. This requirement recognises the position where tax on a revaluation surplus is regarded as likely to be perpetually deferred (because, even if the asset is sold, rollover relief will be available in respect of its replacement and no tax liability is expected to arise on the disposal of the replacement asset). In these circumstances, it may be treated as a permanent difference and not as a timing difference;

(f) if the value of an asset is disclosed in a note because it differs materially from its book amount, the note should also disclose the tax effects, if any, that would arise if the asset were realised at the balance sheet date at the noted value. It may be that, as outlined in (e) above, the difference should be regarded as permanent and the tax effect as nil, because of the availability of rollover relief. This requirement applies equally to disclosure of the value of an asset in the directors' report as to disclosure in a note to the accounts;

(g) if deferred tax is not provided on earnings retained overseas and not disclosed as a potential deferred liability on the grounds that it is not a timing difference, this fact should be stated (see **27.102** above and **27.116** below). Under FRS 2, the following additional disclosures must be given:

(i) where deferred tax has been provided on the unremitted earnings of overseas subsidiaries, then the amount should be disclosed; and

(ii) where deferred tax has not been provided in full, the reason should be given, e.g., that the amounts are considered to be permanently invested overseas and are not intended to be remitted, or the earnings when remitted are not expected to result in a UK tax liability due to double tax relief;

(h) deferred tax on the unremitted earnings of overseas subsidiaries will be accounted for on consolidation only. It will not appear on the parent company's own balance sheet;

(i) if, in assessing its deferred tax position, a company which is a member of a group takes account of any group relief and any payment for that purpose, the assumptions made as to the availability of and payment for group relief should be stated (see **27.137** to **27.141** below).

27.115 It is convenient to combine the information required in **27.114** (a) and (b) above in a single note, as in the following example (see **27.93** to **27.98** for calculation of the amount of a deferred tax asset that may be offset against a deferred tax liability).

Example 27.115

The amounts of deferred tax provided and unprovided in the accounts are:

	Provided		Unprovided	
	2000	1999	2000	1999
	£'000	£'000	£'000	£'000
Capital allowances in excess of depreciation	242	197	501	487
Surplus on revaluation of fixed assets	–	–	640	640
Other	20	18	–	–
	262	215	1,141	1,127
Less: trading losses carried forward	(112)	(70)	–	–
Unrelieved ACT	(100)	(84)	(21)	(76)
	50	61	1,120	1,051

27.116 The following example illustrates the information required by **27.114** (g) above.

Example 27.116

No provision has been made for taxation that would arise in the event of certain overseas subsidiaries and associated companies distributing the balance of their reserves, since these amounts are not expected to be remitted in the foreseeable future.

Published extracts

27.117 The following are extracts from financial statements which reflect deferred tax disclosures.

Extract 27.117.1

Vodafone Airtouch plc

Year ended 31 March 1999

Notes to the Consolidated Financial Statements

17 Provisions for liabilities and charges

	Deferred taxation	Other provisions Restated	Total Restated
	£m	£m	£m
1 April 1998	5.4	5.9	11.3
Profit and loss account	4.6	1.5	6.1
Utilised in the year	–	(7.4)	(7.4)
31 March 1999	10.0	–	10.0

Deferred taxation

The amounts provided and unprovided for deferred taxation are:

| | 1999 | | 1998 | |
| | Amount provided | Amount unprovided | Amount provided | Amount unprovided |
	£m	£m	£m	£m
Accelerated capital allowances	0.4	101.4	0.2	90.7
Gains subject to rollover relief	–	6.7	–	6.7
Other timing differences	9.6	(9.9)	5.2	(17.6)
	10.0	98.2	5.4	79.8

The potential net tax benefit in respect of tax losses carried forward at 31 March 1999 was £18.1m in United Kingdom subsidiaries (1998 – £23.1m) and £52.1m in international subsidiaries (1998 – £57.7m). These losses are only available for offset against future profits arising from the same trade within these companies.

In addition, the Group's share of losses of United Kingdom and international associated undertakings that is available for offset against future trading profits in these entities is £Nil and £55.2m respectively (1998 – £1.2m and £88.0m respectively).

Extract 27.117.2

Logica plc

Year ended 30 June 1999

Notes to the Consolidated Financial Statements

Accounting policies

Deferred taxation

Provision is made for deferred taxation to take account of timing differences between the treatment of certain items for accounts purposes and their treatment for tax purposes. The provision is maintained to the extent that the timing differences are expected, with reasonable probability, to reverse in the foreseeable future.

21 Deferred taxation

| | 1999 | 1998 |
Full provision is made in the accounts for deferred taxation as follows:	£'000	£'000
Short-term timing differences	**−2,943**	**−1,817**
01-Jul	−1,817	−1,145
Translation differences	27	−38
Transfer	−43	83
(Release) in respect of current year	−1,110	−717
30-Jun	**−2,943**	**−1,817**

The deferred taxation asset is included in note 14.

Advance corporation tax

Summary of current position

27.118 Pre 5 April 1999, when UK companies paid a dividend or other qualifying distribution to their shareholders an advance payment of corporation tax (an ACT payment) was payable to the Inland Revenue. Subject to the maximum allowed set-off, ACT payments made could be offset against the corporation tax liability of the accounting period in which the distribution became due and payable.

27.119 From 6 April 1999, ACT was abolished and replaced by a system of 'shadow' ACT (see **27.133** to **27.135** below). Under this system, when a company makes a distribution, it no longer has to pay over an amount of ACT to the Inland Revenue. The shadow ACT system affects all UK companies with surplus ACT on 6 April 1999 because this is the only opportunity for companies to recover any ACT paid in the past which has not been offset against corporation tax. It is possible for a company with surplus ACT (see **27.123** below) to opt out of the shadow ACT regime if it is willing to forego the opportunity of recovering its surplus ACT (this may be the case where a company finds the complexities and record-keeping requirements of the shadow ACT system too onerous). If a company has no unrelieved ACT as at 6 April 1999 but is a member of a group during its accounting period straddling the 6 April 1999 and another company in the group has unrelieved surplus ACT, the group and therefore the company should be in the shadow ACT regime (see **27.133** to **27.135** below).

27.120 As the accounting treatment of ACT is still relevant to some companies, the paragraphs below deal with the main aspects of accounting for ACT, the shadow ACT system and the ability of companies to reclaim surplus ACT.

ACT – main aspects

27.121 Prior to 6 April 1999 ACT was payable on most distributions made by companies to shareholders and the amount of ACT payable was calculated as the amount of the net distribution multiplied by the ACT rate. ACT was accounted for on form CT61 under the quarterly accounting procedure, under which ACT had to be paid within 14 days after the end of each calendar quarter and accounting period. The tax credits on UK dividends received by the paying company in the same quarter were allowed to be used to reduce the amount of ACT that was payable. Where a dividend was paid by a subsidiary company to its parent company, the distribution could be made under a group income election. No ACT was payable in respect of dividends paid under such an election.

27.122 ACT was primarily recovered by being offset against the corporation tax liability arising from the company's taxable profits of the accounting period in which the payment of the dividend was made on which ACT was due.

Example 27.122

Example of tax computation showing ACT setoff

	£
Corporation tax payable in the year	156,000
Less ACT paid in the year	(34,000)
Mainstream corporation tax liability	122,000

27.123 A maximum offset of ACT against a company's corporation tax liability was imposed by the Inland Revenue each year, so situations arose where the payments of ACT in the year (or in past years) exceeded the amount of the offset available under the Inland Revenue rules. These surplus payments of ACT could be:

(a)   carried back and used to reduce the taxable income of any of the previous six years (this would mean a repayment of previously paid tax); or

(b)   surrendered to a subsidiary company with capacity to offset the ACT; or

(c)   carried forward indefinitely to be used to set against the taxable income of future years (called 'surplus ACT').

27.124 From 6 April 1999, companies with surplus ACT have to enter the shadow ACT system introduced by the Inland Revenue in order that they may reclaim the surplus ACT paid in the past (see **27.133** to **27.135** below).

Foreign income dividends

27.125 Prior to 6 April 1999, in certain circumstances, companies could elect to pay a foreign income dividend (FID) instead of, or in addition to, a normal dividend. This allowed companies to pay dividends from distributable foreign profits (net foreign income after all taxes and double tax relief). The effect of treating such dividends as FIDS was to allow companies with distributable foreign profits to recover additional ACT which was in excess of the maximum offset outlined above in **27.123**. FIDs were abolished, together with ACT, from 6 April 1999.

Recoverable advance corporation tax

27.126 FRS 16(20) requires that any unrelieved (i.e., surplus) ACT existing at the date of implementing the standard should be recognised on the balance sheet only to the extent that it is regarded as recoverable. Appendix II of FRS 16 helps in deciding whether ACT should be carried forward as recoverable by stating that regard should be had only to the immediate and foreseeable future. How long this future period should be will depend upon the circumstances of each case, but FRS 16 suggests that where there is no deferred tax account it should normally not extend beyond the next accounting period. This means that, even though the Inland Revenue rules allow an indefinite carry forward, from an accounting perspective no asset will be recognised unless it is foreseen that it is going to be recovered.

27.127 ACT should be offset against a credit balance on the deferred tax account only if, in the period in which the underlying timing differences are expected to reverse, the reversal will create sufficient taxable profits to enable ACT to be recovered under the shadow ACT system.

27.128 Subject to **27.126** and **27.127** above, if the ACT on dividends relating to previous periods is regarded as recoverable but has not yet been recovered, it should be deducted from the deferred tax account if such an account is available for this purpose.

27.129 In the absence of a deferred tax account ACT recoverable should be shown as a deferred asset and should be included in 'Prepayments and accrued income'. If 'Prepayments and accrued income' is included under debtors rather than as a separate main heading, then the recoverable ACT should be included in the amount falling due after more than one year.

Irrecoverable advance corporation tax

27.130 If ACT is not regarded as recoverable, it is called 'irrecoverable ACT' and should be recognised as part of the tax charge (or credit) for the period in the profit and loss account and separately disclosed on the face of the profit and loss account or in a note (FRS 16(20)). See examples in **27.10** above for sample disclosures.

27.131 Likewise, if ACT, that was previously regarded as recoverable (and was either recorded as a separate asset or used to reduce a deferred tax liability) becomes irrecoverable, it is required to be charged in the profit and loss account as a separately disclosed component of the tax charge.

27.132 If ACT has been written off in the past as irrecoverable and subsequently becomes recoverable, then such ACT is required to be credited in the profit and loss account as a separately disclosed component of the tax charge.

Shadow ACT

27.133 From 6 April 1999, ACT was abolished and replaced by a system of shadow ACT. This shadow system allows companies which have surplus ACT carried forward (or ACT which has been written off as irrecoverable under accounting rules but is still available for recovery under Inland Revenue rules) to reduce future corporation tax payments in the same way as they would have been able to if the system of ACT had not been abolished. There are many rules which apply to the shadow ACT system and it has been designed to be no more generous than the old ACT system. Its effect is to ensure that ACT that was previously irrecoverable becomes recoverable only to the extent that it would have become recoverable under the old ACT system.

27.134 The principal elements of the shadow ACT system are as follows:

(a) companies calculate the shadow ACT payable on all dividends paid net of dividends received (as they would have before the abolishment of ACT), but no actual payments of ACT are made. The calculation is complex (and is not described here) as, from 6 April 1999, even though the rate of shadow ACT is 20% of the net distribution, the actual tax credit on dividends received is 10% of the grossed-up distribution. Once calculated, this notional figure of ACT payable is called 'shadow' ACT;

(b) companies will calculate ACT set-off as normal (see **27.123** above), which will be utilised in the following order:
   (i) shadow ACT arising in the year;
   (ii) shadow ACT carried forward from prior years;
   (iii) shadow ACT carried back from future years (subject to time limit restrictions);
   (iv) any surplus ACT brought forward from periods up to 5 April 1999.

Companies can therefore reduce their tax liabilities by using the brought forward ACT surplus if the shadow ACT does not utilise all the set-off in the year.

27.135 If any surplus ACT which had previously been written off through the profit and loss account as irrecoverable ACT is utilised then, as per **27.132** above, the credit to the profit and loss account should be shown separately either on the face of the profit and loss account or disclosed in a note. At the end of each accounting period, the recoverability of the surplus ACT in the company needs to be assessed. The table in **27.136** below summarises the position.

Summary of surplus ACT accounting treatments

27.136 A summary of the accounting treatment relating to surplus ACT is as follows:

ACT situation	Accounting treatment
1. Surplus ACT has been recognised in the accounts as an asset in the past and now:	
(a) It is still deemed recoverable;	(a) Keep recognising asset.
(b) It is deemed irrecoverable.	(b) Write off asset to P&L account and disclose separately.
2. Surplus ACT exists but has not been recognised in the accounts in the past as was deemed irrecoverable. If now:	
(a) it is still deemed irrecoverable;	(a) No adjustment needed.
(b) it is deemed to be recoverable.	(b) Credit P&L account disclosing separately and recognise asset.

Group relief

Introduction

27.137 Group relief is available to certain qualifying UK groups of companies and consortia, whereby trading losses of one company can be set against taxable profits of another for the same accounting period. The company which has incurred and surrendered the losses loses all right to any relief in respect of them. The surrender may be made for any consideration or none, provided due regard is paid to the interests of any minority shareholders or creditors who may be affected. The most usual arrangement is for the receiving company to make a payment equal to the tax that it will save, but alternative arrangements sometimes seen are for the loss to be surrendered for no consideration at all, and for a payment to be made equal to the full amount of the losses rather than just the tax saving. The tax legislation provides that a payment for group relief (up to the amount of the losses surrendered) shall not be taken into account in computing the taxable profits or losses of the paying or receiving company or be regarded as a distribution. It is still open to the authorities (Inland Revenue/HM Customs and Excise) to argue that the payment is not for group relief, but rather for the acquisition of goods/services giving rise to the loss or is a means of distributing funds to the shareholders. Such a question is a matter of fact and it will be necessary to assess all the evidence in a particular case.

Accounting for group relief

27.138 A question that arises for subsidiary companies which have received or surrendered group relief is how the relevant transactions should be recorded in the profit and loss account. It should be noted that the matter does not arise for a holding company in the normal circumstance where it produces a consolidated profit and loss account only, since all the entries cancel out on consolidation.

27.139   Although not stated in FRS 16, it is recommended that group relief payments and receipts should be included as part of the tax charge for the year in the profit and loss account and be separately disclosed in the taxation note in the accounts.

27.140 Examples **27.140** and **27.141** below illustrate appropriate presentations adopting this approach and disclosure required. The examples assume that £100,000 of tax losses have been surrendered to a profit-making company and that, in case A, no payment (contribution) is made, in case B, payment equivalent to the tax relief is made and, in case C, payment equivalent to the losses surrendered is made. A corporation tax rate of 30 per cent is assumed.

Example 27.140

Profit-making company

	A	B	C
	£'000	£'000	£'000
Profit on ordinary activities before taxation	300	300	300
Tax on profit on ordinary activities	(60)	(90)	(160)
Profit for the financial year	240	210	140
Note 4 – Tax on profit on ordinary activities Corporation tax based on the profit for the year at 30%	60	60	60
Group relief payable	0	30	100
Tax charge for year on profit on ordinary activities	60	90	160
Loss-making company			
Loss on ordinary activities before taxation	(100)	(100)	(100)
Tax on loss on ordinary activities	–	30	100
Loss for the financial year	(100)	(70)	–
Note 4 – Tax on loss on ordinary activities Corporation tax credit based on the loss for the year at 30%	–	–	–
Group relief surrendered	–	30	100
Tax credit for year relating to loss on ordinary activities	–	30	100

27.141 An alternative approach, which, in practice, is acceptable, is to deal with the matter within the taxation note as illustrated below.

Example 27.141

Profit-making company

Of the tax on profit on ordinary activities of £90,000, £30,000 has been relieved by the surrender of losses by another group company [in exchange for a payment of the same amount].

Loss-making company

The tax benefit of £30,000 arising from the losses incurred has been surrendered to another group company [in exchange for a payment of the same amount].

Special circumstances affecting taxation

Introduction

27.142 The Act requires particulars to be given of any special circumstances which affect liability in respect of taxation of profits, income or capital gains for the financial year or for succeeding financial years. [Sch 4: 54(2)] There is a similar requirement in FRS 3. [FRS 3(23)] Generally, circumstances which should be disclosed are those which result in the tax charge for the year being materially higher or lower than would normally be expected, and items such as losses carried forward or ACT written off as irrecoverable which are available to reduce the tax liabilities on the profits of future years. However, where there are two or more circumstances which all have a material effect on the liability for the year, they should all be disclosed, even though the combined effect of them leaves the tax charge for the year at a normal level.

27.143 One specific circumstance which is referred to in SSAP 15 is where timing differences have arisen in the period but deferred tax has not been provided because no asset or liability is expected to crystallise.

27.144 Examples of the more common taxation situations that require disclosure are given in **27.145** to **27.149** below.

Current year's losses

27.145 Where a company has incurred a loss (as adjusted for tax purposes), it is appropriate to recognise a credit for tax in the profit and loss account to the extent that:

(a) repayment of tax can be obtained by carrying back the loss to reduce the taxable profit of the previous year; or

(b) the loss can be surrendered to another group company under the group relief arrangements (see **27.137** to **27.141** above); or

(c) the loss can be set against a liability arising in respect of a credit or of a gain which has not passed through the profit and loss account; or

(d) the loss can be set against other timing differences to reduce a deferred tax liability that is expected to crystallise; or

(e) exceptionally, it can be foreseen with reasonable certainty that the loss can be set off against profits of the next accounting period.

27.146   If credit cannot be taken for tax on all the losses incurred in the foregoing ways, then the difference should be disclosed as losses which are available to set against future profits, since this is a special circumstance which will affect the tax liability of future financial years. The note should also explain why the tax credit is unrecognised.

> ### Example 27.146
>
> The tax relief available in respect of the loss for the current year is restricted to the corporation tax paid in respect of the previous financial year. Unrelieved losses of £260,000 are carried forward and are available to reduce the tax liability in respect of future profits.

Prior years' losses brought forward

27.147   Where a company's taxable profit is reduced by the application of losses brought forward for which credit has not been taken previously, the resulting reduced tax charge should be explained.

> ### Example 27.147
>
> Tax on profit on ordinary activities has been reduced by tax relief of £18,000 in respect of prior years' losses brought forward.

Significant disallowable items

27.148   Although some items which are properly treated as revenue expenditure are disallowable for tax purposes (e.g., entertaining expenses), it is rare for their effect on the tax liability to be sufficiently large to require disclosure. A problem which is likely to be more significant is that losses incurred by a company operating in one country cannot normally be set off against profits earned by other group companies elsewhere.

> ### Example 27.148
>
> The tax liability is unduly high in relation to the group profit on ordinary activities before tax, because losses of £179,000 were incurred by a foreign subsidiary for which no tax relief is immediately available. Unrelieved losses of the foreign subsidiary amounting to approximately £306,000 may be set against its future profits, but will cease to be available for this purpose at various dates over the next five years.

Irrecoverable advance corporation tax

27.149 ACT which has not been recovered otherwise may be carried forward indefinitely and set against future corporation tax liabilities. The amount of ACT written off as irrecoverable or utilised in the year should be disclosed separately as an expense or credit in the profit and loss account or in the tax note (FRS 16(20)) (see the examples in **27.10** above).

Future developments

FRED 19

27.150 FRED 19 was issued in August 1999 and proposes to replace the current partial provision basis for deferred tax with a form of full provisioning. This exposure draft follows on from the March 1995 discussion paper and April 1998 preliminary proposal which also recommended the adoption of the full provision method.

27.151 FRED 19 proposes an incremental liability approach, which provides for deferred tax on timing differences which exist at the balance sheet date and are capable of reversal in future periods. Provision will only be made when the deferred tax meets the definition of an asset or liability in its own right (i.e., there is an obligation to receive or transfer economic benefits in the future). The critical point is that deferred tax should only be provided for as a liability when the reporting entity has an obligation to pay more tax in future as a result of past events.

27.152 In the past, the full provision method has been criticised because it can lead to the build up of large liabilities that fall due only far in the future. To mitigate this, FRED 19 proposes that material deferred tax balances should be discounted and respondents were asked their views as to whether this would be the preferred method.

27.153 One of ASB's objectives appears to be international harmonisation since the partial provisioning basis has lost favour in the international world because it anticipates future events and is viewed as being inconsistent with other areas of accounting. However, the proposals in FRED 19 are not in line with International Accounting Standard 12 (IAS 12) as that standard adopts a temporary difference approach rather than FRED 19's incremental liability approach. The temporary difference approach identifies the tax that would be payable if the balance sheet carrying amounts of each of the assets and liabilities of the entity were recovered or settled in the future. Additionally, FRED 19 proposes discounting which is not permitted under IAS 12. Thus, when IAS 12 is compared to the proposed approach in FRED 19, differences arise and reconciliations between the two accounting standards will still be necessary.

27.154 FRED 19 states that deferred tax should be provided on all timing differences which have originated but not reversed at the balance sheet date, subject to some exceptions. It then goes on to give detailed guidance on some specific areas. These are:

(a) Revaluations (see **27.155** below);

(b) Gains on sale of assets (see **27.156** to **27.157** below);

(c) Unremitted earnings (see **27.158** to **27.159** below);

(d) Discounting (see **27.160** to **27.162** below); and

(e) Recognition in accounts (see **27.163** to **27.166** below).

Revaluations

27.155 The general rule is that NO deferred tax will be provided for as a result of a revaluation policy. However, where there is a binding sale agreement to sell the revalued asset AND the expected gain or loss on sale has been recognised AND no rollover relief will be (or it is more likely than not that it will not be) claimable on disposal, then a provision for the tax on the gain that will be payable on the sale should be made. Where holdover relief is given such that taxation of the gain is postponed for up to ten years, the above rule in respect of rollover relief does not apply, i.e., no provision for tax on a gain would need to be made. It is expected that the ASB will amend this requirement to allow tax to be provided on revaluation gains which have been included in the profit and loss account, for example, insurance companies, as a component of performance.

Gains on sale of assets

27.156 Where an asset has been sold, (whether or not it was previously revalued) and the proceeds of the sale will be taxable in a different period to that in which the accounting entries have been made, deferred tax should be provided to the extent that rollover relief will not be claimable. This does not extend to other types of relief, such as hold-over relief.

27.157 If it is more likely than not that rollover relief will be available at some point within the qualifying time-frame then the conditions which have to be met, and an estimate of the tax that would become payable if they are not met, needs to be disclosed in the accounts.

Unremitted earnings

27.158 If any of a company's subsidiaries, associates or joint ventures decide to pay over part of their earnings to the company then these amounts normally fall to be taxable in the UK. If the dividends have been accrued for in the company's profit and loss account, a timing difference will exist if they are only recognised in the UK company's tax computation when it becomes finally entitled to receive them (i.e., in future periods).

27.159 Deferred tax will only be provided for under the FRED when either:

(1) dividends from subsidiaries, associates or joint ventures are accrued in the parent's/investor's books (as described above); or

(2) a binding agreement to distribute past earnings in the future exists (expected to be rare).

(1) will affect both individual company and consolidated accounts as the additional tax in the individual company is a liability which is external to the group. However, (2) will only affect consolidated accounts as the additional tax is an external liability which only arises on consolidation.

As it is unlikely that there will be many occasions under which case (2) applies, in most circumstances the deferred tax provision comprises only tax that will become payable on receipt of dividends accrued at the balance sheet date (taking account of double taxation relief).

Discounting

27.160 In the preface to FRED 19, the ASB states that there is disagreement amongst the members as to whether discounting should be required, where the effect of it is material. The disagreement, in the main, relates to accelerated capital allowances where it is argued, inter alia, that the cashflow has already happened, so any future tax effects cannot be discounted as they are not cashflows. Therefore, even though discounting has been included in the FRED, the ASB is waiting for respondents' views before making a final decision.

27.161 Discounting is undoubtedly the hardest requirement of the standard, asking for every timing difference's deferred tax balance to be discounted when the effect is material. In many cases, balances will be short-term, and will not require discounting. However, for balances which are longer term than 'normal', it appears that the discounting process has to be undertaken just to establish whether or not the effect of discounting is material.

27.162 The proposals are to use a government bond post-tax yield that matures in the same period as the timing difference reverses. Any unwinding of the discount and changes in the discount rate must be shown in the profit and loss account as a financial item next to interest in the profit and loss account. The amount would be shown separately from other interest either on the face of the profit and loss account or in a note, irrespective of where the original deferred tax charge/credit was reflected. An example of how discounting would be applied under the proposals in FRED 19 is shown below.

Example 27.162

Discounting

A company has a timing difference of £100,000 at 31/12/99. It is due to reverse in 2 equal amounts in 2004 and 2009.

If no discounting:

Timing difference	£100,000
Deferred tax	
£100,000 × tax rate (30%)	= £30,000

£30,000 is the deferred tax liability until 2004 when it reduces to £15,000 (i.e., £50,000 x 30%–assuming tax rate does not change)

If discounting is applied:

In year ended 1999, deferred tax liability	= £22,191
(see calculation below)	

	2004	2009
Timing difference reversal	(£50,000)	(£50,000)
Tax due @ 30%	£15,000	£15,000
Government bid yield	6.35	5.73
Discount Factor (using bid yield less tax of 30%)	0.805	0.675
	(5 yrs)	(10 yrs)
	£12,068	£10,123
Total discounted tax liability =		**£22,191**

In 2000, need to calculate the unwinding of the discount using the same government bid yields for one year less.

	2004	2009
Timing difference reversal	(£50,000)	(£50,000)
Tax due @ 30%	£15,000	£15,000
Government bid yield	6.35	5.73
Discount Factor (using bid yield less tax of 30%)	0.840	0.702
	(4 yrs)	(9 yrs)
	£12,600	£10,529
Total discounted tax liability =		**£23,129**

Unwinding of the discount = £23,129 – £22,191 = £938 (interest charge in 2000)

It is, of course, necessary in following years to calculate discounted deferred tax balances for timing differences which arise in those later years, and also to ensure that the post tax government bid yield figures remain up to date.

Recognition in accounts

27.163 The deferred tax for a period, and adjustments to amounts arising in previous periods, should be recognised in the profit and loss account, except to the extent that they are attributable to a gain or loss that is or has been recognised in the statement of total recognised gains and losses. To the extent that they are attributable to a gain or loss recognised in the statement of total recognised gains and losses, they should also be recognised in that statement. For example, deferred tax relating to a revalued asset that is contracted to be sold in the future, should be recognised in the statement of total recognised gains and losses, alongside the revaluation surplus.

27.164 It is intended that deferred tax assets and liabilities should be offset in the balance sheet only to the extent that the assets and liabilities relate to taxes levied by the same tax authority and to the extent that the entity has a legally enforceable right to offset current tax assets against current tax liabilities.

27.165 Net deferred tax liabilities should be classified as 'provisions for liabilities and charges' in the balance sheet. Net deferred tax assets should be classified as debtors, as a separate subheading of debtors where material. Deferred tax assets and liabilities should be separately disclosed on the face of the balance sheet if the amounts are so material in the context of the total net current assets, or net assets that, in the absence of such disclosure, readers may misinterpret the accounts.

27.166 Deferred tax assets should be recognised when, on the basis of all available evidence, it is more likely than not that suitable taxable profits will be available in the future from which the future reversal of the underlying timing differences can be deducted. The FRED discusses at length which profits are deemed 'suitable'. In summary, if the future reversal of deferred tax liabilities does not cover the deferred tax assets, then other profits, based on historical and relevant information need to be estimated. If the availability of future profits at the time of the deferred tax asset reversing is in doubt, then no asset should be recognised. If circumstances change, and the recoverability of the asset becomes probable, then the deferred tax asset is recognised at that point, the credit entry being made to the current performance statement and not as a prior year adjustment. It can be assumed that the future reversal of any deferred tax liabilities recognised at the balance sheet date will give rise to taxable profits. To the extent that those profits will be suitable for the deduction of the reversing deferred tax asset, the asset can always be regarded as recoverable.

Future standard?

27.167 It is not yet possible to confirm in what form FRED 19 will become an FRS.

28 Reporting the substance of transactions

28 Reporting the substance of transactions

Introduction

Current accounting requirements

28.1   Until the issue of the ASB's Statement of Principles in final form (December 1999 – see chapter 3), the key foundation statement within UK accounting was SSAP 2 *Disclosure of accounting policies,* issued in 1971. SSAP 2 lists four fundamental accounting concepts: going concern, accruals, consistency and prudence. However, as early as 1964, a fifth concept was evident in official UK literature. In that year, the ICAEW issued Recommendation on Accounting Principles 23, requiring hire purchase and other instalment credit transactions to be accounted for, not according to legal form, but according to substance. That same 'substance over form' concept was central to the development, in the early 1980s, of SSAP 21 *Accounting for leases and hire purchase contracts.* After many years of debate and development, the ASB issued FRS 5 *Reporting the substance of transactions* in April 1994, making the application of this accounting for substance concept a generalised requirement applicable in all circumstances where there is no more specific accounting rule.

28.2   Prior to the issue of FRS 5, with the exception of leases and hire purchase contracts, UK accounting requirements reflected legal form. For many years, this did not cause any major problems, since the legal form of a transaction generally provided a sound basis for its accounting. Throughout the 1980s, however, many 'off balance sheet accounting' schemes were developed that deliberately separated form and substance. By accounting only in accordance with strict legal form, the result often failed to reflect in full the assets and liabilities upon which income flows were based, notably, many loans were excluded from balance sheets. A wide recognition that these 'creative accounting' structures were not ultimately to the benefit of companies or their investors led first the ICAEW, and then the ASB's predecessor body, the ASC, to commence work on a general substance-based accounting standard. This led to the issue of ED 42 in 1988 and ED 49 in 1990.

28.3   At the same time that this work was being undertaken, the EU Seventh Directive on company law (consolidated accounts) was enacted into GB legislation. The resulting law, the Companies Act 1989, included a new definition of 'subsidiary undertaking', which contributed towards the reduction in scope for off balance sheet schemes involving a 'controlled non-subsidiary'. Many such entities, which fell outside the earlier definition of a subsidiary, fell within the new legal definition of a subsidiary undertaking and thus within the legal requirement for full consolidation. In particular, the element of the subsidiary undertaking definition that is based on the existence of a participating interest, together with the actual exercise of a dominant influence, has been effective in dealing with many cases where one entity holds a significant minority shareholding in, and exercises control over, another entity (see chapter 23).

28.4   Building on ED 49, the ASB continued to develop an accounting standard dealing with the substance of transactions. However, the complexity of the subject matter, the need to consider fully the legal implications and the wide range of industry groups affected by the proposed changes meant that the process took a significant period of time. In October 1991, the ASB issued a bulletin dealing specifically with its proposals for the contentious issue of securitised assets. By February 1993, a full draft of an accounting standard, FRED 4 *Reporting the substance of transactions*, was issued. Finally, after further refinement, FRS 5 was issued on 14 April 1994. In the main, FRS 5 was mandatory for accounting periods ending on or after 22 September 1994 – there were some transitional arrangements.

28.5

> Implementation of FRS 5 thus began to take place towards the end of 1994, as companies prepared financial statements for September 1994, and later, year ends. The issue of FRS 5 had a significant effect on, for example:
>
> (a)   consignment stock arrangements within the motor industry;

> (b) securitisations of various monetary receivables, and loan transfers, in the financial services industry; and
>
> (c) netting of assets and liabilities by insurance brokers, market makers and reinsurance companies.

FRS 5: scope, objective and summary requirements

28.6   FRS 5 applies to 'all transactions of a reporting entity whose financial statements are intended to give a true and fair view of its financial position and profit or loss (or income and expenditure) for a period' irrespective of whether they report under the Act or otherwise. [FRS 5(11)] The term 'transaction' includes a group or series of legally distinct elements that together achieve a particular commercial effect.

28.7   FRS 5 does not exempt any industry groups from its requirements, but does exempt certain types of transactions. These are: [FRS 5(12)]

(a)   forward contracts and futures (such as those for foreign currencies or commodities);

(b)   foreign exchange and interest rate swaps;

(c)   contracts where a net amount will be paid or received based on the movement in a price or an index (sometimes referred to as 'contracts for differences');

(d)   expenditure commitments (such as purchase commitments) and orders placed, until the earlier of delivery or payment; and

(e)   employment contracts.

The logic behind these exemptions is twofold:

(a)   the ASB is working on a separate project to look at financial instruments and derivatives, including their role as hedging instruments and within treasury management generally; and

(b)   contracts for future performance such as purchase commitments could, if the principles of FRS 5 were applied, result in assets and liabilities being recorded at the time an order was placed or contract signed and not at the time of delivery or payment.

In addition, where the substance of a transaction falls within the scope of another standard, as well as falling within FRS 5, the standard containing the more specific guidance should be applied. See paragraphs **28.12** to **28.15** below.

28.8 More recently, the need to apply FRS 5 to PFI transactions has stimulated debate over the application of FRS 5 to circumstances where a dedicated asset is used to provide long-term services to a specific customer. This debate concluded with the issue in September 1998 of an additional application note to FRS 5.

28.9 The summary objective of FRS 5 is that 'a reporting entity's financial statements should report the substance of the transactions into which it has entered'. [FRS 5(14)] This is achieved if financial statements represent faithfully the commercial effect of transactions that they purport to represent.

28.10 FRS 5 is written in general terms. This means that its requirements apply to all transactions. However, for the vast majority of routine transactions, substance and form will be the same and the FRS does not alter the established method of accounting. The FRS is chiefly relevant to those transactions where substance and legal form differ or where the substance is not readily apparent. Common situations include those listed in the table below.

Feature	Examples
Legal title deliberately separated from underlying benefits.	• consignment stock; • factored debts; • use of special purpose vehicles.
Options granted where the exercise of the option can be considered a virtual certainty.	• sale with 'put and call' options to repurchase.
A series of transactions designed so that the commercial effect can only be appreciated when the series is taken as a whole.	• securitisations; • project financing; • circular finance structures; • take-or-pay agreements.

28.11 Although the objective is to ensure that the substance of an entity's transactions are reported in its financial statements, the FRS does not simply require this and stop there. Instead it goes on to give, in addition to the overall requirement for substance, specific rules which if followed will, in the ASB's view, lead to the substance of transactions being portrayed in financial statements. These rules are under five headings, as follows.

Heading and relevance	FRS 5
Recognition – a transaction results in the 'acquisition' of an asset or a liability or both.	Recognition is required when 'recognition criteria' are met. *FRS 5 paragraph 20 contains general recognition criteria.*
Ceasing to recognise – a transaction results in the 'disposal' of an asset; a corollary is that proceeds received do not represent a liability.	Removal from the financial statements, or derecognition, is required when 'derecognition criteria' are met. *FRS 5 paragraphs 21 to 24 contain general criteria for continued recognition, derecognition of an entire asset and partial derecognition in special cases; paragraphs 66 to 74 provide additional explanation.*
Linked presentation – an asset does not qualify for derecognition, but non-recourse finance is received which can only be repaid out of funds generated by the asset. Such finance is shown alongside the related asset on the face of the balance sheet and not as a separate liability.	Linked presentation is required when two general and six detailed conditions are met. *FRS 5 paragraph 26 contains general conditions, paragraph 27 contains detailed conditions, and paragraphs 76 to 88 provide additional explanation.*
Offset – conditions required for assets and matching liabilities to be offset.	Offset is required only where the individual asset and liability cease to meet the definition of 'asset' and 'liability'. *FRS 5 paragraph 29 contains both the general rule and detailed conditions. Paragraphs 89 to 91 provide limited additional guidance.*
Quasi-subsidiaries – a quasi-subsidiary, although not a legal subsidiary undertaking, is controlled by the 'parent', and is a source of benefits or risks that are similar to a legal subsidiary.	Where the reporting entity conducts business through a 'quasi-subsidiary', the substance of transactions entered into by the quasi-subsidiary should be included in the consolidated accounts. Where conditions for linked presentation are met, the quasi-subsidiary should be included on that basis. *FRS 5 paragraphs 32 to 38, and 95 to 103 deal with identification, accounting for and disclosure of quasi-subsidiaries.*

Relationship of FRS 5 with other standards

28.12   Since FRS 5 applies general principles to all transactions, there will be occasions when the application of FRS 5 will overlap with another accounting standard or legal requirement. FRS 5 states that: 'Where the substance of a transaction or the treatment of any resulting asset or liability falls not only within the scope of this FRS but also directly within the scope of another FRS, a Statement of Standard Accounting Practice ("SSAP"), or a specific statutory requirement governing the recognition of assets or liabilities, the standard or statute that contains the more specific provision(s) should be applied'. [FRS 5(13)]

28.13   One example is pension obligations, for which SSAP 24 represents a more specific standard, resulting in:

(a)   pension liabilities not appearing gross on the employer's balance sheet; and

(b)   a pension fund not being consolidated as a quasi-subsidiary.

A sale and repurchase transaction between a company and its pension fund, say, of the company's head office, would, however, be dealt with under FRS 5.

28.14   One area that gives rise to some difficult judgements is accounting for leases under SSAP 21. The approach of SSAP 21 can be described as an 'all or nothing' approach, i.e., a leased asset and related obligation to pay rentals remain wholly off-balance sheet until the '90%' threshold is passed. At this point, the full fair value of the asset, and an equal liability, is displayed on balance sheet. This approach contrasts with that adopted in FRS 5 (and in the ASB's Statement of Principles) which allows for an asset to be analysed into different rights (the 'property rights' approach). Thus, it is possible to recognise only those rights that have been acquired; in effect, this approach ceases to distinguish between finance and operating leases and would require the present value of all lease obligations to be recorded on balance sheet. A discussion paper proposing this treatment for leases has been issued, see **29.102** et seq. below. While SSAP 21 remains the extant standard the key question is whether the requirements of FRS 5 override those of SSAP 21. A practical approach, based on the guidance referred to in the previous paragraph, is that:

(a)   a stand-alone lease transaction that falls wholly within the parameters of SSAP 21 should initially be evaluated under the criteria of SSAP 21, including the 90 per cent net present value test;

(b) where the classification under SSAP 21 appears to contradict other substance-based features of the lease, e.g., the net present value test indicates that the lease is an operating lease, but the lessor nevertheless fulfils the role of a lender, then all features of the lease should be reviewed in the light of FRS 5 to determine whether there is sufficient evidence to rebut the SSAP 21 classification;

(c) where a transaction has more complex features, e.g., a financing arrangement that includes a lease component where the series of related transactions are not wholly covered by the parameters of SSAP 21, the requirements of FRS 5 should be applied to the entire transaction.

28.15   FRS 5 (see **28.14** above) gives specific authority for a SSAP 21 classification to be challenged where the result clearly contradicts the substance of the transaction. In other areas, FRS 5 may also be relevant where a transaction is designed deliberately to avoid the requirements of another standard.

Specific requirements of FRS 5

Analysis of transactions

28.16   The key to accounting in accordance with the objective of FRS 5 is to begin by obtaining a full understanding of the rationale of a transaction as a whole, including the role of each party, and the commercial logic for their involvement. FRS 5 thus requires:

(a) realistic appreciation of why a transaction exists and why each party is involved: 'In determining the substance of a transaction, all its aspects and implications should be identified and greater weight given to those more likely to have a commercial effect in practice' [FRS 5(14)];

(b) placing a transaction in context: 'A group or series of transactions that achieves or is designed to achieve an overall commercial effect should be viewed as a whole' [FRS 5(14)];

(c) assessment of what a transaction achieved: 'To determine the substance of a transaction it is necessary to identify whether the transaction has given rise to new assets or liabilities for the reporting entity and whether it has changed the entity's existing assets or liabilities' [FRS 5(16)];

(d) identification of the 'risk-takers': 'Evidence that an entity has rights or other access to benefits (and hence has an asset) is given if the entity is exposed to the risks inherent in the benefits, taking into account the likelihood of those risks having a commercial effect in practice'. [FRS 5(17)] Similarly: 'Evidence that an entity has an obligation to transfer benefits (and hence has a liability) is given if there is some circumstance in which the entity is unable to avoid, legally or commercially, an outflow of benefits' [FRS 5(18)];

(e) realistic appraisal of conditional events: 'Where a transaction incorporates one or more options, guarantees or conditional provisions, their commercial effect should be assessed in the context of all the aspects and implications of the transaction in order to determine what assets and liabilities exist' [FRS 5(19)] and 'in determining the substance of a transaction, ... greater weight given to those more likely to have a commercial effect in practice' [FRS 5 (14)].

28.17 In practice, the following analysis will assist in understanding the commercial effects of the transaction:

(a) obtain all relevant documents and agreements, including side letters that impact on the likely course of events. Documents should always be in final form and include monetary details where relevant;

(b) identify the role played by each party to the transaction (in particular, the 'equity participants' to a transaction) and the reason for their involvement. It is reasonable to suppose that a financial institution will limit its interest to that of financier: an assertion to the contrary should be supported by clear evidence. If a transaction appears to lack logic from the point of view of one or more participants, then it is likely that either not all the relevant parts of the transaction have been identified or the commercial effect of some aspect of the transaction has been incorrectly assessed;

(c) assess the likely course of action (including options): place greater emphasis on the probable course of events and, accordingly, little or no emphasis on unlikely events. The consequences of liquidation of one of the parties should only be considered where this is a likely event;

(d) test the transaction's responsiveness, and the return for each participant, to marginal changes in variables: interest rates, asset values and the timing of events. This provides useful insight into the role of the parties involved, e.g., whether a participant obtains a risk-taker's return or a financier's return.

28.18 The effect of a transaction on an entity's assets and liabilities will depend on the starting point, i.e., whether an asset or liability already appears on balance sheet. In summary, the possible outcomes are as follows.

After transaction	Before transaction	No asset is recorded	Asset is recorded
Entity does not have asset		No entry	Full or partial derecognition (see **28.33** below)
Entity has asset		Recognition (see **28.23** below)	Linked presentation (if conditions met) (see **28.45** below) or Offset asset and liability (if conditions met) (see **28.52** below) or Continued gross presentation

28.19   In practice, the two most commonly encountered situations are as follows.

Situation 1:   An entity does not have any existing asset, but is party to a transaction where an asset is financed by a third party.

Practical issue: Should the entity recognise both an asset and liability or neither?

Approach: Isolate the variables such as risk of change in asset values and the existence of interest or an equivalent charge. If either accrues to or is borne by the entity, it is likely that both asset and liability exist (see **28.24** below for detailed tests).

Situation 2:   An entity has an existing asset and receives cash.

Practical issue: Does the cash represent proceeds of sale or a source of finance?

Approach: The following logic chart indicates the order in which the tests of FRS 5 should be applied:

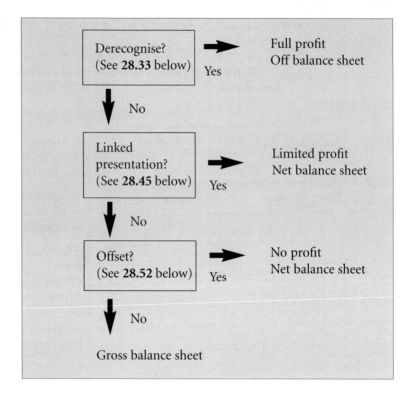

Recognition and derecognition

28.20 FRS 5 deals separately with recognition and derecognition. However, both involve two stages:

(a) identifying assets and liabilities: consideration of the definition of asset and liability to determine whether an asset or liability has been acquired or assumed, or transferred to others;

(b) applying recognition and derecognition tests: application of various tests to determine whether the asset or liability identified qualifies for inclusion in or exclusion from the balance sheet.

Meaning of 'significant'

28.21 Wherever FRS 5 uses the term 'significant' to qualify benefits or risks, it should be taken to refer to the benefits and risks that are likely to occur in practice; not in relation to the total possible benefits and risks. For example, a provider of loan finance may contribute 90 per cent of a transaction's value, but have little or no risk if they rank preferentially to the contributor of the remaining 10 per cent, and expected losses are below 10 per cent of the transaction's value.

Definitions of 'assets' and 'liabilities'

28.22 The definitions of 'assets' and 'liabilities' are as follows.

[FRS 5(2), (3) and (4)]

(a) *Assets*: 'Rights or other access to future economic benefits controlled by an entity as a result of past transactions or events'.

(b) *Control in the context of an asset*: 'The ability to obtain the
future economic benefits relating to an asset and to restrict the
access of others to those benefits'.

(c) *Liabilities*: 'An entity's obligations to transfer economic benefits
as a result of past transactions or events'.

Recognition

28.23 Two stages have been identified (see **28.20** above) in determining
whether, as a result of a transaction, a new asset requires recognition
(or an existing asset is to be increased). The stages are considered
below as follows.

- Stage 1 – Application of identification tests:

  - whether benefits have been transferred (see **28.24**
  below);

  - whether control exists (see **28.25** below).

- Stage 2 – Application of recognition tests (see **28.27** below).

28.24 The prime practical test of an asset having been acquired or assumed
is whether, as a result of a transaction, an entity becomes entitled to
(or exposed to the risks inherent in) the benefits that make up the
asset. The test can be analysed as follows.

Stage of analysis	Implications / Action required
1. Identify what assets are affected by the transaction.	• Assets may be non-monetary, such as property or stock, or monetary. • Although analysis is normally carried out for each asset, it may be necessary to analyse connected assets together.
2. For each asset, identify the benefits that make up the asset.	• Ultimately, economic benefits will be cash flows – from the use or realisation of the asset.
3. Identify the risk of change in the benefits – both positive and negative.	• For monetary assets, the main risk is the timing of cash flows. Risk that the cash flow will not occur (credit risk) is usually less relevant. • For non-monetary assets, in addition to the timing risk, there is the risk that the asset's value will change and affect the amount of any subsequent cash flow. Risks associated

	with asset performance, and obsolescence, are more difficult to measure and are of secondary importance.
4. Identify the entity that holds the asset before the transaction occurs.	• The entity having an asset will be the 'equity participant', i.e., the party exposed to the principal risks of change to the benefits that comprise an asset. • In determining whether an entity has an asset, it is often helpful to approach from the other direction, i.e., whether the entity has a matching liability to make payments as a result of the acquisition of the asset. Since the main risk of change to a liability is the timing of payment, the existence of a time-related interest charge (or an equivalent charge called by another name) is evidence that a liability exists and thus a matching asset exists.
5. Determine whether, as a result of the transaction, the party holding the asset has changed.	• For a transfer of an asset to have occurred, there must be a transfer of risks associated with the asset. The position after the transaction must thus be assessed using the pretransaction position as a reference point. For example, an entity that ends up holding 50 per cent of an asset's risks may have too few to justify that an acquisition has occurred (if it started at nil); conversely, it may have too many to justify that a disposal has occurred (if it started at 100 per cent). • The emphasis on whether a transfer of risks has occurred is especially relevant where risks are divided between two or more parties, such that there is no single party having all the risks either before or after the transaction.

28.25   The definition of an asset also requires that access to future economic benefits is controlled by the entity. Control is the means by which an entity ensures that the benefits accrue to itself and not to others. It thus involves ability to define and alter the mechanism by which the allocation of benefits is made. In short, it is the ability to determine what happens to the asset and when.

28.26   Control can be distinguished from management. While control necessarily involves the ability to obtain economic benefits (and restrict the access of others), management may involve the directing of the use of an asset without deriving any direct benefit. While control and management usually lie with the same party, this need not be so. Perhaps the most common example is that of an investment manager who provides expertise in the buying and selling of assets in a portfolio in return for a fee. Control of the portfolio within the meaning of FRS 5, however, lies with those to whom the benefits flow, i.e., the investors in the fund, who will have the right to direct where their benefits shall flow. The only circumstance where an investment manager may be considered to control a portfolio is where the manager is also a significant investor in the fund.

28.27 Once it is determined that an asset or liability exists, the second stage of recognition involves application of two recognition tests: [FRS 5(20)]

> 'Where a transaction results in an item that meets the definition of an asset or liability, that item should be recognised in the balance sheet if –
>
> (a) there is sufficient evidence of the existence of the item (including, where appropriate, evidence that a future inflow or outflow of benefit will occur), and
>
> (b) the item can be measured at a monetary amount with sufficient reliability.'

28.28 In essence, these criteria are the same as those in chapter 5 of the ASB's Statement of Principles 'Recognition in financial statements'. In summary, the conditions require:

(a) the asset and/or liability recognised constitutes an 'element' (see **28.29** below);

(b) there is evidence of occurrence (see **28.30** below); and

(c) there is reliability of measurement (see **28.31** below).

Constitutes an 'element'

28.29 Although the terms 'asset' and 'liability' are defined in FRS 5, the definitions are the same as those in chapter 4 of the Statement of Principles 'The elements of financial statements'. This chapter deals in greater detail with the meaning of terms used in the definitions, such as 'rights or other access', 'future economic benefits', 'controlled by the entity', 'obligations', etc. In cases of doubt, reference should be made to the Statement of Principles.

Evidence of occurrence

28.30 Past events, which trigger recognition, by their nature provide different degrees of persuasiveness that a change has occurred. The following points are relevant:

(a) the event that triggers recognition must have occurred prior to the balance sheet date, e.g., a transaction has occurred with an external party, performance or part performance has been achieved under a contract, changes in the market price of the asset occurring after the balance sheet date accrue (gain) or are borne (loss) by the 'acquiring' entity, etc.;

(b) while arm's-length transactions provide conclusive evidence of change, a non-arm's-length transaction may require additional disclosure or a modified form of recognition so that its substance is faithfully reflected;

(c) a decision to enter into a transaction or contract does not, of itself, provide sufficient evidence to justify recognition.

Reliability of measurement

28.31   Reliability of measurement is dependent on the amount of evidence available about two factors: the timing of conversion to monetary amounts and the size of the amounts. The following points are relevant:

(a) an item that generates a cash flow in the future may need to be discounted to arrive at its value at the balance sheet date;

(b) possible variations in future outcome may result in materially different future potential cash flows. Where such uncertainty exists, the single number used for incorporation in the financial statements should represent the minimum level of benefits expected to flow.

28.32   FRS 5(65) states that 'less reliability of measurement is acceptable' when recognising liabilities than recognising assets and 'it follows that, particularly for liabilities, where a reasonable estimate of the amount of an item is available, the item should be recognised'.

Derecognition

28.33   The stages of analysis described in **28.23** to **28.26** above for recognition of an asset are also relevant as the first stage when considering whether a transaction has resulted in an entity ceasing to have an asset or liability.

28.34   As with recognition, the conditions for derecognition are also based on chapter 5 of the ASB's Statement of Principles. In summary, derecognition occurs when an asset or liability is eliminated, for example, an asset is sold or a loan is repaid. In some cases, certain rights in assets and liabilities are eliminated whilst others remain intact. In such cases, an asset may need to be partially derecognised, or a different asset recognised. The hurdles set out in FRS 5 that have to be passed before an asset is fully derecognised are tougher than the tests that have to be met for initial recognition.

28.35   A derecognition commonly involves the receipt of proceeds. Identifying what the proceeds represent is an important step in the analysis, for example, a receipt of cash might represent the proceeds of sale of an asset or it might represent the receipt of a loan secured on the asset. The outcome is potentially more complex than for recognition. FRS 5 deals with three separate possible outcomes:

(a) no derecognition: the transaction has not resulted in any change;

(b) total derecognition: the transaction provides an effective disposal;

(c) partial derecognition: an asset is replaced by a different asset.

No derecognition

28.36 FRS 5 requires that:
[FRS 5(21)]

> 'Where a transaction involving a previously recognised asset results in no significant change in–
>
> (a) the entity's rights or other access to benefits relating to that asset, or
>
> (b) its exposure to the risks inherent in those benefits,
>
> the entire asset should continue to be recognised. In particular this will be the case for any transaction that is in substance a financing of a previously recognised asset, unless the conditions for a linked presentation ... are met, in which case such a presentation should be used.'

Example 28.36

On 31 December 1999 X plc sells debtors totalling £10,000 to Y Ltd. X plc receives £8,000 for the sale. As proceeds are received from the debtors, X immediately transfers them into Y's bank account. On 31 March 2000 Y reassigns all outstanding debtors to X and X pays to Y an amount calculated as (i) £8,000 less amounts received from debtors, plus (ii) a charge being base rate plus 1% applied to the £8,000 as reduced by receipts from debtors. At 31 December 1999, X will include the debtors on its balance sheet as assets and the £8,000 as a loan.

28.37 'Significant' has to be judged in relation to the risks and benefits that are likely to occur in practice rather than in relation to the total possible risks and benefits.

28.38 Consider example **28.36** further with the following revised arrangements taking place on 31 March 2000 instead of those described above. The outstanding debtors are not reassigned to X. The payment that X makes to Y comprises (i) a charge being (as before) base rate plus 1% applied to the £8,000 as reduced by receipts from debtors together with (ii) an amount, capped at £1,000, equal to bad debts. It might be thought that X has transferred significant risk because after three months the

> maximum bad debts it can suffer is limited to 10% of the orig-
> inal debtor balance. However, if on 31 December 1999, bad
> debts were expected to be £500 then X has retained significant
> risks and thus derecognition of the debtors is not appropriate.

Total derecognition

28.39   FRS 5 requires that:
[FRS 5(22)]

> 'Where a transaction involving a previously recognised asset trans-
> fers to others–
>
> (a)   all significant rights or other access to benefits relating to that
>   asset, and
>
> (b)   all significant exposure to the risks inherent in those benefits,
>
> the entire asset should cease to be recognised.'

> In example **28.36** above consider varying the circumstances so
> that, on 31 December 1999, X plc sells debtors totalling £10,000
> to Y Ltd. X plc receives £9,000 for the sale. As proceeds are
> received from debtors X immediately transfers them into Y's
> bank account. There are no further cash flows or transactions
> in respect of the debtors. Under this scenario, X plc can treat
> the £9,000 receipt as proceeds arising on the sale of debtors.

28.40   Total derecognition thus depends on the effective removal of both
control and exposure of risk of change in benefits. Removal of control alone with continued exposure to some risks prevents total derecognition, although partial derecognition (see **28.43** below) may still
be appropriate.

28.41   In addition to the removal of an asset, it is further necessary for derecognition to demonstrate that any funds received in respect of the
asset do not constitute either a liability (requiring continued gross
presentation) or a form of non-recourse finance that meets the conditions for linked presentation but which does not qualify for
removal from the balance sheet (see **28.45** below).

28.42   As above, 'significant' has to be judged in relation to the risks and
benefits that are likely to occur in practice rather than in relation to
the total possible risks and benefits.

Partial derecognition

28.43   FRS 5 recognises three 'special cases' where total derecognition is not
justified, but the description, classification and amount of an asset
may require change, or a liability may need to be recognised, as a
result of a transaction. The three circumstances are:

(a) a transfer of a measurable part of an asset: a simple example would be the disposal of a fixed proportion of both capital and interest of a loan such that future cash flows, profits and losses are shared. The principle also applies if two benefit streams, each with its own risks, can be separated. For example, the disposal of rights to capital payment of a loan, but retention of interest coupons;

(b) a transfer for part of an asset's life: where an asset is genuinely sold, but with an agreement to repurchase in a substantially depreciated form, the vendor no longer has the original asset but has a residual interest in the asset. It is a requirement that the repurchase can only be of a substantially depreciated form of the asset. This is unlikely to occur with an asset such as property, which would be accounted for as a sale and repurchase (see **28.81** below), but would be appropriate for an asset such as a motor car. For example, a car is sold, but the dealer agrees to repurchase at a fixed price after three years. A sale is recorded, but an asset (stock) and a liability equal to the present value of the obligation to repurchase is retained on the balance sheet.

Extract 28.43.1

Perry Group plc

Year ended 31 December 1998

14. Stocks

	Group	
	1998	1997
	£'000	£'000
Goods for resale	30,014	27,600
Vehicles subject to repurchase agreements	16,820	15,658
Interest bearing consignment vehicles	2,498	4,801
	49,332	48,059

Strictly, FRS 5 requires the original cost of the asset to be apportioned between that sold and that retained. [FRS 5(74)] In practice, a reasonable approximation may be found by assuming that the cost of the residual asset is equal to the repurchase liability.

> **Extract 28.43.2**
>
> **Perry Group plc**
>
> **Year ended 31 December 1998**
>
> Accounting policies (extract)
>
> **Stocks**
>
> Vehicle stocks have been valued at the lower of cost and net realisable value. Parts stocks are valued at cost which is arrived at principally on a weighted average or a 'first in, first out' basis. Provisions are made against obsolete and surplus stock. Vehicles on consignment from manufacturers that are the subject of interest or other charges are included at cost. Vehicles which are the subject of repurchase agreements are included at the agreed repurchase price. In both cases the associated liability is recorded in creditors.

(c) control of an asset is transferred, but some risk is retained. For example, an investment in a subsidiary is sold, but the consideration includes an earn-out arrangement related to future profits of the former subsidiary. The investment is derecognised (providing the earn-out arrangement does not entitle the vendor to too large a proportion of the subsidiary's future profits), but a new asset (debtor) is recorded equal to a prudent best estimate of the amount receivable. A second example would be the sale of equipment subject to a warranty of its condition at the time of sale or a guarantee of its residual value; the vendor would cease to show the equipment as an asset, but would recognise a liability for the expected cost of meeting the warranty or guarantee. Any profit taken is restricted by the same amount.

28.44 Item (c) in **28.43** above deals with warranties in respect of non-monetary assets. Warranties in respect of monetary assets require separate consideration. In general, the sale of an asset where the seller provides a warranty does not prevent a sale being recorded, provided that the warranty relates only to the condition of the asset at the time of sale, e.g., that individual monetary assets within a large portfolio each meet set conditions; consequently, the seller will only be required to make provision for the expected cost of meeting warranty claims. Conversely, a warranty that relates to events occurring after sale (e.g., the failure of a debtor to make a due payment) indicates that a key risk has not passed to the purchaser and no derecognition is justified.

Linked presentation

28.45   Linked presentation is relevant where non-recourse finance has been received, which is repayable only out of the proceeds of the asset(s) financed. The commercial effect for the reporting entity must be that it is committed to the disposal of the asset, but that the sale process is not yet complete. Receipt of non-recourse finance is thus the first stage of a two-stage disposal of the asset. The seller may receive further profit from the second stage of disposal, but is not required to return proceeds received. Linked presentation is not appropriate for any asset which remains in use by the seller or which the seller can reacquire. Where detailed conditions are met, the finance is shown deducted from the gross amount of the asset on the face of the balance sheet. Legally, the seller's asset is the net amount. The argument in favour of this treatment is that:

(a)   since a major proportion of the benefits generated by the asset will be used to service the suppliers of finance, the reporting entity no longer has access to all the future benefits generated by the asset;

(b)   the reporting entity does not have a liability for the full amount of the finance, since repayment is limited to benefits generated by the asset being financed;

(c)   nevertheless, the reporting entity does retain significant risk of variation in the benefits that make up the asset, e.g., residual profits which are expected to remain after finance is repaid, and which accrue to the reporting entity, are generally sufficient to absorb all likely downside variation in benefits and will be increased by any upside variation.

28.46   Linked presentation therefore provides a presentation that shows the net asset on the balance sheet, supported by disclosure on the face of the balance sheet of the asset on a gross basis, less non-recourse finance received. It will never be acceptable to relegate the disclosure of gross asset and matching finance to a note to the balance sheet.

28.47   The conditions for linked presentation are contained in two separate paragraphs of FRS 5:

•   two summary conditions [FRS 5(26)]; and

•   six detailed conditions [FRS 5(27)].

The two paragraphs are related as follows.

Summary conditions (FRS 5 paragraph 26)	Detailed conditions (FRS 5 paragraph 27)
(a) 'the finance will be repaid only from proceeds generated by the specific item it finances (or by transfer of the item itself) and there is no possibility whatsoever of a claim on the entity being established other than against funds generated by that item (or the item itself)'	(a) 'the finance relates to a specific item (or portfolio of similar items) and, in the case of a loan, is secured on that item but not on any other asset of the entity' (b) 'the provider of the finance has no recourse whatsoever, either explicit or implicit, to the other assets of the entity for losses and the entity has no obligation whatsoever to repay the provider of finance' (c) 'the directors of the entity state explicitly in each set of financial statements where a linked presentation is used that the entity is not obliged to support any losses, nor does it intend to do so' (d) 'the provider of the finance has agreed in writing (in the finance documentation or otherwise) that it will seek repayment of the finance, as to both principal and interest, only to the extent that sufficient funds are generated by the specific item it has financed and that it will not seek recourse in any other form, and such agreement is noted in each set of financial statements where a linked presentation is used' (e) 'if the funds generated by the item are insufficient to pay off the provider of the finance, this does not constitute an event of default for the entity'
(b) 'there is no provision whatsoever whereby the entity may either keep the item on repayment of the finance or reacquire it at any time'	(f) 'there is no provision whatsoever, either in the financing arrangement or otherwise, whereby the entity has a right or an obligation either to keep the item upon repayment of the finance or (where title to the item has been transferred) to re-acquire it at any time. Accordingly: (i) where the item is one (such as a monetary receivable) that directly generates cash, the provider of the finance will be repaid out of the resulting cash receipts (to the extent these are sufficient); or (ii) where the item is one (such as a physical asset) that does not directly generate cash, there is a definite point at which either the item will be sold to a third party and the provider of the finance repaid from the proceeds (to the extent these are sufficient) or the item will be transferred to the provider of the finance in full and final settlement'.

28.48   Further guidance on the use of linked presentation is given in FRS 5. [FRS 5(28), (76)–(88) and (91)] The following general points can be made.

(a)   In the balance sheet, the gross amount for the asset should be shown with linked finance deducted on the face of the balance sheet within a single asset caption. It is not sufficient to show the asset and finance by way of note. [FRS 5(26)]

(b)   In the profit and loss account, a true and fair view will normally be provided if the profit and loss account discloses only the net amount of income or expense for each period, with disclosure of the gross components by way of note. Where, in view of the amounts involved, a true and fair view is not provided by this form of disclosure, then a gross presentation should be adopted on the face of the profit and loss account. [FRS 5(28) and (88)]

(c)   Initial profit may be recognised under linked presentation, but only to the extent that non-returnable proceeds received exceed the previous carrying value of the item. [FRS 5(28) and (87)] In subsequent periods, income and expense related to the performance of the gross asset should be recognised as it arises.

> Where the asset is a fixed asset, the profit and loss account normally includes only the net gain or loss on 'disposal'. Where the asset is a current asset, such as a development property, the approach used in SSAP 9 for the recognition of profit on long-term contracts (see chapter 16) will be relevant; on this basis, the profit and loss account should reflect appropriate amounts of turnover and cost of sales and the resulting gross asset be disclosed within debtors (rather than stocks).

(d)   Linked presentation can only be used for single assets or portfolios of similar assets. For this purpose, a portfolio must consist of assets falling within a single balance sheet caption. It cannot be used where finance relates to any kind of business unit or for items that generate the funds required to repay finance only by being used in conjunction with other assets of the entity. [FRS 5(82)] This means that linked presentation may not be used for any assets that continue to be used within the seller's operations, e.g., retail sites, hotels, ships, and aircraft.

(e)   Where linked presentation is to be used for a non-monetary asset, the conditions require that a date is set at which either the asset is sold or the asset is transferred to the provider of non-recourse finance in final settlement. [FRS 5 (27)(f)(ii)]

(f)   Recourse includes all of the following:
[FRS 5(83)]

    (i)   agreement to repurchase non-performing items;

    (ii)   substitution of good items for bad;

    (iii) a guarantee of performance, proceeds or other support (unless qualifying as a warranty of condition at the point of transfer – see **28.44** above);

    (iv) a put option forcing a return transfer;

    (v)   a swap of some or all of the amounts generated by the item for a separately determined payment;

    (vi) a penalty on a related ongoing agreement that effectively passes the cost of bad items back to the selling entity.

It is however possible to apply a partial linked presentation where part of the finance received is non-recourse. [FRS 5(84)] (See the example in **28.87** below.)

(g)   Provision for repurchase includes all of the following: [FRS 5(86)]

    (i)   a put or call option held by either party to effect re-purchase of the asset or the entity that holds title to the asset;

    (ii)   an understanding between the parties that repurchase will occur.

Where the asset is held in a quasi-subsidiary, the presumption of control over the quasi-subsidiary includes the ability to require return of the asset, unless the terms of the arrangement clearly provide otherwise.

(h)   Use of the linked presentation does not constitute an application of the offset rules to two gross items. Where the conditions of FRS 5 are met, the entity's legal asset is a single net asset, being the net amount after non-recourse finance is deducted, but the realisation of the asset depends upon the performance of the gross components. [FRS 5(26) and (27)] Disclosure of the gross amounts making up the net asset represents provision of additional information about the asset necessary in order to give a true and fair view.

28.49

Three situations which may meet the conditions for linked presentation are:

(a)   securitisation of a closed portfolio of monetary assets having a limited life, such as mortgages (see discussion of Application note D in **28.88** below). Where a securitisation (e.g., of credit card receivables) allows new assets to be added to the securitisation pool, and the repayment of those new assets contributes towards the repayment of the original finance, then the conditions in FRS 5 will not be met. [FRS 5(26)(a) and (27)(d)];

> (b) factoring of debts involving non-recourse finance (see discussion of Application note C in **28.86** and the example in **28.87** below);
>
> (c) receipt of non-recourse finance in respect of the disposal of an asset, such as a development property, where a final purchaser has not yet been identified. To achieve linked presentation, the property should have been legally transferred, such that the seller may receive further profits on the onward future sale of the property, but is not required to return proceeds already received. Also, the seller may neither continue to use the property within its operations nor reacquire the property.

28.50 In situations (a) and (c) in **28.49** above, the asset financed is usually transferred to a non-subsidiary special purpose company, which will be required to include the gross asset and gross liability on its own balance sheet; however, in the accounts of the selling entity (both company and consolidated), the conditions for linked presentation are met (indeed, total derecognition may be possible in the seller's own company financial statements). If the company holding the asset was a legal subsidiary and was unable to use linked presentation in its own accounts, then FRS 2 *Accounting for subsidiary undertakings* would require that all the subsidiary's assets and liabilities be fully consolidated, thus defeating the ability to use a linked presentation in the selling company's consolidated accounts (see also FRS 5 paragraph 102).

28.51 The following example illustrates linked presentation.

Extract 28.51

The Great Universal Stores plc
Year ended 31 March 1999

Group balance sheet (extract)

	Notes	1999 £m	1999 £m	1998 (restated) note 1) £m	1998 £m
CURRENT ASSETS					
Stocks	18		501.7		313.7
Debtors – due within one year	19		1,714.3		1,749.0
– due in more than one year	19		537.5		730.8
Securitised receivables	20	413.9		–	
Less: non-recourse borrowings		(400.0)		–	
			13.9		–
Investments at cost	21		32.7		29.2
Bank balances and cash			253.6		852.5
			3,053.7		3,675.2

Creditors	– amounts falling due			
	within one year	22	(2,654.9)	(1,188.0)
	– amount due on			
	acquisition of Metromail		–	(511.4)
Net current assets			398.8	1,975.8

20. SECURITISED RECEIVABLES

On 25 March 1999 General Guarantee Finance Limited ('GGF'), the major trading subsidiary within the Finance Division, sold £421m of hire purchase receivables to Automobile Loan Finance (No 1) Limited ('ALF1'). That company issued debt to finance the purchase of the hire purchase receivables, the written terms of which provide no recourse to GGF. Neither GGF nor any other member of the Group is obliged, or intends, to support any losses in respect of the securitised receivables. GGF may offer further hire purchase receivables for purchase by ALF1.

Receipts of interest and principal from GGF's customers in respect of the securitised receivables are used to repay ALF1's obligations on its issued debt and to pay its administrative expenses. Any excess income is payable to GGF and this amounted to £0.6m in the current year. ALF1 is a quasi-subsidiary of the Group. The key elements of its balance sheet at 31 March 1999, which form the basis of the linked presentation in the consolidated balance sheet, are:

	£m
Securitised receivables:	
Due within one year	189.6
Due in more than one year	224.3
	413.9
Non-recourse borrowings:	
Due in more than one year	400.0

ALF1 also has £21m of subordinated debt which is eliminated in the Group accounts. ALF1's gross financial income and expenses and cash inflows from operating activities were not material in the current year.

Offset

28.52   Offsetting is the process of aggregating debit and credit balances and including only the net amount in the balance sheet. The general principle of FRS 5 is that: 'Assets and liabilities should not be offset. Debit and credit balances should be aggregated into a single net item where, and only where, they do not constitute separate assets and liabilities'. [FRS 5(29)] This condition is further amplified in, and offset made conditional on meeting, three specific conditions, which are discussed in **28.53** to **28.59** below.

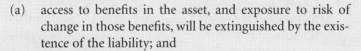

In summary, the conditions are intended to ensure that:

(a) access to benefits in the asset, and exposure to risk of change in those benefits, will be extinguished by the existence of the liability; and

(b) exposure to the obligation in the liability, and risk of change in that obligation, will be extinguished by the existence of the asset.

Condition 1

28.53 *Condition 1*: 'The reporting entity and another party owe each other determinable monetary amounts, denominated either in the same currency, or in different but freely convertible currencies. For this purpose a freely convertible currency is one for which quoted exchange rates are available in an active market that can rapidly absorb the amount to be offset without significantly affecting the exchange rate'. [FRS 5(29)(a)]

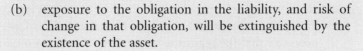

This condition would allow the offset of balances carrying different rates of interest, but balances due to and from different parties can never be offset.

Condition 2

28.54 *Condition 2*: 'The reporting entity has the ability to insist on a net settlement. In determining this, any right to insist on a net settlement that is contingent should be taken into account only if the reporting entity is able to enforce net settlement in all situations of default by the other party'. [FRS 5(29)(b)]

28.55 A common example where this condition is relevant occurs where a bank, which would be the reporting entity in this instance, holds a right to enforce a net settlement of a specified deposit and loan which is contingent on the customer being in breach of certain covenants, or where debit and credit balances with different companies in a group may be offset in the event of default.

28.56 Ultimately, whether there exists an ability for the reporting entity to 'enforce net settlement in all situations of default by the other party' is a legal issue. As a minimum, it should be possible to verify that net settlement would survive the insolvency of the counter-party. (See **28.57** below.)

Condition 3

28.57 *Condition 3*: 'The reporting entity's ability to insist on a net settlement is assured beyond reasonable doubt. It is essential that there is no possibility that the entity could be required to transfer economic benefits to another party whilst being unable to enforce its own access to economic benefits. For this to be the case it is necessary that the debit balance matures no later than the credit balance. It is also necessary that the reporting entity's ability to insist on a net settlement would survive the insolvency of the other party'. [FRS 5(29)(c)] Where either the reporting entity or the other party is a group, it is important that insistence on a net settlement can be achieved and would survive the insolvency of any of the separate legal entities that constitute the other party. [FRS 5(90)]

28.58 The explanatory paragraphs of the FRS regard this condition as met, provided, at its own discretion, the reporting entity can ensure that the debit balance matures no later than the credit balance. This can be achieved by the reporting entity having the ability to accelerate the maturity of the debit balance or deferring the maturity of the credit balance.

28.59 A common application that arises regarding offset is whether a positive balance at a bank by one subsidiary can be offset in the consolidated accounts with a negative balance at the same bank by another subsidiary. The above criteria will require that the group has the right to settle obligations to the bank on a net basis.

Hedging

28.60   FRS 5 does not deal with hedging, since the issues involved are potentially very wide ranging. However, in many cases, the ability to account realistically for a hedge transaction will depend on two or more items being presented together within financial statements. For example, a company may have a sterling loan, together with a sterling/dollar swap contract that has been acquired as an effective hedge to switch exposure from sterling into dollar currency movements; arguably, the most appropriate presentation of these items will be as a single balance sheet liability denominated in dollars and a single interest charge also denominated in dollars. FRS 13 calls for a number of disclosures (see chapter 21) including: interest rate risk disclosure (the disclosure is after taking account of the swap; currency risk disclosures (the disclosure is after taking account of the swap); and fair value disclosures (the fair value of the loan and the swap have to be disclosed separately). An FRS is being developed to prescribe the accounting treatment of the loan and swap (see chapter 21).

Quasi-subsidiaries

28.61 Prior to the Companies Act 1989, in which the current definition of subsidiary undertaking was introduced, it was common practice for groups to avoid consolidation of certain assets and liabilities by placing them in 'controlled non-subsidiaries'. While the 1989 change in law resulted in many of these structures falling within the scope of legal subsidiary undertakings, there remained some scope for companies to place assets and liabilities in another entity (or 'vehicle') that did not meet the legal definition of a subsidiary undertaking, but where the commercial effect of the transactions between company and vehicle were no different from that which would have resulted had the vehicle been a subsidiary. FRS 5 introduced a definition of 'quasi-subsidiary', and rules on how to account for them, in order to bring these remaining entities into the consolidated accounts.

28.62 The definitions of 'quasi-subsidiary' and 'control of another entity' are set out below.

  (a) *quasi-subsidiary*: 'A quasi-subsidiary of a reporting entity is a company, trust, partnership or other vehicle that, though not fulfilling the definition of a subsidiary, is directly or indirectly controlled by the reporting entity and gives rise to benefits for that entity that are in substance no different from those that would arise were the vehicle a subsidiary' [FRS 5(7)];

  (b) *control of another entity*: 'The ability to direct the financial and operating policies of that entity with a view to gaining economic benefit from its activities' [FRS 5(8)].

28.63 Further guidance on the identification of a quasi-subsidiary is given in FRS 5. [FRS 5(32)–(34) and (95)–(98)] In summary, the following is evidence that a vehicle is a quasi-subsidiary of a company, since control as defined above exists:

  (a) while the company is not entitled to all the gross benefits in the vehicle (e.g., due to the claims of creditors on the assets of the vehicle), it fulfils the role of equity participant because it bears the risk of change in benefits in the vehicle;

  (b) the legal owners, although they may have the ability to make certain decisions, do not derive any benefit from those decisions;

  (c) all significant decisions and transactions are dealt with according to a predetermined agreement (contractual or otherwise) to which the company was a party. In this situation, the party possessing control will be the one that gains the benefits arising from the net assets of the entity.

28.64   The following will not normally be a quasi-subsidiary:

(a)   a pension fund, since although there may be significant representation of the company management on the fund's board of trustees, the impact of decisions made by the trustees accrues mainly to the pension scheme members and not to the company;

(b)   a vehicle where the company has a 'participating interest', but it has been satisfactorily judged that the company does not 'actually exercise a dominant influence over it'. [s260]

The amendment of company law in the Companies Act 1989, specifically the definition of subsidiary undertaking, and the subsequent issue by the ASB of interpretative guidance, resulted in many 'controlled non-subsidiary' structures being brought on balance sheet, since they qualified as legal subsidiary undertakings. In particular, the element of the subsidiary undertaking definition that is based on the existence of a participating interest, together with the actual exercise of a dominant influence, has been effective in dealing with the many cases where one entity holds a significant minority shareholding in another entity. In view of this, and the common definition of 'control of another entity' (see **28.62** above) in both FRS 2 and FRS 5, it is unlikely that a minority shareholding which is judged not to be a subsidiary undertaking under FRS 2 would fall within the definition of quasi-subsidiary in FRS 5.

28.65   There are two possible methods of accounting for a quasi-subsidiary:

(a)   the normal method is to treat the quasi-subsidiary as if it were a legal subsidiary. [FRS 5(35), (36) and (99) – 817(101)] This requires:

(i)   full consolidation in consolidated accounts of assets, liabilities, profits, losses and cash flows;

(ii)   application of the accounting principles set out in the Act and FRS 2, e.g., elimination of unrealised profits, and use of consistent accounting policies. FRS 5 notes that exclusion from consolidation will only be permissible on two grounds: immateriality (thus falling outside the scope of the FRS) and where the interest in the quasi-subsidiary is held with a view to subsequent resale. The existence of severe long-term restrictions which impair control is likely to exclude a company from falling within the definition of a quasi-subsidiary. Different activities do not justify exclusion from consolidation (see chapter 23);

      (iii)   where the 'parent' has no legal subsidiaries and therefore does not prepare group accounts, it is nevertheless required to prepare 'consolidated' accounts dealing with the quasi-subsidiary, presented with equal prominence to the parent's individual accounts;

(b)   FRS 5 also deals with the inclusion of a quasi-subsidiary in an originator's consolidated accounts on a linked presentation basis where the quasi-subsidiary holds a single asset, or a single portfolio of similar assets, such that the linked presentation conditions are met from the perspective of the group irrespective of whether the quasi-subsidiary uses a gross or linked presentation in its own accounts [FRS 5(37) and (102)].

> By inference, where assets are held in a legal subsidiary, rather than a quasi-subsidiary, linked presentation will not be possible in the parent's consolidated accounts. By definition, the legal subsidiary is controlled by the legal parent. Thus, unless a valid reason for exclusion from consolidation exists, the parent is required by the Act and FRS 2 to consolidate the subsidiary's accounts, thus use of a linked presentation in the parent's group accounts is only possible where the subsidiary has used a linked presentation in its own accounts. In practice, the subsidiary holding the asset is unlikely to be entitled to use a linked presentation (see **28.50** above).

28.66   It was noted above in the discussion on linked presentation (see **28.48**(b) above), that where linked presentation is used in a balance sheet, FRS 5 allows some flexibility as to whether the profit and loss account shows information on a gross or net basis (with gross information by way of note). Use of a net basis on the face of the profit and loss account is acceptable, provided that it does not prevent a true and fair view being given.

Disclosure

28.67   The general rule of FRS 5 is that financial statements should be sufficiently detailed in respect of a transaction to enable the user to understand its commercial effect irrespective of whether an asset or liability has been recognised. [FRS 5(30) and (31)] Additional disclosure to that normally achieved by the classification and note disclosure required by the Act and other accounting standards may be needed in two cases:

(a)   where the reporting entity is a party to a transaction which does not give rise to any assets or liabilities being recorded on its balance sheet; or

(b)   where a complex transaction results in assets and liabilities that differ in nature from those normally included in the statutory balance sheet captions, e.g., an asset may not be available as security for the general liabilities of the entity or certain liabilities may only be repayable to the extent of an asset on which they are secured.

28.68 For a quasi-subsidiary, FRS 5 requires:
[FRS 5(38) and (103)]

  (a) disclosure of the fact that a quasi-subsidiary is included;

  (b) a clear distinction between information in respect of the statutory group and a quasi-subsidiary; and

  (c) a summary of the quasi-subsidiary's financial statements to be given in the notes to the consolidated accounts. This should show each major balance sheet, profit and loss account, STRGL and cash flow heading for which there is a material item, together with comparative figures. Where the reporting entity has more than one quasi-subsidiary of a similar nature, the information may be combined if it would otherwise be unduly voluminous.

28.69 Although, at first sight, the disclosure in respect of a quasi-subsidiary appears burdensome, the fact that many quasi-subsidiaries are created to hold a single asset, or portfolio of similar assets, which is funded through the issue of a single class of loans, results in a simple statement showing two items: the asset of the quasi-subsidiary and the matching loan.

28.70 Where a linked presentation is used for a portfolio of assets held within a quasi-subsidiary, e.g., mortgage assets, it is likely that the mortgage assets will be continually generating cash receipts, but that this cash will only be used to repay borrowings periodically. Consequently, at any balance sheet date, the quasi-subsidiary may hold two classes of assets: mortgage assets and cash. Similarly, in addition to the capital value of loans, it may have accrued interest payable but not yet paid. The question then arises whether these assets and liabilities should be disclosed under separate captions in the originator's balance sheet. FRS 5 does not make reference to this situation, since it is assumed that the amount of cash and/or interest payable will be immaterial. Where the amounts are, in fact, material, the most suitable presentation, consistent with the principles of linked presentation, will be to disclose total assets and total liabilities of the quasi-subsidiary together on the face of the originator's balance sheet, with disclosure of the elements by way of note.

Example 28.70

Balance sheet presentation may be as follows:

	£'000	£'000
Securitised debtors receivable	258	
Less: non-recourse borrowings	(196)	
		62

with note disclosure analysing the securitised debtors receivable as, say:

	£'000
Securitised debtors receivable	186
Cash received from debtors	72
	258

and analysing the non-recourse borrowings as, say:

	£'000
Capital value of borrowings	154
Interest payable on the borrowings	42
	196

Alternatively, the presentation on the face of the balance sheet might have been as follows:

	£'000	£'000	£'000
Securitised debtors receivable		186	
Cash received from debtors		72	
		258	
Less: non-recourse borrowings:			
Capital	154		
Interest	42		
		196	
			62

28.71   For linked presentation, FRS 5 requires, in addition to the disclosure on the face of the balance sheet of the asset on a gross basis, less non-recourse finance received, disclosure of:

(a)   the fact that the entity is not obliged to support any losses and nor does it intend to do so; [FRS 5(27)] and

(b)   in the notes to the accounts, the gross components of the net profit (recognised in the profit and loss account). [FRS 5(28)]

28.72 In addition to the general disclosure requirements described above, which come from the main body of FRS 5, the application notes to FRS 5, under the heading 'required accounting' stipulate the disclosures required in each of the applications illustrated. Thus, for example, application note C explains that where a debt factoring meets neither the derecognition nor linked presentation criteria, and so both an asset (debtors) and liability (proceeds received from the factor) are presented on the balance sheet, the notes should nevertheless disclose the amount of factored debts outstanding at the balance sheet date.

Application to specific examples

Application notes

28.73 FRS 5 includes specific guidance on six areas within 'Application notes'. These cover consignment stock, sale and repurchase agreements, factoring of debts, securitised assets, loan transfers and PFI. The paragraphs below consider these application notes. In addition, guidance is included on employee share ownership trusts (see **28.103** below) and undisclosed agencies (see **28.117** below).

28.74 Each Application note is structured in three sections, as follows.

(a) *Features*: identifies the key features normally found within transactions that are relevant to the accounting analysis.

(b) *Analysis*: considers each of the features in turn to identify benefits, and risk of change in benefits, and thus provide a basis for classifying the transaction as requiring recognition, derecognition or linked presentation.

(c) *Required accounting*: sets out the required accounting treatment that follows from the above classification.

28.75 Each Application note concludes with a summary table of indicators that will assist in classification. Reference should be made to the Application notes, which are not reproduced in this chapter.

Consignment stock

28.76 Consignment stock is considered in FRS 5 Application note A in the context of stock held on a sale or return basis by a motor dealer. FRS 5 is relevant in determining whether, prior to the transfer of legal title, the dealer is required to record stock as an asset on its balance sheet, together with an associated matching liability to pay for the stock.

28.77   The focus of Application note A is whether an asset (i.e., stock)
is controlled by a dealer. In most practical cases, arrangements
for allowing a dealer to have access to stock held by other dealers ensures that the dealer cannot exclude others from access to
stock, thus there is normally evidence that individual items of
stock are not controlled by a single dealer. However, research
indicates that the arrangement for financing consignment stock
will be highly relevant. For example, although a dealer may not
have paid a deposit equal to the value of consignment vehicles
directly to the manufacturer or distributor, he may be required
to pay interest (or an equivalent time-dependent charge equivalent to interest) to a provider of finance who has paid the
deposit on the dealer's behalf. Under FRS 5, the existence of an
interest charge demonstrates that the dealer bears the timing
risk of vehicle stocks. Since this risk is generally more significant
than the risk of a change in vehicle list prices, the dealer is
required to record a liability on balance sheet from the time that
the interest charge commences (which may be after an initial
interest-free period). Where a liability is brought on balance
sheet, it follows that a matching asset will also be recorded. This
asset represents the deposit paid to the manufacturer or distributor on the dealer's behalf, which gives the dealer rights to
access a certain number of vehicles from the pool of vehicles
held by all dealers, and will generally be recognised in stock.

Extract 28.77

Perry Group plc

Year ended 31 December 1998

Accounting policies (extract)

Stocks
Vehicle stocks have been valued at the lower of cost and net realisable
value. Parts stocks are valued at cost which is arrived at principally on
a weighted average or a 'first-in, first-out' basis. Provisions are made
against obsolete and surplus stock. Vehicles on consignment from
manufacturers that are the subject of interest or other charges are
included at cost. Vehicles which are the subject of repurchase agreements are included at the agreed repurchase price. In both cases the
associated liability is recorded in creditors.

14. Stocks

	Group	
	1998	1997
	£'000	£'000
Goods for resale	**30,014**	27,600
Vehicles subject to repurchase agreements	**16,820**	15,658
Interest-bearing consignment vehicles	**2,498**	4,801
	49,332	48,059

28.78   Relevant practical tests are summarised in the following table.

Tests	Indicates on balance sheet	Indicates off balance sheet
Test 1 – deposit paid by dealer.	A deposit paid by the dealer will already appear on the dealer's balance sheet. Consequently, FRS 5 will have no further impact.	
Test 2 – finance charge paid by dealer.	Dealer pays interest (by whatever name) on the value of consignment stock.	Consignment stock is provided on an interest-free basis.
Test 3 – dealer controls asset:		
• Transfers between dealers.	• Few transfers.	• Significant transfers.
• Adoption at the end of the consignment period.	• Significant number of actual adoptions.	• Adoption not normally enforced.
• Changes in list price during consignment period.	• Not passed to dealer.	• Passed to dealer.

> In practice, the different tests are likely to suggest different treatments in respect of the same transaction and a balance has to be struck. As explained above, the existence of a finance charge means that an asset and liability should be recognised on the dealer's balance sheet.

28.79   Neither linked presentation nor offset is likely to be available for consignment stock that is brought on balance sheet, because:

(a)   the FRS 5 conditions for linked presentation will not be met, since consignment terms allow for the vehicle to be retained by the dealer;

(b)   the FRS 5 conditions for offset will not be met, since, while the dealer has a theoretical legal right of set-off, this must be disregarded because it could only be achieved by returning all vehicles, effectively terminating the agreement.

28.80   Application note A does not consider the position of the manufacturer or distributor of vehicles. The key issue will be when the manufacturer or distributor should record a sale and thus derecognise stocks on its balance sheet. Prior to FRS 5, normal practice was to record a sale on a legal basis, i.e., only when the dealer either sold stock to a customer or otherwise adopted the vehicle. This treatment was also consistent with the treatment for tax purposes, whereby VAT is not payable on vehicles until legal sale occurs. Under a typical arrangement, there is some support within FRS 5 for three possible dates on which a sale could be recorded:

(a)   the date that stock is consigned to the dealer. Although stock is legally returnable, there is little evidence in practice that the right of return is ever used. Also, a deposit equal to the value of stock will usually have been received from the dealer or on the dealer's behalf. The effect is that the most significant expected risk of change in benefits, i.e., the timing risk, is passed to the dealer network at that date. Against this, there is generally a contractual limit to the number of vehicles that dealers can be required to take on consignment and a commercial limit to the number of vehicles that dealers will expect to sell in any period. Also, where a particular model proves difficult to sell by all dealers, there is evidence that a manufacturer or distributor will provide assistance through discounts to stimulate sales;

(b)   the date that interest starts to be paid by a dealer. Symmetry between the date that a dealer recognises an asset and liability and a manufacturer or distributor derecognises their asset is an elegant concept. However, as was noted above, the asset that the dealer brings on balance sheet is unlikely to be an exclusive right to control identifiable vehicles. Rather, it is the recognition that a deposit has been paid, giving the dealer right to access a certain number of vehicles from a pool of stock. Thus, although timing risk is borne by the dealer from this date, the dealer's asset is different to that of the manufacturer or distributor;

(c)   the date that the dealer adopts stock or sells it to a customer. This date is the most prudent of the three and carries with it the certainty that risk of change in benefits has been transferred to others.

In view of uncertainty under (a) and (b), it is suggested that (c) will usually be the most appropriate date for derecognition by a manufacturer or distributor.

Sale and repurchase transactions

28.81 Sale and repurchase agreements are considered in FRS 5 Application note B. This considers two types of transaction: the sale and potential repurchase of an existing asset and the future purchase of an asset that has been acquired on an entity's behalf by a third party. The note concludes with two illustrations to assist in classification.

28.82 There are three possible outcomes to a transaction under this Application note:

(a) the substance is that of a secured loan requiring gross presentation of the original asset and treatment of receipts as a finance liability;

(b) the substance is that of an outright sale allowing derecognition of the original asset and treatment of receipts as proceeds of sale; and

(c) there is no longer access to the original asset, but the seller has a new asset. An example would be the sale of a new motor vehicle, but with a commitment to repurchase the used vehicle at a fixed price in three years' time. FRS 5 paragraph 23 describes this situation (see **28.43** (b) above) and Application note B21 describes the accounting entries that follow.

28.83 It is likely that some sale and repurchase transactions will involve leases such that the transaction falls within the scope of both SSAP 21 and FRS 5. As noted in **28.12** above, the general rule is that the transaction should be dealt with according to whichever standard contains the more specific provisions.

Example 28.83

A company, which holds the freehold to a property, leases the property under a 125-year lease to an investment vehicle. The company provides an unconditional agreement to repurchase, after five years, either the lease or the company holding the lease for a fixed sum, which provides investors in the vehicle with a guaranteed return.

Although the granting of a 125-year lease is covered by SSAP 21, the inclusion of a repurchase provision (after such a small proportion of the lease's life and at a predetermined price), which is, in reality, likely to be exercised, falls under FRS 5. Since FRS 5 contains the more specific provisions, it should be applied. The result will be that the property and proceeds received will continue to be shown by the original company on a gross basis.

28.84 Linked presentation is unlikely ever to be possible for a sale and repurchase transaction, since any repurchase feature will breach the condition that 'there is no provision whatsoever whereby the entity may either keep the item on repayment of the finance or reacquire it at any time' (see **28.47** above). [FRS 5(26)(b)]

28.85 Offset is unlikely ever to be possible, since a sale and repurchase agreement typically relates to a physical asset such as property or stock, while the proceeds received is a monetary liability. Thus, the condition requiring that 'the reporting entity and another party owe each other determinable monetary amounts' will not be met (see **28.53** above). [FRS 5(29)(a)]

Factoring of debts

28.86 Factoring of debts, and the related practice of invoice discounting, is considered in FRS 5 Application note C. The note concludes with two illustrations to assist in classification.

28.87 In addition to derecognition and separate (gross) presentation, it may be possible to achieve a linked presentation where all (or part) of the funds received are non-recourse. Where only part of the funds received are non-recourse, linked presentation may be applied to that part only, leaving the balance of funds received to be disclosed within liabilities.

Example 28.87

An entity has debtors of £100,000 on which expected bad debts are £4,000. The entity receives finance of £90,000, of which £80,000 is non-recourse. Provided all the conditions for linked presentation are met, disclosure on the face of the balance sheet would be as follows:

	£'000
Current assets	
Debts subject to financing arrangements:	
Gross debts (less provision for bad debts)	96
Less: non-returnable amounts received	80
	16

In addition to the £80,000 non-recourse finance disclosed in this way, the remaining balance of finance received, £10,000, will appear as a liability within creditors.

Securitised assets

28.88 Securitised assets are considered in FRS 5 Application note D. The note applies to all kinds of securitised assets: household mortgages, other receivables such as credit accounts, hire purchase loans and trade debts, and non-monetary assets such as property and stock. The note identifies three separate issues for consideration:

(a) accounting in the originating entity's own accounts (both single and multi-originator programmes);

(b) accounting in the vehicle that holds the securitised assets (the 'issuer'); and

(c) accounting in the originating entity's group accounts.

28.89 The commercial form of most securitisations result in two accounting issues to be decided:

(a) whether accounting in the originating entity's own accounts should be on the basis of derecognition or linked presentation;

(b) whether accounting in the originator's group accounts should be on the basis of linked presentation or separate (gross) presentation.

28.90 Application note D8(b) deals with the provision of warranties by the originator. The sale of an asset where the seller provides a warranty does not prevent a sale being recorded, provided that the warranty relates only to the condition of the asset at the time of sale, e.g., individual monetary assets within a large portfolio each meet set conditions; consequently, the seller will only be required to make provision for the expected cost of meeting warranty claims. Conversely, a warranty that relates to events occurring after sale, e.g., the failure of a debtor to make a due payment, indicates that significant risk has remained with the seller, so that derecognition would not be appropriate.

28.91 It was noted in **28.49**(a) above that securitisation of an 'open' portfolio does not qualify for linked presentation. For example, where a securitisation of credit card receivables allows cash collections to be reinvested in new purchases by credit card customers, then repayment of an initial non-recourse funding liability will be made partially from the creation of new balances. This breaches the condition in FRS 5 that 'the provider of the finance has agreed in writing (in the finance documentation or otherwise) that it will seek repayment of the finance, as to both principal and interest, only to the extent that sufficient funds are generated by the specific item it has financed and that it will not seek recourse in any other form'. [FRS 5(27)(d) and Application note D12]

28.92 The existence of swap contracts and interest rate caps between the originator and the issuer gave rise to much debate during the final stages of the development of FRS 5. Where an issuer holds fixed rate mortgage assets, that are financed with high-quality variable rate debt, it will be necessary for the issuer to protect lenders from the risk of changes in interest rates. The fact that mortgages amortise over the repayment period means that market rate swap contracts are not currently available. Thus, the originator will be the only party willing to act as counter-party to such a contract.

28.93 Initially, it was held that such a swap contract would breach the condition that 'the provider of finance has no recourse whatsoever'. The notes explaining the development of the FRS, issued as appendix 3 to FRS 5, state that the ASB 'decided with reluctance and as a pragmatic and provisional response to the issue, to permit use of a linked presentation in the originator's accounts notwithstanding the presence of an interest rate swap between the originator and the issuer in a securitisation provided certain strict criteria are met. ... In reaching this decision, the Board took into account the interaction of its decision with the present framework for regulating banks'. The strict criteria are set out in Application note D11. The decision was an interim measure and is to be reviewed in the light of developments in securitisations and of progress made in the ASB's project on measurement of derivatives.

28.94 By comparison, since there exists a market for interest rate caps, the ASB will only allow linked presentation where there is an interest rate cap between originator and issuer (and the conditions of Application note D11 are met) if the securitisation was entered before 22 September 1994. Thereafter, the existence of an interest rate cap will generally prevent linked presentation from being used.

28.95 It was noted in **28.50** above that the use of linked presentation in the originator's consolidated accounts will generally only be possible where the vehicle holding the securitised asset(s) is not a legal subsidiary of the originator. If the vehicle was a legal subsidiary, and used gross presentation in its own accounts, then FRS 2 would require aggregation of all the subsidiary's assets and liabilities, thus defeating the ability to use a linked presentation in the selling company's consolidated accounts.

Loan transfers

28.96 Loan transfers are considered in FRS 5 Application note E. The note deals with the transfer of interest bearing loans to an entity other than a special purpose vehicle (which falls within 'factoring' above).

28.97 The legal basis of transfer, i.e., novation, assignment or sub-participation, will be relevant in identifying whether benefits and risk of change in benefits have been transferred. Three outcomes are possible: derecognition, continued gross presentation and linked presentation.

Private finance initiative

28.98 Under PFI, instead of a public sector body self-supplying services that require the creation or maintenance of an asset which it legally owns, the private sector takes responsibility for the services, including design, build, finance and operation of any asset which is essential to their delivery. A contract specifies the level of service required over the period of the contract and a unitary payment mechanism linked to such factors as service volume, capacity, availability, performance and levels of usage. FRS 5 (and possibly SSAP 21) is relevant in determining whether, for accounting purposes, the purchaser has an asset in the capital asset and a corresponding liability to pay the operator. Take-or-pay and related project finance arrangements give rise to similar considerations.

28.99   Application note F includes the following stages of analysis.

(a)   Consider whether any element of the unitary payment is in substance in respect of separately identifiable services. If so, these are disregarded.

(b)   Where the residual element of the payment does not include any service, i.e., it is in respect of the provision of an asset, then SSAP 21 will be the more specific standard. The application note includes guidance on the application of the '90 per cent test', choice of discount rate and assessment of minimum lease payments.

(c)   Where the residual element of the payment includes both asset and non-separable services, analysis under FRS 5 should focus on the degree to which each party bears the variations in profits (or losses) relating to the asset and any non-separable services. Seven risks are described: demand, third-party revenue, penalties for underperformance, changes in operating costs, determining the nature of the property, obsolescence and changes in technology, and residual value. The discussion suggests that demand risk and penalties will generally be the most significant.

28.100   Analyses which rely on variations in the operator's return on equity should not be used for the following reasons:

(a)   the proportion of equity finance, compared to debt, in most PFI transactions is small, such that the return on equity is susceptible to small variations in inputs; and

(b)   there are no agreed parameters for varying the input risks such as costs, time delays, penalty lapses, etc.

Similarly, analyses which seek to attribute a money value to each risk, and then deduce the party which should record the asset by reference to the one with the majority of risks, should be viewed with some suspicion since:

(a)   the attribution of a money value to each risk will be highly subjective; and

(b) the approach of FRS 5 is not to allocate an entire asset to the party with the majority of risks, but rather to allocate an asset proportionately based on each party's access to benefits and risks.

28.101 In summer 1999 the Treasury Taskforce on private finance issued a revised version of its Technical Note No.1, entitled *How to account for PFI transactions*. The objective of the Treasury Note is to provide additional practical guidance for certain public sector bodies on the application of the ASB's Application Note. The Treasury Note advocates both a qualitative and a quantitative analysis of transactions. The qualitative analysis is to be carried out first and it is only where this is inconclusive that the quantitative analysis should be considered.

28.102 Where the quantitative analysis is to be performed under the Treasury Note, an argument that demand risk is insignificant, and so should be ignored, should be challenged; it should not be confused with the situation where demand risk does exist but has been hedged. In particular, paragraph F29 of the ASB's Application Note F states that:

> 'Where the PFI payments do not vary substantially with demand or usage of the property (although they may vary with other factors), the purchaser will be obliged to pay for the output or capacity of the property (e.g., prison places, hospital beds) whether or not it is needed (i.e., whether or not there are sufficient prisoners or patients). This is evidence that the property is the purchaser's asset and the purchaser has a liability to pay for it. In particular, if the purchaser, in substance, is obliged to pay a minimum amount (i.e., there is no genuine commercial possibility of non-payment) whether or not it will need the property, and the minimum amount more than covers the cost of the property, this is evidence that the property is an asset of the purchaser. In making this assessment of demand risk, any penalties or reductions in payments for non-availability of the property should be ignored; these relate to whether the property is in a state fit for use and do not affect the incidence of demand risk.'

Employee share ownership trusts

28.103 UITF Abstract 13 *Accounting for ESOP trusts* requires that until the time when shares held in an ESOP trust vest unconditionally in specific employees, they should be included as assets in the sponsoring company's balance sheet.

Summary requirement

28.104 UITF Abstract 13 applies the principles of FRS 5 *Reporting the substance of transactions* to employee share ownership plan trusts. Where the sponsoring company has *de facto* control of shares held within an ESOP trust, and bears their benefits or risks, the company is required to recognise those shares as assets in its own balance sheet under the heading 'own shares'.

Control of an ESOP by the sponsoring company

28.105 Although the trustees of an ESOP trust must act at all times in accordance with the interests of trust beneficiaries, most ESOP trusts are specifically designed to serve the purposes of the sponsoring company. For example, the trust is set up by the sponsoring company, to remunerate its employees, in accordance with annual information on entitlement received from the sponsoring company. Further, the trustees are generally not empowered to undertake any other activities. There is consequently minimal risk of any conflict arising between the duties of the trustees and the interest of the company. Where this is so, there will be nothing to prevent implementation of the company's wishes in practice and this will amount to *de facto* control by the company. Such control will be evidenced by the commercial effect of the arrangement, which is that the sponsoring company is, for all practical purposes, in the same position as if it had acquired the shares directly. For example, the sponsoring company may have loaned or given the finance for shares to be purchased, or provided guarantees or is paying interest on a loan from a third-party. The company is thus exposed to falls in the value of shares and also benefits from increases in value through its ability to provide enhanced benefits to its employees.

Accounting requirement

28.106 Shares held in a trust which are not yet gifted, gifted conditionally or put under option should be included as assets of the sponsoring company. This will include unallocated shares, shares on which employees have been granted options or allocated shares which vest with employees only after they complete a set period of employment. Note that UITF Abstract 13 does not conclude that the trust is a quasi-subsidiary. Rather, it concludes that the trust assets are assets of the sponsoring company. It treats the trust as though it were a branch of the sponsoring company.

28.107 Shares gifted unconditionally to specific employees should not be included as assets of the sponsoring company, even if they are still held within an ESOP trust. This will include shares held under a profit-sharing trust for a tax-efficient period where dividends are passed through to employees.

Balance sheet treatment

28.108 Shares held within an ESOP trust which qualify as assets should be classified as 'own shares' as prescribed in the Companies Act formats.

Where shares are held for the continuing benefit of the sponsoring company's business, they will be included as fixed assets; otherwise, they will be current assets. In the most common situation treatment will be as a fixed asset and shares will be carried at cost less provisions for permanent diminution in value although there is nothing to prevent a company from revaluing the shares. In addition, where shares are conditionally gifted to employees, or under option at less than carrying value, shares should be written down to residual value (i.e., nil, in the case of a gift, or else the option price) over the period to which service relates or to the date on which the gift becomes unconditional, if shorter.

28.109   Where a trust is funded by a loan from the sponsoring company, there will be no further liability to be recorded, the debtor in the sponsoring company being cancelled by the creditor in the ESOP. However, where the trust is funded by an external loan which is guaranteed, formally or informally, by the sponsoring company, then a liability should be recognised by the company.

Profit and loss account treatment

28.110   The profit and loss account should reflect charges for a permanent diminution in shares held as a fixed asset (or write-down to net realisable value of shares held as a current asset), amortisation of carrying value to residual value (as described in **28.108** above) and financing and administrative charges on an accruals basis.

28.111   The trust will have a choice: it can either receive the dividends declared on the shares it holds, or it can waive the right to those dividends. Where it has waived its right to dividends no adjustments are needed to the profit and loss account. Where, on the other hand, the trust continues to receive dividends, those dividends should not be recognised as income in the sponsoring company's profit and loss account. Instead the dividends should be deducted from the aggregate of dividends paid and proposed. If material, the deduction should be disclosed on the face of the profit and loss account, otherwise it should be disclosed in a note. Further issues regarding the treatment in the profit and loss account are discussed in **9.190** et seq. above.

Earnings per share

28.112   Shares held by an ESOP trust, to the extent they have not vested unconditionally in employees, are treated for earnings per share purposes as though they had been cancelled. Thus, they are excluded from the denominator. As discussed in **28.111** above, any dividend income on those shares is excluded in arriving at profit attributable to ordinary shareholders and is thus also excluded from the numerator.

Disclosure

28.113 Sufficient information should be disclosed in the financial statements of the sponsoring company to enable readers to understand the significance of the ESOP trust in the context of the sponsoring company. This should include:

(a)   a description of the main features of the ESOP trust, including the arrangements for distributing shares to employees;

(b)   the manner in which the costs are dealt with in the profit and loss account;

(c)   the number and market value of shares held by the ESOP trust and whether dividends on those shares have been waived; and

(d)   the extent to which these shares are under option to employees or have been conditionally gifted to them.

28.114 Appendix 2 to UITF Abstract 13 includes illustrative examples.

28.115 The following extract illustrates the presentation seen in financial statements.

Extract 28.115

The EMI Group plc
Year ended 31 March 1999

Balance sheet (extract)

| | | | Group | | Company | |
| | | 1999 | 1998 (restated) | 1999 (restated) | 1998 | |
	Notes	£m	£m	£m	£m
Fixed Assets					
Music copyrights	11	373.6	372.2	–	–
Goodwill	12	11.6	–	–	–
Tangible fixed assets	13	348.7	356.1	26.4	26.3
Investments: subsidiaries	14	–	–	6,148.6	6,319.0
Investments: joint venture (HMV Media Group)	14	–	–	96.5	87.5
Investments: associates	14	5.0	5.3	0.6	0.6
Other fixed asset investments	14	53.2	50.9	28.5	28.5
Investments: own shares	15	19.9	19.5	19.9	19.5
		812.0	804.0	6,320.5	6,481.4

15. Investments: own shares

The EMI Group General Employee Benefit Trust (EBT) was established to hedge the future obligations of the Group in respect of shares awarded under the Senior Executive Incentive Plan, the EMI Music Long-Term Incentive Plan and other share-based plans. The

---

Trustee of the EBT, EMI Group Trustees (Guernsey) Limited, purchases the Company's Ordinary Shares in the open market with financing provided by the Company, as required, on the basis of regular reviews of the anticipated share liabilities of the Group.

The cost of the shares expected to be awarded under each plan is amortised evenly over the period from the original grant of the particular award to the time of vesting. This is normally a period of not less than three years.

Group and Company	Shares held in trust	Nominal value	Cost	Amortisation	Net book value
	Number	£m	£m	£m	£m
At 31 March 1998	9,618,855	1.3	44.9	(25.4)	19.5
Shares purchased	308,797	–	1.6	–	1.6
Awarded by the EBT	(2,036,179)	(0.2)	(10.3)	10.3	–
Amortisation in the period	–	–	–	(1.2)	(1.2)
At 31 March 1999	**7,891,473**	**1.1**	**36.2**	**(16.3)**	**19.9**

At 31 March 1999, the outstanding loan by the Company to the EBT to finance the purchase of Ordinary Shares was £37.6m (1998: £52.7m). The market value at 31 March 1999 of the Ordinary Shares held in the EBT, which are listed in the UK, was £34.9m (1998: £47.8m).

28.116   One problem encountered in practice with UITF 13 is in identifying which is the 'sponsoring company'. Rather unhelpfully, the term is not defined in the UITF abstract. The assumption in the abstract is that the sponsoring company is the company employing the employees who are granted options, the company providing the finance or guarantee in respect of third-party finance used by the ESOP trust and the company over whose shares the options are granted. In a group situation this may not be so.

Example 28.116

A plc is a listed company with two subsidiaries, B Ltd and C Ltd. The group operates a long-term incentive plan for senior employees. A plc set up an ESOP trust and gave the trust money so that it could go into the market and purchase 400 ordinary shares in A plc. On the day that the shares were purchased the shares were provisionally allocated to employees in all three companies as follows:

Employees of	No. of shares
A plc	200
B Ltd	100
C Ltd	100

The actual number of shares that will vest in the employees will depend on the achievement of performance criteria. B Ltd and C Ltd each reimburse A plc for the cost of 100 shares.

In this instance, given that some employees from each of A, B and C will receive shares in A plc and the relevant shares have been paid for by the respective companies, it would appear reasonable for all three companies to be regarded as sponsoring companies. It is suggested that 200 shares are included in A's balance sheet (under 'own shares') and that 100 shares are included in each of B and C's balance sheet – they will be classified as 'shares in group undertakings'.

If A plc provided the funding for all 400 shares and was not going to be reimbursed in any way by B and C then it is suggested that A plc would include all 400 shares in its financial statements and that neither B nor C would recognise any of the shares in their financial statements. If so, although A plc would write 200 shares (in respect of its employees) off over the performance period, it would have to write the other 200 down to nil immediately in its own individual company accounts because it will get no benefit. In the group accounts all 400 would be written down to nil over the performance period.

Undisclosed agencies

28.117   It is common practice in a wide variety of businesses to operate through the medium of agencies. The rationale for using agencies may vary, as will the degree to which the customer is aware of the agency arrangements. Travel agencies, for example, usually make it clear on the customer booking forms that the contractual relationship is between the customer and the travel company, not the travel agent. On the other hand, agency arrangements may be undisclosed. For example:

(a)   a company wishing to lease equipment to customers may enter into an arrangement with a financier whereby the financier assumes the legal rights and obligations of the company's agreement with the customer. The paperwork (invoices, correspondence, etc.) indicates, however, that the customer has entered into a contract with the company itself;

(b)   a subsidiary transfers its business to the parent company, but the subsidiary's name is still used for trading purposes (in effect, creating an agency).

The issue arises as to whether the agent is required to record the transactions in its books. In particular, in (b) above, the subsidiary may seek to file accounts as a dormant company.

28.118   The legal position is that the only form of agency which is effective in allowing the removal of the transactions from the agent's books is a disclosed agency, i.e., the agent should state clearly on all paper-work that it is acting as agent and the name of the principal. Alternatively, if these matters are not disclosed, the company is holding itself out as principal and therefore incurs legal obligations, which means the transactions should be reflected in the accounts. FRS 5 requires us also to look at the substance of transactions and the economic benefit accruing to the company acting as agent. According to FRS 5, where a transaction results in an item that meets the definition of an asset or liability, that item should be recognised in the balance sheet if there is sufficient evidence of its existence and it can be measured with sufficient reliability. Conversely, where the agent has no benefits or obligations which meet the definition of an asset or liability, no balance sheet entry is required. As a general rule, the accounting treatment which should be adopted is as follows:

(a) where the agency arrangements are fully disclosed to the customer and the agent has no economic interest in the transactions, they should not be recorded and, provided there are no other transactions, it will be appropriate for the agent to prepare dormant company accounts. There may, however, be a contractual duty to maintain memorandum accounts on behalf of the principal;

(b) where the agency arrangements are undisclosed, the agent should record the original transaction, followed by a disposal to the financier, provided that the conditions for derecognition under FRS 5 are met. Derecognition requires that all significant rights or other access to benefits relating to an asset and all significant exposure to the risks inherent in those benefits have been transferred to a third party. For a trading transaction, the minimum entries are thus equal amounts within turnover and cost of sales.

29 Leasing

29 Leasing

Summary of changes since the previous issue of this publication

Para.	Topic	Summary
29.10	Discussion paper *Leases: Implementation of a New Approach*	The central proposal of the the discussion paper is that accounting for leases should be approached in accordance with the normal principles of asset and liability recognition as set out in the statement of principles. Thus the current distinction between finance and operating leases would disappear and financial statements would reflect the economic reality which is that the obligations which exist under operating leases are no different to those created by finance leases.

Introduction

SSAP 21 Accounting for leases and hire purchase contracts

29.1 The accounting treatment of leases, both by lessors and lessees, is dealt with in SSAP 21 *Accounting for leases and hire purchase contracts*. In some cases, the accounting requirements and disclosures are complex and, for this reason, the SSAP is supported by guidance notes, which give more detailed guidance on how the statement should be applied, including illustrations and discussion of problem areas. Although the guidance notes are not part of the SSAP, and therefore do not have mandatory status, they should be regarded for all practical purposes as if they were part of the SSAP.

29.2 The key distinction to be made in accounting for leases is whether the lease in question is a simple short-term hire arrangement (operating lease), whereby rentals are dealt with in the profit and loss account, but with little or no balance sheet effect, or whether the lease is akin to an arrangement for financing the use of fixed assets (finance lease), where the accounts presentation will depart from the legal form of the transaction and be based on the economic substance, i.e., as if the asset had indeed been purchased by the user.

29.3

> Since the balance sheet effect of classification of a lease either as a finance lease or an operating lease is significantly different, lessees (supported by the lessor) may be anxious to see a lease classified as an operating lease. As a consequence, the classification of a lease based on an analysis both of the lease agreement and actual behaviour will play an important part in determining how the lease should be accounted for.

The relationship of SSAP 21 with FRS 5

29.4   The approach of SSAP 21 can be described as an 'all or nothing' approach, i.e., a leased asset and the related obligation to pay rentals remain wholly off balance sheet until a threshold is passed. At this point, the full fair value of the asset, and an equal liability, is displayed on balance sheet. This approach contrasts with that adopted in FRS 5 *Reporting the substance of transactions* (based in turn on the ASB's Statement of Principles), which allows for an asset to be analysed into different rights (the 'property rights' approach). The ASB has issued a discussion paper *Leases: Implementation of a New Approach* which sets out proposals for replacing SSAP 21 with an approach based on recognition of liabilities for all leases on a consistent basis. This approach would recognise only those rights that have been acquired and cease to distinguish between finance and operating leases; requiring the present value of all lease obligations to be recorded on the balance sheet (see **29.102** below).

29.5   In the meantime, the key question is whether the requirements of FRS 5 override those of SSAP 21. FRS 5 states that: 'Where the substance of a transaction or the treatment of any resulting asset or liability falls not only within the scope of this FRS but also directly within the scope of another FRS, a Statement of Standard Accounting Practice (SSAP), or a specific statutory requirement governing the recognition of assets or liabilities, the standard or statute that contains the more specific provision(s) should be applied'. [FRS 5(13)] The explanatory paragraphs also state that: 'The relationship between SSAP 21 *Accounting for lease and hire purchase contracts* and FRS 5 is particularly close. In general, SSAP 21 contains the more specific provisions governing accounting for stand-alone leases that fall wholly within its parameters, although the general principles of the FRS will also be relevant in ensuring that leases are classified as finance or operating leases in accordance with their substance. However, for some lease arrangements, and particularly for those that are merely one element of a larger arrangement, the FRS will contain the more specific provisions. An example is a sale and leaseback arrangement where there is also an option for the seller/lessee to repurchase the asset; in this case the provisions of FRS 5's Application Note B are more specific than those of SSAP 21'. [FRS 5(45)]

29.6

In practice, therefore:

(a) a stand-alone lease transaction that falls wholly within the parameters of SSAP 21 should initially be evaluated under the criteria of SSAP 21;

(b) where the classification under SSAP 21 appears to contradict other substance based features of the lease, e.g., the net present value test indicates that the lease is an operating lease but the lessor nevertheless fulfils the role of a lender, then all features of the lease should be reviewed in the light of FRS 5 to determine whether there is sufficient evidence to rebut the SSAP 21 classification;

(c) where a transaction that has more complex features, e.g., a financing arrangement that includes a lease component where the series of related transactions are not wholly covered by the parameters of SSAP 21, the requirements of FRS 5 should be applied to the entire transaction.

Definitions

29.7 SSAP 21 contains 17 definitions. Of these, the definitions of 'finance lease', 'operating lease' and 'hire purchase contract' set out below are most relevant to an understanding of the accounting treatment of leases.

29.8 Of the remaining definitions, reference to SSAP 21 maybe required, e.g., 'minimum lease payments', 'fair value', etc.

Finance lease

29.9 A finance lease is a lease that transfers substantially all the risks and rewards of ownership of an asset to the lessee. It should be presumed that such a transfer of risks and rewards occurs if at the inception of a lease the present value of the minimum lease payments, including any initial payment, amounts to substantially all (normally 90 per cent or more) of the fair value of the leased asset. The present value should be calculated by using the interest rate implicit in the lease. If the fair value of the asset is not determinable, an estimate of it should be made. [SSAP 21(15)]

29.10 Notwithstanding the fact that a lease meets the above conditions, the presumption that it should be classified as a finance lease may, in exceptional circumstances, be rebutted if it can be clearly demonstrated that the lease in question does not transfer substantially all the risks and rewards of ownership (other than legal title) to the lessee. Correspondingly, the presumption that a lease which fails to meet the above conditions is not a finance lease may, in exceptional circumstances, be rebutted. [SSAP 21(16)]

Operating lease

29.11 An operating lease is a lease other than a finance lease. [SSAP 21(17)]

Hire purchase contract

29.12 A hire purchase contract is a contract for the hire of an asset which contains a provision giving the hirer an option to acquire legal title to the asset upon the fulfilment of certain conditions stated in the contract. [SSAP 21(18)]

Accounting by lessees

Approach and materiality

29.13 The approach required by SSAP 21 is that a finance lease should be capitalised by the lessee, i.e., both an asset (the rights to use the asset) and a liability (an obligation to make future payments) appear on the lessee's balance sheet. If the lease is an operating lease, the rental payable is taken into account only as it arises.

29.14   As with all accounting standards, SSAP 21 need not be applied to immaterial items and, in many cases, this consideration may justify accounting for finance leases as operating leases. The guidance notes suggest that the relevant criterion is the size of the leases in aggregate in the context of the size of the lessee and that regard should be had to the effect which capitalisation would have on the financial statements as a whole. Thus, consideration should be given to the effect on total fixed assets, total borrowings, the gearing ratio and the profit or loss for the year. If capitalisation of finance leases would not have a material effect on any of these items, then the leases need not be capitalised.

29.15 Where leases entered into by a lessee are material, the most difficult problem is to determine whether or not a lease falls within the definition of a finance lease. This problem is discussed in the following section.

Classification of leases

29.16   The core criteria differentiating a finance lease from an operating lease is that a finance lease transfers substantially all of the risks and rewards of ownership of the asset to the lessee (see **29.9** and **29.10** above for the full definition). The SSAP then goes on (unhelpfully, some might say with hindsight) to provide a 'rebuttable presumption' that the distinguishing line occurs where, at the inception of the lease, the present value of the minimum lease payments (including any initial payment) amounts to more or less than 90 per cent of the fair value of the leased asset. The intention is thus that the '90 per cent test' provides an important source of evidence; however, where other evidence contradicts the '90 per cent test', an overall evaluation should be based on all the evidence taken together (see **29.4** to **29.6** above).

29.17   By comparison with the US definition, the SSAP 21 definition does not include any test based on time (e.g., testing whether the lease period exceeds, say, 75 per cent of the asset's useful life) or the likelihood of transfer of title at the end of the lease period. However, these factors may contribute to the evidence that may be used to challenge the result of the '90 per cent test' as indicated by paragraph 135 of the guidance notes to SSAP 21 which state that:

> 'exceptionally, it may not be practicable to determine the lease classification based on consideration of whether the present value of the minimum lease payments amounts to 90% or more of the fair value of the leased asset; … . For example if the lessee has the use of an asset for the period in which substantially all the economic benefits can be derived from the asset, then a finance lease is indicated.'

29.18   In practice, since the pressure from accounts preparers is usually in favour of classifying the lease as an operating lease, there will be instances where the '90 per cent test' is exceeded (indicating the lease is a finance lease), but where other evidence is used to support treatment as an operating lease.

29.19   This is often the case for property leases where the present value of rentals under property leases amount to more than 90 per cent of the fair value. Generally two arguments are raised in support of the conclusion that such leases are operating. The first is that the economic life of the asset is expected to be significantly longer than the life of the lease, and the second that the lessor has retained a significant reward, this being the right to increase the rentals under a rent review option.

29.20   By comparison, where the '90 per cent test' indicates with a sufficiently clear margin that the lease is an operating lease, there may be a less robust attempt to rebut the presumption that the lease is an operating lease; as a generality, auditors have not challenged this disparity of approach. This feature is particularly apparent in leases of motor cars where, due to the predictable nature of residual values, the balance of risk/reward between lessee and lessor falls short of the 90:10 ratio; in reality, however, all genuine risk of variation in residual values is often borne by the lessee. As a further very broad generalisation, leases where the lessor is a bank or financial institution are likely to demonstrate features that, in substance, amount to a finance lease; by comparison, where the lessor's business includes dealing in, or operating, the type of assets that are the subject of the lease, then it is more plausible that the lease will include operating lease features, since the lessor will be both able and willing to accept risks associated with the asset's value and performance.

29.21 Evaluation of a lease will require an examination of the lease agreement, including any supporting schedules and side letters, particularly where these include the monetary amounts of rental payments and arrangements for the return and disposal of the asset. It follows that a blank lease agreement, i.e., without a schedule of rental payments, cannot be adequately assessed. In summary, the most relevant evidence will be found from clauses dealing with:

(a) rental payments and rebates (normally contained in a schedule to the lease agreement) to which the '90 per cent test' may be applied; and

(b) arrangements that apply where the lease runs its normal full term, e.g., the existence of options, balloon payments, guarantees, process for disposal of the asset, etc.

29.22 Clauses dealing with the following issues will be of less relevance:

(a) maintenance and insurance (not normally a significant element of overall cost); and

(b) arrangements for termination that are unlikely to be applicable in practice, e.g., following insolvency of the lessee or failure to pay rentals when due.

29.23 In applying the '90 per cent test', the following points are based on the definitions of SSAP 21:

(a) the fair value of the leased asset is normally its purchase cost on a cash basis, but any grants that would be receivable towards its purchase should be deducted. If the fair value cannot be determined accurately, it should be estimated;

(b)   the minimum lease payments are the minimum payments over the lease term (excluding charges for services and taxes), together with any residual amounts guaranteed by the lessee or a party related to him;

(c)   the lease term is the initial lease period plus any further periods for which the lessee has the option to continue the lease and which it is reasonably certain at the inception of the lease that he will exercise;

(d)   where a lease gives the lessee an option for early termination, any calculation of the minimum lease payments which assumes the exercise of that option should include any penalties associated with the termination;

(e)   the present value of the minimum lease payments should be calculated using the interest rate 'implicit in the lease'. The interest rate implicit in the lease is defined as the discount rate which, when applied at the inception of the lease to the amounts which the lessor expects to receive and retain, produces a present value equal to the fair value of the leased asset. Since the amounts which the lessor expects to receive and retain include any residual value of the asset even though that value is not guaranteed, calculation of the interest rate implicit in the lease requires a knowledge on the part of the lessee of the lessor's estimate of that residual value. If, as is likely, this information is not available to the lessee, it is not possible to determine the interest rate implicit in the lease. If the rate is not determinable, then the rate which the lessee would be expected to pay on a similar lease should be used. Where a rate supplied by a lessor appears higher than a market rate, a check calculation should be performed, using a market rate to test the sensitivity of the result to the discount rate.

The '90 per cent test' is framed as a one-directional assumption, i.e., if net present value exceeds 90 per cent, then it is presumed that the lease is finance. It is not stated in SSAP 21 that a net present value less than 90 per cent leads to a presumption of an operating lease. In particular, where a net present value narrowly falls under the 90 per cent level, greater emphasis should be placed on other factors, such as the existence of options and the asset's useful life compared to the lease term. In practice, classification as an operating lease is more easily achieved where the net present value falls below 90 per cent by a reasonable margin.

29.24   In most cases, either the lessee or lessor will be able to provide calculations of net present value based on computer models. Where this is not available, or where an independent calculation of net present value is needed, the following formulae may be used.

29.25   The general formula for expressing a monetary sum from one date (a terminal value) to an earlier date (a present value) is:

Present value (£) = Terminal value (£) × Discount factor

29.26   For a single sum, the discount factor will be:

Discount factor = $(1+i)^{-n}$

where: i = periodic rate of interest; and
   n = the number of periods between present and terminal dates.

29.27   For a series of equal payments, each occurring at the end of a period, the discount factor will be:

$$\frac{1 - (1 + i)^{-n}}{i}$$

where: i = periodic rate of interest; and
   n = number of payments, each at the end of a period.

Where a series of n payments occur at the beginning of each period, this should be treated as a single payment at time zero, followed by a series of n–1 payments at the end of each period.

29.28   Where payment dates coincide with annual periods, then the annual rate of interest may be used. Where, however, payments are monthly or quarterly, the annual rate of interest should first be expressed at a monthly or quarterly rate. For a monthly rate, the formula will be:

Monthly interest rate = $(1+i)^{1/12} - 1$

where: i = annual rate of interest.

For a quarterly rate, the formula will be:

Quarterly interest rate = $(1+i)^{1/4} - 1$

where: i = annual rate of interest.

29.29   The following example demonstrates the calculation of net present value.

Example 29.29

Information

An asset with a fair value of £13,500 is to be leased. The minimum guaranteed payments under the lease are £15,600 payable as follows: deposit payable at commencement £350; followed by 35 monthly

---

payments of £350; followed by a single balloon payment at the end of the 36th month of £3,000. The annual rate of interest implicit in the lease is eight per cent.

Workings

(1) Monthly rate of interest $= (1.08)^{1/12} - 1$
$= 0.006434$ or 0.6434%

(2) Discount factor for 35 monthly payments at 0.6434% per month
$= (1 - (1.006434)^{-35})/0.006434$
$= 31.2495$

(3) Discount factor for a single payment at the end of three years
$= (1.08)^{-3}$
$= 0.7938$

Calculation of net present value:

Payment	Undiscounted value	Discount factor	Present value
	£		£
Deposit	350	1.0000	350
35 monthly rentals	350 each	31.2495	10,937
Balloon rental	3,000	0.7938	2,381
Total net present value			13,668

Conclusion

Net present value	£13,668
Fair value of asset	£13,500
Net present value as a percentage of fair value	101%

Since the net present value exceeds 90 per cent of the asset's fair value, the lease should be classified as a finance lease. If, alternatively, the balloon rental was an optional payment so that it could be excluded from guaranteed minimum payments, then the net present value would fall by £2,381 to £11,287. This represents 83.6 per cent of the asset's fair value, which would allow classification as an operating lease.

29.30 One alternative method of applying the '90 per cent test', suggested within the guidance notes to SSAP 21, is to approach the test from the other direction and consider whether the present value of any amounts which the lessor expects to receive, but which do not form part of the minimum lease payments of the lessee, exceeds 10 per cent of the fair value of the leased asset.

Most commonly, the only amount to be considered for this purpose will be the estimated residual value of the asset at the end of the lease term (less any amounts which, because they are guaranteed by the lessee, are included as part of the minimum lease payments); if the present value of this residual value is less than 10 per cent of the fair value of the asset, it will usually imply that the lease is a finance lease. This is expressed in terms of the 'reward' retained. It could also be expressed in terms of residual value expected by the lessor which is at risk. Whether we consider the risk or reward, this approach does not solve the problem that the amount to be taken into account is the amount the lessor expects to receive, i.e., the lessor's estimate of the residual value; this will generally not be known to the lessee. It will only be possible to estimate residual value reasonably where the asset is one, e.g., a motor vehicle, in which there is a ready market throughout its life.

29.31 The following example illustrates how to calculate the present value of the estimated residual value.

Example 29.31

Information

The lessor of a motor car estimates that, at the end of the primary period, the vehicle will have a residual value equal to 30 per cent of its original cost. At that date, the vehicle will be sold and the proceeds allocated as follows:

(a) if proceeds exceed 30 per cent of cost, the lessor receives the estimate of residual value and the lessee receives the excess;

(b) if proceeds fall short of the estimate, but exceed 20 per cent of cost, then the lessor will receive all the proceeds plus a compensation payment from the lessee so that the lessor receives, in aggregate, the estimate of residual value; and

(c) if proceeds fall short of 20 per cent of original cost, then the lessor will receive all the proceeds plus a compensation payment from the lessee limited to 10 per cent of the original cost.

The lease has an implicit interest rate of 9 per cent.

Analysis

The effect of the above arrangements is that the lessor's risk in respect of the residual value at the end of the third year is equal to 20 per cent of the original cost (if the proceeds are nil the lessor will receive 10 per cent in comparison to 30 per cent expected). By discounting this percentage from the end of year three to the beginning of the lease, we can test whether the present value of the risk retained amounts to more than 10 per cent of original cost, thereby supporting treatment as an operating lease.

Workings

Discount factor for a single payment at the end of three years

$$= (1.09)^{-3}$$
$$= 0.7722$$

Net present value of guarantee

Guarantee x discount factor

$$= 20\% \text{ of cost} \times 0.7722$$
$$= 0.1544 \text{ or } 15.44\% \text{ of cost}$$

Conclusion

Since the answer easily exceeds 10 per cent, the net present value of payments guaranteed by the lessee must be less than 90 per cent of the asset's fair value. The lease thus appears to qualify as an operating lease.

In reality, however, the risk of a three year old motor car falling in value by one-third is very remote, especially when averaged across a fleet of vehicles; the true risk to the lessor is, therefore, negligible. In such circumstances, FRS 5 would require such a transaction to be treated as a financing transaction. This would represent a change from previous practice, where this type of lease was often accepted as an operating lease.

29.32   The SSAP 21 definition of 'lease term' includes 'any further terms for which the lessee has the option to continue to lease the asset, with or without further payment, which option it is reasonably certain at the inception of the lease that the lessee will exercise'. [SSAP 21(19)] In justifying the inclusion of a secondary lease period, the phrase 'reasonably certain' should be interpreted strictly. It is not sufficient that the optional renewal terms should appear advantageous to the lessee at the time of the inception of the lease, since uncertainties relating to rates of interest, technological developments and economic circumstances should be taken into account. Clearly, these uncertainties become more significant the longer the period before the option is exercisable. Unless the initial lease period is very short, it is unlikely that reasonable certainty of renewal will exist other than on the payment of a nominal rental only. Thus, in practice, the determination of whether or not a lease is a finance lease will normally be made by reference only to the lease period for which the lessee is irrevocably committed at the inception of the lease.

29.33   'Break clauses', i.e., clauses offering the lessee an opportunity to return equipment and cancel remaining rentals, may be included in a lease. Where, in order to classify a lease as an operating lease, a lessee places reliance on its ability to invoke a break clause and thus limit the lease term to the period then ended, it will be important to ensure that:

(a)   there is genuine likelihood of the break clause being used; and

(b)   all financial consequences of a decision to break the contract are taken into consideration.

29.34   The classification of the lease should be based on the most likely course of events. There are instances where an artificial break clause is inserted purely in order to meet the operating lease definition, but where there is no commercial possibility of the break clause being invoked. For example, a clause may allow the lessee to terminate a three-year lease after one month of operation, but, in return, requires the lessee to pay a penalty of 75 per cent of the asset's cost. Although the penalty payment falls short of the '90 per cent test', there is no commercial possibility of a lessee paying 75 per cent of the cost of an asset in return for one month's use. Accordingly, such a break clause should be disregarded.

29.35   Similar considerations apply when evaluating 'upgrade options', whereby a lessee can return existing equipment provided that they enter into a new lease. In particular, the impact on new lease rentals should be considered. For example, a lessor may seek to recover remaining rentals on the old lease by increasing the rentals on new equipment. To the extent that classification of the old lease assumes exercise of an upgrade option, any increase in rentals on the new lease should be regarded as part of the guaranteed minimum payments under the old lease.

Accounting for finance leases

29.36   At the inception of a finance lease, both the leased asset and the related lease obligation should be recorded in the balance sheet at the present value of the minimum lease payments. In most cases, the fair value of the asset is a close approximation of the present value of the minimum lease payments; where the leased asset is also offered on a cash sale basis, the cash price might be a suitable measure of the present value. Alternatively, the contract terms or rates quoted by finance houses may indicate a suitable discount rate which may be used to calculate a present value.

29.37   Leased assets should be described as such in the balance sheet, to distinguish them from owned assets.

29.38   Leased assets should be depreciated over the shorter of the lease term or their estimated useful lives. The principle is that depreciation should be based on the period over which the lessee expects to use the asset. Thus, in determining the lease term for this purpose, it is acceptable to include secondary periods for which the lessee has the option to continue to lease the asset, with or without further payment, which option it is reasonably certain at the inception of the lease that the lessee will exercise. Similarly, where the lease includes a bargain purchase option (e.g., a hire purchase contract) which it is reasonably certain at the inception of the lease that the lessee will exercise, the depreciable life of the asset to the lessee will extend beyond the contractual lease term and will amount to the asset's estimated useful life.

29.39   The difference between the total minimum lease payments and their present value at the inception of the lease represents a finance charge. This should be allocated to accounting periods over the term of the lease, so as to produce a constant rate of interest (or a reasonable approximation to it) on the remaining balance of the lease obligation. This is achieved by apportioning each rental payment between a finance charge and a reduction of the lease obligation. SSAP 21 does not specify particular methods which are to be used for this purpose; however, the guidance notes do set out three methods which are often used in practice. These are:

- actuarial method;

- sum of digits method; and

- straight-line method.

These are considered in more detail in **29.42** to **29.44** below.

29.40   In some circumstances, the availability of grants and capital allowances to the lessor will mean that an asset can be offered on a finance lease at a rental which gives a total for the minimum lease payments which is actually less than the fair value of the asset. In such a case, recording the lease obligation at the fair value of the leased asset would give rise to a negative finance charge, which is specifically prohibited by SSAP 21. Consequently, the leased asset and the obligations under the lease should be recorded at the start of the lease at the total of the minimum lease payments. This will result in no finance charge being suffered by the lessee.

29.41   The guidance notes suggest that where a lease contains variation clauses which adjust the rentals to take account of movements in base rates of interest or changes in taxation, no adjustment need normally be made to the calculations which are carried out at the start of the lease. Any increase or reduction in rentals should be accounted for as an increase or reduction in finance charges in the period in which it arises. Where the reduction in rentals exceeds the future finance charges, the excess should be applied to reduce future depreciation charges. Thus, in most cases, any difference between the rental assessed at the start of the lease and the actual amount payable may be dealt with in the profit and loss account for the period covered by the particular payment. In exceptional circumstances where a very large change in rental for a significant period is involved, it may be thought necessary to spread the aggregate difference over the remainder of the lease period by the same method as was used to allocate the finance charges initially (e.g., by the sum of the digits method).

Actuarial method

29.42 This method achieves an accurate apportionment of interest cost over the term of the lease. Often, the information necessary to adopt this basis is provided to the lessee by the lessor. Alternatively, microcomputer spreadsheets generally have suitable functions for such calculations to be performed.

Sum of digits method

29.43 This is also referred to as the 'Rule of 78'. In most cases, the method produces an acceptable approximation of the results obtained by the actuarial method, but is simpler to apply. It is probably the method most frequently used in practice.

Example 29.43

An asset is leased under a finance lease for a three-year period, with 12 quarterly rental payments; the total finance charge amounts to £10,000.

(a) If rentals are paid quarterly in arrears

The digit assigned for the first period will be 12 and, for the last period, 1.

Period	Quarter	Digit	Finance charge allocation	£
Year 1	1	12	£10,000 × 12/78	1,539
	2	11	£10,000 × 11/78	1,410
	3	10	£10,000 × 10/78	1,282
	4	9	£10,000 × 9/78	1,154
Year 2	1	8	£10,000 × 8/78	1,026
	2	7	£10,000 × 7/78	897
	3	6	£10,000 × 6/78	769
	4	5	£10,000 × 5/78	641
Year 3	1	4	£10,000 × 4/78	513
	2	3	£10,000 × 3/78	385
	3	2	£10,000 × 2/78	256
	4	1	£10,000 × 1/78	128
		78		10,000

> (b)   If rentals are paid in advance
>
> Since there is no capital outstanding during the final quarter of the last year, there is no finance charge allocation to that quarter. Consequently, the digit for the last period will be zero; for the first period, 11. The sum of the digits becomes 66.

Straight-line method

29.44   The finance charge is spread equally over the period of the lease. Thus, if it were applied in the circumstances of the example in **29.43** above, the finance charge would be £833 (i.e., £10,000/12) in each quarter. This method does not attempt to produce a constant periodic rate of charge and does not, therefore, comply with SSAP 21. It is only appropriate, on grounds of simplicity, if the difference between the figures thus produced and those which would be produced by one of the above methods would not be material to the financial statements. This is unlikely to be the case where the aggregate amount of finance leases is large relative to the size of the company.

Accounting for operating leases

29.45   Rentals payable under an operating lease should be charged on a straight-line basis over the lease term, even if the payments are not made on that basis, unless another systematic and rational basis is more appropriate. For example, where the rentals of an asset are based on the actual usage of that asset, or are revised periodically to reflect the efficiency of the asset or current market rates, the rentals actually payable may be an appropriate measure.

29.46   Property leases give rise to two situations where the basis of rental payments may differ from the basis of charging the profit and loss account, i.e., rental holidays and vacancy following removal to new premises.

Rental holidays, reverse premiums and other lessee incentives

29.47   A lessor may grant a rent-free period, e.g., as an inducement at the start of a new lease. Similar incentives include an up front cash payment (a reverse lease premium) or a contribution to certain lessee costs (such as fitting out or relocation). The UITF has issued UITF Abstract 12 *Lessee accounting for reverse lease premiums and similar incentives*, which recognises that a lessor will offer benefits for one purpose only: inducing a tenant to enter a lease by reducing the lessor's return from the lease.

29.48   UITF Abstract 12 confirms that, whatever form they may take, any benefits received and receivable by a lessee as an incentive to sign a lease should be spread on a straight-line basis over the lease term or, if shorter than the full lease term, to the review date on which the rent is first adjusted to the prevailing market rate.

29.49

> A rental review mechanism should be evaluated carefully; there will be many examples of rental reviews which do not result in an adjustment to prevailing market rate, e.g., an upward only review based on predetermined percentage increases.

29.50 UITF Abstract 12 became effective for accounting periods ending on or after 23 December 1994 in respect of lease agreements commencing in the current or preceding period. It was necessary to adjust comparative figures for such leases. Adoption for earlier leases is permitted but not required. The abstract supersedes that part of the guidance given in paragraph 16 of the guidance notes to SSAP 21, which suggests that the total rentals should be charged 'over the period in which the asset is in use'.

29.51

> Initial application of UITF Abstract 12 to existing leases had the effect of reducing retained profits brought forward, and increasing future profits, by the amount of benefits related to the remaining years of a lease term. The impact of this effect may be constrained by the availability of reserves brought forward and the potential impact that a reduction may have on borrowing covenants.

29.52 The UITF Abstract 12 acknowledges that there may be exceptional circumstances where it is possible to rebut the presumption that an incentive is in substance part of the lessor's market return. For example, this might apply to a lessor wishing to redevelop a valuable site who may, in addition to finding a sitting tenant new accommodation for a market rent, pay sizeable compensation for terminating the old lease.

29.53 The UITF Abstract 12 also recognises that it is possible to demonstrate that amortisation on a straight-line basis over the lease term or to an earlier review date could be misleading. For example, this might apply to a low-start rental which reflects occupation of a retail unit in an incomplete development which, on later completion, will attract a larger number of customers and provide a greater range of services to tenants.

29.54 In either of the situations referred to in **29.52** and **29.53** above, an alternative systematic and rational basis may be used, with disclosure of:
[UITF Abstract 12(8)]

(a) an explanation of the specific circumstances that render the required treatment misleading;

(b) a description of the policy adopted and the amounts involved; and

(c) the effect on the results for the current and preceding periods.

29.55   When evaluating whether a lessor derives a market return from a lease, it should be borne in mind that a market return may vary according to factors such as the size and prestige of the tenant.

29.56   Where an incentive takes the form of a contribution to lease costs of vacated property, care is needed to determine whether UITF Abstract 12 applies. Where the new lessor accepts the total risk of remaining rental payments (providing the lessor with access to the potential benefit of occupation and rental income from alternative tenants), this will amount to a disposal of the lessee's interest in the old lease and the abstract will not have any effect, e.g., the new lessor agrees to pay all rentals on a remaining five-year lease, irrespective of when, or if, the property is let to a new tenant. By comparison, where a lessor makes a contribution to costs, but the lessee retains the risk of remaining rentals, the abstract will require the contribution to costs to be dealt with as a benefit which is subject to the abstract's requirements. For example, where a new lessor agrees to pay two years' rent on a lease with five years remaining, and which is expected to take two years to find a tenant, then the lessee should treat the two-year contribution as an incentive falling within the scope of UITF Abstract 12, even though there may be a provision for two years' vacant property cost which is charged immediately (see **29.57** below).

Vacant property

29.57   The need to provide for rentals on a lease where the property has been vacated is within the scope of FRS 12 'provisions'. FRS 12 requires the recognition of a provision where:

(a) there is a present obligation resulting from a past event;

(b) there is a probable outflow of benefits; and

(c) the outflow can be measured with sufficient reliability.

Condition (a) is met through the existence of the lease, which is a legal contract and gives rise to a legal obligation to pay future rentals. At the point the property is vacated, the benefit derived from occupation ceases. Conditions (b) and (c) are met, since the payment of rentals is both precise and enforceable by law. However, the best estimate of the provision will reflect market conditions at the balance sheet date, i.e., the rental cost of as many future periods as the lessee is likely to pay for until it is reasonably certain that the leasehold interest will be sold or sublet. The provision, which should be considered separately for each property and not on a portfolio basis, should also take account of other ongoing expenses (such as rates and costs of security) together with any costs associated with vacating the property (such as moving costs). Where the lessee moves to a new property on which there is a rental holiday, it will not be appropriate to spread the vacant property cost over the rental holiday period unless there is a clear link between the two leases, e.g., the lessor of both properties is the same.

Accounting for hire purchase contracts

29.58 Generally, hire purchase contracts have all the characteristics of finance leases and should be accounted for as such. They should be accounted for as operating leases only if the contract is such that substantially all the risks and rewards of ownership do not pass to the hirer at the inception of the contract. Such a situation might arise if, at the conclusion of the lease period, the hirer's right to acquire legal title to the asset was on condition that he paid an amount equal to the then market value of the asset which was not insignificant in relation to its original cost. Contracts of this nature are very rare.

Accounting for sale and leaseback and similar transactions

29.59 A sale and leaseback transaction is a linked arrangement whereby the owner of an asset sells that asset and immediately leases it back from the purchaser. The subject of the sale and leaseback is commonly a property, but may be another fixed asset.

29.60 The leaseback may be a finance lease, if it meets the criterion that substantially all the risks and rewards of ownership remain with the lessee, or it may be an operating lease (in which case, significant risks and rewards of ownership will have been transferred to, and remain with, the purchaser). A long lease of a property at a fixed annual rental may be a finance lease, since the present value of the reversionary interest in the property is likely to be very small. On the other hand, a short lease or one which incorporates provision for regular rent reviews would usually be an operating lease. The lease should be accounted for as a finance lease or as an operating lease in the manner described above.

29.61

> Care should be taken in applying the '90 per cent test' to a leaseback transaction. A result which falls narrowly under 90 per cent is unlikely to result in transfer of sufficient risks such that the lessee no longer has substantially all the risks and rewards of asset ownership. It should be remembered that classification of a leaseback as an operating lease amounts to treating the sale and leaseback as a disposal, which should be capable of support from the overall substance of the arrangement.

29.62 Accounting for the proceeds of sale of the asset will depend on the relationship of three factors: the sale proceeds, the previous book value of the asset and the fair value of the asset.

29.63 If the fair value at the date of sale is below book value, then a permanent diminution in value has taken place and the book value must be reduced accordingly by an immediate charge to profit and loss account.

29.64 If the related leaseback is a finance lease, the substance of the transaction is that no disposal of property has taken place and therefore no gain or loss on disposal should be recognised. The difference between the sale price and the book value (or fair value if lower) should be carried forward and amortised over the same period as that in which the leased asset is depreciated (i.e., the shorter of the lease term and the estimated useful life of the asset).

29.65 If the related leaseback is an operating lease, it is necessary to determine the fair value of the asset and compare this with the contract sale price. Because the sale and lease transactions are connected, the sale may be arranged at other than fair value, with the effect of any difference being recognised in the rentals payable. The appropriate accounting is as follows:

(a) if the sale price is equal to the fair value, any profit or loss on sale should be recognised in the profit and loss account immediately;

(b) if the sale price is above the fair value, the profit to be recognised immediately should be restricted to any excess of the fair value over the book value; the excess of the sale price over the fair value will be reflected in higher rental charges and should, therefore, be carried forward and amortised over the period to the first rent review or over the period of the lease if there is no rent review;

(c) if the sale price is below the fair value, then fair value may be ignored; any excess of the sale price over the book value should be recognised immediately. However, if the sale price is below the book value, the shortfall will be compensated by lower rentals in the lease agreement and it may therefore be carried forward and charged to profits over the period to the first rent review or over the period of the lease if there is no rent review. (It should be noted that the fair value cannot be below book value, since the book value of the asset must first be adjusted as indicated in **29.63** above.)

29.66 The following examples illustrate these rules.

Example 29.66

(a) **Sale price above fair value (see 29.65(b) above)**

	£
Book value	100
Fair value	110
Sale price	125
Profit to be recognised	10
Profit to be deferred	15

(b) **Sale price below fair value (see 29.65(c) above)**

	Asset A	Asset B
	£	£
Book value	100	100
Fair value	125	110
Sale price	110	95
Profit to be recognised	10	–
Apparent loss to be deferred if compensated by below market rentals	–	(5)

29.67 Similar considerations to those contained in the preceding paragraphs are also relevant to other arrangements involving the use of leases where legal title and risks and rewards of ownership may be separated, e.g., lease and leaseback arrangements, lease with a future commitment to repurchase the lessee company, etc. Transactions which do not fall wholly within the scope of SSAP 21 are considered in **29.5** and **29.6** above.

Disclosures

29.68 The disclosure requirements of SSAP 21 for lessees are summarised in the following paragraphs.

Accounting policies

29.69 The policies adopted for accounting for operating leases and finance leases should be stated. An example of an appropriate note is included in the model financial statements of Delto PLC set out in chapter 46.

Finance leases

29.70 Disclosures required in respect of finance leases are as follows.

(a) The gross amount, related accumulated depreciation and total depreciation allocated for the period in respect of assets held under finance leases, by each major class of asset, should be shown. A suggested description for capitalised leased assets is 'assets held under finance leases and hire purchase contracts'. Alternatively, these amounts may be included in similar items in respect of owned fixed assets; in which case, the net amount of assets held under finance leases and the depreciation allocated for the period in respect of such leased assets included in the overall totals should be disclosed. (This alternative treatment is illustrated in the model financial statements of Delto PLC – see chapter 46.)

(b) The amount of lease obligations (net of future finance charges) should be disclosed separately either on the face of the balance sheet or in the notes, analysed between amounts payable within one year, in the second to fifth years inclusive, and amounts payable thereafter. Where the analysis is shown separately from amounts shown for other liabilities, it may be presented as an analysis of the gross obligations, with the future finance charges being separately deducted from the total. A suggested description of the net lease obligations is 'obligations under finance leases and hire purchase contracts'. In the model financial statements of Delto PLC (see chapter 46), the information is included with amounts for other borrowings. An example of the alternative presentation is set out in **29.71** below.

(c) The aggregate finance charges for the period should be disclosed.

(d) The amount of any commitments for finance leases entered into at the balance sheet date but whose inception occurs after the year end should be shown (see **29.72** for an example).

29.71 The presentation of obligations under finance leases and hire purchase contracts required by SSAP 21 (see **29.70**(b)) is illustrated below. The requirements of FRS 4 (as modified by FRS 13) should also be given (see **17.82**).

Example 29.71

Obligations under finance leases and hire purchase contracts

	2000 £'000	1999 £'000
Minimum lease payments payable		
Within one year	22	19
Between one and five years	104	101
After five years	16	14
	142	134
Less: Finance charges allocated		
to future periods	18	16
	124	118

29.72 The example below illustrates the disclosure of commitments for finance leases entered into at the balance sheet date but whose inception occurs after the year end (see **29.70** (d) above).

Example 29.72

The group has entered into a contract to lease an asset under a finance lease, whereby the asset will be delivered and rental obligations commence in February 2001. The minimum payments under the lease total £25,000, payable over five years.

Operating leases

29.73 Disclosures required in respect of operating leases are as follows:

(a) the lease payments which the lessee is committed to make during the next year should be disclosed. These commitments should be analysed between those relating to lease terms which expire within that year, those which expire in the second to fifth years inclusive and those which continue for over five years from the balance sheet date; commitments in respect of leases of land and buildings should be shown separately from other operating leases. An example of an appropriate note is shown in the model financial statements of Delto PLC (see chapter 46);

(b) the total operating lease rentals charged to the profit and loss account during the period should be disclosed, analysed between hire of plant and machinery and other operating leases.

Statutory disclosure requirements

29.74 The Act requires particulars to be given of any other financial commitments which have not been provided for and are relevant to assessing the company's state of affairs. [Sch 4: 50(5)] This disclosure is met by requirements in **29.70** (d) and **29.73** (a) above.

Accounting by lessors

Approach and materiality

29.75 The approach required by SSAP 21 to finance leases is to recognise the substance of the transaction, i.e., that the lessor is providing finance to the lessee to enable him to obtain the use of a specific asset. Consequently, the asset recognised by the lessor under a finance lease is the amount receivable from the lessee, rather than the asset which is the subject of the lease. Under an operating lease, the lessor treats the leased asset as a fixed asset and the rentals received as income.

29.76 Although SSAP 21 does not apply to immaterial items, most lessors carry out leasing business as a significant activity and it is therefore unlikely that the standard will not apply on the grounds of immateriality.

Classification of leases

29.77 The circumstances under which a lease is presumed to be a finance lease are the same for a lessor as for a lessee (see **29.16** to **29.35** above). However, there may be differences in circumstances, including differences in the cash flows arising, which may result in the lessor treating a lease in a different manner from the lessee; in particular, leases which are regarded as finance leases by lessors may be operating leases as far as lessees are concerned. The principal matters which give rise to these differences are summarised below:

(a) in determining the minimum lease payments, a lessee takes account only of payments to be made by him or by a party related to him, whereas the lessor also takes account of amounts to be received from independent third parties. A lessor may be able to arrange at or before the commencement of the lease that, at its conclusion, the asset will be sold to a third party at a guaranteed minimum price; he would take account of any such guaranteed residual value in determining the minimum lease payments;

(b) although the interest rate implicit in the lease and the fair value of the leased asset may not be known to the lessee, they will be known to the lessor. In determining the interest rate implicit in the lease, the lessor will take account of amounts receivable from all sources, including grants receivable and the incidence of tax relief.

Accounting for finance leases

29.78   The net investment in the lease should be recorded in the balance sheet as a debtor. Initially, the net investment is normally the cost to the lessor of the leased asset. As with any other debtor balance, consideration should be given to its collectibility and provision made for any anticipated losses. In considering collectibility, regard should be had not only to amounts expected to be received from the lessee but also to amounts which may be recovered by sale of the leased asset. The net investment in the lease is reduced over the lease period by the proportion of rental income which is treated as repayment of the debtor balance.

29.79   The rentals (net of any charges for services, etc.) received by the lessor should be apportioned between finance income to the lessor and repayment of the debtor balance. Over the whole period of the lease, the finance income equals the gross earnings from the lease, i.e., the amount by which the total of the receipts expected by the lessor exceeds the cost of the leased asset. The receipts expected by the lessor consist of the total rentals payable by the lessee, together with any residual value of the asset which is receivable by the lessor, whether or not that residual value is guaranteed. The cost of the asset is the net cost after deducting any grants receivable by the lessor.

29.80   The gross earnings should normally be allocated to accounting periods over the term of the lease so as to produce a constant rate of return (or a reasonable approximation to it) on the lessor's net cash investment in the lease. This allocation should take account not only of the cost of the asset and the rentals received but also of all cash flows associated with the lease (such as tax cash flows arising from capital allowances claimed by the lessor). The net cash investment at any given time is:

(a)   the net investment at the start of the lease (i.e., the cost of the asset less related grants); plus

(b)   the following related payments:

    (i)   taxation payments on the rental income;
    (ii)   interest payments on related borrowings; and

(c)   profit taken out of the lease; less

(d)   the following related receipts:

    (i)   rentals received (excluding charges for services, etc.);
    (ii)   interest received on any cash surplus;
    (iii)   taxation receipts, including reductions in taxation liabilities as a result of capital allowances on the leased asset (to the extent that these are given to the lessor); and
    (iv)   any amount received for the sale of the asset at the end

of the lease term or, if no amount is received, its residual value (if any) at that time.

29.81 The guidance notes to SSAP 21 set out two methods which are commonly used to allocate gross earnings so as to give a constant rate of return on the net cash investment:

- actuarial method after tax; and

- investment period method.

29.82 Under the 'actuarial method after tax', a rate is calculated which, when applied to the net cash invested in the lease, makes the total return over the whole period during which cash flows occur in respect of the lease equal to the gross earnings determined as above.

29.83 Under the 'investment period method', the net cash invested is calculated as for the actuarial method. The gross earnings are then allocated to those periods in which the lessor has positive cash invested. This allocation is made in proportion to the net cash invested in each period.

29.84 The two methods will generally lead to very similar results. The main difference will occur where the net cash invested becomes negative at some stage. In these circumstances, the investment period method gives a more prudent result. In both cases, the calculations are complex. As a result, it is likely that lessors will have developed or acquired computer tools to assist in the calculations. Consequently, no examples are produced here. However, examples of calculations using each method are given in the guidance notes to SSAP 21.

29.85 Where, under Inland Revenue statement of practice, capital allowances are not given to the lessor, the impact on the lessor's net cash investment of tax effects will be reduced. Similarly, hire purchase contracts which are considered to be finance leases will not normally give rise to cash flows for the lessor, as a result of such items as capital allowances. Consequently, an allocation of gross earnings so as to give a constant rate of return on the net investment (i.e., the balance sheet carrying value of the debtor before any provision for bad and doubtful debts) will usually be an acceptable approximation to an allocation based on net cash investment. The guidance notes to SSAP 21 contain examples of two methods: the actuarial method before tax and the sum of digits method, which may be appropriate for hire purchase contracts. These methods were dealt with in **29.42** and **29.43** above.

29.86 Initial direct costs, such as commission, legal fees, selling costs, etc., which are incurred by the lessor in arranging a lease, may be deferred and apportioned over the period of the lease on a systematic and rational basis or they may be written off as incurred. Apportionment may be achieved by treating the costs as a deduction from gross earnings before the earnings are allocated to accounting periods.

29.87 Where grants are received against the purchase price of assets acquired for leasing, they should be credited to income over the period of the lease. This will occur automatically by applying the methods of allocating finance income set out above. In most cases, some or all of the benefit of receipt of a grant will be passed on to the lessee in the form of reduced rentals. Where a grant is tax free, this may result in the lessor's profit and loss account showing a loss before tax and a profit after tax in respect of that lease. For accounting periods ending before 22 June 1997, SSAP 21 allowed, as an option to treating the grant as tax-free income, the grossing up of the grant at the appropriate tax rate by adding the appropriate amount both to pre-tax profits and to the tax charge for the period. However, for periods ending on or after 22 June 1997, an amendment to SSAP 21, issued in February 1997, removes this option. More generally, UITF Abstract 16 *Income and expenses subject to non-standard rates of tax,* issued at the same time as the amendment to SSAP 21, prohibits the practice of grossing up items of profit before tax, and tax charges, on all transactions which are subject to non-standard tax rates. This prohibition has been repeated in FRS 16 which supersedes UITF Abstract 16 and is effective for periods ending on or after 23 March 2000.

Accounting for operating leases

29.88 Assets leased under operating leases should be recorded as fixed assets and depreciated over their useful lives. The method of depreciation should reflect the pattern of usage of the asset, e.g., a straight-line basis where the asset is used evenly over its life or a usage basis where the pattern of rental is uneven (see **29.91** and **29.92** below).

29.89 Rental income, excluding charges for services such as insurance and maintenance, should be recognised on a straight-line basis over the lease term, even though the payments are not made on that basis, unless another systematic and rational basis is more representative of the way in which the benefit of the leased asset is receivable (e.g., where rentals are based on usage).

29.90 Initial direct costs in arranging the lease may either be written off immediately or deferred and amortised over the lease term.

29.91 The result of recognising operating lease income on a straight-line basis and the depreciation on a straight-line basis as set out above may be recognition of a loss in early years, even on a profitable lease, and higher profits in later years. The new Finance and Leasing

Association SORP recognises that when an asset is leased for a substantial portion of its economic life it has some of the attributes of a financial asset. The method of depreciation which is consistent with viewing the asset as having many of the attributes of a financial asset is one which reflects the time value of money, the annuity method. This results in a lower depreciation charge in earlier years and a more constant net profit after interest.

29.92　The SORP therefore permits lessors to use the annuity method of depreciation for assets leased under operating leases where:

(a)　the asset is let on a lease that is for a substantial portion of the total economic life of the asset;

(b)　the terms of the lease adequately protect the lessor against early cancellation; and

(c)　adequate income is retained in the lease to cover future uncertainties in respect of the realisation of residual values.

29.93　The ASB are expected to endorse this approach of charging 'economic depreciation' as a temporary measure pending the replacement of SSAP 21 with a new standard (see **29.102** below).

Accounting by manufacturers and dealers

29.94　Where a manufacturer or dealer offers leasing terms as an option to normal selling terms (termed, in the USA, a 'sales-type lease'), a question arises as to whether or not an immediate selling profit should be recognised when the asset is first leased. The answer will depend on whether there has, in effect, been a disposal of that asset. This in turn will depend whether the lease is an operating or finance lease.

29.95　In the case of an operating lease, the manufacturer or dealer has retained the asset with a view to using it to generate rental income. Consequently, no selling profit should be recognised and the asset should be included in the balance sheet initially at its purchase price or production cost.

29.96　In the case of a finance lease, there are two types of income associated with the contract: a profit on the 'sale' of the asset and finance income over the period of the lease. The selling profit should be recognised at the commencement of the lease. However, the amount of selling profit should be restricted to the excess of the fair value of the asset (i.e., its normal selling price reflecting appropriate discounts and current market conditions) over its cost to the lessor (net of grants receivable by the lessor). As the lessor will often allow some degree of discount on the normal selling price in order to obtain the overall deal, the assessment of the fair value of the asset should be calculated to ensure that the finance income under the lease is based on a normal rate of interest.

Disclosures

29.97 The disclosure requirements of SSAP 21 for lessors are summarised in the following paragraphs.

Accounting policies

29.98 The policies adopted for accounting for operating leases and finance leases and, in detail, the policy for recognising finance lease income should be disclosed.

Finance leases

29.99 The following should be disclosed:

(a) the net investment in finance leases (subdivided between finance leases and hire purchase contracts) at the balance sheet date; this amount should be included under debtors and a suitable description is 'Amounts receivable under finance leases (and hire purchase contracts)';

(b) the cost of assets acquired for the purpose of letting under finance leases; and

(c) the aggregate rentals receivable in the accounting period in respect of finance leases.

Operating leases

29.100 The following should be disclosed:

(a) the gross amount and related accumulated depreciation charges of assets held for use in operating leases; and

(b) the aggregate rentals receivable in the accounting period in respect of operating leases.

Comparison with International Accounting Standards

29.101 IAS 17 (revised) *Accounting for leases* is similar to SSAP 21. Significant differences are:

(a) definition of a finance lease: the IAS definition does not contain any rebuttable presumption equivalent to the '90 per cent test';

(b) lessor recognition of income: lessors are required to recognise income on the net investment method. The net cash investment method is not recognised;

(c) the IAS level of note disclosures is higher.

Future developments

Revision of SSAP 21

29.102   In December 1999 the ASB issued a discussion paper *Leases: Implementation of a New Approach*. This is the position paper developed by the G4+1 group which comprises the national accounting standard-setters of the UK, Australia, Canada, New Zealand and the USA, together with the IASC. This paper builds on the group's special report *Accounting for Leases: A New Approach* issued in 1996. Both papers recognise that, under the various frameworks used in these countries, the present distinction between finance and operating leases is arbitrary and does not reflect the economic reality which is that the obligations which exist under operating leases are no different to those created by finance leases. The ASB supports the central proposal of the paper that all leases should be dealt with on a consistent basis. There are some areas where the Board has a different view to that expressed in the paper, but it believes that in the interests of achieving international harmonisation at this stage the paper should be presented as originally prepared. The ASB intends to proceed with a revision of SSAP 21 on the basis of this paper. Internationally taking these proposals further may proceed at a slower pace.

29.103   The central proposal of the discussion paper is that accounting for leases should be approached in accordance with the normal principles of asset and liability recognition as set out in the statement of principles.

Proposed scope

29.104   It is proposed that the scope of a revised leasing standard be wider than the current scope of SSAP 21. It would apply additionally to leases of intangible assets including exploration rights and licensing agreements such as film rights. Although the original 1996 paper suggested a de minimus period of one year below which capitalisation would be avoided, the discussion paper proposes no minimum time period and refers instead to the general concept of materiality applying to all standards.

29.105   Executory contracts (see **17.161** above) and contracts for services are excluded from the scope of the discussion paper. However, where a contract for services also provides for access to property, the two elements should be separated and the property element accounted for as a lease. This is the approach that FRS 5 requires in relation to PFI contracts.

29.106   One question raised in the proposals is whether properties used as 'investment' properties should be included in the proposals. In general, in the UK, leases over land and buildings held for investment purposes are currently viewed as operating leases. Thus the lessor shows the property in its balance sheet at current open market value. The general recommendations of the discussion paper would lead such lessors to record a financial asset and a residual interest (see **29.121** below). The proposals conclude that leases over land and buildings should be within the scope of a new standard, but that current information on market values should be preserved, a point specifically supported by the ASB. One solution proposed is to report the interest in residual value each period as the difference between the lease receivable and fair value.

Accounting by lessees

29.107 The paper proposes that 'Assets and liabilities should be recognised by a lessee in relation to the rights and obligations conveyed by a lease when the lessor has substantially performed its obligation to provide the lessee with access to the leased property for the lease term.' In general the lessor will be deemed to have 'substantially performed' its obligation when the leased property is delivered or otherwise made available to the lessee, not when the lease is signed.

29.108 The asset and corresponding liability would be recorded at the present value of the minimum payments required by the lease plus the fair value of any residual value guarantee. Although not explicitly stated, it is assumed that the rentals paid would subsequently be allocated between repayment of the liability and interest charge so as to produce a constant periodic rate of charge on the remaining obligation, as per the current SSAP 21 requirement for finance lease obligations.

29.109 Leases can include various additional terms and the discussion paper includes chapters dealing with 'leases with optional features' and 'lessees' interests in residual values'. The overall recommendations in respect of accounting for these features is summarised as:

(a) Options to renew or cancel the lease – the term of a lease would be assumed to be the minimum possible under the lease and any cost of exercising an option to cancel would be included in the minimum lease payments. The conditions attached to some cancellation or renewal options effectively restrict the lessee's ability to exercise the option, e.g., cancellation is only permitted if a lease for a new asset is entered into. In these circumstances the initial recognition of the asset and liability should reflect that the lease will not be cancelled.

(b) A renewal or purchase option that has significant value which can be reliably measured should be accounted for separately from the rights to use the property for the non-cancellable period. A portion of the minimum lease payments would be deemed payment for the option.

(c) Contingent rentals based upon additional usage also represent an option to 'purchase more' of an asset and again where freely exercisable would not be anticipated.

(d) Contingent rentals based on the lessee's profits or revenue again would not be recognised until the contingencies are met. However, if the minimum payments are clearly unrepresentative of the property rights conveyed by the lease, the fair value of the rights should be recognised as assets and liabilities.

(e) Additional assets and liabilities arising from the exercise of a renewal option would be accounted for when the option is exercised. Similarly, contingent rentals would be recognised when their payment is triggered.

(f) Lessee guarantees of residual value or rights to receive a surplus or pay a shortfall on sale – if it is practical to value the guarantee or agreement, the initial asset and liability recorded will be the present value of the lease payments plus the fair value of the guarantee.

Contingent rentals and options

29.110 The general proposals outlined above apply the normal asset and liability recognition principles and the resulting asset and liability reflect the flexibility afforded by any options included in the lease. However, in two respects the paper proposes to deviate from the liability recognition principle and require recognition of a liability and corresponding asset even though the legal obligation arises only if the entity continues to operate in the future. These are the proposals that:

(a) a renewal option should be assumed to be exercised when an entity is compelled to renew the lease. The factors which might indicate compulsion to renew include those such as:

(i) the uniqueness of purpose of location of the asset;
(ii) its importance to the continuance of the business;
(iii) the costs associated with relocation and replacement; and
(iv) the willingness of the lessee to bear these costs.

(b) where the lease includes a large proportion of contingent rentals such that 'the minimum payments are clearly unrepresentative of the property rights conveyed by the lease', the fair value of the rights should be recognised as assets and liabilities.

29.111 At present under SSAP 21 the lease term is taken to include further terms for which the lessee has the option to continue to lease the asset, with or without further payment, which option it is reasonably certain at the inception of the lease that the lessee will exercise.

29.112 The proposals would result in a reduction in the asset and liability currently reflected under finance leases where further terms have been assumed.

Rent review clauses

29.113 Some leases, particularly property leases in the UK, provide for review of rentals in line with prices. These represent an obligation of uncertain amount. The view supported by the discussion paper is that on initial recognition, an estimate of the contingent obligation should be included which should be updated at each balance sheet date. The ASB supports the alternative view presented that a reliable estimate of the amount payable cannot be made and the asset and liability should be adjusted only when the rents are revised.

Lessees' interests in residual values

29.114 Currently if a residual value guarantee results in all the risks and rewards, including changes in residual value, passing to the lessee, the total fair value of the asset and corresponding liability are recognised by the lessee. The discussion paper proposals are such that if a residual value guarantee results in all risks and rewards passing to the lessee, but only a 'net' payment/receipt of the shortfall/excess is made with respect to the residual value, a lower asset and liability excluding the estimated residual value, but including the fair value of the guarantee, is recognised.

29.115 The reason for proposing this treatment rather than including the 'total' asset is that it can be applied to more complex guarantee arrangements. In practice it may be difficult to arrive at a fair value for the guarantee. One method is to compare the rental payments of the lease with those that would be seen under a lease without the guarantee.

29.116 An alternative view to the valuation of the guarantee is the provisions approach under which the amount included is the probable amount payable under the guarantee.

29.117 Any changes in the value of the residual value guarantee after initial recognition would be reflected by adjustments to the asset and liability.

Discount rates

29.118 Under SSAP 21 the discount rate used to arrive at the present value of the lease payments is the rate implicit in the lease. However, this is the rate that when applied to the amounts the *lessor* expects to receive equals the fair value of the asset. Where the lessor bears the risk in relation to residual value this rate reflects not only the credit risk in respect of the lessee, but also the risk in relation to the residual value. For this reason the discussion paper recommends that the rate applied by the lessee to arrive at the present value of rentals should be:

(a) an estimate of the lessee's incremental borrowing rate for a loan of similar term and with the same security as is provided by the lease; or

(b) the rate implicit in the lease when it is known by the lessee and represents a reasonable approximation for the rate in (a).

Sale and leaseback

29.119 The discussion paper rightly concludes that a sale and leaseback cannot be viewed as an arm's length transaction and should be accounted for under the 'one transaction' approach under which a gain would be recognised in respect of that portion of the asset which has been disposed of; the remaining asset would be shown at a proportion of the previous carrying value.

29.120 Under what is termed the 'two transaction' approach, which is discussed but not supported by the paper, the outcome would be that the portion of the asset retained would be recorded at current fair value.

Accounting by lessors

29.121 The basic recommendation for lessors is that on initial recording of the lease two components would be recorded:

(a) a financial asset being the rentals receivable; and

(b) a non-financial asset representing an interest in the residual asset (guaranteed or unguaranteed) at the end of the lease.

29.122 This recommendation is made on the basis that separate recognition of the two components in respect of the leased asset better reflects the different risks associated with the two components; full disclosure would be made of any residual value guarantees and similar arrangements.

29.123 In some circumstances, discussed in **29.130** below, the recommendations in the paper would permit a gain to be recognised on inception of the lease. Where no gain is recognised the previous carrying amount of the asset would be split between the lease receivable and the residual asset. This allocation would be based on discounting the cashflows associated with the two components at discount rates reflecting the different risks.

Subsequent measurement

29.124 Subsequent profit recognition on the rentals receivable would be using an appropriate interest method; the ASB supports the net cash investment basis for the UK, as at present. The paper also discusses the net investment method which is likely to be used internationally.

29.125 Receivable assets that include elements of contingent rentals should be remeasured during the lease term to current expected values with a corresponding gain or loss recognised immediately in the profit and loss account. However, if the increase in rentals represents a higher usage which would affect the residual value, the carrying amount of the residual value would be reduced.

29.126 The residual interest asset is initially recorded at the present value of the estimated residual value at the end of the lease. Over the lease term the carrying amount would be increased by 'unwinding' the discount. This interest would be recognised in the profit and loss account.

Optional features

29.127 These would be considered in the same way as for the lessee. On initial recognition of the lease the lessor would assume that the lease would be terminated at the earliest date the lessee has the right to terminate.

29.128 When a renewal or purchase option is exercised by the lessee, the lessor should record the additional rentals receivable and correspondingly reduce the residual interest.

29.129 If the minimum payments required by the lease are unrepresentative of the value of the property rights conveyed, the lessor should record a financial asset equivalent to the fair value of such rights. This corresponds to the asset and liability that it is proposed the lessee should recognise (see **29.109** above).

Recognition of gains at the beginning of the lease

29.130 Under SSAP 21 a lessor is not permitted to recognise a gain on inception of a lease except in the case of a manufacturer or dealer (see **29.94** above). The discussion paper recommends that this continues where:

    (a)   there is evidence of the increase in value of assets as a result of the lease; and

(b)   the increase can be reliably measured.

29.131   More significantly the paper recommends that this be extended so that a gain can also be recognised in other cases if the carrying amount of the property subject to the lease is demonstrably lower than its fair value, e.g., a property which had been held for a number of years at historic cost.

29.132   Any gain permitted to be recognised would be restricted to reflect the proportion of the asset being transferred under the lease.

30 Pension costs

30 Pension costs

Summary of changes since the previous issue of this publication

Para.	Topic	Summary
30.67	FRED 20 *Retirement benefits*	Proposes radical changes for defined benefit schemes leading to increased volatility in the balance sheet as actuarial gains and losses are recognised immediately in the STRGL and scheme assets are valued at fair values.

Introduction

Types of pension scheme

30.1 Over the last few decades, occupational pension schemes which provide benefits for employees on their retirement have become almost universal for employers in the UK. The usual pattern is for both employee and employer to pay regular amounts, based on a percentage of the employee's salary.

30.2 There are two main types of occupational pension scheme in the UK:

(a) defined benefit schemes (also called final salary schemes), in which the rules specify the benefits to be paid (usually based on the employee's average or final pay), the scheme being financed accordingly; and

(a) defined contribution schemes (commonly called money purchase schemes), where the rate of contribution is normally specified in the rules. The individual member's benefits are determined by reference to contributions paid into the scheme in respect of that member, usually increased by an amount based on the investment return on those contributions.

30.3   In a defined contribution scheme, the employer's cost comprises the contributions payable.

30.4   For a defined benefit scheme, the situation is more complex, since the benefits to be paid are dependent on the average or final pay of the employee and the remaining lifetime of pensioner members of the scheme. The impossibility of predicting the pensions, benefits and investment returns on contributions means that the pension cost for each financial year can only be fully determined when the scheme is being wound up. In the meantime, it has to be assessed by actuarial calculation. Such actuarial reviews are normally made every three years.

Costs of pensions and other post-retirement benefits

30.5   Prior to the introduction of SSAP 24, pension costs in the accounts of employing companies were almost universally determined on the basis of funding, i.e., the amount of contributions payable into the scheme each year by the employer. However, for defined benefit schemes, funding requirements may vary considerably from valuation to valuation as a consequence of changes in the various factors, such as investment returns, salary levels and staff turnover. The result was that cost could fluctuate from year to year and not match the provision of benefits with the service of the employee. To eliminate such distortions, which became increasingly evident as many occupational pension schemes moved into substantial surplus in the early 1980s, the ASC developed SSAP 24, which became effective for UK companies for financial periods commencing on or after 1 July 1988. SSAP 24 is currently under review and the ASB has issued two discussion papers and a FRED on the subject (see **30.67** et seq. below). Until a new accounting standard is issued, SSAP 24 remains the current accounting standard.

30.6   SSAP 24 addresses pensions, but suggests that its principles might be equally applicable to the cost of providing other post-retirement benefits. This suggestion, although effectively withdrawn for some time by Technical Release (TR) 756, was given 'force' in 1992, when the UITF issued UITF Abstract 6 *Accounting for post-retirement benefits other than pensions* (see **30.53** to **30.57** below).

30.7   The ASB amended SSAP 15 *Accounting for deferred tax* in December 1992, to allow the same recognition criteria to be applied to deferred tax in respect of pensions and other post-retirement benefits as are applied to the obligations themselves (see chapter 27 above).

Accounting requirements of SSAP 24

Basic principles

30.8   The accounting objective of SSAP 24 is that the employer should recognise the expected cost of providing pensions on a systematic and rational basis over the period during which he derives benefit from the employees' services. [SSAP 24(77)] For defined contribution schemes, the charge against profits should be the amount of contributions payable to the pension scheme in respect of the accounting period. [SSAP 24(78)] For defined benefit schemes, the pension cost should be calculated using actuarial valuation methods providing the actuary's best estimate of the cost of the promised benefits. [SSAP 24(79)] The SSAP recognises two elements of pension cost for a defined benefit scheme: the regular cost and variations from the regular cost. These terms are considered more fully in **30.9** to **30.27** below.

Regular cost

30.9   SSAP 24 states that 'the method of providing for expected pension costs over the service lives of employees in the scheme should be such that the regular pension cost is a substantially level percentage of the current and future pensionable payroll in the light of current actuarial assumptions'. [SSAP 24(79)] The explanatory note defines regular pension cost as 'the consistent ongoing cost recognised under the actuarial method used'. [SSAP 24(20)] Actuaries view regular pension cost as being the standard contribution rate calculated on an acceptable actuarial method (see **30.10** below) before allowing for any surplus or deficit (where such a rate exists). However, the SSAP recognises as an acceptable alternative that regular cost can mean the stable contribution rate for regular contributions, expressed as a percentage of pensionable earnings, provided it makes full provision for the expected benefits over the anticipated service lives of employees. [SSAP 24(20)]

Actuarial methods

30.10   There are a number of actuarial methods which are encountered in practice. The main methods are:

- projected unit method;
- current unit method;
- entry age method;
- attained age method; and
- aggregate method.

30.11 The projected unit, entry age and attained age methods will usually form an acceptable basis for the determination of pension cost under SSAP 24. Indeed, the projected unit method is the approach favoured by the 1995 discussion paper and the FRED (see **30.67** et seq. below). The current unit and any method applied on a discontinuance basis will generally not be acceptable, the former because it does not take into account final salaries and the latter because it assumes that the scheme is to be wound up. The aggregate method, as strictly defined, does not deal properly with those items of surplus or deficit which do not fall to be spread. Therefore, it cannot, in general, be used to calculate pension cost. If the method is used loosely enough to comply with SSAP 24, it should probably be described as an attained age method. However, it should be recognised that a number of variations of actuarial methods exist such that categorisation should not be seen as being definitive. The essential feature of any actuarial valuation method used to calculate pension cost under SSAP 24 is that it should be such that the regular pension cost (the consistent ongoing cost recognised under the actuarial method used) is a substantially level percentage of the current and future pensionable payroll in the light of the current actuarial assumptions. The choice of assumptions will vary according to the membership profile of the scheme, the actuarial method used and the judgement of the actuary. It is important to ensure that the assumptions and method as a whole are compatible with the accounting objective of SSAP 24 and should lead to the actuary's best estimate of the cost of providing the pension benefits.

Variations from regular cost

30.12 Variations from regular cost may occur if the experience of the scheme varies from the assumptions made by the actuary. Variations may arise from:

(a) experience surplus or deficiencies, where the assumptions made by the actuary, e.g., on salary inflation or return on investments, have not been borne out in practice;

(b) the effect of changes in assumptions or actuarial method on the actuarial value of accrued benefits as calculated at the previous valuation;

(c) retroactive changes in conditions of membership or changes in benefits, e.g., admission of part-time employees; and

(d) increases to pensions in payment or to deferred pensions for which provision has not previously been made.

[SSAP 24(21)]

30.13 Such variations should generally not be treated as a prior period adjustment, but spread forward over the average remaining service lives of current employees in the scheme. However, there are exemptions from this general rule. These are discussed in **30.17** to **30.27** below.

30.14 UITF Abstract 18 *Pension costs following the 1997 tax changes in respect of dividend income* was issued by the UITF in December 1997 and is effective for accounting periods ending on or after 23 December 1997. The abstract addressees the loss that arises in the financial statements of employers sponsoring defined benefit schemes as a result of the Finance (No. 2) Act 1997, which removed the right of pension schemes to reclaim a tax credit on dividend income. The abstract indicates that the loss of the right to reclaim the tax credit does not, of itself, fall outside of the normal scope of the actuarial assumptions (see **30.20** below). It is simply a change in the expected return on assets, similar to those arising from changes in tax rates. Hence, the loss should be spread forward over the expected remaining service lives of current employees in the scheme, whatever the financial position of the scheme and regardless of any additional contributions that are made.

30.15 Although requiring regular cost to be a substantially level percentage of pensionable payroll, no guidance is given in SSAP 24 as to the means of amortising variations other than requiring them to be allocated over average remaining service lives. This is one of the areas addressed in the 1995 discussion paper but which ceases to be relevant under the immediate recognition proposals of FRED 20 (see **30.67** et seq. below). In their computations of pension cost, it is common to see actuaries amortise variations from regular cost in a number of different ways. Three main approaches may be identified:

(a) spreading variations as a percentage of payroll;

(b) straight-line amortisation of the capital amount with interest on the reducing balance; and

(c) the mortgage method whereby equal amounts of interest and capital are charged or credited each year.

30.16 On a theoretical basis, it can be argued that amortisation of a variation as a percentage of payroll is to be preferred. Regular cost is calculated on this basis and it is therefore logical to calculate the variations in the same way. However, whichever method of amortising variations is applied, it is important to consider the long-term effects on pension costs, because a short-term advantage by the use of a particular method may

> give rise to unacceptable fluctuations in the cost profile. In particular, methods should be avoided which give rise to a pension cost which fluctuates from negative to positive. Whichever method of amortisation is applied, it is recommended that it be disclosed.

30.17 In certain circumstances, SSAP 24 permits or requires an alternative treatment for such variations (see **30.18** to **30.26** below).

Significant reduction in the number of employees

30.18 To the extent that contributions are adjusted to eliminate a surplus or deficit arising as a result of a significant reduction of the number of employees covered by the company's pension arrangements, the surplus or deficit should not be spread forward as noted in **30.13** above. SSAP 24 identifies two mutually exclusive treatments in such a situation:

(a) A reduction in contributions arising from a significant reduction in employees should be recognised over the period of any consequential reduction in funding. If, therefore, the actuary advises that funding be reduced over a period of two years to eliminate such a surplus, the surplus should be recognised during the two years following his recommendation and not spread over a longer period. Although SSAP 24 does not explicitly state that the same treatment should be followed in respect of a deficit it would be inconsistent not to do so. The provision in **30.20** would support such an approach.

(b) The treatment of a surplus or deficit in (a) above would not be followed where such treatment would be inconsistent with FRS 3 in relation to the sale or termination of an operation; in such a case, SSAP 24 requires that the pension cost or credit should be recognised immediately to the extent necessary to comply with the provisions of FRS 3 relating to the consequences of a decision to sell or terminate an operation (see **9.164** above). [SSAP 24(81)]

30.19 Thus, if an employer made a substantial reduction in its workforce, any resulting change in funding should be recognised in the profit and loss account in the period over which the change in funding occurs, which may extend over a number of accounting periods. However, to the extent that the pension surplus or deficit arises from a reduction in employees resulting from the sale or termination of an operation, it should be taken into account in arriving at the provision required in respect of the sale or termination and included in the profit and loss on sale or termination. This may result in the setting up of a pension prepayment (or provision) to be released as any lower (higher) future funding level recommended to take account of the surplus (deficit) is offset against (included in) pension cost in subsequent years.

Material deficit

30.20 If there is a material deficit, prudence may require that the deficit be recognised over a period shorter than the employees' average remaining service lives. [SSAP 24(82)] The SSAP envisages this as being of strictly limited application, where a major event or transaction not allowed for in the actuarial assumptions and outside their normal scope has necessitated the payment of significant additional contributions to the scheme, e.g., where there has been a complete failure of a major investment made by the scheme. [SSAP 24(28)]

Refunds

30.21 Taxed refunds paid by the pension scheme trustees to the employing company under the Finance Act 1986 can either be spread forward or credited when they occur. [SSAP 24(83)] The accounting treatment adopted for such refunds should be disclosed. [SSAP 24(88)] This option to recognise a surplus immediately applies where a refund is paid and only to the extent of the refund. It does not apply to any contribution reduction or holiday agreed under the legislation as part of a plan to reduce the surplus.

30.22 Because of the formalities which have to be completed before a refund is payable to the employer, it is quite possible that the amount of the refund will be finally determined and paid in an accounting period after that in which the application to the relevant authorities has been made. SSAP 24 makes it clear that such a refund may only be credited to the profit and loss account when it is received. This should be interpreted in a very restricted way. It is not acceptable to anticipate the amount as a debtor. However, it may be necessary, in order to present a true and fair view, to refer to the matter of a refund and its amount in the pensions note if a refund of a significant amount has been applied for and is expected to be credited in the following accounting period.

30.23 There seems little conceptual merit to this exception to the general spreading rule. The ASB's 1995 discussion paper (see **30.67** et seq. below) suggests that a refund should be treated as a negative pension contribution and adjusted against any pension item in the balance sheet, rather than being credited to the profit and loss account. The FRED does not explicitly discuss refunds but the effect of any contribution or refund would be to increase or decrease the net pension asset or liability and not to impact the performance statements.

30.24 Such refunds are subject to 40 per cent tax at source and the tax cannot be offset or refunded. The employer receives only the net payment, the tax having been paid to the Inland Revenue by the scheme administrator. If the refund is accounted for as it occurs, it should normally be credited to the profit and loss account on a gross basis, with the tax deducted forming part of the taxation charge for the year. If the refund arose as a result of an extraordinary event, an unlikely situation following the issue of FRS 3, then the net refund should be included within extraordinary items with separate disclosure of the tax effect.

Discretionary and ex gratia payments

30.25 Most occupational pension schemes are a legal and contractual obligation on the part of the employer and the benefits on retirement are specified. However, the capital cost of discretionary and *ex gratia* pensions increases not allowed for by the actuary and not covered by a surplus should be recognised in the profit and loss account in the period in which they are initially granted. [SSAP 24(85)] In practice, many actuaries do take such increases into account in their valuation assumptions and this should be encouraged. The alternative could have a material impact on profits in years when such increases are granted.

30.26 The capital cost of granting *ex gratia* pensions should also be recognised in the profit and loss account in the period in which such pensions are granted, to the extent not covered by a surplus. [SSAP 24(84)] If such a pension is paid by the employer and not the scheme, then the full cost must be charged to the profit and loss account even where a surplus exists in the scheme.

Summary

30.27 The treatments of variations from regular cost are summarised in the table below.

Source of variation	Spread over expected future service lives	Immediate debit/credit to the profit and loss account
Experience surpluses or deficiencies, e.g., better investment return than assumed (see **30.12** to **30.13**)	Yes	No
Changes in actuarial assumptions or method of valuation (see **30.12** to **30.13**)	Yes	No
Capital cost of pension increases and *ex gratia* pensions not allowed for in actuarial assumption to the extent not covered by a surplus (see **30.12** to **30.13** and **30.25** to **30.26**)	No	Yes
Refund of surplus to company under the Finance Act 1986 (see **30.12** to **30.13** and **30.21**)	Optional	Optional
Significant reduction in workforce (see **30.12** to **30.13** and **30.18** to **30.19**)	No	Reduction in funding recognised as it occurs
Significant reduction in workforce resulting from sale or termination of an operation (see **30.12** to **30.13** and **30.18** to **30.19**)	No	Consistency with FRS 3 required
Material deficit due to a major event or transaction not allowed for by the actuary outside the usual scope and requiring significant additional contributions (see **30.12** to **30.13** and **30.20**)	Prudence may require use of a period shorter than expected future service lives	No

Interest

30.28   Although SSAP 24 touches briefly on interest and discounting it does not set any standard practice. [SSAP 24(40)] It notes that the interest effects of short-term timing differences are unlikely to be material, but that, for long-term differences, interest may need to be recognised.

30.29

> Any surplus or deficit in a pension scheme generates further income or costs to be borne by the employing company and it has been widely recognised that computation of interest on provisions and prepayments is appropriate, provided that the amount of any such surplus or deficit has been discounted by the actuary in his calculations of the amount. This interest should be presented as part of the pension cost, as its nature is so different from what is normally recognised as interest receivable or payable and because it forms part of the actuarial assessment of pension cost. If interest is ignored in the computation of pension cost, then it will become part of the variation from regular cost and be spread forward instead of coming through in the year in which it is earned or incurred.

Subsequent valuations

30.30

> Actuarial valuations are generally performed every three years. Thus, subsequent valuations are likely to identify new variations, when variations calculated at the previous valuation are still being amortised. Although SSAP 24 does not address this topic, there are two basic accounting choices:
>
> (a)   to spread forward the surpluses or deficits at previous valuations on their original bases of amortisation, spreading any new variation which has arisen since the latest valuation over the estimated remaining service lives of employees at the latest valuation date. This means that the pension cost may include a number of variations being amortised; and
>
> (b)   to assess the total surplus or deficit at the latest valuation date, combining the previous surpluses or deficits which have not been amortised with any which has arisen since the last valuation and spread forward the total variation over the expected remaining service lives of current employees.

30.31   Method (a) in **30.30** above is perhaps theoretically more correct. It results in greater complexity, both in keeping track of the differing variations and in the level of disclosure required if both the spreading method and period are disclosed for each variation. Method (b) has the advantage of simplicity, the amount being spread over the expected remaining service lives being the aggregate of the surplus or deficit identified in the latest valuation and the accrual or prepayment recognised in the balance sheet resulting from the earlier valuation. In practice, the second method is more likely to be adopted. The uncertainties inherent in assessing pension cost are such that it would be difficult to argue that the first approach is superior.

30.32   The second approach was favoured in the ASB 1995 discussion paper (see **30.67** below). The question is not relevant to FRED 20 as surpluses and deficits are recognised immediately under its proposals.

Transitional provisions

30.33   SSAP 24 applies to accounting periods beginning on or after 1 July 1988, so it should have been implemented some years ago in most companies. However, the effect of the transitional provisions, which permitted departure from the normal spreading rule, may still be there. In addition, UITF Abstract 6 (see **30.53** to **30.57** below) requires the transitional rules of SSAP 24 to be applied to post-retirement benefits other than pensions. For these reasons, the transitional provisions are discussed below.

30.34   A cumulative adjustment may have arisen in respect of prior years at the date when SSAP 24 was first applied. This represented the actuarial value of the surplus or deficit of pension fund assets less liabilities on an ongoing basis, as adjusted by any existing provision for unfunded pension costs or pension prepayments. When first applying the SSAP, such an adjustment could either be treated in accordance with the other provisions of the statement (i.e., normally spread forward) or treated as a cumulative adjustment in accordance with the provisions of FRS 3 (i.e., prior period adjustment).

30.35   In practice, three methods of dealing with the cumulative adjustment on implementation emerged:

(a)   the surplus or deficit was identified at the beginning of the accounting period when the SSAP was first implemented and spread forward over the expected remaining service lives of employees from that date. Those parts that could not be spread forward were dealt with as discussed in **30.17** to **30.27** above (i.e., recognised in the period or over a period less than the expected remaining service lives);

(b)   the surplus or deficit arising at the previous valuation was spread forward from the previous valuation date over the estimated expected service lives of employees at the valuation date, as though SSAP 24 became effective from that date. Items that could not be spread forward were dealt with as discussed in **30.17** to **30.27** above. Prior period figures were adjusted accordingly; or

(c)   the surplus or deficit at the implementation date was identified and credited or debited to profit and loss account as a single prior period adjustment, with the corresponding prepayment or creditor being amortised.

30.36   Methods (a) and (b) in **30.35** above both apply the normal spreading rules of SSAP 24. However under method (a), the prior period pension charge may not have been comparable. Method (c) has been widely adopted by companies with large pension scheme surpluses. It is argued that overfunding in the past has meant too high a charge to the profit and loss account and that the surplus should be written back to that account. One major disadvantage of taking credit for a surplus in this way may arise if any subsequent actuarial valuation reveals that the level of surplus as shown in the balance sheet is in excess of that calculated by the actuary. In such circumstances, it can be argued that prudence and the Act require that the surplus be written down through the profit and loss account and this may have a material effect on the company's results in the year of the valuation. Method (b) would seem to be the most consistent with FRS 3 and the way in which other standards have been implemented. It also has the advantage of ensuring compliance with the Act by providing corresponding amounts which are not provided under methods (a) or (c), the SSAP having been interpreted as not requiring them.

30.37   Use of method (c) in **30.35** above requires that the prepayment or creditor be amortised in some way. SSAP 24 requires that the cumulative adjustment should be spread over the remaining service lives of current employees or accounted for as a prior period adjustment. [SSAP 24(53)] The 'or' appears to allow the prepayment or creditor arising as a result of method (c) to be amortised over a period other than remaining service life. One approach used in practice is to release the prepayment or creditor so as to give a pension charge equal to regular cost.

30.38   Disclosure of the method of application of transitional provisions was required in the period in which SSAP 24 was first implemented.

Negative pension costs

30.39 It is possible for a surplus to be so large that once spread the variation exceeds the regular cost, giving a theoretical negative pension cost. In practice, such a situation is most likely to arise where a scheme is substantially overfunded. Views are divided as to whether a negative pension cost is appropriate. The difficulty relates to the pension scheme being a separate legal entity outside the corporate structure and is allied to the concept of realised profit under the Act and SSAP 2 *Disclosure of accounting policies*. SSAP 2 states, in relation to prudence, 'revenue and profits are not anticipated, but are recognised by inclusion in the profit and loss account only when realised in the form either of cash or of other assets the ultimate cash realisation of which can be assessed with reasonable certainty....' [SSAP 2(14)]

30.40 Under this interpretation, the surplus is seen as an overpayment in the past which will reduce the cost of providing employees' pensions in the future, but is not realised unless it is repaid as a refund of surplus. The view is that the surplus is tied up in the scheme's investments and that the profits and losses on those investments belong to (or are suffered by) the scheme. The employers' interest is what it costs to maintain the fund at an adequate level. If this view is taken, where the pension cost calculation is negative, the accounting cost is taken as zero on the grounds of prudence. As, in such circumstances, the company is very likely to be taking a contribution holiday, cost and funding will be the same.

30.41 However, the alternative view is that the results of the scheme are part of those of the company and that negative pension cost is quite logical. Indeed, it is argued that not to recognise a negative cost would appear to place an arbitrary limitation on the requirements of SSAP 2 regarding the spreading of variations. The ASB 1995 discussion paper (see **30.67** below) accepts that, in principle, negative costs could arise, but that the pension asset that arises as a result of the negative cost should be capped by reference to the recoverable amount. FRED 20 would also allow a net credit to the performance statements, albeit split between the STRGL and the operating costs and finance costs areas of the profit and loss account, subject to a cap on the defined benefit asset based on the amount that can be recovered through reduced contributions in the future or through refunds from the scheme (see **30.67** et seq. below).

Group pension schemes

Single group scheme

30.42 It is common for companies within the same group to contribute to a single group pension scheme. In such circumstances, the actuary examines the actuarial liability of the group as a whole, rather than the liabilities of the individual companies. A contribution rate is therefore calculated as a percentage of payroll which applies to all group companies within the scheme and contribution rates on an individual company basis are not provided. SSAP 24 permits the use of a common group rate for contributions payable by sponsoring employers, provided that the subsidiary indicates that its contributions are based on the pension cost across the group as a whole. [SSAP 24(52) and (90)] It also allows for reduced disclosure in the financial statements of subsidiaries which are members of group schemes, on the grounds that it may not be possible to estimate the pension obligations for which a particular group company is responsible (see **30.64** below). [SSAP 24(90)]

Group with more than one pension scheme

30.43

> For those groups with a number of schemes, the situation is not so straightforward. Pension costs for companies under the control of the main holding company may well vary according to the particular scheme to which a participating subsidiary contributes. In effect, there may be common group rates not for the group overall but for sub-groups, determined by participation in the individual schemes. In such circumstances, pension costs should be determined for each company and sub-group with its own scheme and the full requirements of SSAP 24 should be applied to those companies and intermediate holding companies. The consolidated accounts will reflect the overall group situation, with disclosures on a combined basis, with the proviso that surpluses and deficiencies must not be set off against each other. [SSAP 24(89)] In such circumstances, the accounts may need to show both a pension prepayment and provision.

Centrally imposed contribution rates

30.44

> It is not unusual for holding companies to impose on subsidiaries whose employees belong to a group scheme a standard contribution rate which is unchanged by any variations from regular cost advised by the scheme's actuary. This is common in the manufacturing industry, where it is important for costing and management accounting purposes to avoid variances in unit costs caused by fluctuations from regular pension cost.

30.45   In such circumstances, the standard contribution will have been established as the regular cost and will satisfy the requirement of SSAP 24 in this respect for each of the individual subsidiary companies. Where a pension scheme is in surplus and the actuary recommends a reduction in funding and an associated variation in regular cost, the holding company will continue to collect the regular cost from subsidiaries while paying the scheme the recommended rate. The difference between that amount and the sum collected from subsidiaries will constitute a realised profit in the holding company. Conversely, if the scheme is in deficit, and the holding company effectively pays more to the scheme than the regular cost, the difference will constitute a realised loss to the holding company. On consolidation, these 'profits' and 'losses' will be eliminated and any variation advised by the actuary will be reflected in the group accounts.

30.46   Such an approach could create considerable tax problems, as tax relief is given to contributions to a pension fund. A payment by a trading subsidiary to a parent is not a payment to a pension fund. Furthermore, where there is a surplus, companies will be paying more than the actuary's recommended rate. Care, therefore, needs to be taken to ensure that tax reliefs are not lost.

Takeovers

30.47   SSAP 24 provided no guidance in the area of takeovers, but provisions are included in FRS 7 *Fair values in acquisition accounting* (see chapter 24).

30.48   FRS 7 contains two requirements concerning pension schemes and other post-retirement arrangements following an acquisition:

(a)   a surplus or deficiency in a funded scheme, or accrued obligations in an unfunded scheme, should be recognised as an asset or a liability of the acquiring group. These assets and liabilities are in substitution for existing prepayments or provisions that have accumulated in the accounts of the acquired entity under the requirements of SSAP 24. A pension scheme (or other post-retirement scheme) asset should, however, only be recognised to the extent that the acquired or acquiring entity is able to benefit from the surplus [FRS 7(19)];

(b)   changes made by an acquirer to the pension arrangements of an acquired scheme should be dealt with as post-acquisition items (i.e., accounted for under SSAP 24 as it applies to ongoing schemes). Thus, the actuarial valuation at the date of acquisition should not include provision for a change in benefits or in the number of employees post-acquisition [FRS 7(20)]; and

(c) the acquirer should apply its own judgement in determining assumptions such as: interest rates, inflation and investment returns; the likely turnover of staff; and future salary increases [FRS 7(73)].

Overseas subsidiaries

30.49 Companies or groups with overseas subsidiaries should ensure that, wherever possible, the pension costs are brought in line with SSAP 24. SSAP 24 and SFAS 87 (the US standard) will, for many companies, be incompatible, because SFAS 87 adopts a 'balance sheet approach' as opposed to the 'profit and loss account approach' of SSAP 24. Where there are material pension costs in US subsidiaries, for consolidation purposes, they should be recalculated to comply with SSAP 24. The SSAP recognises that it may be difficult and expensive to obtain the necessary actuarial information and therefore impractical to make the consolidation adjustment. In such circumstances, the SSAP requires as a minimum the disclosure of the amount charged to the profit and loss account and the basis of the charge in respect of such overseas subsidiaries. However, as regards post-retirement benefits other than pensions (see **30.53** to **30.57** below), compliance with SFAS 106 (the US standard) is deemed by UITF Abstract 6 to satisfy the principles of SSAP 24.

Centralised and industry-wide schemes

30.50 SSAP 24 is directed towards the employing companies, with the implicit assumption that the actuarial valuation will cover the employees of the employing company or group of companies. The standard does not address the issues where the employer participates in a centralised scheme, i.e., a scheme operated on behalf of several unrelated employers or, in an industry-wide scheme, a centralised scheme for non-associated employers in a particular industry.

30.51 Many industry-wide schemes are operated on a money purchase basis. In these circumstances, the pension cost charge will be the contributions payable by the company to the fund in the same way as for any other defined contribution scheme. Sometimes, centralised schemes are defined benefit schemes where contribution rates are calculated separately for each employer, making the employer's pension cost easily identifiable as the contribution levels are actuarially assessed on the basis of the individual contributor's workforce. Some centralised schemes operated on a defined benefit basis have a number of factors which distinguish them from the usual single employer or group scheme. The individual employer is in a participating situation but does not control the funding rate nor directly influence the benefits. Most importantly, the actuary determines the liabilities for the scheme as a whole and does not reflect the liabilities relating to the employees of the individual participating employers, which might be very different. The practical implications of this situation are that the actuarial liabilities, that would exist if the sponsoring employer funded its own scheme, and the amounts paid to the centralised scheme in respect of the employees of a participating employer do not necessarily coincide.

30.52   As a result of the absence of actuarial valuations relating to individual employers and the imposition of a centrally calculated contribution rate, for some members of the scheme the charges being paid may be in excess of the theoretical actuarial liability and for some they may be less. However, in respect of the employer's accounts, the contributions payable to the scheme will represent, for the purposes of SSAP 24, the pension cost to the employing company. Only if the scheme as a whole is subject to variation will funding and cost differ. The reasoning for this 'pragmatic' approach is based upon the common situation whereby trustees of such schemes take a long-term view of contribution rates and do not refund surpluses or they take holidays or they require deficits to be made good in the short term.

Other post-retirement benefits

UITF Abstract 6 Accounting for post-retirement benefits other than pensions

30.53   The UITF issued UITF Abstract 6 *Accounting for post-retirement benefits other than pensions* in November 1992. UITF Abstract 6 addresses the accounting requirements and disclosures required in respect of those obligations arising for employers who provide post-retirement health care or other benefits. Although such arrangements are rare (at present) in the UK, they are common in some other countries, e.g., the USA. UK holding companies with overseas subsidiaries may need to consider providing for such commitments in their group accounts, even if they have no material obligations in the UK.

30.54   For example, companies may provide employees with medical insurance which continues, at the company's expense, when the employees retire. Such benefits are analogous to an unfunded pension and UITF Abstract 6 requires the cost of such benefits to be accrued over the working life of the employees.

30.55 UITF Abstract 6 requires SSAP 24 principles as to measurement and disclosure to be applied in relation to all post-retirement benefits in financial statements relating to accounting periods ending on or after 23 December 1994. The long lead-in period recognised that the measurement of such obligations may pose difficulties. Transitional provisions required certain disclosures to be made in financial statements for accounting periods ending on or after 23 December 1992, but before 23 December 1994, where employers had not yet applied the principles of SSAP 24 to post-retirement benefits.

30.56 To simplify matters for UK parent undertakings with subsidiaries that follow the requirements of the US standard, UITF Abstract 6 allows that 'measurement in accordance with (SFAS 106 *Employers accounting for post-retirement benefits other than pensions*), including use of the transitional 20 year spreading option, will be deemed to satisfy SSAP 24 principles for full provisions'.

30.57 UITF Abstract 6 requires employers to adopt the transitional provisions of SSAP 24 when they change their accounting policy to account for post-retirement benefits other than pensions, in accordance with the principles of SSAP 24. [SSAP 24(92)] Generally, this will require the unprovided obligation to be recognised by means of a prior period adjustment, in line with FRS 3, or spread forward over the expected remaining service lives of current employees (see **30.33** to **30.38** above). The method chosen should be disclosed.

Disclosure requirements

Defined contribution schemes

30.58 The following information should be given by way of note to the accounts:
[SSAP 24(87)]

(a) the nature of the scheme (i.e., defined contribution);

(b) the accounting policy;

(c) the pension cost charged for the period; and

(d) any outstanding or prepaid contributions at the balance sheet date.

Defined benefit schemes

30.59 The following information should be given by way of note to the accounts:
[SSAP 24(88)]

(a) the nature of the scheme (i.e., defined benefit);

(b) whether it is funded or unfunded;

(c) the accounting policy and, if different, the funding policy (an example of this is given in the model financial statements of Delto PLC – see chapter 46);

(d) whether the pension cost and provision (or asset) are assessed in accordance with the advice of a professionally qualified actuary and, if so, the date of the most recent formal actuarial valuation or later formal review used for this purpose. If the actuary is an employee or officer of the reporting company, or of the group of which it is a member, this fact should be disclosed;

(e) the pension cost charge for the period, together with explanations of significant changes in the charge compared to that in the previous accounting period (e.g., the effect of the 1997 tax changes in respect of dividend income for pension schemes (see **30.14** above) [UITF Abstract 18(8)]);

(f) any provisions or prepayments in the balance sheet resulting from a difference between the amounts recognised as cost and the amounts funded or paid directly;

(g) the amount of any deficiency on a current funding level basis, indicating the action, if any, being taken to deal with it in the current and future accounting periods;

(h) an outline of the results of the most recent formal actuarial valuation or later formal review of the scheme on an ongoing basis;

(i) any commitment to make additional payments over a limited number of years;

(j) the accounting treatment adopted in respect of a refund made under the Finance Act 1986 where a credit appears in the financial statements in relation to it; and

(k) details of the expected effects on future costs of any material changes in the group's and/or company's pension arrangements.

30.60 An outline of the results of the most recent formal actuarial valuation or later formal review of the scheme on an ongoing basis (see **30.59**(h) above) should include disclosure of:

(a) the actuarial method used and a brief description of the main actuarial assumptions;

(b) the market value of scheme assets at the date of their valuation or review;

(c)   the level of funding expressed in percentage terms; and

(d)   comments on any material actuarial surplus or deficiency indicated by (c) above.

30.61   The actuarial method and assumptions disclosed should be those used to calculate the pension costs for SSAP 24 purposes and may differ from those used for funding purposes. The SSAP requires that the actuarial assumptions and method, taken as a whole, should be compatible and should lead to the actuary's best estimate of the cost of providing the pension benefits promised. [SSAP 24(79)] It is not necessarily true to say that the funding assumptions are 'best estimates', as the company may have some non-neutral funding objective in mind. The Institute and Faculty of Actuaries has issued GN 17 *Accounting for pension costs under SSAP 24*. Paragraph 23 notes that: 'The method and assumptions used for SSAP 24 may well differ from those used for funding purposes because of factors which may be relevant to funding but which are not relevant to SSAP 24. The actuary should be prepared to explain to his client any difference between the approaches for funding and SSAP 24'. Paragraph 24 goes on to note that for SSAP 24 purposes: 'It is not inappropriate to adopt assumptions which, taken together, are somewhat more likely to lead to surplus rather than to deficiency at future valuations, this being in accordance with the accounting concept of prudence. However it is not satisfactory to include significant margins which are likely to lead to future surpluses or deficits which are material ...'.

30.62

SSAP 24 appears to allow that the level of funding expressed in percentage terms may or may not include future salary increases (see **30.60**(c) above). To avoid ambiguity, the disclosure should indicate whether or not such increases are included. The example of disclosure given in the appendix to the SSAP does include such increases.

Companies and groups with more than one scheme

30.63   SSAP 24 states that disclosure should be made on a combined basis, unless a proper understanding of the accounts requires disclosure of information concerning individual schemes. Where there is a deficiency on a current funding level basis in any group scheme, this may not be offset against a surplus in another. [SSAP 24(89)]

Group schemes

30.64   Subsidiary companies whose employees are members of a group scheme (see **30.42** to **30.49**) and whose holding company is registered in the UK are exempt from the disclosures listed in **30.59**(g) and **30.59**(h) above. They should, however, disclose the nature of the group scheme, indicating, where appropriate, that contributions are based on pension costs across the group as a whole. They should also state the name of the holding company in whose financial statements particulars of the actuarial valuation of the group scheme are contained. [SSAP 24(90)]

Overseas schemes

30.65 Where consolidation adjustments are impractical because of the difficulty and cost of obtaining the relevant information, disclosure should be made of the amount charged to the profit and loss account and its basis. [SSAP 24(91)]

Illustrative disclosures

30.66 Illustrative disclosures are given in the appendix to SSAP 24 and in Delto plc (see chapter 46). The following disclosure is taken from the financial statements of Safeway plc.

Extract 30.66

Safeway plc

3 April 1999

Notes to financial statements

24.3 Pension Schemes

The group maintains pension schemes for all eligible full-time and part-time employees. Scheme funds are administered by Trustees and are independent of group finances. Investment of pension scheme assets in group companies is not permitted by the Trustees.

The principal scheme, the Safeway Pension Scheme, is a defined benefit scheme. The pension cost relating to the scheme is assessed in accordance with the advice of independent actuaries and is such as to spread the cost of pensions over the working lives of the employees who are scheme members.

The latest valuation of the scheme was carried out as at 1 April 1998 using the projected unit method. The assumptions which have the most significant effect on the results of the valuation are those relating to the rate of return on investments and the rates of increase in salaries, pensions and dividends. It was assumed that retail price inflation would be 3.5% per annum, that the investment return would be 7.5% per annum, that salary increases would average 5.5% per annum, that pensions (in excess of the Guaranteed Minimum Pension) would increase at the rate of 3.5% per annum and that dividends on United Kingdom equity investments would increase at 3.5% per annum.

The actuarial value of the assets was assessed by assuming that 60% of the market value of the assets was invested in the FTSE Actuaries All

---

Share Index with the remaining 40% invested in the securities under-lying the FTSE Actuaries Over 5 years Index Linked Gilt Index. Anticipated future dividend income, coupon payments, sale and redemption proceeds were then discounted to the valuation date at the valuation rate of return.

At the date of the latest actuarial valuation, the market value of the assets of the scheme (excluding members' Additional Voluntary Contributions) was £786.5 million and the actuarial value of the assets was sufficient to cover 114% of the benefits that had accrued to members, after allowing for expected future increases in earnings. The excess is being eliminated as a uniform annual percentage of pen-sionable pay over 11 years, this being the approximate average remaining service life of scheme members.

Contributions to group pension schemes are charged to the profit and loss account so as to spread the cost of pensions at a substantially level percentage of payroll costs over employees' working lives with the group.

The total pension cost for the year amounted to £19.2 million (1998 – £17.1 million). This reflected a regular cost of £26.0 million (1998 – £23.4 million) and a credit of £6.8 million (1998 – £6.3 million). The credit relates primarily to the amortisation of the excess of assets over liabilities in the principal scheme, as described above. The pension-able payroll for the year in the principal scheme was £213.6 million (1998 – £190.3 million).

Directors' report

Pension Fund

Full details of the group's pension schemes are set out in Note 24.3 shown earlier. Pension scheme funds are administered by Trustees and are independent of group finances. There is no investment in the shares of the Company nor do the pension schemes own any property occupied by the group.

The Safeway Pension Scheme is open to all permanent full-time and part-time employees of the group. The Scheme provides benefits additional to those from the State Basic Pension Scheme, whilst enabling members to be contracted-out of the State Earnings Related Pension Scheme. In addition to the normal retirement pension based on pay and length of service at retirement, there are further benefits payable when members die in service.

Future developments

Revision of SSAP 24

Background

30.67 Various reviews of SSAP 24 have identified perceived shortcomings in SSAP 24, the two key problems being the flexibility provided to preparers of financial statements (giving them the ability to adjust results on a short-term basis), and the inadequate disclosure requirements (typically an employer with a scheme in surplus records a provision in its financial statements as the balance sheet simply reflects the balancing figure between contributions paid and SSAP 24 costs charged).

30.68 The ASB has issued two discussion papers, one in each of 1995 and 1998. Initially, proposals were aimed at addressing the problems with SSAP 24 noted above (1995). However, following moves internationally (in IAS 19 *Employee benefits*) to a market basis for valuing scheme assets and the move to such a basis in the UK for valuations for minimum funding requirement (MFR) and transfer value purposes, a more radical change was proposed in 1998. FRED 20 *Retirement benefits* was issued in 1999 and continues with the proposals of the last discussion paper, reducing the options it gave in relation to the recognition of the actuarial gains and losses and of past service costs, and revisiting the rate used to discount the actuarial liability. The proposals, in FRED 20, represent radical changes from the current requirements of SSAP 24 in respect of defined benefit schemes, leading to increased volatility in the balance sheet as actuarial gains and losses are recognised immediately and scheme assets are valued at fair values. Accounting for defined contribution schemes is unchanged from SSAP 24, i.e. the P&L is charged with the contributions payable for the period.

Accounting approach

30.69 The objectives of the FRED are to ensure that:

(a) the employer's financial statements reflect the assets and liabilities arising from retirement benefit obligations and any related funding, measured at fair value;

(b) operating costs of providing retirement benefits are recognised in the periods the benefits are earned by employees, and finance costs and any other changes in value of the assets and liabilities are recognised in the periods in which they arise; and

(c) the financial statements contain adequate disclosures.

30.70 The proposals in FRED 20 in respect of defined benefit schemes may be summarised as:

(a) scheme assets to be valued at fair value at the balance sheet date (see **30.71** below);

(b) the defined benefit scheme liability to be valued using the projected unit method and discounted using an AA corporate bond rate of an equivalent currency and term to the scheme liability (see **30.73** and **30.74** below);

(c) the net defined benefit pension asset or liability, after attributable deferred tax, to be shown after other net assets in the balance sheet. A surplus should only be recognised as an asset to the extent that the employer can benefit through reduced contributions in the future or through refunds from the scheme. Any overpaid/unpaid contributions are represented as a debtor/creditor due within one year;

(d) the P&L charge to be split between:
   (i) operating costs – current service cost, past service costs and gains or losses on settlements and curtailments;
   (ii) financing costs – interest costs and <u>expected</u> return on assets;
   (iii) FRS 3(20) exceptional items – to the extent any gains or losses on settlements and curtailments relate to those items;

(e) actuarial gains and losses to go to the STRGL (these include differences between actual and expected return on scheme assets and, in relation to scheme liabilities, changes in actuarial assumptions and differences between those assumptions and actual experience);

(f) past service costs to be charged in the P&L over the period in which they vest. If they vest immediately they are recognised immediately; and

(g) gains and losses on settlements and curtailments to be recognised in the P&L once the settlement or curtailment is certain (i.e., the employer is **demonstrably committed** if a loss, and other parties **irrevocably committed** if a gain).

A considerable level of disclosure is also prescribed, some of which was not required by SSAP 24, e.g., a five year record of actuarial gains and losses recognised in the STRGL.

Value of pension scheme assets

30.71 FRED 20 proposes that scheme assets be included at their fair value at the employer's balance sheet date. Thus, in this respect, it will be necessary to update the actuarial valuation each year. There is no provision for the use of an averaged price to smooth out short-term variances in values.

30.72 Expected return on scheme assets is calculated as: Expected long-term rate of return multiplied by market value (both values are taken as at the start of the period).

Pension liabilities

30.73 The other side of the equation is the calculation of the pension liability. The AA corporate bond rate, which the FRED requires to be used to discount the liability, will be derived by the actuary from gilt rates, for example gilt rate plus 1%. This rate will usually be lower than the discount rate used under SSAP 24 (which will have assumed a higher proportion of equity return) and thus is likely to lead to the current service cost under the FRED being higher than the regular cost under SSAP 24 – this will form part of the operating costs. The AA corporate bond rate is also likely to be lower than the expected rate of return on plan assets under the FRED so that the net finance charge in respect of the pension scheme (assuming it is not in deficit) is likely to be a credit as the expected return on assets will be higher than the interest cost relating to the liability.

30.74 The AA corporate bond rate represents a key change from the recommendations of the 1998 discussion paper. That suggested the expected return on a matching portfolio of assets (matching the liability in terms of risk and term) in order to arrive at a synthetic 'market value' for the obligation. As discussed in paragraphs 11 to 20 of Appendix V of the FRED, subsequent research showed that the correlation between salary increases and equity returns was not as high as had been assumed. Returning to basics, the ASB took the view that the discount rate should reflect the time value of money (a risk free rate) and the risks associated with the uncertainty of the ultimate cash payments due. The use of an AA corporate bond rate includes a small premium to reflect this risk and accords with IAS 19.

Recognition of actuarial gains and losses

30.75 FRED 20 addresses the volatility arising from variances between actual and expected outcomes by passing actuarial gains and losses through the STRGL. This does not avoid volatility in the balance sheet. Thus the proposals of FRED 20 may impact loan covenants or limits on borrowings linked to net assets. The implications for distributable profits is considered in **30.79** to **30.81** below. It should be noted that the FRED 20 approach minimises volatility in the P&L but does not remove it. Changes in market rates will be reflected in year on year changes in long-term expected percentage returns on assets and long-term AA corporate bond rates. In addition, market changes in the fair value of scheme assets year on year will flow through to the value of the expected return on those assets in the P&L.

30.76 SSAP 24 requires the effect of material actuarial deficiencies or surpluses to be spread for accounting purposes over the expected remaining service lives of the current employees in the scheme. As a minimum, IAS 19 requires net cumulative unrecognised actuarial gains and losses exceeding a '10 per cent corridor' (i.e., 10% of the greater of the gross assets or gross liabilities of the scheme) to be recognised over the expected remaining service lives of employees participating in the plan, with non-recognition of actuarial gains and losses within the 10 per cent corridor. However, the IAS allows systematic methods of faster recognition, provided they are applied consistently from period to period and between gains and losses. Such a systematic method could include immediate recognition of all gains and losses. Indeed in the discussion on the development of IAS 19, the Board of the International Accounting Standards Committee noted 'The Board found the immediate recognition approach attractive. However, the Board believes that it is not feasible to use this approach for actuarial gains and losses until the Board resolves substantial issues about performance reporting. When the Board makes further progress with those issues, it may decide to revisit the treatment of actuarial gains and losses.' The subject of performance reporting is being addressed in a separate international G4+1 project; a discussion paper setting out the proposals was issued by ASB in 1999 (see chapters 9 and 11).

Past service costs

30.77 Another change from SSAP 24 which has attracted widespread comment has been the proposed treatment of past service costs. These arise when the pension liability relating to employee service in prior periods increases due to the introduction or improvement of benefits beyond that to which the employer is already statutorily, contractually or implicitly committed. Under SSAP 24 these would normally be written off over the remaining service lives of employees. [SSAP 24(31)]

30.78 FRED 20 proposes that past service costs would be charged to the P&L over the period of vesting. In most UK pension schemes such increases vest immediately, so the cost would be charged immediately in the P&L account even if funded from a surplus. The one exception relates to the use of that part of the surplus not recognised due to the capping restrictions (see **30.70**(c) above). In such a case that part of the surplus would be deducted from the past service costs in the P&L account with separate disclosure in the notes.

Distributable profits

30.79 Appendix III of FRED 20 addresses the effect on distributable profits. The appendix appears to take the view that the actuarial gains and losses are not realised profits and losses for the purposes of the

Companies Act ('the Act') so that the impact on distributable profits in this respect is restricted to plcs. The net assets test of s264 of
the Act, referred to by the FRED, restricts distributable profits to the
extent that a plc has net accumulated unrealised losses (see chapter
33).

30.80   Appendix III to the FRED appears to permit the deficit to be measured on a discontinuance basis with 'additional disclosure' given of
the additional amount of the deficit on a 'normal' FRED 20 basis.
The word 'appears' is used here as it is not clear whether the appendix can override bold text standards in the body of the FRED. The
appendix makes the point that the 'Companies Act balance sheet'
ends after the liability on a discontinued basis not after the full liability, and reserves are measured on the same basis.

30.81   This approach is justified on the basis 'that the employer has the discretion to reduce the projected deficit by curtailing benefits or, in
the ultimate, closing the scheme.' [FRED 20, appendix III, paragraph 8] This seems at odds with paragraph 26 of the FRED which
states that 'It is not appropriate to assume a reduction in benefits
below those currently promised on the grounds that the employer
will curtail the scheme at some time in the future.'

Transitional provisions

30.82   The only specific transitional provisions in the FRED relate to the
five-year history of actuarial gains and losses passed through the
STRGL. These do not need to be created retrospectively. [FRED
20(78)]

30.83   Gains and losses arising on the initial application of the proposals
in the FRED should be dealt with as a prior year adjustment. [FRED
20(78)] Thus, it would be necessary to restate comparative figures to
reflect the scheme surplus or deficit at the end of the prior period
and to restate the P&L and STRGL to reflect the gains and losses on
a FRED 20 basis. This raises the interesting question of how the
expected and actual rates of return, discount rate and other assumptions should be set retrospectively. Would it be permissible simply
to calculate the FRED 20 gains and losses on an 'actual' basis, so that
all gains and losses in the restated comparatives are P&L items, or
should an expected and actual split be applied? In the latter case it
would seem appropriate to give a history of the gains and losses
recorded in the STRGL if only for the comparative period.

30.84   If the ASB are of the view that actuarial gains and losses are not
realised profits and losses (see **30.79** above), how should the prior
period adjustment be analysed between realised and unrealised? For
long-standing schemes it would clearly be totally impracticable to

go back to the introduction of the pension scheme seeking to identify actuarial gains and losses on a FRED 20 basis.

How FRED 20 articulates the primary financial statements

30.85 The following table summaries the double entry envisaged by FRED 20.

	Profit and loss account	STRGL	Plan Assets	Plan Obligation	Unamortised past service cost
B/f			x	(x)	x
Contributions			A		
Current service cost	B			(B)	
Interest cost on obligation	C			(C)	
Expected return on assets – (income)	(C)		C		
Actuarial gain/ (loss) on plan assets		D	D		
Actuarial gain/ (loss) on obligation		D		D	
Past service cost – vest immediately	E			(E)	
Past service cost – not vesting immediately				(F)	F
Amortisation of past service cost	F				F
Losses on curtailments/ settlements	G		(G)	G	(G)
Gains on curtailments/ settlements	(H)		(H)	H	(H)
Benefits paid			(I)	I	
Profit and loss hit	X				
STRGL hit		X			
C/f			J	(J)	J

A   Any unpaid contributions fall within creditors due within one year, NOT as part of the pension scheme asset/ liability.

B   Based on the most recent actuarial valuation at the beginning of the period, with the financial assumptions updated to reflect conditions at that date. Include in the appropriate statutory heading for pension costs in the profit and loss account.

C   Based on the most recent actuarial valuation at the beginning of the period, with the financial assumptions updated to reflect conditions at that date. Include net as a financial item adjacent to interest. (FRED 20 does not specify whether it must be shown separately on the face of the P&L nor whether it can be aggregated with the unwinding of the discount under FRS 12(48).)

D   For scheme assets, reflects differences between actual and expected return. On scheme liabilities, reflects difference between assumptions and actual experience and also changes in assumptions.

E   Past service costs arise when benefits are improved (e.g., widow(er) benefit introduced). Does not relate to increases already committed to – they would be actuarial gains and losses on scheme liability (see D). Recognise immediately if they vest immediately, otherwise recognise over the period in which they do vest (see F). If funded by a surplus which could not previously be recognised (due to recoverability constraints) show net of surplus in the P&L with separate disclosure in the notes.

F   If past service costs do not vest immediately, so that they are to be recognised over the period of vesting, it is unclear where the unrecognised debit' goes. It is presumed it is included within the balance sheet as part of the net pension asset/liability as per IAS 19.

G   Losses on curtailments/settlements not allowed for in actuarial assumptions should be recognised in the P&L account once the employer is demonstrably committed. Include in arriving at operating profit unless caused by an FRS 3(20) event in which case include in the appropriate FRS 3(20) exceptional item.

H   Gains on curtailments/settlements not allowed for in actuarial assumptions should be recognised in the P&L account once all parties are irrevocably committed. Include in arriving at operating profit unless caused by an FRS 3(20) event in which case include in the appropriate FRS 3(20) exceptional item.

I   Benefits paid reduces both plan assets and the obligation.

J   The defined benefit net asset/liability (net of any deferred tax balance) should be shown separately on the face of the balance sheet after all other net assets.

31 Government grants

31   Government grants

Summary of changes since the previous issue of this publication

Para.	*Topic*	*Summary*
31.24	*Accounting by Recipients for Non-reciprocal Transfers, Excluding Contribution by Owners*	Paper issued by the G4+1 international group of accounting standard setters addressing various types of contributions such as gifts, donations, government grants and taxes.

Introduction

SSAP 4 Accounting for government grants

31.1   The accounting treatment of government grants is dealt with in SSAP 4, which was first issued in 1974 and substantially revised in 1990, following changes in company law and an increase in the forms of assistance available.

Definition

31.2   Government grants are defined by the standard as assistance by government in the form of cash or assets in return for past or future compliance with certain conditions relating to the operating activities of the enterprise. [SSAP 4(22)]

31.3   Government, for these purposes, includes local, national or international government and government agencies and similar bodies. [SSAP 4(21)]

31.4   Other forms of government assistance, e.g., the provision of a free consultancy service, are not grants.

Accounting requirements

General requirements

31.5   The general requirement of SSAP 4 is that grants should be recognised in the profit and loss account so as to match them with the expenditure towards which they are intended to contribute. The following specific requirements are given:
[SSAP 4(23)]

(a)   where grants are made to give immediate financial support to an entity or to reimburse costs previously charged to profit, they should be recognised in the profit and loss account in the period in which they become receivable;

(b)   a grant made to finance the general activities of an enterprise or compensate for a loss of income should be recognised in the profit and loss account in the period in respect of which it is paid;

(c)   where grants are made as a contribution towards expenditure on fixed assets, they should be recognised over the expected useful economic lives of the related assets.

31.6   These requirements are all subject to the general provision that a grant should not be recognised until the conditions for its receipt have been complied with and there is reasonable assurance that it will be received. [SSAP 4(24)]

Grants made as a contribution to fixed assets

31.7   SSAP 4 requires grants made as a contribution towards expenditure on a fixed asset to be recognised over the expected useful economic life of the asset. The two methods of achieving this are:

(a)   to treat the grant as deferred income which is credited to the profit and loss account over the expected useful economic life of the asset on a basis consistent with the depreciation policy; or

(b)   to deduct the grant from the purchase cost of the related asset, with a consequent reduction in the annual depreciation charge.

31.8   SSAP 4 considers both of these methods to be acceptable and prior to the Companies Act 1981 the use of either of these methods was permitted. However, the Companies Act 1981 introduced certain provisions, now included in the 1985 Act, which, in counsel's opinion, have the effect of prohibiting the use of the second method, i.e., deducting the grant from the purchase cost of the asset.

31.9   Although SSAP 4 still considers both methods of recognising the grant as valid, the appropriate balance sheet treatment of a grant for an entity which produces accounts in compliance with the Act is to treat the grant as deferred income and amortise it to the profit and loss account on a basis consistent with the depreciation policy.

31.10 The requirements of SSAP 4 will be met through use of the 'netting' method by entities who do not have to compile accounts under the requirements of the Act.

31.11

One situation where it is appropriate to use the netting method for contributions made from one entity to another is seen in the utility companies, e.g., the electricity and water companies. When private development companies, e.g., house builders, build new sites, they make a payment to the utility companies as a contribution to the costs of establishing the necessary assets to service the site. These are costs of the development company necessarily incurred to bring the site to a saleable state. In these circumstances, it is appropriate for the utility companies to record the assets at the total cost to establish the assets less the costs attributable to and paid for by the development company. This approach entails invoking the 'true and fair' override and giving the disclosure required by UITF 7 (see **5.11** above). An example of a company choosing to net off grants against related infrastructure assets is United Utilities plc:

Extract 31.11

United Utilities plc

31 March 1999

Accounting policies, (h) Grants and Contributions

Capital contributions towards infrastructure assets are deducted from the cost of those assets. This is not in accordance with Schedule 4 to the Companies Act 1985 under which the infrastructure assets should be stated at their purchase price or production cost and the capital contributions treated as deferred income and released to the profit and loss account over the useful life of the corresponding assets. The directors are of the opinion that, although provision is made for depreciation of infrastructure assets (see note (g) above), these assets have no finite economic lives and the capital contributions would therefore remain in the balance sheet in perpetuity. The treatment otherwise required by the Companies Act 1985 would not present a true and fair view of the group's effective investment in infrastructure assets. The financial effect of this accounting policy is set out in note 11.

Grants receivable in respect of other tangible fixed assets are treated as deferred income, which is credited to the profit and loss account over the estimated economic lives of the related assets.

31.12 Where a grant is received as a contribution towards expenditure on an asset which is assessed as having no finite economic life, e.g., land, the grant cannot be recognised over the useful economic life of the asset. In these cases, the grant will normally remain as a deferred income balance and only be recognised in the profit and loss account when the related asset is sold. The deferred income balance will be brought into the calculation of the profit or loss on sale of the asset.

31.13 A grant received as a contribution to an asset which is assessed as having a finite life is always recognised in the profit and loss account over the economic life. This is the case even where there is a nil depreciation charge on the asset due to the estimated residual value being not materially different from its carrying amount.

Potential repayment

31.14 In many cases, the grant-making body has the right to require repayment of all or part of a grant paid if the conditions under which it was made have not been complied with. The potential liability should only be provided for to the extent that repayment is probable, in line with the requirements of FRS 12 *Provisions, contingent liabilities and contingent assets* (see chapter 17). Any charge should be set off against any unamortised deferred income relating to the grant, with any excess being taken to the profit and loss account.

Determining the related expenditure

31.15 Matching a grant received to the related expenditure is normally straightforward, as the terms of the grant describe it as a contribution towards a specified expenditure. Difficulties arise where the terms of the grant are not sufficiently precise, e.g., where they refer to 'assistance with a project'. In these cases, it will normally be appropriate to consider the circumstances which give rise to the payment of instalments of the grant. If the payment is made on the basis of the achievement of an objective, the grant should be matched with the identifiable costs of obtaining that objective. [SSAP 4(9)]

31.16 If sufficiently persuasive evidence exists that the actual expenditure towards which the grant is to contribute is different from that on which the payments are based, it is appropriate to match the grant with the expenditure to which it is intended to relate. Such evidence may be found in the application for the grant, subsequent correspondence or negotiations with the grant-making body. [SSAP 4(10)]

31.17 Where a grant is based on the achievement of a non-financial objective, such as the creation of jobs for a certain period, the grants should be matched with the costs of creating and maintaining the jobs, taking into account the incidence of these costs which are generally higher at the start-up. [SSAP 4(11)]

Non-cash grants

31.18   Grants are sometimes given by way of donation of non-cash assets. For example, as an incentive for a business to build a factory, a local authority may grant a long leasehold interest at a peppercorn rent. Such non-cash assets should be included in the balance sheet at their fair value and the corresponding credits shown as deferred income. [SSAP 4(16)]

Taxation of grants

31.19   Many grants are taxed as income on receipt. The accounting for such grants should not be influenced by the tax treatment. Taxable grants which are deferred in accordance with the principles stated above give rise to timing differences which should be accounted for in accordance with SSAP 15.

31.20   As regards tax-free grants which are available to the lessor against the purchase price of assets, SSAP 21 specifies that these should be spread over the period of the lease and that the grant should be treated as non-taxable income. [SSAP 21(41)] The option to gross up the grant and include the grossed up amount in arriving at profit before tax has been removed by the ASB in its amendment to SSAP 21 (dated February 1997) and, as a result, is not permitted for financial years ending on or after 22 June 1997.

Disclosure requirements

Grants

31.21   The required disclosures with respect to grants, assistance in the form of cash or assets, are:

(a)   the accounting policy adopted; [SSAP 4(28)(a)] and

(b)   the effects of the government grants on the results for the period and, where appropriate, on the financial position of the enterprise. [SSAP 4(28)(b)]

Other forms of assistance

31.22   For other forms of government assistance, e.g., consultancy or advisory services, if the receipt of assistance materially affects the results for the period, then the nature of that assistance should be disclosed and, to the extent that the effects on the financial statements can be measured, an estimate of such effects should also be given. [SSAP 4(28)(c)]

Potential liabilities

31.23   Where potential liabilities exist to repay the grant in certain circumstances, then these should be disclosed, if necessary, in accordance with the requirements of FRS 12. [FRS 12(91)]

Future developments

31.24   In January 2000, the ASB issued for comment a special report, *Accounting by Recipients for Non-reciprocal Transfers, Excluding Contribution by Owners*, produced by G4+1 international group of accounting standard setters. Non-reciprocal transfers defined by the paper include various types of contributions such as gifts, donations, government grants and taxes. They may be received in cash, in kind, or as a reduction of liability.

31.25   The position taken by the paper is that the approach for reporting non-reciprocal transfers based on the matching of related revenues and expenses (i.e., the approach currently employed by SSAP 4 in accounting for government grants) should not be adopted where it conflicts with application of the definitions and recognition criteria for assets and liabilities in IASC's *Framework for Preparing and Presentation of Financial Statements* or the ASB's *Statement of Principles for Financial Reporting* – it's UK equivalent. Usually this would imply that transfers are recognised as income when they become receivable.

32 Related-party transactions, including directors' loans

32 Related-party transactions, including directors' loans

Introduction

Sources of disclosure requirements

32.1   Disclosure of transactions with related parties is required by:

(a)   statute;

(b)   the Listing Rules; and

(c)   FRS 8 *Related party disclosures.*

32.2   The disclosures required by the Act, the Listing Rules, the Rules of the London Stock Exchange and FRS 8 are dealt with in **32.5** to **32.36**, **32.37** to **32.48**, **32.49**, and **32.50** to **32.91** below respectively.

32.3   The requirements of the listing rules and of the rules of the London Stock Exchange that are addressed here are only those relating to the disclosures required in the annual financial statements of listed or AIM companies. It should be noted that there are additional requirements in certain cases, e.g., to notify the UK Listing Authority or, for AIM companies, the London Stock Exchange in writing of the proposed transaction. Reference should be made to the Listing Rules (for listed companies) or the rules of the London Stock Exchange (for AIM companies).

32.4   FRS 8 *Related party disclosures* was issued in 1995. The FRS notes that, in certain instances, it will extend existing disclosure requirements; in other instances, the statutory and the Listing Rules requirements go beyond the FRS. [FRS 8(23)] Examples of extensions to statutory disclosure requirements include:

(a)   the FRS does not exempt transactions of the reporting entity carried out in the normal course of business (see **32.61** below);

(b)   there is no fixed *de minimis* below which related-party transactions need not be reported (see **32.74** below);

(c)   the fact that a majority of the board resolve that a transaction is not material is not conclusive (see **32.17** and **32.74** below).

Statutory disclosures of transactions with directors

Persons affected

32.5 Disclosure is required of relevant transactions with:

(a) persons who were directors, including 'shadow directors', of the company or its holding company, at any time during the financial year; and

(b) persons connected with them.

32.6 A shadow director is a person in accordance with whose directions or instructions other directors are accustomed to act.

32.7 Persons connected with a director include:
[s346]

(a) his spouse;

(b) his child under the age of 18 (including a stepchild or illegitimate child);

(c) a company with which he is associated, i.e., he and other persons connected with him are interested in 20 per cent or more of the company's equity share capital or are entitled to exercise 20 per cent or more of the votes at a general meeting. A director is treated as being entitled to exercise votes if they may be exercised by a company under his control (i.e., either a company in which he or a person connected with him is entitled to exercise some of the voting power and he, persons connected with him and the other directors of the company together can exercise more than half the voting power or, alternatively, a company in which he or a person connected with him is interested in part of the equity share capital and he, persons connected with him and the other directors of the company together are interested in more than half of that share capital). In this subparagraph references to a company include a body corporate;

(d) a person acting in his capacity as trustee of a trust whose beneficiaries include the director or anyone falling within (a) to (c) above (including a trustee of a discretionary trust which includes the persons as potential beneficiaries but excluding a trustee under an employees' share scheme or a pension scheme);

(e) a person acting in his capacity as partner of the director or of anyone falling within (a) to (d) above;

(f) a Scottish firm in which the director or anyone falling within (a) to (d) above is a partner; and

(g)   a Scottish firm in which a Scottish firm falling within (f) above is a partner.

32.8   A person is not treated as being 'connected with a director' if that person is himself a director of the company.

Transactions which require disclosure

32.9   The following transactions should be disclosed if they were made for any person affected (as described in **32.5** to **32.7** above) by the company or any of its subsidiaries:
[Sch 6: 15 and 16]

(a)   loans;

(b)   quasi-loans (i.e., arrangements whereby the company pays or agrees to pay sums on behalf of the person affected to be reimbursed at a later date, e.g., credit card transactions);

(c)   credit transactions (i.e., leasing transactions, hire purchase transactions, conditional sales and other sales on deferred payment terms);

(d)   guarantees or provisions of security for any loans, quasi-loans or credit transactions made by a third party;

(e)   any agreement to enter into any of the above transactions; and

(f)   any other transaction or arrangement in which the person affected had directly or indirectly a material interest (see **32.15** and **32.16** below for the definition of material interest).

32.10   It is specifically enacted that disclosure is required even if:
[Sch 6: 19]

(a)   the transaction or arrangement is prohibited under the Act (the prohibitions with regard to loans, etc. in favour of directors and connected persons are discussed in **32.26** to **32.30** below);

(b)   the person for whom it was made was not a director or connected person at the time it was made; or

(c)   the company making the transaction is a subsidiary company which was not a subsidiary at the time it was made.

32.11   Disclosure is required unless the transaction or arrangement was not entered into during the financial year and did not subsist at any time during it. [Sch 6: 18]

32.12 The Act does not define a loan, but a definition which has received judicial approval is 'a sum of money lent for a time to be returned in money or money's worth'. Thus, an essential ingredient of a loan is that there should be an intention of the parties that it should be repaid at some future time. On this basis, an amount drawn by a director on account of remuneration (e.g., of a bonus which only becomes payable when approved at the annual meeting) would not be classified as a loan. Similarly, advances of sums which are intended to meet expenses to be incurred on the company's business are not loans. However, every case must be considered on its merits and regard had to the substance of the transaction. If a sum advanced to a director purports to be on account of remuneration, then PAYE ought to be applied at the time of payment and, if this is not done, then the payment may assume the characteristics of a loan. Similarly, advances made on account of expenses which are clearly in excess of any amount which a director could reasonably be expected to incur within a reasonable time are probably entered into in order to give the director concerned the benefit of the use of the money and should therefore be classified as loans. In any case, amounts advanced may require the approval of shareholders (see **32.27**(e) below).

32.13 Any transaction with a director or with a person connected with him is treated as a transaction in which that director is interested, but disclosure is not required if:

(a) a director is interested in a transaction or arrangement with another company only by virtue of being a director of that other company (this would not apply if he was also a shareholder of that company); or

(b) it is in respect of a director's contract of service [Sch 6: 18].

32.14 A loan from a director to his company or to a subsidiary company is a 'transaction or arrangement' which must be disclosed, unless it can be excluded as not material, as discussed in **32.15** and **32.16** below.

32.15 Transactions and arrangements which should be disclosed under **32.9**(f) above are restricted to those in which the director's interest is 'material', but there are some differences of view as to how materiality should be judged in this context.

32.16 It is suggested that the best way to approach the matter is to consider the guidance on materiality given in FRS 8 and consider whether disclosure of the transactions might reasonably

> be expected to influence decisions made by the users of the financial statements (see **32.74** below). What is required is the disclosure of significant information concerning the existing relationship between the company and its directors and of matters which might affect this relationship in the future. On this basis, it is not necessary to disclose a director's interest in a transaction on the grounds that the interest is material to the transaction as a whole if the transaction itself is insignificant; on the other hand, an item should not be excluded from disclosure merely because the amount involved is small in relation to the amounts included in the accounts, such as turnover or profit.

32.17 The Act specifically provides that if a majority of the directors (excluding the director whose interest is under consideration) resolve that an interest in a particular transaction or arrangement is not material, then that is conclusive and the interest need not be disclosed under the requirement in **32.9**(f) above. [Sch 6: 17] However, this would not, of itself, preclude the transaction from falling to be disclosed under FRS 8 (see **32.74** below).

Permitted exemptions from the statutory disclosures

32.18 In addition to the exemptions in **32.13** and **32.14** above, other exemptions from the requirement in **32.9**(f) above (to disclose transactions or arrangements in which a director has a material interest) are:

(a) transactions entered into by a company in the ordinary course of business and on an arm's-length basis (i.e., on terms not less favourable to the company and the group than would have been obtained if there had been no director's interest). [Sch 6: 20] (There is some doubt as to whether this exemption applies where the company is not a member of a group);

(b) transactions entered into by a company which is a member of a group and either it is wholly owned or no other group member (other than the company or a subsidiary of the company) is involved in the transaction, where the interest of the director in the transaction or arrangement has arisen only because the director is associated with the company [Sch 6: 21]; and

(c) transactions in which any director was interested if the aggregate value of the transactions for that director made after the commencement of the financial year, together with any liability outstanding in respect of transactions entered into before the beginning of that year, did not exceed £1,000 or, if they did exceed £1,000, did not exceed the lower of £5,000 or one per cent of the net assets of the company at the year end. [Sch 6: 25]

32.19   There is also an exemption from disclosure of credit transactions, guarantees of credit transactions and agreements to enter into credit transactions in respect of any individual director if the aggregate outstanding balance of such transactions entered into for that director and persons connected with him did not exceed £5,000 at any one time during the financial year. [Sch 6: 24] Only reduced disclosures are required for loans or quasi-loans between two companies where one is a wholly owned subsidiary of the other or both are wholly owned subsidiaries of another company. In such cases, only the disclosures in **32.20**(a), (b) and (c) below are required. [Sch 6: 23]

Particulars to be disclosed

32.20   The particulars to be disclosed are:
[Sch 6: 22]

(a)   the principal terms of the transaction;

(b)   a statement that the loan, guarantee, transaction, etc. was made or subsisted during the financial year;

(c)   the name of the person for whom it was made (if the person is a connected person, the name of the director with whom he is connected must also be given);

(d)   in the case of a loan made or to be made, the amount of the liability in respect of principal and interest at the beginning and end of the financial year, the maximum amount of the liability during the financial year, any interest due which has not been paid and the amount of any provision made against the loan or accrued interest;

(e)   where a company has guaranteed or provided security for a loan, the amount for which the company was liable at the beginning and end of the financial year, the maximum potential liability and the amount of any actual liability incurred;

(f)   in the case of quasi-loans and credit transactions, the value of the transaction; and

(g)   in the case of any other transaction or arrangement in which a director had a material interest, the name of the director concerned, the nature of the interest and the value of the transaction or arrangement.

32.21   The value of a transaction or arrangement is the value which would be attached on an arm's-length basis in the ordinary course of business to the goods or services which are the subject of the transaction. If the transaction is a loan or guarantee, it is the principal of the loan or the amount guaranteed or secured. [s340]

32.22 The above rules are summarised in Appendix VII of this manual.

32.23 An example of disclosure of a transaction in which a director has a material interest is given below.

> ### *Example 32.23*
>
> C.P. Plastics Limited (a member of the group) has, during the year, contracted to purchase its plastic raw material requirements over the next three years from Plastic Products Limited. Mr J. Docker, a director of Delto PLC, owns a significant proportion of the equity share capital of Plastic Products Limited. Based on forecast production schedules and prices agreed for the year ending 31 December 2000, the company will purchase materials valued at approximately £1.2 million in 2000. The value of the contract for the years 2001 and 2002 will depend on a price formula tied to the direct production costs incurred by Plastic Products Limited.

Loans to directors

Restrictions on loans to directors

32.24 The legislation concerning restrictions on loans to and similar transactions with or on behalf of directors and persons connected with them is contained in ss330 to 347.

32.25 There are civil remedies and criminal penalties (including up to two years' imprisonment) for breaches of these requirements.

32.26 The Act provides that:
[s330]

(a) a company shall not make a loan to a director or to a director of its holding company or guarantee or provide security in connection with a loan made by any person to such a director;

(b) a 'relevant' company shall not make a loan or quasi-loan or enter into a credit transaction or guarantee or provide security in connection with a loan, quasi-loan or credit transaction to its director or director of its holding company or to a person 'connected' with such a director. A 'relevant' company is defined by the Act as a company which is either a public limited company or a member of a group which includes a public limited company [s331(6)];

(c) a company shall not arrange for the assignment to it or the assumption by it of any rights, obligations or liabilities under a transaction which, if the company had entered into it, would have been prohibited by (a) and (b) above;

(d)   a company shall not take part in any arrangement whereby another person enters into a transaction described in (a), (b) and (c) above and in return that person obtains some benefit from the company or another company in the group.

Exemptions

32.27   The following are excepted from the rules in **32.26** above concerning restriction of loans to and similar transactions with directors:

(a)   loans to directors if the aggregate amount to any director does not exceed £5,000 [s334];

(b)   loans and quasi-loans to, and credit transactions in respect of, a holding company and entering into guarantees or providing security to a third party in connection with loans, quasi-loans and credit transactions in respect of a holding company [s336];

(c)   relevant companies making loans and quasi-loans to, or guarantees for, a fellow group company where the connection is only that the director of one company is associated with the other [s333];

(d)   credit transactions, and guarantees and security in connection with credit transactions, up to £10,000 or where entered into in the normal course of business and on normal commercial arm's-length terms [s335];

(e)   provision to a director of a company (but not to a director of its holding company) of funds to meet expenditure for the purposes of the company or to enable him to perform his duties as an officer of the company. The provision must either be approved in advance at a general meeting or made on conditions that, unless it is approved at or before the next annual general meeting, it will be repaid within the six months thereafter. In a relevant company, the provision must not exceed £20,000 [s337]; and

(f)   quasi-loans aggregating not more than £5,000 which are required to be repaid within two months [s332].

32.28

A loan made to an employee before he is appointed to the board is not of itself illegal, since it is the making of a loan to a director, rather than the existence of the loan, which is addressed by the Act. However, once the employee becomes a director, any increase in the loan due to further advances or the accruing of interest would be subject to the restrictions.

32.29

Money carried by a director on behalf of a company is often not provision of funds to that director. For example, cash (or traveller's cheques) given to a director to settle company expenses

> incurred on an overseas visit, but which is not available for the director's own use, will, in many cases, not fall to be disclosed, because the director obtains no benefit from carrying such cash. However, if the money had been paid into the director's bank account, he could benefit from it and thus the transaction would fall to be disclosed as a provision of funds.

32.30 There are additional exemptions for money lending companies which are summarised along with the above rules in Appendix VI.

Transactions with officers other than directors

Statutory disclosure requirements

32.31 The notes to the accounts should disclose information in respect of arrangements made by the company or any of its subsidiaries for persons who were officers of the company at any time during the financial year, but who were not directors. [s232]

32.32 Under the Act, an officer includes a director, manager or secretary of a corporate entity. [s744] Courts have laid different interpretations on what constitutes a manager, but in the case *Re a Company* (1980) 1 All ER 284, the judge stated: 'The expression "manager" should not be too narrowly construed. It is not to be equated with a managing or other director or a general manager. As I see it, any person who in the affairs of a company exercises a supervisory control which reflects the general policy of the company for the time being or which is related to the general administration of the company is in the sphere of management'. Although it is not clearly stated in the Act, it seems that an auditor of the company will be considered by the courts to be an officer.

32.33 The information to be disclosed is the aggregate amount, for all officers other than directors, outstanding at the end of the financial year under each of the following headings:
[Sch 6: 28 and 29]

- loans;

- quasi-loans; and

- credit transactions.

32.34 In each case, guarantees and securities for these items and agreements to enter into such arrangements are to be included under the appropriate heading.

32.35 The number of officers for whom they were made in each case should also be stated.

32.36   If the aggregate of such arrangements outstanding at the end of the financial year in respect of any individual officer does not exceed £2,500, then the arrangements in respect of that officer may be excluded from the amounts disclosed.

Listing Rules requirements

Contracts of significance and transactions with controlling shareholders

32.37   The Listing Rules require listed companies to disclose the following: [Listing Rules 12.43(q), (r) and (s)]

(a)   particulars of any contract of significance (see **32.38** below for the definition) subsisting during the period, to which the company, or one of its subsidiary undertakings, is a party and in which a director of the company is or was materially interested (the requirement to disclose the fact if there has been no such contract was removed with effect from 1 July 1996);

(b)   particulars of any contract of significance between the company, or one of its subsidiary undertakings, and a controlling shareholder (see **32.39** below for the definition) subsisting during the period; and

(c)   particulars of any contract for the provision of services to the company or any of its subsidiary undertakings by a controlling shareholder subsisting during the period; an exception is allowed if the services provided are those which it is the principal business of the shareholder to provide and the contract is not a 'contract of significance'.

32.38   A 'contract of significance' is defined as one which represents in amount or value (or, as the case may be, in annual amount or value) a sum equal to one per cent or more, calculated on a group basis where relevant, of:
[Listing Rules 12.44]

(a)   in the case of a capital transaction or a transaction of which the principal purpose or effect is the granting of credit, the aggregate of the group's share capital and reserves; or

(b)   in other cases, the total annual purchases, sales, payments or receipts, as the case may be, of the group.

32.39   A 'controlling shareholder' is defined as any person (or persons acting jointly by agreement whether formal or otherwise) who is:
[Listing Rules 3.13]

(a)   entitled to exercise, or control the exercise of, 30 per cent or more of the rights to vote at general meetings of the company; or

(b)   able to control the appointment of directors who are able to exercise a majority of votes at board meetings.

Associates (see **32.47** and **32.48** below for definitions) of a controlling shareholder will, unless the contrary is established to the satisfaction of the UK Listing Authority, be presumed to be acting jointly or by agreement with that controlling shareholder.

32.40   The UK Listing Authority does not specify how this information is to be given, but it is usual to comply with the UK Listing Authority requirements in the directors' report. However, if a 'contract of significance' requires disclosure as a material contract under the statutory rules or FRS 8, it should also be disclosed in the financial statements or cross-referenced to the directors' report in the notes to the financial statements.

Small related-party transactions

32.41   The Listing Rules also require listed companies to make disclosure of 'small related-party transactions' (see **32.42** below for the definition). [Listing Rules 12.43(t)] The information to be disclosed is: [Listing Rules 11.8(c)]

(a)   the identity of the related party;

(b)   the value of the consideration for the transaction; and

(c)   all other relevant circumstances.

32.42   A 'small related-party transaction' is a transaction with a related party where each of the percentage ratios referred to in the Listing Rules paragraph 10.5 (i.e., assets, profits, turnover, consideration to market capitalisation, and gross capital) is less than five per cent, but one or more exceeds 0.25 per cent. [Listing Rules 11.8] For a transaction exceeding any of these five per cent limits, the Listing Rules require a circular to be sent to shareholders containing specified information and shareholder approval for the transaction to be obtained. [Listing Rules 11.4] In computing the above ratios, it is necessary to aggregate all transactions which are entered into by the company (or any of its subsidiary undertakings) with the same related party (and any of its associates) in any 12- month period and which have neither been approved by shareholders nor described in a circular complying with specified requirements. [Listing Rules 11.9]

32.43   A 'transaction with a related party' means: [Listing Rules 11.1]

    (a)   a transaction (other than a transaction of a revenue nature in the ordinary course of business) between a company, or any of its subsidiary undertakings, and a related party;

    (b)   any arrangements pursuant to which a company, or any of its subsidiary undertakings, and a related party each invests in, or provides finance to, another undertaking or asset; or

    (c)   a transaction (other than a transaction of a revenue nature in the ordinary course of business) between a company, or any of its subsidiary undertakings and any person who, or other entity which exercises significant influence over the company.

32.44   A 'related party' means:
[Listing Rules 11.1]

    (a)   a substantial shareholder;

    (b)   any person who is (or was within the 12 months preceding the date of the transaction) a director or shadow director of the company or of any other company which is (and, if he has ceased to be such, was while he was a director or shadow director of such other company) its subsidiary undertaking or parent undertaking or a fellow subsidiary undertaking of its parent undertaking; or

    (c)   an associate of a related party within (a) or (b) above.

32.45   A 'substantial shareholder' means any person (excluding a bare trustee) who is, or was within the 12 months preceding the date of the transaction, entitled to exercise or to control the exercise of 10 per cent or more of the votes able to be cast on all or substantially all matters at general meetings of the company (or any other company which is its subsidiary undertaking or parent undertaking or is a fellow subsidiary undertaking of its parent undertaking). [Listing Rules 11.1]

32.46   Prior to Amendment No. 13 to the Listing Rules (effective from 11 January 1999), where potential conflicts existed between the interests of the company and those of a controlling shareholder (or associate) (see **32.39** above), the company was required to demonstrate that contractual arrangements were in place to avoid detriment to the general body of shareholders of the company and that decisions as to the enforcement of those contractual arrangements were taken independently of the controlling shareholder. Amendment No. 13 removed these rules, instead requiring full disclosure in the listing particulars of the existence of any controlling shareholder and how the company is satisfied that it is capable of carrying on its business independently of, and at arm's-length from, the controlling shareholder.

32.47 An 'associate' means in relation to either a director or a substantial shareholder who is an individual:
[Listing Rules 11.1]

(a) that individual's spouse or child (together 'the individual's family');

(b) the trustees (acting as such) of any trust of which the individual or any of the individual's family is a beneficiary or discretionary object (other than a trust which is either an occupational pension scheme, as defined in s207 Financial Services Act 1986, or an employees' share scheme, which does not, in either case, have the effect of conferring benefits on persons all or most of whom are related parties);

(c) any company in whose equity shares the individual or any member or members (taken together) of the individual's family or the individual and any such member or members (taken together) are directly or indirectly interested (or have a conditional or contingent entitlement to become interested) so that they are (or would on the fulfilment of the condition or the occurrence of the contingency be) able:

(i) to exercise or control the exercise of 30 per cent or more of the votes able to be cast at general meetings on all, or substantially all, matters; or

(ii) to appoint or remove directors holding a majority of voting rights at board meetings on all, or substantially all, matters.

For these purposes, where more than one director of the listed company, its parent undertaking or any of its subsidiary undertakings is interested in the equity shares of another company, then the interests of those directors and their associates will be aggregated when determining whether such a company is an associate of the director.

32.48 An 'associate' means in relation to a substantial shareholder which is a company:
[Listing Rules 11.1]

(a) any other company which is its subsidiary undertaking, parent undertaking or fellow subsidiary undertaking of the parent undertaking;

(b) any company whose directors are accustomed to act in accordance with the substantial shareholder's directions or instructions; and

(c) any company in the capital of which the substantial shareholder, and any other company under (a) or (b) taken together, is (or would on the fulfilment of a condition or the occurrence of a contingency be) interested in the manner described in **32.47**(c) above.

Alternative investment market companies

32.49 AIM companies are required to disclose, in their next published accounts, details of transactions with related parties (including the identity of the related party, the value of the consideration for the transaction and all other relevant circumstances) where any of the percentage ratios exceeds 0.25 per cent. [Rules of the London Stock Exchange 16.25] The percentage ratios are broadly similar to those noted in **32.42** above, except that the third ratio is based on consideration to assets instead of being based on turnover. [Rules of the London Stock Exchange 16.23(b)] A related party is defined in the rules of the London Stock Exchange (definitions section) in similar terms to those in **32.44** above. In computing these ratios, it is necessary to aggregate with the current transaction all transactions which are entered into with the same related party (or person connected with them) in the 12 months prior to the date of the latest transaction. [Rules of the London Stock Exchange 16.27]

Financial Reporting Standard 8

Introduction

32.50 The ASB issued FRS 8 *Related party disclosures* in 1995. The FRS requires disclosure of a material transaction undertaken by the reporting entity with a related party, irrespective of whether a price is charged. Disclosure of control is required where the reporting entity is controlled by another party, irrespective of whether a transaction has taken place. The objective of the FRS is 'to ensure that financial statements contain the disclosures necessary to draw attention to the ***possibility*** [our emphasis] that the reported financial position and results may have been affected by the existence of related parties and by material transactions with them'. [FRS 8(1)]

Definition of related parties

32.51 The FRS defines two or more parties as related when at any time during the financial period (see **32.52** below):
[FRS 8(2.5)(a)]

(a) one party has either direct or indirect control of the other party; or

(b) the parties are subject to common control from the same source (see **32.58** below); or

(c) one party has influence over the financial and operating policies of the other party to an extent that that other party might
be inhibited from pursuing at all times its own separate interests; or

(d) the parties, in entering a transaction, are subject to influence
from the same source to such an extent that one of the parties
to the transaction has subordinated its own separate interests
(see **32.59** below).

Control is the ability to direct the financial and operating policies of
an entity with a view to gaining economic benefits from its activities.
[FRS 8(2.2)] Examples of those parties deemed or presumed to be
related parties are provided in **32.53** and **32.55** below. However, this
is not intended to be an exhaustive list of related parties.

32.52

The phrase 'at any time during the financial period' implies
that all transactions in a financial period with a related party
need to be considered even if the control or influence giving
rise to the relationship was not present at the date of the transaction. [FRS 8(2.5)] Such an approach is consistent with the
Act which requires disclosure of transactions, etc. entered into
with a person who was at any time in the financial year a director of the company or its holding company (see **32.5** above).
Thus, for example, under FRS 8, if two parties are subject to
influence from the same source to such an extent that for a particular transaction one of the parties to that transaction has
subordinated its own separate interests, then all transactions
between those two parties in the financial period are related-
party transactions.

32.53 For the avoidance of doubt, certain parties are deemed to be related.
They include:
[FRS 8(2.5)(b)]

(a) the reporting entity's ultimate and intermediate parent undertakings, subsidiary undertakings and fellow subsidiary undertakings;

(b) the reporting entity's associates and joint ventures;

(c) the investor or venturer in respect of which the reporting entity
is an associate or a joint venture;

(d) directors of the reporting entity and the directors of its ultimate and intermediate parent undertakings (directors include
shadow directors); and

(e) pension funds for the benefit of employees of the reporting
entity or of any entity that is a related party of the reporting
entity.

32.54 Certain parties are presumed to be related parties of the reporting entity, unless it can be demonstrated that neither party has influenced the financial and operating policies of the other in such a way as to inhibit the pursuit of separate interests. Such parties include: [FRS 8(2.5)(c)]

(a) the key management of the reporting entity and the key management of its parent undertaking or undertakings (key management are those persons in senior positions having authority or responsibility for directing or controlling the major activities and resources of the reporting entity);

(b) a person owning or able to exercise control over 20 per cent or more of the voting rights of the reporting entity, whether directly or through nominees;

(c) each person acting in concert in such a way as to be able to exercise control or influence over the reporting entity (persons acting in concert are persons who, pursuant to an agreement or understanding (whether formal or informal), actively cooperate, whether by the ownership by any of them of shares in an undertaking or otherwise, to exercise control or influence over that undertaking; influence to be considered in terms of inhibiting the reporting entity from pursuing at all times its own separate interests); and

(d) an entity managing or managed by the reporting entity under a management contract.

32.55 Additionally, certain other parties are, because of their relationship with related parties of an entity, also presumed to be related parties of that reporting entity. They include:

(a) members of the close family of any individual falling under parties mentioned in **32.51**, **32.53** and **32.54** above; and

(b) partnerships, companies, trusts and other entities in which any individual or member of the close family in **32.51**, **32.53** and **32.54** above has a controlling interest.

32.56

> The lack of a qualifying 'unless it can be demonstrated ....' is interesting. Since the other parties are presumed rather than deemed to be related, there is an implication that the presumption is rebuttable. Although not stated, this would appear to be on the same grounds as noted in **32.54** above. [FRS 8(2.5)(d)]

32.57 The definition of a person's close family is much more far reaching than that contained in legislation in relation to a director (see **32.7** above). Close members of the family of an individual are those family members, or members of the same household, who may be expected to influence, or be influenced by, that person in their dealings with the reporting entity. The earlier exposure draft (FRED 8) used the term 'immediate family' and listed the family members that would normally be caught by that term. In recognition of the fact that the emphasis should be on influence rather than the immediacy of the family relationship, the ASB chose to substitute close family for immediate family, in line with IAS 24. The phrase 'members of the same household' reflects the view of the ASB that 'related parties in this context are not necessarily confined to the individual's legal family'.

Common control

32.58   Entities under common control are deemed to be related parties, as the controlling entity could cause them to transact or not transact with each other or stipulate the particular terms of a transaction. Thus, for either of the controlled parties, there is a possibility that the relationship could have a material effect on their reported financial position and results. Common control is deemed to exist when both parties are subject to control from boards having a controlling nucleus of directors in common. [FRS 8(13)]

Common influence

32.59   FRED 8, the exposure draft that preceded FRS 8, caught as related parties two parties where one was subject to control and another to influence from the same source. This did not survive in FRS 8, but was modified to require common influence and the subordination, by one party, of its own separate interests. This has a number of repercussions, in that common influence, by itself, does not make two entities related parties and that two related parties of a third entity are not necessarily related parties of each other. Thus, the following relationships do not of themselves constitute related-party relationships:
[FRS 8(14) and FRS 8, appendix IV(7)]

(a)   two parties that are associated companies of the same investor;

(b)   two parties where one is a subsidiary undertaking and the other an associate of the same investor (note that if the investor is an individual, there is a presumption that the subsidiary and associate in this case are related, as the investor is an individual, is a related party to the associate and has a controlling interest in the subsidiary – see **32.55** above);

(c)   two entities that simply have a director in common and not a controlling nucleus of directors in common (see **32.58** above).

Subordinated interests

32.60

> An individual may be the director of one company (A) and own a controlling interest in another (B); if so, A and B are presumed to be related parties. [FRS 8(2.5)(d)(ii)] If the individual uses his influence as a director of A to obtain discounts from a third-party supplier for B, there may be a related-party transaction reportable in B's financial statements. The reporting entity (B) has received assets (in the form of the discount) not from A or the individual but the third party. However, the individual may have influenced the third party to subordinate its own separate interests and offer discounts that it would otherwise not have given. If so, the third party and B are deemed to be related by FRS 8 and the transaction would require disclosure, if material, in B's accounts and possibly in the third party's. [FRS 8(2.5)(a)(iv)]

Definition of related-party transactions

32.61 As noted previously, FRS 8 requires disclosure of all material related-party transactions. A related-party transaction is: 'The transfer of assets or liabilities or the performance of services by, or for a related party irrespective of whether a price is charged'. There is no exemption simply because transactions are in the normal course of the reporting entity's business or at arm's length.

> **Extract 32.61**
>
> **Tesco plc 1999**
>
> **Note 30 Related party transactions**
>
> During the year there were no material transactions or amounts owed or owing with any of the Group's key management or members of their close family.
>
> During the year the Group traded with its five joint ventures, Shopping Centres Limited, BLT Properties Limited, Tesco British Land Property Partnership, Tesco Personal Finance Group Limited and Tesco Personal Finance Life Limited. The main transactions during the year were:
>
> (i) Equity funding of £28m (£26m in Tesco Personal Finance Group Limited and £2m in Tesco Personal Finance Life Limited).
>
> (ii) Equity funding of £21m and the sale of two properties to Tesco British Land Property Partnership worth £33m. Additionally the Group made rental payments of £13m (1998 – nil) to Tesco British Land Property Partnership.
>
> (iii) The Group made rental payments of £3m (1998 – £3m) and £11m (1998 – £9m) to Shopping Centres Limited and BLT Properties Limited respectively. In addition, BLT Properties Limited purchased a

property from Spenhill Properties Limited (a fellow Group company) for £7m.

(iv) The Group has charged Tesco Personal Finance Limited (a 100% subsidiary of Tesco Personal Finance Group Limited) an amount totalling £10m in respect of services, loan interest and assets transferred, of which £9m was outstanding at 27 February 1999. Tesco Personal Finance Limited received fees totalling £11m from the Group for managing certain financial products, £3m of which was outstanding at 27 February 1999.

(v) The Group made loans totalling £20m to Tesco Personal Finance Group Limited.

32.62 It is not uncommon for a parent or group company to guarantee the borrowings of another group company or for a shareholder/director to guarantee the borrowings of his company. Statute requires disclosure of guarantees made by a company in regard to its own borrowings or those of other parties (see **21.30** above). The definition of a related-party transaction in **32.51** above is such that a reporting entity receiving the benefit of a guarantee from a related party would, if it was material, be required to disclose that guarantee. An example of such a disclosure is given below. This is reinforced in the ASB's FRSSE, which specifically notes that personal guarantees given by directors in respect of borrowings by the reporting entity should be disclosed.

Example 32.62

Mr Lincoln, the managing director, has guaranteed the bank overdraft of the company by granting the bank a charge over a property owned by him. The overdraft has an authorised limit of £60,000.

32.63 The payment of a dividend to a related party would constitute a related-party transaction and disclosure would be required if it were material. However, in some cases, the information may already be disclosed and additional disclosure would be unnecessary to meet the requirements of FRS 8. For example, if disclosure is made:

(a) Of the fact that the reporting entity is wholly owned;

(b) That the ownership has not changed in the year; and

(c) Of details of the dividend paid and proposed,

it would not be necessary to state explicitly that the dividend had been paid to the owner.

The scope of FRS 8

32.64 The FRS applies to all financial statements intended to give a true and fair view. There is no exemption for small entities which are following FRS 8 rather than choosing to adopt the FRSSE. However, there are exemptions from disclosure of certain related-party transactions, as follows:
[FRS 8(3)]

(a) in consolidated financial statements, of any transactions or balances between group entities that have been eliminated on consolidation;

(b) of pension contributions paid to a pension fund;

(c) of emoluments in respect of services as an employee of the reporting entity;

(d) in a parent's own financial statements when those statements are presented together with its consolidated financial statements; and

(e) in the financial statements of subsidiary undertakings, 90 per cent or more of whose voting rights are controlled within the group, of transactions with entities that are part of the group or investees of the group qualifying as related parties, provided that the consolidated financial statements in which the subsidiary is included are publicly available. Note that the exemption is only in relation to transactions with fellow group entities or investees of the group. Disclosure is still required of material transactions with other related parties, such as directors. Also, it is only applicable to subsidiary undertakings and not quasi-subsidiaries as defined in FRS 5. [FRS 5(7)]

32.65

FRS 8 requires that reporting entities should state the fact if they take advantage of exemption (e) in **32.64** above. However, it does not specify what is meant by publicly available. It would appear to cover not only those cases where, by law, the financial statements must be publicly available (e.g., by filing at Companies House), but also those instances where the parent chooses to make consolidated financial statements publicly available on a reasonable basis. In the latter case, the subsidiary should disclose that fact and the address from which the financial statements may be obtained.

32.66 Some commentators have noted an apparent discrepancy between the exemptions in FRS 8 paragraphs 3(a) and 3(c) ((a) and (e) in **32.64** above). The former, dealing with consolidated accounts, exempts balances and transactions eliminated on consolidation. The latter, dealing with the accounts of a 90 per

cent subsidiary, exempts transactions with fellow group entities, but makes no mention of exempting disclosure of balances. Two points may be made in this respect. Firstly, FRS 8
indicates that the term 'transactions' incorporates related balances and that the exemption in 3(c) would thus extend to such
balances. [FRS 8(6)] Secondly, the Act's balance sheet formats
specifically require amounts owed to or due from group undertakings to be shown separately (although the need for a more
detailed analysis under Sch 4 para 59 was deleted by the
Companies Act 1985 (Miscellaneous Accounting
Amendments) Regulations 1996 (SI 1996 No 189)) and such
disclosure could be said to meet the requirements of the FRS
on an aggregated basis. However, it may be desirable to give
details of individual balances with group undertakings where
they are material.

32.67 The exemption for 90 per cent or more subsidiaries requires
consolidated accounts to be publicly available that include the
subsidiary. However, FRS 8 does not explicitly state that the
consolidated accounts should incorporate all the group entities
or investees. Take, as an example, a company A that has two
subsidiaries, B and C. Each of B and C has a subsidiary, D and
E respectively (see chart below). Only B is required to, and
does, prepare consolidated financial statements that are publicly available. Can D, B's 90 per cent or more subsidiary, claim
the exemption in FRS 8 paragraph 3(c) in respect of transactions with A, C and E?

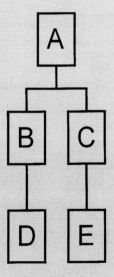

Taken literally, the requirements of the exemption have been
met: 90 per cent or more of D's voting rights are controlled
within both the group headed by B and the group headed by A,

and it is included in B's consolidated financial statements that are publicly available. The intention behind the exemption is explained in FRS 8 paragraph 9 and paragraphs 11 to 13 of appendix IV to FRS 8. Disclosure of the nature of the relationship and the fact that the exemption has been invoked is such as to alert the reader of the financial statements to the possible existence of related-party transactions. In addition, the ASB considered that 'the ultimate holding company is named in the notes to the financial statements and those wishing to find out more information about the group could do so provided that consolidated financial statements were "publicly available" '. The implication appears to be that consolidated financial statements should be available at the ultimate holding company level. This would appear to argue that the spirit of the exemption is such that the condition should read 'provided that the consolidated financial statements of that group in which the subsidiary is included are publicly available'. In our example, therefore, D could not claim the exemption in respect of transactions with A, C and E, as consolidated financial statements including that part of the group are not prepared.

32.68   The FRS does not require disclosure of the relationship and transactions between a reporting entity and certain parties arising simply as a result of the normal role of those other parties. These include: [FRS 8(4)]

(a)   providers of finance in the course of their business in that regard;

(b)   utility companies; and

(c)   government departments and their sponsored bodies,

      even though they may circumscribe the freedom of action of an entity or participate in its decision-making process; and

(d)   a customer, supplier, franchiser, distributor or general agent with whom an entity transacts a significant volume of business.

32.69

It may be the case that a supplier operates a system of inducements (e.g., loans or bank guarantees) in exchange for a customer agreeing to source supplies solely from that supplier. This of itself will not normally create a related-party relationship. However, consideration will need to be given to whether the agreement allows the supplier to direct the financial or operating policies of the customer. For example, is the customer free to terminate the agreement, if more favourable terms are available elsewhere, subject to a reasonable penalty?

32.70   The above exemptions apply only to transactions with related parties and not to disclosure of control.

32.71   The explanatory section of the FRS notes that the related-party disclosure provisions do not apply in circumstances where to comply with them conflicts with the reporting entity's duties of confidentiality arising by the operation of the law. For example, banks are obliged by law to observe a strict duty of confidentiality in respect of their customers' affairs and the FRS would not override the obligation to preserve the confidentiality of customers' dealings. [FRS 8(16)] However, operation of the law would not include the effects of terms stipulated in a contract.

Group accounts

32.72   The FRS does not specifically address the question of who is a related party in respect of group accounts. Two approaches would seem to be possible. The first is to disclose transactions with parties who are related parties of the group as a whole, which, by implication, means considering the group in its role as reporting entity and considering which parties are related to it under FRS 8. The alternative is to provide a straight aggregation of related-party disclosures from the accounts of the group undertakings and of the transactions with related parties of the parent (there are unlikely to be any disclosures in the parent's own accounts, given the exemption in FRS 8 paragraph 3(b)). The first approach appears to follow more closely the intention of the FRS and also the approach taken by the Act. Thus, a director of a subsidiary company would be deemed to be a party related to that company for the purposes of its own financial statements but may be deemed, on a rebuttable basis, to be a related party as part of the key management of the group for the purposes of the group financial statements.

Transactions with other group undertakings

32.73   When an undertaking becomes a subsidiary part way through the parent's financial period, it is a related party of the other group undertakings for the whole of that financial period. Only those transactions between the new subsidiary and the rest of the group arising on or after the date of acquisition will be eliminated on consolidation, allowing disclosure exemption (a) in **32.64** above to be used. Any material transactions arising between the new subsidiary and the rest of the group prior to the date of acquisition should be disclosed in the consolidated financial statements. If exemption (e) in **32.64** above were applicable to the new subsidiary, then neither pre-acquisition nor post-acquisition transactions with the group would be required to be disclosed in the subsidiary's own financial statements. Where an undertaking ceases to be a subsidiary part way through a parent's financial period, any transactions between that undertaking and its former fellow group undertakings occurring between the date of it ceasing to be a subsidiary and the end of the financial period would not be eliminated on consolidation and, if material, would require disclosure in the consolidated financial statements as related-party transactions. In the undertaking's own financial statements, all material transactions with the group would require disclosure, as it was a related party in the period and exemption (e) in **32.64** above would not apply, as it was no longer a subsidiary at the period end.

Materiality

32.74   FRS 8 identifies a number of approaches to materiality in the context of related-party transactions. [FRS 8(20)]

'Transactions are material when their disclosure might reasonably be expected to influence decisions made by the users of general purpose financial statements. The materiality of related party transactions is to be judged, not only in terms of their significance to the reporting entity, but also in relation to the other related party when that party is:

(a)   a director, key manager or other individual in a position to influence, or accountable for stewardship of, the reporting entity; or

(b)   a member of the close family of any individual mentioned in (a) above; or

(c)   an entity controlled by any individual mentioned in (a) or (b) above.'

32.75   Thus, FRS 8 considers:

(a)   the significance to the reporting entity; and

(b)   the significance to the related party; but primarily

(c)   whether disclosure might reasonably be expected to influence decisions made by the users of general purpose financial statements.

Requirement (c) may give a lower level of materiality than (a) or (b).

32.76   The ASB's FRSSE, in considering related-party transactions notes only that materiality of a related-party transaction should be judged in terms of its significance to the reporting entity.

32.77

In considering the materiality of transactions to individuals, the following should be borne in mind:

(a) materiality is both a qualitative and quantitative judgement. A transaction may be relatively small, but of significance to the individual. Materiality for an individual may be considerably lower than that used for the reporting entity;

(b) an indication of 'significance' may be gained by considering the possible reaction of the Inland Revenue if it became aware of the matter;

(c) in determining what is material to the individual, consideration should be given to what might be regarded by the outside world as unreasonable or worthy of public scrutiny, for example, a transaction which may be seen as immaterial in the context of the personal wealth of a particular individual could be regarded as material by public opinion;

(d) transactions are not excluded simply because they are at 'arm's length' or in the normal course of business. Disclosure is required of **all** material related-party transactions, whether 'normal' or 'abnormal'. However, consideration of such aspects will be of relevance when considering the qualitative aspects of materiality;

(e) a user is likely to be interested not simply in the value of the transaction but also in transactions which enhance a related party's influence over the entity or which reflect on the general governance of the entity;

(f) disclosure is not required for emoluments in respect of services as an employee of the reporting entity (see **32.64** above).

Disclosure of related-party transactions

32.78 FRS 8 requires disclosure of material transactions undertaken by the reporting entity with a related party, irrespective of whether a price is charged. The disclosures required include:

(a) the names of the transacting related parties;

(b) a description of the relationship between the parties;

(c) a description of the transactions;

(d) the amounts involved;

(e)   any other elements of the transactions necessary for an under-standing of the financial statements;

(f)   the amounts due to or from related parties at the balance sheet date and provision for doubtful debts due from such parties at that date; and

(g)   amounts written off in the period in respect of debts due to or from related parties.

Example 32.78

During the year, the group purchased from C.P. Plastics Ltd, an asso-ciated company, £220,000 (1999 – £200,000) of finished goods at nor-mal trade price and a freehold property in Holborn at an independent open market value of £1,500,000 (1999 – nil). At the financial year end, £50,000 (1999 – £30,000) was due to C.P. Plastics Ltd in respect of finished goods. This amount is included within creditors due within one year.

Extract 32.78

Associated Nursing Services plc 1999

28 Related Party Transactions (extract)

The following companies are deemed to be related parties by virtue of the fact the Associated Nursing Services plc manages their day-to-day operations and has influence over their financial and operating policies.

Assured Care Centres plc

Associated Nursing Services plc has a management contract to man-age the Borehamwood Nursing Home and Close Care Units at two different sites.

Assured Close Care Centres plc

Associated Nursing Services plc had a management contract to man-age Close Care Units at two different sites. These Close Care Units have now been sold by Assured Close Care Centres, and ANS no longer has any management contracts with this company.

Grosvenor Care plc

Associated Nursing Services plc has a management contract to man-age the Haven Nursing Home.

Nightingale Nursing Homes plc

Associated Nursing Services plc has a management contract to man-age the Nightingale Nursing Home.

Summerville Nursing Homes plc

Associated Nursing Services plc has a management contract to man-age the Summerville Nursing Home.

No director of Associated Nursing Services plc held any beneficial interests in the share capital of the related parties during the year.

During the year the following amounts were charged to related parties for the following services:

Year ended 31 March 1999

	Management fees £000's	Construction fees £000's	Other £000's	Total £000's
Assured Care Centres plc	46	–	–	46
Assured Close Care Centres plc	8	–	–	8
Grosvenor Care plc	23	–	5	28
Nightingale Nursing Homes plc	20	–	5	25
Summerville Nursing Homes plc	28	–	5	33
	125	–	15	140

Year ended 31 March 1998

	Management fees £000's	Construction fees £000's	Other £000's	Total £000's
Assured Care Centres plc	113	–	–	113
Assured Close Care Centres plc	24	–	–	24
Grosvenor Care plc	34	–	–	34
Nightingale Nursing Homes plc	20	–	–	20
Summerville Nursing Homes plc	34	97	–	131
	225	97	–	322

Year ended 31 March 1999

	Management fees £000's	Construction fees £000's	Other £000's	Total £000's
Grosvenor Care plc	27	122	3	152
Nightingale Nursing Homes plc	3	25	2	30
Summerville Nursing Homes plc	141	14	2	157
	171	161	7	339

Year ended 31 March 1998

	Management fees £000's	Construction fees £000's	Other £000's	Total £000's
Grosvenor Care plc	27	122	–	149
Nightingale Nursing Homes plc	3	43	2	48
Summerville Nursing Homes plc	141	14		155
	171	179	2	352

32.79 FRS 8 requires disclosure of material related party transactions in the 'financial statements'. If this disclosure or part of it is made in some other place within the annual report (e.g., the directors' report, remuneration report, or OFR) it must be cross-referenced to in the notes to the accounts to comply with FRS 8. This was emphasised by the Financial Reporting Review Panel in its findings in respect of the 1997 accounts of H&C Furnishings (now Harveys Furnishings). Harveys Furnishings plc subsequently revised its 1997 accounts by including a supplementary note in its 1998 accounts which contained the amendment reproduced below.

> **Extract 32.79**
>
> **Harveys Furnishings (formerly H&C Furnishings) 1998 (extract from supplementary note to the 1997 financial statements)**
>
> **Note 23 Transactions with directors and related parties**
>
> Details of related party transactions and employee share options are set out in the directors' report on pages 15 to 16 and 18 respectively and form part of these financial statements. The aggregate gains made by directors on the exercise of share options amounted to £126,977.

32.80 Transactions with related parties may be disclosed on an aggregated basis (aggregation of similar transactions by type of related party), unless disclosure of an individual transaction, or connected transactions, is necessary for an understanding of the impact of the transactions on the financial statements of the reporting entity or is required by law. Aggregation should not be done in such a way as to obscure the importance of significant transactions. Hence, purchases or sales of goods should not be aggregated with purchases or sales of fixed assets. Nor should a material related-party transaction with an individual be concealed in an aggregated disclosure. [FRS 8(21)] Thus, for example where a number of companies are under common ownership, it would normally be acceptable to aggregate transactions of a similar type with the other companies, but not transactions with the owner.

Example 32.80

The company is controlled by Mr Smith, who owns all of the issued share capital of the company. Mr Smith also owns all of the issued share capital of A Limited and of B Limited. The aggregate amounts of the company's trade with A Limited and B Limited in the year were:

(a) services purchased £120,000 (1999 – £115,000);

(b) purchase of raw materials £250,000 (1999 – £200,000);

(c) sales of finished goods £200,000 (1999 – £210,000).

The above transactions were on normal terms.

At the financial year end, the aggregate amount:

(a) due to A Limited and B Limited, included within creditors due within one year, was £50,000 (1999 – £40,000);

(b) due from A Limited and B Limited was £30,000 (1999 – £45,000).

Disclosure of control

32.81 Where the reporting entity is controlled by another party, disclosure of that control is required irrespective of whether any transactions have taken place between the reporting entity and the controlling parties. Disclosure is required of:

- the related-party relationship;

- the name of the other party; and, if different

- the name of the ultimate controlling party.

Example 32.81

The company is controlled by Mr. Lincoln, the managing director, who owns 80 per cent of the issued share capital of the company.

32.82 Although FRS 8 refers to a controlling party, this need not be an individual person or company. The reporting entity may be controlled by two or more parties acting in concert pursuant to an agreement or understanding (formal or informal).

32.83 If the controlling party or ultimate controlling party is not known, that fact should be disclosed. Disclosure is not required if there is no controlling party or ultimate controlling party.

32.84   FRS 8 does not address the situation where there are a number of intermediate controlling parties. As a minimum, disclosure should be made of the ultimate controlling party and the immediate controlling party.

32.85   The disclosure of control required by FRS 8 is in addition to that required by Sch 5 (see **4.35** to **4.39** above).

> ### Example 32.85
>
> In the opinion of the directors, the company's ultimate parent company and ultimate controlling party is Saffron Sarl, a company incorporated in Luxembourg. The parent undertaking of the largest group, which includes the company and for which group accounts are prepared, is Sapphire Limited, a company incorporated in Great Britain. The parent undertaking of the smallest such group is Ruby Limited, a company incorporated in New Zealand. Copies of the group financial statements of Sapphire Limited are available from Companies House, Crown Way, Maindy, Cardiff CF4 3UZ. Copies of the group financial statements of Ruby Limited are available from The Registrar of Companies, Companies House, Wellington, New Zealand. The company's immediate controlling party is Pearl Ltd.

32.86   While the Act does not specify the date in respect of which the disclosures on parent undertakings are to be given, FRS 8's provisions on the disclosure of control could be interpreted more widely as requiring disclosure of information on all controlling parties from the beginning of the period up until the date of approval of the financial statements.

> ### Extract 32.86
>
> **Canary Wharf plc 1999 (extract)**
>
> **27 Ultimate Parent Undertaking and Related Party Transactions**
>
> Until 6 April 1999 the company's ultimate parent undertaking was C.W. Investments Limited Partnership, a Cayman Islands undertaking. The limited partnership was dissolved immediately after the shares of the company were admitted for listing on the London Stock Exchange on 1 April 1999.
>
> The smallest and largest group into which the accounts of the company for the year ended 30 June 1999 are consolidated are the company's consolidated accounts embodied herein.

32.87   Where disclosure of control required by FRS 8 is made in the directors' report or any other part of the annual report outside the main body of the accounts (e.g., control by directors disclosed in directors' report to comply with Sch 7 requirement to give certain details of directors' interests in the shares of the company and other group companies), it should be cross-referenced in the notes to the accounts (see **32.79** above).

Comparative figures

32.88 The standard is silent on the question of comparative figures. The press release which accompanied FRS 8 made it clear that comparatives would not be expected in the first year of implementation. Thereafter, under the Act, companies are required to give comparative figures for related-party transactions. [Sch 4: 58(3)]

32.89 This raises an interesting question, i.e., what are the comparatives for related-party disclosures? A number of areas of uncertainty may be identified:

(a)   a party is a related party this year, but was not last year. Do transactions with that party last year, even though it was not a related party in that period, need to be disclosed as comparatives?

(b)   a party was a related party last year, but is not this year. Do transactions with that party last year need to be disclosed?

(c)   where transactions are aggregated by type of related party, should the aggregated comparatives be in respect of only those related parties that are related parties this year (which again raises points (a) and (b) above) or the totals as disclosed in the prior year's accounts?

32.90 The purpose of the disclosures required by FRS 8 is to draw attention to the possibility that the financial statements have been affected by related-party transactions. The transactions that may have affected the current period's results are those with parties that were related in the current period. The appropriate comparative, i.e., transactions that may have affected the comparative period's results, would therefore be transactions with parties that were related in the comparative period. Under this approach, the financial statements should disclose:

(a)   the impact on this year's figures of transactions with parties who are related this year; and

(b)   as a comparative, the impact on last year's figures of transactions with parties who were related last year.

Where this is deemed to give insufficient explanation, then additional disclosure may be given.

32.91 This can perhaps best be illustrated by considering some illustrative examples.

Example 32.91.1

A party is related this year, but not in the comparative period

In the context of accounts to be produced by X Limited:

Q   Sales were made to A both this year and last year. If A is related this year, but was not related last year, should comparatives be disclosed?

A   Comparatives need not be disclosed, as the transactions will not have affected the comparative period's results. Where the absence of comparatives may create confusion, then additional explanation might be given stating that, while transactions were made in the prior period, they are not disclosed, as the related-party relationship did not exist in that period.

Example 32.91.2

A party was related last year, but is not related in the current period

In the context of accounts to be produced by X Limited:

Q   Sales were made to A both this year and last year. If A was related last year, but is not related this year, should last year's sales be disclosed again? If so, should this year's sales also be disclosed even though A is not related?

A   Last year's sales should be disclosed again, since they may have affected the comparative figures in the accounts. This year's sales need not, however, be disclosed, since A is no longer related. Where the inclusion of comparatives but no current period figures may create confusion, then additional explanation might be given stating that, while transactions were made in the current period, they are not disclosed, as the related-party relationship did not exist in that period.

Example 32.91.3

A party is related both years, but has not transacted in both years

In the context of accounts to be produced by X Limited:

Q   A is a related party both this year and last year. Sales were made to A this year, but not last year. Fixed assets were purchased from A last year, but not this year. What comparatives are required?

A   Clearly this year's sales, and the nil comparatives, will need to be disclosed. Last year's fixed asset transactions (for which there is no equivalent this year) should be disclosed again, since they may have affected the comparative figures in the accounts.

33 Requirements concerning share capital and distributions

33 Requirements concerning share capital and distributions

Summary of changes since the previous issue of this publication

Para.	*Topic*	*Summary*
33.89	*Company Formation and Capital Maintenance*	Consultation paper issued as part of the company law review process. Among other matters it proposes a move to no par value shares for private companies.
33.96	Determination of realised profits and distributable profits	Draft technical release 6/99 issued by the ICAEW. Its proposals include, in certain circumstances, that marked to market gains constitute realised profits.

Introduction

33.1 This chapter summarises the main aspects of the Act relating to:

(a) the issue of share capital;

(b) the repurchase or redemption of share capital;

(c) the granting of financial assistance;

(d) distributions; and

(e) reduction of share capital.

The requirements relating to the disclosure of share capital and reserves in financial statements, together with the accounting for that purpose under FRS 4, are dealt with in chapter 18.

Issue of share capital

33.2 The Act contains regulations regarding the issue of share capital. [ss80–116] A summary of the major provisions follows below.

Several of the provisions are complex and, where necessary, reference should be made to the Act.

33.3 Shares may not be allotted at a discount. [s100] This means that shares cannot be issued, as fully paid, for consideration less than their nominal value.

33.4 The board of directors may not allot 'relevant securities' (see **33.5** below) unless it is given authority to do so by the company's Articles or by an ordinary resolution of the company. [s80] Normally, such authority may not exceed five years. The board of directors of a private company may be given authority for an indefinite period, or a period in excess of five years, by an elective resolution of the company. [s80A] (An elective resolution requires 21 days' notice and unanimous approval.)

33.5 'Relevant securities' are:

(a) shares in the company other than shares shown in the Memorandum to have been taken by the subscribers to it or shares allotted in pursuance of an employees' share scheme; and

(b) any right to subscribe for, or to convert any security into, shares in the company (other than shares so allotted).

An allotment of relevant securities includes the grant of a right to subscribe, convert, etc. but does not then include the subsequent allotment of shares pursuant to such a right.

33.6 Ordinary shares or securities convertible into ordinary shares (other than those to be allotted in pursuance of an employees' share scheme) to be allotted for cash must first be offered pro rata to existing holders of shares or securities of the same class on terms similar to or more favourable than those on which they are to be offered to others (pre-emption rights). [s89] A number of other shares are also affected. [ss89 and 94] Private companies can exclude pre-emption rights altogether by means of a provision in their Memorandum or Articles. [s91] Where directors are authorised to issue shares (see **33.4** above), a company can, by special resolution, permit the directors to issue shares under that authority without regard to pre-emption rights. [s95]

33.7 No share of a public company can be allotted unless one quarter of its nominal value and the whole of any premium is paid up. [s101]

33.8 A public company cannot allot shares otherwise than for cash (except in connection with a takeover or merger) unless the consideration has been valued within the previous six months. The valuation report required for this purpose will usually be given by the auditor, who may rely on the valuation of an expert (see **43.26** below). [s103]

Purchase or redemption of own shares

General requirements

33.9   The Act contains provisions which permit limited companies to redeem or purchase their own shares. [ss159–181] The relevant sections are summarised in **33.10** to **33.26** below.

33.10   A company may redeem or purchase its own shares only if so authorised by its Articles. [s159]

33.11   Shareholder approval is required for the purchase as follows:

(a)   off-market purchase: the terms of the proposed contract must be authorised by a special resolution before the contract is entered into; for a public company, this resolution must specify the date on which the authority expires, which must not be more than 18 months from the date of the resolution [s164];

(b)   market purchase: authority must be obtained from the company in general meeting; the authority:

(i)   may be restricted to a specific class of share capital or may be a general authority to purchase its own shares;
(ii)   may be conditional or unconditional;
(iii) must state the maximum number of shares to be acquired;
(iv)   must state the maximum and minimum prices to be paid; and
(v)   must specify the date on which it expires, which must not be more than 18 months from the date of the resolution [s166].

33.12   A purchase is 'off-market' if a company purchases its own shares otherwise than on a recognised investment exchange (RIE) or if they are purchased on a RIE but are not subject to a marketing arrangement on that exchange. A purchase that is not off-market is called a 'market purchase'. [s163]

33.13   The power to issue redeemable shares or to purchase a company's own shares is limited by the requirement that there must always be a member of the company who holds non-redeemable shares. [ss159(2) and 162(3)]

33.14 Shares may not be redeemed or purchased unless they are fully paid. [s159(3)]

33.15 Shares redeemed or purchased must be cancelled; such cancellation does not reduce the authorised share capital. [s160(4)]

33.16 Except in the case of private companies (see **33.20** below), shares may only be redeemed or purchased out of distributable profits or out of the proceeds of a new issue made for that purpose. To the extent that the redemption or purchase of the nominal value of the shares is made out of distributable profits or exceeds the proceeds of a new issue of shares, a transfer must be made to the capital redemption reserve (see **33.22** to **33.26** below). [ss160(1)(a), 170 and 171(1)] See **33.40** below as regards distributable profits for this purpose for investment companies.

33.17 With the exceptions given in **33.18** and **33.20** below, any premium payable on the redemption or purchase of shares (i.e., the difference between the redemption (purchase) proceeds and the nominal value of the shares) must be paid out of the distributable profits of the company. [s160(1)(b)]

33.18 Where shares which have been redeemed or purchased were issued at a premium, any premium payable on their redemption or purchase may be paid out of the proceeds of a fresh issue of shares made for the purpose up to the lesser of:

(a)   the amount of the premium originally received by the company on the issue of the shares redeemed or purchased; and

(b)   the current balance on share premium account (including any premium on the new shares) [s160(2)].

33.19 The effect is that the amount which can be charged against share premium is the lower of:

(a)   the original premium received; and

(b) the balance on share premium account; and

(c) the proceeds of a fresh issue.

Thus where there is no fresh issue, no amount may be charged to share premium.

> The operation of the above rule can give some apparently confusing results. Having the proceeds of the new issue of the shares equal to the redemption (or purchase) amount is not sufficient on its own to avoid the need to make a transfer out

of distributable profits. Consider the following three examples: in each of them, the transfer out of distributable profits represents the difference between the amount by which the redemption proceeds exceeds the nominal value of the shares redeemed and the share premium which arose when the shares were issued. This will not always be the case, since the balance on the share premium account, including that arising on the new issue of shares, may be lower than the share premium which arose when the shares were first issued and, as such, would cause the transfer out of distributable profits to be even greater; consider the fourth example for an illustration of this.

Example 33.19.1

New shares with a nominal value of £10,000 were issued for £40,000. Shares having a nominal value of £10,000, which were originally issued for £40,000, are redeemed or purchased for £40,000. The capital and reserves section of the balance sheet before the transactions was as follows:

	£
Issued share capital	50,000
Share premium	30,000
Distributable profits	60,000
	140,000

The relevant journal entries are as follows:

	Debit £	Credit £
Called up share capital	10,000	
Share premium account *(see note below)*	30,000	
Cash		40,000
Cash	40,000	
Called up share capital		10,000
Share premium		30,000

To record the redemption (purchase) of 10,000 £1 shares at £4.00 per share and the issue of 10,000 new £1 shares for £4.00 per share to fund the redemption (purchase).

The capital and reserves section of the balance sheet after the transactions is as follows:

	£
Issued share capital	50,000
Share premium	30,000
Distributable profits	60,000
	140,000

In this example, the balance on the share premium account at the date of redemption, including the premium that arose on the new issue of shares, totals £60,000 (£30,000 + £30,000) and the share premium that originally arose on the issue of the shares now redeemed totals £30,000. The lower of the two is £30,000. Therefore, the premium on redemption can be funded out of the share premium account rather than out of distributable profits up to a maximum of £30,000. The premium on redemption is £30,000 (i.e., redemption proceeds of £40,000 less the nominal value of the shares redeemed of £10,000) and so the whole redemption premium is funded out of share premium account.

Example 33.19.2

New shares with a nominal value of £10,000 were issued for £40,000. Shares having a nominal value of £10,000, which were originally issued at par, are redeemed or purchased for £40,000. The capital and reserves section of the balance sheet before the transactions was as follows:

	£
Issued share capital	50,000
Share premium	30,000
Distributable profits	60,000
	140,000

The relevant journal entries are as follows:

	Debit £	Credit £
Called up share capital	10,000	
Distributable profits (see note below)	30,000	
Cash		40,000
Cash	40,000	
Called up share capital		10,000
Share premium		30,000

To record the redemption (purchase) of 10,000 £1 shares at £4.00 per share, including the transfer out of distributable profits to fund the premium payable on redemption (purchase), and the issue of 10,000 new £1 shares for £4.00 per share.

The capital and reserves section of the balance sheet after the transactions is as follows:

	£
Issued share capital	50,000
Share premium	60,000
Distributable profits	30,000
	140,000

In this example, the balance on the share premium account at the date of redemption, including the premium that arose on the new issue of shares, totals £60,000 (consisting of the £30,000 premium on the new issue of shares, together with the £30,000 balance on the share premium account immediately before the new issue; this latter amount is included in the calculation even though it arose on an issue of shares other than those to be redeemed). The share premium that originally arose on the issue of the shares now redeemed, however, is nil. The lower of the two is nil. Therefore, none of the premium on redemption can be funded out of the share premium account and it must all be funded out of distributable profits (even though the company had a balance on its share premium account). The premium on redemption is £30,000 (i.e., redemption proceeds of £40,000 less the nominal value of the shares redeemed of £10,000) and this must come out of distributable profits.

Example 33.19.3

New shares with a nominal value of £10,000 were issued for £40,000. Shares having a nominal value of £5,000, which were originally issued for £20,000, are redeemed or purchased for £40,000. The capital and reserves section of the balance sheet before the transactions was as follows:

	£
Issued share capital	65,000
Share premium	15,000
Distributable profits	60,000
	140,000

The relevant journal entries are as follows:

	Debit £	Credit £
Called up share capital	5,000	
Share premium account *(see note below)*	15,000	
Distributable profits *(see note below)*	20,000	
Cash		40,000
Cash	40,000	
Called up share capital		10,000
Share premium		30,000

To record the redemption (purchase) of 10,000 £0.50 shares at £4.00 per share, including the transfer out of distributable profits of £20,000 to fund the premium payable on redemption (purchase) in excess of the premium received on the issue of the shares, and the issue of 10,000 new £1 shares for £4.00 per share.

The capital and reserves section of the balance sheet after the transactions is as follows:

	£
Issued share capital	70,000
Share premium	30,000
Distributable profits	40,000
	140,000

In this example, the balance on the share premium account at the date of redemption, including the premium that arose on the new issue of shares, totals £45,000 and the share premium that originally arose on the issue of the shares now redeemed totals £15,000. The lower of the two is £15,000. Therefore, the premium on redemption can be funded out of the share premium account rather than out of distributable profits up to a maximum of £15,000. The premium on redemption is £35,000 (i.e., redemption proceeds of £40,000 less the nominal value of the shares redeemed of £5,000) and so £15,000 of the redemption premium is funded out of share premium account and the balance of £20,000 is funded out of distributable profits.

Example 33.19.4

New shares with a nominal value of £30,000 were issued for £40,000. Shares having a nominal value of £5,000, which were originally issued for £20,000, are redeemed or purchased for £40,000. The capital and reserves section of the balance sheet before the transactions was as follows:

	£
Issued share capital	80,000
Share premium	–
Distributable profits	60,000
	140,000

Although share premium arose on the issue of the shares now being redeemed, there is no balance in the share premium account, because it was all used to fund a bonus issue of shares two years ago.

The relevant journal entries are as follows:

	Debit £	Credit £
Called up share capital	5,000	
Share premium account (see note below)	10,000	
Distributable profits (see note below)	25,000	
Cash		40,000
Cash	40,000	
Called up share capital		30,000
Share premium		10,000

To record the redemption (purchase) of 10,000 £0.50 shares at £4.00 per share, including the transfer out of distributable profits of £25,000 to fund the premium payable on redemption (purchase) in excess of the balance on the share premium account, and the issue of 30,000 new £1 shares for £1.33 per share.

> The capital and reserves section of the balance sheet after the transactions is as follows:
>
> | | £ |
> |---|---|
> | Issued share capital | 105,000 |
> | Share premium | – |
> | Distributable profits | 35,000 |
> | | 140,000 |
>
> In this example, the balance on the share premium account at the date of redemption (nil), including the premium that arose on the new issue of shares (£10,000), totals £10,000 and the share premium that originally arose on the issue of the shares now redeemed totals £15,000. The lower of the two is £10,000. Therefore, the premium on redemption can be funded out of the share premium account rather than out of distributable profits up to a maximum of £10,000. The premium on redemption is £35,000 (i.e., redemption proceeds of £40,000 less the nominal value of the shares redeemed of £5,000) and so £10,000 of the redemption premium is funded out of share premium account and the balance of £25,000 is funded out of distributable profits.

Private companies and permissible capital payments

33.20 If authorised by its Articles to do so, a private company may redeem or purchase its shares out of capital. [s171] The capital portion, referred to as the permissible capital payment, is defined as the price of redemption or purchase less the sum of any distributable profits and the proceeds of any new issue of shares made for the purpose of the redemption or purchase. Where the aggregate of the permissible capital payment plus the proceeds of a new issue is greater than the nominal amount of the shares redeemed or purchased, the excess may be applied to reduce the amount of any capital redemption reserve, share premium account, fully paid share capital of the company or revaluation reserve. To the extent that the aggregate of the permissible capital payment plus the proceeds of a new issue are less than the nominal amount of the shares redeemed or purchased, a transfer must be made to the capital redemption reserve (see **33.22** below).

In summary:

	£
Price of redemption/purchase	X
Less: Balance of distributable profits	(X)
Less: Proceeds of fresh issue	(X)
Permissible capital payment (if positive)	X

The effect of these requirements is that any balance of distributable profits is first utilised to pay the cost of redemption or purchase. Once distributable profits are exhausted, a private company (with the appropriate authority) may reduce its capital.

Example 33.20.1

Shares having a nominal value of £100,000 are redeemed or purchased for £80,000. The company has no distributable profits. Therefore, the relevant figures are calculated as follows:

	£
Cost of purchase	80,000
Less: Distributable profits	NIL
Proceeds of fresh issue	NIL
Permissible capital payment	80,000

	£
Nominal value of purchase	100,000
Less: Proceeds of fresh issue	NIL
Permissible capital payment	80,000
Transfer to capital redemption reserve	20,000

The relevant journal entries are as follows:

	Debit £	Credit £
Called up share capital	100,000	
Cash		80,000
Capital redemption reserve		20,000

To record the redemption (purchase) of 100,000 £1 shares at £0.80 per share out of capital and to transfer the excess nominal value of such shares to the capital redemption reserve.

Example 33.20.2

New shares with a nominal value of £100,000 were issued for £250,000. Shares having a nominal value of £500,000 are redeemed or purchased for £700,000. The capital and reserves section of the balance sheet before the transactions was as follows:

	£
Issued share capital	1,000,000
Share premium (none of this arose on the shares now redeemed)	1,000,000
Distributable profits	300,000
	2,300,000

The relevant figures are calculated as follows:

	£
Price paid for redemption	700,000
Less: distributable profits	(300,000)
Less: proceeds of new issue	(250,000)
Permissible capital payment	150,000
Nominal value of shares redeemed	500,000
Less: permissible capital payment	(150,000)
Less: proceeds of new issue	(250,000)
Transfer to capital redemption reserve	(100,000)

The relevant journal entries are as follows:

	Debit £	Credit £
Profit and loss account (distributable reserves)	200,000	
Called up share capital	500,000	
Cash		700,000
Cash	250,000	
Called up share capital		100,000
Share premium		150,000
Profit and loss account (distributable reserves)	100,000	
Capital redemption reserve		100,000

To record the redemption (purchase) of 500,000 £1 shares at £1.40 per share, the issue of 100,000 new £1 shares for £2.50 per share and to transfer an amount equal to the difference between the nominal value of the shares redeemed (purchased) and the aggregate of the proceeds of the fresh issue and the permissible capital payment to the capital redemption reserve.

33.21 The following safeguards must be met before a payment out of capital can lawfully be made: [ss173–176]:

(a) the payment must be approved by a special resolution;

(b) the directors must make a statutory declaration (see **43.39** below);

(c) a report by the company's auditors must be annexed to the directors' declaration (see **43.40** below);

(d) a notice of the proposed capital payment, giving the informa- tion specified in s175, must be published in the *Gazette* and either published in a national newspaper or given by written notice to each creditor within a week of the date of the resolution. [s175] 'The Gazette' means, as respects companies registered in England and Wales, the *London Gazette* and, as respects companies registered in Scotland the *Edinburgh Gazette*. [s744] Creditors and members may apply to the court within five weeks of the date of the resolution for the resolution to be cancelled. The payment must not be made less than five weeks or more than seven weeks after the date of the resolution.

Capital redemption reserve

33.22   Where shares are redeemed or purchased wholly out of distributable profits, the Act requires a transfer to be made to the capital redemption reserve. [s170] In such a case, the amount of the required transfer is the amount by which the company's share capital is diminished on cancellation of the shares, i.e., the nominal value of the shares.

Example 33.22

Shares having a nominal value of £100,000 (and which were originally issued for £120,000) are redeemed or purchased for £130,000. The relevant journal entries are as follows:

	Debit £	Credit £
Profit and loss account (distributable reserves)	130,000	
Cash		130,000
Called up share capital	100,000	
Capital redemption reserve		100,000

To record the redemption (purchase) of 100,000 £1 shares at £1.30 per share and to transfer the nominal value of such shares to the capital redemption reserve.

Note: The capital redemption reserve would be the same even if the shares were purchased at a discount to nominal value.

33.23   Where the redemption or purchase is financed wholly or partly by a new issue of shares, the transfer required is reduced by the proceeds of the new issue. The transfer required should be further reduced to the extent that the company can make a permissible capital payment (see **33.20** and **33.21** above).

In summary, the transfer from distributable profits to capital redemption reserve is:

	£
Nominal value of shares purchased/redeemed	X
Less: Proceeds of fresh issue	(X)
Less: Permissible capital payment (if any, for a private company)	(X)
Amount of transfer	X

Note: In addition to this reduction in distributable profits, any premium payable must also be dealt with as explained in **33.17** above.

33.24   A strict reading of the Act could lead to a reduction in capital if the maximum amount of a new issue is used to fund the premium on the redemption of shares and the residual amount of the proceeds of the new issue is less than the nominal value of the shares being redeemed. [s170] (See **33.18** above) This shortfall occurs because the Act requires a transfer to the capital redemption reserve of the amount by which the proceeds of the fresh issue is less than the nominal value of the shares redeemed or purchased. [s170] This requirement ignores the extent to which the premium on redemption is funded by the fresh issue. If capital levels are to be maintained, then the reference to 'aggregate amount of proceeds' should be taken as being reduced to the extent that the fresh issue finances the premium on redemption. [s170]

Example 33.24

Shares with a nominal value of £50,000 were issued for £100,000. The shares were issued to finance the redemption of shares with a nominal value of £100,000. The shares, which were originally issued at a premium of £5,000, were redeemed for £120,000.

Balance sheet prior to redemption

	£
Issued share capital	300,000
Share premium (includes £5,000 arising on the issue of shares to be redeemed)	20,000
	320,000
Distributable profits	130,000
	450,000

Redemption of shares

	Nominal	Premium
	£	£
Redemption costs to be financed	100,000	20,000
Maximum amount that can finance the premium on redemption is the lower of the premium originally received on the shares being redeemed (£5,000) and the balance on the share premium account after the new issue (£70,000)		5,000
Balance of premium financed from distributable profits		15,000
Redemption of nominal value financed by the balance of fresh issue proceeds (£100,000 – £5,000)	95,000	
Balance of nominal value not financed by fresh issue proceeds	5,000	

Balance sheet after redemption – following the strict reading of s170

The aggregate proceeds of £100,000 are not less than the £100,000 nominal value of the shares redeemed therefore no transfer is required to the capital redemption reserve. This results in the creditors' buffer, the aggregate of share capital and share premium, being reduced by £5,000.

	£
Issued share capital (£300,000 – £100,000 + £50,000)	250,000
Share premium (£20,000 – £5,000 + £50,000)	65,000
	315,000
Distributable profits (£130,000 – £15,000)	115,000
	430,000

Balance sheet after redemption – reading s170 to require a transfer of £5,000 to the capital redemption reserve

The excess of the nominal value of the redeemed shares over the proceeds of the fresh issue, net of the portion used to finance the share premium, is £5,000.

	£
Issued share capital (£300,000 – £100,000 + £50,000)	250,000
Share premium (£20,000 – £5,000 + £50,000)	65,000
Capital redemption reserve	5,000
	320,000
Distributable profits (£130,000 – £15,000 – £5,000)	110,000
	430,000

33.25

The Act states that redeemable shares may only be redeemed out of distributable profits of the company or out of the proceeds of a fresh issue of shares made for the purposes of the redemption. [s160(1)] Accordingly, this would suggest that the transfer of £5,000 to the capital redemption reserve in the above example is required (since the proceeds of the fresh issue fall short of the redemption proceeds by £20,000, thus requiring £20,000 of the redemption proceeds to be funded by distributable profits). A company not wishing to make a transfer in these circumstances should take legal advice.

Purchasing or redeeming share capital denominated in a foreign currency

33.26

A difficulty is encountered where a company that has previously issued foreign currency share capital wishes to redeem, cancel or purchase some or all of those shares. This can be illustrated by the following example.

Example 33.26

A company issues 1,000 shares for $1 each. The shares each have a nominal value of $1. The company's functional (or local) currency is sterling. The exchange rate ruling when the shares were issued was $2:£1.

Several years later, the company purchases those shares for $1 each and then cancels the shares. Assume at this date the exchange rate is (i) $1.50:£1 and (ii) $2.50:£1.

On issue, the share capital of $1,000 would be translated to £500.

Assume that the company does not retranslate the share capital in subsequent years' accounts. Therefore, at the date of purchase and cancellation, the share capital is still recorded at £500.

However, the $1,000 paid to purchase the shares translates to either (i) £667 or (ii) £400.

Two questions arise which can be demonstrated by looking at the double-entry, which is:

	$1.50:£1		$2.50:£1	
	Debit	Credit	Debit	Credit
	£	£	£	£
Called up share capital	500		500	
?	167			100
Cash		667		400
Distributable profits	?		?	
Capital redemption reserve		?		?

The first question is which account is debited with £167 or credited with £100?

The second question is how much should be transferred out of distributable profits to capital redemption reserve: £500 or £677/£400?

On the first question, it is necessary to consider whether the share premium account might be available for any debit. Assuming the shares were not originally issued at a premium, the share premium account is not available to fund the debit and it would, therefore, seem logical for the entry to be to distributable profits. In the case of the credit entry, again it seems logical for the entry to be to distributable profits, provided that the shares were originally issued for cash or near cash. Indeed, if the shares were redeemable, FRS 4 would require the amount to be debited/credited to profit and loss account.

The answer to the second question tends to suggest that the transfer to the capital redemption reserve ought to be the $ amount of share capital translated at the historic exchange rate (i.e., a transfer of £500). However, we understand that some legal advice has suggested that, under the Act's capital maintenance rules, the transfer to the capital redemption reserve should be the nominal value of the shares translated at the exchange rate ruling at the date of the redemption or purchase, i.e., £677/£400.

Therefore, if a company has foreign currency share capital and wishes to redeem or purchase the shares, it should take legal advice.

If the answer to the first question is distributable profits, a related question is whether distributable profits should be affected each year by that year's exchange difference (see **33.69** below).

Expenses of purchasing ordinary shares

33.27

In recent years, there has been an increasing incidence of companies purchasing, for cancellation, some of their ordinary shares in the market. There is no guidance on how to account for the expenses incurred in purchasing these shares. It would appear appropriate to charge the expenses directly against reserves, since the other entries in respect of the purchase are also made directly to shareholders' funds.

Financial assistance for acquisition of own shares

General prohibition

33.28 With certain exceptions, including those outlined below, it is unlawful for a company to give financial assistance directly or indirectly (i.e., loan, gift, guarantee, indemnity or security, etc.) for the purpose of the acquisition of its shares or those of its holding company or for the purpose of reducing or discharging any liability incurred in the acquisition of such shares. [s151] The Act defines 'reducing or discharging a liability' as wholly or partly restoring the person's financial position to what it was before the acquisition took place. [s152(3)]

33.29 This prohibition is wide and would include, for example, giving the person a gift of cash or granting the person a loan specifically to replace the cash of its own that it had used to buy the shares.

33.30 This prohibition does not apply where: [s153]

   (a) the lending of money is part of the ordinary business of the company and the money is lent in the ordinary course of business; or

   (b) the provision of financial assistance is made for the purpose of an employees' share scheme; or

   (c) the provision of financial assistance by the company or its subsidiaries is to enable or facilitate transactions in the company's shares between (and involving the acquisition of beneficial ownership of those shares by) employees or former employees or their spouses, widows(ers) or infant children or stepchildren; or

   (d) the loan is made to bona fide employees (not directors) to enable them to purchase shares in the company or its holding company to be held by them by way of beneficial ownership; or

   (e) the principal purpose of the transaction is not to give financial assistance for the purpose of the acquisition of shares, or is incidental to some larger purpose, and the assistance is given in good faith in the interests of the company.

33.31 However, a public company may only give financial assistance under **33.30**(a) to (d) above if its net assets are not thereby reduced or, to the extent the net assets are reduced, the assistance is provided out of distributable profits. [s154]

Private companies

33.32 The prohibition on the giving of financial assistance imposed by s151 does not apply to a private company, provided the company fulfils certain requirements for safeguarding the interests of creditors and shareholders. [ss156–158] The principal limitation imposed on any financial assistance given which does not fall into the exemptions given by s153 is that the company has net assets which are not reduced by the financial assistance or, to the extent that the net assets are reduced, the assistance shall be made out of distributable profits. [s155] The safeguards which must be met before the financial assistance can lawfully be given include:

(a) approval of the assistance by special resolution in general meeting (unless the company is a wholly owned subsidiary);

(b) a statutory declaration by the directors (see **43.37** below); and

(c) a report by the company's auditors on the directors' statutory declaration (see **43.37** below).

33.33 The financial assistance must not be given before the expiry of four weeks from the date on which the special resolution was passed (unless all the members of the company entitled to attend and vote on the special resolution voted in favour of it) nor must it be given later than eight weeks after the date on which the statutory declaration was given. [ss157 and 158] Thus, where financial assistance is to be given at regular intervals (e.g., payments of interest and principal over a prolonged period), a statutory declaration supported by an auditors' report will have to be given at the appropriate regular intervals to enable repeated financial assistance to be given in compliance with the Act.

33.34 Loans and other financial assistance which may be made by a company under the above rules must not include any loans, etc. to directors which are prohibited by s330 (see **32.24** to **32.29** above).

33.35 Where a private company taking advantage of the relaxations for private companies is doing so in order to give assistance for the acquisition of shares in its parent, there are additional conditions that must be met. [ss155–158] These additional conditions include:

(a) the parent whose shares are being or have been acquired is also a private company;

(b) a private company cannot give assistance for the acquisition of shares in its private parent if that parent has a subsidiary which is a public company and that public company is a parent to the company giving the assistance;

(c) special resolutions and statutory declarations have to be given by the company giving the assistance, by the company whose shares are being or have been acquired and by any other company which is an intermediate holding company of the company giving the assistance (except, with respect to the special resolution, any company which is a wholly owned subsidiary).

Profits available for distribution

Introduction

33.36 The provisions of the Act regarding the payment of dividends and other distributions relate to individual companies only and not to groups.

33.37 The Act defines which profits are distributable and the circumstances in which they may be legally distributed. [ss263–281] A distribution for these purposes is defined as any distribution of a company's assets to members except by way of:

(a) an issue of fully or partly paid bonus shares;

(b) redemption or purchase of a company's own shares out of capital (including the proceeds of any fresh issue of shares) or out of unrealised profits in accordance with the Act;

(c) certain reductions of capital; and

(d) distribution of assets in a winding-up.

Rules regarding the payment of dividends

33.38 A private company can, subject to any other restriction imposed by law, distribute the whole of its accumulated realised profits (not previously distributed or capitalised) less its accumulated realised losses (not previously written off in a reduction or reorganisation of capital). It is not required by statute to take account of unrealised losses. However, as indicated below, a provision is usually to be treated as a realised loss. [s263(3)] The restrictions imposed by common law duties may also mean that, in practice, unrealised losses cannot be ignored (see **33.42** below).

33.39 A public company cannot distribute its realised profits without first making good any excess of unrealised losses over unrealised profits. It can make a distribution only if the distribution does not reduce the company's net assets below the aggregate of the called up share capital and undistributable reserves. [s264]

33.40 An investment company (as defined in the Act) is subject to special rules which, in general, allow it to make distributions out of the accumulated realised revenue profits less revenue losses, both realised and unrealised, provided that the distribution does not reduce its assets to less than one and a half times its liabilities. [s66] Liabilities include provisions for liabilities or charges. In most circumstances, these rules allow an investment company to ignore capital losses, whether realised or unrealised, when making a distribution. [s265] In October 1999 the government issued Statutory Instrument SI 1999 No 2770 which introduced a change to the Act enabling investment companies to use capital profits to repurchase their own shares. This change does not affect the prohibition in the Act on all other distributions out of capital profits for such companies. The change is effective 8 November 1999.

33.41   An insurance company is subject to the same restrictions as any other company. There is an additional proviso that any amount properly transferred to the profit and loss account from a surplus on its long-term business fund shall be treated as a realised profit, any deficit in that fund shall be treated as a realised loss and any other profit or loss in that business shall be disregarded. [s268]

33.42   It is not necessarily enough simply to comply with the Act's requirements as to the payment of dividends. The Act specifically preserves any existing rules of law, or any provision of a company's Memorandum or Articles, restricting dividends. [s281] It is a fundamental rule of law that dividends may not be paid out of capital. So, for example, a dividend based on accounts which show available profits (see **33.44** to **33.55** below) would be *ultra vires* if made after subsequent losses have eliminated the profits, although the requirements of the Act have ostensibly been met. Similarly, directors' common law duties (to act with reasonable skill and care in what they believe to be the best interests of the company) would generally preclude them from paying an imprudent dividend. Directors who make an unlawful dividend may be held personally liable to account for it to the company.

33.43   The Act makes a shareholder liable to repay a distribution if, at the time of the distribution, he knew, or had reasonable grounds for believing, that the distribution was in contravention of the Act. [s277] Thus, a company that has paid an illegal dividend may have to recognise a debtor in its financial statements in respect of the amount recoverable from members. [s277]

Relevant accounts

33.44   In order to determine whether a distribution may be lawfully made by a company in accordance with the rules mentioned above (see **33.38** to **33.43**), reference must be made to the following items stated in the company's 'relevant accounts':

(a)   profits, losses, assets and liabilities;

(b)   provisions of any kind mentioned in Sch 4 (depreciation, diminution in value of assets, retentions to meet liabilities, etc.) [Sch 4: 88 and 89]; and

(c)   share capital and reserves (including undistributable reserves).

Where a small company is following Sch 8, it will still need to take account of provisions of any kind mentioned in Sch 4; these will be the provisions mentioned in Sch 8. [Sch 4: 88 and 89 and Sch 8: 57 and 58]

33.45   A distribution is deemed unlawful unless the following statutory requirements about relevant accounts have been complied with. [s270(5)]

33.46   Relevant accounts for this purpose are the company's last annual accounts as laid before the members in general meeting or sent to them if the company has dispensed with the laying of accounts and reports under s252 (see **4.13** above). However, if the profits available for distribution as shown by these accounts are found to be insufficient to pay a proposed distribution, 'interim accounts' may be used for this purpose. Also, where a distribution is proposed to be declared during the company's first accounting reference period, or before any accounts are laid in respect of that period, 'initial accounts' may be used.

33.47   In the case of interim or initial accounts prepared by a private company, there are no formal requirements as to the form and content of the accounts, other than that they must enable a reasonable judgement to be made as to the amounts of the items mentioned in **33.44** above. [s270(4)] Management accounts are acceptable for this purpose, providing they have been prepared using the measurement rules necessary to give a true and fair view of the above items. They should be prepared using the same accounting policies used or planned to be used in the preparation of the annual accounts and the directors will need to follow the prudence concept to ensure adequate provision is made for depreciation, diminution in value of assets, liabilities, etc. Such accounts need not be audited or filed with the Registrar of Companies.

33.48   Where interim accounts are prepared by a public company, they must be 'properly prepared' but need not be audited. A copy must be sent to the Registrar of Companies. [s272]

33.49   'Properly prepared' means that the interim accounts comply with s226 (duty to prepare individual accounts), the balance sheet has been signed by a director on behalf of the board and the profit and loss account and balance sheet give a true and fair view. However, such interim accounts need not include matters which are not material for determining by reference to the items in **33.44** above whether the proposed distribution can be lawfully made. [ss272(2) and 273(2)]

33.50 Many of the additional disclosures required by the Act and accounting standards would not be required as a result of the exemption discussed in **33.49** above. For example the disclosure of such items as fixed asset movements, directors' remuneration, cash flow statement, statement of total recognised gains and losses, analysis of stocks, particulars of the tax charge, segmental analysis, which would be required in the annual accounts, would not be necessary. Similarly, it is not necessary to give comparatives.

33.51 Where initial accounts are prepared by a public company, the company's auditors must report whether, in their opinion, those initial accounts have been 'properly prepared' (see **43.24** below). 'Properly prepared' has the same meaning as in **33.49** above. The initial accounts, together with the auditors' report, must be filed with the Registrar of Companies.

33.52 If the audit report on the annual or, for a public company, initial, accounts contains a qualification, the auditors must state in writing, either at the time of their report or subsequently, whether in their opinion the matter in respect of which the report is qualified is material for determining whether the distribution would be in contravention of the relevant section (see **43.14** to **43.23** below). [ss271(4) and 273(5)]

33.53 If the qualification concerns annual accounts, the auditors' statement must be laid before the company in general meeting or sent to the members if the company has dispensed with the laying of accounts and reports. If the qualification concerns initial accounts, the statement must be sent to the Registrar of Companies.

33.54 A 'fundamental uncertainty' paragraph in the auditors' report does not constitute a qualification. Directors should, nevertheless, consider the possible consequences of that uncertainty on their dividend policy if they are considering making a distribution.

33.55 Where a company has already made a distribution or has otherwise entered into an arrangement (e.g., the purchase or redemption of shares or the giving of financial assistance for the purchase of its shares) which reduces its distributable reserves as shown in the relevant accounts, appropriate account must be taken of the reduction in the reserves when determining the amount of any remaining reserves which are available for distribution. [s274] This requirement does not prohibit successive distributions being made based upon the same relevant accounts, but requires the directors to aggregate earlier distributions with those proposed when determining whether a distribution may be made.

Definition of realised profits and losses

33.56 Realised profits and losses in relation to a company's accounts are defined as those profits or losses which fall to be treated as realised in accordance with principles generally accepted at the time those accounts are prepared. [s262(3)] In addition, the Act specifically provides that certain items are to be treated as realised or unrealised.

33.57 The guidance in **33.58** to **33.81** below may be helpful in distinguishing between realised and unrealised profits.

33.58 When determining whether an item is realised, particular regard should be had to the prudence concept: profits should not be anticipated and should only be recognised in the profit and loss account when realised in the form either of cash or of other assets the ultimate cash realisation of which can be assessed with reasonable certainty; losses should be provided for whether the amount is known with certainty or is a best estimate in the light of the information available.

33.59 The following guidance on realised profits is based on the guidance given by the CCAB in their statement TR 481:
[ICAEW Members' Handbook Statement 2.402]

   (a)   a profit which is required by accounting standards to be recognised in the profit and loss account should normally be treated as a realised profit, unless the accounting standard indicates otherwise;

   (b)   a profit will normally be a realised profit if the accounting policy adopted is not the subject of an accounting standard and if that policy is consistent with the accounting principles stated in the Act and with the accruals and prudence concepts set out in SSAP 2; and

   (c)   in exceptional circumstances, a profit may be recognised in the profit and loss account in accordance with an accounting policy which is contrary to an accounting standard. Such a profit is realised if the policy is consistent with the accounting principles stated in the Act and with the accruals and prudence concepts of SSAP 2.

33.60 The CCAB in its guidance statement TR 482 on distributable profits states:

(a) valuations or contingencies included in the notes to the accounts but not incorporated therein have no effect on the amount of distributable profits; and

(b) there is no requirement that distributions can only be made out of distributable profits described as such in the accounts.

(Both TR 481 and TR 482 are currently under review – see **33.96** below.)

33.61 On the basis of the prudence concept and the rules laid down in Sch 4, a surplus arising from a revaluation of any fixed asset should be regarded as unrealised. Sch 4 requires the measure of the surplus to be the difference between the revalued amount and the historical cost amount after provisions for depreciation and diminution in value. [Sch 4: 34]

33.62 Provisions for liabilities or charges and provisions for depreciation or diminution in value of assets, other than a write-down in value of a fixed asset appearing on a revaluation of all fixed assets (or of all fixed assets other than goodwill) of the company, are realised losses. [s275(1)]

33.63 In order that companies can avail themselves of the exception in **33.62** above in circumstances where only certain assets (e.g., properties) have been revalued, assets which have not been revalued can be treated as being revalued for the purposes of this section if the directors are satisfied that their aggregate value is not less than the aggregate amount at which they are stated in the accounts. If the directors are so satisfied, the effect of this exception is to permit a provision for diminution in value of a fixed asset to be treated as an unrealised loss, provided there is appropriate disclosure in the relevant accounts. [s275(4), (5) and (6)]

33.64 When a fixed asset is revalued to an amount above the historical cost carrying amount, the revaluation surplus is an unrealised profit. Depreciation of a revalued asset in excess of the depreciation of that asset based on original cost is charged in the profit and loss account and thus is a realised loss. Consequently, the Act provides that an amount of the revaluation surplus equal in value to the depreciation in excess of that based on the asset's original cost is treated as if it were a realised profit. Thus, it will be appropriate to make a transfer annually from undistributable to distributable reserves (i.e., from revaluation reserve to the profit and loss account). [s275(2)]

33.65 If the directors cannot determine whether a particular profit or loss made before 22 December 1980 is realised or unrealised, they may treat any profit as realised and any loss as unrealised. [s263(5)]

33.66 Development costs shown as an asset in the balance sheet shall be treated as a realised loss, unless the directors can justify the costs carried forward not being so treated and a note to the accounts explains the circumstances relied upon to justify the decision of the directors. [s269] The CCAB advises, in its statement on distributable profits, that development costs carried forward in accordance with SSAP 13 will normally provide the directors with such justification.

33.67 If a distribution is made of a non-cash asset, any unrealised profit relating to that asset is treated as a realised profit for the purpose of determining the lawfulness of the distribution and that amount may be transferred from the revaluation reserve to the profit and loss account. [s276]

33.68 SSAP 20 advises that all exchange gains taken through the profit and loss account, other than those relating to unsettled long-term monetary items, are realised, although the foreword to the SSAP does state that it does not deal specifically with the determination of distributable profits. The decision of the House of Lords in the *Marine Midland* case in 1983 has put into doubt whether any translation gain can be construed as a profit before a foreign currency balance is actually converted into a local currency. Consequently, legal advice should be taken wherever translation gains or losses are crucial to the distributability of reserves.

33.69 Where a company issues foreign currency share capital, the question arises as to whether distributable profits should be increased or reduced each year by the amount of the 'translation difference' on the share capital, irrespective of whether the company actually retranslates the share capital each year. In the example in **33.26** above, it is suggested that, on cancellation or redemption of foreign currency share capital, distributable reserves are affected by the translation difference (£167/£100). Should redeemable shares affect distributable profits year by year (by retranslating at the rate of exchange ruling on the balance sheet date) or only at the date of redemption? It would seem to be inappropriate to affect distributable profits year by year only where shares are redeemable. However, if shares are not redeemable and the company has no intention to buy the shares back and cancel them, there are no potential cash flows; in such a case, it does not seem logical to retranslate the shares and to impact distributable profits. A different treatment depending on whether shares are redeemable or not does not seem to be appropriate. A company with foreign currency

> share capital for which such movements could be significant to its ability to make distributions should take legal advice on this issue.

33.70 Appendix 2 to SSAP 22 and appendix V to FRS 10 (which reproduces, with little change, appendix 2 to SSAP 22) advise that the write-off of goodwill in a company's own accounts, done as a matter of accounting policy rather than because of an actual diminution in value, does not give rise to an immediate reduction in realised reserves; rather, it will be appropriate to charge the elimination initially to a suitable unrealised reserve and thereafter to transfer systematically from unrealised to realised reserves an amount equivalent to the write-off under the amortisation method.

33.71 For accounting periods ending on or after 23 December 1998, FRS 10 requires negative goodwill to be recognised and separately disclosed on the face of the balance sheet, immediately below the goodwill heading, and then recognised in the profit and loss account over an appropriate period (see **13.51** above). Under the transitional rules in FRS 10, negative goodwill arising in earlier periods may be left in reserves. Appendix 2 to SSAP 22 and appendix V to FRS 10 discuss such negative goodwill, advising that, in a company's own accounts, it should be credited initially to an unrealised reserve, from which it may be transferred to realised reserves in line with the depreciation or realisation of the assets acquired in the business combination which gave rise to the goodwill in question.

33.72

> Under UITF Abstract 17, a company operating a bonus or option scheme is required to make a charge in its profit and loss account based on the fair value of the shares at the date of award, being the date of conditional grant of shares or rights to shares. Where new shares are to be issued by the company, the other half of the entry is reported in the reconciliation of movements in shareholders' funds; it is appropriate to present this as 'shares to be issued' within the other reserves statutory heading in the balance sheet. At the date the shares are issued, any difference between the cash subscribed for the shares and the fair value at date of grant of rights should be credited to reserves other than the share premium account. This advice is on the basis that the services of the employee do not, as a matter of law, form part of the consideration received for the shares issued; the UITF has been advised that this would be the usual legal interpretation of such transactions. Exceptionally, the terms of a transaction might lead to a different legal interpretation and companies may need to take legal advice on this issue. The UITF has not commented on whether the credit to 'reserves other than the share premium account' would be

> regarded as available for distribution. Since the credit arises
> when the shares are issued, it is suggested that the credit would
> be available for distribution. Until the shares are issued, the
> amount accruing in 'shares to be issued' should be regarded as
> non-distributable.

Inter-company transactions

33.73 Whether or not a distribution can be made is dependent upon the level of distributable profits of the company, not of the group. Accordingly, questions can arise about certain inter-company transactions and whether or not they increase the amount of a company's distributable profits. The issues that arise include:

(a) a company selling an asset to another group company; and

(b) dividends from a subsidiary to its parent.

These are discussed briefly in turn below.

33.74 A company may be carrying an asset, e.g., a property or shares in a subsidiary, in its books at an amount which is below its market value. If the asset were sold to another group company at market value, would the resulting profit be distributable? The answer, unfortunately, is not simple and legal advice should be sought. For example, if the asset is sold to a company with net liabilities, with the consideration being added to an inter-company account with no realistic possibilities that it can ever be settled, it is probable that the profit arising in the selling company will be regarded as unrealised. Similarly, if the selling company makes a loan to the purchasing company in order that the latter company can purchase the asset, it is unlikely that the selling company can regard the profit as distributable if the purchasing company could not otherwise afford the asset and could not get a loan from a party other than the selling company. On the other hand, if the purchasing company is profitable and buys the asset using surplus cash, the selling company's profit is likely to be regarded as realised.

33.75 Where a group company considers selling an asset to another group company, legal advice should be sought on the question of whether the sale gives rise to distributable profits.

33.76 Where a subsidiary has distributable profits, the profits can only be distributed to shareholders in the ultimate parent company if they are first passed from the subsidiary to the ultimate parent company, via any intermediate parent companies. There are two issues to consider with regard to inter-company dividends: the method of payment and the timing of recognition in the receiving company's financial statements. On the first point, TR 482 explains that a parent should regard dividends as realised whether they are paid or are passed through a current account, provided that, in the latter case, an appropriate reassessment of the realisable value of the current account balance is made.

33.77 Where, for the foreseeable future, the only way that a subsidiary will be able to settle its inter-company account is by borrowing from its parent, it is unlikely that the parent could regard the dividend receivable as a realised profit.

33.78 TR 482 points out that exchange control or other restrictions may affect the ability of overseas subsidiaries to remit dividends to the UK and that dividends receivable should only be treated as realised when their eventual receipt can be assessed with reasonable certainty.

33.79 On the question of timing, TR 482 points out that, although it is not normal practice to take credit for dividends unless the dividend was declared before the receiving company's year end, dividends receivable from subsidiaries and associates normally breach this rule. According to TR 482, dividends receivable from subsidiaries and associates in respect of accounting periods ending on or before that of the parent company are normally accrued in the parent's financial statements, even if declared by the subsidiary or associate after the parent's year end (and are regarded as realised or not in accordance with the above comments).

33.80 In June 1996, however, the European Court gave a judgment on a case on this topic. The Court's ruling dealt only with the specific details of the case in hand and did not consider wider aspects. The ruling was that where:

(a) one company (the parent company) is the sole or majority shareholder in another company (the subsidiary) and controls it;

(b) under national law, the parent company and the subsidiary form a group;

(c) the financial years of the two companies coincide;

(d) the subsidiary's annual accounts for the financial year in question were adopted by the general meeting before completion of the audit of the parent company's annual accounts for that year;

(e) the subsidiary's annual accounts for the financial year in question, as adopted by its general meeting, show that on the subsidiary's balance sheet date, i.e., the last day of that financial year, the subsidiary appropriated profits to the parent company; and

(f)   the national court is satisfied that the subsidiary's annual accounts for the financial year in question give a true and fair view of its assets and liabilities, financial position and profit or loss,

it is not contrary to the EU Fourth Directive for the national court to consider that the profits in question must be entered in the parent company's balance sheet for the financial year in respect of which they were appropriated by the subsidiary.

33.81   The judgment is not phrased in such a way that it is only if all the above conditions are met that a parent company can lawfully recognise a dividend receivable from its subsidiary. However, it is unclear whether the dividend receivable can be recognised in any circumstances other than those outlined in **33.80** above.

Deemed distributions

33.82   In the case of *Aveling Barford Ltd* v *Perion and Others* (1989) 5 BCC 677, a company sold a property for less than its market value to another company. Both companies were controlled by the same individual. The court held that the sale at an undervalue was a return of capital and as such was *ultra vires,* since the selling company had no distributable reserves.

33.83   Thus, it follows that, where a company sells an asset for less than its market value, the amount by which the market value exceeds the proceeds may be a deemed distribution. If so, it is essential to consider whether the selling company has sufficient distributable profits. The rule in **33.67** above is particularly pertinent. The effect of the rule can be seen in the following example.

Example 33.83

B Limited, a wholly owned subsidiary of A Limited, sells an asset to A Limited. The consideration for the sale is £10,000, being the book value of the asset in B Limited's financial statements. The market value of the asset at the date of sale is £25,000. Thus, B Limited is deemed to have made a distribution to A Limited of £15,000.

Consider two scenarios: one where B Limited, at the date of sale, has realised profits less realised losses netting to losses of £2,000; the second where B Limited, at the date of sale, has realised profits less realised losses netting to a profit of £1.

At first glance, it would appear that B Limited does not have sufficient distributable profits to fund the deemed distribution legally in either scenario. However, now consider what would happen if B Limited revalued the asset to its market value immediately before its sale to A Limited.

	Scenario 1 £	Scenario 2 £
Distributable profits immediately before sale	(2,000)	1
Revaluation reserve available to be treated as distributable	15,000	15,000
Net distributable profits	13,000	15,001
Deemed distribution/loss on sale	(15,000)	(15,000)
Net distributable profits after the sale	(2,000)	1

Thus, it can be seen that in the above example, by revaluing and using the rule in **33.67** above, the deemed distribution is legal while the company has at least £1 of distributable profits prior to the revaluation. However, if the company has negative distributable profits before the sale, then revaluing will not help; the distribution is still illegal.

Thus, where a company sells an asset at its book value (which is less than its market value), it does not have to have distributable profits equal to the full deemed distribution; it only needs to have some, positive, distributable profits and the deemed distribution will be covered by the revaluation surplus that would arise if the asset were revalued.

Where a company wishes to sell an asset for less than its book value (and assuming that market value is greater than book value), there would need to be distributable profits, excluding any potential revaluation, of an amount at least equal to the amount by which the sales value is below book value.

The rule in **33.67** above applies only where a revaluation is recognised in a company's financial statements. FRS 15, however, will require the revaluation of all or none of the assets in a particular class. Companies may therefore not wish to incorporate revaluations in their financial statements once FRS 15 becomes effective. If the spirit of the legislation is adhered to, i.e., there would be sufficient distributable reserves if the asset were revalued, it is hoped that this might suffice for establishing the legality of the distribution. Nevertheless, companies may wish to take legal advice on this point if they do not want to put a revaluation through in their financial statements.

Reduction of capital under a Court Order

33.84 Companies Act 1985 s135 provides for a company to reduce its capital through passing a special resolution, and applying to the Court for confirmation. A typical capital reduction will involve the transfer of share premium either to a special reserve (e.g., to provide a reserve for the elimination of goodwill prior to FRS 10) or to cover past losses. The Court will have regard to the protection of creditors and will require the company to give an undertaking which will take one of two forms:

(a) that the company will not distribute the special reserve until all creditors outstanding at the time of the undertaking have been paid; or

(b) that the company will only distribute the special reserve, pound for pound, as new capital is issued.

33.85 Two questions arise regarding the status of the reserve arising from the capital reduction:

(a) whether it is a distributable reserve; and

(b) whether it is a realised profit in accordance with Companies Act 1985 s262.

33.86 The view often expressed by legal advisors is that the reserve is a profit available for distribution from the date of the special resolution. This follows the traditional legal view that all items on a balance sheet are either an asset or a liability. Capital is a liability to shareholders. Hence the vote by shareholders to waive their right to an amount of capital represents the forgiveness of a liability, and thus a profit arises. The terms of the Court Order confirm this in that the company undertakes not to distribute the profit until certain events have taken place. It follows that once those events have occurred, the company is free to distribute the profit.

33.87 However, this view does not take account of two factors:

(a) under the UK accounting model set out in the Statement of Principles, a balance sheet contains three elements: assets, liabilities and equity. Capital is equity, and changes in equity are reported as movements in shareholders' funds, and not within the performance statements;

(b) realisation of profits, and hence their availability to be regarded as distributable under Companies Act 1985 s262, is an economic concept requiring a change to an asset or liability as understood within the accounting model. For example, a revaluation reserve is linked to a particular asset, and becomes realised when the asset is sold or depreciated.

33.88 From a legal point of view, the terms of undertakings required by the Court indicate the Court's acceptance that the reserve is distributable subject to the terms of the undertaking. On this basis, a reserve arising from a capital reduction may be regarded as distributable. However, from an accounting viewpoint, the reserve is not realised in the normal sense. Where an auditor is requested to give an opinion that such a reserve is a realised profit in accordance with Companies Act 1985 s262 he should not do so, but should instead refer to the legal status of the reserve and the Court's acceptance of it as distributable.

Future developments

Company law reform

33.89   In March 1998, the Government announced a fundamental review of company law which should result in an up-to-date framework that promotes the competitiveness of UK companies and so contributes to national prosperity (see chapter 2). In October 1999, the Company Law Review Steering Group issued three consultation documents, including the one on *Company Formation and Capital Maintenance*. The document makes detailed proposals for the statutory provisions on the allotment of shares; increase, maintenance and reduction of share capital; financial assistance by a company for the acquisition of its own shares and other capital maintenance matters which would replace those of the Companies Act 1985.

33.90   The main proposal is a move to no par value shares for private companies and, if the second EC directive can be amended, for public companies also. Under such proposals the net proceeds on issue of shares would go to a single undistributable reserve, subscribed share capital, rather than to the share capital and share premium account.

33.91   Other proposals include major relaxation of the rules governing the reduction of share capital and removal of restrictions on financial assistance for private companies. Instead of the present requirement for a company to seek court approval for any reduction of its share capital, it is proposed to replace this by a requirement that a capital reduction should be decided by a special resolution of the company, and that to protect creditors the directors should be required to make a formal declaration of solvency. Additionally, for public companies, in order to comply with the second EC directive, creditors would be given the opportunity, at their initiative, to challenge the reduction in court. Although views are sought on complete removal of restrictions on financial assistance for the acquisition of a company's own shares for private companies, the document invites suggestions for alternative methods of relaxation of these rules.

Other proposed changes to the Act

33.92   In January 1998, the DTI issued a consultative document *The Euro: Redenomination of Share Capital,* in which it invited comments on whether changes to the Act are necessary to facilitate redenomination of par values of shares. The driving force behind the issue of the consultative document was the introduction of the euro and the possibility that companies might wish to redenominate their shares into euros either in advance of any UK decision to join the single currency or, in the event of UK membership, before the end of the transitional period. Clearly, the issue is also relevant to the redenomination of shares into any other currency.

33.93 Following the consultation, in September 1998 Lord Simon, Minister for Trade and Competitiveness in Europe, announced new legislation giving companies a simpler legal mechanism for redenominating share capital. The proposed legislation will also provide that the minimum share capital of a public company may be denominated in any currency, not just sterling.

33.94 In May 1998 the DTI issued a further consultative document, this time on share buybacks. The purpose of this consultative document is to invite views on whether the current law, which requires a company purchasing its own shares to cancel them, should be changed to permit companies to purchase and hold in treasury for subsequent resale up to 10 per cent of their issued share capital. If this change is made, it is proposed that the right to vote attaching to shares held in treasury would have to be suspended and that a transfer should be made, equal to the carrying value of the purchased shares, from a distributable reserve to a non-distributable reserve. The payment of dividends in respect of shares held in treasury should also be suspended. A number of related issues arise, such as whether shareholders should be required to approve the resale, and pre-emption rights should apply to the resale of treasury shares. These and other issues are set out in the consultative document. As was indicated by the DTI in December 1999, responses received to the first consultative document were mostly in favour of the proposed changes and the next stage will be the publication for consultation of the draft amending legislation. It will propose restricting the facility of treasury shares to companies which are traded on the London Stock Exchange or another recognised investment exchange such as AIM.

33.95 The UITF has considered an amendment to UITF Abstract 13 *Accounting for ESOP trusts*, under which shares held in an ESOP would be disclosed as a deduction from shareholders' funds and not as an asset. Although the majority of responses to the proposed change in balance sheet presentation were positive, the UITF decided not to proceed with the proposed amendments to UITF 13 and further related changes to UITF 17 at this stage. Instead, a fuller review of accounting for employee share options will be undertaken as part of the ASB's equity project. The ASB has indicated that it hopes to issue a discussion paper on this topic in the course of 2000.

Distributable profits

33.96   In July 1999, the Institute of Chartered Accountants in England and Wales issued a draft statement of guidance on the determination of realised profits and distributable profits which would replace previous guidance contained in the TR 481 and TR 482 (see **33.59** and **33.60** above). The draft statement acknowledges that the concepts of prudence and 'accruals' are now not the only basis for the recognition of realised profits and that changes in the financial and economic environment since SSAP 2 was issued have led to the acceptance of the principles that, in certain circumstances, marked to market gains may constitute realised profits.

34 Small and medium-sized companies

34 Small and medium-sized companies

Summary of changes since the previous issue of this publication

Para.	*Topic*	*Summary*
34.81	Consultative document *Raising the Thresholds Levels for SMEs*	Proposes increasing the thresholds for statutory accounting exemptions.
34.83	Consultative document *The Statutory Audit Requirement for Smaller Companies*	Reviews the thresholds below which companies will not require an audit.
34.85	*Developing the Framework*	The consultation document from the company law review makes a number of proposals for change to the small company reporting regime.

Introduction

Exemptions available

34.1 This chapter considers the exemptions available to small and medium-sized companies and groups in respect of the annual accounts that are sent to members. The Companies Act 1985 (Accounts of Small and Medium-sized Companies and Minor Accounting Amendments) Regulations 1997 (SI 1997 No 220), which were issued to clarify the requirements applicable to small companies, apply to annual accounts approved on or after 1 March 1997 and to auditors' reports in respect of those accounts. However, transitional provisions allow the changes to be disregarded for periods ending on or before 24 March 1997; in which case, the previous requirements may be followed. The provisions of the FRSSE are briefly considered in **34.63** to **34.80** below. The statutory exemptions that permit abbreviated accounts to be filed with the Registrar of Companies are dealt with in chapter 35.

34.2 The exemptions from disclosure applicable to small and medium-sized entities fall into two categories: exemptions from the requirements of the Act (see **34.18** to **34.42** below) and exemptions from accounting standards (FRSs and SSAPs) (see **34.43** to **34.47** below).

34.3 Certain small companies are also exempt from the obligation to have their annual accounts audited. This exemption is dealt with in **34.48** to **34.62** below.

Exemptions from disclosure requirements

Definitions

34.4 The Act's definitions of small and medium-sized companies and small and medium-sized groups are contained in s247 and s249 respectively and are discussed in **34.5** to **34.11** and **34.12** to **34.17** below. Even if a company or group qualifies as small or medium-sized, it may still not be entitled to the exemptions from the disclosure requirement of the Act if it is an ineligible entity (see **34.18** to **34.20** below).

Individual companies

34.5 A company qualifies as small or medium-sized in relation to a financial year if the qualifying conditions are met:

(a) in the case of the company's first financial year, in that year; and

(b) in the case of any subsequent financial year, in that year and the preceding year.

34.6 A company shall be treated as qualifying as small or medium-sized in relation to a financial year:

(a) if it so qualified in relation to the previous financial year under **34.5** above or was treated as so qualifying under (b) below; or

(b) if it was treated as so qualifying in relation to the previous year by virtue of (a) above and the qualifying conditions are met in the year in question.

34.7 The qualifying conditions are met by a company in a year in which it does not exceed two or more of the following criteria.

		Small company	Medium-sized company
1.	Turnover Note (a)	£2,800,000	£11,200,000
2.	Balance sheet total Note (b)	£1,400,000	£5,600,000
3.	Average number of employees Note (c)	50	250

Notes

(a) If the financial year is not a year, the turnover figure is to be proportionately adjusted.

(b) Total of all assets without any deduction for liabilities.

(c) Average to be determined on a monthly basis using the method stated in Sch 4 para 56(2) and (3) (see **9.183** above).

34.8   For any company, other than a newly incorporated company, the conditions in **34.7** above must have been satisfied for at least two consecutive years before the company can qualify. However, a company which both qualified as small or medium-sized and met the size criteria in the previous year does not cease to be so qualified if it fails to meet the appropriate size criteria in one year. If, having failed the criteria one year, the company meets the criteria the next year, it will continue to be treated as small or medium-sized. If it fails to meet the criteria in two consecutive years, it ceases to be qualified and must then meet the criteria for a further two consecutive years before it can regain its status as small or medium-sized. A newly incorporated company will qualify as small or medium-sized in its first financial year if it meets the appropriate criteria in **34.7** above in that year.

34.9   The following example illustrates the application of the above rules to a company whose first financial year ended on 31 December 1996.

Year	Size criteria	Permitted to file abbreviated accounts as:	Explanation
1996	Small	Small	Initial year of incorporation.
1997	Medium-sized	Small	Having qualified as small and having met the small qualifying conditions in 1996, it does not cease to qualify as a result of one year's failure to meet the criteria.
1998	Small	Small	Even though it failed to meet the small criteria in 1997, it was treated as qualifying as small in that year and has met the small size criteria this year.
1999	Medium-sized	Small	Having been treated as qualifying and having met the small qualifying conditions in 1998, it does not cease to qualify as a result of one year's failure to meet the criteria.
2000	Large	Medium-sized	Even though it failed to meet the small size criteria in 1999, it has met the criteria as medium-sized in each of the preceding two years and thus continues to qualify as medium.
2001	Large	No concession	It has failed to meet either the small or medium-sized criteria in two consecutive years.
2002	Medium-sized	No concession	Having ceased to qualify as medium-sized, it must now meet the criteria for two consecutive years to be reinstated.
2003	Small	Medium-sized	It has met the medium-sized criteria for two consecutive years.

34.10   A parent company can only qualify as small in relation to a financial year if the group headed by it qualifies as a small group and can only qualify as a medium-sized company in a financial year if the group qualifies as a medium-sized group. [s247A(3)]

34.11

Thus, if a parent qualified as a small company, but the group was medium-sized, the parent would only be entitled to the exemptions available to a medium-sized company when preparing individual accounts. The size criteria for groups are given in **34.15** below.

Groups

34.12   A group qualifies as small or medium-sized in relation to a financial year if the qualifying conditions are met:

(a)   in the case of the parent company's first financial year, in that year; and

(b)   in the case of any subsequent financial year, in that year and the preceding year.

34.13

There is no equivalent of **34.10** above as regards a group. Thus, theoretically, a group may be small, even if the parent is medium-sized, or medium-sized, even if the parent is 'large'. For example, if the subsidiaries are very small, the group may qualify on a 'gross' basis although the parent exceeds the qualifying conditions for a company and hence the group fails on a 'net' basis because the qualifying conditions for a company are the same as those for a group on a 'net' basis (see **34.17** below for the meaning of 'gross' and 'net' bases).

34.14   A group shall be treated as qualifying as small or medium-sized in relation to a financial year:

(a)   if it so qualified in relation to the previous financial year under **34.12** above or was treated as so qualifying under (b) below; or

(b)   if it was treated as so qualifying in relation to the previous year by virtue of (a) above and the qualifying conditions are met in the year in question.

34.15   The qualifying conditions are met by a group in a year in which it does not exceed two or more of the following criteria.

	Small group	Medium-sized group
1. Aggregate turnover	£2,800,000 net, or £3,360,000 gross	£11,200,000 net, or £13,440,000 gross
2. Aggregate balance sheet total	£1,400,000 net, or £1,680,000 gross	£5,600,000 net, or £6,720,000 gross
3. Aggregate number of employees	50	250

34.16 The aggregate figures shall be determined by aggregating the relevant figures for each member of the group (see **34.7** above).

34.17 'Net' means with set-off and other adjustments required by Sch 4A (i.e., elimination of intra-group turnover, balances and profits or losses) and 'gross' means without those set-offs and other adjustments. A company may satisfy the relevant requirement on the basis of either the net or the gross figure.

Exemptions from statutory disclosure requirements

Introduction

34.18 The exemptions from the disclosure requirements of the Act may be divided into two groups: those exemptions that apply to both small and medium-sized companies (see **34.21** to **34.25** below) and those exemptions that apply to small companies only (see **34.26** to **34.35** below).

34.19 A company is not entitled to the exemptions if it is, or was at any time during the financial year:
[s247A(1)]

- a public company;

- a banking or insurance company;

- an authorised person under the Financial Services Act 1986; or

- a member of an ineligible group.

34.20 A group is ineligible if any of its members is:
[s 247A(2)]

(a) a public company or a body corporate (e.g., a foreign company) which (not being a company) has power under its constitution to offer its shares or debentures to the public and may lawfully exercise that power [ss735 and 740];

(b)   an authorised institution under the Banking Act 1987;

(c)   an insurance company to which Part II of the Insurance Companies Act 1982 applies; or

(d)   an authorised person under the Financial Services Act 1986.

Exemptions applicable to small and medium-sized companies and groups

34.21   Small or medium-sized companies do not have to disclose:

(a)   remuneration paid to auditors for non-audit work [SI 1991 No 2128 reg 4]; and

(b)   whether the accounts have been prepared in compliance with applicable accounting standards and particulars of any material departure [ss246(2) and 246A(2)].

34.22   These two exemptions apply to both the annual accounts which must be sent to members and to the abbreviated accounts that may be filed with the Registrar of Companies instead of the annual accounts.

34.23   A parent company is exempt from the requirement to prepare group accounts if the group, of which it is the parent, qualifies as a small or medium-sized group and it is not an ineligible group (see **34.20** above). [s248] SI 1996 No 189 removed the requirement for the auditors to state in their report that the company was entitled to the exemption. However, if the directors make use of the exemption, without being entitled to do so, the auditors are required to state that fact in their report (see **39.98** below). [s237(4A)]

34.24   The removal of the requirement for the auditors to state in their report that the company was entitled to the exemption appears to mean that if a small or medium-sized group chooses to produce consolidated accounts, then there is no longer a 'mechanism' that would allow the parent's individual profit and loss account to be excluded from the annual accounts.

34.25   The definitions of ineligible entities (see **34.19** and **34.20** above) may lead to a situation where an intermediate parent is not entitled to prepare accounts as a small or medium-sized company but can avoid preparing group accounts because the group it heads is not ineligible.

Example 34.25

A Ltd is a intermediate parent company with a UK subsidiary, B Ltd. A Ltd has a parent undertaking incorporated in the USA (X Inc) which has power under its constitution to offer its shares or debentures to the public and may lawfully exercise that power. A Ltd is a

> member of an ineligible group (i.e., the group headed by X Inc) and hence not entitled to the exemptions for a small or medium-sized company. However, X Inc is not a member of the group headed by A Ltd and hence does not breach (a) in **34.20** above.

Exemptions applicable to small companies

34.26 The Companies Act 1985 (Accounts of Small and Medium-sized Companies and Minor Accounting Amendments) Regulations 1997 (SI 1997 No 220) were issued to clarify the requirements applicable to small companies. They apply to annual accounts approved on or after 1 March 1997 and to directors' and auditors' reports in respect of those accounts. However, transitional provisions allow the changes to be disregarded for periods ending on or before 24 March 1997; in which case, the previous requirements may be followed.

34.27 SI 1997 No 220 creates a stand-alone 'small company schedule' which details the provisions applicable to a small company's accounts. The previous approach set out the general accounting provisions in Sch 4 and then detailed the exemptions to those provisions in Sch 8. After revision by SI 1997 No 220, the guidance in the Act comprises:

(a) Sch 8 – form and content of accounts prepared by small companies for members;

(b) Sch 8A – form and content of accounts of small companies delivered to the Registrar of Companies (see chapter 35);

(c) s246 – details of exemptions applicable to small companies in respect of disclosures required by Schs 5, 6 and 7 to the Act.

34.28 If companies take advantage of these exemptions, the directors must state that fact in the directors' report (see **34.30** below) and on the face of the balance sheet (see **34.36** below) as appropriate. There is no longer a requirement for the directors to state the grounds, in their opinion, on which the company is entitled to the exemptions.

Directors' report

34.29 The directors' report for a small company need not disclose:

- the fair review of the business [s234(1)(a)];
- the amount to be paid as a dividend [s234(1)(b)];
- significant differences in asset values [Sch 7: 1(2)];
- post-balance sheet events [Sch 7: 6(a)];
- future developments [Sch 7:6(b)];
- research and development activities [Sch 7: 6(c)];
- branches outside the UK [Sch 7: 6(d)];
- employee involvement [Sch 7: 11].

34.30 If advantage is taken of these exemptions, that fact must be stated in the directors' report. [s246(8)]

> ### *Example 34.30*
>
> **Directors' report – accounts for members**
>
> This report has been prepared in accordance with the special provisions relating to small companies under s246 Companies Act 1985.

> This statement is required only if exemptions relating to the directors' report have been taken. The exemptions relating to the accounts and the exemptions relating to the directors' report are considered separately.

Balance sheet

34.31 Schedule 8 contains a format 1 and a format 2 balance sheet. These are derived from the two balance sheet formats in Sch 4, with many of the subheadings (to which Arabic numbers are assigned) aggregated and renamed. Schedule 8 also requires a reduced amount of supplementary balance sheet information compared to that required by Sch 4. The format changes from Sch 4 are considered below. The applicability of the exemptions to a group balance sheet is considered in **34.35** below.

(a) Fixed assets:

    (i) intangible assets – 'development costs', 'concessions, patents, etc.' and payments on account are aggregated under a single heading 'other intangible assets';

    (ii) tangible assets – 'plant and machinery', 'fixtures, fittings, tools and equipment', 'payments on account and assets in the course of construction' are aggregated under a single heading 'plant and machinery, etc.';

    (iii) investments – 'other loans' and 'own shares' are aggregated under a single heading 'others'. Shares in group undertakings are combined with participating interests and loans to group undertakings are combined with loans to participating interests.

(b) Current assets:

    (i) stocks – 'raw materials and consumables', 'work in progress' and 'finished goods and goods for resale' are aggregated under a single heading 'stocks';

    (ii) debtors – amounts owed by group undertakings is combined with amounts owed by participating interests.

'Other debtors', 'called up share capital not paid' and 'prepayments and accrued income' are aggregated under a single heading 'others';

(iii) investments – 'own shares' and 'other investments' are aggregated under a single heading 'other investments'.

(c) Creditors: amounts owed to group undertakings is combined with amounts owed to participating interests. 'Debenture loans', 'payments received on account', 'bills of exchange payable', 'other creditors, including taxation and social security' and 'accruals and deferred income' are aggregated under a single heading 'other creditors'.

(d) Provisions for liabilities and charges: need not analyse between 'pensions and similar obligations', 'taxation, including deferred income' and 'other provisions'.

(e) Other reserves: need not analyse between 'capital redemption reserve', reserve for own shares', 'reserves provided for by the Articles of Association' and 'other reserves'.

34.32 The following supplementary balance sheet disclosures of Sch 4 are not repeated in Sch 8:

(a) difference between carrying amount and the 'relative alternative amount' (see **16.6** above);

(b) particulars of any contingent right to the allotment of shares;

(c) particulars of debentures issued;

(d) particulars of debentures of the company held by a nominee or trustee on behalf of the company;

(e) analysis of land and buildings between freehold, long leasehold and short leasehold;

(f) the amount of provision for deferred taxation;

(g) the terms of payment or repayment and interest payable in respect of debts falling due, in all or part, more than five years from the end of the financial year. (Note that it is still necessary to disclose the amount of debts falling due all or in part after five years, although this may be given in aggregate rather than for each item in creditors);

(h) the nature of security given in respect of 'creditors';

(i) loans given as financial assistance for the purchase of the company's own shares.

Profit and loss account

34.33 Schedule 8 contains four standard profit and loss account formats which are unchanged from those required by Sch 4. However, there is a reduced level of supplementary disclosure required by Sch 8 compared to that required by Sch 4. The following supplementary profit and loss account disclosures of Sch 4 are not repeated in Sch 8:

(a) interest on bank loans and overdrafts and loans of any other kind;

(b) special circumstances affecting the tax charge or liability;

(c) the charge for UK corporation tax;

(d) the effect of double taxation relief;

(e) the charge for UK income tax;

(f) the amount of overseas tax on profits and capital gains;

(g) analysis of turnover by class or market, instead the percentage of turnover attributable to non-UK markets is to be disclosed;

(h) the average number of employees in aggregate and by category; and

(i) the aggregate wages and salaries, social security costs and other pension costs.

Other disclosures

34.34 Schedules 5 and 6 apply to a small company, subject to certain exemptions. [s246(3)] The disclosures in these schedules not required of a small company include: [s246(3)(b)]

(a) financial years of subsidiary undertakings with non-coterminous year ends [Sch 5: 4];

(b) number of directors exercising share options and receiving shares under long-term incentive schemes [Sch 6: 1(2)(b)];

(c) details of highest paid director's emoluments, etc. [Sch 6: 2]; and

(d) excess retirement benefits of directors and past directors [Sch 6: 7].

In addition, small companies may disclose the total of the three separate aggregates required by Sch 6. [Sch 6: 1(a), (c) and (d)] That is, they need only disclose the aggregate of: [s246(3)(a)]

(a) aggregate emoluments paid to or receivable by directors in respect of qualifying services;

(b) aggregate amounts paid, received or receivable under long-term incentive schemes in respect of qualifying services; and

(c) aggregate value of company contributions paid, or treated as paid, to a pension scheme in respect of directors' qualifying services.

Group accounts prepared by a small company

34.35 If the parent qualifies as small, then, by implication, the group must also be small (see **34.10** above) and the parent is therefore not required to produce group accounts (see **34.23** above). However, if group accounts are prepared, then they may be prepared in accordance with Sch 8 rather than Sch 4. Thus, the exemptions in **34.31** to **34.34** above would apply to the group accounts, except that fixed asset investments should show separately 'shares in group undertakings', 'interests in associated undertakings' and 'other participating interests'. [s248A(3)] The group accounts need not give the information required by the provisions of s246(3), although they will still be required in the individual accounts (see **34.23** and **34.34** above). [s248A(4)] There is no provision to file abbreviated group accounts (see **35.16** below).

Directors' statement on the face of the balance sheet

34.36 The fact must be stated on the face of the balance sheet, if advantage is taken of the exemptions in s246(2) or (3) or s248A by a small company or small group (i.e., the exemptions in **34.21**(b) and **34.31** to **34.35** above). [s246(8) and s248A(5)]

> **Example 34.36**
>
> These accounts have been prepared in accordance with the special provisions relating to small companies under s246 Companies Act 1985.

> This statement is required only if exemptions relating to the accounts have been taken. The exemptions relating to the accounts and the exemptions relating to the directors' report are considered separately.

Effect of statutory exemptions for small companies on disclosures required by accounting standards

34.37 Certain of the statutory disclosures of Sch 4, from which small companies are exempted by following Sch 8, are also required by SSAPs or FRSs. The question thus arises whether a small company is still required to make such a disclosure under the accounting standards.

Foreword to Accounting Standards, issued by the ASB in June 1993, states that:

'Where accounting standards prescribe information to be contained in financial statements, such requirements do not override exemptions from disclosure given by law to, and utilised by, certain companies.'

34.38 It seems clear, not surprisingly, that if a company is exempt from a statutory disclosure, because it falls within a certain category, it is also exempt from an identical disclosure required by an accounting standard. The situation is not so clear where accounting standards require related disclosures or further disclosures in respect of items where there is a statutory exemption. These areas are considered below as they relate to the small company exemptions.

Deferred tax

34.39 Schedule 8 omits Sch 4 para 47 and therefore does not require small companies to disclose the provision for deferred taxation. However, the SSAP 15 disclosure requirements go beyond simply disclosing the amount provided. SSAP 15 requires an analysis of the deferred tax balance between its major components, the disclosure of transfers to and from the deferred tax provision and the disclosure of the amount of unprovided deferred tax, analysed between major components. This latter requirement provides additional, useful information. These additional SSAP 15 disclosures should be given.

34.40 SSAPs 8 and 15 require the disclosure of the deferred tax element of the profit and loss account tax charge for the year. Schedule 8 omits Sch 4 para 54 and does not require small companies to disclose particulars of the tax charge. Disclosure of the deferred tax element, in isolation from the other main elements of the tax charge, appears to be of little benefit and, when taken in conjunction with the 'spirit' of omitting a requirement to disclose particulars of tax, implies that, in most instances, the omission of the disclosure would not be a significant departure from the SSAPs.

Particulars of tax

34.41 As mentioned above, Sch 8 does not repeat Sch 4 para 54, which requires disclosure of tax particulars. Certain of these particulars are also required by SSAP 8 (corporation tax charge, relief for overseas taxation and overseas taxation). Applying the foreword (see **34.37** above), a small company is not required to disclose an item under an accounting standard when it is exempt from making that disclosure by law.

34.42 SSAP 8 also requires disclosure of certain other particulars namely tax on franked investment income and irrecoverable ACT. For the same reasons as noted in **34.40** above, there seems to be little benefit in disclosing these particulars. For periods ending on or after 23 March 2000 SSAP 8 is superseded by FRS 16 (see chapter 27).

Exemptions from accounting standards

Introduction

34.43 Eligible entities adopting the FRSSE become exempt from applying all other accounting standards (i.e., SSAPs and FRSs) and UITF Abstracts, known collectively as 'Big GAAP' (generally accepted accounting practice). However, if the FRSSE is not adopted, FRS 1 (revised 1996) *Cash flow statements*, SSAP 13 *Accounting for research and development* and SSAP 25 *Segmental reporting* all provide some degree of exemption based upon size.

Cash flow statements

34.44 Companies entitled to the filing exemptions applicable to small companies are entirely exempt from the requirements of FRS 1. This exemption is extended to entities which would have been classed as small had they been companies under UK companies legislation.

Research and development

34.45 Certain types and sizes of company are exempted from disclosing under SSAP 13 details of the research and development charge for the period and from analysing the charge between the current year and amounts amortised from deferred expenditure. These exemptions apply to companies that:

(a) are not a public limited company, bank, insurance company or an authorised person under the Financial Services Act 1986 or a parent company that has such a company as a subsidiary; and

(b) satisfy the criteria, multiplied by 10, for defining a medium-sized company (see **34.47** below).

Segmental reporting

34.46   SSAP 25 requires segmental disclosures additional to those required by companies legislation (see **20.11** et seq above). These additional disclosures are not required provided the reporting entity:

(a)   is not a public limited company, the parent of a public limited company, a banking or insurance company or group and;

(b)   satisfies the criteria, multiplied by 10, for defining a medium-sized company (see **34.47** below).

Medium-sized company limits multiplied by a factor of 10

34.47   The medium-sized criteria (see **34.7** above) multiplied by a factor of 10 are:

Turnover	£112 million
Balance sheet total	£56 million
Number of employees	2,500

Thus, a company or group that exceeds more than one of these criteria will not be entitled to the exemptions discussed in **34.45** and **34.46** above.

Exemption from the obligation to have annual accounts audited

Introduction

34.48   The dropping of the requirement for certain very small companies to have their annual accounts audited has been the subject of discussion for many years, the APC having issued an audit brief on the subject in 1979. In April 1993, the DTI issued a consultative document dealing with the audit and accounting requirements for very small companies and, in his Budget speech on 30 November 1993, the Chancellor of the Exchequer announced revised proposals which led ultimately to the issue in July 1994 of SI 1994 No 1935, the Companies Act 1985 (Audit Exemption) Regulations 1994 (the Regulations), which introduced ss249A–E.

34.49   These Regulations provided for two levels of exemption for all eligible companies. Companies that met the 'total exemption conditions' were exempt from the requirement to have their annual accounts audited. Companies that met the 'report conditions' were exempt from the audit requirement, but instead needed to obtain an accountants' report.

34.50   The Companies Act 1985 (Audit Exemption) (Amendment) Regulations 1997 (the Amendment Regulations) SI 1997 No 936 increased the amount of turnover that a company may have and still take advantage of the 'total exemption provisions'. This extension to the total exemption limit renders the audit exemption report obsolete for all but eligible charitable companies. The amendment applies to financial years ending on or after 15 June 1997.

34.51   With the exception of the matters relating to groups and dormant companies (see **34.57** and **34.58** below), the other conditions to qualify for exemption and the cases where exemption is not available remain unchanged by the Amendment Regulations.

34.52   Reports by reporting accountants for the purpose of the Regulations are dealt with in chapter 45 (see **45.14** to **45.23** below).

Criteria for exemptions

34.53   For all companies, except companies that are charities, to meet the 'total exemption conditions' the company's turnover must not exceed £350,000 for periods ending on or after 15 June 1997. For companies that are charities, the company's turnover must not exceed £90,000 for periods ending on or after 15 June 1997. For companies that are charities to meet the 'report conditions', the company's turnover must not exceed £250,000. 'Gross income' is substituted for 'turnover' for charitable companies. [s249A]

In addition, to meet either set of conditions:
[s249B(1) and (1A)]

(a)   the company must qualify as a small company for the year, for the purposes of the abbreviated accounts exemptions;

(b)   the company's balance sheet total must not exceed £1,400,000;

(c)   the company must not have been at any time during the year:

    (i)   a parent company or a non-dormant subsidiary undertaking;

    (ii)   a public company;

    (iii)   a banking or insurance company;

    (iv)   an authorised person or an appointed representative under the Financial Services Act 1986;

    (v)   an insurance broker enrolled by the Insurance Brokers Registration Council;

    (vi)   a special register body as defined in s117(1) Trade Union and Labour Relations (Consolidation) Act 1992 or an employers' association as defined in s122 of that Act.

34.54 It should be noted that the exclusion above refers to subsidiary undertakings and not subsidiary companies. The definition of a 'subsidiary undertaking' and an 'undertaking' in the Act are such that a company that is a subsidiary of a body corporate, or partnership, or an unincorporated association carrying on a trade or business (with or without a view to profit) is precluded from claiming the above exemptions. [ss258 and 259] Whether or not a company owned by a trust falls into this category is unclear and it is suggested that legal advice be sought in relation to the particular circumstances in any case where this applies. (See **34.57** below for the treatment of members of small groups.)

34.55 As noted in **34.53** above, for financial years ending prior to 15 June 1997, qualifying companies with turnover in excess of £90,000 but not more than £350,000 had the option of filing accounts with an 'audit exemption report' prepared by a 'reporting accountant'. The extension to the total exemption limit renders the audit exemption report obsolete for all but eligible charitable companies.

34.56 Members holding 10 per cent or more of the issued share capital (or any class) may require that the company has an audit for a financial year by depositing a written notice at the company's registered office not later than one month before the year end.

Treatment of small groups

34.57 For financial years ending on or after 15 June 1997, the changes made by the Amendment Regulations enable a company (including charitable companies), which would otherwise be disqualified from claiming exemption from audit because it was a parent company or non-dormant subsidiary undertaking for any period during the financial year, to claim exemption from audit if the group of which it is a member meets all of the following conditions throughout the financial year into which the period of group membership falls: [s249B(1B) and (1C)]

(a) the group qualifies as a small group for the purposes of s249; and is not, at the time of preparing accounts, and was not, at any time in the financial year, an ineligible group (see **34.12** to **34.17** and **34.20** above);

(b) the group's aggregate turnover in that year is not more than £350,000 net (or £420,000 gross); and

(c) the group's aggregate balance sheet total for that year is not more than £1.4 million net (or £1.68 million gross).

Treatment of dormant companies

34.58   The Amendment Regulations confirm that exemption from audit is available to dormant companies under either the audit exemption provisions or the dormant company provisions (see **4.57** to **4.65** above). [s250] Use of the audit exemption provisions can be advantageous, because they do not require the passing of a special resolution. This amendment is retrospective and is deemed to have had effect since the commencement of the original audit exemption provisions on 11 August 1994. [s249A(6A)]

Charitable companies

34.59   The raising of the audit exemption limit for small companies to an annual turnover of £350,000 does not apply to companies which are also charities. Accordingly, eligible charitable companies with annual gross income of between £90,000 and £250,000 will require an audit exemption report if they opt not to have an audit. However, small charitable companies which are parent companies or subsidiary undertakings are included in the change, conceding exemption from audit if the group of which they are members is a small group meeting the conditions in **34.57** above. Thus, for financial years ending on or after 15 June 1997, membership of a small group that meets the conditions of s249B will not preclude charitable companies from utilising the audit exemptions. [s249B(1B) and (1C)]

Disclosures in annual reports and accounts

34.60   The balance sheet of a company taking advantage of either of the audit exemptions has to include a statement by the directors to the effect that:

(a)   the company is eligible to take advantage of the exemption;

(b)   no notice has been deposited at the company's registered office by members holding 10 per cent or more of the issued share capital requiring that the company has an audit for the financial year (see **34.56** above); and

(c)   the directors acknowledge their responsibilities for:

    (i)   ensuring that the company keeps proper accounting records; and

    (ii)   preparing accounts which give a true and fair view.

> ### Example 34.60
>
> These annual accounts have not been audited because the company is entitled to the exemption provided by *s249A(1)* Companies Act 1985 and no notice under s249B(2) has been deposited at the company's

> registered office requiring the company to obtain an audit of the accounts.
>
> The directors acknowledge their responsibilities for ensuring that the company keeps accounting records that comply with s221 Companies Act 1985. The directors also acknowledge their responsibilities for preparing accounts which give a true and fair view of the state of affairs of the company as at the end of the financial year and of its profit or loss for the financial year in accordance with s226 Companies Act 1985, and which otherwise comply with the requirements of that Act relating to accounts, so far as applicable to the company.
>
> *N.B. Italicised text refers to companies which are not charities. For a company that is a charity, this should be replaced with 's249A(2)'.*

34.61   The statement referred to in **34.60** above must be given on the face of the balance sheet above the signature required by s233 (approval and signing of accounts – see **4.4** above).

34.62   The requirement to provide a statement of directors' responsibilities in SAS 600 does not apply to financial statements prepared under the Regulations, as they are not subject to an audit. Therefore, such a statement could be omitted or abbreviated by cross-referring to the directors' statement on the face of the balance sheet.

A Financial Reporting Standard for smaller entities

Background

34.63   The ASB first issued the FRSSE on 6 November 1997. The FRSSE is applicable to companies and groups that qualify as small under the Act and analogous entities. The FRSSE allowed immediate adoption, but its application is optional.

34.64   The FRSSE was developed following a lengthy consultation process. The first draft was included within the report of a CCAB working party published in December 1995. The recommendations in the report were broadly accepted by the ASB, which issued an exposure draft in December 1996 and the final standard on 6 November 1997.

34.65   As part of a periodic update procedure, revised standards have been issued on 10 December 1998 and 2 December 1999, which update the standard for the aspects of FRSs and UITF Abstracts relevant to smaller entities issued since the last update. The current revised

FRSSE is standard in respect of relevant financial statements relating to accounting periods ending on or after 23 March 2000 (see **34.74** and **34.76** below).

Scope

34.66 The FRSSE may be applied to all financial statements, intended to give a true and fair view of the financial position and profit or loss, of all entities that are small companies or groups as defined in companies legislation and entitled to the exemptions available in the legislation for small companies when filing accounts with the Registrar of Companies. The FRSSE may also be applied to entities that would fall within that definition had they been incorporated under companies legislation (excluding building societies).

34.67 The requirement that the entity be entitled to the exemptions in legislation, rather than being based simply on qualification as small (i.e., simply on size), precludes the entities in **34.19** above (i.e., entities such as public companies, banking or insurance companies, authorised persons under the Financial Services Act 1986 or members of an ineligible group) from applying the FRSSE.

34.68 The scope paragraph of the FRSSE notes that adoption of the FRSSE is not available for those entities required to prepare their accounts in accordance with SORPs existing when the FRSSE was issued. This is because existing SORPs are drafted on the basis that the financial statements concerned comply with accounting standards. Future SORPs may make reference to adoption of the FRSSE. SORPs and equivalent guidance developed or revised after the issue of the FRSSE may specify the circumstances, if any, when the FRSSE may be adopted. The most significant group of entities in this position are charities.

Adoption of the FRSSE

34.69 Eligible entities adopting the FRSSE become exempt from applying all other accounting standards (i.e., SSAPs and FRSs) and UITF Abstracts, known collectively as 'Big GAAP'. If an entity chooses not to adopt the FRSSE it remains subject to Big GAAP.

34.70 When an entity has chosen to adopt the FRSSE, its financial statements are required to disclose that they have been prepared in accordance with it. For companies taking advantage of other statutory exemptions available to small companies, this can be done by adding the relevant words to the statutory statement on the balance sheet (see **34.36** above), as signed by the directors.

Example 34.70

These accounts have been prepared in accordance with the special provisions relating to small companies under s246 Companies Act 1985 and with the Financial Reporting Standard for Smaller Entities *(effective March 2000)*.

N.B. Italicised text refers to the latest revision of the FRSSE, which is standard in respect of financial statements relating to accounting periods ending on or after 23 March 2000. (see **34.65** *above).*

Content of the FRSSE

34.71 The FRSSE collects together in one document, and in simplified form, those accounting standards and other requirements that are applicable to smaller entities. The measurement bases in the FRSSE are the same as, or a simplification of, those in existing standards. However, in many cases, the disclosure requirements of the accounting standards included as part of the FRSSE have been significantly reduced.

34.72 Appendices V and VI of the FRSSE give comprehensive details of the sources used in its compilation and the changes to and simplifications of that source material.

34.73 Areas of simplification of measurement bases specifically detailed by the FRSSE include:

(a) finance leases: allocation of interest on a straight-line basis may provide a reasonable approximation to a constant periodic rate of charge over the period of the lease;

(b) arrangement fees in respect of borrowings: where an arrangement fee does not represent a significant additional cost of finance, when compared to the interest payable over the term of the borrowing, it should be charged to the profit and loss account immediately it is incurred;

(c) setting 20 years as an absolute maximum, rather than a presumed maximum that may be rebutted, for the useful economic lives assigned to intangible assets and goodwill arising on the acquisition of unincorporated businesses. This removes the opportunity to choose a longer life where justified and so removes also the consequent need for annual exercises to check impairment by forecasting and discounting future cash flows;

(d) removing the exception that allows the recognition of internally developed intangible assets with market values and revaluation of any intangible asset with a market value;

(e) omitting the detailed requirements for calculating value in use (as part of recoverable amount) and subsequent monitoring of cash flows for five years following an impairment review where recoverable amount has been based on value in use.

34.74 The revised FRSSE (effective March 2000) added the following further simplifications when addressing the issues raised by FRS 12 and FRS 15:

(a) where revalued, tangible fixed assets are to be carried at market value or best estimate thereof, unless judged inappropriate by the directors in which case current value may be used. FRS 15 requires current value to be used;

(b) valuations may be performed by an experienced valuer, whereas FRS 15 refers to a qualified valuer;

(c) residual values and useful economic lives to be reviewed regularly, rather than annually, and revised when necessary rather than when expectations are significantly different from previous estimates as required by FRS 15;

(d) the detailed rules in FRS 12 relating to discount rates have been omitted from the revised FRSSE.

34.75 Standard disclosures not required if the FRSSE is adopted include:

(a) the requirement to analyse turnover, costs, results and exceptional items into continuing operations, acquisitions and discontinued operations;

(b) the requirement for a note of historical cost profits and losses;

(c) the requirement for a reconciliation of shareholders' funds;

(d) the requirement to disclose amounts of research and development charged to the profit and loss account;

(e) the requirement to disclose amounts of foreign exchange gains and losses charged to the profit and loss account;

(f) certain of the disclosures regarding defined benefit pension schemes; and

(g) when considering disclosure of related-party transactions with the entity, there is no requirement to consider the materiality of transactions to the related party. Only materiality to the entity need be considered.

The FRSSE omits most of the detailed disclosure requirements of FRS 10 and FRS 11. FRS 9 is not addressed by the FRSSE, except that (as with FRS 2) the reader is cross-referred to it if group accounts are being prepared. UITF Abstracts 18, 19 and 22 were not addressed by the FRSSE because they were not considered relevant to smaller entities. Only the basic accounting principles of UITF Abstracts 20 and 21 were incorporated into the FRSSE.

34.76   With the exception of the nature and financial effect of contingent liabilities (unless remote) and probable contingent assets, the revised FRSSE (effective March 2000) omits the detailed disclosure requirements of FRS 12. Most of the detailed disclosure requirements of FRS 15 have also been omitted from the revised FRSSE. FRSs 13 and 14, and three other amendments to FRS 5 and UITFs 15 and 21, are not addressed by the revised FRSSE (effective March 2000) because they were not considered relevant to smaller entities.

34.77   The FRSSE explicitly states that personal guarantees given by directors in respect of borrowings by the reported entity should be disclosed in the notes to the accounts. This statement emphasises that transactions of this nature are required to be disclosed in accordance with FRS 8 (see **32.62** above).

Consolidated financial statements under the FRSSE

34.78   Where a reporting entity is adopting the FRSSE and preparing consolidated financial statements, it should regard as standard the accounting practices and disclosure requirements set out in FRSs 2, 6 and 7 and, as they apply in respect of consolidated financial statements, FRSs 5, 9, 10 and 11.

Guidance on items not included in the FRSSE

34.79   The FRSSE notes that in cases where a matter is not dealt with by the FRSSE, preparers of accounts should have regard to other accounting standards and UITF Abstracts ('Big GAAP'), not as mandatory documents, but as a means of establishing current practice, as financial statements will generally be prepared using accepted practice.

Updating the FRSSE and the effect of new standards and abstracts

34.80   The FRSSE will continue to be updated and revised periodically by the ASB to reflect developments in financial reporting relevant to small entities. To this end, the ASB has set up a subcommittee, the 'Committee on Accounting for Smaller Entities' (CASE), to advise on issues affecting small companies and recommend future revisions and modifications to the FRSSE, including those arising from new or revised standards and abstracts. By adopting the FRSSE, small entities will exempt themselves from following all new standards and abstracts issued in future, unless those standards and abstracts specifically detail that those entities applying the FRSSE are not exempt from the new provisions.

Future developments

Raising the thresholds levels for SMEs

34.81   In March 1999, the DTI issued a consultative document *Raising the Thresholds Levels for SMEs*. The document sought views on whether the thresholds detailed above should be increased to the maximum level permissible within the EEC directives. It outlined the potential for the turnover thresholds to be increased to £4.8 million for small companies and £19.2 million for medium-sized companies. The balance sheet total has the potential to be raised to £2.4 million for small companies and £9.6 million for medium-sized entities. The employee thresholds would remain unchanged.

34.82   The consultation period ended on 30 June 1999. However, no response has yet been issued by the DTI since the consultation process has been linked to the issue of audit exemption for smaller entities (see **34.83** below). Revised legislation is expected in the second quarter of 2000.

34.83   In October 1999, the DTI issued the consultation document *The Statutory Audit Requirement for Smaller Companies*. The issue addressed by the document was 'whether the balance of costs and benefits supports a mandatory requirement for an external audit for companies of a certain size' (see **34.48** to **34.61** above for current requirements). On 4 April 2000, the DTI announced that, subject to parliamentary approval, qualifying companies with annual turnover below £1 million would soon be able to take advantage of full exemption from audit. It is anticipated that the new regulations will apply to financial years ending after 31 July 2000. The government also stated their intention to raise this limit further in the future, to £4.8 million, the maximum allowed under EU legislation. This further increase will be delayed until the final recommendations of the company law review are received.

Company law review

34.84   The consultation document from the Company Law Review Steering Group issued in March 2000 *Developing the Framework* asked for comments on a number of proposals for change to the small company reporting regime.

34.85   These proposals included:

   (a)   A simplified format for reports and accounts for smaller companies reducing disclosure below that required by Schedule 8 of the Act. However, as part of this simplification process, the ability to file abbreviated accounts (see chapter 35) would be abolished.

(b) The small company qualification thresholds be increased to the maximum allowed under EU directive being:

    (i)   turnover no more than £4.8 million;

    (ii) balance sheet total no more than £2.4 million;

    (iii) number of employees no more than 50.

(c) Audit exemption available to 'micro' companies meeting two out of three of the following criteria:

    (i)   turnover no more than £1 million;

    (ii) balance sheet total no more than £0.5 million;

    (iii) number of employees no more than 25.

(d) The accounts of small companies not qualifying as micro companies being subject to Independent Professional Review rather than audit.

(e) The category of, and hence very limited exemptions available to, medium-sized companies be abolished.

(f) The time-limit for preparation and filing of small company accounts should be reduced to seven months, with an aim of bringing this down to five months in due course.

34.86 The consultation period for the above proposals ends on 15 June 2000.

35 Abbreviated accounts

35 Abbreviated accounts

Summary of changes since the previous issue of this publication

Para.	*Topic*	*Summary*
35.23	*Developing the Framework*	The consultation document from the company law review makes a number of proposals for change to the small company reporting regime.

Introduction

35.1 This chapter considers the exemptions available to small and medium-sized companies in respect of the accounts to be delivered to the Registrar of Companies. The exemptions available in respect of the annual accounts which are to be presented to members are considered in chapter 34. This chapter reflects SI 1997 No 220, the Companies Act 1985 (Accounts of Small and Medium-sized Companies and Minor Accounting Amendment) Regulations 1997, which were issued to clarify the requirements applicable to small companies. They apply to annual accounts approved on or after 1 March 1997 and to auditors' reports in respect of those accounts. However, transitional provisions allow the changes to be disregarded for periods ending on or before 24 March 1997; in which case, the previous requirements may be followed.

35.2 In most cases, the accounts delivered to the Registrar of Companies will be the same as those required under the Act to be laid before the company in a general meeting. [s241] Certain companies, however, which qualify as small or medium-sized may take advantage of some or all of the exemptions given under the Act and file 'abbreviated accounts' with the Registrar. [ss246–247A] This will require the preparation of another set of financial statements solely for this purpose, with differing levels of disclosure, depending upon whether the entity is classified as small or medium-sized. Companies may not consider it worthwhile to take advantage of the exemption, particularly given that small companies may now reduce the level of disclosure made in the annual accounts which are presented to members.

35.3   The term 'modified accounts' was used in the original text of the Act to identify the accounts which may be filed instead of full accounts. This term was dropped as a consequence of amendments made to the Act by the Companies Act 1989. Normal practice has continued to use the term 'abbreviated accounts' and this term is now incorporated within s247B, which addresses the special auditors' report required on such accounts.

Entitlement to file abbreviated accounts

35.4   The qualifying conditions to be met by a small or medium-sized company are explained in chapter 34.

35.5   A company is not entitled to file abbreviated accounts if it is, or was at any time during the financial year to which those accounts relate: [s247A(1)]

(a) a public company;

(b) a banking company (i.e., an authorised institution under the Banking Act 1987);

(c) an insurance company (i.e., as defined by the Insurance Companies Act 1982);

(d) an authorised person under the Financial Services Act 1986; or

(e) a member of an ineligible group.

35.6   A group is ineligible if any of its members is a public company or a body corporate not registered under the Companies Acts (e.g., a foreign company) which has the power to offer its shares or debentures to the public, or a banking company, or an insurance company or an authorised person under the Financial Services Act 1986. [s247A(2)]

35.7   A dormant company may avail itself of the filing exemptions of a small company, even if it is a member of an ineligible group, if it is exempt from the obligation to appoint auditors (see **4.57** above). [s250(4)(a)]

Form and content of abbreviated accounts

Summary of requirements

35.8   The accounts must be an abbreviated version of the full financial statements required to be laid before the company in a general meeting. SI 1997 No 220 creates a stand-alone 'small company schedule' which details the provisions applicable to a small company's accounts. The previous approach set out the general accounting provisions in Sch 4 and then detailed the exemptions to those provisions in Sch 8. After revision by SI 1997 No 220, the guidance in the Act comprises:

(a) Sch 8 – form and content of accounts prepared by small companies for members;

(b) Sch 8A – form and content of accounts of small companies delivered to the Registrar of Companies;

(c) s246 – details of exemptions applicable to small companies in respect of disclosures required by Schs 5, 6 and 7 to the Act.

The exemptions applicable to the accounts of medium-sized companies delivered to the Registrar are now contained in s246A.

The documents and information required are as follows:

	Small company (s246 and Sch 8A)	Medium-sized company (s246A)
Full auditors' report	Need not be delivered, but the audit report on the financial statements sent to members must be reproduced in full or part in the special auditors' report in specified circumstances (see below).	
Special auditors' report	This report, to be prepared by the auditors, must state that, in their opinion, the company is entitled to deliver abbreviated accounts and that they have been properly prepared in accordance with the relevant provisions. The text of the auditors' report on the financial statements sent to members must be reproduced, in full or in part, in specified circumstances (see **43.5** to **43.13** below). Such a report is not required if the company takes advantage of the provisions of s249A (exemption from the obligation to appoint auditors – see **34.48** above). However, if an accountants' report is required under s249A(2) (i.e., certain small charities with a turnover between £90,000 and £250,000), then that report must be filed with the abbreviated accounts. This could be misleading, as the audit exemption report is on the full financial statements prepared for members and refers to different requirements to those used in abbreviated accounts. To avoid possibly misleading the reader, the form of report set out in the example in **43.12** below could be filed with the abbreviated accounts.	

Statement of directors' responsibilities	Not required. However, in some cases, it may be necessary to reproduce, in full or in part, an audit report on the full financial statements which does not include the statement of directors' responsibilities. In such circumstances, it may assist a reader of the auditors' special report on the abbreviated accounts if the statement of directors' responsibilities included in the full financial statements is reproduced. This can be done by adding appropriate wording to the end of the special report (see **43.11** below).	
Directors' report	Not required.	Copy required without modification.
Balance sheet	Abbreviated version required (see **35.10** below).	Copy required without modification.
Statement on the face of the balance sheet that advantage is taken of exemptions	A statement that advantage is taken of the exemptions to be placed above the director's signature on the balance sheet (see **35.13** below for example).	
Profit and loss account	Not required.	Abbreviated version required (see **35.14** below).
Accounting policies	Required to be disclosed, including the basis of translation of foreign currency amounts into sterling. [Sch 4: 36 and 58(1), Sch 8: 36 and 51(1), Sch 8A: 4 and 9(1)] However, exemption is given from the requirement of Sch 4 para 36A (disclosure of compliance with accounting standards). [s246(2) and (5) and s246A(2)] Where the accounts for members have been prepared in accordance with the Financial Reporting Standard for Smaller Entities (FRSSE) a statement to this effect should be included in the accounting policies. This clarification was first established by the FRSSE (effective March 2000).	

Other statutory disclosures in the notes to the accounts required by Sch 4	Only the following information is required to be given by **s246** and Sch 8A: • share capital; [Sch 8A: 5] • particulars of allotments [Sch 8A: 6] • details of fixed asset movements, so far as the information relates to items with a letter or Roman numeral; [Sch 8A: 7] • particulars of debts; [Sch 8A: 8] • corresponding amounts. [Sch 8A: 9(2) and 9(3)]	Required to be disclosed without modification with the exception that particulars of turnover by class of business and geographical markets need not be given. [s246A(3)(b)]
Other statutory disclosures in the notes to the accounts required by Sch 5 and s231(4) and (6)	Only the following information is required to be given by s246: • information on subsidiaries, etc. required by Sch 5, excluding Schs 5: 4, 6 and 10; • ultimate holding company; [Sch 5: 12] • fact if advantage is taken of the exemption in s231(3) (disclosure seriously prejudicial); • disclosures required by s231(6) if advantage is taken of s231(5) where the disclosures required by Sch 5 would result in information of excessive length.	Required to be disclosed without modification.

Other statutory disclosures in the notes to the accounts required by Sch 6	Only the following information is required to be given by s246: • loans and transactions with directors and officers. [Sch 6: Parts II and III]	Required to be disclosed without modification.
Audit and non-audit work remuneration	Disclosure of amount of auditors remuneration is not required s246.	Required to be disclosed without modification.
	Disclosure of remuneration for non-audit work is not required. [SI 1991 No 2128]	Disclosure of remuneration for non-audit work is not required. [SI 1991 No 2128]
Disclosures required by accounting standards	There is currently some discussion as to the applicability of the disclosure requirements of accounting standards to abbreviated accounts (see **35.18** to **35.21** below).	

35.9   An example of abbreviated accounts for a parent company which qualifies as a small company (which requires the group of which it is the parent group to qualify as a small group – see **34.10** above) follows **35.22** below.

Abbreviated balance sheet

35.10   There are two abbreviated balance sheet formats permitted by Sch 8A for a small company. They are derived from the Sch 4 formats by aggregating the headings to which a Arabic number is assigned in Sch 4. The balance sheet or the notes to the accounts must disclose separately the amounts of debtors falling due after one year and, where format 2 is used, the amounts of creditors falling due within one year and after more than one year.

35.11   The abbreviated balance sheet must be signed on behalf of the board of directors by a director of the company. [s246(7)]

Statement that advantage is taken of exemptions

35.12 A statement that advantage is taken of the exemptions conferred by s246 or s246A is required on the balance sheet above the signature.

35.13 An example of such a statement is as follows.

Example 35.13

These accounts have been prepared in accordance with the special provisions relating to *small companies under s246 Companies Act 1985* with respect to the delivery of individual accounts.

N.B. *Italicised text refers to small companies. For medium-sized companies, it should be replaced with 'medium-sized companies under s246A Companies Act 1985'.*

Abbreviated profit and loss account

35.14 The abbreviated profit and loss account for a medium-sized company must correspond to the company's profit and loss account prepared under s226, with the exception that the items listed below may be combined as one item under the heading 'Gross profit or loss'.

Formats 1 and 3:   turnover, cost of sales, other operating income.

Formats 2 and 4:   turnover, changes in stocks, own work capitalised, raw materials and consumables, other external charges and other operating income.

Parent company and group accounts

35.15 A parent company is exempt from the requirement to prepare group accounts if the group qualifies for the exemptions as a small or medium-sized group and it is not an ineligible group (see **35.6** above). [s248]

35.16 There is no statutory provision for a small or medium-sized parent company to file abbreviated group accounts instead of its abbreviated individual accounts. If such a company wishes to produce annual accounts for members including group accounts the annual accounts must also include individual accounts including the parent's profit and loss account and supporting notes. It could then file abbreviated individual accounts by omitting all group accounts information.

35.17   It should be emphasised that a parent company which files abbreviated accounts will need to disclose a great deal of information concerning each of its subsidiaries and other significant investment holdings as required by Sch 5. In particular, except where the parent company's accounts are included in the accounts of a larger group, the abbreviated accounts must disclose with respect to each subsidiary undertaking and holding of 20 per cent or more the aggregate of its capital and reserves at the end of its financial year and its profit or loss for that year.

Applicability of accounting standards to abbreviated accounts

35.18   There is currently some discussion as to the applicability of the disclosure requirements of accounting standards to abbreviated accounts. Obviously, standards relating to measurement that have been applied to the accounts prepared for members will apply to the abbreviated accounts, as the abbreviated balance sheet and, for medium-sized companies, profit and loss account are produced by abbreviating, not recalculating, the corresponding statements in the financial statements produced for members.

35.19   It is generally agreed that small company abbreviated accounts need not comply with the disclosure requirements of accounting standards. Two main reasons are put forward for this view. Firstly, following the changes made by SI 1997 No 220 (see **35.1** above), the Act largely specifies what the abbreviated accounts should contain rather than, as before, starting with the financial statements prepared for members and identifying what could be removed (see **35.8** above). Secondly, accounting standards only apply to financial statements that give a true and fair view and a small company's abbreviated accounts do not, e.g., there is no profit and loss account.

35.20   There is no such general agreement among commentators on the question of medium-sized abbreviated accounts. Some commentators argue that medium-sized abbreviated accounts should be the financial statements prepared for members subject only to the exemptions allowed by the Act. Others argue that the abbreviated accounts need not include disclosures which are not specified by the Act, as abbreviated accounts are not required to give a true and fair view. APB Bulletin 1997/1 *The special auditors' report on abbreviated accounts in Great Britain* appears to support this latter view, as it notes: 'Legal advice has indicated that, although they must be properly prepared in accordance with the relevant provisions, the abbreviated accounts are not required to give a true and fair view (in practice they will not do so)'.

35.21 As there is no apparent requirement for abbreviated accounts to give a true and fair view, they need not include disclosures not required by the relevant requirements of the Act, e.g., disclosures made voluntarily or solely in accordance with accounting standards. Thus, abbreviated accounts may exclude the cash flow statement, the statement of total recognised gains and losses and related-party disclosures under FRS 8. It should be noted that the disclosures required by Sch 6, Parts II and III (loans and transactions with directors and officers) are required in the abbreviated accounts for both small and medium-sized companies.

Example of abbreviated accounts for a small company

35.22 The following set of accounts illustrates the form of abbreviated accounts of a parent company which qualifies as a small company. Note that, as discussed in **34.10** above, this requires the group to qualify as a small group and, as discussed in **43.11** below, no statement of directors' responsibilities is given.

Company Registration Number 3456789

DELTO (SMALL COMPANY) LIMITED

Abbreviated accounts 31 December 1999

AUDITORS' REPORT TO DELTO (SMALL COMPANY) LIMITED PURSUANT TO SECTION 247B OF THE COMPANIES ACT 1985

We have examined the abbreviated accounts on pages 2 to 4 together with the financial statements of DELTO (SMALL COMPANY) Limited prepared under s226 Companies Act 1985 for the year ended 31 December 1999.

Respective responsibilities of directors and auditors

The directors are responsible for preparing the abbreviated accounts in accordance with ss246(5) and (6) Companies Act 1985. It is our responsibility to form an independent opinion as to the company's entitlement to deliver abbreviated accounts prepared in accordance with those sections and whether the abbreviated accounts have been properly prepared in accordance with those provisions and to report our opinion to you.

Basis of opinion

We have carried out the procedures we considered necessary to confirm, by reference to the audited financial statements, that the company is entitled to deliver abbreviated accounts and that the abbreviated accounts have been properly prepared from those financial statements. The scope of our work for the purpose of this report does not include examining or dealing with events after the date of our report on the full financial statements.

Opinion

In our opinion the company is entitled under ss247, 247A and 249 Companies Act 1985 to deliver abbreviated accounts prepared in accordance with ss246(5) and (6) Companies Act 1985, in respect of the year ended 31 December 1999, and the abbreviated accounts on pages 2 to 4 have been properly prepared in accordance with those provisions.

Verry & Fire
Chartered Accountants and
Registered Auditors
31 March 2000

Thrift House,
Cheapside,
London
EC2V 5TH

Page 1

DELTO (SMALL COMPANY) LIMITED

BALANCE SHEET
31 December 1999

	Note	1999 £	1998 £
FIXED ASSETS			
Tangible assets	2	135,248	136,875
Investments	3	2,000	2,000
		137,248	138,875
CURRENT ASSETS			
Stocks		232,890	212,005
Debtors	4	153,030	181,321
Cash at bank and in hand		100	100
		386,020	393,426
CREDITORS: amounts falling due within one year	5	314,775	335,005

NET CURRENT ASSETS		71,245	58,421
TOTAL ASSETS LESS CURRENT LIABILITIES		208,493	197,296
CREDITORS: amounts falling due after more than one year	5	(30,000)	(32,000)
PROVISIONS FOR LIABILITIES AND CHARGES		(2,300)	(1,560)
		176,193	163,736
CAPITAL AND RESERVES			
Called up share capital	6	50,000	50,000
Share premium account		10,000	10,000
Revaluation reserve		25,000	25,000
Profit and loss account		91,193	78,736
		176,193	163,736

These accounts have been prepared in accordance with the special provisions relating to small companies under section 246 of the Companies Act 1985 with respect to the delivery of individual accounts.

Signed on behalf of the Board of Directors

J. Tramp, Director
Page 2 31 March 2000

DELTO (SMALL COMPANY) LIMITED
NOTES TO THE BALANCE SHEET
Year ended 31 December 1999

1. ACCOUNTING POLICIES

Accounting convention

The financial statements are prepared under the historical cost convention as modified by the revaluation of freehold properties.

Consolidation

The company has taken advantage of the exemption granted under s248 Companies Act 1985 not to prepare group accounts, as the group qualifies as a small group. *[N.B. Paragraph 1(4) of Sch 5 Companies Act 1985 requires the reason for the company not being required to produce group accounts to be stated.]*

Tangible fixed assets

Depreciation is not provided on freehold land. On other assets, it is provided on cost or revalued amount in equal instalments over the estimated lives of the assets. The annual rates of depreciation are as follows:

Freehold buildings	2%
Plant and equipment	10%
Motor vehicles	25%

Stocks

Stocks are stated at the lower of cost and net realisable value. Cost represents materials, direct labour and appropriate overheads.

[Include any other accounting policies including reference to preparing accounts for members in accordance with the FRSSE where the company has done so.]

2. TANGIBLE FIXED ASSETS

	£
Cost or valuation	
At 1 January 1999	304,850
Additions	12,600
Disposals	(2,500)
At 31 December 1999	314,950
Accumulated depreciation	
At 1 January 1999	164,030
Provision	18,172
Disposals	(2,500)
At 31 December 1999	179,702
Net book value	
At 31 December 1999	135,248

Page 3

3. INVESTMENTS

Investments represent the cost of acquiring all of the ordinary share capital of XYZ Limited, a company registered in England and Wales. The share capital and reserves of XYZ Limited at 31 December 1999 were £72,100 and its profit for the year then ended was £4,222.

4. DEBTORS

Debtors include a loan of £5,000 (1998 – £5,000) which falls due after more than one year.

5. CREDITORS

The company has given security in respect of the following bank loans and overdrafts:

	1999 £	1998 £
Falling due within one year	45,244	38,033
Falling due after one year	30,000	32,000

Creditors falling due within one year include £27,505 (1998 – £21,360) owed to Mr Black, a director.

6. CALLED UP SHARE CAPITAL

	1999 £	1998 £
Authorised – 100,000 shares of £1 each	100,000	100,000
Allotted and fully paid – 50,000 shares of £1 each	50,000	50,000

Future developments

35.23 The consultation document from the Company Law Review Steering Group issued in March 2000 *Developing the Framework* asked for comments on a number of proposals for change to the small company reporting regime. These proposals include a simplified format for reports and accounts for smaller companies reducing disclosure below that required by Schedule 8 of the Act (see chapter 34). However, as part of this simplification process, the ability to file abbreviated accounts would be abolished. The consultation period for the above proposals ends on 15 June 2000.

36 Summary financial statements

36 Summary financial statements

Summary of changes since the previous issue of this publication

Para.	Topic	Summary
36.19	Discussion Paper *Year end financial reports: improving communication*	Proposes that the minimum content requirements of the Summary Financial Statements should be the same as those for preliminary announcements, and that they should be supplied by default to all shareholders.
36.20	Consultation document *Developing the framework*	A consultation document from the company law review. The proposals include making preliminary announcements a statutory requirement and hence removing the need for summary financial statements.

Introduction

36.1   The facility for listed companies to issue summary financial statements rather than the full financial statements was introduced by the Companies Act 1989 and the Companies (Summary Financial Statement) Regulations 1990 (SI 1990 no 515) and was initially restricted to the financial statements sent to members. This restriction was relaxed in 1992, so that listed companies may now send copies of a summary financial statement to shareholders, debenture holders and other persons entitled to receive notice of general meetings ('entitled persons') if it has obtained the entitled person's consent and provided the company's Articles or debenture trust deed or governing instrument do not require the full financial statements to be sent to entitled persons. The rules relating to summary financial statements were further revised in 1995 to make it easier for companies to ascertain the wishes of entitled persons. [s251 and SI 1995 No 2092]

36.2   An entitled person gives his consent:

    (a)   if he notifies the company in writing that he wishes to receive a summary financial statement instead of the full financial statements and does not subsequently countermand the instruction; or

    (b)   if he fails to reply to a 'relevant consultation' notice from the company giving him the opportunity to elect to receive summary financial statements, provided that several requirements have been observed, particularly the inclusion with that notice of both full and summary financial statements for a financial year preceding that for which the election is invited; or

    (c)   if he fails to reply to a consultation by notice from the company inviting him to elect to receive summary financial statements. There is no need for full and summary financial statements for a financial year to be sent, but the notice must indicate what the summary financial statements will contain and state that they will not contain sufficient information to allow as full an understanding as would be provided by the full accounts and reports.

36.3   It is no longer necessary to send a reply-paid card to the entitled person with the annual summary financial statement in order to enable the full annual accounts and reports to be requested. However, the summary financial statement must contain a clear, conspicuous statement of how members and debenture holders can:

    (a)   obtain, free of charge, a copy of the company's last full accounts and reports; and

    (b)   elect to receive the full accounts and reports instead of the summary financial statements in all future years.

A failure to respond to a consultation cannot annul an earlier expression of a desire to receive the full financial statements.

Form and content of a summary financial statement

Introduction

36.4   The form and content of a summary financial statement is specified by the Companies (Summary Financial Statement) Regulations 1995 (SI 1995 No 2092). The statement should:

    (a)   include a summary directors' report, profit and loss account and balance sheet. Comparative figures are required in the summary profit and loss account and balance sheet;

    (b)   state that it is only a summary of information in the company's annual accounts and directors' report;

(c)   state the name of the director who signed the statement fol-
      lowing its approval by the board;

(d)   include a statement in a prominent position, to the effect that
      the summary financial statements do not contain sufficient
      information to allow a full understanding of the results and
      state of affairs of the company/group as would be provided by
      the full annual accounts and reports, and that members and
      debenture holders requiring more detailed information have
      the right to obtain, free of charge, a copy of the company's last
      full accounts and reports (see example in **36.5** below);

(e)   contain a clear, conspicuous statement of how members and
      debenture holders can obtain, free of charge, a copy of the com-
      pany's last full accounts and reports and of how members and
      debenture holders can elect to receive the full accounts and
      reports instead of the summary financial statements in all
      future years (see example in **36.6** below);

(f)   contain the auditors' opinion as to consistency with the annual
      accounts and directors' report and compliance with the legislation;

(g)   state whether the auditors' report on the annual accounts was
      unqualified or qualified. If qualified, the statement should set
      out the auditors' report in full, together with any further mate-
      rial needed to understand the qualification; and

(h)   state whether the auditors' report on the annual accounts con-
      tained any reservations about accounting records or obtaining
      necessary information and, if so, set them out in full.

36.5   An example of a statement to the effect that the summary financial
statements do not contain sufficient information to allow a full
understanding of the results and state of affairs is set out below. It
should be noted that, while this statement was once prescribed and
could not be amended, this is no longer the case. SI 1995 No 2092
sets out what is to be covered by the statement, but does not prescribe the words to be used. The statement should appear in a prominent position.

> ### Example 36.5
>
> This summary financial statement does not contain sufficient infor-
> mation to allow as full an understanding of the results of the group and
> state of affairs of the company or of the group as would be provided by
> the full annual accounts and reports. Members and debenture holders
> requiring more detailed information have the right to obtain, free of
> charge, a copy of the company's last full accounts and reports

36.6   The statement of how members and debenture holders can obtain,
free of charge, a copy of the company's last full accounts and reports,

and of how they may elect in writing to receive full accounts and reports in place of the summary financial statements for all future years, should be clear and conspicuous. An example of such a statement is set out below.

> **Example 36.6**
>
> Members and debenture holders who wish to receive, free of charge, a copy of the full annual accounts and reports for the year ended [date] or who wish to receive full accounts and reports in place of the summary financial statements for all future years should write to the company's registrars at [address of registrars] stating their requirements.

36.7   The contents of the summary directors' report, profit and loss account and balance sheet for a company that prepares accounts under Sch 4 are discussed in **36.11** to **36.15** below. Special provisions relate to banking and insurance companies and groups.

36.8   The audit report for a summary financial statement is discussed in **43.48** to **43.53** below.

36.9   The Act and the regulations set a minimum level of information. They do not prevent additional information being added. Indeed, the Listing Rules require that the earnings per share figure should also be given in the summary financial statements.

36.10   The impact of FRS 3 and FRS 4 on the profit and loss account and balance sheet may lead to other headings being added to the summary profit and loss account and summary balance sheet. For example:

(a)   operating profit;

(b)   aggregate of exceptional items shown after operating profit in the full profit and loss account;

(c)   alternative earnings per share figures;

(d)   amount of shareholders' funds, minority interests and dividends attributable to equity and non-equity interests; and

(e)   amount of convertible debt.

Summary directors' report

36.11   The directors' report should include the whole, or a summary, of the text of those parts of the full directors' report concerning the following:

(a) fair review of the development of the business and the position at the year end;

(b) the amount recommended to be paid as dividend, if not disclosed in the summary profit and loss account;

(c) particulars of important post balance sheet events;

(d) likely future developments in the business; and

(e) a list of persons who were directors at any time during the period.

Summary profit and loss account

36.12 The summary profit and loss account for an individual company should show the items below in the order set out and, in each case, under an appropriate heading (allowing alternative descriptions to be used):

(a) turnover;

(b) income from shares in group undertakings and participating interests;

(c) the net figure of other interest receivable and similar income and interest payable and similar charges;

(d) the profit or loss on ordinary activities before taxation;

(e) tax on profit or loss on ordinary activities;

(f) the profit or loss on ordinary activities after taxation;

(g) extraordinary income and charges after tax;

(h) profit or loss for the financial year;

(i) aggregate amount of dividends paid and, if not disclosed in the summary directors' report, proposed;

(j) aggregate directors' emoluments; and

(k) earnings per share (required by the Listing Rules).

36.13 If the annual accounts are group accounts, the summary financial statement should include a summary consolidated profit and loss account. This should give the items noted in **36.12** above, subject to the following modifications:

(a) substitute 'income from interest in associated undertakings' for 'income from shares in group undertakings and participating interests';

(b) insert 'minority interests' after 'the profit or loss on ordinary activities after taxation'; and

(c) show 'extraordinary income and charges after tax' net of the minority interest in that figure.

Summary balance sheet

36.14 The summary balance sheet should show, under an appropriate heading, a single item for each of the headings to which a letter is assigned in the balance sheet formats set out in Sch 4 (see **36.15** below). If the company is required to produce group accounts, only a summarised consolidated balance sheet is required. If an alternative position is permitted in the formats, the summary balance sheet should use the same position as the full balance sheet.

36.15 Summary balance sheet formats:

Format 1

Called up share capital not paid (if not included within 'debtors' in the full balance sheet)

Fixed assets

Current assets

Prepayments and accrued income (if not included within 'debtors' in the full balance sheet)

Creditors: amounts falling due within one year

Net current assets/(liabilities)

Total assets less current liabilities

Creditors: amounts falling due after more than one year

Provisions for liabilities and charges

Accruals and deferred income (if not included within creditors)

Minority interests (if a consolidated balance sheet)

Capital and reserves

Minority interests (alternative position)

Format 2

Assets

Called up share capital not paid (if not included within 'debtors' in the full balance sheet)

Fixed assets

Current assets

Prepayments and accrued income (if not included within 'debtors' in the full balance sheet)

Liabilities

Capital and reserves

Minority interests (if a consolidated balance sheet)

Provisions for liabilities and charges

Creditors (showing separately amounts due within one year and amounts due after one year)

Accruals and deferred income (if not included within creditors).

Corresponding amounts

36.16   Corresponding amounts are required for every item shown in the summary profit and loss account and summary balance sheet, both company and group. The regulations do not specify that corresponding figures be given in respect of the summary directors' report, but it would seem appropriate that they be given for the proposed dividend if that item is disclosed in the summary directors' report rather than the summary profit and loss account.

Examples

36.17   An example of a summary financial statement follows. An example of an appropriate auditors' report is given at **43.48** below.

Example 36.17A

DELTO (SFS) PLC
SUMMARY FINANCIAL STATEMENT
Year ended 31 December 1999

This summary financial statement is only a summary of information in the company's annual accounts and directors' report. It does not contain sufficient information to allow as full an understanding of the results of the group and state of affairs of the company or of the group as would be provided by the full annual accounts and reports. Members and debenture holders requiring more detailed information have the right to obtain, free of charge, a copy of the company's last full accounts and reports for the period ended 31 December 1999.

Members and debenture holders who wish to receive, free of charge, a copy of the full annual accounts and reports for the year ended 31 December 1999, or who wish to receive full accounts and reports in place of the summary financial statements for all future years, should write to the company's registrars at the address shown below stating their requirements. The registrars are Aardvark Nominees Ltd, Serendipity House, Taunton, Devon, England.

SUMMARY DIRECTORS' REPORT

Business Review

Delto (SFS) PLC is the holding company of a group of companies engaged in the manufacture of accessories for the motor trade and costume jewellery.

Despite difficult trading conditions in the motor industry throughout 1999, the directors are pleased to be able to report pre-tax profits up at £2.2 million, compared with £0.85 million for the preceding year, an increase of 164 per cent. Turnover from our continuing business increased by 11 per cent to £35.1 million, due to the exceptionally buoyant demand for our products in North America.

On 30 June 1999, shareholders approved the acquisition for £2 million cash of all the issued share capital of C.P. Plastics Limited, manufacturer of plastic trim for the motor trade. Primarily due to a sharp downturn in the automotive market which could not have been foreseen at the time of the takeover, the company only achieved an operating profit of £22,000 compared with the £30,000 forecast.

Profits retained in the year amounted to £1.1 million. Properties were revalued, giving rise to a £0.5 million deficit. This has led to shareholders' funds increasing by £0.6 million during 1999.

Important post-balance sheet events

A fire destroyed production facilities in Meriden after the end of the financial year. While insurance cover exceeds the net book value of the assets destroyed, the replacement cost of facilities is expected to require considerable additional investment, which cannot be quantified at this time.

Likely future developments in the business

Your directors are optimistic about the long-term prospects for continued growth. The fire at Meriden will significantly affect the completion of orders for bumpers in the first half of 2000, but the replacement of these facilities in the third quarter should result in the resumption of sales, with no permanent loss of business anticipated.

Names of Directors

J. Tramp, Chairman; M. Driver, Managing Director; A. Vagrant FCA; J. Docker; F. Sharp; A. Blackguard.

page 1

DELTO (SFS) PLC

SUMMARY CONSOLIDATED PROFIT AND LOSS ACCOUNT
for the year ended 31 December 1999

	1999 £'000	1998 £'000
TURNOVER	43,180	39,200
OPERATING PROFIT	1,770	1,540
Income from interests in associated undertakings	200	120
Interest payable and similar charges less other interest receivable and similar income	(300)	(330)
PROFIT ON ORDINARY ACTIVITIES BEFORE TAX	2,240	850
Tax on profit on ordinary activities	(770)	(500)
PROFIT ON ORDINARY ACTIVITIES AFTER TAX	1,470	350
Minority interests	20	20
PROFIT FOR THE FINANCIAL YEAR	1,450	330
Dividends paid and proposed	(320)	(244)
Directors' emoluments:	128	121
Earnings per share (Basic and Diluted):	16.9p	2.9p

SUMMARY CONSOLIDATED BALANCE SHEET
as at 31 December 1999

	1999 £'000	1998 £'000
FIXED ASSETS	8,630	9,171
CURRENT ASSETS	14,140	13,438
CREDITORS: amounts falling due within one year	(7,080)	(6,901)
NET CURRENT ASSETS	7,060	6,537
TOTAL ASSETS LESS CURRENT LIABILITIES	15,690	15,708
CREDITORS: amounts falling due after more than one year	(1,390)	(1,770)
PROVISIONS FOR LIABILITIES AND CHARGES	(900)	(1,070)
	13,400	12,868
CAPITAL AND RESERVES	13,180	12,668
Minority interests	220	200
	13,400	12,868

> The auditors' report on the annual accounts was unqualified and did not contain any statement under s237(2) (accounting records or returns inadequate or accounts not agreeing with records and returns) or s237(3) (failure to obtain necessary information and explanations).
>
> Approved by the Board of Directors and signed in their behalf on 5 April 2000 by J. Tramp, Director.
>
> *Page 2*

36.18 Bass plc, in its Annual Review for the year to 30 September 1999 published as a document accompanying its full financial statements, included a summary financial statement. Part of that summary financial statement follows below.

Extract 36.18

profit and loss

	1999	1998	1997
	£m	£m	£m
Adjusted earnings per share	62.3p	57.4p	55.5p
Dividend per share	32.3p	30.0p	27.5p
Turnover	4,686	4,609	5,254
Costs	(3,878)	(3,890)	(4,473)
Share of associates' profit	16	39	20
Operating profit	824	758	801
Exceptional items: major	(110)	183	(237)
other	(2)	(10)	–
Interest	(140)	(97)	(87)
Profit before tax	572	834	477
Tax	(177)	(179)	(212)
Profit after tax	395	655	265
Minority interests	(8)	(5)	(15)
Earnings	387	650	250
Dividends	(277)	(240)	(244)
Retained for reinvestment	110	410	6

cash flow

	1999	1998	1997
	£m	£m	£m
Operations	986	938	1,051
Net capital expenditure	(501)	(587)	(599)
Trade loans	32	27	29
Dividends from associates	10	3	–
Operating cash flow	527	381	481
Interest	(130)	(105)	(91)
Dividends	(250)	(250)	(206)

Taxation	(174)	(152)	(165)
Normal cash flow	(27)	(126)	19
Major disposals/(acquisitions)	–	489	385
Net cash flow	(27)	363	404
Return of capital	(30)	(801)	–
Net debt acquired	(5)	(991)	(3)
Net debt	(1,995)	(1,950)	(555)

net worth

	1999	1998	1997
	£m	£m	£m
Fixed assets	6,335	5,576	5,027
Current assets	1,405	1,396	1,631
Short-term creditors	(1,803)	(1,989)	(1,470)
Net current (liabilities)/assets	(398)	(593)	161
Total assets less current liabilities	5,937	4,983	5,188
Long-term creditors	(2,231)	(2,012)	(1,180)
Provisions	(266)	(272)	(123)
Minority interests	(127)	(122)	(116)
Net assets	3,313	2,577	3,769
Shareholders' funds	3,313	2,577	3,769

This summary financial statement was approved by the Board on 7 December 1999 and signed on its behalf by Sir Ian Prosser and Richard North. It does not contain sufficient information to provide as full an understanding of the results and state of affairs of the Group as that contained in the Annual Report & Financial Statements 1999. That report may be obtained, free of charge, by completing the relevant section of the enclosed proxy card and returning it to Lloyds TSB Registrars.

The auditors have issued an unqualified report on the financial statements containing no statement under Section 237(2) or 237(3) of the Companies Act 1985.

Future developments

ASB discussion paper – Year End Financial Reports: Improving Communication

36.19 The ASB published this paper in February 2000. In its review of the position of summary financial statements in the overall reporting package, the ASB is proposing that the minimum content requirements of the summary financial statement should be the same as those for preliminary announcements, and that they should be supplied by default to all shareholders. The full financial statements would be filed and available to shareholders on request. Recognising that summary financial statements, if expanded to coincide in content with preliminary statements, might become not only longer but also more complex, the ASB suggests that the need to supply ordinary shareholders with understandable information might be better met by giving them the option of receiving a simplified financial review in place of the summary financial statements.

Company law review consultation document - Modern Company Law for a Competitive Economy: Developing the Framework

36.20 Published in March 2000, this paper refers to the ASB's paper (**36.19** above). It welcomes the ASB's proposals for the better uses by companies of the summary financial statements option, and also the possibility of new ASB guidance on the subject. However, the DTI's proposals also include making preliminary announcements a statutory requirement. With that in mind, the paper recognises that there could also be a case for simply withdrawing the summary financial statements option altogether as they may be merely an additional complication giving little benefit once the regime includes statutory prelims.

36.21 The proposed timetable thereafter is for a further consultation document in November 2000 and then a final report in spring 2001.

37 Preliminary announcements

37 Preliminary announcements

Summary of changes since the previous issue of this publication

Para.	*Topic*	*Summary*
37.22	Consultation document *Developing the framework*	A consultation document from the company law review. The proposals include making preliminary announcements a statutory requirement and hence removing the need for summary financial statements.
37.23	Discussion paper *Year-end financial reports: improving communication*	Proposes that the minimum content requirements of the Summary Financial Statements should be the same as those for preliminary announcements, and that they should be supplied by default to all shareholders.

Introduction

37.1 There is no legal requirement for companies to issue a preliminary statement of annual results and dividends.

Listing Rules requirements

Announcement of annual results

37.2 A listed company must notify the Company Announcements Office, without delay after board approval, of the matters relating to its preliminary statement of annual results set out in **37.3** to **37.8** below. [Listing Rules 12.40]. Following the January 2000 revision of the Listing Rules the notification in respect of accounting periods beginning on or after 23 December 1999 should be within 120 days of the accounting period end.

Preliminary statement of annual results

37.3 A preliminary statement of the annual results must:
[Listing Rules 12.40(a)]

(a) have been agreed with the company's auditors;

(b) show the figures in the form of a table, consistent with the presentation to be adopted in the annual accounts for that financial year, including at least the items required for a half-yearly report (see **37.4** below);

(c) if the auditors' report is likely to be qualified, give details of the nature of the qualification; and

(d) include any significant additional information necessary for the purpose of assessing the results being announced.

37.4 The following figures in table form must be included in the preliminary statement:
[Listing Rules 12.40(a)(ii) and 12.52]

(a) a profit and loss account comprising the following:

(i) net turnover;

(ii) operating profit or loss;

(iii) interest payable less interest receivable (net);

(iv) profit or loss before taxation and extraordinary items;

(v) taxation on profits on ordinary activities (UK taxation and, if material, overseas and share of associated undertakings' taxation to be shown separately);

(vi) profit or loss on ordinary activities after tax;

(vii) minority interests;

(viii) profit or loss attributable to shareholders, before extraordinary items;

(ix) extraordinary items (net of taxation);

(x) profit or loss attributable to shareholders;

(xi) rates of dividend(s) paid and proposed and amount absorbed thereby; and

(xii) earnings per share expressed as pence per share;

(b) a balance sheet;

(c) a cash flow statement; and

(d) comparative figures in respect of (a) to (c) for the corresponding period in the preceding financial year.

37.5   A 'grey' area surrounds the question of whether, in addition to basic earnings per share, a listed company has to disclose diluted earnings per share in its preliminary announcement. Listing Rule 12.52 (discussed in **37.4** above) refers only to

> 'earnings per share expressed as pence per share', which could be either basic or diluted earnings per share. The ASB Statement on Preliminary Announcements (see **37.14** to **37.21** below) interprets this as referring to both basic and diluted earnings per share, hence it would seem appropriate to disclose both amounts.

37.6 The UK Listing Authority may authorise the omission from a preliminary statement of any information if it considers that disclosure of such information would be contrary to the public interest or seriously detrimental to the company, provided that, in the latter case, such omission would not be likely to mislead users of the preliminary statement. The request for omission must be in writing with the responsibility placed on the company to ensure the correctness and relevance of the facts on which the request is based. [Listing Rules 12.40(a)(ii) and 12.59]

37.7 In addition, the UK Listing Authority may authorise the omission from a preliminary statement of any information if it considers such omissions necessary or appropriate. [Listing Rules 12.40(a)(ii) and 12.59]

Announcement of dividends

37.8 A listed company must notify the Company Announcements Office, without delay after board approval, of any decision to pay or make any annual dividend or other distribution on listed equity securities or to withhold any dividend or interest payment on listed securities, giving details of:
[Listing Rules 12.40(c)]

(a) the exact net amount payable per share;

(b) the payment date;

(c) the record date (where applicable); and

any foreign income dividend election, together with any income tax treated as paid at the lower rate and not repayable.

Auditors' involvement

37.9 The Listing Rules require that the preliminary statement of the annual results 'must have been agreed with the company's auditors'. Additionally, if the auditors' report is likely to be qualified, the preliminary statement must 'give details of the nature of the qualification' (see **37.3** above). The guidance in **40.21** to **40.29** below explains the position of the auditors; this guidance is not affected by the recommendations of the Statement on Preliminary Announcements published by the ASB in July 1998 (see **37.14** to **37.21** below).

37.10 Preliminary announcements contain comparable information covering the preceding financial year and these figures should be regarded as constituting non-statutory accounts. The Act requires that where a company or group publishes non-statutory accounts (i.e., any balance sheet or profit and loss account relating to any financial year of the company otherwise than as part of the company's statutory accounts, such as a preliminary announcement of annual results which contains information which can be regarded as a balance sheet or profit and loss account), it should publish with them a statement indicating:
[s240]

(a) that the accounts are not the company's statutory accounts;

(b) whether statutory accounts dealing with any financial year with which the non-statutory accounts purport to deal have been delivered to the Registrar of Companies;

(c) whether the auditors have made a report in respect of the statutory accounts and, if so, whether the report was qualified or contained a statement under s237(2) or (3) (i.e., accounting records or returns inadequate, accounts not agreeing with records and returns or failure to obtain necessary information and explanations) or whether any report made for the purposes of s249A(2) (report by a reporting accountant on the accounts of certain small companies) was qualified.

The company must not publish the auditors' report under s235 or any report made for the purposes of s249A(2) (report by a reporting accountant on the accounts of certain small companies) with the non-statutory accounts.

37.11 The term 'publishes' in this context means that the company publishes, issues or circulates the document or otherwise makes it available for public inspection in a manner calculated to invite any member of the public to read it. [s240(4)]

37.12 The examples below suggest forms of words which satisfy the requirements, in the case of unqualified audit reports, and make clear the status of the numbers.

> ### *Example 37.12.1*
>
> **Announcement based on audited accounts (unqualified audit reports)**
>
> The financial information set out above does not constitute the company's statutory accounts for the years ended 31 March 2000 or 1999, but is derived from those accounts. Statutory accounts for 1999 have been delivered to the Registrar of Companies and those for 2000 will be delivered following the company's annual general meeting. The auditors have reported on those accounts; their reports were unqualified and did not contain statements under s237(2) or (3) Companies Act 1985.

> ### *Example 37.12.2*
>
> **Announcement based on draft accounts (unqualified audit report)**
>
> The financial information set out in the announcement does not constitute the company's statutory accounts for the years ended 31 March 2000 or 1999. The financial information for the year ended 31 March 1999 is derived from the statutory accounts for that year which have been delivered to the Registrar of Companies. The auditors reported on those accounts; their report was unqualified and did not contain a statement under s237(2) or (3) Companies Act 1985. The statutory accounts for the year ended 31 March 2000 will be finalised on the basis of the financial information presented by the directors in this preliminary announcement and will be delivered to the Registrar of Companies following the company's annual general meeting.
>
> *Note: In this example 'draft accounts' should be interpreted as 'audit is at an advanced stage' (see guidance in 40.21 to 40.29 below).*

Alternative investment market companies

37.13   Companies with securities which have been admitted to AIM are not required under the Stock Exchange Rules to issue a preliminary statement of annual results and dividends, but may choose to do so.

Best practice

ASB Statement on Preliminary Announcements

37.14   Many companies have expanded the disclosures in their preliminary announcements beyond the requirements of the Listing Rules. However, current practices vary significantly. In order to improve the timeliness, quality and relevance of these communications and aid comparability with previous published accounts, the ASB issued a Statement on Preliminary Announcements in July 1998. The

Statement applies to all entities that are required to issue preliminary statements of annual results. It is commended to companies as a statement of best practice and thus compliance with it is voluntary.

37.15 The Statement emphasises the importance of the timeliness of preliminary announcements and hence encourages companies to issue them within 60 days of the year end. The ASB acknowledges, however, that this might not be practicable for all companies.

37.16 The Statement reiterates the requirements in the Listing Rules in respect of distribution of a preliminary announcement (i.e., that it has to be notified to the UK Listing Authority, which then disseminates it on the Regulatory News Service, and that the UK Listing Authority has to be the first party to receive the announcement). However, while ensuring compliance with the rules, companies are encouraged to make this information available to wider audiences without delay (e.g., using electronic means such as the Internet).

37.17 The Listing Rules require the company's auditors to agree with the release of the preliminary announcement. The overriding consideration is that the information in the preliminary announcements should be reliable and not subject to later alterations. This should be balanced against the potential danger of holding onto price-sensitive information. It is recommended that the audit, if not complete, should be at an advanced stage (see **40.21** to **40.29** below) at the date of the preliminary announcement. It is considered to be helpful to state clearly in the announcement that, where this is the case, the audit report has yet to be signed.

37.18 It is recommended that a preliminary announcement should include a narrative commentary, a summarised profit and loss account, a statement of recognised gains and losses, a summarised balance sheet and a summarised cash flow statement. The information should be presented in a succinct manner, though the specified headings are to act as a recommended minimum only and directors are encouraged to give more detail where they believe it to be helpful.

37.19 The recommended minimum level of disclosure is:

(a) for the profit and loss account:

    (i) turnover;
    (ii) operating profit or loss;
    (iii) interest payable less interest receivable (net);
    (iv) profit or loss on ordinary activities before tax;
    (v) tax on profit or loss on ordinary activities;
    (vi) profit or loss on ordinary activities after tax;
    (vii) minority interests;
    (viii) profit or loss for the period;
    (ix) dividends paid and proposed;

(b)   for the balance sheet:

  (i)   fixed assets;
  (ii)   current assets:
    • stocks;
    • debtors;
    • cash at bank and in hand;
    • other current assets;

  (iii) creditors: amounts falling due within one year;
  (iv)   net current assets/liabilities;
  (v)   total assets less current liabilities;
  (vi)   creditors: amounts falling due after more than one year;
  (vii) provisions for liabilities and charges;
  (viii) capital and reserves;
  (ix)   minority interests;

(c)   for the cash flow statement:

  (i)   headings required by FRS 1 (revised);
  (ii)   reconciliation of operating profit to operating cash flow;
  (iii) reconciliation of the movement of cash in the year with the movement in net debt.

37.20   Other detailed recommendations are as follows.

(a)   The commentary should enable users to appreciate the main factors influencing the company's performance during the financial year and its position at the year end. It is not intended to be as detailed as an operating and financial review, though the directors should consider whether the key issues normally addressed in the operating and financial review should be included in the preliminary announcement.

(b)   Salient features of the second half-year should be discussed. Companies are also encouraged to provide second half-year results, though they are given flexibility as to the extent and manner in which the second half-year results are presented.

(c)   Segmental information should be provided where it is significant to the understanding of the results.

(d)   Accounting policies should be consistent with those in the full financial statements which have yet to be published.

(e)   Comparative figures should be presented for the previous full financial year.

(f)   Information on acquisitions and discontinued operations, exceptional items and earnings per share should be provided in line with FRS 3.

37.21 The Statement does not require disclosures required by FRSs and SSAPs which are not specifically mentioned in the Statement. Some additional disclosures will, however, be required, including:

(a) the period covered by the report;

(b) the date on which it is approved by the directors.

Future Developments

Company law review

37.22 The consultative document published in March 2000 as part of the company law review suggested that the year-end reporting package should be re-focused so as to improve timeliness of information and to provide small private shareholders equality with the City in access to information. Under the proposals, there will be a statutory requirement for listed companies to publish a set of accounts, whose content will be based on the present prelims, within 70 days of the accounting period-end and to send it to all shareholders without delay (see **36.20** above). A full report and accounts will be filed at Companies House within 90 days of accounting period end and will be available to shareholders on request.

37.23 The document proposes that companies will be encouraged to make use of electronic communications, e.g., to place their prelims and full report and accounts on their website; but it goes further in posing the question as to whether companies should be required to do so. The proposals are different from those set out in the ASB discussion paper *"Year-end financial reports: improving communications"* (February 2000) which leaves the role and status of the prelims unchanged (see also **4.162** and **36.19** above).

38　Interim financial reports

38 Interim financial reports

Summary of changes since the previous issue of this publication

Para.	*Topic*	*Summary*
38.2 to 38.22	*Listing Rules*	Amendment 14 to the Listing Rules changed the contents of half-yearly reports and the period within which they are required to be notified to CAO. These changes are effective for reports published in respect of accounting periods beginning on or after 23 December 1999. The same amendment also introduced a new route for listing innovative high growth companies which includes a requirement for quarterly reporting.

Introduction

38.1   There is no legal requirement for companies to prepare an interim financial report. Interim accounts for distribution purposes are addressed in **33.46** to **33.49** above.

Listing Rules requirements

38.2   A company which has listed shares must prepare a report (the half-yearly report), on a group basis where relevant, on its activities and profit or loss for the first six months of each financial year. [Listing Rules 12.46]

38.3   If a company changes its accounting reference date, it must notify the Company Announcements Office without delay. Where the change in accounting reference date results in the extension of the accounting period to more than 14 months, the company must prepare and publish a second interim report, either at the old accounting reference date or at an alternative date within the last six months of the accounting period to cover the period commencing the day after the end of the first interim period to the chosen date. [Listing Rules 12.60]

38.4   Following the revision of the Listing Rules in January 2000, the half-yearly report in respect of accounting periods beginning on or after 23 December 1999 must be published within 90 days of the end of the period to which it relates. In exceptional circumstances, the UK Listing Authority may grant an extension of this time limit. [Listing Rules 12.48]

38.5   A company must publish the half-yearly report by notifying it to the Company Announcements Office, without delay after board approval. [Listing Rules 12.49] In addition, the report must be sent to the shareholders or placed, as a paid advertisement, in at least one national paper. [Listing Rules 12.50]

38.6   The half-yearly report should consist of figures and an explanatory statement relating to the group's activities and profit or loss during the relevant period. [Listing Rules 12.51] The figures to be presented (in table form) are:
[Listing Rules 12.52]

   (a)   a profit and loss account comprising the following:
      (i)   net turnover;
      (ii)   operating profit or loss;
      (iii) interest payable less interest receivable (net);
      (iv)   profit or loss before taxation and extraordinary items;
      (v)   taxation on profits on ordinary activities (UK taxation and, if material, overseas and share of associated undertakings' taxation to be shown separately);
      (vi)   profit or loss on ordinary activities after tax;
      (vii) minority interests;
      (viii) profit or loss attributable to shareholders, before extraordinary items;
      (ix)   extraordinary items (net of taxation);
      (x)   profit or loss attributable to shareholders;
      (xi)   rates of dividend(s) paid and proposed and amount absorbed thereby; and
      (xii) earnings per share expressed as pence per share;

   (l)   a balance sheet;

   (m   a cash flow statement; and

   (d)   comparative figures in respect of (a) to (c) for the corresponding period in the preceding financial year.

38.7   Where items set out in **38.6** above are unsuited to the company's activities, appropriate adjustments should be made. [Listing Rules 12.53]

38.8

> A 'grey' area surrounds the question of whether, in addition to
> basic earnings per share, a listed company has to disclose
> diluted earnings per share in its interim report. Listing Rule
> 12.52 (discussed in **38.6** above) refers only to 'earnings per
> share expressed as pence per share', which could be either basic
> or diluted earnings per share. The ASB statement *Interim
> reports* (see **38.28** to **38.46** below) interprets this as referring to
> basic earnings per share, yet encourages companies which
> choose to present in their annual financial statements addi-
> tional amounts per share based on another level of earnings to
> disclose these additional amounts in their interim statements.
> This encouragement will certainly cover the diluted earnings
> per share, since it is a requirement of FRS 14 *Earnings per share*
> to disclose diluted earnings per share whenever basic earnings
> per share is provided. On balance, taking into account the
> uncertainty as to the exact requirement of the Listing Rules
> and the encouragement in the ASB's statement *Interim reports*,
> it would seem appropriate to disclose both amounts (see also
> **10.17** to **10.19** above).

38.9   The Listing Rules [Listing Rules 12.47] require that the accounting
        policies and presentation applied to interim figures should be con-
        sistent with those applied to the latest published annual accounts,
        unless:

    (a)   the accounting policies and presentation are to be changed in
           the subsequent annual financial statements to ensure consis-
           tency with company law and accounting standards; or

    (b)   the UK Listing Authority otherwise agrees to a change in
           accounting policies and/or presentation.

38.10   If the accounting policies and presentation are changed to ensure
        consistency with company law and accounting standards, the
        changes and the reasons for them should be disclosed in the interim
        report. [Listing Rules 12.47]

38.11   The disclosure required by Listing Rule 12.47 can be given in the
        note setting out the basis of preparation of the interim financial
        statements. The following example suggests one way in which this
        requirement can be met.

> **Example 38.11**
>
> With the following exceptions, the interim accounts, which are unau-
> dited, have been prepared on the basis of the accounting policies set
> out in the 1998 group accounts:
>
> (a)   following the adoption of FRS 9 *Associates and joint ventures*,
>   further disclosures have been provided in respect of the results,

assets, liabilities and cash flows of the group's interests in joint ventures and associates. The comparative figures for 1998 have been restated accordingly, resulting in an increase in both operating profit and the interest charge of £x for the full year and £x for the first half;

(b) following the adoption of FRS 10 *Goodwill and intangible assets*, goodwill arising on acquisitions will be capitalised and amortised over its estimated useful economic life. Goodwill previously eliminated against reserves has not been reinstated;

(c) FRS 11 *Impairment of fixed assets and goodwill* has been adopted, although it has had no effect on the period being reported on;

(d) FRS 14 *Earnings per share* has been adopted, although it has had no effect on the period being reported on, other than the disclosure of diluted earnings per share. This has not previously been published, as it is not materially different from basic earnings per share.

38.12 The question arises as to whether Listing Rule 12.47 means that a disclosure standard like FRS 13 *Derivatives and other financial instruments: disclosures* should be implemented in the interim statements (see chapter 21). In general, new accounting standards usually only affect interim figures if there are changes to recognition, measurement or presentation. An exception to this would be a disclosure of a 'special factor' required under Listing Rule 12.56 (see **38.15** below). Similarly, a disclosure might be appropriate under the best practice provisions as set out in the ASB statement *Interim reports* (see **38.28** to **38.46** below) either as part of the management commentary or as supplementary information.

38.13 The UK Listing Authority may authorise the omission from a half-yearly report of certain of the items of information set out in **38.6** above (see list below), together with their comparatives, if it considers that disclosure of such information would be contrary to the public interest or seriously detrimental to the company, provided that, in the latter case, such omission would not be likely to mislead users of the half-yearly report. The request for omission must be in writing, with the responsibility placed on the company to ensure the correctness and relevance of the facts on which the request is based. The items of information that may be omitted under this procedure are:

(a) net turnover;

(b) profit or loss before taxation and extraordinary items; and

(c)   rates of dividend(s) paid and proposed and amount absorbed thereby.

[Listing Rules 12.58]

38.14   Where the figures in the half-yearly report have been audited or reviewed by auditors pursuant to the APB guidance on review of interim financial information, the auditors' report should be reproduced in full. [Listing Rules 12.54]. In addition to this requirement, where the figures in the half-yearly report have not been audited or reviewed pursuant to APB Bulletin 1999/4, the Bulletin encourages directors to describe interims as 'neither audited nor reviewed' (see **40.30** to **40.36** below, which deal with *interim review* reports).

38.15   The half-yearly report should contain an explanatory statement which includes:

[Listing Rules 12.56]

(a)   any significant information enabling investors to make an informed assessment of the trend of the group's activities and profit or loss;

(b)   an indication of any special factors which have influenced those activities and the profit or loss during the period;

(c)   enough information to enable a comparison to be made with the corresponding period of the preceding financial year; and

(d)   so far as possible, a reference to the group's prospects in the current financial year.

(See also **6.82** above as regards interims and year 2000 issues.)

38.16   The UK Listing Authority may authorise the omission from a half-yearly report of any information (in addition to the items of information already mentioned in **38.13** above) if it considers such omissions necessary or appropriate. [Listing Rules 12.59]

38.17   Where the requirements of the Listing Rules in relation to half-yearly reports are unsuited to the company's activities or circumstances, the UK Listing Authority may require suitable adaptations to be made. [Listing Rules 12.57]

38.18   Some interim profit announcements contain comparable information covering the preceding financial year and these figures should be regarded as constituting non-statutory accounts. The rules regarding the publication of such information are dealt with in **4.133** to **4.135** above.

38.19 Best practice in interim reporting has advanced beyond the requirements of the Listing Rules. The ASB's statement *Interim reports* is covered in **38.28** to **38.46** below.

Innovative high growth companies

38.20 Amendment 14 to the Listing Rules (January 2000) introduced a concessionary route for listing innovative high growth companies without a three year record. This concession comes at a cost of additional continuing obligations, including a requirement to publish a quarterly report on activities. The report should be prepared on a group basis where relevant, and should contain financial and non-financial data, together with explanatory notes, relating to the business operations and the results of the issuer for the reporting period. [Listing Rules 25.13]

38.21 There are some special rules relating to the first year of listing. The first quarterly report shall cover the first three months, the half-yearly report shall cover the first six months and the third quarterly report shall cover the first nine months of the financial year. A fourth quarterly report will not be required if the fourth quarter ends with the financial year end. [Listing Rules 25.14]

38.22 Quarterly reports should be prepared in accordance with the provisions on half-yearly reports as explained in 38.2 to 38.19 above. Where the figures in the quarterly report have been audited or reviewed by auditors pursuant to guidance published by the APB on review of interim financial information, the report of the auditors must be reproduced in full. [Listing Rules 25.15]

Alternative investment market companies

38.23 Companies that have securities which have been admitted to AIM should prepare a half-yearly report within four months of the end of the relevant period and send a copy to the Company Announcements Office. [Stock Exchange Rules 16.19(f)]

> There is no specific guidance on the half-yearly report's form and content, but it is usual for it to be similar to those prepared by listed companies (see **38.2** to **38.19** above).

Current best practice in interim reporting

Introduction

38.24 As mentioned in **38.19** above, best practice in interim reporting has advanced beyond the requirements of the Listing Rules.

38.25 The Cadbury report recommended that interim financial reports should be expanded to increase their value to users. Specific recommendations included the inclusion of balance sheet information and that consideration be given to including cash flow information.

38.26 The Cadbury report also recommended that the ASB, in conjunction with the London Stock Exchange, should clarify the accounting principles which companies should follow in preparing interim financial reports.

38.27 In response to the Cadbury initiative, the Financial Reporting Committee of the ICAEW drew up a consultative paper. Building on the proposals in this paper, the ASB has developed a statement *Interim reports*, September 1997 (see **38.28** to **38.46** below for a summary of the main recommendations of the statement).

ASB Statement on interim reports

38.28 The ASB statement *Interim reports* applies to all entities that are either required to provide interim reports or do so voluntarily. It is commended to companies as a statement of best practice and hence it is for voluntary compliance only. The statement encourages companies to make their interims available within 60 days after the interim period end.

38.29 It is recommended that an interim report should include a narrative commentary, summarised profit and loss account, statement of total recognised gains and losses (where relevant), summarised balance sheet and summarised cash flow statement. The interim accounts should be prepared on a consistent and comparable basis with the annual accounts.

38.30 The recommended minimum headings are:

(a)   for the profit and loss account:

    (i)   turnover;
    (ii)   operating profit or loss;
    (iii) interest payable less interest receivable (net);
    (iv) profit or loss on ordinary activities before tax;
    (v)   tax on profit or loss on ordinary activities;
    (vi) profit or loss on ordinary activities after tax;
    (vii) minority interests;
    (viii) profit or loss for the period;
    (ix) dividends paid and proposed;

(b)   for the balance sheet:
    (i)   fixed assets;
    (ii)   current assets;

- stocks;
- debtors;
- cash at bank and in hand;
- other current assets;

(iii) creditors: amounts falling due within one year;

(iv) net current assets/liabilities;

(v) total assets less current liabilities;

(vi) creditors: amounts falling due after more than one year;

(vii) provisions for liabilities and charges;

(viii) capital and reserves;

(ix) minority interests;

(c) for the cash flow statement:

(i) headings required by FRS 1 (revised 1996);

(ii) reconciliation of operating profit to operating cash flow and reconciliation of the movement of cash in the period with the movement in net debt.

38.31 Other detailed recommendations are as follows:

(a) *the commentary* should be sufficient to enable users to appreciate the main factors influencing the company's performance during the period and its position at the period end. The focus should be on areas of change and key issues normally referred to in the operating and financial review should be considered;

(b) *acquisitions and discontinued operations* should be disclosed separately on the face of the profit and loss account in accordance with FRS 3;

(c) *segmental analysis* of turnover and profit/loss before interest should be provided in a manner similar to that disclosed in the annual report;

(d) *exceptional items* should be recognised and disclosed in the profit and loss account of the interim period in which they occur;

(e) *earnings per share*, both basic and any additional where provided in the annual financial statements, should be derived from the results for the interim period;

(f) recognition of the *value changes of assets* held at valuation will depend upon the nature of the assets and the difficulty of obtaining valuations;

(g) *comparative figures* for the profit and loss account and cash flow statement should be provided for both the corresponding interim period and the previous financial year;

(h) *comparative figures* for the balance sheet should be provided for the previous financial year.

38.32 The ASB statement suggests that disclosures required by FRSs and SSAPs but not specifically mentioned in the statement could be omitted. Some additional disclosures will, however, be required:

(a) the period covered by the report;

(b) the date on which it is approved by the directors; and

(c) the extent to which the information it contains has been audited or reviewed.

Measurement of interim results

38.33 One of the issues that arises when preparing interim financial reports is whether such reporting should involve the same accounting principles as are used at the year end or whether different principles should be applied.

38.34 There are two fundamentally different approaches: the 'discrete' period approach and the 'integral' approach. The discrete period approach treats each interim period as an accounting period in isolation, whereas the integral approach treats the interim period as part of the annual period and attempts to relate the interim results to the expected results for the year. The essential difference between the two approaches is that, under the integral method, items are allocated to interim periods based on estimates of the total revenue and expenses. Consequently, profits fluctuate less under the integral approach than under the discrete approach.

38.35 The ASB statement recommends the discrete approach. The only exceptions to this principle are:

(a) taxation – the interim tax charge should be based on an estimate of the likely effective tax rate for the year (see **38.36** to **38.46** below); and

(b) expenses/income determined on an annual basis (e.g., contractual supplier volume discount should be calculated as a proportion of the expected annual discount).

The result is a 'combined' approach, under which interim reports are prepared under the discrete approach, in the same manner as annual financial statements, but 'integral' adjustments are made to ensure that the interim financial reports are not misleading.

Tax charge in interim financial statements

38.36 As noted above, listed companies are required to prepare a half-yearly or interim report reflecting a charge for UK and overseas taxation in arriving at the half-year profit (or loss) on ordinary activities after taxation. Questions arise as to how this tax charge should be calculated. Applying the discrete approach to the tax charge will not result in a meaningful figure, since it will not take account of capital allowances and other adjustments that affect the effective annual rate. Therefore, the ASB statement *Interim reports* recommends that the tax rate to be applied to the interim profit or loss on ordinary activities should be based so far as practicable on the effective annual tax rate. If group profits are being reported, the effective annual tax rate of the group should be applied to the interim profits of the group. The application of this principle is dealt with below.

Calculation of effective annual tax rate

39.37 The calculation of the effective annual tax rate is based on the formula (expressed as a percentage):

$$\frac{\text{Estimated annual tax charge or credit}}{\text{Estimated annual profit or loss on ordinary activities before taxation}}$$

38.38 In applying this formula, the following should be taken into account:

(a)   the estimated annual tax charge or credit should be calculated using the same degree of prudence as would be applied in the annual financial statements and should follow the rules laid down in FRS 16 (see chapter 27). The treatment of losses is considered in **38.41** to **38.45** below;

(b)   permanent and timing tax differences should be recognised rateably over the year as a whole;

(c)   exceptional items and the related tax should be excluded from the calculations. Exceptional gains or losses in the second half of the year should not be anticipated, unless the events which give rise to such gains or losses are virtually certain to occur.

38.39 The effective tax rate thus calculated should then be applied to the interim profit or loss on ordinary activities (subject to the restrictions mentioned in the paragraphs below arising from trading losses or losses brought forward).

38.40 The following example illustrates the application of the above rules to a routine set of circumstances.

> **Example 38.40**
>
> £
>
> Profit before taxation for the interim period   500,000
>
> The estimated results for the full year are as follows:

Profit before tax	1,500,000
Capital allowances in excess of depreciation	
(assuming no deferred tax is required)	(400,000)
Disallowed expenses	100,000
Taxable profit	1,200,000
Tax payable at 30% of £1,200,000	360,000
The effective annual tax rate is:	
£360,000/£1,500,000, i.e., 24%	
The tax charge to be included in the	
interim statement is:	
£500,000 @ 24%	£120,000

Note that it is not necessary (and not practicable) to estimate the capital allowances available for the interim period.

Treatment of losses

38.41 Difficult questions sometimes arise in regard to the treatment of losses.

38.42 The company may accumulate tax losses or suffer a trading loss in one or both halves of a year. If the tax losses can be used (e.g., by applying them against profits of the previous year) or it is estimated with reasonable certainty that there will be sufficient profits in the full year to absorb the losses, then the estimated effective annual tax charge (or the amount recoverable) should be apportioned over the two half-years by reference to accounting profits or losses. No credit should be taken for tax to be recovered if sufficient profits are neither available nor predictable.

38.43 The following chart gives guidance on the availability of losses in calculating the interim period's tax charge.

Are there losses brought forward from prior years?			
Yes		No	
Trading results for interim period		Trading results for interim period	
Trading loss	Profit	Trading loss	Profit
Credit for trading losses and losses brought forward should not be taken into account, except in the rare instance where sufficient profits in the remaining period can be predicted with reasonable certainty to absorb such losses.	Credit for losses brought forward should be applied to the extent that forecast annual profits will absorb the losses, the relief to be taken pro rata over the full year. The example in **38.44** below demonstrates this rule.	Credit for recovery of prior years' taxes by carryback of interim period's trading losses and first year allowances can be taken into account. No consideration should be given to forecast profits or losses in remaining period, unless they can be predicted with reasonable certainty.	No consideration should be given to forecast losses in the remaining period, unless they can be predicted with reasonable certainty.

38.44 If, in the example in **38.40** above, the company had trading losses brought forward of £400,000, this would have the effect of reducing the estimated taxable profit for the year to £800,000, which at 30 per cent gives a tax liability of £240,000. The effective annual rate becomes £240,000/£1,500,000, i.e., 16 per cent, and the tax liability on the interim period is £500,000 at 17.6 per cent, i.e., £80,000.

38.45 The rule for limitation of loss utilisation against the results of the first half-year set out in **38.42** above is demonstrated in the following example.

Example 38.45

	£
First half-year taxable profits	100,000
Expected second half-year tax loss	(40,000)
Tax loss brought forward	(75,000)
Loss utilisation is as follows:	
First half-year profit	100,000
Less: loss utilised (restricted to 100,000 – 40,000)	(60,000)
Taxable profit	40,000
Second half-year loss	40,000
Taxable profits in the year	NIL
Resulting tax charge for the year	NIL

Comparative figures

38.46 The comparative figures should be based on the actual tax rate for the previous full year. Companies may not wish to alter previously published figures. However, where the actual tax rate is significantly different from the rate used in last year's interim statement, restatement using the actual rate should be encouraged.

Combined Code on Corporate Governance: provisions in relation to interims

38.47 The Combined Code principle D.1 states that the board should present a balanced and understandable assessment of the company's position and prospects. Code provision D.1.2 emphasises that this applies inter alia to interim reports. (See chapter 7 as regards corporate governance generally and appendix IV for the Combined Code.)

Review of interim financial reports by auditors

38.48 Although there is no requirement for half-yearly reports of listed companies to be audited (see **38.14** above), the auditors are frequently asked by the directors to review these statements before they are published and sent to their members. Such reviews are dealt with in **40.30** to **40.36** below.

39 Reports on audited financial statements

39 Reports on audited financial statements

Summary of changes since the previous issue of this publication

Para.	Topic	Summary
39.24	FRSSE 2000	Reflecting in audit report the version of the FRSSE which applies for any given year.
39.27	Identification of nationality of law and accounting standards	Indicating in audit report nationality of law and accounting standards under which the financial statements have been prepared, in accordance with an agreement between the International Forum for Accountancy Developments and leading global regulators.
39.27	APB Bulletin 1999/5 *The Combined Code: requirements of auditors under the Listing Rules of the London Stock Exchange*	Changes to wording of responsibilities statement in audit report arising from audit, review and read responsibilities of auditors.
39.37	Identification of nationality of auditing standards	Indicating in audit report nationality of auditing standards under which the financial statements have been audited. This is in response to an agreement between the International Forum for Accountancy Developments and leading global regulators.
39.43, 39.132, 39.146	SAS 601 *Imposed limitation of audit scope*	Auditors should refuse to accept an engagement where the scope of their work is limited to the extent that a disclaimer of opinion will be likely to result.

39.193, 39.195	SAS 160 (Revised) *Other information in documents containing audited financial statements*	Requires auditors to read other information and consider their actions where misstatements and/or inconsistencies are identified.

General requirements

SAS 600 Auditors' reports on financial statements

39.1   In May 1993, the APB issued SAS 600 *Auditors' reports on financial statements*. The auditing standards contained in SAS 600 are reproduced in the paragraphs below in **bold** type. They represent the basic principles and essential procedures with which auditors are required to comply. Apparent failures by auditors to comply with them are liable to be enquired into by the appropriate committee established under the authority of the relevant accountancy body and disciplinary or regulatory action may result. SAS 600 is accompanied by explanatory material which is designed to assist auditors in interpreting and applying auditing standards.

39.2   SAS 600 applies to all audit reports which express an opinion in terms of whether the financial statements give a true and fair view or where statutory or other specific requirements prescribe the use of such terms as 'presents fairly' or 'properly prepared in accordance with'.

39.3   The term 'financial statements' used in SAS 600 is defined as 'the balance sheet, profit and loss account (or other form of income statement), statements of cash flows and total recognised gains and losses, notes and other statements and explanatory material, all of which are identified in the auditors' report as being the financial statements'. [SAS 600(9)] The view given in the financial statements is derived from a combination of fact and judgement and consequently cannot be characterised as either 'absolute' or 'correct'. When reporting on financial statements, therefore, auditors provide a level of assurance which is reasonable in that context, but equally cannot be absolute. Consequently, it is important that the reader of financial statements is made aware of the context in which the auditors' report is given. Therefore, the requirements of SAS 600 are intended to achieve informative reporting by auditors within the reporting obligations on auditors.

Companies Act requirements

39.4   The majority of audit reports issued are reports on companies incorporated under the Companies Acts and the relevant legislation is contained in the Companies Act 1985.

39.5   Company audits can only be undertaken by an auditor who is registered with a recognised supervisory body. The ICAEW is recognised to register and supervise its members as auditors and keeps a list of registered auditors available to the public.

39.6 'Registered auditors' are required to make a report to the members of the company on all annual accounts of which copies are laid before the company in general meeting during their tenure of office. If a private company elects not to hold an annual meeting, then the auditors must still report on the accounts sent to the members. For the purposes of the Act, annual accounts comprise balance sheets and profit and loss accounts and the information required by the Act to be given in the notes to them.

39.7 The auditors' report must state their opinion on whether the annual accounts:

(a) have been properly prepared in accordance with the Act; and

(b) give a true and fair view of the state of affairs of the company as at the end of the financial year and of its profit or loss for the financial year. [s235] However special considerations apply to auditors' reports on banking and insurance companies and on companies which qualify for and claim exemption as a 'small company' (see **42.10**, **42.13** and **39.86** below respectively).

39.8 The auditors have a further duty to carry out such investigations as will enable them to form an opinion as to whether or not:

(a) proper accounting records have been kept by the company and proper returns adequate for the audit have been received from branches not visited;

(b) annual accounts are in agreement with the accounting records and returns,

and must consider whether the information given in the directors' report is consistent with those accounts. If the auditors are of the opinion that any of the above requirements have not been met, they must state that fact in their report. [ss235 and 237]

39.9 If the disclosures required by Sch 6 (directors' emoluments and other benefits and directors' loans and transactions) have not been given in the financial statements, the auditors must include in their report, so far as they are reasonably able to do so, a statement giving the required particulars. [s237]

39.10 The auditors also have a duty to report if they have not obtained all the information and explanations they require for the purposes of their audit. [s237]

39.11 The absence of any statement on the above matters in the auditors' report is, therefore, equivalent to an assurance that the auditors have satisfied themselves on those matters.

Position of the audit report

39.12   The explanatory material in SAS 600 states that it will aid communication with the reader if the auditors' report is placed before the financial statements and, where the directors set out their responsibilities themselves, if this description is immediately before the auditors' report. While explanatory material is not mandatory, it is indicative of good practice and therefore directors (or their equivalent) should be encouraged to position the auditors' report in this manner.

Form of the audit report

39.13   SAS 600 sets out the form and sections of the auditors' reports, requiring that they **should include the following matters:** [SAS 600(14)]

   (a)   **a title identifying the person or persons to whom the report is addressed;**

   (b)   **an introductory paragraph identifying the financial statements audited;**

   (c)   **separate sections, appropriately headed, dealing with:**

      (i)   **respective responsibilities of directors (or equivalent persons) and auditors;**
      (ii)   **the basis of the auditors' opinion;**
      (iii)   **the auditors' opinion on the financial statements;**

   (d)   **the manuscript or printed signature of the auditors; and**

   (e)   **the date of the auditors' report.**

39.14   Although SAS 600 does not require each of the above elements to be given in the order listed above, it is expected that most auditors will do so, as it is clearly intended to establish a standard format to assist the reader in understanding from the report (which is much enlarged from the standard two-paragraph report previously given) the various matters which are of relevance.

39.15   SAS 600 does not prescribe the wording for each section heading, but there should be headings which indicate the nature of the matters contained in the section concerned. The examples of auditors' reports on financial statements given in the appendix to the standard ('the report examples') suggest the use of the following headings:

   •   'Respective responsibilities of directors and auditors';

- 'Basis of opinion'; and

- 'Opinion',

and these headings have become standard wording where an opinion is expressed. It is also suggested in the report examples that where a report which is other than unqualified is given, the opinion section heading might be expanded to indicate the reason for giving other than an unqualified opinion. This might include wording such as:

- 'Qualified opinion arising from disagreement about ...';

- 'Adverse opinion';

- 'Disclaimer of opinion on view given by financial statements ...'; or

- 'Qualified opinion arising from limitation in audit scope'.

39.16   Each of these elements of the auditors' report are discussed in detail below. Examples of unqualified reports are set out in **39.84** to **39.105** below.

Title and addressee

39.17   SAS 600 requires an introductory title which identifies the addressee. The title should contain an appropriate phrase, such as 'auditors' report', to distinguish the auditors' report from other information accompanying it. Reports issued on the statutory financial statements of companies should be addressed to the members of the company.

> ### Example 39.17
>
> **AUDITORS' REPORT TO THE MEMBERS OF DELTO PLC**

39.18   The report examples attached to SAS 600 are addressed to the 'shareholders' of the company. As the Act requires the auditors to report to the company's members, it would appear to be more correct that statutory audit reports for companies should be addressed to the members and not to the shareholders. This would also deal with the situations where there are no shareholders, e.g., companies limited by guarantee and companies which issue stock rather than shares.

39.19   A change in the company's name during the accounting period, or after the year end but before the accounts are approved, should be disclosed by mentioning the former name in the heading of the report.

> **Example 39.19**
>
> AUDITORS' REPORT TO THE MEMBERS OF DELTO (UK) LTD
> (formerly Delto (Birmingham) Limited)

39.20

> Reports on financial statements other than for companies should be addressed to the individuals or bodies as prescribed by statute or by the terms of the engagement. They should not be addressed to the members, unless the auditor is specifically engaged to do so. Normally, in such circumstances, he will either report to the directors (or their equivalent) or preferably to the entity itself.

Identification of financial statements

39.21   SAS 600 requires the auditors' report to include **'an introductory paragraph identifying the financial statements audited'**. [SAS 600(14b)] Usually, the financial statements are accompanied by other financial information, such as that contained in the directors' report, chairman's statement and historical summaries. Apart from being satisfied that the information given in the directors' report is not inconsistent with the financial statements, the auditors have no responsibility under the Act to provide an opinion on this information. It is important, therefore, to identify clearly the financial statements to which the auditors' opinion relates and this is best done by identifying by numbers the pages which contain the financial statements. The report examples do not include a heading for the explanatory paragraph and it is suggested that no such heading be created, as it would serve little purpose. The term 'scope paragraph' previously used by auditors should not be used.

39.22   In accordance with the policy adopted by the ASB and supported by the APB, the audit report should normally refer to 'financial statements' instead of the 'accounts and notes'. Reference in the directors' report should also be to financial statements. However, consistency of terminology is desirable and if the directors insist on using a term like 'accounts and notes' to describe the company's financial statements, then the audit report should do the same.

39.23

> The explanatory material suggests that the introductory paragraph may refer to the accounting convention and accounting policies followed. A footnote to one of the report examples suggests that a reference to the convention draws attention to the fact that the values reflected in the financial statements are not current but historical and, where appropriate, to the fact that there is a mixture of past and recent values. However,

> given that the vast majority of accounts are prepared under the historical cost convention modified by the revaluation of certain fixed assets, a reference to the accounting convention would appear to add little to the readers' understanding of the financial statements that is not readily apparent when reading the notes to the accounts; accordingly, such a reference would appear to be unnecessary, except where the auditors conclude that a significant departure from the historical cost convention warrants it.

Companies complying with the FRSSE

39.24 APB Bulletin 1997/3 *The FRSSE: guidance for auditors* states that in view of the relevance of the use of the FRSSE to an appreciation of the financial statements, auditors are encouraged to refer to it in the introductory paragraph of their report.

> ### Example 39.24
>
> We have audited the financial statements on pages 9 to 22, which have been prepared in accordance with the Financial Reporting Standard for Smaller Entities (effective March 2000) and under the accounting policies set out on page 9.

39.25 As the FRSSE is updated on a regular basis, it is helpful to indicate, as shown in the above example, which version is being applied.

Responsibilities of directors and auditors

39.26 SAS 600 requires the auditors' report to include a separate section stating the respective responsibilities of directors (or equivalent persons) and auditors. [SAS 600(20)] In this section:

'(a) **Auditors should distinguish between their responsibilities and those of the directors by including in their report:**

(i) a statement that the financial statements are the responsibility of the reporting entity's directors;

(ii) a reference to a description of those responsibilities when set out elsewhere in the financial statements or accompanying information; and

(iii) a statement that the auditors' responsibility is to express an opinion on the financial statements.

(b) **Where the financial statements or accompanying information (for example the directors' report) do not include an adequate statement of directors' relevant responsibilities, the auditors' report should include a description of those responsibilities.'**

39.27 The report examples indicate (a)(i) is fulfilled by stating that 'the company's directors are responsible for the preparation of financial statements' and that (a)(iii) is fulfilled by stating that 'it is our responsibility to form an independent opinion, based on our audit, on the financial statements prepared by the directors and to report our opinion to you'. Some additional wording, over and above that required under SAS 600 above, is included in our example wording in **39.84, 39.96,** and **40.4** below, in order to identify the nationality of the accounting standards and law under which the financial statements have been prepared. This is in response to an agreement by the International Forum for Accountancy Developments with leading global regulators and a concern that it is not always clear from reports which standards are being followed.

APB Bulletin 1999/5 and listed companies

The wording of the auditors' responsibilities statement in **40.4** below is longer than that in **39.84** and **39.96** below, since APB Bulletin 1999/5 *The Combined Code: requirements of auditors under the Listing Rules of the London Stock Exchange*, recommends auditors of listed companies, for financial periods ending on or after 23 December 1999, to include in the statement of responsibilities a description of their 'audit, review and read' responsibilities. In a footnote to that Bulletin, the APB also encourages auditors of entities other than listed companies to include a full description of the auditors' responsibilities. However, the Bulletin does not provide any examples of wording for responsibilities statements for entities other than listed companies, so it is a matter of choice as to whether such entities should include additional wording until the APB provides specific guidance in this area. In the probably unlikely event that such an entity should wish to include additional wording, a suggested text, which may be appropriate until such time as specific guidance appears from the APB, is given in the following example.

> **Example 39.27**
>
> **Extract from audit report for a group which is not listed**
>
> **Respective responsibilities of directors and auditors**
>
> As described on page 10, the company's directors are responsible for the preparation of financial statements, which are required to be prepared in accordance with applicable United Kingdom law and accounting standards. It is our responsibility to form an independent opinion, based on our audit, on those statements and to report our opinion to you as described below.
>
> We report to you our opinion as to whether the financial statements give a true and fair view and are properly prepared in accordance with the Companies Act 1985. We also report to you if, in our opinion, the

> directors' report is not consistent with the financial statements, if the company has not kept proper accounting records, if we have not received all the information and explanations we require for our audit or if information specified by law regarding directors' remuneration and transactions with the company and other members of the group is not disclosed.
>
> We read the other information contained in the annual report and consider whether it is consistent with the audited financial statements. We consider the implications for our report if we become aware of any apparent misstatements or material inconsistencies with the financial statements.

39.28   What normally constitutes an adequate description of company directors' responsibilities in the context of a company's statutory financial statements is given in the explanatory material to SAS 600. According to that explanatory material, such a description will normally be considered adequate when it includes directors' responsibilities to:

(a)   prepare in accordance with company law financial statements for each financial year which give a true and fair view of the company's (or group's) state of affairs at the end of the year and profit or loss for the year then ended;

(b)   select suitable accounting policies and then apply them on a consistent basis, making judgements and estimates that are prudent and reasonable;

(c)   state whether applicable accounting standards have been followed, subject to any material departures disclosed and explained in the financial statements (this applies only to large companies, i.e., companies which are not small or medium-sized companies as defined by the Act);

(d)   apply the going concern basis, unless it is not appropriate to presume that the company will continue in business (only necessary where no separate statement on going concern is made by the directors);

(e)   keep proper accounting records;

(f)   safeguard the assets of the company (or group) and take reasonable steps for the prevention and detection of fraud and other irregularities.

These responsibilities apply to most corporate entities, but will need to be adapted for different legal requirements applicable to entities not subject to the Act.

39.29   For reporting entities other than companies, the adequacy of the description should be assessed by reference to statutory or other specific requirements with which the principals or management of those entities are required to comply.

39.30   Situations may arise where the directors (or equivalent persons) are not minded to include all of the responsibilities listed above in their description which would normally be considered necessary to constitute adequate disclosure. In such circumstances, the auditors should give consideration as to what is normally considered adequate for the type of entity and where there are omissions include appropriate details in their report. In most cases, directors will agree to include a full description of their responsibilities when they appreciate that the alternative is a statement in the audit report giving the required particulars.

39.31   The following example for a company incorporated under the Companies Act is based on the example given in SAS 600. [SAS 600 Appendix 3] It is suitable for inclusion in the directors' statement of responsibilities or in the auditors' report when the directors do not include a description of their responsibilities.

Example 39.31

Company law requires the directors to prepare financial statements for each financial year which give a true and fair view of the state of affairs of the company as at the end of the financial year and of the profit or loss of the company for that period. In preparing those financial statements, the directors are required to

(a)   select suitable accounting policies and then apply them consistently;

(b)   make judgements and estimates that are reasonable and prudent;

(c)   state whether applicable accounting standards have been followed, *subject to any material departures disclosed and explained in the financial statements* (applies to large companies only);

(d)   prepare the financial statements on the going concern basis, unless it is inappropriate to presume that the company will continue in business (only necessary where no separate statement on going concern is made by the directors).

The directors are responsible for keeping proper accounting records which disclose with reasonable accuracy at any time the financial position of the company and to enable them to ensure that the financial statements comply with the Companies Act 1985. They are also responsible for safeguarding the assets of the company and hence for taking reasonable steps for the prevention and detection of fraud and other irregularities.

Note:
It is suggested that the words in *italics* be included only if there is a

---

material departure from applicable accounting standards. Otherwise, they may give a misleading impression that there has been a material departure in circumstances in which there is no departure.

Where the auditors are forced to include the above description in their report, they are required also to make the statements referred to in **39.26** (a)(i) and (iii) above. It is suggested that (a)(i) be dealt with at the beginning of the section on the responsibilities of directors and auditors and (a)(iii) at the end.

See **39.97** below for situations in which group accounts are prepared.

39.32   Directors are required to give a description rather than a statement of their responsibilities and therefore it is acceptable to have as an alternative to a separate statement a section of the directors' report headed up as 'Directors' responsibilities'. In such circumstances, however, it is recommended that such a section is the final section of the directors' report, so as to be next to the auditors' report which follows it. Any modifications suggested by the directors will need to be considered to determine whether they undermine the adequacy of the description.

39.33   It is to be hoped that the APB can issue a Practice Note to give guidance on descriptions of responsibilities for entities which are not companies. The following example of a statement of responsibility is suitable for an entity (in this case, a sole proprietor) whose reporting requirements are not governed by legislation or constitution and the auditors are asked to report in 'true and fair' terms.

Example 39.33

The proprietor is responsible for the preparation of financial statements which give a true and fair view. In preparing them, the proprietor is required to select suitable accounting policies and then apply them consistently, make judgements and estimates that are reasonable and prudent, and to prepare the financial statements on the going concern basis, unless it is inappropriate to presume that the proprietor will continue in business. The proprietor is also responsible for taking reasonable steps for the prevention and detection of fraud and other irregularities.

39.34   An appendix to SAS 600 refers to the term 'statement of directors' responsibilities' and it is suggested that this is the most appropriate heading where there is a separate statement.

Circumstances requiring an alternative to a true and fair opinion

39.35   In some circumstances, auditors may be required to report whether the financial statements have been properly prepared in accordance with regulations or other requirements, but are not required to report on whether they give a true and fair view. Where special circumstances exist, the reporting entity may be required by regulations or other requirements to adopt policies or accounting bases which do not permit a true and fair view to be given. The explanatory material supporting SAS 600 makes it clear that, in such cases, the auditors should refer to these circumstances in the paragraphs dealing with the respective responsibilities of the directors and auditors (unless the requirements are included in a separate statement given by the directors) and may draw attention to them in the basis of opinion section of their report. The auditors' opinion would normally be expressed in terms of whether the financial statements are 'properly prepared in accordance with ... '. The accounting policy note in the financial statements should be comprehensive and give details of any departures from fundamental accounting concepts and significant departures from accounting standards.

Basis of auditors' opinion

39.36   SAS 600 requires the auditors to explain, in a separate section, **'the basis of their opinion, by including in their report:**
[SAS 600(24)]

(a)   **a statement as to their compliance or otherwise with auditing standards, together with the reasons for any departure therefrom;**

(b)   **a statement that the audit process includes:**

    (i)   **examining, on a test basis, evidence relevant to the amounts and disclosures in the financial statements;**

    (ii)   **assessing the significant estimates and judgements made by the reporting entity's directors in preparing the financial statements;**

    (iii)   **considering whether the accounting policies are appropriate to the reporting entity's circumstances, consistently applied and adequately disclosed;**

(c)   **a statement that they planned and performed the audit so as to obtain reasonable assurance that the financial statements are free from material misstatement, whether caused by fraud or other irregularity or error, and that they have evaluated the overall presentation of the financial statements.'**

39.37   Where the auditors are required by statute to follow other auditing standards which are comparable to those issued by the APB (e.g., the

Code of Audit Practice for Local Authorities and the National Health Service in England and Wales), the auditors are to refer to these standards. See chapter 42 below (specifically **42.110** to **42.124**), where the auditors are required to report under IASs or generally accepted auditing standards in the USA. Some additional wording, over and above that required under SAS 600 above, is included in our example wording in **39.84**, **39.96** and **40.4** below, in order to identify the nationality of the auditing standards under which the financial statements have been audited. This is in response to an agreement between the International Forum for Accountancy Developments and leading global regulators.

39.38 In exceptional circumstances, the auditors may depart from auditing standards in order to carry out the objectives of the audit more effectively. In such cases, the reasons for the departure must be given in the audit report. Unless a departure from an auditing standard affecting significant information in the financial statements can be justified, it constitutes a limitation in the scope of the audit and will result in a qualified opinion or a disclaimer of opinion (see **39.128** and **39.130** below).

Added emphasis

39.39 An additional paragraph at the end of the 'Basis of opinion' section should be included in the audit report to:

(a) refer to a fundamental uncertainty as required by SAS 600 (see **39.70** below); or

(b) highlight other important matters which the auditors regard as relevant to a proper understanding of the basis of their opinion (e.g., an unusual accounting policy or significant post balance sheet event). It is expected that such matters will be rare.

39.40 The expression 'emphasis of matter' is not included in SAS 600 and should no longer be used. The term which has been used by the APB to refer to an additional paragraph is an 'added emphasis'.

Auditors' opinion

39.41 In a separate section of the audit report dealing with the auditors' opinion, the auditors' report is required by SAS 600 to **'contain a clear expression of opinion on the financial statements and on any further matters required by statute or other requirements applicable to the particular engagement'**. [SAS 600(30)] The opinion is **'based on review and assessment of the conclusions drawn from evidence obtained in the course of the audit'**. [SAS 600(2)]

39.42 The auditors' opinion is expressed in the context of the particular accounting requirements applicable to the financial statements and normally includes giving an opinion on whether the financial statements give a true and fair view and whether or not those accounting requirements have been met. In most cases, compliance with accounting standards is necessary for giving a true and fair view. For statutory audits of many commercial enterprises incorporated in Great Britain, the opinion is expressed in terms of whether the financial statements give a true and fair view of the financial position and profit or loss and whether they have been properly prepared in accordance with the Act. The position of small companies which take advantage of following Sch 8 is discussed in **39.86 to 39.90** below.

39.43   Where the auditors cannot express an opinion, either because of a limitation in the scope of the auditors' examination or because the auditors disagree with the treatment or disclosure of a matter in the financial statements, a qualified opinion, disclaimer of opinion or adverse opinion is given. Further sections of this chapter discuss in detail and give examples of each type of opinion. Note that following the issue of SAS 601 *Imposed limitation of audit scope*, auditors have a duty to consider whether those who appoint them will impose a limitation on the scope of their work, which they consider likely to result in the need to issue a disclaimer of opinion. In these circumstances, the auditors should not accept that engagement, unless required to do so by statute.

Reporting periods

39.44   If the period reported upon is other than a year, it is preferable to refer in the opinion to the precise period, e.g., 'for the six months then ended' and not 'for the period then ended'.

Reporting on 'profit or loss'

39.45   The Act requires that the profit and loss account gives a true and fair view of the profit or loss for the financial year. The opinion should refer to a profit for the year or to a loss for the year, depending on whether the item in the profit and loss formats entitled 'profit or loss for the financial year' (i.e., after tax and extraordinary items) is a profit or a loss.

Identification of the auditors

Name and signature of the auditors

39.46   SAS 600 requires the auditors' report to include **'the manuscript or printed signature of the auditors'**. [SAS 600(14d)] This standard complements the legal requirement of s236 for audit reports of companies incorporated under the Act to state the names of the auditors and for the copy of the audit report which is delivered to the

Registrar of Companies also to be signed by them. Normally, it will be in the name of a firm; in which case, the person signing it must be authorised to sign it on the firm's behalf (an authorised person must be a 'responsible individual' under audit regulations). In practice, one manually signed copy of the audit report to be filed with the Registrar is delivered to the company and additional copies have the signature photocopied or otherwise reproduced.

Auditors' qualifications and address

39.47   To assist identification, the auditors' qualifications and the location of their office are normally given. The office address is usually shown opposite the title 'Registered auditors'. It is suggested that where a letterhead is used, the statement of directors' responsibilities be set out on the previous page.

39.48   Audit reports of companies incorporated under the Act and of any other entity requiring a registered auditor must state the name of the registered auditor and be signed in that name. Where an accounting firm is registered under its own name, rather than individually for each partner, it is permissible to use either the singular term 'Registered auditor' or the plural 'Registered auditors'. In such circumstances, chartered accountants are entitled to sign as 'Chartered accountants and Registered auditors'.

39.49   Note that it is very important to check the constitution of entities in case they specify that audit reports are to be audited by a registered auditor (a person eligible for appointment as a company auditor under s25 Companies Act 1989). Additional information reports (see **45.28** to **45.33** below) and Isle of Man and Channel Island companies are not required to be audited by registered auditors.

39.50   ICAEW audit regulations apply to all 'audits' as defined in the regulations. The definition of an audit is the exercise of expressing an opinion on financial statements, or extracts of financial statements, where that opinion is required by one of the following[1]:

(a)   under the Companies Act 1985, opinions on:

   (i)   annual financial statements [s235];
   (ii) revised annual financial statements and directors' reports [ss245, 245A and 245B];
   (iii) abbreviated accounts [Sch 8A];
   (iv) summary financial statements [s251];
   (v)   exemptions from preparing group accounts [s248];
   (vi) distributions [ss271(4) and 273(4)];
   (vii) reregistration of a private company as a public company [s43(3)(b)];
   (viii) redemption or purchase by a private company of its own shares out of capital [s173(5)];

        (ix)   financial assistance for acquisition of a private company's own shares [s156(4)];

    (b)   under legislation governing:

        (i)   building societies;

        (ii)   credit unions;

        (iii)   registered charities;

        (iv)   industrial and provident societies;

        (v)   friendly societies;

        (vi)   persons (including firms and companies) authorised under legislation relating to the conduct of audit business; and

        (vii) pension schemes.

[1]Note that the full definition of 'audit' is wider than shown above as it brings in legislation issued in Northern Ireland and the Republic of Ireland. The audit regulations should be referred to for the full definition.

39.51   Other Acts, including the Companies Act 1985, require reports to be given by a registered auditor, but the reports are not an expression of an opinion on all or part of the financial statements. One such example is the report on the transfer of non-cash assets to a public company. [s104] This is not a report on the financial statements, so would not fall within the scope of these regulations. However, a report on the initial accounts of a company wishing to make a distribution would be within these regulations, because it is a report on financial statements. [s273(4)] The definition of 'audit' does not include an independent accountant's report required by the Act. [s249C] Nor does it include a report required as part of a public offer of securities (prospectus) required by investment business legislation.

39.52   Where they apply, the audit regulations require that any auditors' report in respect of an audit client or any reports which are to be given by the auditors in respect of that audit client shall state the name of the firm and be signed in the name of the firm. In addition to any other description of the firm, the words 'Registered auditor' or 'Registered auditors' shall appear after such signature. Where reports are required by a qualified accountant (who is not necessarily the auditor), they need not include the words 'Registered auditor(s)' after the signature.

Signing and dating of the auditors' report

39.53   SAS 600 requires the auditors' report on an entity's financial statements to include the date of their report. This date **'is the date on which the auditors signed their report expressing an opinion on**

those statements'. [SAS 600(76b)] Furthermore, SAS 600 states that the '**auditors should not express an opinion on financial statements until those statements and all other financial information contained in a report of which the audited financial statements form a part have been approved by the directors, and the auditors have considered all necessary available evidence**'. [SAS 600(76a)]

39.54   The explanatory material indicates that, before signing (in manuscript) and dating their report, the auditors should have:

(a)   received a copy of the financial statements and other accompanying documents in the form approved by the directors for release;

(b)   reviewed all documents which they are required to consider in addition to the financial statements (e.g., the directors' report, chairman's statement or other review of an entity's affairs which accompany the financial statements); and

(c)   completed all procedures necessary to form an opinion on the financial statements (and any other opinions required by law or regulation), including a review of post balance sheet events.

Strictly, a 'review' is required only for the directors' report and certain specified matters in connection with UK Listing Authority Listing Rules. Other information issued with the audited financial statements is required to be 'read' by the auditors in the light of the knowledge they have acquired during the audit in accordance with SAS 160 (revised).

39.55   The explanatory material also indicates that the documents approved by the directors may be in the form of final drafts from which printed documents will be prepared and that subsequent production of printed copies of the financial statements does not constitute the creation of a new document. Copies of the report produced for the circulation to members or others of the statutory financial statements may therefore reproduce a printed version of the auditors' signature, showing the date of actual signature. However, before signing their report on the basis of the draft documents, the explanatory material goes further to explain that the auditors should 'consider whether the form of the draft financial statements is sufficiently clear for them to assess the overall financial statement presentation'. Where this is not the case, the auditors should defer signing until it is possible for them to do so.

39.56   Under SAS 600, the date of the auditors' report should not be before either the date on which the directors have approved the financial statements or the date of approval of other documents, such as the directors' report, chairman's statement or review of the entity's affairs which the auditors are required to review.

39.57   The explanatory material to SAS 600 states that, where the date of the auditors' report is later than that on which the directors approved the financial statements, the auditors should:

(a)   obtain assurance that the directors would have approved the financial statements on that later date (e.g., by obtaining confirmation from specified individual members of the board to whom authority has been delegated for this purpose); and

(b)   ensure their procedures for reviewing subsequent events cover the period up to that date.

SAS 600 does not require the assurance which is obtained to be given in writing, but it is recommended that, if it is given orally, it is documented as part of the auditors' post balance sheet events review.

39.58   The dating of the auditors' report informs the reader that the auditors have considered the effect on the financial statements of events or transactions of which they are aware which occurred up to that date. SAS 600 states that the auditors, therefore, plan the conduct of audits to take account of the need to ensure, before expressing an opinion on the financial statements, that the directors have approved the financial statements and any accompanying financial information and that the auditors have completed a sufficient review of post balance sheet events.

39.59

A problem which arises in practice is that auditors and their clients are keen to date the financial statements (and accompanying documents) and the auditors' report on the same date. Various solutions have been suggested. These include:

(a)   making arrangements for the financial statements and accompanying documents to be passed to the auditors, for signing their report, on the date on which they are approved;

(b)   the directors at their board meeting giving their approval conditional on any final amendments being agreed by a subcommittee or by nominated directors who would give their approval on the same day as the auditors sign their report;

(c)   before the financial statements are in final printed form, the auditors signing a report at the meeting at which the financial statements are approved by the directors in final draft form. The signed report shown in the final printed form is then regarded as a reproduction of the previously signed version;

(d)   the auditors asking the directors to contact them on the date of approval of the financial statements and accompanying documents so that the auditors can sign a report in respect of identical documents.

39.60 It is to be regretted that the APB has created the need for such 'solutions'. They would be unnecessary if SAS 600 permitted auditors to put an effective date against their report which is the same as the date of approval by the directors. Unfortunately, such an obvious solution does not appear to be recognised by SAS 600.

39.61 Another problem which arises in practice is the requirement of SAS 600 for the report to include 'the manuscript or printed signature of the auditors'. This appears to preclude the issue or publication of reports with no auditors' signature.

39.62 The Act requires a manually signed copy of the auditors' report to be delivered to the Registrar of Companies. Where the auditors sign their report in a form from which final printed copies are produced, they may sign copies of their report for identification purposes in order to provide the Registrar with a signed copy to accompany the financial statements. No further procedures need to be followed at that later date.

39.63 The date of the audit opinion should normally be placed adjacent to or immediately below the name and qualifications of the auditors.

Unqualified audit reports

Definition

39.64 An unqualified audit report is one in which the opinion expressed by the auditors is based on a judgement that the financial statements give a true and fair view (where applicable) and have been prepared in accordance with relevant accounting or other requirements. In forming this judgement, the auditors must be satisfied in all material respects that:

(a) appropriate accounting policies have been consistently applied in the preparation of the financial statements;

(b) the financial statements have been prepared in accordance with relevant legislation, regulations or applicable accounting standards (and that any departures are justified and adequately explained in the financial statements); and

(c) all information relevant to a proper understanding of the financial statements has been adequately disclosed.

39.65 If the auditors have reservations as to any of the above matters, an unqualified opinion should not be expressed. It is essential, therefore, that the wording of an opinion is precise, brief and without reference to any matters which may be contained in other sections of the audit report, such as highlighting specific information contained in the financial statements, as such reference might be interpreted as a qualification in the mind of the reader when none is intended.

Compliance with relevant accounting requirements

39.66   The explanatory material indicates that it is likely that a court would infer that financial statements which meet the Act's requirements for financial statements to give a true and fair view will follow, rather than depart from, accounting standards and that any departure would be sufficiently abnormal to require justification. Therefore, general compliance with accounting standards is necessary to meet the requirement of company law that the directors prepare annual accounts which give a true and fair view of a company's (or group's) state of affairs and profit or loss.

39.67   Particulars of any material departure from accounting standards which the auditors agree are necessary to give a true and fair view must still be explained, together with the financial effects of the departure, unless this is impracticable or misleading in the context of giving a true and fair view. This matter is discussed in more detail below (see **39.136** to **39.140**).

Primary statements

39.68   Reference to the term 'financial statements' in the auditors' opinion includes not only the balance sheet and profit and loss account required by the Act but also the additional primary statements of cash flows and total recognised gains and losses required in certain circumstances by FRSs 1 and 3. Where required by an accounting standard, these additional primary statements are normally deemed necessary for the annual accounts to give a true and fair view of the state of affairs and profit or loss, as required by the Act. Therefore, it is unnecessary for the auditors' opinion to refer specifically to primary statements required by accounting standards. Indeed, the explanatory material within SAS 600 goes further and states that it may also be misleading to the reader of the auditors' report, in that it may appear to detract from the role of the additional primary statements in supporting the information contained in the company's balance sheet and profit and loss account so as to give a true and fair view as required by the law.

39.69   Where the auditors are requested to report separately on one or more primary statements, they need to check that, in doing so, no impression is given that the primary statement(s) referred to is other than integral to the financial statements as a whole and that it is clear that the primary statement is necessary to give a true and fair view of the state of affairs and profit or loss for statutory purposes. It is unlikely in practice that such requests will occur, but, if they do arise it is suggested that the directors be asked to make these points in the financial statements.

Inherent uncertainty

39.70   Prior to the issue of SAS 600, matters which gave rise to inherent uncertainty were grounds for qualification of the auditors' opinion. This is no longer the case. The requirements of SAS 600 are as follows: [SAS 600(54)]

> '(a)   **In forming their opinion on financial statements, auditors should consider whether the view given by the financial statements could be affected by inherent uncertainties which, in their opinion, are fundamental.**
>
> (b)   **When an inherent uncertainty exists which:**
>
>> (i)   **in the auditors' opinion is fundamental; and**
>>
>> (ii)   **is adequately accounted for and disclosed in the financial statements,**
>
> **the auditors should include an explanatory paragraph referring to the fundamental uncertainty in the section of their report setting out the basis of their opinion.**
>
> (c)   **When adding an explanatory paragraph, auditors should use words which clearly indicate that their opinion on the financial statements is not qualified in respect of its contents.'**

39.71   SAS 600 makes clear that provided a fundamental uncertainty is both adequately accounted for and disclosed in the financial statements, the auditors' reference to it does not represent a qualification of their opinion. Accordingly, reference to the uncertainty should be made in a separate paragraph which sets out the basis of their opinion, not in the 'opinion' section of the audit report, and the paragraph should conclude with a statement that the auditors' opinion is not qualified in respect of the uncertainty.

39.72   The explanatory material to SAS 600 states that the separate paragraph should describe the matter giving rise to the fundamental uncertainty and its possible effects on the financial statements, including (where practicable) quantification, and where quantification is not possible, the auditors should include a statement to that effect. It would seem, therefore, that adequate disclosure in the notes to the accounts can be limited to particulars of the circumstances giving rise to the uncertainty. There are likely to be instances where the directors will wish to include in the notes to the accounts full disclosure of not only the detailed circumstances but also the possible effects, including quantification. While reference may be made to the notes to the accounts to minimise duplication, such a reference is not a substitute for sufficient description of the fundamental uncertainty so that the reader can appreciate the principal points at issue and their implications.

39.73 SAS 600 defines an uncertainty as inherent when its 'resolution is dependent upon uncertain future events outside the control of the reporting entity's directors at the date the financial statements are approved'. [SAS 600(12)] An uncertainty is fundamental 'when the magnitude of its potential impact is so great that, without clear disclosure of the nature and implications of the uncertainty, the view given by the financial statements would be seriously misleading'. [SAS 600(13)] When judging the magnitude of an inherent uncertainty's potential impact, the auditors should consider:

(a) the risk that the estimate included in the financial statements may be subject to change;

(b) the range of possible outcomes; and

(c) the consequences of those outcomes on the view shown in the financial statements.

39.74 When forming their opinion on the adequacy of the accounting treatment of inherent uncertainties, the explanatory material to SAS 600 states that the auditors should consider:

(a) the appropriateness of the accounting policies dealing with uncertain matters;

(b) the reasonableness of the estimates included in the financial statements in respect of inherent uncertainties; and

(c) the adequacy of disclosures.

In effect, the auditors must consider whether the requirements of FRS 12 *Provisions, contingent liabilities and contingent assets* have been complied with (see chapter 17).

39.75 Most audits involve a number of inherent uncertainties which the auditors must evaluate as to whether, individually or collectively, their ultimate outcome could materially affect the view given by the financial statements. Many involve the valuation of assets (e.g., collectibility of debts and sale of stocks above cost) and liabilities (e.g., provision for warranties or contract penalties). Normally, the auditors are able to obtain sufficient audit evidence by assessing whether there is sufficient evidence to support an opinion as to the reasonableness of management's accounting estimates of their value. In such cases, the uncertainties are not regarded as fundamental and no reference need be made to them in the financial statements.

39.76   Auditors can only evaluate the adequacy of the accounting treatment and disclosure based on evidence available at the date they form their opinion. Where, because of a limitation in the scope of their work, the auditors do not receive evidence which exists (or reasonably could be expected to exist) pertaining to an inherent uncertainty, they should issue a qualified opinion or disclaimer of opinion.

39.77   Where the accounting policies or estimates included in the financial statements are materially misstated, or the disclosures relating to the uncertainty are inadequate, the auditors should issue a qualified or adverse opinion.

39.78   To highlight the importance of a fundamental uncertainty, SAS 600 suggests the use of an appropriate subheading differentiating the explanatory paragraph from other matters included in the section describing the basis of the auditors' opinion. Such an appropriate subheading might be 'uncertainty relating to litigation' or 'going concern'.

Example 39.78

Basis of opinion

We conducted our audit ...

We planned and performed our audit ...

Uncertainty relating to Inland Revenue enquiry

In forming our opinion, we have considered the adequacy of the disclosure made in note 2 to the accounts concerning an Inland Revenue enquiry into the tax affairs of the company. Until the enquiry is completed, it is not possible to estimate, with any reasonable degree of certainty, any ultimate liability which may fall upon the company. Consequently, no liability has been included in the financial statements. Our opinion is not qualified in this respect.

Opinion

In our opinion, the financial statements give a true and fair view of the state of the company's affairs at 31 March 2000 and of its profit for the year then ended and have been properly prepared in accordance with the Companies Act 1985.

Uncertainties about going concern

39.79   One of the fundamental accounting principles prescribed by the Act is that a company shall be presumed to be carrying on business as a going concern (i.e., the company will continue in operational existence for the foreseeable future). In November 1994, the APB issued SAS 130 to establish standards and provide guidance for auditors in respect of their consideration of and reporting on the going concern basis as part of their work on audited financial statements. SAS 130 and the forms of audit report required in circumstances in which there are concerns about the going concern basis are dealt with in chapter 41.

Major litigation

39.80 Another circumstance which is likely to give rise to a fundamental uncertainty is one which involves major litigation. In forming their opinion as to the adequacy of the accounting treatment and disclosure of the uncertainty, the auditors should consider:

(a) the completeness of information from the solicitors involved in the litigation, detailing the nature of the plaintiff's claim, counterclaims and the solicitors' assessment of the likely outcome;

(b) quantification and evaluation of the maximum risk to the company should the court rule in favour of the plaintiff;

(c) the reasonableness of management's estimates of probable loss which will be suffered and the appropriateness of any provisions accrued in the accounts in accordance with FRS 12 *Provisions, contingent liabilities and contingent assets*;

(d) the disclosures in the notes to the accounts regarding the litigation;

(e) updated discussions to determine the position as at the date the opinion is to be expressed; and

(f) written representations from management.

39.81 Where the auditors conclude from the above assessment that the litigation is major, that the accounting policy dealing with uncertain matters is appropriate and that the estimates included in the financial statements and disclosure are reasonable and adequate, the auditors need not qualify their opinion, but should refer in their report to the fundamental uncertainty.

Example 39.81

AUDITORS' REPORT ...

Basis of opinion

We conducted our audit ...

We planned and performed our audit ...

Uncertainty relating to litigation

In forming our opinion, we have considered the adequacy of the disclosures made in note 23 which explain the status of litigation against the company for an alleged breach of environmental regulations. The future settlement of this litigation could result in additional liabilities.

> It is not possible to quantify the effects, if any, of the resolution of this uncertainty. Our opinion is not qualified in this respect.
>
> **Disclosure in the financial statements**
>
> *Note 23 to the accounts*
>
> *Claim against the company*
>
> A claim has been lodged against the company in respect of a major contract. The claim calls for rectification and for substantial compensation for alleged damage to the customer's business. The directors have made provision of £100,000 for the estimated cost of rectification, but no provision for compensation, as that part of the claim is being strongly resisted. It is not possible to determine with reasonable accuracy the ultimate cost of rectification and compensation, if any, which may become payable.

39.82   The final sentence in the example note to the accounts should be included whenever quantification is not possible. Where the auditors conclude that the estimates included in the financial statements are materially misstated or that there is limitation in scope of the audit, again the possibilities of 'except for', disclaimer and adverse opinions cannot be ruled out.

39.83   Where major litigation could threaten the whole future of the business, consideration should also be given to inherent uncertainty about going concern.

Examples of unqualified reports

Single company

39.84   An example of the wording of an unqualified report by a firm of chartered accountants to the members of a single company incorporated under the Companies Act is set out below. For listed companies, refer to chapter 40.

> ### *Example 39.84*
>
> **AUDITORS' REPORT TO THE MEMBERS OF XYZ LIMITED**
>
> We have audited the financial statements on pages 9 to 22 which have been prepared under the accounting policies set out on page 9.
>
> **Respective responsibilities of directors and auditors**
>
> As described on page 7, the company's directors are responsible for the preparation of financial statements, which are required to be prepared in accordance with applicable United Kingdom law and accounting standards. It is our responsibility to form an independent

opinion, based on our audit, on those statements and to report our opinion to you.

Basis of opinion

We conducted our audit in accordance with United Kingdom auditing standards issued by the Auditing Practices Board. An audit includes examination, on a test basis, of evidence relevant to the amounts and disclosures in the financial statements. It also includes an assessment of the significant estimates and judgements made by the directors in the preparation of the financial statements and of whether the accounting policies are appropriate to the company's circumstances, consistently applied and adequately disclosed.

We planned and performed our audit so as to obtain all the information and explanations which we considered necessary in order to provide us with sufficient evidence to give reasonable assurance that the financial statements are free from material misstatement, whether caused by fraud or other irregularity or error. In forming our opinion, we also evaluated the overall adequacy of the presentation of information in the financial statements.

Opinion

In our opinion, the financial statements give a true and fair view of the state of the company's affairs as at 31 March 2000 and of its profit [loss] for the year then ended and have been properly prepared in accordance with the Companies Act 1985.

(Signature and name of auditors)

Chartered Accountants and Registered Auditors   (Address)

(Date)

Note: It should be noted that reference is not made to 'cash flows' in the opinion paragraph. Note also that the wording is altered in the circumstances described in **39.86** to **39.89** below.

39.85   In order to keep other example reports to a reasonable length, only the relevant paragraphs which illustrate a particular point are shown in the subsequent examples.

Small companies

39.86   Companies which qualify as small companies are permitted to prepare their annual reports and accounts to members with considerably reduced disclosures in the financial statements and directors' report (see chapter 34). The regulations which set out the disclosure requirements are contained in Sch 8 to the Act.

39.87   The financial statements of a small company that opts to follow Sch 8 should still show a true and fair view and the auditors should report as to whether or not that is the case. Accordingly, the form of report to be used should follow SAS 600 and include an opinion on whether there is a true and fair view. It is helpful to indicate that the company is following the provisions of the Act applicable to small companies, which can be done by adding 'applicable to small companies' to the end of the opinion paragraph as shown below.

Example 39.87

Opinion

In our opinion, the financial statements give a true and fair view of the state of the company's affairs as at 31 March 2000 and of its profit [loss] for the year then ended and have been properly prepared in accordance with the provisions of the Companies Act 1985 applicable to small companies.

39.88   If the company is following the FRSSE, the introductory paragraph of the audit report should make this clear, as shown in the example in **39.24** above.

39.89   The current Sch 8, which sets out required disclosures rather than exemptions from disclosure, does not include the provisions from a previous version of Sch 8 which indicated that:

(a)   the omission of any information under the small company exemptions did not of itself prevent the financial statements from giving a true and fair view; and

(b)   where a company entitled to the exemptions had taken advantage of them, the auditors were only required to state 'whether in their opinion the annual accounts have been properly prepared in accordance with the provisions of this Act applicable to small companies'.

Accordingly, if the auditors now consider that the financial statements do not show a true and fair view because of compliance with Sch 8, they should qualify their report to that effect. The footnote to report example 5 of SAS 600, which describes the use of the opinion that omits a reference to 'true and fair', is now out of date.

39.90   See **39.98** below where the parent company of small group wishes to take advantage of the exemption from the requirement to prepare group accounts.

Non-trading companies on which a true and fair view opinion is given

39.91   Where a company has not traded or entered into other transactions during the year and the preceding year, a balance sheet should be prepared. A note in the financial statements should indicate that the company has not traded and has made neither profit nor loss in the financial year and the preceding year. In these circumstances, the opinion would be as follows.

> ### Example 39.91
>
> **Opinion**
>
> In our opinion, the financial statements give a true and fair view of the state of the company's affairs as at 31 March 2000 and of the result for the year then ended and have been properly prepared in accordance with the Companies Act 1985.

39.92 Alternatively, a heading 'Profit and loss account' can be followed by a statement indicating that the company has not traded and has made neither profit nor loss in the financial year and the preceding year. In these circumstances, an unqualified audit report should be the same as the above example.

39.93 It should be noted that a profit and loss account is necessary for the first year in which a company does not trade, since the corresponding amounts for the preceding year must be disclosed.

39.94   An argument which may arise is that, in such circumstances, the 'normal' wording contained in the 'basis of opinion' set out in the report examples could be altered. However, it is suggested that no revision be made, as it is an attempt not to describe the individual audit but audits in general.

39.95 A non-trading company may qualify as a dormant company and resolve not to appoint auditors; in which case, no auditors' report is appended to the financial statements and no statement of directors' responsibilities need be given.

Group of companies

39.96 An example full audit report for a group which is not listed is given below. An example full audit report for a listed group is given in chapter 40.

> ### Example 39.96
>
> **AUDITORS' REPORT TO THE MEMBERS OF XYZ LIMITED**
>
> We have audited the financial statements on pages 9 to 22 which have been prepared under the accounting policies set out on page 9.
>
> **Respective responsibilities of directors and auditors**
>
> As described on page 7, the company's directors are responsible for the preparation of financial statements, which are required to be prepared in accordance with applicable United Kingdom law and

accounting standards. It is our responsibility to form an independent opinion, based on our audit, on those statements and to report our opinion to you.

Basis of opinion

We conducted our audit in accordance with United Kingdom auditing standards issued by the Auditing Practices Board. An audit includes examination, on a test basis, of evidence relevant to the amounts and disclosures in the financial statements. It also includes an assessment of the significant estimates and judgements made by the directors in the preparation of the financial statements and of whether the accounting policies are appropriate to the circumstances of the company and the group, consistently applied and adequately disclosed.

We planned and performed our audit so as to obtain all the information and explanations which we considered necessary in order to provide us with sufficient evidence to give reasonable assurance that the financial statements are free from material misstatement, whether caused by fraud or other irregularity or error. In forming our opinion, we also evaluated the overall adequacy of the presentation of information in the financial statements.

Opinion

In our opinion, the financial statements give a true and fair view of the state of affairs of the company and the group as at 31 March 2000 and of the profit [loss] of the group for the year then ended and have been properly prepared in accordance with the Companies Act 1985.

(Signature and name of auditors)

Chartered Accountants and Registered Auditors   (Address)

(Date)

39.97   An example of the wording that should normally be included in a statement of directors' responsibilities for a group is shown below.

> ## Example 39.97
>
> Company law requires the directors to prepare financial statements for each financial year which give a true and fair view of the state of affairs of the company and the group as at the end of the financial year and of the profit or loss of the group for that period. In preparing those financial statements, the directors are required to:
>
> (a)   select suitable accounting policies and then apply them consistently;
>
> (b)   make judgements and estimates that are reasonable and prudent;

(c)   state whether applicable accounting standards have been followed, *subject to any material departures disclosed and explained in the financial statements* (applies only to large groups);

(d)   prepare the financial statements on the going concern basis, unless it is inappropriate to presume that the group will continue in business (applies only where no separate statement on going concern is made by the directors).

The directors are responsible for keeping proper accounting records, for safeguarding the assets of the group and for taking reasonable steps for the prevention and detection of fraud and other irregularities.

Note: It is suggested that the words in *italics* be included only if there is a material departure from applicable accounting standards.

Parents of small or medium-sized groups not producing group accounts

39.98   The Companies Act 1985 (Miscellaneous Accounting Amendments) Regulations 1996 (SI 1996 No 189), have repealed the requirement for directors of parent companies of small or medium-sized groups, who wish to take advantage of the exemption from preparing group accounts, to obtain an auditors' report confirming that the company is entitled to the exemption. However, if the directors of a company take advantage of the exemption and, in the auditors' opinion, they were not entitled to, the auditors are required to state that fact in their report. Such a statement will normally result in an adverse opinion.

Example 39.98

Adverse opinion in respect of absence of group accounts

As stated in the directors' report on page y/in note x, the directors of the company have taken advantage of the exemption from preparing group accounts conferred by s248 Companies Act 1985 in respect of small and medium-sized groups. The company has a controlling share in an unincorporated undertaking which, in our opinion, should be consolidated if group accounts were prepared. The directors have assessed the criteria for the exemption from preparing group accounts on the basis that the undertaking would be included by way of the equity method of accounting. If the undertaking were consolidated, the aggregate turnover of the group would be £15,500,000 and its aggregate balance sheet total would be £8,400,000, both of which exceed the criteria set out in the Companies Act 1985 for the group to qualify as small or medium-sized. Accordingly, in our opinion, the directors are not entitled to take advantage of the exemption from preparing group accounts.

In view of the failure to include group accounts, in our opinion, the financial statements do not give a true and fair view of the state of affairs of the group as at 31 March 2000 and of the profit of the group for the year then ended and accordingly have not been prepared in accordance with the Companies Act 1985. In our opinion, the financial statements give a true and fair view of the company's affairs at 31 March 2000 and of its profit for the year then ended.

(Signature and name of auditors)

Chartered Accountants and Registered Auditors   (Address)

(Date)

Note: To give such a report, it is important that the directors are on record as stating that the reason for not preparing group accounts is that they are taking advantage of the exemption conferred by s248. The auditors should not be seen to be making a statement on the directors' behalf that they themselves are not prepared to make.

Reference to other auditors

39.99   SAS 510 *The relationship between principal auditors and other auditors* states that the group auditors have sole responsibility for their audit opinion and no reference should be made to the fact that any subsidiary or associated company has been audited by other auditors.

Subsidiaries with different accounting dates

39.100   No reference need be made in the audit report where subsidiaries use different accounting dates from that of the holding company, as long as appropriate disclosures are made in the notes to the accounts.

Unincorporated concerns

39.101   An example of an opinion suitable for financial statements of unincorporated concerns which are intended to show a true and fair view of profit or loss and financial position is as follows.

Example 39.101

Opinion

In our opinion, the financial statements give a true and fair view of the state of the ['club's', 'trust's', etc. as appropriate] affairs as at 31 March 2000 and of its profit [or net income, net revenue, results, excess of income over expenditure, etc. as appropriate] for the year then ended.

39.102   In addition, the terms of appointment of the auditors may sometimes require them to confirm that the form and content of the

financial statements comply with rules contained in the statutes or
other regulations which govern the concern.

Example 39.102

... for the year then ended and have been properly prepared in accordance with the trust deed.

Price-adjusted accounts

39.103 The preparation of supplementary current cost accounts is no longer
mandatory and no accounting standard is in force to give guidance
on their preparation. However, auditors may, in special cases, be
asked to report on price-adjusted accounts.

39.104 The explanatory material to SAS 600 states that the introductory section may refer to the accounting convention. An example in respect
of price-adjusted accounts is given in **39.105** below.

39.105 The example below illustrates the report required on a set of main
historical cost accounts, together with a set of supplementary current
cost accounts on which the auditor has been requested to report in
terms of their compliance with the principles, policies and methods
described in the accounts.

Example 39.105

We have audited:

(a) the financial statements on pages 9 to 22, which have been prepared under the historical cost convention [as modified by the
revaluation of certain fixed assets] and the accounting policies
set out on page 12; and

(b) the supplementary current cost accounts set out on pages 23
to 28, which have been prepared in accordance with the current
cost principles, accounting policies and methods set out on
pages 26 to 28.

Respective responsibilities of directors and auditors

As described on page 8, the company's directors are responsible for
the preparation of the financial statements, which are required to be
prepared in accordance with applicable United Kingdom law and
accounting standards, and supplementary current cost accounts. It is
our responsibility to form independent opinions, based on our audit,
on those statements and supplementary accounts and to report our
opinions to you.

Basis of opinions

We conducted our audit ...

We planned our audit ...

> **Opinions**
>
> In our opinion, the financial statements give a true and fair view of the state of the company's affairs as at 31 March 2000 and of its profit [loss] for the year then ended and have been properly prepared in accordance with the Companies Act 1985.
>
> In our opinion, the supplementary current cost accounts have been properly prepared in accordance with the current cost principles, accounting policies and methods set out on pages 26 to 28.

Audit reports which are not unqualified

Introduction

39.106 Where circumstances arise which result in the auditors being unable to express an unqualified opinion, their report must be modified.

39.107 Before giving a report which is not unqualified, the auditors should discuss the financial statements with management and make their position clear, so that management may, where possible, take steps to provide any necessary information which the auditors may require or to amend the financial statements so that form of report can be avoided.

39.108 Since audit reports must be stated in terms chosen to fit the circumstances of each case, it is impracticable to suggest standard wording. The examples which are cited in this manual are for illustrative purposes only.

39.109 The audit report should describe the reasons for a report being other than unqualified and should quantify the effects on the financial statements whenever this is practicable. The report examples also indicate that the opinion section should be clearly headed up to advise a reader that the opinion is qualified, e.g., by indicating 'Adverse opinion', 'Qualified opinion arising from disagreement about accounting treatment', 'Qualified opinion arising from omission of cash flow statement'.

39.110 A qualified opinion should also cover all material matters on which the auditors have reservations.

39.111 Where a note to the accounts explains the problem in detail, the explanatory paragraph may include a reference to the note in order to minimise repetition. However, reference to the note is not a substitute for sufficient description of the circumstances such that a reader appreciates the principal points at issue and their implications for an understanding of the financial statements.

39.112 If the entity for which the auditors are issuing a qualified report is a company incorporated under the Companies Act 1985 and a distribution is envisaged, the company must obtain from the auditors a written statement whether in their opinion the matter giving rise to the qualification is material for determining whether the distribution would contravene the legislation (see chapter 43).

Materiality

39.113 It is not appropriate to qualify an audit report unless the matters involved are material in relation to the financial statements. For the purposes of SAS 600, a matter is material if its omission or misstatement would reasonably influence the decisions of a user of the financial statements.

39.114 Materiality may be judged on the basis of the financial statements taken as a whole, any individual primary statement or individual items within them (e.g., profit before taxation, current assets less current liabilities, share capital and reserves).

39.115 The concept of materiality applies not only to monetary misstatements but also to disclosure requirements and adherence to appropriate accounting principles and statutory requirements. Although the Act permits certain disclosures to be excluded where they are not material, it requires other disclosures (see **39.184** below) which, if not made in the financial statements, must be given in the auditors' report, regardless of the size of the amounts involved.

39.116 The ICAEW has issued a Technical Release, TECH 32/96, which gives guidance on the interpretation of materiality in financial reporting. It should be noted that TECH 32/96 provides guidance to preparers, rather than auditors, of financial statements and other information. It is also relevant to consider materiality in qualitative as well as quantitative terms. In this respect, it should be noted that the Financial Reporting Review Panel, in May 1998, formed a view in respect of RMC Group Plc that a fine would be regarded as material on qualitative grounds. A fine of £5 million paid by the company in 1995 was not disclosed as an exceptional item in the financial statements, as it had been judged by the directors and auditors as not material. It had been disclosed in previous years as a contingent liability. As is indicated in TECH 32/96, guidance for auditors is provided by SAS 220 *Materiality and the audit*, which was issued by the APB. When evaluating the effect of misstatements, SAS 220 states that if the directors refuse to adjust the financial statements and the results of extended audit procedures do not enable the auditors to conclude that the aggregate of uncorrected misstatements is not material, they consider the implications for their report. [SAS 220(14)] It is possible that in the period ahead UK standards and guidance may be strengthened to reflect recent changes in the USA which have developed in response to concerns expressed by the Securities and Exchange Commission about 'a culture of gamesmanship' associated with financial reporting leading to companies putting earnings management above all other considerations.

Circumstances giving rise to reports other than unqualified

39.117 SAS 600 identifies three types of audit reports which are other than unqualified: 'except for', adverse and disclaimer of opinions. They can be shown diagrammatically as follows.

	Disagreement (explanatory paragraph in the opinion section)	Limitation of scope (explanatory paragraph in the basis of opinion section)
Material	Qualified ('Except for')	Qualified ('Except for')
So material or pervasive	Adverse ('In view of the effect')	Disclaimer ('Because of the possible effect')

39.118 The phrase 'other than unqualified' is used because the description 'qualified opinion' cannot, for the purpose of SAS 600, be applied to disclaimer of and adverse opinions. The reason for this is that IASs use the term qualified opinion only for 'except for' reports.

39.119 The type of report depends upon the nature of the circumstances and the auditors' judgement as to whether the effect of the matter is sufficiently material to the financial statements to require the opinion to be qualified in respect of the matter, or could be or is so material to the financial statements as a whole that a disclaimer of opinion or adverse opinion must be expressed. It is suggested, however, that before issuing disclaimers of and adverse opinions, the auditors should consider whether the use of a qualified opinion would give a user of the financial statements better communication of the auditors' reservation and its implications.

39.120 SAS 600 gives the following circumstances as the basis of a qualified opinion:

(a)   a limitation in the scope of the auditors' examination; or

(b)   a disagreement with the treatment or disclosure of a matter in the financial statements,

and, in the auditors' judgement, the effect of the matter is or may be material to the financial statements and therefore those financial statements do not give a true and fair view of the matters on which the auditors are required to report or do not comply with relevant accounting or other requirements.

Limitation in scope of audit

39.121 SAS 600 deals with the circumstances and reporting requirements when there is a limitation in the scope of the auditors' examination. The requirements are the same whether a limitation is imposed on the auditors or is outside the control of the auditors or directors, as it results in the auditors obtaining insufficient evidence necessary to form an opinion on particular components of the financial statements which, in the auditors' opinion, are material to an understanding of the financial statements. The requirements of SAS 600 are:
[SAS 600(68)]

'When there has been a limitation on the scope of the auditors' work that prevents them from obtaining sufficient evidence to express an unqualified opinion:

(a) **the auditors' report should include a description of the factors leading to the limitation in the opinion section of their report;**

(b) **the auditors should issue a disclaimer of opinion when the possible effect of a limitation on scope is so material or pervasive that they are unable to express an opinion on the financial statements;**

(c) **a qualified opinion should be issued when the effect of the limitation is not so material or pervasive as to require a disclaimer, and the wording of the opinion should indicate that it is qualified as to the possible adjustments to the financial statements that might have been determined to be necessary had the limitation not existed.'**

39.122 When planning their work, auditors consider potential errors in, or assertions underlying, the financial statements and develop procedures which are expected to provide sufficient evidence to be satisfied that the financial statements are free of material misstatement. Where there are limitations imposed by circumstances that prevent those procedures being performed to their satisfaction, the auditors should consider carrying out reasonable alternative procedures. In considering whether a limitation results in a lack of evidence necessary to form an opinion, the auditors should assess:

(a) the quantity and type of evidence which may reasonably be expected to be available to support the particular figure or disclosure in the financial statements; and

(b) the possible effect on the financial statements of the matter for which insufficient evidence is available. When the possible effect is, in the opinion of the auditors, material to the financial statements, there will be insufficient evidence to support an opinion.

39.123 Inherent uncertainties do not arise from, or give rise to, a limitation on the auditors' work and are considered in **39.70** to **39.83** above.

39.124 SAS 600 (see **39.121**(a) above) requires a description of the factors leading to the limitation to be included in the opinion section of the audit report. However, all the report examples in the appendix to SAS 600 which deal with limitations in scope of audit include the description of the factors in the section dealing with the basis of opinion. This position would appear to be the most logical place for the description. It does mean, however, that auditors need to remember that for reports indicating disagreement, the explanatory paragraph is included in the opinion section, while for reports indicating limitation of scope, the explanatory paragraph is in the basis of opinion section.

39.125 The description of the factors should enable the reader to distinguish between:

(a) the limitations imposed on the auditors (e.g., accounting records not made available to the auditors or directors prevent auditors from carrying out a procedure considered necessary by the auditors, such as attendance at stocktaking); and

(b) limitations outside the control of the auditors or directors (e.g., timing of auditors' appointment prevents attendance at stocktaking and there is no alternative form of evidence).

39.126 When reporting under the Act, the auditors should also report the fact that, in respect of the limitation relating to the areas affected, they have not obtained all the information and explanations that they considered necessary for the purposes of their audit. The report examples include this statement in a separate paragraph at the end of the opinion section of their report.

39.127 The report examples also include in the same paragraph in the opinion section a statement that the auditors were unable to determine whether proper accounting records had been 'maintained'. The examples in this manual use the word 'kept' rather than 'maintained', so as to meet the exact requirements of the Act.

'Qualified' opinions

39.128 A 'qualified opinion' should be given where, as a result of a limitation in their audit, the auditors have insufficient evidence to form an opinion on one or more matters which together are assessed as material to the financial statements, but not to the degree that the auditors are unable to express an opinion on the financial statements. SAS 600 does do not prescribe wording to introduce the qualified opinion, but the explanatory material indicates that the qualification should be expressed in terms of 'except for the effects of any adjustments that might have been found to be necessary had the limitation not affected the evidence available'.

39.129 A material limitation in the scope of the audit will prevent the auditors from making a positive assertion in the 'basis of opinion' section that they have conducted their audit in accordance with auditing standards and that they have planned and performed their audit to obtain all the information and explanations they consider necessary. Accordingly, it will be necessary to modify these statements in a manner shown in the following illustrations.

Example 39.129.1

Basis of opinion

We conducted our audit in accordance with United Kingdom auditing standards issued by the Auditing Practices Board, except that the scope of our work was limited as explained below.

An audit includes examination, on a test basis, of evidence relevant to the amounts and disclosures in the financial statements. It also includes an assessment of the significant estimates and judgements made by the directors in the preparation of the financial statements and of whether the accounting policies are appropriate to the company's circumstances, consistently applied and adequately disclosed.

We planned our audit so as to obtain all the information and explanations which we considered necessary in order to provide us with sufficient evidence to give reasonable assurance that the financial statements are free from material misstatement, whether caused by fraud or other irregularity or error. However, the evidence available to us was limited because of a state of war in .... and consequently we could not attend the stocktake at .... to verify stocks included in the balance sheet at £........... . There were no other satisfactory audit procedures that we could adopt to confirm that stocks were properly recorded. Any adjustment to this figure would have a consequential effect on the profit for the year.

In forming our opinion, we also evaluated the overall adequacy of the presentation of information in the financial statements.

Qualified opinion arising from limitation in audit scope

Except for any adjustments to the financial statements that might have been found to be necessary had we been able to obtain sufficient evidence concerning stocks, in our opinion, the financial statements

---

give a true and fair view of the state of the company's affairs as at 31 March 2000 and of its profit [loss] for the year then ended and have been properly prepared in accordance with the Companies Act 1985.

In respect alone of the limitation on our work relating to stocks:

(a)   we have not obtained all the information and explanations that we considered necessary for the purposes of our audit; and

(b)   we were unable to determine whether proper accounting records have been kept.

Example 39.129.2

Basis of opinion

We conducted our audit in accordance with United Kingdom auditing standards issued by the Auditing Practices Board, except that the scope of our audit was limited as explained below.

An audit includes examination, on a test basis, of evidence relevant to the amounts and disclosures in the financial statements. It also includes an assessment of the significant estimates and judgements made by the directors in the preparation of the financial statements and of whether the accounting policies are appropriate to the company's circumstances, consistently applied and adequately disclosed.

We planned our audit so as to obtain all the information and explanations which we considered necessary in order to provide us with sufficient evidence to give reasonable assurance that the financial statements are free from material misstatement, whether caused by fraud or other irregularity or error. However, the evidence available to us was limited in respect of fixed assets in the course of construction of £...... which include the cost of own labour capitalised amounting to £....... . The labour costs are based on the directors' estimates of time spent by them and certain employees on the construction work, which are unsupported by time records. There were no satisfactory audit procedures that we could adopt to confirm that labour costs have been properly capitalised. Any adjustment to this figure would have a consequential effect on the profit for the year.

In forming our opinion, we also evaluated the overall adequacy of the presentation of information in the financial statements.

Qualified opinion arising from limitation in audit scope

Except for any adjustments to the financial statements that might have been found to be necessary had we been able to obtain sufficient evidence concerning labour costs capitalised in fixed assets in the course of construction, in our opinion, the financial statements give a true and fair view of the state of the company's affairs as at 31 March 2000 and of its profit [loss] for the year then ended and have been properly prepared in accordance with the Companies Act 1985.

1413

> In respect alone of the limitation on our work relating to fixed assets in the course of construction:
>
> (a) we have not obtained all the information and explanations that we considered necessary for the purposes of our audit; and
>
> (b) we were unable to determine whether proper accounting records have been kept.

Disclaimers of opinion

39.130 A 'disclaimer' arises where the possible effect of the limitation is so material or pervasive to the financial statements that they could, as a whole, be misleading. This would occur where the auditors have not been able to obtain sufficient evidence to support, and accordingly are unable to express, an opinion on the financial statements. Accordingly, the auditors will not be able to state whether the financial statements give a true and fair view and comply with the relevant legislation. It is possible that a number of matters considered together may be so pervasive in their effect that a disclaimer is required.

39.131 A disclaimer is appropriate where:

(a) there are pervasive deficiencies in the accounting records such that it is not practicable to prepare meaningful financial statements; or

(b) there are serious deficiencies in audit evidence, other than the accounting records, affecting so many important parts of the financial statements that the auditors are unable to express any meaningful opinion on them; or

(c) management representations are an essential element in the auditors' ability to express an opinion on the financial statements and they have strong reasons to doubt management's integrity.

39.132 In March 1999, the APB issued SAS 601 *Imposed limitation of audit scope*. It introduced two new standards as follows.

(a) If the auditors are aware, before accepting an audit engagement, that the directors of the entity, or those who appoint its auditors, will impose a limitation on the scope of their work which they consider likely to result in the need to issue a disclaimer of opinion on the financial statements, they should not accept that engagement, unless required to do so by statute (SAS 601.1).

(b) If the auditors become aware, after accepting an audit engagement, that the directors of the entity, or those who appointed them as its auditors, have imposed a limitation on the scope of their work which they consider likely to result in the need to issue a disclaimer of opinion on the financial statements, they should request the removal of the limitation. If the limitation is not removed, they should consider resigning from the audit engagement (SAS 601.2).

39.133 One of the main aims of SAS 601 is to prevent certain auditors being complicit in arrangements that are designed to enable an entity to meet the form of legal or regulatory requirements but evade complying with the substance of those obligations.

39.134 SAS 600 does not prescribe wording to introduce the disclaimer. The report examples suggest that the opinion section be headed up 'Opinion: disclaimer on view given by financial statements' and that the section commences with the phrase 'Because of the possible effect'. The following example includes a more straightforward heading.

Example 39.134

Basis of opinion

...

Disclaimer of opinion on view given by financial statements

Because of the possible effect of the limitation in the evidence available to us, we are unable to form an opinion as to whether the financial statements give a true and fair view of the state of the company's affairs as at 31 March 2000 and of its profit [loss] for the year then ended and whether the financial statements have been properly prepared in accordance with the Companies Act 1985.

In respect of the limitation on our work:

(a)   we have not obtained all the information and explanations that we considered necessary for our audit; and

(b)   we were unable to determine whether proper accounting records have been kept.

39.135 In SAS 600's report example number 9, which illustrates a disclaimer of opinion, the suggested wording includes the following: 'In respect alone of the limitation on our work in relation to stocks:….'. However, in practice, such wording would suggest that a qualified opinion arising from limitation in scope and using the term 'except for' would have been sufficient, rather than a disclaimer of opinion, which indicates a far more pervasive problem. For this reason the example in **39.134** above omits these words.

The report examples of a disclaimer of opinion conclude with the statement: 'In all other respects, in our opinion, the financial statements have been properly prepared in accordance with the Companies Act 1985'. This statement is not included in the foregoing example, because it seems of little or no value. If the auditors cannot determine whether the financial statements meet the fundamental requirements of the Act that they give a true and fair view, the fact that they comply with other requirements seems too insignificant to be worth saying.

Disagreement with accounting treatment or disclosure

39.136 Where the auditors disagree with the accounting treatment or disclosure of matters in the financial statements, they will have obtained sufficient information regarding a particular matter and have formed an opinion that the treatment is not fairly presented or that the disclosure is inadequate or misstates the facts. The requirements of SAS 600 in this regard are:
[SAS 600(74)]

'Where the auditors disagree with the accounting treatment or disclosure of a matter in the financial statements and, in the auditors' opinion, the effect of that disagreement is material to the financial statements:

(a) the auditors should include in the opinion section of their report:

    (i) a description of all substantive factors giving rise to the disagreement;

    (ii) their implications for the financial statements;

    (iii) whenever practicable, a quantification of the effect on the financial statements;

(b) when the auditors conclude that the effect of the matter giving rise to disagreement is so material or pervasive that the financial statements are seriously misleading, they should issue an adverse opinion;

(c) in the case of other material disagreements, the auditors should issue a qualified opinion indicating that it is expressed except for the effects of the matter giving rise to the disagreement.'

39.137 When an audit report is qualified for reasons of disagreement, the opinion section of the report should include an introductory paragraph giving a description of the reasons for the qualification and the effects on the financial statements. While it may be appropriate to make reference to the notes to the financial statements regarding the qualifying matter, the auditors' reasons for qualifying and the effects should be included in the audit report, so that the reader can appreciate the principal points of difference.

'Qualified' opinions

39.138 A 'qualified opinion' is appropriate where the auditors disagree with the treatment or disclosure of one or more matters which are material to the financial statements, but they are not so material or pervasive that the financial statements as a whole are misleading. The qualification of the opinion should be expressed by stating that the financial statements give a true and fair view 'except for the effects of the matter giving rise to the disagreement'. The use of the phrase 'except for the above' is normally insufficiently precise.

> ### *Example 39.138*
>
> **Qualified opinion arising from disagreement about accounting treatment**
>
> (Explanatory paragraph describing the disagreement and quantifying its effect on the financial statements)
>
> Except for the absence of the provision described above, in our opinion, the financial statements give a true and fair view of the state of the company's affairs as at 31 March 2000 and of its profit [loss] for the year then ended and have been properly prepared in accordance with the Companies Act 1985.

Adverse opinions

39.139 An 'adverse opinion' is appropriate in circumstances where the auditors disagree on matters (exceptionally on a single matter) in the financial statements which are so material or pervasive that the auditors conclude that the financial statements are seriously misleading.

> ### *Example 39.139*
>
> **Adverse opinion**
>
> (Explanatory paragraph describing the disagreement and quantifying its effect on the financial statements)
>
> In view of the effect of the failure to provide for the losses described above, in our opinion, the financial statements do not give a true and fair view of the state of the company's affairs as at 31 March 2000 and of its profit [loss] for the year then ended and accordingly have not been properly prepared in accordance with the Companies Act 1985.

39.140 The example of an adverse opinion given in the appendix to SAS 600 concludes with a statement that: 'In all other respects, in our opinion the financial statements have been properly prepared in accordance with the Companies Act 1985'. This statement seems inappropriate, because when the auditors form the opinion that the financial statements do not give a true and fair view, the fact that they may comply with other requirements seems too insignificant to be worth saying.

Qualified opinion on part of the financial statements

39.141 A qualified opinion on the balance sheet will usually result in a similar qualification being given on the remainder of the financial statements.

39.142 There may, however, be circumstances where although the auditors must qualify their opinion on the profit and loss account, an opinion can still be given on the balance sheet (e.g., where there is a scope limitation or disagreement affecting the financial position at the beginning of the year). An example of a qualified opinion on part of the financial statements is given in **39.164** below.

Multiple qualification

39.143 Multiple qualifications arise in exceptional circumstances where there are two or more qualifying matters. Each matter must be explained in the opinion section and their combined effect must be considered in deciding whether a multiple qualification, disclaimer or adverse opinion is appropriate. Where there are a large number of qualifying matters included in a multiple qualification, the use of numbered paragraphs often makes the audit report easier for the reader to understand. An example of a multiple qualification is given in **39.207** below.

Examples of limitation of scope of audit

Introduction

39.144 Circumstances leading to a limitation in the scope of audit can arise from limitations imposed on the auditors (see **39.132** above regarding SAS 601 *Imposed limitation of audit scope*) or from limitations which are outside the control of the auditors or directors. Such circumstances include:

(a)   auditors instructed not to carry out audit procedures;

(b)   information not made available to the auditors;

(c)   proper accounting records not kept;

(d)　incompleteness of recording of transactions;

(e)　limitations arising in the first year of appointment as auditors.

39.145　In the subsections which follow, each of the above circumstances is discussed in detail and examples of audit reports are given.

Auditors instructed not to carry out audit procedures

39.146　Companies which are subject to the Act are prohibited from imposing restrictions on the scope of the audit, although other entities may seek to do so. However, auditors of companies and other entities fall within the scope of SAS 601 *Imposed limitation of audit scope*. Where the auditors are prevented from carrying out the procedures they consider necessary, and are unable to carry out acceptable alternative procedures, in particular, where the limitation in scope may result in the need to issue a disclaimer of opinion, they have regard to the guidance given in SAS 601, which may result in not accepting the engagement, or having once accepted, subsequently resigning from it (see **39.132** above). If, having considered SAS 601, they remain in appointment they must qualify their report appropriately. It is not sufficient merely to state in the report that they have not obtained all the information and explanations they require, but must describe the restrictions imposed and the effect on the financial statements.

39.147　Organisations such as sole traders, partnerships, clubs, trusts, etc., which are not required by law to have an audit, sometimes wish to restrict the normal audit scope. If the restrictions are so extensive as to prevent the auditors from forming an opinion on the financial statements as a whole, they should not accept the audit engagement in line with guidance given in SAS 601 (see **39.132** above).

Information not made available to auditors

39.148　The Act requires the officers of the company to give the auditors such information and explanations as the auditors consider necessary for the performance of their duties. An officer of a company who knowingly or recklessly gives information to the auditors which is misleading, false or deceptive is guilty of a criminal offence. [s399A]

39.149　The Act also imposes a duty on a British subsidiary and its auditors to give to the auditors of the parent company such information and explanations as they may reasonably require to carry out their duties. [s399A] If the subsidiary is incorporated outside Great Britain, the parent company auditors may request the parent to take such steps as are reasonably open to it to obtain from that subsidiary the information and explanations required by the auditors.

39.150   Where information and explanations are not forthcoming, the auditors are required to state that fact in their report. [s237(3)] Auditors should also have regard to the guidance given in SAS 601 *Imposed limitation of audit scope* (see **39.132** above) which may result in their resignation as auditors.

39.151   In order to form an opinion on the consolidated financial statements, the auditors of the parent company need to be satisfied with all material information included in the statements which relates to subsidiaries which they have not audited. If they are not satisfied that an adequate audit has been performed on information derived from subsidiaries not audited by them, and if they have not been given sufficient information and explanations to overcome their reservations, they will need to qualify/disclaim their opinion in respect of such amounts included in the consolidated financial statements. These should be disclosed, preferably by way of reference to a note identifying the assets, liabilities and profits or losses of the subsidiaries concerned.

Example 39.151

Basis of opinion

We conducted our audit in accordance with United Kingdom auditing standards issued by the Auditing Practices Board, except that the scope of our work was limited as explained below.

An audit includes examination, on a test basis, of evidence relevant to the amounts and disclosures in the financial statements. It also includes an assessment of the significant estimates and judgements made by the directors in the preparation of the financial statements and of whether the accounting policies are appropriate to the circumstances of the company and the group, consistently applied and adequately disclosed.

We planned our audit so as to obtain all the information and explanations which we considered necessary in order to provide us with sufficient evidence to give reasonable assurance that the financial statements are free from material misstatement, whether caused by fraud or other irregularity or error. However, the evidence available to us was limited, because the auditors of Deltois SA, a recently acquired wholly owned subsidiary, were not appointed until after the financial year end and they have not completed their audit. Accordingly, the amounts included in the accompanying consolidated financial statements in respect of this subsidiary of £...... profit and £...... net assets are based on unaudited management accounts. There were no other satisfactory audit procedures that we could adopt to verify these amounts.

In forming our opinion, we also evaluated the overall adequacy of the presentation of information in the financial statements.

> **Qualified opinion arising from limitation in audit scope**
>
> Except for any adjustments to the financial statements that might have been found to be necessary had we been able to obtain sufficient evidence concerning the management accounts of the above-mentioned subsidiary, in our opinion, the financial statements give a true and fair view of the state of the group's affairs as at 31 March 2000 and of the profit [loss] of the group for the year then ended and have been properly prepared in accordance with the Companies Act 1985. In our opinion, the financial statements give a true and fair view of the state of the company's affairs as at 31 March 2000.
>
> In respect alone of the limitation on our work relating to the management accounts of Deltois SA, we have not obtained all the information and explanations that we considered necessary for the purposes of our audit.
>
> Note: Reference is not made to inability to determine whether proper accounting records have been kept because, under the Act, the auditors are only required to state the fact where they are of the opinion that the company has not kept proper accounting records.

Proper accounting records not kept

39.152 Accounting records should:

(a)   be sufficient to show and explain the company's transactions;

(b)   disclose with reasonable accuracy the company's financial position at any time; and

(c)   enable the directors to ensure that any balance sheets and profit and loss accounts which they are required to prepare comply with the Act [s221].

39.153 In particular, accounting records should contain:

(a)   entries from day to day of all sums of money received and expended and the matters in respect of which the receipts and expenditure take place;

(b)   a record of the assets and liabilities of the company; and

(c)   where the company's business involves dealing in goods:

   (i)   statements of stock held at the end of each financial year;
   (ii)   all statements of stocktakings from which those statements of stock have been prepared; and
   (iii) except in the case of goods sold by way of ordinary retail trade, statements of all goods sold and purchased in sufficient detail to identify the goods and the buyers and sellers.

39.154 For an interpretation of these requirements, reference should be made to the statement of guidance issued by the ICAEW in Technical Release FRAG 5/92. The key points of the guidance on the obligation of companies to keep accounting records under the Act include the following:

(a)   the Act requires that accounting records should be such as to 'disclose with reasonable accuracy, at any time, the financial position at that time'. The words 'at any time' emphasise the need to keep accounting records up to date and do not impose an obligation to keep accounting records capable of disclosing the financial position as at any time in the past;

(b)   the requirement that accounting records must be kept up to date does not mean that they should be updated instantaneously, but that they are updated within a reasonable time;

(c)   the financial position is not limited to the cash position. It comprises the assets and liabilities including provisions for matters such as depreciation, bad debts and other losses that are often only made at the end of an accounting period. Clearly this requires the stock figure to be assessable at any time. However, continuous records are not essential if the position can be assessed with sufficient reliability from other accounting records, including, in appropriate cases, interim stocktakes;

(d)   accounting records must be preserved for prescribed periods. Any programmed instructions, documentation or hardware necessary to convert the records to a usable form must be available for the same period.

39.155 A common circumstance giving rise to the failure of a company to keep proper accounting records is the incomplete recording of transactions, which is discussed further in **39.161** to **39.162** below. Other circumstances giving rise to failure to keep proper accounting records include falsification of information in the accounting records and the hiding, misfiling or destruction (deliberate or otherwise) of the accounting records. These circumstances will usually result in the auditors not obtaining all the information and explanations which they require. The Act will then require them to report their opinion that proper accounting records have not been kept and that they have not obtained all the information and explanations they required. If the deficiencies are so material or pervasive that the financial statements could be misleading, then a disclaimer of opinion would be required; where the deficiencies are confined to a particular area, a qualified opinion may be appropriate. The example below illustrates a disclaimer of opinion resulting from accounting records destroyed by fire.

Example 39.155

Basis of opinion

We conducted our audit in accordance with United Kingdom auditing standards issued by the Auditing Practices Board, except that the scope of our work was limited as explained below.

An audit includes examination, on a test basis, of evidence relevant to the amounts and disclosures in the financial statements. It also includes an assessment of the significant estimates and judgements made by the directors in the preparation of the financial statements and of whether the accounting policies are appropriate to the company's circumstances, consistently applied and adequately disclosed.

We planned our audit so as to obtain all the information and explanations which we considered necessary in order to provide us with sufficient evidence to give reasonable assurance that the financial statements are free from material misstatement, whether caused by fraud or other irregularity or error. However, the evidence available to us was limited, because a fire on 7 April 2000 at the company's computer centre destroyed the accounting records concerning debtors, creditors and stocks. The financial statements therefore include significant amounts based on estimates. In these circumstances, we were unable to carry out all the auditing procedures necessary to obtain adequate assurance regarding the amounts appearing in the balance sheet for debtors at £....., creditors at £...... and stocks at £....... Any adjustments to these figures would have a consequential effect on the profit for the year.

In forming our opinion, we also evaluated the overall adequacy of the presentation of information in the financial statements.

Disclaimer of opinion on view given by financial statements

Because of the possible effect of the limitation in evidence available to us, we are unable to form an opinion as to whether the financial statements give a true and fair view of the state of the company's affairs as at 31 March 2000 or of its profit [loss] for the year then ended and whether the financial statements have been properly prepared in accordance with the Companies Act 1985.

In respect of the limitation on our work, we have not obtained all the information and explanations that we considered necessary for the purposes of our audit. In our opinion, proper accounting records have not been kept in respect of debtors, creditors and stocks.

39.156 As the records have been destroyed, it is inappropriate in the above example for the auditors to state that they were unable to determine whether proper accounting records have been kept.

39.157 When reporting on a group, there is need to remember that the reporting requirement relates to the company and not the group. When qualifying an audit report on a group set of financial statements in respect of accounting records, the related opinion should read: 'In our opinion proper accounting records have not been kept by the company in respect of ...'.

39.158 The Act also requires the auditors to report where, in their opinion, proper returns adequate for their audit have not been received from branches not visited by them. [s237]

Service organisations

39.159 SAS 480 *Service organisations*, which is effective for audits of financial statements for periods beginning on or after 23 December 1998, states that 'if a service organisation maintains all or part of a user entity's accounting records, user entity auditors should assess whether the arrangements affect their reporting responsibilities in relation to accounting records arising from law or regulations'. [SAS 480.5] The guidance in SAS 480 states that when a user entity incorporated under company law arranges for a service organisation to maintain its accounting records, the contractual arrangements can only be regarded as appropriate if they establish the company's legal ownership of the records and provide for access to them at any time by the directors or officers of the company and by its auditors.

39.160 An issue that is highlighted in SAS 480 is that the wording of the Act appears to be prescriptive and to require the company itself to keep accounting records. Whether a company 'keeps' accounting records (as opposed to 'causes accounting records to be kept') will depend upon the particular terms of the outsourcing arrangement and the extent to which the company retains ownership of, has access to or holds copies of those records. Where there is doubt as to whether arrangements are such as to enable the company to meet its statutory obligations, auditors are advised that they may wish to encourage the directors to take legal advice before issuing their report on the financial statements.

Incompleteness of recording of transactions

39.161 While auditors can never obtain absolute assurance that all transactions entered into by a company have been recorded in the accounting records, they normally will be able to carry out sufficient tests of transactions, balances and controls and to perform analytical reviews, in particular of profit margins and costs, to enable them to conclude that the recording of transactions is complete. In the circumstances of many small companies which are owner-dominated, there may be few, if any, controls on which the auditors can rely and they will need to obtain management's representations as to the completeness and correctness of the recording of transactions. Where the auditors are satisfied that management is actually in a position to know that the assurances it gives are accurate and where evidence from their audit tests indicates that the accounting records are complete, they should make no reference in their report either to the representations received or to the less formal system of internal control in operation, as such references might be construed as a qualification.

39.162 Where adequate assurance cannot be obtained (e.g., where many transactions are made for cash, there is no system of control which can be relied on for audit purposes and gross margins are not in line with expectations), the auditors should give a qualified opinion or disclaim their opinion in extreme cases where the uncertainties are so material or pervasive. When reporting under the Act, they should also state that they have not obtained all the information and explanations which they consider necessary for the purposes of their audit. The example below illustrates a qualified opinion due to an inability to substantiate cash sales.

Example 39.162

Basis of opinion

We conducted our audit in accordance with United Kingdom auditing standards issued by the Auditing Practices Board, except that the scope of our work was limited as explained below.

An audit includes examination, on a test basis, of evidence relevant to the amounts and disclosures in the financial statements. It also includes an assessment of the significant estimates and judgements made by the directors in the preparation of the financial statements and of whether the accounting policies are appropriate to the company's circumstances, consistently applied and adequately disclosed.

We planned our audit so as to obtain all the information and explanations which we considered necessary in order to provide us with sufficient evidence to give reasonable assurance that the financial statements are free from material misstatement, whether caused by fraud or other irregularity or error. However, the evidence available to us was limited, because £98,500 of the company's recorded turnover comprises cash sales. There was no system of control over such sales on which we could rely for the purposes of our audit and there were no other satisfactory audit procedures that we could adopt to confirm that cash sales were properly recorded.

In forming our opinion, we also evaluated the overall adequacy of the presentation of information in the financial statements.

Qualified opinion arising from limitation in audit scope

Except for any adjustments to the financial statements that might have been found to be necessary had we been able to obtain sufficient evidence concerning cash sales, in our opinion, the financial statements give a true and fair view of the state of the company's affairs as

---

at 31 March 2000 and of its profit [loss] for the year then ended and have been properly prepared in accordance with the Companies Act 1985.

In respect alone of the limitation on our work relating to cash sales:

(a) we have not obtained all the information and explanations that we considered necessary for the purposes of our audit; and

(b) we were unable to determine whether proper accounting records have been kept.

39.163 The use of a 'properly prepared' report is not a mechanism which enables auditors to avoid qualifying on grounds of incompleteness of recording of transactions.

Limitations arising in the first year of appointment as auditors

39.164 Where the auditors have not audited the financial statements of the previous year, they cannot rely on them for the assurance that they require regarding the opening balances, without making further enquiries. The most efficient way of obtaining the necessary assurance will often be by consultation with the outgoing auditors and possibly by a review of the audit working papers. Where they cannot obtain assurance in this way, they may not be able to carry out all the necessary verification work, since they will usually have been appointed after the start of the financial year. In such circumstances, they may have reservations as to the fairness of the profit and loss account, but should be satisfied that the balance sheet is fairly stated. The example below illustrates the situation where opening stocks were not audited, giving rise to a qualified opinion.

> ### *Example 39.164*
>
> **Basis of opinion**
>
> We conducted our audit in accordance with United Kingdom auditing standards issued by the Auditing Practices Board, except that the scope of our work was limited as explained below.
>
> An audit includes examination, on a test basis, of evidence relevant to the amounts and disclosures in the financial statements. It also includes an assessment of any significant estimates and judgements made by the directors in the preparation of the financial statements and of whether the accounting policies are appropriate to the company's circumstances, consistently applied and adequately disclosed.
>
> We planned our audit so as to obtain all the information and explanations which we considered necessary in order to provide us with sufficient evidence to give reasonable assurance that the financial

statements are free from material misstatement, whether caused by fraud or other irregularity or error. However, the evidence available to us was limited, because we were not appointed auditors until 3 June 1999 and did not report on the financial statements for the year ended 31 March 1999. In consequence, we were unable to carry out auditing procedures necessary to obtain adequate assurance regarding the quantities and condition of stocks appearing in the balance sheet at 31 March 1999 at £236,000. Any adjustment to this figure would have a consequential effect on the profit for the year ended 31 March 2000.

In forming our opinion, we also evaluated the overall adequacy of the presentation of information in the financial statements.

Qualified opinion arising from limitation in audit scope

In our opinion, the financial statements give a true and fair view of the state of the company's affairs as at 31 March 2000. Except for any adjustments to the financial statements that might have been found to be necessary had we been able to obtain sufficient evidence concerning stocks at the beginning of the year, in our opinion, the financial statements give a true and fair view of the company's profit [loss] for the year then ended and have been properly prepared in accordance with the Companies Act 1985.

In respect alone of the limitation on our work relating to stocks:

(a)   we have not obtained all the information and explanations that we considered necessary for the purposes of our audit; and

(b)   we were unable to determine whether proper accounting records have been kept.

Examples arising from disagreement

Introduction

39.165   Circumstances which give rise to disagreement include:

(a)   disagreement as to the accounting policies followed;

(b)   disagreement as to facts or amounts shown in the financial statements;

(c)   disagreement as to manner or extent of disclosure of facts or amounts in the financial statements;

(d)   failure to comply with relevant legislation or other requirements; and

(e)   omission of primary statements.

39.166   In the subsections which follow, each of these categories is discussed in detail and examples of audit reports are given.

Disagreement as to accounting policies followed

39.167 In deciding whether an accounting policy is appropriate to the circumstances of the business, the auditors must first be satisfied that the application of the policy will give a true and fair view. They will also need to consider whether the policy departs significantly from:

(a)   accounting standards;

(b)   accepted practice where a policy is not covered by an accounting standard; or

(c)   other relevant accounting requirements, such as those contained in the Act and UITF Abstracts.

Departure from accounting standards

36.168 Although there is no specific requirement for companies' financial statements to comply with accounting standards, Sch 4 requires companies which do not qualify as small or medium-sized to state in the financial statements whether they have been prepared in accordance with applicable accounting standards and give particulars of and reasons for any material departure from them. [Sch 4: 36A]

39.169 Ordinarily, compliance with UK accounting standards (FRSs and SSAPs) is necessary in order to give a true and fair view. If a company's financial statements depart from accounting standards, it is unlikely that the auditors will be able to agree with the departure. Their concurrence with a material departure would be justified if it could be demonstrated that compliance with a standard would not give a true and fair view, the alternative treatment does give a true and fair view and adequate disclosure has been made concerning the departure.

39.170 A material departure from the accounting requirements of the Act is permitted by the true and fair view override of s226(5) and by s227(6), which requires that the particulars of any such departure, the reasons for it and its effect are given in a note to the accounts. UITF Abstract 7 interprets the disclosure requirements of the Act as follows:

(a)   'particulars of any such departure': a statement of the treatment which the Act would normally require in the circumstances and a description of the treatment actually adopted;

(b)   'the reasons for it': a statement as to why the treatment prescribed would not give a true and fair view;

(c)   'its effect': a description of how the position shown in the accounts is different as a result of the departure, normally with quantification, except where quantification is evident in the accounts or when the effect cannot reasonably be quantified; in which case, the directors should explain the circumstances.

39.171 In the rare circumstances where the auditors concur with a material departure and it has been adequately disclosed in the financial statements in the manner described above, they need not make reference to it in their report.

39.172 Where the auditors disagree with a material departure, SAS 600 requires that their report should describe all substantive factors giving rise to the disagreement and quantify, whenever practicable, the effect on the financial statements. The following example illustrates an opinion resulting from a departure from an accounting standard (FRS 9).

Example 39.172.1

Qualified opinion arising from disagreement about accounting treatment

The company follows the policy of including in the financial statements only the dividends received from XYZ Limited, its associated company. This is not in accordance with Financial Reporting Standard 9 *Associates and joint ventures*. If the company had equity accounted XYZ Limited, in accordance with that accounting standard, the group profit on ordinary activities after taxation shown in the consolidated profit and loss account would have been increased by £290,000 and the group's interest in XYZ Limited and the group reserves, as shown in the consolidated balance sheet, would have been increased by £1,830,000.

Except for the failure to account for the associated company in the manner described above, in our opinion, the financial statements give a true and fair view...

The following example illustrates a departure from an accounting standard (SSAP 13) and the Act that is not quantifiable.

Example 39.172.2

Qualified opinion arising from disagreement about accounting treatment

Included in the development costs shown as intangible assets on the balance sheet is an amount of £...... relating to pit development costs which is being written off to profit and loss account as the related production is sold. This is not in accordance with Statement of Standard Accounting Practice 13 *Accounting for research and development* which only permits development expenditure to be carried forward in the balance sheet to the extent that its future recovery can reasonably be regarded as assured. As explained in note 8 to the accounts, the revenue to be derived from the pit is dependent upon the quality of slate block extracted. Since the quality of block extracted has not been consistent, it is not possible to determine with reasonable

---

certainty whether the balance of deferred expenditure will be recovered from future revenues after taking account of extraction and other production costs. In these circumstances, we are unable to quantify the effect of the departure from the accounting standard.

Except for the failure to account for development costs in the manner described above, in our opinion, the financial statements give a true and fair view of the state of the company's affairs at 31 March 2000 and of its loss for the year then ended and have been properly prepared in accordance with the Companies Act 1985.

The following example illustrates a departure from an accounting standard (FRS 2) and the Act that is not quantifiable – the failure to prepare consolidated group financial statements.

Example 39.172.3

Qualified opinion arising from disagreement about accounting treatment

As explained in note 1, the financial statements of the company do not include consolidated financial statements for its group as required by s227 Companies Act 1985 and Financial Reporting Standard 2 *Accounting for subsidiary undertakings*. As a consequence, the financial statements do not give the information required by generally accepted accounting practice about the economic activities of the group of which the company is the parent. It is not practicable to quantify the effects of this departure. Accordingly, in our opinion, a true and fair view of the group is not given.

In our opinion, the financial statements give a true and fair view of the state of the company's affairs at (date) and of its profit [loss] for the year then ended and, except for the fact that consolidated financial statements have not been prepared, the financial statements have been properly prepared in accordance with the Companies Act 1985.

The following example illustrates a departure from an accounting standard (FRS 2) and the Act. In this example, the auditors are able to give some financial information on the effects of the departure.

Example 39.172.4

Qualified opinion arising from failure to consolidate subsidiary

As explained in note x, the subsidiary undertaking, Delto Europe Limited, has been excluded from consolidation on the basis that the interest of the parent company is held exclusively with a view to resale. The investment was acquired on 25 April 1960 and had previously been included in the consolidated financial statements. In our opinion, this subsidiary should be included in the consolidation as required by s227 Companies Act 1985 and Financial Reporting Standard 2 *Accounting for subsidiary undertakings*. Had the subsidiary been consolidated, the investment in and amounts owed to/by the unconsolidated subsidiary stated in the consolidated balance sheet at £...... would have been replaced by increases in various assets and liabilities with a corresponding net increase/decrease in consolidated reserves of £...... and the consolidated profit for the financial year would have been increased/decreased by £......

In our opinion, the financial statements give a true and fair view of the state of affairs of the company at 31 March 2000. Except for the failure to consolidate the subsidiary as described above, in our opinion, the financial statements give a true and fair view of the state of affairs of the group at 31 March 2000 and of its profit for the year then ended and have been properly prepared in accordance with the Companies Act 1985.

Notes: The above assumes that consolidated financial statements have been prepared dealing with other subsidiary undertakings.

If there are any other significant features of the financial statements which would have been affected by the failure to consolidate, then these should also be disclosed.

The following example illustrates a departure from an accounting standard (SSAP 19) that is not quantifiable.

Example 39.172.5

Qualified opinion arising from disagreement about accounting treatment

The company follows the policy of including investment properties in the balance sheet at cost. This is not in accordance with Statement of Standard Accounting Practice 19 *Accounting for investment properties*, which requires that such properties be included at open market value. Any surpluses that arise from valuations would increase the amounts shown in the balance sheet for investment properties and revaluation reserve. Any deficits that arise from valuations would decrease the amount shown in the balance sheet for investment properties. Such deficits would also, to the extent that the revalued amount is not less than the original cost of the investment property, reduce the amount shown in the balance sheet for revaluation reserve; to the extent that the revalued amount is less than the original cost of the investment property, the deficit would reduce the profit on ordinary activities before taxation. In the absence of valuations of the company's investment properties, it is not practicable to quantify the effects of the departure.

Except for the failure to account for investment properties in the manner described above, in our opinion, the financial statements give a true and fair view of the state of the company's affairs as at 31 March 2000 and of the profit [loss] for the year then ended and have been properly prepared in accordance with the Companies Act 1985.

> Note: The above opinion assumes that no investment properties have been sold in the financial year. If properties have been sold, the explanation would need to be expanded to explain the further effect on the profit and loss account.

39.173 The above examples assume that the financial statements of companies which do not qualify as small or medium-sized disclose that, apart from the stated departure, they comply with applicable accounting standards and have given the particulars of and reasons for the departure. When the financial statements do not provide this information as required by the Act, the auditors must refer to the departure and also qualify on the grounds of non-compliance with this specific requirement of the Act.

> **Example 39.173**
>
> **Qualified opinion arising from disagreement about accounting treatment**
>
> The company follows the policy of including investment properties in the balance sheet at cost. This is not in accordance with Statement of Standard Accounting Practice 19 *Accounting for investment properties,* which requires that such properties be included at open market value. Any surplus or deficit arising from a valuation would increase or decrease, respectively, the amounts shown in the balance sheet for investment properties and revaluation reserve. In the absence of a valuation being made of the company's investment properties, it is not practicable to quantify the effects of the departure.
>
> The financial statements do not disclose whether they have been prepared in accordance with applicable accounting standards and the particulars of the above material departure from those standards and the reasons for it, as required by Sch 4 para 36A Companies Act 1985.
>
> Except for the failure to account for investment properties and provide disclosures concerning the departure from applicable accounting standards in the manner described above, in our opinion, the financial statements give a true and fair view of the state of the company's affairs as at 31 March 2000 and of its profit [loss] for the year then ended and have been properly prepared in accordance with the Companies Act 1985.
>
> Note: The Act exempts companies which qualify as small or medium-sized from giving disclosure in respect of compliance with applicable accounting standards.

Departure from accepted practice where the policy is not covered by an accounting standard or other relevant accounting requirements

39.174 The development of accounting in the UK has resulted in a diversity of accounting practices, with varying degrees of acceptability. While the issue of accounting standards has done much to reduce the number of acceptable accounting practices, there still remain some areas where different accounting practices are generally accepted.

39.175 The role of the UITF is to issue Abstracts (consensus pronouncements) to assist in areas where an accounting standard or a Companies Act provision exists, but where unsatisfactory or conflicting interpretations have developed. Although a UITF Abstract does not have the status of an accounting standard, the ASB has, nonetheless, stated that 'it should be considered to be part of the corpus of practices forming the basis for determining what constitutes a true and fair view' and 'unless the ASB has indicated that it dissents from the consensus ... the consensus is ... to be regarded as accepted practice and all companies will be expected to conform to it, if necessary by changing previously adopted accounting policies, unless the consensus explicitly states otherwise'.

39.176 Failure to comply with a UITF Abstract which has a material effect on the financial statements will give rise to a qualification of the auditors' opinion (or an adverse opinion) in the same manner as a departure from an accounting standard, as explained in **39.168** to **39.173** above.

39.177 Guidance as to the acceptability of accounting policies can be found by reference to the sources of information described in chapter 2.

39.178 If a company follows an accounting policy which is not the subject of an accounting standard and which the auditors consider is not appropriate to the circumstances of the business, their report should refer to the policy with which they disagree and should indicate the treatment they consider appropriate. They should quantify, wherever practicable, the effects on the financial statements in a manner similar to the examples given above.

Disagreement as to facts or amounts shown in financial statements

39.179 During the course of an audit, information may be obtained which the auditors conclude conflicts with the facts or amounts shown in the financial statements. Where the discrepancy is due to an error, there should be no disagreement, since the company will normally alter the financial statements if the facts or amounts are material. There are, however, other instances where evaluation of the evidence leads the auditors to a conclusion which is different from that of the company. These often relate to the valuation of assets or liabilities. It is the auditors' duty to exercise their independent judgement and where a disagreement is considered material to an appreciation of the financial statements, a qualified or adverse opinion should be given.

> **Example 39.179**
>
> **Qualified opinion arising from disagreement about value of investment**
>
> The shares in Delto Limited, which is in liquidation, are shown in the balance sheet at cost of £123,000. The liquidator has stated that it is unlikely that the company will be able to pay its debts in full and, in our opinion, full provision should be made against this investment. Accordingly, in our opinion, the amounts shown in the financial statements for fixed asset investments, profit and loss reserve and profit for the financial year are overstated by £123,000.
>
> Except for the failure to provide for the loss in value of the above investment, in our opinion, the financial statements give a true and fair view ...

39.180 As already indicated, the evidence available to support an estimate can only be persuasive and never conclusive. Unless the evidence available is significantly less than the auditors are entitled to expect (in which case, they should qualify on the grounds of limitation in the scope of their work and that they have not obtained all the information and explanations which they require), the auditors must exercise their judgement on the basis of the information available. If, on that evidence, they reach a conclusion which is different from that of the directors, they should give a qualified opinion on the grounds of disagreement or issue an adverse opinion.

39.181 The notes form part of the financial statements for the purposes of the Act, but disclosures in the notes cannot correct or amend accounts which show a differing view. Therefore, if a note materially alters the view otherwise given by the accounts, it will be necessary to qualify the audit report.

39.182 For example, if a note to the accounts indicates that investments include £123,000 which is not expected to be recovered but that, pending the final report of the liquidators, no provision has been made, the audit report should still be qualified in the manner shown in the example in **39.179** above.

Disagreement as to the adequacy of disclosure

39.183 If the financial statements fail to disclose information which is required to be disclosed by accounting standards or significant information which the auditors believe is essential to a true and fair view, their report should be qualified on grounds of disagreement or an adverse opinion given. The report should clearly indicate the nature of the omitted information and should provide the omitted information if it is practicable to do so.

Failure to comply with relevant legislation or other requirements

Companies Act disclosures concerning directors and officers

39.184 The Act requires certain information concerning emoluments and other benefits of directors and others to be disclosed in a note to the accounts and, in addition, provides that, if it is not given, the auditors should give it in their report so far as they are reasonably able to do so. [s237(4)]

39.185 The information covered by this requirement is that required by Sch 6, namely:

(a) details of directors' remuneration, pensions and compensation for loss of office [Sch 6: Pt I];

(b) particulars of loans, quasi-loans and other dealings in favour of directors [Sch 6: Pt II];

(c) particulars of transactions, arrangements and agreements with directors and officers [Sch 6: Pt III].

39.186 Considerations in respect of reporting on listed companies are dealt with in chapter 40. Directors' remuneration is dealt with in chapter 8.

Other Companies Act disclosures

39.187 Schedules 4 and 5 require many other items to be separately disclosed either in the accounts or in the notes. In some circumstances, the auditors may consider that the financial statements give a true and fair view in spite of the omission of certain statutory disclosures, but they will still be required to indicate that the financial statements have not been properly prepared in accordance with the Act. In these circumstances, there is no statutory requirement to provide the omitted information in the audit report. However, SAS 600 states that where the auditors disagree with the disclosure of a matter, the effect of which is material to the financial statements, the effect of the disagreement should be quantified, whenever practicable. Normally, directors will agree to include any omitted disclosures in the financial statements when they understand that such omissions will be included in the auditors' report.

> ### *Example 39.187.1*
>
> **Qualified opinion arising from non-disclosure of compliance with accounting standards**
>
> The company has not stated whether the financial statements have been prepared in accordance with applicable accounting standards as

required by the Companies Act 1985. In our opinion, the financial statements have been prepared in accordance with applicable accounting standards, but the financial statements do not make this disclosure as required by the Act.

In our opinion, the financial statements give a true and fair view of the company's state of affairs as at 31 March 2000 and of its profit for the year then ended. Except for the non-disclosure of the matter described above, the financial statements have been properly prepared in accordance with the Companies Act 1985.

Note: The Act exempts companies or groups which qualify as small or medium-sized from giving disclosure of compliance with applicable accounting standards.

Example 39.187.2

Qualified opinion arising from disagreement about extent of disclosure and limitation of audit scope

The comparable cost and accumulated depreciation determined under the historical cost accounting rules in respect of revalued fixed tangible assets or the differences between those amounts and the corresponding amounts shown in the balance sheet have not been disclosed as required by Sch 4 para 33(3) Companies Act 1985 and by Financial Reporting Standard 15 *Tangible fixed assets*. This information has not been made available to us.

Except for the omission of the information described above, in our opinion, the financial statements give a true and fair view of the state of the company's affairs as at 31 March 2000 and of its profit [loss] for the year then ended and have been properly prepared in accordance with the Companies Act 1985.

In respect alone of the limitation on our work relating to revalued fixed assets:

(a) we have not obtained all the information and explanations we considered necessary for the purposes of our audit; and

(b) in our opinion, proper accounting records have not been kept in respect of the cost and accumulated depreciation of revalued fixed assets.

39.188 Exceptional circumstances may arise when a board declines to give the required information on the grounds that it is likely to be seriously prejudicial to the business of the company or one of its subsidiary undertakings. A particular example arises where the company has applied to the Secretary of State for exemption in accordance with the Act.

In such circumstances the auditors may decide that it is not appropriate for them to disclose the omitted information.

Example 39.188

Qualified opinion arising from disagreement about extent of disclosure

As explained in note 15, the information concerning overseas investments acquired during the year has not been disclosed as required by Sch 5 para 7 Companies Act 1985.

In our opinion, the financial statements give a true and fair view of the state of the company's affairs as at 31 March 2000 and of its profit [loss] for the year then ended and, except for the omission of the disclosure concerning overseas investments described above, have been properly prepared in accordance with the Companies Act 1985.

Note: The note referred to in the audit report should explain the reason for non-disclosure of the information (i.e., it would be seriously prejudicial to the business of the company/one of the company's subsidiary undertakings) and that application has been made to the Secretary of State for exemption under the 1985 Act. In this example, the opinion on the true and fair view shown by the financial statements is not impaired by omission of this required disclosure.

Financial statements not in agreement with accounting records

39.189 When the balance sheet and profit and loss account are not in agreement with the accounting records and returns, the auditors are required to state that fact in their report. [s237] This should be done in the opinion section.

39.190 Usually, the company records all approved audit adjustments, so that the accounting records agree with the financial statements. However, care should be taken to ensure that all adjustments made at the consolidation level, except those normal consolidating adjustments necessary to eliminate inter-company investments, balances and profits and to achieve consistency of accounting policies within the group, are recorded in the accounting records of the applicable companies.

Directors' report not consistent with the financial statements

39.191 The Act imposes a duty on the auditors to consider whether the information given in the directors' report relating to the financial year is consistent with the financial statements and, if there is an inconsistency, to state that fact in the audit report. [s235(3)]

39.192 It is rare for there to be a straightforward difference between figures appearing in the audited financial statements and corresponding figures quoted in the directors' report. Sometimes, however, inconsistency arises from loose or ambiguous wording in the directors' report. For example, a reference in the directors' report to the profit before taxation of £A, where £A is, in fact, the operating profit and the profit on ordinary activities before taxation disclosed in the profit and loss account is significantly lower because of a large exceptional item, would result in an inconsistency between the directors' report and the profit and loss account.

39.193 The most difficult area of possible inconsistency arises from the narrative content of the directors' report; in particular, the fair review of the development of the business of the company and of its position at the year end. Sometimes, the inconsistency arises from the use of a different basis of preparation of data for purposes of the directors' report from that used in the financial statements and the different basis is not disclosed. The auditors must distinguish between, firstly, purportedly factual statements which are inconsistent with the information in the financial statements, and secondly, expressions of judgement which place an interpretation on the financial statements with which they disagree. While they will try to get both changed, they should only refer to the matter in their report when they are satisfied that there is inconsistency. However, they should consider carefully the need to take further action, as indicated in SAS 160 (Revised) *Other information in documents containing audited financial statements.*

39.194 It is seldom necessary for the auditors to report on inconsistency, since the directors will usually agree to amend their report to remove the inconsistency. When an inconsistency remains, the opinion section should explain the nature of the inconsistency and the resulting difference in a paragraph following the opinion on the financial statements.

Example 39.194

Opinion   (Opinion on the financial statements)

Inconsistency between the financial statements and the directors' report

In our opinion, the information given in paragraph 7 of the directors' report is not consistent with these financial statements. That

> paragraph states without amplification that the company's trading resulted in a profit before tax of £X. The profit and loss account, however, states that the company incurred an operating loss for the year of £Y and a profit from the sale of land of £Z.
>
> Note that this form of report is not a qualified report for the purposes of ss240(3)(d) or 271(4) of the Act, or s49(3)(c) of the Companies (Amendment) Act 1983 and s19(2)(d) of the Companies (Amendment) Act 1986 in the Republic of Ireland, as the opinion on the financial statements is unaffected.

Other information (other than that in the directors' report) not consistent with the financial statements

39.195 As explained in **39.21** above, auditors have no responsibility under the Act to provide an opinion on the other information accompanying the financial statements. However, SAS 160 (Revised) *Other information in documents containing audited financial statements* requires auditors to read the other information in the light of the knowledge they have acquired during the audit. They are not required to verify any of the other information.

39.196 If auditors become aware of any apparent misstatements in the other information, or identify any material inconsistencies with the financial statements, they should seek to resolve the situation through discussion with the directors. However, if they are unable to resolve it with the directors, the auditors consider requesting the directors to consult with a qualified third party, such as the entity's lawyers.

39.197 If subsequently the auditors still consider an amendment is necessary to the other information, and the directors refuse to make it, then whilst there is no statutory duty to make reference to the inconsistencies in their audit report (unlike for information contained in directors' reports, see **39.191** above), the auditors consider including in the audit report an explanatory paragraph describing the apparent misstatement or material inconsistency. In these circumstances, where the auditors have no issues with the financial statements themselves, an explanatory paragraph does not give rise to a qualified opinion.

39.198 When determining whether to add such an explanatory paragraph to the audit report, auditors may need to take legal advice, including advice on whether they would be protected by qualified privilege from a defamation claim if they were to refer to the matters in their report or subsequently.

Statutory financial statements not drawn up by reference to a valid accounting reference date

39.199 Companies sometimes prepare financial statements to a date which is not a valid accounting reference date under s224, and the directors may ask the auditors to report on such statements. The auditors' attitude to this request will depend on the purpose for which the statements are required. If they are required for any purpose other than to lay before the members in general meeting (e.g., for the information of bankers), they should carry out their audit in the normal way, with the exceptions that the report should be addressed to the company and not to the members of the company and they should not report as to whether the financial statements have been properly prepared in accordance with the Act.

39.200 If statutory financial statements are intended but an invalid accounting reference date is used, the auditors should point out to the directors that they are not acceptable for this purpose. Should the directors be unable or unwilling to correct the position and insist on presenting such financial statements as statutory accounts, then the financial statements could not be said to have been properly prepared in accordance with the Act and the auditors should qualify their report accordingly.

Example 39.200

Qualified opinion: invalid accounting reference date

The financial statements are not drawn up to the company's accounting reference date as required by ss223, 224 and 226 Companies Act 1985.

In our opinion, the financial statements give a true and fair view of the state of the company's affairs as at 31 March 2000 and of its profit [loss] for the 20 months then ended and, except that they are not drawn up to the company's accounting reference date, have been properly prepared in accordance with the Companies Act 1985.

Corresponding amounts

39.201 The auditors' opinion as to the truth and fairness of the financial statements relates only to amounts reported in relation to the period covered by those statements and does not extend to the corresponding amounts. However, the Act requires the disclosure of corresponding amounts for all items in a company's balance sheet and profit and loss account and that these amounts must be adjusted if necessary to be comparable with the amounts for the current financial year. The auditors' responsibility under the Act in respect of corresponding amounts is therefore to consider whether the amounts disclosed as corresponding amounts are the amounts which appeared in the previous year's financial statements or have been properly restated to be comparable with the amounts for the current year. [Sch 4: 4(2)] Restatement will normally be appropriate only in the circumstances outlined in FRS 3, i.e., to reflect a change in accounting policy or the correction of a fundamental error. Where corresponding amounts have been adjusted, particulars of the adjustments and the reasons for them should be shown in the notes to the accounts.

39.202 The auditors would normally qualify their opinion if they are not satisfied that the corresponding amounts are comparable. This might arise either:

(a)   when they consider that the corresponding amounts should have been restated (e.g., to reflect a change in accounting policy), but this has not been done, or that the corresponding amounts have been restated in an unjustifiable manner; or

(b)   when the previous financial statements were other than unqualified and they consider that the corresponding amounts are not, or may not be, comparable with those of the current period. It is unlikely that, in such circumstances, an adverse opinion would be appropriate.

Example 39.202

Qualified opinion arising from failure to restate corresponding amounts

As explained in note 5, the company has changed its accounting policy in respect of stocks, to include appropriate production overheads which had previously been excluded. The stock records at 31 March 1998 were not prepared in sufficient detail to enable the stocks at that date to be restated in accordance with the new policy. Accordingly, the corresponding amounts shown in the profit and loss account in respect of cost of sales, gross profit and profit before and after taxation are not comparable with the figures for the current period. Also, the corresponding amounts for changes in stocks and work in progress in the reconciliation of operating profit to net cash flow from operating activities (note x) are not comparable with the figures for the current period.

In our opinion, the financial statements give a true and fair view of the state of the company's affairs as at 31 March 2000 and of its profit [loss] for the year then ended and, except for the failure to restate the above prior year amounts in accordance with the change in accounting policy, have been properly prepared in accordance with the Companies Act 1985.

39.203

As with other qualifications, the auditors should quantify the effects of the misstatement on the previous year's financial statements, if this is practicable. It is sometimes not practicable to quantify these effects because it is not possible to determine the correct restated amount for the previous year, following a change in accounting policy. When this situation occurs, it may be helpful to the reader of the financial statements to disclose in a note what the current year's result would have been under the old accounting policy. If the company is unwilling to do this, the auditors should consider providing the information in their report.

39.204 It should not be assumed that an audit report which is other than unqualified in one year automatically results in a qualification of the corresponding amounts in the following year. If the matters which caused the report which is other than unqualified in the previous year have been resolved during the current year and properly reflected in the financial statements, no reference to the previous report is normally necessary. The most common circumstances are discussed below.

(a) The auditors disagreed with an accounting policy adopted by the client. The report should normally be qualified in the current year also, unless the policy has been changed to meet the auditors' view; in which case, the corresponding amounts should be restated.

(b) The auditors disagreed with a treatment which had the effect of transferring profit between the previous period and the one now being audited (e.g., as to the valuation of closing stocks of raw materials). The report should normally be qualified, because the auditors' disagreement concerns a matter which affects the profit of the current year; the qualification should make clear the effect on the corresponding amounts also.

(c) The auditors disagreed as to the amount to be included in respect of a material asset or liability. In the following year, the disagreement may be resolved either because the matter has been determined or because the auditors or the client have changed their view in the light of current information. In the circumstances, no qualification of the corresponding amounts is appropriate, but if the resolution has a material effect on the results of the year and the preceding one, the auditors will need to be satisfied that suitable disclosure is made. In exceptional circumstances, it might be necessary to deal with the matter as a correction of a fundamental error. If the matter has not been determined and both auditors and client adhere to their original views, the qualification must be repeated, but it is desirable to refer to the previous qualification so as to make it clear that the problem did not arise in the current period.

(d) The auditors qualified on the grounds of a limitation in the scope of the audit affecting profit, but gave an opinion on the balance sheet. In this case, the auditors are uncertain as to whether the comparable amounts in the profit and loss account are comparable and they would therefore qualify their report. The qualification relates to compliance with the Act only, since the true and fair view in respect of the current year is unaffected.

Example 39.204

Qualified opinion arising from limitation in audit scope

The corresponding amounts in the current period's financial statements are derived from the financial statements for the year ended 31 March 1999. In our report on those financial statements, we stated that we were unable to express an opinion on the profit for the year ended on that date because we were unable to substantiate the amount of stock at 1 April 1998. Accordingly, the corresponding amounts shown for the profit for the year ended 31 March 1999 may not be comparable with the figures for the current period.

In our opinion, the financial statements give a true and fair view of the state of the company's affairs as at 31 March 2000 and of its profit [loss] for the year then ended and, except for any adjustments that might have been found necessary had we been able to obtain sufficient evidence concerning the matter described above, have been properly prepared in accordance with Companies Act 1985.

Omission of primary statements

39.205 The omission of a primary statement normally results in the financial statements not giving a true and fair view of the state of affairs and profit or loss. Although the Act specifically requires the accounts to include a balance sheet and profit and loss account, the Act also requires the financial statements to include additional information necessary to give a true and fair view; therefore, the omission of a primary statement such as the cash flow statement will normally result in a failure to comply with the Act. An example of a qualified opinion arising from the omission of a cash flow statement is as follows.

Example 39.205

Qualified opinion arising from omission of cash flow statement

As explained in note 2, the financial statements do not contain a cash flow statement as required by Financial Reporting Standard 1 *Cash flow statements*. Net cash flows for the year ended 31 March 2000

> amounted to £3,578,000 outflow and, in our opinion, information
> about the company's cash flows is necessary for a proper understand-
> ing of the company's state of affairs and profit [loss].
>
> Except for the failure to provide information about the company's
> cash flows, in our opinion, the financial statements give a true and
> view ...

39.206   There may be extreme circumstances in which the auditors may conclude that the omission of a primary statement is so material that the
financial statements are seriously misleading. In such circumstances,
the auditors should issue an adverse opinion.

Example of a multiple qualification

Scope limitation and disagreement

39.207   The following is an example of a multiple qualification which
includes a scope limitation arising from inability to substantiate cash
sales and disagreement as to the facts shown in the financial statements.

> ### Example 39.207
>
> **Basis of opinion**
>
> We conducted our audit in accordance with United Kingdom audit-
> ing standards issued by the Auditing Practices Board, except that the
> scope of our work was limited as explained below.
>
> An audit includes examination, on a test basis, of evidence relevant to
> the amounts and disclosures in the financial statements. It also
> includes an assessment of the significant estimates and judgements
> made by the directors in the preparation of the financial statements
> and of whether the accounting policies are appropriate to the com-
> pany's circumstances, consistently applied and adequately disclosed.
>
> We planned our audit so as to obtain all the information and expla-
> nations which we considered necessary in order to provide us with
> sufficient evidence to give reasonable assurance that the financial
> statements are free from material misstatement, whether caused by
> fraud or other irregularity or error. However, the evidence available to
> us was limited because £98,500 of the company's recorded turnover
> comprises cash sales. There was no system of control over such sales
> on which we could rely for the purposes of our audit and there were
> no other satisfactory audit procedures that we could adopt to confirm
> that cash sales were properly recorded.
>
> In forming our opinion, we also evaluated the overall adequacy of the
> presentation of information in the financial statements.

Qualified opinion arising from limitation in audit scope and disagreement about accounting treatment

Trade debtors include a balance of £85,712 owed by a customer which is in liquidation and against which no provision has been made. In our opinion, the company, as an unsecured creditor, will not receive full payment and a provision of at least £80,000 should have been made.

Except for:

(a)   the failure to provide for the loss mentioned above; and

(b)   any adjustments that might have been found to be necessary had we been able to obtain sufficient evidence concerning cash sales,

in our opinion, the financial statements give a true and fair view of the state of the company's affairs as at 31 March 2000 and of its profit [loss] for the year then ended and have been properly prepared in accordance with the Companies Act 1985.

In respect alone of the limitation on our work relating to cash sales:

(a)   we have not obtained all the information and explanations that we considered necessary for the purposes of our audit; and

(b)   we were unable to determine whether proper accounting records had been kept.

40 Reports on listed companies

40 Reports on listed companies

Summary of changes since the previous issue of this publication

Para.	*Topic*	*Summary*
40.1 40.4	APB Bulletin 1999/5 *The Combined Code: requirements of auditors under the Listing Rules of the London Stock Exchange*	Changes to wording of responsibilities statement in audit report arising from 'audit, review and read' responsibilities of auditors. Also changes in respect of compliance with provisions of Combined Code and in relation to board's statements on internal controls. Changes effective for accounting periods ending on or after 23 December 1999.
40.4	Identification of nationality of law and accounting standards	Indicating in audit report nationality of law and accounting standards under which the financial statements have been prepared, in accordance with an agreement between the International Forum for Accountancy Developments and leading global regulators.
40.4	Identification of nationality of auditing standards	Indicating in audit report nationality of auditing standards under which the financial statements have been audited. This is in response to an agreement between the International Forum for Accountancy Developments and leading global regulators.
40.21	Amendment 14 to Listing Rules	The rules regarding timing and content of preliminary announcements were updated in January 2000 for accounting periods beginning on or after 23 December 1999.

40.30   APB Bulletin 1999/4   New review report wording
             Review of interim   introduced in July 1999.
             financial information

40.1   The guidance in this chapter is applicable to financial periods ending on or after 23 December 1999. This corresponds with the effective date of APB Bulletin 1999/5 *The Combined Code: requirements of auditors under the Listing Rules of the London Stock Exchange*. This chapter addresses reporting on the annual report, preliminary announcement or interim financial information of a listed company. It does not deal with other reports that may be required by the UK Listing Authority.

General requirements

40.2   In general, the reporting requirements described in chapter 39 apply to listed companies. However, some additional considerations were introduced in respect of auditors' reports for audits of listed companies for financial periods ending on or after 31 December 1998. These considerations were introduced by way of APB Bulletin 1998/10 *Corporate governance reporting and auditors' responsibilities statements*. This Bulletin has since been superseded by APB Bulletin 1999/5 as referred to in **40.1** above. The considerations relate primarily to the description of auditors' responsibilities as explained below.

40.3   Annual reports of many listed companies have been increasing in content and complexity for a number of years. In some cases, the audited financial statements now form a relatively low proportion of the total content of the annual report. In response to this development, the APB believes that it is important that the auditors' differing responsibilities with respect to the various elements of the annual report should be properly explained. APB Bulletin 1999/5 encourages the inclusion in the annual report of listed companies of a description of auditors' responsibilities which is more detailed than that set out in SAS 600. While this statement may be given separately, it is expected that it will normally be included in the auditors' report on the financial statements, as illustrated in the example in **40.4** below. This makes sense, as a section on respective responsibilities already exists within the auditor's report under SAS 600 and it is useful for the members of the company to see the description of the auditors' responsibilities when they read the auditor's report.

40.4   APB Bulletin 1999/5 states that the key elements of such a statement of auditors' responsibilities relate to the requirements of:

(a)   statute and auditing standards with respect to the audit of the financial statements;

(b) statute and the Listing Rules where the auditors are only required to report by exception;

(c) the Listing Rules for auditors to review the statement concerning the company's compliance with certain provisions of the Combined Code; and

(d) auditing standards to read the 'other information' in the annual report.

The purpose is solely to explain what the auditors' responsibilities are; it is not intended to either extend or narrow the responsibilities of auditors.

Example 40.4

AUDITORS' REPORT TO THE MEMBERS OF XYZ PLC

We have audited the financial statements on pages 25 to 43, which have been prepared under the accounting policies set out on page 28.

Respective responsibilities of directors and auditors

The directors are responsible for preparing the annual report, including as described on page 23, preparation of the financial statements, which are required to be prepared in accordance with applicable United Kingdom law and accounting standards. Our responsibilities, as independent auditors, are established by statute, the Auditing Practices Board, the UK Listing Authority and by our profession's ethical guidance.

We report to you our opinion as to whether the financial statements give a true and fair view and are properly prepared in accordance with the Companies Act 1985. We also report to you if, in our opinion, the directors' report is not consistent with the financial statements, if the company has not kept proper accounting records, if we have not received all the information and explanations we require for our audit, or if information specified by law or the Listing Rules regarding directors' remuneration and transactions with the company and other members of the group is not disclosed.

We review whether the corporate governance statement on page 20 reflects the company's compliance with the seven provisions of the Combined Code specified for our review by the UK Listing Authority and we report if it does not. We are not required to consider whether the board's statements on internal control cover all risks and controls, or form an opinion on the effectiveness of the group's corporate governance procedures or its risk and control procedures.

We read the other information contained in the annual report, including the corporate governance statement, and consider whether it is consistent with the audited financial statements. We consider the implications for our report if we become aware of any apparent misstatements or material inconsistencies with the financial statements.

> **Basis of audit opinion**
>
> We conducted our audit in accordance with United Kingdom auditing standards issued by the Auditing Practices Board. An audit includes examination, on a test basis, of evidence relevant to the amounts and disclosures in the financial statements. It also includes an assessment of the significant estimates and judgements made by the directors in the preparation of the financial statements and of whether the accounting policies are appropriate to the circumstances of the company and the group, consistently applied and adequately disclosed.
>
> We planned and performed our audit so as to obtain all the information and explanations which we considered necessary in order to provide us with sufficient evidence to give reasonable assurance that the financial statements are free from material misstatement, whether caused by fraud or other irregularity or error. In forming our opinion, we also evaluated the overall adequacy of the presentation of information in the financial statements.
>
> **Opinion**
>
> In our opinion, the financial statements give a true and fair view of the state of affairs of the company and the group as at 31 March 2000 and of the profit of the group for the year then ended and have been properly prepared in accordance with the Companies Act 1985.
>
> Chartered Accountants and Registered Auditors   (Address)
> (Date)

40.5   The example report above is largely based on that in appendix 3 of APB Bulletin 1999/5, but is in respect of a group, rather than a single company, as the majority of listed companies prepare group accounts. Reference is made to the 'Companies Act 1985' in the third paragraph, as the term 'Companies Act' (as used in the APB example) is undefined in English law and is strictly incorrect.

40.6

> A problem arises in respect of AIM companies and listed companies which avail themselves of an exemption from the requirement to publish a statement of compliance with the Combined Code provisions (see chapter 7). APB Bulletin 1999/5 appears to apply to all listed companies and thus requires a fuller description of the auditors' responsibilities, even though, for some listed companies, a statement of compliance or an auditor review of specified provisions is not required. Until the APB clarifies this situation, it is suggested that, for such companies, the effect on the audit report depends on whether the company has disclosed the fact that they are availing themselves of an exemption or not.

> ### *Example 40.6*
>
> (a) When directors explain that they have availed themselves of an exemption (as per **7.12** above), the third paragraph in the section 'Respective responsibilities of directors and auditors' in the example in **40.4** above ('the responsibilities section') will be removed and the fourth paragraph amended to remove the corporate governance reference.
>
> (b) When directors have availed themselves of an exemption, but do not make disclosures explaining their eligibility, the third paragraph of the auditors' responsibilities is replaced with the following: 'We are not required to review any corporate governance disclosures for UK Listing Authority purposes, as the company has availed itself of an exemption from the requirement to publish a statement of compliance with the Combined Code.'
>
> The words '...including the corporate governance statement...' in the fourth paragraph in the responsibilities statement are removed.
>
> (c) For AIM companies, the third paragraph of the responsibilities section will be removed, as will the reference to corporate governance in the fourth paragraph.

40.7   Listed and AIM companies are required to include additional information specified in the continuing obligations of the Listing Rules for listed companies and Chapter 16 of the Stock Exchange Rules for AIM companies. As a matter of client service, auditors will wish to bring to the attention of the directors (including, where appropriate, non-executive directors) their obligation to fulfil these requirements. Where breaches come to the auditors' attention, it is also useful to suggest that they be drawn to the attention of the company's brokers, as they have a role with regard to communication with the market. The auditors should also consider the implications for their audit report if they become aware of apparent misstatements or material inconsistencies with the financial statements. SAS 160 sets out relevant standards and guidance and APB Bulletin 1999/5 *The Combined Code: requirements of auditors under the Listing Rules of the London Stock Exchange* includes the recommendation that auditors need to read other information in the annual report, as well as a suggested audit report wording to be included in the respective responsibilities section.

Requirements of the Listing Rules of the UK Listing Authority

40.8   The Listing Rules of the UK Listing Authority impose review and reporting requirements on listed companies and their auditors in respect of:

- corporate governance statements;

- reports by the Board on directors' remuneration;

- going concern statements;

- preliminary announcements;

- interim financial information.

Each of these is considered in separate sections below.

Corporate governance statements

40.9   The corporate governance disclosure requirements for listed companies with accounting periods ending on or after 23 December 1999
are dealt with in chapter 7. There is no formal requirement for auditors to report on companies' corporate governance narrative statements made under Listing Rule 12.43A(a). Listing Rule 12.43A does
specifically require the statement of compliance made under Listing
Rule 12.43A(b) to be reviewed by the auditors before publication
insofar as it relates to Code provisions A.1.2, A.1.3, A.6.1, A.6.2,
D.1.1, D.2.1 and D.3.1 of the Combined Code..

40.10   APB guidance for auditors in respect of corporate governance disclosures is given in APB Bulletin 1999/5 *The Combined Code: requirements of auditors under the Listing Rules of the London Stock
Exchange.* APB Bulletin 1999/5 superseded a number of previous
APB Bulletins, one of which was 1998/10 *Corporate governance
reporting and auditors' responsibilities statements.* Prior to the issue of
APB Bulletin 1998/10, the APB's view was that auditors would always
issue a report on the results of their review of the statement of compliance with the Cadbury Code and they strongly recommended that
an auditors' report be included within the annual report and
accounts, either as a separate review report or included within the
auditors' report on the financial statements. Following the publication of the Combined Code, and taking account of the growth in the
content and complexity of annual reports, the APB decided that it
would be appropriate for annual reports of listed companies to contain a more comprehensive description of auditors' responsibilities
than is required by SAS 600 (see **40.3** above). Also, in view of the relatively narrow scope of the auditors' review in comparison to the
total corporate governance disclosures (only seven out of 45 Code
provisions are reviewed) and the lack of a UK Listing Authority
requirement for auditors to review the directors' narrative statement,
the APB believes that it is no longer appropriate for auditors' to
review reports on corporate governance disclosures to be published
in the annual report.

40.11   However, where the auditors become aware of any Code provision (specified for their review) with which the company has not complied they check whether the departure is described in the directors' statement of compliance. If the disclosure is properly made, including the reasons for the departure, the auditors do not refer to this in their report. But if proper disclosure has not been made, the auditors report this in the opinion section of their report. This does not give rise to a qualification of the opinion on the financial statements and to make this clear the auditors' comments should be included under a sub-heading "Other matter" within the opinion section of the report. An example is given in paragraph 53 of APB Bulletin 1999/5.

Example 40.11

Opinion

In our opinion the financial statements give a true and fair view of the state of the company's affairs as at 31 March 2000 and of its profit for the year then ended and have been properly prepared in accordance with the Companies Act 1985.

Other matter

We have reviewed the board's description of its process for reviewing the effectiveness of internal control set out on page 10 of the annual report. In our opinion the board's comments concerning … do not appropriately reflect our understanding of the process undertaken by the board because … .

40.12   It is important that the audit report reference to the page(s) of the annual report on which the corporate governance statement is located is clear. The reference is in the third paragraph of the responsibilities section of the audit report (see **40.4** above). If the annual report includes a 'stand-alone' compliance statement, e.g., which states 'the company has complied with all the provisions of the Combined Code except as described below', the audit report should refer to the page on which the compliance statement is located. If the compliance statement spans two pages, then both pages need to be referred to.

40.13   It is more complicated where the annual report contains a compliance statement that refers to non-compliances which are spread throughout the text of the narrative statement. In these circumstances the audit report reference depends on whether the non-compliances relate to any of the seven provisions specified for our review by the Listing Rules.

(a) If the non-compliances do relate to, or include, any of the seven provisions specified for our review by the Listing Rules, then the audit report needs to refer not only to the compliance statement itself, but also to the pages where the non-compliance disclosure is made in respect of any of those seven provisions. It need not refer to any pages that disclose non-compliance with provisions other than the seven specified for our review by the Listing Rules.

(b) If the non-compliances do not relate to any of the seven provisions specified for our review by the Listing Rules, then the audit report need refer only to the page(s) where the compliance statement is located (i.e., the statement saying 'the company has complied with all the provisions of the Combined Code except as disclosed otherwise.').

40.14

APB Bulletin 1999/5 indicates that prior to the release of the annual report and accounts the auditors communicate and discuss the factual findings of their review with the directors. This is best done on a confidential basis. The following example sets out, in the absence of any exceptions, an appropriate form of private report to issue to the directors.

Example 40.14

REVIEW REPORT TO THE DIRECTORS OF [XYZ PLC] BY [ABC AND CO] ON CORPORATE GOVERNANCE MATTERS

In addition to our audit of the financial statements, we have reviewed the directors' statements on page(s)... on the company's compliance with the seven provisions of the Combined Code specified for our review by the UK Listing Authority and their adoption of the going concern basis in preparing the financial statements. The objective of our review is to draw attention to non-compliance with those parts of Listing Rules 12.43A(b) and 12.43(v) specified for our review.

Basis of opinion

We carried out our review in accordance with guidance issued by the Auditing Practices Board. That guidance does not require us to perform the additional work necessary to, and we do not, express any opinion on the effectiveness of either the group's system of internal controls or the company's corporate governance procedures or on the ability of the group to continue in operational existence.

Opinion

With respect to the directors' statements on going concern and internal control on page(s) ..., in our opinion, the directors have provided the disclosures required by the Listing Rules referred to above and such statements are not inconsistent with the information of which we are aware from our audit work on the financial statements.

> Based on enquiry of certain directors and officers of the company, and examination of relevant documents, in our opinion, the directors' statement on page ... appropriately reflects the company's compliance with the other Code provisions of the Combined Code specified for our review by Listing Rule 12.43A.
>
> Chartered Accountants   (Address)
> (Date)

Reports by the board on directors' remuneration

40.15   Listing Rule 12.43A(c) of the UK Listing Authority requires listed companies (other than those with only debt securities or fixed income shares listed, overseas companies and investment companies (including investment trusts) and venture capital trusts with no executive directors), to provide a report by the board to the shareholders giving details of directors' remuneration (see chapter 8). Overseas companies with a primary listing must, however, give the statement required by Listing Rule 12.43A(c)(vii) on the unexpired term of any directors' service contract of a director proposed for election or re-election at the forthcoming annual general meeting and, if any director proposed for election or re-election does not have a directors service contract, a statement to that effect.

40.16   Listing Rule 12.43A also requires that the scope of the auditors' report on the financial statements must cover the disclosures made pursuant to paragraphs 12.43A(c)(ii),(iii), (iv), (ix) and (x). If these disclosures are included only in the report to the shareholders by the board on directors' remuneration, without an appropriate cross-reference being included in the financial statements which indicates unambiguously which disclosures fall within the scope of the audit, it will be necessary to modify the introductory paragraph of the auditors' report so that the disclosures are specifically included within the scope of the report.

> ### *Example 40.16*
>
> We have audited the financial statements on pages 12 to 26, which have been prepared under the accounting policies set out on page 12. We have also audited the information which is specified by the UK Listing Authority to be audited in respect of any directors' remuneration, share options, long-term incentive schemes and pension entitlements and which is set out in paragraphs 6 to 10 of the report to shareholders by the board on directors' remuneration on pages 4 to 7.

40.17   If the information required to be audited by the UK Listing Authority is not capable of being clearly described, e.g., because it is widely interspersed with other information that need not be, and has not been, audited, it may, as a last resort, be necessary to reproduce the detailed disclosures within the auditors' report.

40.18 The auditors are required to state in their report on the financial statements if, in their opinion, the company has not complied with the requirements of Listing Rule 12.43A(c)(ii),(iii), (iv), (ix) and (x) and, in such cases, must include in their report, so far as they are reasonably able to do so, a statement giving the required particulars. APB Bulletin 1999/5 recommends, where the company has not complied with the requirements, that the opinion section of the auditors' report be worded along the following lines.

Example 40.18

Opinion

In our opinion, the financial statements give a true and fair view of the state of the company's affairs as at 31 March 2000 and of the profit of the group for the year then ended and have been properly prepared in accordance with the Companies Act 1985.

Other matter

The Listing Rules of the UK Listing Authority require us to report any instances when the company has not complied with certain of the disclosure requirements set out in the Rules. In this connection, we report that, in our opinion, the company has not complied with the requirements of paragraph 12.43A(c)(ix)(b)(ii) of those Rules, because the board's report on directors' remuneration, as referred to on page 15, does not disclose the right of [insert name of director] to retire at age 55 on a full pension.

Qualification on these grounds is unlikely to be necessary. In most cases, directors will agree to the necessary disclosure being included in the notes to the accounts when they appreciate that the alternative is a statement in the audit report giving the required particulars.

Going concern statements

40.19 Directors of listed companies that are required to comply with Listing Rule 12.43(v) are required to include in the annual report and accounts a statement that the business is a going concern, with supporting assumptions or qualifications as necessary, as interpreted by the guidance on going concern and financial reporting for directors of listed companies registered in the UK. The statement should be reviewed by the auditors before publication.

40.20 Chapter 41 discusses in more detail reports on the appropriateness of the going concern basis. Chapter 7 discusses statements by the directors.

Preliminary announcements

40.21 Under the Listing Rules, listed companies must issue a preliminary announcement of their annual results (see chapter 37). The announcement must be issued without delay after board approval and in any event, for statements published in respect of accounting periods beginning on or after 23 December 1999, within 120 days of the end of the financial period to which it relates. (See chapter 37 for further details including exemptions.) The preliminary statement must:

(a) have been agreed with the company's auditors;

(b) show the figures in the form of a table, consistent with the presentation to be adopted in the annual accounts for that financial year, including at least the items required for a half-yearly report;

(c) if the auditors' report is likely to be qualified, give details of the nature of the qualification; and

(d) include any significant additional information necessary for the purpose of assessing the results being announced.

40.22 The auditors have no statutory right or duties in regard to these preliminary announcements, but the UK Listing Authority requires the information published to have been agreed with the auditors. Thus, although the information is routinely described as unaudited, any significant difference between the preliminary announcement and the audited financial statements would be a matter for concern. The auditors should therefore request the opportunity to examine the announcement before it is issued, to check that it reflects fairly the relevant information that will be included in the financial statements. Auditors are therefore in a difficult position in circumstances where they do not agree with an announcement which is about to be made or has been made or where they think it is misleading. If this occurs and management does not wish to make the necessary changes, it is useful to draw the matter to the attention of the chairman of the audit committee and ask that the company's brokers be consulted. If a problem still remains, it may be appropriate to seek legal advice.

40.23 The Listing Rules do not address situations where the auditors' report does, or will, contain an explanatory paragraph dealing with a fundamental uncertainty. The APB provides guidance for auditors in APB Bulletin 1998/7 *The auditors association with preliminary announcements.* The Bulletin states that the auditors do not agree to the preliminary announcement unless the directors have explained the fundamental uncertainty in the preliminary announcement. This is because a fundamental uncertainty is significant additional information necessary for the purpose of assessing the results being announced. There is no need for the preliminary announcement to refer to the auditors in this context.

40.24   If the auditors conclude that there is a significant level of concern about the company's ability to continue as a going concern and this matter is not appropriately disclosed in the preliminary announcement, the going concern standards state that it is unlikely that the auditors will be willing to agree to that announcement. [SAS 130(53)]

40.25   Therefore, if there is significant concern about the going concern basis, the auditors should request that wording which conveys the underlying uncertainty be included in the preliminary announcement. If the company's management are unhappy with including such wording, the auditors may wish to discuss the matter with the non-executive directors and the company's brokers.

40.26   When giving details about a qualification of the auditors' report, care needs to be taken to check compliance with the Act, which states that an auditors' report on the statutory accounts may not be published with non-statutory accounts. [s240]

40.27   APB Bulletin 1998/7 states that if the precise details of the matters giving rise to a qualified opinion or explanatory paragraph are critical to a full appreciation of the auditors' report, the APB strongly recommends that auditors should not normally agree to a preliminary announcement containing information about a qualification before the matter has been resolved.

40.28   APB Bulletin 1998/7 also states that auditors do not agree to the preliminary announcement until its entire content has been formally approved by the board or by a duly authorised committee of the board. The Bulletin recommends that the auditors should make explicit their agreement to the issue of the preliminary announcement by issuing a letter to the directors. An example letter based on that given in appendix 1 of APB Bulletin 1998/7 follows.

Example 40.28

Example letter to directors indicating auditors' agreement with preliminary announcement

[Date]

Dear Sirs

Preliminary announcement for the year ended [date]

In accordance with the terms of our engagement letter dated [ ], we have reviewed the attached proposed preliminary announcement of XYZ plc for the year ended [ ]. Our work was conducted having regard to Bulletin 1998/7 issued by the Auditing Practices Board. As directors, you are responsible for preparing and issuing the preliminary announcement.

Our responsibility is solely to give our agreement to the preliminary announcement having carried out the procedures specified in the Bulletin as providing a basis for such agreement. In this regard, we agree to the preliminary announcement being notified to the UK Listing Authority.

[As you are aware we are not in a position to sign our report on the annual financial statements, as they have not yet been approved by the directors and we have not yet... *[insert significant procedures that are yet to be completed, e.g., completing the subsequent events review and obtaining final representations from directors...]*. Consequently, there can be no certainty that we will be in a position to issue an unmodified audit opinion on financial statements consistent with the results and financial position reported in the preliminary announcement.]

Yours faithfully

Chartered Accountants and Registered Auditors   (Address)

(Date)

Notes:

The above wording assumes that the statutory financial statements and audit of them are close to finalisation and no qualification or modification of the audit opinion is contemplated. The wording should be adapted to reflect the specific circumstances of each assignment.

40.29 The example in APB Bulletin 1998/7 includes the following additional sentences at the end of the last paragraph: 'However, at the present time, we are not aware of any matters that may give rise to a modification to our report. In the event that such

> matters do come to our attention we will inform you immedi-
> atel'. They have been excluded from the example in **40.28** above
> on the grounds that they go further in both reporting and
> establishing subsequent obligations than auditors are required
> to.

Interim financial information

40.30   Although there is no requirement for half-yearly reports of listed companies to be either audited or reviewed, the auditors are frequently asked by the directors to review these statements before they are published and sent to the members. It is important, in such circumstances, that the scope of the auditors' work, which will probably be some form of limited review, should be agreed with the client in advance and be the subject of a letter of engagement.

40.31   Where the auditors are asked to report their findings orally in the first instance, they should confirm these findings in a letter to the directors.

40.32   Listing Rule 12.54 of the UK Listing Authority requires that where the half-yearly report of a listed company has been reviewed by auditors pursuant to the APB guidance (which is currently contained within APB Bulletin 1999/4 *Review of interim financial information*), the review report of the auditor must be reproduced in full. The following is an example of an unqualified review report and is based on the wording in APB Bulletin 1999/4.

Example 40.32

INDEPENDENT REVIEW REPORT TO XYZ PLC[3]

Introduction

We have been instructed by the company to review the financial information[5] set out on pages 4 to 10 and we have read the other information contained in the interim report and considered whether it contains any apparent misstatements or material inconsistencies with the financial information.

Directors' responsibilities

The interim report, including the financial information contained therein, is the responsibility of, and has been approved by, the directors. The Listing Rules of the UK Listing Authority require that the accounting policies and presentation applied to the interim figures should be consistent with those applied in preparing the preceding annual accounts except where any changes, and the reasons for them, are disclosed.[6]

Review work performed

We conducted our review in accordance with guidance contained in Bulletin 1999/4 issued by the Auditing Practices Board. A review consists principally of making enquiries of group[1] management and applying analytical procedures to the financial information and underlying financial data and based thereon, assessing whether the accounting policies and presentation have been consistently applied unless otherwise disclosed.[2] A review excludes audit procedures such as tests of controls and verification of assets, liabilities and transactions. It is substantially less in scope than an audit performed in accordance with Auditing Standards and therefore provides a lower level of assurance than an audit. Accordingly, we do not express an audit opinion on the financial information.

Review Conclusion

On the basis of our review we are not aware of any material modifications that should be made to the financial information as presented for the six months ended 31 March 2000.

Chartered Accountants[4]   (Address)

(Date)

Notes:

1   The word 'group' will be deleted in a situation where there are no subsidiary companies.

2   Where there is a change in accounting policy and the auditors do not consider that the accounting policy change has been properly reflected in the financial information they consider the implications for their review report.

3   The report should be addressed to the company rather than the members or directors on the basis of legal advice obtained by the APB.

4   Because this engagement is not an audit, the term 'Registered auditors' should not be used.

5   The term 'financial information' refers to that selected information within the interim report, identified by reference to page numbers, which auditors agree with directors will be reviewed by them. That selected information would exclude year 2000 disclosures. An alternative wording for the introductory paragraph to ensure that this is clear might be as follows: 'We have been instructed by the company to review the financial information set out in pages 4 to 10, excluding note 6 in relation to year 2000 matters, and we have read the other information contained in the interim report and considered whether it contains any apparent misstatements or material inconsistencies with the financial information.'

> 6   Note that for AIM companies the directors' responsibilities under Chapter 16 of the Rules of the London Stock Exchange are simply to prepare a half-yearly report. So in view of this, for an AIM company, the second sentence of the directors' responsibilities paragraph should be deleted.

40.33   Where there is a fundamental uncertainty which has been appropriately disclosed in the financial information, the auditors should insert an additional paragraph in their review report.

Example 40.33

Extract from INDEPENDENT REVIEW REPORT TO XYZ PLC

Review work performed

We conducted our review in accordance with guidance contained in Bulletin 1999/4 issued by the Auditing Practices Board. A review consists principally of making enquiries of [group] management and applying analytical procedures to the financial information and underlying financial data and based thereon, assessing whether the accounting policies and presentation have been consistently applied unless otherwise disclosed. A review excludes audit procedures such as tests of controls and verification of assets, liabilities and transactions. It is substantially less in scope than an audit performed in accordance with Auditing Standards and therefore provides a lower level of assurance than an audit. Accordingly, we do not express an audit opinion on the financial information.

Fundamental uncertainty

In arriving at our review conclusion, we have considered the adequacy of disclosures made in the financial information concerning the possible outcome of litigation against B Limited, a subsidiary undertaking of the company, for an alleged breach of environmental regulations. The future settlement of this litigation could result in additional liabilities and the closure of B's business, whose net assets included in the summarised balance sheet total £Y and whose profit before tax for the year is £Z. Details of the circumstances relating to this fundamental uncertainty are described in Note 10.

Review Conclusion

On the basis of our review we are not aware of any material modifications that should be made to the financial information as presented for the six months ended 31 March 2000.

40.34   Where the auditors disagree with an accounting treatment, they should qualify their review conclusions.

> ### Example 40.34
>
> **Qualified review conclusion arising from disagreement about accounting treatment**
>
> (Explanatory paragraph describing the disagreement and its effect on the financial information)
>
> On the basis of our review, with the exception of the matter described in the preceding paragraph we are not aware of any material modifications that should be made to the financial information as presented for the six months ended 31 March 2000.

40.35 APB Bulletin 1999/4 indicates that financial information in interim reports should be described as 'reviewed' only if a review in accordance with APB Bulletin 1999/4 has been carried out and the financial information is clearly identified within the interim report. Otherwise, the interim financial information should be described as 'neither audited nor reviewed'. In rare circumstances where interims *are* audited, they should be described as such and the audit report, including any qualifications, should be reproduced in full. [Listing Rule 12.54]

40.36 Auditors may, on occasion, be asked to carry out specific agreed-upon procedures as an alternative to a review, or the directors may approach the auditors for advice and guidance on specific financial issues such as appropriateness of accounting policies they propose to adopt. In such circumstances the auditors first agree the procedures to be carried out with the directors, or the audit committee, and then report within that context. Such engagements are outside the scope of Bulletin 1999/4 and the report should not be reproduced within the published interim report.

Communication between external auditors and audit committees

40.37 In June 1998, the APB published an audit briefing paper, which sets out what it sees as best practice in this area. The APB believes that effective communication between external auditors and audit committees is a key element in corporate governance and hopes that its briefing paper will be of assistance to members of audit committees and others involved in corporate governance. This area may become more significant in the UK in the future, following new rules and standards issued in the USA as a result of the influential Blue Ribbon report on the effectiveness of audit committees.

41 Reports on the appropriateness of the going concern basis

41 Reports on the appropriateness of the going concern basis

Summary of changes since the previous issue of this publication

Para.	Topic	Summary
41.84	*Statement of Principles* and FRED 21 *Accounting Policies*	Proposals will not have any effect on the interpretation of the going concern presumption

Introduction

The going concern basis

41.1   Most financial statements are prepared on the basis that the entity will continue in operational existence for the foreseeable future (i.e., on the going concern basis). This means that there is no intention or necessity to liquidate or curtail significantly the scale of operation of the entity. The Act and SSAP 2 state that an entity is presumed to be carrying on business as a going concern unless the financial statements state otherwise.

41.2   Directors of listed companies incorporated in the UK that are required to comply with Listing Rule 12.43(v) of the London Stock Exchange are required to include in the annual report and accounts a statement that the business is a going concern, with supporting assumptions or qualifications as necessary, as interpreted by the guidancc on going concern and financial reporting for directors of listed companies registered in the UK. The statement should be reviewed by the auditors before publication (see chapter 40). It is particularly important that the statement is not inconsistent with any disclosures regarding going concern in either the financial statements or the auditors' report thereon. To avoid such inconsistency, the statement can usefully include a cross reference to the relevant note in the financial statements.

41.3   The implication of the going concern basis is that assets are recorded on the basis that the entity will be able to recover, through use or realisation, the recorded amounts in the normal course of business and liabilities are recorded on the basis that they will be discharged in the normal course of business.

41.4   When a company is not a going concern, it is unlikely to realise assets on a forced sale at the amounts at which they are recorded. Also, additional liabilities (such as those arising from breach of contract and redundancies caused by cessation of operations) may need to be recognised and long-term assets and liabilities will need to be reclassified as current. In such circumstances, financial statements prepared on the going concern basis will be inappropriate, as they will normally not give a true and fair view. Where auditors disagree with the preparation of financial statements on the going concern basis, they should issue an adverse audit opinion (see **41.77** below).

41.5   As a consequence of ss226 and 227, which require directors to prepare financial statements which give a true and fair view, directors should satisfy themselves as to whether the going concern basis is appropriate.

41.6   In special circumstances, e.g., where the directors conclude that the entity is not a going concern, compliance with the provisions of the Act, even when supplemented by additional information, may be inconsistent with the requirement to give a true and fair view. In such cases, the directors should consider departing from the going concern basis of accounting to the extent necessary to give a true and fair view, but disclosure must be made in a note of the particulars of the departure, the reasons for it and its effect (see **5.8** to **5.12** above). [ss226(5) and 227(6) and UITF Abstract 7(4)]

41.7

> Although the Act and SSAP 2 state that the going concern presumption is one of the fundamental accounting concepts, there is no accounting framework for reporting by directors in this area. This is unfortunate because, following the issue of SAS 130 *The going concern basis in financial statements*, it is likely that auditing standards will be used as a guide to interpreting the requirements of the Act. It is to be hoped that the ASB will consider this issue in the future, with a view to issuing an accounting standard specifying the appropriate accounting and disclosure.

41.8   It is important that where there is concern as to the going concern status of the entity, the members are informed adequately of the basis on which the directors have satisfied themselves that the financial statements prepared on the going concern basis give a true and fair view. In those cases where there is concern about the ability of the entity to continue as a going concern and the financial statements do not include appropriate disclosures, the auditors will need to consider whether the financial statements give a true and fair view and whether their audit opinion should be qualified in respect of disagreement with the adequacy of the disclosure of the matter giving rise to the concern.

41.9 Audited financial statements prepared on the going concern basis without any reference by the auditors to any concerns or uncertainties in their report are not a guarantee that the entity will remain in operational existence for the foreseeable future. The preparation and auditing of financial statements involves the formation of judgements, one of which relates to the going concern status; these judgements are exercised at the date of approval of the financial statements. Any judgement made, while reasonable at the time, can be valid only at that time and can be overturned by subsequent events.

Auditing standards on going concern

SAS 130 The going concern basis in financial statements

41.10 In November 1994, the APB issued SAS 130 *The going concern basis in financial statements*. Auditors are required to comply with the requirements of the SAS in respect of audits of financial statements for financial years ending on or after 30 June 1995.

41.11 SAS 130 applies to the going concern aspects of audits of financial statements which are required to be properly prepared in accordance with the Act and which are intended to give a true and fair view. The SAS also applies, in the absence of legal or other provisions to the contrary, to financial statements of other entities, including those in the public sector. It does not establish standards or provide guidance about going concern in any other context, such as an engagement to report on the future viability of a company or on any report made by directors in compliance with the London Stock Exchange Listing Rule 12.43(v) and the Combined Code. Such statements on going concern are dealt with in chapter 7.

41.12 The going concern standards are accompanied by explanatory material which is designed to assist auditors in interpreting and applying auditing standards. Where going concern standards contained in SAS 130 are reproduced in the paragraphs below, they are indicated by **bold** type.

41.13 Apparent failures by auditors to comply with going concern standards are liable to be enquired into by the appropriate committee established under the authority of the relevant accountancy body and disciplinary or regulatory action may result.

Application to groups

41.14 The standards and guidance given in SAS 130 apply to groups as well as to individual entities. It may be appropriate, on the grounds of immateriality, for consolidated financial statements to be prepared on a going concern basis even though it would be inappropriate for the financial statements of one or more members of the group (other than the parent) to be prepared on the going concern basis. When reporting on the parent entity's consolidated financial statements, auditors should consider the circumstances that apply to the group as a whole. [SAS 130(51) and (52)]

Preliminary announcements

41.15 The London Stock Exchange Listing Rules require that an announcement of preliminary results be agreed with the company's auditors before it is notified to the Stock Exchange. If the auditors conclude that there is a significant level of concern about the company's ability to continue as a going concern and this matter is not appropriately disclosed in the preliminary announcement, the going concern standards state that it is unlikely that the auditors will be willing to agree to that announcement. [SAS 130(53)]

41.16   Therefore, if there is significant concern about the going concern basis, the auditors should request that wording which conveys the underlying uncertainty be included in the preliminary announcement. If the company's management are unhappy with including such wording, the auditors may wish to discuss the matter with the non-executive directors and the company's brokers. Going concern considerations for listed companies are also discussed in chapter 40.

Considerations in respect of going concern

41.17 The basic principle set out in SAS 130 is that: **'When forming an opinion as to whether financial statements give a true and fair view, the auditors should consider the entity's ability to continue as a going concern, and any relevant disclosures in the financial statements'.** [SAS 130(2)]

41.18 To this end, SAS 130 states that:
[SAS 130(21)]

'The auditors should assess the adequacy of the means by which the directors have satisfied themselves that:

(a) it is appropriate for them to adopt the going concern basis in preparing the financial statements; and

(b) the financial statements include such disclosures, if any, relating to going concern as are necessary for them to give a true and fair view.

For this purpose:

(i) the auditors should make enquiries of the directors and examine appropriate available financial information; and

(ii) having regard to the future period to which the directors have paid particular attention in assessing going concern, the auditors should plan and perform procedures specifically designed to identify any material matters which could indicate concern about the company's ability to continue as a going concern'.

Foreseeable future

41.19 SSAP 2 uses the term 'foreseeable future' in the definition of going concern, but this term is not defined in SSAP 2 or in the Act. However, in assessing going concern, the directors will need to determine the period that they regard as 'foreseeable future'. This period will depend on the specific circumstances at a point in time, including the nature of the company's business, its associated risks and external influences.

41.20 The nature of this exercise involves the directors looking forward and there will be some future period to which they will pay particular attention in assessing going concern. It is not possible to specify a minimum length for this period; it is recognised, in any case, that any such period would be artificial and arbitrary, since, in reality, there is no 'cut-off point' after which there should be a sudden change in the approach adopted by the directors. The length of the period is likely to depend upon such factors as:

(a) the nature of the entity, including its size or complexity; and

(b) the entity's reporting and budgeting systems.

41.21 Recognising that the foreseeable future will vary from entity to entity, SAS 130 does not lay down a specific minimum period to which directors and auditors should consider in assessing going concern. Nevertheless, the explanatory text of the standard states that: 'Where the period considered by the directors has been limited, for example, to a period of less than one year from the date of approval of the financial statements, the directors will have determined whether, in their opinion, the financial statements require any additional disclosure to explain adequately the assumptions that underlie the adoption of the going concern basis'. [SAS 130(13)]

41.22 Such guidance is unsatisfactory, because it seems to imply that, in the normal course of events, members of an entity are provided with some form of assurance that it will continue in operational existence for the period up until the date of issue of the following year's financial statements.

41.23 In reality, however, for many entities, a reasonable foreseeable future may be based on its financial year (i.e., the period to the next balance sheet date). However, a period of less than six months from the date of approval of the financial statements may be unreasonably short. Other matters, such as the length of the trading cycle, may also be factors in determining what should be the minimum period which the directors and auditors should reasonably consider in assessing the going concern basis.

41.24 Directors are recommended to disclose in the financial statements the period that they regard as the foreseeable future when this period is less than one year from the date of approval of the financial statements, because the reference in the auditors' report that is required in the absence of such disclosure (see **41.75** below) is likely to give the matter more prominence. In such circumstances, directors are also advised to prepare a board paper, justifying the length of the foreseeable future; alternatively, they could minute their consideration of the matter. Such written records would assist the directors in their considerations in respect of going concern and may also protect their position should the entity subsequently fail.

The auditors' assessment of going concern and the related disclosures

41.25 In relation to going concern, the auditors will need to:

(a) consider the appropriateness of the going concern assumption adopted by the directors in the preparation of the financial statements;

(b) consider the adequacy of the disclosures, if any, in the notes to the financial statements in respect of going concern; and

(c) assess whether the information upon which the directors have based their assessment and the directors' reasoning constitute sufficient appropriate audit evidence and whether they concur with the directors' judgement about the extent of additional disclosure.

41.26 The procedures referred to in **41.25** above require the auditors to consider not only the present circumstances under which the company is operating but also all the available information relating to future events. In particular, the auditors will need to consider whether the period to which the directors have paid particular attention when considering going concern is reasonable in the entity's circumstances.

41.27 The extent of audit evidence which will be judged sufficient and appropriate will depend on the circumstances of the entity and, in particular, on the matters described in **41.20** above and **41.36** below. The auditors should consider whether the extent of their audit evidence is appropriate.

Reporting on the financial statements

Introduction

41.28 Under SAS 130, the following situations can arise:

(a) there is no significant level of concern about the entity's ability to continue as a going concern (unqualified report);

(b) there is a significant level of concern about the entity's ability to continue as a going concern, but the circumstances are explained fully in the notes to the accounts (unqualified report with added emphasis);

(c) there is concern, but not of such significance as to be required to be highlighted in the auditors' report, about the entity's ability to continue as a going concern (unqualified report, provided that there is adequate disclosure by the directors in the financial statements);

(d) there is concern about the entity's ability to continue as a going concern, but the circumstances are not explained fully in the notes to the accounts (qualified on grounds of disagreement regarding disclosure);

(e) the auditors are unable to obtain such information and explanations as they consider necessary from the entity's management (qualified on grounds of limitation of scope);

(f) the period to which the directors have paid particular attention in assessing the going concern basis is less than one year from the date of approval of the financial statements, but the directors have disclosed that fact (unqualified);

(g) the period to which the directors have paid particular attention in assessing the going concern basis is less than one year from the date of approval of the financial statements and the directors have not disclosed that fact (qualified on grounds of disagreement regarding disclosure);

(h) the auditors disagree with the preparation of the financial statements on the going concern basis (adverse opinion); and

(i)   the financial statements, in order to give a true and fair view, are prepared on a basis other than the going concern basis (unqualified report given adequate disclosure, but consider added emphasis paragraph).

41.29

> The distinction between a significant concern and a 'concern which is not of such significance as to be required to be highlighted in the auditors' report' is a novel and unwelcome concept, particularly in view of the fact that the APB has not provided any detailed guidance in this area. See **41.54** to **41.57** below, which deal with the cases where this may be applicable.

41.30   The following paragraphs set out the reporting requirements for each set of circumstances described in **41.28** above.

No significant concern about the entity's ability to continue as a going concern

41.31   This situation will be the most common which will be encountered. If there is no significant level of concern about the entity's ability to continue in operational existence for the foreseeable future and the foreseeable future regarded by the directors extends to at least one year from the date of approval of the financial statements, then there is no requirement for the directors to make any disclosure in the financial statements regarding going concern. Similarly, in such circumstances, there is no need for the auditors' report to make any reference to the going concern basis.

41.32   Nevertheless, Stock Exchange companies following the Combined Code will include in the annual report (usually in a statement separate from the financial statements) a statement on the appropriateness of the going concern basis, even when the directors are satisfied that the company will continue in operational existence for the foreseeable future. Other companies (particularly large private companies and 'public interest' companies) may wish to follow this practice (see **7.87** above).

41.33   However, neither the directors nor the auditors should come to the conclusion that the entity will continue in operational existence for the foreseeable future without considering, at the time at which the financial statements are approved, the entity's specific circumstances, including the nature of the entity's business, its associated risks and external influences. In making their assessments, the directors and auditors should take account of all relevant information of which they are aware at the time.

41.34   Where the period considered by the directors has been limited, e.g., to a period of less than one year from the date of approval of the financial statements, the directors will have determined whether, in their opinion, the financial statements require any additional disclosure to explain adequately the assumptions that underlie the adoption of the going concern basis.

41.35   The basis for the auditors' procedures is the information upon which the directors have based their assessment and the directors' reasoning. The auditors assess whether this constitutes sufficient appropriate audit evidence for their purpose and whether they concur with the directors' judgement about the need for, and nature of, additional disclosures.

41.36   The following factors, in particular, may affect the information available to the auditors and whether the auditors consider this information constitutes sufficient audit evidence for the purposes of their audit:

(a)   the nature of the entity (e.g., its size and the complexity of its circumstances). The larger or more complex the entity, the more sophisticated is likely to be the information available and needed to support the assessment of whether it is appropriate to adopt the going concern basis;

(b)   whether the information relates to future events and, if so, how far into the future those events lie. The information relating to the period falling after one year from the balance sheet date is often prepared in far less detail and subject to a greater degree of estimation than the information relating to periods ending on or before one year from the balance sheet date.

41.37   The example below (taken from situation 1 of appendix 2 to SAS 130) provides an illustration of a situation where the directors consider that there are no special disclosures required in the financial statements and where the auditors can concur with this position and neither qualify their auditors' opinion nor add an explanatory paragraph to their report.

Example 41.37

The situation is that of a company with uncomplicated circumstances, but with a significant bank overdraft.

Having completed their audit, the auditors consider that:

(a)   the results of their procedures confirm their preliminary assessment that there is not a significant level of concern about the ability of the company to continue as a going concern;

(b)   the information in the financial statements, and that received during their preparation and audit, does not suggest that there is a significant level of concern about the ability of the company to continue as a going concern;

> (c)   having reconsidered the directors' outline plans for the future, the plans do not appear to be inconsistent with the other information of which the auditors are aware; and
>
> (d)   there is no reason to disagree with the directors' view, based on their discussions with the bankers, that it is likely that the bankers will renew an overdraft facility that meets the anticipated needs of the company by a reasonable margin.
>
> The directors consider that no special disclosures are required in the financial statements. The auditors agree and, accordingly, the auditors do not consider it necessary to qualify their audit opinion or to add an explanatory paragraph to their audit report.

41.38   Clearly, in the circumstances described in the example in **41.37** above, a great deal of judgement is expected from directors and auditors.

41.39   It is recommended that, in larger companies (e.g., listed and 'public interest' entities), the directors should create a written record of their deliberations, which could take the form of a board paper and a specific board minute. The record could usefully include the significant factors that the directors have placed weight upon in their deliberations and the length of the foreseeable future which they have considered. They will also find it useful to record that they have given consideration to whether the factors set out in paragraphs 24 to 42 and the appendix to the Joint Working Group's guidance for directors could become significant in the foreseeable future. These factors are described under the headings:

- forecasts and budgets;
- borrowing requirements;
- liability management;
- contingent liabilities;
- products and markets;
- risk management; and
- financial adaptability.

41.40   The entity's procedures will be influenced primarily by the excess of the financial resources available to the entity over the financial resources that it requires. The entity's procedures need not always be elaborate to provide sufficient appropriate audit evidence. For example, auditors may not always need to examine budgets and forecasts for this purpose. This is particularly likely to be the case in respect of entities with uncomplicated circumstances. Many smaller entities fall into this category. Thus, for example:

(a) regarding the systems or other means for timely identification of warnings of future risks and uncertainties, the directors might consider that it is appropriate simply to keep abreast of developments within their individual business and their business sector. In the circumstances, the auditors might concur with the directors; or

(b) the directors might not, as a matter of course, prepare periodic cash flow and other budgets, forecasts or other management accounts information apart from the accounting records required by law and outline plans for the future. In the directors' view, this might be acceptable when the business is stable. In the circumstances, the auditors might concur with the directors. Hence, the auditors' procedures regarding budgets, forecasts and related issues might comprise discussion of the directors' outline plans in the light of other information available to the auditors.

Significant level of concern about the entity's ability to continue as a going concern, but the circumstances are explained fully

41.41 SAS 130 states that: **'Where the auditors consider that there is a significant level of concern about the entity's ability to continue as a going concern, but do not disagree with the preparation of the financial statements on the going concern basis, they should include an explanatory paragraph when setting out the basis of their opinion. They should not qualify their opinion on these grounds alone, provided the disclosures in the financial statements of the matters giving rise to the concern are adequate for the financial statements to give a true and fair view'.** [SAS 130(42)]

41.42 Thus, if there is a significant level of concern about the entity's ability to continue as a going concern, the form of the auditors' report will depend on the adequacy of the disclosures in the financial statements.

41.43 Situations where it may be more likely for the directors and auditors to conclude that there is a significant level of concern about the entity's ability to continue as a going concern include those where indications of the following are present:

(a) financial;

    (i) an excess of liabilities over assets;
    (ii) net current liabilities;
    (iii) necessary borrowing facilities have not been agreed;
    (iv) default on terms of loan agreements, and potential breaches of covenants;
    (v) significant liquidity or cash flow problems;

(vi) major losses or cash flow problems which have arisen since the balance sheet date and which threaten the entity's continuing existence;

(vii) substantial sales of fixed assets not intended to be replaced;

(viii) major restructuring of debt;

(ix) denial of (or reduction in) normal terms of trade by suppliers;

(x) major debt repayment falling due where refinancing is necessary to the entity's continuing existence;

(xi) inability to pay debts as they fall due;

(b) operational;

(i) fundamental changes in the market or technology to which the entity is unable to adapt adequately;

(ii) externally forced reductions in operations (e.g., as a result of legislation or regulatory action);

(iii) loss of key management or staff, labour difficulties or excessive dependence on a few product lines where the market is depressed;

(iv) loss of key suppliers or customers or technical developments which render a key product obsolete;

(c) other:

(i) major litigation in which an adverse judgment would imperil the entity's continued existence;

(ii) issues which involve a range of possible outcomes so wide that an unfavourable result could affect the appropriateness of the going concern basis; and

(iii) the impact of the year 2000 issue being sufficient to threaten the entity's ability to continue as a going concern.

41.44

> The auditors' assessment as to whether there is significant concern will need to take account of the directors' plans and the financial adaptability of the entity. Normally, significant concern will arise when, taking all the evidence as a whole, the auditor concludes that the possibility of the entity not being able to continue in operational existence for the foreseeable future is not remote and is a significant risk.

41.45 Where auditors conclude that there is a significant level of concern, SAS 130 advises that auditors will not normally regard disclosures as adequate unless the following matters are included in the financial statements:

[SAS 130(44)]

(a) a statement that the financial statements have been prepared on the going concern basis;

(b)   a statement of the pertinent facts;

(c)   the nature of the concern;

(d)   a statement of the assumptions adopted by the directors, which should be clearly distinguishable from the pertinent facts;

(e)   (where appropriate and practicable) a statement regarding the directors' plans for resolving the matters giving rise to the concern; and

(f)   details of any relevant actions by the directors.

41.46   SAS 130 also states that the guidance on disclosure referred to in **41.45** above does not constitute an accounting standard. [SAS 130(44)] However, the implication of the guidance is that auditors will be unwilling to regard financial statements as giving a true and fair view unless such disclosures are included in the notes to the financial statements. SAS 130 paragraph 44 should, therefore, be regarded by directors as a quasi-accounting standard which they would be wise to follow.

41.47   Other issues which should be considered by directors are the location of going concern basis disclosures and how they should be headed up. It is recommended that where there is significant concern about the ability of the entity to continue as a going concern the disclosures should normally be included towards the beginning of the notes to the accounts under a heading such as 'going concern' or 'basis of preparation of the financial statements'; they should not normally be 'lost' within the minor notes.

41.48   Examples of situations where there is significant concern about the ability of the entity to continue as a going concern, but the notes to the accounts disclose the position adequately, are set out below. The example is based on uncertainty regarding the continuing support of the bank.

> ### Example 41.48
>
> **Extract from the notes to the financial statements**
>
> *Note 1 Basis of preparation of the financial statements*
>
> The company meets its day-to-day working capital requirements through an overdraft facility which is repayable on demand.
>
> The nature of the company's business is such that there can be considerable unpredictable variation in the timing of cash inflows. The directors have prepared projected cash flow information for the

current financial year and the first half of the following financial year (approximately 13 months from the date of approval of these financial statements).

On the basis of this cash flow information and discussions with the company's bankers, the directors have formed a judgement at the time of approving the financial statements that there may be periods when the company's overdraft exceeds the facility currently agreed and that which the directors expect will be agreed on 15 June 2000, when the company's bankers are due to consider renewing the facility for a further six months. However, the directors believe that the company's bankers will continue to support it, as they have done so in similar situations in the past. On this basis, the directors consider it appropriate to prepare the financial statements on the going concern basis. The financial statements do not include any adjustments that would result from a withdrawal of support by the company's bankers.

Extract from the 'Basis of opinion' section of the unqualified auditors' report

Going concern

In forming our opinion, we have considered the adequacy of the disclosures made in note 1 to the accounts concerning the uncertainty, as to the continuation of support by the company's bankers. In view of the significance of this uncertainty, we consider that it should be drawn to your attention, but our opinion is not qualified in this respect.

41.49   APB Bulletin 1998/5 *The year 2000 issue – supplementary guidance for auditors* includes guidance concerning the impact of the year 2000 issue on the going concern basis. This indicates that if the auditors consider that there is a significant level of concern about the entity's ability to continue as a going concern, but do not disagree with the preparation of the financial statements on the going concern basis, they include an explanatory paragraph in the 'Basis of opinion' section of their report, referring to the uncertainty. They do not qualify their report on these grounds alone, provided the disclosures in the financial statements of the matters giving rise to the concern are adequate for the financial statements to give a true and fair view.

41.50   In assessing cash flow information, directors and auditors should focus their attention on what could reasonably be expected to happen. In the example in **41.48** above the possibility that the bankers will not continue to support the company is not remote and gives rise to significant concern.

41.51   A matter of some importance for auditors is that the relevant specimen extracts from the auditors' reports in the appendices to SAS 130 do not include in the 'Basis of opinion' section any reference to any adjustments that would result if the underlying uncertainty is not resolved. This is presumably because this matter is set out in the notes to the accounts and the auditors conclude that there is adequate disclosure in this respect. However, where such wording is not included in the notes to the accounts, it is recommended that it be included as a final sentence to the basis of opinion section.

Example 41.51

The financial statements do not include any adjustments that might result from a withdrawal of the overdraft facility by the company's bankers.

41.52 Such an approach (i.e., disclosure by directors) would appear to be preferable to that set out in the appendices to SAS 600, which suggest that a reference to the non-inclusion of adjustments should always be made in an added emphasis paragraph dealing with an inherent uncertainty relating to the going concern basis.

41.53 Another interesting matter is that the emotive subheading 'fundamental uncertainty', suggested originally in SAS 600, is no longer given. This is understandable, as such a subheading may, in some cases, be self-fulfilling prophecy. The subheading 'going concern' seems much more appropriate.

Concern, but not significant enough to be highlighted in the audit report

41.54 Although not specifically discussed in the going concern standards or accompanying guidance, the commentary in situation 2 of example 1 in appendix 2 of SAS 130 indicates that there may be circumstances where the auditors consider that there is 'concern' (e.g., the possibility of non-renewal of overdraft facilities is not remote) but not a 'significant level of concern', but the concern is such that it may require the notes to the accounts to give disclosure of the matter in order to give a true and fair view.

Example 41.54

The situation is that of a company with uncomplicated circumstances, but with a significant bank overdraft.

The auditors' past experience and preliminary planning procedures reveal that the company has, on several occasions in the past few years, exceeded its agreed bank facility. In the past, the bankers have not withdrawn the facility, but the auditors are aware that the company's relationship with the bankers is worsening. In these circumstances, the bankers have for some time requested and received each quarter management accounts covering the year to date.

Towards the end of the audit, the auditors examine the most recent management accounts. In particular, they consider whether the management accounts and any assumptions underlying their preparation are inconsistent with other information of which they are aware. The directors have started to implement a cost reduction exercise and this appears to be reasonable and proceeding according to plan. The management accounts show that the company is so far managing to remain within its current overdraft facility and the directors' outline plans (which take account of the cost reduction exercise) indicate that the company should be able to continue to do so.

The auditors scrutinise the company's correspondence and notes of conversations between the directors and the bankers, who examine the draft financial statements and the most recent management accounts. The auditors also examine a letter which they have requested the directors to obtain from the bankers regarding maintenance and renewal of overdraft facilities. The letter (addressed to the directors with a copy sent by the bankers directly to the auditors) contains a number of normal banking caveats. From the comments made in the letter, it is evident that:

(a)   the bankers have not made a decision about the continuance of the facilities;

(b)   the bankers will continue to monitor the facilities in the light of information which becomes available to them; and

(c)   (subject to the foregoing) the bankers will consider renewal of the facility on the agreed review date, which falls after the date on which the directors plan to approve the financial statements.

On this basis, the auditors decide that:

(a)   in the absence of indications that the facility may be exceeded in the 12-month period to the anniversary of the date of approval of the financial statements which they are auditing; and

(b)   together with the results of other audit work, they consider that there is concern about the ability of the company to continue as a going concern, but not of such significance as to require to the highlighted in the audit report.

In this particular case, the possibility that adequate overdraft facilities will not be renewed is not remote. Because the financial statements contain disclosures such as those shown below, the auditors conclude that no mention of the concern is required in their report on the financial statements.

> **Extract from 'Borrowings' note to the accounts**
>
> *Bank facilities*
>
> The company meets its day-to-day working capital requirements through an overdraft facility which is repayable on demand and renewable on an annual basis, the next renewal date being 31 August 2000. The directors are satisfied that, at the time of approval of the financial statements, there is no significant concern that the company will be unable to operate within the facility currently agreed and within that expected to be agreed on 31 August 2000.

41.55   The situation referred to in **41.54** above draws a very fine distinction between 'concern' and 'significant level of concern', which, because it is not addressed in the standards themselves, can cause much confusion among auditors and their clients.

41.56   It is suggested, therefore, that this approach (i.e., not highlighted in the audit report) should be used only in cases where the auditors conclude that, although there is no significant risk regarding the entity's ability to continue in operational existence for the foreseeable future, the risk is more than remote. Hence, if the directors and auditors consider the concern/risk to be remote (e.g., because the company appears to be working within plans agreed and monitored by the company's bankers), no disclosure is required in the financial statements.

41.57   In the absence of any clear guidance on what should be included in the financial statements, it is suggested that a note sets out the pertinent facts and a statement of the assumptions adopted by the directors. The APB's example appears to suggest that, in such circumstances, the matter can be included in a minor note and given a heading appropriate to the particular part of the financial statements, e.g., 'Creditors: amounts falling due within one year'. It also appears to suggest that, in such circumstances, the wording of the note does not need to include the phrase 'going concern' or refer to 'uncertainty'. It is therefore suggested that, in such circumstances, auditors resist the temptation to force the inclusion of such wording in the notes to the accounts, as to do so would give mixed messages whereby the directors would give a 'red flag' while the audit report does not do so. If they believe such wording is necessary, they may need to conclude that they have significant concern and therefore include an added emphasis in their report.

Concern (including significant concern) about the entity's ability to continue as a going concern and the disclosures in the financial statements are not adequate

41.58 If the auditors believe that the disclosures, if any, in the financial statements relating to going concern are not adequate for the financial statements to give a true and fair view (i.e., they do not include the details set out in **41.45** above), they should issue a qualified opinion expressing disagreement with the disclosures of the relevant matters in the financial statements.

41.59 Where the auditor disagrees with the disclosure of a matter, he is required to describe all the substantive factors giving rise to the disagreement, their implications for the financial statements and quantification of the effect where practicable. [SAS 600(74)] An example of appropriate disclosures where there is significant concern about the ability of the entity to continue as a going concern is set out below.

Example 41.59

Extract from the notes to the accounts

Note 1 Basis of preparation of the financial statements

The directors are currently negotiating with lenders to the group for new terms for amounts borrowed totalling £2.3 million. In addition, the directors' plans for raising funds of approximately £1.8 million from a share issue by the company are at an advanced stage. Both matters have already been announced publicly.

The financial statements have been prepared on the going concern basis which assumes that the company and its subsidiaries will continue in operational existence for the foreseeable future.

The validity of this assumption depends on the successful conclusion of the negotiations with the group's lenders and the raising of additional funds by a share issue. Certain of these arrangements will require the approval of shareholders in a general meeting. The financial statements do not include any adjustments that might result if negotiations were not concluded successfully.

While the directors are presently uncertain as to the outcome of both the matters mentioned above, they believe that it is appropriate for the financial statements to be prepared on the going concern basis.

Extract from the auditors' report

Qualified opinion arising from disagreement about an accounting treatment and the adequacy of disclosure in the financial statements

In our opinion, the financial statements should disclose the fact that the company and certain of its subsidiaries have not complied with covenants relating to certain of their borrowings. Under the terms of these covenants, there have been defaults relating to certain of the

---

group's borrowings, as a consequence of which the related borrowings become repayable on demand. These related borrowings should have been reclassified as amounts falling due within one year, which would have reduced the figures recorded in the consolidated balance sheet for 'net current assets' and 'Creditors: amounts falling due after more than one year' by £5.4 million. Similarly, the equivalent amounts recorded in the parent company balance sheet would have been reduced by £2.1 million.

Except for the absence of the disclosures, and the failure to reclassify the relevant borrowings, referred to in the paragraph above, in our opinion, the financial statements give a true and fair view of the state of affairs of the company and the group as at 31 March 2000 and have been properly prepared in accordance with the Companies Act 1985. In our opinion, the financial statements give a true and fair view of the profit of the group for the year ended 31 March 2000.

41.60 The example in **41.59** above is based on example 3 in appendix 2 to SAS 130. The SAS 130 example also includes in its report an added emphasis paragraph. Such a paragraph has not been included in the above example because the combined effect is to confuse the reader. This confusion arises because the added emphasis paragraph states that the opinion is not qualified in respect of the matter highlighted, but then goes on to state that certain aspects of the disclosures give rise to a qualification.

41.61 In practice, it is unlikely that auditors will be placed in a position to qualify their report, since the directors are likely to include any relevant disclosures in the notes to the accounts if the alternative is a qualified auditors' report which discloses the missing information.

41.62 Where there is concern about the going concern basis which the auditors would not wish to highlight (i.e., the concern is not significant) but the disclosures in the financial statements are inadequate, a qualification can also arise.

Example 41.62

Extract from the auditors' report

Qualified opinion arising from disagreement as to the adequacy of a disclosure in the financial statements

In our opinion, the financial statements should disclose the following matters.

The company meets its day-to-day working capital requirements through an overdraft facility which is repayable on demand and renewable on an annual basis, the next renewal date being 31 August 2000.

> We understand from the directors that they are satisfied that, at the time of approval of the financial statements, there is no significant concern that the company will be unable to operate within the facility currently agreed and within that expected to be agreed on 31 August 2000. On this basis, the directors consider it appropriate to prepare the financial statements on the going concern basis.
>
> Except for the absence of the disclosure referred to in the paragraph above, in our opinion, the financial statements give a true and fair view of the company's state of affairs as at 31 March 2000 and have been properly prepared in accordance with the Companies Act 1985. In our opinion, the financial statements give a true and fair view of the company's profit for the year ended 31 March 2000.

41.63 An important point to bear in mind is that a concern which is not a significant concern can be described in a minor note to the accounts.

Limitation on the scope of the auditors' work

41.64 Circumstances may arise when the auditors decide that their uncertainty about the going concern basis arises not from inherent uncertainty but from a limitation in the scope of their work. Such circumstances can include situations where:

(a) in the auditors' opinion, the directors have performed insufficient procedures given the circumstances of the entity;

(b) the uncertain nature of future events could affect the going concern status and the directors fail to provide written confirmations regarding the directors' assessment that the company is a going concern and in support of any relevant disclosures when the auditors consider that such representations are critical to obtaining appropriate audit evidence;

(c) the auditors conclude that the future period to which the directors have paid attention is not reasonable in the company's circumstances;

(d) the directors have not made any year 2000 impact analysis.

In each of the above circumstances, or in a combination of them, the auditors will need to consider a qualified opinion based on a limitation on the scope of their work.

41.65 To prevent a multiplicity of auditors' reports qualified on this basis, it is suggested that where the auditors' preliminary review of the going concern position indicates a possible problem, they discuss the problem with the directors with a view to the directors taking remedial action to avoid an audit qualification.

41.66 Examples of the situations where the auditors are unable to perform sufficient procedures are set out below. The first example relates to borrowing facilities.

Example 41.66

Basis of opinion

We conducted our audit in accordance with United Kingdom auditing standards issued by the Auditing Practices Board, except that the scope of our work was limited as explained below.

An audit includes examination, on a test basis, of evidence relevant to the amounts and disclosures in the financial statements. It also includes an assessment of the significant estimates and judgements made by the directors in the preparation of the financial statements and of whether the accounting policies are appropriate to the circumstances of the company and the group, consistently applied and adequately disclosed.

We planned our audit so as to obtain all the information and explanations which we considered necessary in order to provide us with sufficient evidence to give reasonable assurance that the financial statements are free from material misstatement, whether caused by fraud or other irregularity or error. However, the evidence available to us was limited, because we were unable to obtain information regarding the existence and terms of borrowing facilities amounting to £20 million (referred to in note 10 to the accounts) and the intention of the lender relating thereto. The availability of the borrowing facilities is necessary for the company to be in a position to repay loans, amounting to £15 million, that fall due for repayment on 30 June 2001. There were no other satisfactory audit procedures that we could adopt to verify these facilities. If adequate borrowing facilities are not available, the company may cease to trade and the going concern basis would then be inappropriate. In these circumstances, adjustments might be required to write down assets, take account of additional liabilities and to reclassify long-term assets and liabilities as current.

In forming our opinion, we also evaluated the overall adequacy of the presentation of information in the financial statements.

Qualified opinion arising from limitation in audit scope

Except for any adjustments to the financial statements that might have been found to be necessary had we been able to obtain sufficient evidence concerning the existence and terms of the borrowing facilities referred to above and the intention of the lender relating thereto, in our opinion, the financial statements give a true and fair view of the state of affairs of the company and the group as at 31 March 2000 and of the profit [loss] of the group for the year then ended and have been properly prepared in accordance with the Companies Act 1985.

> In respect alone of the limitation on our work relating to the borrowing facilities referred to above, we have not obtained all the information and explanations that we considered necessary for the purposes of our audit.

41.67

> The key point to note about the qualification in **41.66** above is that it arises not as a result of inherent uncertainty but from inability to obtain audit evidence. In practice, auditors are likely, in many cases, to view a going concern problem as an inherent uncertainty, particularly where third parties (e.g., bankers) are involved.

41.68 APB Bulletin 1998/5 *The year 2000 issue – supplementary guidance for auditors* indicates that if the directors have not undertaken any impact analysis, then, unless the auditors are satisfied that the year 2000 issue can reasonably be expected to have no significant implications for the entity's ability to continue as a going concern, they discuss with the directors the grounds for their use of the going concern basis. In accordance with SAS 130, the auditors qualify their opinion, on the grounds of a limitation in scope, if they consider that the directors have not taken adequate steps to satisfy themselves that it is appropriate for them to adopt the going concern basis.

> ### Example 41.68
>
> **Basis of opinion**
>
> We conducted our audit in accordance with United Kingdom auditing standards issued by the Auditing Practices Board, except that the scope of our work was limited as explained below.
>
> An audit includes .....
>
> We planned our audit so as to obtain all the information and explanations which we considered necessary in order to provide us with sufficient evidence to give reasonable assurance that the financial statements are free from material misstatement, whether caused by fraud or other irregularity or error.
>
> However, the directors have not made any assessment of the impact of the year 2000 problem on the company. Based on our knowledge of the business of the company, it appears possible that the risks and uncertainties associated with the year 2000 problem could give rise to significant concern over its ability to continue in business as a going concern. In the absence of any assessment by the directors, we have been unable to consider the impact, if any, of the year 2000 problem on the financial statements and, in particular, on the directors' assessment that it is appropriate to adopt the going concern basis in preparing the financial statements.

In forming our opinion, we also evaluated the overall adequacy of the presentation of information in the financial statements.

Qualified opinion arising from limitation in audit scope

Except for any adjustments to the financial statements that might have been found to be necessary had we been able to obtain sufficient evidence concerning the impact of the year 2000 problem on the company, in our opinion, the financial statements give a true and fair view of the state of the company's affairs as at 31 March 2000 and of its profit for the year then ended and have been properly prepared in accordance with the Companies Act 1985.

OR [1]

Opinion: disclaimer on view given by the financial statements

Because of the possible effect of the limitation in evidence available to us, we are unable to form an opinion as to whether the financial statements give a true and fair view of the state of the company's affairs as at 31 March 2000 and of its profit for the year then ended. In all other respects, in our opinion, the financial statements have been properly prepared in accordance with the Companies Act 1985.

In relation only to the limitation on the scope of our work relating to going concern and the year 2000 problem, we have not obtained all the information and explanations that we considered necessary for the purpose of our audit.

[1] Note: A disclaimer of opinion is only appropriate in cases where the possible effect of the limitation of audit scope is so material or pervasive that the auditors are unable to express any opinion.

41.69 An example of the situation where the auditors are unable to obtain written representations which they regard as critical appropriate audit evidence (a situation which is unlikely to arise frequently) is set out below.

Example 41.69

Basis of opinion

We conducted our audit in accordance with United Kingdom auditing standards issued by the Auditing Practices Board, except that the scope of our work was limited as explained below.

An audit includes examination, on a test basis, of evidence relevant to the amounts and disclosures in the financial statements. It also includes an assessment of the significant estimates and judgements made by the directors in the preparation of the financial statements and of whether the accounting policies are appropriate to the circumstances of the company and the group, consistently applied and adequately disclosed.

We planned our audit so as to obtain all the information and explanations which we considered necessary in order to provide us with sufficient evidence to give reasonable assurance that the financial statements are free from material misstatement, whether caused by fraud or other irregularity or error. However, the directors did not provide us with written representations regarding future plans which they have discussed with us and which we believe may be significant to the ability of the company to continue to trade. These plans may affect the financial resources that the company could require in the future. There were no other satisfactory audit procedures that we could adopt to verify these facilities. If the company ceases to trade, the going concern basis would then be inappropriate. In these circumstances, adjustments might be required to write down assets, take account of additional liabilities and to reclassify long-term assets and liabilities as current.

In forming our opinion, we also evaluated the overall adequacy of the presentation of information in the financial statements.

Qualified opinion arising from limitation in audit scope

Except for any adjustments to the financial statements that might have been found to be necessary had we been able to obtain sufficient evidence concerning the company's future plans referred to above, in our opinion, the financial statements give a true and fair view of the state of affairs of the company and the group as at 31 March 2000 and of the profit [loss] of the group for the year then ended and have been properly prepared in accordance with the Companies Act 1985.

In respect alone of the limitation on our work relating to the company's future plans, we have not obtained all the information and explanations that we considered necessary for the purposes of our audit.

Unreasonableness of the period regarded by the directors as the foreseeable future

41.70 Situations will arise where the auditors consider that the period regarded by the directors as the foreseeable future is unreasonable in all the circumstances.

41.71

In situations where the period regarded by the directors is patently unreasonable, a disclaimer of opinion, rather than a qualified opinion, will normally be appropriate.

Example 41.71

Basis of opinion

We conducted our audit in accordance with United Kingdom auditing standards issued by the Auditing Practices Board, except that the scope of our work was limited by the matter set out below.

An audit includes examination, on a test basis, of evidence relevant to the amounts and disclosures in the financial statements. It also includes an assessment of the significant estimates and judgements made by the directors in the preparation of the financial statements and of whether the accounting policies are appropriate to the circumstances of the company and the group, consistently applied and adequately disclosed.

We planned our audit so as to obtain all the information and explanations which we considered necessary in order to provide us with sufficient evidence to give reasonable assurance that the financial statements are free from material misstatement, whether caused by fraud or other irregularity or error. However, the period to which the directors have paid particular attention in assessing going concern was, as indicated in note 2 to the accounts, two months from the date of approval of the financial statements. In our opinion, in all the circumstances, such a period is not sufficient to assess and determine whether the going concern basis is appropriate. There were no practical auditing procedures we could adopt to ascertain the likely financial position and therefore the company's ability to continue trading for the foreseeable future.

Disclaimer of opinion on view given by the financial statements

Because of the possible effect of the limitation in the evidence available to us, we are unable to form an opinion as to whether the financial statements give a true and fair view of the state of the company's affairs as at 31 March 2000 and of its profit [loss] for the year then ended and whether the financial statements have been properly prepared in accordance with the Companies Act 1985.

In respect of the limitation on our work relating to the going concern basis, we have not obtained all the information and explanations that we considered necessary for the purpose of our audit.

41.72   In other situations, the auditors may decide that a qualified opinion is appropriate.

Example 41.72

Basis of opinion

We conducted our audit in accordance with United Kingdom auditing standards issued by the Auditing Practices Board, except that the scope of our work was limited by the matter set out below.

An audit includes examination, on a test basis, of evidence relevant to the amounts and disclosures in the financial statements. It also includes an assessment of the significant estimates and judgements made by the directors in the preparation of the financial statements and of whether the accounting policies are appropriate to the circumstances of the company and the group, consistently applied and adequately disclosed.

We planned our audit so as to obtain all the information and explanations which we considered necessary in order to provide us with
sufficient evidence to give reasonable assurance that the financial
statements are free from material misstatement, whether caused by
fraud or other irregularity or error. However, the period to which the
directors have paid particular attention in assessing going concern
was, as indicated in note 2 to the accounts, four months from the date
of approval of the financial statements. In our opinion, in all the circumstances, such a period is not sufficient to assess and determine
whether the going concern basis is appropriate. There were no practical auditing procedures we could adopt to ascertain the likely financial position and therefore the company's ability to continue trading
for the foreseeable future.

Qualified opinion arising from limitation in audit scope

Except for any adjustments to the financial statements that might
have been found to be necessary had we been able to obtain sufficient
evidence concerning going concern, in our opinion, the financial
statements give a true and fair view of the state of the company's
affairs as at 31 March 2000 and of its profit [loss] for the year then
ended and have been properly prepared in accordance with the
Companies Act 1985.

In respect alone of the limitation on our work relating to the going
concern basis, we have not obtained all the information and explanations that we considered necessary for the purpose of our audit.

Disclosure of the period regarded by the directors as the foreseeable future

41.73 SAS 130 states that: 'Where the period considered by the directors
has been limited, for example, to a period of less than one year from
the date of approval of the financial statements, the directors will
have determined whether, in their opinion, the financial statements
require any additional disclosure to explain adequately the assumptions that underlie the adoption of the going concern basis'.
[SAS 130(13)] An example of such a disclosure is set out below.

Example 41.73

In accordance with their responsibilities as directors, the directors
have considered the appropriateness of the going concern basis for
the preparation of the financial statements.

After making enquiries, the directors have a reasonable expectation
that the company has adequate resources to continue in operational
existence for the current financial year to 31 March 2000. For this
reason, they continue to adopt the going concern basis in preparing
the financial statements.

41.74 In such circumstances, the auditors may form a view that an un-qualified audit report is appropriate.

Non-disclosure where the foreseeable future regarded by the directors is less than twelve months from the date of approval of the financial statements

41.75 The auditors' assessment of going concern is based upon the information upon which the directors have based their assessment. [SAS 130(14)] Accordingly, it is important for a user of the financial statements to be aware if the period considered by the directors (and thus the auditors) has been limited. To this end, SAS 130 states that: **'If the period to which the directors have paid particular attention in assessing going concern is less than one year from the date of approval of the financial statements, and the directors have not disclosed that fact, the auditors should do so within the section of their report setting out the basis of their opinion, unless the fact is clear from any other references in their report. They should not qualify their opinion on the financial statements on these grounds alone'.** [SAS 130(45)]

Example 41.75

Extract from 'Basis of opinion'

In forming our opinion, we also evaluated the overall adequacy of the presentation of information in the financial statements. In this regard, we draw your attention to the fact that the directors have not disclosed that the period to which they have paid particular attention in assessing going concern is less than one year from the date of approval of these financial statements. The period considered by the directors was six months from the date of approval of the financial statements. Our opinion is not qualified in this respect.

41.76 Modification of a report on this basis is likely to be rare, because the directors are likely to agree to disclose this fact in the financial statements rather than have it referred to in the auditors' report.

The auditors disagree with the preparation of the financial statements on the going concern basis

41.77 In some circumstances, the directors may decide to prepare the financial statements on a going concern basis even though the going concern presumption is inappropriate. In such cases, disclosure of the matters giving rise to the conclusion will be insufficient for the financial statements to give a true and fair view if the effect on the financial statements prepared on that basis is so material or pervasive as to cause the financial statements to be seriously misleading.

SAS 130 states that: **'Where the auditors disagree with the prepara-tion of the financial statements on the going concern basis, they should issue an adverse audit opinion'.** [SAS 130(49)]

Example 41.77

The directors have prepared the financial statements on a going con-cern basis. We do not believe that the going concern basis is appro-priate, because, following the company's failure to make a scheduled repayment to one of its bankers on 31 July 2000, the company's prin-cipal bankers have demanded, under the terms of the various borrowing agreements, repayment in full of loans amounting to £80 million. The bankers have indicated that they are not willing to open discussions on renegotiating banking facilities and we do not believe that the company has access to sufficient resources from other sources to repay the borrowings. The bank loans are secured on the company's factory, warehouse and head office building; if the bank were to appoint a receiver to realise these assets, the company would be unable to continue to operate.

If the company ceased to be a going concern:

(a)   it is unlikely to be able to realise assets at the amounts at which they are stated in the financial statements;

(b)   additional liabilities may need to be recognised; and

(c)   long-term assets and liabilities will need to be reclassified as current.

It is not possible to quantify the financial impact of the company ceasing to be a going concern.

In view of the inappropriateness of the going concern basis as described above, in our opinion, the financial statements do not give a true and fair view of the state of the company's affairs as at 31 March 2000 and of its profit [loss] for the year then ended and accordingly have not been properly prepared in accordance with the Companies Act 1985.

41.78   In the above circumstances, an adverse opinion, rather than an 'except for' opinion, would normally be appropriate.

41.79   Auditors will need to exercise considerable judgement in deciding the level of concern about the ability of a company to continue to operate as a going concern. It will be in extreme circumstances that the auditors will conclude that the concern will be so great as to invalidate the use of the going concern basis.

Financial statements prepared on a basis other than the going concern basis

41.80   When the directors consider that the company is not a going concern, they will usually seek legal advice and may decide to prepare the financial statements on an alternative basis. SAS 130 states that: **'In rare circumstances, in order to give a true and fair view, the directors may have prepared financial statements on a basis other than that of a going concern. If the auditors consider this other basis to be appropriate in the specific circumstances, and if the financial statements contain the necessary disclosures, the auditors should not qualify their audit opinion in this respect'.** [SAS 130(54)]

41.81   However, in such circumstances, the auditors may wish, without qualifying their opinion, to refer in their report to the basis on which the financial statements are prepared. [SAS 130(55)]

Example 41.81

Basis of opinion

We conducted our audit in accordance with United Kingdom auditing standards issued by the Auditing Practices Board. An audit includes examination, on a test basis, of evidence relevant to the amounts and disclosures in the financial statements. It also includes an assessment of the significant estimates and judgements made by the directors in the preparation of the financial statements and of whether the accounting policies are appropriate to the company's circumstances, consistently applied and adequately disclosed.

We planned and performed our audit so as to obtain all the information and explanations which we considered necessary in order to provide us with sufficient evidence to give reasonable assurance that the financial statements are free from material misstatement, whether caused by fraud or other irregularity or error. In forming our opinion, we also evaluated the overall adequacy of the presentation of information in the financial statements.

We draw your attention to note 1 to the accounts which states that the financial statements have been prepared on the basis that the company is no longer a going concern. Our opinion is not qualified in this respect.

In practice, however, it is often difficult to prepare financial statements on a basis other than the going concern basis and, therefore, the auditor will only rarely be able to adopt this approach. In such circumstances, the auditor may decide that, because of the inherent uncertainties relating to the amounts included in financial statements prepared on a basis other than the going concern basis, the auditors' opinion will need to be modified to include an explanatory paragraph dealing with a fundamental uncertainty.

Judgements by directors and auditors

41.82 The new regime requires much judgement on the part of directors and auditors. These judgements, which will impact on all of the guidance set out in this chapter, will not be easy for a number of reasons:

(a) much of the evidence relating to going concern will at best be persuasive rather than conclusive;

(b) the appraisal of any budgets and plans cannot take account of unexpected events;

(c) virtually all business entails some risk;

(d) in the absence of a detailed protocol between bankers and the APB, it is difficult to correlate the extent of the assurances which bankers may give with the various situations set out above.

41.83 It is suggested that the greater the concern about the ability of the entity to continue in business, the greater the extent of assurance auditors will require in respect of bank facilities. It should be recognised that bankers are frequently reluctant to commit such facilities in writing and therefore an appraisal of such facilities can usually take account of the tone of recent correspondence and intimations made by bankers at meetings at which notes are taken.

Future developments

41.84 The ASB's *Statement of Principles* and FRED 21 *Accounting Policies* were published in December 1999. FRED 21 proposes the withdrawal of SSAP 2 *Disclosure of accounting policies*. SSAP 2 introduced and defined four 'fundamental accounting concepts', one of which was going concern. Since then these concepts have been reflected in the EU Accounting Directives and in companies legislation.

41.85 The explanatory note to SSAP 2 explained that the concepts were not intended to stand for all time, but were 'capable of variation and evolution' as accounting thought and practice moved forward.

41.86 The *Statement of Principles* reflects the changes in accounting thought and practice since SSAP 2 was issued and whilst it discusses the fundamental accounting concepts, it no longer refers to them as such. However, it is clear that the notion of going concern is still regarded as part of the bedrock of accounting.

41.87 The proposals of FRED 21 would not actually have any effect on the interpretation of the going concern presumption, but the references in this chapter to SSAP 2 will change to reflect the new Financial Reporting Standard on accounting policies once it is issued.

42 Other audit reports

42 Other audit reports

Summary of changes since the previous issue of this publication

Para.	*Topic*	*Summary*
42.11	APB Practice Note 19 *Banks in the United Kingdom*	Guidance on the application of Auditing Standards to the audit of banks in the UK. Also guidance to assist the reporting accountants of a bank in reporting on matters specified by the Financial Services Authority ('the FSA') in its capacity as banking supervisor.
42.18	APB Practice Note 20 *The audit of insurers in the United Kingdom*	Guidance on the treatment of equalisation reserves in insurers' financial statements and reports on regulatory returns.
Throughout	Identification of nationality of law and standards	Indicating in the audit report the nationality of law and standards under which financial statements have been prepared and audited, in accordance with an agreement between the International Forum for Accountancy Developments and leading global regulators.
Throughout	APB Bulletin 1999/5 *The Combined Code: requirements of auditors under the Listing Rules of the London Stock Exchange*	Changes to the wording of the responsibilities statement in the audit report arising from "audit, review and read" responsibilities of auditors.
42.80	Tech 12/99 *The audit of friendly societies*	Guidance relating to the form of audit reports on the accounts of friendly societies.
42.92	Accounting Requirements for Registered Social Landlords General Determination 2000	Guidance on preparation of accounts for registered social landlords (RSLs).

42.93	Revised SORP *Accounting by registered housing associations*	The aim of the SORP is to narrow the areas of difference in accounting practice in the financial statements of housing associations and to provide guidance on the formats and accounting policies which enable housing associations to comply with the accounting requirements of the Accounting Requirements for Registered Social Landlords General Determination 2000.
42.104	SI 1999/248 *The building societies (contents of accounts) regulations 1999*	The statutory requirement for building societies to publish a statement of source and application of funds has been repealed for financial years ending on or after 23 March 1999. From that date, building societies are required, by FRS 1, to provide a cash flow statement. This resulted in an amendment to APB Practice Note 18 *The audit of building societies in the United Kingdom.*
42.132	FRED 21 *Accounting policies*	Proposes additional disclosures where a significant part of an entity's activities falls within the scope of a SORP.

Introduction

42.1   Many of the examples of other audit reports given in this chapter are restricted to the wording of the opinion section. For appropriate wording required in the other sections of the audit report, reference should be made to the examples given in **39.84**, **39.96** and **40.4** above, which illustrate the full wording of an unqualified audit report for a single company, an unlisted group and a listed group respectively.

Financial statements drawn up to a date other than the financial year end and not purporting to relate to the company's financial year

42.2   There may be special circumstances where the auditors are engaged to audit the financial statements of a company drawn up to a date other than the financial year end and which do not purport to relate to the company's financial year. This section does not deal with cases where directors ask auditors to review half-yearly reports (interim reports) of listed companies, which are discussed in chapter 40. Nor does it deal with 'non-statutory accounts', which are discussed in **42.7** below.

42.3   The audit report should be addressed to the directors. An example of the opinion paragraph is set out in Example **42.3.1** below, where the auditor is requested to report in true and fair terms. Example **42.3.2** below illustrates wording suitable for inclusion in the directors' statement of responsibilities, or in the auditors' report when the directors do not include a description of their responsibilities. This suggested wording is based on some of the wording in the explanatory material included in SAS 600, but account is taken of the fact that there are no statutory reporting requirements which are appropriate to these circumstances. However, some reference to the keeping of proper accounting records, safeguarding of assets and steps to prevent and detect fraud and other irregularities is suggested, as this helps eliminate any subsequent misunderstandings about scope of auditors' and directors' respective responsibilities. In practice it may be appropriate to add further points in the description of the directors' responsibilities to take account of any specific responsibilities which relate to the issue of the financial statements for a period which is different to statutory accounts.

Example 42.3.1

Opinion

In our opinion, the financial statements give a true and fair view of the state of the company's affairs as at 31 March 2000 and of its profit [loss] for the nine months then ended.

Example 42.3.2

The directors are responsible for the preparation of the financial statements which give a true and fair view of the state of affairs of the company at the period end and of the profit or loss of the company for that period. In preparing those financial statements the directors:

(a) select suitable accounting policies and then apply them consistently;

(b) make judgements and estimates that are reasonable and prudent; and

(c) prepare the financial statements on the going concern basis, unless it is inappropriate to presume that the company will continue in business (only necessary where no separate statement on going concern is made by the directors).

> The directors are responsible for keeping proper accounting records, safeguarding the assets of the company and taking reasonable steps for the prevention and detection of fraud and other irregularities.

42.4   No mention is made in the above report of compliance with the Act, since the financial statements are not the 'statutory accounts' prepared for filing purposes or for laying before the members. However, consideration needs to be given as to whether the financial statements give adequate disclosure and comply with applicable accounting standards so as to present a true and fair view. If disclosures required by the Act are omitted, the auditors need to consider whether the omitted information is necessary for a true and fair view and, if it is, they should consider giving a qualified or adverse opinion. For example, information regarding the remuneration of directors may not be necessary for a true and fair view, whereas information about long-term debt probably is. It is also suggested that the following wording be included in the opening notes to the financial statements: 'These financial statements are drawn up to a date other than the financial year end and do not purport to relate to the company's financial year' (s240 statement). This is suggested in order to avoid any misunderstanding that the financial statements could be either statutory or non-statutory accounts, within the meaning of s242 and s240 of the Act respectively. This would be particularly advisable where the financial statements could be construed as 'published as defined by s240(4)'.

Accounts prepared for commercial agreements and non-statutory accounts

42.5   Accountants are frequently appointed to report on accounts prepared for a specific commercial transaction. The Audit Brief *Special reports of accountants*, which was issued by the APC in 1984, gives guidance on reports on particular aspects of financial activity (e.g., a statement of sales for a period), but does not really consider the situation where accountants are asked to report on more complete sets of accounts. The Audit Brief stresses that accountants should avoid giving 'certificates', as the term implies a high degree of factual certainty which an examination of records cannot normally provide and also does not allow for a qualified opinion. Review opinions are not often considered acceptable by the parties to the transaction, as such opinions are unclear as to the extent to which procedures have been performed and may not give the addressees of the report the level of assurance they are looking for.

42.6   Occasionally, accountants may be asked to perform 'agreed upon procedures'. If so, it is important that the procedures are very clearly specified and the accountants give a factual statement of the results of the procedures performed rather than an opinion.

42.7 If not performing 'agreed upon procedures', accountants should normally arrange that they are appointed to perform an audit in accordance with auditing standards. In such circumstances it would be prudent for the auditor to establish with the directors that the financial statements, or information, will not be published non-statutory accounts within the meaning of s240(4) of the Act. If there is any possibility that they may be so construed then there should be an opening note to the financial statements which includes a s240 statement as illustrated in **42.4** above. Section 240 of the Act makes it clear that where non-statutory accounts are published no auditors' report under s235 should be published with them. This is to avoid the potentially confusing situation where two sets of accounts, i.e., the statutory accounts (for filing and general meeting purposes) and the non-statutory accounts (which relate or purport to relate to the company's financial year) are in the public domain, both having a true and fair opinion associated with them. So, where the non-statutory accounts may be published, it would be more appropriate to express an opinion in terms of 'properly prepared in accordance with the stated accounting policies'.

42.8 Whatever form of opinion is given, the principles of SAS 600 should be applied and there should be disclosure of the respective responsibilities of the preparers of the information and the auditors. For preparers, no responsibilities which arise from statute should be referred to (see example wording in **42.3** above). Any limitations on the scope of the work should also be made clear. Note that where the special circumstances of the reporting entity either require or permit adoption of accounting policies which would not normally permit a true and fair view to be given, reference would be made to those circumstances in the paragraphs of the report dealing with respective responsibilities of the preparers and the auditors, unless the matter is included in a separate statement given by the directors. The auditor may draw attention to them in the basis of opinion section of the report. This guidance is in accordance with paragraph 28 of SAS 600 *Auditors' reports on financial statements.*

42.9 The accountants should consider carefully to whom their report should be addressed and to whom they wish to owe a duty of care. Normally, it is appropriate to report to only one party to a transaction and advise the other parties to obtain their own independent advice. In cases of doubt, legal or professional advice should be obtained.

Banking companies

42.10   The provisions of the Act for the accounts of banking companies and groups were amended by the Companies Act 1985 (Bank Accounts) Regulations 1991 (SI 1991 No 2705, which incorporated into UK law the provisions of the EU Bank Accounts Directive.

42.11   Where a banking company prepares its individual accounts or the parent company of a banking group prepares its group accounts, the audit report required, including the opinion, is the same as that required for the generality of companies incorporated under the Companies Act, as illustrated in **39.84** and **39.96** above (see chapter 40 as regards listed companies). In May 1999 the APB issued Practice Note 19 *Banks in the United Kingdom*. The Practice Note contains guidance on the application of Auditing Standards to the audit of banks in the UK. In addition it contains guidance intended to assist the reporting accountants of a bank in reporting on matters specified by the Financial Services Authority (the FSA) in its capacity as banking supervisor. Guidance is also given on the conduct of auditors' and reporting accountants' periodic meetings with, and direct reports to, the FSA. The auditors of a UK incorporated bank have a specific statutory duty to give written notice to the FSA when they resign, or decide not to seek reappointment, or decide to issue a report which is other than unqualified on the bank's accounts.

42.12   It should be remembered that banking companies are not entitled to the exemptions available to small and medium-sized companies. Their directors' statements of responsibility should therefore indicate that the directors are required to state whether applicable accounting standards have been followed. Accounting best practice for banks is set out in the five British Bankers' Association (BBA) Statements of Recommended Practice (SORPs). These are not mandatory and so non-compliance by a bank with a SORP recommendation would be expected to give rise to a qualification in the audit report only if the auditor believes that the financial statements do not give a true and fair view.

Insurance companies

Statutory accounts

42.13   Schedule 9A contains the special provisions of the Act regarding the form and content of annual accounts of insurance companies and groups. These regulations incorporate into UK law the requirements of the EU Insurance Undertakings Accounts Directive.

42.14   An insurance company must prepare its individual accounts and the parent company of an insurance group must prepare its group accounts in accordance with Sch 9A. They are not permitted to prepare accounts in accordance with Sch 4.

42.15   An insurance group is defined in the Act as a group where the parent company is an insurance company or where:
[s255A]

   (a)   the parent company's principal subsidiary undertakings are wholly or mainly insurance companies; and

   (b)   the parent company does not itself carry on any material business apart from the acquisition, management and disposal of interests in subsidiary undertakings.

42.16   Where an insurance company prepares its individual accounts, or the parent company of an insurance group prepares its group accounts, in accordance with Sch 9A, the audit report format, including the opinion, is the same as for the generality of companies incorporated under the Companies Act (see chapter 39 and also chapter 40 as regards listed companies).

42.17   Insurance companies carrying on credit business or property, consequential loss, marine and aviation (but not marine cargo) or nuclear business in excess of the *de minimis* limits are required to include equalisation provisions calculated on a statutory basis in their financial statements. Insurance groups and non-insurance groups with one or more insurance subsidiaries are similarly required to include equalisation provisions in their financial statements.

42.18   APB Practice Note 20 *The audit of insurers in the United Kingdom*, issued in August 1999 provides guidance on the treatment of equalisation reserves in insurers' financial statements. Equalisation reserves do not represent liabilities at the balance sheet date and may not apply to all companies in a group. Nevertheless, the APB (which took legal advice on this matter) does not consider it appropriate, in the generality of cases, for group accounts to exclude equalisation reserves established at company level, either in order to standardise accounting policies for the group or for the group accounts to show a true and fair view.

42.19   Equalisation reserves should be included at liabilities item C5 in the Sch 9A accounts format and the amount of such reserves should therefore be separately disclosed in the financial statements. In addition, the financial statements should contain disclosure of the basis on which equalisation reserves are established and their financial effect on the results for the period.

42.20   Where there is adequate disclosure, along the lines of that recommended in the Association of British Insurers (ABI) SORP on accounting for insurance business, issued in December 1998, and the equalisation reserves established in accordance with the appropriate legislation are material to the audit opinion, the following paragraph should be included in the basis of opinion section of the auditors' report, but the report should normally express an unqualified opinion on the financial statements.

Example 42.20

Equalisation reserves

Our evaluation of the presentation of information in the financial statements has had regard to the statutory requirement for insurance companies to maintain equalisation reserves. The nature of equalisation reserves, the amounts set aside at [date] and the effect of the movement in those reserves during the year on the balance on the general business technical account and profit [loss] before tax, are disclosed in notes x and y respectively.

42.21   It should be noted that although the balance sheet and profit and loss account format headings and the ABI recommended disclosures refer to equalisation provisions, it is appropriate to refer to equalisation reserves in the audit report, as they do not represent 'liabilities' in the conventional sense at the balance sheet date.

42.22   The ICAEW issued FRAG 3/93 in February 1993 to provide guidance on information to be given in financial statements of non-life insurers in respect of claims provisions in cases of material uncertainty. It recommended that any material inherent uncertainties are disclosed in the financial statements and that where such material inherent uncertainties are material to the accounts as a whole, the auditors should consider carefully the content of the audit report in the light of the particular circumstances and the extent of the disclosures and explanations by the directors in the financial statements.

42.23   Insurance companies are not entitled to the disclosure exemptions available to small and medium-sized companies.

42.24   It is the responsibility of the directors to prepare the annual regulatory return to the primary insurance regulator, currently the Financial Services Authority on behalf of the Insurance Directorate of HM Treasury in compliance with the Insurance Companies (Accounts and Statements) Regulations 1996 as amended.

42.25   The audited regulatory return is required to be delivered to the FSA within six months after the end of the company's accounting reference period and it is the directors' responsibility to ensure that this deadline is met. The FSA has published proposals to bring forward this deadline for regulatory returns prepared in relation to financial periods ending on or after 31 December 2001.

Auditors' reports on regulatory returns

42.26 APB Practice Note 20 *The audit of insurers in the United Kingdom* was issued in August 1999. It provides detailed guidance, the major points of which are summarised below.

42.27 It is recommended that the report be addressed to the directors.

42.28 Except where there are no financial statements prepared for an insurer operating through a UK branch rather than as UK limited company, the auditors' work is not a separate audit of the regulatory return in accordance with auditing standards but a set of additional procedures, in accordance with APB Practice Note 20, which, in conjunction with the evidence drawn from the audit work on the financial statements, enable the auditors to report on the regulatory return.

42.29 The regulatory return contains much detailed disclosure of segmental information that analyses the underwriting account by accounting class, business category or risk group. APB Practice Note 20 notes that auditors should apply materiality in relation to the business as a whole, not in relation to the particular accounting class, business category or risk group in which an item is reported, except when considering figures which are required by the regulations to be derived from a prescribed source elsewhere in the return or to be calculated on a specified basis when no concept of materiality applies.

42.30 Auditors are required to report whether the directors' certificate has been properly prepared in accordance with the regulations and whether it was not unreasonable for the directors to have made the statements therein. Each statement in the directors' certificate must be considered separately for reasonableness. Where the directors cannot confirm a particular matter, they should omit it and add a supplementary note to the return to state this fact. The auditors have no obligations to report on omissions; however, the matters giving rise to the omission of a particular statement in the directors' certificate may give rise to statutory duty to report to a regulator.

42.31 The directors' certificate is required to include a list of published guidance on systems of control over the company's business with which it complied at the end of the year, when it is reasonable to believe both that the company continued to comply with that guidance and it will continue to do so in the future. The directors' certificate should also include a list of published guidance that has been followed in preparing the regulatory return.

42.32   Failure of the insurer to comply with any such guidance does not give rise to a reporting obligation in the auditors' report on the regulatory return. However, it may give rise to a statutory duty for the auditor to report directly to the FSA on the grounds that the non-compliance may constitute a breach of the sound and prudent management criteria for insurers and therefore represent grounds for intervention by the FSA. APB Practice Note 20 provides guidance on the auditors' statutory duty to report directly to the FSA.

42.33   Where the audit report contains a fundamental uncertainty paragraph, the auditors are required to state whether, in their opinion, that uncertainty is material to determining whether the company had available assets in excess of its required minimum margin, required European Economic Area (EEA) minimum margin or required UK minimum margin, as the case may be. A fundamental uncertainty paragraph is not a qualification and therefore this opinion in relation to the solvency margin should be included in the fundamental uncertainty paragraph of the auditors' report, not the opinions paragraph.

42.34   It is possible that an insurer may have such a significant surplus of assets over liabilities as shown in the FSA return that the effect of the fundamental uncertainty is unlikely to materially affect that surplus. However, any uncertainty that is such as to be considered fundamental is likely to be material to determining whether the company had available assets in excess of its required minimum margin, required EEA minimum margin or required UK minimum margin, as the case may be.

42.35   Auditors of life insurers are not required to report on the directors' certificates in relation to the following:

(a)   consistency of the company's investment policy and practice for internal linked funds with any representations made to policyholders or potential policyholders; and

(b)   compliance with *Money Laundering – Guidance Notes for Insurance and Retail Products.*

42.36   If the life insurer has obtained a s68 order, it will need to be referred to in the respective responsibilities paragraph and also in the bases of opinions paragraph, if it refers to implicit items.

42.37   The example report for a composite insurer includes the matters relevant to both general and life insurers.

42.38   Appropriate wordings for the auditors' reports on the annual regulatory returns are set out in the following examples (taken from APB Practice Note 20). If the company has no s68 orders, the relevant additions to the audit report should not be included.

42.39   When reporting on an insurance company's regulatory return, the illustrative reports should be adapted to meet the circumstances of that individual company, taking account of the notes set out below.

Example 42.39.1

Example auditors' report on regulatory return – general insurance company

(This illustrative auditors' report should be tailored in accordance with the notes set out beneath the examples)

XYZ GENERAL INSURANCE COMPANY LIMITED

Global business/UK branch business

Financial year ended 31 March 2000

Report of the auditors to the directors pursuant to regulation 29 of the Insurance Companies (Accounts and Statements) Regulations 1996

We have examined the following documents prepared by the company pursuant to section 17 of the Insurance Companies Act 1982 ('the Act') and the Insurance Companies (Accounts and Statements) Regulations 1996 ('the Regulations'):

(a)   Forms [9 to 13, 15 to 17, 20 to 39], including supplementary notes thereto ('the forms');

(b)   the statements required by regulations 19, 20 21 and 23, on pages x to x ('the statements'); and

(c)   the certificate signed in accordance with regulation 28(a) on pages x to x ('the certificate').

In the case of the certificate, our examination did not extend to paragraph [ ] in relation to the statements required by regulations 24 and 26, concerning shareholder controllers and general business ceded.

Respective responsibilities of the company and its auditors

The company is responsible for the preparation of an annual return (including the Forms, statements and certificate) under the provisions of the Act and the Regulations. [*The requirements of the Regulations have been modified by [an] order[s] issued under section 68 of the Act on .... 199X and .... 199X.*] Under regulation 5, the Forms and statements are required to be prepared in the manner specified by the Regulations and to state fairly the information provided on the basis required by the Regulations.

It is our responsibility to form an independent opinion as to whether the Forms and statements meet these requirements and, in the case of the certificate, whether it was or was not unreasonable for the persons giving the certificate to have made the statements therein and to report our opinions to you.

Bases of opinions

We conducted our work in accordance with Practice Note 20 *The audit of insurers in the United Kingdom* issued by the Auditing Practices Board. Our work included examination, on a test basis, of evidence relevant to the amounts and disclosures in the Forms and statements. The evidence included that previously obtained by us relating to the audit of the financial statements of the company for the financial year on which we reported on [*date*]. It also included an assessment of the significant estimates and judgements made by the company in the preparation of the Forms and statements.

We planned and performed our audit so as to obtain all the information and explanations which we considered necessary in order to provide us with sufficient evidence to give reasonable assurance that the Forms and statements are free from material misstatement, whether caused by fraud or other irregularity or error, and comply with regulation 5.

In the case of the certificate, the work performed involved a review of the procedures undertaken by the signatories to enable them to make the statements therein and does not extend to an evaluation of the effectiveness of the company's internal control systems.

Opinions

In our opinion:

(a)   the Forms and statements fairly state the information provided on the basis required by the Regulations [*as modified*] and have been properly prepared in accordance with the provisions of those Regulations; and

(b)   according to the information and explanations received by us:

(i)   the certificate has been properly prepared in accordance with the provisions of the Regulations; and

(ii)   it was not unreasonable for the persons giving the certificate to have made the statements therein.

(Signature and name of auditors)

Chartered Accountants and Registered Auditors   (Address)

(Date)

Example 42.39.2

Example auditors' report on regulatory return – life company

(This illustrative auditors' report should be tailored in accordance with the notes set out beneath the examples)

XYZ LIFE INSURANCE COMPANY LIMITED

Global business/UK branch business

Financial year ended 31 March 2000

Report of the auditors to the directors pursuant to regulation 29 of the Insurance Companies (Accounts and Statements) Regulations 1996

We have examined the following documents prepared by the company pursuant to section 17 of the Insurance Companies Act 1982 ('the Act') and the Insurance Companies (Accounts and Statements) Regulations 1996 ('the Regulations'):

(a)   Forms [9, 10, 13 to 17 and 40 to 45], including the supplementary notes thereto ('the Forms');

(b)   the statement required by regulation 23 on pages x to x ('the statement'); and

(c)   the certificate signed in accordance with regulation 28(a) on pages x to x ('the certificate').

In the case of the certificate, our examination did not extend to:

(a)   paragraph [ ] in relation to the statements required by regulations 24 and 31, concerning shareholder controllers and the appointed actuary;

(b)   paragraph [ ], concerning the investment policy and practice of internal linked funds, required by paragraph 4(d) of Schedule 6; and

(c)   paragraph [ ] insofar as it relates to controls with respect to money laundering.

Respective responsibilities of the company and its auditors

The company is responsible for the preparation of an annual return (including the forms, statement and certificate) under the provisions of the Act and the Regulations. [*The requirements of the Regulations have been modified by [an] order[s] issued under section 68 of the Act on .....199X and ...... 199X.*] Under regulation 5, the Forms and statement are required to be prepared in the manner specified by the Regulations and to state fairly the information provided on the basis required by the Regulations.

It is our responsibility to form an independent opinion as to whether the forms and statement meet these requirements and, in the case of the certificate, whether it was or was not unreasonable for the persons giving the certificate to have made the statements therein and to report our opinions to you.

Bases of opinions

We conducted our work in accordance with Practice Note 20 *The audit of insurers in the United Kingdom* issued by the Auditing Practices Board. Our work included examination, on a test basis, of evidence relevant to the amounts and disclosures in the Forms and statement. The evidence included that previously obtained by us relating to the audit of the financial statements of the company for the financial year on which we reported on [*date*]. It also included an assessment of the significant estimates and judgements made by the company in the preparation of the Forms and statement.

We planned and performed our audit so as to obtain all the information and explanations which we considered necessary in order to provide us with sufficient evidence to give reasonable assurance that the Forms and statement are free from material misstatement, whether caused by fraud or other irregularity or error and comply with regulation 5.

In the case of the certificate, the work performed involved a review of the procedures undertaken by the signatories to enable them to make the statements therein and does not extend to an evaluation of the effectiveness of the company's internal control systems.

In giving our opinion, we have relied on:

(a) the certificate of the actuary on page x with respect to the mathematical reserves and the required minimum margin; [*and*

(b) *the identity and value of implicit items as they have been admitted in accordance with regulation 23(5) of the Insurance Companies Regulations 1994 by virtue of an order issued under section 68 of the Act on ....*]

Opinions

In our opinion:

(a) the Forms and statement fairly state the information provided on the basis required by the Regulations [*as modified*]; and have been properly prepared in accordance with the provisions of those Regulations; and

(b) according to the information and explanations received by us:

(i) the certificate has been properly prepared in accordance with the provisions of the Regulations; and

        (ii) it was not unreasonable for the persons giving the certificate to have made the statements therein.

(Signature and name of auditors)

Chartered Accountants and Registered Auditors   (Address)

(Date)

Example 42.39.3

Example auditors' report on regulatory return – composite insurer

(This illustrative auditors' report should be tailored in accordance with the notes set out beneath the examples)

XYZ COMPOSITE INSURANCE COMPANY LIMITED

Global business/UK branch business

Financial year ended 31 March 2000

Report of the auditors to the directors pursuant to regulation 29 of the Insurance Companies (Accounts and Statements) Regulations 1996

We have examined the following documents prepared by the company pursuant to section 17 of the Insurance Companies Act 1982 ('the Act') and the Insurance Companies (Accounts and Statements) Regulations 1996 ('the Regulations'):

(a)   Forms [9 to 17 and 20 to 45], including the supplementary notes thereto ('the Forms');

(b)   the statements required by regulations 19, 20, 21 and 23 on pages x to x ('the statements'); and

(c)   the certificate signed in accordance with regulation 28(a) on pages x to x ('the certificate').

In the case of the certificate, our examination did not extend to:

(a)   paragraph [ ] in relation to the statements required by regulations 24, 26 and 31, concerning shareholder controllers, general business ceded and the appointed actuary;

(b)   paragraph [ ], concerning the investment policy and practice of internal linked funds, required by paragraph 4(d) of Schedule 6; and

(c)   paragraph [ ] insofar as it relates to controls with respect to money laundering.

Respective responsibilities of the company and its auditors

The company is responsible for the preparation of an annual return (including the Forms, statements and certificate) under the provisions of the Act and the Regulations. [*The requirements of the Regulations have been modified by [an] order[s] issued under section 68 of the Act on .....199X and ...... 199X.*] Under regulation 5, the Forms and statements are required to be prepared in the manner specified by the Regulations and to state fairly the information provided on the basis required by the Regulations.

It is our responsibility to form an independent opinion as to whether the Forms and statements meet these requirements and, in the case of the certificate, whether it was or was not unreasonable for the persons giving the certificate to have made the statements therein and to report our opinions to you.

Bases of opinions

We conducted our work in accordance with Practice Note 20 *The audit of insurers in the United Kingdom* issued by the Auditing Practices Board. Our work included examination, on a test basis, of evidence relevant to the amounts and disclosures in the Forms and statements. The evidence included that previously obtained by us relating to the audit of the financial statements of the company for the financial year on which we reported on [*date*]. It also included an assessment of the significant estimates and judgements made by the company in the preparation of the Forms and statements.

We planned and performed our audit so as to obtain all the information and explanations which we considered necessary in order to provide us with sufficient evidence to give reasonable assurance that the Forms and statements are free from material misstatement, whether caused by fraud or other irregularity or error and comply with regulation 5.

In the case of the certificate, the work performed involved a review of the procedures undertaken by the signatories to enable them to make the statements therein and does not extend to an evaluation of the effectiveness of the company's internal control systems.

In giving our opinion, we have relied on:

(a)   the certificate of the actuary on page x with respect to the mathematical reserves and the required minimum margin for long-term business; [*and*

(b)   *the identity and value of implicit items as they have been admitted in accordance with regulation 23(5) of the Insurance Companies Regulations 1994 by virtue of an order issued under section 68 of the Act on ....*]

Opinions

In our opinion:

(a)   the Forms and statements fairly state the information provided on the basis required by the Regulations [*as modified*] and have been properly prepared in accordance with the provisions of those Regulations; and

(b)   according to the information and explanations received by us:

(i)   the certificate has been properly prepared in accordance with the provisions of the Regulations; and

(ii) it was not unreasonable for the persons giving the certificate to have made the statements therein.

(Signature and name of auditors)

Chartered Accountants and Registered Auditors   (Address)

(Date)

Notes to examples 42.39.1 to 42.39.3

The following notes from APB Practice Note 20 should be taken into account when tailoring the above example reports.

(a)   The forms that are cited should be those that are relevant to the company concerned. For example, the report for a general insurance company that does not discount its outstanding claims provision should not refer to Form 30.

(b)   The exclusions relating to the directors' certificate referred to at the end of the scope paragraph should omit reference to any of these items that do not appear in the directors' certificate, for example, the regulation 26 statement will only be present in the return for a UK company as defined.

(c)   Section 68 orders modifying the form or rules governing the preparation of the regulatory return prepared by the company will be referred to in the respective responsibilities paragraph (words in square brackets), with the words 'as modified' (also indicated by the use of square brackets) being inserted in the opinions sections.

(d)   Where a company writing long-term business has a s68 order allowing it to recognise an implicit item in the return, this is dealt with by the reference in the bases of opinions section and does not require the insertions referred to in (c). If a company writing long-term business does not have such an order, the relevant part of the bases of opinions paragraph should be omitted.

(e) There is no need for the auditors' report to refer to s68 orders modifying the application of the asset valuation rules.

(f) The specimen reports reflect the fact that there is currently no extant guidance that is likely to be referred to in paragraph 5 of the directors' certificate which expressly states that it does not need to be audited. If such guidance were to be published and referred to in the certificate, the exclusions at the end of the scope paragraph would need to be expanded accordingly.

(g) The sentence in the bases of opinions paragraph referring to the audit of the financial statements is normally appropriate. If, however, financial statements have not been prepared and audited, it should be omitted. Auditors may add further details of the work undertaken.

(h) If part or all of the return has to be resubmitted, the auditors' report on the resubmitted documents will be modelled upon the specimen reports, but adapted to reflect the particular documents being resubmitted. In the case of the complete resubmission of a return, appropriate wording for inclusion in the scope paragraph is as follows:

'These documents have been amended pursuant to section 22(5) of the Act. This report replaces the report of the auditors, dated [.......XX] which was issued in respect of the original documents and which is now withdrawn.'

In the case of a partial resubmission, the report should indicate that the documents being reported upon have been prepared as amended documents pursuant to s22(5) of the Act to replace the corresponding documents on which the auditors reported on [..........XX].

Investment businesses

42.40 The requirements for auditors to report to regulators on annual financial statements and various prescribed matters pertaining to investment businesses are set out in the rule books of the Financial Services Authority (the Securities and Investments Board rulebook as was) and of the self-regulatory organisations (SROs). Additional guidance on auditors' reporting responsibilities and the format of audit reports has been issued by the APB as part of Practice Note 1 *Investment business.* A copy of this Practice Note should normally be obtained and read before the commencement of the audit of an investment business. Note that Practice Note 1 is currently being revised by the APB and is likely to be reissued during 2000 as Practice Note 21 *The audit of investment businesses in the United Kingdom.* When issued in final form, this will supersede Practice Note 1.

42.41   The detailed requirements differ according to the regulator and the type of investment business carried on, but essentially the auditors are required to report on:

(a)   whether the auditors have obtained all the information and explanations considered necessary for their audit;

(b)   annual financial statements which are required to show a true and fair view and be drawn up in accordance with accounting requirements laid down by the regulator;

(c)   compliance throughout the period with the regulator's requirements for accounting records and systems; in particular, with the rules relating to client money and/or investments;

(d)   compliance with financial resources requirements;

(e)   whether the investment business has complied with the client assets rules at all relevant dates.

The APB has agreed with the regulators a common format for auditors' reports as set out in Practice Note 1.

42.42   The auditors are usually required to report on the annual financial statements in true and fair view terms. Some regulators, such as the Securities and Futures Authority (SFA), require a copy of the Companies Act statutory accounts to be submitted with the regulatory returns and the auditors' report thereon, and the reference to the true and fair view is to the annual statutory accounts. However, where this is not the case, the auditors should generally annex a copy of the statutory accounts and refer to these in their report to the regulators along the lines of 'the ...., together with the annual statutory accounts, give a true and fair view'. If this is not possible, the auditors should compare the financial statements prepared for the regulator with the financial statements prepared for other statutory purposes, to identify any items which are not included in the former. They should consider each of these items and decide whether it is necessary for a true and fair view. If it is, they should request that it be disclosed as additional information in the financial statements prepared for the regulator. All such items may be disclosed in a separate section entitled 'Additional information considered necessary for a true and fair view'.

42.43   Where information is required purely as a statutory formality (such as auditors' remuneration), it is unlikely to be judged necessary for a true and fair view.

42.44   Where financial statements are prepared only for a regulator, regard should be paid to the information which would need to be disclosed if the investment business were preparing Companies Act accounts;

professional judgement should be exercised in determining whether the disclosure of items is necessary for a true and fair view.

42.45 Reporting on (c) and (e) in **42.41** above would be unsatisfactory, unless the relevant rules or regulations impose on management detailed criteria as to the controls they are required to maintain or at least as to the objectives they must achieve. In the absence of such clear regulations, what constitutes an adequate internal control system is a judgement which is made by management based largely on cost/benefit considerations. The Practice Note sets out guidance on the responsibilities of management in this area in paragraphs 7 and 20 and these can be summarised as follows:

The directors are responsible for establishing and maintaining adequate accounting and internal control systems. In fulfilling that responsibility, estimates and judgements must be made to assess the expected benefits and related costs of management information and of control procedures. The objective is to provide reasonable but not absolute assurance that assets are safeguarded against loss, that transactions are executed in accordance with established authorisation procedures and are recorded properly and to enable the management to conduct the business in a prudent manner. Because of inherent limitations in any accounting and internal control system, errors or irregularities may occur and not be detected. Also, projection of any evaluation of the systems to future periods is subject to the risk that management information and control procedures may become inadequate because of changes in conditions or that the degree of compliance with those procedures may deteriorate.

42.46 Reports to regulators are prepared solely for their use and that of any person with whom they are permitted to share information. The common format of the audit report states:

'Our report is provided to .... in its capacity as a regulator under the Financial Services Act 1986.'

42.47 Following discussion by the APB with the Financial Services Authority (FSA) regulatory bodies, it has been agreed that reports provided solely to regulators in the financial services sector, e.g., the SFA, Personal Investment Authority (PIA), Investment Management Regulatory Organisation (IMRO) and Securities and Investments Board (SIB), are private reports and that the provisions of SAS 600 do not apply. A paper issued by the APB following the discussions states:

'The Board issued Practice Note 1 *Investment business* in June 1992. Section 1 of the Practice Note includes example forms of routine reports by auditors of investment businesses to SIB and the SROs, which were agreed with the regulators before the issue.

The need for inclusion of statements of the responsibilities of directors and auditors was reviewed by the working party, in the context of the recommendations which were then being considered by the Board. The conclusion of that review was that reports by auditors to regulators should not then include such statements:

(a) the reports are addressed to the regulator concerned and include a statement that they are issued solely for the use of the regulator in its capacity as such. Other than the possibility that the report may be made available to other third parties using the statutory "gateways" for disclosure of information by the regulator, there is therefore no likelihood that the reports would properly be made available to others;

(b) although the reports include an opinion on financial statements, they are not primarily reports on "general purpose" financial statements, whose use may be considerably wider than initially proposed.'

42.48   The private nature of reports to regulators should be made clear in both the engagement letter with the client and in the regulatory report itself, e.g., by using the phrase: 'Our report is provided to [SFA] in its capacity as a regulator under the Financial Services Act 1986'.

42.49   Fundamental uncertainties under SAS 600 are required to be explained in the section of the audit report which sets out the basis of the audit opinion. As no such section will exist in regulatory audit reports relating to FSA entities, care should be taken when dealing with fundamental uncertainties. In most cases, the uncertainty will be in respect of the true and fair view shown by the accounts and the most appropriate treatment would be the insertion of an explanatory paragraph after the heading 'Financial statements' but before the phrase 'In our opinion' in the report.

Pension schemes

42.50   The Occupational Pension Schemes (Requirement to obtain Audited Accounts and a Statement from the Auditor) Regulations 1996 (SI 1996 No 1975) ('the Audited Accounts Regulations') lay down rules for the contents of financial statements of all occupational pension schemes that are required to produce audited accounts under pensions regulations.

42.51   In addition, the SORP *Financial reports of pension schemes* provides guidance on the accounting for pension schemes. The Audited Accounts Regulations require the accounts to contain a statement as to whether they have been prepared in accordance with the SORP and, if not, an indication of where there are any material departures from those guidelines. Although SORPs are not mandatory, the legislative support described above, taken together with the due process required by the ASB's code of practice for the development of the SORP, create a strong presumption that in all but exceptional cases it is necessary to follow the guidance in the SORP in order that the financial statements should give the true and fair view required by law.

42.52 The Audited Accounts Regulations require the auditors' report to deal with the following matters:

(a) to report as to whether in the auditors' opinion the requirements of regulations 3(a) and (b) have been satisfied, i.e., whether, in the auditors' opinion, the financial statements show a true and fair view of the financial transactions of the scheme during the scheme year and of the amount and disposition of the assets at the end of the scheme year and of the liabilities of the scheme (other than liabilities to pay pensions and benefits after the end of the scheme year) and contain the information specified in the Schedule to the Audited Accounts Regulations;

(b) to state whether or not in the auditors' opinion contributions have been paid in accordance with the schedule of contributions or payment schedule and, if the statement is negative or qualified, to state the reasons. This statement is referred to in the 'Audited Accounts Regulations as the 'Auditors' Statement about Contributions'.

Where there is no schedule of contributions or payment schedule in relation to the whole or part of the scheme year, the Audited Accounts Regulations require the auditors' statement about contributions to state whether or not in the auditors' opinion contributions payable to the scheme during that year (or during that part of the year when there is no schedule of contributions or payment schedule) have been paid in accordance with the scheme rules or contracts under which they were payable and (where appropriate) with the recommendation of the actuary. If the auditors' statement is negative or qualified, the reasons must be stated.

42.53 SAS 600 *Auditors' reports on financial statements* requires that the responsibilities of auditors should be distinguished from those of directors. It requires that a description of directors' responsibilities should be adequately described in the financial statements or accompanying information or, failing this, in the auditors' report. In the case of trusts, such as pension schemes, the equivalent requirement would be for a description of the trustees' responsibilities in relation to the financial statements.

42.54 The wording of any note on trustees' responsibilities will need to take into account the particular circumstances of the scheme. The examples given may provide the basis of a note describing the responsibilities of pension scheme trustees in relation to the financial statements in the broad generality of cases. The example of an audit report (Example **42.54.2** below) includes wording to identify the nationality of the accounting standards and law under which the financial statements have been prepared (see **39.27** above). It assumes that the opinions on the financial statements and on the contributions are given separately and an extended 'audit, review, read' report is to be given (see **39.27** above). It is understood that the separate opinions approach is likely to be recommended as part of a revision to Practice Note 15 *The audit of occupational pension schemes in the United Kingdom.*

Example 42.54.1

Statement of trustees' responsibilities

The financial statements are the responsibility of the trustees and are required to comply with applicable United Kingdom law and accounting standards. Pension scheme regulations require the trustees to make available to scheme members, beneficiaries and certain other parties, audited financial statements for each scheme year which:

(a) show a true and fair view of the financial transactions of the scheme during the scheme year and of the amount and disposition at the end of that year of the assets and liabilities, other than liabilities to pay pensions and benefits after the end of the scheme year; and

(b) contain the information specified in the Schedule to the Occupational Pension Schemes (Requirement to obtain Audited Accounts and a Statement from the Auditor) Regulations 1996, including a statement whether the financial statements have been prepared in accordance with the Statement of Recommended Practice *Financial reports of pension schemes.*

The trustees have supervised the preparation of the financial statements [by ...... *third-party administrators*] and have agreed suitable accounting policies, to be applied consistently, making any estimates and judgements on a prudent and reasonable basis.

The following paragraph applies for a defined benefit scheme where a schedule of contributions is in place – see alternative paragraphs below for a money purchase scheme; or for a defined benefit scheme where a schedule of contributions is not yet in place under the transitional rules.

The trustees are responsible under pensions legislation for ensuring that there is prepared, maintained and from time to time revised a schedule of contributions showing the rates of contributions payable

---

towards the scheme by or on behalf of the employer and the active members of the scheme and the dates on or before which such contributions are to be paid. The trustees are also responsible for keeping records in respect of contributions received in respect of any active member of the scheme and for procuring that contributions are made to the scheme in accordance with the schedule of contributions [, the scheme rules and the recommendations of the actuary].[1]

The trustees also have a general responsibility for ensuring that adequate accounting records are kept and for taking such steps as are reasonably open to them to safeguard the assets of the scheme and to prevent and detect fraud and other irregularities.

Alternative penultimate paragraph for money purchase schemes

The trustees are responsible under pensions legislation for ensuring that there is prepared, maintained and from time to time revised a payment schedule showing the rates of normal contributions payable towards the scheme by or on behalf of the employer and the active members of the scheme and the dates on or before which such contributions are to be paid. The trustees are also responsible for keeping records in respect of contributions received in respect of any active member of the scheme and for procuring that contributions are made to the scheme in accordance with the payment schedule [, the scheme rules [and the recommendations of the actuary]]. [2]

Alternative penultimate paragraph for a defined benefit scheme where a schedule of contributions is not yet in place under the transitional rules

The trustees are responsible under pensions legislation for keeping records in respect of contributions received in respect of any active member of the scheme and for procuring that contributions are made to the scheme in accordance with the scheme rules [or contracts under which they are payable] and with the recommendations of the actuary.

[1, 2] *The trust deed and rules of many schemes require auditors also to report on whether contributions have been paid to the scheme in accordance with the rules of the scheme and with the recommendations of the actuary, where one is appointed, and the references to these make it clear that compliance with the rules and recommendations is in the first instance a matter for the trustees.*

[The above statement of responsibility may be included within the trustees' report or as a separate statement immediately preceding the auditors' report.

Where the scheme is managed by a corporate trustee but the client prefers to refer in the annual report to 'trustees' (in the plural), the annual report should include an explanation of the term, e.g.:

'Throughout the annual report and accounts, 'trustees' means XYZ Limited'.]

Example 42.54.2

Where trustees provide a description of their responsibilities

REPORT OF THE AUDITORS TO THE TRUSTEES OF THE XYZ PENSION SCHEME

We have audited the financial statements on pages 8 to 15, which have been prepared on the basis of the accounting policies set out on pages 9 and 10.

Respective responsibilities of trustees and auditors

As described on page 6, the scheme's trustees are responsible for obtaining audited financial statements, which comply with applicable United Kingdom law and accounting standards and for making available certain other information about the scheme in the form of an annual report. They are also responsible for procuring that contributions are made to the scheme in accordance with the *schedule of contributions certified by the actuary/payment schedule (amend as appropriate)*. Our responsibilities, as independent auditors, are established by statute, the Auditing Practices Board and our profession's ethical guidance.

We report to you our opinion as to whether the financial statements show a true and fair view and contain the information specified in the Schedule to the Occupational Pension Schemes (Requirement to obtain Audited Accounts and a Statement from the Auditor) Regulations 1996 made under the Pensions Act 1995. We also provide a statement about contributions, in which we report to you our opinion as to whether contributions have been paid in accordance with the *schedule of contributions certified by the actuary/payment schedule (amend as appropriate)*. We report to you if we have not received all the information and explanations that we require for our audit.

We read the other information contained in the annual report and consider the implications for our report if we become aware of any apparent misstatements or material inconsistencies with the financial statements

Basis of audit opinion and statement about contributions

We conducted our audit in accordance with United Kingdom auditing standards issued by the Auditing Practices Board. An audit includes examination, on a test basis, of evidence relevant to the amounts and disclosures in the financial statements. It also includes an assessment of the significant estimates and judgements made by or on behalf of the trustees in the preparation of the financial statements, and of whether the accounting policies are appropriate to the scheme's circumstances, consistently applied and adequately disclosed.

We planned and performed our audit so as to obtain all the information and explanations which we considered necessary in order to provide us with sufficient evidence to give reasonable assurance that the financial statements are free from material misstatement, whether caused by fraud or other irregularity or error. In forming our opinion we also evaluated the overall adequacy of the presentation of the information in the financial statements.

Our work also included examination, on a test basis, of evidence relevant to the amount of contributions payable to the scheme and the timing of those payments in order to provide us with reasonable assurance that contributions have been paid in accordance with the *schedule of contributions certified by the actuary on [date]/payment schedule (amend as appropriate).*

Statement about contributions under the scheme

In our opinion contributions payable to the scheme during the year ended 31 March 2000 have been paid in accordance with the *schedule of contributions certified by the actuary on [date]/payment schedule (amend as appropriate).*

Opinion

In our opinion the financial statements show a true and fair view of the financial transactions of the scheme during the scheme year ended 31 March 2000, and of the amount and disposition at that date of the assets and liabilities, other than liabilities to pay pensions and benefits after the end of the scheme year, and contain the information specified in the Schedule to the Occupational Pension Schemes (Requirement to obtain Audited Accounts and a Statement from the Auditor) Regulations 1996 made under the Pensions Act 1995.

(Signature and name of auditors)

Chartered Accountants and Registered Auditors   (Address)

(Date)

Example 42.54.3

Where trustees do not provide a description of their responsibilities

The text contained in Example 42.54.1 should be substituted in the previous example audit report in place of the paragraph under 'Respective responsibilities of trustees and auditors' where the trustees themselves do not describe their responsibilities in relation to the financial statements

42.55 The above examples should be tailored to suit the particular circumstances of a pension scheme by reviewing the provisions relating to the financial statements and accounting records contained in:

(a)   the trust deed; and

(b)   contractual arrangements with third parties assisting in scheme administration.

42.56   It is important to bear in mind that there is no requirement for trustees to describe their responsibilities. SAS 600 sets standards for auditors, not trustees. While it would be preferable for trustees to acknowledge their responsibilities explicitly in their annual report, they should not be pressured into doing so. The simple alternative is to extend the audit report.

42.57   The guidance given above has been developed to provide auditors with advice for the purposes of complying with SAS 600. Trustees seeking specific guidance on their legal responsibilities should be advised to consult a lawyer.

Charities

Introduction

42.58   Section 42 of the Charities Act 1993 empowers the Secretary of State to prescribe regulations concerning the format and content of a charity's statement of accounts. The Charities (Accounts and Reports) Regulations 1995 (SI 1995 No 2724) ('the Regulations') were published in October 1995 and came into force on 1 March 1996. They apply to non-corporate charities, with a few exceptions, and to incorporated charities with respect to the annual report (i.e., the directors' report). The Regulations apply to accounting periods of a charity commencing on or after 1 March 1996. The SORP *Accounting by charities* was published by the Charities Commission in October 1995 and superseded SORP 2. The SORP is currently in the process of being updated and an exposure draft has been issued. The final revised SORP is likely to be published later in 2000.

42.59   The Regulations include provisions on the form of report the auditor should use where a statement of accounts has been prepared under s42(1) Charities Act 1993. The APB issued Practice Note 11 *The audit of charities* in October 1996 to give guidance to auditors.

42.60   The appropriate wording for an audit report on a charity depends on the constitution of the charity concerned and the terms of the audit engagement. The operation of the Charity Commission does not extend to Northern Ireland or Scotland, so references in the auditors' report to respective responsibilities of trustees and auditors, and the wording of the opinion paragraph, will differ according to the country in which charities are established.

Addressee of the report

42.61 Reports on the financial statements of charities incorporated under the Companies Acts or Friendly Societies Acts should be addressed to the members. If the charity is registered under the Acts governing industrial and provident societies, the audit report is required to be addressed to the charity itself. Audit reports on friendly and industrial and provident societies are further discussed in **42.77** to **42.85** below.

42.62 In the case of unincorporated charities in England and Wales, the Regulations specify that the auditors' report should be addressed to the trustees, unless the auditor has been appointed by the Charity Commission, when the report should be addressed to the Commission. If the charity's governing document requires the auditors' report to be addressed to a person or persons other than those identified by the applicable legislation, the auditors should address separate reports to each party.

42.63 Where charities are not governed by statute, the audit report will be addressed to the persons appointing the auditor (usually the trustees) and the form and content of the report will be determined by the auditors' terms of engagement. The terms of engagement may be specified in the deed constituting the charity or may be fixed by the persons appointing the auditors. For example, the appropriate report might be simply that, in the auditors' opinion, the financial statements have been prepared in compliance with the regulations of the charity.

Trustees' statement of responsibilities

42.64 The trustees' statement of responsibilities for a charity incorporated under the Companies Acts should be based on the directors' statement of responsibilities for a company (see chapter 39), but be modified to include additional responsibilities, if any, which they may have under the charity's constitution. For a non-corporate charity, the trustees' responsibilities should be based on those set out in the documents under which the charity is constituted, such as the trust deed, and also the Charities Act 1993 and regulations made thereunder (see **42.58** above). The SORP *Accounting by charities*, which applies to corporate and non-corporate charities (currently being updated, see **42.58** above), sets out requirements for the trustees, including a duty to prepare an annual report and accounts.

Unqualified 'true and fair' opinion

42.65 An example of an unqualified audit report for an incorporated charity is as follows.

Example 42.65

AUDITORS' REPORT TO THE MEMBERS OF XYZ CHARITY LIMITED

We have audited the financial statements on pages 5 to 31, which have been prepared under the accounting policies set out on pages 10 to 13.

Respective responsibilities of trustees and auditors

As described on page 3, the trustees, who are also the directors of the charity for the purposes of company law, are responsible for the preparation of financial statements, which are required to be prepared in accordance with applicable United Kingdom law and accounting standards. It is our responsibility to form an independent opinion, based on our audit, on the financial statements and to report our opinion to you.

Basis of opinion

We conducted our audit in accordance with United Kingdom auditing standards issued by the Auditing Practices Board. An audit includes examination, on a test basis, of evidence relevant to the amounts and estimates and judgements made by the trustees in the preparation of the financial statements and of whether the accounting policies are appropriate to the charitable company's circumstances, consistently applied and adequately disclosed.

We planned and performed our audit so as to obtain all the information and explanations which we considered necessary in order to provide us with sufficient evidence to give reasonable assurance that the financial statements are free from material misstatement, whether caused by fraud or other irregularity or error. In forming our opinion, we also evaluated the overall adequacy of the presentation of information in the financial statements.

Opinion

In our opinion, the financial statements give a true and fair view of the charitable company's state of affairs as at 31 March 2000 and of its incoming resources and application of resources, including its income and expenditure, in the year then ended and have been properly prepared in accordance with the Companies Act 1985.

(Signature and name of auditors)

Chartered Accountants and Registered Auditors   (Address)

(Date)

42.66 An example of an unqualified report for an unincorporated charity in England and Wales, preparing financial statements under s42(1) Charities Act 1993 (which requires a true and fair view), is as follows.

Example 42.66

AUDITORS' REPORT TO THE TRUSTEES OF XYZ CHARITY

We have audited the financial statements on pages 5 to 31, which have been prepared under the accounting policies set out on pages 10 to 13.

Respective responsibilities of trustees and auditors

As described on page 3, you are responsible as trustees for the preparation of the financial statements, which are required to be prepared in accordance with applicable United Kingdom law and accounting standards. It is our responsibility to form an independent opinion, based on our audit, on those statements and to report our opinion to you. We have been appointed as auditors under s43 Charities Act 1993 and report in accordance with regulations made under s44 of that Act.

Basis of opinion

We conducted our audit in accordance with United Kingdom auditing standards issued by the Auditing Practices Board. An audit includes examination, on a test basis, of evidence relevant to the amounts and disclosures in the financial statements. It also includes an assessment of the significant estimates and judgements made in the preparation of the financial statements and of whether the accounting policies are appropriate to the charity's circumstances, consistently applied and adequately disclosed.

We planned and performed our audit so as to obtain all the information and explanations which we considered necessary in order to provide us with sufficient evidence to give reasonable assurance that the financial statements are free from material misstatement, whether caused by fraud or other irregularity or error. In forming our opinion, we also evaluated the overall adequacy of the presentation of information in the financial statements.

Opinion

In our opinion, the financial statements give a true and fair view of the charity's state of affairs as at 31 March 2000 and of its incoming resources and application of resources in the year then ended and have been properly prepared in accordance with the Charities Act 1993, reg 3[1] of the Charities (Accounts and Reports) Regulations 1995 and the trust deed.

(Signature and name of auditors)

Chartered Accountants and Registered Auditors   Address

(Date)

> 1   Regulation 4 in the case of a common investment fund or a common deposit fund which is deemed to be a charity by virtue of s24(8), including that subsection as applied by s25(2) Charities Act 1993.

42.67   Whether auditors can give an unqualified 'true and fair' opinion on the financial statements of charities will depend, among other things, on whether the financial statements depart significantly from the recommendations given in the SORP *Accounting by charities*. With the exception of universities and housing associations, the SORP is intended to be applicable to all charities, regardless of their constitution, size or complexity. However, the SORP adds that 'it is recognised that some of the recommendations may not be applicable to all charities because of the nature of the particular charity or ... the limited classes or size of the transactions or assets involved' and it leaves 'discretion to the trustees of each charity to apply the recommendations according to the character of their charity and the significance of the figures involved'. The APB states, in Practice Note 11, that there is a strong presumption that, in all but exceptional circumstances, it is necessary to follow the guidance set out in the SORP in order to give a true and fair view.

42.68   In accordance with s43 Charities Act 1993, certain charities are permitted to obtain an independent examination of their accounts instead of an annual audit. The purpose of this section is to enable small charities to avoid costs by having their accounts examined by someone other than a registered auditor. This is similar to the exemption from audit available to incorporated charities under the Companies Acts (see **43.12** and **45.20** below). The Charity Commission has issued Directions and Guidance Notes (CC56: *The Carrying Out of an Independent Examination*) which sets out the Commission's expectations and directions.

42.69   In practice, auditors may take the view that the report required of an independent examiner will be interpreted by the reader as amounting to an audit opinion in substance without the opportunity to do the work that needs to precede such an opinion. They may decide that the risks attaching to such an engagement are such that they will not accept appointment as independent examiner but only as auditor.

Reports which are other than unqualified

42.70   The principles governing reports for charities which are other than unqualified are the same as for other enterprises. Appendix 6 to Practice Note 11 gives some specimen reports with qualified opinions.

42.71 A particular problem faced by a number of charities, particularly small ones, is ensuring that all income to which they are entitled is correctly accounted for. The old Auditing Guideline *Charities* took the position that, even where the auditors are satisfied that the system of accounting and control is reasonable in the circumstances, the auditors may appropriately qualify their opinion on the ground that 'the charity, in common with many others of similar size and organisation, derives a substantial proportion of its income from voluntary donations which cannot be fully controlled until they are entered in the accounting records, and are not therefore susceptible to independent audit verification'. The Auditing Guideline has been superseded by Practice Note 12 and the basis for, and form of, this qualification is no longer appropriate.

42.72 The charities SORP and Practice Note 11 recognise that trustees of a charity cannot be held responsible for the security of money or other assets which are intended for its use until that money or assets are within the control of the charity. The Practice Note indicates that, for example, where informal fund raising groups raise money or other resources for charitable purposes on a voluntary basis, without knowledge of any particular charity, criteria for recognising income are not met until the funds raised are notified to the recipient charity. In general, therefore, neither the trustees nor auditors have an obligation to estimate the extent of income from such sources before this point. The Practice Note states that the combination of testing of and reliance on internal controls and, where appropriate, analytical review procedures and substantive testing of accounting records normally provide the auditors with sufficient, appropriate evidence on which they can determine whether the income included in a charity's financial statements is, in all material respects, complete. If the auditors are unable to obtain satisfactory evidence in any material respect, they consider the implications for their report in accordance with the principles set out in SAS 600.

Reports on summarised financial statements

42.73 Some charities include summarised accounts in their publications. The charities SORP (currently being updated, see **42.58** above) requires that such summarised accounts should always be accompanied by a statement signed on behalf of the trustees, that they are a summary of information extracted from the annual accounts and should contain information relating to both the statement of financial activities and the balance sheet.

42.74 The charities SORP also requires that summarised accounts should also contain a warning statement such as that in the following example.

Example 42.74

These summarised accounts may not contain sufficient information to allow for a full understanding of the financial affairs of the charity. For further information, the full annual accounts, the auditors' report on those accounts and the trustees' annual report should be consulted; copies of these can be obtained from [address].

The statement should give the date on which the annual accounts were approved and, for charities registered in England and Wales, state whether or not the annual report and accounts have been submitted to the Charity Commission and, in the case of charitable companies, state whether or not the accounts have been delivered to the Registrar of Companies.

42.75 The accompanying statement should also state whether or not the full annual accounts from which the summary is derived have as yet been audited. If they have been, a statement by the auditor giving an opinion as to whether or not the summarised accounts are consistent with the full annual accounts should be included in the summarised accounts.

42.76 An example of an auditors' statement on summarised financial statements is as follows.

Example 42.76

AUDITORS' STATEMENT TO THE TRUSTEES OF XYZ CHARITY

We have examined the summarised financial statements set out in pages … to …

Respective responsibilities of trustees and auditors

You are responsible as trustees for the preparation of the summarised financial statements. We have agreed to report to you our opinion on the summarised financial statements' consistency with the financial statements, on which we reported to you on [date].

Basis of opinion

We have carried out the procedures we consider necessary to ascertain whether the summarised financial statements are consistent with the full financial statements from which they have been prepared.

Opinion

In our opinion, the summarised financial statements are consistent with the full financial statements for the year ended 31 March 2000.

(Signature and name of auditors)

Chartered Accountants and Registered Auditors   Address

(Date)

Friendly and Industrial and Provident Societies

Friendly societies

42.77   The auditors' responsibilities and reporting requirements relating to friendly societies are governed by the Friendly Societies Act 1992 and regulations made under it. The regulations governing the preparation of the annual accounts of friendly societies for years ended on or after 31 December 1995 are the Friendly Societies (Accounts and Related Provisions) Regulations 1994 (SI 1994 No 1983).

42.78   Auditors of friendly societies are required to make a report to the members stating whether the annual accounts have been properly prepared in accordance with the Friendly Societies Act 1992 and the regulations made under it and, in particular, whether:

(a)   the income and expenditure account gives a true and fair view of the income and expenditure of the society or branch for the financial year;

(b)   the balance sheet gives a true and fair view of the state of the affairs of the society or branch as at the end of the financial year; and

(c)   (if appropriate) the group accounts of an incorporated friendly society gives a true and fair view of the state of affairs as at the end of the financial year of the society and any subsidiaries of the society.

42.79   In their report to the members, the auditors are also required to make a report on the report of the committee of management, stating whether, in the auditors' opinion, it has been prepared in accordance with the Friendly Societies Act 1992 and the regulations made under it and whether the information given in the report of the committee of management is consistent with the accounting records and the annual accounts for the financial year.

Example 42.79

Opinion

In our opinion, the financial statements give a true and fair view of the state of affairs of the society as at 31 March 2000 and of the income and expenditure of the society for the year then ended and have been properly prepared in accordance with the Friendly Societies Act 1992 and the regulations made under it.

In our opinion, the Report of the Committee of Management on pages ... to ... has been prepared in accordance with the Friendly Societies Act 1992 and the regulations made under it and the information given therein is consistent with the accounting records and the financial statements for the year.

42.80   The ICAEW issued a Technical Release,Tech 12/99 *The audit of friendly societies*, in 1999. It highlights some issues relating to the form of audit reports on the accounts of friendly societies and gives example audit report wordings.

42.81   Under Section 79(1) of the 1992 Act, auditors are required to report to the Commission on whether:

(a)   the accounting records;

(b)   the system of control of the business and records; and

(c)   the system of inspection and report

comply with Section 68 of the 1992 Act. Section 68 is broadly concerned with the proper recording of transactions and of assets and liabilities in the accounting records, and the controls in place to ensure that the society's activities are conducted in accordance with the 1992 Act and the decisions of the Committee of Management.

42.82   If the auditors determine that any of the above are below the standard required for compliance with Section 68, the Section 79 report should be qualified and details provided of the reasons for the shortfall.The Society is also required to report on these matters to the Commission under Section 68, and the matters covered by the Section 68 and Section 79 reports are expected to be the same.

Example 42.82

Opinion

In our opinion, during the year ended 31 March 2000:

(a)   [except for the matters set out in paragraphs … to … of the appendix to this report] the accounting records complied with the requirements of Section 68 of the Friendly Societies Act 1992.

(b)   [except for the matters set out in paragraphs … to … of the appendix to this report] the system of control of the business and records of the society complied with the requirements of Section 68 of the Friendly Societies Act 1992.

(c)   [except for the matters set out in paragraphs … to … of the appendix to this report] the system of inspection and report complied with Section 68 of the Friendly Societies Act 1992.

Industrial and provident societies

42.83   The auditors' responsibilities and reporting requirements relating to industrial and provident societies which are registered under the Industrial and Provident Societies Act 1965 are governed by the Friendly and Industrial and Provident Societies Act 1968. The

Deregulation (Industrial and Provident Societies) Order 1996 (SI 1996 No 1738) sets out criteria which, if met, may enable a society to elect for an exemption from audit. Reporting and disclosure requirements relating to group accounts of Industrial and Provident Societies are set out in the Industrial and Provident Societies (Group Accounts) Regulations 1969 (SI 1969 No 1037). Whilst these regulations initially state a requirement for a consolidated balance sheet and consolidated revenue account, they also give wide discretion to the Committee of the Society to prepare the accounts in a form other than that required if, in the opinion of the Committee, the equivalent information can be more readily appreciated by the Societies' members.

42.84 For industrial and provident societies requiring a full audit, the auditors are required to make a report to the society or branch, stating whether the revenue account(s) and balance sheet comply with the requirements of the Friendly and Industrial and Provident Societies Act 1968 and the appropriate regulations and whether in the auditors' opinion:

(a) the revenue account(s) gives a true and fair view of the income and expenditure of the society or branch as a whole and, in the case of each account which deals with a particular business, a true and fair view of the income and expenditure of that business; and

(b) the balance sheet gives a true and fair view of the state of affairs of the society or branch.

Example 42.84.1

Opinion

In our opinion, the financial statements give a true and fair view of the state of the society's affairs as at 31 March 2000 and of its income and expenditure for the year then ended and have been properly prepared in accordance with the requirements of the Industrial and Provident Societies Acts 1965 to 1978.

Suitable amendment to the above opinion would be required where group accounts have been prepared.

Example 42.84.2

Opinion

In our opinion, the financial statements give a true and fair view of the state of the society's and group's affairs as at 31 March 2000 and of the income and expenditure of the group for the year then ended and have been properly prepared in accordance with the requirements of the Industrial and Provident Societies Acts 1965 to 1978 and the Industrial and Provident Societies (Group Accounts) Regulations 1969.

Suitable amendment to the opinion in Example **42.84.1** above would be required where there are separate revenue accounts which deal with particular businesses conducted by the society.

Example 42.84.3

Opinion

In our opinion, the financial statements give a true and fair view of the state of the society's affairs as at 31 March 2000 and of the income and expenditure of the society as a whole and of the particular businesses dealt with thereby for the year then ended and have been properly prepared in accordance with the requirements of the Industrial and Provident Societies Acts 1965 to 1978.

42.85 As with audits under the Companies Act, the auditors will have to carry out such investigations as will enable them to form an opinion as to whether the society has kept proper accounting records and whether the financial statements are in agreement with them. An important additional legal requirement which goes beyond those of the Companies Act is to determine whether the society has maintained a satisfactory system of control over its transactions. Additionally, if the auditors form a negative opinion on any of these matters, they must so state in their report. It is suggested that this additional (and unusual) responsibility be dealt with in the section on respective responsibilities of trustees and auditors. For instance, the auditors could add the words 'we are also required to form an opinion on whether the society has maintained a satisfactory system of control over its transactions and to state in our report if we are of the opinion that it is not satisfactory'.

Educational institutions

Higher education institutions (England)

42.86 Auditors' responsibilities and the reporting requirements relating to higher education institutions in England are governed by the Education Reform Act 1988, the Higher and Further Education Act 1992 and, where relevant, the Companies Act. They are further defined in the Financial Memorandum between the institutions and the Higher Education Funding Council for England (HEFCE) and the HEFCE's Audit Code of Practice. The accounting requirements for higher education institutions are given in the SORP *Accounting in higher education institutions* ('the SORP'), which came into force for financial statements relating to accounting periods ending on or after 31 July 1994. The SORP is currently being updated and an exposure draft detailing the changes is due to be issued in 2000. It is likely to apply to accounting periods ending on or after 31 July 2000, subject to gaining agreement on a common SORP with the Further Education sector.

42.87 Under the Audit Code of Practice, the auditors are required to report whether:

(a) the financial statements give a true and fair view of the state of the institution's affairs and of its income and expenditure and statement of cash flow for the year, taking into account relevant statutory and other mandatory disclosure and accounting requirements, and HEFCE requirements;

(b) funds from whatever source administered by the institution for specific purposes have been properly applied to those purposes and, if relevant, managed in accordance with relevant legislation;

(c) funds provided by the HEFCE have been applied in accordance with the Financial Memorandum and any other terms and conditions attached to them;

(d) the SORP has been complied with; and

(e) (*where the institution is incorporated under the Companies Act*) the financial statements comply with the Companies Act 1985 and, where appropriate, the SORP.

Auditors are also required to report, by exception, where they are not satisfied that:

(a) proper accounting records are being kept by the institution;

(b) the financial statements agree with the accounting records; and

(c) they have obtained all the information and explanations they think are necessary for the purpose of the audit.

42.88 The audit report should be addressed to the governing body of the institution. An appropriate form of wording for accounts, based on the guidance issued by the HEFCE, is given in the example below.

Example 42.88

REPORT OF THE AUDITORS TO THE [GOVERNING BODY] OF [INSTITUTION]

We have audited the financial statements on pages ... to ..., which have been prepared under the accounting policies set out on page ... .

Respective responsibilities of the [Governing Body] and auditors

As described on page ..., the [Governing Body] is responsible for ensuring that financial statements are prepared in accordance with applicable United Kingdom law and accounting standards. It is our responsibility to form an independent opinion, based on our audit, on those statements and to report our opinion to you.

Basis of opinion

We conducted our audit in accordance with United Kingdom auditing standards issued by the Auditing Practices Board, and the Audit Code of Practice issued by the Higher Education Funding Council for England. An audit includes examination, on a test basis, of evidence relevant to the amounts and disclosures in the financial statements. It also includes an assessment of the significant estimates and judgements made by the [Governing Body] in the preparation of the financial statements, and of whether the accounting policies are appropriate to the [Institution's] circumstances, consistently applied and adequately disclosed.

We planned and performed our audit so as to obtain all the information and explanations which we considered necessary in order to provide us with sufficient evidence to give us reasonable assurance that the financial statements are free from material misstatement, whether caused by fraud or other irregularity or error. In forming our opinion, we also evaluated the overall adequacy of the presentation of information in the financial statements.

Opinion

In our opinion:

(a) the financial statements give a true and fair view of the state of affairs of the [Institution] [and its subsidiaries] at 31 July 19... and of the surplus of income over expenditure and cash flows for the year then ended and have been properly prepared in accordance with [the Companies Act (*if appropriate*) and where appropriate the] [Statement of Recommended Practice: Accounting in Higher Education] [and *relevant instrument of incorporation (e.g., Royal Charter, Education Reform Act, etc.)*];

(b) funds from the Higher Education Funding Council for England [and Further Education Funding Council (*if appropriate*) and Teacher Training Agency (*if appropriate*)], grants and income for specific purposes and from other restricted funds administered by the [Institution] have been applied only for the purposes for which they were received;

(c) income has been applied in accordance with the [*relevant instrument of incorporation*] governing the [Institution] and, where appropriate, with the Financial Memorandum dated [........] with the Higher Education Funding Council for England.

(Signature and name of auditors)

Chartered Accountants and Registered Auditors   (Address)

(Date)

42.89 The HEFCE guidance indicates that the introductory paragraph may refer to the accounting convention followed. However, given that the majority of accounts are prepared under the historical cost convention modified by the revaluation of certain fixed assets, a reference to the accounting convention would appear to add little to the reader's understanding of the financial statements that is not readily apparent when reading the notes to the accounts; accordingly, such a reference would appear to be unnecessary, except where the auditors conclude that a significant departure from the historical cost convention warrants it.

42.90 The model description of the responsibilities of governing bodies issued by the HEFCE is set out in the following example.

Example 42.90

Responsibilities of the [Governing Body] of [Institution]

In accordance with the [*relevant instrument of incorporation (e.g., Royal Charter, Education Reform Act, etc.)*], the [Governing Body] of [Institution] is responsible for the administration and management of the affairs of the [Institution] and is required to present audited financial statements for each financial year.

The [Governing Body] is responsible for keeping proper accounting records which disclose with reasonable accuracy at any time the financial position of the [Institution] and to enable it to ensure that the financial statements are prepared in accordance with the [*relevant instrument of incorporation*], the [Statement of Recommended Practice: Accounting in Higher Education Institutions], [the Companies Act] and other relevant accounting standards. In addition, within the terms and conditions of a Financial Memorandum agreed between the Higher Education Funding Council for England and the [Governing Body] of [Institution], the [Governing Body], through its designated office holder, is required to prepare financial statements for each financial year which give a true and fair view of the state of affairs of the [Institution] and of the surplus or deficit and cash flows for that year.

In causing the financial statements to be prepared, the [Governing Body] has to ensure that:

(a) suitable accounting policies are selected and applied consistently;

(b) judgements and estimates are made that are reasonable and prudent;

(c) applicable accounting standards have been followed, subject to any material departures disclosed and explained in the financial statements;

(d)   financial statements are prepared on the going concern basis, unless it is inappropriate to presume that the [Institution] will continue in operation.

The [Governing Body] has taken reasonable steps to:

(a)   ensure that funds from the Higher Education Funding Council for England are used only for the purposes for which they have been given and in accordance with the Financial Memorandum with the Funding Council and any other conditions which the Funding Council may from time to time prescribe;

(b)   ensure that there are appropriate financial and management controls in place to safeguard public funds and funds from other sources;

(c)   safeguard the assets of the [Institution] and to prevent and detect fraud;

(d)   secure the economical, efficient and effective management of the [Institution's] resources and expenditure.

Registered social landlords

42.91   Registered social landlords (RSLs) (being those organisations that are registered with a relevant regulatory body such as the Housing Corporation in England) may be constituted in various ways, including industrial and provident societies, companies limited by guarantee and unincorporated organisations such as charities. The auditors' opinion will be expressed in true and fair terms and compliance with the relevant legislation.

42.92   RSLs are required to prepare their accounts in accordance with the Housing Act 1996, if registered in England or Wales, or the Housing Associations Act 1985, if registered in Scotland, and the orders and determinations made under those Acts. RSLs registered in England should, for periods ending on or after 31 March 1998 but before 31 March 2000, comply with the Accounting Requirements for Registered Social Landlords General Determinations 1997 and 1998, and for those periods ending on or after 31 March 2000, comply with the Accounting Requirements for Registered Social Landlords General Determination 2000. RSLs registered in Wales comply with the Accounting Requirements for Social Landlords registered in Wales General Determination 1996 (although a new Accounting Requirements General Determination is expected later in 2000); RSLs registered in Scotland previously complied with the Registered Housing Associations (Accounting Requirements) (Scotland) Order 1993 but for accounting periods beginning on or after 1 April 1999 comply with the Registered Housing Associations (Accounting Requirements) (Scotland) Order 1999; and RSLs registered in Northern Ireland comply with the Registered Housing Associations (Accounting Requirements) Order (Northern Ireland) 1993.

42.93 In March 1999, the National Federation of Housing Associations, the Welsh Federation of Housing Associations and the Scottish Federation of Housing Associations issued a revised SORP *Accounting by registered housing associations* which applies to accounting periods ended on or after 23 March 2000. This replaced the SORP issued in February 1994. The aim of the SORP is to narrow the areas of difference in accounting practice in the financial statements of housing associations and to provide guidance on the formats and accounting policies which enable housing associations to comply with the accounting requirements of the Accounting Requirements for Registered Social Landlords General Determination 1997 and 1998 (which are about to be superseded by the Accounting Requirements for Registered Social Landlords General Determination 2000 – see **42.92** above). The revised SORP has addressed the requirements of FRS 11 and FRS 15 which have had a major impact on the accounting policies and procedures of registered social landlords, particularly in respect of the capitalisation of development overheads, subsequent expenditure and interest, and providing for depreciation.

42.94 Most RSLs are incorporated under the Industrial and Provident Societies Act 1965. The wording of the audit report for such societies is set out in the example below. The wording of reports on societies established under other legislation or in non-corporate form should refer to the appropriate laws and regulations.

Example 42.94

AUDITORS' REPORT TO THE MEMBERS OF XYZ REGISTERED SOCIAL LANDLORD

We have audited the financial statements on pages 8 to 20, which have been prepared under the accounting policies set out on page 8.

Respective responsibilities of the board[1] and auditors

As described on page 6, the board is responsible for the preparation of financial statements, which are required to be prepared in accordance with applicable United Kingdom law and accounting standards. It is our responsibility to form an independent opinion, based on our audit, on those statements and to report our opinion to you.

Basis of opinion

We conducted our audit in accordance with United Kingdom auditing standards issued by the Auditing Practices Board. An audit includes the examination, on a test basis, of evidence relevant to the amounts and disclosures in the financial statements. It also includes an assessment of the significant estimates and judgements made by the board in the preparation of the financial statements and of whether accounting policies are appropriate to XYZ Association's circumstances, consistently applied and adequately disclosed.

We planned and performed our audit so as to obtain all the information and explanations which we considered necessary in order to provide us with sufficient evidence to give reasonable assurance that the financial statements are free from material misstatement, whether caused by fraud or other irregularity or error. In forming our opinion, we also evaluated the overall adequacy of the presentation of information in the financial statements.

Opinion

In our opinion, the financial statements give a true and fair view of the state of XYZ Association's affairs at 31 March 2000 and of its surplus for the year then ended and have been properly prepared in accordance with the Industrial and Provident Societies Acts 1965 to 1978, Schedule 1 to the Housing Act 1996 and the Accounting Requirements for Registered Social Landlords General Determination 2000[2].

(Signature and name of auditors)

Chartered Accountants and Registered Auditors   (Address)

(Date)

1   The term 'board' should be taken to mean the body charged with the overall responsibility of managing an RSL and includes the term 'committee of management'. An alternative term could be used if considered appropriate.

2   For an RSL registered in England (see **42.92** above).

42.95   The following wording is suitable for inclusion in the board's statement of responsibilities, for an RSL registered under the Industrial and Provident Societies Act 1965, or in the auditors' report when the board does not include a statement of its responsibilities. This should be modified as appropriate to take account of other laws and regulations, if any, that affect the RSL.

> ### *Example 42.95*
>
> The Industrial and Provident Societies Acts and registered social housing legislation require the board to prepare financial statements for each financial year which give a true and fair view of the state of affairs of the XYZ Association as at the end of the financial year and of the surplus or deficit for that period. In preparing these financial statements, the board is required to:
>
> (a)   select suitable accounting policies and then apply them consistently;
>
> (b)   make judgements and estimates that are reasonable and prudent;

> (c)   state whether applicable accounting standards have been fol-
>   lowed, subject to any material departures disclosed and
>   explained in the financial statements; and
>
> (d)   [where no separate statement on going concern is made by the
>   board] prepare the financial statements on the going concern
>   basis, unless it is inappropriate to presume that the Association
>   will continue in business.
>
> The board is responsible for keeping proper accounting records
> which disclose with reasonable accuracy at any time the financial
> position of the Association and to enable it to ensure that the finan-
> cial statements comply with the requirements of Industrial and
> Provident Societies Acts 1965 to 1978, Schedule 1 to the Housing Act
> 1996 and the Accounting Requirements for Registered Social
> Landlords Determination 2000[1]. It has general responsibility for tak-
> ing reasonable steps to safeguard the assets of the Association and to
> prevent and detect fraud and other irregularities.
>
> 1   For an RSL registered in England (see **42.92** above).

42.96   The APB has issued Practice Note 14 *The audit of registered social
landlords in the United Kingdom* to give guidance to auditors on the
audit of social housing in the UK. The Practice Note was developed
by the APB in consultation with the bodies that regulate RSLs: the
Housing Corporation, the Department of the Environment for
Northern Ireland, Scottish Homes and Housing for Wales.

Statements on internal financial control

42.97   Auditors of RSLs are required, under the Friendly and Industrial and
Provident Societies Act 1968 or the Housing Act 1996, to carry out
such investigations as will enable them to form an opinion as to
whether the RSL has maintained a satisfactory system of control over
its transactions and to report by exception that if they are of the
opinion that the RSL has failed to comply with this requirement to
state that fact in their report.

42.98   The Housing Corporation has issued Circular R2 18/96 *Internal
financial control and financial reporting* which has tailored the
'Cadbury' guidance on internal control and financial reporting for
directors of listed companies to RSLs and provides guidance consistent with some of the requirements in this respect for directors of
listed companies.

42.99   The Housing Corporation's guidance requires every RSL with over
50 homes to include, within its annual report, a statement about the
RSL's system of internal financial control. Auditors are required to
review that statement to enable them to conclude that:

(a) the board has provided the disclosures required by the guidance; and

(b) the board's comments are not inconsistent with the information of which they are aware from their audit of the financial statements.

42.100 Auditors of RSLs should seek to establish which guidance issued by the APB they should follow. Recently, all past guidance issued has been combined in APB Bulletin 1999/5 *The Combined Code: Requirements of Auditors Under the Listing Rules of the London Stock Exchange* (see chapter 40). However, it is by no means clear whether this particular guidance is appropriate in the case of RSLs (see footnote 1 to the example audit report wording in Example **42.101** below). Reports should be addressed to the RSL and are therefore not normally included in the auditors' report on the financial statements.

42.101 The board's statement on the system of internal financial control should contain as a minimum:

(a) an acknowledgement that the board is responsible for the RSL's system of internal financial control;

(b) an explanation that such a system can provide only reasonable and not absolute assurance against material misstatement or loss;

(c) a description of the key procedures which the board has established and which are designed to provide effective internal financial control;

(d) confirmation that the board has reviewed the effectiveness of the system of internal financial control; and

(e) information about those weaknesses in internal financial control that have resulted in material losses, contingencies or uncertainties which require disclosure in the financial statements or in the auditors' report on the financial statements.

Example 42.101

REVIEW REPORT TO XYZ RSL BY [NAME OF AUDITORS] ON THE STATEMENT OF INTERNAL FINANCIAL CONTROL

In addition to our audit of the financial statements, we have reviewed the board's statement on page(s) ... on the Association's compliance with the Housing Corporation's circular *Internal financial control and financial reporting* ('the circular'). The objective of our review is to enable us to conclude that the board has provided the disclosure required by the circular and that the board's comments are not inconsistent with the information of which we are aware from our audit work on the financial statements.

Basis of opinion

We carried out our review in accordance with guidance issued by the Auditing Practices Board. That guidance does not require us to perform the additional work necessary to, and we do not, express any opinion on the effectiveness of the Association's system of internal financial control.

Opinion

With respect to the board's statement on internal [financial] control on page ...*, in our opinion, the board has provided the disclosures required by the circular and the statement is not inconsistent with the information of which we are aware from our audit work on the financial statements.

(Signature)

Chartered Accountants   (Address)

(Date)

Notes:

The wording above is based on that set out in the APB Bulletin 1996/3[1].

If the board makes a statement on internal control which goes beyond the requirements of the circular, the words '(other than [their opinion on effectiveness] [and] [statements going beyond internal financial control] which [is] [are] outside the scope of our report)' (as appropriate in the circumstances) should be added where indicated by '*' and the word 'financial' in square brackets should be deleted.

[1] APB Bulletin 1996/3 has been superseded by APB Bulletin 1999/5 which is aimed at listed companies. However, the Housing Corporation has not issued a new circular to update the recommendation to prepare the report in accordance with Bulletin 1996/3. Auditors should wait until the Housing Corporation update their guidance, if indeed they do so, before changing the wording of the audit report.

Building societies

42.102   The auditors' responsibilities for and the reporting requirements of building societies are governed by the Building Societies Act 1986 and regulations made under it. Guidance on the auditors' responsibilities is given in the APB Practice Note 18 *The audit of building societies in the United Kingdom*.

42.103 Given the relatively limited number of building societies, guidance on reporting on them is not included in this manual. Example reports can be found in Practice Note 18. Note that the statutory requirement for building societies to publish a statement of source and application of funds has been repealed for financial years ending on or after 23 March 1999. From that date, building societies are required, by FRS 1, to provide a cash flow statement (see chapter 19). This has meant a consequential amendment to the wording of the audit opinion as set out in Practice Note 18.

42.104 The opinion in the audit report set out in Practice Note 18 consists of four parts. The first part reads as follows:

> '(a) the financial statements [annual accounts] give a true and fair view of the state of affairs of the society [and of the group] as at ...., of the income and expenditure of the society [and of the group] for the year then ended and of the manner in which the business of the society [group] has been financed and in which the society's [group's] financial resources have been used during the year.'

Because of the above mentioned repealed requirement, and the new requirement to provide a cash flow statement, part (a) of the opinion, as shown above, should terminate at the word 'ended' on the fourth line, i.e., omitting the text 'and of the manner in which the business of the society [group] has been financed and in which the society's [group's] financial resources have been used during the year'. This is directly in line with the approach adopted in SAS 600 *Auditors' reports on financial statements*.

Local authorities

42.105 Reference should be made to the appendix to the Audit Commission's *Code of Audit Practice for Local Authorities and the National Health Service in England and Wales,* and to the Accounts Commission for Scotland's equivalent, for a discussion of the reporting considerations for local authorities. For examples of suggested standard report wording, reference should be made to the latest relevant technical bulletins issued by the Audit Commission (England and Wales) and the Accounts Commission for Scotland. While reports for local authorities are referred to as audit certificates, auditors are required to express an opinion rather than actually 'certify' information. In applying the reporting standards, auditors are required to take account of the specific statutory and regulatory framework which applies to the audit of local authority financial statements. Both the Audit Commission and the Accounts Commission for Scotland issue recommended wording for auditors' reports on financial statements.

42.106   In England and Wales only, as well as reporting on the annual financial statements of a local authority, there is also a requirement for an audit opinion to be given on the authority's annual Best Value Plan. This requirement is reflected in the aforementioned Code of Audit Practice. This opinion needs to include whether there are grounds to refer either aspects of the authority's services, or the authority itself, to the Audit Commission's Inspectorate or to the Secretary of State (or, in Wales, the National Assembly for Wales). Such referrals would arise from identifying 'failing services' or a 'failing' authority. As for accounts reporting, the Audit Commission issues guidance and a standard report format for this Best Value audit opinion.

Reports on UK financial statements stated in foreign currency

42.107   A UK form of audit report on financial statements expressed in sterling will normally be the only report issued in respect of UK subsidiaries of foreign companies. In exceptional circumstances, the auditors may be called upon to report on a second set of financial statements expressed in the currency of the country of the foreign parent. This version should always contain both the sterling figures and the translated foreign currency figures. Alternatively, the separate foreign currency financial statements should be attached to the sterling financial statements. The auditors' report should express an opinion on the truth and fairness of the sterling financial statements only, but should contain assurances as to the translation. The basis of opinion section of the report should identify the accounting and auditing standards as being those of the UK.

42.108   The example of an opinion shown below assumes the use of US dollars as the foreign currency.

Example 42.108

AUDITORS' REPORT TO THE DIRECTORS OF XYZ LIMITED

We report on the financial statements on pages 3 to 15, which have been prepared in accordance with applicable United Kingdom law and accounting standards and the accounting policies set out on pages 4 and 5.

Respective responsibilities of directors and auditors

As described on page 2, the directors are responsible for .....

Basis of opinion

We have conducted our audit in accordance with United Kingdom auditing standards issued by the Auditing Practices Board. An audit includes.....

> We planned and performed.....
>
> **Opinion**
>
> In our opinion, the financial statements expressed in pounds sterling give a true and fair view of the state of the company's affairs as at 31 March 2000 and of its profit [loss] for the year then ended and have been properly prepared in accordance with the Companies Act 1985. In our opinion, the financial statements expressed in US dollars have been properly translated on the bases described in note 2.

42.109   Such financial statements should contain an accounting policy note on foreign currency translation along the following lines.

> ***Example 42.109***
>
> The translation of the financial statements into US dollars is included solely for convenience and they are stated, as a matter of arithmetical computation only, on the following bases:
>
> [State bases]
>
> This translation should not be construed as meaning that the sterling amounts actually represent, or have been or could be converted into, US dollars.

Reports on financial statements using standards of other countries

42.110   Special attention is required in cases where the needs of the engagement are not met by the statutory financial statements and the auditors are requested by the client to issue a second version in a format normally used in another country or in accordance with another country's accounting standards. In order to avoid the confusion which could arise from the existence of two versions of the financial statements (possibly even showing different profit figures), any second version should comply with UK accounting standards and only be modified in respect of format and the inclusion of a translation of the sterling amounts into the currency of the other country.

42.111   In very exceptional circumstances (e.g., because they are required to be filed with regulatory or governmental agencies of a foreign country, such as the Securities and Exchange Commission (SEC), and for purposes of consolidation in a foreign group), it may be appropriate to report on a second version prepared in accordance with another country's accounting standards. In such limited circumstances, the secondary financial statements should disclose in a note the existence of the

UK statutory financial statements and reconcile the differences between the two. The reconciliation should disclose the individual and combined effects on:

- net operating results for the year, and
- shareholders' interests.

42.112   Where the reserves as shown by the secondary statements which are apparently available for distribution to shareholders by way of dividend exceed those shown as legally distributable as shown in the UK statutory financial statements, attention should be drawn to this fact in the notes to the secondary statements.

42.113   Where there are no differences between the secondary and UK statements other than language or format, the secondary financial statements should disclose the existence of the UK statutory financial statements and explain that there are no other differences of substance.

42.114   There is an increasingly common practice for audit reports on financial statements to identify whether United Kingdom or other national or international accounting and auditing standards have been applied (see chapter 39). This information should certainly be specified in the auditors' report on the secondary statements and is likely to be included in the primary statements in any case. The form and content of the audit report should be consistent with that of the country whose accounting standards have been used.

42.115   The following example unqualified audit report in US form is appropriate where the auditors have been asked by the US parent company to report on secondary financial statements for consolidation purposes. The secondary financial statements contain both sterling and US dollar amounts and comply with the SEC requirement to provide three-year statements of income, retained earnings and cash flows.

Example 42.115

INDEPENDENT AUDITORS' REPORT TO THE DIRECTORS OF XYZ LIMITED

We have audited the accompanying balance sheets of XYZ Limited as of 31 March 2000 and 1999, and the related statements of income, retained earnings and cash flows for each of the three years in the period ended 31 March 2000, all expressed in pounds sterling. These financial statements are the responsibility of the company's management. Our responsibility is to express an opinion on these financial statements based on our audits.

We conducted our audits in accordance with auditing standards generally accepted in the United States of America. Those standards require that we plan and perform the audit to obtain reasonable assurance about whether the financial statements are free of material misstatement. An audit includes examining, on a test basis, evidence supporting the amounts and disclosures in the financial statements. An audit also includes assessing the accounting principles used and significant estimates made by management, as well as evaluating the overall financial statement presentation. We believe that our audits provide a reasonable basis for our opinion.

In our opinion, the financial statements referred to above, expressed in pounds sterling, present fairly, in all material respects, the financial position of XYZ Limited at 31 March 2000 and 1999, and the results of its operations and its cash flows for each of the three years in the period ended 31 March 2000 in conformity with generally accepted accounting principles of the United States of America. Our audits also comprehended the translation of pounds sterling amounts into US dollar amounts for purposes of consolidation with the financial statements of Parent Company Inc. In our opinion, such translation has been made in conformity with accounting principles generally accepted in the United States of America, as set forth in Statement of Financial Accounting Standards No. 52, applicable to foreign currency financial statements incorporated in financial statements of an enterprise by consolidation.

42.116 It should be noted that, under US auditing standards, there is no detailed statement of directors' responsibilities and the audit report does not have subheadings within it. No amendments should be made to bring the above report in line with the UK reporting standards, as otherwise the auditors would be unable to state that 'we conducted our audits in accordance with auditing standards generally accepted in the United States of America'.

42.117 There are a number of significant differences between UK and US auditing and accounting standards. Auditors should not assume that if their audit complies with UK requirements they can report under US auditing standards. They should check that they have taken into account all relevant US auditing requirements as set out in the US American Institute of Certified Public Accountants (AICPA) Professional Standards manuals. US accounting standards differ from UK accounting standards to varying degrees and ensuring that all applicable US GAAP items are addressed can be a complex process, which may necessitate seeking advice from a US GAAP specialist.

42.118 Where the translated amounts have been made using a basis different from that set out in SFAS 52, the last paragraph in the example in **42.115** above should be worded as follows.

Example 42.118

Our audits also comprehended the translation of certain pounds sterling amounts into US dollars and, in our opinion, such translation has been made in conformity with the basis stated in Note X. Such US dollar amounts are presented solely for the convenience of readers in the United States of America.

Note X: Basis of translation

Amounts in the accompanying financial statements are stated in pounds sterling, the currency of the country in which the company is incorporated. The translation into US dollars of certain amounts in the consolidated financial statements is for convenience only and has been made at the rate of $1.xxx to £1. This translation should not be construed as a representation that the pounds sterling amounts actually represented have been, or could be, converted into dollars at this or any other rate.

Reports prepared in accordance with International Standards on Auditing

42.119 Auditors may be asked to report in accordance with International Standards on Auditing (ISAs). This would not be appropriate for a company incorporated under the UK Companies Acts, but may be acceptable for other entities, including companies incorporated in other jurisdictions.

42.120 Auditors who report under ISAs should ensure they are familiar with requirements of those standards: there are some differences from UK auditing standards. An example of an unqualified report based on that in ISA 700 is given below.

Example 42.120

AUDITOR'S REPORT TO THE SHAREHOLDERS OF ABC COMPANY

We have audited the accompanying[1] balance sheet of the ABC Company as of 31 March 2000, and the related statements of income and cash flows for the year then ended. These financial statements are the responsibility of the company's management. Our responsibility is to express an opinion on these financial statements based on our audit.

We conducted our audit in accordance with [International Standards on Auditing][2]. Those Standards require that we plan and perform the

---

audit to obtain reasonable assurance about whether the financial statements are free of material misstatement. An audit includes examining, on a test basis, evidence supporting the amounts and disclosures in the financial statements. An audit also includes assessing the accounting principles used and significant estimates made by management, as well as evaluating the overall financial statement presentation. We believe that our audit provides a reasonable basis for our opinion.

In our opinion, the financial statements give a true and fair view of [or 'present fairly, in all material respects'][3] the financial position of the company as of 31 March 2000, and of the results of its operations and its cash flows for the year then ended in accordance with [International Accounting Standards][4] and comply with the requirements of [relevant statutes or law].

Signature of the auditor

(Address)

(Date)[5]

Notes:

1 The reference can be by page numbers.

2 Or refer to relevant national standards or practices.

3 The terms 'true and fair' and 'present fairly, in all material respects' are equivalent.

4 Or refer to relevant national standards.

5 The auditor should date the report as of the completion date of the audit. The auditor should not date the report earlier than the date on which the financial statements are signed or approved by management.

42.121   While not required by ISAs, to avoid confusion from the use of different standard-setting regimes, the audit should normally be conducted in accordance with ISAs and the financial statements should normally be prepared in accordance with International Accounting Standards (IASs), unless this conflicts with the local statutes or laws. Hybrid reports, combining, say, UK accounting standards and IASs for audit purposes, should generally be avoided. It should be noted that there are some very significant differences between UK accounting standards and IASs.

42.122   The meaning of 'completion date of the audit' will be interpreted differently in different countries. In some countries, such as the USA, it may be interpreted as the date of cessation of field work. In the UK, however, it will generally be interpreted as the date of completion of the subsequent events review and on which the audit report is signed.

42.123 As can be seen from the example, ISA reports do not have paragraph headings and only limited descriptions of the directors' responsibilities. It is useful to ask the directors to include in the financial statements a statement of directors' responsibilities, so as to clarify the respective roles of the directors and the auditors.

42.124 ISA 700 sets out the various forms of qualifications and of added emphasis of matter paragraphs. The ISA indicates that the addition of a paragraph emphasising a going concern problem or significant uncertainty is ordinarily adequate to meet the auditor's reporting responsibilities regarding such matters (similar to UK auditing standards). However, ISA 700 suggests that in extreme cases, such as situations involving multiple uncertainties that are significant to the financial statements, the auditor may consider it appropriate to express a disclaimer of opinion instead of adding an emphasis of matter paragraph.

Opinions for partnerships

42.125 When auditing a partnership the auditors' opinion should indicate whether the financial statements have been 'properly prepared in accordance with the accounting policies stated on page x'. Such opinions will be inappropriate where the auditor has not conducted a full audit. In those circumstances an Accountant's Report will be more appropriate.

42.126 It is not uncommon that the partners in a professional practice consciously prepare accounts which do not comply fully with UK accounting standards. This may be because of some particular requirement of a partnership deed, a desire to effect an equitable financial relationship between partners or because of taxation considerations. Where the departures from accounting standards are material, auditors would need to qualify any audit report given in 'true and fair' terms, and continue to do so, so long as the breaches remain material.

42.127 An alternative to the qualified 'true and fair' opinion is to issue a 'properly prepared' opinion. This opinion may be appropriate where:

(a) an audit has been conducted in accordance with auditing standards issued by the Auditing Practices Board; and

(b) the financial statements make it clear that the partnership is not required to prepare accounts which give a true and fair view; and

(c) the accounting policies adopted by the partnership are clearly set out together with, where appropriate, a detailed description of departures from accounting standards. It is not enough merely to state that the financial statements do not accord with accounting standards.

42.128 The 'properly prepared' opinion will be appropriate only for financial statements prepared in the circumstances indicated. It will not be appropriate for financial statements which adopt wholly inappropriate accounting policies or which contain insupportable judgements. In these circumstances, a qualification may be necessary irrespective of the type of audit opinion being given. Note that a 'properly prepared' opinion cannot be issued unless an audit (as defined in **42.127** above) has been undertaken.

42.129 It follows from the above that all reports on partnerships should now take one of the following three prescribed forms:

(a) *Accountants' report on unaudited accounts:* this style of report takes a number of forms depending on the particular situation. Guidance on these reports can be found in Chapter 45. Whilst there is no requirement to express an audit opinion, auditors check that the accounting policies are clearly communicated.

(b) *'True and Fair' opinion on audited accounts:* some professional practices require a true and fair opinion. In these cases a full audit is required, and the report wording should be in accordance with the guidance set out in SAS 600 *Auditors' reports on financial statements.* In practice the audit report is likely to be qualified on the basis of limitation of scope and on grounds of disagreement with accounting policies, as the partnership may be unwilling to comply with all accounting standards.

(c) *'Properly prepared in accordance with accounting policies' opinion on audited accounts:* the wording of the opinion is set out in the following example. It will be necessary to include a statement of responsibilities of the board in the partnership accounts, located before the auditors' report and disclosures of accounting policies.

Example 42.129

AUDITORS' REPORT TO THE PARTNERS OF XYZ & CO

We have audited the financial statements on pages 9 to 22 which have been prepared under the accounting policies set out on page 9.

Respective responsibilities of the [Board] and auditors

As described on page 7, the [Board] is responsible for the preparation of financial statements. It is our responsibility to form an independent opinion, based on our audit, on those statements and to report our opinion to you.

Basis of opinion

We conducted our audit in accordance with United Kingdom auditing standards issued by the Auditing Practices Board. An audit includes examination, on a test basis, of evidence relevant to the amounts and disclosures in the financial statements. It also includes an assessment of the significant estimates and judgements made by the [Board] in the preparation of the financial statements and of whether the accounting policies adopted by the [Board] are appropriate to the particular circumstances of the Partnership and have been consistently applied and adequately disclosed.

We planned and performed our audit so as to obtain all the information and explanations which we considered necessary in order to provide us with sufficient evidence to give reasonable assurance that the financial statements are free from material misstatement, whether caused by fraud or other irregularity or error. In forming our opinion, we also evaluated the overall adequacy of the presentation of information in the financial statements on the basis of the accounting policies adopted.

Opinion

In our opinion, the financial statements have been properly prepared in accordance with the accounting policies set out on page 9.

(Signature and name of auditors)

Chartered Accountants   (Address)

(Date)

42.130   An example of the wording that should normally be included in a statement of responsibilities of the board is shown below.

Example 42.130

STATEMENT OF RESPONSIBILITIES OF THE [BOARD]

[Under the Partnership Deed, the Partnership is obliged to produce financial statements on an annual basis. In practice, this responsibility is undertaken by the Board.] The Board organises the preparation of the financial statements which are properly prepared in accordance with the accounting policies adopted by the Partnership.

In so doing the [Board] is required to:

(a)   select suitable accounting policies and apply them consistently;

(b)   make judgements and estimates that are reasonable and prudent; and

(c)   prepare the accounts on a going concern basis, unless that basis is deemed to be inappropriate.

The [Board] is responsible for ensuring that proper accounting records are kept which disclose with reasonable accuracy at any time the financial position of the Partnership, and enable the [Board] to ensure that the financial statements comply with the Partnership Deed. They are also responsible for safeguarding the assets of the Partnership and hence for taking reasonable steps for the prevention and detection of fraud and other irregularities.

[The wording of this statement and the reference to it in our auditors' report should be modified in line with the precise obligations under the Partnership Deed. In some firms it will be the Senior Partner, a management committee, or the whole partnership which will be charged with the responsibilities ascribed above to the Board.]

42.131   An example of the wording of the disclosure of accounting policies is shown below.

Example 42.131

ACCOUNTING POLICIES

The partnership is not required legally or otherwise to present financial statements which give a true and fair view. The partners have adopted UK accounting standards except where, for reasons of equity or other considerations, they believe it is inappropriate to do so. The principal policies adopted are set out below together with an indication of where these depart from accounting standards.

(a)   Basis of Accounting

The financial statements are prepared under the historical cost convention.

Etc.

> All accounting policies which deviate from accounting standards should be disclosed as doing so in a prominent, detailed and clear manner.
>
> The statement in the first sentence above ('The partnership is not required . . . ') should be included.

Future developments

FRED 21 *Accounting policies*

42.132   The Accounting Standards Board (ASB) has published for public comment proposals for disclosures relating to compliance with Statements of Recommended Practice (SORPs). SORPs recommend accounting practices for specialised sectors, and supplement accounting standards and other legal and regulatory requirements in the light of the special factors prevailing or transactions undertaken in a particular sector. Currently, as should be clear from looking at the examples in this chapter, the relevant SORP sometimes requires that the audit report for the particular entity should mention compliance with the SORP. The ASB's proposals are set out in a supplement to the exposure draft FRED 21 *Accounting policies,* published in December 1999.

42.133   One of the proposals in FRED 21 is that an entity will assess, in selecting accounting policies, whether accepted industry practices are appropriate to its particular circumstances. The FRED notes that such practices will be particularly persuasive if developed by public consultation through the SORP-making process. It has been suggested to the ASB that the usefulness of information in an entity's financial statements is enhanced if users are made aware of the extent to which an entity complies with a SORP, and the reasons for any departures. Accordingly, the Supplement to FRED 21 proposes additional disclosures where a significant part of an entity's activities falls within the scope of a SORP. This is an area which should be kept under review.

43 Special reports required by companies legislation

43 Special reports required by companies legislation

Introduction

43.1 The introduction to the reporting standards indicates that much of the guidance provided can be adapted to auditors' reports on financial information other than financial statements. The APB (with assistance from the ICAEW) has issued Practice Note 8 *Reports by auditors under company legislation in the United Kingdom*, which gives guidance on the application of the principles of SAS 600 to reports by auditors under the Act. The examples in this chapter are, where appropriate, in line with the Practice Note.

43.2 APB Practice Note 8 states that reports on other information should follow the structure set out in SAS 600 and include a description of the basis of the opinion expressed. A statement of the respective responsibilities (of directors and auditors) ought ordinarily also to be included, unless:

(a) the directors have no responsibilities concerning the presentation to shareholders of the information on which the auditors report, so that the auditors report direct to the shareholders rather than attesting to a report made by the directors; or

(b) the auditors' report is addressed to the company or the directors and is intended primarily for private use. However, where the auditors are aware that their report is intended for wide distribution, they may nevertheless wish to include a description of the respective responsibilities so that a third-party reader of their report is aware of the general nature of those responsibilities.

43.3 Such a description is useful even where the auditors are aware that their report is intended solely for the use of the directors. The presence of a description of responsibilities is, therefore, not to be construed as awareness of third-party reliance.

43.4 The guidance set out in **39.52** above on the use of the designation 'Registered auditor' or 'Registered auditors' must also be followed.

Special report on abbreviated accounts

43.5   Chapter 35 explains the circumstances under which the directors
may deliver abbreviated accounts to the Registrar of Companies.
Accounts so delivered must be accompanied by a copy of a special
auditors' report in which the auditors must state that in their opinion:

(a)   the company is entitled to deliver abbreviated accounts prepared in accordance with the relevant provisions to the registrar; and

(b)   the abbreviated accounts to be delivered are properly prepared
in accordance with the relevant provisions.

No special auditors' report is required by statute in respect of abbreviated accounts if the company is exempt by virtue of s249A (certain
categories of small companies) from the obligation to appoint auditors (see **34.48** to **34.62** above), nor does it apply if the company is
exempt from the obligation to appoint auditors by virtue of s250
(dormant companies).

43.6   If the auditors cannot report positively on these matters, abbreviated
accounts cannot be delivered to the Registrar of Companies. This
may arise where the auditors have qualified the full financial statements or referred to a fundamental uncertainty and the qualifying
matter or fundamental uncertainty relates to one or more of the
determinants for exemption. The auditors will need to assess the
maximum effect of the qualification or fundamental uncertainty on
the figures of turnover, total assets and number of employees. Where
the determinants are exceeded or where the effect of the qualification
or fundamental uncertainty cannot be quantified, the auditors
should inform the client that they will be unable to issue a report in
a form which would permit the company to file abbreviated accounts
with the Registrar.

43.7   The Companies Act 1985 (Accounts of Small and Medium-sized
Companies and Minor Accounting Amendments) Regulations 1997
(SI 1997 No 220) removed, for abbreviated accounts prepared on or
after 1 March 1997, the requirement for the special report to reproduce the full text of the auditors' report on the full annual financial
statements if it was unqualified.

43.8   If the auditors' report on the full annual financial statements was
qualified, the special report is required to set out the qualified report
in full, together with any further material necessary to understand
the qualification. This would require reproducing the full text of any
notes to the accounts which have been referred to in the audit report.
If the auditors' report on the full financial statements contained a

statement under s237(2) (accounts, records or returns inadequate or accounts not agreeing with records or returns) or s237(3) (failure to obtain necessary information and explanations), the special report is required to set out the statement in full.

43.9   The previous paragraph sets out minimum requirements for the special auditors' report. APB Bulletin 1997/1 *Abbreviated accounts in Great Britain* recommends that when the auditors' report on the full financial statements is unqualified but contains an explanatory paragraph regarding a fundamental uncertainty, the explanatory paragraph (together with any further material necessary to understand it) is included in the special auditors' report.

Example 43.9

AUDITORS' REPORT TO XYZ LIMITED PURSUANT TO SECTION 247B OF THE COMPANIES ACT 1985

We have examined the abbreviated accounts on pages 2 to 4, together with the financial statements of XYZ Limited prepared under s226 Companies Act 1985 for the year ended 31 March 2000.

The directors are responsible for preparing the abbreviated accounts in accordance with *s246(5) and (6) Companies Act 1985*[1]. It is our responsibility to form an independent opinion as to the company's entitlement to deliver abbreviated accounts prepared in accordance with *those sections*[2] and whether the abbreviated accounts have been properly prepared in accordance with those provisions and to report our opinion to you.

Basis of opinion

We have carried out the procedures we considered necessary to confirm, by reference to the audited financial statements, that the company is entitled to deliver abbreviated accounts and that the abbreviated accounts have been properly prepared from those financial statements. The scope of our work for the purpose of this report does not include examining or dealing with events after the date of our report on the full financial statements.

Opinion

In our opinion, the company is entitled under *ss[247 and 247A]*[3]/ *[247, 247A and 249]*[4] Companies Act 1985 to deliver abbreviated accounts prepared in accordance with *s246(5) and (6) Companies Act 1985*[1], in respect of the year ended 31 March 2000 and the abbreviated accounts on pages 2 to 4 have been properly prepared in accordance with those provisions[5].

(Signature and name of auditors)

Chartered Accountants and Registered Auditors   (Address)

(Date)

Notes:

1   For medium-sized companies, replace with 's246A(3) Companies Act 1985'.

    For small companies it is assumed that advantage is taken of the exemptions in both s246(5) and (6) in producing the abbreviated accounts. If advantage is taken of the exemptions in only one of these subsections in producing the abbreviated accounts, the references in the report should be changed accordingly.

2   For medium-sized companies, replace with 'that section'.

3   For companies which are not parent companies.

4   For companies which are parent companies.

5   If the s235 auditors' report on the full financial statements was qualified, it should be set out in full here under an additional heading 'Other information', together with any further material necessary to understand the qualification.

    If the s235 audit report contained a statement under s237(2) (proper accounting records) or s237(3) (obtaining information and explanations), that statement should be included in full in the special report. Again, an additional heading of 'Other information' would be required and an appropriate introduction to the statement would be: 'On [date], we reported as auditors to the members of the company on the financial statements prepared under s266 Companies Act 1985 and our report included the following paragraph:'.

    If the s235 auditors' report was unqualified but contained an explanatory paragraph regarding a fundamental uncertainty, that paragraph, appropriately introduced, should be included together with any further material necessary to understand it under the heading 'Other information'. An appropriate introduction would be: 'On [date], we reported as auditors to the members of the company on the financial statements prepared under s266 Companies Act 1985 and our report included the following paragraph:'.

43.10

The wording in the above example is slightly different to that included in APB Bulletin 1997/1. In particular, it gives an indication in the opinion of the sections in the Companies Act under which the company is entitled to deliver abbreviated accounts, and the year being reported on.

43.11   In many cases, the statement of directors' responsibilities is not included in the auditors' report on the full financial statements.

> If that report was qualified and is accordingly reproduced in the auditors' special report on abbreviated accounts, it may assist a reader of the special report if the statement of directors' responsibilities included in the full financial statements is reproduced. This can be done by adding appropriate wording to the end of the special report.

Example 43.11

The statement of directors' responsibilities referred to in our audit report on the full financial statements, referred to above, was as follows:

[Insert text of statement of directors' responsibilities. It is helpful to put such text in quotation marks and to slightly inset it to distinguish it from the accompanying special report].

43.12 Under the audit exemption regulations, charitable companies with gross income between £90,000 and £250,000 may opt for an 'audit exemption report' rather than an audit report (see **45.14** to **45.23** below). Such charities are required to file a copy of the audit exemption report with the abbreviated accounts. This could be misleading, as the audit exemption report is on the full accounts prepared for members and is required to state whether the accounts have been drawn up in a manner consistent with the requirements of s249C(6). Abbreviated accounts do not meet such a requirement, as they are prepared in accordance with s246. To avoid possibly misleading the reader, the form of report set out in the following example could be filed with the abbreviated accounts.

Example 43.12

ACCOUNTANTS' REPORT TO THE DIRECTORS ON THE UNAUDITED ACCOUNTS OF XYZ LIMITED

We have reported to the members on the accounts prepared under s226 Companies Act 1985 for the year ended [date] and our report is reproduced below. Such a report is required under s242 Companies Act 1985 to be delivered to the Registrar even if the accounts being delivered are abbreviated accounts and not the full accounts prepared for the shareholders.

[Accountants' report under s249A(2) to be reproduced here – see **45.20** below.]

43.13 This does not affect the requirement for the directors to make a statutory statement on the balance sheet, indicating that the company is taking advantage of the audit exemption, immediately above the statement required on the balance sheet indicating that the company is taking advantage of the entitlement to file abbreviated accounts.

Auditors' statement in connection with a distribution

43.14 The amounts which are legally available for distribution are determined by reference to the relevant accounts, which are normally the last annual accounts prior to the distribution. If the audit report on those accounts was qualified and a distribution is envisaged, the company must obtain from the auditors a written statement whether, in their opinion, the matter giving rise to the qualification is material for determining whether the distribution would contravene the legislation. [s271(4)] For the purposes of this section (but unlike SAS 600), the term 'qualified' must include 'adverse' and 'disclaimer of opinion'. It is, therefore, unfortunate that the term 'qualified' has different meanings under the reporting standards and the Act. Another problem is that, as confirmed by legal advice taken by the APB at the time of preparing SAS 600, an added emphasis describing a fundamental uncertainty does not constitute a qualification. Clearly, however, such an added emphasis is a matter which the company should take account of in determining distributions.

43.15 No such auditors' statement is required where the directors of a company have taken advantage of the exemption conferred by s249A (certain categories of small companies) from the obligation to appoint auditors (see **34.48** to **34.62** above).

43.16 The statement may be made either at the time of the audit report or subsequently, but a copy of it must be laid before the company in general meeting. It may therefore be convenient to make the necessary statement as an addition to the opinion section in the audit report, as in the following example.

> ### *Example 43.16*
>
> In our opinion, the matter(s) in respect of which our report is qualified is (are) not material for determining by reference to these financial statements whether the distribution of £....... proposed by the company would contravene s263 Companies Act 1985.
>
> Note: It is necessary to consider whether it is appropriate to include the word 'not'.

43.17 An example of a statement made separately from the audit report is as follows.

Example 43.17

AUDITORS' STATEMENT TO MEMBERS OF XYZ LIMITED PURSUANT TO SECTION 271(4) OF THE COMPANIES ACT 1985

We have audited the financial statements of XYZ Limited for the year ended 31 March 2000 in accordance with United Kingdom auditing standards issued by the Auditing Practices Board and have expressed a qualified opinion thereon in our report dated 20 May 2000.

Basis of opinion

We have carried out such procedures as we considered necessary to evaluate the effect of the qualified opinion for the determination of profits available for distribution.

Opinion

In our opinion, the matter(s) in respect of which our report was qualified is (are) not material for determining by reference to those financial statements whether the distribution of £....... proposed by the company would contravene s263 Companies Act 1985.

(Signature and name of auditors)

Chartered Accountants and Registered Auditors   (Address)

Date

43.18   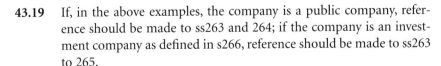 A description of responsibilities is not included because the auditors are not attesting to a statement made by the directors. The example (example 7) included in APB Practice Note 8 does not include such a description. However, it is the directors' obligation to ensure that, where appropriate, they obtain the necessary statement from the auditors and lay it before the company in general meeting. This is most easily done by asking for it to be included in the audit report. Directors of subsidiaries should be alert to the need to arrange this, as illegal dividends can arise where dividends are paid up through the group without taking account of the Act's requirements.

43.19   If, in the above examples, the company is a public company, reference should be made to ss263 and 264; if the company is an investment company as defined in s266, reference should be made to ss263 to 265.

43.20   The above examples are preferred to the examples given in APB Practice Note 8, as they are more in line with the wording of the Act.

43.21　If the statement refers specifically to the dividend proposed in the accounts, as in the above examples, then it seems that before an interim dividend can be paid for the following year, the auditors must make a further statement and it must be laid before the company in general meeting. As an alternative, the original auditors' statement may be expressed in terms of the company's ability to make potential distributions up to a specific level. This would also be appropriate where the amount of dividend has not yet been determined. A suitable form of wording would be as follows.

> **Example 43.21**
>
> In our opinion, the matter(s) in respect of which our report is qualified is (are) not material for determining by reference to these financial statements whether distributions by the company totalling not more than £...... would contravene s263 Companies Act 1985.

43.22　 This wording effectively requires the auditors to state the amount of the company's distributable reserves after taking account of the effect of the qualification. The auditors will need to be careful to consider the status of any special reserves the company may have. It would not be appropriate to give this form of opinion if it had not been possible to quantify the effects of the qualification, as may be the case with a limitation in audit scope.

43.23　For this purpose 'material' means that the effect of the matter which is the subject of the qualification is or may be such as to reduce the amount of distributable profits below that legally required to make a distribution of the sum under consideration.

Report on initial accounts

43.24　Where a public company intends to make a distribution before the end of its first accounting reference period, it must prepare initial accounts which have been properly prepared or so prepared subject only to matters which are not material for determining whether the proposed distribution would contravene the law. [s273] The initial accounts must be accompanied by the auditors' report, stating whether, in the auditors' opinion, the accounts have been 'properly prepared'. If the opinion is qualified, the auditors must also state whether the matter giving rise to the qualification is material for determining whether the distribution would contravene the relevant section of the Act (see **43.14** to **43.23** above for specimen wording). As properly prepared means that the balance sheet and profit and loss account give a true and fair view, the auditors will need to carry out an audit in accordance with auditing standards. An example of such a report is as follows.

Example 43.24

AUDITORS' REPORT TO THE DIRECTORS OF DELTO PLC UNDER SECTION 273(4) OF THE COMPANIES ACT 1985

We have audited the initial accounts on pages 2 to 10, which have been prepared under the accounting policies set out on pages 2 and 3.

Respective responsibilities of directors and auditors

The company's directors are responsible for the preparation of the initial accounts, which must be properly prepared in accordance with applicable United Kingdom law and accounting standards, subject only to matters which are not material for determining whether the proposed distribution contravenes the Companies Act 1985. In preparing those accounts, the directors are required to:

(a)   select suitable accounting policies and apply them consistently;

(b)   make judgements and estimates that are reasonable and prudent;

(c)   state whether applicable accounting standards have been followed; and

(d)   prepare the financial statements on the going concern basis unless it is not appropriate to presume that the company will continue in business.

The Directors have general responsibility for taking such steps as are reasonably open to them to safeguard the assets of the Company and to prevent and detect fraud and other irregularities.

It is our responsibility to form an independent opinion, based on our audit, on those accounts and to report our opinion to you.

Basis of opinion

We conducted our audit in accordance with United Kingdom auditing standards issued by the Auditing Practices Board. An audit includes examination, on a test basis, of evidence relevant to the amounts and disclosures in the initial accounts. It also includes an assessment of the significant estimates and judgements made by the directors in the preparation of the initial accounts and of whether the accounting policies are appropriate to the company's circumstances, consistently applied and adequately disclosed.

We planned and performed our audit so as to obtain all the information and explanations which we considered necessary in order to provide us with sufficient evidence to give reasonable assurance that the initial accounts are free from material misstatement, whether caused by fraud or other irregularity or error. In forming our opinion, we also evaluated the overall adequacy of the presentation of information in the initial accounts.

> **Opinion**
>
> In our opinion the initial accounts for the period from 15 June 1999, the date of incorporation, to 31 March 2000 have been properly prepared within the meaning of s273(2) Companies Act 1985.
>
> (Signature and name of auditors)
>
> Chartered Accountants and Registered Auditors   (Address)
>
> Date

Valuation report on non-cash assets

Introduction

43.25 There are two situations where the Act requires a public company to obtain a valuation report from a person qualified to act as auditor of the company as to the value placed on non-cash assets to be acquired by the company. The valuation reports required in these situations are dealt with under the headings below. A potential problem which auditors should be aware of is that, even though such reports are for the benefit of the shareholders, the Securities and Exchange Commission appear to regard them as grounds for impairment of the auditors' independence. They would therefore insist that the auditors stand down after giving such a report. Auditors of companies which are, or could conceivably become, SEC registrants should avoid giving such reports.

Shares allotted in exchange for non-cash consideration

43.26 A public company may not allot shares for a non-cash consideration unless a report as to the value of the consideration has been made within six months prior to the share allotment by an independent person qualified to be the auditor of the company. [s103(1)] A copy of the report must be sent to the allottee. These restrictions do not apply to takeover and merger situations.

43.27 The Act requires the valuer's report to state:
[s108]

(a)   the nominal value of the shares to be issued;

(b)   the amount of any premium payable on them;

(c)   the description of the consideration, the method used to value it and the date of the valuation;

(d)   the extent to which the nominal value of the shares and any premiums are to be treated as paid up:

       (i)   by the consideration;

       (ii) by cash;

(e)   that it appears reasonable to him to accept the valuation by another person (if applicable);

(f)   that (whoever made the valuation) the method of valuation was reasonable in all the circumstances;

(g)   that it appears that there has been no material change in the value of the consideration since the date of valuation;

(h)   that on the basis of valuation, the value of the consideration together with any cash received by the company is not less than the aggregate of the nominal value and the premium on shares which are treated as paid up by the consideration and the cash.

43.28   The valuer may use an outside expert with the requisite knowledge and experience to value all or part of the consideration. Where this is done, the report must state that fact and:

(a)   state the name of the valuer and give details of his knowledge and experience to carry out the valuation;

(b)   describe that part of the consideration valued by him and the method used to value it and the date of the valuation.

43.29   APB Practice Note 8 sets out the elements that should be incorporated in the independent accountants' report. A suitable valuation report is given below. This report assumes the following facts. Delto PLC proposes to allot 250,000 ordinary shares of £1 each under a contract with XYZ Ltd to acquire vending machines, transport vehicles and customer routes in the Midlands. Delto PLC has ascribed a value of £4 to each ordinary share to be treated as fully paid up. The auditors have obtained a valuation report on the fixed assets from professional valuers and the auditors have been able to place a value on the customer routes.

Example 43.29

INDEPENDENT ACCOUNTANTS' REPORT TO DELTO PLC FOR THE PURPOSES OF SECTION 103(1) OF THE COMPANIES ACT 1985

We report on the value of the consideration for the allotment to XYZ Ltd of 250,000 ordinary shares, having a nominal value of £1 each, to be issued at a premium of £3 per share. The whole of the nominal value and share premium is to be treated as fully paid up by the consideration.

The consideration for the allotment to XYZ Ltd is as follows:

(a) vending machines and transport vehicles as listed in Schedule A of said agreement;

(b) rights to service customers as described in Schedule B of said agreement.

Basis of opinion

The vending machines and transport vehicles were valued at £850,000 as at 30 October 1999, on the basis of net current replacement cost taking into account the condition and remaining useful life of the equipment, by Worthmore and Co, Chartered Surveyors. We believe it reasonable to accept such a valuation.

The rights to service customers, forming the remainder of the consideration, were valued by us as at 13 October 1999 at £200,000. The method used was to estimate the discounted value of income expected to be earned from the vending machines kept at customers' premises.

Opinion

In our opinion, the methods of valuation used in the above valuations were reasonable in all the circumstances and there appears to have been no material change in the value of either part of the consideration since the valuations were made.

On the basis of these valuations, in our opinion, the value of the total consideration is not less than £1,000,000, being the aggregate of the nominal value and premium on shares which are treated as paid up by the consideration.

(Signature and name of accountants)

Chartered Accountants   (Address)

(Date)

43.30   A description of responsibilities is not included, because the auditors are not attesting to a statement made by the directors. The example (example 12) included in APB Practice Note 8 does not include such a description.

43.31   The report is required to be made by an independent accountant and not necessarily by the auditor and therefore the title 'Registered auditor' can be omitted.

Non-cash assets acquired from subscribers or members

43.32   Where a public company is to acquire, within two years of its date of incorporation or re-registration as a public company, a non-cash

asset from a subscriber to its Memorandum or from a member of the company at the date of re-registration, and the consideration to be given equals one-tenth or more of the nominal value of the company's share capital, the Act requires:
[s104]

(a) the assets to be transferred to the company and any consideration to be paid by the company other than in cash to be valued by someone qualified to be the auditor of the company;

(b) a report on the valuation to be delivered to the company during the six months preceding the date of the agreement;

(c) the terms of the agreement to be approved by an ordinary resolution of the company; and

(d) copies of the resolution and report to be circulated to the members not later than the giving of the notice of the meeting at which the resolution is proposed.

43.33 The provisions concerning the use of outside experts' valuations are identical to those in s108 described in **43.28** above and the auditors should check that a copy of any such valuation is delivered to the company within the appropriate timescale.

43.34 APB Practice Note 8 sets out the elements that should be incorporated in the independent accountants' report. The content of the report is the same as that required under s103(1) (see **43.26** to **43.31** above) with the following changes:

(a) provisions dealing with shares are replaced by a requirement to state the consideration to be received (describing the asset in question and the amount to be received in cash) and the consideration to be given by the company, specifying the amount to be given in cash;

(b) instead of the statement required in **43.27**(h) above, a statement that on the basis of the valuation, in the opinion of the auditors, the value of the consideration received by the company is not less than the value of the consideration to be given by it;

(c) the heading should refer to s104(4) rather than to s103(1).

Example 43.34

INDEPENDENT ACCOUNTANTS' REPORT TO XYZ PLC FOR THE PURPOSE OF SECTION 104(4) OF THE COMPANIES ACT 1985

We report on the transfer of non-cash assets to XYZ PLC ('the company') by subscribers to the company's memorandum of association.

The consideration to be received by the company is the freehold building situated at ... (address).

The consideration to be given by the company is ... (number) shares, having a nominal value of £1 each, in LMN PLC.

Basis of opinion

The freehold building was valued on the basis of its open market value by J. Phipps, a Fellow of the Royal Institution of Chartered Surveyors, on 13 October 1999 and, in our opinion, it is reasonable to accept such a valuation.

The shares in LMN PLC were valued by us on 2 October 1999 on the basis of the price shown in the Stock Exchange Daily Official List at 2 October 1999.

Opinion

In our opinion, the methods of valuation were reasonable in all the circumstances. There appears to us to have been no material change in the value of the consideration received and given since the dates at which the valuations were made.

On the basis of the valuations, in our opinion, the value of the consideration to be received by the company is not less than the consideration to be given by the company.

(Signature and name of accountants)

Chartered Accountants   (Address)

(Date)

43.35   A description of responsibilities is not included, because the auditors are not attesting to a statement made by the directors. The example (example 13) included in APB Practice Note 8, does not include such a description.

43.36   The report is required to be made by an independent accountant and not necessarily by the auditor and therefore the title 'Registered auditor' can be omitted.

Report on financial assistance for acquisition of own shares

43.37   Private companies are allowed to give financial assistance for the purchase of shares in the company, provided certain conditions and procedures are complied with (see **33.32** to **33.35** above). [s155] These include a statutory declaration by the directors that they have formed the opinion that there will, immediately following the date on which the assistance is provided, be no grounds on which the company could be found unable to pay its debts, and that the company will be able to pay its debts as they fall due during the year immediately following that date or, if it is intended to wind up the company, within twelve months of that date, that the company will be able to pay all its debts in full. As a further safeguard, the Act requires that this declaration shall have annexed to it a report addressed to the directors by the auditors of the company stating that they have enquired into the state of affairs of the company and are not aware of anything to indicate that the opinion expressed by the directors is unreasonable in all the circumstances.

Example 43.37

AUDITORS' REPORT TO THE DIRECTORS OF XYZ LIMITED PURSUANT TO SECTION 156(4) OF THE COMPANIES ACT 1985

We have examined the attached statutory declaration of the directors dated 15 June 1999 in connection with the proposal that the company should give financial assistance for the purchase of ... (number) of the company's ordinary shares.

Basis of opinion

We have enquired into the state of the company's affairs in order to review the bases for the statutory declaration.

Opinion

We are not aware of anything to indicate that the opinion expressed by the directors in their declaration as to any of the matters mentioned in s156(2) Companies Act 1985 is unreasonable in all the circumstances.

(Signature and name of auditors)

Chartered Accountants and Registered Auditors   (Address)

(Date)

A description of respective responsibilities is not included, because the directors deal adequately with their responsibilities in the attached statutory declaration.

43.38 There is no provision in the Act for auditors to issue such a report which is either qualified or makes reference to a fundamental uncertainty. Accordingly, the DTI argues that the report by the auditors should be 'unmodified' or, if that is not possible, not be given.

Report on purchase or redemption of own shares out of capital

43.39   Private companies are permitted to purchase or redeem their own shares, subject to certain conditions and procedures, out of capital. [s171] Where any part of the payment is to be made out of capital, the Act requires a statutory declaration by the directors which must state the amount of the 'permissible capital payment' (see **33.20** above) and that, in their opinion, there are no grounds on which the company could be found unable to pay its debts immediately following the date of the payment and that the company will be able to carry on business as a going concern (and accordingly pay its debts as they fall due) throughout the following year. [s173(3)] The amount of the permissible capital payment required to be stated in the declaration must be determined by the directors by reference to accounts prepared as at a date within a period of three months ending with the date on which the statutory declaration is made and must be reduced by any distributions lawfully made after the date of those accounts. [s172] Such accounts need not be audited.

43.40   The directors' statutory declaration must have annexed to it a report by the company's auditors addressed to the directors, stating that the auditors have inquired into the company's state of affairs, that the amount specified as the permissible capital payment has, in the auditors' opinion, been properly determined and that the auditors are not aware of anything to indicate that the opinion expressed by the directors in their declaration is unreasonable in all the circumstances. [s173(5)] If the auditors are unable to issue such a report without qualification, the company cannot legally purchase or redeem any of its shares out of capital.

Example 43.40

AUDITORS' REPORT TO THE DIRECTORS OF XYZ LIMITED PURSUANT TO SECTION 173(5) OF THE COMPANIES ACT 1985

We have examined the attached statutory declaration of the directors dated 15 June 1999 in connection with the company's proposed purchase of 5,000 ordinary shares by a payment out of capital and reserves.

Basis of opinion

We have enquired into the state of the company's affairs in order to review the bases for the statutory declaration.

Opinion

In our opinion, the amount of £250,000 specified in the statutory

---

> declaration of the directors as the permissible capital payment for the shares to be purchased is properly determined in accordance with ss171 and 172 Companies Act 1985.
>
> We are not aware of anything to indicate that the opinion expressed by the directors in their declaration as to any of the matters mentioned in s173(3) Companies Act 1985 is unreasonable in all the circumstances.
>
>
> (Signature and name of auditors)
>
> Chartered Accountants and Registered Auditors   (Address)
>
> (Date)

Statement required on reregistration as a public company

43.41 A private company wishing to reregister as a public company must deliver to the Registrar of Companies various documents, including: [s43(3)]

(a) a copy of the balance sheet as at a date not more than seven months before the application to reregister, together with an unqualified audit report in relation to that balance sheet; and

(b) a copy of a written statement by the company's auditors that, in their opinion, the relevant balance sheet shows that at that date the amount of the company's net assets was not less than the aggregate of its called up share capital and undistributable reserves.

43.42 Undistributable reserves include the share premium account, the capital redemption reserve, any excess of accumulated unrealised profits over accumulated unrealised losses (so far as not previously written off in a reduction or reorganisation of capital duly made) and any other reserves which the company is prohibited from distributing by any enactment or by its Memorandum or Articles.

43.43 If the balance sheet to be delivered is contained in a copy of the statutory financial statements on which an unqualified audit report (see **43.44** below) is included, no further report by the auditors is required to satisfy the requirements of **43.41**(a) above. An example of the report required by **43.41**(b) in such circumstances is set out below.

> **Example 43.43**
>
> **AUDITORS' STATEMENT TO XYZ LIMITED FOR THE PURPOSE OF SECTION 43(3)(b) OF THE COMPANIES ACT 1985**
>
> We have examined the balance sheet of XYZ Limited as at 31 March 2000 which formed part of the financial statements for the year then ended audited by us/ABC and Co.
>
> **Basis of opinion**
>
> The scope of our work for the purpose of this statement was limited to an examination of the relationship between the company's net assets and its called up share capital and undistributable reserves as stated in the audited balance sheet in connection with the company's proposed reregistration as a public company.
>
> **Opinion**
>
> In our opinion, the balance sheet at 31 March 2000 shows that the amount of the company's net assets was not less than the aggregate of its called up share capital and undistributable reserves.
>
> (Signature and name of auditors)
>
> Chartered Accountants and Registered Auditors   (Address)
>
> (Date)

43.44 An audit report is treated as unqualified even though it contains a qualification, providing that it contains a statement that the matter giving rise to the qualification is not material for the purpose of determining whether at the balance sheet date the amount of the company's net assets was not less than the aggregate of its called up share capital and undistributable reserves. An example of such a statement is set out below. It is expressed as an opinion, since it indicates the exercise of judgement on the part of the auditors. It is suggested that such a statement should be inserted after the final paragraph of the example in **43.43** above.

> **Example 43.44**
>
> We audited the financial statements of XYZ Limited for the year ended 31 March 2000 in accordance with United Kingdom auditing standards issued by the Auditing Practices Board and expressed a qualified opinion thereon. In our opinion, the matter giving rise to our qualification is not material for determining by reference to the balance sheet at 31 March 2000 whether at that date the net assets of the company were not less than the aggregate of its called up share capital and undistributable reserves.

43.45   If the audit report is qualified and the auditors are unable to make the statement set out in **43.41**(b) above, the company will be unable to reregister as a public company.

43.46   If the balance sheet was not prepared for a financial year, the form of report required is that, in the auditors' opinion, the balance sheet has been properly prepared in accordance with the provisions of the Companies Act 1985 applied as if the balance sheet were prepared for the company's financial year. A statement regarding net assets, similar to that set out in **43.43** above will also be required. However, the reference to the balance sheet forming part of the audited financial statements will clearly not be appropriate.

Example 43.46

AUDITORS' REPORT TO XYZ LIMITED FOR THE PURPOSE OF SECTION 43(3)(c) OF THE COMPANIES ACT 1985

We have audited the balance sheet and related notes on pages 4 to 6.

Respective responsibilities of directors and auditors

As described on page 2, the company's directors are responsible for the preparation of the balance sheet. It is our responsibility to form an independent opinion, based on our audit, and to report our opinion to you.

Basis of opinion

We conducted our audit in accordance with United Kingdom auditing standards issued by the Auditing Practices Board. An audit includes examination, on a test basis, of evidence relevant to the amounts and disclosures. It also includes an assessment of the significant estimates and judgements made by the directors and of whether the accounting policies are appropriate to the company's circumstances, consistently applied and adequately disclosed.

We planned and performed our audit so as to obtain all the information and explanations which we considered necessary in order to provide us with sufficient evidence to give reasonable assurance that the balance sheet is free from material misstatement, whether caused by fraud or other irregularity or error. In forming our opinion, we also evaluated the overall adequacy of the presentation of information in the balance sheet.

Opinion

In our opinion, the balance sheet has been properly prepared in accordance with the provisions of the Companies Act 1985 which would have applied had the balance sheet been prepared for a financial year of the company.

(Signature and name of auditors)

Chartered Accountants and Registered Auditors   (Address)

(Date)

43.47

> The example in **43.46** above does not include a 'true and fair view' opinion, even though such an opinion is suggested by example 9 in APB Practice Note 8, because such an opinion would imply that all accounting standards have been followed. However, the Act requires only a balance sheet to be presented.

Auditors' statement on a summary financial statement

43.48 When a summary financial statement is sent to members in place of the full directors' report and annual accounts, it must include a statement of opinion by the company's auditors as to whether the summary is consistent with the annual accounts and directors' report and complies with the Act and the regulations made under it. [s251] The following is an example based on the wording of the appendix to APB Bulletin 1999/6 *The auditors' statement on the summary financial statement*, issued in December 1999 (which has superseded that in example 5 in APB Practice Note 8).

Example 43.48

AUDITORS' STATEMENT TO THE MEMBERS OF DELTO PLC

We have examined the summary financial statement set out on page 2.

Respective responsibilities of directors and auditors

The directors are responsible for preparing the [*summarised annual report*][1]. Our responsibility is to report to you our opinion on the consistency of the summary financial statement with the full annual accounts and directors' report, and its compliance with the relevant requirements of section 251 of the Companies Act 1985 and the regulations made thereunder. We also read the other information contained in the [*summarised annual report*][1] and consider the implications for our report if we become aware of any apparent misstatements or material inconsistencies with the summary financial statement.

Basis of opinion

We conducted our work in accordance with Bulletin 1999/6 *The Auditors' Statement on the Summary Financial Statement* issued by the Auditing Practices Board.

Opinion

In our opinion, the summary financial statement is consistent with the full annual accounts and directors' report of Delto PLC for the year ended 31 March 2000 and complies with the applicable requirements of section 251 of the Companies Act 1985, and the regulations made thereunder.

(Signature and name of auditors)

Chartered Accountants and Registered Auditors   (Address)

(Date)[2]

1   Insert the title of the document containing the summary financial statement.

2   Where this date is after the date of the auditors' report on the annual accounts, the following words are included: 'We have not considered the effects of any events between the date on which we signed our report on the annual accounts (insert date) and the date of this statement.'

43.49   The earlier example and wording contained in SAS 600 has also been superseded and should not be used.

43.50   If the auditors' report on the full annual accounts is qualified, the auditors state that fact and reproduce the qualified audit report in their statement on the summary financial statement. Any further material needed to understand the qualified report should also be set out [s251(4)(c)] – this would include any explanatory information that was included in a note to the full financial statements.

43.51   Section 251 and the regulations do not deal with unqualified auditors' reports that contain an explanatory paragraph referring to a fundamental uncertainty. Nevertheless, Bulletin 1999/6 makes it clear that in such situations the auditors should refer to the fundamental uncertainty in their statement on the summary financial statement. The reference should be sufficiently detailed for the reader to obtain a proper understanding of the issue or issues involved – again, this would include any explanatory information that was included in a note to the full financial statements.

Example 43.51

Referring to a fundamental uncertainty:

Our report on the group's full financial statements included an explanatory paragraph concerning a fundamental uncertainty arising from the outcome of possible litigation against B Limited, a subsidiary of the company, for an alleged breach of environmental regulations. Details of the circumstances relating to this fundamental uncertainty are described in note ... of the summary financial statement. Our opinion on the full financial statements is not qualified in this respect.

43.52   Two other matters relevant to the auditors are required to be stated in the summary financial statement, namely:

(a)   whether the auditors' report on the annual accounts was unqualified or qualified (if it was qualified, the report must be set out in full, together with any further material needed to understand the qualification);

(b)   whether the auditors' report on the annual accounts contained a statement under s237(2) (i.e., the accounting records or returns are inadequate or the accounts do not agree with the records and returns) or s237(3) (i.e., the auditors have not obtained all the information or explanations which are necessary). If so, the statement must be set out in full.

However, the wording of the Act indicates that these are to be included in the summary financial statement rather than in the auditors' statement.

43.53   Bulletin 1999/6 differentiates between the summary financial statement (a statement prepared in accordance with section 251 of the Companies Act and the regulations made under it) and the other information contained within the issued document (the 'summarised annual report'). The auditors form their opinion on the summary financial statement which is identified in the audit report by reference to page numbers. The auditors read the other information and seek to resolve any apparent misstatements therein and/or inconsistencies with the summary financial statement. If the required amendments are not made, the auditors consider the implications for their statement.

Report on revised accounts and directors' reports

43.54   The Act grants directors the authority to revise annual accounts or directors' reports which do not comply with the Act and also gives the Secretary of State, or a person authorised by him, power to apply to the court for an order requiring the directors to revise defective accounts. [ss245 and 245A] The procedures for the voluntary revision of accounts by the directors are set out in the Companies (Revision of Defective Accounts and Report) Regulations 1990 (SI 1990 No 2570) ('the Regulations'). The only revisions which may be made are those necessary to correct errors in the original accounts and directors' reports.

43.55   Annual accounts and directors' reports may be corrected by complete replacement or by the issue of a supplementary note. The Regulations contain no conditions which require one form or the other to be used and therefore the directors may use whichever appears more appropriate to the circumstances leading to the revision. In both instances, the accounts or report are to be prepared as if prepared and approved by the directors as at the date of the original annual accounts or directors' report. The auditors' opinion on the view given by the revised accounts is given as at the date on which the original accounts were approved.

43.56 The example below, based on the examples in APB Practice Note 8, illustrates the report required when the directors choose to effect the revision by replacement of the original accounts.

Example 43.56

AUDITORS' REPORT TO THE MEMBERS OF XYZ LIMITED

We have audited the revised financial statements on pages 12 to 24, which have been prepared under the accounting policies set out on pages 15 and 16. The revised financial statements replace the original financial statements approved by the directors on 5 June 1999.

Respective responsibilities of directors and auditors

As described on page 10, the directors are responsible for the preparation of financial statements, which are required to be prepared in accordance with applicable United Kingdom law and accounting standards. It is our responsibility to form an independent opinion, based on our audit, on these financial statements and to report our opinion to you. We are also required to report whether in our opinion the original financial statements failed to comply with the requirements of the Companies Act 1985 in the respects identified by the directors.

Basis of opinions

We conducted our audit in accordance with United Kingdom auditing standards issued by the Auditing Practices Board. An audit includes examination, on a test basis, of evidence relevant to the amounts and disclosures in the financial statements. It also includes an assessment of the significant estimates and judgements made by the directors in the preparation of the financial statements and of whether the accounting policies are appropriate to the company's circumstances, consistently applied and adequately disclosed. The audit of revised financial statements includes the performance of additional procedures to assess whether the revisions made by the directors are appropriate and have been properly made.

We planned and performed our audit so as to obtain all the information and explanations which we considered necessary in order to provide us with sufficient evidence to give reasonable assurance that the revised financial statements are free from material misstatement, whether caused by fraud or other irregularity or error. In forming our

---

opinion, we also evaluated the overall adequacy of the presentation of information in the revised financial statements.

Opinions

In our opinion, the revised financial statements give a true and fair view, seen as at the date the original financial statements were approved, of the state of the company's affairs as at 31 March 1999 and of its profit for the year then ended and have been properly prepared in accordance with the provisions of the Companies Act 1985 as they have effect under the Companies (Revision of Defective Accounts and Report) Regulations 1990.

In our opinion, the original financial statements for the year ended 31 March 1999 failed to comply with the requirements of the Companies Act 1985 in the respects identified by the directors in the statement contained in note 1 to these financial statements.

(Signature and name of auditors)

Chartered Accountants and Registered Auditors   (Address)

(Date)

If the company was listed, account would need to be taken of APB Bulletin 1999/5 *The Combined Code: requirements of auditors under the Listing Rules of the London Stock Exchange* (see chapter 40).

43.57   If the directors' responsibilities with respect to revised financial statements are not set out in a separate statement, the auditors should include a description in their report

> ***Example 43.57***
>
> Under s245 Companies Act 1985, the directors have the authority to revise financial statements or a directors' report if they do not comply with the Act. The revised financial statements must be amended in accordance with the Companies (Revision of Defective Accounts and Report) Regulations 1990 and in accordance therewith do not take account of events which have taken place after the date on which the original financial statements were approved. The Regulations require that the revised financial statements show a true and fair view as if they were prepared and approved by the directors as at the date of the original financial statements.

43.58   The example below, based on the examples in APB Practice Note 8, illustrates the report required when the directors choose to effect the revision by supplementary note.

Example 43.58

AUDITORS' REPORT TO THE MEMBERS OF XYZ LIMITED

We have audited the revised financial statements of XYZ Limited for the year ended 31 March 1999. The revised financial statements replace the original financial statements approved by the directors on 5 June 1999 and consist of the attached supplementary note, together with the original financial statements which were circulated to members on 20 June 1999.

Respective responsibilities of directors and auditors

.....

Basis of opinion

.....

Opinions

In our opinion, the revised financial statements give ... (as for previous example – see **43.56** above).

In our opinion, the original financial statements for the year ended 31 March 1999 failed to comply with the requirements of the Companies Act 1985 in the respects identified by the directors in the supplementary note.

(Signature and name of auditors)

Chartered Accountants and Registered Auditors   (Address)

(Date)

43.59 If revision is made only to the directors' report, auditors are required to report whether the information in the revised directors' report is consistent with the annual financial statements.

Example 43.59

AUDITORS' REPORT TO MEMBERS OF XYZ LIMITED

We have considered the information given in the revised directors' report for the year ended 31 March 1999 on pages 2 to 4. The revised report replaces the original report approved by the directors on 5 June 1999 and consists of the attached supplementary note, together with the original report which was circulated to members on 20 June 1999. It has been prepared under the Companies (Revision of Defective Accounts and Report) Regulations 1990 and accordingly does not take account of events which have taken place after the date on which the original report was approved.

Respective responsibilities of directors and auditors

The directors are responsible for the preparation of their revised report. It is our responsibility to report to you whether the revised directors' report is consistent with the annual financial statements.

Basis of opinion

In our opinion, the information in the revised directors' report is consistent with the annual financial statements for the year ended 31 March 1999 which were circulated to members on 20 June 1999.

(Signature and name of auditors)

Chartered Accountants and Registered Auditors   (Address)

(Date)

44 Other special reports

44 Other special reports

Introduction

44.1   Accountants are frequently asked to give reports to official or quasi-official bodies and to contracting parties. Examples are reports on investment grants, insurance for consequential loss, circulation of periodicals, royalties, government contracts and borrowing powers under a trust deed. Quite often, the report is contained in a printed form. Occasionally, the form of the report has been agreed between the accounting institutes and the body concerned, in which case, it is likely to be acceptable to the accountants. In some other cases, however, the wording may not be acceptable and accountants must either amend the standard form or completely rewrite the report in a form in which they are prepared to give it.

44.2   Chapter 42 gives guidance on reports on accounts prepared for commercial agreements. For other types of special report, the following should be considered.

(a)   An engagement letter should be agreed between the accountants and their client which limits the accountants' liability.

(b)   An addressee should be specified.

(c)   The report should indicate the sole purpose for which it has been prepared.

(d)   The procedures performed by the accountants should be clearly specified.

(e)   The phrase 'performed such procedures as we considered necessary to obtain sufficient evidence' should be avoided, as it is too open-ended.

(f)   If the term 'review' is used, it should be clearly specified what procedures are included within the review. It should also be made clear that an audit has not been performed.

(g)   The report should be redrafted in accordance with reporting standards if it falls within the definition of an audit report expressed in terms such as 'true and fair view', 'presents fairly' or 'properly prepared in accordance with'.

(h)   The directors, or their equivalent, should be asked to indicate their approval of the matters reported on before the accountants sign off.

(i)   The opinion should be limited to matters which fall within the area of competence of accountants (e.g., comparison with the books and records) and should not extend to matters outside their professional function as accountants.

(j)   Where possible, the procedures to be performed should be agreed with the client and summarised in the report. The opinion should then be prefaced with 'On the basis of the above procedures ...'.

(k)   In place of words like 'correct', the accountants should use words such as 'reasonable in material respects'.

(l)   The accountants should avoid stating that information is 'accurate', but can confirm that it has been accurately extracted from the accounting records.

(m)   Where the accountants know of misleading information, they should not associate themselves with it.

(n)   The accountants should avoid 'certifying' anything as they give a report, not a certificate. Where a statutory requirement obliges the accountant to give a certificate, they can usually overcome this by certifying the scope of their work.

> **Example 44.2**
>
> We certify that we have examined the .....

(o)   The accountants should decline to give a report if they consider that they cannot discharge what is expected from them under an agreement to which they are not a party.

(p)   The report should be confined to confirming accounting information and should not extend to interpreting such information. For example, they should avoid expressing an opinion on whether:

   (i)   a company is a going concern;
   (ii)   it can continue to pay its debts as they fall due; or
   (iii) interest on a loan can be serviced.

(q)   The wording of the report should be considered carefully where it may otherwise be inappropriately construed that a high level of assurance can be taken.

44.3   In the case of (p)(iii) in **44.2** above, where the client is an individual, the accountants should confine their report to confirming the client's gross income as shown in the accounting records of his business or as declared for tax purposes. In addition, they should state that, as they cannot confirm the extent of the client's outgoings, their report is given without any financial responsibility on their part. In some cases, the client will be reluctant to disclose his total remuneration to the third party. In these cases, the report should be confined to confirming that the client's gross income as shown in the accounting records of his business or as disclosed to the Inland Revenue exceeds a stated amount which is agreed with the client.

44.4   Engagement terms for the report (including, where appropriate, a jurisdiction clause, a liability cap and an indemnity against liability arising from the accountant being supplied with false information) should be agreed. Where it is known that the report will be relied on by third parties, the engagement letter which contains an 'aggregate cap' should be attached to the report.

44.5   The report should normally be sent to the client for despatch to the official body.

44.6   The guidance given in **39.52** above on the use of the designation 'Registered auditor' or 'Registered auditors' should also be followed

44.7   The International Federation of Accountants (IFAC) is currently developing a standard on assurance engagements. This is, therefore, an area where developments in the period ahead are likely to influence the format of reports upon which specific standards or guidance have not already been issued.

44.8   Accountants may be asked to provide a level of assurance which is inappropriate because criteria have not been developed for the subject matter, the matter reported on is beyond their competence or there is no opportunity given to convey matters which are relevant to the level of assurance, if any, which can be taken. Situations where inappropriate wording may be specified include requests to provide assurance on systems, prospective information, or on matters which it is unusual for accountants to report upon. In many cases it may be appropriate to provide an 'agreed upon procedures' report which sets out the procedures performed and the factual findings, but which does not convey an opinion or any assurance.

Insurance certificate

44.9   As a basis for setting consequential loss premiums, some insurance companies require the auditors to complete a certificate in which they are required to 'certify' the amount of gross profit and wages for the preceding financial year. The auditors should refuse to complete such a certificate. Instead, they should ensure that such information is set out in a return which is approved by the client. They should then prepare a report, addressed to the client, along the following lines.

Example 44.9

ACCOUNTANTS' REPORT TO THE DIRECTORS OF XYZ LIMITED

We have examined the figures set out in part X of the attached return, the terms of policy no. 48666, and the accounting records of XYZ Limited for the year ended 31 March 2000.

Basis of opinion

The scope of our work was limited to checking whether the figures have been computed from the amounts recorded in the accounting records on the basis of the definitions stated in the policy.

Opinion

In our opinion, the amounts of gross profit and wages shown in the return have been computed from the amounts recorded in the accounting records on the basis of the definitions stated in the policy.

Report on tenants' service charges

44.10   Section 21 of the Landlord and Tenant Act 1985, as amended by the Landlord and Tenant Act 1987, requires certain landlords, at the request of a tenant or tenants' association, to give the tenant(s) a written summary of the costs which are relevant to the service charges payable by the tenant(s). If there are more than four flats in the building or the relevant costs relate also to another building, this summary must be 'certified by a qualified accountant' as being in his opinion:

(a)   a fair summary of those costs set out in a way which shows how they are or will be reflected in demands for service charges; and

(b)   sufficiently supported by accounts, receipts and other documents which have been produced to the accountant.

44.11   APB Practice Note 14 *The audit of registered social landlords in the United Kingdom* indicates that the examination by a qualified accountant of service charge accounts will take the form of an audit. An appropriate form of report is as follows.

Example 44.11

AUDITORS' REPORT TO THE TENANTS OF UTOPIAN COURTS

We have audited the service charge account set out on pages 2 to 4.

Respective responsibilities of the board and auditors

Under the Landlord and Tenant Act 1985, the board is responsible for the preparation of the service charge account in respect of the costs in respect of Utopian Courts. It is our responsibility to form an independent opinion, based on our audit, on the service charge account and to report our opinion to you.

Basis of opinion

We conducted our audit in accordance with United Kingdom auditing standards issued by the Auditing Practices Board. An audit includes examination, on a test basis, of evidence relevant to the costs summarised in the service charge account. It also includes an assessment of the significant estimates and judgements made by the board in the preparation of the service charge account.

We planned and performed our audit so as to obtain all the information and explanations which we considered necessary in order to provide us with sufficient evidence to give reasonable assurance that the service charge account is a fair summary of the costs relating to Utopian Court and is sufficiently supported by the accounts, receipts and other records of XYZ Registered Social Landlord.

Opinion

In our opinion, the service charge account presents a fair summary of the costs for the year ended 30 June 1999, is sufficiently supported by the accounts, receipts and other records of XYZ Registered Social Landlord and has been prepared in accordance with s21(5) Landlord and Tenant Act 1985 and clause 10 of the tenancy agreement dated 23 June 1989 between the tenant and XYZ Registered Social Landlord.

44.12   The above example is not exactly the same as that in APB Practice Note 14, which is presented as a combination of an examination report and audit report. The wording in the above example is considered more appropriate if the examination required by the Landlord and Tenant Act 1985 is undertaken as an audit.

44.13   In 1998, the ICAEW reprimanded and fined a firm of chartered accountants for failing to report properly on the service charge costs relating to leasehold properties. The leasehold service charge accounts failed to show how repair costs had been reflected in service charges, the correct periods when payments were made and the amounts of funds credited to tenants. An article published in *Audit News* (issue 25) sets out some of the more obvious pitfalls in respect of accounting for leaseholders and how they can be avoided.

Report to debenture and loan stock trustees

44.14 Most trust deeds covering the issue of debenture and loan stocks impose restrictions on the activities of the company in order to safeguard the interests of the stockholders. These restrictions include limits on the amounts and categories of borrowings, based on defined formulae. The trust deeds usually require the company's auditors or an appointed auditor to report on specific information relating to the borrowing limits, either at any time requested by the trustees or at specified regular intervals or as a precondition to the issue of further debt.

44.15 The form of the auditors' report is determined by the trust deed, but the following should be taken into account:

(a) Trust deeds frequently require the auditors to 'certify' information, but this is rarely possible and the auditors should therefore express an opinion on, rather than certify, the information. In circumstances in which the trustees are unwilling to accept a report which does not incorporate the words 'we certify that', an appropriate compromise may be the words 'We certify that in our opinion ....';

(b) If there are problems of interpretation of a trust deed and it is not possible to assess the intention of the original drafters, the auditors may be able to reach agreement with the company and trustees as to what was intended and how any ambiguity in the trust deed should be interpreted. If there is a dispute regarding a question of legal interpretation, the auditors should consider taking their own legal advice;

(c) A problem which occurs is the interpretation of the date as at which the auditors should be reporting. The trustees may ask for the report to be given at the end of the company's financial year. At that date, the latest audited accounts available (on which the borrowing limits will be calculated) will be those for the previous financial year. Although a report based on those accounts will enable the requirements of trust deeds to be met, it does mean that the information on which the auditors report is seriously out of date. To overcome this, the trustees may request that the report includes a statement of the borrowing limits as at the date on which the new audited accounts become available and compare those limits to a directors' certificate of the borrowings at the same date.

(d) Consideration should be given to limiting liability to third parties. At the time of writing, the ICAEW Audit Faculty has established a working party on reliance by banks which is likely to
provide guidance on reporting for the purposes of debenture
trust deeds. In the meantime, accountants should consider
carefully whether they wish to give such reports, in view of the
potential risks if the trustees do not accept a liability cap.

44.16 Specimen reports are included in the APC Audit Brief *Reports to
debenture and loan stock trustees,* but it is stressed that they are likely
to require amendment to ensure that the auditors report is in accordance with the trust deed and complies with the principles established by SAS 600 where appropriate. Among other matters, the
Audit Brief gives guidance on interpreting trust deeds and circumstances leading to qualification.

Reporting under the Banking Act 1987

44.17 Besides the reporting requirements of the Companies Act which
apply to banking companies, there are also reporting requirements
arising from the Banking Act 1987. In May 1999, APB issued Practice
Note 19 *Banks in the United Kingdom* (superseding the APC Auditing
Guideline of the same name) giving guidance for auditors on the
related reporting considerations.

45 Reports on unaudited financial statements

45 Reports on unaudited financial statements

Introduction

45.1 In addition to acting as auditors, professional accountants are also frequently called on to act in different capacities in relation to financial information. Typically, they may be called on to compile (prepare) financial statements or to compare them with accounting records without carrying out an audit. Following the issue of the audit exemption regulations in July 1994, accountants are asked to carry out such work on those small companies that neither require an audit nor a report from a reporting accountant (see **34.48** to **34.62** above).

45.2 It is important that whenever financial information with which professional accountants are associated is made available to third parties, they should be left in no doubt as to the extent to which the accountants are responsible for the quality of the information provided. Therefore, it is best practice for every set of financial statements made available to third parties to be accompanied by an accountants' report which clearly identifies the client and the scope and purpose of the accountants' engagement. An exception might be made if an accountant prepares on behalf of the directors the financial statements of a dormant company which has resolved not to appoint auditors. It is also useful for the terms of the accountants' engagement to make it clear that the engagement does not constitute an audit.

Compilation reports

45.3 The Audit Faculty of the ICAEW issued guidance in Audit 1/95 on reports on accounts compiled (prepared) by accountants. The guidance extends to accounts of trusts, joint ventures, partnerships, not-for-profit organisations and audit exempt companies where no audit or s249A(2) report is required.

45.4 The guidance states that accountants should ensure that the users of the accounts are aware of the extent of their involvement with the accounts, so that users do not derive unwarranted assurance or, alternatively, may gain some comfort that the accounts have been prepared by a chartered accountant.

45.5 Where the involvement of the accountants is not apparent (e.g., management accounts printed on blank paper), the accountant may agree with the client that no report will be given and should make clear to the client in the engagement letter that the client must not represent to third parties that the accounts have been prepared by the accountant.

45.6 Where the accountants prepare accounts on their firm's headed paper, a report making clear the accountants' role should be attached. Where the accountant has additional reporting responsibilities imposed by statute or agreement (e.g., the accountant performs an audit or a s249A(2) reporting engagement), the report required by those additional responsibilities is the only report needed.

45.7 For an audit exempt company, with no additional responsibilities and no other opinion required, wording along the following lines should be used.

Example 45.7

ACCOUNTANTS' REPORT ON THE UNAUDITED ACCOUNTS TO THE DIRECTORS OF XYZ LIMITED

As described on the balance sheet, you are responsible for the preparation of the accounts for the year ended ...., set out on pages ... to ..., and you consider that the company is exempt from an audit [and a report under s249A(2) Companies Act 1985]*. In accordance with your instructions, we have compiled these unaudited accounts in order to assist you to fulfil your statutory responsibilities, from the accounting records and information and explanations supplied to us.

* If a charitable company.

45.8 In circumstances other than for audit exempt companies, where no other report or opinion is required, wording along the following lines should be used.

Example 45.8

ACCOUNTANTS' REPORT ON THE UNAUDITED ACCOUNTS TO THE PARTNERS OF XYZ MEDICAL PRACTICE

As described on page ..., you have approved the accounts for the year ended .... set out on pages ... to ... . In accordance with your instructions, we have compiled these unaudited accounts from the accounting records and information and explanations supplied to us.

45.9 The report should not be described as an audit report and the word 'audit' should not be used to describe the assignment in the financial statements or in correspondence or bills. Also, the accountants should not describe themselves as 'registered auditors'. It is enough that they describe themselves for the purpose of such reports as 'Chartered Accountants'.

45.10 There may be situations where, although they are not carrying out an audit, the accountants have been asked to do certain work of an auditing nature (e.g., to verify investments or count cash). To avoid any misunderstanding by a reader, they should not include any reference to these tests in their report, but should describe the work done in a separate letter to the client.

45.11 Statutory financial statements are still required from smaller companies and such financial statements are required to give a true and fair view and comply with the other provisions of the Act. They should, therefore, comply with the accounting provisions of the Act and applicable accounting standards. In the case of other entities, there can be circumstances where it is appropriate to depart from accepted principles (e.g., the financial statements of a social club might be more meaningful to members if they were drawn up on a cash basis). Such departures should be clearly explained in the financial statements and referred to in the accountants' report. Also, the accounting policies adopted should be made clear either in the accounts or in the notes.

45.12 If the client will not accept adjustments which the accountants wish to make (e.g., a provision for bad debts) and these are significant to a fair presentation of the financial statements, it may, depending on the circumstances, be appropriate to deal with the matter by setting out the facts in their report.

Example 45.12

ACCOUNTANTS' REPORT ON THE UNAUDITED ACCOUNTS TO THE DIRECTORS OF XYZ LIMITED

As described on the balance sheet, you are responsible for the preparation of the accounts for the year ended ...., set out on pages ... to ..., and you consider that the company is exempt from an audit. In accordance with your instructions, we have compiled these unaudited accounts in order to assist you to fulfil your statutory responsibilities, from the accounting records and information and explanations supplied to us.

Problem relating to the accounting treatment for bad debts

In carrying out our procedures, it has come to our attention that the balance sheet total of debtors includes a debt of £ ..... which is in

---

respect of a company that has gone into administration. XYZ Limited has no security for this debt. The directors have made no provision against the debt and have expressed the view that it will be recovered in full. Although we are not required to perform, and have not performed, any procedures to corroborate the directors' views, in the circumstances, we are of the opinion that a provision of £ ..... should be made against this debt, with the result that the profit before taxation should be reduced by the same amount.

45.13 The accountants must not under any circumstances be associated with financial statements which they believe give a misleading view, without giving sufficient explanation of the facts in their report. If, during their work, they have obtained knowledge of significant information which, if not disclosed, would make the financial statements materially misleading, they should insist that such information be disclosed. Failing this, they should not allow their names, or that of their firm, to be associated with the financial statements.

Reports for the purposes of section 249A(2) of the Act

Introduction

45.14 In July 1994, the Companies Act 1985 (Audit Exemption) Regulations 1994 (SI 1994 No 1935) ('the 1994 Regulations') were issued. The 1994 Regulations provide for two levels of exemption. Companies that meet the 'total exemption conditions' are exempt from the requirement to have their annual accounts audited. Companies that meet the 'report conditions' are also exempt from the audit requirement, but instead need to obtain an accountants' report. The exemption conditions and the disclosures required by directors in annual accounts are dealt with in paragraphs **34.48** to **34.62** above. Reports on companies which are not audited or subject to a s249A(2) report are dealt with in **45.3** to **45.13** above.

45.15 On 15 April 1997, the Companies Act 1985 (Audit Exemption) (Amendment) Regulations 1997 (SI 1997 No 3080) came into force. One of the effects of these regulations is that, for annual accounts for periods ending on or after 15 June 1997, the only companies that are required to obtain an audit exemption report, if they have opted for an exemption from audit, are charities with gross income between £90,000 and £250,000 (see **34.59** above).

Reports by reporting accountants

Companies Act requirements

45.16 The Act (as amended by the 1994 Regulations) requires the reporting accountants to state whether in their opinion:

[s249C]

(a) the accounts of the company are in agreement with the accounting records of the company;

(b) having regard only to, and on the basis of, the information contained in the accounting records, the accounts have been drawn up in a manner consistent with:

    (i) s226(3) and Sch 4;
    (ii) s231 and Sch 5 paras 7 to 9A and 13(1), (3) and (4); and
    (iii) s232 and Sch 6,

    where appropriate modified by s246(2) and (3), so far as applicable to the company; and

(c) having regard only to, and on the basis of, the information contained in the accounting records, the company satisfied the requirements of s249A(4) (or, where the company is a charity, of that subsection as modified by s249A(5)) for the financial year, and did not fall within s249B(1)(a) to (f) at any time within the financial year.

The Companies Act 1985 (Audit Exemption) (Amendment) Regulations 1997 (SI 1997 No 936) made various amendments to s249A (see **45.15** above), including the repeal of s249A(5). However, s249C was not correspondingly amended to remove the requirement for the accountants' report to refer, where a company is a charity, to s249A(4) as modified by s249A(5). In practice, to make sense, the reporting accountants should not refer to modification by s249A(5) and the example report in **45.20** below does not do so.

45.17 The report should also state the name of the reporting accountant and be signed by him.

Statement of Standards for Reporting Accountants

45.18 In October 1994, the APB issued a Statement of Standards for Reporting Accountants entitled *Audit exemption reports* ('the Statement of Standards') setting out the work to be performed and the form of reports to be made by reporting accountants under the 1994 Regulations. The Statement of Standards requires that if the reporting accountants are satisfied that the results of their procedures provide a reasonable basis on which to express an affirmative opinion on each of the matters specified by the Act, they should issue a report including such an opinion.

45.19 The Statement of Standards requires that such reports include:

(a) a title identifying the shareholders of the company as the persons to whom the report is addressed;

(b)   an introductory paragraph identifying the accounts reported on;

(c)   a statement that the directors are responsible for the preparation of the accounts;

(d)   a description of the basis of the reporting accountants' opinion;

(e)   the reporting accountants' opinion;

(f)   the name and signature of the reporting accountants; and

(g)   the date of the report.

45.20   An example of the wording of an unqualified accountants' report for a charitable company for the purposes of s249A(2) of the Act, based on the wording in the Statement of Standards is set out below.

Example 45.20

ACCOUNTANTS' REPORT TO THE MEMBERS ON THE UNAUDITED ACCOUNTS OF XYZ LIMITED

We report on the accounts for the year ended .... set out on pages ... to ... .

Respective responsibilities of directors and reporting accountants

As described on the balance sheet, the company's directors are responsible for the preparation of the accounts and they consider that the company is exempt from an audit. It is our responsibility to carry out procedures designed to enable us to report our opinion.

Basis of opinion

Our work was conducted in accordance with the Statement of Standards for Reporting Accountants and so our procedures consisted of comparing the accounts with the accounting records kept by the company and making such limited enquiries of the officers of the company as we considered necessary for the purposes of this report. These procedures provide only the assurance expressed in our opinion. These procedures do not constitute an audit. Accordingly, we do not express an audit opinion on the accounts. Therefore, our report does not provide any assurance that the accounting records and the accounts are free from material misstatement.

Opinion

In our opinion:

(a)   the accounts are in agreement with the accounting records kept by the company under s221 Companies Act 1985;

(b)   having regard only to, and on the basis of, the information contained in those accounting records:

> (i) the accounts have been drawn up in a manner consistent with the accounting requirements specified in s249C(6) of the Act; and
>
> (ii) the company satisfied the conditions for exemption from an audit of the accounts for the year specified in s249A(4) of the Act and did not, at any time within that year, fall within any of the categories of companies not entitled to the exemption specified in s249B(1).
>
>
> (Signature and name of reporting accountants)
>
> Reporting Accountants   (Address)
>
> (Date)

45.21   Although the Statement of Standards refers to 'shareholders', the term 'members' should be used as this is the term used in the Act (s249A(2)).

45.22   This regime has been criticised because there is no explicit requirement for the reporting accountant to consider the appropriateness of the accounting policies. However, accountants have a professional responsibility not to allow their name to be associated with accounts which may be misleading. Therefore, although reporting accountants are not required to search for such matters, should they become aware, for any reason, of any matters which they believe should be brought to the attention of the members (and the matter is not adequately dealt with in the accounts), they should include an explanatory paragraph in their report. An example, which describes the matters giving rise to concern more clearly than the example included in the Statement of Standards, is set out below.

> ## *Example 45.22*
>
> **ACCOUNTANTS' REPORT TO THE MEMBERS ON THE UNAUDITED ACCOUNTS OF XYZ LIMITED**
>
> We report on the accounts for the year ended .... set out on pages ... to .... .
>
> **Respective responsibilities of directors and reporting accountants**
>
> As described on the .....
>
> **Basis of opinion**
>
> Our work was conducted .....

Problem relating to the accounting treatment of bad debts

In carrying out our procedures, it has come to our attention that the balance sheet total of debtors includes a debt of £ ..... which is in respect of a company that has gone into administration. XYZ Limited has no security for this debt. The directors have made no provision against the debt and have expressed the view that it will be recovered in full. Although we are not required to perform, and have not performed, any procedures to corroborate the directors' views, in the circumstances, we are of the opinion that a provision of £ ..... should be made against this debt, with the result that the profit before taxation should be reduced by the same amount. Our statutory opinion below is not required to be qualified in this respect because, for statutory purposes, it is sufficient that the accounts are in agreement with the accounting records. However, we believe that this is a matter of which the members should take account when reading the accounts.

Opinion

In our opinion .....

(Signature and name of reporting accountants)

Reporting Accountants   (Address)

(Date)

45.23 In extreme circumstances, where the matter cannot be adequately dealt with by means of qualifying the opinion (or by other appropriate modifications of the statutory reporting accountants' report), the reporting accountant should not issue any report and should withdraw from the engagement.

Investment advertisements

45.24 The auditors may be requested by management to approve profit announcements or other documents on the grounds that they fall within the meaning of 'investment advertisements' for the purposes of the Financial Services Act 1986. In such cases, the auditors should have regard to *Investment Business Regulations and Guidance* (July 1997) issued by the ICAEW, Institute of Chartered Accountants of Scotland (ICAS) and Institute of Chartered Accountants in Ireland (ICAI). The auditors should:

    (a) indicate to the client that if there is doubt as to whether the document is an investment advertisement, legal advice should be sought;

    (b) proceed with an assignment to give approval only if the firm is authorised to carry on investment business and the requirements for the approval of investment advertisements of the body which has authorised the firm are met.

45.25 These requirements include the need for prescribed wording to be included within the investment advertisement. An example of a statement containing such wording is as follows.

> ### *Example 45.25*
>
> The directors of (name of entity) accept responsibility for the contents of this advertisement, which have been approved by (name of accounting firm) a firm authorised by the Institute of Chartered Accountants in England and Wales to carry on investment business.
>
> Note: If there is doubt whether the advertisement is an investment advertisement, the statement of approval could be modified by including after the word 'which' the words 'may be an investment advertisement. The contents'.

45.26 Where only part of the information contained in a document constitutes an investment advertisement, it is suggested that the above wording is preceded by the following sentence.

> ### *Example 45.26*
>
> The information contained in pages 2 to 4 of this [identify document] constitutes an investment advertisement within the meaning of s57(2) Financial Services Act 1986.

45.27 Depending on the investment advertisement, additional wordings may be required. For example, if it contains information about the past performance of an investment, the following wording should be included: 'The past is not necessarily a guide to the future'. The relevant financial rules should be consulted on such wordings. Also, before approving any statement, the practising firm's compliance department must be consulted as to the most recent rules and the appropriateness of giving such approval.

Additional information reports

45.28 It is quite common for companies to ask for additional information on revenue and expenses to be attached to the statutory financial statements for consideration by the directors of the company or the Inland Revenue. In such circumstances, auditors have in the past provided additional information reports expressed in positive 'presented fairly' or 'presented fairly in all material respects' terms. Unfortunately, such reports now fall within the scope of the reporting standards and will therefore need to be lengthier and more complex than was previously the case. See **45.30** below for guidance where the directors do not wish the auditors to give a report.

Example 45.28

AUDITORS' REPORT TO THE DIRECTORS OF XYZ LIMITED

We have examined the additional information set out on pages 16 and 17 in conjunction with our audit of the statutory financial statements set out on pages 5 to 14. This additional information is supplementary to, and prepared using the same accounting policies as, the statutory financial statements and should be read in conjunction therewith.

Respective responsibilities of directors and auditors

As described on page 3, the company's directors are responsible for the preparation of the financial statements which are required to be prepared in accordance with applicable United Kingdom law and accounting standards. It is our responsibility to form an opinion, based on our audit, on those financial statements and to report our opinion to you. The directors are also responsible for the preparation of any additional financial information. Our responsibility is to examine that additional information and to report whether in relation to the financial statements taken as a whole it is presented fairly in all material respects.

Basis of opinion

We conducted our audit in accordance with United Kingdom auditing standards issued by the Auditing Practices Board. An audit includes examination, on a test basis, of evidence relevant to the amounts and disclosures in the financial statements. It also includes an assessment of the significant estimates and judgements made by the directors in the preparation of the financial statements, of whether the accounting policies are appropriate to the company's circumstances, consistently applied and adequately disclosed and of whether any additional financial information is consistent with the financial statements.

Our opinion on the additional financial information in relation to the statutory financial statements taken as a whole is based on the work done in our audit of the statutory financial statements as described above.

Opinion

In our opinion, the additional information in relation to the statutory financial statements taken as a whole is presented fairly in all material respects.

(Signature and name of auditors)

Chartered Accountants   (Address)

(Date)

45.29 Reference to 'Registered Auditors' is not made, as the report is not required to be given by the auditors. Such reports should not be addressed to the members, as it would cause confusion as to which report is the statutory report.

45.30 In practice, such reports will appear unwieldy. Therefore, in most cases, where the directors wish to provide additional information but do not require the auditors to provide a report on it, it is recommended that an introductory statement along the lines of the following example be made on a page preceding the additional information.

> ***Example 45.30***
>
> **Additional information**
>
> The additional information on pages ... to ... has been prepared from the accounting records of the company. While it does not form part of the statutory financial statements, it should be read in conjunction with them and the auditors' report thereon.

45.31 It is emphasised that the above statement is an introductory statement by the company, rather than a report by the auditors. Accordingly, it should not be signed by the auditors and should not be headed 'Accountants'/Auditors' report' or 'Additional information report'.

45.32 While auditors would not have a responsibility to audit this information, they should review it in accordance with SAS 160 *Other information in documents containing audited financial statements* to satisfy themselves that it is not materially inconsistent and does not undermine the view shown by those statements.

45.33 Good practice would put the package of the statutory financial statements and the additional financial information in the following order:

(a) statement of directors' responsibilities;

(b) auditors' report on the statutory financial statements;

(c) statutory financial statements;

(d) additional information – introductory statement (or report on additional financial information, if given);

(e) additional information.

Preliminary announcements

45.34 These are dealt with in chapter 40.

Review reports on interim financial information

45.35 These are dealt with in chapter 40.

Small companies

45.36 At the time of writing, a recent DTI announcement has indicated that, subject to parliamentary approval, the audit exemption limit (discussed in detail in chapter 34) will be increased to an annual turnover of £1m and, potentially, to £4.8m at a later date. One possibility, currently being considered by the company law review Steering Group is that, for companies with turnover between £1m and £4.8m, the audit should be replaced by a lighter, less costly form of assurance (the Independent Professional Review). The form that the required review report would then take is also currently under discussion.

46 Model report and financial statements

46   Model report and financial statements

Introduction

46.1   The last section of this chapter illustrates the report and financial statements of a hypothetical listed company, Delto PLC, which owns a group of manufacturing companies, showing the recommended style and layout. The purpose is to illustrate style and layout only. A single model cannot, of course, illustrate the disclosure requirements for all situations. A comprehensive check list of disclosures for such a company can be found in Appendices II and V.

46.2   The requirements of Sch 4 impose a considerable degree of rigidity on the format and headings. However, advantage should be taken of such flexibility as is allowed by the Act to achieve the presentation which will be most useful to the reader. In any event, the requirement to show a true and fair view may, in rare cases, require departure from the standard formats.

46.3   The financial statements are, of course, the responsibility of the directors and the auditor expresses his opinion on them. Although the auditor may have participated in the accountancy work and/or drafted the financial statements, it is the client who ultimately decides the accounting policies to be adopted. The client may also have preferences as to the format to be adopted or the extent to which disclosure may be made in the notes rather than on the face of the accounts. The auditor must respect his client's wishes in these respects, provided he is satisfied that all legal requirements have been complied with and particularly that the financial statements give a true and fair view. If he is not so satisfied, he will be unable to issue an unqualified report.

46.4   The 'Delto PLC' model report and financial statements are representative of the information contained in the published financial statements of a listed company. The arrangement of information follows the order which is commonly adopted, but it is, of course, open to the company to amend the package by, for example:

(a)   excluding any of the optional sections, i.e., contents, directors' listing, chairman's statement, salient features and financial calendar, and statistical record;

(b)   changing the order of the financial statements and auditors' report; or

(c)   presenting the consolidated and parent company balance sheets on one page.

Some considerations of style and language

Language

46.5   Simple and concise language which will be understandable to all readers of the financial statements should be used.

Use of capital letters

46.6   The indiscriminate use of capital letters prevents attention being focused on significant words and should be avoided.

Period covered by financial statements

46.7   Each balance sheet forming part of the financial statements should disclose prominently the date at which it is prepared. The directors' report, the remaining statements forming the financial statements and the first page of the notes to the accounts should disclose prominently the precise period covered. In all statements, the amounts for the current period and the preceding one should be identified at the top of each column. Where both the current and preceding accounting periods are of 12 months, the year in which the period ends is sufficient identification.

Example 46.7

DELTO PLC
BALANCE SHEET – 31 March 2000

	2000	*1999*
	£'000	*£'000*
FIXED ASSETS		
Tangible assets	720	695

46.8   It is important that, in any set of financial statements in which the length of period covered by the current and comparative figures is different, a precise description of the period should be shown over the appropriate columns. This is necessary to alert the reader that the comparative figures are not comparable without taking into account the time differences.

Example 46.8

DELTO PLC
PROFIT AND LOSS ACCOUNT
Year ended 31 March 2000

	2000 £'000	Six months ended 31 March 1999 £'000
Turnover	36,615	14,998

46.9 The use of the term 'period ended (date)' without further amplification is uninformative and should not be used. Examples of good description include:

Example 46.9

Period from 15 February 1999 to 31 December 1999

15 February 1999 (date of incorporation) to 31 December 1999

13 months ended 31 March 2000

53 weeks ended 1 April 2000

Notes to the accounts

46.10 Accounts on their own rarely provide all the financial information required to show a true and fair view. The Act specifies certain information to be shown either in the balance sheet and profit and loss account or in the notes to the accounts and further requires that any additional information which is necessary to give a true and fair view must be provided. Thus, the notes form an integral part of the financial statements.

46.11 The Act does not dictate the manner or arrangement in which the notes are to be shown. The preparer of financial statements should adopt a presentation that will provide the reader with an orderly arrangement of information which can be easily referenced to the relevant items. The following approach is recommended.

(a) Notes should be placed after the accounts.

(b) Notes should be numbered and cross-referenced to the relevant item(s) in the accounts.

(c) Each note should be given a heading which identifies the subject matter of the disclosure.

(d)   Notes relating to specific account balances should be shown in the order in which they appear in the accounts.

Cross-referencing between notes

46.12   Difficulties of understanding may be caused by relegating the supporting detail of one balance sheet or profit and loss account item to more than one note. This should be avoided as far as possible, but, where necessary, the relevant notes should be cross-referenced.

Rounding and reducing figures

46.13   There are two main reasons for it being sensible to round and reduce figures:

(a)   if they are stated to the last pound, an illusory degree of accuracy is suggested;

(b)   there is difficulty in understanding very large numbers.

46.14   It is therefore suggested that rather than detail such as:

	£
Raw materials and consumables	1,851,784
Work in progress	7,933,241
Finished goods and goods for resale	5,839,473
	15,624,498

the presentation should be:

	£'000
Raw materials and consumables	1,852
Work in progress	7,933
Finished goods and goods for resale	5,839
	15,624

Use of brackets

46.15   Opinions differ as to when figures should be bracketed and no set rules can be said to apply to all circumstances. To obtain some consistency, the following guidelines are suggested.

46.16   Where brackets are required to make mathematical sense out of a listing of numbers, the items which are mathematically opposite in direction to the nature of items in the list should be bracketed. For example, in a listing of expenses, a rebate credit or bad debt recovery should be bracketed.

46.17   If two items are subtotalled and their descriptions clearly indicate the mathematical direction of the amounts, it would usually be acceptable to omit brackets.

Example 46.17.1

	2000 £'000	1999 £'000
Profit on ordinary activities before taxation	173	123
Tax on profit on ordinary activities	89	55
Profit on ordinary activities after taxation	84	68

Example 46.17.2

	2000 £'000	1999 £'000
Contract work in progress	1,283	937
Less payments on account	400	674
	883	263

46.18 Where comparative figures are positive in one year and negative the next year, both the description of the appropriate item and amount should be bracketed.

Example 46.18

	2000 £'000	1999 £'000
(Loss)/profit on ordinary activities before taxation	(84)	123
Tax (credit)/charge on (loss)/profit on ordinary activities	45	(155)
Loss on ordinary activities after taxation	(39)	(32)

46.19 Generally, adverse balances in the balance sheet and profit and loss account should be bracketed, e.g., loss on ordinary activities before taxation, loss on ordinary activities after taxation, net current liabilities, debit balance on profit and loss account, etc.

Model report and financial statements

46.20 The following example illustrates the report and financial statements of a hypothetical listed company, DELTO PLC (see **46.1** above).

Company Registration No. 1234567

DELTO PLC

Report and Financial Statements

31 March 2000

DELTO PLC

REPORT AND FINANCIAL STATEMENTS 2000

CONTENTS | **Page**

* Not prepared for the purposes of this manual.

1

DELTO PLC

REPORT AND FINANCIAL STATEMENTS 2000

NOTICE OF MEETING

Notice is hereby given that the Annual General Meeting of Delto PLC. will be held at The Connaught Rooms, Great Queen Street, London, WC2 on Thursday, 17 August 2000 at 12.00 noon for the following purposes:

1. To receive the financial statements for the year ended 31 March 2000, together with the reports of the directors and auditors thereon.

2. To declare a final ordinary dividend.

3. To re-elect directors.

4. To re-appoint the auditors and to authorise the directors to fix their remuneration.

5. To transact any other ordinary business of the company.

By Order of the Board

A. EVANS

8 July 2000   Secretary

Notes:

1. A member entitled to attend and vote at this meeting is entitled to appoint a proxy or proxies to attend and vote instead of him or her. A proxy need not be a member of the company. Proxy forms must be lodged with the registrars not later than 48 hours before the time fixed for the meeting.

2. Copies of all directors' service contracts are available for inspection during business hours at the company's registered office, Swift House, Cheapside, London EC2V 5TH and on the day of the Annual General Meeting at The Connaught Rooms, Great Queen Street, London, WC2 from 11.45 a.m. until the conclusion of that meeting. A map (*not reproduced in this example*) showing the location of The Connaught Rooms is shown overleaf.

3. Messrs Delto and Decker are due to retire by rotation and offer themselves for re-election.

    Biographical details, as required by The Combined Code provision A.6.2, of directors submitted for re-election could be given here. These have not been reproduced in this example.

    The Secretary may wish to include in the notice of meeting the wording of the actual resolutions to be placed before the members. The wording in 1 to 5 above represents the minimum requirement in respect of ordinary business. If there are any non-routine or special resolutions, the associated wording in the notice of meeting should be entirely accurate and sufficient for the members to fully understand the nature of said resolutions – in such cases, it would normally be advisable to include the actual wording of the resolution in the notice.

2

DELTO PLC

OFFICERS AND PROFESSIONAL ADVISERS

DIRECTORS

J Delto	(Chairman)
M Driver	(Chief Executive)
A Carter FCA	
A Blake	(Non-executive)
J Decker	
F Sharp	(Non-executive)
A Worth	(Non-executive)

SECRETARY

A Evans FCIS

REGISTERED OFFICE

Swift House
Cheapside
London
EC2V 5TH

BANKERS

Universal Bank Limited

SOLICITORS

Busola Peabody & Co.

REGISTRARS

B & D Registrars Limited
3 London Wall
London
EC2M 5PH

AUDITORS

Lindsay & Robinson
Chartered Accountants
Swift House
Cheapside
London
EC2V 5TH

3

DELTO PLC

SALIENT FEATURES AND FINANCIAL CALENDAR

	2000 £'000	1999 £'000
TURNOVER	42,196	49,240
PROFIT AFTER TAXATION	950	891
EARNINGS PER ORDINARY SHARE	7.1p	7.2p
DIVIDENDS PER ORDINARY SHARE	7.2p	7.0p

RESULTS

First half year	Announcement mid-November
Results for the year	Announced early-July
Report and financial statements	Circulated mid-July

DIVIDENDS

Ordinary dividends:

Interim	Declared mid-November
	Paid early-January
Final	Proposed mid-May
	Paid early-September

4

OPERATING AND FINANCIAL REVIEW (extract)

DERIVATIVES AND OTHER FINANCIAL INSTRUMENTS

The following is based upon the illustrative disclosures in appendix III of FRS 13. In practice the narrative will be specific to the business. It has been assumed that the narrative disclosures are provided in the operating and financial review. As such, the notes to the financial statements will need to contain a cross-reference to the disclosures below.

It is envisaged that the discussion set out below will usually be preceded by a general discussion of, inter alia, the entity's activities, structure and financing. This discussion will typically consider the financial risk profile of the entity as a whole as a prelude to the narrative disclosures required by the FRS.

The group's financial instruments, other than derivatives, comprise borrowings, long-term loans, commercial paper, cash and liquid resources and various items, such as trade debtors, trade creditors, etc., that arise directly from its operations. The main purpose of these financial instruments is to raise finance for the group's operations.

The group also enters into derivatives transactions (principally interest rate swaps and forward foreign currency contracts). The purpose of such transactions is to manage the interest rate and currency risks arising from the group's operations and its sources of finance.

It is, and has been throughout the period under review, the group's policy that no trading in financial instruments shall be undertaken.

The main risks arising from the group's financial instruments are interest rate risk, liquidity risk and foreign currency risk. The Board reviews and agrees policies for managing each of these risks and they are summarised below. These policies have remained unchanged since April 1999.

Interest rate risk

The group finances its operations by a mixture of retained profits, bank borrowings, long-term loans and commercial paper. The group borrows in the desired currencies at both fixed and floating rates of interest and then uses interest rate swaps to generate the desired interest profile and to manage the group's exposure to interest rate fluctuations. The group's policy is to keep between 58 per cent and 63 per cent of its borrowings, including preference shares issued by the group, at fixed rates of interest. At the year-end, 62.2 per cent of the group's borrowings were at fixed rates after taking account of interest rate swaps. Also included within the financial liabilities of the company are other creditors, accruals and deferred income of £245,000 (2.3 per cent of the total) which do not bear any interest.

Liquidity risk

As regards liquidity, the group's policy has throughout the year been that, to ensure continuity of funding, at least 18 per cent of its borrowings, including preference shares issued by the group, should mature in more than five years. At the year-end, 19.1 per cent of the group's borrowings were due to mature in more than five years.

Short-term flexibility is achieved by overdraft facilities.

Foreign currency risk

The group has significant overseas subsidiaries which operate in the USA and continental Europe. Their revenues and expenses are denominated substantially in US dollars and various European currencies respectively. In order to protect the group's sterling balance sheet from the movements in these currencies and the sterling exchange rate, the group finances its net investment in these subsidiaries by means of borrowings in their respective functional currencies.

About one-third of the sales of the group's UK businesses are to customers in continental Europe. These sales are priced in sterling but invoiced in the currencies of the customers involved. The group's policy is to eliminate all currency exposures on sales at the time of sale through forward currency contracts. All the other sales of the UK businesses are denominated in sterling.

DELTO PLC

DIRECTORS' REPORT

The directors present their annual report and the audited financial statements for the year ended 31 March 2000.

ACTIVITIES

Delto PLC is the parent company of a group of companies engaged in the manufacture of accessories for the motor trade and costume jewellery.

REVIEW OF DEVELOPMENTS

Group results

Turnover from continuing operations increased by £3.3 million (8.6%) from £38.6 million to £41.9 million. The comparison with 1998/99 is affected by the fact that Gems 4' U was acquired on, and its results consolidated from, 30 September 1998 and that Shed Technology Limited was acquired on, and its results consolidated from, 30 September 1999. Operating profit for continuing operations increased by £0.42 million (19.6%) from £2.15 million to £2.57 million. This improvement follows from the ongoing reorganisation and restructuring of both the motor products and jewellery divisions following recent acquisitions. The costs of the reorganisation were £296,000 (1999 – £234,000). These amounts have been charged in arriving at operating profit, as the reorganisation did not have a material effect on the nature and focus of the group's operations.

A geographical analysis of operating profits from ordinary activities is given below:

	2000		1999	
	£'000	%	*£'000*	%
United Kingdom	1,026	40.0	887	41.6
Other European Countries	588	22.9	522	24.5
North America	954	37.1	722	33.9
	2,568	100	2,131	100

Exceptional items include a gain on sale of fixed assets of £202,000 (1999 – £216,000) and a loss on sale and termination of the home plastics division of £8,000 (1999 – £42,000).

Discontinued operations

The directors have previously stated their intention to discontinue the group's housewares operations. The majority of the disposals required to carry out this strategy were undertaken last year. This year the group has completed the disposal of the domestic plastics operations with the sale of Plastic Manufacturing Company Ltd.

Acquisition

Shareholders approved the acquisition of a further 60% of the issued share capital of Shed Technology Ltd on 30 September 1999 for £208,000 increasing the group's interest to 80%. This subsidiary manufactures and assembles prefabricated retail and light industrial buildings. Its contribution to turnover and operating profits is disclosed in the financial statements.

6

DELTO PLC

DIRECTORS' REPORT

REVIEW OF DEVELOPMENTS (continued)

Motor Products Division

This division is a major producer of accessories for the motor trade in the EU and in the USA, with manufacturing plants in the UK, Belgium and the USA producing a wide range of products for the car industry.

Total sales of the division showed only a slight increase on last year. The effects of the reorganisation programme, however, which has been implemented over the last three years, helped operating profits to improve by 6.1% from £1.8 million to £1.9 million.

Jewellery Division

The Jewellery Division manufactures costume jewellery which is sold to leading department stores and jewellery chains in the UK and the rest of Western Europe and also through the division's own retail outlets in the USA.

Sales and profits of this division exceeded all expectations, turnover increasing by 35.7% to £7.8 million from £5.7 million and operating profits by 69.9% to £0.6 million from £0.4 million. This success is attributed to our line of teenage trinkets introduced at the end of 1998/99, the full benefits of which are reflected in this year's results.

Financial position

Shareholders' funds were increased by £1.1 million to £14.9 million – the loss for the year was £0.02 million, other recognised gains were £1.0 million (net) and shares issued represented an increase in funds of £0.1 million. With working capital at £9.8 million the directors believe the group is soundly based to take advantage of opportunities for additional growth through further acquisition of companies in our core businesses.

DIVIDENDS

The final dividend recommended by the directors is 4.24p per ordinary share, which together with the interim dividend paid of 3p per ordinary share, gives a total dividend for the year of 7.24p compared with 7.0p last year.

RESEARCH AND DEVELOPMENT

The group continues an active programme of research and development, the costs of which in the year amounted to £150,000 (1999 – £140,000). We believe that the new line of shock-resistant bumpers introduced in 1999 will prove to be one of the main sources of turnover for the Motor Division in the coming year. Our increased order book, which is due mainly to this product, should be reflected in next year's results.

We attribute much of the success of our Jewellery Division to the constant review and updating of product lines to capitalise on the rapid changes in fashions.

IMPORTANT EVENT OCCURRING AFTER THE END OF YEAR

A fire destroyed production facilities in Meriden after the end of the year. The financial implications of this loss are disclosed in note 39 to the accounts.

FUTURE PROSPECTS

Your directors are optimistic about the long-term prospects for continued growth. The destruction of production facilities mentioned in the preceding paragraph, and in note 39 to the accounts, will significantly affect the completion of orders for bumpers in the first half of 2000/01. The replacement of these facilities in the third quarter should result in the resumption of sales with no permanent loss of business expected.

7

DELTO PLC

DIRECTORS' REPORT

YEAR 2000 ISSUES

While UITF 20 remains effective, entities should, in the directors' report, OFR (where prepared), or any equivalent statement, consider the potential impact and extent of the year 2000 problem on their business and operations and make the following disclosures:

(a) the risks and uncertainties associated with the year 2000 problem. If the entity has not made an assessment of this problem or has not determined its materiality, that fact.

(b) the entity's general plans to address the year 2000 issues relating to its business and operations and, if material, its relationships with customers, suppliers and other relevant parties.

(c) whether the total estimated costs of these plans, including amounts to be spent in future periods, have been quantified and, where applicable, an indication of the total costs likely to be incurred, with an explanation of the basis on which the figures are calculated (e.g., the treatment of internal costs and replacement expenditure).

Clearly, the disclosures should now be in the context of 31 December 1999 having passed. Entities would, typically, include details of the impact (and potential future impact), if any, the problem has had (may have) on their business, the costs incurred in addressing the problem to date and an indication of any further costs likely to be incurred. As the narrative will be specific to the business no example wording has been given here.

IMPACT OF CHANGEOVER TO THE EURO

Either in the directors' report, or in the OFR (where prepared), or any equivalent statement included in the annual report published by the entity, UITF 21 Accounting issues arising from the proposed introduction of the euro *recommends that where the potential impact is likely to be significant to the entity, information and discussion should be given, including an indication of the total costs likely to be incurred.*

As the narrative will be specific to the business no example wording has been given here.

DIRECTORS AND THEIR INTERESTS

The present membership of the Board is set out below. All directors served throughout the year. In accordance with the company's Articles of Association, Messrs Delto and Decker retire by rotation and, being eligible, offer themselves for re-election at the AGM. Details of directors' service contracts with the company are given in the Report of the Board to the Shareholders on Directors' Remuneration.

The directors' interests in the ordinary shares of the company at 31 March 2000 and at 1 April 1999:

	Beneficial holdings		Share options	
	2000	1999	2000	1999
	No.	*No.*	*No.*	*No.*
J Delto (Chairman)	235,000	235,000	–	–
M Driver (Chief Executive)	160,000	145,000	72,000	73,000
J Decker	28,350	15,000	46,020	52,600
A Carter	–	–	23,000	19,240
F Sharp (Non-executive)	–	–	–	–
A Blake (Non-executive)	–	–	–	–
A Worth (Non-executive)	–	–	–	–

Mr F Sharp also held at both dates a non-beneficial interest in 320,000 ordinary shares.

Further details relating to directors' share options, including options granted or exercised in the year, are given in note 6a to the accounts.

The directors had no interests in the company's loan stock or in the shares of its subsidiaries.

Model report and financial statements

8

DELTO PLC

DIRECTORS' REPORT

There have been no changes in directors' interests between the year end and 8 July 2000.

Except as stated in note 38, none of the directors had any interests in any material contract during the year relating to the business of the group.

(Note: Particulars of directors' holdings of shares and debentures may be disclosed in the notes to the accounts.)

SUBSTANTIAL INTERESTS

At 8 July 2000 the following interests in three per cent or more of the issued ordinary share capital had been notified to the company:

	Number of Ordinary shares
Shedwell & Barnes Life Assurance Company and its subsidiaries	700,000

DONATIONS

During the year the group made the following donations:

Political purposes – Conservative Party	£1,000
Charitable purposes	£3,500

EMPLOYEE INVOLVEMENT

Quarterly meetings are held with employee representatives to discuss sales, financial position and prospects. Opportunity is given at these meetings for senior executives to be questioned about matters which concern the employees.

A monthly magazine is distributed to all employees which includes articles on the group's performance and plans.

We encourage the involvement of employees in the performance of the company through the employee share scheme (note 26).

EMPLOYMENT OF DISABLED PERSONS

The company and its subsidiaries have continued the policy regarding the employment of disabled persons. Full and fair consideration is given to applications for employment made by disabled persons having regard to their particular aptitudes and abilities. During the year, 35 disabled persons were employed compared to 31 in the preceding year. Appropriate training is arranged for disabled persons, including retraining for alternative work of employees who become disabled, to promote their career development within the organisation.

1628

9

DELTO PLC

DIRECTORS' REPORT

SUPPLIER PAYMENT POLICY

It is group policy to agree and clearly communicate the terms of payment as part of the commercial arrangement negotiated with suppliers and then to pay according to those terms based upon the timely receipt of an accurate invoice. The company supports and the UK based businesses follow the CBI Prompt Payers Code. A copy of the code can be obtained from the CBI at Centre Point, 103 New Oxford Street, London, WC1A 1DU.

Delto Plc holds the investments in the group companies, does not trade itself and does not have suppliers within the meaning of the Companies Act 1985. However, the directors believe it would be helpful to give the disclosures on a group basis. Trade creditor days of the group for the year ended 31 March 2000 were 29.5 days, calculated in accordance with the requirements set down in the Companies Act 1985. This represents the ratio, expressed in days, between the amounts invoiced to the group by its suppliers in the year and the amounts due, at the year end, to trade creditors within one year.

AUDITORS

Lindsay & Robinson have expressed their willingness to continue in office as auditors and a resolution to reappoint them will be proposed at the forthcoming Annual General Meeting.

Approved by the Board of Directors
and signed on behalf of the Board

A Evans

Secretary 8 July 2000

10

CORPORATE GOVERNANCE

The Combined Code, as appended to the Listing Rules, was based on the report of the Hampel Committee. It sets out Principles of Good Corporate Governance and Code provisions which consolidate the work of the earlier Cadbury and Greenbury Committees. Section 1 of the Code is applicable to companies.

A narrative statement on how the company has applied the Principles and a statement explaining the extent to which the provisions in the Code have been complied with appear below.

NARRATIVE STATEMENT

The Code establishes 14 Principles of Good Governance which are split into the four areas described below.

Directors

The company is controlled through the Board of Directors which comprises four executive and three independent non-executive directors. As the Chairman is mainly responsible for the running of the Board, he has to ensure that all directors receive sufficient relevant information on financial, business and corporate issues prior to meetings. The Chief Executive's responsibilities focus on running the group's businesses and implementing group strategy. All directors are able to take independent professional advice in furtherance of their duties if necessary.

The Board has a formal schedule of matters reserved to it and meets monthly. It is responsible for overall group strategy, acquisition and divestment policy, approval of major capital expenditure projects and consideration of significant financing matters. It monitors the exposure to key business risks and reviews the strategic direction of individual trading subsidiaries, their codes of conduct, their annual budgets, their progress towards achievement of those budgets and their capital expenditure programmes. The Board also considers environmental and employee issues and key appointments. It also ensures that all directors receive appropriate training on appointment and then subsequently as appropriate. A budget is established for this purpose. All directors, in accordance with the Code, will submit themselves for re-election at least once every three years.

The Board has established a number of standing committees. Each committee operates within defined terms of reference. The principal committees are the Operations Committee, which operates as a general executive management committee, the Audit Committee, the Remuneration Committee and a Nominations Committee. Trading companies have separate boards of directors. The minutes of their meetings and of the standing committees are circulated to and reviewed by the Board of Directors.

Although the Board believes it is a 'small' Board in the context of the Code and therefore does not need to establish a Nominations Committee, it considers that such a Committee, which makes recommendations to the Board on all new board appointments, will reassure shareholders as to the suitability of chosen directors. Its members have agreed to meet at least once a year and will also advise on general Board composition.

11

CORPORATE GOVERNANCE

Those attending and the frequency of Board and Committee meetings during the year were as follows:

Board Meetings	12	**Nominations Committee**	1
J Delto (Chairman)		A Blake (chair)	
M Driver (Chief Executive)		F Sharp	
A Carter		A Worth	
A Blake (non-executive)			
J Decker		**Audit Committee**	4
F Sharp (non-executive)		A Blake (chair)	
A Worth (non-executive)		F Sharp	
		A Worth	
Operations Committee	6	**Remuneration Committee**	1
M Driver (chairman)		F Sharp (chairman)	
A Carter		A Blake	
J Decker		A Worth	

The Board of Directors considers that Mr Sharp and Mr Worth are independent of management and, in making this decision, have had regard to guidance issued by several of the company's largest institutional investors.

Directors' remuneration

The Remuneration Committee, under the chairmanship of Mr Sharp, measures the performance of the executive directors and key members of senior management as a prelude to recommending their annual remuneration, bonus awards and awards of share options to the Board for final determination. The group's Senior Human Resources Officer attends its meetings and serves as a technical adviser to the Committee, but is not actually a member. The remuneration of the non-executive directors is recommended by Mr Decker and Mr Driver and takes account of the time spent on Committee matters. The final determinations are made by the Board as a whole but no director plays a part in any discussion about his, or her, own remuneration. The Committee consults the Chairman and the Chief Executive about its proposals and has access to professional advice from inside and outside the company.

The Report of the Board to the Shareholders on Directors' Remuneration is set out on pages 14 and 15 and includes details of directors' incentive payments and the related performance criteria.

Relations with shareholders

The company encourages two way communication with both its institutional and private investors and responds quickly to all queries received. The Chief Executive and the Finance Director attended 24 meetings with analysts and institutional shareholders in the year ended 31 March 2000. All shareholders have at least twenty working days' notice of the Annual General Meeting at which all directors and Committee chairs are introduced and available for questions.

12

CORPORATE GOVERNANCE

Accountability and audit

Financial reporting

Detailed reviews of the performance and financial position of every product line are included in the Operating and Financial Review (*not included in this illustrative report*). The Board uses this, together with the Chairman's statement (*not included in this illustrative report*) and the Directors' Report on pages 5 - 9, to present a balanced and understandable assessment of the company's position and prospects. The directors' responsibility for the financial statements is described on page 17.

Internal control

The group has adopted the transitional approach to the internal control aspects of the Combined Code as set out in the letter from the London Stock Exchange to listed companies dated 27 September 1999 and reports as follows:

Wider aspects of internal control

The board confirms that it has established the procedures necessary to implement the guidance 'Internal Control: Guidance for Directors on the Combined Code'[1]./The board expects to have the procedures in place in August 2000 necessary to implement the guidance 'Internal Control: Guidance for Directors on the Combined Code'. This takes account of the time that needs to be taken to put in place the procedures which the board has agreed should be established. These include holding a risk management workshop, attended by all board members, together with prioritising change issues, the group's objectives and risks, and determining a control strategy for each of the significant risks. Where appropriate, actions are agreed to improve the management of these risks. A risk management policy document is also being sent to all employees setting out the board's attitude to risk to the achievement of the business objectives. The monthly management information is also being improved with the addition of some key risk indicators.[2,3]

The board has changed its meeting calendar and agenda so that risk management and internal control will be considered on a regular basis during the year and there will be a full risk and control assessment before reporting on the year ending 31 March 2001.[4]

Internal financial control

The directors are responsible for the group's system of internal financial control. Such a system can provide only reasonable but not absolute assurance against material misstatement or loss. The key control procedures are described under the following five headings:

- **Financial information**

  The group has a comprehensive system for reporting financial results to the Board; each operating unit prepares monthly results with a comparison against budget. The Board reviews these for the group as a whole and determines appropriate action.

- **Quality and integrity of personnel**

  The group's policies are detailed in the 'Corporate Policy Manual', to which all operating units are required to adhere.

- **Operating unit controls**

  Key controls over major business risks include reviews against performance indicators and exception reporting. The operating units make regular assessments of their exposure to major business risks and the extent to which these risks are controlled, which are considered during internal audit visits.

- **Computer systems**

  The group has established controls and procedures over the security of data held on computer systems and put in place comprehensive disaster recovery arrangements. These arrangements are tested regularly and reviewed by the group's internal audit department.

- **Controls over central functions**

  A number of the group's key functions, including treasury and taxation, are dealt with centrally. Each of

13

CORPORATE GOVERNANCE

these functions has detailed procedures manuals and is required to report to the Board on a monthly basis. These central functions are also subject to self-assessment and visits by the group's internal auditors.

The Board has conducted a review of the effectiveness of the system of internal financial control for the year ended 31 March 2000 and has taken account of material developments which have taken place since the year end. The review was performed on the basis of the criteria set out in the Guidance for Directors 'Internal Control and Financial Reporting' issued in December 1994.[5,6]

Audit Committee and auditors

The Audit Committee, comprising the non-executive directors, has specific terms of reference which deal with its authority and duties. It meets four times a year with the external auditors attending by invitation. The Committee receives and considers reports relating to the monitoring of the adequacy of the group's internal controls, the suitability of its accounting policies and financial reporting, the audit arrangements and matters arising from the external auditors' work. It makes recommendations to the Board on these matters and also regarding the scope, authority and resources of the internal audit function. The chairman of the Audit Committee makes a report to the Board following each committee meeting.

Going concern basis

After making enquiries, the directors have formed a judgement, at the time of approving the financial statements, that there is a reasonable expectation that the group has adequate resources to continue in operational existence for the foreseeable future. For this reason the directors continue to adopt the going concern basis in preparing the financial statements. This statement also forms part of the Operating and Financial Review (*not included in this illustrative report*).

COMPLIANCE STATEMENT

The Listing Rules require the Board to report on compliance with the forty-five Code provisions throughout the accounting period. Save for the exceptions outlined below, the company has complied throughout the accounting period ended 31 March 2000 with the provisions set out in Section 1 of the Code. The exceptions to the Code and the resulting changes to the company's corporate governance procedures to comply with specified code provisions were as follows:

A.2.1   No senior independent non-executive director has been formally appointed as the Board believes that, given the current structure and existing independent directors, appointing a senior independent director is not necessary or appropriate at the current time. This will be monitored and if circumstances change such that the Board feels it appropriate to appoint a senior independent director, it will do so in the future.

B.1.7   Executive directors' contract periods have been set at two years (once existing three year contracts have expired), not the required one year. The Board considers that this is appropriate given their seniority and value to the company.

B.2.2   The Remuneration Committee comprises the three non-executive directors. Only two of these directors are deemed to be independent, not all three as required by the Code. This is due to Mrs Blake, a non-executive on the Remuneration Committee, being the sister-in-law of the Chief Executive and hence not meeting the requirement to be free from other relationships which could materially interfere with the exercise of independent judgement.

[1] This assumes that the company has not been able to comply in full with the Turnbull disclosure regime for the accounting period ending on or after 23 December 1999, but has been able to put in place procedures necessary to implement the guidance.

[2] This assumes that the company is still putting in place its procedures. The explanation is intended to provide meaningful, high-level information which does not give a misleading impression.

[3] Where there is no internal audit function it may be useful to state the following (although it is not mandatory to do so): 'The board has considered the need for internal audit, but has decided that because of the size of the company it cannot be justified at present. The board will review this decision next year.' However, a company would be required to disclose if it did not have an internal audit function and had not reviewed the need for one.

[4] This disclosure is not required but directors may decide that it is useful to refer to the review process for reporting on the next year.

[5] The Rutteman internal financial control disclosures are required on the basis that the company is not yet in full compliance with the Turnbull disclosure regime.

[6] It should be borne in mind that the internal control statement will be subject to review by the external auditor.

14

REPORT OF THE BOARD TO THE SHAREHOLDERS ON DIRECTORS' REMUNERATION

Remuneration Committee

The Committee consists solely of three non-executive directors: Messrs Sharp and Worth and Mrs Blake, under the chairmanship of Mr Sharp. None of the committee has any personal financial interests (other than as shareholders), conflicts of interests arising from cross-directorships or day-to-day involvement in running the business. The Committee consults the Chairman and the Chief Executive about its proposals and has access to professional advice from inside and outside the company. The Committee makes recommendations to the Board. No director plays a part in any discussion about his or her own remuneration.

Remuneration policy

Executive remuneration packages are prudently designed to attract, motivate and retain directors of the high calibre needed to maintain the company's position as a market leader and to reward them for enhancing value to shareholders. The performance measurement of the executive directors and key members of senior management and the determination of their annual remuneration package is undertaken by the Committee. The remuneration of the non-executive directors is determined by the Board within the limits set out in the Articles of Association.

There are four main elements of the remuneration package for executive directors and senior management:

(a)   basic annual salary (including directors' fees) and benefits;

(b)   annual bonus payments which cannot exceed 40% of basic salary;

(c)   share option incentives; and

(d)   pension arrangements.

Executive directors are entitled to accept appointments outside the company providing the Chairman's permission is sought and fees in excess of £20,000 from all such appointments are accounted for to the company.

Basic salary

An executive director's basic salary is determined by the Remuneration Committee at the beginning of each year and when an individual changes position or responsibility. In deciding appropriate levels the Committee considers the group as a whole and relies on objective research which gives up-to-date information on a comparator group of companies which comprises the top ten companies by capitalisation within the sector. Basic salaries were reviewed in February 1999 with increases taking effect from 1 April 1999. They were again reviewed in February 2000 and increased by 2% from 1 April 2000. Executive directors' contracts of service which include details of remuneration will be available for inspection at the Annual General Meeting.

Annual bonus payments

The Committee establishes the objectives that must be met for each financial year if a cash bonus is to be paid. In setting appropriate bonus parameters the Committee refers to the objective research on comparator groups of companies as noted above. The Committee believes that any incentive compensation awarded should be tied to the interests of the company's shareholders and that the principal measure of those interests is total shareholder return. Account is also taken of the relative success of the different parts of the business for which the executive directors are responsible and the extent to which the strategic objectives set by the Board are being met. The maximum performance related bonus that can be paid is 40% of basic annual salary. Incentive payments for the year ended 31 March 2000 varied between 22% and 26%. This reflects the improvement of the company from being eighth to fifth within its sector in terms of capitalisation. The strategic objectives, control system and indicators are also aligned to total shareholder return.

Share options

The Board, acting on the recommendations of the Remuneration Committee, proposes a new share option scheme (the 2000 Restricted Share Scheme), full details of which are given in the Annual General Meeting document and for which the approval of the shareholders will be sought. The reason for the change is to incentivise the executive directors and to enable them to benefit in the increased market capitalisation of the company. The Remuneration Committee will have responsibility for supervising the new Scheme and the grant of options under its terms.

DELTO PLC

REPORT OF THE BOARD TO THE SHAREHOLDERS ON DIRECTORS' REMUNERATION

The performance criterion that must be met requires the company's share price to outperform the FTSE All Share Index over a period of three years or more from the date the option was granted. To avoid an option becoming exercisable through a sudden price fluctuation the test must also be met for six successive months at the end of the period. Thereafter the option may be exercised for the rest of its ten year life without further test. Executive directors' existing share options were granted under the terms of the 1992 Employee Share Option Scheme which is open to all employees with more than three years' service. Under that scheme options are allocated to qualifying employees by reference to profit for the year and basic salary. The exercise of options granted under the 1992 scheme is not dependent upon performance criteria. Following the approval and implementation of the 2000 Restricted Share Scheme, the executive directors will cease to be eligible to acquire new options under the 1992 Employee Share Option Scheme. No option is offered at a discount.

The Committee has minuted a decision that, given the company's circumstances, the members in Annual General Meeting need not be invited to approve other aspects of the remuneration policy set out in this report. The Chairman of the Committee will, however, be available to answer questions on any aspect of the remuneration policy at the Annual General Meeting.

Directors' pension arrangements

Executive directors are members of the company pension scheme. Their dependants are eligible for dependants' pensions and the payment of a lump sum in the event of death in service. The pension arrangements provide for a pension on retirement of 2/3 basic annual salary after 30 years' eligible service. No other payments to directors are pensionable. To the extent that a director's benefits from the company scheme are restricted by Inland Revenue limits, payments are made to a funded unapproved retirement benefit scheme. The pension costs of directors are charged in the profit and loss account over their estimated service lives based upon actuarial advice. The changes in pension entitlements arising in the financial year, required to be disclosed by the UK Listing Authority, are given in note 6a to the accounts. There have been no changes in the terms of directors' pension entitlements during the year. There are no unfunded pension promises or similar arrangements for directors.

Directors' contracts

All directors have three-year service contracts. However, in the Board Meeting on 27 November 1999 it was decided to set directors' contract periods at two years. All existing directors remain on their current contract terms until the current contract expires. If re-elected they will move to a two year contract. The company may have a contractual obligation to pay compensation for the unexpired portion of a director's contract, if it is terminated early. No other payments are made for compensation for loss of office. Messrs Delto and Decker are due to retire by rotation and offer themselves for re-election.

Non-executive directors

All non-executive directors have specific terms of engagement and their remuneration is determined by the Board within the limits set out in the Articles of Association and based upon independent surveys of fees paid to non-executive directors of similar companies. The fee paid to each non-executive director in the year was £18,000. The non-executives receive a further fee of £5,000 for additional work performed for the company in respect of time spent working on Remuneration and Audit Committees. Non-executive directors cannot participate in any of the company's share option schemes. Non-executive directors are not eligible to join the company's pension scheme.

Details of directors' remuneration and share options

This report should be read in conjunction with note 6a to the accounts which also constitutes part of this report giving full details of the amounts in the remuneration package of each director and details of each director's share options.

By order of the Board

A Evans

Company Secretary

8 July 2000

If the detailed remuneration disclosures (included in note 6 to the accounts in this example) are included within the remuneration report, they should be specifically included in the scope of the auditors' opinion or there should be an unambiguous cross-reference indicating that they form part of the audited financial statements.

16

STATEMENT OF DIRECTORS' RESPONSIBILITIES

Company law requires the directors to prepare financial statements for each financial year which give a true and fair view of the state of affairs of the company and the group as at the end of the financial year and of the profit or loss of the group for that period. In preparing those financial statements, the directors are required to:

- select suitable accounting policies and then apply them consistently;

- make judgements and estimates that are reasonable and prudent; and

- state whether applicable accounting standards have been followed, subject to any material departures disclosed and explained in the financial statements.

The directors are responsible for keeping proper accounting records which disclose with reasonable accuracy at any time the financial position of the company and to enable them to ensure that the financial statements comply with the Companies Act 1985. They are also responsible for the group's system of internal financial control, for safeguarding the assets of the group and hence for taking reasonable steps for the prevention and detection of fraud and other irregularities.

By order of the Board

A. Evans, Secretary

8 July 2000

No reference is made to the going concern basis here, due to the inclusion of a going concern report by the directors (in the corporate governance statement).

DELTO PLC

AUDITORS' REPORT TO THE MEMBERS OF DELTO PLC

We have audited the financial statements on pages 18 to 59 which have been prepared under the accounting policies set out on pages 26 to 28.

Respective responsibilities of directors and auditors

The directors are responsible for preparing the Annual Report, including as described on page 16 the preparation of the financial statements, which are required to be prepared in accordance with applicable United Kingdom law and accounting standards. Our responsibilities, as independent auditors, are established by statute, the Auditing Practices Board, the UK Listing Authority and by our profession's ethical guidance.

We report to you our opinion as to whether the financial statements give a true and fair view and are properly prepared in accordance with the Companies Act 1985. We also report to you if, in our opinion, the directors' report is not consistent with the financial statements, if the company has not kept proper accounting records, if we have not received all the information and explanations we require for our audit, or if information specified by law or the Listing Rules regarding directors' remuneration and transactions with the company and other members of the group is not disclosed.

We review whether the corporate governance statement on page 13 reflects the company's compliance with the seven provisions of the Combined Code specified for our review by the UK Listing Authority, and we report if it does not. We are not required to consider whether the board's statements on internal control cover all risks and controls, or form an opinion on the effectiveness of the group's corporate governance procedures or its risk and control procedures.

We read the other information contained in the Annual Report, including the corporate governance statement, and consider whether it is consistent with the audited financial statements. We consider the implications for our report if we become aware of any apparent misstatements or material inconsistencies with the financial statements.

Basis of audit opinion

We conducted our audit in accordance with United Kingdom auditing standards issued by the Auditing Practices Board. An audit includes examination, on a test basis, of evidence relevant to the amounts and disclosures in the financial statements. It also includes an assessment of the significant estimates and judgements made by the directors in the preparation of the financial statements, and of whether the accounting policies are appropriate to the circumstances of the company and the group, consistently applied and adequately disclosed.

We planned and performed our audit so as to obtain all the information and explanations which we considered necessary in order to provide us with sufficient evidence to give reasonable assurance that the financial statements are free from material misstatement, whether caused by fraud or other irregularity or error. In forming our opinion we also evaluated the overall adequacy of the presentation of information in the financial statements.

Opinion

In our opinion the financial statements give a true and fair view of the state of affairs of the company and the group as at 31 March 2000 and of the profit of the group for the year then ended and have been properly prepared in accordance with the Companies Act 1985.

Lindsay & Robinson (*signature and name*)   Swift House
Chartered Accountants and Registered Auditors   Cheapside
8 July 2000   London, EC2V 5TH

18

DELTO PLC

CONSOLIDATED PROFIT AND LOSS ACCOUNT
Year ended 31 March 2000

	Note	2000 £'000	2000 £'000	1999 £'000
TURNOVER				
Continuing operations		41,088		38,592
Acquisitions		820		
		41,908		
Discontinued operations		288		10,648
Total turnover	3,4		42,196	49,240
Cost of sales	4		(29,390)	(37,824)
Gross profit			12,806	11,416
Net operating expenses	4		(10,238)	(9,285)
OPERATING PROFIT				
Continuing operations		2,516		2,147
Acquisitions		52		
		2,568		
Discontinued operations		(2)		(26)
less utilisation of prior year provisions		2		10
Group operating profit	3,4,5		2,568	2,131
Share of operating profit of associates			66	110
Total operating profit			2,634	2,241
Profit on sale of fixed assets in continuing operations			202	216
Provision for loss on operations to be discontinued			–	(12)
Loss on disposal of discontinued operations	2		(18)	(96)
less utilisation of prior year provisions			10	54
PROFIT ON ORDINARY ACTIVITIES BEFORE INTEREST			2,828	2,403
Investment income	7		310	428
Amounts written off investments			–	(80)
Interest payable and similar charges	8		(1,314)	(1,130)
PROFIT ON ORDINARY ACTIVITIES BEFORE TAXATION			1,824	1,621
Tax on profit on ordinary activities	9		(874)	(730)
PROFIT ON ORDINARY ACTIVITIES AFTER TAXATION			950	891
Equity minority interests			(96)	(52)
Non-equity minority interest			(24)	(24)
PROFIT FOR THE FINANCIAL YEAR			830	815
Dividends paid and proposed – including amounts in respect of non-equity shares	11		(851)	(818)
Loss for the financial year			(21)	(3)
Basic earnings per ordinary share	12		7.10p	7.20p
Diluted earnings per ordinary share	12		7.09p	7.20p

19

DELTO PLC

CONSOLIDATED PROFIT AND LOSS ACCOUNT

STATEMENTS OF MOVEMENTS ON RESERVES

	Share premium account £'000	Revalua- tion reserve £'000	Foreign exchange translation £'000	Profit and loss account £'000	Total £'000
THE GROUP					
Balance at 1 April 1999	1,230	1,200	1,112	7,627	11,169
Loss for the year	–	–	–	(21)	(21)
Goodwill transferred to the profit and loss account in respect of disposal of business	–	–	–	10	10
Foreign exchange differences on the translation of net equity investments in foreign enterprises	–	–	288	–	288
Foreign exchange differences on borrowings hedging net equity investments in foreign enterprises	–	–	(84)	–	(84)
Transfer of amount equivalent to additional depreciation on revalued assets	–	(60)	–	60	–
Transfer of realised revaluation reserve	–	(123)	–	123	–
Surplus on revaluation of fixed assets	–	800	–	–	800
Scrip dividend	11	–	–	–	11
Shares issued	78	–	–	–	78
Balance at 31 March 2000	1,319	1,817	1,316	7,799	12,251
THE COMPANY					
Balance at 1 April 1999	1,230	–	–	3,322	4,552
Loss for the year	–	–	–	(747)	(747)
Scrip dividend	11	–	–	–	11
Shares issued	78	–	–	–	78
Balance at 31 March 2000	1,319	–	–	2,575	3,894

20

DELTO PLC

CONSOLIDATED BALANCE SHEET
31 March 2000

	Note	2000 £'000	1999 £'000
FIXED ASSETS			
Intangible assets	13	2,431	2,543
Tangible assets	14	13,250	12,464
Investments	15	749	652
		16,430	15,659
CURRENT ASSETS			
Stocks	16	8,904	9,188
Pension fund asset due beyond one year	37	1,140	1,264
Debtors	17	7,832	7,694
Investments	18	2,608	658
Cash at bank and in hand		600	1,874
		21,084	20,678
CREDITORS: amounts falling due within one year	19	(11,329)	(11,129)
NET CURRENT ASSETS		9,755	9,549
TOTAL ASSETS LESS CURRENT LIABILITIES		26,185	25,208
CREDITORS: amounts falling due after more than one year			
Redeemable convertible preference shares in			
Deltoled Finance NV	21	(2,316)	(2,198)
Other creditors	20	(5,413)	(5,249)
PROVISIONS FOR LIABILITIES AND CHARGES	24	(2,628)	(3,142)
MINORITY INTERESTS			
Equity minority interests		(766)	(662)
Non-equity minority interests	25	(200)	(200)
NET ASSETS		14,862	13,757
CAPITAL AND RESERVES			
Called up share capital	26	2,611	2,588
Share premium account		1,319	1,230
Revaluation reserve		1,817	1,200
Other reserves		1,316	1,112
Profit and loss account		7,799	7,627
SHAREHOLDERS' FUNDS		14,862	13,757
Attributable to equity shareholders		14,570	13,465
Attributable to non-equity shareholders		292	292

These financial statements were approved by the Board of Directors on 8 July 2000.
Signed on behalf of the Board of Directors.

J Delto–Director

21

DELTO PLC

BALANCE SHEET
31 March 2000

	Note	2000 £'000	1999 £'000
FIXED ASSETS			
Investments	15	10,676	13,222
CURRENT ASSETS			
Debtors	17	218	42
Cash at bank and in hand		230	136
		448	178
CREDITORS: amounts falling due within one year	19	(1,727)	(1,362)
NET CURRENT LIABILITIES		(1,279)	(1,184)
TOTAL ASSETS LESS CURRENT LIABILITIES		9,397	12,038
CREDITORS: amounts falling due after more than one year	20	(2,892)	(4,898)
NET ASSETS		6,505	7,140
CAPITAL AND RESERVES			
Called up share capital	26	2,611	2,588
Share premium account		1,319	1,230
Profit and loss account		2,575	3,322
SHAREHOLDERS' FUNDS		6,505	7,140
Attributable to equity shareholders		6,213	6,848
Attributable to non-equity shareholders		292	292

These financial statements were approved by the Board of Directors on 8 July 2000.
Signed on behalf of the Board of Directors.

J Delto
Director

22

DELTO PLC

CONSOLIDATED CASH FLOW STATEMENT
Year ended 31 March 2000

	Note	2000 £'000	1999 £'000
Net cash inflow from operating activities	27	3,848	3,216
Dividends received from associates		20	20
Returns on investments and servicing of finance	28	(963)	(700)
Taxation	28	(930)	(906)
Capital expenditure and financial investment	28	(749)	(494)
Acquisitions and disposals	28	76	(2,424)
Equity dividends paid		(806)	(750)
Cash inflow/(outflow) before use of liquid resources and financing		496	(2,038)
Management of liquid resources	28	(1,950)	96
Financing	28	1,240	(256)
Decrease in cash in the period		(214)	(2,198)

Reconciliation of net cash flow to movement in net debt (Note 29)

	Note	2000 £'000	2000 £'000	1999 £'000	1999 £'000
Decrease in cash in the period		(214)		(2,198)	
Cash (inflow)/outflow from (increase)/ decrease in debt and lease financing		(1,060)		398	
Cash outflow/(inflow) from increase/ (decrease) in liquid resources		1,950		(96)	
Change in net debt resulting from cash flows			676		(1,896)
Loans and finance leases acquired with subsidiary			(14)		(1,286)
Loans and finance leases disposed with subsidiary			12		10
New finance leases			(116)		(100)
Redemption premium on convertible preference shares			(118)		(104)
Translation difference			(258)		(197)
			182		(3,573)
Net debt at 1 April			(7,150)		(3,577)
Net debt at 31 March			(6,968)		(7,150)

23

DELTO PLC

STATEMENT OF TOTAL RECOGNISED GAINS AND LOSSES
Year ended 31 March 2000

	2000 £'000	1999 £'000
Profit for the financial year	830	815
Surplus arising on revaluation of fixed assets	800	–
Currency translation differences on foreign currency net investments	204	(308)
Total recognised gains and losses relating to the year	1,834	507

24

NOTE OF HISTORICAL COST PROFITS AND LOSSES
Year ended 31 March 2000

	2000 £'000	1999 £'000
Profit on ordinary activities before taxation	1,824	1,621
Realisation of property valuation gains of prior years	123	–
Difference between the historical cost depreciation charge and the actual depreciation charge for the year calculated on the revalued amount	60	60
Historical cost profit on ordinary activities before taxation	2,007	1,681
Historical cost profit for the year retained after taxation, minority interests and dividends	162	57

DELTO PLC

**RECONCILIATION OF MOVEMENT IN CONSOLIDATED SHAREHOLDERS'
FUNDS**
Year ended 31 March 2000

	2000 £'000	1999 £'000
Profit for the financial year	830	815
Dividends	(851)	(818)
	(21)	(3)
Other recognised gains and losses relating to the year	1,004	(308)
Issue of shares	112	1,396
Goodwill transferred to profit and loss account in respect of the disposal of a business	10	97
Net addition to shareholders' funds	1,105	1,182
Opening shareholders' funds	13,757	12,575
Closing shareholders' funds	14,862	13,757

26

NOTES TO THE ACCOUNTS
Year ended 31 March 2000

1. **ACCOUNTING POLICIES**

The financial statements are prepared in accordance with applicable accounting standards. The particular accounting policies adopted by the directors are described below.

Accounting convention

The financial statements are prepared under the historical cost convention as modified by the revaluation of freehold properties.

Basis of consolidation

The consolidated financial statements incorporate the financial statements of the company and all its subsidiaries.

Acquisitions and disposals

On the acquisition of a business, including an interest in an associated undertaking, fair values are attributed to the group's share of net separable assets. Where the cost of acquisition exceeds the fair values attributable to such net assets, the difference is treated as purchased goodwill and capitalised in the balance sheet in the year of acquisition. Prior to the implementation of FRS 10 (in the year ended 31 March 1999), purchased goodwill was written off directly to reserves and has not been reinstated.

The profit or loss on the disposal or closure of a previously acquired business includes the attributable amount of any purchased goodwill relating to that business not previously charged through the profit and loss account.

The results and cash flows relating to a business are included in the consolidated profit and loss account and the consolidated cash flow statement from the date of acquisition or up to the date of disposal.

Goodwill and Intangible fixed assets

For acquisitions of a business, including an interest in an associated undertaking purchased goodwill is capitalised in the year in which it arises and amortised over its estimated useful life up to a maximum of 20 years with a full year's charge for amortisation in the year of acquisition. The directors regard 20 years as a reasonable maximum for the estimated useful life of goodwill since it is difficult to make projections exceeding this period.

Capitalised purchased goodwill in respect of subsidiaries is included within intangible fixed assets. Capitalised purchased goodwill relating to associates is included within the carrying value of the associate.

Goodwill which arose on the acquisition of a business, including an interest in an associated undertaking, prior to the implementation of FRS 10 which was written off to the profit and loss reserve as a matter of accounting policy, remains eliminated in that reserve and will be charged or credited in the profit and loss account as appropriate on the subsequent disposal of the business to which it relates.

Patents and trademarks are valued at cost on acquisition and are depreciated in equal annual amounts over their estimated useful economic lives (5–20 years).

Tangible fixed assets

Depreciation is not provided on freehold land. On other assets it is provided to write off the cost or revalued amounts less estimated residual value (based on prices prevailing at the date of acquisition or revaluation) in equal annual instalments over the estimated useful economic lives of the assets. The estimated useful economic lives are as follows:

Land and buildings

Freehold buildings and long leasehold land and buildings	50 years
Short leasehold property	Period of lease

DELTO PLC

NOTES TO THE ACCOUNTS
Year ended 31 March 2000

1. **ACCOUNTING POLICIES (continued)**

   Plant and machinery

Leased assets	The shorter of the term of the lease and the useful economic life of the asset
Plant and machinery	4–20 years
Electronic equipment	5 years
Motor vehicles	5 years
Fixtures, fittings, tools and equipment	3–10 years

The company capitalises directly attributable interest on all tangible fixed assets in the course of construction. Rates of capitalisation depend on whether a specific loan has been taken out (when the actual interest rate and interest paid are used), or whether the construction has been financed by general borrowings (when a weighted average rate is calculated on all non-specific borrowings). The rates used for capitalisation purposes in the year are as follows:

For the office building construction	actual rate of 7.5%
For the factory construction	weighted average rate of 8.1%

Investments

Except as stated below, investments held as fixed assets are stated at cost less provision for any impairment.

In the consolidated accounts, shares in associated undertakings are accounted for using the equity method. The consolidated profit and loss account includes the group's share of the pre-tax profits and attributable taxation of the associated undertakings based on audited financial statements for the financial year. In the consolidated balance sheet, the investment in associated undertakings is shown at the group's share of the net assets of the associated undertakings. Goodwill arising on the acquisition of an associate is capitalised as part of the carrying amount in the consolidated balance sheet and amortised over its estimated useful life. Prior to the implementation of FRSs 9 and 10, such goodwill was written off to reserves as a matter of accounting policy. (See note above on Goodwill and Intangible fixed assets.)

Stocks

Stocks and work in progress, other than long-term contracts, are stated at the lower of cost and net realisable value. Cost comprises materials, direct labour and a share of production overheads appropriate to the relevant stage of production. Net realisable value is based on estimated selling price less all further costs to completion and all relevant marketing, selling and distribution costs.

Long-term contracts

Long-term contract balances represent costs incurred on specific contracts, net of amounts transferred to cost of sales in respect of work recorded as turnover, less foreseeable losses and payments on account not matched with turnover. Contract work in progress is recorded as turnover on the following bases: on contracts which provide for delivery of own manufactured units or components, turnover is recorded when deliveries are made to customers; on other contracts and in respect of the installation phase of delivery type contracts, turnover is determined by reference to the value of work carried out to date. No profit is recognised until the contract has advanced to a stage (normally when work exceeds 25 per cent. completion) where the total profit can be assessed with reasonable certainty. Provision is made for the full amount of foreseeable losses on contracts. Income arising from settlement of contract claims is recorded when final negotiations have been completed and the amount of the settlement is considered to be collectible.

Deferred taxation

Deferred taxation is provided in full on timing differences relating to pension and other post retirement benefits calculated at the rates at which it is expected that tax will arise. Deferred taxation is provided on other timing differences, arising from the different treatment of items for accounting and taxation

28

NOTES TO THE ACCOUNTS
Year ended 31 March 2000

1.   **ACCOUNTING POLICIES (continued)**

urposes, which are expected to reverse in the future without replacement, calculated at the rates at which it is expected that tax will arise.

Foreign exchange

Transactions denominated in foreign currencies are translated into the functional currency at the rates ruling at the dates of the transactions. Monetary assets and liabilities denominated in foreign currencies at the balance sheet date are retranslated at the rates ruling at that date. These translation differences are dealt with in the profit and loss account.

The financial statements of foreign subsidiaries are translated into sterling at the closing rates of exchange and the differences arising from the translation of the opening net investment in subsidiaries at the closing rate and matched long-term foreign currency borrowings are taken direct to reserves.

Leases

Assets held under finance leases and hire purchase contracts are capitalised at their fair value on the inception of the leases and depreciated over the shorter of the period of the lease and the estimated useful economic lives of the assets. The finance charges are allocated over the period of the lease in proportion to the capital amount outstanding and are charged to the profit and loss account.

Operating lease rentals are charged to profit and loss in equal annual amounts over the lease term.

Pension and other post retirement benefits

The expected costs of providing pensions and other post retirement benefits, as calculated periodically by professionally qualified actuaries, is charged to the profit and loss account so as to spread the cost over the service lives of employees in the schemes operated within the group in such a way that the pension cost is a substantially level percentage of current and expected future pensionable payroll.

Capital instruments

Capital instruments are accounted for and classified as equity or non-equity share capital, equity or non-equity minority interests and debt according to their form. Convertible debt is separately disclosed and regarded as debt unless conversion actually occurs. Provision is made for the accrued premium payable on redemption of redeemable debt or non-equity interests.

Research and Development

Research and development expenditure is charged to the profit and loss account as incurred.

Financial Instruments

Derivative instruments utilised by the group are interest rate swaps and forward exchange contracts. The group does not enter into speculative derivative contracts. All such instruments are used for hedging purposes to alter the risk profile of an existing underlying exposure of the group in line with the group's risk management policies. Amounts payable or receivable in respect of interest rate swaps are recognised as adjustments to interest expense over the period of the contracts.

Termination payments made or received are spread over the life of the underlying exposure in cases where the underlying exposure continues to exist. In other cases termination payments are taken to the profit and loss account.

Transactions denominated in foreign currencies are recorded at the rate ruling on the date of the transaction, unless matching forward foreign exchange contracts have been entered into, in which case the rate specified in the relevant contract is used. At the balance sheet date unhedged monetary assets and liabilities denominated in foreign currencies are translated at the rate of exchange ruling at that date.

DELTO PLC

NOTES TO THE ACCOUNTS
Year ended 31 March 2000

2. **ACQUISITIONS, DISPOSALS AND GOODWILL**

Acquisitions

A further 60% of the issued share capital of Shed Technology Limited was acquired on 30 September 1999 for a consideration of £208,000 increasing the group's interest to 80%. This acquisition has been accounted for using the acquisition method of accounting. The amount of goodwill arising as a result of the acquisition is £64,000. This has been capitalised on the group balance sheet. The consideration included £70,000 payable on 30 September 2002 contingent upon the two directors of Shed Technology (Mr Shadwell and Mr Heathcote) remaining with the company until that date. Operating profits were charged with £46,000 in respect of a provision for costs expected to be incurred in respect of restructuring, reorganising and integrating Shed Technology Limited. Of this amount £24,000 was utilised in the period.

The profits after taxation of Shed Technology Limited, and the amount attributable to the minority interest, were as follows:

	Profit after tax and minority interest £'000
Results prior to acquisition	
1 April 1999 to the date of acquisition	50
Preceding financial year ended 31 March 1999	100

The following table summarises the adjustments made to the book value of the major category of assets and liabilities acquired to arrive at the fair values included in the consolidated financial statements at the date of acquisition. The cash flow effects of the acquisition are given in note 32.

	Book amount £'000	Revalua- tion £'000	Alignment of accounting policies £'000	Fair value to the group £'000
Tangible fixed assets	55	14	(2)	67
Investments	20	–	–	20
Current assets	182	(16)	(8)	158
Creditors and provisions	(82)	(5)	(10)	(97)
Taxation	(2)	42	12	52
	173	35	(8)	200
Minority interests				(40)
				160
Goodwill				64
				224

30

NOTES TO THE ACCOUNTS
Year ended 31 March 2000

2.   ACQUISITIONS, DISPOSALS AND GOODWILL (continued)

	£'000
Consideration	
Cash	138
Deferred	70
Cost of existing 20% investment transferred from fixed asset investments	16
	224

Disposals

The disposal of the group's housewares operations was completed when Plastic Manufacturing Company Limited was sold on 5 May 1999. The loss on disposal, which was determined including attributable goodwill, was £18,000 of which £10,000 was provided in 1998/99. The results of the company have been shown under discontinued operations. The cash effects of the disposal are given in note 33.

Goodwill

Goodwill capitalised in the current financial year under the accounting policy stated in note 1 amounted to £64,000 (1999 – £2,466,000) in respect of the acquisition of Shed Technology Limited. Goodwill of £10,000 (1999 – £97,000) attributable to Plastic Manufacturing Company Limited was taken into account in calculating the loss on the disposal of that company. The cumulative amount of goodwill charged to reserves as a matter of accounting policy prior to the implementation of FRS 10 is £1,206,000 (1999 – £1,216,000), net of amounts attributable to companies sold. This includes £15,000 (1999 – £15,000) relating to associates (see note 15).

3.   ANALYSES OF TURNOVER, OPERATING PROFIT AND NET ASSETS

Analyses by class of business of turnover, operating profit and net assets are stated below:

	Turnover		Operating profit		Net assets	
	2000 £'000	1999 £'000	2000 £'000	1999 £'000	2000 £'000	1999 £'000
Class of business						
Continuing operations:						
Motor products	33,322	32,868	1,884	1,775	12,869	12,689
Jewellery	7,766	5,724	632	372	8,968	8,108
Construction – Acquisition	820	–	52	–	240	–
	41,908	38,592	2,568	2,147	22,077	20,797
Discontinued operations:						
Housewares	288	10,648	–	(16)	–	320
	42,196	49,240	2,568	2,131	22,077	21,117
Net borrowings					(6,968)	(7,150)
Other fixed asset investments					382	354
Associated undertakings					367	298
Minority interests					(996)	(862)
					14,862	13,757

DELTO PLC

NOTES TO THE ACCOUNTS
Year ended 31 March 2000

3. ANALYSES OF TURNOVER, OPERATING PROFIT AND NET ASSETS (continued)

	Turnover		Operating profit		Net assets	
	2000 **£'000**	**1999** **£'000**	**2000** **£'000**	**1999** **£'000**	**2000** **£'000**	**1999** **£'000**
Geographical analysis by location						
United Kingdom	20,990	29,228	1,026	887	11,313	12,019
Other European countries	8,426	8,150	588	522	3,896	3,452
North America	12,780	11,862	954	722	6,868	5,646
	42,196	49,240	2,568	2,131	22,077	21,117

	2000 **£'000**	**1999** **£'000**
Geographical analysis of turnover by destination		
United Kingdom	18,500	26,851
Other European countries	10,596	9,766
North America	13,100	12,623
	42,196	49,240

Items appearing in the consolidated profit and loss account below the operating profit line are not analysed by class of business or geographical segment.

4. ANALYSES OF CONTINUING AND DISCONTINUED OPERATIONS

	2000 **Continuing** **£'000**	**2000** **Dis-** **continued** **£'000**	**2000** **Total** **£'000**	**1999** **Continuing** **£'000**	**1999** **Dis-** **continued** **£'000**	**1999** **Total** **£'000**
Turnover	41,908	288	42,196	38,592	10,648	49,240
Cost of sales	29,158	232	29,390	27,370	10,454	37,824
Gross profit	12,750	56	12,806	11,222	194	11,416
Net operating expenses						
Distribution costs	7,092	30	7,122	6,374	134	6,508
Administrative expenses	3,266	28	3,294	3,007	76	3,083
Other operating income	(176)	(2)	(178)	(306)	–	(306)
	10,182	56	10,238	9,075	210	9,285
Operating profit	2,568	–	2,568	2,147	(16)	2,131

The total figures for continuing operations in 1999/2000 include the following amounts relating to acquisitions: turnover £820,000, cost of sales £592,000, gross profit £228,000, net operating expenses £176,000 (namely distribution costs £118,000 and administrative expenses £58,000) and operating profit £52,000.

32

NOTES TO THE ACCOUNTS
Year ended 31 March 2000

5.   OPERATING PROFIT

	2000 £'000	1999 £'000
Operating profit is after charging:		
Depreciation and other amounts written off tangible and intangible fixed assets:		
Owned assets	1,144	1,034
Leased assets	178	174
Goodwill amortisation	126	123
Rentals under operating leases		
Hire of plant and machinery	160	214
Other operating leases	384	334
Research and development	150	140
Exceptional software modification costs in respect of the year 2000	40	20
Exceptional expenditure incurred in preparing for the changeover to the euro	35	15
Auditors' remuneration		
– Group audit fees	70	70
– Company audit fees	4	3
– Other services – UK	20	8
– Overseas	6	6

6.   INFORMATION REGARDING DIRECTORS AND EMPLOYEES

6(a)   DIRECTORS REMUNERATION

	Fees £'000 2000	Basic salaries £'000 2000	Annual bonuses £'000 2000	Benefits in kind £'000 2000	Total £'000 2000	Total £'000 1999
Executive Directors						
J Delto	25	113	25	–	163	148
M Driver	25	98	25	75	223	210
J Decker	25	96	23	–	144	131
A Carter	25	107	24	–	156	138
Non-executive Directors						
F Sharp	23	–	–	–	23	22
A Blake	23	–	–	–	23	22
A Worth	23	–	–	–	23	22
Total	169	414	97	75	755	693

The executive directors are paid basic salaries and can also earn an annual incentive payment based on increases in total shareholder return and the relative success of the different parts of the business for which the executive directors are responsible. These payments are restricted to 40% of basic salary.

DELTO PLC

NOTES TO THE ACCOUNTS
Year ended 31 March 2000

6(a)   DIRECTORS REMUNERATION (continued)

The benefits in kind received by Mr M Driver related to the occupation, without payment of rent, of accommodation in Central London under a licence agreement granted by the company. The benefit, based on the estimated market value, was £75,000.

Directors' pensions

	Increase in accrued pension during the year excluding any increase for inflation	Transfer value of increase	Accumulated total accrued pension at 31 March 2000	Accumulatd total accrued pension at 31 March 1999
	£'000	**£'000**	**£'000**	**£'000**
J Delto	5	62	71	63
M Driver	4	38	25	19
J Decker	2	15	12	9
A Carter	3	33	40	35

The four executive directors are members of the company defined benefit pension scheme and accrued benefits during the year under that scheme (1999 – four). The pension entitlement shown above is that which would be paid annually on retirement based on services to 31 March 2000. Further information as to the terms of the scheme are given in the Report of the Board to the Shareholders on Directors' Remuneration.

The transfer value has been calculated on the basis of actuarial advice in accordance with Actuarial Guidance Note GN11 less directors' contributions. Members of the scheme have the option to pay Additional Voluntary Contributions; neither the contributions nor the resulting benefits are included in the above table.

34

NOTES TO THE ACCOUNTS
Year ended 31 March 2000

6(a)   DIRECTORS REMUNERATION (continued)

Directors' share options

Directors	Number of options				Exercise price	Market price at exercise date	Date from which exercisable	Expiry date
	1 April 1999	Granted	Exercised	31 March 2000				
M Driver	15,000	–	15,000	–	96p	108p	31/4/98	31/4/2000
M Driver	20,000	–	–	20,000	105p	–	31/4/99	31/4/2001
M Driver	38,000	–	–	38,000	110p	–	31/4/2000	31/4/2002
M Driver	–	14,000	–	14,000	120p	–	31/4/2001	31/4/2003
J Decker	13,350	–	13,350	–	96p	108p	31/4/98	31/4/2000
J Decker	20,000	–	–	20,000	105p	–	31/4/99	31/4/2001
J Decker	19,250	–	–	19,250	110p	–	31/4/2000	31/4/2002
J Decker	–	6,770	–	6,770	120p	–	31/4/2001	31/4/2003
A Carter	19,240	–	–	19,240	110p	–	31/4/2000	31/4/2002
A Carter	–	3,760	–	3,760	120p	–	31/4/2001	31/4/2003
	144,840	24,530	28,350	141,020				

The above options are held under the 1992 Employee Share Option Scheme the terms of which grant options at nil cost based upon the group performance for the year and basic salary. No options lapsed during the year. The market price of the company's shares at 31 March 2000 was 117p and the range during the year ended 31 March 2000 was 98p to 119p. Aggregate gains made by directors on the exercise of share options were £3,402 (1999 – £3,700) including a gain of £1,800 (1999 – £2,050) by Mr M Driver.

6(b)   INFORMATION REGARDING EMPLOYEES

Employees	2000 No.	1999 No.
Average number of persons employed by the group in the year:		
Production	1,561	1,254
Sales and distribution	621	605
Administration	228	216
	2,410	2,075

35

DELTO PLC

NOTES TO THE ACCOUNTS
Year ended 31 March 2000

6(b) **INFORMATION REGARDING EMPLOYEES** (continued)

	2000 £'000	1999 £'000
Staff costs incurred during the year in respect of these employees were:		
Wages and salaries	22,910	18,840
Social security costs	2,210	1,840
Other pension costs	1,400	1,250
	26,520	21,930

7. **INVESTMENT INCOME**

	2000 £'000	1999 £'000
Income from other fixed asset investments	16	76
Other interest receivable and similar income	252	336
Amounts receivable in respect of interest rate swaps	44	–
(Loss)/profit on sale of other fixed asset investments	(2)	2
Profit on sale of current asset investments	–	14
	310	428

8. **INTEREST PAYABLE AND SIMILAR CHARGES**

	2000 £'000	1999 £'000
Debentures	4	2
Loans	512	354
Bank overdraft and other borrowings	448	397
Finance leases	90	96
Convertible redeemable preference shares (note 21)	260	246
Amounts (receivable)/payable in respect of interest rate swaps	–	35
	1,314	1,130

	2000 £'000	1999 £'000
The amount payable in respect of the convertible redeemable preference shares comprises:		
– dividends	142	142
– redemption premium	118	104

1655

36

NOTES TO THE ACCOUNTS
Year ended 31 March 2000

9. **TAX ON PROFIT ON ORDINARY ACTIVITIES**

	2000 £'000	1999 £'000
United Kingdom corporation tax at 30% (1999 – 31%) based on the profit for the year	468	514
Adjustments in respect of prior periods	(40)	(114)
	428	400
Relief for overseas taxation	(316)	(406)
	112	(6)
Income tax	3	9
Deferred taxation	36	14
Overseas taxation	695	679
Associated companies	28	34
	874	730

The introduction of FRS 16 has meant that dividends, interest and other amounts payable and receivable are now shown net of any attributable tax credit. If the resulting restatement of comparative figures is material (assumed not to be the case in these specimen accounts) there should be brief explanatory disclosure.

The UK tax charge for the year has been reduced as follows:		
Capital allowances in excess of depreciation not dealt with in the deferred tax provision	(40)	(5)
Profit on sale of fixed assets covered by reliefs	(54)	(33)
Loss on sale of operation	(4)	(23)
The overseas tax charge has been increased by losses carried forward	172	(66)

10. **PROFIT OF PARENT COMPANY**

As permitted by Section 230 of the Companies Act, the profit and loss account of the parent company is not presented as part of these accounts. The parent company's profit for the financial year amounted to £104,000 (1999 – £972,000).

11. **DIVIDENDS**

	2000 £'000	1999 £'000
Interim paid–3.0p per ordinary share (1999–3.0p)	346	344
Final proposed–4.24p per ordinary share (1999–4.0p)	491	460
Ordinary dividends on equity shares	837	804
4.86% cumulative preference dividend on non-equity shares	14	14
	851	818

Shareholders were given the opportunity of receiving newly issued ordinary shares, as an alternative to cash, in respect of the interim dividend. The number of shares offered was based on their market value when the dividend was declared (15 November 1999), being 108.58p. The holders of 453,320 shares accepted the offer (see note 26).

DELTO PLC

NOTES TO THE ACCOUNTS
Year ended 31 March 2000

12. **EARNINGS PER ORDINARY SHARE**

Basic earnings per share is calculated by dividing the earnings attributable to ordinary shareholders by the weighted average number of ordinary shares during the year.

Diluted earnings per share is calculated by adjusting the weighted average number of ordinary shares in issue on the assumption of conversion of all dilutive potential ordinary shares. The group has only one category of dilutive potential ordinary shares, those share options granted where the exercise price is less than the average price of the company's ordinary shares during the year.

	2000	1999
Profit for the financial year (£'000)	830	815
Preference share dividend (£'000)	(14)	(14)
Basic and diluted earnings attributable to ordinary shareholders (£'000)	816	801
Weighted average number of ordinary shares ('000)	11,490	11,120
Effect of dilutive share options	20	10
Adjusted weighted average number of ordinary shares ('000)	11,510	11,130
Earnings per share	7.10p	7.20p
Diluted earnings per share	7.09p	7.20p

13. **INTANGIBLE FIXED ASSETS**

	Goodwill £'000	Patents and trademarks £'000	Total £'000
The group			
Cost			
At 1 April 1999	2,466	250	2,716
Additions in the year	64	–	64
At 31 March 2000	2,530	250	2,780
Accumulated amortisation			
At 1 April 1999	123	50	173
Charge for the year	126	50	176
At 31 March 2000	249	100	349
Net book value			
At 31 March 2000	2,281	150	2,431
At 31 March 1999	2,343	200	2,543

Model report and financial statements

DELTO PLC

NOTES TO THE ACCOUNTS
Year ended 31 March 2000

14. TANGIBLE FIXED ASSETS

	Land and Buildings £'000	Plant and machinery £'000	Fixtures, fittings, tools and equipment £'000	Totals £'000
The group				
Cost or valuation				
At 1 April 1999	6,382	13,638	2,374	22,394
Foreign exchange translation differences	137	334	57	528
Acquired with subsidiary	27	40	–	67
Disposed of with subsidiary	(42)	(270)	–	(312)
Additions	156	1,324	–	1,480
Disposals	(414)	(1,024)	–	(1,438)
Adjustment arising on revaluation	(136)	–	–	(136)
At 31 March 2000	6,110	14,042	2,431	22,583
Accumulated depreciation				
At 1 April 1999	1,304	7,372	1,254	9,930
Foreign exchange translation differences	34	130	31	195
Adjustment arising on revaluation	(936)	–	–	(936)
Charge for the year	150	707	415	1,272
Disposed of with subsidiary	(12)	(168)	–	(180)
Disposals	(118)	(830)	–	(948)
At 31 March 2000	422	7,211	1,700	9,333
Net book value				
At 31 March 2000	5,688	6,831	731	13,250
At 31 March 1999	5,078	6,266	1,120	12,464
Comparable amounts determined according to the historical cost convention				
Cost	4,818	14,042	2,431	21,291
Accumulated depreciation	(947)	(7,211)	(1,700)	(9,858)
Net book value				
At 31 March 2000	3,871	6,831	731	11,433
At 31 March 1999	3,878	6,266	1,120	11,264

39

DELTO PLC

NOTES TO THE ACCOUNTS
Year ended 31 March 2000

14. **TANGIBLE FIXED ASSETS (continued)**

The net book value of land and buildings comprises:

	2000 £'000	1999 £'000
Freehold	5,041	4,021
Long leasehold	562	967
Short leasehold	85	90
	5,688	5,078

FRS 15 *Tangible Fixed Assets* has been implemented and it has been decided that all freehold land and buildings will now be held at a valuation. All such assets were given a full valuation on 31 March 2000 on the basis of existing use value, by Messrs K. T. and Co., Chartered Surveyors. The revised net book value includes £167,000 of directly attributable acquisition costs. The net book value of freehold land and buildings determined according to the historical cost convention is £3,224,000. Leasehold land and buildings continue to be held at depreciated historical cost.

Included in land and buildings are property in course of construction amounting to £130,000 (1999 – nil) and land valued at £300,000 (1999 – £350,000) which are not depreciated.

Included within land and buildings cost carried forward are finance costs of £113,000 (1999 – £104,000) which have been capitalised. £9,000 has been capitalised in the period which is based on a specific loan rate of 7.5% and a capitalisation rate of 8.1% based on a weighted average of general borrowings which have also been used to finance the construction.

The net book value of the group's plant and machinery includes £948,000 (1999 – £1,110,000) in respect of assets held under finance leases and hire purchase contracts.

15. **INVESTMENTS HELD AS FIXED ASSETS**

The group – associated undertakings	Goodwill £'000	Share of net assets £'000	Total £'000
At 1 April 1999	–	298	298
Exchange difference	–	7	7
Additions	4	40	44
Disposals	–	(2)	(2)
Profits retained for the year	–	20	20
Amortisation for the year	–	–	–
At 31 March 2000	4	363	367

Details of goodwill arising on the acquisition of associates written off direct to profit and loss reserve as a matter of accounting policy prior to the adoption of FRSs 9 and 10 is given in note 2. The goodwill amortisation charge in respect of associates acquired was £200. It is included within the share of associates' operating profit of £66,000 in the profit and loss account.

Model report and financial statements

DELTO PLC

NOTES TO THE ACCOUNTS
Year ended 31 March 2000

15. **INVESTMENTS HELD AS FIXED ASSETS (continued)**

The group	Other investments £'000
Cost	
At 1 April 1999	386
Exchange difference	16
Additions	12
Disposals	(2)
Transfer to investment in subsidiaries	(16)
Acquired with subsidiary	20
Disposed of with subsidiary	(2)
At 31 March 2000	414
Provisions	
At 31 March 2000 and 1 April 1999	(32)

Net book value	Associates	Other investments	Total
At 31 March 2000	367	382	749
At 1 April 1999	298	354	652

The company	Shares in subsidiary undertakings £'000	Loans to subsidiary undertakings £'000	Total £'000
Cost			
At 1 April 1999	8,208	5,014	13,222
Additions	–	1,572	1,572
Repaid	–	(3,318)	(3,318)
At 31 March 2000	8,208	3,268	11,476
Provisions			
At 1 April 1999	–	–	–
Provided in year	–	(800)	(800)
At 31 March 2000	–	(800)	(800)
Net book value			
At 31 March 2000	8,208	2,468	10,676
At 31 March 1999	8,208	5,014	13,222

All of the above investments (group and company) are unlisted.

DELTO PLC

NOTES TO THE ACCOUNTS
Year ended 31 March 2000

16. **STOCKS**

	The group	
	2000 **£'000**	**1999** **£'000**
Raw materials and consumables	1,753	1,866
Work in progress	2,551	2,560
Finished goods and goods for resale	4,600	4,762
	8,904	9,188

Work in progress includes net long-term contracts as follows:

Net costs less foreseeable losses	110	–
Applicable payments on account	(10)	–
	100	–

The replacement cost of raw materials and consumables held by the group at 31 March 2000 was £76,000 greater (1999 – £93,000 greater) than the amount at which they are stated in the financial statements; there were no significant differences between the replacement cost and the values shown for other stock categories.

17. **DEBTORS**

	The group		The company	
	2000 **£'000**	**1999** **£'000**	**2000** **£'000**	**1999** **£'000**
Trade debtors				
Due within one year	5,422	5,782	–	–
Due after more than one year	574	422	–	–
Amounts recoverable on contracts	74	–	–	–
Amounts owed by subsidiary undertakings	–	–	20	18
Amounts owed by associated undertakings	64	14	–	–
Other debtors	1,180	1,002	198	24
Prepayments and accrued income	518	474	–	–
	7,832	7,694	218	42

42

NOTES TO THE ACCOUNTS
Year ended 31 March 2000

18. **INVESTMENTS HELD AS CURRENT ASSETS**

	The group	
	2000	**1999**
	£'000	**£'000**
Investments – listed on recognised stock exchanges		
In Great Britain	10	10
Overseas	26	48
	36	58
Cash deposits with terms in excess of seven days	2,572	600
	2,608	658
Market value of listed investments at 31 December	42	70

A taxation liability of £1,500 for the group would arise if the listed investments were sold at the stated market values.

19. **CREDITORS: AMOUNTS FALLING DUE WITHIN ONE YEAR**

	The group		The company	
	2000	**1999**	**2000**	**1999**
	£'000	**£'000**	**£'000**	**£'000**
Bank loans and overdrafts (note 22)	2,570	2,220	446	282
Obligations under finance leases and				
hire purchase contracts (note 22)	122	172	–	–
Payments received on account	10	4	–	–
Trade creditors	3,776	3,766	–	–
Bills of exchange payable	670	704	–	58
Amounts owed to associated companies	14	6	–	–
Taxation and social security	1,704	1,854	740	534
Other creditors	979	830	35	2
Accruals and deferred income	979	1,099	–	12
Proposed dividend (note 11)	505	474	506	474
	11,329	11,129	1,727	1,362

DELTO PLC

NOTES TO THE ACCOUNTS
Year ended 31 March 2000

20. **CREDITORS: AMOUNTS FALLING DUE AFTER MORE THAN ONE YEAR**

	The group		The company	
	2000	1999	2000	1999
	£'000	£'000	£'000	£'000
Debenture loans, loan stock and other loans				
(note 22)	548	548	–	–
Bank loans (note 22)	3,778	3,664	16	18
Obligations under finance leases and hire purchase				
contracts (note 22)	842	880	–	–
Amounts owed to subsidiary undertakings	–	–	2,876	4,880
Other creditors	62	16	–	–
Accruals and deferred income	183	141	–	–
	5,413	5,249	2,892	4,898
Guaranteed redeemable convertible preference				
shares (note 21)	2,316	2,198		
	7,729	7,447		

21. **GUARANTEED REDEEMABLE CONVERTIBLE PREFERENCE SHARES**

On 30 July 1997, Deltoled Finance NV, a subsidiary company incorporated in the Netherlands Antilles, issued 20,000 7.1% guaranteed redeemable convertible preference shares with a paid up value of £100 per share. Delto PLC have guaranteed the shares on a subordinated basis and they are each convertible into 50 ordinary shares of Delto PLC at a price of 1.50p per ordinary share at any time prior to 1 August 2018. The shares outstanding at that date will be redeemed on 14 August 2018 at their issue price or in specified circumstances on earlier revocation of the guarantee. The shares may be redeemed on 1 August 2002 at the preference shareholders' option at a redemption price of 127.5 % of the paid up value of the shares. Provision is made for the possible premium on redemption and included within the carrying amount of the shares. At 31 March 2000 the amount accrued was £316,000 (1999 – £198,000). The shares have been treated as liabilities in accordance with FRS 4 as the group has an obligation to transfer liabilities in connection with the shares. The dividend on the shares and the possible premium on redemption have been charged in interest payable (note 8).

Model report and financial statements

DELTO PLC

NOTES TO THE ACCOUNTS
Year ended 31 March 2000

22. BORROWINGS

	The group		The company	
	2000	1999	2000	1999
	£'000	£'000	£'000	£'000
Debenture loans 5% 1995/2005	64	64	–	–
Unsecured loan notes – 8% 2006	140	140	–	–
Unsecured loan notes – 5.7% 2001	172	172	–	–
Unsecured loan notes – 7.75% 2002	172	172	–	–
Bank overdraft	798	1,836	446	282
Bank loans	5,550	4,048	16	18
	6,896	6,432	462	300
Obligations under finance leases and hire purchase contracts	964	1,052	–	–
Redeemable convertible preference shares (note 21)	2,316	2,198	–	–
	10,176	9,682	462	300
Due within one year	2,692	2,392	446	282
Due after more than one year	7,484	7,290	16	18
	10,176	9,682	462	300

An analysis of the maturity of group debt is given in note 23(a). The company's bank loan disclosed above is due within one and two years.

	The group		The company	
	2000	1999	2000	1999
	£'000	£'000	£'000	£'000
Amounts wholly repayable after five years:				
Loan notes 8% 2006	140	140	–	–
Debenture loans 5% – 1995/2005	64	64	–	–
Amounts repayable by instalments some of which fall due after five years:				
Bank loans: Instalments due after five years	1,168	896	–	–
Finance leases and hire purchase contracts				
Instalments due after five years	356	374	–	–
Aggregate of amounts wholly repayable after five years and instalments due after five years	1,728	1,474	–	–

The debenture loans 5% 1995/2005 are secured by first mortgage on the freehold factory premises of the UK subsidiary companies. The long-term bank loan bears interest at 2% above the bank's base rate. The bank loans and overdrafts are secured by fixed and floating charges on the assets of the group. Obligations under finance leases and hire purchase contracts are secured by related leased assets and bear finance charges at rates ranging from 7% to 12% per annum. Delto PLC has guaranteed £2,940,000 (1999 – £2,030,000) of the bank loans to subsidiary companies.

DELTO PLC

NOTES TO THE ACCOUNTS
Year ended 31 March 2000

23.   FINANCIAL INSTRUMENTS

The group's polices as regards derivatives and financial instruments are set out in the Operating and Financial Review on page 4 and the accounting policies on pages 36-38. The group does not trade in financial instruments.

Short-term debtors and creditors have been omitted from all disclosures other than the currency profile.

Details of non-equity shares issued by the group are given in notes 21 and 26.

23(a) MATURITY PROFILE OF FINANCIAL LIABILITIES

	2000			1999		
	Bank borrowings and debentures £'000	**Other £'000**	**Total £'000**	**Bank borrowings and debentures £'000**	**Other £'000**	**Total £'000**
Within one year or less or on demand	2,570	–	2,570	2,220	–	2,220
More than one year but not more than two years	1,680	376	2,056	808	189	997
More than two years but not more than five years	1,274	355	1,629	2,304	474	2,778
More than five years	1,372	356	1,728	1,100	374	1,474
Gross financial liabilities	6,896	1,087	7,983	6,432	1,037	7,469

In the maturity analysis of the group financial liabilities 'Other' includes liabilities shown as other creditors, accruals and deferred income, and obligations under finance leases and hire purchase contracts falling due after more than one year in note 20.

The 7.1% guaranteed redeemable convertible preference shares issued by Deltoled Finance NV and included within borrowings in note 22 are redeemable in 2002 at the holders' option (see note 21).

The 4.86% cumulative preference shares issued by Delto Plc are not redeemable (see note 26).

The group had the following undrawn committed borrowing facilities at 31 March:

Expiry date	**2000 £'000**	**1999 £'000**
In one year or less	678	456
In more than one year but not more than two years	233	965
In more than two years	678	324
Total	1,589	1,745

NOTES TO THE ACCOUNTS
Year ended 31 March 2000

23(b) **INTEREST RATE PROFILE**

The following interest rate and currency profiles of the group's financial liabilities and assets are after taking into account interest rate swaps entered into by the group.

Currency	Total	Floating rate financial liabilities	Fixed rate financial liabilities	Non-interest bearing financial liabilities	Fixed rate financial liabilities — Weighted average interest rate	Fixed rate financial liabilities — Weighted average period for which the rate is fixed	Non-interest bearing financial liabilities — Weighted average period until maturity
	£'000	£'000	£'000	£'000	%	Years	Years
At 31 March 2000							
Sterling	3,346	1,796	1,426	124	6.0	3.5	2.4
US$	2,942	1,115	1,729	98	5.4	1.9	1.9
Euro	1,695	1,047	625	23	4.3	1.7	2.3
Gross financial liabilities	7,983	3,958	3,780	245	5.4	2.5	2.2
At 31 March 1999							
Sterling	4,226	2,923	1,176	127	7.5	2.9	2.8
US$	1,734	894	820	20	5.8	1.5	2.2
Other	1,509	761	738	10	4.7	0.9	2.4
Gross financial liabilities	7,469	4,578	2,734	157	6.2	1.9	2.6

Interest on floating rate liabilities is based on the relevant national inter bank rates.

The sterling preference shares issued by the group pay a fixed dividend, which is not hedged, of:
- 7.1% guaranteed redeemable convertible preference shares issued by Deltoled Finance NV (see note 21).
- 4.86% cumulative preference shares issued by Delto Plc (see note 26).

DELTO PLC

NOTES TO THE ACCOUNTS
Year ended 31 March 2000

23(b) INTEREST RATE PROFILE (continued)

Financial Assets

Currency	Total	Floating rate financial assets	Fixed rate financial assets	Non-interest bearing assets Equity investments	Other non-interest bearing financial assets
	£'000	£'000	£'000	£'000	£'000
At 31 March 2000					
Sterling	2,390	1,199	689	225	277
US$	1,281	943	–	113	225
Euro	493	341	–	80	72
Gross financial assets	4,164	2,483	689	418	574
At 31 March 1999					
Sterling	2,281	1,053	622	249	357
US$	737	609	–	93	35
Other	290	190	–	70	30
Gross financial assets	3,308	1,852	622	412	422

Financial assets comprise cash in hand and at bank of £0.6m (1999 – £1.87m), fixed asset investments other than associates of £0.38m (1999 – £0.35m), current assets investments of £2.6m (1999 – £0.66m) and trade debtors due in more than one year of £0.57m (1999 – £0.42m). Non-interest bearing assets, other than £0.38m (1999 – £0.35m) of unlisted shares, are fully liquid and have no maturity period.

Interest on floating rate bank deposits is based on the relevant national inter bank rate and is fixed in advance for periods up to six months. The weighted average rate and period for fixed rate deposits are 3.7% and 5 months (1999 – 5.2% and 7 months).

23(c) FAIR VALUES OF FINANCIAL ASSETS AND LIABILITIES

Primary financial instruments held for use in the group's operations	2000 Carrying amount	2000 Estimated fair value	1999 Carrying amount	1999 Estimated fair value
	£'000	£'000	£'000	£'000
Cash at bank, in hand and other liquid investments	3,172	3,172	2,474	2,474
Long-term investments	382	390	354	357
Current asset investments	36	42	58	70
Trade debtor due in more than one year	574	505	422	371
Gross financial assets	4,164	4,109	3,308	3,272

Model report and financial statements

48

DELTO PLC

NOTES TO THE ACCOUNTS
Year ended 31 March 2000

23(c) FAIR VALUES OF FINANCIAL ASSETS AND LIABILITIES (continued)

Primary financial instruments issued to finance the group's operations	2000		1999	
	Carrying amount	Estimated fair value	Carrying amount	Estimated fair value
	£'000	£'000	£'000	£'000
Bank borrowings	6,348	6,192	5,884	5,942
Debentures	548	540	548	543
Finance leases	842	830	880	870
Other liabilities	245	240	157	154
Gross financial liabilities	7,983	7,802	7,469	7,509
7.1% guaranteed redeemable convertible preference shares	2,316	2,650	2,198	2,456
4.86% cumulative preference shares issued by Delto Plc	292	281	292	275
Derivative financial instruments held to manage the interest rate and currency profile				
Interest rate swaps	–	14	–	(8)
Forward foreign exchange contracts	–	(10)	–	4

Market values have been used to determine the fair values of all swaps, foreign currency contracts and listed instruments issued or held. The fair values of all other items have been calculated by discounting expected cash flows at prevailing interest rates at the year end.

DELTO PLC

NOTES TO THE ACCOUNTS
Year ended 31 March 2000

23(d) HEDGING

As explained in the operating and financial review on page 4, the group's policy is to hedge the following exposures:

- interest rate risk – using interest swaps and forward foreign currency contracts; and

- structural and transactional currency exposures, and currency exposures on future expected sales – using forward foreign currency contracts.

Gains and losses on instruments used for hedging are not recognised until the exposure that is being hedged is itself recognised. Unrecognised gains and losses on instruments used for hedging, and the movements therein, are as follows:

	2000 Gains	2000 Losses	2000 Total net gains/ losses	1999 Gains	1999 Losses	1999 Total net gains/ losses
	£'000	£'000	£'000	£'000	£'000	£'000
Unrecognised gains and losses at 1 April 1999 (1998)	5	(9)	(4)	4	(12)	(8)
Gains and losses arising in previous years that were recognised in the year	2	(5)	(3)	4	(5)	(1)
Gains and losses arising before 1 April 1999 (1998) that were not recognised in the year	3	(4)	(1)	–	(7)	(7)
Gains and losses arising in the year that were not recognised in the year	8	(3)	5	5	(2)	3
Unrecognised gains and losses on hedges at 31 March	11	(7)	4	5	(9)	(4)
Gains and losses expected to be recognised in the next financial year	7	(5)	2	2	(5)	(3)
Gains and losses expected to be recognised after the next financial year	4	(2)	2	3	(4)	(1)

23(e) CURRENCY PROFILE

The main functional currencies of the group are sterling, the US dollar and various European currencies now participating in the euro. The following analysis of net monetary assets and liabilities shows the group's currency exposures after the effects of forward contracts and other derivatives used to manage currency exposure. The amounts shown represent the transactional (or non-structural) exposures that give rise to the net currency gains and losses recognised in the profit and loss account. Such exposures comprise the monetary assets and monetary liabilities of the group that are not denominated in the operating (or 'functional') currency of the operating unit involved, other than certain non-sterling borrowings treated as hedges of net investments in overseas operations.

50

DELTO PLC

NOTES TO THE ACCOUNTS
Year ended 31 March 2000

23(e) CURRENCY PROFILE (continued)

| | **2000** | | | | **1999** | | | |
	Sterling	US $	Other European currencies	Total	Sterling	US $	Other European currencies	Total
	£'000	£'000	£'000	£'000	£'000	£'000	£'000	£'000
Sterling	–	20	15	35	–	13	10	23
US $	–	–	(19)	(19)	–	–	(4)	(4)
Other European currencies	9	8	–	17	4	6	–	10
Total	9	28	(4)	33	4	19	6	29

24. PROVISIONS FOR LIABILITIES AND CHARGES

The group	Pensions and similar obligations £'000	Deferred taxation £'000	Reorganis-ations and disposals £'000	Product guarantees £'000	Total £'000
Balance at 1 April 1999	1,271	373	604	894	3,142
Subsidiaries acquired/sold	–	2	–	(8)	(6)
Profit and loss account charge	1,276	36	140	328	1,780
Exchange differences	28	(2)	28	28	82
Applied	(1,762)	(6)	(440)	(162)	(2,370)
Balance at 31 March 2000	813	403	332	1,080	2,628

Pensions and similar obligations (see note 37).

Deferred taxation
The amounts of deferred taxation provided and unprovided in the accounts are as follows:

The group	Provided 2000 £'000	Provided 1999 £'000	Not provided 2000 £'000	Not provided 1999 £'000
Capital allowances in excess of depreciation	602	528	40	5
Other timing differences	(412)	(446)	–	–
Taxation on valuation surplus	–	–	545	372
Pension fund prepayment	213	291	–	–
	403	373	585	377

No provision has been made for taxation that would arise in the event of the overseas subsidiaries distributing the balance of their reserves as these amounts are retained for investment in the business.

DELTO PLC

NOTES TO THE ACCOUNTS
Year ended 31 March 2000

24. **PROVISIONS FOR LIABILITIES AND CHARGES (continued)**

Reorganisation and disposals

The provision for reorganisation costs stands at £332,000 at the year end. This represents expected further directly attributable costs of the integration into the group of Shed Technology Ltd which was purchased during the year (see note 2 above) and the ongoing reorganisation of the motor product and jewellery divisions following acquisitions in recent years. It is expected that these costs will all be incurred during the next financial year.

Product guarantees

A provision of £1,080,000 has been recognised for expected claims against product guarantees on products sold during the last three financial years. It is expected that most of this expenditure will be incurred in the next financial year, and all will be incurred within two years of the balance sheet date. The provision has not been discounted since the effect of discounting is not material.

25. **MINORITY INTERESTS**

The non-equity minority interest comprises 200,000, £1, 12% Cumulative redeemable preference shares in Deltoled Finance NV. The shares do not entitle the holders to any rights against other group companies. The shares are redeemable on 31 March 2011 at par.

26. **CALLED UP SHARE CAPITAL**

| | 2000 | | 1999 | |
	Number of shares	£'000	Number of shares	£'000
Authorised				
Ordinary shares of 20p each	15,000,000	3,000	15,000,000	3,000
4.86% Cumulative preference shares of 10p each	20,000,000	2,000	20,000,000	2,000
		5,000		5,000
Called up, allotted and fully paid				
Ordinary shares of 20p each	11,593,259	2,319	11,479,160	2,296
4.86% Cumulative preference shares of 10p each	2,918,467	292	2,918,467	292
		2,611		2,588

The 4.86% Cumulative preference shares of 10p each entitle the holder to receive a cumulative preferential dividend at the rate of 4.86% on the paid up capital and the right to a return of capital plus a premium of 1.25p for each 10p of paid up capital at either a winding up or a repayment of capital. The preference shares do not entitle the holders to any further rights or other participation in the profits or assets of Delto PLC nor do they carry any voting rights.

52

DELTO PLC

NOTES TO THE ACCOUNTS
Year ended 31 March 2000

26. **CALLED UP SHARE CAPITAL (continued)**

Under the company's 1992 Employee Share Option Scheme, employees held options at 31 March 2000 for 534,026 unissued ordinary shares (1999 – 514,988) as follows:

Number of shares	Option price per share £	Option period ending
235,374	1.05	30 April 2001
178,040	1.10	30 April 2002
120,612	1.20	30 April 2003

During the year 120,612 £1.20 options were granted and 101,574 options were exercised as noted below.

Shares issued in the year were:	Nos.	Nominal Value	Consideration £
Employee share option scheme at £1.05	8,350	1,670	8,768
Employee share option scheme at £0.96	93,224	18,645	89,495
	101,574	20,315	98,263
Shares issued in respect of share dividend	12,525	2,505	13,600
	114,099	22,820	111,863

27. **RECONCILIATION OF OPERATING PROFIT TO NET CASH INFLOW FROM OPERATING ACTIVITIES**

	2000 £'000	1999 £'000
Operating profit	2,568	2,131
Depreciation and amortisation charges	1,448	1,331
Decrease in stocks	388	758
Decrease in pension fund asset	124	54
Decrease in debtors	102	338
Decrease in creditors	(150)	(420)
Decrease in provisions	(632)	(976)
Net cash inflow from operating activities	3,848	3,216

DELTO PLC

NOTES TO THE ACCOUNTS
Year ended 31 March 2000

28. **ANALYSIS OF CASH FLOWS FOR HEADINGS NETTED IN THE CASH FLOW STATEMENT**

	Note	2000 £'000	1999 £'000
Returns on investments and servicing of finance			
Interest and other investment income received		266	414
Interest paid		(945)	(834)
Interest element of finance lease rentals payments		(90)	(96)
Dividend paid on convertible preference shares	8	(142)	(142)
Dividends paid to minority interests		(52)	(42)
		(963)	(700)
Taxation			
UK corporation tax paid (including advance corporation tax)		(274)	(354)
Overseas tax paid		(656)	(552)
		(930)	(906)
Capital expenditure and financial investment			
Payments to acquire tangible fixed assets		(1,429)	(1,072)
Receipts from sales of fixed assets		692	616
Purchase of fixed asset investments		(12)	(38)
		(749)	(494)
Acquisitions and disposals			
Purchase of subsidiary undertaking	32	(138)	(2,482)
Net cash/(overdrafts) acquired with subsidiary	32	10	(918)
Sale of subsidiary undertaking	33	240	910
Net (cash)/overdrafts disposed of with subsidiary	33	8	66
Purchase of associate undertakings	15	(44)	–
		76	(2,424)
Management of liquid resources			
Net increase in 7-day deposits		(1,972)	72
Sale of current asset investments		22	24
		(1,950)	96
Financing			
Issue of ordinary share capital		112	24
Issue of shares to minorities		4	18
New borrowings		5,710	3,812
Sale and leaseback of plant and machinery		72	100
Repayment of borrowings		(4,444)	(4,018)
Capital element of finance lease rental payments		(206)	(192)
Redemption of minorities		(8)	–
		1,240	(256)

Model report and financial statements

DELTO PLC

NOTES TO THE ACCOUNTS
Year ended 31 March 2000

29. ANALYSIS OF NET DEBT

	1999 £'000	Cash Flow	Acquisitions and disposals exc cash and overdrafts	Other non-cash changes	Exchange movement	2000 £'000
Cash in hand and at bank	1,874	(1,240)	–	–	(34)	600
Overdraft	(1,836)	1,026	–	–	12	(798)
		(214)				
Redeemable convertible shares	(2,198)	–	–	(118)	–	(2,316)
Debt due after one year	(4,212)	(170)	–	214	(158)	(4,326)
Debt due within one year	(384)	(1,096)	(2)	(214)	(76)	(1,772)
Finance leases	(1,052)	206	–	(116)	(2)	(964)
		(1,060)				
Current asset investments	658	1,950	–	–	–	2,608
Total	(7,150)	676	(2)	(234)	(258)	(6,968)

30. CASH FLOW RELATING TO EXCEPTIONAL ITEMS

The operating cash outflows include under discontinued activities an outflow of £2,000, which relates to the £12,000 exceptional provision for loss on disposal of discontinued operations made in the 1999 accounts.

31. NON-CASH TRANSACTIONS

During the year the group entered into finance lease arrangements in respect of assets with a total capital value at the inception of the leases of £116,000 (1999 – £100,000) and charged £118,000 (1999 – £104,000) for the possible premium on redemption of the 7.1% guaranteed redeemable convertible preference shares of Deltoled Finance NV (see note 21).

DELTO PLC

NOTES TO THE ACCOUNTS
Year ended 31 March 2000

32.   **PURCHASE OF SUBSIDIARY UNDERTAKINGS**

Net assets acquired:	2000 £'000	1999 £'000
Tangible fixed assets	67	2,774
Investments	20	28
Stocks	80	1,044
Debtors	54	2,288
Cash at bank and in hand	24	2
Pension fund asset	–	1,318
Creditors	(47)	(1,618)
Taxation	54	(134)
Bank overdraft	(14)	(920)
Provisions	(22)	(594)
Loans and finance leases	(14)	(1,286)
Deferred tax	(2)	(144)
Minority interest	(40)	(172)
	160	2,586
Goodwill	64	2,466
	224	5,052
Satisfied by:		
Shares allotted	–	1,372
Loan notes	–	14
Cash	138	2,482
Deferred consideration	70	–
Cost of existing investment transferred from fixed assets	16	1,184
	224	5,052

The subsidiary undertaking acquired during the year contributed £48,000 to the group's net operating cash flows, paid £104,000 in respect of net returns on investment and servicing of finance, paid £20,000 in respect of taxation and utilised £150,000 for investing activities. See note 2 for further details of the 1999/2000 acquisition. Comparative figures relate to the acquisition of Gems 4'U Ltd. on 30 September 1998.

Model report and financial statements

DELTO PLC

NOTES TO THE ACCOUNTS
Year ended 31 March 2000

33. SALE OF SUBSIDIARY UNDERTAKINGS

	2000 £'000	1999 £'000
Tangible fixed assets	132	356
Goodwill	10	97
Investments	2	–
Stocks	202	729
Debtors	52	438
Creditors	(42)	(230)
Taxation	–	(18)
Bank overdraft	(8)	(66)
Provisions	(30)	–
Loans and finance leases	(12)	(10)
Deferred tax	–	(56)
Minority interest	–	(234)
	306	1,006
Loss on disposal	(18)	(96)
	288	910
Satisfied by:		
Cash	240	910
Deferred consideration	48	–
	288	910

See note 2 for further details of the 1999/2000 disposal. Comparative figures relate to the sale of a number of subsidiaries operating in the group's housewares division (now discontinued).

DELTO PLC

NOTES TO THE ACCOUNTS
Year ended 31 March 2000

34. CAPITAL COMMITMENTS

	The group		The company	
	2000 **£'000**	**1999** **£'000**	**2000** **£'000**	**1999** **£'000**
Contracted for but not provided *(include costs to be incurred in* *preparing for the changeover to the* *euro when they fall within the* *requirement of companies legislation* *to give particulars of financial* *commitments relevant to assessing* *the company's state of affairs)*	250	750	50	50

35. CONTINGENT LIABILITIES

	The group		The company	
	2000 **£'000**	**1999** **£'000**	**2000** **£'000**	**1999** **£'000**

Guarantees in respect of loans and
  redeemable convertible preference
  shares (note 21)
	–	–	5,256	4,228

Performance bonds	546	383	–	24

36. OPERATING LEASE COMMITMENTS

At 31 March 2000 the group was committed to making the following payments during the next year in respect of operating leases:

	Land and buildings **2000** **£'000**	Other **2000** **£'000**	Land and buildings **1999** **£'000**	Other **1999** **£'000**
Leases which expire:				
Within one year	24	32	34	32
Within two to five years	156	128	92	114
After five years	248	2	214	12
	428	162	340	158

DELTO PLC

NOTES TO THE ACCOUNTS
Year ended 31 March 2000

37. PENSION SCHEMES

The group operates funded defined benefit schemes for all qualifying employees. The assets of the schemes are held in separate trustee administered funds. The total cost of retirement benefits for the group was £1.4 million (1999 – £1.25 million) of which £420,000 (1999 – £311,000) relates to overseas schemes.

The UK scheme is subject to triennial valuation by independent actuaries, the last valuation being carried out as at 31 March 1999, using the projected unit credit method, in which the actuarial liability makes allowances for projected earnings. The following actuarial assumptions were applied:

Investment returns   8.5% per annum

Salary growth   6.5% per annum

Pension increases   4.0% per annum

At the last actuarial valuation date, the market value of the assets of the UK scheme was £15.1 million and this actuarial value was sufficient to cover 120% of the benefits which had accrued to members, after allowing for expected future increases in earnings. The employer's contribution rate over the average remaining service lives of the members of the scheme takes account of the surplus disclosed by the valuation.

There are two defined benefit schemes operating in North America. The Gems 4' U scheme was valued at the 30 September 1998 on the acquisition of the company. The market value of the assets at that valuation was £2.7 million which covered 149% of the benefits which had accrued to members, after allowing for expected future increases in earnings. The actuarial surplus of the assets over the accrued benefits of £1.3 million was taken to reserves and was included within the acquisition balance sheet of Gems 4' U as at 30 September 1998. This asset has been reduced by the pension charge for Gems 4' U which, after offsetting the interest credit on the asset, was £124,000 (1999 – £54,000). The pension costs of the group's remaining US pension schemes, amounting to £246,000 (1999 – £209,000), have been determined in accordance with the accounting standards of that country. The group's US subsidiaries provide health care and life assurance benefits for substantially all current and retired full-time employees. The unfunded liability in respect of eligible employees has been determined in accordance with US accounting standard FAS 106, as permitted by UITF 6, and is fully provided for in the accounts.

Provisions include £63,000 (1999 – £550,000) being the excess of accumulated pension costs over the amounts funded and £750,000 (1999 – £721,000) in respect of post retirement health care and life assurance benefits.

38. RELATED PARTY TRANSACTIONS

Mr J Delto is the lessor in a contract expiring in 2001 whereby factory premises have been leased to the company at an annual rental of £220,000.

During the year the group purchased from its associated companies £220,000 (1999 – £200,000) of finished goods at normal trade prices and sold to its associated companies £124,000 (1999 – £92,000) of finished goods and raw materials at normal trade prices. At the financial year end £14,000 (1999 – £6,000) was due to associated companies in respect of finished goods and £64,000 (1999 – £14,000) was due from associated companies in respect of finished goods and raw materials. These amounts are included within creditors due within one year and debtors respectively.

39. EVENT OCCURRING AFTER THE END OF YEAR

On 15 May 2000, facilities for the production of motor products at Meriden were destroyed by fire. While insurance cover carried by the group exceeds the net book value of the assets destroyed, the replacement cost of new facilities is expected to require a large additional investment which cannot be quantified at this time. Reconstruction of these facilities should be completed by February 2001.

DELTO PLC

NOTES TO THE ACCOUNTS
Year ended 31 March 2000

40. **ADDITIONAL INFORMATION ON SUBSIDIARIES AND ASSOCIATED UNDERTAKINGS**

Subsidiary undertakings

	Country of registration and operation	Activity	Portion of ordinary shares held %
Automotive Products			
*C. P. Plastics Ltd.	Scotland	Manufacturer of plastic accessories	100
Metals Ltd.	England and Wales	Manufacturer of metal accessories	100
Plastic Inc.	USA	Manufacturer of plastic accessories	75
*Delto Sales Ltd.	England and Wales	Sales and distribution	100
J. Delto Ltd.	England and Wales	Property and management for the group	100
Jewellery products			
Delto Fashions Ltd.	England and Wales	Manufacturer of costume jewellery	100
Delto (Gems) Ltd.	England and Wales	Retailers	100
*Delto Gems Corp.	USA	Retailers	98
*Gems 4'U Corp.	USA	Manufacturers and retailers	80
Construction			
*Shed Technology Ltd.	England and Wales	Manufacturers and assembler of prefabricated buildings	80

Finance Companies			**Portion held %**
Deltoled Finance NV	Netherland Antilles	Finance company	100

Associated undertakings

	Class of capital	Total issued capital	Par value £'000	Portion held %
Automotive products				
*Metal Bashing Ltd.	'A' Ordinary of £1	36	36	100
	'B' Ordinary of 10p	540	54	–
	Debenture loan	600	600	–
*Deltoion Ltd.	Ordinary of £1	55	55	40

All associated undertakings are registered and operate in England and Wales and their principal activities are manufacturers of automotive parts and accessories.

With the exception of companies marked with an asterisk, all shareholdings are in the name of Delto PLC. All subsidiaries have been included in the consolidation. With the exception of Deltoled Finance NV, where the group holds 82% of the voting rights, the proportion of voting rights of subsidiaries held by the group is the same as the proportion of shares held.

Appendix I List of terms and abbreviations

ABI	Association of British Insurers
the Act	Companies Act 1985, as amended
ACCA	Association of Chartered Certified Accountants
AGM	Annual general meeting
AIM	Alternative investment market
APB	Auditing Practices Board, successor body to the APC
APC	Auditing Practices Committee, which formulated auditing standards and guidelines prior to the formation of the APB
ARD	Accounting reference date
ARP	Accounting reference period
ASB	Accounting Standards Board, which issues FRSs, FREDs, etc.
ASC	Accounting Standards Committee, which formulated SSAPs for approval by councils of the accountancy bodies until August 1990
Cadbury Code	Code of Best Practice, issued by the Cadbury Committee
Cadbury Committee	Committee on the Financial Aspects of Corporate Governance
CASE	Committee on Accounting for Smaller Entities, a subcommittee of the ASB to advise on issues affecting small companies and recommend future revisions and modifications to the FRSSE, including those arising from new or revised standards and abstracts
CCAB	Consultative Committee of Accountancy Bodies, consisting of the ACCA, CIMA, CIPFA, ICAI, ICAS and ICAEW
CIMA	Chartered Institute of Management Accountants
CIPFA	Chartered Institute of Public Finance and Accountancy
CISCO	City Group for Smaller Companies
Code of Best Practice	Code of Best Practice issued by the Cadbury Committee
Combined Code	The principles of good governance and the code of best practice provisions issued by the London Stock Exchange derived by the Hampel Committee from the Committee's final report and from the Cadbury and Greenbury reports.
DRC	Depreciated replacement cost
DTI	Department of Trade and Industry

EASDAQ	European Association of Securities Dealers Automated Quotation Systems
ED	Exposure Draft, issued by the ASC
EEA	European Economic Area
eps	Earnings per share
ESOP	Employee share ownership plan
EU	European Union
EUV	existing use value
FAS	Financial Accounting Standard (USA)
FASB	Financial Accounting Standards Board (USA)
FID	Foreign income dividend
FIFO	First in, first out
FRAG	Financial Reporting and Auditing Group (of the ICAEW)
FRED	Financial Reporting Exposure Draft, issued by the ASB
FRRP	Financial Reporting Review Panel
FRS	Financial Reporting Standard, issued by the ASB
FRSSE	Financial Reporting Standard for Smaller Entities issued by the ASB
FSA	Financial Services Authority
FS Act	Financial Services Act 1986
FT-SE 100	Financial Times Stock Exchange top 100 best-performing companies (share index)
G4 + 1	A grouping of national standard-setters, together with the IASC
GAAP	Generally accepted accounting practice
GN	Guidance Note, issued by the Institute and Faculty of Actuaries
Greenbury Committee	Study Group on Directors' Remuneration
Hampel Committee	Committee on Corporate Governance
HEFCE	Higher Education Funding Council for England
IAS	International Accounting Standard
IASC	International Accounting Standards Committee
ICAEW	The Institute of Chartered Accountants in England & Wales
ICAI	The Institute of Chartered Accountants in Ireland
ICAS	The Institute of Chartered Accountants of Scotland
ICSA	Institute of Chartered Secretaries and Administrators
IMRO	Investment Management Regulatory Organisation
IOSCO	International Organisation of Securities Commissions

IRR	internal rate of return
ISA	International Standard on Auditing
ISMA	International Securities Market Association Ltd
JANE	Joint arrangement that is not an entity
LIBOR	London Inter-Bank Offer Rate
LIFFE	London International Financial Futures and Options Exchange
LIFO	Last in, first out
Listed company	A company, any class of whose securities is listed (i.e., admitted to the Official List of the UK Listing Authority)
Listing Rules	The listing rules made by the competent authority (see UK Listing Authority) for the purposes of Part IV of the FS Act and in the exercise of its functions in respect of the admission of securities to the Official List otherwise than in accordance with Part IV of the FS Act
LTIP	Long-term investment plan
MFR	Minimum funding requirement
NASDAQ	National Association of Securities Dealers Automated Quotation-System
NI	National Insurance
OEIC	Open ended investment company
OFR	Operating and financial review
P & L	Profit and loss
PAYE	Pay as you earn
PFI	Private finance initiative
PIA	Personal Investment Authority
reporting standards	SAS 600 *Auditors' reports on financial statements*
Review Panel	Financial Reporting Review Panel
RICS	The Royal Institution of Chartered Surveyors
RIE	Recognised investment exchange
ROI	Return on investment
RPI	Retail price index
RSL	Registered social landlord
Rutteman guidance	The guidance on internal financial control and reporting, issued by the Rutteman Working group in 1994. It is still applicable where the transitional approach to Turnbull is adopted but will be fully superseded when Turnbull becomes fully effective
SAS	Statement of Auditing Standards
SAYE	Save as you earn
SEC	Securities and Exchange Commission (USA)

SFA	Securities and Futures Authority
SFAS	Statement of Financial Accounting Standards, issued by the FASB
SI	Statutory instrument – the government order which amends or supplements legislation. In the context of this manual, these will normally be amendments to the Companies Acts
SIB	Securities and Investments Board
SOF	Statement of finance
SORP	Statement of Recommended Practice, which gives guidance on current best practice on topics that are not of major or fundamental importance
SRO	Self-regulatory organisation
SSAP	Statement of Standard Accounting Practice, issued by the ASC
TR	Technical Release
TSR	Total shareholder return
Turnbull Committee	The Working Party set up by the ICAEW to provide guidance to assist listed companies to implement the new requirements of the Combined Code relating to internal control
Turnbull guidance	The final guidance issued by the Turnbull working Party in September 1999 which supports Combined Code Principle D.2 and Provisions D.2.1 and D.2.2
UK Listing Authority	The FSA acting in its capacity as the competent authority for the purposes of Part IV of the FS Act and in the exercise of its functions in respect of the admission of securities to the Official List otherwise than in accordance with Part IV of the FS Act
UITF	Urgent Issues Task Force of the ASB
UITF Abstract	Consensus pronouncements issued by the UITF
VAT	Value added tax

Appendix II Checklist of disclosure requirements

1   Introduction

This checklist lists the disclosure requirements required in the financial statements of companies in the United Kingdom. It includes those requirements in force for periods ending on or after 31 March 2000.

Corporate governance disclosures required by the Listing Rules of the UK Listing Authority are excluded from this checklist and given in a separate checklist at appendix V.

The list is applicable to companies preparing accounts in compliance with schedule 4 of the Act. It includes the general requirements of chapter 12 of the Listing Rules, but not those applicable to specific industries as set out in other chapters of the Listing Rules.

The checklist highlights the statutory exemptions available to small companies in the annual reports that they present to members by including those disclosures in shaded boxes (see also chapter 31). The checklist does not incorporate the FRSSE.

References to 'listed companies' in the checklist are to companies admitted to the Official List.

Referencing

The checklists have been referenced to the relevant Accounting Standard or section of the Companies Act 1985. The referencing convention in the column headed 'Ref' is as shown below.

SP 25:3	Statement of Standard Accounting Practice 25, paragraph 3
FRS 1:3	Financial Reporting Standard 1, paragraph 3
UITF 20:11	UITF Abstract 20, paragraph 11
S4:3	Paragraph 3 of Schedule 4 of the Companies Act 1985
s234	Section 234 of the Companies Act 1985
LR12.43(n)	UK Listing Authority Listing Rules paragraph 12.43(n)
SAS600.2	Statement of Auditing Standards 600.2
ICA 1.201	*Members' Handbook*, section 1.201
AB 95/1:20	Audit Bulletin 95/1, paragraph 20
RSE16.19(e)	Rules of the London Stock Exchange paragraph 16.19(e)

Contents

2   Directors' Report

No.	*Disclosure*	*Ref*

Activities and results

2.1	The principal activities of the company and its subsidiaries during the year; and any significant change in those activities.	s234(2)
2.2	A fair review of the development of the company's/(group's) business during the year and its position at the year end.	s234(1)
2.3	Amounts (if any) recommended to be paid as dividends.	s234(1)
2.4	Particulars of important events affecting the company or its subsidiary undertakings which occurred after the year end. (If this information is given in the notes to the accounts, cross-refer to it in the directors' report.)	S7:6(a)
2.5	Indication of likely future developments in the business.	S7:6(b)
2.6	Indication of any research and development activities.	S7:6(c)
2.7	For listed companies an explanation (either in the directors' report or in the notes) of any material difference between the trading results shown in the accounts and those given in any published forecast.	LR12.43(b)

Directors

2.8	The names of persons who were directors of the company during the financial year.	s234(2)
2.9	For each person who was a director of the company at the year end:	S7:2A
	(1) the number of shares in or amounts of debentures of the company or any group company (specifying it) in which he was interested (including nil interest) at the year end, according to the register;	
	(2) for each director who had an interest at the year end, particulars as in (1) above at the beginning of the financial year or date of appointment if later.	
	(Information to be given either in the directors' report or on the notes.)	
2.10	For each director of the company at the year end, disclose (either in the directors' report or in the notes) the number of shares in and amount of debentures of each group company for which any subscription rights (options) were granted to or exercised by him, or members of his immediate family (excluding family members who are directors), during the year.	S7:2B

No.	Disclosure	Ref
	SI 1985 No 802 lists certain exceptions from the requirement to disclose directors' interests under 2.9 and 2.10 in the report of a wholly owned subsidiary.	
	UITF Abstract 10 recommends that specified information, concerning options applicable to individual directors, together with market price information at the year end and at the date of exercise, be disclosed. Separate figures would be given for each item for each exercise price and/or date combination. This information is required for certain listed companies by LR12.43A(c)(iii) and the detailed requirements are given in appendix V, paragraph 14(iii). Other than as required by S7:2B (see above) the disclosures in UITF Abstract 10 are not mandatory for other companies.	UITF 10
2.11	For listed UK-incorporated companies, the beneficial and non-beneficial interests of each director of the company, disclosed to the company under the Companies Act 1985, as at the end of the financial year under review together with any changes in those interests between the financial year end and a date not more than one month prior to the notice date of the general meeting at which the accounts are to be laid or, if no change, a statement of that fact.	LR12.43(k)

Capital

No.	Disclosure	Ref
2.12	Where the company has an interest in its own shares by purchase, forfeiture or surrender in lieu of forfeiture, acquisition by company's nominee or by another with company financial assistance with the company having a beneficial interest, or by having a lien or charge on its own shares:	S7:7,8
	(1) the number and nominal value of shares purchased, or otherwise acquired or charged by the company during the year;	
	(2) the aggregate consideration paid for shares purchased during the year and reasons for the purchase;	
	(3) the maximum number and nominal amount of such shares acquired or charged (whether or not during year) held at anytime during the year;	
	(4) the number and nominal amount of such shares acquired or charged which were disposed of during the year and the amount or value of the consideration;	
	(5) if shares are charged, the amount of the charge;	
	(6) where the number and nominal value of shares are to be stated above, the percentage of the called-up share capital which such shares represent.	
2.13	For listed companies, information as specified in 2.12 above, where, since the year end, the company has purchased or entered into options or contracts to purchase its own shares other than on the open market or by tender offer.	LR12.43(n)

No.	Disclosure	Ref
2.14	For listed companies, particulars of the nature and extent of the interests of any person, other than a director, as required to be disclosed to the company in accordance with ss198 to 208. Disclose as at a date not more than one month prior to the notice of meeting or a statement that there are no such shareholders. (Information to be given in the directors' report or notes.)	LR12.43(l)
2.15	For listed companies, particulars of any shareholders' authority existing at year end for the purchase of the company's own shares.	LR12.43(n)
2.16	For listed companies, where the company purchased or proposes to purchase its own shares otherwise than through the market or by tender or partial offer to all shareholders, disclose the names of the sellers, or proposed sellers.	LR12.43(n)

Fixed assets

No.	Disclosure	Ref
2.17	Any substantial difference between market value and balance sheet value of fixed asset interests in land of company and subsidiaries.	S7:1(2)

Employees

Disclosures in 2.18 and 2.19 are required where the company employs more than 250 persons in the UK on a weekly average in the year.

No.	Disclosure	Ref
2.18	Company policy for: (1) giving full and fair consideration of employment applications by disabled persons; (2) continuing employment and training of employees who have become disabled; and (3) training, career development and promotion of disabled persons.	S7:9(3)
2.19	Action taken to introduce, maintain or develop arrangements with employees to: (1) provide employees systematically with information on matters concerning them as employees; (2) consult employees or their representatives on a regular basis when decisions are taken which are likely to affect their interests; (3) encourage involvement of employees in company performance through an employee share scheme or by other means; (4) achieve employee awareness of financial and economic factors affecting the company's performance.	S7:11(3)

No.	Disclosure	Ref

Political and charitable gifts

2.20	Where political and charitable donations made to UK residents by a company and/or its subsidiary undertakings (wholly owned subsidiaries of a company incorporated in Great Britain are exempted when preparing their own accounts) exceed £200:	S7:3, 4, 5

    (1) aggregate of such charitable donations;

    (2) aggregate of such political donations; and

    (3) amount and identity of each individual or party given political donations exceeding £200.

Trustee investments

2.21	If partners or members of staff of the auditors (or a person closely connected with either) are trustees of trusts that have a shareholding in the company and the aggregate of such interest is 1 per cent or more of the issued capital, the trust investment should be shown in the accounts, Directors' report or in the audit report.	ICA 1.201, 4.46(c)

Branches

2.22	An indication of the existence of branches of the company outside the United Kingdom.	S7:6(d)

Signing of directors' report

2.23	Name of director or company secretary who signed the directors' report.	s234A
2.24	In addition, if applicable, small companies are required to give a statement to the effect that they have taken advantage of the special provisions of Part VII of the Companies Act 1985 relating to small companies.	s246(8)

Policy on payment of creditors

The disclosures under 2.25 to 2.27 inclusive are required of plcs and of any of their subsidiaries not qualifying as small or medium-sized by virtue of s247.

In 2.25 to 2.27, a person is a supplier of a company if at any time:

- *he is owed an amount in respect of goods and services supplied; and*

- *that amount would be included under the heading corresponding to Item E4 in Format 1 (trade creditors falling due within one year) if accounts were prepared at that time in accordance with Schedule 4 and using a Format 1 balance sheet.*

In 2.25 and 2.27 references to suppliers are references to persons who are or may become suppliers.

No.	*Disclosure*	*Ref*
2.25	With respect to the financial year immediately following that covered by the directors' report:	S7:12
	(1) Whether it is company policy in respect of some or all suppliers:	
	(a) to follow a code or standard on payment practice; and if so, the name of the code or standard and the place where information about and copies of the code or standard may be obtained;	
	(b) to settle the terms of payment with those suppliers when agreeing the terms of each transaction: to ensure those suppliers are made aware of the terms of payment; and to abide by terms of payment.	
	(2) Policy in respect of payment of those suppliers if not as mentioned above.	
2.26	If company's policy differs for different suppliers or classes of supplier; identify the suppliers or classes of suppliers to which the different policies apply.	S7:12
2.27	For periods ending after 24 March 1997 the number of days which bears to the number of days in the financial year the same proportion as X bears to Y where X = the aggregate of the amounts which were owed to trade creditors at the end of the year; and Y = the aggregate of the amounts in which the company was invoiced by suppliers during the year.	S7:12

Year 2000 problem

2.28	In the directors' report, OFR or other statement included in the annual report published by the entity:	UITF 20:11
	(1) the risks and uncertainties associated with the year 2000 problem;	
	(2) the fact if an assessment has not been made of the problem or if the entity has not determined its materiality;	
	(3) the general plans to address the year 2000 issues relating to the business and operations and, if material, its relationships with customers, suppliers, and other relevant parties;	
	(4) whether the total estimated costs of these plans, including amounts to be spent in future periods, have been quantified; and	
	(5) where applicable, an indication of the total costs likely to be incurred, with an explanation of the basis on which the figures are calculated (e.g., the treatment of internal costs and replacement expenditure).	

No.	*Disclosure*	*Ref*
	Euro	
2.29	Where the potential impact is likely to be significant give information and discussion including an indication of the total costs likely to be incurred. Disclosure may be in the directors' report, OFR or other statement included in the annual report published by the entity.	UITF 21:18

3   General requirements

No.	Disclosure	Ref

Content of accounts

3.1	Particulars (describe the treatment required by the Act and that actually adopted), reasons (why prescribed treatment does not give a true and fair view) and effects of departure (how the position is different, normally with quantification) from the requirements of Schedule 4 or Schedule 4A in order to give a true and fair view. Include in or cross refer to note of compliance with applicable accounting standards (see 3.12).	s226(5) s227(6) UITF 7
3.2	Sufficient disclosure to understand the commercial effect of a transaction. The application notes (A to F) to FRS 5 also specify disclosures required in respect of those specific transactions. (*N.B. for the vast majority of transactions this will not involve additional disclosure.*)	FRS 5:30, 92
3.3	Publish a listed parent company's own accounts if they contain significant additional information to that shown in its consolidated accounts.	LR12.42(c)

Comparatives

3.4	Comparative amounts for all disclosure items except: (1) investment class and ownership proportion of subsidiaries; associates; joint ventures and other significant investments; (2) details of accounting treatment of acquisitions; (3) movements in fixed assets, reserves, provisions and charges; (4) directors' loans, quasi-loans and other disclosable dealings.	S4:58(3) S4:4(1)
3.5	Particulars of and reasons for any adjustments to prior year's financial statements to make them comparable with current year.	S4:4(2) S4:58(2)

Accounts format

3.6	Particulars of, and reasons for, a change in the format of either the balance sheet or the profit and loss statement.	S4:2
3.7	Where items which are assigned Arabic numerals in the formats have been combined in the accounts, include individual amounts in notes.	S4:3(4)
3.8	Omit headings or subheadings which have nil amounts for both current and previous years.	S4:3(5)

No.	Disclosure	Ref

Directors' signatures and approval

3.9	Name of signing director on balance sheet.	s233(3)
	Above the signature a statement, if applicable, to the effect that advantage has been taken of the special provisions of Part VII of the Companies Act 1985 relating to small companies.	s246(1A)
3.10	Date on which the board approved the financial statements.	SP 17:26

Accounting policies

3.11	Particulars, reasons and effects of any departures from principles of going concern, consistency, prudence, accruals and separate determination of amounts.	S4:15, SP 2:17
3.12	Statement as to whether the accounts have been prepared in accordance with applicable accounting standards and particulars and reasons for any material departure from them. (Not required if a small or medium company/group.) Cross-reference to note on true and fair override, if applicable (see 3.1).	S4:36A s246(1)
3.13	Particulars, reasons and financial effects of departure from an accounting standard.	Foreword to Accounting Standards
3.14	For group accounts, particulars (include the different accounting policies used) reasons and effect of not adjusting the value of assets and liabilities included in the consolidation to accord with the accounting rules used for the group accounts (where the adjustments are material for giving a true and fair view).	FRS 2:41 S4A:3(2)
3.15	For group accounts, where there are material differences of accounting rules between the parent's individual accounts and its group accounts, state those differences and reasons in the group accounts.	S4A:4
3.16	Accounting policies regarding:	
	(1) depreciation method and useful lives or depreciation rates used for each class of depreciable asset;	FRS 15:100
	(2) finance costs – where a policy of capitalisation is adopted;	FRS 15:31
	(3) translation method and treatment of foreign currency balances;	SP 20:59 S4:58(1)
	(4) stocks and long-term contracts, in particular the method of ascertaining turnover and attributable profit;	SP 9:32
	(5) research and development;	SP 13:30

No.	Disclosure	Ref
	(6) goodwill – where goodwill remains eliminated against reserves:	
	(a) the accounting policy followed in respect of that goodwill;	FRS 10:71(a)
	(b) the fact that this goodwill had been eliminated as a matter of accounting policy and would be charged or credited in the profit and loss account on subsequent disposal of the business to which it related;	FRS 10:71(a)
	(7) government grants;	SP 4:28
	(8) operating and finance leases;	SP 21:57, 60
	(9) recognition of finance lease income;	SP 21:60
	(10) accounting for pension schemes; and the funding policy for defined benefit schemes if different from the accounting policy;	SP 24:87, 88
	(11) accounting for post retirement benefits other than pensions;	UITF 6
	(12) accounting for deferred tax implications of pensions and other post-retirement benefits;	SP 15:32A
	(13) elimination of effects of hyper-inflation and reasons if UITF Abstract 9 methods are not used;	UITF 9
	(14) derivatives and other financial instruments; and	FRS 13:73 to 76
	(15) any other accounting policy used to determine amounts material in determining profit or loss and financial position.	S4:36 SP 2:18
3.17	Fact, if the period to which the directors have paid particular attention in assessing going concern is less than one year from the date of approval of the financial statements.	SAS 130: 13, 45

Joint arrangement that is not an entity

No.	Disclosure	Ref
3.18	Joint arrangement that is not an entity or a structure with the form but not the substance of a joint venture – account for own assets, liabilities and cash flows in the investor's entity accounts and consolidated accounts.	FRS 9:18, 24

4 Profit and loss account

No.	*Disclosure*	*Ref*

General

4.1	Effect of including in the profit and loss account any material amount relating to any preceding year.	S4:57(1)
4.2	Items to be shown on the face of the profit and loss account (see also 4.4 and 4.5):	
	(1) Turnover	FRS 3:14
	(a) For group accounts, share of joint venture turnover but not as part of group turnover.	FRS 9:21
	(b) For group accounts, associate turnover must be clearly distinguished from group turnover if a total combining group turnover and associate turnover has been given as a memorandum item.	FRS 9:27
	(2) Operating profit	FRS 3:14
	(a) For group accounts, share of joint venture operating result, immediately after group operating result, any amortisation or write down of goodwill arising on acquiring the joint venture should be charged at this point and disclosed.	FRS 9:21, 27
	(b) For group accounts, share of associate operating result immediately after group operating result and share of joint venture operating result (if any), any amortisation or write down of goodwill arising on acquiring the joint venture should be charged at this point and disclosed.	FRS 9:27
	(3) Exceptional profits or losses on the sale or termination of an operation.	FRS 3:20
	(4) Exceptional costs of a fundamental reorganisation or restructuring having a material effect on the nature and focus of the reporting entity's operations.	FRS 3:20
	(5) Exceptional profits or losses on the disposal of fixed assets.	FRS 3:20
	(a) For group accounts, share of any FRS 3:20 exceptional items or of interest of joint ventures separately from amounts relating to the group.	FRS 9:21, 27
	(b) For group accounts, share of any FRS 3:20 exceptional items or of interest of associates separately from amounts relating to the group.	FRS 9:27
	(6) Profit or loss on ordinary activities before taxation.	S4:3(6)
	(7) Extraordinary profit/loss for financial year.	FRS 3:22
	(8) Dividends paid and proposed (including withholding taxes, but excluding any other taxes). (Where the amounts relating to non-equity shares are immaterial and hence not given on the face of the P&L the relevant caption should make clear that such amounts are included.)	S4:3(7), FRS 16:8, FRS 4:59, 100

No.	Disclosure	Ref
	(9) Any other appropriations of profit in respect of non-equity shares. (Where the amounts relating to non-equity shares are immaterial and hence not given on the face of the P&L the relevant caption should make clear that such amounts are included.)	FRS 4:59, 100
	(10) Transfers to/from reserves.	S4:3(7)
	(11) For group accounts, any supplementary information in respect of joint ventures given in the profit and loss account, except for any items below profit before tax, must be shown clearly separate from amounts for the group and must not be included in group totals.	FRS 9:22
	(12) For group accounts, at or below the level of profit before tax, include the investor's share of the relevant amount for joint ventures within the amounts for the group and for items below this level disclose the amounts relating to joint ventures.	FRS 9:21, 27
	(13) For group accounts, at or below the level of profit before tax, include the investor's share of the relevant amount for associates within the amounts for the group and for items below this level disclose the amounts relating to associates	FRS 9:27
	Items (1) and (2) should be analysed between continuing, acquisitions and discontinued operations on the face of the profit and loss.	FRS 3:14, 20, 3
	Items (3) to (5) above should be analysed between continuing and discontinued operations on the face of the profit and loss and where practicable the analysis should identify the amounts arising in respect of acquisitions.	
4.3	Items to be shown either on the face of the profit and loss account or in the notes (dividends, interest or other income receivable should include withholding taxes but exclude any other taxes):	S4:F FRS 16:9
	(1) other operating income;	S4:F
	(2) income from shares in group undertakings;	S4:F
	(3) income from participating interests (in consolidated accounts, replace by two items: 'Income from interests in associated undertakings' and 'Income from other participating interests');	S4:F, S4A:21
	(4) income from other fixed asset investments (show income from group undertakings separately);	S4:F
	(5) other interest receivable and similar income (show interest from group undertakings separately);	S4:F
	(6) amounts written off investments;	S4:F
	(7) interest payable and similar charges (show amount payable to group undertakings separately).	S4:F
	Separately from other interest, either on the face of the profit and loss account or in the notes, the unwinding	FRS 12:47

No.	Disclosure	Ref
	of the discount on provisions which should be included as a financial item adjacent to interest;	
(8)	tax on profit or loss on ordinary activities;	S4:F
(9)	profit or loss on ordinary activities after taxation:	S4:F
(10)	minority interest – ordinary activities;	S4A:17
(11)	extraordinary income;	S4:F
(12)	extraordinary charges;	S4:F
(13)	extraordinary profit or loss;	S4:F
(14)	tax on extraordinary profit or loss, with separate identification of deferred tax;	S4:F
(15)	minority interest – extraordinary;	S4A: 17
(16)	other taxes not shown under above items;	S4:F
(17)	profit or loss for the financial year;	S4:F
(18)	aggregate amount of any dividends proposed;	S4:3(7)(c)
(19)	for group accounts, at or below the level of profit before tax, include the investor's share of the relevant amount for joint ventures within the amounts for the group and for items below this level disclose the amounts relating to joint ventures;	FRS 9:21, 27
(20)	for group accounts, at or below the level of profit before tax, include the investor's share of the relevant amount for associates within the amounts for the group and for items below this level disclose the amounts relating to associates;	FRS 9:27
(21)	on the face of the profit and loss account, if material, or in a note, the dividend income arising on shares held in a ESOP trust which has been deducted from the aggregate of dividends paid and proposed.	UITF 13: 8(g), FRS 14:81
4.4	**For formats 1 and 3**, disclose either on the face of the profit and loss account or in the notes:	
(1)	cost of sales;	S4:F
(2)	gross profit or loss (format 1 only);	S4:F
(3)	distribution costs;	S4:F
(4)	administrative expenses.	S4:F
4.5	**For formats 2 and 4**, disclose either on face of the profit and loss or in the notes:	
(1)	change in stocks of finished goods and in work in progress;	S4:F
(2)	own work capitalised;	S4:F
(3)	raw materials and consumables;	S4:F
(4)	other external charges;	S4:F

No.	*Disclosure*	*Ref*
	(5) staff costs: (a) wages and salaries, (b) social security costs, (c) other pension costs	S4:F
	(6) depreciation and other amounts written off tangible and intangible fixed assets;	S4:F
	(7) exceptional amounts written off current assets;	S4:F
	(8) other operating charges.	S4:F
4.6	The separate components of any net profit or loss recognised in respect of linked items. Disclosure should be on the face of the profit and loss account if necessary for a true and fair view.	FRS 5:28, 88

Discontinued and acquired operations

4.7	Turnover and operating profit for current period analysed between continuing operations, acquisitions and discontinued operations on the face of the profit and loss account,	FRS 3:14
4.8	Analysis of each statutory heading between turnover and operating profit between continuing operations, acquisitions and discontinued operations by way of note if not given on the face of the profit and loss account.	FRS 3:14
4.9	Method and assumptions used if interest or tax are allocated between continuing and discontinued operations.	FRS 3:14
4.10	Where it is not practicable to determine post-acquisition results to the end of the current period, an indication of the contribution of the acquisition to turnover and operating profit. If an indication of the contribution of an acquisition to the results of the period cannot be given, this fact and the reason should be explained.	FRS 3:16, FRS 6:29
4.11	Utilisation of provisions in respect of operating losses and the loss on sale or termination of a discontinued operation should be disclosed on the face of the profit and loss account immediately below the relevant items. The results of the discontinued operation being included within each of the statutory format headings.	FRS 3:18

Income – other disclosures

4.12	Rents receivable in respect of operating leases.	SP 21:60
4.13	Rents receivable in respect of finance leases.	SP 21:60
4.14	Nature and effects of government grants and other government assistance on the results for the period and/or the financial position.	SP 4:28

No.	Disclosure	Ref

Depreciation and diminution in value

4.15	Total charge for depreciation and diminution in value of tangible and intangible fixed assets where formats 1 or 3 are used.	S4:F
4.16	Total depreciation charge by major class of asset held under finance lease or hire purchase contracts, or if leased assets are combined with owned fixed assets, disclose the total depreciation in respect of leased assets.	SP 21:49, 50
4.17	Provision for diminution in value of fixed assets and any such provisions written back which are not shown on the face of the profit and loss account.	S4:19
4.18	Where the depreciation method has changed, the effect and reason for the change.	FRS 15:102
4.19	The effect of a change during the period in either the estimate of useful economic lives or the estimate of residual values.	FRS 15:100
4.20	Particulars, reason and effect of departure from legal requirement to depreciate investment properties.	SP 19:17 S226(5)
4.21	Where depreciation is based on revalued amounts and the depreciation shown on the face of the profit and loss account under Formats 2 and 4 or in the notes under Formats 1 and 3 is based on historical cost, the additional depreciation (based on the revaluation surplus) which has been charged to the profit and loss account.	S4:32
4.22	(1) The amount of goodwill amortised and charged to the profit and loss account.	FRS 10:53
	(2) Goodwill relating to associates or joint ventures written off in the period due to impairment.	FRS 9:38
4.23	The amount of purchased goodwill attributable to a business disposed of and included in the calculation of the profit and loss on disposal or the fact and the reason if it is not possible to ascertain or reasonably apportion such goodwill.	UITF 3

Directors' remuneration for periods ending on or after 31 March 1997

The statutory disclosures in respect of directors' remuneration were changed by SI 1997 No 570 for financial years ending on or after 31 March 1997. Paragraphs 4.25 to 4.31 inclusive address periods ending on or after 31 March 1997.

No.	Disclosure	Ref
	For the purposes of paragraphs 4.25 to 4.28 and 4.30:	
	(1) *Any information (other than the aggregate amount of gains made by directors on the exercise of share options) shall be treated as shown if it is capable of being readily ascertained from other information which is shown.*	S6:1(6)
	(2) *Emoluments paid or receivable or share options granted in respect of a person's accepting office as a director shall be treated as emoluments paid or receivable or share options granted in respect of his services as a director.*	S6:1(6)
	For the purposes of paragraphs 4.25 to 4.30:	
	(3) *Pension scheme has the meaning assigned to retirement benefit scheme by s611 ICTA 1988. This is generally interpreted as extending to unfunded pension arrangements.*	S6:13(3)
	For the purposes of paragraphs 4.25 to 4.28:	
	(4) *In the case of a hybrid scheme (where benefits become payable based on the higher of the money purchase benefits or the defined benefits) the company may assume the scheme is money purchase or defined benefit according to which seems more likely at the end of the financial year.*	S6:1(7)
	(5) *Qualifying services mean services as a director of the company and, while director, services as a director of any of its subsidiary undertakings or otherwise in connection with the management of the affairs of the company or any of its subsidiary undertakings.*	S6:1(5)
	(6) *Company contribution in relation to a pension scheme and a director means any payment (including insurance premiums) made, or treated as made, to the scheme in respect of the director by a person other than the director.*	S6:1(5)
	(7) *Share option means a right to acquire shares.*	S6:1(5)
	(8) *Long-term incentive schemes means an agreement or arrangement under which money or other assets may become receivable by a director and where at least one qualifying condition with respect to service or performance cannot be fulfilled within a single financial year. Specifically excluded are:*	S6:1(4)
	(a) *bonuses the amount of which falls to be determined by reference to service or performance within a single financial year;*	
	(b) *compensation for loss of office, payments for breach of contract and other termination payments; and*	
	(c) *retirement benefits.*	
4.24	(1) Aggregate emoluments paid to or receivable by directors in respect of qualifying services.	S6:1(1)(a)
	Emoluments of a director include *salary, fees and bonuses, sums paid by way of expense allowances subject to UK income tax, and the money value of any other benefits receivable otherwise than in cash.*	S6:1(3)

No.	Disclosure	Ref
	Emoluments do not include:	S6:1(3)
	(a) the value of share options granted or gains made on the exercise of such options;	
	(b) any company contributions paid or treated as paid under a pension scheme;	
	(c) any money or other assets paid to or received or receivable under any long-term incentive scheme.	
(2)	For listed or AIM companies; aggregate amount of the gains made by directors on the exercise of share options *(calculated as the difference between the market price of the shares on the day on which the option was exercised and the price actually paid for the shares).*	S6:1(1)(b)
(3)	For listed or AIM companies; the aggregate of the following:	
	(a) the amount of money paid to or receivable by directors under long-term incentive schemes in respect of qualifying services; and	S6:1(1)(c)
	(b) the net value of assets (other than money and share options) received or receivable by directors under long-term incentive schemes in respect of qualifying services.	S6:1(1)(c)
(4)	For companies that are not listed or AIM companies; the aggregate of the following:	
	(a) the amount of money paid to or receivable by directors under long-term incentive schemes in respect of qualifying services; and	S6:1(1)(c)
	(b) the net value of assets (other than money, shares and share options) received or receivable by directors under long-term incentive schemes in respect of qualifying services.	S6:1(1)(c), S6:1(2)
	A small company may give the total of aggregate amounts required by 4.24(1), (4) and 4.26(1) instead of giving those three figures separately.	s246(3)(a)
4.25	For companies that are not listed or AIM companies; the number of each of the following (if any) shall be shown:	S6:1(2)(b)
	(1) the directors who exercised share options;	S6:1(2)(b)
	(2) the directors in respect of whose qualifying services shares were received or receivable under long-term incentive schemes.	S6:1(2)(b)
4.26	(1) Aggregate value of company contributions paid or treated as paid to a pension scheme in respect of directors' qualifying services which are contributions by reference to which the rate or amount of any money purchase benefits that may become payable will be calculated.	S6:1(1)(d)

No.	Disclosure	Ref
	(2) The number of directors (if any) to whom retirement benefits are accruing under each of the following types of scheme in respect of qualifying services:	S6:1(1)(e)
	(a) money purchase schemes; (b) defined benefit schemes.	S6:1(1)(e)
4.27	Where the aggregate of the amounts reported under 4.25 are £200,000 or more:	
	(1) how much of the total of those aggregates as is attributable to the highest paid director *(i.e., the director to whom is attributable the greatest part of the total of the aggregate shown under 4.25 above);*	S6:2(1)
	(2) the amount of the aggregate contributions disclosed under 4.27 attributable to the highest paid director;	S6:2(1)
	(3) where the highest paid director has performed qualifying services during the year which attract defined benefits:	
	(a) the amount at the end of the year of that director's accrued pension and,	S6:2(2)
	(b) where applicable, the amount at the end of the year of the accrued lump sum. *(Disclosure should only be made of a lump sum to which the director is automatically entitled on retirement. It does not relate to a lump sum payable by way of commutation of rights to an annual pension.)*	S6:2(2) S6:2(5)
	(N.B. Comparatives are not required in respect of this disclosure for financial years ending before 31 March 1998.)	SI 1997/570 Reg 3(2)
	(4) For companies that are not listed or AIM companies; whether the highest paid director:	S6:2(3)
	(a) exercised any share options; and (b) received shares or has shares receivable under a long-term incentive scheme in respect of qualifying services.	
	(It is not necessary to state that fact if there are no transactions to be disclosed.)	S6:2(4)
4.28	Aggregate of excess retirement benefits paid to or receivable by directors and past directors.	S6:7(1) and (2)
	In each case the excess is calculated by reference to the benefits to which they were entitled on the later of 31 March 1997 and the date the benefits first became payable. Amounts paid or receivable need not be included in the aggregate amount if the funding of the scheme was such that the amounts were, or could have been, made without recourse to additional contributions and the amounts were paid or receivable on the same basis to all persons entitled to the present payment of retirement benefits under the scheme.	

No.	Disclosure	Ref
4.29	Compensation to directors and past directors for loss of office:	S6:8(1)
	(1) aggregate amount (amounts to include non-cash benefits);	
	(2) the nature of any non-cash benefits.	
	N.B.	
	(1) Compensation for loss of office includes payments in respect of breach of contract.	S6:8(4)
	(2) Any information (other than the aggregate amount of gains made by directors on the exercise of share options) shall be treated as shown if it is capable of being readily ascertained from other information which is shown.)	S6:1(6)(a), S6:8(5)
4.30	For consideration paid to or receivable by third parties for making available the services of any person as a director of the company or, while director, as a director of any of its subsidiary undertakings or in connection with the management of the affairs of the company or any of its subsidiary undertakings:	S6:9
	(1) aggregate amount (including non-cash benefits);	
	(2) the nature of any non-cash benefits.	

Employees

No.	Disclosure	Ref
4.31	Monthly average number of persons employed in the year and the number so employed in each category selected by the directors.	S4:56(1)
4.32	Aggregate amounts for the year of:	
	(1) wages and salaries;	S4:56(4)
	(2) social security costs;	S4:56(4)
	(3) other pension costs.	S4:56(4)
	(In formats 2 and 4 the above may appear on the face of the profit and loss account.)	

Pensions

No.	Disclosure	Ref
4.33	Pension cost charge in the year, explaining for defined benefit schemes any significant changes in the pension cost charge as compared with the previous period.	SP 24:87, 88 UITF 18:8
4.34	The amount charged to the profit and loss account and the basis of the charge, where a group has foreign pension schemes which have commitments which are very different from those customary in the UK and it is impractical (due to difficulties and cost of obtaining actuarial information) to adjust to SSAP 24 basis.	SP 24:91

No.	Disclosure	Ref

Other expenses

4.35	Interest payable or similar charges in respect of:	
	(1) bank loans and overdrafts (excluding group loans); and	S4:53(2)
	(2) other loans (exclude interest on loans from group companies); and	S4:53(2)
	(3) finance charges allocated for the year in respect of finance leases.	SP 21:53
4.36	Separately within or adjacent to 'interest payable and similar charges', gains or losses on repurchase or early settlement of debts.	FRS 4:64
4.37	Operating lease charges:	SP 21:55
	(1) for hire of plant and machinery;	
	(2) for hire of other assets.	
4.38	Where reverse premiums and similar incentives to enter into a lease are not accounted for using the standard treatment for the reasons specified in UITF Abstract 12:	UITF 12
	(1) an explanation of the specific circumstances that render the standard treatment specified by UITF Abstract 12 misleading;	
	(2) a description of the basis used and amounts involved;	
	(3) a note of the effect on the results for the current and corresponding period of any departure from the standard treatment.	
4.39	(1) Auditors' remuneration (including expenses) and the nature of any non-cash benefits for the company audit.	s390A
	(2) Auditors' remuneration (including expenses) and the nature of any non-cash benefits for the group audit.	s390A & S4A:1(1)
4.40	Non-audit fees paid to the auditors and their associates.	s390B
4.41	Research and development expense, analysed between:	SP 13:31
	(1) current year's expenditure; and	
	(2) amounts amortised from deferred expenditure.	
	The information in 4.42 above does not need to be given by any company or other entity (provided it is not a public limited company, bank or insurance company or a parent company which has as a subsidiary any of these types of companies) which satisfies the Act's current criteria, multiplied in each case by 10, for defining a medium-sized company.	SP 13:22

No.	Disclosure	Ref

Taxation

No.	Disclosure	Ref
4.42	Special circumstances affecting the tax charge/credit for the period or future periods with quantification. Include circumstances relating to tax attributable to FRS 3:20 exceptional items in 4.2 above.	FRS 3:23 S4:54(2)
4.43	Effects of a fundamental change in the basis of taxation shown separately on the face of the profit and loss account as part of the tax charge/credit for the period.	FRS 3:23
4.44	The basis used to apportion tax between extraordinary items and FRS 3:20 exceptional items listed in 4.2 above if different from that suggested by FRS 3.	FRS 3:24
4.45	Amounts comprising the taxation charges on ordinary activities and on extraordinary items:	
	(1) UK corporation tax; (before double tax relief) analysed between the estimate for the current period and any adjustments in respect of prior periods	S4:54(3) FRS 16:17
	(2) changes in amount of ACT recoverable;	FRS 16:20
	(3) overseas taxation relief	S4:54(3)
	(4) UK corporation tax net of overseas tax relief;	S4:54 (3) FRS 16:17
	(5) foreign tax analysed between the estimate for the current period and any adjustments in respect of prior periods.	S4:54 (3) FRS 16:17
4.46	Amount of unprovided deferred tax in respect of the period, analysed into its major component.	SP 15:35
4.47	The amount within the annual tax charge arising from adjustments to deferred tax resulting from changes in tax rates and tax allowances.	SP 15:36
4.48	That deferred taxation has not been provided on earnings retained overseas, if applicable.	SP 15:44
4.49	Where a group company takes account of group relief, the assumptions made as to the availability of group tax relief and payment for group relief.	SP 15:43
4.50	Non-taxpaying entities entitled to transitional relief following the removal of their right to reclaim tax credits should disclose the nature and amount of the relief separately. Such relief may be presented as part of the income to which it relates.	

Exchange movements

No.	Disclosure	Ref
4.51	(1) Net amount of exchange gains and losses on foreign currency borrowings less deposits, showing separately:	SP 20:60

No.	*Disclosure*	*Ref*
	(a) the amount charged/credited to the profit and loss account;	
	(b) amount offset in reserves where borrowings provide a hedge against equity investments in foreign enterprises; and	
	(c) amount of tax charges and credits taken to reserves in respect of borrowings providing a hedge against equity investments in foreign enterprises.	UITF 19:9
	(2) The net movement on reserves arising from exchange differences.	SP 20:60

Exceptional items

4.52	For exceptional items:	
	(1) description of each item;	S4:57(3) FRS 3:19
	(2) for items other than as noted in 4.2, include within relevant statutory headings and attribute to continuing or discontinued operations as appropriate with the amount of each item disclosed separately by way of note or on the face of the profit and loss account if necessary for a true and fair view.	FRS 3:19
4.53	The effect of the exceptional items in 4.2 above on the taxation and minority interest figures.	FRS 3:20
4.54	For each material acquisition and other acquisitions in aggregate, any exceptional profit or loss post acquisition determined using fair values recognised on acquisition should be disclosed as required by FRS 3 and identified as relating to the acquisition.	FRS 6:30

Extraordinary items

4.55	Description of each extraordinary item.	S4:57, FRS 3:22

Dividends

4.56	Aggregate dividends for each class of share including total amount in respect of each of:	FRS 4:59, 100
	(1) dividends on equity shares;	
	(2) participating dividends; and	
	(3) other dividends on non-equity shares.	

Minority interests

4.57	Analyse profit and loss charge between equity and non-equity minority interest.	FRS 4:60

No.	Disclosure	Ref

Prior period adjustments

4.58 For changes in accounting policies or correction of fundamental errors:

    (1) where practicable the effect of prior period adjustments on the preceding period's results; and   **FRS 3:29**

    (2) the cumulative effect of the adjustments at the foot of the statement of total recognised gains and losses for the current period;   **FRS 3:29**

    (3) particulars of and reasons for prior period adjustments;   **S4:58(2)**

    (4) effect on the current year's results. If the effect on the current year is immaterial or similar to the effect on the prior year a simple statement will suffice. Fact and reasons if it is not practicable to give effect on the current year.   **UITF 14**

Earnings per share

FRS 14 is mandatory for periods ending on or after 23 December 1998 for entities whose ordinary shares or potential ordinary shares are publicly traded, that are in the process of issuing ordinary shares or potential ordinary shares in public securities markets or that choose to disclose EPS. Whilst the provisions of FRS 14 are drafted principally in terms of amounts per share as components of net profit; the requirements also apply, as far as appropriate, to other amounts per share (e.g., net assets per share).   **FRS 14**

Where both the parent's and consolidated financial statements are presented, the disclosures called for by FRS 14 are required only on the basis of consolidated information.

4.59 Basic and diluted earnings per share on the face of the profit and loss account: **FRS 14:69**

    (1) For each class of ordinary share that has a different right to share in the net profit for the period.   **FRS 14:69**

    (2) With equal prominence for all periods presented.   **FRS 14:69**

    (3) Even if the amounts disclosed are negative.   **FRS 14:70**

4.60 Amounts used as the numerators in calculating basic and diluted earnings per share, and a reconciliation of those amounts to the net profit or loss for the period.   **FRS 14:71**

4.61 Weighted average number of ordinary shares used as the denominators in calculating basic and diluted earnings per share, and, excepting figures given in respect of different classes of ordinary share, a reconciliation of these denominators to each other.   **FRS 14:71**

4.62 If an entity discloses an additional eps figure based upon a reported component of net profit other than net profit or loss for the period attributable to ordinary shareholders: **FRS 14:74**

No.	Disclosure	Ref
	(1) It should be calculated using the weighted average number of ordinary shares determined in accordance with FRS 14.	FRS 14:73
	(2) It should be calculated on a consistent basis over time.	FRS 14:74
	(3) A reconciliation to the amount required by FRS 14 either adjacent to the FRS 14 eps disclosure or referenced from it. Such reconciliation to include:	FRS 14:74 FRS 3:25
	(a) a list of the items for which adjustment is being made;	FRS 14:74
	(b) their individual effect on the calculation.	FRS 14:74
	(4) Any additional eps should not be more prominent than the FRS 14 eps.	FRS 14:74
	(5) The reason for the additional eps either adjacent to the FRS 14 eps disclosure or referenced from it.	FRS 14:74 FRS 3:25
	(6) If both an additional basic and an additional diluted eps are given they should appear with equal prominence.	FRS 14:74
	The above disclosures will also satisfy the requirements of FRS 3:25.	
4.63	The fact where calculations of basic and diluted eps are restated for changes in the number of shares without a corresponding change in resources (including changes after the year end but before the financial statements are approved).	FRS 14:63
4.64	The fact if no restatement is made in respect of a share consolidation combined with a special divided which has the overall commercial effect of a share repurchase at fair value.	FRS 14:64
4.65	A description of ordinary share transactions or potential ordinary share transactions occurring after the balance sheet date which are of such importance that non-disclosure would affect the ability of the users of the financial statements to make proper evaluations and decisions. Examples of such transactions are given in FRS 14:67. Disclosure not required if shares are accounted for in accordance with FRS 14:63 (i.e., calculation per share restated as there is no corresponding change of resources – see 4.63 above).	FRS 14:66
4.66	The fact that eps and dividend per share are restated and clearly distinguished from non-adjusted data in historical summaries where eps are restated to be consistent with FRS 14:63.	FRS 14:76, 77
4.67	Whether or not required by FRS 4, FRS 14 encourages the disclosure of terms and conditions that affect the measurement of basic and diluted earnings per share. These terms and conditions may determine whether any potential ordinary shares are dilutive and, if so, the effect on the weighted average number of shares outstanding and any consequent adjustments to the net profit attributable to ordinary shareholders.	FRS 14:72

No.	Disclosure	Ref

Joint ventures

4.68   If consolidated accounts are not prepared then, unless the company is exempt from preparing consolidated accounts, or would be if it had subsidiaries, show the following information by producing a separate set of financial statements or by showing the relevant amounts, together with the effects of including them, as additional information to the company's own financial: **FRS 9:48**

(1) share of joint venture turnover but not as part of group turnover;   **FRS 9:21**

(2) share of joint venture operating result, immediately after group operating result, any amortisation or write down of goodwill arising on acquiring the joint venture should be charged at this point and disclosed;   **FRS 9:21, 27**

(3) share of any FRS 3:20 exceptional items or of interest separately from amounts relating to the group;   **FRS 9:21, 27**

(4) at or below the level of profit before tax, include the investor's share of the relevant amount for joint ventures within the amounts for the group and for items below this level disclose the amounts relating to joint ventures;   **FRS 9:21, 27**

(5) any supplementary information given in the profit and loss account, except for any items below profit before tax, must be shown clearly separate from amounts for the group and must not be included in group totals.   **FRS 9:22**

Associates

4.69   If consolidated accounts are not prepared then, unless the company is exempt from preparing consolidated accounts, or would be if it had subsidiaries, show the following information by producing a separate set of financial statements or by showing the relevant amounts, together with the effects of including them, as additional information to the company's own financial: **FRS 9:48**

(1) associate turnover must be clearly distinguished from group turnover if a total combining group turnover and associate turnover has been given as a memorandum item;   **FRS 9:27**

(2) share of associate operating result immediately after group operating result and share of joint venture operating result (if any), any amortisation or write down of goodwill arising on acquiring the joint venture should be charged at this point and disclosed;   **FRS 9:27**

(3) share of any FRS 3:20 exceptional items or of interest should be shown separately from amounts relating to the group;   **FRS 9:27**

(4) at or below the level of profit before tax, include the investor's share of the relevant amount for associates within the amounts for the group and for items below this level disclose the amounts relating to associates.   **FRS 9:27**

No.	Disclosure	Ref

Note of historical cost profits and losses

4.70   Immediately following the profit and loss account or statement of total recognised gains and losses reconciling reported profit/loss on ordinary activities before taxation to the equivalent historical cost amount and showing the retained profit/loss for the year on a historical cost basis.

FRS 3:26

Reconciliation of movement in shareholder's funds

4.71   Note to the accounts reconciling opening and closing shareholders' funds for the period.

FRS 3:28

Parent's profit and loss account

4.72   If the group accounts exclude the profit and loss account of the parent company, state that the exemption conferred by s230 applies and give the parent company's profit or loss for the financial year.

s230

Recognition of impairment loss

4.73   Recognise impairment losses in the profit and loss account, included under the relevant statutory heading in the profit and loss account with disclosure as an exceptional item if appropriate, unless they relate to previously revalued fixed assets (see 4.74).

FRS 11:14, 67

4.74   Recognition of impairments losses of revalued fixed assets:

FRS 11:63

     (1) in the profit and loss account, included under the relevant statutory heading in the profit and loss account with disclosure as an exceptional item if appropriate, if caused by a clear consumption of economic benefits; otherwise

FRS 11:63, 67

     (2) in the STRGL (separately on the face of the statement) until carrying amount reaches depreciated historical cost; then

FRS 11:63, 67

     (3) in the profit and loss account, included under the relevant statutory heading in the profit and loss account with disclosure as an exceptional item if appropriate, to the extent that reaches depreciated historical cost exceeds carrying value.

FRS 11:63, 67

Reversal of impairment loss

4.75   Reversal of an impairment loss on tangible fixed assets, investments in subsidiaries, associates and joint ventures should be recognised in the profit and loss account, unless arising on a previously revalued fixed asset (see 4.76).

FRS 11:56

4.76   Reversal of an impairment loss on a revalued fixed asset should be recognised in the profit and loss account to the

FRS 11:66

No.	*Disclosure*	*Ref*

extent that the original impairment loss (adjusted for subsequent depreciation) was so recognised. The remaining balance of the reversal of an impairment should be recognised in the STRGL.

Provisions

4.77 In the profit and loss account the expense relating to a provision may be presented net of the amount recognised for a reimbursement.

FRS 12:57

5 Balance sheet

No.	*Disclosure*	*Ref*

General

5.1   On the face of the balance sheet: **S4:F**

     (1)   Called up share capital not paid (alternatively may be shown under 'Debtors' either on the face of the balance sheet or in the notes).

     (2)   Fixed assets, with separate headings for:

         (a)   intangible assets;
         (b)   tangible assets;
         (c)   investments.

     (3)   Current assets, with separate headings for:

         (a)   stocks;
         (b)   debtors;
         (c)   investments;
         (d)   cash at bank and in hand.

     (4)   Prepayments and accrued income (alternatively may be shown under 'Debtors' either on the face of the balance sheet or in the notes).

     (5)   Creditors: amounts falling due within one year (format 1 only).

     (6)   Net current assets (liabilities) (format 1 only).

     (7)   Total assets less current liabilities (format 1 only).

     (8)   Creditors: amounts falling due after more than one year (format 1 only).

     (9)   Creditors (format 2 only).

    (10)   Provisions for liabilities and charges.

    (11)   Accruals and deferred income (alternatively may be shown under 'Creditors' headings (5), (7), (8) above either on the face of the balance sheet or in the notes).

    (12)   In consolidated accounts, minority interests (alternatively may be shown after 'Capital and Reserves').   **S4A:17**

    (13)   Capital and reserves, with separate headings for:

         (a)   called up share capital (show separately amount of allotted share capital and amount of called up share capital that has been paid up);   **S4:F(12)**

         (b)   share premium account;

         (c)   revaluation reserve (a title other than 'revaluation reserve' may be used;   **S4:34(2)**

         (d)   other reserves;

         (e)   Profit and loss account.

    (14)   Total amount of shareholders' funds.

No.	Disclosure	Ref
	(15) Where linked presentation has been used disclose the gross amounts of the item and the finance on the face of the balance sheet.	
	(16) Convertible debt to be stated separately from other liabilities. If immaterial disclosure may be made in the notes but the caption on the balance sheet should make clear that convertible debt is included.	FRS 4:25, 54, 100
	(17) Amount of shareholders' funds attributable to equity interests and amount attributable to non-equity interests. If immaterial disclosure may be made in the notes but the caption on the balance sheet should make clear that non-equity interests are included.	
	(18) Amount of minority interests attributable to equity interests and amount attributable to non-equity interests. If immaterial disclosure may be made in the notes but the caption on the balance sheet should make clear that non-equity interests are included.	
5.2	Disclose any differences in the nature of an item compared with items usually included under the relevant balance sheet headings.	

Assets generally

No.	Disclosure	Ref
5.3	Where a policy of capitalisation of finance costs is adopted, the financial statements should disclose:	FRS 15:31
	(1) the aggregate finance costs included in the cost of tangible fixed assets (this may be different to interest);	
	(2) finance costs capitalised during the period;	
	(3) finance costs recognised in the profit and loss account during the period; and	
	(4) the capitalisation rate used to determine the amount of finance costs capitalised during the period.	
5.4	Interest included in the production cost of an asset.	S4:26
5.5	For listed companies, interest capitalised in the financial year and the amount and treatment of any related tax relief.	LR12.43(c)
5.6	Where there is no record of purchase price or production cost for an asset, or it cannot be obtained without unreasonable expense or delay, particulars of the assets valued at the amount shown in the earliest available record. (Disclosure only required the first time this basis is used.)	S4:28
5.7	Where stocks or fungible assets are valued using FIFO, LIFO, weighted average cost or a similar method to these, the difference (if material) between the balance sheet value of those stocks/fungible assets (including investments) and their replacement cost at the balance sheet date.	S4:27
5.8	Where the alternative accounting rules have been used to value assets:	
	(1) the balance sheet items affected and basis of valuation of each such item;	S4:33

No.	Disclosure	Ref
	(2) for all such items (except stocks) the comparable historical cost amounts or the difference between historical cost amounts and balance sheet values (for cost and depreciation).	S4:33
5.9	Where the difference between total debt repayments and loan proceeds has been treated as an asset, the amount of the unamortised balance.	S4:42

Fixed assets – intangible assets

No.	Disclosure	Ref
5.10	On the face of the balance sheet or in the notes:	S4:F
	(1) development costs;	
	(2) concessions, patents, licences, trademarks and similar rights and assets;	
	(3) goodwill;	
	(a) positive purchased goodwill to be capitalised and classified as an asset;	FRS 10:7, 48
	(b) negative goodwill should be shown separately on the face of the balance sheet immediately after positive goodwill;	FRS 10:7, 48
	(c) a subtotal showing the net amount of the positive and negative goodwill.	FRS 10:7, 48
	(4) Payments on account in respect of intangible assets.	
	Small companies need only show (1) goodwill and (2) other intangible assets.	
5.11	The reasons for capitalising development costs and the write off period.	S4:20
5.12	If capitalised development costs are not treated as a realised loss for purposes of determining distributable profits, then state that the amount is not so treated and explain circumstances which justify the directors' decision.	s269(2)(b)
5.13	Movements on deferred development expenditure and amounts brought forward and carried forward.	SP 13:32
5.14	Methods used to value intangible assets.	FRS 10:52
5.15	Separately for positive goodwill, negative goodwill and each class of capitalised intangible asset on the balance sheet:	FRS 10:53
	(1) cost or revalued amount at the beginning of the financial period and at the balance sheet date;	FRS 10:53 S4:42
	(2) cumulative amount of provisions for amortisation or impairment at the beginning of the financial period and at the balance sheet date;	FRS 10:53 S4:42
	(3) aggregate movements in cost or valuation, separately disclosing additions, disposals, revaluations and transfers;	FRS 10:53 S4:42

No.	Disclosure	Ref
	(4) aggregate movements in provisions for amortisation and impairment, separately disclosing disposals, transfers, amortisation, impairment losses, reversals of past impairment losses and amounts of negative goodwill written back in the financial period; and	FRS 10:53 S4:42
	(5) the net carrying amount at the balance sheet date.	FRS 10:53
5.16	In respect of amortisation of goodwill and intangible assets:	
	(1) the methods;	FRS 10:55
	(2) periods of amortisation;	FRS 10:55 S4:21
	(3) the reason for choosing those periods;	FRS 10:55 S4:21
	(4) if the amortisation period is changed in the year, the reason and effect, if material, for the change;	FRS 10:56
	(5) if the amortisation method is changed in the year, the reason and effect, if material, for the change;	FRS 10:57
	(6) grounds for rebutting the 20 year presumption where goodwill or intangible asset is amortised over a period exceeding 20 years from the date of acquisition or is not amortised. (This should be a reasoned explanation based upon the specific factors contributing to the durability of the acquired business or intangible asset.)	FRS 10:58
5.17	Where goodwill in the financial statements of companies is not amortised:	FRS 10:59
	(1) the financial statements should state that they depart from the specific requirement of companies legislation to amortise goodwill over a finite period for the overriding purpose of giving a true and fair view;	FRS 10:59
	(2) in sufficient detail to convey to the reader of the financial statements the circumstances justifying the use of the true and fair override (see 3.1 above):	FRS 10:59 UITF 7

	(a) particulars of the departure;
	  (b) the reasons for it; and
	  (c) its effect.	

	(3) The reasons for the departure should incorporate the explanation of the specific factors contributing to the durability of the acquired business or intangible asset required by the previous paragraph.	FRS 10:59
5.18	If a class of assets has been revalued:	
	(1) the year in which revalued, the values and the bases of valuation;	FRS 10:61 S4:43
	(2) original cost or original fair value of the assets;	FRS 10:61
	(3) amount of any provision for amortisation that would have been recognised had the assets been valued at their original cost or original fair value; and	FRS 10:61

No.	Disclosure	Ref
	(4) if revalued in the year, the name and qualifications of the valuer.	FRS 10:62 S4:43
5.19	Period in which negative goodwill is being written back in the profit and loss account.	FRS 10:63
5.20	If negative goodwill exceeds the fair value of the non-monetary assets:	FRS 10:64
	(1) the amount and source of the excess negative goodwill;	
	(2) explanation of the period(s) in which it (the excess negative goodwill) is being written back.	
5.21	(1) Where goodwill previously eliminated against reserves is reinstated on implementing FRS 10:	FRS 10:70
	(a) original cost of goodwill; (b) amounts attributed to prior period amortisation; (c) amounts attributed to prior period impairment.	
	(2) Where goodwill remains eliminated against reserves:	FRS 10:71
	(a) The cumulative amount of positive goodwill eliminated against reserves and negative goodwill added to reserves net of any goodwill attributable to businesses disposed of before the balance sheet date.	FRS 10: 71(a) S4:14, 16
	In the UK, disclosure of amounts pertaining to an overseas business need not be given if it would be seriously prejudicial to the business and official agreement has been obtained. For acquisitions before 23 December 1989 (in Northern Ireland, 1 April 1990), disclosure need not be made if the information necessary to calculate the amount with material accuracy is unavailable or cannot be obtained without unreasonable expense or delay. The exclusion of such amounts and the grounds for the exclusion should be stated.	SI 1990/355
	(b) The eliminated goodwill should not be shown as a debit balance on a separate goodwill write-off reserve but should be offset against the profit and loss account or another appropriate reserve. The amount by which the reserve has been reduced by the elimination of goodwill (or increased by the addition of negative goodwill) should not be shown separately on the face of the balance sheet.	FRS 10:71(b)
5.22	In the reporting period in which the business with which the goodwill eliminated against reserves was acquired is disposed of or closed:	FRS 10:71(c)
	(1) as a component of the profit or loss on disposal or closure, the attributable amount of goodwill, to the extent that it has not previously been charged in the profit and loss account;	

No.	Disclosure	Ref

(2) the fact and reason where it is impractical or impossible to ascertain the goodwill attributable to a business that was acquired before 1 January 1989.

Fixed assets – tangible assets

5.23 On the face of the balance sheet or in the notes: — S4:F

(1) land and buildings;

(2) plant and machinery;

(3) fixtures and fittings, tools and equipment; and

(4) payments on account and assets under construction.

Small companies need only show (1) land and buildings; and (2) plant and machinery etc.

5.24 Amounts of land and buildings which are freehold, long leaseholds (not less than 50 years unexpired) and short leaseholds. — S4:44, 83

5.25 For each class of fixed asset: — S4:42 FRS 15:100

(1) aggregate cost or valuation at the beginning of the financial period and at the balance sheet date;

(2) aggregate movement in cost or valuation, differentiating between additions, disposals, revaluations and transfers;

(3) aggregate accumulated provision for depreciation or diminution in value at the beginning of the financial period and at the balance sheet date;

(4) aggregate movement in the provisions, differentiating between depreciation provisions made in the year, disposal, revaluation and transfer adjustments, impairment losses and reversals of past impairment losses and other adjustments.

(5) the net carrying amount at the beginning of the financial period and at the balance sheet date. — FRS 15:100

5.26 For non-specialised properties included at a valuation (on the basis of existing use value (EUV)), disclose the open market value (OMV) where it is materially different from EUV and the reasons for the difference. — FRS 15:33

5.27 Where a class of fixed assets is revalued but it is impossible to obtain a reliable valuation of an asset (within that class) held outside the UK or the Republic of Ireland the carrying amount of the tangible fixed asset and the fact that it has not been revalued must be stated. — FRS 15:61

5.28 Where any class of tangible fixed assets of an entity has been revalued the following information should be disclosed in each reporting period: — FRS 15:74

No.	Disclosure	Ref
	(1) for each class of revalued assets:	
	(a) the name and qualifications of the valuer(s) or the valuer's organisation and a description of its nature;	S4:43
	(b) the basis or bases of valuation (including whether notional directly attributable acquisition costs have been included or expected selling costs deducted);	S4:43
	(c) the date and amounts of the valuations;	S4:43
	(d) where historical cost records are available, the carrying amount that would have been included in the financial statements had the tangible fixed assets been carried at historical cost less depreciation;	
	(e) whether the person(s) carrying out the valuation is (are) internal or external to the entity;	
	(f) where the directors are not aware of any material change in value and therefore the valuation(s) have not been updated (as described in paragraphs 45, 46 and 50), a statement to that effect; and	
	(g) where the valuation has not been updated, or is not a full valuation, the date of the last full valuation.	
	(2) In addition for revalued properties:	
	(a) where properties have been valued as fully-equipped operational entities having regard to their trading potential, a statement to that effect and the carrying amount of those properties; and	
	(b) the total amount of notional directly attributable acquisition costs (or the total amount of expected selling costs deducted), included in the carrying amount, where material.	
5.29	Where, on implementation of FRS 15 an entity does not adopt a policy of revaluation, but the carrying amount of its tangible fixed assets reflects previous revaluations, and the entity chooses to retain the book amounts, disclose:	FRS 15:104
	(1) the fact that the transitional provisions of the FRS are being followed;	
	(2) that the valuation has not been updated; and	
	(3) the date of the last revaluation and amount.	S4:43
5.30	For revalued investment properties disclose:	
	(1) the carrying value and investment revaluation reserve;	SP 19:15

No.	Disclosure	Ref
	(2) the names of the valuers or their qualifications, and where the valuer is an employee or officer of the company or group, a statement of that fact;	SP 19:12 S4:43
	(3) bases of valuation (should be at open market value);	SP 19:12 S4:43
	(4) changes in value as a movement on investment revaluation reserve; and	SP 19:13
	(5) reasons and effect of failure to depreciate.	SP 19:17 s226, s227
5.31	The gross amount and related accumulated depreciation of assets held under finance leases and hire purchase contracts by each major class of asset, or if combined with owned fixed assets, the net amount held under finance leases.	SP 21:49, 50
5.32	Where assets are leased to other parties under operating leases give the gross value of assets and related accumulated depreciation.	SP 21:59

Fixed assets – investments

No.	Disclosure	Ref
5.33	On the face of the balance sheet or in the notes:	S4:F
	(1) Shares in group undertakings;	S4:F
	(2) Loans to group undertakings;	S4:F
	(3) Participating interests (in group accounts, this item is replaced by 'Interests in associated undertakings' and 'Other participating interests');	S4:F, S4A:21
	(3.1) In group accounts, share of the net assets of associates including goodwill arising on the acquisition of associates (less any write down or amortisation). The net amount of goodwill should be disclosed separately	FRS 9:29
	(3.2) In group accounts, share of the net assets of its joint ventures including goodwill arising on the acquisition of joint ventures (less any write down or amortisation). Disclose separately on the face of the balance sheet share of gross assets and liabilities of joint venture in amplification of net amount The net amount of goodwill should be disclosed separately	FRS 9:21, 29
	(4) Loans to undertakings in which the company has a participating interest;	S4:F
	(5) Other investments other than loans;	S4:F
	(6) Other loans; and	S4:F
	(7) Own shares (including shares held by ESOP for the continuing benefit of the sponsoring company's business where shares are recognised as assets of the company).	UITF 13

No.	Disclosure	Ref
	Small companies need only show (1) Shares in group undertakings and participating interests (in consolidated balance sheet replaced by 'Shares in group undertakings', 'Interests in associated undertakings' and 'Other participating interests'); (2) Loans to group undertakings and undertakings in which the company has a participating interest; (3) Other investments other than loans; and (4) Others.	
5.34	For each class of investment:	
	(1) aggregate cost or valuation at the beginning of the financial period and at the balance sheet date;	S4:42
	(2) aggregate movement in cost or valuation, differentiating between additions, disposals, revaluations and transfers;	S4:42
	(3) aggregate accumulated provision for diminution in value at the beginning of the financial period and at the balance sheet date;	S4:42
	(4) aggregate movement in provisions, differentiating between provisions made in the year, disposal adjustments and other adjustments.	S4:42
5.35	Where fixed assets investments are stated at an alternative valuation basis other than market value, the method of valuation adopted and reasons for doing so.	S4:31

Subsidiary undertakings and other significant holdings

No.	Disclosure	Ref
5.36	Fact if quasi-subsidiaries are included within consolidated financial statements, the effect of inclusion and a summary of the financial statements of each quasi-subsidiary or on a combined basis for quasi-subsidiaries of a similar nature.	FRS 5:38, 103
	If the company has a quasi-subsidiary but no subsidiaries and therefore does not prepare group financial statements, it should provide in its financial statements consolidated financial statements of itself and the quasi-subsidiary, presented with equal prominence to the reporting entity's individual financial statements.	FRS 5:35
	Where the company has a quasi-subsidiary, the substance of the transactions entered into by the quasi-subsidiary should be reported in consolidated financial statements.	FRS 5:15
5.37	Where the directors have restricted Schedule 5 disclosures (information about subsidiaries, etc.) to unconsolidated subsidiaries and to material undertakings, because full compliance would result in information of excessive length, a statement of that fact. (*N.B. full information is required to be annexed to the next annual return.*)	s231(6)

No.	Disclosure	Ref
5.38	Where Schedule 5 disclosures pertaining to related undertakings have been omitted (with the agreement of the Secretary of State) because the disclosure would be seriously prejudicial to the business, a statement of that fact.	s231(4)
5.39	Where consolidated accounts are produced state, for each subsidiary undertaking, whether it is included in the consolidation.	S5:15(4) FRS 2:26
5.40	Where consolidated accounts are produced state the conditions specified in s258(2) or (4) under which each undertaking is considered a subsidiary of its immediate parent. This need not be given if the group holds the majority of the voting rights and the immediate parent undertaking holds the same proportion of shares in the undertaking as it holds voting rights.	S5:15(5)
5.41	Where consolidated accounts are produced and the undertaking is a subsidiary only because the parent has a participating interest in it and exercises a dominant influence, the basis of the parent's dominant influence.	FRS 2:34
5.42	Where at the end of the year the company (group) held shares in a subsidiary, the group held shares in an associate, or the company (group) had other significant holdings (i.e., exceeded 20 per cent or more of nominal value of any class of shares or the value exceeded 20 per cent of the investing company's (group's) assets, disclose the following:	S5:1, 2, 7, 8, 15, 16, 22, 23, 24, 26, 27
	(1) name of the undertaking;	S5:1, 8, 15, 22, 24, 27
	(2) country of incorporation or, if unincorporated, the address of its principal place of business;	S5:1, 8, 15, 22, 24, 27
	(3) identity and proportion of the nominal value of each class of shares held. (Where group accounts are not prepared distinguish between shares in subsidiaries held by or on behalf of the parent company and shares in subsidiaries attributed to the parent which are held by or on behalf of a subsidiary undertaking.) (In group accounts, distinguish holdings in subsidiaries, associated companies and other significant holdings between direct holdings of the parent and those of the group);	S5:2, 8, 16, 22, 24, 27
	(4) the proportion of voting rights of principal subsidiaries (held by the parent and its subsidiaries) whose results or financial position principally affect the figures in the consolidated accounts.	FRS 2:33

No.	Disclosure	Ref
5.43	If a member of a qualifying undertaking:	S5:9A, 28A
	(1) name and legal form of the undertaking;	
	(2) address of qualifying undertakings registered office or, if no registered office, its head office.	
	If a qualifying partnership:	
	(3) whether a copy of qualifying partnerships last full accounts is to be or has been appended to the company's account filed with the registrar; or	
	(4) the name of the body corporate that has dealt with the qualifying partnership on a consolidated basis in it's group accounts. (Need not be given if advantage is taken of exemption in regulation 7 of the Partnerships and Unlimited Companies (Accounts) Regulations 1993 and that fact disclosed.)	
5.44	The nature of the business of each principal subsidiary whose results or financial position principally affect the figures in the consolidated accounts.	FRS 2:33
5.45	Where group accounts are not prepared, for each material subsidiary and other significant holdings (held at the financial year end) (i.e., exceeded 20 per cent or more of nominal value of any class of shares or the value exceeded 20 per cent of the investing company's (group's) assets):	S5:3, 9
	(1) the total of its capital and reserves at the end of its financial year; and	
	(2) its profit and loss for that year.	
	(Information need not be given for:	
	(1) holdings of less than 50 per cent where the undertaking is not required to deliver and does not otherwise publish its balance sheet for the relevant financial year;	
	(2) Holdings of 20 per cent or more (not being subsidiaries) if the reporting company is exempt from producing group accounts by virtue of s228 and the investment in such undertakings is disclosed in the notes on an equity valuation;	
	(3) Subsidiary undertakings if the reporting company is exempt from producing group accounts by virtue of s228;	
	(4) subsidiary undertakings if investment included in company's accounts by way of equity method of valuation.)	
5.46	Where consolidated accounts are produced state; for each significant holding (held at the financial year end) (i.e., exceeded 20 per cent or more of nominal value of any class of shares or the value exceeded 20 per cent of the investing company's (group's) assets) and for subsidiaries excluded	S5:17, 25, 28

No.	Disclosure	Ref
	from consolidation (excluding consolidated subsidiaries, equity accounted associated undertakings, proportionately consolidated joint ventures and unconsolidated subsidiaries included by equity method):	
	(1) the total of its capital and reserves at the end of its financial year; and	
	(2) its profit or loss for that year.	
	(Information need not be given if the holding is less than 50 per cent and the undertaking is not required to deliver and does not otherwise publish its balance sheet for the relevant financial year.)	
5.47	Where a company has subsidiary undertakings and group accounts are not prepared:	
	(1) state the reason; if all subsidiaries are excluded by the exceptions given in s229, give applicable exclusion for each subsidiary;	S5:1(4), (5)
	(2) state that the company's financial statements present information about it as an individual undertaking and not about its group;	FRS 2:22
5.48	Where the company has not prepared consolidated financial statements because it is exempt under s228 Companies Act 1985 (part of a larger group) state that the company is exempt from the obligation to prepare and deliver group accounts; and give the name of parent which draws up the group accounts and its country of incorporation or, if unincorporated, the address of its principal place of business.	s228(2)
5.49	Where group accounts are not prepared, for each subsidiary disclosed under 5.45 with a year end different to that of the parent give the date of its last year-end, prior to the parent's year-end.	S5:4
5.50	For each consolidated subsidiary, included on a basis of information prepared to a different date or accounting period from that of the parent, disclose:	FRS 2:44
	(1) the name of the subsidiary;	
	(2) the accounting date or period of the subsidiary; and	
	(3) the reason for using the different date or period.	

Parent company

5.51	If the company is a subsidiary undertaking, the name of the ultimate parent company; and if known, its country of incorporation.	S5:12, 31
5.52	If the company is a subsidiary undertaking, in respect of the parent which heads the largest group in which the company is a member and for which group accounts are prepared and also in respect of the parent of the smallest such group:	S5:11, 30

No.	Disclosure	Ref
	(1) the name of the parent;	
	(2) the country of incorporation; if unincorporated, the address of its principal place of business; and	
	(3) the addresses from which copies of the group accounts which are available to the public can be obtained.	
5.53	If the reporting company is listed and a subsidiary, the parent company's participation in any vendor consideration placing made during the year in respect of shares issued by the company.	LR12.43(p)

Disclosures in respect of subsidiary undertakings excluded from consolidation

No.	Disclosure	Ref
5.54	Where group accounts are required, for subsidiaries excluded from consolidation:	
	(1) the names of the subsidiaries excluded;	S5:15(4) FRS 2:26
	(2) the reasons for exclusion from consolidation;	S5:15(4) FRS 2:26
	(3) particulars of balances between excluded subsidiaries and the rest of the group;	FRS 2:31(a)
	(4) the nature and extent of transactions of the excluded subsidiaries with the rest of the group;	FRS 2:31(b)
	(5) for an excluded subsidiary not equity accounted, any amounts included in the consolidated accounts in respect of dividends received and receivable from that subsidiary and any write-down in the period of the investment in and amounts due from that subsidiary.	FRS 2:31(c)
	The above disclosures may be made on an aggregate basis in some instances.	FRS 2:32
5.55	For a subsidiary undertaking excluded from consolidation because of different activities, include in the consolidated financial statements the separate financial statements of the undertaking. Summarised information may be provided for undertakings that individually, or in combination with those with similar operations, do not account for more than 20 per cent of any one or more of operating profits, turnover or net assets of the group (measured by including all excluded subsidiaries).	FRS 2:31(d)
5.56	In the year in which a previously excluded subsidiary is included in consolidation because severe restrictions have ceased and the parent's rights have been restored:	FRS 2:28
	(1) the amount of unrecognised profit or loss that accrued during the period of restriction; and	
	(2) the amount previously charged for impairment that needs to be written back as a result of restrictions ceasing.	

No.	Disclosure	Ref

Related undertakings [participating interests/associates]

No.	Disclosure	Ref
5.57	For each proportionally consolidated joint venture: (1) name of the joint venture; (2) address of its principal place of business; (3) factors on which joint management is based; (4) proportion of capital of the joint venture held by the group; (5) for non-coterminous year ends, the joint venture's financial year last ended before the year end of the company.	S5:21
5.58	Any supplementary information in respect of joint ventures given in the balance sheet must be shown clearly separate from amounts for the group and must not be included in group totals.	FRS 9:22
5.59	Where consolidated accounts are not prepared then, unless the company is exempt from preparing consolidated accounts, or would be if it had subsidiaries show the following information by producing a separate set of financial statements or by showing the relevant amounts, together with the effects of including them, as additional information to the company's own financial statements:	FRS 9:48
	(1) as a separate fixed asset investment the investor's share of the net assets of its joint ventures;	FRS 9:21, 29
	(2) goodwill arising on the acquisition of joint ventures (less any write down or amortisation) should be included in the carrying amount for joint ventures but disclosed separately;	FRS 9:21, 29
	(3) share of gross assets and liabilities of joint venture in amplification of net amount; and	FRS 9:21
	(4) any supplementary information given in the balance sheet must be shown clearly separate from amounts for the group and must not be included in group totals.	FRS 9:22
5.60	Where consolidated accounts are not prepared then unless the company is exempt from preparing consolidated accounts, or would be if it had subsidiaries show the following information by producing a separate set of financial statements or by showing the relevant amounts, together with the effects of including them, as additional information to the company's own financial statements:	FRS 9:48
	(1) as a separate fixed asset investment the investors share of the net assets of its associates;	FRS 9:29
	(2) goodwill arising on the acquisition of associates (less any write down or amortisation) should be included in the carrying amount associates but disclosed separately.	FRS 9:29

No.	*Disclosure*	*Ref*
5.61	Distinguish amounts due to/from associates or joint ventures between loans and trading balances.	FRS 9:55

Other investments

No.	*Disclosure*	*Ref*
5.62	In respect of listed investments:	
	(1) aggregate amount;	S4:45(1)
	(2) aggregate market value of those investments where it differs from the carrying amount;	S4:45(2)
	(3) both the market value and the stock exchange value of investments if market value shown in the accounts is greater than the latter.	S4:45(2)
5.63	Nominal value of own shares held.	S4:F (Note 4)

Stocks

No.	*Disclosure*	*Ref*
5.64	On the face of the balance sheet or in the notes:	S4:F
	(1) raw materials and consumables;	
	(2) work in progress;	
	(3) finished goods and goods for resale; and	
	(4) payments on account.	
	Small companies need only show (1) stocks and (2) payments on account.	
5.65	In respect of long-term contracts:	SP 9:30
	(1) within debtors, as 'amounts recoverable on contracts', the excess of recorded turnover over payments on account;	
	(2) within creditors, as 'payments on account', the excess of such payments over amounts after being (i) matched with turnover and (ii) offset against long-term contract balances;	
	(3) within stocks, as 'long-term contract balances', the net costs of long-term contracts after transfers to cost of sales less foreseeable losses and payments on account not matched with turnover, showing separately (i) net cost less foreseeable losses and (ii) payments on account; and	
	(4) within provisions for liabilities or creditors, any excess of provisions for foreseeable losses over costs incurred after transfers to cost of sales.	

Debtors

No.	*Disclosure*	*Ref*
5.66	On the face of the balance sheet or in the notes:	S4:F
	(1) trade debtors;	

No.	Disclosure	Ref
	(2) amounts owed by group undertakings;	
	(3) amounts owed by participating interests;	
	(4) other debtors;	
	(5) called up share capital not paid (if not shown as a separate item on the balance sheet); and	
	(6) prepayments and accrued income (if not shown as a separate item on the balance sheet).	
	Small companies need only show (1) trade debtors; (2) amounts owed by group undertakings and undertakings in which the company has a participating interest; (3) others.	
5.67	Amounts falling due after more than one year for each category of debtors.	S4:F(5)
	Small companies need only disclose the aggregate debtors due after more than one year.	
5.68	Debtors due after more than one year, if so material in context of total net current assets, on the face of the balance sheet.	UITF 4
5.69	Where assets are leased to other parties under finance leases:	
	(1) net investment in finance leases and hire purchase contracts;	SP 21:58
	(2) cost of assets acquired for letting under finance leases.	SP 21:60
5.70	Any prepaid pension contributions or prepayments resulting from a difference between amounts recognised as cost and amounts funded or paid directly, analysed between defined contribution schemes and defined benefit schemes.	SP 24:87, 88
5.71	Aggregate amount of loans made to provide financial assistance for purchase of the company's own shares.	S4:51(2)

Current asset investments

No.	Disclosure	Ref
5.72	On the balance sheet or in the notes:	S4:F
	(1) shares in group undertakings;	
	(2) own shares (including shares held by ESOP recognised as assets of the company) (nominal value to be shown separately);	UITF 13 S4:F(4)
	(3) other investments.	
	Small companies need only show (1) shares in group undertakings; (2) other investments.	
5.73	In respect of, listed current asset investments:	S4:4
	(1) aggregate amount;	

No.	*Disclosure*	*Ref*

(2) aggregate market value of those investments where it differs from the stated amount;

(3) both the market value and the stock exchange value of investments if market value used in the accounts is greater than the latter.

Creditors: amounts falling due within one year and after more than one year

5.74	On the face of the balance sheet or in the notes:	S4:F
	(1) debenture loans, showing convertible loans separately;	S4:F(7)
	(2) bank loans and overdrafts;	
	(3) payments received on account not shown as deductions from stocks;	
	(4) trade creditors;	
	(5) bills of exchange payable;	
	(6) amounts owed to group undertakings;	
	(7) amounts owed to undertakings in which the company has a participating interest;	
	(8) other creditors, including taxation and social security (showing the amount for taxation and social security separately);	S4:F(9)
	(9) Accruals and deferred income (if not shown separately on the balance sheet); and	
	Recognise as own liabilities any borrowing of an ESOP trust guaranteed, formally or informally, by the sponsoring employer.	UITF 13
	In a format 2 balance sheet amounts falling due within one year and after one year shall be shown for each item in creditors and for the aggregate of all these items.	S4:F(13)
	Small companies need only show (1) bank loans and overdrafts; (2) trade creditors; (3) amounts owed to group undertakings and undertakings in which the company has a participating interest; (4) other creditors.	
	In a format 2 balance sheet small companies need only analyse the aggregate creditors figure between creditors falling due within one year and those falling due after one year.	
5.75	Any outstanding pension contributions or provisions resulting from a difference between amounts recognised as cost and amounts funded or paid directly, analysed between defined contribution schemes and defined benefit schemes.	SP 24:87, 88
5.76	Where the company has given security in respect of any debt included under each item shown under 'creditors':	S4:48(4)

No.	Disclosure	Ref
	(1) aggregate amount of any debt included under that item; and	
	(2) nature of the securities given.	
5.77	For each item in 'creditors' which falls due after more than one year the aggregate of:	S4:48(1)
	(1) amount of any instalments falling due after five years in respect of debts which are payable or repayable by instalments; and	
	(2) amount of any debts not payable or repayable by instalments which fall due after five years.	
	Small companies need only give the above analysis in aggregate for all items in creditors.	
5.78	For each debt in which any amount is payable after five years, the payment terms and interest rate (a general indication of terms and rates may be given where the number of debts would result in a statement of excessive length).	S4:48(2)
5.79	Debt to be analysed between amounts falling due as shown below.	FRS 4:33 FRS 13:77
	(1) in one year or less or on demand;	
	(2) in more than one year but not more than two years;	
	(3) in more than two years but not more than five years; and	
	(4) in more than five years.	
5.80	If maturity of debt is assessed by reference to refinancing facilities the amount of debt so treated and the earliest date on which the lender could demand repayment in the absence of the facilities should be disclosed.	FRS 4:36
5.81	Redemption dates and amounts in respect of convertible debt. Conversion dates and number and class of shares into which the debt may be converted. Whether conversion is at option of issuer or holder.	FRS 4:62
5.82	Legal nature of any instrument if different from normal debt. Any difference between balance sheet value and the amount payable.	FRS 4:63
5.83	Where the company's debentures are held by a nominee for the company, the nominal amount and the amount at which they are stated in the company's accounting records.	S4:41(3)
5.84	For debentures issued during the year the amount, description and consideration received for each class issued.	S4:41(1)
5.85	Separately from other liabilities, on the balance sheet or in the notes, the amount of finance lease obligations (net of future finance charges).	SP21:51

No.	Disclosure	Ref
5.86	Finance lease obligations, (either given for lease obligations (see note below) or, if combined with other obligations, by an equivalent analysis of that total – see 5.74 above), showing the amounts payable: (1) in the next year; (2) in the second to fifth years; and (3) thereafter. If the analysis is given separately for finance lease obligations it may alternatively be analysed using the gross obligations, with future finance charges being deducted from the total.	SP 21:52

Provisions for liabilities and charges

No.	Disclosure	Ref
5.87	On the face of the balance sheet or in the notes: (1) pensions and similar obligations; (2) taxation, including deferred taxation (3) other provisions (giving particulars of any material provisions included in other provisions).	S4:F S4:46(3)
5.88	For each provision shown on the balance sheet or in the notes where any amount has been transferred to or from that provision: (1) amounts at beginning and end of year; (2) amounts transferred to or from the provision; and (3) source and application of amounts transferred.	S4:46, 58
5.89	For each class of provision:	FRS 12:89
	(1) the carrying amount at the start of the period;	FRS 12:89
	(2) the carrying amount at the end of the period;	FRS 12:89
	(3) additional provision made in the period including increases to existing provisions;	FRS 12:89
	(4) amounts used during the period (i.e., incurred and charges against the provision);	FRS 12:89
	(5) unused amounts reversed in the period;	FRS 12:89
	(6) increase in the period in the discounted amount due to the passage of time and the effect of changes in the discount rate.	FRS 12:89
	Comparative information for the above is not required.	FRS 12:89 Sch 4:58(3)
5.90	For each class of provision (1) brief description of the nature of the obligation and expected timing of any resulting transfers of benefit;	FRS 12:90
	(2) indication of the uncertainties about the amount or timing of those transfers of economic benefits. Where necessary to provide adequate information the major	FRS 12:90, 51

No.	Disclosure	Ref
	assumptions made concerning the future events that may affect the amount required to settle an obligation;	
	(3) the amount of any expected reimbursement, stating the amount of any asset that has been recognised for that expected reimbursement.	FRS 12:90
5.91	For each material acquisition and other acquisitions in aggregate, movements on provisions or accruals for costs related to the acquisition(s) analysed between amounts used for the specific reasons for which they were created and the amounts released unused.	FRS 6:32
5.92	Provision for deferred taxation stated separately from any provision for other taxation.	S4:47

Deferred taxation

No.	Disclosure	Ref
5.93	In respect of deferred tax:	SP 15:37
	(1) deferred tax balance and its major components;	SP 15:38
	(2) transfers to or from deferred tax;	
	(3) the amount of unprovided deferred tax analysed into its major components.	SP 15:40
5.94	Where the potential deferred tax on a revalued asset is not shown because the revaluation does not constitute a timing difference, state that fact and that tax has therefore not been quantified.	SP 15:41
5.95	The tax effects, if any, of an asset being realised at the value shown in a note, when that value differs materially from its book amount.	SP 15:42

Minority interests

No.	Disclosure	Ref
5.96	Description of rights of non-equity minority interests against other group companies.	FRS 4:61

Share capital

No.	Disclosure	Ref
5.97	Authorised share capital.	S4:38(1)
5.98	Number and aggregate nominal value of each class of shares allotted (where more than one class has been allotted).	S4:38:1
5.99	Where any part of allotted share capital is redeemable:	S4:38(2)
	(1) earliest and latest redemption dates;	
	(2) whether redemption is compulsory or at the option of the company or of the shareholder; and	
	(3) amount of redemption premium payable.	
5.100	For each class of shares allotted during the period:	S4:39

No.	Disclosure	Ref
	(1) classes of shares allotted;	
	(2) for each class of shares, the consideration received, number allotted, and aggregate nominal value.	
5.101	For listed companies, where securities having an equity element have been issued for cash to persons other than to the company's equity shareholders in proportion to their equity share holdings, without approval by the company's shareholders:	LR12.43(o)
	(1) the names of the allottees, if less than six;	
	(2) a brief generic description of the allottees, if more than five; and	
	(3) the market price of the securities concerned on the date on which the terms of the issue were fixed.	
5.102	For any contingent right to allotment of shares (including options, rights and convertible securities):	S4:40
	(1) number, description and amount of shares for which such rights are exercisable; and	
	(2) exercise period and price to be paid.	
5.103	For each class of shares with fixed cumulative dividends in arrears:	S4:49
	(1) the amount of any arrears; and	
	(2) period of arrears.	
5.104	For listed companies, any arrangement under which a shareholder has waived or agreed to waive any dividends.	LR12.43(e)
5.105	The number and description of share capital of the company held by its subsidiaries (see s23 Companies Act 1985, as regards membership of holding company).	S5:6, 20
5.106	Brief summary of rights of each class of share and of classes to be issued for warrants or convertible debt. Certain equity shares exempted.	FRS 4:56, 57, 58

Reserves

No.	Disclosure	Ref
5.107	On the face of the balance sheet or in the notes:	S4:F
	(1) capital redemption reserve;	
	(2) reserve for own shares;	
	(3) reserves provided for by the articles of association; and	
	(4) other reserves.	
5.108	For each reserve where there has been an amount transferred to or from that reserve:	S4:46
	(1) amounts at beginning and end of year;	

No.	Disclosure	Ref
	(2) amounts transferred to or from the reserve; and	
	(3) source and application of amounts so transferred.	
5.109	The deferred tax arising in respect of movements on reserves.	SP 15:39
5.110	Treatment for tax purposes of amounts credited or debited to revaluation reserve.	S4:34(4)
5.111	In respect of exchange differences (see also 4.51):	
	(1) the net movement on reserves arising from exchange differences;	SP 20:60
	(2) amount offset in reserves where borrowings provide a hedge against equity investments in foreign enterprises; and	SP 20:60
	(3) amount of tax charges and credits taken to reserves in respect of borrowings providing a hedge against equity investments in foreign enterprises.	UITF 19:9
5.112	Where significant statutory, contractual or exchange control restrictions on distributions by subsidiaries materially limit the parent's access to distributable profits, disclose the nature and extent of the restrictions.	FRS 2:53
5.113	Extent of significant statutory, contractual or exchange control restrictions on the ability of an associate or joint venture to distribute its reserves (other than those shown as non-distributable).	FRS 9:54
5.114	Analysis of non-equity interests in shareholders funds relating to each class of non-equity shares and series of warrants for non-equity shares.	FRS 4:55

Impairment loss – other disclosures (see also 4.74 above)

No.	Disclosure	Ref
5.115	In the accounting periods after an asset has suffered impairment:	FRS 11:68
	(1) for assets held at historic cost the impairment loss should be included within cumulative depreciation; the costs of the asset should not be reduced;	FRS 11:68(a)
	(2) for revalued assets held at market value the impairment loss should be included within the revalued carrying amount;	FRS 11:68(b)
	(3) for revalued assets held at depreciated replacement cost an impairment loss:	FRS 11:68(c)
	(a) charged to the profit and loss account should be included within cumulative depreciation, the carrying amount of the asset should not be reduced;	
	(b) charged to the STRGL should be deducted from the carrying amount.	

No.	Disclosure	Ref
5.116	The discount rate used, where an impairment loss is measured by reference to value in use of a fixed asset or IGU. If a risk free rate is used, some indication of the risk adjustments made to cash flows.	FRS 11:69
5.117	The reasons for the reversal of an impairment loss and any changes in the assumptions upon which the calculation of recoverable amount is based, where an impairment loss recognised in a prior period reverses in the current period.	FRS 11:70
5.118	The previously unrecognised impairment and its subsequent reversal where an impairment loss would have been recognised in a previous period had forecast cash flows been more accurate but the impairment has now reversed and that reversal is permitted to be recognised.	FRS 11:71
5.119	The length of the projection period and the justifying circumstances, where, in the measurement of value in use, the projection period, before a steady or declining long-term growth rate has been assumed, extends to more than five years.	FRS 11:72
5.120	The growth rate assumed and the circumstances justifying it, where, in the measurement of value in use, the long-term growth rate used has exceeded the average long-term growth rate for the country or countries in which the business operates.	FRS 11:73
5.121	Impairments recognised when FRS 11 is first implemented are not the result of a change in accounting policy and should be recognised in accordance with FRS 11 and not as prior period adjustments.	FRS 11:75

6   Cash flow statement

No.	*Disclosure*	*Ref*
	Cash flow statements (FRS 1 revised)	
6.1	Include the following standard headings:	FRS 1:7
	(1) operating activities;	FRS 1:11, 12 FRS 9:61(b)
	(2) dividends from joint ventures and associates;	FRS 1:12(a) FRS 9:21, 30, 61(a)
	(3) returns on investments and servicing of finance;	FRS 1:13 to 15
	(4) taxation;	FRS 1:16 to 18
	(5) capital expenditure and financial investment;	FRS 1:19 to 21
	(6) acquisitions and disposals;	FRS 1:22 to 24
	(7) equity dividends paid;	FRS 1:25
	(8) management of liquid resources;	FRS 1:26 to 28
	(9) financing (the amounts of any financing cash flows received for or paid to equity accounted entities should be disclosed separately).	FRS1:29 to 32
	The first seven headings should be in the sequence set out above. The last two headings may be combined under a single heading provided the cash flows relating to each are shown separately and separate subtotals are given.	FRS 1:7
	Include under normal headings any other cash flows between the investor and its joint ventures/associates. None of the other cash flows of the joint ventures/associates should be included	FRS 9:21, 30
6.2	As a note or adjoining the cash flow statement, a reconciliation between operating profit reported in the profit and loss account and the net cash flow from operating activities, showing separately movements in stocks, debtors and creditors related to operating activities and other differences between cash flow and profits. Unless FRS 9 has been adopted, the reconciliation should show separately the difference between dividends received and results taken into account for equity accounted entities. *(The note is not part of the cash flow statement: if adjoining the cash flow statement it should be labelled and kept separate.)*	FRS 1:12, 58 & 59 FRS 9: 61(c)

No.	Disclosure	Ref
6.3	As a note or adjoining the cash flow statement, a reconciliation between the movement in cash and the movement in net debt. The changes in net debt should be analysed from the opening to the closing components showing separately:	FRS 1:33
	(a) cash flows;	
	(b) acquisition/disposals of subsidiaries;	
	(c) other non-cash changes;	
	(d) changes in market value and exchange rate movement.	
	Give sufficient detail to allow the cash and other components of net debt to be traced back to the balance sheet. *(The note is not part of the cash flow statement: if adjoining the cash flow statement it should be labelled and kept separate.)*	
6.4	Cash flows related to exceptional or extraordinary items under the appropriate standard heading according to the nature of each item. The cash flows relating to exceptional/extraordinary items should be identified in the cash flow or notes to it and the relationship between the cash flows and the originating exceptional/extraordinary item should be explained to allow the user to understand the effect of the underlying transactions on the entity's cash flows.	FRS 1:37, 63
6.5	Where exceptional cash flows are not related to anything treated as exceptional in the profit and loss account sufficient disclosure to explain their cause an nature.	FRS 1:38, 63
6.6	Where the group has acquired or disposed of a subsidiary, a summary of the effects of the acquisition or disposal, indicating how much of the consideration comprised cash.	FRS 1:45, FRS 6:33
6.7	The material effects on amounts reported under each standard heading of cash flows in respect of a subsidiary acquired or disposed of in the period. This should be done by dividing cash flows between continuing and discontinued operations and acquisitions.	FRS 1:45
6.8	Material non-cash transactions if necessary for an understanding of the underlying transactions.	FRS 1:46
6.9	The amounts and circumstances where restrictions prevent the transfer of cash from one part of the business to another.	FRS 1:47
6.10	Comparatives except for the notes analysing changes in the balance sheet amounts comprising net debt and the note of the material effects of acquisitions and disposals of subsidiaries on each of the standard headings.	FRS 1:48

7   Statement of total recognised gains and losses

No.	Disclosure	Ref
7.1	A primary statement showing the total recognised gains and losses and its components, being the gains and losses recognised in the period insofar as they are attributable to shareholders.	FRS 3:27
7.2	If a statement is not being given as there have been no gains and losses other than profit or loss for the period then a statement of that fact should be made immediately below the profit and loss account.	FRS 3:57
7.3	Material recognised movements between the amount attributable to different classes of shareholders which do not affect shareholders' funds.	FRS 3:58
7.4	Investment companies should disclose the amount of finance costs and any gains or losses on repurchase of debt included in the statement of total recognised gains and losses. Accounting policy for allocating finance costs between revenue and capital should also be disclosed.	FRS 4:52
7.5	Where consolidated accounts are prepared, show separately for each heading the share of the joint ventures' total recognised gains and losses either in the statement or in a note referred to from the statement.	FRS 9:21, 28
7.6	Where consolidated accounts are prepared, show separately for each heading the share of the associates' total recognised gains and losses either in the statement or in a note referred to from the statement.	FRS 9:28
7.7	Where consolidated accounts are not prepared then, unless the company is exempt from preparing consolidated accounts, or would be if it had subsidiaries, show separately for each heading the share of the joint ventures' total recognised gains and losses either in the statement or in a note referred to from the statement by producing a separate set of financial statements or by showing the relevant amounts, together with the effects of including them, as additional information to the company's own financial statements.	FRS 9:21, 28, 48
7.8	Where consolidated accounts are not prepared then, unless the company is exempt from preparing consolidated accounts, or would be if it had subsidiaries, show separately for each heading the share of the associates' total recognised gains and losses either in the statement or in a note referred to from the statement by producing a separate set of financial statements or by showing the relevant amounts, together with the effects of including them, as additional information to the company's own financial statements.	FRS 9:28, 48

No.	*Disclosure*	*Ref*

Recognition of impairment loss

7.9	Recognition of impairments losses of revalued fixed assets (see also 4.73 and 5.115 above):	FRS 11:63
	(1) in the profit and loss account, included under the relevant statutory heading in the profit and loss account with disclosure as an exceptional item if appropriate, if caused by a clear consumption of economic benefits; otherwise	FRS 11:63, 67
	(2) in the STRGL (separately on the face of the statement) until carrying amount reaches depreciated historical cost; then	
	(3) in the profit and loss account, included under the relevant statutory heading in the profit and loss account with disclosure as an exceptional item if appropriate, to the extent that reaches depreciated historical cost exceeds carrying value.	

Reversal of impairment loss

7.10	Reversal of an impairment loss on a revalued fixed asset should be recognised in the profit and loss account to the extent that the original impairment loss (adjusted for subsequent depreciation) was so recognised. The remaining balance of the reversal of an impairment should be recognised in the STRGL (see also 4.75 above).	FRS 11:66
7.11	The tax attributable to a gain or loss should be recognised directly in the statement of total recognised gains and losses if the gain or loss is or has been recognised directly in the statement.	FRS 16:6
7.12	The following major components of the current tax expense (or income) for the period in the statement of total recognised gains and losses should be disclosed separately:	FRS 16:17
	(a) UK or Republic of Ireland tax (depending on the companies legislation in accordance with which the entity is reporting); and	
	(b) foreign tax.	
	Both (a) and (b) should be analysed to distinguish tax estimated for the current period and any adjustments recognised in respect of prior periods. The domestic tax should be disclosed before and after taxation relief.	

8 Other disclosures

No.	*Disclosure*	*Ref*

Contingencies and commitments

8.1	For each class of contingent liability unless the possibility of any transfer in settlement is remote:	FRS 12:91
	(1) A brief description of the nature of the contingent liability.	FRS 12:91
	(2) An estimate of its financial effect, measured in accordance with FRS 12:36–55.	FRS 12:91
	(3) An indication of the uncertainties relating to the amount or timing of any outflow.	FRS 12:91
	(4) The possibility of any reimbursement.	FRS 12:91
	(5) The fact where any of the information in (2), (3) and (4) is not disclosed because is not practicable to do so.	FRS 12:91, 96
8.2	Where a provision and a contingent liability arise from the same set of circumstances the disclosures required by 5.84, 5.85 and 8.1 should be made in such a way as to show the link between the provision and the contingent liability.	FRS 12:93
8.3	For contingent assets where an inflow of economic benefit is probable:	FRS 12:94
	(1) A brief description of the nature of the contingent asset at the balance sheet date.	FRS 12:94
	(2) An estimate of its financial effect, measured in accordance with FRS 12:36–55.	FRS 12:94
	(3) The fact where the information in (2) is not disclosed because is not practicable to do so.	FRS 12:94, 96
	The disclosures in respect of a contingent asset should avoid giving misleading indications of the likelihood of a profit arising.	FRS 12:95
8.4	Where some or all of the disclosures required by FRS 12: 89–94 (included in 5.88, 5.89, 8.1, 8.2 and 8.3 above) in respect of provisions, contingent liabilities or contingent assets are not given because to do so would prejudice seriously the position of the entity (assuming disclosure is not required by law):	FRS 12:97
	(1) General nature of the dispute.	FRS 12:97
	(2) Fact that and reason why the information has not been disclosed.	FRS 12:97
8.5	Particulars of any charge on the company's assets to secure the liabilities of any other person, including, where practicable, the amount secured.	S4:50(1)
8.6	For unprovided contingent liabilities:	S4:50(2)

No.	Disclosure	Ref
	(1) the legal nature;	
	(2) the amount or estimated amount of the liability; and	
	(3) if secured, details of the security provided.	
8.7	Total amount of capital expenditures contracted for.	S4:50(3)
8.8	The potential liability that a government grant will be repaid in specified circumstances, unless possibility is remote.	SP 4:29
8.9	Other financial commitments which have not been provided for and are relevant to assessing the company's state of affairs.	S4:50(5)
8.10	Particulars of any pension commitments included under any provision in the balance sheet and such commitments not provided for. Give separate particulars of any commitments so far as they relate to pensions payable to former directors.	S4:50(4)
8.11	A description of the nature of all pension schemes (both defined benefit and defined contribution schemes).	SP 24:87, 88
8.12	For defined benefit schemes:	SP 24:88
	(1) whether it is funded or unfunded;	
	(2) whether the pension cost and provision (or asset) have been assessed by a professionally qualified actuary and, if so, the date of the most recent formal valuation or later formal review;	
	(3) where the actuary is an employee or officer of the company, a statement to this effect;	
	(4) any deficiency on a current funding level basis, indicating the action, if any, being taken to deal with it in the current and future periods;	
	(5) an outline of the results of the most recent formal actuarial valuation or later formal review of the scheme on an on-going basis, including:	
	(a) the actuarial method used and brief description of the main actuarial assumptions;	
	(b) the market value of scheme assets at the date of valuation;	
	(c) the level of funding in percentage terms;	
	(d) comments on any material actuarial surplus or deficiency indicated by the level of funding;	
	(6) any commitment to make additional payments over a limited number of years;	
	(7) the accounting treatment of a refund made in accordance with the provisions of UK Finance Act 1986 or equivalent law where a credit appears in the accounts in relation to it; and	

No.	Disclosure	Ref
	(8) details of expected effects on future costs of any material changes in pension arrangements.	
8.13	If a subsidiary participating in a group pension scheme:	SP 24:90
	(1) this fact and the nature of the group scheme;	
	(2) indicate, where appropriate, that contributions are based on group pension costs; and	
	(3) where disclosures required in (4) and (5) of question 8.10 are not given because the parent is registered in the UK or the Republic of Ireland, state the name of the holding company in whose financial statements the details of the scheme's actuarial valuation are disclosed.	
8.14	Where post-retirement benefits other than pensions are not provided for under SSAP 24 principles:	UITF 6
	(1) description of the nature of the benefits to which employees are entitled and approximate number of eligible employees;	
	(2) estimate of the liability or a statement that no reliable estimate can be made;	
	(3) whether the liability will attract tax relief when paid and an estimate of the relief if practicable; and	
	(4) amount of expense recognised in the period, and an indication if materially different from amount that would have been shown on an accruals basis.	
8.15	Disclose separately guarantees and other financial commitments mentioned in 8.5, 8.6, 8.7, 8.9 or 8.10 undertaken on behalf of or for the benefit of:	S4:59A
	(1) parent company and fellow subsidiary undertakings;	
	(2) subsidiary undertakings; and	
	(3) other parties.	
8.16	Lease payments which lessee is committed to make during the next year under operating leases, analysed between those which expire within one year, within two to five years inclusive, and over five years from the balance sheet date and showing separately those in respect of land and buildings and other operating leases.	SP 21(56)
8.17	Any commitments entered into at the balance sheet date in respect of finance leases which start after the year end.	SP 21:54

Post balance sheet events

8.18	For each material non-adjusting post balance sheet event:	
	(1) nature of the event;	SP 17:24
	(2) an estimate of the financial effect (before taking account of taxation), or a statement that it is not practicable to make such an estimate, and	

No.	*Disclosure*	*Ref*
	(3) the taxation implications where necessary for a proper understanding of the financial position.	SP 17:2

Transactions and arrangements with officers

8.19	For transactions, or arrangements to enter into transactions, made by the company or its subsidiaries with persons who were officers (other than directors) during the year (amounts not exceeding £2,500 for any officers are excluded).	S6:29
	(1) the aggregate amounts outstanding at the end of the year in relation to (a) loans, (b) quasi-loan, and (c) credit transactions (including guarantees and securities in respect of each category); and	
	(2) the number of officers for whom each of the above types of transactions were made.	S6:28

Transactions and arrangements with directors

8.20	For each disclosable transaction and arrangement entered into by the company, or a subsidiary thereof, with a director of the company, or its holding company or for persons connected with the directors, at any time in the financial year:	S6:22
	(1) its principal terms;	S6:22
	(2) a statement that the transaction was made or subsisted during the financial year; and	S6:22(2)
	(3) the name of the person for whom it was made; where that person is a connected person, give the name of the director with whom he is connected.	S6:22(2)
8.21	In addition, for each disclosable loan, agreement for a loan, assignment or assumption of a loan or loan by another person who obtained benefit from the company/group:	S6:22(2)
	(1) amount due, including principal and interest, at the beginning and end of the year;	
	(2) maximum amount of the liability during the year;	
	(3) unpaid interest; and	
	(4) amount of any provision made in respect of failure or anticipated failure to pay any part of the loan or interest.	
8.22	In addition, for each disclosable guarantee or assignment or assumption of security:	S6:22(2)
	(1) amount which the company was liable under the guarantee or security at the beginning and end of the year;	
	(2) maximum amount which the company may become so liable;	

No.	Disclosure	Ref
	(3) amounts paid and liability incurred in fulfilling the guarantee or discharging the security, including any loss incurred by reason of the enforcement of the guarantee or security.	
8.23	For disclosable transactions, arrangements or agreement, other than those relating to loans, guarantees or securities, the value of the transactions, arrangements or agreements.	S6:22(2)(f)

Contracts with directors and controlling shareholders

No.	Disclosure	Ref
8.24	For listed companies, particulars of any contracts of significance subsisting during or at the end of the financial year in which a director of the company is or was materially interested. (Prior to 1 July 1996 a statement that there has been no such contract is required if applicable.)	LR12.43(q)
8.25	For listed companies, particulars of any contracts of significance between the company, or one of its subsidiaries, and a controlling shareholder (where a company is a parent, determination of contracts of significance is to be made on a consolidated basis).	LR12.43(r)
8.26	For listed companies, particulars of any contracts for services to the company or any subsidiaries by a controlling shareholder, unless such a contract is for services which are the principal business of the shareholder and the contract does not meet the criteria which define a 'contract of significance'.	LR12.43(s)
8.27	For listed companies, details of small related party transactions.	LR12.43(t)

Segmental reporting

No.	Disclosure	Ref
8.28	For companies which carry on substantially different classes of business or supply substantially different geographical markets:	S4:55, SP 25:34
	(1) turnover for each class of business and geographical market;	
	(2) profit or loss before taxation for each class of business;	
	(3) turnover derived from external customers and turnover derived from other segments;	
	(4) geographical segment results before taxation, minority interest and extraordinary items;	
	(5) net assets by class of business and geographical segment.	
	If a small company has supplied geographical markets outside the UK the percentage of turnover attributable to those markets.	

No.	Disclosure	Ref
8.29	(1) The following information segmentally for associated undertakings which account for at least 20 per cent of the entity's total results or 20 per cent of its total net assets, the entity's share of (1) associate's results before taxation, minority interest and extraordinary items; and (2) associate's net assets. (The reason for non-disclosure and a brief description of the omitted businesses, if this information is not given because it is prejudicial to the business of the associate.)	SP 25:36
	(2) In consolidated segmental analysis clearly distinguish share of joint venture turnover from group turnover and joint venture operating profit from group operating profit.	FRS 9:21, 27
	(3) In consolidated segmental analysis clearly distinguish share of associate turnover from group turnover and associate operating profit from group operating profit.	FRS 9:27
	The information in 8.28(2) to (5) and 8.29(1) above is required of a company or other entity which:	
	(1) Is a public limited company or has a public limited company as a subsidiary.	SP 25:41
	(2) Is a banking or insurance company or group.	
	(3) Exceeds the Act's current criteria, multiplied in each case by 10, for defining a medium-sized company.	
	The information need not be given if the company is a subsidiary (but is not a public limited company, banking or insurance company) if its parent provides segmental information in accordance with SSAP 25.	
8.30	Where segmental information is not given because it is prejudicial to the interest of the company, state that fact.	SP 25:4, S4:55(5)
8.31	Fact and explanation if an acquisition, sale or termination has a material impact on a major business segment.	FRS 3:15, FRS 6:28

Acquisitions

No.	Disclosure	Ref
8.32	For each business combination (acquisition or merger) made in the financial year:	
	(1) names of the combining entities;	FRS 6:21
	(2) name of acquired undertaking or, where a group was acquired, the name of the parent acquired;	S4A:13(2)
	(3) whether the acquisition has been accounted for by the acquisition or merger method;	S4A:13(2) FRS 6:21
	(4) the date of combination.	
	The information required by S4A:13 need not be given in respect of overseas businesses if it is seriously prejudicial to the business and agreement has been obtained from the Secretary of State.	

No.	Disclosure	Ref
8.33	For each material acquisition and other acquisitions in aggregate:	
	(1) a table showing for each class of acquired assets and liabilities:	
	(a) book values immediately before acquisition;	S4A:13(5), FRS 6:25
	(b) fair value adjustments (analysed between revaluations, adjustments to achieve consistency of accounting policies, other significant adjustments) giving reasons for the adjustments;	S4A:13(5), FRS 6:25
	(c) fair values at the date of acquisition;	S4A:13(5), FRS 6:25
	(d) the amount of purchased goodwill or negative goodwill arising on the acquisition;	S4A:13(5), FRS 6:25
	(e) provision for reorganisation/restructuring costs included in the liabilities of the acquired entity, and related asset write downs, made in the 12 months up to the date of acquisition should be identified separately;	FRS 6:26
	(2) State fact and give reason if the fair values of the assets, liabilities or consideration are on a provisional basis. Subsequent material adjustments to provisional values, with corresponding adjustments to goodwill should be disclosed and explained;	FRS 6:27
	(3) the cost of reorganising, restructuring and integrating the acquisitions;	FRS 6:31
	(4) composition and fair value of consideration;	S4A:13(3), FRS 6:24
	(5) nature of deferred or contingent purchase consideration;	FRS 6:24
	(6) if contingent consideration, range of possible outcomes and principal factors effecting outcome.	FRS 6:24
8.34	For each material acquisition, profit after tax and minority interest of the acquired entity for the period from the beginning of its financial year to the date of acquisition, giving the date its financial year began, and for its previous financial year.	FRS 6:35
8.35	For each substantial acquisition:	FRS 6:36
	(1) a summarised profit and loss account and statement of total recognised gains and losses for the period from the beginning of its financial year to the effective date of acquisition, giving the date its financial year began. The minimum disclosure for the summarised profit and loss is turnover, operating profit, FRS 3:20 exceptionals, profit before tax, taxation, minority interest and extraordinary items;	

No.	*Disclosure*	*Ref*
	(2) profit after tax and minority interest for the acquired entity's previous financial year.	
8.36	For mergers:	S4A:13(3) and (6); FRS 6:22
	(1) analysis of principal components of profit and loss and statement of total recognised gains and losses into:	
	(a) period post-merger;	
	(b) for each party to the merger, amounts for the period up to the date of the merger;	
	(c) for each party to the merger, amounts for the previous financial year.	
	(Minimum disclosure in respect of profit and loss turnover, operating profit and exceptional items, split between continuing discontinued and acquisitions; profit before tax, tax and minority interest; and extraordinary items.)	
	(2) composition and fair value of consideration;	
	(3) aggregate book value of net assets of each party at date of merger;	
	(4) nature and amount of significant accounting adjustments made to net assets to achieve consistency of accounting policies and an explanation on any significant adjustments made to the net assets as a consequence of the merger;	
	(5) adjustments made to the consolidated reserves as a result of the merger.	
8.37	The circumstances where an undertaking has become, or ceased to be, a subsidiary other than as a result of a purchase or exchange of shares.	FRS 2:49

Disposals

No.	*Disclosure*	*Ref*
8.38	Where group accounts are being prepared, for each disposal made during the financial year:	S4A:15
	(1) the name of the undertaking, or name of parent disposed of;	
	(2) the extent to which the profit or loss in the group accounts is attributable to the undertaking disposed of; and	
	(3) disclosure in respect of overseas businesses disposed of need not be given if it is seriously prejudicial to the business and agreement has been obtained from the Secretary of State.	S4A:16
8.39	Where group accounts are being prepared and a material undertaking has ceased to be a subsidiary in the period:	FRS 2:48
	(1) the name of the undertaking;	
	(2) any ownership interest retained; and	

No.	Disclosure	Ref
	(3) where it ceased to be a subsidiary other than by disposal of part of the interest held by the group, an explanation of the circumstances.	
8.40	Profit or loss on each material disposal of a previously acquired business or business segment.	FRS 10:54

Tax on reserves of overseas subsidiaries

8.41	Where consolidated financial statements include overseas subsidiaries:	FRS 2:54 SP 15:44
	(1) the extent to which deferred tax has been accounted for in respect of future remittances of accumulated reserves of overseas subsidiaries; and	
	(2) where deferred tax has not been provided in respect of all such reserves, the reason for not fully providing.	

Linked presentation

8.42	Where linked presentation is used.	
	(1) state explicitly that the entity is not obliged to support any losses, nor does it intend to do so;	FRS 5:27(c)
	(2) note agreement of financier to seek repayment of finance (principal and interest) only to the extent that sufficient funds are generated by the specific item it has financed and that it will not seek recourse in any other form.	FRS 5:27(d)

ESOP trusts

8.43	Sufficient information to understand significance of ESOP in context of sponsoring company. Include:	UITF 13
	(1) main features of ESOP including arrangements for distributing shares to employees;	
	(2) manner in which costs are dealt with in profit and loss account;	
	(3) number and market value of shares held by ESOP and whether dividend waived;	
	(4) extent to which shares are under option to employees, or have been conditionally gifted to them.	

AIM companies

8.44	(1) Name and address of both the nominated adviser and the nominated broker.	RSE 16.19(e)
	(2) Identity of related party, value of consideration and other relevant circumstances if a specified percentage ratio exceeds 0.25 per cent. Ratios normally based on assets, profits, consideration to assets and consideration to market capitalisation.	RSE 16.25

No.	Disclosure	Ref

Related party disclosures – FRS 8

8.45   The name of controlling party and of ultimate controlling party, if different, and the related party relationship. If the controlling party or ultimate controlling party is not known, disclose that fact. Disclosure required irrespective of whether any transactions have taken place between the parties.

FRS 8:5

8.46   Material transactions undertaken with a related party to include:

(1) the names of the transacting related parties;

(2) a description of the relationship between the parties;

(3) a description of the transactions;

(4) the amounts involved;

(5) any other elements of the transactions necessary for an understanding of the financial statements;

(6) the amounts due to or from related parties at the balance sheet date and the provisions for doubtful debts due from such parties at that date; and

(7) amounts written off in the period in respect of debts due to or from related parties.

Transactions with related parties may be disclosed on an aggregated basis (aggregation of similar transactions by type of related party) unless disclosure of an individual transaction, or connected transactions, is necessary for an understanding of the impact of the transactions on the financial statements of the reporting entity or is required by law

FRS 8:6

Aggregation should not be done in such a way as to obscure the importance of significant transactions. Hence, purchases or sales of goods should not be aggregated with purchases or sales of fixed assets. Nor should a material related party transaction with an individual be concealed in an aggregated disclosure.

FRS 8:21

Associates and joint ventures

The disclosures in 8.47 to 8.53 need not be given if the company is exempt from producing consolidated accounts, or would be if it had subsidiaries.

8.47   For all principal associates and joint ventures:

(1) names;

FRS 9:52

(2) proportion of issued shares in each class held by the group, indicating any special rights or constraints attaching to them;

FRS 9:52

No.	Disclosure	Ref
	(3) the accounting period or date of the financial statements if they differ from those of the investing group;	FRS 9:52
	(4) an indication of the nature of the business.	FRS 9:52
8.48	Matters/notes relating to the financial statements of the associates/joint ventures, or which would have been noted had the investor's accounting policies been followed, that are material to understanding the effect on the investor of its investments (e.g., share of jointly incurred contingent liabilities and share of capital commitments).	FRS 9:53
8.49	Why the facts of a case rebut either the presumption that the company:	FRS 9:56
	(1) is exercising significant influence over the operating and financial policies of another entity where it holds 20 per cent or more of the voting rights of that entity; or	FRS 9:56
	(2) has a participating interest where it holds 20 per cent or more of the shares.	FRS 9:56
8.50	Where the investment in associates exceeds a 15 per cent threshold (as defined) the aggregate of the share in its associates of:	FRS 9:58(a)
	(1) turnover (unless already included as a memorandum item);	
	(2) fixed assets;	
	(3) current assets;	
	(4) liabilities due within one year;	
	(5) liabilities due after one year or more.	
8.51	Where the investment in joint ventures exceeds a 15 per cent threshold (as defined) the aggregate of the share in its joint ventures of:	FRS 9:58(b)
	(1) fixed assets;	
	(2) current assets;	
	(3) liabilities due within one year;	
	(4) liabilities due after one year or more.	
8.52	Where the investment in any associate or joint venture exceeds a 25 per cent threshold (as defined) give the name of the associate/joint venture and the investor's share of the amounts below. If the associate/joint venture accounts for nearly ALL the amounts included for that class of investment, only the aggregate, not the individual, information need be given, provided that this is explained and the associate or joint venture identified:	FRS 9:58(c)
	(1) turnover;	
	(2) profit before tax;	

No.	Disclosure	Ref

(3) taxation;

(4) profit after tax;

(5) fixed assets;

(6) current assets;

(7) liabilities due within one year;

(8) liabilities due after one year or more.

8.53   In addition to the disclosures in 8.50 to 8.52 above, further analysis should be given where this is necessary to understand the nature of the total amounts disclosed. In deciding into which balance sheet headings the amounts should be analysed, regard should be had to the nature of the businesses and, therefore, which are the most relevant and descriptive balance sheet amounts to disclose. It may be important to give an indication of the size and maturity profile of the liabilities held.   **FRS 9:58**

Derivatives and other financial instruments

The disclosures in 8.54 to 8.65 relate to normal corporates as defined below. Separate disclosures are set by FRS 13 for banks and for non-bank financial institutions. The latter can choose whether to provide disclosures akin to corporates or those akin to banks.

'Normal corporates' is an entity which has any of its capital instruments listed or publicly traded on a stock exchange or market and which is not one of the following:

(1) a financial institution or financial institution group;

(2) an entity that is applying the Financial Reporting Standard for Smaller Entities;

(3) an insurance company or group.

A financial institution is defined as an entity whose principal activity is to carry one or more of the following activities:

(1) acceptance of deposits or other repayable funds from the public;

(2) lending;

(3) financial leasing;

(4) money transmission services;

(5) issuing and administering means of payment (e.g., credit cards, travellers' cheques and bankers' drafts);

(6) guarantees and commitments;

(7) trading for own account or for account of customers, or investing for own account, in money market instruments (cheques, bills, certificates of deposit, etc.), foreign exchange, financial futures and options, exchange and interest rate instruments, transferable securities;

No.	Disclosure	Ref

(8) participation in share issues and the provision of services related to such issues;

(9) advice to undertakings on capital structure, industrial strategy, and related questions and advice and services relating to mergers and the purchase of undertakings;

(10) money broking;

(11) portfolio management and advice;

(12) safekeeping and administration of services.

A financial institution group is defined as a group where the parent company is a financial institution, or the parent does not carry on any material business apart from the acquisition, management and disposal of interests in subsidiary undertakings and its principal subsidiaries are wholly or mainly entities that are financial institutions.

Narrative disclosures (should deal with all financial assets, financial liabilities and cash-settled commodity contracts except those specifically excluded from the scope of the FRS).

8.54 To be provided in the notes to the accounts or OFR with a cross-reference in the notes to the financial statements to the exact location within OFR: — **FRS 13:23**

(1) an explanation of the role that financial instruments have had during the period in creating or changing the risks that the entity faces in its activities (e.g., nature and purpose for which financial instruments are held or issued, instruments used for risk management purposes, instruments used for trading or speculation); — **FRS 13:13**

(2) an explanation of objectives, policies and strategies for holding or issuing financial instruments, as agreed by the directors (e.g., fixed/floating split, maturity and currency profile of financial assets and liabilities, hedging policies in respect of transaction and translation exposures); — **FRS 13:13**

(3) a description of transactions and risks that have been hedged, including their timing, and instruments used for that purpose, distinguishing between those that have been hedge accounted for and those that have not; — **FRS 13:21**

(4) any significant changes in explanations provided for the previous accounting period, including the reasons for the changes; — **FRS 13:16**

(5) any significant changes to the role of financial instruments in the period between the balance sheet date and the date of approval of the financial statements; — **FRS 13:18**

(6) an explanation of how the year end figures reflect the position during the period and, where these figures are materially unrepresentative of the entity's position during the period or of its agreed objectives, policies and strategies, an explanation of the extent to which this is the case. — **FRS 13:20**

No.	*Disclosure*	*Ref*

Numerical disclosures (to be provided in the notes to the accounts). Short-term debtors and creditors should be either included in all disclosures or excluded from all disclosures (other than currency profile). An explanation of how such items have been dealt with should be provided. — FRS 13:6

Interest rate profile

8.55 An analysis of the aggregate carrying amount of financial liabilities by principal currency, showing separately those at fixed interest rates, those at floating interest rates and those on which no interest is paid. In preparing the analysis: — FRS 13:26

(1) take account of non-optional derivatives whose effect is to alter the interest or currency basis of the financial liabilities (e.g., interest rate swaps, currency swaps and forwards); — FRS 13:26

(2) exclude any financial liabilities and derivatives that cannot be adequately reflected in the analysis and provide the summary of their main effects instead; — FRS 13:26

(3) disclose non-equity shares issued by the entity separately; — FRS 13:8

(4) disclose the weighted average interest rate of the fixed rate financial liabilities; — FRS 13:30

(5) disclose the weighted average period for which interest rates on fixed rate liabilities are fixed; — FRS 13:30

(6) disclose the weighted average period until maturity for financial liabilities on which no interest is paid; — FRS 13:30

(7) disclose the benchmark rate for determining interest payments for the floating rate financial liabilities; — FRS 13:30

(8) where there are material financial assets, analyse them separately, consistently with the above analysis of the financial liabilities. — FRS 13:32

Currency profile

8.56 An analysis of the net amount of monetary assets and liabilities at the balance sheet date showing the amount denominated in each currency, analysed by reference to the functional currencies of the operations involved. In preparing the analysis: — FRS 13:34

(1) focus on principal functional currencies and currencies in which the monetary items are denominated; — FRS 13:34

(2) exclude monetary assets and liabilities denominated in the same currency as the functional currency of the operations involved; — FRS 13:34

(3) exclude SSAP 20 hedges (i.e., foreign currency borrowings used to finance or hedge foreign equity investments which meet the offset criteria under SSAP 20); — FRS 13:34

No.	*Disclosure*	*Ref*
	(4) take account of derivatives contributing to the matching of foreign currency exposures and disclose the main effect of those that have not been taken into account;	FRS 13:34
	(5) deal with the non-equity shares issued by the entity in the same way as with financial liabilities but disclose them separately;	FRS 13:8
	(6) include short-term debtors and creditors in the analysis even where these are excluded from all other disclosures.	FRS 13:6

Maturity profile (liquidity)

8.57	A maturity profile of the carrying amount of financial liabilities (determined by reference to the earliest date on which payment can be required or on which the liability falls due) showing amounts falling due:	FRS 13:38
	(1) in one year or less, or on demand;	
	(2) in more than one year but not more than two years;	
	(3) in more than two years but not more than five years; and	
	(4) in more than five years.	
	In preparing this analysis deal with non-equity shares issued by the entity as with financial liabilities but disclose them separately.	FRS 13:8
8.58	A maturity analysis of any material undrawn committed borrowing facilities (including only those conditional facilities for which all conditions are met at the balance sheet date) showing those amounts expiring:	FRS 13:40
	(1) in one year or less;	
	(2) in more than one year but not more than two years; and	
	(3) in more than two years.	

Fair values

8.59	For each category of financial assets and liabilities either:	FRS 13:44,
	(1) the aggregate fair value at the balance sheet date together with the aggregate carrying amount; *or*	
	(2) the aggregate fair value of items with a positive fair value and, separately, the aggregate fair value of items with a negative fair value, in both cases as at the balance sheet date and in each case accompanied by the relevant aggregate carrying amount.	
	In preparing this disclosure:	

No.	*Disclosure*	*Ref*
	(1) include cash-settled commodity contracts;	FRS 13:64
	(2) disclose non-equity shares issued by the entity separately;	FRS 13:8
	(3) where the fair value is not materially different from the carrying amount, the carrying amount may be used as the fair value;	FRS 13:48
	(4) disclose method and any significant assumptions used in determining fair value.	FRS 13:51
8.60	Where it is not practicable to estimate with sufficient reliability the fair value of any financial asset or financial liability, or category of them, that is not traded on an organised market in a standard form:	FRS 13:53
	(1) a description of the financial asset or liability and its carrying amount;	
	(2) the reasons why it is not practicable for the reporting entity to estimate the fair value with sufficient reliability;	FRS 13:53
	(3) information about the principal characteristics of the underlying financial asset or liability that is pertinent to estimating its fair value and the market for such instruments, unless the disclosure is likely, in the opinion of directors, to be seriously prejudicial to the entity's interests (in which case disclose this fact and the reasons for the omission).	FRS 13:53

Instruments held for trading

No.	*Disclosure*	*Ref*
8.61	For financial assets, financial liabilities and cash-settled commodity contracts held for trading:	FRS 13:57, FRS 13:64
	(1) the net gain or loss from trading which has been included in the profit and loss account during the period, analysed by type of financial instrument. (Alternatively, this analysis can be provided by business activity, risk or in such other way as is consistent with the entity's management of this activity, in which case a description of the types of financial instruments involved, for each line of that analysis, should also be given);	
	(2) the period-end fair value of financial assets and separately of financial liabilities;	FRS 13:57
	(3) where the period-end position is materially unrepresentative of the entity's typical position during the period, the average fair value calculated using daily figures or, where these are not available, the most frequent interval that an entity's systems generate for management, regulatory or other purposes.	FRS 13:57

No.	*Disclosure*	*Ref*

Hedging disclosures

8.62 For gains and losses on financial assets, financial liabilities and cash-settled commodity contracts for which hedge accounting has been used (excluding hedging gains and losses accounted for by adjusting the carrying amount of a fixed asset recognised on the balance sheet): — FRS 13:59, FRS 13:60, FRS 13:64

   (1) the cumulative aggregate gains and losses unrecognised at the balance sheet date (items for which no fair value disclosures are given need not be dealt with in this disclosure);

   (2) the cumulative aggregate gains and losses carried forward in the balance sheet at the balance sheet date, pending their recognition in the profit and loss account; — FRS 13:59

   (3) the extent to which unrecognised gains and losses and gains and losses carried forward are expected to be recognised in the profit and loss account in the next period; — FRS 13:59

   (4) gains and losses included in the profit and loss account which arose in previous years and were either unrecognised or carried forward at the start of the reporting period; — FRS 13:59

   (5) gains and losses recognised in the profit and loss account in the period as a result of termination of hedge accounting on re-classification of hedging instruments. — FRS 13:62

8.63 Not all disclosures in 8.59 to 8.62 need be given in respect of cash-settled commodity contracts where: — FRS 13:65

   (1) an entity participates in an illiquid commodity market; *and*

   (2) it can demonstrate that the market is dominated by very few participants; *and*

   (3) the disclosure at the time that its financial statements become publicly available is likely to move the market significantly; *and*

   (4) in the directors' opinion, the disclosure would be seriously prejudicial to the interests of the entity,

in which case the fact that the disclosure has not been given and the reasons for the omission should be stated.

Market price risk – encouraged only

8.64 For all financial instruments, cash-settled commodity contracts and, if significant all other items carrying market price risk, numerical disclosures that show the magnitude of market price risk arising over the period, using a technique or other basis that is consistent with the way the entity manages its risk exposures. (Where different approaches are — FRS 13:66

No.	Disclosure	Ref
	used in different parts of the business, separate disclosure should be given for each part.) The disclosure should be supplemented by:	
	(1) an explanation of the method used and of the main parameters and assumptions underlying the data provided;	FRS 13:69
	(2) an explanation of the objective of the method used and of the limitations that may result in the information not fully reflecting the market price risk of the assets and liabilities involved;	FRS 13:69
	(3) reasons for any material changes in the amount of the reported market price risk when compared with that reported for the previous period;	FRS 13:69
	(4) where material changes are made to the method, or key assumptions and parameters, the reasons for the change and the previous period's information restated using the basis adopted in the current period.	FRS 13:71
8.65	Discussion of the approach to market price risk so as to set the numerical information in context and to assist in its interpretation.	FRS 13:67

9 Statement of directors' responsibilities

No.	Disclosure	Ref
9.1	An adequate description of directors' responsibilities to include the following points:	SAS 600.3
	(1) requirement for directors' to prepare true and fair financial statements;	
	(2) directors to select suitable accounting policies, apply them on a consistent basis and make judgements and estimates that are prudent and reasonable;	
	(3) state whether suitable accounting standards have been followed subject to material departures being disclosed and explained in the financial statements (only required of large companies – see 3.12 above);	
	(4) financial statements prepared on a going concern basis unless it is not appropriate to presume that the company will continue in business (not required where there is a separate statement by the directors on going concern);	
	(5) responsibility for keeping proper accounting records, safeguarding the assets and taking reasonable steps for the prevention and detection of fraud and other irregularities.	

10   Auditors' report

No.	Disclosure	Ref
10.1	Particulars of inconsistencies between the information presented in the directors' report and the annual accounts.	s235(3)
10.2	Where proper accounting records have not been kept, or proper returns from branches not visited by the auditor have not been received, or accounts are not in agreement with accounting records and returns, a statement of that fact.	s237(2)
10.3	Where the auditor has been unable to obtain all the information and explanations necessary for the audit, a statement of that fact.	s237(3)
10.4	(1) Where information required by Schedule 6 to the Companies Act 1985 (directors' emoluments and other benefits, transactions with directors and officers) is not disclosed in the accounts include the required information in the audit report.	s237(4)
	(2) Where there are material undisclosed related party transactions or an undisclosed control relationship that are required to be disclosed under FRS 8 include the relevant information in the opinion section of the audit report whenever practicable.	SAS 460:42
10.5	Ensure that the audit report states: (1) the firm's name; (2) qualification (e.g., registered auditor); and (3) address.	s236
10.6	Ensure that the audit report includes: (1) a title indicating to whom the report is addressed; (2) an introductory paragraph indicating the financial statements audited; (3) respective responsibilities of directors and auditors; (4) the basis of the auditors' opinion; (5) the auditors opinion on the financial statements; (6) the manuscript or printed signature of the auditors; (7) the date of the auditors' report; (8) appropriate headings.	SAS 600.2
10.7	A description of directors' relevant responsibilities if an adequate description is not given elsewhere in the financial statements and accompanying information (see 9.1 above).	SAS 600.3
10.8	Fact, if the period to which the directors have paid particular attention in assessing going concern is less than one year from the date of approval of the financial statements and that is not disclosed in the financial statements (see 3.17 above).	SAS 130:45

No.	*Disclosure*	*Ref*
10.9	State fact if directors have taken advantage of the exemption for small or medium-sized groups from producing group accounts and they are not entitled to that exemption.	s237(4A)
10.10	For listed companies refer to appendix V as regards:	
	(1) a more comprehensive statement of auditors responsibilities (paragraph 10);	
	(2) going concern (paragraph 11);	
	(3) internal control statement (paragraph 12);	
	(4) directors' statement of compliance with the combined code (paragraph 13);	
	(5) directors' remuneration (paragraph 17 and note ****).	
10.11	Identify :	
	(a) the nationality of the accounting standards and law under which the financial statements have been prepared; and	
	(b) the nationality of the auditing standards under which the financial statements have been audited.	
	This is in response to an agreement between the International Forum for Accountancy Developments and leading global regulators.	

Appendix III Companies Act 1985 – accounts formats

Balance sheet – Format 1

A   Called up share capital not paid (1)

B   Fixed assets
   I   Intangible assets
       1   Development costs
       2   Concessions, patents, licences, trade marks and similar rights and assets (2)
       3   Goodwill (3)
       4   Payments on account
   II   Tangible assets
       1   Land and buildings
       2   Plant and machinery
       3   Fixtures, fittings, tools and equipment
       4   Payments on account and assets in course of construction
   III   Investments
       1   Shares in group undertakings
       2   Loans to group undertakings
       3   Participating interests (*)
       4   Loans to undertakings in which the company has a participating interest
       5   Other investments other than loans
       6   Other loans
       7   Own shares (4)

C   Current assets
   I   Stocks
       1   Raw materials and consumables
       2   Work in progress
       3   Finished goods and goods for resale
       4   Payments on account
   II   Debtors (5)
       1   Trade debtors
       2   Amounts owed by group undertakings
       3   Amounts owed by undertakings in which the company has a participating interest.
       4   Other debtors
       5   Called up share capital not paid (1)
       6   Prepayments and accrued income (6)
   III   Investments
       1   Shares in group undertakings
       2   Own shares (4)
       3   Other investments
   IV   Cash at bank and in hand

D   Prepayments and accrued income (6).

E   Creditors: amounts falling due within one year
    1   Debenture loans (7)
    2   Bank loans and overdrafts
    3   Payments received on account (8)
    4   Trade creditors
    5   Bills of exchange payable
    6   Amounts owed to group undertakings
    7   Amounts owed to undertakings in which the company has a participating interest
    8   Other creditors including taxation and social security (9)
    9   Accruals and deferred income (10)

F   Net current assets (liabilities) (11)

G   Total assets less current liabilities

H   Creditors: amounts falling due after more than one year
    1   Debenture loans (7)
    2   Bank loans and overdrafts
    3   Payments received on account (8)
    4   Trade creditors
    5   Bills of exchange payable
    6   Amounts owed to group undertakings
    7   Amounts owed to undertakings in which the company has a participating interest
    8   Other creditors including taxation and social security (9)
    9   Accruals and deferred income (10)

I   Provisions for liabilities and charges
    1   Pensions and similar obligations
    2   Taxation, including deferred taxation
    3   Other provisions

J   Accruals and deferred income (10)
Minority interests (**)

K   Capital and reserves
    I   Called up share capital (12)
    II   Share premium account
    III Revaluation reserve
    IV   Other reserves
        1   Capital redemption reserve
        2   Reserve for own shares
        3   Reserves provided for by the articles of association
        4   Other reserves
    V   Profit and loss account
Minority interests (**)

References in ( ) are explained below

Balance Sheet – Format 2

Assets

A   Called up share capital not paid (1)

B   Fixed assets
  I   Intangible assets
     1   Development costs
     2   Concessions, patents, licences, trade marks and similar rights and assets (2)
     3   Goodwill (3)
     4   Payments on account
  II   Tangible assets
     1   Land and buildings
     2   Plant and machinery
     3   Fixtures, fittings, tools and equipment
     4   Payments on account and assets in course of construction
  III   Investments
     1   Shares in group undertakings
     2   Loans to group undertakings
     3   Participating interests (*)
     4   Loans to undertakings in which the company has a participating interest
     5   Other investments other than loans
     6   Other loans
     7   Own shares (4)

C   Current assets
  I   Stocks
     1   Raw materials and consumables
     2   Work in progress
     3   Finished goods and goods for resale
     4   Payments on account
  II   Debtors (5)
     1   Trade debtors
     2   Amounts owed by group undertakings
     3   Amounts owed by undertakings in which the company has a participating interest
     4   Other debtors
     5   Called up share capital not paid (1)
     6   Prepayments and accrued income (6)

Liabilities

A   Capital and reserves
  I   Called up share capital (12)
  II   Share premium account
  III   Revaluation reserve
  IV   Other reserves
     1   Capital redemption reserve
     2   Reserve for own shares
     3   Reserves provided for by the articles of association
     4   Other reserves
  V   Profit and loss account
  Minority interests

B   Provisions for liabilities and charges
     1   Pensions and similar obligations
     2   Taxation, including deferred taxation
     3   Other provisions

C   Creditors (13)
     1   Debenture loans (7)
     2   Bank loans and overdrafts
     3   Payments received on account (8)
     4   Trade creditors
     5   Bills of exchange payable
     6   Amounts owed to group undertakings
     7   Amounts owed to undertakings in which the company has a participating interest.
     8   Other creditors including taxation and social security (9)
     9   Accruals and deferred income (10)

D   Accruals and deferred income (10)

III Investments
    1 Shares in group undertakings
    2 Own shares (4)
    3 Other investments
IV Cash at bank and in hand

D   Prepayments and accrued income (6).

Note: Liabilities may alternatively be shown below assets, beside assets (in a two columnar layout) or on a separate page.

References in ( ) are explained below.

Notes on the balance sheet formats

(1)   Called up share capital not paid.

    This item may be shown in either of the two positions given in Formats 1 and 2.

(2)   Concessions, patents, licences, trade marks and similar rights and assets.

    Amounts in respect of assets shall only be included in a company's balance sheet under this item if either:

    (a) the assets were acquired for valuable consideration and are not required to be shown under goodwill; or

    (b) the assets in question were created by the company itself.

(3)   Goodwill.

    Amounts representing goodwill shall only be included to the extent that the goodwill was acquired for valuable consideration.

(4)   Own shares.

    The nominal value of the shares held shall be shown separately.

(5)   Debtors.

    The amount falling due after more than one year shall be shown separately for each item included under debtors.

(6)   Prepayments and accrued income.

    This item may be shown in either of the two positions given in Formats 1 and 2.

(7)   Debenture loans.

    The amount of any convertible loans shall be shown separately.

(8)   Payments received on account.

    Payments received on account of orders shall be shown for each of these items in so far as they are not shown as deductions from stocks.

(9)   Other creditors including taxation and social security.

    The amount for creditors in respect of taxation and social security shall be shown separately from the amount for other creditors.

(10) Accruals and deferred income.

    The two positions given for this item in Format 1 at E9 and H9 are an alternative to the position at J, but if the item is not shown in a position corresponding to that at J it may be shown in either or both of the other two positions (as the case may require).

The two positions given for this item in Format 2 are alternatives.

(11) Net current assets (liabilities).

In determining the amount to be shown for this item any amounts shown under 'prepayments and accrued income' shall be taken into account wherever shown.

(12) Called up share capital.

The amount of allotted share capital and the amount of called up share capital which has been paid up shall be shown separately.

(13) Creditors.

Amounts falling due within one year and after one year shall be shown separately for each of these items and for the aggregate of all of these items.

(*) Participating interests.

In consolidated accounts this item shall be replaced by two items 'Interests in associated undertakings' and 'Other participating interests'.

(**) Minority interests.

The two positions given in Format 1 for this item are alternatives.

Profit and loss account – format 1 (17)

1   Turnover
2   Cost of sales (14)
3   Gross profit or loss
4   Distribution costs (14)
5   Administrative expenses (14)
6   Other operating income
7   Income from shares in group undertakings
8   Income from participating interests (***)
9   Income from other fixed asset investments (15)
10 Other interest receivable and similar income (15)
11 Amounts written off investments
12 Interest payable and similar charges (16)
13 Tax on profit or loss on ordinary activities
14 Profit or loss on ordinary activities after taxation
    Minority interests
15 Extraordinary income
16 Extraordinary charges
17 Extraordinary profit or loss
18 Tax on extraordinary profit or loss
    Minority interests
19 Other taxes not shown under the above items
20 Profit or loss for the financial year

References in ( ) are explained below

Profit and loss account - Format 2

1   Turnover
2   Change in stocks of finished goods and in work in progress

3   Own work capitalised
4   Other operating income
5   (a)   Raw materials and consumables
    (b)   Other external charges
6   Staff costs:
    (a)   wages and salaries
    (b)   social security costs
    (c)   other pension costs
7   (a)   Depreciation and other amounts written off tangible and intangible fixed assets
    (b)   Exceptional amounts written off current assets
8   Other operating charges
9   Income from shares in group undertakings
10 Income from participating interests (***)
11 Income from other fixed asset investments (15)
12 Other interest receivable and similar income (15)
13 Amounts written off investments
14 Interest payable and similar charges (16)
15 Tax on profit or loss on ordinary activities
16 Profit or loss on ordinary activities after taxation
    Minority interests
17 Extraordinary income
18 Extraordinary charges
19 Extraordinary profit or loss
    Minority interests
20 Tax on extraordinary profit or loss
21 Other taxes not shown under the above items
22 Profit or loss for the financial year

References in ( ) are explained below

Profit and loss account – Format 3 (17)

A   Charges
    1   Cost of sales (14)
    2   Distribution costs (14)
    3   Administrative expenses (14)
    4   Amounts written off investments
    5   Interest payable and similar charges (16)
    6   Tax on profit or loss on ordinary activities
    7   Profit or loss on ordinary activities after taxation
        Minority interests
    8   Extraordinary charges
    9   Tax on extraordinary profit or loss
        Minority interests
    10 Other taxes not shown under the above items
    11 Profit or loss for the financial year

B   Income
    1   Turnover
    2   Other operating income
    3   Income from shares in group undertakings
    4   Income from participating interests (***)
    5   Income from other fixed asset investments (15)
    6   Other interest receivable and similar income (15)
    7   Profit or loss on ordinary activities after taxation
        Minority interests

8   Extraordinary income
      Minority interests
9   Profit or loss for the financial year

References in ( ) are explained below

Profit and loss account - Format 4

A   Charges
      1   Reduction in stocks of finished goods and in work in progress
      2   (a) Raw materials and consumables
            (b) Other external charges
      3   Staff costs:
            (a) wages and salaries
            (b) social security costs
            (c) other pension costs
      4   (a) Depreciation and other amounts written off tangible and intangible
                  fixed assets
            (b) Exceptional amounts written off current assets
      5   Other operating charges
      6   Amounts written off investments
      7   Interest payable and similar charges (16)
      8   Tax on profit or loss on ordinary activities
      9   Profit or loss on ordinary activities after taxation
            Minority interests
      10   Extraordinary charges
      11   Tax on extraordinary profit or loss
            Minority interests
      12   Other taxes not shown under the above items
      13   Profit or loss for the financial year

B   Income
      1   Turnover
      2   Increase in stocks of finished goods and in work in progress
      3   Own work capitalised
      4   Other operating income
      5   Income from shares in group undertakings
      6   Income from participating interests (***)
      7   Income from other fixed asset investments (15)
      8   Other interest receivable and similar income (15)
      9   Profit or loss on ordinary activities after taxation
            Minority interests
      10   Extraordinary income
            Minority interests
      11   Profit or loss for the financial year

References in ( ) are explained below.

Notes on the profit and loss account formats

(14) Cost of sales: distribution costs: administrative expenses.

   These items shall be stated after taking into account any necessary provisions for
   depreciation or diminution in value of assets.

(15) Income from other fixed asset investments: other interest receivable and similar
   income.

Income and interest derived from group undertakings shall be shown separately from income and interest derived from other sources.

(16) Interest payable and similar charges.

The amount payable to group undertakings shall be shown separately.

(17) Formats 1 and 3.

The amount of any provisions for depreciation and diminution in value of tangible and intangible fixed assets falling to be shown under items 7(a) and A4(a) respectively in Formats 2 and 4 shall be disclosed in a note to the accounts in any case where the profit and loss account is prepared by reference to Format 1 or Format 3.

(***) Income from participating interests.

In consolidated accounts this item shall be replaced by two items, 'Income from interests in associated undertakings' and 'Income from other participating interests'.

Appendix IV   The Combined Code – Principles of good governance and code of best practice

Derived by the Committee on Corporate Governance from the Committee's Final Report and from the Cadbury and Greenbury Reports.

Preamble

1. In the Committee's final report we said that, in response to many requests, we intended to produce a set of principles and code which embraced Cadbury, Greenbury and the Committee's own work. This Combined Code fulfils that undertaking.

2. The Combined Code is now issued in final form, and includes a number of changes made by The London Stock Exchange, with the Committee's agreement, following the consultation undertaken by the Exchange on the Committee's original draft.

3. The Combined Code contains both principles and detailed code provisions. We understand that it is the intention of the London Stock Exchange to introduce a requirement on listed companies to make a disclosure statement in two parts.

4. In the first part of the statement, the company will be required to report on how it applies the principles in the Combined Code. We make clear in our report that we do not prescribe the form or content of this part of the statement, the intention being that companies should have a free hand to explain their governance policies in the light of the principles, including any special circumstances applying to them which have led to a particular approach. It must be for shareholders and others to evaluate this part of the company's statement.

5. In the second part of the statement the company will be required either to confirm that it complies with the Code provisions or – where it does not – provide an explanation. Again, it must be for shareholders and others to evaluate such explanations.

6. In our report we make clear that companies should be ready to explain their governance policies, including any circumstances justifying departure from best practice; and that those concerned with the evaluation of governance should do so with common sense and with due regard to companies' individual circumstances.

7. We also make clear in our report that it is still too soon to assess definitively the results of the Cadbury and, more especially, the Greenbury codes. We see this Combined Code as a consolidation of the work of the three committees, not as a new departure. We have therefore retained the substance of the two earlier codes except in those few cases where we take a different view from our predecessors. We should in particular like to make clear, in relation to the detailed

provisions in the Listing Rules on directors' remuneration, that we envisage no change except where we take a different view from the Greenbury committee. With two exceptions, relating to the status of the remuneration committee, and the compensation payable to an executive director on loss of office, these changes are minor.

8. Section 1 of the Combined Code contains the corporate governance principles and code provisions applicable to all listed companies incorporated in the United Kingdom. These would be covered by the statement referred to in paragraphs 3–5 above, which will be required by the Listing Rules. Section 2 contains principles and code provisions applicable to institutional shareholders with regard to their voting, dialogue with companies and evaluation of a company's governance arrangements. These are not matters which are appropriate for the Listing Rules to include within the disclosure requirement. Nevertheless we regard Section 2 of the Combined Code as an integral part of our recommendations; we commend it to the organisations representing institutional shareholders and we hope that at least the major institutions will voluntarily disclose to their clients and the public the extent to which they are able to give effect to these provisions.

9. We have not included in the Combined Code principle D.IV in Chapter 2 of our final report, which reads as follows:

> 'External Auditors. The external auditors should independently report to shareholders in accordance with statutory and professional requirements and independently assure the board on the discharge of its responsibilities under D.I and D.II above in accordance with professional guidance.'

We say in paragraph 6.7 of the report that we recommend neither any additional prescribed requirements nor the removal of any existing requirements for auditors in relation to governance or publicly reported information, some of which derive from the Listing Rules. This recommendation is accepted by the London Stock Exchange. But the existing requirements for auditors will be kept under review, as a matter of course, by the responsible organisations.

COMMITTEE ON CORPORATE GOVERNANCE
June 1998

Part 1 Principles of good governance

Section 1 Companies

A. Directors

The Board

1. Every listed company should be headed by an effective board which should lead and control the company.

Chairman and CEO

2. There are two key tasks at the top of every public company – the running of the board and the executive responsibility for the running of the company's business. There should be a clear division of responsibilities at the head of the company which will ensure a balance of power and authority, such that no one individual has unfettered powers of decision.

Board Balance

3. The board should include a balance of executive and non-executive directors (including independent non-executives) such that no individual or small group of individuals can dominate the board's decision taking.

Supply of Information

4. The board should be supplied in a timely manner with information in a form and of a quality appropriate to enable it to discharge its duties.

Appointments to the Board

5. There should be a formal and transparent procedure for the appointment of new directors to the board.

Re-election

6. All directors should be required to submit themselves for re-election at regular intervals and at least every three years.

B. Directors' remuneration

The Level and Make-up of Remuneration

1. Levels of remuneration should be sufficient to attract and retain the directors needed to run the company successfully, but companies should avoid paying more than is necessary for this purpose. A proportion of executive directors' remuneration should be structured so as to link rewards to corporate and individual performance.

Procedure

2. Companies should establish a formal and transparent procedure for developing policy on executive remuneration and for fixing the remuneration package of individual directors. No director should be involved in deciding his or her own remuneration.

Disclosure

3. The company's annual report should contain a statement of remuneration policy and details of the remuneration of each director.

C. Relations with shareholders

Dialogue with Institutional Shareholders

1. Companies should be ready, where practicable, to enter into a dialogue with institutional shareholders based on the mutual understanding of objectives.

Constructive Use of the AGM

2. Boards should use the AGM to communicate with private investors and encourage their participation.

D. Accountability and audit

Financial Reporting

1. The board should present a balanced and understandable assessment of the company's position and prospects.

Internal Control

2. The board should maintain a sound system of internal control to safeguard shareholders' investment and the company's assets.

Audit Committee and Auditors

3. The board should establish formal and transparent arrangements for considering how they should apply the financial reporting and internal control principles and for maintaining an appropriate relationship with the company's auditors.

Part 1 Principles of good governance

Section 2 Institutional shareholders

E. Institutional investors

Shareholder Voting

1. Institutional shareholders have a responsibility to make considered use of their votes.

Dialogue with Companies

2. Institutional shareholders should be ready, where practicable, to enter into a dialogue with companies based on the mutual understanding of objectives.

Evaluation of Governance Disclosures

3. When evaluating companies' governance arrangements, particularly those relating to board structure and composition, institutional investors should give due weight to all relevant factors drawn to their attention.

Part 2 Code of best practice

Section 1 Companies

A. Directors

A.1 The Board

Principle

Every listed company should be headed by an effective board which should lead and control the company.

Code Provisions

A.1.1   The board should meet regularly.

A.1.2   The board should have a formal schedule of matters specifically reserved to it for decision.

A.1.3   There should be a procedure agreed by the board for directors in the furtherance of their duties to take independent professional advice if necessary, at the company's expense.

A.1.4   All directors should have access to the advice and services of the company secretary, who is responsible to the board for ensuring that board procedures are followed and that applicable rules and regulations are complied with. Any question of the removal of the company secretary should be a matter for the board as a whole.

A.1.5   All directors should bring an independent judgement to bear on issues of strategy, performance, resources (including key appointments) and standards of conduct.

A.1.6   Every director should receive appropriate training on the first occasion that he or she is appointed to the board of a listed company, and subsequently as necessary.

A.2 Chairman and CEO

Principle

There are two key tasks at the top of every public company – the running of the board and the executive responsibility for the running of the company's business. There should be a clear division of responsibilities at the head of the company which will ensure a balance of power and authority, such that no one individual has unfettered powers of decision.

Code Provision

A.2.1   A decision to combined the posts of chairman and chief executive officer in one person should be publicly justified. Whether the posts are held by different people or by the same person, there should be a strong and independent non-executive element on the board, with a recognised senior member other than the chairman to whom concerns can be conveyed. The chairman, chief executive and senior independent director should be identified in the annual report.

A.3 Board Balance

Principle

The board should include a balance of executive and non-executive directors (including independent non-executives) such that no individual or small group of individuals can dominate the board's decision taking.

Code Provisions

A.3.1   The board should include non-executive directors of sufficient calibre and number for their views to carry significant weight in the board's decisions.

Non-executive directors should comprise not less than one third of the board.

A.3.2   The majority of non-executive directors should be independent of manage-ment and free from any business or other relationship which could materi-ally interfere with the exercise of their independent judgement. Non-executive directors considered by the board to be independent in this sense should be identified in the annual report.

A.4 Supply of Information

Principle

The board should be supplied in a timely manner with information in a form and of a quality appropriate to enable it to discharge its duties.

Code Provision

A.4.1   Management has an obligation to provide the board with appropriate and timely information, but information volunteered by management is unlikely to be enough in all circumstances and directors should make fur-ther enquiries where necessary. The chairman should ensure that all direc-tors are properly briefed on issues arising at board meetings.

A.5 Appointments to the Board

Principle

There should be a formal and transparent procedure for the appointment of new directors to the board.

Code Provision

A.5.1   Unless the board is small, a nomination committee should be established to make recommendations to the board on all new board appointments. A majority of the members of this committee should be non-executive direc-tors and the chairman should be either the chairman of the board or a non-executive director. The chairman and members of the nomination committee should be identified in the annual report.

A.6 Re-election

Principle

All directors should be required to submit themselves for re-election at regular inter-vals and at least every three years.

Code Provisions

A.6.1   Non-executive directors should be appointed for specified terms subject to re-election and to Companies Act provisions relating to the removal of a director, and reappointment should not be automatic.

A.6.2   All directors should be subject to election by shareholders at the first oppor-tunity after their appointment, and to re-election thereafter at intervals of no more than three years. The names of directors submitted for election or re-election should be accompanied by sufficient biographical details to enable shareholders to take an informed decision on their election.

B. Directors' remuneration

B.1 The Level and Make-up of Remuneration

Principle

Levels of remuneration should be sufficient to attract and retain the directors needed to run the company successfully, but companies should avoid paying more than is necessary for this purpose. A proportion of executive directors' remuneration should be structured so as to link rewards to corporate and individual performance.

Code Provisions

Remuneration policy

B.1.1 The remuneration committee should provide the packages needed to attract, retain and motivate executive directors of the quality required but should avoid paying more than is necessary for this purpose.

B.1.2 Remuneration committees should judge where to position their company relative to other companies. They should be aware what comparable companies are paying and should take account of relative performance. But they should use such comparisons with caution, in view of the risk that they can result in an upward ratchet of remuneration levels with no corresponding improvement in performance.

B.1.3 Remuneration committees should be sensitive to the wider scene, including pay and employment conditions elsewhere in the group, especially when determining annual salary increases.

B.1.4 The performance-related elements of remuneration should form a significant proportion of the total remuneration package of executive directors and should be designed to align their interests with those of shareholders and to give these directors keen incentives to perform at the highest levels.

B.1.5 Executive share options should not be offered at a discount save as permitted by paragraphs 13.30 and 13.31 of the Listing Rules.

B.1.6 In designing schemes of performance-related remuneration, remuneration committees should follow the provisions in Schedule A to this Code.

Service Contracts and Compensation

B.1.7 There is a strong case for setting notice or contract periods at, or reducing them to, one year or less. Boards should set this as an objective, but they should recognise that it may not be possible to achieve it immediately.

B.1.8 It is necessary to offer longer notice or contract periods to new directors recruited from outside, such periods should reduce after the initial period.

B.1.9 Remuneration committees should consider what compensation commitments (including pension contributions) their directors' contracts of service, if any, would entail in the event of early termination. They should, in particular, consider the advantages of providing explicitly in the initial contract for such compensation commitments except in the case of removal for misconduct.

B.1.10 Where the initial contract does not explicitly provide for compensation commitments, remuneration committees should, within legal constraints, tailor their approach in individual early termination cases to the wide variety of circumstances. The board aim should be to avoid rewarding poor performance while dealing fairly with cases where departure is not due to poor performance and to take a robust line on reducing compensation to reflect departing directors' obligations to mitigate loss.

B.2 Procedure

Principle

Companies should establish a formal and transparent procedure for developing policy on executive remuneration and for fixing the remuneration packages of individual directors. No director should be involved in deciding his or her own remuneration.

Code Provisions

B.2.1 To avoid potential conflicts of interest, boards of directors should set up remuneration committees of independent non-executive directors to make recommendations to the board, within agreed terms of reference, on the company's framework of executive remuneration and its cost; and to determine on their behalf specific remuneration packages for each of the executive directors, including pension rights and any compensation payments.

B.2.2 Remuneration committees should consist exclusively of non-executive directors who are independent of management and free from any business or other relationship which could materially interfere with the exercise of their independent judgement.

B.2.3 The members of the remuneration committee should be listed each year in the board's remuneration report to shareholders (B.3.1 below).

B.2.4 The board itself or, where required by the Articles of Association, the shareholders should determine the remuneration of the non-executive directors, including members of the remuneration committee, within the limits set in the Articles of Association. Where permitted by the Articles, the board may however delegate this responsibility to a small sub-committee, which might include the chief executive officer.

B.2.5 Remuneration committees should consult the chairman and/or chief executive officer about their proposals relating to the remuneration of other executive directors and have access to professional advice inside and outside the company.

B.2.6 The chairman of the board should ensure that the company maintains contact as required with its principal shareholders about remuneration in the same way as for other matters.

B.3 Disclosure

Principle

The company's annual report should contain a statement of remuneration policy and details of the remuneration of each director.

Code Provisions

B.3.1   The board should report to the shareholders each year on remuneration. The report should form part of, or be annexed to, the company's annual report and accounts. It should be the main vehicle through which the company reports to shareholders on directors' remuneration.

B.3.2   The report should set out the company's policy on executive directors' remuneration. It should draw attention to factors specific to the company.

B.3.3   In preparing the remuneration report, the board should follow the provisions in Schedule B to this Code.

B.3.4   Shareholders should be invited specifically to approve all new long-term incentive schemes (as defined in the Listing Rules) save in the circumstances permitted by paragraph 13.13A of the Listing Rules.

B.3.5   The board's annual remuneration report to shareholders need not be a standard item of agenda for AGMs. But the board should consider each year whether the circumstances are such that the AGM should be invited to approve the policy set out in the report and should minute their conclusions.

C. Relations with shareholders

C.1 Dialogue with Institutional Shareholders

Principle

Companies should be ready, where practicable, to enter into a dialogue with institutional shareholders based on the mutual understanding of objectives.

C.2 Constructive Use of the AGM

Principle

Boards should use the AGM to communicate with private investors and encourage their participation.

Code Provisions

C.2.1   Companies should count all proxy votes and, except where a poll is called, should indicate the level of proxies lodged on each resolution, and the balance for and against the resolution, after it has been dealt with on a show of hands.

C.2.2   Companies should propose a separate resolution at the AGM on each substantially separate issue and should in particular propose a resolution at the AGM relating to the report and accounts.

C.2.3   The chairman of the board should arrange for the chairmen of the audit, remuneration and nomination committees to be available to answer questions at the AGM.

C.2.4   Companies should arrange for the Notice of the AGM and related papers to be sent to shareholders at least 20 working days before the meeting.

D. Accountability and audit

D.1 Financial Reporting

Principle

The board should present a balanced and understandable assessment of the company's position and prospects.

Code Provisions

D.1.1　The directors should explain their responsibility for preparing the accounts and there should be a statement by the auditors about their reporting responsibilities.

D.1.2　The board's responsibility to present a balanced and understandable assessment extends to interim and other price-sensitive public reports and reports to regulators as well as to information required to be presented by statutory requirements.

D.1.3　The directors should report that the business is a going concern, with supporting assumptions or qualifications as necessary.

D.2 Internal Control

Principle

The board should maintain a sound system of internal control to safeguard shareholders' investment and the company's assets.

Code Provisions

D.2.1　The directors should, at least annually, conduct a review of the effectiveness of the group's system of internal controls and should report to shareholders that they have done so. The review should cover all controls, including financial, operational and compliance controls and risk management.

D.2.2　Companies which do not have an internal audit function should from time to time review the need for one.

D.3 Audit Committee and Auditors

Principle

The board should establish formal and transparent arrangements for considering how they should apply the financial reporting and internal control principles and for maintaining an appropriate relationship with the company's auditors.

Code Provisions

D.3.1　The board should establish an audit committee of at least three directors, all non-executive, with written terms of reference which deal clearly with its authority and duties. The members of the committee, a majority of whom should be independent non-executive directors, should be named in the report and accounts.

D.3.2　The duties of the audit committee should include keeping under review the scope and results of the audit and its cost effectiveness and the independence and objectivity of the auditors. Where the auditors also supply a substantial volume of non-audit services to the company, the committee should keep the nature and extent of such services under review, seeking to balance the maintenance of objectivity and value for money.

Part 2 Code of best practice

Section 2 Institutional shareholders

E. Institutional investors

E.1 Shareholder Voting

Principle

Institutional shareholders have a responsibility to make considered use of their votes.

Code Provisions

E.1.1 Institutional shareholders should endeavour to eliminate unnecessary variations in the criteria which each applies to the corporate governance arrangements and performance of the companies in which they invest.

E.1.2 Institutional shareholders should, on request, make available to their clients information on the proportion of resolutions on which votes were cast and non-discretionary proxies lodged.

E.1.3 Institutional shareholders should take steps to ensure that their voting intentions are being translated into practice.

E.2 Dialogue with Companies

Principle

Institutional shareholders should be ready, where practicable, to enter into a dialogue with companies based on the mutual understanding of objectives.

E.3 Evaluation of Governance Disclosures

Principle

When evaluating companies' governance arrangements, particularly those relating to board structure and composition, institutional investors should give due weight to all relevant factors drawn to their attention.

Schedule A: Provisions on the design of performance-related remuneration

1. Remuneration committees should consider whether the directors should be eligible for annual bonuses. If so, performance conditions should be relevant, stretching and designed to enhance the business. Upper limits should always be

considered. There may be a case for part payment in shares to be held for a significant period.

2. Remuneration committees should consider whether the directors should be eligible for benefits under long-term incentive schemes. Traditional share option schemes should be weighed against other kinds of long-term incentive scheme. In normal circumstances, shares granted or other forms of deferred remuneration should not vest, and options should not be exercisable, in under three years. Directors should be encouraged to hold their shares for a further period after vesting or exercise, subject to the need to finance any costs of acquisition and associated tax liability.

3. Any new long-term incentive schemes which are proposed should be approved by shareholders and should preferably replace existing schemes or at least form part of a well considered overall plan, incorporating existing schemes. The total rewards potentially available should not be excessive.

4. Payouts or grants under all incentive schemes, including new grants under existing share option schemes, should be subject to challenging performance criteria reflecting the company's objectives. Consideration should be given to criteria which reflect the company's performance relative to a group of comparator companies in some key variables such as total shareholder return.

5. Grants under executive share option and other long-term incentive schemes should normally be phased rather than awarded in one large block.

6. Remuneration committees should consider the pension consequences and associated costs to the company of basic salary increases and other changes in remuneration, especially for directors close to retirement.

7. In general, neither annual bonuses nor benefits in kind should be pensionable.

Schedule B: Provisions on what should be included in the remuneration report

1. The report should include full details of all elements in the remuneration package of each individual director by name, such as basic salary, benefits in kind, annual bonuses and long-term incentive schemes including share options.

2. Information on share options, including SAYE options, should be given for each director in accordance with the recommendations of the Accounting Standards Board's Urgent Issues Task Force Abstract 10 and its successors.

3. If grants under executive share option or other long-term incentive schemes are awarded in one large block rather than phased, the report should explain and justify.

4. Also included in the report should be pension entitlements earned by each individual director during the year, disclosed on one of the alternative bases recommended by the Faculty of Actuaries and the Institute of Actuaries and included in the Stock Exchange Listing Rules. Companies may wish to make clear that the transfer value represents a liability of the company, not a sum paid or due to the individual.

5. If annual bonuses or benefits in kind are pensionable the report should explain and justify.

6. The amounts received by, and commitments made to, each director under 1, 2 and 4 above should be subject to audit.

7.   Any service contracts which provide for, or imply, notice periods in excess of one year (or any provisions for pre-determined compensation on termination which exceed one year's salary and benefits) should be disclosed and the reasons for the longer notice periods explained.

Appendix V   Corporate governance disclosure checklist

Introduction

This checklist sets out the disclosures on corporate governance matters that are required to be included in the annual reports and accounts of listed companies. It reflects the UK Listing Authority's reporting requirements and its interpretations extant in March 2000. The Combined Code on Corporate Governance is effective for accounting periods ending on or after 31 December 1998.

The checklist also reflects 'The guidance for Directors on Internal Control and the Combined Code' ('Turnbull'), the letters dated 10 December 1998 and 27 September 1999 from the London Stock Exchange on the transitional and implementation arrangements for the Turnbull guidance, and the guidance issued to auditors by the Auditing Practices Board in Bulletin 1999/5 – *The Combined Code: Requirements of Auditors under the Listing Rules of the London Stock Exchange.*

Section 12 below on the internal control statement includes alternatives relating to:

(a) pre-adoption of Turnbull;

(b) the transitional approach to Turnbull; and

(c) full implementation of Turnbull.

Corporate governance disclosure requirements are subject to change and before reporting a check should be performed as to whether any such changes have taken place.

The items in the checklist should be treated as mandatory unless there is indication to the contrary. Where there are transitional arrangements or requirements yet to come into force these are explained. It should be borne in mind that this checklist does not deal with the Companies Act disclosure requirements.

Exemptions for certain listed companies

Under the Listing Rules, various exemptions from the corporate governance disclosures are available for various categories of companies. Refer to paragraphs **7.11** to **7.19** above for details of these exemptions and suggested wordings to be used where companies avail themselves of them.

The exemptions available vary for each of the categories of companies. Given the complexity of the rules in this area and the possibility of change, it is worth the company secretary checking the position with the Listing Authority, if a company wishes to continue availing itself of an exemption.

AIM companies

Companies that have securities traded on the Alternative Investment Market (AIM) are required to prepare annual reports and accounts in accordance with chapter 16 of the rules of the London Stock Exchange (which should not be confused with the Listing Rules). These rules do not require AIM companies to comply with the post-Combined Code disclosures and nor did they previously require AIM companies to comply with the Cadbury or Greenbury recommendations. Refer to paragraphs **7.20** to **7.21** above as regards the applicability of the Combined Code disclosures to AIM companies and the type of disclosure that might be made where the directors voluntarily provide corporate governance disclosures.

	Location in annual report and accounts	Included (Yes/No)
1 Statement of appliance of the Principles of the Combined Code A narrative statement of how the company has applied the Principles set out in Section 1 of the Combined Code, providing explanation which enables the company's shareholders to evaluate how the Principles have been applied. A brief bland statement will not suffice and such statements could be treated as a rule breach. Directors should arrange for a check to be carried out to satisfy themselves that all 14 Principles are covered in the narrative. We advise directors to include the internal control statement in (or cross-refer it to) the narrative statement describing how the Principles are applied. Also, for companies which are not reporting under Turnbull in full (see section 12 below), it is advisable that the description of how Principle D.2 on internal control is applied should relate only to internal financial control. Where such companies do respond to the encouragement in the 1994 Rutteman guidance to report on the wider aspects of internal control, this should be explained so as to assist the readers' understanding. *Listing Rules, paragraph 12.43A(a).* *London Stock Exchange letter dated 27 September 1999 explaining the implementation arrangements for the internal control aspects of the Combined Code.* *Guidance for directors on internal control and financial reporting issued in December 1994.*	Corporate governance statement or directors' report.*	
2 Statement of compliance with the Code provisions in the Combined Code A statement as to whether or not the company has complied throughout the accounting period with the Code provisions set out in Section 1 of the Combined Code, disclosing any provisions with which it has not complied throughout the period under review, including the part of the period during which non-compliance	Corporate governance statement or directors' report.*	

	Location in annual report and accounts	Included (Yes/No)
continued and the reasons therefore. Suggested wording is as follows:		
'Throughout the year ended xx/xx/xx the company has been in compliance with the Code Provisions set out in Section 1 of the Combined Code on Corporate Governance issued by the UK Listing Authority.'		
For years ending before 23 December 1999 (when the company is not following the transitional approach to Turnbull), following the letter from the Exchange dated 10 December 1998 (see section 12 below), we suggest that directors include a sentence along the following lines in their statement of compliance:		
'As permitted by the UK Listing Authority, the company has complied with Code provision D.2.1 on internal control by reporting on internal financial control in accordance with the guidance for directors on internal control and financial reporting that was issued in December 1994.'		
However, if the company/group is adopting the transitional approach to Turnbull as outlined in the letter from the Exchange dated 27 September 1999 (see section 12 below), then companies should refer to this fact, either in their internal control statement or in the compliance statement. Appropriate wording could be:		
'The company/group has adopted the transitional approach for the internal control aspects of the Combined Code as set out in the letter from the London Stock Exchange dated 27 September 1999.'		
Listing Rules, paragraph 12.43A(b).		
London Stock Exchange letters dated 10 December 1998 and 27 September 1999.		
3 Assessment of the company's position and prospects Presentation by the Board of a balanced and understandable assessment of the company's position and prospects. *Combined Code – Principle D.1.*	Chairman's statement, operating and financial review or directors' report.*	

	Location in annual report and accounts	Included (Yes/No)
4 Combining the posts of chairman and chief executive officer A decision to combine the posts of chairman and chief executive officer in one person should be publicly justified. Such justification is **not** required to be in the annual report and accounts, although we believe that it will be regarded as best practice to disclose the justification here. *Combined Code – provision A.2.1.*	Corporate governance statement or directors' report.*	
5 Identifying the chairman, chief executive and the senior independent director The chairman, chief executive and senior independent director should be identified in the annual report. *Combined Code – provision A.2.1.*	Corporate governance statement, details of directors or directors' report.*	
6 Identifying the independent directors The non-executive directors considered by the board to be independent of management and free from any business or other relationship which could materially interfere with the exercise of their independent judgement should be identified in the annual report. (See **7.31** above.) *Combined Code – provision A.3.2.*	Corporate governance statement, details of directors or directors' report.*	
7 Identifying the nomination committee members The chairman and members of the nomination committee should be identified in the annual report. A majority of the members of the nomination committee should be non-executive directors and the chairman should be either the chairman of the board or a non-executive director. The recommendation in the Combined Code to establish a nomination committee does not apply where the board is small. The term 'small' is not defined within the Combined Code. Where the board is deemed to be 'small' appropriate explanation can usefully be given when explaining how Principle A.5 has been applied – see section 1 above. *Combined Code – provision A.5.1.*	Corporate governance statement, details of directors or directors' report.*	

	Location in annual report and accounts	Included (Yes/No)
8 Identifying the audit committee members The members of the audit committee should be named in the annual report and accounts. The audit committee should comprise at least three directors, all non-executive. A majority of the committee members should be independent non-executive directors. The audit committee should have written terms of reference which deal clearly with its authority and duties. *Combined Code – provision D.3.1.*	Corporate governance statement, details of directors or directors' report.*	
9 Statement of directors' responsibilities in respect of the financial statements A brief statement of directors' responsibilities for the financial statements. Unlike the Cadbury Code, the Combined Code does not specify where in the annual report and accounts this responsibilities statement should be located. However, paragraph 4 of SAS 600 states that, 'It will aid communication with the reader if ... and, where the directors set out their responsibilities themselves, if this description is immediately before the auditors' report.' The Combined Code contains no prescribed contents for the directors' responsibilities statement. However, paragraph 21 of SAS 600 states that the statement should cover:	Immediately before the auditors' report on the financial statements.**	
(1) the legal requirement for directors to prepare financial statements for each financial year which give a true and fair view of the state of affairs of the company (or group) as at the end of the financial year and of the profit or loss for the year then ended;		
(2) the directors requirement in preparing financial statements to select suitable accounting policies and then apply them on a consistent basis, making judgements and estimates that are prudent and reasonable;		
(3) (large companies only – all listed companies will meet the definition of large) the directors requirement in		

	Location in annual report and accounts	Included (Yes/No)
preparing financial statements to state whether applicable accounting standards have been followed, subject to any material departures disclosed and explained in the notes to the accounts. (This does not obviate the need for a formal statement in the notes to the accounts disclosing whether the financial statements have been prepared in accordance with applicable accounting standards);		
(4) (where no separate statement on going concern is made by the directors – this should therefore not apply to listed companies) the directors requirement in preparing financial statements to prepare the financial statements on the going concern basis unless it is not appropriate to presume that the company/group will continue in business;		
(5) the responsibility of the directors for keeping proper accounting records, for safeguarding the assets of the company (or group), and for taking reasonable steps for the prevention and detection of fraud and other irregularities. Note 12 to the Cadbury Code (which was not mandatory) also contained guidance on the points to be included in the directors' responsibility statement – the points are the same as the SAS 600 points above but excluding point (4). Note 12 to the Cadbury Code, however, called for confirmation by the directors that they had complied with points (2) and (3) above (rather than simply stating what is the responsibility). In the absence of guidance in the Combined Code on the required contents, it is suggested that a directors' responsibility statement that complies with SAS 600, whether or not it also complies with Note 12 to the Cadbury Code, would satisfy the recommendation in provision D.1.1 of the Combined Code. *Combined Code, provision D.1.1 and Statement of Auditing Standards 'Auditors' reports on financial statements' (SAS 600).*		

	Location in annual report and accounts	Included (Yes/No)
10 Statement of auditors' responsibilities A statement by the auditors of their responsibilities. (See chapter 40.) The key elements of such a statement of auditors' responsibilities relate to the requirements of: (1) statute and Auditing Standards with respect to the audit of the financial statements; (2) statute and the Listing Rules where the auditors are only required to report by exception; (3) the Listing Rules for auditors to review the statement concerning the company's compliance with seven specified provisions of the Combined Code; and (4) Auditing Standards to read the 'other information' in the annual report. For companies with subsidiaries, the wording should reflect group considerations. It is also preferable to refer to the Companies Act 1985. APB Bulletin 1999/5 states that a description of the auditors' responsibilities may be included either as a separate statement or as a section within the audit report. Since such a description will encompass the auditors' review of the company's compliance with the seven specified provisions of the Combined Code, it will remove the need for the publication of a separate auditors' report on this review. APB Bulletin 1999/5 does envisage, however, a factual report for the directors on the auditors' review for Listing Rule purposes. This report would be a private report not intended for publication. Leading accountancy firms have given undertakings to global regulators to change their audit reports to include details of the nationality of auditing and accounting standards used in preparing and auditing the accounts. This is in	In the auditors' report on the financial statements (our preference) or set out in a separate section within the annual report.**	

	Location in annual report and accounts	Included (Yes/No)
response to the International Forum of Accountancy Development's (IFAD) request to help cross-border investors be more aware of standards being used. *Combined Code – provision D.1.1.* *APB Bulletin 1999/5 The Combined Code: Requirements of auditors under the Listing Rules of the London Stock Exchange.*		
11 Going concern Statement by the directors on whether, after making enquiries: (1) they have a reasonable expectation that the company will continue in operational existence for the foreseeable future and have therefore used the going concern basis in preparing the financial statements; (2) they have identified factors which cast doubt on the ability of the company to continue in operational existence for the foreseeable future but they consider that it is appropriate to use the going concern basis in preparing the financial statements; or (3) they consider that the company is unlikely to continue in operational existence for the foreseeable future and therefore the going concern basis is not an appropriate one on which to draw up the financial statements. The statement will be supported by assumptions or qualifications as necessary. The statement by the directors should not be inconsistent with the disclosures regarding going concern either in the financial statements or the auditors' report thereon. APB Bulletin 1999/5 indicates that where going concern matters are discussed in the financial statements, one method of achieving consistency is for the directors' statement to include a cross-reference to the relevant note in the financial statements.	Operating and financial review or (as is our preference) included in the corporate governance statement with an indication that it also constitutes part of the OFR (if one is included).**	

	Location in annual report and accounts	Included (Yes/No)
Code provision D.1.3 of the Combined Code, interpreted by the guidance for directors 'Going concern and financial reporting' published in November 1994. *Listing Rules, paragraph 12.43(v).* *APB Bulletin 1999/5.*		
12 Internal control statement Combined Code Principle D.2 states 'The Board should maintain a sound system of internal control to safeguard share-holders' investment and the company's assets'. Under Code provision D.2.1 directors should, at least annually, conduct a review of the effectiveness of the group's system of internal controls and should report to shareholders that they have done so. The review should cover all controls, including financial, operational and compliance controls and risk man-agement. The Listing Rules require the board to disclose if it has failed to con-duct such a review. Under Code provision D.2.2, companies that do not have an internal audit func-tion should from time to time review the need for one. Turnbull interprets 'from time to time' as referring to an annual review requirement. If such a review is not conducted annually, this should be stated (normally in the compliance statement as this is a breach of provision D.2.2). Prior to September 1999, companies were allowed to report only on internal financial controls in relation to D.2.1. At the end of September 1999 the Turnbull working party published guidance for directors on the Combined Code. The guidance focuses on the wider aspects of internal control and allows full compli-ance with D.2.1 (see **7.66** to **7.80** above). The letter from the London Stock Exchange dated 27 September 1999 specifies how this guidance should be implemented in order to satisfy the Listing Rules, and gives details of its implementation arrangements.	Corporate governance statement or directors' report cross-referred to narrative appliance statement.*	

	Location in annual report and accounts	Included (Yes/No)
(A) PRE-ADOPTANCE OF TURNBULL For accounting periods ending before 23 December 1999, a company's statement of compliance will satisfy the requirements of Listing Rule paragraph 12.43A(b) in respect of Code Provision D.2.1 if it reports on its internal financial controls in accordance with the guidance for directors on internal controls and financial reporting that was issued by the Rutteman Working Group in December 1994. A company that has adopted this approach should indicate in its statement of compliance that it has done so (see section 2 above). The disclosures required under Rutteman are described in section B below. **(B) TRANSITIONAL APPROACH TO TURNBULL** In this situation, which may exist for many companies for the first accounting period ending on or after 23 December 1999 and up to 22 December 2000, a statement should be made that the transitional approach is being adopted. One of the two following disclosures should be made by the directors, as a minimum, in respect of the application of Code Principle D.2: (a) a statement that they have established the procedures necessary to implement the guidance – *Internal Control: Guidance for Directors on the Combined Code*; or (b) an explanation of when they expect to have those procedures in place. Additionally, in respect of Code provision D.2.1, the directors should report on their internal financial controls pursuant to the (Rutteman) guidance for directors on internal control and financial reporting that was issued in December 1994. In order to comply with the 1994 Rutteman guidance, directors should include a statement on the system of		

	Location in annual report and accounts	Included (Yes/No)
internal financial control covering the period of the financial statements and taking account of material developments between the balance sheet date and the date on which the financial statements are signed, including:		
(1) an acknowledgement by the directors that they are responsible for the company's/group's system of internal financial control;		
(2) an explanation that such a system of internal financial control can provide only reasonable and not absolute assurance against material misstatement or loss;		
(3) a description of the key procedures that the directors have established and which are designed to provide effective internal financial control, having regard to paragraph 11 of the 1994 guidance for directors and the section of the guidance entitled 'Criteria for assessing effectiveness';		
(4) a confirmation that the directors (or a board committee) have reviewed the effectiveness of the system of internal financial control; and		
(5) where weaknesses in internal financial control have resulted in material losses, contingencies or uncertainties which require disclosure in the financial statements or auditors' report, the statement should:		
(a) describe what corrective action has been taken or is intended to be taken; or (b) explain why no changes are considered necessary.		
Where the company is a parent company preparing group financial statements, the directors' statement regarding internal financial control should be in respect of the group as a whole. The 1994 guidance (paragraph 14) states that directors may wish, and are encouraged, to extend their statement to cover their responsibility		

	Location in annual report and accounts	*Included (Yes/No)*
for wider aspects of internal control rather than just internal financial control. However, we would urge caution in this area. If companies are planning to report on the wider aspects of internal control whilst still adopting the transitional approach, then this should be clearly explained.		
We advise directors to avoid expressing any form of opinion on the control system on the grounds that there is no requirement to express an opinion.		
We also advise directors to include the control statement in (or refer it to) the main statement describing how the Principles are applied.		
A company or group which adopts this transitional approach should indicate within its corporate governance disclosures that it has done so. We suggest the inclusion of the following sentence either at the beginning of the statement on internal control or in the compliance statement:		
'The company/group [as appropriate] has adopted the transitional approach for the internal control aspects of the Combined Code as set out in the letter from the London Stock Exchange to listed companies dated 27 September 1999.'		
(C) FULL IMPLEMENTATION OF TURNBULL		
Companies which are adopting the guidance in full early (or for accounting periods ending on or after 23 December 2000) should, as a minimum, disclose where applicable:		
(a) that there is an ongoing process for identifying, evaluating and managing the significant risks faced by the company, that it has been in place for the year under review and up to the date of approval of the annual report and accounts, that it is regularly reviewed by the board and accords with the Turnbull guidance;		

	Location in annual report and accounts	Included (Yes/No)
(b) a summary of the process the board (where applicable, through its committees) has applied in reviewing the effectiveness of the system of internal control (e.g., reports from management, the role of the audit committee and other relevant committee(s), the role of the internal audit function and the annual assessment of the system); and		
(c) the process it has applied to deal with material internal control aspects of any significant problems disclosed in the annual report and accounts.		
The summary of the process the board/committee has applied in reviewing the effectiveness of the system of internal control should encompass:		
(a) scope and frequency of reports received/reviewed in the year; and		
(b) the process for annual assessment.		
It is also recommended that the annual assessment of the system of internal control should provide sound, appropriately documented support for the statements on internal control.		
It is suggested that a check should be made of the Operating and Financial Review and other parts of the annual report in case they disclose significant problems. If there is any doubt whether or not an item could be regarded as significant and no disclosure is made, it is also suggested that there should be a board minute setting out the directors' rationale for the decision they have made.		
Where a board cannot make one or more of the above disclosures, it should state this fact and provide an explanation.		
Other required disclosures are:		
(a) an acknowledgement by the board that it is responsible for the company's system of internal control and for reviewing its effectiveness;		
(b) an explanation that such a system is designed to manage rather than		

	Location in annual report and accounts	Included (Yes/No)
eliminate the risk of failure to achieve business objectives, and can only provide reasonable and not absolute assurance against material misstatement or loss; and (c) where material joint ventures and associates have not been dealt with as part of the group for the purposes of applying the guidance, a statement of this fact. The guidance recommends the board to ensure that its disclosures provide meaningful, high-level information and do not give a misleading impression. It also suggests that the board may wish to provide additional information in the annual report to assist understanding of the company's risk management processes and system of internal control. For groups of companies, the review of effectiveness of internal control and the report to the shareholders should be from the perspective of the group as a whole. A common situation that might arise for companies that have adopted the transitional approach in the previous period is that they cannot state that there was an ongoing process for the whole period. Our suggested wording would be: 'The board is unable to state that the process has been in place for the first x months of the year as this period was needed to put in place the procedures which the board agreed should be established.' Internal Control: Guidance for Directors on the Combined Code *issued in September 1999 by the Turnbull Working Party.* *Combined Code – Principle D.2 and provisions D.2.1 and D.2.2.* *Letters from the London Stock Exchange dated 10 December 1998 and 27 September 1999.* *Guidance for directors on internal control and financial reporting issued in December 1994.*		

		Location in annual report and accounts	Included (Yes/No)
	APB Bulletin 1999/5 and, in particular, paragraph 37 which interprets what should be included in the summary of the process.		
13	**Auditors' review on the directors' statement of compliance with the Code provisions of the Combined Code** Auditors are required to review the directors' statement of compliance with the Combined Code in so far as it relates to provisions A.1.2, A.1.3, A.6.1, A.6.2, D.1.1, D.2.1 and D.3.1. In addition, the Listing Rules require the directors' statement on going concern (section 11 above) to be reviewed by the auditors before publication. APB Bulletin 1999/5 assumes that the new expanded responsibility statement in the auditors' report obviates the need to publish an auditors' review report on governance disclosures. Our view is that a private review report for the directors is useful support for the directors and helps remove the possibility of misunderstanding about the auditors' role in this area. APB Bulletin 1999/5 (and in particular the guidance on the auditors' responsibilities statement) indicates that auditors need to report if the statement of compliance with the Combined Code does not properly disclose a departure from one of the seven provisions specified for their review. Such a report will be provided by way of an additional paragraph in the auditors' report on the financial statements. This could be worded as follows: 'Other matter We have reviewed the board's description of its process for reviewing the effectiveness of internal control set out on page . . of the annual report. In our opinion the board's comments concerning ... do not	The auditors' report on the financial statements.*	

	Location in annual report and accounts	*Included (Yes/No)*
appropriately reflect our understanding of the process undertaken by the board because ...' *Listing Rules, paragraph 12.43A.* *APB Bulletin 1999/5.*		
14 Report to shareholders on directors' remuneration Report to the shareholders by the Board. *Listing Rules paragraph 12.43A(c) and Combined Code – provision B.3.1.* The report must contain:	Separate report to shareholders (remuneration report).***	
(1) A statement of the company's policy on executive directors' remuneration, drawing attention to factors specific to the company. *Listing Rules paragraph 12.43A(c)(i) and Combined Code – Principle B.3 and provision B.3.2* Although Principle B.3 of the Combined Code says no more than there should be a statement of remuneration policy, Code provision B.3.2 states that statement on policy 'should draw attention to factors specific to the company'. In addition, the Hampel Committee in its final report, paragraph 4.15, commented that, 'We have reviewed the value of a general statement of remuneration policy. A number of companies have met the letter of this requirement with anodyne references to the need to "recruit, retain and motivate" or to pay "market rates". We consider that a policy statement is potentially helpful, to set the context for the more detailed information; we hope that companies will provide more informative statements, drawing attention to factors specific to the company.' To this end the disclosure on general policy could usefully cover	Remuneration report.**	

	Location in annual report and accounts	*Included (Yes/No)*
those matters set out in paragraph 5.5 of the Greenbury Report that are relevant to the company. These are: (a) the total level of remuneration; (b) the main components and the arrangements for determining them, including the division between basic and performance-related components; (c) the comparator groups of companies considered; (d) the main parameters and rationale for any annual bonus schemes, including caps; (e) the main parameters and rationale for any share option or other long-term incentive schemes; (f) how performance is measured, how rewards are related to it, how the performance measures relate to longer-term company objectives and how the company has performed over time relative to comparator companies; (g) the company's policy on allowing executive directors to accept appointments and retain payments from sources outside the company; (h) the company's policy on contracts of service and early termination; (i) the pension and retirement benefit schemes for directors, including the type of scheme, the main terms and parameters, what elements of remuneration are pensionable, how the Inland Revenue pensions cap has been accommodated, and whether the scheme is part of, or separate from, the main company scheme. In setting out the company's policy on executive directors' remuneration it will often not be necessary to cover all of the above points.		

	Location in annual report and accounts	Included (Yes/No)
(2) The amount of each element in the remuneration package for the period under review of each director by name, including, but not restricted to, basic salary and fees, the estimated money value of benefits in kind, annual bonuses, deferred bonuses, compensation for loss of office and payments for breach of contract or other termination payments, together with the total for each director for the period under review and for the corresponding prior period, and any significant payments made to former directors during the period under review. These details should be presented in tabular form, unless inappropriate, together with explanatory notes as necessary. *Listing Rules paragraph 12.43A(c)(ii) and Combined Code – Principle B.3 and paragraph 1 of Schedule B to the Combined Code.*	Note to the audited financial statements (with a cross-reference to the remuneration report) or remuneration report (with a cross-reference to the notes to the accounts if Schedule 6 information is combined with this disclosure).****	
(3) Information on share options, including SAYE options, for each director by name in accordance with the recommendations of the Accounting Standards Board's Urgent Issues Task Force Abstract 10 (UITF Abstract 10). This information should be presented in tabular form together with explanatory notes as necessary. UITF Abstract 10 recommends that the following information concerning options applicable to individual directors, together with market price information at the year end and at the date of exercise, be disclosed for each director and for each combination of exercise price and date: (a) the number of shares under option at the beginning of the year (or date of appointment if later); (b) the number of shares under option at the end of the year;	Directors' report, or a note to the audited financial statements (in either case with a cross-reference to the remuneration report) or remuneration report (with cross-references to either the directors' report or the notes to the accounts). ****	

	Location in annual report and accounts	Included (Yes/No)
(c) the number of options: 　(i) granted 　(ii) exercised 　(iii) lapsed unexercised during the year; (d) the exercise prices; (e) the dates from which the options may be exercised; (f) the expiry dates; (g) the cost of the options (if any); (h) for any options exercised during the year, the market price of the shares at the date of exercise; (i) a concise summary of any performance criteria conditional upon which the options are exercisable; *(Note that paragraph 4 of Schedule A to the Combined Code states that 'Payouts or grants under all incentive schemes, including new grants under existing share option schemes, should be subject to challenging performance criteria reflecting the company's objectives ...')* (j) the market price of the shares at the end of the year, together with the range during the year (high and low). *Listing Rules paragraph 12.43A(c)(iii) and Combined Code – Principle B.3 and paragraphs 1 and 2 of Schedule B to the Combined Code.*		
(4) Details of any long-term incentive schemes, other than share options, details of which have been disclosed under 14(3) above, including: (a) the interests of each director by name in the long-term incentive schemes at the start of the period under review; (b) entitlements or awards granted and commitments made to each director under such schemes during the period, showing which	Directors' report, or a note to the audited financial statements (with a cross-reference to the remuneration report) or remuneration report (with a cross-reference to the notes to the accounts if Schedule 6 information is combined with this disclosure).****	

		Location in annual report and accounts	Included (Yes/No)
	crystallise either in the same year or subsequent years; (c) the money value and number of shares, cash payments or other benefits received by each director under such schemes during the period; and (d) the interests of each director in the long-term incentive schemes at the end of the period. *See also section 15 below.* *Listing Rules paragraph 12.43A(c)(iv) and Combined Code – Principle B.3 and paragraph 1 of Schedule B to the Combined Code.*		
(5)	Explanation and justification of any element of remuneration, other than basic salary (excluding benefits in kind), which is pensionable. *Listing Rules paragraph 12.43A(c)(v) and paragraph 5 of Schedule B to the Combined Code.*	Remuneration report.**	
(6)	Details of any director's service contract with a notice period in excess of one year or with provisions for pre-determined compensation on termination which exceeds one year's salary and benefits in kind, giving the reasons for such notice period. *Listing Rules paragraph 12.43A(c)(vi) and paragraph 7 of Schedule B to the Combined Code.*	Remuneration report.**	
(7)	The unexpired term of any service contract of a director proposed for election or re-election at the forthcoming annual general meeting and, if any director proposed for election or re-election does not have a service contract, a statement to that effect. *Listing Rules paragraph 12.43A(c)(vii).*	Remuneration report.**	

	Location in annual report and accounts	Included (Yes/No)
(8) A statement of the company's policy on the granting of options or awards under its employees' share schemes and other long-term incentive schemes, explaining and justifying any departure from that policy in the period under review and any change in the policy from the preceding year. *See also 14(12) below.* *Listing Rules paragraph 12.43A(c)(viii).*	Remuneration report.**	

(9) For defined benefit pension schemes (as defined in Part I of Schedule 6 to the Companies Act 1985):
(a) details of the amount of the increase during the period under review (excluding inflation) and of the accumulated total amount at the end of the period in respect of the accrued benefit to which each director would be entitled on leaving service or is entitled to having left service during the period under review;
(b) and either:
  (i) the transfer value (less directors' contributions) of the relevant increase in accrued benefit (to be calculated in accordance with Actuarial Guidance Note GN 11 but making no deduction for any underfunding) as at the end of the period (also see section 18 below); or
  (ii) so much of the following information as is necessary to make a reasonable assessment of the transfer value in respect of each director:
    • current age;
    • normal retirement age;
    • the amount of any contributions paid or
	Note to the audited financial statements (with a cross-reference to remuneration report) or remuneration report (with a cross-reference to the notes to the accounts if schedule 6 information is combined with this disclosure).****	

	Location in annual report and accounts	Included (Yes/No)
payable by the director under the terms of the scheme during the period under review; • details of spouse's and dependants' benefits; • early retirement rights and options, expectations of pension increases after retirement (whether guaranteed or discretionary); and • discretionary benefits for which allowance is made in transfer values on leaving and any other relevant information which will significantly affect the value of the benefits. Voluntary contributions and benefits should not be disclosed. *Listing Rules paragraph 12.43A(c)(ix) and Combined Code – Principle B.3 and paragraph 4 of Schedule B to the Combined Code.*		
(10) For money purchase pension schemes (as defined in Part I of Schedule 6 to the Companies Act 1985) details of the contribution or allowance payable or made by the company in respect of each director during the period under review. *Listing Rules paragraph 12.43A(c)(x) and Combined Code – Principle B.3.*	Note to the audited financial statements (with a cross-reference to remuneration report) or remuneration report (with a cross-reference to the notes to the accounts if schedule 6 information is combined with this disclosure).****	
(11) The names of the members of the remuneration committee. *Combined Code – provision B.2.3.*	Remuneration report.**	

		Location in annual report and accounts	*Included (Yes/No)*
	(12) An explanation and justification where grants under executive share option or other long-term incentive schemes are awarded in one large block rather than phased. *See also 14(8) above.* *Paragraph 3 of Schedule B to the Combined Code.* To the extent that the specified disclosures are included in the notes to the audited financial statements rather than the report itself, the report should include appropriate cross-references so that those elements included in the notes also constitute part of the report (see notes ****).	Remuneration report.**	
15	**Information on long-term incentive schemes** For long-term incentive schemes in which the only participant is a director of the issuer (or an individual whose appointment as a director of the issuer is in contemplation) and the arrangement is established specially to facilitate, in unusual circumstances, the recruitment or retention of the relevant individual, the following information should be disclosed in the first annual report published by the issuer following the date on which the individual becomes eligible to participate in the arrangement: (1) the name of the sole participant; (2) the date on which the individual first became eligible to participate in the arrangement; (3) explanation of why the circumstances in which the arrangement was established were unusual; (4) the conditions to be satisfied under the terms of the arrangement; (5) the maximum award(s) under the terms of the arrangement, or if there is no maximum, the basis on which awards will be determined; (6) either the full text of the scheme	In the separate report on directors' remuneration (see 14 above) or elsewhere in the annual report and accounts.*	

	Location in annual report and accounts	Included (Yes/No)
or a description of its principal terms;		
(7) where directors of the company are trustees of the scheme or have a direct or indirect interest in the trustees, details of such trusteeship or interest;		
(8) statement that the provisions (if any) relating to:		
(a) the persons to whom, or for whom, securities, cash or other benefits are provided under the scheme (the 'participants');		
(b) limitations on the number or amount of the securities, cash or other benefits subject to the scheme;		
(c) the maximum entitlement for any one participant;		
(d) the basis for determining a participant's entitlement to, and the terms of, securities, cash or other benefit to be provided and for the adjustment thereof (if any) in the event of a capitalisation issue, rights issue or open offer, subdivision or consolidation of shares or reduction of capital or any other variation of capital;		
cannot be altered to the advantage of participants without the prior approval of shareholders in general meeting (except for minor amendments to benefit the administration of the scheme, to take account of a change in legislation or to obtain or maintain favourable tax, exchange control or regulatory treatment for participants in the scheme or for the company operating the scheme or for members of its group);		
(9) statement as to whether benefits under the scheme will be pensionable and, if so, the reasons for this.		
Listing Rules paragraph 12.43(u).		
APB Bulletin 1999/5.		

	Location in annual report and accounts	Included (Yes/No)
16 **Waiver of emoluments** Details of any arrangement under which a director of the company has waived or agreed to waive any emoluments from the company or any subsidiary undertaking; where a director has agreed to waive future emoluments, details of such waiver together with those relating to emoluments which were waived during the period under review. *Listing Rules paragraph 12.43(d).*	In the separate report on directors' remuneration (see 14 above) or elsewhere in the annual report and accounts.*	
17 **Auditors' report on specified directors' remuneration disclosures** Statement by the auditors if in their opinion the company has not complied with any of the requirements of paragraph 12.43A(c)(ii), (iii), (iv), (ix) and (x) of the Listing Rules (see 14(2), (3), (4), (9) and (10) above). In such a case, the auditors should include in their report on the financial statements, so far as they are reasonably able to do so, a statement of the required particulars. *Listing Rules paragraph 12.43A.*	Auditors' report on the financial statements.**, ****	
18 **Remuneration report** Where companies disclose the transfer value of the increase in directors' accrued pension benefits (see section 14(9)(b)(i) above), they may wish to make clear that the transfer value represents a liability of the company, not a sum paid or due to the individual. The above wording is taken from paragraph 4 of Schedule B to the Combined Code. However, in some cases the wording may not be correct. We suggest that the following wording is preferable: 'The transfer values disclosed above do not represent a sum paid or payable to the individual director. Instead they represent a potential liability of the company/pension scheme†.' †'Company' will be appropriate if the scheme is unfunded and 'pension scheme' will be appropriate if the scheme is funded. *Paragraph 4 of Schedule B to the Combined Code.*	Remuneration report.**	

	Location in annual report and accounts	Included (Yes/No)
19 Notice of AGM	Notice of AGM.**	
(1) All directors should be subject to election by shareholders at the first opportunity after their appointment. *Combined Code – provision A.6.2.*		
(2) Directors are required to submit themselves for re-election at regular intervals and at least every three years. *Combined Code principle A.6 and provision A.6.2.*	Notice of AGM.**	
(3) The names of directors submitted for election or re-election should be accompanied by sufficient bio graphical details to enable shareholders to take an informed decision on their election. *Combined Code – provision A.6.2.*	Notice of AGM or notes to notice of AGM.*	
(4) The Board has to consider each year whether the circumstances are such that the AGM should be invited to approve the policy set out in the board's annual remuneration report. Where the AGM is to be invited to approve the policy in a year there will be a resolution required in the notice of AGM. *Combined Code – provision B.3.5.*	Notice of AGM.*	
(5) Companies should propose a separate resolution at the AGM on each substantially separate issue and should in particular propose a resolution at the AGM relating to the report and accounts. *Combined Code – provision C.2.2.*	Notice of AGM.*	
(6) The chairman of the board should arrange for the chairmen of the audit, remuneration and nomination committees to be available to answer questions at the AGM. Where they are to be at the AGM the company might wish to disclose this in the annual report and accounts or in the notice of AGM or notes thereto. *Combined Code – provision C.2.3.*	Notice of AGM, notes to notice of AGM or corporate governance statement.*	

	Location in annual report and accounts	Included (Yes/No)
(7) Shareholders should be invited to approve all new long-term incentive schemes (other than as permitted by paragraph 13.13A of the Listing Rules). *Combined Code – provision B.3.4 and paragraph 3 of Schedule A to the Combined Code.*	Notice of AGM.**	
(8) Companies should arrange for the Notice of AGM and related papers to be sent to shareholders at least 20 working days before the meeting. *Combined Code – provision C.2.4.*		
20 Institutional investors Although not required by the UK Listing Authority, institutional investors may wish to indicate the extent to which they support Section 2 of the Combined Code and any steps taken (or to be taken) to apply it. *Combined Code – Section 2.*	Corporate governance statement or directors' report.*	

Notes:

*   There are no requirements or recommendations that state specifically where in the annual report and accounts these items should be disclosed.

**   There are requirements or recommendations that specifically state where in the annual report and accounts these items should be disclosed.

***   The Listing Rules require the report to the shareholders by the board to be included in the annual report and accounts.

**** It is recommended that only those disclosures that are required by the Listing Rules to be within the scope of the auditors' report on the accounts (i.e., the requirements of paragraphs 12.43A(c)(ii), (iii), (iv), (ix) and (x) of the Listing Rules) should be included in the notes to the accounts. To avoid duplication and to satisfy the Listing Rules requirement that the disclosures are included in the remuneration report, the remuneration report should include a cross-reference to the relevant information included in the accounts.

The disclosures required by the revised Part 1 of Schedule 6 to the Companies Act 1985 (disclosure of directors' remuneration) are required to be included in the notes to the accounts. The new legislation provides that (other than in respect of the aggregate of gains made on the exercise of options, in respect of retirement benefits of directors and former directors and in respect of sums paid to third parties) information shall be treated as shown if it is capable of being readily ascertained from other information which is shown. The Companies Act disclosures can therefore be combined with those required by the Listing Rules to minimise duplication; although when combined appropriate cross-references should be included in the remuneration report or notes to the accounts (since the Listing Rule disclosures are required to be in the remuneration report and the Companies Act disclosures are required to be in the notes to the accounts).

Where companies include the disclosures relating to directors' remuneration, share options, long-term incentive schemes and pension entitlements in the remuneration report and incorporate the disclosures in the audited financial statements by means of a cross-reference, the cross-reference must be unambiguous as to which disclosures are within the scope of the audit if the auditors are not to modify the introductory paragraph of their report on the financial statements. Example wording for a suitable cross-reference to the disclosures required by both the Act and the Listing Rules is as follows:

Disclosures on directors' remuneration*, share options*, long-term incentive schemes*, pension contributions* and pension entitlements* required by the Companies Act 1985 and those specified for audit by the UK Listing Authority are on pages 20† and 21† within the remuneration report and form part of these audited financial statements.

*   Delete any not relevant to the company.

†   The page references must be unambiguous. It is assumed in this example that all of the information required to be audited is on pages 20 and 21 and that these pages contain no other information. Where these pages contain information that has not been audited, the reference would need to be more specific, e.g., 'paragraphs 6 to 10 of the remuneration report on pages 19 to 21'.

Where companies include the disclosures relating to directors' remuneration, share options, long-term incentive schemes and pension entitlements in the remuneration report with the audited financial statements either containing no cross-reference to the disclosures or a cross-reference that is ambiguous as to which disclosures fall within the scope of audit, the auditors should modify the introductory paragraph of their report on the financial statements to indicate unambiguously in that paragraph which disclosures fall within the scope of audit. Example wording is as follows:

We have audited the financial statements on pages 12 to 26 which have been prepared under the accounting policies set out on page 12. We have also audited the information which is specified by the UK Listing Authority to be audited in respect of any directors' remuneration*, share options*, long-term incentive schemes* and pension entitlements* and which is set out in paragraphs 6† to 10† of the report to shareholders by the Board on directors' remuneration on pages 4 to 7‡.

*   Delete any not relevant to the company.

†   The references must be unambiguous

---

‡ The Act's disclosures on directors' remuneration are required to be included in the financial statements. Thus, where a company includes the Act's disclosures in the remuneration report, the company will be required to include in the financial statements an unambiguous cross-reference to those disclosures. If the company is unable to draft an unambiguous cross-reference it will have to include the Act's disclosure requirements within the financial statements rather than include them in the remuneration report. This example wording therefore assumes that the unambiguous cross-reference or lack of cross-reference is in respect of the Listing Rule disclosures only.

If the information required to be audited by the UK Listing Authority is not capable of being clearly described, e.g., because it is widely interspersed with other information that need not be, and has not been, audited, the APB, in its Bulletin 1999/5 suggests that it may be necessary to describe the particulars that have been audited within the auditors' report. Our view is that this should arise only as a last resort.

Appendix VI Table of permitted transactions concerning directors under ss332 to 338 of the Companies Act 1985

Transactions, agreements, arrangements and guarantees between a company (or its subsidiary) and a director of the company (or a person connected with the director) in relation to loans, quasi-loans and credit transactions are generally prohibited [s330], except as noted below. (Other transactions, etc., are generally permitted, except that special rules apply to directors' service contracts [s319] and substantial transfers of non-cash assets between companies and directors [s320].)

Loans, quasi-loans and credit transactions which are permitted are:

Permitted for:	Loans	Quasi-loans	Credit transactions
Any company	A company may make a loan to a director if the aggregate amount does not exceed £5,000. [s334] A company may provide a director with funds (up to £20,000 in the case of a public company or member of a group which includes a public company) to meet expenditure for the purposes of the company or to enable him to perform his duties. Approval of the company in general meeting is required, failing which the loan etc., is repayable within six months. [s337]		
Public company or member of a group which includes a public company	Not permitted (except as above).	Only if reimbursable within two months, and the total for the director does not exceed £5,000. [s332] Not permitted to a connected person.	Either: (i) where transaction is under normal commercial terms; or (ii) where the total for the director does not exceed £10,000. [s335]
Private company not a member of a group which includes a public company	Not permitted to a director (except as above). May be made to a connected person.	Permitted.	Permitted.
Money lending company	Either: (i) where loan etc., is under normal commercial terms, with upper limit of £100,000 per director (no upper limit for a recognised bank or for a private company not being a member of a group which includes a public company); or (ii) where loan etc., is in the ordinary course of business, on terms available to other employees and is in connection with the purchase or improvement of the director's main residence, with an upper limit of £100,000 per director. [s338]	No special rules	

Notes:

1. Definitions may be found in the Act of the terms 'quasi-loans' and 'credit transactions' [s331], 'money lending company' [s338], 'relevant amount' [s339], and 'value' of transaction and arrangements [s340].

2. 'Director' includes 'shadow director', i.e., one on whose instructions the directors are accustomed to act (excluding professional advice).

3. Other minor exemptions may be found in ss333 and 336.

Appendix VII Table of disclosures of transactions concerning directors

(Information required by s232 and Part II of Schedule 6 to the Act)

The particulars indicated by the table below should be disclosed by way of notes to the accounts in relation to each transaction, agreement, arrangement or guarantee (or security given) whether permitted or not between a company (or its subsidiary) and a director of the company (or a person connected with the director) in respect of loans, quasi-loans, credit transactions and other transactions. Directors include shadow directors. Corresponding amounts are not required.

Particulars to be disclosed	Loans	Quasi-loans	Credit transactions	Guarantee (for security)	Other material transactions except service contracts *
1 The principal terms of the transaction, etc., including: 2 a statement that the transaction, etc., was made or subsisted during the year; 3 the name of the director (and, where applicable, the connected person);	Yes	Yes	Yes – except where the aggregate outstanding sum for a director (including connected persons) did not exceed £5,000 during the financial year.	Yes	Yes – except where the aggregate interest in each transaction with a director (including connected persons) did not exceed the higher of either: (i) the lower of £5,000 and 1 per cent of net asset value; or (ii) £1,000 during the financial year.
4 the nature of the director's interest in the transaction (including a deemed interest in relation to a connected person);	N/A	N/A	N/A	N/A	Yes – except as above.
5 the amount due (including interest) at the beginning and end of the financial year; 6 the maximum amount due during the financial year; 7 the amount of unpaid interest; 8 the amount of any provision;	Yes	No – but see 9 below	No	No – but see 10–12 below	No
9 the value of the transaction, etc.;	No – but see 5–8 above	Yes	Yes – except as above	No – but see 10–12 below	Yes – except as above
10 the amounts guaranteed (secured) at the beginning and end of the financial year; 11 the maximum liability guaranteed (secured); and 12 any amounts paid or incurred since the inception of the guarantee (security).	No	No	No	Yes	No

If the financial statements do not give this information the auditor must give it in his report (s237(4)).

* A transaction is not material for these purposes if the director's interest is not material in the opinion of the majority of the other directors (Sch 6 paragraph 17(2)). This will not of itself prevent such a transaction being disclosed under FRS 8.

Note: There are specific exemptions relating to banking companies and a number of further minor exemptions which are not covered by the table above.

Requirements of FRS 8

FRS 8 would also require disclosure of transactions with directors or shadow directors, the close family of directors or shadow directors; and entities in which directors, shadow directors or their close family have a controlling interest. The disclosures required by FRS 8 are discussed in chapter 32 starting at **32.50** above. Comparatives are required.

Appendix VIII Summary of small and medium-sized company exemptions

Exemption	GAAP 2001	Conditions	Limits to be satisfied			Comments
			B/S total limit	T/O limit	Other limit	
Companies Act						
May file small company abbreviated accounts.	35.2 and 35.5 to 35.7	Qualifies as a small company (see note 1 below).	£1.4m	£2.8m	<50 employees	Exemption applies to company accounts not group accounts.
May produce reduced disclosure annual accounts for members.	34.18 to 34.42	Qualifies as a small company (see note 1 below).	£1.4m	£2.8m	<50 employees	Exemption applies to both company accounts and, with slight modifications, to group accounts.
May file medium-sized company abbreviated accounts.	35.2 and 35.5 and 35.7	Qualifies as a medium-sized company (see note 1 below).	£5.6m	£11.2m	<250 employees	Exemption applies to company accounts not group accounts.
Exempted from disclosure of: • **fees for non-audit services;** • **compliance with applicable accounting standards.**	34.21	Qualifies as small or medium-sized company (see note 1 below).	£5.6m	£11.2m	<250 employees	Applies to both annual accounts and to abbreviated accounts filed with registrar.
Exempted from preparing group accounts.	34.23	Qualifies as a small or medium-sized group (see note 2 below).	net – £5.6m gross – £6.72m	net – £11.2m gross – £13.44m	<250 employees	
Exempted from audit	34.48	Qualifies as a small company (see notes 1 and 3 below).	£1.4m	£0.35m	<50 employees	

Note 1:

To qualify as small or medium-sized a company must not be a plc, a banking or insurance company, or an authorised person under the Financial Services Act 1986 (FSA 86) or a member of an ineligible group (see **34.20** and **35.5** above). In addition, to qualify initially, the qualifying conditions must be met two years running or, for the first set of accounts, in the first financial year. Having qualified as small or medium-sized, a company is allowed a year's grace before ceasing to be so qualified. The qualifying conditions require two of the three size criteria to be met. If the company is a parent its group must also be small or medium-sized as appropriate.

Note 2:

To qualify as small or medium-sized, a group must not include as a member a plc or a body corporate (e.g., a foreign company) able to offer its shares or debentures to the public, a banking or insurance company, or an authorised person under the FSA 86 (groups that include one or more of the foregoing are ineligible groups). The qualifying conditions require two of the three size criteria to be met on either a net or a gross basis. The qualifying conditions must be met for the same period as a company.

Note 3:

To qualify for audit exemption the company must not be a plc, a banking or insurance company, insurance broker, an authorised person or an appointed representative under the FSA 86, trade union, an employers' association, a parent company or a non-dormant subsidiary undertaking. For periods ending on or after 15 June 1997 the exclusion for parent companies and non-dormant subsidiary undertakings may be ignored if the group meets certain criteria (see **34.57** above). Further restrictions apply to companies that are charities (see **34.53** above). There must be no objection from members holding in total more than 10 per cent of the issued share capital or 10 per cent of a particular class of share.

Accounting standards

Exempted from producing a company cash flow statement.	19.9 and 34.44	Entitled to exemptions for small companies when filing accounts. [FRS 1 (Revised 1996): (5g)]	£1.4m	£2.8m	<50 employees	
Exempted from producing a group cash flow statement.	19.9 and 19.11	Group would have qualified as small if it had been a company incorporated under UK legislation. [FRS 1 (Revised 1996): (5g)]	£1.4m	£2.8m	<50 employees	
Exempted from certain disclosures required by SSAPs 13 and 25.	34.45 and 34.46	Qualifies as medium-sized, having multiplied the criteria in each case by 10. Not a plc, banking or insurance company or authorised person for FSA 86; or a parent of such a company.	£56m	£112m	<2500 employees	

Appendix IX   Useful website addresses

Accountancy Magazine	– http://www.accountancymag.co.uk
Accounting Standards Board	– http://www.asb.org.uk
Association of Chartered Certified Accountants	– http://www.acca.co.uk
Auditing Practices Board	– http://www.apb.org.uk
The UK Listing Authority, a division of the Financial Services Authority	– http://www.fsa.gov.uk/ukla/
Chartered Institute of Management Accountants	– http://www.cima.org.uk
Chartered Institute of Public Finance and Accountancy	– http://www.cipfa.org.uk
CISCO	– http://www.cisco.org.uk
Deloitte & Touche	– http://www.deloitte.co.uk
Department of Trade and Industry	– http://www.dti.gov.uk
Financial Accounting Standards Board	– http://www.fasb.org
Financial Reporting Council	– http://www.frc.org.uk
Financial Reporting Review Panel	– http://www.frrp.org.uk
Her Majesty's Stationery Office – Acts of Parliament, Statutory Instruments and draft Statutory Instruments	– http://www.legislation.hmso.gov.uk
Institute of Chartered Accountants in England and Wales	– http://www.icaew.co.uk
Institute of Chartered Accountants in Ireland	– http://www.icai.ie
Institute of Chartered Accountants of Scotland	– http://www.icas.org.uk
Institute of Chartered Secretaries and Administrators	– http://www.icsa.org.uk/
International Accounting Standards Committee	– http://www.iasc.org.uk
The European Union	– http://europa.eu.int
The Stationery Office – links to official documents	– http://www.official-documents.co.uk
The International Federation of Accountants	– http://www.ifac.org
Institute of Directors	– http://www.iod.co.uk
Financial Services Authority	– http://www.fsa.gov.uk/
London Stock Exchange	– http://www.londonstockexchange.com/

Appendix X   Testing for impairment

(Reproduced text from FRS 11 is shown in italics.)

Full impairment review

Impairment is measured by comparing the carrying value of an asset, or group of assets (income-generating unit), with its recoverable amount. Recoverable amount is the higher of the amounts that can be obtained from selling (net realisable value) or using the asset (value in use).

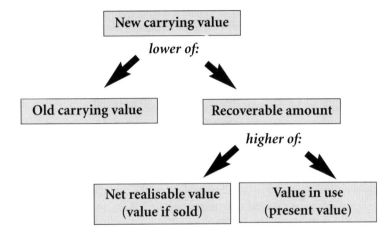

In practice, it is extremely unlikely that a ready market exists for most businesses or business divisions.

> This guidance therefore assumes that no net realisable value can be established for many assets or any goodwill and that the impairment review will therefore comprise of a comparison of existing carrying value with value in use.

Value in use is defined as: the present value of the future cash flows obtainable as a result of an asset's continued use, including those resulting from its ultimate disposal. [FRS 11(2)]

The calculation of value in use can be broken down into a four stage process. This appendix looks at the impairment review in terms of the four stages in the calculation of value in use and the subsequent fifth stage which is the comparison to carrying value and allocation of any impairment:

Calculation	Stage 1:	Identify income-generating units
	Stage 2:	Estimate expected future cash flows
	Stage 3:	Determine appropriate discount rate
	Stage 4:	Discount expected cash flows and total to arrive at value in use
Comparison	Stage 5:	Compare value in use to carrying value and allocate any impairment

Stage 1 Identify 'income-generating units' (IGUs)

Income-generating units should be identified by dividing the total income of the entity into as many largely independent income streams as practicable. [FRS 11(27)]

To perform impairment reviews as accurately as possible:

- the groups of assets and liabilities that are considered together should be as small as is reasonably practicable; but

- the income stream underlying the future cash flows of one group should be largely independent of other income streams of the entity and should be capable of being monitored separately.

Income-generating units are therefore identified by dividing the total income of the business into as many largely independent income streams as is reasonably practicable in the light of the information available to management. [FRS 11(28)]

In general terms, the income streams identified are likely to follow the way in which management monitors and makes decisions about continuing or closing the different lines of business of the entity. Unique intangible assets, such as brands and mastheads, are generally seen to generate income independently of each other and are usually monitored separately. Hence income streams can often be used to identify income-generating units. Other income streams may be identified by reference to major products or services. [FRS 11(29)]

Income-generating units are defined by allocating the assets and liabilities of the reporting entity (excluding deferred tax balances, interest-bearing debt, dividends payable and other items relating wholly to financing) to the identified income streams. Certain assets and liabilities that are directly involved in the production and distribution of individual products may be attributed directly to one unit. [FRS 11(30)]

Although FRS 11 paragraph 30 only refers to deferred tax balances, the exclusion extends to all tax balances. The exclusion of current tax is implicit in FRS 11 paragraph 33 which excludes working capital items that generate cash flows equal to their carrying value.

Examples of identifying income generating units

Example 1 Interchangeable products

A publisher owns a particular publishing title. The title is sold in both paper and electronic form. In general customers will purchase either the paper or the electronic version, not both, depending upon their own circumstances. Demand for one therefore affects demand for the other.

The assets used for production of both paper and electronic versions of the title comprise one income-generating unit.

Example 2 Spare capacity

A company owns a warehouse to store its products. When the company has spare warehouse capacity it sells the capacity externally. The income from selling warehouse space externally only arises when there happens to be spare capacity and is not a largely independent income stream.

The warehouse represents one income-generating unit.

Example 3 Service companies

Service companies such as telecom companies will have substantial assets to support their services. The arrangement and use of the assets will generally indicate appropriate IGUs.

Other service companies, especially if office buildings are leased, may have very few net assets. In such companies the importance of identifying IGUs is not in determining how to allocate assets to the IGUs, but, in being able to make accurate estimates of levels of demand for the various services provided.

If a company provides regional services and economic decisions are taken by region, it may be appropriate to identify each region as a separate IGU. In contrast, if unprofitable regional offices are supported because overall coverage is necessary to the business as a whole, then 'countrywide' IGUs may be appropriate

Examples of income-generating units provided by FRS 11

Example 1 Network

A transport company runs a network comprising trunk routes fed by a number of supporting routes. Decisions about continuing or closing the supporting routes are not based on the returns generated by the routes in isolation but on the contribution made to the returns generated by the trunk routes.

An income-generating unit comprises a trunk route plus the supporting routes associated with it because the cash inflows generated by the trunk routes are not independent of the supporting routes.

Example 2 Production at different sites

A manufacturer can produce a product at a number of different sites. Not all the sites are used to full capacity and the manufacturer can choose how much to make at each site. However, there is not enough surplus capacity to enable any one site to be closed. The cash inflows generated by any one site therefore depend on the allocation of production across all sites.

The income-generating unit comprises all the sites at which the product can be made.

Example 3 Production with different stages

An entity comprises three stages of production, A (growing and felling trees), B (creating parts of wooden furniture) and C (assembling the parts from B into finished goods). The output of A is timber that is partly transferred to B and partly sold in an external market. If A did not exist, B could buy its timber from the market. The output of B has no external market and is transferred to C at an internal transfer price. C sells the finished product in an external market and the sales revenue achieved by C is not affected by the fact that the three stages of production are all performed by the entity (unlike example 1, where the sales revenue of the trunk routes is affected by the existence of supporting routes run by the same entity).

A forms an income-generating unit and its cash inflows should be based on the market price for its output. B and C together form one income-generating unit because there is no market available for the output of B. In calculating the cash outflows of the income-generating unit B+C, the timber received by B from A should be priced by reference to the market, not any internal transfer price.

Example 4 Chain of service or retail sites

A restaurant chain has a large number of restaurants across the country. The cash inflows of each restaurant can be individually monitored and sensible allocations of costs to each restaurant can be made.

Each restaurant is an income-generating unit by itself. However, any impairment of individual restaurants is unlikely to be material. A material impairment is likely to occur only when a number of restaurants are affected together by the same economic factors. It may therefore be acceptable to consider groupings of restaurants affected by the same economic factors rather than each individual restaurant.

Immaterial income-generating units

Example 4 from FRS 11 raises the issue of immaterial income-generating units. It states that, if a company has a large number of IGUs, material impairment is only likely to occur when a number of the IGUs are affected by the same economic factors, in which case it may therefore be acceptable to consider groupings of units.

For a company in such a situation, it is not acceptable simply to consider the company as one IGU. IGUs should be grouped into the smallest groups for which any impairment could be material. The IGUs should be grouped to ensure that IGUs subject to similar economic factors are reviewed together. The types of factors which could be relevant include:

- location: city centre/out-of-town developments/small town/rural;
- geographical location – south-west/south-east/etc.;
- demographic characteristics: levels of demand for new housing development/ development in process;
- competitors: number of competitors in the vicinity/expansion plans of competitors.

Allocating assets and liabilities, including central assets, to income generating units

Central assets, such as group or regional head offices, and working capital may have to be apportioned across the units on a logical and systematic basis. The resulting income-generating units will be complete and non-overlapping, so that the sum of the carrying amounts of the units equals the carrying amount of the net assets (excluding tax and financing items) of the entity as a whole. [FRS 11(30)]

If it is not possible to apportion certain central assets meaningfully ... these assets may be excluded ... However, an additional impairment review should be performed on the excluded central assets. In this review, the income-generating units to which the central assets contribute should be combined and their combined carrying amount (including that of the central assets) should be compared with their combined value in use. [FRS 11(32)]

In a company where the opening or closure of any one IGU does not have a significant impact on the head office assets or services required, e.g., in a restaurant or retail company with a large number of income generating units, a meaningful apportionment of head office assets seems difficult. However, where the closure of an IGU would have a significant impact on head office resources (e.g., by justifying staff reductions or a move to smaller premises), more likely in the case of a company with only two or three IGUs, apportionment would perhaps be more meaningful.

The basis of apportionment should be decided for each entity but some possibilities are:

- for a service organisation – number of staff employed in each IGU;
- turnover per IGU;
- total carrying value per IGU.

Where central assets are allocated to individual IGUs, when estimating cash flows of the unit, central costs will be allocated on the same basis.

The additional step to the impairment review required when central assets and costs are not allocated is demonstrated by the example provided in stage 5.

Allocating goodwill to income-generating units

Capitalised goodwill should be attributed to (or apportioned between) income-generating units or groups of similar units. If they were acquired as part of the same investment and are involved in similar parts of the business, individual units identified for the purpose of monitoring the recoverability of assets may be combined with other units to enable the recoverability of the related goodwill to be assessed. [FRS 11(34)]

Goodwill is allocated to IGUs in the same way as are the assets and liabilities of the entity. However, where several similar IGUs are acquired together in one investment, the units may be combined to assess the recoverability of goodwill. [FRS 11(35)]

Examples of similar and dissimilar IGUs

Example 1 similar IGUs

The acquired entity owns 10 restaurants. Each restaurant is a separate IGU. For the purpose of reviewing goodwill, the IGUs are similar and can be combined thus avoiding apportionment of goodwill to each unit.

Example 2 dissimilar IGUs

The acquired entity comprises a publishing title and a retail outlet. These are dissimilar IGUs and therefore goodwill should be allocated to each IGU.

Further guidance:

Allocation of goodwill to IGUs – see stage 5 below.

Example of allocation of head office assets to income-generating units – see FRS 11: Examples 5–6.

Stage 2 Estimate expected future cash flows

The expected future cash flows of the income-generating unit, including any allocation of central overheads but excluding cash flows relating to financing and tax, should be based on reasonable and supportable assumptions. The cash flows should be consistent with the most up-to-date budgets and plans that have been formally approved by management. Cash flows for the period beyond that covered by formal budgets and plans should assume a steady or declining growth rate. Only in exceptional circumstances should (a) the period before a steady or declining growth rate is assumed extend to more than five years or (b) the steady or declining growth rate exceed the long-term average growth rate for the country or countries in which the business operates. [FRS 11(36)]

The UK post-war average growth in gross domestic product, expressed in real terms, is 2.25 per cent (source: Financial Statement and Budget Report March 1998, HM Treasury).

In exceptional circumstances, the use of a long-term growth rate that is higher than the average country growth rate may be Justified. This may, e.g., be the case where:

(a) *the long-term growth rate for the relevant industry is expected to be significantly higher than the relevant country growth rate; and*

(b) *the business under review is expected to grow as rapidly as the industry as a whole, taking into account the likelihood of new competitors entering such an industry. [FRS 11(37)]*

Subject to paragraph 39 below, future cash flows should be estimated for income-generating units or individual fixed assets in their current condition. They should not include:

(a) *future cash outflows or related cost savings (e.g., reductions in staff costs) or benefits that are expected to arise from a future reorganisation for which provision has not yet been made; or*

(b) *future capital expenditure that will improve or enhance the income-generating units or assets in excess of their originally assessed standard of performance or the related future benefits of this future expenditure. [FRS 11(38)]*

In the case of a newly acquired income-generating unit such as a subsidiary, the purchase price will reflect the synergies and other opportunities for making more effective use of the assets as a result of the acquisition. In some of these cases, in order to obtain the benefits from its investment, it may be necessary for the purchaser to undertake related capital expenditure and reorganisations. Consequently, in assessing the future cash flows of the investment, the costs and benefits of such reorganisations and capital expenditure anticipated at the time of performing impairment reviews up to the end of the first full year after acquisition and consistent with budgets and plans at that time may be taken into account in those and subsequent impairment reviews, to the extent that the investment or reorganisations are still to be incurred. [FRS 11(39)]

Failure to undertake capital investment or a reorganisation according to the planned schedule may call into question the validity of continuing to forecast that the investment or reorganisation will be undertaken in the future and may be an indication of impairment as discussed in paragraphs 8–13. The costs and benefits of the investment or reorganisation would then have to be omitted from forecasts performed for subsequent impairment reviews. Additionally, the monitoring of cash flows required by paragraph 54 may indicate that impairment has already occurred. [FRS 11(40)]

> **Example 1 Capital expenditure included in cash flow forecasts**
>
> The assets of the IGU comprise a factory and plant and machinery. The factory is expected to last 50 years, but will need a new roof in 30 years, and the machinery needs to be replaced every 10 years. The company expects to be able to reduce costs per unit of production by extending the factory to double production in a few years time.
>
> The replacement expenditure for the 50 years should be included in the cash flows, but neither the expenditure to double the size of the factory nor the additional income and revenue expenditure consequent on that expansion should be included.

Stage 3 Determine appropriate discount rate

The discount rate used should be an estimate of the rate that the market would expect on an equally risky investment. It should exclude the effects of any risk for which the cash flows have been adjusted and should be calculated on a pre-tax basis. [FRS 11(41)]

Estimates of this market rate may be made by a variety of means including reference to:

(a)   the rate implicit in market transactions of similar assets;

(b)   the current weighted average cost of capital (WACC) of a listed company whose cash flows have similar risk profiles to those of the income-generating unit; or

(c)   the WACC for the entity but only if adjusted for the particular risks associated with the income-generating unit. [FRS 11(42)]

In practice, a rate under (a) will seldom be available due to the unique nature of different transactions.

For (b), there may be few listed companies that offer a readily usable comparison since listed companies are likely to have a wider product/service base, wider markets and potentially lower risk profile.

If method (c) is used the following matters are of note.

- Where the cash flow forecasts assume a real growth rate that exceeds the long-term average growth rate for more than five years, it is likely that the discount rate will be increased to reflect a higher level of risk.

- The discount rates applied to individual income-generating units will always be estimated such that, were they to be calculated for every unit, the weighted average discount rate would equal the entity's overall WACC. [FRS 11(43)]

When basing the discount rate on WACC, if a company has only one IGU, the WACC for the company can be used. Where a company comprises a number of IGUs, the discount rate for any IGU will be higher or lower depending on the relative difference in risk elements such as durability, transferability, liquidity, asset versatility regarding strategic re-deployment and other factors. For example, a higher rate of return is generally associated with intangible assets which may currently contribute significantly to the profitability but bear the highest degree of risk. However, as noted in FRS 11, the weighted average discount rates for all IGUs should equal the overall WACC.

Using a discount rate equal to the rate of return that the market would expect on an equally risky investment is a method of reflecting the risk associated with the cash flows in the value in use measurement. It is likely that this method will be the easiest method of reflecting risk. However, an acceptable alternative is to adjust the cash flows for risk and to discount them using a risk-free rate (e.g., a government bond rate). Whichever method of reflecting risk is adopted, care must be taken that the effect of risk is not double-counted by inclusion in both the cash flows and the discount rate. [FRS 11(45)]

If the cash flows to be discounted are expressed in current prices, a real discount rate will be used. If the cash flows are expressed in expected future prices, a nominal discount rate will be used. [FRS 11(46)]

Converting from a post-tax to a pre-tax discount rate

The required pre-tax rate of return is simply the rate of return that will, after tax has been deducted, give the required post-tax rate of return. Because the tax consequence of different cash flows may be different, the pre-tax rate of return is not always the post-tax rate of return grossed up by a standard rate of tax. The effect of discounting pre-tax cash flows at a pre-tax discount rate should be similar to the effect of discounting post-tax cash flows at a post-tax discount rate. [FRS 11, App 1 paras 2–3]

Two difficulties are:

(a) that benchmark discount rates, such as WACC, are generally post-tax rates; and

(b) where a company has conducted an impairment test on a post-tax basis (in particular, some companies may have carried out such a test because FRED 15 proposed the use of that basis), it will expect an impairment test on a pre-tax basis to give a consistent result.

In practice, estimating a suitable pre-tax rate is far from straightforward. Under FRED 15, the exposure draft which preceded FRS 11, a post-tax rate was applied to post-tax cash flows; while the forecasting of post-tax cash flows was more complex, the estimation of a discount rate was less complex. Under FRS 11, a pre-tax rate is applied to pre-tax cash flows; while the estimation of cash flows is easier, the estimation of a suitable discount rate is more difficult.

Guidance in FRS 11, Appendix 1 suggests that:

(a) the true benchmark for the impairment test result is the post-tax basis;

(b) a suitable pre-tax discount rate is a rate which achieves a result consistent with the post-tax basis;

(c) a simple grossing-up of the post-tax rate is only likely to be reliable where the pattern of tax cash flows is similar to the pattern of pre-tax operating cash flows.

An assessment of a pre-tax rate must therefore take into account the tax status of the assets in an IGU and the timing of tax cash flows.

How high would the discount rate need to be before an impairment situation were reached?

> Prior to making detailed estimates it may be worthwhile carrying out a simplified test to establish a rough idea of the level of discount rate above which impairment would be recognised, i.e., the apparent rate of return (ARR) when value in use equals carrying value. (If the discount rate that would demonstrate impairment proves to be clearly unrealistically high, then it can be assumed that no impairment has occurred and that more rigorous testing need not be carried out.)

This simple test is only appropriate where it is possible to assume that:

(a) there will be a steady growth rate in operating cash flows from the current year into perpetuity; and

(b) the pattern of tax cash flows is such that pre-tax discount rates can be found by grossing up post-tax rates at an average tax rate.

The ARR will be a pre-tax discount factor which, when applied to current cash flow taken to perpetuity, produces a present value equal to the carrying value of the IGU. This is then compared with WACC adjusted to reflect steady growth in cash flows, inflation, and tax. The resulting discount factors are to enable a rough and ready comparison to be made, and do not represent valid discount rates for any other purpose.

1 Calculate Apparent Rate of Return

$$\text{ARR} = \frac{\text{Current annual cash flow}}{\text{Carrying value of IGU}}$$

2 Calculate target pre-tax discount range (applicable to current cash flow)

$$\text{Target rate} = (WACC - g - i) \times \frac{1}{1 - t}$$

Where:

WACC = Weighted average cost of capital

g = steady growth rate

i = inflation

t = average tax rate

Notes:

1   Since all figures are subject to estimate, it is advisable to produce a range of possible rates.

2   A minor adjusting factor i x g should also be deducted from WACC. This has been omitted on the grounds of immateriality.

3   The calculation, in particular the treatment of tax, is to provide a rough guide only. The method is not a substitute for a more detailed calculation of a suitable pre-tax discount rate.

4   Adjustment of the discount rate for growth is a substitute for building growth into the cash flows. It should not be confused with a real rate of return which would adjust for inflation only.

3 Compare ARR with target range.

If ARR is clearly above the possible range of appropriate target discount rates then no further calculation to support carrying value is necessary, since discounting cash flows at a rate within the target range will produce a value in use which is greater than the carrying value.

However, if ARR falls close to or below the target discount range, then this test has not produced conclusive evidence of no impairment and therefore a full impairment test must be carried out.

Example: Use of target range

A non-quoted company has an income generating unit as follows:

Current operating cash flow before tax	£3.1m
Carrying value (including goodwill and head office costs, excluding tax and finance)	£12.0m
Current growth in cash flows	6.8%

Other information:

WACC of similar quoted company	14.0%
WACC of unquoted company (say, higher than quoted company by $2^1/_2$–$4^1/_2$%)	$16^1/_2$-$18^1/_2$%
Prudent long-term growth	2.5%
Bank of England inflation target	2.5%
Average tax rate	30.0%

$$\text{ARR} = \frac{3.1}{12} = 25.8\%$$

2 Target discount range:

$$\text{Lower} = (0.165 - 0.025 - 0.025) \times \frac{1}{1 - 0.3} = 16.4\%$$

$$\text{Upper} = (0.185 - 0.025 - 0.025) \times \frac{1}{1 - 0.3} = 19.3\%$$

3 Since ARR is comfortably higher than the target discount range, there is evidence that discounting current cash flow at a rate within the target discount range would produce a value in use that is higher than the IGU's carrying value, therefore no further impairment testing is required for this IGU.

Further issues on converting from a post-tax to a pre-tax discount rate – tax deductibility of assets and timing of allowances

Two factors which will impact on the relationship between pre- and post-tax return are whether assets are deductible for tax, i.e., are capital/writing down allowances available, and the timing of any such allowances.

Examples of calculating pre-tax from post-tax discount rate

Example 1 Tax deductible asset

Assume:

- An IGU with a single asset.
- The asset generates cash flows for five years and is then worth nil.
- Cash flows are taxed at a standard rate of 30 per cent.

- Tax allowances are given at 25% writing down allowance per year with a final year balancing credit.

	Year 0	Year 1	Year 2	Year 3	Year 4	Year 5
Pre-tax cash flow (asset cost)	(620.00)	160.00	170.00	180.00	200.00	210.00
W/down allowance given on balance of:		155.00	116.25	87.19	65.39	196.17
W/down allowance		46.50	34.88	26.16	19.62	58.85
Tax on cash flow		(48.00)	(51.00)	(54.00)	(60.00)	(63.00)
Post-tax cash flow		158.50	153.88	152.16	159.62	205.85

Post-tax return 10 per cent (IRR of post-tax cash flows including original cost).

Actual pre-tax return 14.01 per cent (IRR of pre-tax cash flows including original cost).

The relationship between pre-tax and post-tax return in the example above can be compared with that achieved through simply grossing up for the rate of tax.

A post-tax rate of 10 per cent grossed up for a standard tax rate of 30 per cent equates to a pre-tax rate of 14.28 per cent. [10 per cent/(1-0.3)]. The reason for the difference between this and the rate of 14.01 per cent seen in the example is that the tax deductions for the asset are not even over its life.

In an IGU comprised of a group of assets acquired at different times it is likely that the overall pattern of tax deduction for assets will even out and the actual pre-tax rate of return will then be closer to a simple grossed up post-tax rate.

Example 2 Asset not deductible for tax

Assume:

- An IGU has only one asset not allowable for tax.
- Tax on cash flows is at 30 per cent.
- The asset generates cash for five years and is then worth nil.

	Year 0	Year 1	Year 2	Year 3	Year 4	Year 5
Pre-tax cash flow (asset)	(1,000)	356	370	380	390	400
Tax on cash flow		(107)	(111)	(114)	(117)	(120)
Post-tax cash flow		249	259	266	273	280
Discounted at 10%		226	214	200	186	174

Post-tax return 10 per cent (IRR of post-tax cash flows including original expenditure).
Actual pre-tax return 25.33 per cent (IRR of pre-tax cash flows including original expenditure).

Example 3 Asset not deductible for tax – effect of differing life

The same assumptions as above, i.e.,

- The IGU has only one asset not deductible for tax
- Tax on cash flows is at 30 per cent.

- But this time the asset is assumed to have 10, 15 and 20 years life (and be worth nil at the end of that life).

A post-tax return of 10 per cent equates to the following pre-tax return rates:

Assumed life	Pre-tax return
10 years	18.80%
15 years	16.83%
20 years	15.37%

The above examples 2 and 3 give an indication of the impact that the non-deductibility of an asset for tax has on the relationship of post-tax to pre-tax rates based on differing asset lives.

Normally a non-deductible asset such as goodwill or an other intangible will be used within a group of other assets. The impact of such a non-deductible asset on the pre-tax return for the IGU will depend on its size relative to the carrying value of the IGU and, as demonstrated, its expected life.

Cost of capital used for internal investment decisions

Many companies have determined a cost of capital to be used to carry out internal assessments of projects and investments. This may be a starting point for determining an appropriate discount rate, although it will often not equate exactly to the rate the market would require for a similar investment. There may be a number of reasons for this. For example:

(a) management may set a higher internal rate to compensate for possible overoptimism of projections. It may be possible to identify the extent of this 'compensation' and therefore adjust the internal rate to arrive at an appropriate discount rate.

(b) if capital is limited, a higher internal rate may be set to ensure that the limited resources are used only for the most profitable projects, i.e., what is known as 'capital rationing'.

(c) the internal rate may be lower than the true cost of capital because it has been calculated by looking at the cost of direct debt financing, with insufficient or no consideration of equity return and total cost of capital.

Cost of debt

The more highly geared a company, the more that company's WACC will tend towards the cost of debt.

Examples of the effect of debt: equity ratio on WACC

Example 1

Assume

- cost of equity is 25 per cent – 35 per cent.
- cost of debt is 10 per cent (Note 1)

WACC at various gearing levels [gearing = debt/(debt+equity)]

Gearing 50%   WACC = 17.5% – 22.5%
Gearing 75%   WACC = 13.75% – 16.25%
Gearing 90%   WACC = 11.5% – 12.5%

Note:
In order to demonstrate how WACC moves towards cost of debt at different gearing levels, this example has assumed a single cost of debt across gearing levels. In reality however, as the gearing ratio rises so the risk attached to debt increases and the cost of debt rises, as does the cost of equity. WACC will not as implied by this example keep falling as the gearing ratio rises. WACC will be lowest for any particular company at its optimum gearing ratio. Above that ratio the increasing cost of debt will mean that WACC will begin to rise again.

For a highly geared company, the cost of debt for finance raised specifically for a particular acquisition should provide an indication of the relative level of risk for that acquisition; it may also be possible to use the cost of debt as the starting point for determining the discount rate to be used for the IGUs in that acquisition.

In the unusual situation where debt has been raised for a specific project and that debt is ring-fenced, the cost of debt would be an appropriate discount rate for that IGU.

Stage 4   Discount expected cash flows and total to arrive at value in use

The formulae for calculating value in use are derived from three formulae:

Single cash flow

$$\text{Present value of a single cash flow occurring in } n \text{ years} = \frac{Cash\ flow}{(1 + d)^n}$$

Series of cash flows

$$\text{Present value of } n \text{ annual cash flows} = Cash\ flow \times \frac{1 - (1 + d)^{-n}}{d}$$

Perpetuity

$$\text{Present value of annual cash flow to perpetuity} = \frac{Cash\ flow}{d}$$

Where d = discount rate.

Notes:

1   In the first (single cash flow) formula, the cash flow is an actual cash flow. The discount rate will therefore be a nominal rate, matching the cash flow by including a compatible estimate of the effect of inflation.

2   In the second (series) and third (perpetuity) formulae, it is assumed that all cash flows are the same, with the first cash flow occurring at the end of year 1. Where these cash flows will increase due to growth and inflation, this effect can be achieved by using a cash flow for year 1, and reducing the nominal discount rate by both growth and inflation rates. Where actual cash flow for the previous period is used, it will first be necessary to increase it by the first year's growth and

inflation in order to find cash flow at the end of year 1. (This adjustment of the discount rate for growth is a substitute for building growth into the cash flows. It should not be confused with a real rate of return which would adjust for inflation only.)

3   At a discount rate of 20 per cent, a perpetuity can be assumed to approximate to 20 years or more, and at 10 per cent to 35 years or more, since any amounts beyond those horizons will be immaterial.

Situation 1 Assumed steady growth in cash flows to perpetuity

The calculation is based on the perpetuity formula. Cash flow is for year 1, thus where the previous year's actual cash flow is used it is first necessary to increase it to reflect growth and inflation in year 1.

$$\text{Value in use} = \frac{CF_0}{d_a} (1 + g)(1 + i)$$

Where:

CF_0 = actual cash flow for previous period

i = annual inflation rate

g = annual growth rate in cash flows

d_a = pre-tax discount rate adjusted to reflect inflation and growth in cash flows.

Situation 2 Cash flows forecast for five years, and assumed steady growth thereafter

The calculation is the sum of individual present values for the first five years, plus a perpetuity from year 6 onwards re-expressed from year 5 back to present value at time 0.

Value in use = Present value of each cash flow for years 1–5

+ Present value of cash flows for year 6 onwards

$$= \frac{CF_1}{1+d_n} + \frac{CF_2}{(1+d_n)^2} + \frac{CF_3}{(1+d_n)^3} + \frac{CF_4}{(1+d_n)^4} + \frac{CF_5}{(1+d_n)^5} + \frac{CF_5(1+g)(1+i)}{d_a \times (1+d_n)^5}$$

Where:

CF_n = Cash flow in n^{th} year

i = annual inflation rate after year 5

g = annual growth rate in cash flows after year 5

d_n = pre-tax nominal discount rate

d_a = pre-tax discount rate adjusted to reflect growth and inflation in cash flows

Note:

The sixth term in the formula, $\dfrac{CF_5(1+g)(1+i)}{d_a \times (1+d_n)^5}$, is a compound of two functions:

$\dfrac{CF_5(1 + g)(1 + i)}{d_a}$ is the present value of cash flows from year 6 onwards

---

expressed as a present value at the beginning of year 6; further adjustment to multiply by $\dfrac{1}{(1+d_n)^5}$ re-expresses this as a present value at the beginning of year 1.

Example 1 Cash flows forecast for two years

Assume:

- Cash flow for year 1   £20m
- Cash flow for year 2   £24m
- Assumed steady growth thereafter   2.5%
- Inflation   2.5%
- Nominal pre-tax discount rate   15%
- Adjusted pre-tax discount rate   10%

Value in use $= \dfrac{£20m}{1.15} + \dfrac{£24m}{1.15^2} + \dfrac{£24m \times 1.025 \times 1.025}{0.1 \times 1.15^2} = £275m$

Stage 5 Compare value in use with carrying value and allocate any impairment

The carrying amounts of the IGUs under review should be calculated as the net of the carrying amount of the assets, liabilities and goodwill allocated to the unit. [FRS 11(47)]

To the extent that the carrying value exceeds the recoverable amount, the unit is impaired. In the absence of an obvious impairment of specific assets the impairment should be allocated:

(a)   first, to any goodwill in the unit;

(b)   thereafter, to any capitalised intangible assets in the unit; and

(c)   finally, to the tangible assets in the unit, on a pro rata or more appropriate basis. [FRS 11(48)]

In this allocation, which aims to write down the assets with the most subjective valuations first, no intangible asset with a readily ascertainable market value should be written down below its net realisable value. Similarly, no tangible asset with a net realisable value that can be measured reliably should be written down below its net realisable value. [FRS 11(49)]

Example 1 Comparison of carrying value to value in use

Income generating unit:	A	B	Unallocated central assets and cash flows	Total
Carrying values:				
Net assets directly involved	£100m	£150m		£250m
Head office assets			£90m	£90m
Goodwill			£40m	£40m
Total				£380m
Value in use	£200m	£140m	(£20m)	£320m

(a) Comparing the individual units an impairment of £10m is identified in unit B. This will be recognised pro-rata against assets in unit B, assuming no intangibles are carried in unit B.

(b) Looking at the company as a whole a total impairment of £60m is identified.

We have seen that £10m attaches to unit B. Following the allocation order £40m is allocated to goodwill, the remainder, £10m, is allocated to head office assets; this does not write them down below NRV. If head office assets were being carried at NRV then the £10m would be allocated between assets in units pro-rata or as otherwise indicated.

Reviewing goodwill not allocated to units

Goodwill is allocated to income-generating units in the same way as are the assets and liabilities of the entity. However, where several similar income-generating units are acquired together in one investment, the units may be combined to assess the recoverability of the goodwill. The income-generating units are first reviewed individually for the purposes of assessing the recoverability of any capitalised intangible assets and tangible fixed assets and then, as illustrated in example below, the combined unit is reviewed to assess the recoverability of the goodwill. [FRS 11(35)]

Example: Alternative approach to allocation of goodwill to income-generating units. [FRS 11 Example 7]

An entity acquires a business comprising three income-generating units, A, B and C. After five years, the carrying amount of the net assets in the income-generating units and the purchased goodwill compares with the value in use as follows (there is no reliable estimate of net realisable value for any of the income-generating units or the business as a whole):

Income-generating unit	A	B	C	Goodwill	Total
Carrying amount (£m)	80	120	140	50	390
Value in use (£m)	100	140	120		360

An impairment loss of £20 million is recognised in respect of income-generating unit C reducing its carrying amount to £120 million and the total carrying amount to £370 million. A further impairment loss of £10 million is then recognised in respect of the goodwill.

Allocation when acquired businesses are merged with existing operations

Where an acquired business is merged with an existing business and results in an income-generating unit that contains both purchased and (unrecognised) internally generated goodwill:

(a) *the value of the internally generated goodwill of the existing business at the date of merging the businesses should be estimated and added to the carrying amount of the income-generating unit for the purposes of performing impairment reviews;*

(b)   any impairment arising on merging the businesses should be allocated solely to the purchased goodwill within the newly acquired business;

(c)   subsequent impairments should be allocated pro rata between the goodwill of the acquired business and that of the existing business;

(d)   the impairment allocated to the existing business should be allocated first to the (notional) internally generated goodwill; and

(e)   only the impairments allocated to purchased goodwill (and, if necessary, to any recognised intangible or tangible assets) should be recognised in the financial statements. [FRS 11(50)]

Example: Allocation of impairment losses when an acquired business is merged with existing operations [FRS 11 Example 8]

Assumptions:

An entity acquires for £60 million a business having net assets with a total fair value of £40 million, resulting in purchased goodwill of £20 million. The acquired business is merged with an existing operation that has net assets with a fair value of £100 million and a carrying amount of £70 million. The value in use of the existing operation at the time of the acquisition is £150 million, implying that the existing operation had internally generated goodwill of £50 million.

Five years later, the carrying amount of the net assets of the combined income-generating unit is £105 million and the carrying amount of the purchased goodwill is £10 million (goodwill is being amortised over 10 years). Value in use is £119 million and there is no reliable estimate of net realisable value.

Calculation of impairment loss	*£m*
Carrying amount of net assets	105
Carrying amount of goodwill	10
Notional carrying amount of internally generated goodwill at the date of acquisition (assuming notional amortisation on same basis as for purchased goodwill)	25
Total	140
Value in use	119
Impairment	21

The impairment is allocated on a pro rata basis (2:5) to the purchased goodwill and internally generated goodwill, resulting in the recognition of an impairment loss of £6 million and purchased goodwill being written down to £4 million.

If value in use were £98 million, the resulting total impairment loss of £42 million would be allocated first to the goodwill (purchased and notional amount of internally generated) of £35 million, then to any intangible assets, then to the tangible fixed assets in the income-generating unit, resulting in the recognition of an impairment loss of £17 million (write-down of purchased goodwill £10 million, write-down of intangible and tangible assets £7 million).

Further guidance

Subsequent monitoring of cash flows, see FRS 11 paragraphs 54–55.

Reversal of past impairments, see FRS 11 paragraphs 60–62.

Appendix XI   Weighted Average Cost of Capital (WACC)

Calculating WACC

The WACC can be defined as the weighted average of the returns required by each of a company's classes of securities. The WACC (post-tax) can be illustrated in its simplest form as follows:

$$\text{WACC} = \left(\begin{array}{l} \text{proportion of} \\ \text{equity} \end{array} \times \begin{array}{l} \text{cost of} \\ \text{equity} \end{array} \right) + \left(\begin{array}{l} \text{proportion of} \\ \text{debt} \end{array} \times \begin{array}{l} \text{cost of} \\ \text{debt} \end{array} \right)$$

or:

$$\text{WACC} = \frac{V_e}{V_e + V_d} \times K_e + \frac{V_d}{V_e + V_d} \times K_d \times (1 - T)$$

where:

V_e = Market value of equity V_d = Market value of debt

K_e = cost of equity K_d = cost of debt

T = effective corporate rate of tax.

There are a number of theoretical approaches to deriving the various constituents of a WACC. Some of the most practical and commonly used approaches are discussed below. Some sources of information to assist in estimating some of the components of the models are listed at the end of this appendix.

Cost of equity ('K_e')

Capital asset pricing model ('CAPM')

One of the most common approaches to estimating a cost of equity is the CAPM. This model is based on the premise that, on average, investors in equity shares expect to receive an extra return over risk-free assets, to compensate for the additional risk inherent in such shares.

It can be set out as below:

$K_e = R_f + ß * (R_m - R_f)$

R_f	Risk free rate
ß	Beta
$(R_m - R_f)$	Market Risk Premium.

Arbitrage pricing theory ('APT')

CAPM is based on a single 'risk factor', the beta, which measures the level of market risk of a minority investment in a particular listed company (i.e., it is a measure of the volatility of a particular share price or investment return) in relation to the returns of a broad market portfolio of leading listed companies. Market risk includes inflation, interest rates, fiscal policy, state of economy, etc. Arbitrage pricing theory (APT) can be considered an extension of CAPM to incorporate certain additional risk factors which may affect a cost of equity. One of the main practical problems in using APT is that there is no consensus as to what these risk factors are. Most models attempt to link risk to macro-economic factors such as interest rates, inflation or yield spreads.

The resulting equity return only reflects market risk. Adjustment for additional non-market risks particular to the company in question (such as size, lack of diversity, access to capital markets, etc.) must then be made to the extent these are not already reflected in the cash flows. These are a matter of informed investment judgement.

Other

Other methods may include more intuitive approaches, based on, for example, observations of rates of return evidenced in market transactions. This can be highly subjective but can be important as a safety cross-check.

Cost of debt ('K_d')

The cost of debt can be derived by looking at the cost to the company of its interest bearing debt. In general all interest bearing debt (ignore non-interest bearing debt) used to finance the business should be included, although short-term 'working capital' (e.g., overdrafts) which are not part of the ongoing financing requirements of the company should not be included. Where the company holds quoted debt instruments, K_d can be estimated with reference to the market yields on those securities.

Debt / Equity ratio ('V_d / V_e')

The debt/ equity ratio of a company is the ratio of the *market value* of debt, V_d, to the *market value* of equity, V_e. In developing this ratio it is necessary to determine an economically appropriate capital structure for the company. This will provide a *target ratio*. Strictly, because the beta risk factor already reflects the actual gearing of the listed stock in question, it should be 'de-geared' before application of the target gearing for the business unit.

This target ration is the appropriate combination of the various sources of financing that optimises the value of the company and, specifically, the value of the equity.

A *target ratio* needs to be developed for two reasons:

1   the current capital structure may not reflect the structure expected to prevail over the company's medium to long-term future. This may be the case if, e.g., a recent transaction has distorted the current capital structure, or management would logically plan to change the mix of debt and equity; and

2   it may be difficult to obtain the current market value of V_e. It is more appropriate to estimate the target ratio rather than attempt to estimate V_e and the current ratio.

Taxation ('T')

The effective corporate tax rate should be used in the calculation of WACC. This reduces the cost of debt based on the fact that interest on debt is an allowable deduction against corporation tax.

WACC estimated as above is a post-tax rate. Converting from a post-tax to a pre-tax rate was discussed in appendix 1.

Quoted companies

Calculating WACC for a quoted company is a relatively simple exercise. As noted above the most difficult element to determine is normally the cost of equity, K_e, for which most entities will use the CAPM:

$$K_e = R_f + \text{ß} * (R_m - R_f)$$

Common sources for all of these factors are provided at the end of this appendix.

Most independent studies indicate that the market equity return over the risk-free rate for the smallest 20–30 per cent of listed shares is somewhat higher than the average due to a lack of size. A premium may be added to reflect this.

Unquoted companies

It can be a more difficult and judgmental exercise to determine WACC for an unlisted company because of the lack of readily available comparable market data. Risk premiums can vary substantially – up to 40–50 per cent – which therefore makes the adjustment for non-market risk from the comparable cost of equity in a listed company to that appropriate to the business in question highly subjective. Companies may therefore wish to consider taking specialist advice when they need to determine such a discount factor. Although there are no clear universally accepted methods for determining WACC for an unquoted company, one possible route that may be considered is (i) to take an industry average beta factor for quoted companies, or beta factor of a quoted company with most similar risk profile. However, with the exception of many larger successful businesses (or businesses with strong profit potential) which are likely to be suitable for listing, this can be a very crude starting point. (ii) Make the major judgmental adjustment to reflect any additional non-market risk due to the nature of products or market the unquoted company is considered to have, including the lack of marketability.

Example 1   Estimate of WACC for an unquoted company

Assume the company is in the retail food sector.

Cost of long-term debt 12 per cent

Using the CAPM the cost of equity is expressed as:

$$K_e = R_f + \text{ß} * (R_m - R_f)$$

The following values have been assigned to these factors:

$R_f = 5.1\%$ Average yield to redemption of UK gilts over 15 years – per Financial Times UK Gilts prices 14 September 1998.

$ß = 0.8$ Based on betas for listed companies in food retailing business – London Business School risk measurement service July – September 1998 (average taken from three measures given 0.82, 0.8 and 0.78).

$(R_m - R_f) = 5.5\%$ Average return over last 20 years – 1998 BZW Equity – Gilt Study Exhibit 2.1.

For a listed company in the food retailing industry the cost of equity could therefore be estimated as:

$K_e = 5.1\% + 0.8 \times 5.5\% = 9.5\%$.

A further premium (possibly substantial) is then required to reflect non-market risks that are peculiar to the particular business compared to the listed comparable company. These involve: size, product and market diversity, market share, access to capital markets, maturity, etc. Accordingly, the range in which such an additional risk premium may fall is necessarily wide and it is not possible to give anything other than the broadest guidance. With a listed cost of equity at 10 per cent, and venture capital start-ups around 50 per cent, an appropriate rate of return will clearly depend on a careful risk analysis of the differences between the comparable company and the business in question.

Sources of information

Detailed below are some of the more common sources for the parameters used in the estimation of a WACC.

R_f *The risk-free rate of return*

The redemption yields on long-term UK gilts are often used as a guide to the risk-free rate or return, with terms matching the investment period.

- Financial Times.
- Datastream (on-line service).
- Bloomberg Financial Markets.

ß Beta

- London Business School, Risk Measurement Service, published quarterly.
- Datastream (on-line service).
- Bloomberg Financial Markets.
- Barra.

$R_m - R_f$ *The market risk premium or ERP*

- Barclays Capital Equity Gilt Study, published annually.
- Ibbotson SBBI Report (see Ibbotson website).
- Investment banks.

Appendix XII   A summary of UK financial reporting (31 March 2000)

Financial Reporting Standards

Title	Effective for periods
FRS 1 Revised *Cash flow statements*	Ending on or after 23 March 1997
FRS 2 *Accounting for subsidiary undertakings*	Ending on or after 23 December 1992
FRS 3 *Reporting financial preformance*	Ending on or after 22 June 1993. Insurance company amendment issued June 1993
FRS 4 *Capital instruments*	Ending on or after 22 June 1994
FRS 5 *Reporting the substance of transactions*	Ending on or after 22 September 1994. Application Note F on PFI transactions effective 10 September 1998
FRS 6 *Acquisitions and mergers*	Business combinations first accounted for in periods commencing on or after 23 December 1994
FRS 7 *Fair Values in acquisition accounting*	Business combinations first accounted for in periods commencing on or after 23 December 1994
FRS 8 *Related party disclosures*	Commencing on or after 23 December 1995
FRS 9 *Associates and joint ventures*	Ending on or after 23 June 1998
FRS 10 *Goodwill and intangible assets*	Ending on or after 23 December 1998
FRS 11 *Impairment of fixed assets and goodwill*	Ending on or after 23 December 1998
FRS 12 *Provisions, contingent liabilities and contingent assets*	Ending on or after 23 March 1999
FRS 13 *Derivatives and other financial instruments: disclosures*	Ending on or after 23 March 1999
FRS 14 *Earnings per share*	Ending on or after 23 December 1998
FRS 15 *Tangible fixed assets*	Ending on after 23 March 2000
FRS 16 *Current taxation*	Ending on after 23 March 2000
Financial Reporting Standard for Smaller Entities (FRSSE) (effective March 2000)	Ending on or after 23 March 2000. Reflects standards to FRS 15

Other Statements issued by ASB

Title	Status
Operating and financial review	Voluntary, no effective date
Interim statements	Voluntary, no effective date
Preliminary announcements	Voluntary, no effective date

ASB Foundation Statements

Title	Status
Statement of aims	Issued 1991
Explanatory foreword to accounting standards	Issued 1993
Statement of principles for financial reporting	Issued 1999

Statements of Standard Accounting Practice (SSAPs), issued by the ASB's predecessor body and adopted/amended by the ASB

SSAP 1	*Superseded by FRS 9 and FRSSE 1999*
SSAP 2	Disclosure of accounting policies
SSAP 3	*Superseded by FRS 14*
SSAP 4	Accounting for government grants
SSAP 5	Accounting for value added tax
SSAP 6	*Superseded by FRS 3*
SSAP 7	*Superseded by SSAP 16*
SSAP 8	*Superseded by FRS 16 (with effect from periods ending on or after 23 March 2000)*
SSAP 9	Stocks and long-term contracts
SSAP 10	*Superseded by FRS 1*
SSAP 11	*Superseded by SSAP 15*
SSAP 12	*Superseded by FRS 15, except for FRSSE users (with effect from periods ending on or after 23 March 2000)*
SSAP 13	Accounting for research and development
SSAP 14	*Superseded by FRS 2*

SSAP 15	Accounting for deferred tax
	Amended December 1992 in respect of post-retirement benefits for financial statements prepared on or after 17 December 1992
SSAP 16	*Withdrawn. Guidance available in 'Accounting for the effects of changing prices: a Handbook'*
SSAP 17	Accounting for post balance sheet events
SSAP 18	*Superseded by FRS 12 except for FRSSE users*
SSAP 19	Accounting for investment properties
	Amended July 1994 in respect of amounts charged to profit and loss account for periods ending on or after 22 September 1994
SSAP 20	Foreign currency translation
SSAP 21	Accounting for lease and hire purchase contracts
	Amended February 1997 to prohibit grossing-up for periods ending on or after 22 June 1997
SSAP 22	*Superseded by FRS 10 and FRSSE 1999*
SSAP 23	*Superseded by FRS 6*
SSAP 24	Accounting for pension costs
SSAP 25	Segmental reporting

UITF Abstracts issued and still in force

Title	Effective for periods
4 *Presentation of long-term debtors in current assets*	Ending on or after 23 August 1992
5 *Transfers from current assets to fixed assets*	Ending on or after 23 December 1992
6 *Accounting for post-retirement benefits other than pensions*	Ending on or after 23 December 1994 (full provision); 23 December 1992 (disclosures)
7 *True and fair view override disclosures*	Ending on or after 23 December 1992
9 *Accounting for operations in hyper-inflationary economies*	Ending on or after 23 August 1993
10 *Disclosure of directors' share options*	Non-mandatory status – unless a listed company
11 *Capital instruments: issuer call options*	Ending on or after 23 October 1994
12 *Lessee accounting for reverse premiums and similar incentives*	Ending on or after 23 December 1994 in respect of leases commending in the current or preceding period
13 *Accounting for employee share ownership plan (ESOP) trusts*	Ending on or after 22 June 1995. Amended by FRS 14 in respect of own shares held in an ESOP for periods ending on or after 23 December 1998

14 *Disclosure of changes in accounting policy*	Ending on or after 23 December 1995
15 *Disclosure of substantial acquisitions*	As for FRS 6
17 *Employee share schemes*	Ending on or after 22 June 1997
18 *Pension costs following the 1997 tax changes in respect of dividend income*	Ending on or after 23 December 1997
19 *Tax on gains and losses on foreign currency borrowings that hedge an investment in a foreign enterprise*	Ending on or after 23 March 1998
20 *Year 2000 issues: accounting and disclosures*	Ending on or after 23 March 1998
21 *Accounting issues arising from the proposed introduction of the euro*	Ending on or after 23 March 1998
22 *Acquisition of a Lloyd's business or similar insurance activities*	Ending on or after 23 December 1998
23 *Application of the transitional rules in FRS 15* (issued 18 May 2000)	Ending on or after 23 March 2000

ASB current projects

Project	Status
FRED 19 *Accounting for deferred tax*	Comment period expired
FRED 20 *Retirement benefits*	Comment period expired
FRED 21 *Accounting policies*	Comment period expired
Discussion Paper *Derivatives* (July 1996)	Measurement/hedging: UK taking part in joint international working group
Discussion Paper *Reporting financial performance: proposals for change* (June 1999)	International (G4+1) group paper circulated in UK. Progress dependent on international movement and changes to EU directives
Discussion paper *Leases: implementation of a new approach* (December 1999)	Comment period expired
Discussion Paper *Business combinations* (December 1998)	US FASB paper circulated in UK for comment. UK taking no action at present
Discussion paper *Year-end financial reports: inproving communication*	Comment period expired 19 May 2000
Working paper *Discounting in financial reporting* (April 1997)	Will remain as ASB reference paper. No further publication intended

Index

Entries are in word-by-word alphabetical order, in which spaces between words are taken into account: 'trade unions' therefore comes before 'trademarks'.

References are to paragraph.

Index